CRIME IN THE UNITED STATES

CRIME IN THE UNITED STATES

2018

12th EDITION

EDITED BY SHANA HERTZ HATTIS

Lanham • Boulder • New York • London

Published by Bernan Press
An imprint of The Rowman & Littlefield Publishing Group, Inc.
4501 Forbes Boulevard, Suite 200, Lanham, Maryland 20706
www.rowman.com
800-462-6420

Unit A, Whitacre Mews, 26-34 Stannary Street, London SE11 4AB

ISBN: 978-1-59888-989-5
eISBN: 978-1-59888-990-1

∞™ The paper used in this publication meets the minimum requirements
of American National Standard for Information Sciences—Permanence
of Paper for Printed Library Materials, ANSI/NISO Z39.48-1992.

Printed in the United States of America

CONTENTS

SECTION V: LAW ENFORCEMENT PERSONNEL 381

SECTION VI: HATE CRIMES 539

SECTION I

SUMMARY OF THE UNIFORM CRIME REPORTING (UCR) PROGRAM

SECTION I: SUMMARY OF THE UNIFORM CRIME REPORTING (UCR) PROGRAM

Bernan Press is proud to present its 12th edition of *Crime in the United States*. This title was formerly published by the Federal Bureau of Investigation (FBI), but is no longer available in printed form from the government. This edition contains final data from 2015 and 2016, the most current years for which data are available.

During a review of publication processes, UCR Program staff analyzed Web statistics from previous compilations of *Crime in the United States* (*CIUS*) to determine the tables accessed most by users. The program also considered which tables provide data that are now available from other sources. Based on these criteria, the UCR Program streamlined the 2016 edition by reducing the number of tables from 81 to 29. The publication, however, still presents the major topics (offenses known, clearances, and persons arrested) that its readers have come to expect.

This section describes the history of the UCR program, which collects the data used in *Crime in the United States* It also examines the best way to use the data in this publication.

About the UCR Program

The UCR program's primary objective is to generate reliable information for use in law enforcement administration, operation, and management; however, over the course of the program, its data has stood out as one of the country's leading social indicators.

The UCR program is a nationwide, cooperative statistical effort of more than 18,000 city, university and college, county, state, tribal, and federal law enforcement agencies voluntarily reporting data on crimes brought to their attention. Since 1930, the FBI has administered the UCR program and continued to assess and monitor the nature and type of crime in the nation. Criminologists, sociologists, legislators, municipal planners, the media, and other students of criminal justice use the data for varied research and planning purposes. Law enforcement agencies active in the UCR Program represented nearly 98 percent of the total population.

Improvements to the UCR Program

The FBI has currently undergone a renovation of the UCR program and its data. National UCR Program staff has been steadily improving the efficiency and functionality of the program's submission processes, quality control measures, and data maintenance. Planned improvements include the streamlining of all national-level crime data into the National Incident-Based Reporting System (NIBRS), the collection of use-of-force statistics at every demographic level, complete compliance with the Uniform Federal Crime Reporting Act (UFCRA) of 1988, active encouragement of other agencies to participate in the UCR program, and the introduction of the Crime Data Explorer (CDE), which will consolidate the different types of data into a diverse, user-friendly tool.

Note for Users

It is important for UCR data users to remember that the FBI's primary objective is to generate a reliable set of crime statistics for use in law enforcement administration, operation, and management. The FBI does not provide a ranking of agencies; instead, it provides alphabetical tabulations of states, metropolitan statistical areas, cities with over 10,000 inhabitants, suburban and rural counties, and selected colleges and universities. Law enforcement officials use these data for their designed purposes. Additionally, the public relies on these data for information about the fluctuations in levels of crime from year to year, while criminologists, sociologists, legislators, city planners, media outlets, and other students of criminal justice use them for a variety of research and planning purposes. Since crime is a sociological phenomenon influenced by a variety of factors, the FBI discourages data users from ranking agencies and using the data as a measurement of the effectiveness of law enforcement.

To ensure that data are uniformly reported, the FBI provides contributing law enforcement agencies with a handbook that explains how to classify and score offenses and provides uniform crime offense definitions. Acknowledging that offense definitions may vary from state to state, the FBI cautions agencies to report offenses according to the guidelines provided in the handbook, rather than by local or state statutes. Most agencies make a good faith effort to comply with established guidelines.

Variables Affecting Crime: Caution Against Ranking

Until data users examine all the variables that affect crime in a town, city, county, state, region, or college or university, they can make no meaningful comparisons. In each edition of *Crime in the United States*, many entities—including news media, tourism agencies, and other organizations with an interest in crime in the nation—use reported figures to compile rankings of cities and counties. However, these rankings are merely a quick choice made by that data user; they provide no insight into the many variables that mold the crime in a particular town, city, county, state, or region. Consequently, these rankings may lead to simplistic and/or incomplete analyses, which can create misleading perceptions and thus adversely affect cities, counties, and their residents.

3

Considering Other Characteristics of a Jurisdiction

To assess criminality and law enforcement's response from jurisdiction to jurisdiction, data users must consider many variables, some of which (despite having significant impact on crime) are not readily measurable or applicable among all locales. Geographic and demographic factors specific to each jurisdiction must be considered and applied in order to make an accurate and complete assessment of crime in that jurisdiction. Several sources of information are available to help the researcher explore the variables that affect crime in a particular locale. The U.S. Census Bureau data, for example, can help the user better understand the makeup of a locale's population. The transience of the population, its racial and ethnic makeup, and its composition by age and gender, educational levels, and prevalent family structures are all key factors in assessing and understanding crime.

Local chambers of commerce, planning offices, and similar entities provide information regarding the economic and cultural makeup of cities and counties. Understanding a jurisdiction's industrial/economic base, its dependence upon neighboring jurisdictions, its transportation system, its economic dependence on nonresidents (such as tourists and convention attendees), and its proximity to military installations, correctional institutions, and other types of facilities all contribute to accurately gauging and interpreting the crime known to and reported by law enforcement.

The strength (including personnel and other resources) and aggressiveness of a jurisdiction's law enforcement agency are also key factors in understanding the nature and extent of crime occurring in that area. Although information pertaining to the number of sworn and civilian employees can be found in this publication, it cannot be used alone as an assessment of the emphasis that a community places on enforcing the law. For example, one city may report more crime than another comparable city because its law enforcement agency identifies more offenses. Attitudes of citizens toward crime and their crime reporting practices—especially for minor offenses—also have an impact on the volume of crimes known to police.

Making Valid Crime Assessments

It is essential for all data users to become as well educated as possible about understanding and quantifying the nature and extent of crime in the United States and in the jurisdictions represented by law enforcement contributors to the UCR program. Valid assessments are possible only with careful study and analysis of the various unique conditions that affect each local law enforcement jurisdiction.

Some factors that are known to affect the volume and type of crime occurring from place to place are:

- Population density and degree of urbanization
- Variations in composition of population, particularly in the concentration of youth
- Stability of the population with respect to residents' mobility, commuting patterns, and transient factors
- Modes of transportation and highway systems
- Economic conditions, including median income, poverty level, and job availability
- Cultural factors and educational, recreational, and religious characteristics
- Family conditions, with respect to divorce and family cohesiveness
- Climate
- Effective strength of law enforcement agencies
- Administrative and investigative emphases of law enforcement
- Policies of other components of the criminal justice system (that is, prosecutorial, judicial, correctional, and probational policies)
- Residents' attitudes toward crime
- Crime reporting practices of residents

Although many of the listed factors equally affect the crime of a particular area, the UCR program makes no attempt to relate them to the data presented. **The data user is therefore cautioned against comparing statistical data of individual reporting units from cities, counties, metropolitan areas, states, or colleges or universities solely on the basis on their population coverage or student enrollment.** Until data users examine all the variables that affect crime in a town, city, county, state, region, or college or university, they can make no meaningful comparisons.

Historical Background

Since 1930, the FBI has administered the UCR program; the agency continues to assess and monitor the nature and type of crime in the nation. Data users look to the UCR program for various research and planning purposes.

Recognizing a need for national crime statistics, the International Association of Chiefs of Police (IACP) formed the Committee on Uniform Crime Records in the 1920s to develop a system of uniform crime statistics. After studying state criminal codes and making an evaluation of the recordkeeping practices in use, the committee completed a plan for crime reporting that became the foundation of the UCR program in 1929. The plan included standardized offense definitions for seven main offense classifications known as Part I crimes to gauge fluctuations in the overall volume and rate of crime. Developers also instituted the Hierarchy Rule as the main reporting procedure for what is now known as the Summary Reporting System of the UCR program.

Seven main offense classifications, known as Part I crimes, were chosen to gauge the state of crime in the nation. These seven offense classifications included the violent crimes of murder and nonnegligent manslaughter, rape, robbery, and aggravated assault; also included were the property crimes of burglary, larceny-theft, and motor vehicle theft. By congressional mandate, arson was added as the eighth Part I offense category. Data collection for arson began in 1979.

During the early planning of the program, it was recognized that the differences among criminal codes precluded a mere aggregation of state statistics to arrive at a national total. Also, because of the variances in punishment for the same offenses in different states, no distinction between felony and misdemeanor crimes was possible. To avoid these problems and provide nationwide uniformity in crime reporting, standardized offense definitions were developed. Law enforcement agencies use these to submit data without regard for local statutes. UCR program offense definitions can be found in Appendix I.

In January 1930, 400 cities (representing 20 million inhabitants in 43 states) began participating in the UCR program. Congress enacted Title 28, Section 534, of the *United States Code* that same year, which authorized the attorney general to gather crime information. The attorney general, in turn, designated the FBI to serve as the national clearinghouse for the collected crime data. Since then, data based on uniform classifications and procedures for reporting have been obtained annually from the nation's law enforcement agencies.

Advisory Groups

Providing vital links between local law enforcement and the FBI for the UCR program are the Criminal Justice Information Systems Committees of the IACP and the National Sheriffs' Association (NSA). The IACP represents the thousands of police departments nationwide, as it has since the program began. The NSA encourages sheriffs throughout the country to participate fully in the program. Both committees serve the program in advisory capacities.

In 1988, a Data Providers' Advisory Policy Board was established. This board operated until 1993, when it combined with the National Crime Information Center Advisory Policy Board to form a single Advisory Policy Board (APB) to address all FBI criminal justice information services. The current APB works to ensure continuing emphasis on UCR-related issues. The Association of State Uniform Crime Reporting Programs (ASUCRP) focuses on UCR issues within individual state law enforcement associations and also promotes interest in the UCR program. These organizations foster widespread and responsible use of uniform crime statistics and lend assistance to data contributors.

Previous Redesign of UCR

Although UCR data collection was originally conceived as a tool for law enforcement administration, the data were widely used by other entities involved in various forms of social planning by the 1980s. Recognizing the need for more detailed crime statistics, law enforcement called for a thorough evaluative study to modernize the UCR program. The FBI formulated a comprehensive three-phase redesign effort. The Bureau of Justice Statistics (BJS) agency in the Department of Justice responsible for funding criminal justice information projects, agreed to underwrite the first two phases. These phases were conducted by an independent contractor and structured to determine what, if any, changes should be made to the current program. The third phase would involve implementation of the changes identified.

The final report, the *Blueprint for the Future of the Uniform Crime Reporting Program,* was released in the summer of 1985. It specifically outlined recommendations for an expanded, improved UCR program to meet future informational needs. There were three recommended areas of enhancement to the UCR program:

- Offenses and arrests would be reported using an incident-based system

- Data would be collected on two levels. Agencies in level one would report important details about those offenses comprising the Part I crimes, their victims, and arrestees. Level two would consist of law enforcement agencies covering populations of more than 100,000 and a sampling of smaller agencies that would collect expanded detail on all significant offenses

- A quality assurance program would be introduced

In January 1986, Phase III of the redesign effort began, guided by the general recommendations set forth in the *Blueprint*. The FBI selected an experimental site to implement the redesigned program, while contractors developed new data guidelines and system specifications. Upon selecting the South Carolina Law Enforcement Division (SLED), which enlisted the cooperation of nine local law enforcement agencies, the FBI developed automated data capture specifications to adapt the SLED's state system to the national UCR program's standards, and the BJS funded the revisions. The pilot demonstration ran from March 1 through September 30, 1987, and resulted in further refinement of the guidelines and specifications.

From March 1 through March 3, 1988, the FBI held a national UCR conference to present the new system to law enforcement and to obtain feedback on its acceptability. Attendees of the conference passed three overall recommendations without dissent: first, that there be established a new, incident-based national crime reporting system; second, that the FBI manage this program; and third, that an Advisory Policy Board composed of law enforcement executives be formed to assist in directing and implementing the new program. Furthermore, attendees recommended that the implementation of national incident-based reporting proceed at a pace commensurate with the resources and limitations of contributing law enforcement agencies.

Establishing the NIBRS

From March 1988 through January 1989, the FBI developed and assumed management of the UCR program's National Incident-Based Reporting System (NIBRS), and by April 1989, the first test of NIBRS data was submitted to the national UCR program. Over the next few years, the national UCR program published information about the redesigned program in five documents:

- *Uniform Crime Reporting Handbook*, NIBRS Edition (1992) provides a nontechnical program overview focusing on definitions, policies, and procedures of the IBRS

- *Data Submission Specifications* (May 1992) is used by local and state systems personnel, who are responsible for preparing magnetic media for submission to the FBI

- *Approaches to Implementing an Incident-Based System* (July 1992) is a guide for system designers

- *Error Message Manual* (revised December 1999) contains designations of mandatory and optional data elements, data element edits, and error messages

- *Data Collection Guidelines* (revised August 2000) contains a system overview and descriptions of the offense codes, reports, data elements, and data values used in the system

As more agencies inquired about the NIBRS, the FBI, in May 2002, made the *Handbook for Acquiring a Records Management System (RMS) That Is Compatible with the NIBRS* available to agencies considering or developing automated incident-based records management systems. The handbook, developed under the sponsorship of the FBI and the BJS, provides instructions for planning and conducting a system acquisition and offers guidelines on preparing an agency for conversion to the new system and to the NIBRS.

The National UCR Program staff has also presented additional documents, including the *National Incident-Based Reporting System (NIBRS) Technical Specification* (Version 1.1, dated September 17, 2014) and the *National Incident-Based Reporting System (NIBRS) User Manual* (Version 1.0, dated January 17, 2013.)

Originally designed with 52 data elements, the redesigned NIBRS captures up to 57 data elements via 6 types of data segments: administrative, offense, victim property, offender, and arrestee. Although, in the late 1980s, the FBI committed to hold all changes to the NIBRS in abeyance until a substantial number of contributors implemented the system, modifications have been necessary. The system's flexibility has allowed the collection of four additional pieces of information to be captured within an incident: bias-motivated offenses (1990), the presence of gang activity (1997), data for law enforcement officers killed and assaulted (2003), and data on cargo theft (2005). The system has also allowed the addition of new codes to further specify location types and property types (2010).

The FBI began accepting NIBRS data from a handful of agencies in January 1989. As more contributing law enforcement agencies become educated about the rich data available through incident-based reporting and as resources permit, more agencies are implementing the NIBRS. Based on the 2012 data submissions, 15 states submit all their data via the NIBRS and 32 state UCR Programs are certified for NIBRS participation.

Suspension of the *Crime Index* and the *Modified Crime Index*

In June 2004, the CJIS APB approved discontinuing the use of the *Crime Index* in the UCR program and its publications and directed the FBI to publish a violent crime total and a property crime total. The *Crime Index*, first published in *Crime in the United States* in 1960, was the title used for a simple aggregation of the seven main offense classifications (Part I offenses) in the Summary Reporting System. The Modified Crime Index was the number of Crime Index offenses plus arson.

For several years, the CJIS Division studied the appropriateness and usefulness of these indices and brought the matter before many advisory groups including the UCR Subcommittee of the CJIS APB, the ASUCRP, and a meeting of leading criminologists and sociologists hosted by the BJS. In short, the *Crime Index* and the *Modified Crime Index* were not true indicators of the degrees of criminality because they were always driven upward by the offense with the highest number, typically larceny-theft. The sheer volume of those offenses overshadowed more serious but less frequently committed offenses, creating a bias against a jurisdiction with a high number of larceny-thefts but a low number of other serious crimes such as murder and rape.

Recent Developments in UCR Program

In the fall of 2011, the APB recommended, and FBI Director Robert Mueller III approved, changing the definition of rape. Since 1929, in the SRS, rape had been defined as "the carnal knowledge of a female forcibly and against her will," (*UCR Handbook*, 2004, p.19). Beginning with the 2013 data collection, the SRS definition for the violent crime of rape will be: "Penetration, no matter how slight, of the vagina or anus with any body part or object, or oral penetration by a sex organ of another person, without the consent of the victim." This definition can be found in the *Summary Reporting System [SRS] User Manual*, Version 1.0, dated June 20, 2013. The FBI is developing reporting options for law enforcement agencies to meet this requirement, which will be built into the redeveloped data collection system.

In addition to approving the new definition of rape for the SRS, the APB and Director Mueller approved removing the word "forcible" from the name of the offense and also replacing the phrase "against the person's will" with "without the consent of the victim" in other sex-related offenses in the SRS, the NIBRS, the Hate Crime Statistics Program, and Cargo Theft.

In response to a directive by the U.S. Government's Office of Management and Budget, the national UCR Program has expanded its data collection categories for race from four (White, Black, American Indian or Alaska Native, and Asian or Other Pacific Islander) to five (White, Black or African American, American Indian or Alaska Native, Asian, and Native Hawaiian or Other Pacific Islander). Also, the ethnicity categories have changed from "Hispanic" to "Hispanic or Latino" and from "Non-Hispanic" to "Not Hispanic or Latino." These changes are reflected in data presented for 2012.

The national UCR Program staff continues to develop data collection methods to comply with both the William Wilberforce Trafficking Victims Protection Reauthorization Act of 2008 and the Matthew Shepard and James Byrd, Jr. Hate Crime Prevention Act of 2009. As a result, the FBI will begin accepting data on human trafficking as well as data on crimes motivated by "gender and gender identity" bias and "crimes committed by, and crimes directed against, juveniles" from contributors in January 2013.

UNIFORM CRIME REPORTING PROGRAM CHANGES DEFINITION OF RAPE

For the first time in its more than 80-year history of the Uniform Crime Reporting (UCR) Program, the FBI changed the definition of a Part 1 offense. In December 2011, then FBI Director Robert S. Mueller, III, approved revisions to the UCR Program's definition of rape as recommended by the FBI's Criminal Justice Information Services (CJIS) Division Advisory Policy Board (APB), which is made up of representatives from all facets of law enforcement.

Beginning in 2013, rape is defined for Summary UCR purposes as, "Penetration, no matter how slight, of the vagina or anus with any body part or object, or oral penetration by a sex organ of another person, without the consent of the victim." The new definition updated the 80-year-old historical definition of rape which was "carnal knowledge of a female forcibly and against her will." Effectively, the revised definition expands rape to include both male and female victims and offenders, and reflects the various forms of sexual penetration understood to be rape, especially nonconsenting acts of sodomy, and sexual assaults with objects.

"This new, more inclusive definition will provide us with a more accurate understanding of the scope and volume of these crimes," said Attorney General Eric Holder. Proponents of the new definition and of the omission of the term "forcible" say that the changes broaden the scope of the previously narrow definitions by capturing (1) data without regard to gender, (2) the penetration of any bodily orifice, penetration by any object or body part, and (3) offenses in which physical force is not involved. Now, for example, instances in which offenders use drugs or alcohol or incidents in which offenders sodomize victims of the same gender will be counted as rape for statistical purposes.

It has long been the UCR Program's mission to collect and publish data regarding the scope and nature of crime in the nation, including those for rape. Since the FBI began collecting data using the revised definition of rape in January 2013, program officials expected that the number of reported rapes would rise. According to David Cuthbertson, former FBI Assistant Director of the CJIS Division, "As we implement this change, the FBI is confident that the number of victims of this heinous crime will be more accurately reflected in national crime statistics."

Beginning January 1, 2017, the UCR Program discontinued collecting rape data via the SRS according to the legacy definition. Therefore, the 2016 editions of *CIUS* and *Hate Crime Statistics* are the final publications which include the legacy definition of rape. Only rape data submitted under the revised definition will be published for 2017 and subsequent years. This change did not affect agencies that submit rape data via NIBRS.

Expanded Offense Tables

Expanded offense data are the details of the various offenses that the Uniform Crime Reporting Program collects beyond the count of how many crimes law enforcement agencies report. These details may include the type of weapon used in a crime, the type or value of items stolen, and so forth. Expanded homicide data provide supplemental details about murders such as the age, sex, and race of both the victim and the offender, the weapon used in the homicide, the circumstances surrounding the offense, and the relationship of the victim to the offender. In addition, expanded data includes trends (for example, 2-year comparisons) and rates per 100,000 inhabitants.

Expanded offense data, including expanded homicide data, are information collected in addition to the reports of the number of crimes known. As a result, law enforcement agencies can report an offense without providing the supplemental data about that offense. These additional tables can be found at http://www.fbi.gov/about-us/cjis/ucr/crime-in-the-u.s/2013/crime-in-the-u.s.-2013/offenses-known-to-law-enforcement/expanded-offense/expandedoffensemain_final.

About the Editor

Shana Hertz Hattis is a consulting writer-editor for Bernan Press. She holds a master's degree in education from Northwestern University and a bachelor's degree in journalism from the same university. She has previously edited *Vital Statistics of the United States: Births, Life Expectancy, Deaths, and Selected Health Data* and several volumes of *Crime in the United States* for Bernan.

SECTION II

OFFENSES KNOWN TO POLICE

VIOLENT CRIME

- MURDER
- RAPE (REVISED DEFINITION)
- RAPE (LEGACY DEFINITION)
- ROBBERY
- AGGRAVATED ASSAULT

PROPERTY CRIME

- BURGLARY
- LARCENY-THEFT
- MOTOR VEHICLE THEFT
- ARSON

VIOLENT CRIME

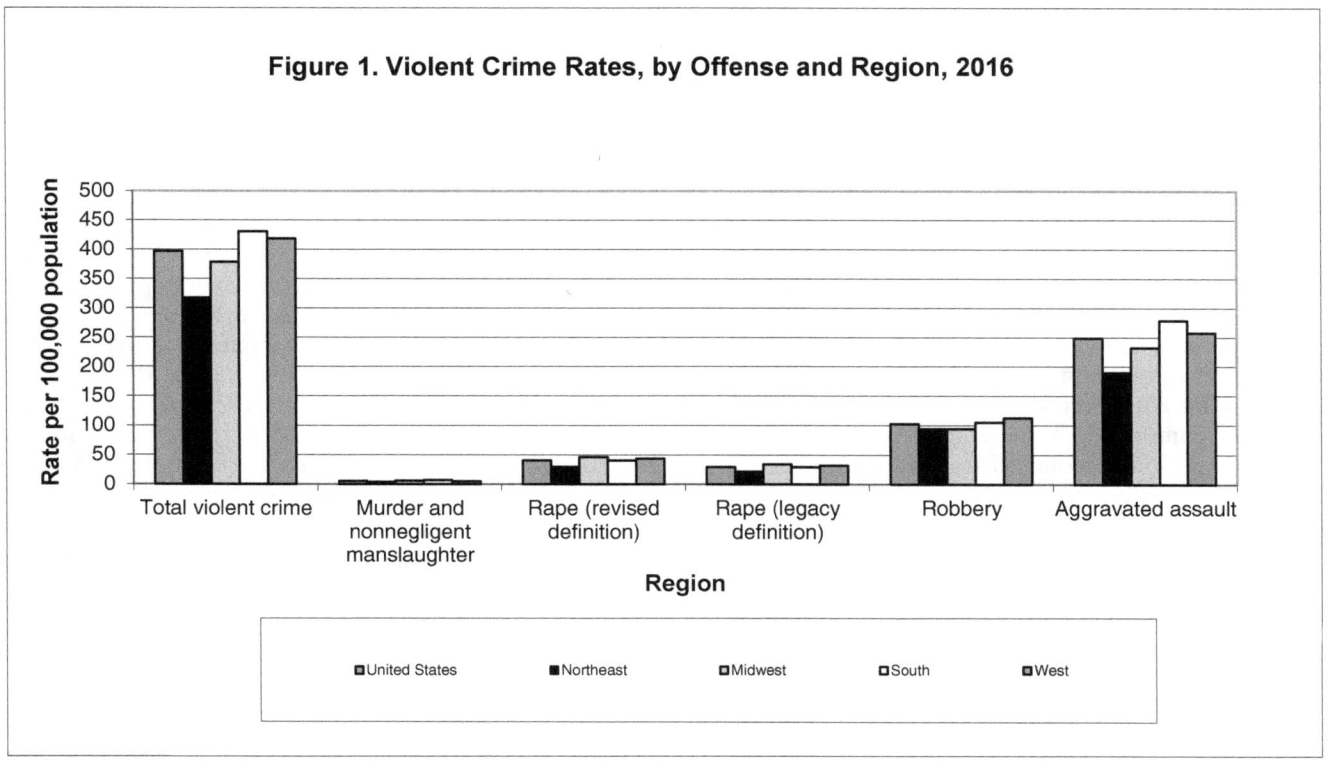

Figure 1. Violent Crime Rates, by Offense and Region, 2016

Rate per 100,000 population

Region

□ United States   ■ Northeast   □ Midwest   □ South   ■ West

Definition

Violent crime consists of four offenses: murder and non-negligent manslaughter, rape, robbery, and aggravated assault. According to the Uniform Crime Reporting (UCR) program, run by the Federal Bureau of Investigation (FBI), violent crimes involve either the use of force or the threat of force.

Data Collection

The data presented in *Crime in the United States* reflect the Hierarchy Rule, which counts only the most serious offense in a multiple-offense criminal incident. In descending order of severity, the violent crimes are murder and nonnegligent manslaughter, rape, robbery, and aggravated assault; these are followed by the property crimes of burglary, larceny-theft, and motor vehicle theft. Arson is also considered a property crime, but the Hierarchy Rule does not apply to the arson offense. In cases in which arson occurs in conjunction with another violent or property crime, the arson and the additional crime are reported. More information on the expanded violent crime tables (which are available online but not included in this publication) can be found in Section I.

IMPORTANT NOTE: RAPE DATA

In 2013, the FBI UCR Program initiated the collection of rape data within the Summary Reporting System under a revised definition. The changes bring uniformity to the offense in both the Summary Reporting System (SRS) and the National Incident-Based Reporting System (NIBRS) by capturing data (1) without regard to gender, (2) including penetration of any bodily orifice by any object or body part, and (3) including offenses where physical force is not involved. The term "forcible" was removed, and the definition changed to the revised UCR definition below.

- Legacy UCR definition of rape: The carnal knowledge of a female forcibly and against her will.

- Revised UCR definition of rape: Penetration, no matter how slight, of the vagina or anus with any body part or object, or oral penetration by a sex organ of another person, without the consent of the victim.

For more information, please see <https://ucr.fbi.gov/crime-in-the-u.s/2013/crime-in-the-u.s.-2013/rape-addendum/rape_addendum_final >.

Beginning January 1, 2017, the UCR Program will discontinue collecting rape data via the SRS according to the historical, legacy definition. Only rape data submitted under the revised definition will be published for 2017 and subsequent years. This change will not affect agencies that submit rape data via NIBRS.

National Volume, Trends, and Rate

In 2016, an estimated 1,248,185 violent crimes occurred in the United States, a 4.1 percent increase from the 2015 estimate. An estimated 386.3 violent crimes were committed per 100,000 inhabitants in 2016, an increase of 3.4 percent since 2015. Aggravated assaults accounted for 64.3 percent of violent crimes, the highest percentage of violent crimes reported to law enforcement. Robbery accounted for 26.7 percent of violent crimes, rape (revised definition) comprised 10.5 percent of violent crimes, rape (legacy definition) accounted for 7.7 percent of violent crimes, and murder accounted for 1.4 percent of violent crimes. (Tables 1 and 1A)

Occurrences of violent crime increased across the board. Murder increased 8.6 percent from 2015 to 2016. Robbery increased by 0.5 percent. Rape (revised definition) increased 2.8 percent, rape (legacy definition) increased 4.2 percent, and aggravated assault increased 4.4 percent. (Tables 1 and 1A)

In longer-term trends, the 2016 estimated violent crime total was 2.6 percent above the 2012 level and 12.3 percent below the 2007 level. The 5-year and 10-year trend data also showed that the violent crime rate decreased 0.4 percent between 2012 and 2016 and decreased 18.1 percent between 2007 and 2016. (Tables 1 and 1A)

In 2016, offenders used firearms in 73.0 percent of the nation's murders, 41.1 percent of robberies, and 25.8 percent of aggravated assaults. (Table 12; Table 13; Table 14; for expanded date, please see <https://ucr.fbi.gov/crime-in-the-u.s/2016/crime-in-the-u.s.-2016/topic-pages/expanded-offense>)

Regional Offense Trends and Rate

The UCR program divides the United States into four regions: the Northeast, the South, the Midwest, and the West. (More details concerning geographic regions are provided in Appendix IV.

THE NORTHEAST

The Northeast accounted for an estimated 17.4 percent of the nation's population in 2016 and an estimated 13.9 percent of its violent crimes. The estimated number of violent crimes decreased 1.2 percent from 2015 to 2016. Murder decreased 0.6 percent in the Northeast, and rape (revised definition) increased 1.4 percent. Rape (legacy definition) increased 2.6 percent. Robberies declined 5.6 percent. Aggravated assaults increased 0.7 percent from 2015. In 2016, there were an estimated 317.1 violent crimes per 100,000 inhabitants. (Table 2)

THE MIDWEST

With an estimated 21.0 percent of the total population of the United States, the Midwest accounted for 20.0 percent of the nation's estimated number of violent crimes in 2016. Violent crime increased in every applicable category. The region had a 5.9 percent increase in violent crime from 2015 to 2016. The estimated number of aggravated assaults increased 7.8 percent, while the estimated number of robberies rose 2.9 percent and the estimated number of murders increased 5.9 percent. The estimated number of rapes (legacy definition) increased 3.1 percent and the estimated number of rapes (revised definition) increased 1.9 percent. The rate of violent crime per 100,000 inhabitants in the Midwest was 378.4, an increase of 4.1 percent from 2015 to 2016. (Table 2)

THE SOUTH

The South, the nation's most populous region, accounted for 37.9 percent of the nation's population in 2016. Approximately 41.1 percent of violent crimes in 2016 occurred in the South. Violent crime increased 3.5 percent, while the estimated number of murders rose 9.1 percent, the estimated number of rapes (revised definition) increased 4.2 percent, and the estimated number of rapes (legacy definition) rose 5.6 percent, robberies increased 1.3 percent, and aggravated assault increased by 4.2 percent. The estimated rate of violent crime in the South was 430.8 incidents per 100,000 inhabitants in 2016. (Table 2)

THE WEST

With 23.7 percent of the nation's population in 2016, the West also accounted for an estimated 25.0 percent of the nation's violent crime. Violent crime in the West increased 6.3 percent from 2015 to 2016. Murders rose 8.0 percent, rapes (revised definition) increased 5.3 percent, rapes (legacy definition) increased 6.8 percent, robberies rose 4.5 percent, and aggravated assault increased 7.2 percent. The region's violent crime rate in 2016 was 418.4 per 100,000 inhabitants. (Table 2)

Population Groups: Trends and Rates

In the UCR program, data are also aggregated into population groups; these groups are described in more detail in Appendix IV. The nation's cities had an overall increase of 4.3 percent in the estimated number of violent crimes from 2015 to 2016. Violent crimes increased in every population group subset. Cities with 1,000,000 or more residents had the greatest increase (7.2 percent), while cities with under 10,000 residents had the smallest increase (0.2 percent). (Table 10)

The law enforcement agencies in the nation's cities collectively reported a rate of 471.6 violent crimes per 100,000 inhabitants in 2016. Law enforcement agencies in the subset of cities with 500,000 to 999,999 inhabitants reported the highest violent crime rate, 861.9 violent crimes per 100,000 inhabitants; the violent crime rate for all cities with 250,000 or more inhabitants was 771.4 per 100,000 inhabitants. Agencies in cities with 10,000 to 24,999 inhabitants reported the lowest violent crime rate (272.6 incidents per 100,000 inhabitants). Law enforcement agencies in the nation's metropolitan counties reported a collective violent crime rate of 267.3 per 100,000 inhabitants, while agencies in nonmetropolitan counties reported a collective rate of 200.6 violent crimes per 100,000 inhabitants. (Table 11)

MURDER

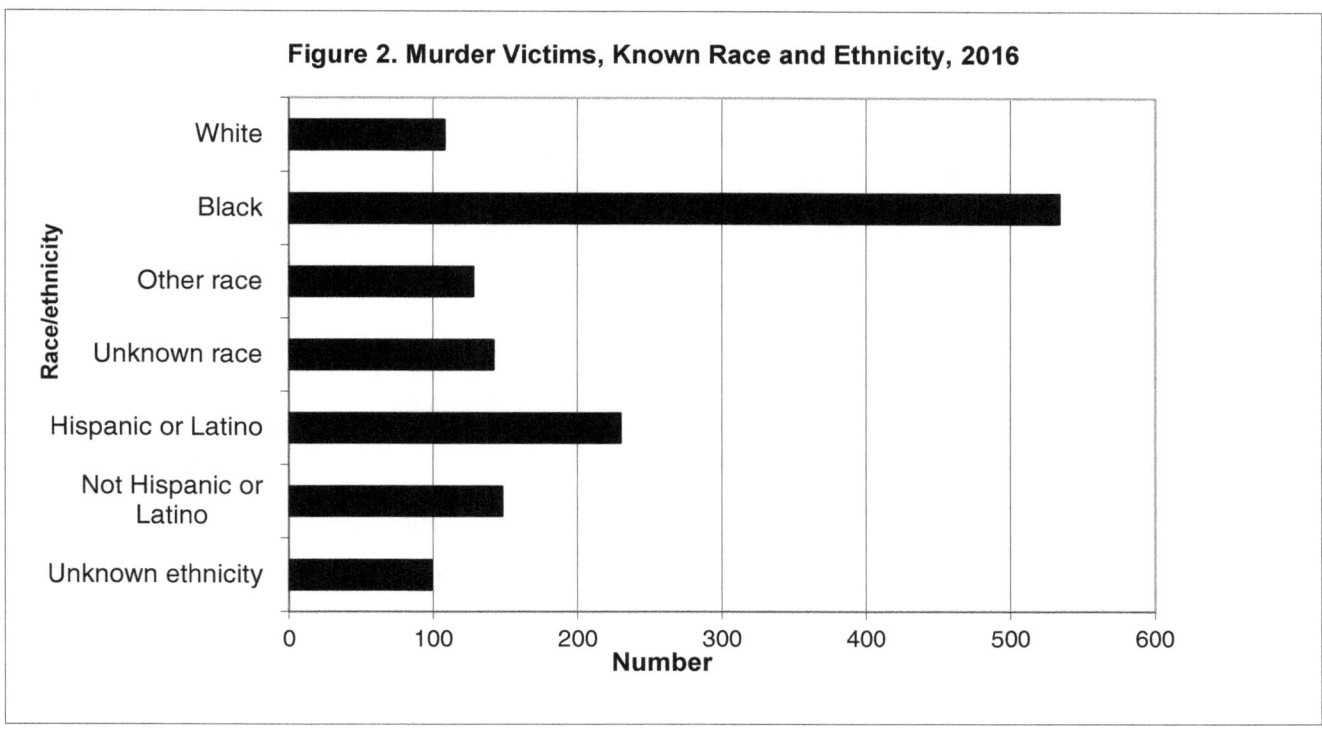

Figure 2. Murder Victims, Known Race and Ethnicity, 2016

Definition

The UCR program defines murder and non-negligent manslaughter as the willful (non-negligent) killing of one human being by another. The classification of this offense is based solely on police investigation, rather than on the determination of a court, medical examiner, coroner, jury, or other judicial body. The UCR program does not include the following situations under this offense classification: deaths caused by negligence, suicide, or accident; justifiable homicides; and attempts to murder or assaults to murder, which are considered aggravated assaults.

Data Collection/Supplementary Homicide Reports (SHR)

The UCR program's *Supplementary Homicide Report* (SHR) provides information about murder victims and offenders by age, sex, and race; the types of weapons used in the murders; the relationships of the victims to the offenders; and the circumstances surrounding the incident. Law enforcement agencies are asked to complete an SHR for each murder reported to the UCR program. Data from SHRs can be viewed in the Expanded Homicide Data section. More information on these reports and the expanded homicide tables can be found in Section I.

National Volume, Trends, and Rates

An estimated 17,250 persons were murdered nationwide in 2016. This number was an 8.6 percent increase from the 2015 estimate, a 16.1 percent increase from the 2012 figure, and a 0.7 percent decrease from the 2007 estimate. The 2016 murder rate, 5.3 offenses per 100,000 inhabitants, was a 7.9 percent increase from the 2015 rate. Murder accounted for 1.4 percent of the overall estimated number of violent crimes in 2016. (Tables 1 and 1A)

Regional Offense Trends and Rates

The UCR program divides the United States into four regions: the Northeast, the South, the Midwest, and the West. (More details concerning geographic regions are provided in Appendix IV.) In 2016, 46.2 percent of murders were reported in the South, the country's most populous region. The Midwest reported 22.5 percent of murders. The West reported 20.0 percent of all murders, while 11.3 percent of murders were reported in the Northeast. (Table 3)

THE NORTHEAST

In 2016, the Northeast accounted for an estimated 17.4 percent of the nation's population and 11.3 percent of its estimated number of murders. With an estimated 1,955 murders, the Northeast saw a 0.6 percent decrease from its 2015 figure. The offense rate for the Northeast was 3.5 murders per 100,000 inhabitants, a 0.7 percent decline from 2015. (Table 2)

THE MIDWEST

The Midwest accounted for an estimated 21.0 percent of the nation's total population and 22.5 percent of the country's estimated number of murders in 2016. The Midwest reported an estimated 3,885 murders in 2016. The region experienced a rate of 5.7 murders per 100,000 inhabitants in 2016, above its 2015 rate of 5.0. (Table 2)

THE SOUTH

The South accounted for an estimated 37.9 percent of the nation's population in 2016 and 46.2 percent of the nation's murders, the highest proportion among the four regions. The estimated 7,961 murders represented a 9.1 percent increase from the 2015 figure. The region's estimated rate of 6.5 murders per 100,000 inhabitants represented an increase of 7.9 percent from the estimated rate for 2015. (Table 2)

THE WEST

The West accounted for an estimated 23.7 percent of the nation's population and 20.0 percent of the estimated number of murders in 2016. The West experienced an estimated 3,449 murders, an 8.0 percent increase from the 2015 estimate. The region's murder rate was 4.5 per 100,000 inhabitants. (Table 2)

Population Groups: Trends and Rates

The UCR program uses the following population group designations in its data presentations: cities (grouped according to population size) and counties (classified as either metropolitan or nonmetropolitan). A breakdown of these classifications is provided in Appendix IV.

From 2015 to 2016, the nation's cities experienced a 12.8 percent increase in homicides. Murders increased in every population group, with the greatest increases occurring in cities with 1,000,000 or more residents (20.3 percent) and cities with 250,000 or more residents (12.9 percent). Metropolitan counties experienced an increase in homicides of 12.3 percent from 2015 to 2016, while nonmetropolitan counties experienced a decrease of 6.7 percent. Suburban areas experienced a 9.8 percent increase. (Table 10)

In 2016, cities collectively had a rate of 6.2 murders per 100,000 inhabitants. Cities with 500,000 to 999,999 inhabitants had the highest murder rate (12.9 murders per 100,000 inhabitants). Cities with under 10,000 inhabitants had the lowest murder rate, with 3.0 murders per 100,000 inhabitants. The homicide rate for metropolitan counties was 3.8 murders per 100,000 inhabitants, while the rate for nonmetropolitan counties was 3.6 murders per 100,000 inhabitants. Suburban areas had a homicide rate of 3.2 per 100,000 inhabitants. (Table 11)

Justifiable Homicide

Certain willful killings must be reported as justifiable, or excusable, homicide. In the UCR program, justifiable homicide is defined as, and is limited to, the following:

- The killing of a felon by a peace officer in the line of duty

- The killing of a felon, during the commission of a felony, by a private citizen

Because these killings are determined by law enforcement investigation to be justifiable, they are tabulated separately from murder and nonnegligent manslaughter. Law enforcement reported 770 justifiable homicides in 2016. Of those, law enforcement officers justifiably killed 435 individuals, and private citizens justifiably killed 331 individuals. (Expanded Homicide Data Tables 14 and 15)

RAPE

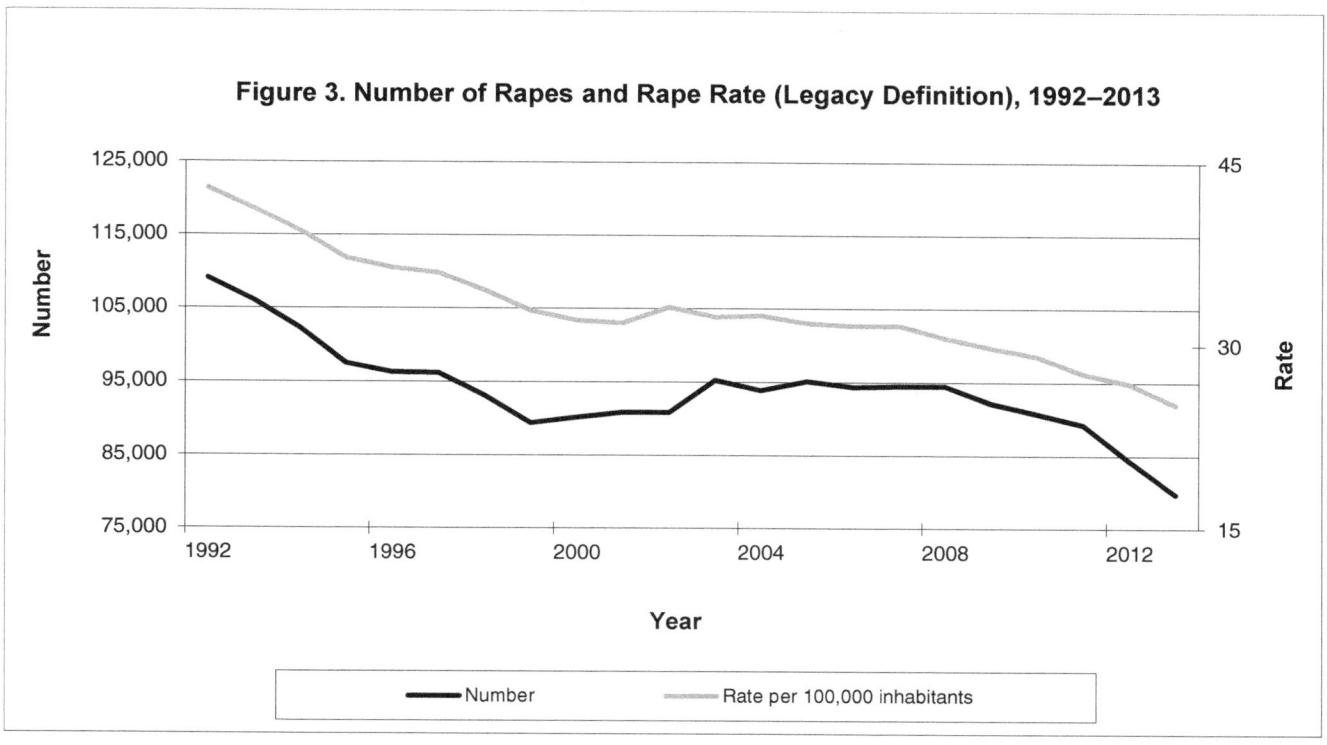

Figure 3. Number of Rapes and Rape Rate (Legacy Definition), 1992–2013

Definition

In 2015, the FBI UCR Program initiated collection of rape data under a revised definition within the Summary Reporting System. Previously, offense data for forcible rape was collected under the legacy UCR definition: the carnal knowledge of a female forcibly and against her will. Beginning with the 2015 data year, the term "forcible" was removed from the offense title, and the definition was changed. The revised UCR definition of rape is: Penetration, no matter how slight, of the vagina or anus with any body part or object, or oral penetration by a sex organ of another person, without the consent of the victim. Attempts or assaults to commit rape are also included; however, statutory rape and incest are excluded. Beginning January 1, 2017, the UCR Program discontinued collecting rape data via the SRS according to the legacy definition. Therefore, the 2016 editions of *CIUS* and *Hate Crime Statistics* are the final publications which include the legacy definition of rape. Only rape data submitted under the revised definition will be published for 2017 and subsequent years. This change did not affect agencies that submit rape data via NIBRS.

All rape data submitted in 2016—whether collected under the revised definition or the legacy definition—are presented in this publication. However, because only two years of rape data have been collected under the revised definition, the overview presented here discusses only legacy definition rape data.

DATA COLLECTION

The UCR Program counts one offense for each victim of a rape, attempted rape, or assault with intent to rape, regardless of the victim's age. Sexual relations without the victim's consent that involves a familial offender are counted as a rape and not an act of incest. All other crimes of a sexual nature are considered to be Part II offenses; as such, the UCR Program collects only arrest data for those crimes. The offense of statutory rape, in which no force is used but the female victim is under the age of consent, is included in the arrest total for the sex offenses category.

National Volume, Trends, and Rates

In 2016, the estimated number of rapes (legacy definition), 95,730, increased 4.9 percent from the 2015 estimate, while the number of rapes (revised definition) was 130,623, a 3.5 percent increase from 2015. The estimated volume of rapes (legacy definition) in 2016 was 4.2 percent higher than in 2012 and 3.0 percent lower than in 2007. For the revised definition, the volume of rapes was 2.8 percent higher than in 2015. (Tables 1 and 1A)

Regional Offense Trends and Rates

The UCR program divides the United States into four regions: the Northeast, the South, the Midwest, and the West. (More details concerning geographic regions are provided in Appendix IV) Regional analysis offers estimates of the volume of rapes, the percent change from the previous year's estimate, and the rate of rape per 100,000 female inhabitants in each region.

NORTHEAST

The Northeast made up 17.4 percent of the U.S. population in 2016. An estimated 16,651 rapes of females (revised definition)—12.7 percent of the national total—occurred in the Northeast. This was an increase of 1.4 percent from the 2015 estimated figure. (Table 2)

MIDWEST

The Midwest accounted for 21.0 percent of the U.S. population in 2016. Of all the rapes (revised definition) in the nation, 24.0 percent occurred in the Midwest in 2016. The 2016 estimate (31,408 rapes) represented an increase of 1.9 percent from the 2015 estimate. (Table 2)

SOUTH

The South, the nation's most populous region, accounted for an estimated 37.9 percent of the nation's population in 2016; the region also accounted for an estimated 37.7 percent of the nation's estimated number of rapes (revised definition). An estimated 49,246 female victims reported rape in the South in 2016, up 4.2 percent from 2015. (Table 2)

WEST

The West accounted for 23.7 percent of the nation's population in 2016. The region also accounted for 25.5 percent of the nation's total number of estimated rapes (revised definition) with an estimated 33,298 offenses. The West saw a 5.3 percent increase in rapes from 2015 to 2016. (Table 2)

Population Groups: Trends and Rates

The UCR program uses the following population group designations in its data presentations: cities (grouped according to population size) and counties (classified as either metropolitan or nonmetropolitan). A breakdown of these classifications is provided in Appendix IV.

From 2015 to 2016, the nation's cities experienced a 3.2 percent increase in rapes (revised definition; see table notes for classification details). Cities with 250,000 to 499,999 inhabitants experienced the greatest increase (7.9 percent). Metropolitan counties experienced a 1.0 percent increase from 2015 to 2016, while nonmetropolitan counties experienced an increase of 1.4 percent. Suburban areas experienced a 1.7 percent increase. (Table 10)

In 2016, cities collectively had a rate of 44.4 rapes (revised definition) per 100,000 inhabitants. Cities with 500,000 to 999,999 inhabitants had the highest rate of rape (62.6 rapes per 100,000 inhabitants). Cities with 10,000 to 24,999 inhabitants had the lowest rate, with 33.7 rapes per 100,000 inhabitants. The rape rate (revised definition) for metropolitan counties was 32.3 per 100,000 inhabitants, and for nonmetropolitan counties, it was 39.1 per 100,000 inhabitants. Suburban areas had a rape rate of 31.5 per 100,000 inhabitants. (Table 11)

ROBBERY

Figure 4. Robberies, by Location and Percent Distribution, 2016

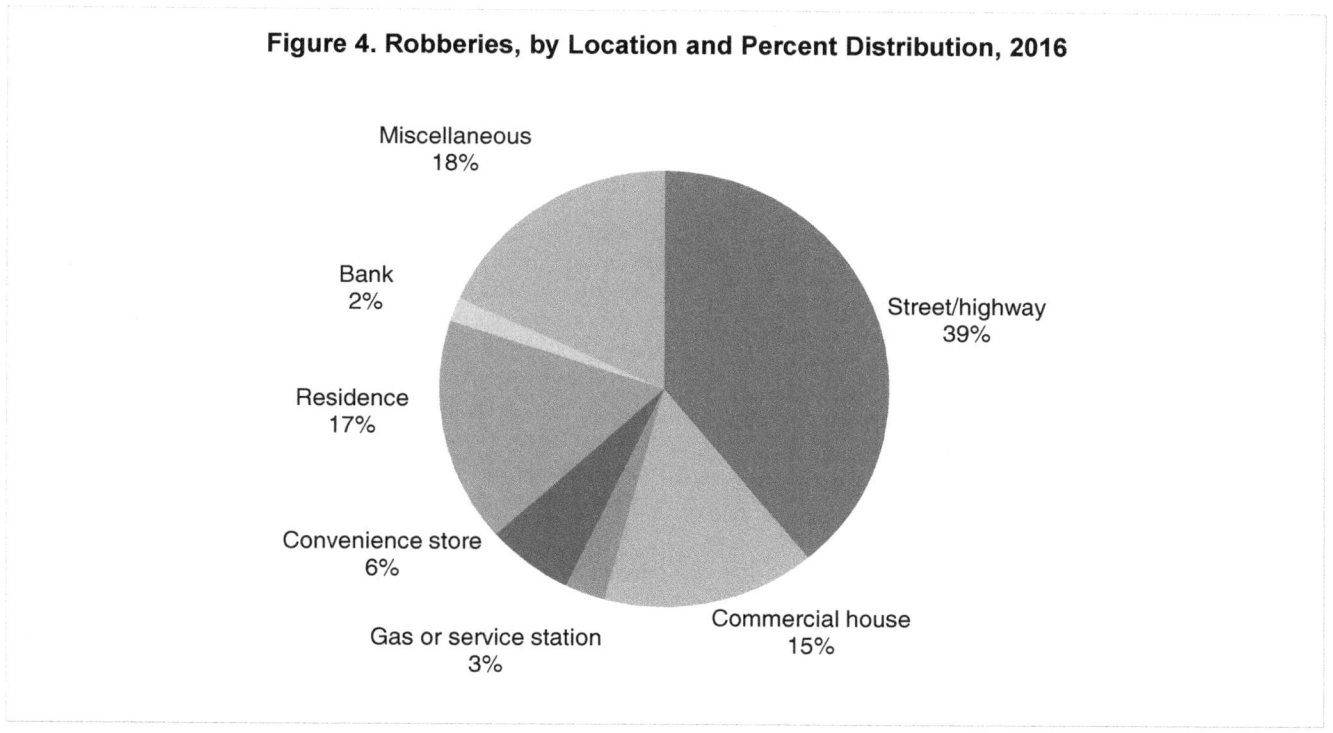

Miscellaneous 18%

Bank 2%

Residence 17%

Convenience store 6%

Gas or service station 3%

Commercial house 15%

Street/highway 39%

Definition

The UCR program defines robbery as the taking or attempt to take anything of value from the care, custody, or control of a person or persons by force or threat of force or violence and/or by putting the victim in fear.

National Volume, Trends, and Rates

In 2016, the estimated robbery total (332,198) increased 1.2 percent from the 2015 estimate. The 5-year robbery trend (2012 data compared with 2016 data) showed a decrease of 6.4 percent. The 2016 estimated robbery rate (102.8 per 100,000 inhabitants) showed an increase of 0.5 percent when compared with the 2015 rate. (Tables 1 and 1A)

Regional Offense Trends and Rates

The UCR program divides the United States into four regions: the Northeast, the South, the Midwest, and the West. (More details concerning geographic regions are provided in Appendix IV.)

NORTHEAST

The Northeast, with an estimated 17.4 percent of the nation's population in 2016, accounted for 16.0 percent of the nation's estimated number of robberies. The estimated number of robberies decreased 5.6 percent

from 2015. The rate for this region was 94.3 robberies per 100,000 inhabitants, down from 100.0 robberies per 100,000 inhabitants in 2015. (Table 2)

MIDWEST

The Midwest accounted for 21.0 percent of the total population of the United States and 19.3 percent of its estimated number of robberies in 2016. An estimated 64,022 robberies occurred in the Midwest in 2016, a 2.9 percent increase from the estimated figure from 2015. The region's robbery rate was 94.2 robberies per 100,000 inhabitants in 2016. (Table 2)

SOUTH

The South, the nation's most highly populated region, accounted for an estimated 37.9 percent of the nation's population and 38.8 percent of the nation's estimated number of robberies in 2016. Robberies accounted for an estimated 128,842 violent crimes in this region in 2016, representing a 1.3 percent increase from the 2015 figure. The 2016 robbery rate in the South was 105.3 per 100,000 inhabitants, up 0.3 percent from 2015. (Table 2)

WEST

The West was home to an estimated 23.7 percent of the nation's population and accounted for 26.0 percent of the nation's estimated number of robberies in 2016. The estimated number of robberies (86,301) in the region in 2016 represented a 4.5 percent increase from the 2015 figure. The rate of robberies per 100,000 inhabitants in the West was 112.6, a 3.4 percent increase from the 2015 rate. (Table 2)

Population Groups: Trends and Rates

The national UCR program aggregates data by various population groups, which include cities, metropolitan counties, and nonmetropolitan counties. A definition of these groups can be found in Appendix IV. The number of robberies in cities as a whole increased by 2.0 percent between 2015 and 2016. Among the population groups labeled *city*, those cities with 1,000,000 or more inhabitants had the greatest increase in the number of robberies (3.4 percent). Nonmetropolitan counties had a 4.9 percent increase in the estimated number of robberies, and metropolitan counties showed a 2.6 percent decrease. The number of robberies in suburban areas rose 0.8 percent. (Table 10)

Among the population groups, the nation's cities collectively had a rate of 136.0 robberies per 100,000 inhabitants. Of the population groups and subsets designated *city*, those with 500,000 to 999,999 inhabitants had the highest rate (277.7 per 100,000 inhabitants), while those with fewer than 10,000 inhabitants had the lowest rate (42.6 per 100,000 inhabitants) of robberies. Of the two county groups, metropolitan counties had a rate of 49.5 robberies per 100,000 inhabitants, while nonmetropolitan counties had a rate of 11.6 robberies per 100,000 inhabitants. Suburban areas had a robbery rate of 52.1 per 100,000 inhabitants. (Table 11)

Offense Analysis

The UCR program collects supplemental data about robberies to document the use of weapons, the dollar loss associated with the offense, and the location types.

ROBBERY BY WEAPON

Firearms were used in 38.1 percent of robberies in 2016. Offenders used knives or cutting instruments in 7.4 percent of these crimes. (Table 19)

LOSS BY DOLLAR VALUE

Based on the supplemental reports from law enforcement agencies, the average loss per robbery was $1,4000. Average dollar losses were the highest for banks, which suffered an average loss of $3,531 per offense. Gas and service stations lost an average of $970 per offense. Commercial houses, which include supermarkets, department stores, and restaurants, had average losses of $1,689 per offense. An average of $1,758 was taken from residences. An average of $732 was lost in each offense against convenience stores. (Table 23)

ROBBERY TRENDS BY LOCATION

Among the location types, street/highway robberies had the only percentage decrease from 2015 to 2016, declining 1.8 percent. Robberies that occurred at convenience stores increased 6.7 percent, while those that occurred at miscellaneous locations increased 5.0 percent. The number of robberies that occurred at commercial houses increased 4.6 percent, while those that occurred at gas or service stations increased 2.1 percent. (Table 23)

By location type, the greatest proportion of robberies in 2016 occurred on streets and highways (38.9 percent). Robbers targeted commercial houses in 15.3 percent of offenses and struck residences in 16.6 percent of offenses. Convenience stores accounted for 6.7 percent of robberies, followed by gas and service stations (6.2 percent) and banks (1.8 percent). (Table 23)

AGGRAVATED ASSAULT

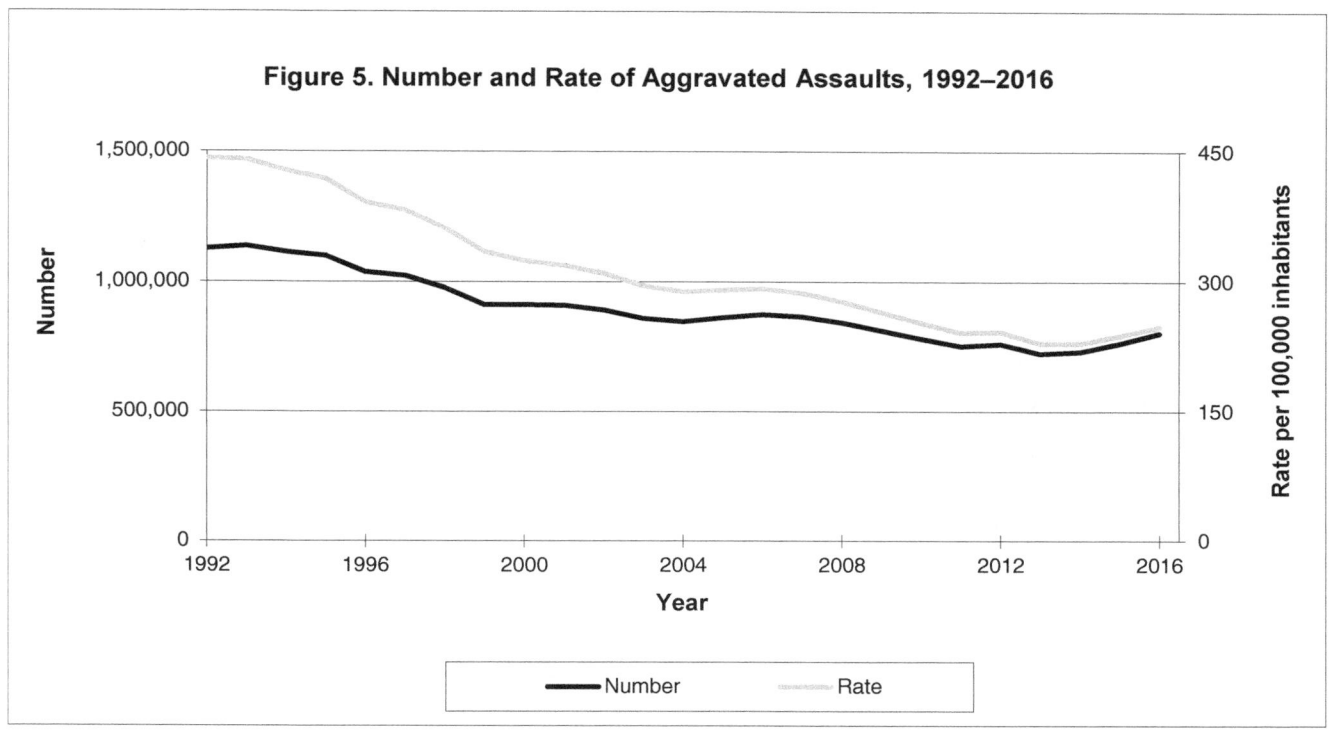

Figure 5. Number and Rate of Aggravated Assaults, 1992–2016

Definition

The UCR program defines aggravated assault as an unlawful attack by one person upon another for the purpose of inflicting severe or aggravated bodily injury. This type of assault is usually accompanied by the use of a weapon or by other means likely to produce death or great bodily harm. Attempted aggravated assaults that involve the display or threat of a gun, knife, or other weapon are included in this crime category because serious personal injury would likely result if these assaults were completed. When aggravated assault and larceny-theft occur together, the offense falls under the category of robbery.

National Volume, Trends, and Rates

In 2016, estimated occurrences of aggravated assaults totaled 803,007, a 5.1 percent increase from the 2015 figure and a 7.3 percent decline when compared with the estimate for 2007. The estimated rate of aggravated assault in 2016 was 248.5 per 100,000 inhabitants, a 13.5 percent decline from 2007. (Tables 1 and 1A)

Among the four types of violent crime offenses (murder, rape, robbery, and aggravated assault), aggravated assault typically has the highest rate of occurrence. This trend continued in 2016. (Table 1)

Regional Offense Trends and Rates

The UCR program divides the United States into four regions: the Northeast, the South, the Midwest, and the West. (More details concerning geographic regions are provided in Appendix IV.)

NORTHEAST

The region with the smallest proportion of the nation's population (an estimated 17.4 percent in 2016) also accounted for the smallest proportion of the nation's estimated number of aggravated assaults (14.0 percent). Occurrences of aggravated assault increased 0.7 percent from 2015 to 2016. The region continued to have the lowest aggravated assault rate in the nation, at 189.7 incidents per 100,000 inhabitants. (Table 2)

MIDWEST

With 21.0 percent of the nation's total population in 2016, the Midwest accounted for approximately 20.7 percent of the nation's estimated number of aggravated assaults. Occurrences of this offense increased 7.8 percent from the estimated total for 2015, rising to an estimated 157,794 incidents. The region's aggravated assault rate, at 232.3 incidents per 100,000 inhabitants, represented a 7.6 percent increase from the 2015 rate. (Table 2)

SOUTH

The South, the nation's most highly populated region, accounted for an estimated 37.9 percent of the nation's population in 2016 and the largest amount of the nation's estimated number of aggravated assaults (44.6 percent). From 2015 to 2016, the estimated number of aggravated assaults increased 4.2 percent to a total of 340,950 incidents. The rate of aggravated assaults increased to 278.7 incidents per 100,000 inhabitants. (Table 2)

WEST

In 2016, the West was home to an estimated 23.7 percent of the nation's population. The region accounted for 25.9 percent of the nation's estimated number of aggravated assaults. From 2015 to 2016, the estimated number of offenses increased 7.2 percent to 197,658 incidents. The rate, estimated at 257.8 offenses per 100,000 inhabitants, represented a 6.0 percent increase from the rate in 2015. (Table 2)

Population Groups: Trends and Rates

From 2015 to 2016, the number of aggravated assaults increased for nearly all cities. Cities with 1,000,000 or more inhabitants experienced the greatest increase (9.5 percent), followed by cities with 500,000 to 999,999

residents (8.7 percent). In metropolitan counties, the number of aggravated assaults rose by 2.8 percent; in nonmetropolitan counties, this number increased by 1.7 percent. Aggravated assaults in suburban areas increased 2.8 percent from 2015 to 2016. (Table 12)

Aggravated assault occurred at an estimated rate of 250.6 offenses per 100,000 inhabitants nationwide. The collective rate for cities was 286.0 aggravated assaults per 100,000 inhabitants. Among city population groups, rates ranged from a high of 510.5 offenses per 100,000 inhabitants (in cities with 500,000 to 999,999 inhabitants) to a low of 180.8 offenses per 100,000 inhabitants (in cities with 25,000 to 49,999 inhabitants). The aggravated assault rate was 183.3 in metropolitan counties and 149.5 in nonmetropolitan counties. It was 170.5 in suburban areas. (Table 11)

Offense Analysis

AGGRAVATED ASSAULT BY WEAPON

Of the aggravated assault offenses for which law enforcement agencies provided expanded data in 2016, 25.8 percent were committed with firearms; 17.6 percent involved knives or other cutting instruments; 31.5 percent involved other weapons, and 25.0 percent involved personal weapons. (Table 19)

PROPERTY CRIME

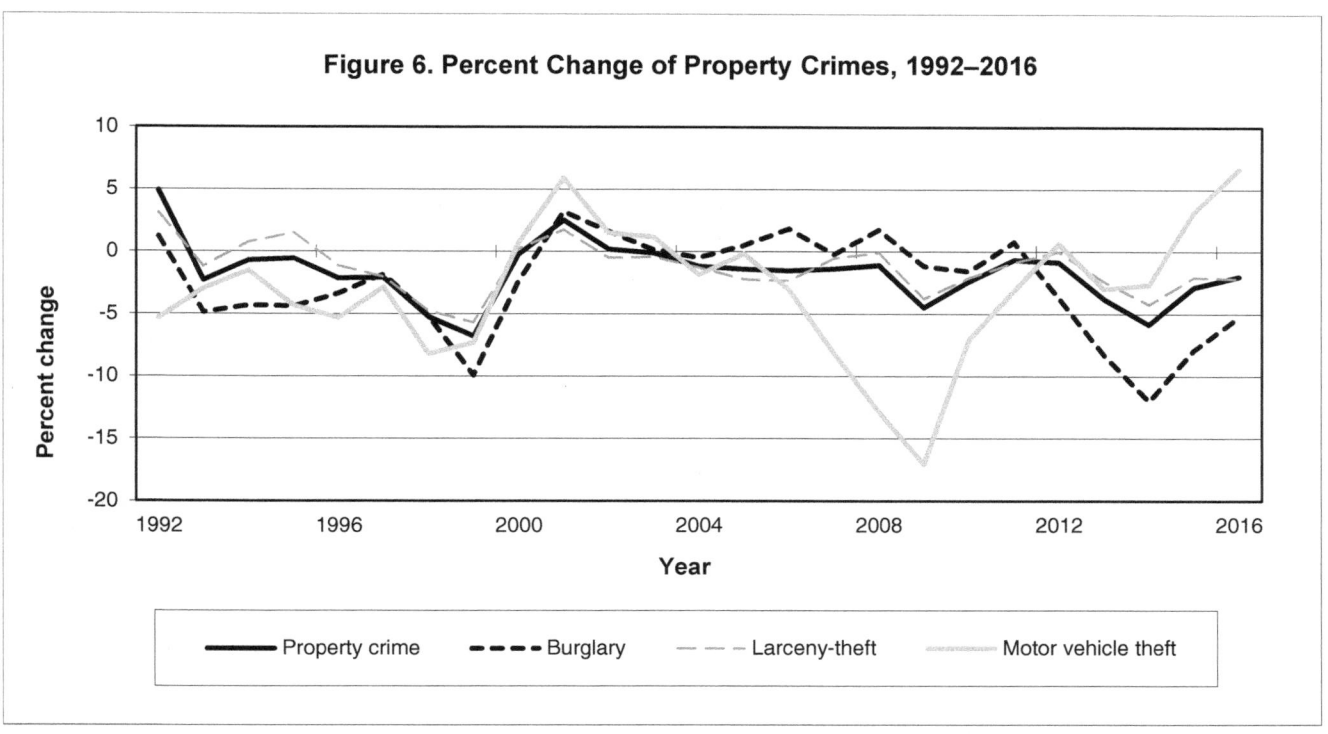

Figure 6. Percent Change of Property Crimes, 1992–2016

Definition

The UCR program's definition of property crime includes the offenses of burglary, larceny-theft, motor vehicle theft, and arson. The object of theft-type offenses is the taking of money or property without the use of force or threat of force against the victims. Property crime includes arson because the offense involves the destruction of property; however, arson victims may be subjected to force. Because of limited participation and the varying collection procedures conducted by local law enforcement agencies, only limited data are available for arson. Arson statistics are included in the trend, clearance, and arrest tables in *Crime in the United States*, but they are not included in any estimated volume data. More information on the expanded arson tables (which are available online but not included in this publication) can be found in Section I.

Data Collection

The data presented in *Crime in the United States* reflect the Hierarchy Rule, which counts only the most serious offense in a multiple-offense criminal incident. In descending order of severity, the violent crimes are murder and nonnegligent manslaughter, rape, robbery, and aggravated assault; these are followed by the property crimes of burglary, larceny-theft, and motor vehicle theft.

The Hierarchy Rule does not apply to the offense of arson.

National Volume, Trends, and Rates

An estimated 7,919,035 property crimes were committed in the United States in 2016, representing a 1.3 percent decrease from the 2015 (2-year trend) estimate, a 12.0 percent decrease from the 2012 (5-year trend) estimate, and a 19.9 percent decrease from the 2007 (10-year trend) estimate. (Tables 1 and 1A)

From 2015 to 2016, motor vehicle theft increased 7.4 percent; from 2007 to 2016, it increased 5.8 percent, and from 2007 to 2016, it decreased 30.4 percent. Larceny-theft decreased 14.5 percent from 2007 to 2016, 8.6 percent from 2012 to 2016, and 1.5 percent from 2015 to 2016. Burglary declined 30.8 percent from 2007, 28.2 percent from 2012, and 4.6 percent from 2015. (Tables 1 and 1A)

The estimated property crime rate per 100,000 inhabitants in 2016 was 2,450.7 incidents per 100,000 people, a 2.0 percent decrease from the 2015 rate, a 14.5 percent decrease from the 2012 rate, and a 25.2 percent decrease from the 2007 rate. The rate of burglaries per 100,000 residents fell 35.4 percent from 2007 to 2016, while the rate for larceny-theft decreased 20.2 percent. The motor vehicle theft rate per 100,000 residents fell 35.1 percent from 2007 to 2016. (Tables 1 and 1A)

Regional Offense Trends and Rates

The UCR program separates the United States into four regions: the Northeast, the Midwest, the South, and the West. (Geographic breakdowns can be found in Appendix IV.) Property crime data collected by the UCR program and aggregated by region reflected the following results.

NORTHEAST

The Northeast region accounted for 17.4 percent of the nation's population in 2016. The region also accounted for 11.5 percent of the nation's estimated number of property crimes in 2016. Law enforcement in the Northeast saw a 4.4 percent decrease in the estimated number of property crimes from 2015 to 2016. The property crime rate for the Northeast, estimated at 1,618.8 incidents per 100,000 inhabitants, was 4.5 percent less than the 2015 rate. (Table 2)

MIDWEST

The Midwest, with 21.0 percent of the U.S. population in 2016, accounted for 19.5 percent of the nation's estimated number of property crimes. Law enforcement in the Midwest saw the number of property crimes decrease 0.7 percent from 2015 to 2016. The rate of property crime in the Midwest in 2016, estimated at 2,273.3 incidents per 100,000 inhabitants, represented a 0.9 percent decrease from the 2015 rate. (Table 2)

SOUTH

The South, the nation's most populous region, accounted for 37.9 percent of the U.S. population in 2016. The region also accounted for an estimated 42.2 percent of the nation's property crimes. The South experienced a 1.4 percent decrease in its estimated number of property crimes from 2015 to 2016. The 2016 property crime rate, an estimated 2,733.7 incidents per 100,000 inhabitants, dropped 2.5 percent from the 2015 rate. (Table 2)

WEST

In 2016, the West accounted for 23.7 percent of the nation's population. The West also accounted for 26.8 percent of the nation's estimated number of property crimes. From 2015 to 2016, the estimated number of property crimes in this region decreased 0.1 percent. The estimated property crime rate in the West in 2016, 2,766.6 incidents per 100,000 inhabitants, was a 1.2 percent decrease from the 2015 rate. (Table 2)

Population Groups: Trends and Rates

The UCR program organizes the agencies that contribute data into population groups, which include cities, metropolitan counties, and nonmetropolitan counties. (Appendix IV provides further details about these groups.) From 2015 to 2016, law enforcement in the nation's cities collectively reported a 1.0 percent decrease in the number of property crimes. Cities with 10,000 or fewer residents had the greatest decline, 3.7 percent. Metropolitan counties also experienced a decrease of 1.9 percent from 2015 to 2016, while property crime in nonmetropolitan counties dropped 5.1 percent. The decrease in suburban areas was 2.1 percent. (Table 10)

The nation's cities collectively had a property crime rate of 2,874.1 incidents per 100,000 inhabitants in 2016. Nonmetropolitan counties had a rate of 1,214.3 incidents per 100,000 inhabitants, and metropolitan counties had a rate of 1,713.9 incidents per 100,000 inhabitants. The rate was 1,933.8 in suburban areas. (Table 11)

Offense Analysis

The estimated dollar loss attributing to property crimes, not including arson, in 2016 was $15.6. Among the individual property crime categories, the dollar losses were an estimated $3.6 billion for burglary, $5.6 billion for larceny-theft, and more than $5.9 billion for motor vehicle theft. In 2016, the average dollar value per motor vehicle stolen in the United States was $7,680. The average dollar value of property taken during burglaries was $2,361, and during larceny-thefts, $999. (Tables 1 and 23)

BURGLARY

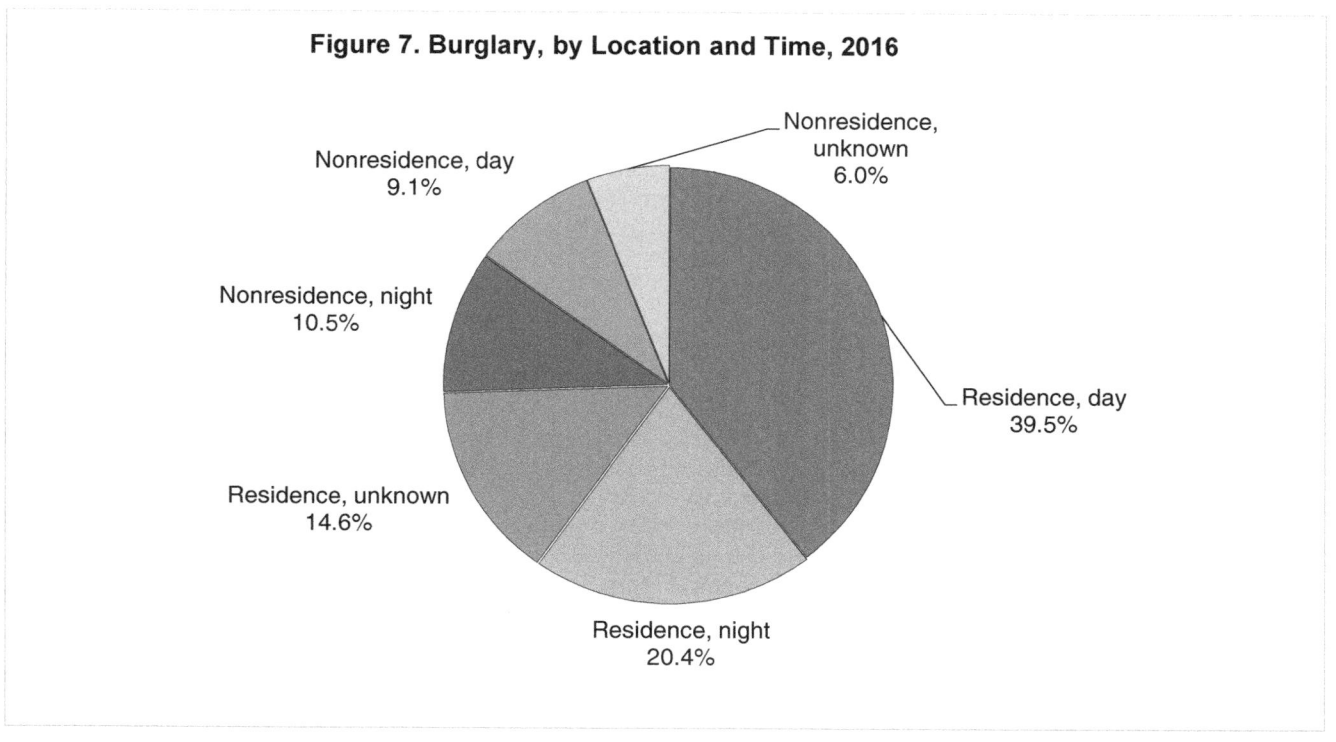

Figure 7. Burglary, by Location and Time, 2016

Nonresidence, day
9.1%

Nonresidence,
unknown
6.0%

Nonresidence, night
10.5%

Residence, day
39.5%

Residence, unknown
14.6%

Residence, night
20.4%

Definition

The UCR program defines burglary as the unlawful entry of a structure to commit a felony or theft. To classify an offense as a burglary, the use of force to gain entry need not have occurred. The program has three subclassifications for burglary: forcible entry, unlawful entry where no force is used, and attempted forcible entry. The UCR definition of "structure" includes, but is not limited to, apartments, barns, house trailers or houseboats (when used as permanent dwellings), offices, railroad cars (but not automobiles), stables, and vessels (such as ships).

National Volume, Trends, and Rate

In 2016, there were an estimated 1,515,096 burglaries—a decrease of 4.8 percent when compared with 2015 data. There was a decrease of 28.2 percent in the number of burglaries in 2016 when compared with the 2012 estimate, and a decrease of 30.8 percent when compared with the 2007 estimate. Burglary accounted for 19.1 percent of the estimated number of property crimes committed in 2016. The burglary rate for the United States in 2016 was 468.9 incidents per 100,000 inhabitants, an 5.2 percent decrease from the 2015 rate. (Tables 1 and 1A)

Regional Offense Trends and Rates

The UCR program divides the United States into four regions: the Northeast, the Midwest, the South, and the

West. (Details regarding these regions can be found in Appendix IV.) An analysis of burglary data by region showed the following details.

NORTHEAST

In 2016, 17.4 percent of the nation's population lived in the Northeast. This region accounted for 9.4 percent of the estimated total number of burglary offenses in the nation in 2016. The region's burglary rate, an estimated 253.9 offenses per 100,000 inhabitants, represented a decrease of 9.7 percent from the 2015 rate. (Table 2)

MIDWEST

The Midwest accounted for 21.0 percent of the nation's population in 2016. This region accounted for 19.8 percent of the nation's estimated number of burglaries. In this region, the estimated number of burglaries dropped 2.4 percent from 2015 to 2016. The Midwest had a burglary rate of 442.1 offenses per 100,000 inhabitants, an 8.3 percent decrease from the 2015 rate. (Table 2)

SOUTH

The South, the nation's most highly populated region (37.9 percent of all inhabitants), had the most burglaries in 2016 (an estimated 684,968); however, this represented a 4.7 percent drop from its estimate in 2015.

With 37.9 percent of the nation's population, this region accounted for 45.2 percent of all burglaries in the United States. The estimated rate of burglary in the South was 560.0 incidents per 100,000 inhabitants, a 5.7 percent decrease from the 2015 rate. (Table 2)

WEST

The West accounted for 23.7 percent of the nation's population in 2016. This region accounted for an estimated 25.5 percent of the nation's burglaries. The region's burglary rate was 504.9, a 4.9 percent increase from the 2015 rate. The total number of burglaries (387,049) represented a 3.9 percent decrease from the 2015 estimate. (Table 2)

Population Groups: Trends and Rates

In addition to analyzing data by region and community type, the UCR program aggregates crime statistics by population groups. Cities are categorized into six groups based on the number of inhabitants; counties are categorized into two groups, metropolitan and nonmetropolitan. (Appendix IV offers further details regarding these population groups.)

An examination of data from law enforcement agencies showed that the nation's cities experienced a collective 4.2 percent decrease in burglaries from 2015 to 2016. Burglaries decreased in all city groups, with cities of 1,000,000 or more inhabitants and cities with 100,000 to 249,999 inhabitants posted the greatest decrease (4.9 percent). The volume of burglaries decreased 5.8 percent in metropolitan counties, 6.5 percent in nonmetropolitan counties, and 5.3 percent in suburban areas. (Table 10)

The UCR program calculates burglary rates for population groups from the information provided by participating agencies that submitted all 12 months of offense data for the year. In 2016, the nation's cities had 503.2 offenses per 100,000 inhabitants. Cities with 500,000 to 999,999 inhabitants had the highest burglary rate at 763.6 incidents per 100,000 inhabitants. Cities with 10,000 to 24,999 inhabitants had the lowest burglary rate—412.0 incidents per 100,000 inhabitants. Metropolitan counties had a rate of 390.4 per 100,000 inhabitants, and nonmetropolitan counties had a rate of 378.7 per 100,000 inhabitants. The rate in suburban areas was 370.5 per 100,000 inhabitants. (Table 11)

Offense Analysis

The UCR program requests that participating law enforcement agencies provide details regarding the nature of burglaries in their jurisdictions, such as type of entry, type of structure, time of day, and dollar loss associated with each offense.

Of all burglaries in 2016, 51.3 percent involved forcible entry, 31.5 percent were unlawful entries (without force), and 5.9 percent comprised forcible entry attempts. (Table 19)

Victims of burglary offenses suffered an estimated $3.6 billion in lost property in 2016; overall, the average dollar loss per burglary offense was $2,316. (Tables 1 and 23)

As in the past, burglars targeted residences more often than nonresidential structures. In 2016, burglaries of residential properties accounted nearly 70 percent of all burglary offenses. Of the burglaries for which time of day could be established, most burglaries of residences (35.9 percent of all reported burglaries) occurred during the day, while most burglaries of nonresidential structures (10.5 percent of all reported burglaries) occurred at night. (Table 23)

LARCENY-THEFT

Figure 8. Larceny-Theft, Percent Distribution, 2016

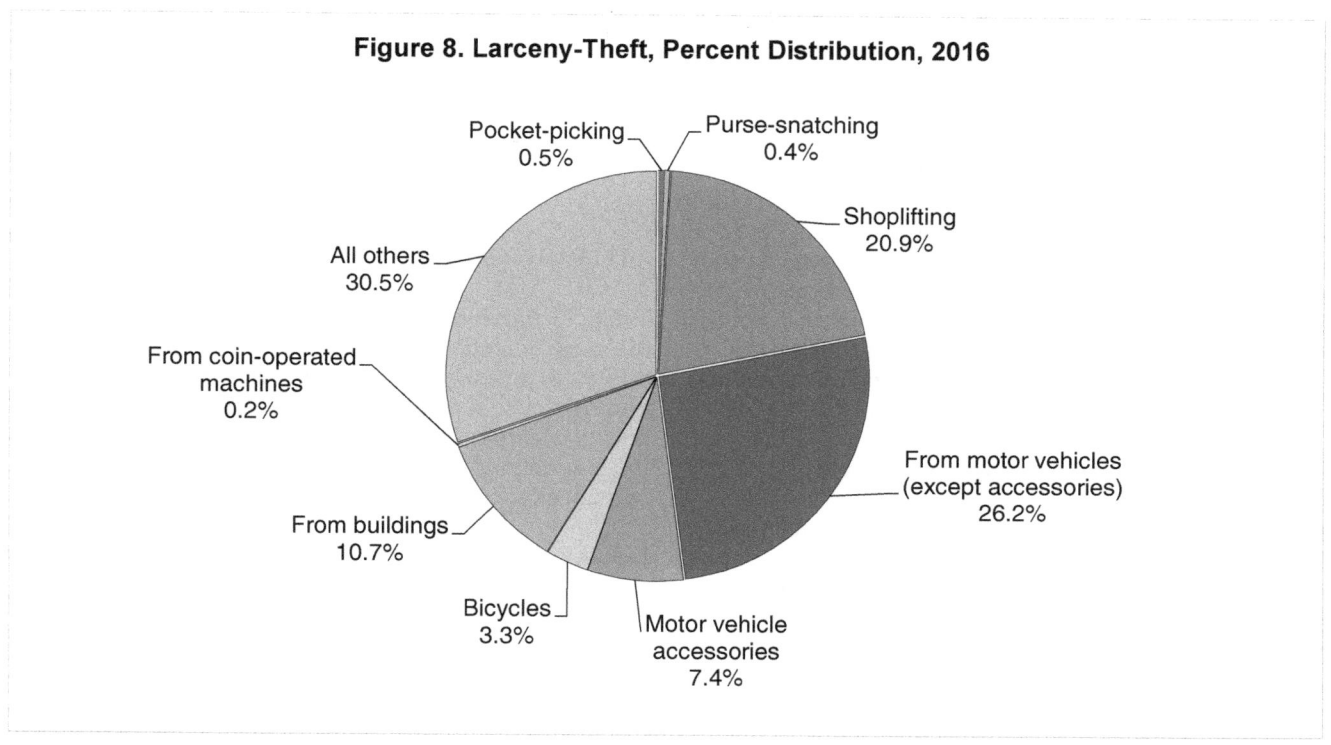

Pocket-picking
0.5%

Purse-snatching
0.4%

Shoplifting
20.9%

All others
30.5%

From coin-operated
machines
0.2%

From motor vehicles
(except accessories)
26.2%

From buildings
10.7%

Bicycles
3.3%

Motor vehicle
accessories
7.4%

Definition

The UCR program defines larceny-theft as the unlawful taking, carrying, leading, or riding away of property from the possession or constructive possession of another. Examples are thefts of bicycles, motor vehicle parts and accessories, shoplifting, pocket picking, or the stealing of any property or article not taken by force and violence or by fraud. Attempted larcenies are included. Embezzlement, confidence games, forgery, check fraud, and so on, are excluded from this category.

National Volume, Trends, and Rates

Larceny-thefts accounted for an estimated 71.2 percent of property crimes in 2016—an estimated 5,638,455 larceny-thefts nationwide. The estimated number of larceny-thefts declined 1.5 from 2015 to 2016. The 2016 estimate showed an 8.6 percent decline compared with the 2007 estimate. The trend data also showed decreases in the larceny-theft rates per 100,000 inhabitants during these periods. The rate of larceny-thefts declined 2.2 percent from 2015 to 2016 and 11.2 percent from 2007 to 2016. (Tables 1 and 1A)

Regional Offense Trends and Rates

The UCR program defines four regions within the United States: the Northeast, the Midwest, the South, and the West. (See Appendix IV for a geographical description of each region.)

NORTHEAST

The Northeast was the region with the smallest proportion (17.4 percent) of the U.S. population in 2016. The region also experienced the fewest larceny-thefts in the country, accounting for only 12.6 percent of all larceny-thefts. The estimated number of offenses in 2016 (709,721) represented a 3.7 percent decline from 2015, and the estimated rate—1,262.6 incidents per 100,000 inhabitants— represented a 3.8 percent decline. (Table 2)

MIDWEST

With 21.0 percent of the U.S. population in 2016, the Midwest accounted for an estimated 19.7 percent of the nation's larceny-thefts. The estimated number of offenses (1,112,596) declined 1.2 percent compared with the 2015 data, and the estimated rate of occurrences (1,637.6 incidents per 100,000 inhabitants) declined 1.3 percent. (Table 2)

SOUTH

With more than one-third of the U.S. population in 2016 (37.9 percent), the South had the nation's highest proportion of larceny-theft offenses: an estimated 42.4 percent.

(Estimated offenses in this region totaled 2,391,288, a 1.3 percent decrease from the 2015 estimate. The South's larceny-theft rate—estimated at 1,955.0 offenses per 100,000 inhabitants—decreased 2.3 percent from the 2015 estimate. (Table 2)

WEST

In 2016, an estimated 23.7 percent of the U.S. population lived in the West. This region was also where 25.3 percent of the nation's estimated number of larceny-thefts took place. Occurrences of larceny-theft decreased 0.9 percent from 2015 to 2016 to an estimated total of 1,424,850 offenses. The region's larceny-theft rate, estimated at 1,858.7 offenses per 100,000 inhabitants, represented a decrease of 2.0 percent from the 2015 rate. (Table 2)

Population Groups: Trends and Rates

In cities, collectively, occurrences of larceny-theft decreased 1.3 percent between 2015 and 2016. Cities with under 10,000 inhabitants experienced the greatest decrease (4.3 percent). Larceny-theft continued to show decline in counties and suburban areas—nonmetropolitan counties experienced the greatest drop in larceny thefts, decreasing 4.8 percent, followed by suburban areas (2.2 percent) and metropolitan counties (1.7 percent),. Some city groups experienced increases, with cities with 1,000,000 or more inhabitants showing the greatest increase, 3.0 percent. (Table 10)

Based on reports of larceny-theft offenses from U.S. law enforcement agencies that submitted 12 months of complete data for 2016, this offense occurred at a rate of 1,756.3 offenses per 100,000 inhabitants. The collective rate for cities was 2,084.1 offenses per 100,000 inhabitants. Among city population groups, cities with 500,000 to 999,000 inhabitants had the highest larceny-theft rate, 2,907.0 incidents per 100,000 inhabitants. Cities with 10,000 to 24,999 inhabitants had the lowest rate, at 1,833.5. In metropolitan counties, the rate was 1,159.9 incidents per 100,000 inhabitants; in nonmetropolitan counties, the rate was 736.2 incidents per 100,000 inhabitants. The rate in suburban areas was 1,406.7 incidents per 100,000 inhabitants. (Table 11)

Offense Analysis

DISTRIBUTION

Table 23 provides a further breakdown of larceny-theft offenses, including shoplifting, thefts from buildings, thefts of motor vehicle accessories, thefts of bicycles, thefts from coin-operated machines, purse snatching, and pocket picking. The "all other" category, which includes the less-defined types of larceny-theft, accounted for 30.3 percent of all offenses in 2016.

LOSS BY DOLLAR VALUE

Larceny-theft offenses cost victims an estimated $5.6 billion dollars in 2016. The average value of property stolen was $999 per offense, $70 more than in 2015. Larceny-theft from buildings had the highest average dollar loss per offense at $1,649. Thefts from motor vehicles (except accessories) had an average dollar loss of $869 per offense; thefts of motor vehicle accessories, $541; purse snatching, $475; pocket picking, $646; thefts from coin-operated machines, $607; thefts of bicycles, $482; and shoplifting, $250. (Tables 1 and 23)

Offenses in which the stolen property was valued at more than $200 accounted for 45.47 percent of all larceny-thefts in 2016, down 0.3 percent from 2015. Table 23 provides further analysis, including the average dollar value per offense of all offenses in the overall category of property crime. (Table 23)

MOTOR VEHICLE THEFT

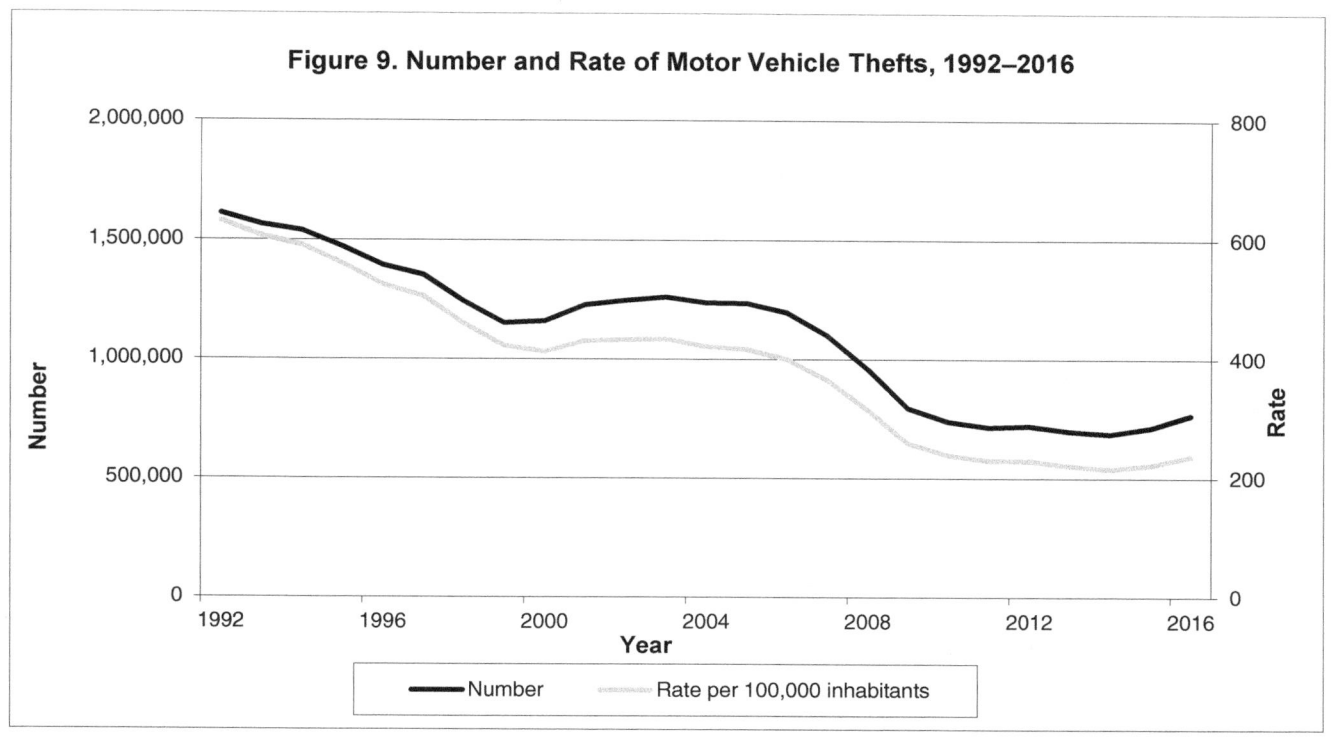

Figure 9. Number and Rate of Motor Vehicle Thefts, 1992–2016

Definition

The UCR program defines motor vehicle theft as the theft or attempted theft of a motor vehicle. The offense includes the stealing of automobiles, trucks, buses, motorcycles, snowmobiles, etc. The taking of a motor vehicle for temporary use by a person or persons with lawful access is excluded.

National Volume, Trends, and Rates

In 2016, an estimated 765,484 motor vehicle thefts took place in the United States. The estimated number of motor vehicle thefts increased 7.4 percent when compared with data from 2015, increased 5.8 percent when compared with 2012 figures, and decreased 30.4 percent when compared with 2007 figures. (Tables1 and 1A)

The estimated rate of motor vehicle theft in 2016 was 236.9 incidents per 100,000 inhabitants. The 2016 rate was 6.6 percent higher than the 2015 rate and 2.8 percent higher than the 2012 rate. The rate decreased 35.1 percent from 2007 to 2016. (Tables 1 and 1A)

Regional Offense Trends and Rates

In order to analyze crime by geographic area, the UCR program divides the United States into four regions:

the Northeast, the Midwest, the South, and the West. (Appendix IV provides a map delineating the regions.) This section provides a regional overview of motor vehicle theft.

NORTHEAST

The Northeast accounted for an estimated 17.4 percent of the nation's population in 2016. The region also accounted for an estimated 7.5 percent of its motor vehicle thefts. An estimated 57,456 motor vehicle thefts occurred in the Northeast in 2016, a 0.9 percent increase in occurrences from 2015. The estimated rate of 102.2 motor vehicle thefts per 100,000 inhabitants in the Northeast in 2016 represented a 0.9 percent increase from the 2015 rate. (Table 2)

MIDWEST

An estimated 21.0 percent of the country's population resided in the Midwest in 2016. The region accounted for 17.2 percent of the nation's motor vehicle thefts. The Midwest had an estimated 131,576 motor vehicle thefts in 2016, an increase of 8.1 percent from the previous year's total. The motor vehicle theft rate was estimated at 193.7 motor vehicles stolen per 100,000 inhabitants, an increase of 7.9 percent from the 2015 rate. (Table 2)

SOUTH

The South, the nation's most populous region, was home to an estimated 37.9 percent of the U.S. population in 2016 and accounted for 35.0 percent of the nation's motor vehicle thefts. The estimated 267,543 motor vehicle thefts in the South was up 6.2 percent from the 2015 estimate. Motor vehicles in the South were stolen at an estimated rate of 218.7 offenses per 100,000 inhabitants in 2016, a rate that was 5.1 percent higher than the 2015 rate. (Table 2)

WEST

With approximately 23.7 percent of the U.S. population in 2016, the West accounted for the highest percentage (40.4 percent) of all motor vehicle thefts in the nation in 2016. An estimated 308,909 motor vehicle thefts occurred in this region, the most in the nation. This number represented a 9.3 percent increase from the previous year's estimate. The region's 2016 rate of 403.0 motor vehicles stolen per 100,000 inhabitants was 8.2 percent higher than the 2015 rate. (Table 2)

Population Groups: Trends and Rates

The UCR program aggregates data by various population groups, which include cities, metropolitan counties, and nonmetropolitan counties. (A definition of these groups can be found in Appendix IV.)

In cities, collectively, the number of motor vehicle thefts increased 1.9 percent from 2015 to 2016. The number of motor vehicle thefts increased in roughly half of all city groups. Cities with fewer than 10,000 residents experienced the greatest rise at 10.0 percent. Nonmetropolitan counties experienced a decrease of 1.6 percent, metropolitan counties experienced an increase of 7.1 percent, and suburban areas experienced a rise of 7.7 percent. (Table 10)

In 2016, cities had a collective motor vehicle theft rate of 286.8 per 100,000 inhabitants. Among the population groups, cities with 500,000 to 999,999 inhabitants experienced the highest rate of motor vehicle thefts with 533.9 motor vehicle thefts per 100,000 inhabitants. Conversely, the nation's smallest cities, those with populations under 10,000, had the lowest rate of motor vehicle theft with 137.2 incidents per 100,000 in population. Within the county groups, metropolitan counties had a rate of 163.7 motor vehicles stolen per 100,000 inhabitants, while nonmetropolitan counties had a rate of 99.4 incidents per 100,000 inhabitants. Suburban areas had a rate of 156.5 per 100,000 inhabitants. (Table 11)

Offense Analysis

Based on the reports of law enforcement agencies, the UCR program estimated the combined value of motor vehicles stolen nationwide in 2016 at approximately $5.9 billion. In 2016, the average dollar value per motor vehicle stolen in the United States was $7,680. (Tables 1 and 23)

ARSON

Definition

The UCR program defines arson as any willful or malicious burning or attempt to burn (with or without intent to defraud) a dwelling house, public building, motor vehicle, aircraft, or personal property of another, etc.

Data Collection

Only fires that investigators determined were willfully set (not fires labeled as "suspicious" or "of unknown origin") are included in this arson data collection. Points to consider regarding arson statistics include:

National offense rates per 100,000 inhabitants do not include arson data; the FBI presents rates for arson separately. Arson rates are calculated based upon data received from all law enforcement agencies that provide the UCR program with data for 12 complete months.

Population Groups: Trends and Rates

The number of arsons reported in cities 2016 was 1.9 percent higher than the number reported in 2015. Among the population groups labeled *city,* the subset with 1,000,000 or more inhabitants reported the largest increases (7.8 percent). Agencies in the nation's metropolitan counties reported a 4.5 percent increase in the number of arsons, while those in nonmetropolitan counties reported a 1.7 percent increase from 2015 to 2016. Those in suburban areas reported a 5.5 percent increase. (Table 10)

Table 1. Crime in the United States, by Volume and Rate Per 100,000 Inhabitants, 1996–2016

(Number, rate per 100,000 population.)

Year	Population[1]	Violent crime[2]		Murder and nonnegligent manslaughter		Rape (revised definition)[3]		Rape (legacy definition)[4]		Robbery		Aggravated assault	
		Number	Rate	Number	Rate	Number	Rate	Number	Rate	Number	Rate	Number	Rate
1996	265,228,572	1,688,540	636.6	19,645	7.4	X	X	96,252	36.3	535,594	201.9	1,037,049	391.0
1997	267,783,607	1,636,096	611.0	18,208	6.8	X	X	96,153	35.9	498,534	186.2	1,023,201	382.1
1998	270,248,003	1,533,887	567.6	16,974	6.3	X	X	93,144	34.5	447,186	165.5	976,583	361.4
1999	272,690,813	1,426,044	523.0	15,522	5.7	X	X	89,411	32.8	409,371	150.1	911,740	334.3
2000	281,421,906	1,425,486	506.5	15,586	5.5	X	X	90,178	32.0	408,016	145.0	911,706	324.0
2001 [5]	285,317,559	1,439,480	504.5	16,037	5.6	X	X	90,863	31.8	423,557	148.5	909,023	318.6
2002	287,973,924	1,423,677	494.4	16,229	5.6	X	X	95,235	33.1	420,806	146.1	891,407	309.5
2003	290,788,976	1,383,676	475.8	16,528	5.7	X	X	93,883	32.3	414,235	142.5	859,030	295.4
2004	293,656,842	1,360,088	463.2	16,148	5.5	X	X	95,089	32.4	401,470	136.7	847,381	288.6
2005	296,507,061	1,390,745	469.0	16,740	5.6	X	X	94,347	31.8	417,438	140.8	862,220	290.8
2006	299,398,484	1,435,123	479.3	17,309	5.8	X	X	94,472	31.6	449,246	150.0	874,096	292.0
2007	301,621,157	1,422,970	471.8	17,128	5.7	X	X	92,160	30.6	447,324	148.3	866,358	287.2
2008	304,059,724	1,394,461	458.6	16,465	5.4	X	X	90,750	29.8	443,563	145.9	843,683	277.5
2009	307,006,550	1,325,896	431.9	15,399	5.0	X	X	89,241	29.1	408,742	133.1	812,514	264.7
2010	309,330,219	1,251,248	404.5	14,722	4.8	X	X	85,593	27.7	369,089	119.3	781,844	252.8
2011	311,587,816	1,206,005	387.1	14,661	4.7	X	X	84,175	27.0	354,746	113.9	752,423	241.5
2012	313,873,685	1,217,057	387.8	14,856	4.7	X	X	85,141	27.1	355,051	113.1	762,009	242.8
2013	316,497,531	1,168,298	369.1	14,319	4.5	113,695	35.9	82,109	25.9	345,093	109.0	726,777	229.6
2014	318,907,401	1,153,022	361.6	14,164	4.4	118,027	37.0	84,864	26.6	322,905	101.3	731,089	229.2
2015 [6]	320,896,618	1,199,310	373.7	15,883	4.9	126,134	39.3	91,261	28.4	328,109	102.2	764,057	238.1
2016	323,127,513	1,248,185	386.3	17,250	5.3	130,623	40.4	95,730	29.6	332,198	102.8	803,007	248.5

Table 1. Crime in the United States, by Volume and Rate Per 100,000 Inhabitants, 1996–2016—Continued

(Number, rate per 100,000 population.)

Year	Property crime		Burglary		Larceny-theft		Motor vehicle theft	
	Number	Rate	Number	Rate	Number	Rate	Number	Rate
1996	11,805,323	4,451.0	2,506,400	945.0	7,904,685	2,980.3	1,394,238	525.7
1997	11,558,475	4,316.3	2,460,526	918.8	7,743,760	2,891.8	1,354,189	505.7
1998	10,951,827	4,052.5	2,332,735	863.2	7,376,311	2,729.5	1,242,781	459.9
1999	10,208,334	3,743.6	2,100,739	770.4	6,955,520	2,550.7	1,152,075	422.5
2000	10,182,584	3,618.3	2,050,992	728.8	6,971,590	2,477.3	1,160,002	412.2
2001 [5]	10,437,189	3,658.1	2,116,531	741.8	7,092,267	2,485.7	1,228,391	430.5
2002	10,455,277	3,630.6	2,151,252	747.0	7,057,379	2,450.7	1,246,646	432.9
2003	10,442,862	3,591.2	2,154,834	741.0	7,026,802	2,416.5	1,261,226	433.7
2004	10,319,386	3,514.1	2,144,446	730.3	6,937,089	2,362.3	1,237,851	421.5
2005	10,174,754	3,431.5	2,155,448	726.9	6,783,447	2,287.8	1,235,859	416.8
2006	10,019,601	3,346.6	2,194,993	733.1	6,626,363	2,213.2	1,198,245	400.2
2007	9,882,212	3,276.4	2,190,198	726.1	6,591,542	2,185.4	1,100,472	364.9
2008	9,774,152	3,214.6	2,228,887	733.0	6,586,206	2,166.1	959,059	315.4
2009	9,337,060	3,041.3	2,203,313	717.7	6,338,095	2,064.5	795,652	259.2
2010	9,112,625	2,945.9	2,168,459	701.0	6,204,601	2,005.8	739,565	239.1
2011	9,052,743	2,905.4	2,185,140	701.3	6,151,095	1,974.1	716,508	230.0
2012	9,001,992	2,868.0	2,109,932	672.2	6,168,874	1,965.4	723,186	230.4
2013	8,651,892	2,733.6	1,932,139	610.5	6,019,465	1,901.9	700,288	221.3
2014	8,209,010	2,574.1	1,713,153	537.2	5,809,054	1,821.5	686,803	215.4
2015 [6]	8,024,115	2,500.5	1,587,564	494.7	5,723,488	1,783.6	713,063	222.2
2015	7,919,035	2,450.7	1,515,096	468.9	5,638,455	1,745.0	765,484	236.9

Note: Although arson data are included in the trend and clearance tables, sufficient data are not available to estimate totals for this offense. Therefore, no arson data are published in this table.
X = Not applicable. 1 Populations are U.S. Census Bureau provisional estimates as of July 1 for each year except 2000 and 2010, which are decennial census counts.   2 The violent crime figures include the offenses of murder, rape (legacy definition), robbery, and aggravated assault.   3 The figures shown in this column for the offense of rape were estimated using the revised UCR definition of rape.   4 The figures shown in this column for the offense of rape were estimated using the legacy UCR definition of rape.   5 The murder and nonnegligent homicides that occurred as a result of the events of September 11, 2001, are not included in this table.   6 The crime figures have been adjusted.

Table 1A. Crime in the United States, Percent Change in Volume and Rate Per 100,000 Inhabitants for 2 Years, 5 Years, and 10 Years, 2007–2016

(Percent change.)

Year	Violent crime[1]		Murder and nonnegligent manslaughter		Rape (revised definition)[2]		Rape (legacy definition)[3]		Robbery		Aggravated assault		Property crime		Burglary		Larceny-theft		Motor vehicle theft	
	Number	Rate	Number	Rate	Number	Rate	Number	Rate	Number	Rate	Number	Rate	Number	Rate	Number	Rate	Number	Rate	Number	Rate
2007–2016	-12.3	-18.1	+0.7	-6.0	X	X	+3.9	-3.0	-25.7	-30.7	-7.3	-13.5	-19.9	-25.2	-30.8	-35.4	-14.5	-20.2	-30.4	-35.1
2012–2016	+2.6	-0.4	+16.1	+12.8	X	X	+12.4	+9.2	-6.4	-9.1	+5.4	+2.4	-12.0	-14.5	-28.2	-30.2	-8.6	-11.2	+5.8	+2.8
2015–2016	+4.1	+3.4	+8.6	+7.9	+3.5	+2.8	+4.9	+4.2	+1.2	+0.5	+5.1	+4.4	-1.3	-2.0	-4.6	-5.2	-1.5	-2.2	+7.4	+6.6

X = Not applicable.   1 The violent crime figures include the offenses of murder, rape (legacy definition), robbery, and aggravated assault.   2 The figures shown in this column for the offense of rape were estimated using the revised UCR definition of rape.   3 The figures shown in this column for the offense of rape were estimated using the legacy UCR definition of rape.

Table 2. Crime,[1] by Region, Geographic Division, and State, 2015–2016

(Number, rate per 100,000 population, percent.)

Area	Population[2]	Violent crime[3]		Murder and nonnegligent manslaughter		Rape (revised definition)[4]		Rape (legacy definition)[5]		Robbery	
		Number	Rate	Number	Rate	Number	Rate	Number	Rate	Number	Rate
United States[6,7,8,9]											
2015	320,896,618	1,234,183	384.6	15,883	4.9	126,134	39.3	91,261	28.4	328,109	102.2
2016	323,127,513	1,283,058	397.1	17,250	5.3	130,603	40.4	95,730	29.6	332,198	102.8
Percent change		+4.0	+3.2	+8.6	+7.9	+3.5	+2.8	+4.9	+4.2	+1.2	+0.5
Northeast[6]											
2015	56,184,737	180,474	321.2	1,967	3.5	16,415	29.2	11,912	21.2	56,202	100.0
2016	56,209,510	178,244	317.1	1,955	3.5	16,651	29.6	12,219	21.7	53,033	94.3
Percent change		-1.2	-1.3	-0.6	-0.7	+1.4	+1.4	+2.6	+2.5	-5.6	-5.7
New England[6]											
2015	14,710,229	42,121	286.3	326	2.2	4,602	31.3	3,374	22.9	9,629	65.5
2016	14,735,525	41,598	282.3	292	2.0	4,505	30.6	3,328	22.6	9,407	63.8
Percent change		-1.2	-1.4	-10.4	-10.6	-2.1	-2.3	-1.4	-1.5	-2.3	-2.5
Connecticut											
2015	3,584,730	7,938	221.4	116	3.2	798	22.3	585	16.3	2,925	81.6
2016	3,576,452	8,123	227.1	78	2.2	763	21.3	561	15.7	2,703	75.6
Percent change		+2.3	+2.6	-32.8	-32.6	-4.4	-4.2	-4.1	-3.9	-7.6	-7.4
Maine											
2015	1,329,453	1,726	129.8	23	1.7	461	34.7	337	25.3	311	23.4
2016	1,331,479	1,648	123.8	20	1.5	412	30.9	300	22.5	266	20.0
Percent change		-4.5	-4.7	-13.0	-13.2	-10.6	-10.8	-11.0	-11.1	-14.5	-14.6
Massachusetts											
2015	6,784,240	26,453	389.9	131	1.9	2,082	30.7	1,538	22.7	5,266	77.6
2016	6,811,779	25,677	376.9	134	2.0	2,128	31.2	1,592	23.4	5,365	78.8
Percent change		-2.9	-3.3	+2.3	+1.9	+2.2	+1.8	+3.5	+3.1	+1.9	+1.5
New Hampshire											
2015	1,330,111	2,692	202.4	15	1.1	644	48.4	468	35.2	475	35.7
2016	1,334,795	2,637	197.6	17	1.3	582	43.6	423	31.7	427	32.0
Percent change		-2.0	-2.4	+13.3	+12.9	-9.6	-9.9	-9.6	-9.9	-10.1	-10.4
Rhode Island[6]											
2015	1,055,607	2,565	243.0	31	2.9	467	44.2	342	32.4	547	51.8
2016	1,056,426	2,524	238.9	29	2.7	442	41.8	328	31.0	540	51.1
Percent change		-1.6	-1.7	-6.5	-6.5	-5.4	-5.4	-4.1	-4.2	-1.3	-1.4
Vermont											
2015	626,088	747	119.3	10	1.6	150	24.0	104	16.6	105	16.8
2016	624,594	989	158.3	14	2.2	178	28.5	124	19.9	106	17.0
Percent change		+32.4	+32.7	+40.0	+40.3	18.7	+19.0	+19.2	+19.5	+1.0	+1.2
Middle Atlantic[6]											
2015	41,474,508	138,353	333.6	1,641	4.0	11,813	28.5	8,538	20.6	46,573	112.3
2016	41,473,985	136,646	329.5	1,663	4.0	12,146	29.3	8,891	21.4	43,626	105.2
Percent change		-1.2	-1.2	+1.3	+1.3	+2.8	+2.8	+4.1	+4.1	-6.3	-6.3
New Jersey											
2015	8,935,421	22,879	256.0	363	4.1	1,373	15.4	1,019	11.4	9,729	108.9
2016	8,944,469	21,914	245.0	372	4.2	1,453	16.2	1,089	12.2	8,984	100.4
Percent change		-4.2	-4.3	+2.5	+2.4	+5.8	+5.7	+6.9	+6.8	-7.7	-7.8
New York[6]											
2015	19,747,183	75,126	380.4	613	3.1	6,141	31.1	4,414	22.4	23,879	120.9
2016	19,745,289	74,285	376.2	630	3.2	6,260	31.7	4,569	23.1	22,316	113.0
Percent change		-1.1	-1.1	+2.8	+2.8	+1.9	+1.9	+3.5	+3.5	-6.5	-6.5
Pennsylvania											
2015	12,791,904	40,348	315.4	665	5.2	4,299	33.6	3,105	24.3	12,965	101.4
2016	12,784,227	40,447	316.4	661	5.2	4,433	34.7	3,233	25.3	12,326	96.4
Percent change		+0.2	+0.3	-0.6	-0.5	+3.1	+3.2	+4.1	+4.2	-4.9	-4.9
Midwest[6]											
2015	67,838,387	242,893	358.0	3,422	5.0	30,827	45.4	22,395	33.0	62,201	91.7
2016	67,941,429	257,109	378.4	3,885	5.7	31,408	46.2	23,080	34.0	64,022	94.2
Percent change		+5.9	+5.7	+13.5	+13.4	+1.9	+1.7	+3.1	+2.9	+2.9	+2.8
East North Central[6]											
2015	46,742,511	168,762	361.0	2,471	5.3	21,268	45.5	15,455	33.1	47,806	102.3
2016	46,755,973	180,827	386.7	2,974	6.4	22,102	47.3	16,199	34.6	49,506	105.9
Percent change		+7.1	+7.1	+20.4	+20.3	+3.9	+3.9	+4.8	+4.8	+3.6	+3.5
Illinois											
2015	12,839,047	49,755	387.5	754	5.9	4,926	38.4	3,602	28.1	15,056	117.3
2016	12,801,539	55,854	436.3	1,054	8.2	4,908	38.3	3,635	28.4	17,827	139.3
Percent change		+12.3	+12.6	+39.8	+40.2	-0.4	-0.1	+0.9	+1.2	+18.4	+18.8
Indiana[6]											
2015	6,612,768	25,373	383.7	370	5.6	2,386	36.1	1,757	26.6	7,081	107.1
2016	6,633,053	26,845	404.7	439	6.6	2,501	37.7	1,851	27.9	7,330	110.5
Percent change		+5.8	+5.5	+18.6	+18.3	+4.8	+4.5	+5.4	+5.0	+3.5	+3.2
Michigan											
2015	9,917,715	41,712	420.6	585	5.9	6,710	67.7	4,782	48.2	7,818	78.8
2016	9,928,300	45,572	459.0	598	6.0	7,125	71.8	5,114	51.5	7,120	71.7
Percent change		+9.3	+9.1	+2.2	+2.1	+6.2	+6.1	+6.9	+6.8	-8.9	-9.0
Ohio[6]											
2015	11,605,090	34,373	296.2	522	4.5	5,441	46.9	3,990	34.4	12,617	108.7
2016	11,614,373	34,877	300.3	654	5.6	5,589	48.1	4,141	35.7	12,523	107.8
Percent change		+1.5	+1.4	+25.3	+25.2	+2.7	+2.6	+3.8	+3.7	-0.7	-0.8

Table 2. Crime,[1] by Region, Geographic Division, and State, 2015–2016—Continued

(Number, rate per 100,000 population, percent.)

Area	Aggravated assault		Property crime		Burglary		Larceny-theft		Motor vehicle theft	
	Number	Rate	Number	Rate	Number	Rate	Number	Rate	Number	Rate
United States[6,7,8,9]										
2015	764,057	238.1	8,024,115	2,500.5	1,587,564	494.7	5,723,488	1,783.6	713,063	222.2
2016	803,007	248.5	7,919,035	2,450.7	1,515,096	468.9	5,638,455	1,745.0	765,484	236.9
Percent change	+5.1	+4.4	-1.3	-2.0	-4.6	-5.2	-1.5	-2.2	+7.4	+6.6
Northeast[6]										
2015	105,890	188.5	951,940	1,694.3	157,910	281.1	737,087	1,311.9	56,943	101.3
2016	106,605	189.7	909,897	1,618.8	142,720	253.9	709,721	1,262.6	57,456	102.2
Percent change	+0.7	+0.6	-4.4	-4.5	-9.6	-9.7	-3.7	-3.8	+0.9	+0.9
New England[6]										
2015	27,564	187.4	257,073	1,747.6	46,260	314.5	193,051	1,312.4	17,762	120.7
2016	27,394	185.9	243,769	1,654.3	42,095	285.7	182,985	1,241.8	18,689	126.8
Percent change	-0.6	-0.8	-5.2	-5.3	-9.0	-9.2	-5.2	-5.4	+5.2	+5.0
Connecticut										
2015	4,099	114.3	65,610	1,830.3	10,286	286.9	48,898	1,364.1	6,426	179.3
2016	4,579	128.0	64,664	1,808.0	10,045	280.9	47,512	1,328.5	7,107	198.7
Percent change	+11.7	+12.0	-1.4	-1.2	-2.3	-2.1	-2.8	-2.6	+10.6	+10.9
Maine										
2015	931	70.0	24,361	1,832.4	4,694	353.1	18,853	1,418.1	814	61.2
2016	950	71.3	21,912	1,645.7	4,003	300.6	17,134	1,286.8	775	58.2
Percent change	+2.0	+1.9	-10.1	-10.2	-14.7	-14.9	-9.1	-9.3	-4.8	-4.9
Massachusetts										
2015	18,974	279.7	114,547	1,688.4	21,826	321.7	84,676	1,248.1	8,045	118.6
2016	18,050	265.0	106,339	1,561.1	19,193	281.8	79,088	1,161.0	8,058	118.3
Percent change	-4.9	-5.3	-7.2	-7.5	-12.1	-12.4	-6.6	-7.0	+0.2	-0.2
New Hampshire										
2015	1,558	117.1	23,453	1,763.2	3,482	261.8	19,076	1,434.2	895	67.3
2016	1,611	120.7	20,194	1,512.9	2,963	222.0	16,360	1,225.7	871	65.3
Percent change	+3.4	+3.0	-13.9	-14.2	-14.9	-15.2	-14.2	-14.5	-2.7	-3.0
Rhode Island[6]										
2015	1,520	144.0	20,038	1,898.2	3,938	373.1	14,714	1,393.9	1,386	131.3
2016	1,513	143.2	20,058	1,898.7	3,788	358.6	14,674	1,389.0	1,596	151.1
Percent change	-0.5	-0.5	+0.1	*	-3.8	-3.9	-0.3	-0.3	+15.2	+15.1
Vermont										
2015	482	77.0	9,064	1,447.7	2,034	324.9	6,834	1,091.5	196	31.3
2016	691	110.6	10,602	1,697.4	2,103	336.7	8,217	1,315.6	282	45.1
Percent change	+43.4	+43.7	+17.0	+17.2	+3.4	+3.6	+20.2	+20.5	+43.9	+44.2
Middle Atlantic[6]										
2015	78,326	188.9	694,867	1,675.4	111,650	269.2	544,036	1,311.7	39,181	94.5
2016	79,211	191.0	666,128	1,606.1	100,625	242.6	526,736	1,270.0	38,767	93.5
Percent change	+1.1	+1.1	-4.1	-4.1	-9.9	-9.9	-3.2	-3.2	-1.1	-1.1
New Jersey										
2015	11,414	127.7	145,701	1,630.6	27,960	312.9	105,963	1,185.9	11,778	131.8
2016	11,105	124.2	138,152	1,544.6	25,284	282.7	101,540	1,135.2	11,328	126.6
Percent change	-2.7	-2.8	-5.2	-5.3	-9.6	-9.7	-4.2	-4.3	-3.8	-3.9
New York[6]										
2015	44,493	225.3	317,225	1,606.4	44,117	223.4	257,837	1,305.7	15,271	77.3
2016	45,079	228.3	305,181	1,545.6	39,821	201.7	250,968	1,271.0	14,392	72.9
Percent change	+1.3	+1.3	-3.8	-3.8	-9.7	-9.7	-2.7	-2.7	-5.8	-5.7
Pennsylvania										
2015	22,419	175.3	231,941	1,813.2	39,573	309.4	180,236	1,409.0	12,132	94.8
2016	23,027	180.1	222,795	1,742.7	35,520	277.8	174,228	1,362.8	13,047	102.1
Percent change	+2.7	+2.8	-3.9	-3.9	-10.2	-10.2	-3.3	-3.3	+7.5	+7.6
Midwest[6]										
2015	146,443	215.9	1,555,516	2,293.0	307,853	453.8	1,125,935	1,659.7	121,728	179.4
2016	157,794	232.3	1,544,531	2,273.3	300,359	442.1	1,112,596	1,637.6	131,576	193.7
Percent change	+7.8	+7.6	-0.7	-0.9	-2.4	-2.6	-1.2	-1.3	+8.1	+7.9
East North Central[6]										
2015	97,217	208.0	1,037,945	2,220.6	211,221	451.9	748,309	1,600.9	78,415	167.8
2016	106,245	227.2	1,034,762	2,213.1	207,962	444.8	742,358	1,587.7	84,442	180.6
Percent change	+9.3	+9.3	-0.3	-0.3	-1.5	-1.6	-0.8	-0.8	+7.7	+7.7
Illinois										
2015	29,019	226.0	256,962	2,001.4	46,846	364.9	192,424	1,498.7	17,692	137.8
2016	32,065	250.5	262,306	2,049.0	47,989	374.9	194,407	1,518.6	19,910	155.5
Percent change	+10.5	+10.8	+2.1	+2.4	+2.4	+2.7	+1.0	+1.3	+12.5	+12.9
Indiana[6]										
2015	15,536	234.9	171,878	2,599.2	34,404	520.3	123,940	1,874.3	13,534	204.7
2016	16,575	249.9	171,759	2,589.8	34,097	514.0	122,931	1,853.3	14,731	222.1
Percent change	+6.7	+6.4	-0.1	-0.4	-0.9	-1.2	-0.8	-1.1	+8.8	+8.5
Michigan										
2015	26,599	268.2	191,191	1,927.8	40,375	407.1	132,019	1,331.1	18,797	189.5
2016	30,729	309.5	189,620	1,909.9	39,568	398.5	129,876	1,308.1	20,176	203.2
Percent change	+15.5	+15.4	-0.8	-0.9	-2.0	-2.1	-1.6	-1.7	+7.3	+7.2
Ohio[6]										
2015	15,793	136.1	303,743	2,617.3	69,994	603.1	216,354	1,864.3	17,395	149.9
2016	16,111	138.7	299,357	2,577.5	66,883	575.9	212,807	1,832.3	19,667	169.3
Percent change	+2.0	+1.9	-1.4	-1.5	-4.4	-4.5	-1.6	-1.7	+13.1	+13.0

Table 2. Crime,[1] by Region, Geographic Division, and State, 2015–2016—Continued

(Number, rate per 100,000 population, percent.)

Area	Population[2]	Violent crime[3]		Murder and nonnegligent manslaughter		Rape (revised definition)[4]		Rape (legacy definition)[5]		Robbery	
		Number	Rate	Number	Rate	Number	Rate	Number	Rate	Number	Rate
Wisconsin[6]											
2015	5,767,891	17,549	304.3	240	4.2	1,805	31.3	1,324	23.0	5,234	90.7
2016	5,778,708	17,679	305.9	229	4.0	1,979	34.2	1,458	25.2	4,706	81.4
Percent change		+0.7	+0.6	-4.6	-4.8	+9.6	+9.4	+10.1	+9.9	-10.1	-10.3
West North Central[6]											
2015	21,095,876	74,131	351.4	951	4.5	9,559	45.3	6,940	32.9	14,395	68.2
2016	21,185,456	76,282	360.1	911	4.3	9,306	43.9	6,881	32.5	14,516	68.5
Percent change		+2.9	+2.5	-4.2	-4.6	-2.6	-3.1	-0.9	-1.3	+0.8	+0.4
Iowa											
2015	3,121,997	8,619	276.1	73	2.3	1,205	38.6	877	28.1	1,050	33.6
2016	3,134,693	9,110	290.6	71	2.3	1,247	39.8	922	29.4	1,148	36.6
Percent change		+5.7	+5.3	-2.7	-3.1	+3.5	+3.1	+5.1	+4.7	+9.3	+8.9
Kansas											
2015	2,906,721	11,483	395.0	126	4.3	1,684	57.9	1,226	42.2	1,823	62.7
2016	2,907,289	11,060	380.4	111	3.8	1,312	45.1	971	33.4	1,671	57.5
Percent change		-3.7	-3.7	-11.9	-11.9	-22.1	-22.1	-20.8	-20.8	-8.3	-8.4
Minnesota											
2015	5,482,435	13,319	242.9	133	2.4	2,321	42.3	1,679	30.6	3,771	68.8
2016	5,519,952	13,394	242.6	101	1.8	2,348	42.5	1,731	31.4	3,728	67.5
Percent change		+0.6	-0.1	-24.1	-24.6	+1.2	+0.5	+3.1	+2.4	-1.1	-1.8
Missouri											
2015	6,076,204	30,292	498.5	503	8.3	2,573	42.3	1,858	30.6	6,383	105.0
2016	6,093,000	31,644	519.4	537	8.8	2,554	41.9	1,884	30.9	6,570	107.8
Percent change		+4.5	+4.2	+6.8	+6.5	-0.7	-1.0	+1.4	+1.1	+2.9	+2.6
Nebraska[6]											
2015	1,893,765	5,167	272.8	62	3.3	885	46.7	648	34.2	994	52.5
2016	1,907,116	5,550	291.0	49	2.6	994	52.1	738	38.7	946	49.6
Percent change		+7.4	+6.7	-21.0	-21.5	+12.3	+11.5	+13.9	+13.1	-4.8	-5.5
North Dakota											
2015	756,835	1,949	257.5	21	2.8	391	51.7	285	37.7	159	21.0
2016	757,952	1,903	251.1	15	2.0	342	45.1	256	33.8	181	23.9
Percent change		-2.4	-2.5	-28.6	-28.7	-12.5	-12.7	-10.2	-10.3	+13.8	+13.7
South Dakota[6]											
2015	857,919	3,302	384.9	33	3.8	500	58.3	367	42.8	215	25.1
2016	865,454	3,621	418.4	27	3.1	509	58.8	379	43.8	272	31.4
Percent change		+9.7	+8.7	-18.2	-18.9	+1.8	+0.9	+3.3	+2.4	+26.5	+25.4
South[6,7,8]											
2015	121,039,206	509,043	420.6	7,300	6.0	47,277	39.1	33,960	28.1	127,149	105.0
2016	122,319,574	526,999	430.8	7,961	6.5	49,246	40.3	35,869	29.3	128,842	105.3
Percent change		+3.5	+2.4	+9.1	+7.9	+4.2	+3.1	+5.6	+4.5	+1.3	+0.3
South Atlantic[6,7,8]											
2015	63,192,408	256,283	405.6	3,824	6.1	21,620	34.2	15,433	24.4	66,792	105.7
2016	63,923,309	258,672	404.7	4,077	6.4	22,333	34.9	16,174	25.3	66,402	103.9
Percent change		+0.9	-0.2	+6.6	+5.4	+3.3	+2.1	+4.8	+3.6	-0.6	-1.7
Delaware											
2015	944,076	4,760	504.2	62	6.6	361	38.2	257	27.2	1,240	131.3
2016	952,065	4,844	508.8	56	5.9	308	32.4	221	23.2	1,359	142.7
Percent change		+1.8	+0.9	-9.7	-10.4	-14.7	-15.4	-14.0	-14.7	+9.6	+8.7
District of Columbia[7]											
2015	670,377	8,538	1,273.6	162	24.2	494	73.7	365	54.4	3,746	558.8
2016	681,170	8,214	1,205.9	139	20.4	532	78.1	401	58.9	3,480	510.9
Percent change		-3.8	-5.3	-14.2	-15.6	+7.7	+6.0	+9.9	+8.1	-7.1	-8.6
Florida											
2015	20,244,914	93,625	462.5	1,041	5.1	7,552	37.3	5,396	26.7	21,137	104.4
2016	20,612,439	88,700	430.3	1,111	5.4	7,598	36.9	5,528	26.8	20,175	97.9
Percent change		-5.3	-6.9	+6.7	+4.8	+0.6	-1.2	+2.4	+0.6	-4.6	-6.3
Georgia[8]											
2015	10,199,398	38,891	381.3	622	6.1	3,257	31.9	2,343	23.0	12,545	123.0
2016	10,310,371	40,990	397.6	681	6.6	3,509	34.0	2,528	24.5	12,205	118.4
Percent change		+5.4	+4.3	+9.5	+8.3	+7.7	+6.6	+7.9	+6.7	-2.7	-3.8
Maryland											
2015	5,994,983	28,185	470.1	538	9.0	1,717	28.6	1,209	20.2	10,111	168.7
2016	6,016,447	28,400	472.0	481	8.0	1,756	29.2	1,266	21.0	10,289	171.0
Percent change		+0.8	+0.4	-10.6	-10.9	+2.3	+1.9	+4.7	+4.3	+1.8	+1.4
North Carolina[6]											
2015	10,035,186	34,734	346.1	517	5.2	2,591	25.8	1,886	18.8	8,821	87.9
2016	10,146,788	37,769	372.2	678	6.7	2,849	28.1	2,086	20.6	9,336	92.0
Percent change		+8.7	+7.5	+31.1	+29.7	+10.0	+8.7	+10.6	+9.4	+5.8	+4.7
South Carolina											
2015	4,894,834	24,448	499.5	407	8.3	2,439	49.8	1,717	35.1	3,950	80.7
2016	4,961,119	24,896	501.8	366	7.4	2,387	48.1	1,711	34.5	4,035	81.3
Percent change		+1.8	+0.5	-10.1	-11.3	-2.1	-3.4	-0.3	-1.7	+2.2	+0.8
Virginia											
2015	8,367,587	16,705	199.6	390	4.7	2,499	29.9	1,767	21.1	4,459	53.3
2016	8,411,808	18,302	217.6	484	5.8	2,737	32.5	1,965	23.4	4,803	57.1
Percent change		+9.6	+9.0	+24.1	+23.5	+9.5	+8.9	+11.2	+10.6	+7.7	+7.1
West Virginia											
2015	1,841,053	6,397	347.5	85	4.6	710	38.6	493	26.8	783	42.5
2016	1,831,102	6,557	358.1	81	4.4	657	35.9	468	25.6	720	39.3
Percent change		+2.5	+3.1	-4.7	-4.2	-7.5	-7.0	-5.1	-4.6	-8.0	-7.5

Table 2. Crime,[1] by Region, Geographic Division, and State, 2015–2016—Continued

(Number, rate per 100,000 population, percent.)

Area	Aggravated assault		Property crime		Burglary		Larceny-theft		Motor vehicle theft	
	Number	Rate	Number	Rate	Number	Rate	Number	Rate	Number	Rate
Wisconsin[6]										
2015	10,270	178.1	114,171	1,979.4	19,602	339.8	83,572	1,448.9	10,997	190.7
2016	10,765	186.3	111,720	1,933.3	19,425	336.1	82,337	1,424.8	9,958	172.3
Percent change	+4.8	+4.6	-2.1	-2.3	-0.9	-1.1	-1.5	-1.7	-9.4	-9.6
West North Central[6]										
2015	49,226	233.3	517,571	2,453.4	96,632	458.1	377,626	1,790.0	43,313	205.3
2016	51,549	243.3	509,769	2,406.2	92,397	436.1	370,238	1,747.6	47,134	222.5
Percent change	+4.7	+4.3	-1.5	-1.9	-4.4	-4.8	-2.0	-2.4	+8.8	+8.4
Iowa										
2015	6,291	201.5	64,688	2,072.0	14,977	479.7	45,328	1,451.9	4,383	140.4
2016	6,644	212.0	65,391	2,086.0	15,030	479.5	45,378	1,447.6	4,983	159.0
Percent change	+5.6	+5.2	+1.1	+0.7	+0.4	-0.1	+0.1	-0.3	+13.7	+13.2
Kansas										
2015	7,850	270.1	80,059	2,754.3	15,619	537.3	57,435	1,975.9	7,005	241.0
2016	7,966	274.0	78,367	2,695.5	14,364	494.1	57,066	1,962.9	6,937	238.6
Percent change	+1.5	+1.5	-2.1	-2.1	-8.0	-8.1	-0.6	-0.7	-1.0	-1.0
Minnesota										
2015	7,094	129.4	121,984	2,225.0	19,299	352.0	94,704	1,727.4	7,981	145.6
2016	7,217	130.7	117,756	2,133.3	18,606	337.1	90,422	1,638.1	8,728	158.1
Percent change	+1.7	+1.0	-3.5	-4.1	-3.6	-4.2	-4.5	-5.2	+9.4	+8.6
Missouri										
2015	20,833	342.9	173,788	2,860.1	34,029	560.0	122,749	2,020.2	17,010	279.9
2016	21,983	360.8	170,549	2,799.4	31,710	520.4	120,544	1,978.4	18,295	300.3
Percent change	+5.5	+5.2	-1.9	-2.1	-6.8	-7.1	-1.8	-2.1	+7.6	+7.3
Nebraska[6]										
2015	3,226	170.3	42,597	2,249.3	6,443	340.2	32,148	1,697.6	4,006	211.5
2016	3,561	186.7	43,163	2,263.3	6,444	337.9	31,994	1,677.6	4,725	247.8
Percent change	+10.4	+9.6	+1.3	+0.6	*	-0.7	-0.5	-1.2	+17.9	+17.1
North Dakota										
2015	1,378	182.1	17,716	2,340.8	3,296	435.5	12,686	1,676.2	1,734	229.1
2016	1,365	180.1	17,402	2,295.9	3,243	427.9	12,195	1,608.9	1,964	259.1
Percent change	-0.9	-1.1	-1.8	-1.9	-1.6	-1.8	-3.9	-4.0	+13.3	+13.1
South Dakota[6]										
2015	2,554	297.7	16,739	1,951.1	2,969	346.1	12,576	1,465.9	1,194	139.2
2016	2,813	325.0	17,141	1,980.6	3,000	346.6	12,639	1,460.4	1,502	173.6
Percent change	+10.1	+9.2	+2.4	+1.5	+1.0	+0.2	+0.5	-0.4	+25.8	+24.7
South[6,7,8]										
2015	327,317	270.4	3,393,611	2,803.7	719,098	594.1	2,422,679	2,001.6	251,834	208.1
2016	340,950	278.7	3,343,799	2,733.7	684,968	560.0	2,391,288	1,955.0	267,543	218.7
Percent change	+4.2	+3.1	-1.5	-2.5	-4.7	-5.7	-1.3	-2.3	+6.2	+5.1
South Atlantic[6,7,8]										
2015	164,047	259.6	1,721,061	2,723.5	352,328	557.5	1,246,078	1,971.9	122,655	194.1
2016	165,860	259.5	1,692,669	2,648.0	330,122	516.4	1,234,761	1,931.6	127,786	199.9
Percent change	+1.1	-0.1	-1.6	-2.8	-6.3	-7.4	-0.9	-2.0	+4.2	+3.0
Delaware										
2015	3,097	328.0	25,545	2,705.8	4,797	508.1	19,555	2,071.3	1,193	126.4
2016	3,121	327.8	26,334	2,766.0	5,023	527.6	19,791	2,078.7	1,520	159.7
Percent change	+0.8	-0.1	+3.1	+2.2	+4.7	+3.8	+1.2	+0.4	+27.4	+26.3
District of Columbia[7]										
2015	4,136	617.0	31,444	4,690.5	2,971	443.2	25,208	3,760.3	3,265	487.0
2016	4,063	596.5	32,716	4,802.9	2,361	346.6	27,382	4,019.8	2,973	436.5
Percent change	-1.8	-3.3	+4.0	+2.4	-20.5	-21.8	+8.6	+6.9	-8.9	-10.4
Florida										
2015	63,895	315.6	570,270	2,816.9	109,268	539.7	420,341	2,076.4	40,661	200.8
2016	59,816	290.2	553,812	2,686.8	100,325	486.7	410,352	1,990.8	43,135	209.3
Percent change	-6.4	-8.1	-2.9	-4.6	-8.2	-9.8	-2.4	-4.1	+6.1	+4.2
Georgia[8]										
2015	22,467	220.3	316,013	3,098.3	68,149	668.2	220,715	2,164.0	27,149	266.2
2016	24,595	238.5	309,770	3,004.5	63,344	614.4	219,625	2,130.1	26,801	259.9
Percent change	+9.5	+8.3	-2.0	-3.0	-7.1	-8.1	-0.5	-1.6	-1.3	-2.3
Maryland										
2015	15,819	263.9	142,547	2,377.8	26,432	440.9	102,701	1,713.1	13,414	223.8
2016	15,874	263.8	137,445	2,284.5	24,692	410.4	100,919	1,677.4	11,834	196.7
Percent change	+0.3	*	-3.6	-3.9	-6.6	-6.9	-1.7	-2.1	-11.8	-12.1
North Carolina[6]										
2015	22,805	227.3	275,915	2,749.5	74,760	745.0	187,732	1,870.7	13,423	133.8
2016	24,906	245.5	277,765	2,737.5	72,082	710.4	190,377	1,876.2	15,306	150.8
Percent change	+9.2	+8.0	+0.7	-0.4	-3.6	-4.6	+1.4	+0.3	+14.0	+12.8
South Carolina										
2015	17,652	360.6	162,830	3,326.6	34,942	713.9	114,778	2,344.9	13,110	267.8
2016	18,108	365.0	160,928	3,243.8	32,976	664.7	114,032	2,298.5	13,920	280.6
Percent change	+2.6	+1.2	-1.2	-2.5	-5.6	-6.9	-0.6	-2.0	+6.2	+4.8
Virginia										
2015	9,357	111.8	157,803	1,885.9	21,542	257.4	128,064	1,530.5	8,197	98.0
2016	10,278	122.2	156,412	1,859.4	20,018	238.0	126,606	1,505.1	9,788	116.4
Percent change	+9.8	+9.3	-0.9	-1.4	-7.1	-7.6	-1.1	-1.7	+19.4	+18.8
West Virginia										
2015	4,819	261.8	38,694	2,101.7	9,467	514.2	26,984	1,465.7	2,243	121.8
2016	5,099	278.5	37,487	2,047.2	9,301	507.9	25,677	1,402.3	2,509	137.0
Percent change	+5.8	+6.4	-3.1	-2.6	-1.8	-1.2	-4.8	-4.3	+11.9	+12.5

Table 2. Crime,[1] by Region, Geographic Division, and State, 2015–2016—Continued

(Number, rate per 100,000 population, percent.)

Area	Population[2]	Violent crime[3]		Murder and nonnegligent manslaughter		Rape (revised definition)[4]		Rape (legacy definition)[5]		Robbery	
		Number	Rate	Number	Rate	Number	Rate	Number	Rate	Number	Rate
East South Central[6]											
2015	18,862,932	81,850	433.9	1,238	6.6	7,640	40.5	5,497	29.1	17,737	94.0
2016	18,940,194	86,674	457.6	1,391	7.3	7,548	39.9	5,455	28.8	18,265	96.4
Percent change		+5.9	+5.5	+12.4	+11.9	-1.2	-1.6	-0.8	-1.2	+3.0	+2.6
Alabama											
2015	4,853,875	22,957	473.0	348	7.2	2,037	42.0	1,449	29.9	4,612	95.0
2016	4,863,300	25,886	532.3	407	8.4	1,916	39.4	1,385	28.5	4,686	96.4
Percent change		+12.8	+12.5	+17.0	+16.7	-5.9	-6.1	-4.4	-4.6	+1.6	+1.4
Kentucky											
2015	4,424,611	9,887	223.5	219	4.9	1,644	37.2	1,165	26.3	3,314	74.9
2016	4,436,974	10,308	232.3	260	5.9	1,641	37.0	1,174	26.5	3,369	75.9
Percent change		+4.3	+4.0	+18.7	+18.4	-0.2	-0.5	+0.8	+0.5	+1.7	+1.4
Mississippi[6]											
2015	2,989,390	8,190	274.0	253	8.5	1,158	38.7	851	28.5	2,312	77.3
2016	2,988,726	8,383	280.5	238	8.0	1,277	42.7	905	30.3	2,397	80.2
Percent change		+2.4	+2.4	-5.9	-5.9	+10.3	+10.3	+6.3	+6.4	+3.7	+3.7
Tennessee											
2015	6,595,056	40,816	618.9	418	6.3	2,801	42.5	2,032	30.8	7,499	113.7
2016	6,651,194	42,097	632.9	486	7.3	2,714	40.8	1,991	29.9	7,813	117.5
Percent change		+3.1	+2.3	+16.3	+15.3	-3.1	-3.9	-2.0	-2.8	+4.2	+3.3
West South Central[6]											
2015	38,983,866	170,910	438.4	2,238	5.7	18,017	46.2	13,030	33.4	42,620	109.3
2016	39,456,071	181,653	460.4	2,493	6.3	19,365	49.1	14,240	36.1	44,175	112.0
Percent change		+6.3	+5.0	+11.4	+10.1	+7.5	+6.2	+9.3	+8.0	+3.6	+2.4
Arkansas											
2015	2,977,853	15,769	529.5	189	6.3	2,008	67.4	1,425	47.9	2,117	71.1
2016	2,988,248	16,461	550.9	216	7.2	2,143	71.7	1,545	51.7	2,120	70.9
Percent change		+4.4	+4.0	+14.3	+13.9	+6.7	+6.4	+8.4	+8.0	+0.1	-0.2
Louisiana											
2015	4,668,960	25,202	539.8	492	10.5	1,733	37.1	1,246	26.7	5,561	119.1
2016	4,681,666	26,502	566.1	554	11.8	1,816	38.8	1,328	28.4	5,576	119.1
Percent change		+5.2	+4.9	+12.6	+12.3	+4.8	+4.5	+6.6	+6.3	+0.3	*
Oklahoma[6]											
2015	3,907,414	16,746	428.6	240	6.1	1,953	50.0	1,418	36.3	3,018	77.2
2016	3,923,561	17,648	449.8	245	6.2	2,039	52.0	1,509	38.5	3,162	80.6
Percent change		+5.4	+5.0	+2.1	+1.7	+4.4	+4.0	+6.4	+6.0	+4.8	+4.3
Texas											
2015	27,429,639	113,193	412.7	1,317	4.8	12,323	44.9	8,941	32.6	31,924	116.4
2016	27,862,596	121,042	434.4	1,478	5.3	13,367	48.0	9,858	35.4	33,317	119.6
Percent change		+6.9	+5.3	+12.2	+10.5	+8.5	+6.8	+10.3	+8.5	+4.4	+2.7
West[6]											
2015	75,834,288	301,773	397.9	3,194	4.2	31,615	41.7	22,994	30.3	82,557	108.9
2016	76,657,000	320,706	418.4	3,449	4.5	33,298	43.4	24,562	32.0	86,301	112.6
Percent change		+6.3	+5.1	+8.0	+6.8	+5.3	+4.2	+6.8	+5.7	+4.5	+3.4
Mountain[6]											
2015	23,492,558	94,784	403.5	917	3.9	12,938	55.1	9,424	40.1	20,236	86.1
2016	23,855,067	102,674	430.4	1,124	4.7	13,126	55.0	9,689	40.6	21,739	91.1
Percent change		+8.3	+6.7	+22.6	+20.7	+1.5	-0.1	+2.8	+1.2	+7.4	+5.8
Arizona											
2015	6,817,565	27,968	410.2	306	4.5	3,109	45.6	2,268	33.3	6,360	93.3
2016	6,931,071	32,583	470.1	380	5.5	3,290	47.5	2,452	35.4	7,055	101.8
Percent change		+16.5	+14.6	+24.2	+22.1	+5.8	+4.1	+8.1	+6.3	+10.9	+9.1
Colorado											
2015	5,448,819	17,348	318.4	173	3.2	3,328	61.1	2,422	44.4	3,315	60.8
2016	5,540,545	18,983	342.6	204	3.7	3,555	64.2	2,619	47.3	3,528	63.7
Percent change		+9.4	+7.6	+17.9	+16.0	+6.8	+5.1	+8.1	+6.3	+6.4	+4.7
Idaho											
2015	1,652,828	3,593	217.4	32	1.9	703	42.5	508	30.7	191	11.6
2016	1,683,140	3,876	230.3	49	2.9	719	42.7	529	31.4	213	12.7
Percent change		+7.9	+5.9	+53.1	+50.4	+2.3	+0.4	+4.1	+2.3	+11.5	+9.5
Montana											
2015	1,032,073	3,647	353.4	38	3.7	572	55.4	405	39.2	210	20.3
2016	1,042,520	3,840	368.3	36	3.5	578	55.4	414	39.7	266	25.5
Percent change		+5.3	+4.2	-5.3	-6.2	+1.0	*	+2.2	+1.2	+26.7	+25.4
Nevada											
2015	2,883,758	20,118	697.6	178	6.2	1,688	58.5	1,232	42.7	6,287	218.0
2016	2,940,058	19,936	678.1	224	7.6	1,733	58.9	1,292	43.9	6,340	215.6
Percent change		-0.9	-2.8	+25.8	+23.4	+2.7	+0.7	+4.9	+2.9	+0.8	-1.1
New Mexico[6]											
2015	2,080,328	13,672	657.2	117	5.6	1,663	79.9	1,218	58.5	2,485	119.5
2016	2,081,015	14,619	702.5	139	6.7	1,526	73.3	1,117	53.7	2,737	131.5
Percent change		+6.9	+6.9	+18.8	+18.8	-8.2	-8.3	-8.3	-8.3	+10.1	+10.1
Utah											
2015	2,990,632	7,138	238.7	57	1.9	1,704	57.0	1,247	41.7	1,329	44.4
2016	3,051,217	7,407	242.8	72	2.4	1,520	49.8	1,116	36.6	1,541	50.5
Percent change		+3.8	+1.7	+26.3	+23.8	-10.8	-12.6	-10.5	-12.3	+16.0	+13.6

Table 2. Crime,[1] by Region, Geographic Division, and State, 2015–2016—Continued

(Number, rate per 100,000 population, percent.)

Area	Aggravated assault		Property crime		Burglary		Larceny-theft		Motor vehicle theft	
	Number	Rate	Number	Rate	Number	Rate	Number	Rate	Number	Rate
East South Central[6]										
2015	55,235	292.8	524,162	2,778.8	126,612	671.2	362,030	1,919.3	35,520	188.3
2016	59,470	314.0	513,087	2,709.0	118,565	626.0	353,470	1,866.2	41,052	216.7
Percent change	+7.7	+7.2	-2.1	-2.5	-6.4	-6.7	-2.4	-2.8	+15.6	+15.1
Alabama										
2015	15,960	328.8	144,785	2,982.9	35,265	726.5	99,182	2,043.4	10,338	213.0
2016	18,877	388.2	143,362	2,947.8	34,065	700.5	97,574	2,006.3	11,723	241.1
Percent change	+18.3	+18.0	-1.0	-1.2	-3.4	-3.6	-1.6	-1.8	+13.4	+13.2
Kentucky										
2015	4,710	106.5	97,545	2,204.6	22,526	509.1	67,143	1,517.5	7,876	178.0
2016	5,038	113.5	97,158	2,189.7	20,834	469.6	66,438	1,497.4	9,886	222.8
Percent change	+7.0	+6.7	-0.4	-0.7	-7.5	-7.8	-1.0	-1.3	+25.5	+25.2
Mississippi[6]										
2015	4,467	149.4	85,785	2,869.6	25,068	838.6	56,446	1,888.2	4,271	142.9
2016	4,471	149.6	82,732	2,768.1	23,354	781.4	55,054	1,842.1	4,324	144.7
Percent change	+0.1	+0.1	-3.6	-3.5	-6.8	-6.8	-2.5	-2.4	+1.2	+1.3
Tennessee										
2015	30,098	456.4	196,047	2,972.6	43,753	663.4	139,259	2,111.6	13,035	197.6
2016	31,084	467.3	189,835	2,854.1	40,312	606.1	134,404	2,020.7	15,119	227.3
Percent change	+3.3	+2.4	-3.2	-4.0	-7.9	-8.6	-3.5	-4.3	+16.0	+15.0
West South Central[6]										
2015	108,035	277.1	1,148,388	2,945.8	240,158	616.0	814,571	2,089.5	93,659	240.3
2016	115,620	293.0	1,138,043	2,884.3	236,281	598.8	803,057	2,035.3	98,705	250.2
Percent change	+7.0	+5.7	-0.9	-2.1	-1.6	-2.8	-1.4	-2.6	+5.4	+4.1
Arkansas										
2015	11,455	384.7	97,391	3,270.5	22,851	767.4	68,720	2,307.7	5,820	195.4
2016	11,982	401.0	97,673	3,268.6	23,771	795.5	66,747	2,233.6	7,155	239.4
Percent change	+4.6	+4.2	+0.3	-0.1	+4.0	+3.7	-2.9	-3.2	+22.9	+22.5
Louisiana										
2015	17,416	373.0	157,708	3,377.8	35,457	759.4	112,520	2,410.0	9,731	208.4
2016	18,556	396.4	154,386	3,297.7	34,667	740.5	109,380	2,336.3	10,339	220.8
Percent change	+6.5	+6.3	-2.1	-2.4	-2.2	-2.5	-2.8	-3.1	+6.2	+6.0
Oklahoma[6]										
2015	11,535	295.2	114,055	2,918.9	28,783	736.6	74,678	1,911.2	10,594	271.1
2016	12,202	311.0	117,037	2,982.9	29,103	741.7	75,779	1,931.4	12,155	309.8
Percent change	+5.8	+5.3	+2.6	+2.2	+1.1	+0.7	+1.5	+1.1	+14.7	+14.3
Texas										
2015	67,629	246.6	779,234	2,840.8	153,067	558.0	558,653	2,036.7	67,514	246.1
2016	72,880	261.6	768,947	2,759.8	148,740	533.8	551,151	1,978.1	69,056	247.8
Percent change	+7.8	+6.1	-1.3	-2.9	-2.8	-4.3	-1.3	-2.9	+2.3	+0.7
West[6]										
2015	184,407	243.2	2,123,048	2,799.6	402,703	531.0	1,437,787	1,896.0	282,558	372.6
2016	197,658	257.8	2,120,808	2,766.6	387,049	504.9	1,424,850	1,858.7	308,909	403.0
Percent change	+7.2	+6.0	-0.1	-1.2	-3.9	-4.9	-0.9	-2.0	+9.3	+8.2
Mountain[6]										
2015	60,693	258.3	662,713	2,820.9	125,323	533.5	470,974	2,004.8	66,416	282.7
2016	66,685	279.5	675,111	2,830.1	122,629	514.1	474,519	1,989.2	77,963	326.8
Percent change	+9.9	+8.2	+1.9	+0.3	-2.1	-3.6	+0.8	-0.8	+17.4	+15.6
Arizona										
2015	18,193	266.9	207,184	3,039.0	38,010	557.5	152,388	2,235.2	16,786	246.2
2016	21,858	315.4	206,432	2,978.4	37,736	544.4	150,275	2,168.1	18,421	265.8
Percent change	+20.1	+18.2	-0.4	-2.0	-0.7	-2.3	-1.4	-3.0	+9.7	+7.9
Colorado										
2015	10,532	193.3	144,044	2,643.6	23,490	431.1	104,532	1,918.4	16,022	294.0
2016	11,696	211.1	151,850	2,740.7	23,903	431.4	108,336	1,955.3	19,611	354.0
Percent change	+11.1	+9.2	+5.4	+3.7	+1.8	+0.1	+3.6	+1.9	+22.4	+20.4
Idaho										
2015	2,667	161.4	28,912	1,749.2	6,124	370.5	20,916	1,265.5	1,872	113.3
2016	2,895	172.0	29,357	1,744.2	6,318	375.4	20,962	1,245.4	2,077	123.4
Percent change	+8.5	+6.6	+1.5	-0.3	+3.2	+1.3	+0.2	-1.6	+11.0	+9.0
Montana										
2015	2,827	273.9	27,276	2,642.8	3,887	376.6	20,966	2,031.4	2,423	234.8
2016	2,960	283.9	27,976	2,683.5	3,934	377.4	21,299	2,043.0	2,743	263.1
Percent change	+4.7	+3.7	+2.6	+1.5	+1.2	+0.2	+1.6	+0.6	+13.2	+12.1
Nevada										
2015	11,965	414.9	77,137	2,674.9	22,360	775.4	43,426	1,505.9	11,351	393.6
2016	11,639	395.9	76,047	2,586.6	18,850	641.1	44,017	1,497.1	13,180	448.3
Percent change	-2.7	-4.6	-1.4	-3.3	-15.7	-17.3	+1.4	-0.6	+16.1	+13.9
New Mexico[8]										
2015	9,407	452.2	77,212	3,711.5	17,084	821.2	51,485	2,474.9	8,643	415.5
2016	10,217	491.0	81,931	3,937.1	17,281	830.4	52,907	2,542.4	11,743	564.3
Percent change	+8.6	+8.6	+6.1	+6.1	+1.2	+1.1	+2.8	+2.7	+35.9	+35.8
Utah										
2015	4,048	135.4	89,797	3,002.6	12,606	421.5	68,464	2,289.3	8,727	291.8
2016	4,274	140.1	90,058	2,951.5	12,836	420.7	67,834	2,223.2	9,388	307.7
Percent change	+5.6	+3.5	+0.3	-1.7	+1.8	-0.2	-0.9	-2.9	+7.6	+5.4

Table 2. Crime,[1] by Region, Geographic Division, and State, 2015–2016—Continued

(Number, rate per 100,000 population, percent.)

Area	Population[2]	Violent crime[3]		Murder and nonnegligent manslaughter		Rape (revised definition)[4]		Rape (legacy definition)[5]		Robbery	
		Number	Rate	Number	Rate	Number	Rate	Number	Rate	Number	Rate
Wyoming											
2015	586,555	1,300	221.6	16	2.7	171	29.2	124	21.1	59	10.1
2016	585,501	1,430	244.2	20	3.4	205	35.0	150	25.6	59	10.1
Percent change		+10.0	+10.2	+25.0	+25.2	+19.9	+20.1	+21.0	+21.2	0.0	+0.2
Pacific[6]											
2015	52,341,730	206,989	395.5	2,277	4.4	18,677	35.7	13,570	25.9	62,321	119.1
2016	52,801,933	218,032	412.9	2,325	4.4	20,172	38.2	14,873	28.2	64,562	122.3
Percent change		+5.3	+4.4	+2.1	+1.2	+8.0	+7.1	+9.6	+8.6	+3.6	+2.7
Alaska											
2015	737,709	5,391	730.8	59	8.0	900	122.0	648	87.8	761	103.2
2016	741,894	5,966	804.2	52	7.0	1,053	141.9	757	102.0	850	114.6
Percent change		+10.7	+10.0	-11.9	-12.4	+17.0	+16.3	+16.8	+16.2	+11.7	+11.1
California											
2015	38,993,940	166,883	428.0	1,861	4.8	12,811	32.9	9,341	24.0	52,862	135.6
2016	39,250,017	174,796	445.3	1,930	4.9	13,702	34.9	10,149	25.9	54,789	139.6
Percent change		+4.7	+4.1	+3.7	+3.0	+7.0	+6.3	+8.7	+7.9	+3.6	+3.0
Hawaii											
2015	1,425,157	3,530	247.7	29	2.0	538	37.8	382	26.8	1,085	76.1
2016	1,428,557	4,417	309.2	35	2.5	619	43.3	447	31.3	994	69.6
Percent change		+25.1	+24.8	+20.7	+20.4	+15.1	+14.8	+17.0	+16.7	-8.4	-8.6
Oregon[6]											
2015	4,024,634	10,680	265.4	110	2.7	1,650	41.0	1,193	29.6	2,163	53.7
2016	4,093,465	10,830	264.6	113	2.8	1,721	42.0	1,261	30.8	2,278	55.6
Percent change		+1.4	-0.3	+2.7	+1.0	+4.3	+2.5	+5.7	+3.9	+5.3	+3.5
Washington[6]											
2015	7,160,290	20,505	286.4	218	3.0	2,778	38.8	2,006	28.0	5,450	76.1
2016	7,288,000	22,023	302.2	195	2.7	3,077	42.2	2,259	31.0	5,651	77.5
Percent change		+7.4	+5.5	-10.6	-12.1	+10.8	+8.8	+12.6	+10.6	+3.7	+1.9
Puerto Rico[9]											
2015	3,473,181	7,629	219.7	584	16.8	165	4.8	123	3.5	4,070	117.2
2016	3,411,307	7,643	224.0	679	19.9	169	5.0	128	3.8	3,201	93.8
Percent change		+0.2	+2.0	+16.3	+18.4	+2.4	+4.3	+4.1	+6.0	-21.4	-19.9

Table 2. Crime,[1] by Region, Geographic Division, and State, 2015–2016—Continued

(Number, rate per 100,000 population, percent.)

Area	Aggravated assault		Property crime		Burglary		Larceny-theft		Motor vehicle theft	
	Number	Rate	Number	Rate	Number	Rate	Number	Rate	Number	Rate
Wyoming										
2015	1,054	179.7	11,151	1,901.1	1,762	300.4	8,797	1,499.8	592	100.9
2016	1,146	195.7	11,460	1,957.3	1,771	302.5	8,889	1,518.2	800	136.6
Percent change	+8.7	+8.9	+2.8	+3.0	+0.5	+0.7	+1.0	+1.2	+35.1	+35.4
Pacific[6]										
2015	123,714	236.4	1,460,335	2,790.0	277,380	529.9	966,813	1,847.1	216,142	412.9
2016	130,973	248.0	1,445,697	2,738.0	264,420	500.8	950,331	1,799.8	230,946	437.4
Percent change	+5.9	+4.9	-1.0	-1.9	-4.7	-5.5	-1.7	-2.6	+6.8	+5.9
Alaska										
2015	3,671	497.6	20,806	2,820.4	3,511	475.9	15,249	2,067.1	2,046	277.3
2016	4,011	540.6	24,876	3,353.0	4,053	546.3	17,766	2,394.7	3,057	412.1
Percent change	+9.3	+8.6	+19.6	+18.9	+15.4	+14.8	+16.5	+15.8	+49.4	+48.6
California										
2015	99,349	254.8	1,024,914	2,628.4	197,404	506.2	656,517	1,683.6	170,993	438.5
2016	104,375	265.9	1,002,070	2,553.0	188,304	479.8	637,010	1,623.0	176,756	450.3
Percent change	+5.1	+4.4	-2.2	-2.9	-4.6	-5.2	-3.0	-3.6	+3.4	+2.7
Hawaii										
2015	1,878	131.8	45,389	3,184.8	6,810	477.8	33,140	2,325.4	5,439	381.6
2016	2,769	193.8	42,753	2,992.7	6,017	421.2	31,082	2,175.8	5,654	395.8
Percent change	+47.4	+47.1	-5.8	-6.0	-11.6	-11.9	-6.2	-6.4	+4.0	+3.7
Oregon[6]										
2015	6,757	167.9	119,752	2,975.5	18,541	460.7	90,514	2,249.0	10,697	265.8
2016	6,718	164.1	121,345	2,964.4	16,866	412.0	91,286	2,230.0	13,193	322.3
Percent change	-0.6	-2.2	+1.3	-0.4	-9.0	-10.6	+0.9	-0.8	+23.3	+21.3
Washington[6]										
2015	12,059	168.4	249,474	3,484.1	51,114	713.9	171,393	2,393.7	26,967	376.6
2016	13,100	179.7	254,653	3,494.1	49,180	674.8	173,187	2,376.3	32,286	443.0
Percent change	+8.6	+6.7	+2.1	+0.3	-3.8	-5.5	+1.0	-0.7	+19.7	+17.6
Puerto Rico[9]										
2015	2,810	80.9	37,717	1,085.9	9,150	263.4	24,493	705.2	4,074	117.3
2016	3,594	105.4	35,201	1,031.9	8,251	241.9	23,163	679.0	3,787	111.0
Percent change	+27.9	+30.2	-6.7	-5.0	-9.8	-8.2	-5.4	-3.7	-7.0	-5.4

Note: Although arson data are included in the trend and clearance tables, sufficient data are not available to estimate totals for this offense. Therefore, no arson data are published in this table.

X = Not applicable.

* = Less than one-tenth of 1 percent.

1 The previous year's crime figures have been adjusted.   2 Population figures are U.S. Census Bureau provisional estimates as of July 1, 2016.   3 The violent crime figures include the offenses of murder, rape (revised definition), robbery, and aggravated assault.   4 The figures shown in this column for the offense of rape were estimated using the revised Uniform Crime Reporting (UCR) definition of rape. See chapter notes for more detail.   5 The figures shown in this column for the offense of rape were estimated using the legacy Uniform Crime Reporting (UCR) definition of rape. See chapter notes for more detail.   6 Agencies within this state submitted rape data according to both the revised UCR definition of rape and the legacy UCR definition of rape.   7 Includes offenses reported by the Metro Transit Police and the District of Columbia Fire and Emergency Services Fire Investigation Unit.   8 This state's agencies submitted rape data according to the legacy UCR definition of rape.   9 The figures submitted by Puerto Rico for rape were not verified and may not be comparable to previous years' data.

Table 3. Crime, by State and Area, 2016

(Number, percent, rate per 100,000 population.)

Area	Population	Violent crime[1]	Murder and nonnegligent manslaughter	Rape (revised definition)[2]	Rape (legacy definition)[3]	Robbery	Aggravated assault	Property crime	Burglary	Larceny-theft	Motor vehicle theft
Alabama											
Metropolitan statistical area	3,716,889										
Area actually reporting	99.2%	20,793	331	1,489	1,084	4,174	14,799	114,605	26,966	78,072	9,567
Estimated total	100.0%	20,949	332	1,498	1,091	4,200	14,919	115,564	27,156	78,771	9,637
Cities outside metropolitan areas	520,422										
Area actually reporting	96.6%	3,551	41	263	187	410	2,837	19,841	4,173	14,332	1,336
Estimated total	100.0%	3,646	42	269	193	421	2,914	20,291	4,275	14,641	1,375
Nonmetropolitan counties	625,989										
Area actually reporting	94.5%	1,220	31	141	95	61	987	7,096	2,490	3,934	672
Estimated total	100.0%	1,291	33	149	101	65	1,044	7,507	2,634	4,162	711
State total	4,863,300	25,886	407	1,916	1,385	4,686	18,877	143,362	34,065	97,574	11,723
Rate per 100,000 inhabitants		532.3	8.4	39.4	28.5	96.4	388.2	2,947.8	700.5	2,006.3	241.1
Alaska											
Metropolitan statistical area	350,298										
Area actually reporting	100.0%	3,751	35	583	439	741	2,392	17,143	2,243	12,620	2,280
Cities outside metropolitan areas	128,053										
Area actually reporting	97.4%	964	2	165	119	71	726	4,069	655	3,101	313
Estimated total	100.0%	989	2	169	123	73	745	4,177	672	3,184	321
Nonmetropolitan counties	263,543										
Area actually reporting	100.0%	1,226	15	301	195	36	874	3,556	1,138	1,962	456
State total	741,894	5,966	52	1,053	757	850	4,011	24,876	4,053	17,766	3,057
Rate per 100,000 inhabitants		804.2	7.0	141.9	102.0	114.6	540.6	3,353.0	546.3	2,394.7	412.1
Arizona											
Metropolitan statistical area	6,583,506										
Area actually reporting	98.3%	27,522	334	2,997	2,238	6,931	17,260	196,398	35,424	143,602	17,372
Estimated total	100.0%	27,789	338	3,025	2,258	6,971	17,455	198,543	35,844	145,152	17,547
Cities outside metropolitan areas	124,210										
Area actually reporting	100.0%	4,342	32	250	184	65	3,995	5,937	1,199	4,069	669
Nonmetropolitan counties	223,355										
Area actually reporting	100.0%	452	10	15	10	19	408	1,952	693	1,054	205
State total	6,931,071	32,583	380	3,290	2,452	7,055	21,858	206,432	37,736	150,275	18,421
Rate per 100,000 inhabitants		470.1	5.5	47.5	35.4	101.8	315.4	2,978.4	544.4	2,168.1	265.8
Arkansas											
Metropolitan statistical area	1,851,896										
Area actually reporting	99.9%	11,573	144	1,315	967	1,711	8,403	68,739	15,650	47,839	5,250
Estimated total	100.0%	11,576	144	1,316	968	1,711	8,405	68,762	15,655	47,856	5,251
Cities outside metropolitan areas	515,688										
Area actually reporting	94.1%	2,925	44	471	343	347	2,063	18,438	4,926	12,537	975
Estimated total	100.0%	3,109	47	500	364	369	2,193	19,599	5,236	13,327	1,036
Nonmetropolitan counties	620,664										
Area actually reporting	96.1%	1,704	24	313	204	38	1,329	8,944	2,766	5,344	834
Estimated total	100.0%	1,776	25	327	213	40	1,384	9,312	2,880	5,564	868
State total	2,988,248	16,461	216	2,143	1,545	2,120	11,982	97,673	23,771	66,747	7,155
Rate per 100,000 inhabitants		550.9	7.2	71.7	51.7	70.9	401.0	3,268.6	795.5	2,233.6	239.4
California											
Metropolitan statistical area	38,426,705										
Area actually reporting	99.9%	170,862	1,880	13,290	9,871	54,288	101,404	983,750	182,895	626,742	174,113
Estimated total	100.0%	170,887	1,880	13,292	9,872	54,296	101,419	983,927	182,929	626,856	174,142
Cities outside metropolitan areas	268,891										
Area actually reporting	100.0%	1,805	8	164	118	310	1,323	9,604	2,243	6,260	1,101
Nonmetropolitan counties	554,421										
Area actually reporting	100.0%	2,104	42	246	159	183	1,633	8,539	3,132	3,894	1,513
State total	39,250,017	174,796	1,930	13,702	10,149	54,789	104,375	1,002,070	188,304	637,010	176,756
Rate per 100,000 inhabitants		445.3	4.9	34.9	25.9	139.6	265.9	2,553.0	479.8	1,623.0	450.3
Colorado											
Metropolitan statistical area	4,845,078										
Area actually reporting	99.9%	17,870	190	3,233	2,391	3,458	10,989	138,992	21,523	98,615	18,854
Estimated total	100.0%	17,882	190	3,235	2,393	3,459	10,998	139,156	21,542	98,740	18,874
Cities outside metropolitan areas	337,897										
Area actually reporting	91.9%	641	10	167	121	48	416	8,641	1,294	6,943	404
Estimated total	100.0%	697	11	181	133	52	453	9,405	1,408	7,557	440
Nonmetropolitan counties	357,570										
Area actually reporting	98.6%	399	3	137	91	17	242	3,243	940	2,010	293
Estimated total	100.0%	404	3	139	93	17	245	3,289	953	2,039	297
State total	5,540,545	18,983	204	3,555	2,619	3,528	11,696	151,850	23,903	108,336	19,611
Rate per 100,000 inhabitants		342.6	3.7	64.2	47.3	63.7	211.1	2,740.7	431.4	1,955.3	354.0
Connecticut											
Metropolitan statistical area	2,961,626										
Area actually reporting	100.0%	7,706	70	685	509	2,629	4,322	60,060	9,054	44,302	6,704
Cities outside metropolitan areas	113,580										
Area actually reporting	100.0%	135	1	21	15	37	76	1,756	248	1,417	91
Nonmetropolitan counties	501,246										
Area actually reporting	100.0%	282	7	57	37	37	181	2,848	743	1,793	312
State total	3,576,452	8,123	78	763	561	2,703	4,579	64,664	10,045	47,512	7,107
Rate per 100,000 inhabitants		227.1	2.2	21.3	15.7	75.6	128.0	1,808.0	280.9	1,328.5	198.7
Delaware											
Metropolitan statistical area	952,065										
Area actually reporting	100.0%	4,843	56	307	220	1,359	3,121	26,333	5,023	19,790	1,520

Table 3. Crime, by State and Area, 2016—Continued

(Number, percent, rate per 100,000 population.)

Area	Population	Violent crime[1]	Murder and nonnegligent manslaughter	Rape (revised definition)[2]	Rape (legacy definition)[3]	Robbery	Aggravated assault	Property crime	Burglary	Larceny-theft	Motor vehicle theft
Cities outside metropolitan areas	None										
Nonmetropolitan counties	None										
Area actually reporting	100.0%	1	0	1	1	0	0	1	0	1	0
State total	952,065	4,844	56	308	221	1,359	3,121	26,334	5,023	19,791	1,520
Rate per 100,000 inhabitants		508.8	5.9	32.4	23.2	142.7	327.8	2,766.0	527.6	2,078.7	159.7
District of Columbia[4]											
Metropolitan statistical area	681,170										
Area actually reporting	100.0%	8,214	139	532	401	3,480	4,063	32,716	2,361	27,382	2,973
Cities outside metropolitan areas	None										
Nonmetropolitan counties	None										
District total	681,170	8,214	139	532	401	3,480	4,063	32,716	2,361	27,382	2,973
Rate per 100,000 inhabitants		1,205.9	20.4	78.1	58.9	510.9	596.5	4,802.9	346.6	4,019.8	436.5
Florida											
Metropolitan statistical area	19,905,117										
Area actually reporting	99.8%	85,184	1,069	7,340	5,356	19,854	56,921	537,956	95,945	399,765	42,246
Estimated total	100.0%	85,327	1,071	7,352	5,365	19,889	57,015	538,945	96,110	400,513	42,322
Cities outside metropolitan areas	146,572										
Area actually reporting	94.3%	929	10	41	29	141	737	5,149	1,159	3,742	248
Estimated total	100.0%	985	11	44	32	149	781	5,459	1,229	3,967	263
Nonmetropolitan counties	560,750										
Area actually reporting	100.0%	2,388	29	202	131	137	2,020	9,408	2,986	5,872	550
State total	20,612,439	88,700	1,111	7,598	5,528	20,175	59,816	553,812	100,325	410,352	43,135
Rate per 100,000 inhabitants		430.3	5.4	36.9	26.8	97.9	290.2	2,686.8	486.7	1,990.8	209.3
Georgia[5]											
Metropolitan statistical area	8,537,584										
Area actually reporting	99.5%	35,058	586	2,975	2,159	11,252	20,245	261,232	52,059	184,537	24,636
Estimated total	100.0%	35,206	588	2,986	2,168	11,297	20,335	262,449	52,298	185,405	24,746
Cities outside metropolitan areas	644,378										
Area actually reporting	89.4%	2,807	53	219	166	641	1,894	24,709	4,962	18,977	770
Estimated total	100.0%	3,132	59	238	182	717	2,118	27,637	5,550	21,226	861
Nonmetropolitan counties	1,128,409										
Area actually reporting	93.0%	2,464	32	262	165	178	1,992	18,309	5,112	12,086	1,111
Estimated total	100.0%	2,652	34	285	178	191	2,142	19,684	5,496	12,994	1,194
State total	10,310,371	40,990	681	3,509	2,528	12,205	24,595	309,770	63,344	219,625	26,801
Rate per 100,000 inhabitants		397.6	6.6	34.0	24.5	118.4	238.5	3,004.5	614.4	2,130.1	259.9
Hawaii											
Metropolitan statistical area	1,160,343										
Area actually reporting	100.0%	3,781	21	459	343	904	2,397	36,333	4,736	26,534	5,063
Cities outside metropolitan areas	None										
Nonmetropolitan counties	268,214										
Estimated total	100.0%	636	14	160	104	90	372	6,420	1,281	4,548	591
State total	1,428,557	4,417	35	619	447	994	2,769	42,753	6,017	31,082	5,654
Rate per 100,000 inhabitants		309.2	2.5	43.3	31.3	69.6	193.8	2,992.7	421.2	2,175.8	395.8
Idaho											
Metropolitan statistical area	1,127,333										
Area actually reporting	100.0%	2,775	28	507	378	170	2,070	21,858	4,307	16,026	1,525
Estimated total											
Cities outside metropolitan areas	255,530										
Area actually reporting	99.1%	587	11	116	85	32	428	4,583	984	3,310	289
	100.0%	592	11	117	86	32	432	4,625	993	3,340	292
Nonmetropolitan counties	300,277										
Area actually reporting	100.0%	509	10	95	65	11	393	2,874	1,018	1,596	260
State total	1,683,140	3,876	49	719	529	213	2,895	29,357	6,318	20,962	2,077
Rate per 100,000 inhabitants		230.3	2.9	42.7	31.4	12.7	172.0	1,744.2	375.4	1,245.4	123.4
Illinois											
Metropolitan statistical area	11,329,203										
Area actually reporting	97.4%	51,812	1,016	4,262	3,172	17,372	29,162	234,747	41,931	173,922	18,894
Estimated total	100.0%	52,414	1,022	4,340	3,231	17,544	29,508	239,672	42,707	177,817	19,148
Cities outside metropolitan areas	829,170										
Area actually reporting	84.2%	2,032	6	311	226	198	1,517	14,538	2,946	11,189	403
Estimated total	100.0%	2,399	7	355	264	235	1,802	17,269	3,499	13,291	479
Nonmetropolitan counties	643,166										
Area actually reporting	88.6%	923	22	189	125	43	669	4,755	1,580	2,924	251
Estimated total	100.0%	1,041	25	213	140	48	755	5,365	1,783	3,299	283
State total	12,801,539	55,854	1,054	4,908	3,635	17,827	32,065	262,306	47,989	194,407	19,910
Rate per 100,000 inhabitants		436.3	8.2	38.3	28.4	139.3	250.5	2,049.0	374.9	1,518.6	155.5
Indiana[6]											
Metropolitan statistical area	5,169,542										
Area actually reporting	84.0%	22,873	370	1,868	1,400	6,857	13,778	134,126	26,691	95,363	12,072
Estimated total	100.0%	24,435	396	2,068	1,546	7,126	14,845	148,420	29,206	105,936	13,278
Cities outside metropolitan areas	522,889										
Area actually reporting	62.7%	774	7	110	81	100	557	9,245	1,381	7,357	507
Estimated total	100.0%	1,236	11	178	134	159	888	14,740	2,202	11,730	808
Nonmetropolitan counties	940,622										
Area actually reporting	60.0%	694	19	143	98	27	505	5,158	1,613	3,158	387
Estimated total	100.0%	1,174	32	255	171	45	842	8,599	2,689	5,265	645

Table 3. Crime, by State and Area, 2016—Continued

(Number, percent, rate per 100,000 population.)

Area	Population	Violent crime[1]	Murder and nonnegligent manslaughter	Rape (revised definition)[2]	Rape (legacy definition)[3]	Robbery	Aggravated assault	Property crime	Burglary	Larceny-theft	Motor vehicle theft
State total	6,633,053	26,845	439	2,501	1,851	7,330	16,575	171,759	34,097	122,931	14,731
Rate per 100,000 inhabitants		404.7	6.6	37.7	27.9	110.5	249.9	2,589.4	514.0	1,853.3	222.1
Iowa											
Metropolitan statistical area	1,857,824										
Area actually reporting	98.8%	6,150	50	884	658	969	4,247	46,230	9,808	32,675	3,747
Estimated total	100.0%	6,192	50	891	663	971	4,280	46,504	9,882	32,856	3,766
Cities outside metropolitan areas	595,688										
Area actually reporting	97.4%	2,094	13	239	175	162	1,680	14,370	3,350	10,238	782
Estimated total	100.0%	2,151	13	246	181	166	1,726	14,760	3,441	10,516	803
Nonmetropolitan counties	681,181										
Area actually reporting	97.5%	748	8	107	75	11	622	4,026	1,665	1,957	404
Estimated total	100.0%	767	8	110	78	11	638	4,127	1,707	2,006	414
State total	3,134,693	9,110	71	1,247	922	1,148	6,644	65,391	15,030	45,378	4,983
Rate per 100,000 inhabitants		290.6	2.3	39.8	29.4	36.6	212.0	2,086.0	479.5	1,447.6	159.0
Kansas											
Metropolitan statistical area	1,970,971										
Area actually reporting	97.9%	8,227	85	887	659	1,451	5,804	56,252	9,453	41,266	5,533
Estimated total	100.0%	8,310	86	898	666	1,460	5,866	57,021	9,579	41,845	5,597
Cities outside metropolitan areas	605,300										
Area actually reporting	95.3%	1,973	11	328	239	178	1,456	16,659	3,234	12,498	927
Estimated total	100.0%	2,068	12	341	251	187	1,528	17,483	3,394	13,116	973
Nonmetropolitan counties	331,018										
Area actually reporting	92.8%	633	12	68	50	22	531	3,583	1,290	1,953	340
Estimated total	100.0%	682	13	73	54	24	572	3,863	1,391	2,105	367
State total	2,907,289	11,060	111	1,312	971	1,671	7,966	78,367	14,364	57,066	6,937
Rate per 100,000 inhabitants		380.4	3.8	45.1	33.4	57.5	274.0	2,695.5	494.1	1,962.9	238.6
Kentucky											
Metropolitan statistical area	2,604,116										
Area actually reporting	100.0%	7,859	176	879	659	2,911	3,893	73,569	14,192	51,591	7,786
Cities outside metropolitan areas	538,773										
Area actually reporting	100.0%	959	14	195	141	298	452	13,676	2,835	9,932	909
Nonmetropolitan counties	1,294,085										
Area actually reporting	100.0%	1,490	70	567	374	160	693	9,913	3,807	4,915	1,191
State total	4,436,974	10,308	260	1,641	1,174	3,369	5,038	97,158	20,834	66,438	9,886
Rate per 100,000 inhabitants		232.3	5.9	37.0	26.5	75.9	113.5	2,189.7	469.6	1,497.4	222.8
Louisiana											
Metropolitan statistical area	3,923,928										
Area actually reporting	99.1%	22,991	497	1,631	1,198	5,198	15,665	134,283	29,366	95,483	9,434
Estimated total	100.0%	23,135	499	1,639	1,205	5,220	15,777	135,537	29,581	96,462	9,494
Cities outside metropolitan areas	248,647										
Area actually reporting	91.6%	1,611	19	75	54	246	1,271	10,561	2,695	7,523	343
Estimated total	100.0%	1,758	21	82	61	268	1,387	11,525	2,941	8,210	374
Nonmetropolitan counties	509,091										
Area actually reporting	97.0%	1,560	33	92	60	85	1,350	7,106	2,081	4,568	457
Estimated total	100.0%	1,609	34	95	62	88	1,392	7,324	2,145	4,708	471
State total	4,681,666	26,502	554	1,816	1,328	5,576	18,556	154,386	34,667	109,380	10,339
Rate per 100,000 inhabitants		566.1	11.8	38.8	28.4	119.1	396.4	3,297.7	740.5	2,336.3	220.8
Maine											
Metropolitan statistical area	789,447										
Area actually reporting	100.0%	1,003	8	225	171	198	572	13,743	2,404	10,881	458
Cities outside metropolitan areas	258,813										
Area actually reporting	100.0%	396	7	116	82	53	220	5,404	839	4,416	149
Nonmetropolitan counties	283,219										
Area actually reporting	100.0%	249	5	71	47	15	158	2,765	760	1,837	168
State total	1,331,479	1,648	20	412	300	266	950	21,912	4,003	17,134	775
Rate per 100,000 inhabitants		123.8	1.5	30.9	22.5	20.0	71.3	1,645.7	300.6	1,286.8	58.2
Maryland											
Metropolitan statistical area	5,866,031										
Area actually reporting	88.1%	25,972	459	1,525	1,103	9,635	14,353	121,542	21,943	88,677	10,922
Estimated total	100.0%	28,003	477	1,711	1,235	10,222	15,593	134,419	24,001	98,686	11,732
Cities outside metropolitan areas	52,622										
Area actually reporting	100.0%	246	3	24	17	58	161	1,823	325	1,451	47
Nonmetropolitan counties	97,794										
Area actually reporting	100.0%	151	1	21	14	9	120	1,203	366	782	55
State total	6,016,447	28,400	481	1,756	1,266	10,289	15,874	137,445	24,692	100,919	11,834
Rate per 100,000 inhabitants		472.0	8.0	29.2	21.0	171.0	263.8	2,284.5	410.4	1,677.4	196.7
Massachusetts											
Metropolitan statistical area	6,713,214										
Area actually reporting	97.6%	24,834	128	2,026	1,512	5,265	17,415	102,464	18,439	76,183	7,842
Estimated total	100.0%	25,319	129	2,070	1,547	5,344	17,776	104,725	18,841	77,877	8,007
Cities outside metropolitan areas	91,574										
Area actually reporting	84.9%	300	4	49	37	18	229	1,370	299	1,028	43
Estimated total	100.0%	353	5	57	44	21	270	1,614	352	1,211	51
Nonmetropolitan counties	6,991										
Area actually reporting	100.0%	5	0	1	1	0	4	0	0	0	0
State total	6,811,779	25,677	134	2,128	1,592	5,365	18,050	106,339	19,193	79,088	8,058
Rate per 100,000 inhabitants		376.9	2.0	31.2	23.4	78.8	265.0	1,561.1	281.8	1,161.0	118.3

Table 3. Crime, by State and Area, 2016—Continued

(Number, percent, rate per 100,000 population.)

Area	Population	Violent crime[1]	Murder and nonnegligent manslaughter	Rape (revised definition)[2]	Rape (legacy definition)[3]	Robbery	Aggravated assault	Property crime	Burglary	Larceny-theft	Motor vehicle theft
Michigan											
Metropolitan statistical area	8,132,404										
Area actually reporting	99.8%	40,537	568	5,310	3,900	6,971	27,688	165,035	34,569	111,303	19,163
Estimated total	100.0%	40,579	568	5,317	3,905	6,979	27,715	165,307	34,612	111,510	19,185
Cities outside metropolitan areas	596,485										
Area actually reporting	91.6%	1,474	7	501	356	71	895	10,647	1,272	9,051	324
Estimated total	100.0%	1,611	8	548	390	78	977	11,623	1,389	9,880	354
Nonmetropolitan counties	1,199,411										
Area actually reporting	98.7%	3,339	22	1,244	809	62	2,011	12,526	3,521	8,376	629
Estimated total	100.0%	3,382	22	1,260	819	63	2,037	12,690	3,567	8,486	637
State total	9,928,300	45,572	598	7,125	5,114	7,120	30,729	189,620	39,568	129,876	20,176
Rate per 100,000 inhabitants		459.0	6.0	71.8	51.5	71.7	309.5	1,909.9	398.5	1,308.1	203.2
Minnesota											
Metropolitan statistical area	4,285,006										
Area actually reporting	100.0%	11,636	84	1,891	1,409	3,610	6,051	99,694	15,244	76,823	7,627
Cities outside metropolitan areas	536,351										
Area actually reporting	100.0%	1,071	9	265	194	93	704	11,809	1,529	9,732	548
Nonmetropolitan counties	698,595										
Area actually reporting	100.0%	687	8	192	128	25	462	6,253	1,833	3,867	553
State total	5,519,952	13,394	101	2,348	1,731	3,728	7,217	117,756	18,606	90,422	8,728
Rate per 100,000 inhabitants		242.6	1.8	42.5	31.4	67.5	130.7	2,133.3	337.1	1,638.1	158.1
Mississippi[6]											
Metropolitan statistical area	1,377,735										
Area actually reporting	81.7%	3,304	103	382	280	1,188	1,631	33,547	7,390	23,892	2,265
Estimated total	100.0%	3,732	111	431	316	1,298	1,892	39,162	8,556	28,063	2,543
Cities outside metropolitan areas	582,351										
Area actually reporting	45.4%	1,171	34	154	115	376	607	12,437	3,562	8,431	444
Estimated total	100.0%	2,602	75	360	273	829	1,338	27,419	7,853	18,587	979
Nonmetropolitan counties	1,028,640										
Area actually reporting	36.3%	718	19	151	99	98	450	5,856	2,518	3,047	291
Estimated total	100.0%	2,049	52	486	316	270	1,241	16,151	6,945	8,404	802
State total	2,988,726	8,383	238	1,277	905	2,397	4,471	82,732	23,354	55,054	4,324
Rate per 100,000 inhabitants		280.5	8.0	42.7	30.3	80.2	149.6	2,768.1	781.4	1,842.1	144.7
Missouri											
Metropolitan statistical area	4,549,686										
Area actually reporting	99.9%	26,940	474	2,151	1,593	6,269	18,046	138,969	24,543	98,114	16,312
Cities outside metropolitan areas	100.0%	26,941	474	2,151	1,593	6,269	18,047	138,978	24,544	98,121	16,313
Area actually reporting	660,363										
Estimated total	99.3%	2,434	32	239	177	240	1,923	21,155	3,641	16,533	981
Nonmetropolitan counties	100.0%	2,450	32	240	178	242	1,936	21,296	3,665	16,643	988
Area actually reporting	882,951										
Estimated total	100.0%	2,253	31	163	113	59	2,000	10,275	3,501	5,780	994
State total	6,093,000	31,644	537	2,554	1,884	6,570	21,983	170,549	31,710	120,544	18,295
Rate per 100,000 inhabitants		519.4	8.8	41.9	30.9	107.8	360.8	2,799.1	520.4	1,978.4	300.3
Montana											
Metropolitan statistical area											
Area actually reporting	367,953										
Estimated total	99.9%	1,306	7	185	137	172	942	13,377	1,823	10,180	1,374
Cities outside metropolitan areas	100.0%	1,307	7	185	137	172	943	13,392	1,824	10,193	1,375
Area actually reporting	100.0%	1,335	11	242	177	68	1,014	7,694	938	6,096	660
Nonmetropolitan counties	453,774										
Area actually reporting	98.9%	1,186	18	150	99	26	992	6,818	1,160	4,957	701
Estimated total	100.0%	1,198	18	151	100	26	1,003	6,890	1,172	5,010	708
State total	1,042,520	3,840	36	578	414	266	2,960	27,976	3,934	21,299	2,743
Rate per 100,000 inhabitants		368.3	3.5	55.4	39.7	25.5	283.9	2,683.5	377.4	2,043.0	263.1
Nebraska[6]											
Metropolitan statistical area	1,240,589										
Area actually reporting	99.2%	4,383	43	719	539	877	2,744	32,557	4,432	24,021	4,104
Estimated total	100.0%	4,398	43	723	543	878	2,754	32,713	4,451	24,143	4,119
Cities outside metropolitan areas	338,960										
Area actually reporting	93.5%	794	4	188	135	55	547	7,716	1,329	6,011	376
Estimated total	100.0%	848	4	200	145	59	585	8,249	1,421	6,426	402
Nonmetropolitan counties	327,567										
Area actually reporting	90.5%	275	2	64	43	8	201	1,992	518	1,289	185
Estimated total	100.0%	304	2	71	50	9	222	2,201	572	1,425	204
State total	1,907,116	5,550	49	994	738	946	3,561	43,163	6,444	31,994	4,725
Rate per 100,000 inhabitants		291.0	2.6	52.1	38.7	49.6	186.7	2,263.3	337.9	1,677.6	247.8
Nevada											
Metropolitan statistical area	2,668,109										
Area actually reporting	100.0%	19,133	209	1,616	1,211	6,292	11,016	71,672	17,652	41,249	12,771
Cities outside metropolitan areas	48,603										
Area actually reporting	100.0%	311	5	49	35	21	236	1,308	327	875	106
Nonmetropolitan counties	223,346										
Area actually reporting	100.0%	492	10	68	46	27	387	3,067	871	1,893	303

Table 3. Crime, by State and Area, 2016—Continued

(Number, percent, rate per 100,000 population.)

Area	Population	Violent crime[1]	Murder and nonnegligent manslaughter	Rape (revised definition)[2]	Rape (legacy definition)[3]	Robbery	Aggravated assault	Property crime	Burglary	Larceny-theft	Motor vehicle theft
State total	2,940,058	19,936	224	1,733	1,292	6,340	11,639	76,047	18,850	44,017	13,180
Rate per 100,000 inhabitants		678.1	7.6	58.9	43.9	215.6	395.9	2,586.6	641.1	1,497.1	448.3
New Hampshire											
Metropolitan statistical area	839,311										
Area actually reporting	99.0%	1,721	10	340	249	327	1,044	11,923	1,580	9,793	550
Estimated total	100.0%	1,733	10	343	252	329	1,051	12,030	1,594	9,881	555
Cities outside metropolitan areas	452,615										
Area actually reporting	89.4%	749	5	200	143	85	459	6,996	1,117	5,624	255
Estimated total	100.0%	839	6	224	161	95	514	7,829	1,250	6,294	285
Nonmetropolitan counties	42,869										
Area actually reporting	93.6%	61	1	14	9	3	43	313	111	173	29
Estimated total	100.0%	65	1	15	10	3	46	335	119	185	31
State total	1,334,795	2,637	17	582	423	427	1,611	20,194	2,963	16,360	871
Rate per 100,000 inhabitants		197.6	1.3	43.6	31.7	32.0	120.7	1,512.9	222.0	1,225.7	65.3
New Jersey											
Metropolitan statistical area	8,944,469										
Area actually reporting	100.0%	21,914	372	1,453	1,089	8,984	11,105	138,152	25,284	101,540	11,328
Cities outside metropolitan areas	None										
Nonmetropolitan counties	None										
State total	8,944,469	21,914	372	1,453	1,089	8,984	11,105	138,152	25,284	101,540	11,328
Rate per 100,000 inhabitants		245.0	4.2	16.2	12.2	100.4	124.2	1,544.6	282.7	1,135.2	126.6
New Mexico[6]											
Metropolitan statistical area	1,386,406										
Area actually reporting	99.3%	10,595	90	1,053	782	2,402	7,050	61,466	12,212	39,082	10,172
Estimated total	100.0%	10,643	90	1,059	786	2,406	7,088	61,774	12,273	39,287	10,214
Cities outside metropolitan areas	399,862										
Area actually reporting	96.9%	2,628	34	273	205	290	2,031	16,171	3,615	11,494	1,062
Estimated total	100.0%	2,710	35	281	211	299	2,095	16,682	3,729	11,857	1,096
Nonmetropolitan counties	294,747										
Area actually reporting	92.9%	1,177	13	173	112	30	961	3,228	1,188	1,638	402
Estimated total	100.0%	1,266	14	186	120	32	1,034	3,475	1,279	1,763	433
State total	2,081,015	14,619	139	1,526	1,117	2,737	10,217	81,931	17,281	52,907	11,743
Rate per 100,000 inhabitants		702.5	6.7	73.3	53.7	131.5	491.0	3,937.1	830.4	2,542.4	564.3
New York[6]											
Metropolitan statistical area	18,370,635										
Area actually reporting	99.4%	71,419	610	5,218	3,864	22,032	43,559	283,107	35,538	233,778	13,791
Estimated total	100.0%	71,584	612	5,246	3,884	22,074	43,652	284,602	35,733	235,018	13,851
Cities outside metropolitan areas	506,786										
Area actually reporting	98.1%	1,297	13	311	227	180	793	11,126	1,927	8,971	228
Estimated total	100.0%	1,324	13	318	233	184	809	11,344	1,965	9,147	232
Nonmetropolitan counties	867,868										
Area actually reporting	100.0%	1,377	5	696	452	58	618	9,235	2,123	6,803	309
State total	19,745,289	74,285	630	6,260	4,569	22,316	45,079	305,181	39,821	250,968	14,392
Rate per 100,000 inhabitants		376.2	3.2	31.7	23.1	113.0	228.3	1,545.6	201.7	1,271.0	72.9
North Carolina[6]											
Metropolitan statistical area	7,938,934										
Area actually reporting	97.6%	30,341	486	2,259	1,673	8,030	19,566	216,973	51,738	152,826	12,409
Estimated total	100.0%	30,715	492	2,290	1,699	8,110	19,823	220,854	52,773	155,488	12,593
Cities outside metropolitan areas	649,752										
Area actually reporting	88.0%	3,418	67	240	179	771	2,340	26,745	7,093	18,539	1,113
Estimated total	100.0%	3,870	76	258	196	876	2,660	30,403	8,063	21,075	1,265
Nonmetropolitan counties	1,558,102										
Area actually reporting	95.3%	3,032	105	286	182	333	2,308	25,253	10,714	13,160	1,379
Estimated total	100.0%	3,184	110	301	191	350	2,423	26,508	11,246	13,814	1,448
State total	10,146,788	37,769	678	2,849	2,086	9,336	24,906	277,765	72,082	190,377	15,306
Rate per 100,000 inhabitants		372.2	6.7	28.1	20.6	92.0	245.5	2,737.5	710.4	1,876.2	150.8
North Dakota											
Metropolitan statistical area	371,557										7,562	981
Area actually reporting	100.0%	1,119	8	214	160	136	761	10,363	1,820		
Cities outside metropolitan areas	201,068									3,441	647
Area actually reporting	99.8%	591	5	86	64	36	464	5,022	934	3,449	648
Estimated total	100.0%	592	5	86	64	36	465	5,033	936		
Nonmetropolitan counties	185,327										
Area actually reporting	100.0%	192	2	42	32	9	139	2,006	487	1,184	335
State total	757,952	1,903	15	342	256	181	1,365	17,402	3,243	12,195	1,964
Rate per 100,000 inhabitants		251.1	2.0	45.1	33.8	23.9	180.1	2,295.9	427.9	1,608.9	259.1
Ohio[6]											
Metropolitan statistical area	9,255,325										
Area actually reporting	91.6%	30,462	574	4,474	3,337	11,543	13,871	237,037	53,589	165,991	17,457
Estimated total	100.0%	31,626	592	4,731	3,534	11,914	14,389	253,645	56,493	178,994	18,158
Cities outside metropolitan areas	1,046,316										
Area actually reporting	81.1%	1,463	25	381	282	334	723	24,090	4,632	18,826	632
Estimated total	100.0%	1,806	31	471	353	412	892	29,716	5,714	23,222	780
Nonmetropolitan counties	1,312,732										
Area actually reporting	94.7%	1,365	29	363	238	187	786	15,145	4,427	10,028	690
Estimated total	100.0%	1,445	31	387	254	197	830	15,996	4,676	10,591	729

Table 3. Crime, by State and Area, 2016—Continued

(Number, percent, rate per 100,000 population.)

Area	Population	Violent crime[1]	Murder and nonnegligent manslaughter	Rape (revised definition)[2]	Rape (legacy definition)[3]	Robbery	Aggravated assault	Property crime	Burglary	Larceny-theft	Motor vehicle theft
State total	11,614,373	34,877	654	5,589	4,141	12,523	16,111	299,357	66,883	212,807	19,667
Rate per 100,000 inhabitants		300.3	5.6	48.1	35.7	107.8	138.7	2,577.5	575.9	1,832.3	169.3
Oklahoma[6]											
Metropolitan statistical area	2,640,800										
Area actually reporting	99.9%	13,864	196	1,577	1,179	2,824	9,267	86,883	20,696	56,351	9,836
Estimated total	100.0%	13,866	196	1,577	1,179	2,824	9,269	86,913	20,702	56,372	9,839
Cities outside metropolitan areas	682,233										
Area actually reporting	99.9%	2,714	28	324	238	311	2,051	22,843	5,563	15,775	1,505
Estimated total	100.0%	2,716	28	324	238	311	2,053	22,863	5,568	15,789	1,506
Nonmetropolitan counties	600,528										
Area actually reporting	91.3%	974	19	126	84	25	804	6,631	2,587	3,304	740
Estimated total	100.0%	1,066	21	138	92	27	880	7,261	2,833	3,618	810
State total	3,923,561	17,648	245	2,039	1,509	3,162	12,202	117,037	29,103	75,779	12,155
Rate per 100,000 inhabitants		449.8	6.2	52.0	38.5	80.6	311.0	2,982.9	741.7	1,931.4	309.8
Oregon[6]											
Metropolitan statistical area	3,431,824										
Area actually reporting	98.7%	9,177	71	1,459	1,076	2,110	5,537	102,894	13,568	77,779	11,547
Estimated total	100.0%	9,278	72	1,483	1,095	2,129	5,594	104,098	13,706	78,729	11,663
Cities outside metropolitan areas	308,081										
Area actually reporting	94.6%	730	10	131	95	113	476	11,246	1,732	8,766	748
Estimated total	100.0%	770	11	137	100	119	503	11,884	1,830	9,264	790
Nonmetropolitan counties	353,560										
Area actually reporting	73.3%	567	22	68	45	22	455	3,930	975	2,413	542
Estimated total	100.0%	782	30	101	66	30	621	5,363	1,330	3,293	740
State total	4,093,465	10,830	113	1,721	1,261	2,278	6,718	121,345	16,866	91,286	13,193
Rate per 100,000 inhabitants		264.6	2.8	42.0	30.8	55.6	164.1	2,964.4	412.0	2,230.0	322.3
Pennsylvania											
Metropolitan statistical area	11,313,467										
Area actually reporting	99.1%	37,232	626	3,535	2,632	11,996	21,075	203,086	31,518	159,219	12,349
Estimated total	100.0%	37,394	627	3,543	2,639	12,038	21,186	204,598	31,708	160,485	12,405
Cities outside metropolitan areas	681,636										
Area actually reporting	95.9%	1,552	10	140	106	162	1,240	9,060	1,378	7,434	248
Estimated total	100.0%	1,609	10	137	103	169	1,293	9,449	1,437	7,753	259
Nonmetropolitan counties	789,124										
Area actually reporting	100.0%	1,444	24	753	491	119	548	8,748	2,375	5,990	383
State total	12,784,227	40,447	661	4,433	3,233	12,326	23,027	222,795	35,520	174,228	13,047
Rate per 100,000 inhabitants		316.4	5.2	34.7	25.3	96.4	180.1	1,742.7	277.8	1,362.8	102.1
Puerto Rico[7]											
Metropolitan statistical area	3,262,275										
Area actually reporting	100.0%	7,362	650	160	121	3,155	3,397	34,107	7,907	22,453	3,747
Cities outside metropolitan areas	149,032										
Area actually reporting	100.0%	281	29	9	7	46	197	1,094	344	710	40
Total	3,411,307	7,643	679	169	128	3,201	3,594	35,201	8,251	23,163	3,787
Rate per 100,000 inhabitants		224.0	19.9	5.0	3.8	93.8	105.4	1,031.9	241.9	679.0	111.0
Rhode Island[6]											
Metropolitan statistical area	1,056,426										
Area actually reporting	100.0%	2,489	28	420	314	539	1,502	19,978	3,787	14,611	1,580
Cities outside metropolitan areas	None										
Nonmetropolitan counties	None										
Area actually reporting	100.0%	35	1	22	14	1	11	80	1	63	16
State total	1,056,426	2,524	29	442	328	540	1,513	20,058	3,788	14,674	1,596
Rate per 100,000 inhabitants		238.9	2.7	41.8	31.0	51.1	143.2	1,898.7	358.6	1,389.0	151.1
South Carolina											
Metropolitan statistical area	4,212,891										
Area actually reporting	99.7%	20,864	303	2,009	1,453	3,488	15,064	135,853	26,498	97,150	12,205
Estimated total	100.0%	20,933	303	2,016	1,459	3,500	15,114	136,379	26,574	97,566	12,239
Cities outside metropolitan areas	205,750										
Area actually reporting	97.2%	1,737	33	147	106	300	1,257	10,856	2,309	8,097	450
Estimated total	100.0%	1,787	34	151	109	309	1,293	11,166	2,375	8,328	463
Nonmetropolitan counties	542,478										
Area actually reporting	99.2%	2,158	29	218	142	224	1,687	13,274	3,994	8,072	1,208
Estimated total	100.0%	2,176	29	220	143	226	1,701	13,383	4,027	8,138	1,218
State total	4,961,119	24,896	366	2,387	1,711	4,035	18,108	160,928	32,976	114,032	13,920
Rate per 100,000 inhabitants		501.8	7.4	48.1	34.5	81.3	365.0	3,243.8	664.7	2,298.5	280.6
South Dakota[6]											
Metropolitan statistical area	416,782										
Area actually reporting	99.3%	1,732	15	309	228	211	1,197	10,354	1,798	7,560	996
Estimated total	100.0%	1,735	15	309	228	211	1,200	10,384	1,802	7,584	998
Cities outside metropolitan areas	219,496										
Area actually reporting	94.6%	1,584	6	152	113	52	1,374	5,254	839	4,042	373
Estimated total	100.0%	1,673	6	159	119	55	1,453	5,554	887	4,273	394
Nonmetropolitan counties	229,176										
Area actually reporting	78.2%	168	5	33	25	5	125	940	243	611	86
Estimated total	100.0%	213	6	41	32	6	160	1,203	311	782	110
State total	865,454	3,621	27	509	379	272	2,813	17,141	3,000	12,639	1,502
Rate per 100,000 inhabitants		418.4	3.1	58.8	43.8	31.4	325.0	1,980.6	346.6	1,460.4	173.6

Table 3. Crime, by State and Area, 2016—Continued

(Number, percent, rate per 100,000 population.)

Area	Population	Violent crime[1]	Murder and nonnegligent manslaughter	Rape (revised definition)[2]	Rape (legacy definition)[3]	Robbery	Aggravated assault	Property crime	Burglary	Larceny-theft	Motor vehicle theft
Tennessee											
Metropolitan statistical area	5,151,809										
Area actually reporting	100.0%	36,002	435	2,261	1,679	7,403	25,903	154,421	31,772	110,354	12,295
Cities outside metropolitan areas	513,895										
Area actually reporting	100.0%	3,326	25	244	177	290	2,767	20,509	3,890	15,469	1,150
Nonmetropolitan counties	985,490										
Area actually reporting	100.0%	2,769	26	209	135	120	2,414	14,905	4,650	8,581	1,674
State total	6,651,194	42,097	486	2,714	1,991	7,813	31,084	189,835	40,312	134,404	15,119
Rate per 100,000 inhabitants		632.9	7.3	40.8	29.9	117.5	467.3	2,854.1	606.1	2,020.7	227.3
Texas											
Metropolitan statistical area	24,814,265										
Area actually reporting	99.7%	112,094	1,382	12,022	8,912	32,508	66,182	708,595	132,040	511,044	65,511
Estimated total	100.0%	112,275	1,382	12,049	8,935	32,551	66,293	710,123	132,303	512,191	65,629
Cities outside metropolitan areas	1,439,521										
Area actually reporting	96.6%	5,470	44	682	497	596	4,148	38,585	8,950	27,759	1,876
Estimated total	100.0%	5,656	46	708	519	614	4,288	39,863	9,250	28,677	1,936
Nonmetropolitan counties	1,608,810										
Area actually reporting	98.9%	3,077	49	604	400	150	2,274	18,758	7,110	10,173	1,475
Estimated total	100.0%	3,111	50	610	404	152	2,299	18,961	7,187	10,283	1,491
State total	27,862,596	121,042	1,478	13,367	9,858	33,317	72,880	768,947	148,740	551,151	69,056
Rate per 100,000 inhabitants		434.4	5.3	48.0	35.4	119.6	261.6	2,759.8	533.8	1,978.1	247.8
Utah											
Metropolitan statistical area	2,725,548										
Area actually reporting	99.4%	6,695	63	1,370	1,010	1,499	3,763	83,517	11,726	62,970	8,821
Estimated total	100.0%	6,721	63	1,375	1,014	1,505	3,778	83,912	11,789	63,255	8,868
Cities outside metropolitan areas	149,141										
Area actually reporting	90.3%	320	2	81	59	20	217	3,185	483	2,508	194
Estimated total	100.0%	354	2	90	66	22	240	3,529	535	2,779	215
Nonmetropolitan counties	176,528										
Area actually reporting	95.5%	317	7	53	34	13	244	2,498	489	1,718	291
Estimated total	100.0%	332	7	55	36	14	256	2,617	512	1,800	305
State total	3,051,217	7,407	72	1,520	1,116	1,541	4,274	90,058	12,836	67,834	9,388
Rate per 100,000 inhabitants		242.8	2.4	49.8	36.6	50.5	140.1	2,951.5	420.7	2,223.2	307.7
Vermont											
Metropolitan statistical area	217,636										
Area actually reporting	100.0%	439	7	74	53	54	304	4,894	747	4,058	89
Cities outside metropolitan areas	203,654										
Area actually reporting	100.0%	322	1	62	42	40	219	3,607	585	2,937	85
Nonmetropolitan counties	203,304										
Area actually reporting	100.0%	228	6	42	29	12	168	2,101	771	1,222	108
State total	624,594	989	14	178	124	106	691	10,602	2,103	8,217	282
Rate per 100,000 inhabitants		158.3	2.2	28.5	19.9	17.0	110.6	1,697.4	336.7	1,315.6	45.1
Virginia											
Metropolitan statistical area	7,366,234										
Area actually reporting	100.0%	16,236	406	2,236	1,628	4,572	9,022	141,037	17,122	114,954	8,961
Cities outside metropolitan areas	259,405										
Area actually reporting	99.9%	848	23	147	104	140	538	6,736	918	5,560	258
Estimated total	100.0%	849	23	147	104	140	539	6,745	919	5,568	258
Nonmetropolitan counties	786,169										
Area actually reporting	100.0%	1,217	55	354	233	91	717	8,630	1,977	6,084	569
State total	8,411,808	18,302	484	2,737	1,965	4,803	10,278	156,412	20,018	126,606	9,788
Rate per 100,000 inhabitants		217.6	5.8	32.5	23.4	57.1	122.2	1,859.4	238.0	1,505.1	116.4
Washington[6]											
Metropolitan statistical area	6,561,914										
Area actually reporting	99.9%	20,475	172	2,786	2,054	5,467	12,050	235,805	44,545	160,783	30,477
Estimated total	100.0%	20,475	172	2,786	2,054	5,467	12,050	235,814	44,546	160,790	30,478
Cities outside metropolitan areas	299,860										
Area actually reporting	97.8%	983	7	195	140	151	630	12,608	2,593	8,804	1,211
Estimated total	100.0%	1,004	7	199	144	154	644	12,894	2,652	9,004	1,238
Nonmetropolitan counties	426,226										
Area actually reporting	100.0%	544	16	92	61	30	406	5,945	1,982	3,393	570
State total	7,288,000	22,023	195	3,077	2,259	5,651	13,100	254,653	49,180	173,187	32,286
Rate per 100,000 inhabitants		302.2	2.7	42.2	31.0	77.5	179.7	3,494.1	674.8	2,376.3	443.0
West Virginia											
Metropolitan statistical area	1,131,010										
Area actually reporting	89.9%	4,030	50	427	309	564	2,989	26,592	6,775	18,050	1,767
Estimated total	100.0%	4,334	52	460	335	597	3,225	29,486	7,377	20,151	1,958
Cities outside metropolitan areas	187,738										
Area actually reporting	59.0%	388	2	28	21	34	324	1,898	314	1,491	93
Estimated total	100.0%	648	3	37	28	58	550	3,220	533	2,529	158
Nonmetropolitan counties	512,354										
Area actually reporting	93.7%	1,476	24	150	99	61	1,241	4,481	1,304	2,809	368
Estimated total	100.0%	1,575	26	160	105	65	1,324	4,781	1,391	2,997	393
State total	1,831,102	6,557	81	657	468	720	5,099	37,487	9,301	25,677	2,509
Rate per 100,000 inhabitants		358.1	4.4	35.9	25.6	39.3	278.5	2,047.2	507.9	1,402.3	137.0

Table 3. Crime, by State and Area, 2016—Continued

(Number, percent, rate per 100,000 population.)

Area	Population	Violent crime[1]	Murder and nonnegligent manslaughter	Rape (revised definition)[2]	Rape (legacy definition)[3]	Robbery	Aggravated assault	Property crime	Burglary	Larceny-theft	Motor vehicle theft
Wisconsin[6]											
Metropolitan statistical area	4,281,462										
Area actually reporting	99.0%	15,475	205	1,532	1,145	4,603	9,135	89,637	15,331	65,137	9,169
Estimated total	100.0%	15,515	205	1,541	1,152	4,608	9,161	90,113	15,411	65,509	9,193
Cities outside metropolitan areas	648,096										
Area actually reporting	99.6%	1,250	14	251	184	66	919	14,410	1,741	12,298	371
Estimated total	100.0%	1,254	14	251	184	66	923	14,471	1,748	12,350	373
Nonmetropolitan counties	849,150										
Area actually reporting	100.0%	910	10	187	122	32	681	7,136	2,266	4,478	392
State total	5,778,708	17,679	229	1,979	1,458	4,706	10,765	111,720	19,425	82,337	9,958
Rate per 100,000 inhabitants		305.9	4.0	34.2	25.2	81.4	186.3	1,933.3	336.1	1,424.8	172.3
Wyoming											
Metropolitan statistical area	180,145										
Area actually reporting	100.0%	413	8	59	43	30	316	5,020	866	3,739	415
Cities outside metropolitan areas	245,821										
Area actually reporting	95.7%	635	10	112	81	26	487	5,091	645	4,167	279
Estimated total	100.0%	663	10	117	86	27	509	5,321	674	4,355	292
Nonmetropolitan counties	159,535										
Area actually reporting	88.4%	314	2	26	19	2	284	989	204	703	82
Estimated total	100.0%	354	2	29	21	2	321	1,119	231	795	93
State total	585,501	1,430	20	205	150	59	1,146	11,460	1,771	8,889	800
Rate per 100,000 inhabitants		244.2	3.4	35.0	25.6	10.1	195.7	1,957.3	302.5	1,518.2	136.6

Note: Although arson data are included in the trend and clearance tables, sufficient data are not available to estimate totals for this offense. Therefore, no arson data are published in this table.
1 The violent crime figures include the offenses of murder, rape (revised definition), robbery, and aggravated assault.   2 The figures shown in this column for the offense of rape were estimated using the revised Uniform Crime Reporting (UCR) definition of rape. See chapter notes for more detail.   3 The figures shown in this column for the offense of rape were estimated using the legacy Uniform Crime Reporting (UCR) definition of rape. See chapter notes for more detail.   4 Includes offenses reported by the Metro Transit Police and the Arson Investigation Unit of the District of Columbia Fire and Emergency Medical Services.   5 This state's agencies submitted rape data according to the legacy UCR definition of rape.   6 Agencies within this state submitted rape data according to both the revised UCR definition of rape and the legacy UCR definition of rape.   7 The figures submitted by Puerto Rico for rape were not verified and may not be comparable to previous years' data.

Table 4. Crime, by Selected Metropolitan Statistical Area, 2016

(Number, percent, rate per 100,000 population.)

Area	Population	Violent crime	Murder and nonnegligent manslaughter	Rape[1]	Robbery	Aggravated assault	Property crime	Burglary	Larceny-theft	Motor vehicle theft
Abilene, TX M.S.A.	169,885									
Includes Callahan, Jones, and Taylor Counties										
City of Abilene	122,523	546	8	70	133	335	4,269	905	3,113	251
Total area actually reporting	100.0%	614	11	79	137	387	4,932	1,104	3,530	298
Rate per 100,000 inhabitants		361.4	6.5	46.5	80.6	227.8	2,903.1	649.9	2,077.9	175.4
Akron, OH M.S.A.[2]	703,561									
Includes Portage and Summit Counties										
City of Akron	197,257	1,216	34	212	415	555	8,646	2,483	5,483	680
Total area actually reporting	96.2%	1,739	41	335	530	833	17,453	3,865	12,599	989
Estimated total	100.0%	1,781	42	344	544	851	18,043	3,963	13,067	1,013
Rate per 100,000 inhabitants		253.1	6.0	48.9	77.3	121.0	2,564.5	563.3	1,857.3	144.0
Albany, GA M.S.A.	152,566									
Includes Baker, Dougherty, Lee, Terrell, and Worth Counties										
City of Albany	74,330	873	16	28	204	625	3,620	888	2,585	147
Total area actually reporting	96.0%	1,098	18	41	237	802	5,553	1,415	3,934	204
Estimated total	100.0%	1,121	18	43	244	816	5,753	1,449	4,084	220
Rate per 100,000 inhabitants		734.8	11.8	28.2	159.9	534.9	3,770.8	949.8	2,676.9	144.2
Albany, OR M.S.A.	122,030									
Includes Linn County										
City of Albany	52,544	43	0	12	21	10	1,512	146	1,256	110
Total area actually reporting	100.0%	139	0	34	33	72	3,283	462	2,564	257
Rate per 100,000 inhabitants		113.9	0.0	27.9	27.0	59.0	2,690.3	378.6	2,101.1	210.6
Albany-Schenectady-Troy, NY M.S.A.	878,166									
Includes Albany, Rensselaer, Saratoga, Schenectady, and Schoharie Counties										
City of Albany	98,617	848	2	59	250	537	3,461	491	2,858	112
City of Schenectady	65,138	595	6	58	146	385	2,100	378	1,525	197
City of Troy	49,876	362	3	25	102	232	1,792	394	1,308	90
Total area actually reporting	100.0%	2,544	18	342	603	1,581	17,647	2,472	14,455	720
Rate per 100,000 inhabitants		289.7	2.0	38.9	68.7	180.0	2,009.5	281.5	1,646.0	82.0
Albuquerque, NM M.S.A.	907,140									
Includes Bernalillo, Sandoval, Torrance, and Valencia Counties										
City of Albuquerque	561,560	6,245	61	381	1,957	3,846	38,528	6,236	24,582	7,710
Total area actually reporting	100.0%	8,173	75	520	2,165	5,413	47,976	8,628	30,113	9,235
Rate per 100,000 inhabitants		901.0	8.3	57.3	238.7	596.7	5,288.7	951.1	3,319.6	1,018.0
Alexandria, LA M.S.A.	154,032									
Includes Grant and Rapides Parishes										
City of Alexandria	47,936	883	11	25	154	693	4,091	1,057	2,765	269
Total area actually reporting	98.8%	1,414	12	76	179	1,147	7,168	1,946	4,740	482
Estimated total	100.0%	1,422	12	77	180	1,153	7,236	1,958	4,793	485
Rate per 100,000 inhabitants		923.2	7.8	50.0	116.9	748.5	4,697.7	1,271.2	3,111.7	314.9
Allentown-Bethlehem-Easton, PA-NJ M.S.A.[3,4]	831,770									
Includes Warren County, NJ and Carbon, Lehigh, and Northampton Counties, PA										
City of Allentown, PA	120,615	552	10	55	274	213	3,337	668	2,387	282
City of Bethlehem, PA[3]	74,869		4	21	58		1,487	213	1,226	48
Total area actually reporting	99.6%		22	160	483			2,195		739
Estimated total	100.0%		22	161	485			2,202		741
Rate per 100,000 inhabitants			2.6	19.4	58.3			264.7		89.1
Altoona, PA M.S.A.	124,942									
Includes Blair County										
City of Altoona	45,158	156	1	23	37	95	821	169	619	33
Total area actually reporting	100.0%	266	1	40	46	179	1,698	238	1,405	55
Rate per 100,000 inhabitants		212.9	0.8	32.0	36.8	143.3	1,359.0	190.5	1,124.5	44.0
Amarillo, TX M.S.A.[2]	263,223									
Includes Armstrong, Carson, Oldham, Potter, and Randall Counties										
City of Amarillo	200,141	1,414	11	162	260	981	9,472	1,797	6,756	919
Total area actually reporting	100.0%	1,560	14	188	269	1,089	10,352	2,004	7,321	1,027
Rate per 100,000 inhabitants		592.7	5.3	71.4	102.2	413.7	3,932.8	761.3	2,781.3	390.2
Ames, IA M.S.A.	97,202									
Includes Story County										
City of Ames	66,333	107	1	39	15	52	1,077	164	867	46
Total area actually reporting	93.0%	141	1	51	16	73	1,517	235	1,203	79
Estimated total	100.0%	158	1	54	17	86	1,640	262	1,293	85
Rate per 100,000 inhabitants		162.5	1.0	55.6	17.5	88.5	1,687.2	269.5	1,330.2	87.4
Anchorage, AK M.S.A.	315,641									
Includes Anchorage Municipality and Matanuska-Susitna Borough										
City of Anchorage	299,097	3,422	28	542	695	2,157	14,649	2,008	10,599	2,042
Total area actually reporting	100.0%	3,519	28	548	709	2,234	15,626	2,070	11,413	2,143
Rate per 100,000 inhabitants		1,114.9	8.9	173.6	224.6	707.8	4,950.6	655.8	3,615.8	678.9

Table 4. Crime, by Selected Metropolitan Statistical Area, 2016—Continued

(Number, percent, rate per 100,000 population.)

Area	Population	Violent crime	Murder and nonnegligent manslaughter	Rape[1]	Robbery	Aggravated assault	Property crime	Burglary	Larceny-theft	Motor vehicle theft
Ann Arbor, MI M.S.A.	361,440									
Includes Washtenaw County										
City of Ann Arbor	117,688	213	1	44	43	125	2,051	242	1,697	112
Total area actually reporting	100.0%	1,147	2	190	186	769	5,956	921	4,597	438
Rate per 100,000 inhabitants		317.3	0.6	52.6	51.5	212.8	1,647.9	254.8	1,271.9	121.2
Anniston-Oxford-Jacksonville, AL M.S.A.	114,790									
Includes Calhoun County										
City of Anniston	22,205	735	7	39	87	602	1,712	712	888	112
City of Oxford	17,066	63	0	0	7	56	763	127	615	21
City of Jacksonville	12,150	123	0	6	16	101	501	140	335	26
Total area actually reporting	99.3%	1,023	8	59	123	833	3,743	1,263	2,298	182
Estimated total	100.0%	1,027	8	59	124	836	3,768	1,268	2,316	184
Rate per 100,000 inhabitants		894.7	7.0	51.4	108.0	728.3	3,282.5	1,104.6	2,017.6	160.3
Appleton, WI M.S.A.	234,069									
Includes Calumet and Outagamie Counties										
City of Appleton	74,439	208	2	30	20	156	1,294	175	1,080	39
Total area actually reporting	100.0%	354	4	60	31	259	3,110	404	2,605	101
Rate per 100,000 inhabitants		151.2	1.7	25.6	13.2	110.7	1,328.7	172.6	1,112.9	43.1
Asheville, NC M.S.A.[3]	451,305									
Includes Buncombe, Haywood, Henderson, and Madison Counties										
City of Asheville	89,546	537	10	48	144	335	4,357	752	3,345	260
Total area actually reporting	99.5%	1,079	23	98	245	713			6,866	722
Estimated total	100.0%	1,085	23	98	247	717			6,918	725
Rate per 100,000 inhabitants		240.4	5.1	21.7	54.7	158.9			1,532.9	160.6
Athens-Clarke County, GA M.S.A.	205,004									
Includes Clarke, Madison, Oconee, and Oglethorpe Counties										
City of Athens-Clarke County	123,934	533	4	53	163	313	4,100	822	3,054	224
Total area actually reporting	100.0%	700	6	78	176	440	5,757	1,145	4,301	311
Rate per 100,000 inhabitants		341.5	2.9	38.0	85.9	214.6	2,808.2	558.5	2,098.0	151.7
Atlanta-Sandy Springs-Roswell, GA M.S.A.	5,790,619									
Includes Barrow, Bartow, Butts, Carroll, Cherokee, Clayton, Cobb, Coweta, Dawson, DeKalb, Douglas, Fayette, Forsyth, Fulton, Gwinnett, Haralson, Heard, Henry, Jasper, Lamar, Meriwether, Morgan, Newton, Paulding, Pickens, Pike, Rockdale, Spalding, and Walton Counties										
City of Atlanta	472,579	5,121	111	136	2,070	2,804	24,804	4,411	16,400	3,993
City of Sandy Springs	107,685	117	3	14	66	34	2,837	532	2,091	214
City of Roswell	95,684	143	2	23	42	76	1,702	228	1,391	83
City of Alpharetta	64,943	35	1	5	20	9	1,308	135	1,129	44
City of Marietta	59,516	233	1	12	117	103	2,282	307	1,825	150
Total area actually reporting	99.7%	23,275	395	1,385	8,324	13,171	173,043	33,252	121,238	18,553
Estimated total	100.0%	23,345	396	1,390	8,346	13,213	173,620	33,364	121,651	18,605
Rate per 100,000 inhabitants		403.2	6.8	24.0	144.1	228.2	2,998.3	576.2	2,100.8	321.3
Auburn-Opelika, AL M.S.A	160,071									
Includes Lee County										
City of Auburn	63,871	210	4	12	31	163	1,125	203	844	78
City of Opelika	30,180	221	7	18	35	161	1,476	233	1,158	85
Total area actually reporting	100.0%	916	22	56	94	744	4,137	885	2,959	293
Rate per 100,000 inhabitants		572.2	13.7	35.0	58.7	464.8	2,584.5	552.9	1,848.6	183.0
Augusta-Richmond County, GA-SC M.S.A.	595,180									
Includes Burke, Columbia, Lincoln, McDuffie, and Richmond Counties, GA and Aiken and Edgefield Counties, SC										
Total area actually reporting	99.9%	2,039	44	214	503	1,278	18,754	3,644	13,931	1,179
Estimated total	100.0%	2,040	44	214	503	1,279	18,761	3,645	13,937	1,179
Rate per 100,000 inhabitants		342.8	7.4	36.0	84.5	214.9	3,152.2	612.4	2,341.6	198.1
Austin-Round Rock, TX M.S.A.	2,054,651									
Includes Bastrop, Caldwell, Hays, Travis, and Williamson Counties										
City of Austin	956,911	3,903	39	751	1,048	2,065	33,545	5,232	26,125	2,188
City of Round Rock	119,308	173	0	31	44	98	2,653	303	2,270	80
Total area actually reporting	99.9%	6,510	70	1,180	1,411	3,849	52,484	8,665	40,428	3,391
Estimated total	100.0%	6,511	70	1,180	1,411	3,850	52,501	8,668	40,441	3,392
Rate per 100,000 inhabitants		316.9	3.4	57.4	68.7	187.4	2,555.2	421.9	1,968.3	165.1
Bakersfield, CA M.S.A.	884,443									
Includes Kern County										
City of Bakersfield	378,788	1,821	32	67	614	1,108	17,138	3,887	10,203	3,048
Total area actually reporting	100.0%	5,128	88	307	1,166	3,567	32,570	8,351	17,742	6,477
Rate per 100,000 inhabitants		579.8	9.9	34.7	131.8	403.3	3,682.5	944.2	2,006.0	732.3
Baltimore-Columbia-Towson, MD M.S.A.	2,797,991									
Includes Anne Arundel, Baltimore, Carroll, Harford, Howard, and Queen Anne's Counties and Baltimore City										

Table 4. Crime, by Selected Metropolitan Statistical Area, 2016—Continued

(Number, percent, rate per 100,000 population.)

Area	Population	Violent crime	Murder and nonnegligent manslaughter	Rape[1]	Robbery	Aggravated assault	Property crime	Burglary	Larceny-theft	Motor vehicle theft
City of Baltimore	618,385	11,010	318	299	5,236	5,157	29,547	7,375	16,855	5,317
Total area actually reporting	100.0%	19,873	395	909	7,743	10,826	78,076	14,986	54,549	8,541
Rate per 100,000 inhabitants		710.3	14.1	32.5	276.7	386.9	2,790.4	535.6	1,949.6	305.3
Bangor, ME M.S.A.	152,658									
Includes Penobscot County										
City of Bangor	32,264	75	0	15	30	30	1,340	180	1,123	37
Total area actually reporting	100.0%	146	0	43	41	62	2,964	584	2,296	84
Rate per 100,000 inhabitants		95.6	0.0	28.2	26.9	40.6	1,941.6	382.6	1,504.0	55.0
Barnstable Town, MA M.S.A.[4]	213,081									
Includes Barnstable County										
City of Barnstable	43,974	199	1	16	15	167	711	133	558	20
Total area actually reporting	100.0%		1	73	35		3,329	850	2,346	133
Rate per 100,000 inhabitants			0.5	34.3	16.4		1,562.3	398.9	1,101.0	62.4
Baton Rouge, LA M.S.A.	833,146									
Includes Ascension, East Baton Rouge, East Feliciana, Iberville, Livingston, Pointe Coupee, St. Helena, West Baton Rouge, and West Feliciana Parishes										
City of Baton Rouge	228,389	2,143	47	123	824	1,149	9,934	2,364	6,907	663
Total area actually reporting	99.7%	4,198	79	278	1,166	2,675	28,229	5,994	20,831	1,404
Estimated total	100.0%	4,207	79	279	1,167	2,682	28,310	6,008	20,894	1,408
Rate per 100,000 inhabitants		505.0	9.5	33.5	140.1	321.9	3,398.0	721.1	2,507.8	169.0
Battle Creek, MI M.S.A	133,914									
Includes Calhoun County										
City of Battle Creek	60,904	594	3	83	64	444	2,325	607	1,629	89
Total area actually reporting	100.0%	1,000	7	178	89	726	4,205	1,065	2,979	161
Rate per 100,000 inhabitants		746.7	5.2	132.9	66.5	542.1	3,140.1	795.3	2,224.6	120.2
Bay City, MI M.S.A.	105,209									
Includes Bay County										
City of Bay City	33,725	205	1	50	25	129	925	291	600	34
Total area actually reporting	100.0%	389	3	109	32	245	1,950	505	1,358	87
Rate per 100,000 inhabitants		369.7	2.9	103.6	30.4	232.9	1,853.5	480.0	1,290.8	82.7
Beaumont-Port Arthur, TX M.S.A.[2]	408,167									
Includes Hardin, Jefferson, Newton, and Orange Counties										
City of Beaumont	118,283	1,316	14	86	379	837	5,065	1,460	3,299	306
City of Port Arthur	55,510	362	5	18	105	234	1,829	580	1,123	126
Total area actually reporting	97.1%	2,308	27	167	573	1,541	10,979	3,034	7,111	834
Estimated total	100.0%	2,342	27	171	581	1,563	11,185	3,083	7,246	856
Rate per 100,000 inhabitants		573.8	6.6	41.9	142.3	382.9	2,740.3	755.3	1,775.3	209.7
Beckley, WV M.S.A	121,287									
Includes Fayette and Raleigh Counties										
City of Beckley	16,940	214	3	14	38	159	1,278	246	984	48
Total area actually reporting	95.7%	491	12	34	57	388	3,144	836	2,161	147
Estimated total	100.0%	506	12	36	59	399	3,323	865	2,301	157
Rate per 100,000 inhabitants		417.2	9.9	29.7	48.6	329.0	2,739.8	713.2	1,897.2	129.4
Bellingham, WA M.S.A	215,331									
Includes Whatcom County										
City of Bellingham	86,005	224	0	61	47	116	4,743	751	3,709	283
Total area actually reporting	100.0%	483	4	124	69	286	6,997	1,388	5,182	427
Rate per 100,000 inhabitants		224.3	1.9	57.6	32.0	132.8	3,249.4	644.6	2,406.5	198.3
Bend-Redmond, OR M.S.A.	180,071									
Includes Deschutes County										
City of Bend	89,244	96	0	17	20	59	2,010	178	1,740	92
City of Redmond	29,164	80	1	13	9	57	973	84	801	88
Total area actually reporting	100.0%	273	2	47	30	194	3,909	438	3,229	242
Rate per 100,000 inhabitants		151.6	1.1	26.1	16.7	107.7	2,170.8	243.2	1,793.2	134.4
Billings, MT M.S.A.	170,245									
Includes Carbon, Golden Valley, and Yellowstone Counties										
City of Billings	111,447	514	0	61	81	372	5,216	723	3,698	795
Total area actually reporting	99.7%	641	3	79	92	467	6,141	912	4,316	913
Estimated total	100.0%	642	3	79	92	468	6,156	913	4,329	914
Rate per 100,000 inhabitants		377.1	1.8	46.4	54.0	274.9	3,616.0	536.3	2,542.8	536.9
Binghamton, NY M.S.A.	243,328									
Includes Broome and Tioga Counties										
City of Binghamton	45,780	353	4	41	93	215	1,844	436	1,306	102
Total area actually reporting	99.7%	703	6	153	146	398	5,165	1,066	3,890	209
Estimated total	100.0%	704	6	153	146	399	5,177	1,068	3,900	209
Rate per 100,000 inhabitants		289.3	2.5	62.9	60.0	164.0	2,127.6	438.9	1,602.8	85.9
Bismarck, ND M.S.A.	129,489									
Includes Burleigh, Morton, Oliver, and Sioux Counties										
City of Bismarck	73,248	212	2	35	29	146	2,472	468	1,715	289

Table 4. Crime, by Selected Metropolitan Statistical Area, 2016—Continued

(Number, percent, rate per 100,000 population.)

Area	Population	Violent crime	Murder and nonnegligent manslaughter	Rape[1]	Robbery	Aggravated assault	Property crime	Burglary	Larceny-theft	Motor vehicle theft
Total area actually reporting	100.0%	380	3	62	34	281	3,676	704	2,523	449
Rate per 100,000 inhabitants		293.5	2.3	47.9	26.3	217.0	2,838.9	543.7	1,948.4	346.7
Blacksburg-Christiansburg-Radford, VA M.S.A.	181,407									
Includes Floyd, Giles, Montgomery, and Pulaski Counties and Radford City										
City of Blacksburg	44,528	43	0	19	3	21	409	62	333	14
City of Christiansburg	22,134	35	0	12	3	20	575	62	505	8
City of Radford	17,504	83	1	22	8	52	316	60	244	12
Total area actually reporting	100.0%	359	5	115	27	212	3,051	470	2,474	107
Rate per 100,000 inhabitants		197.9	2.8	63.4	14.9	116.9	1,681.9	259.1	1,363.8	59.0
Bloomington, IL M.S.A.	189,092									
Includes DeWitt and McLean Counties										
City of Bloomington	78,604	307	0	42	59	206	1,347	224	1,064	59
Total area actually reporting	94.7%	503	3	89	91	320	2,720	464	2,163	93
Estimated total	100.0%	524	3	92	97	332	2,890	491	2,297	102
Rate per 100,000 inhabitants		277.1	1.6	48.7	51.3	175.6	1,528.4	259.7	1,214.8	53.9
Bloomington, IN M.S.A.	166,354									
Includes Monroe and Owen Counties										
City of Bloomington	84,772	378	2	46	70	260	2,703	546	2,011	146
Total area actually reporting	87.6%	491	4	71	81	335	3,967	773	2,950	244
Estimated total	100.0%	520	5	75	85	355	4,207	833	3,106	268
Rate per 100,000 inhabitants		312.6	3.0	45.1	51.1	213.4	2,528.9	500.7	1,867.1	161.1
Boise City, ID M.S.A.	693,703									
Includes Ada, Boise, Canyon, Gem, and Owyhee Counties										
City of Boise	220,749	657	6	143	51	457	5,134	732	4,066	336
Total area actually reporting	100.0%	1,693	17	349	103	1,224	12,282	2,193	9,139	950
Rate per 100,000 inhabitants		244.1	2.5	50.3	14.8	176.4	1,770.5	316.1	1,317.4	136.9
Boston-Cambridge-Newton, MA-NH M.S.A.[4]	4,798,657									
Includes the Metropolitan Divisions of Boston, MA; Cambridge-Newton-Framingham, MA; and Rockingham County-Strafford County, NH										
City of Boston, MA	673,880	4,767	49	278	1,530	2,910	14,489	1,837	11,429	1,223
City of Cambridge, MA	111,030	294	2	28	76	188	2,369	326	1,924	119
City of Newton, MA	89,116	46	0	3	11	32	642	80	544	18
City of Framingham, MA	71,422	211	0	8	18	185	831	122	655	54
City of Waltham, MA	63,613	99	1	12	8	78	688	109	550	29
Total area actually reporting	98.0%		88	1,263	3,399		65,828	9,496	51,258	5,074
Estimated total	100.0%		89	1,291	3,445		67,153	9,729	52,254	5,170
Rate per 100,000 inhabitants			1.9	26.9	71.8		1,399.4	202.7	1,088.9	107.7
Boston, MA M.D.[4]	1,994,514									
Includes Norfolk, Plymouth, and Suffolk Counties										
Total area actually reporting	95.7%		58	632	2,260		30,970	4,471	24,142	2,357
Estimated total	100.0%		59	657	2,302		32,158	4,682	25,032	2,444
Rate per 100,000 inhabitants			3.0	32.9	115.4		1,612.3	234.7	1,255.0	122.5
Cambridge-Newton-Framingham, MA M.D.	2,373,065									
Includes Essex and Middlesex Counties										
Total area actually reporting	99.7%	5,562	25	451	1,060	4,026	29,097	4,291	22,354	2,452
Estimated total	100.0%	5,582	25	453	1,063	4,041	29,193	4,308	22,426	2,459
Rate per 100,000 inhabitants		235.2	1.1	19.1	44.8	170.3	1,230.2	181.5	945.0	103.6
Rockingham County-Strafford County, NH M.D.	431,078									
Includes Rockingham and Strafford Counties										
Total area actually reporting	99.2%	632	5	180	79	368	5,761	734	4,762	265
Estimated total	100.0%	637	5	181	80	371	5,802	739	4,796	267
Rate per 100,000 inhabitants		147.8	1.2	42.0	18.6	86.1	1,345.9	171.4	1,112.6	61.9
Boulder, CO M.S.A.	324,108									
Includes Boulder County										
City of Boulder	109,189	258	0	52	30	176	3,275	559	2,497	219
Total area actually reporting	100.0%	766	1	222	82	461	7,501	1,128	5,875	498
Rate per 100,000 inhabitants		236.3	0.3	68.5	25.3	142.2	2,314.4	348.0	1,812.7	153.7
Bowling Green, KY M.S.A.	170,204									
Includes Allen, Butler, Edmonson, and Warren Counties										
City of Bowling Green	64,561	204	4	51	85	64	2,773	379	2,236	158
Total area actually reporting	100.0%	280	6	74	91	109	3,664	691	2,740	233
Rate per 100,000 inhabitants		164.5	3.5	43.5	53.5	64.0	2,152.7	406.0	1,609.8	136.9
Bremerton-Silverdale, WA M.S.A.	262,877									
Includes Kitsap County										
City of Bremerton	39,862	198	0	29	38	131	1,576	257	1,159	160
Total area actually reporting	100.0%	680	1	112	93	474	6,993	1,458	5,000	535
Rate per 100,000 inhabitants		258.7	0.4	42.6	35.4	180.3	2,660.2	554.6	1,902.0	203.5
Bridgeport-Stamford-Norwalk, CT M.S.A.	935,988									
Includes Fairfield County										

Table 4. Crime, by Selected Metropolitan Statistical Area, 2016—Continued

(Number, percent, rate per 100,000 population.)

Area	Population	Violent crime	Murder and nonnegligent manslaughter	Rape[1]	Robbery	Aggravated assault	Property crime	Burglary	Larceny-theft	Motor vehicle theft
City of Bridgeport	148,180	1,115	10	69	441	595	3,258	667	1,857	734
City of Stamford	130,116	351	2	29	119	201	2,073	268	1,613	192
City of Norwalk	88,989	295	1	18	65	211	1,427	239	1,034	154
City of Danbury	85,335	161	0	30	75	56	1,363	168	1,056	139
City of Stratford	52,841	67	0	6	34	27	1,160	177	867	116
Total area actually reporting	100.0%	2,151	14	175	801	1,161	13,423	2,137	9,686	1,600
Rate per 100,000 inhabitants		229.8	1.5	18.7	85.6	124.0	1,434.1	228.3	1,034.8	170.9
Brownsville-Harlingen, TX M.S.A.	423,865									
Includes Cameron County										
City of Brownsville	185,583	448	4	50	130	264	6,028	917	4,960	151
City of Harlingen	65,913	281	2	35	58	186	2,590	503	2,018	69
Total area actually reporting	100.0%	1,607	8	201	224	1,174	12,101	2,116	9,654	331
Rate per 100,000 inhabitants		379.1	1.9	47.4	52.8	277.0	2,854.9	499.2	2,277.6	78.1
Brunswick, GA M.S.A.	116,597									
Includes Brantley, Glynn, and McIntosh Counties										
City of Brunswick	16,309	164	3	5	36	120	775	196	528	51
Total area actually reporting	100.0%	434	5	27	85	317	3,520	850	2,470	200
Rate per 100,000 inhabitants		372.2	4.3	23.2	72.9	271.9	3,018.9	729.0	2,118.4	171.5
Buffalo-Cheektowaga-Niagara Falls, NY M.S.A.	1,127,663									
Includes Erie and Niagara Counties										
City of Buffalo	257,446	2,857	44	153	1,049	1,611	10,599	2,631	7,133	835
City of Cheektowaga Town	78,100	181	2	22	68	89	2,523	280	2,128	115
City of Niagara Falls	48,675	565	3	14	199	349	2,402	551	1,665	186
Total area actually reporting	100.0%	4,635	55	373	1,566	2,641	27,260	5,206	20,555	1,499
Rate per 100,000 inhabitants		411.0	4.9	33.1	138.9	234.2	2,417.4	461.7	1,822.8	132.9
Burlington, NC M.S.A.	159,667									
Includes Alamance County										
City of Burlington	52,760	392	6	15	71	300	1,833	430	1,309	94
Total area actually reporting	100.0%	625	11	28	99	487	3,744	985	2,570	189
Rate per 100,000 inhabitants		391.4	6.9	17.5	62.0	305.0	2,344.9	616.9	1,609.6	118.4
California-Lexington Park, MD M.S.A.	111,930									
Includes St. Mary's County										
Total area actually reporting	100.0%	227	2	28	31	166	2,075	413	1,591	71
Rate per 100,000 inhabitants		202.8	1.8	25.0	27.7	148.3	1,853.8	369.0	1,421.4	63.4
Cape Coral-Fort Myers, FL M.S.A.	720,949									
Includes Lee County										
City of Cape Coral	179,631	224	5	16	31	172	3,081	632	2,286	163
City of Fort Myers	76,579	947	15	55	161	716	2,163	354	1,589	220
Total area actually reporting	100.0%	2,562	41	249	445	1,827	11,637	2,459	8,359	819
Rate per 100,000 inhabitants		355.4	5.7	34.5	61.7	253.4	1,614.1	341.1	1,159.4	113.6
Cape Girardeau, MO-IL M.S.A.	97,631									
Includes Alexander County, IL and Bollinger and Cape Girardeau Counties, MO										
City of Cape Girardeau, MO	39,738	236	5	10	54	167	1,628	227	1,332	69
Total area actually reporting	100.0%	469	6	21	72	370	2,342	396	1,841	105
Rate per 100,000 inhabitants		480.4	6.1	21.5	73.7	379.0	2,398.8	405.6	1,885.7	107.5
Carson City, NV M.S.A.	54,605									
Includes Carson City										
Total area actually reporting	100.0%	157	1	3	20	133	995	211	698	86
Rate per 100,000 inhabitants		287.5	1.8	5.5	36.6	243.6	1,822.2	386.4	1,278.3	157.5
Casper, WY M.S.A.	82,870									
Includes Natrona County										
City of Casper	61,343	70	0	2	7	61	1,669	255	1,297	117
Total area actually reporting	100.0%	168	0	23	12	133	2,081	389	1,535	157
Rate per 100,000 inhabitants		202.7	0.0	27.8	14.5	160.5	2,511.2	469.4	1,852.3	189.5
Cedar Rapids, IA M.S.A.[4]	267,187									
Includes Benton, Jones, and Linn Counties										
City of Cedar Rapids	131,181	387	4	67	100	216	5,019	995	3,670	354
Total area actually reporting	94.9%	566	5	96	114	351			4,512	456
Estimated total	100.0%	589	5	100	115	369			4,587	468
Rate per 100,000 inhabitants		220.4	1.9	37.4	43.0	138.1			1,716.8	175.2
Chambersburg-Waynesboro, PA M.S.A.	153,940									
Includes Franklin County										
City of Chambersburg	20,770	87	2	14	27	44	630	83	527	20
City of Waynesboro	10,902	29	6	6	6	11	266	43	211	12
Total area actually reporting	100.0%	221	13	52	56	100	2,281	444	1,763	74
Rate per 100,000 inhabitants		143.6	8.4	33.8	36.4	65.0	1,481.7	288.4	1,145.3	48.1
Champaign-Urbana, IL M.S.A.	239,184									
Includes Champaign, Ford, and Piatt Counties										
City of Champaign	87,071	625	3	41	124	457	2,838	728	1,979	131
City of Urbana	42,461	162	4	25	54	79	1,543	327	1,185	31

Table 4. Crime, by Selected Metropolitan Statistical Area, 2016—Continued

(Number, percent, rate per 100,000 population.)

Area	Population	Violent crime	Murder and nonnegligent manslaughter	Rape[1]	Robbery	Aggravated assault	Property crime	Burglary	Larceny-theft	Motor vehicle theft
Total area actually reporting	99.0%	1,048	11	125	214	698	6,108	1,506	4,367	235
Estimated total	100.0%	1,053	11	126	215	701	6,147	1,512	4,398	237
Rate per 100,000 inhabitants		440.2	4.6	52.7	89.9	293.1	2,570.0	632.1	1,838.8	99.1
Charleston, WV M.S.A.	218,036									
Includes Boone, Clay, and Kanawha Counties										
City of Charleston	49,429	767	13	36	152	566	3,939	947	2,694	298
Total area actually reporting	91.6%	1,293	17	90	205	981	8,585	2,061	5,708	816
Estimated total	100.0%	1,341	17	96	210	1,018	9,056	2,157	6,052	847
Rate per 100,000 inhabitants		615.0	7.8	44.0	96.3	466.9	4,153.4	989.3	2,775.7	388.5
Charleston-North Charleston, SC M.S.A.	762,454									
Includes Berkeley, Charleston, and Dorchester Counties										
City of Charleston	135,153	408	11	44	107	246	3,359	417	2,681	261
City of North Charleston	110,490	993	32	89	293	579	6,218	918	4,655	645
Total area actually reporting	99.5%	3,170	72	250	667	2,181	21,566	3,651	15,963	1,952
Estimated total	100.0%	3,188	72	252	670	2,194	21,699	3,670	16,068	1,961
Rate per 100,000 inhabitants		418.1	9.4	33.1	87.9	287.8	2,845.9	481.3	2,107.4	257.2
Charlottesville, VA M.S.A.	230,398									
Includes Albemarle, Buckingham, Fluvanna, Greene, and										
Nelson Counties and Charlottesville City										
City of Charlottesville	46,979	245	1	36	43	165	1,228	170	983	75
Total area actually reporting	100.0%	457	3	89	80	285	3,369	446	2,738	185
Rate per 100,000 inhabitants		198.4	1.3	38.6	34.7	123.7	1,462.3	193.6	1,188.4	80.3
Chattanooga, TN-GA M.S.A.	551,407									
Includes Catoosa, Dade, and Walker Counties, GA and										
Hamilton, Marion, and Sequatchie Counties, TN										
City of Chattanooga, TN	177,801	1,819	26	111	375	1,307	9,752	1,570	7,122	1,060
Total area actually reporting	97.5%	2,938	32	208	493	2,205	17,576	3,081	12,685	1,810
Estimated total	100.0%	2,982	33	211	506	2,232	17,926	3,160	12,921	1,845
Rate per 100,000 inhabitants		540.8	6.0	38.3	91.8	404.8	3,251.0	573.1	2,343.3	334.6
Cheyenne, WY M.S.A.	97,275									
Includes Laramie County										
City of Cheyenne	64,046	172	5	26	15	126	2,427	356	1,873	198
Total area actually reporting	100.0%	245	8	36	18	183	2,939	477	2,204	258
Rate per 100,000 inhabitants		251.9	8.2	37.0	18.5	188.1	3,021.3	490.4	2,265.7	265.2
Chicago-Naperville-Elgin, IL-IN-WI M.S.A.[2]	9,523,022									
Includes the Metropolitan Divisions of Chicago-Naperville-										
Arlington Heights, IL; Elgin, IL; Gary, IN; and Lake County-										
Kenosha County, IL-WI										
City of Chicago, IL	2,725,153	30,126	765	1,589	11,957	15,815	86,960	14,258	61,229	11,473
City of Naperville, IL	148,070	92	0	15	34	43	1,587	141	1,401	45
City of Elgin, IL	112,886	236	2	34	63	137	1,565	218	1,279	68
City of Gary, IN	76,556	460	46	32	212	170	3,617	990	2,229	398
City of Arlington Heights, IL	76,077	58	0	8	14	36	722	79	624	19
City of Evanston, IL	75,716	130	2	6	38	84	1,671	329	1,269	73
City of Schaumburg, IL	74,774	74	0	23	21	30	1,685	108	1,526	51
City of Skokie, IL	64,819	158	1	15	45	97	1,557	228	1,283	46
City of Des Plaines, IL	58,726	45	0	6	11	28	537	91	423	23
City of Hoffman Estates, IL	52,177	55	0	11	15	29	429	52	353	24
Total area actually reporting	96.9%	41,539	958	3,088	15,723	21,770	192,468	30,652	144,323	17,493
Estimated total	100.0%	42,187	967	3,162	15,887	22,171	198,228	31,492	148,887	17,849
Rate per 100,000 inhabitants		443.0	10.2	33.2	166.8	232.8	2,081.6	330.7	1,563.4	187.4
Chicago-Naperville-Arlington Heights, IL M.D.[2]	7,318,619									
Includes Cook, DuPage, Grundy, Kendall, McHenry, and										
Will Counties										
Total area actually reporting	98.0%	37,221	867	2,546	14,474	19,334	156,027	24,872	115,796	15,359
Estimated total	100.0%	37,530	871	2,588	14,561	19,510	158,528	25,263	117,778	15,487
Rate per 100,000 inhabitants		512.8	11.9	35.4	199.0	266.6	2,166.1	345.2	1,609.3	211.6
Elgin, IL M.D.	634,927									
Includes DeKalb and Kane Counties										
Total area actually reporting	98.3%	1,202	14	215	218	755	8,755	1,214	7,232	309
Estimated total	100.0%	1,225	14	218	225	768	8,943	1,243	7,381	319
Rate per 100,000 inhabitants		192.9	2.2	34.3	35.4	121.0	1,408.5	195.8	1,162.5	50.2
Gary, IN M.D.	700,547									
Includes Jasper, Lake, Newton, and Porter Counties										
Total area actually reporting	84.6%	1,652	70	135	605	842	15,338	2,597	11,388	1,353
Estimated total	100.0%	1,908	74	156	658	1,020	17,918	2,940	13,432	1,546
Rate per 100,000 inhabitants		272.4	10.6	22.3	93.9	145.6	2,557.7	419.7	1,917.4	220.7
Lake County-Kenosha County, IL-WI M.D.	868,929									
Includes Lake County, IL and Kenosha County, WI										
Total area actually reporting	96.7%	1,464	7	192	426	839	12,348	1,969	9,907	472
Estimated total	100.0%	1,524	8	200	443	873	12,839	2,046	10,296	497
Rate per 100,000 inhabitants		175.4	0.9	23.0	51.0	100.5	1,477.6	235.5	1,184.9	57.2
Chico, CA M.S.A.	224,973									
Includes Butte County										

Table 4. Crime, by Selected Metropolitan Statistical Area, 2016—Continued

(Number, percent, rate per 100,000 population.)

Area	Population	Violent crime	Murder and nonnegligent manslaughter	Rape[1]	Robbery	Aggravated assault	Property crime	Burglary	Larceny-theft	Motor vehicle theft
City of Chico	91,122	293	0	66	57	170	3,290	499	2,336	455
Total area actually reporting	100.0%	790	4	133	138	515	7,307	1,755	4,531	1,021
Rate per 100,000 inhabitants		351.2	1.8	59.1	61.3	228.9	3,247.9	780.1	2,014.0	453.8
Cincinnati, OH-KY-IN M.S.A.	2,163,182									
Includes Dearborn, Ohio, and Union Counties, IN; Boone, Bracken, Campbell, Gallatin, Grant, Kenton, and Pendleton Counties, KY; and Brown, Butler, Clermont, Hamilton, and Warren Counties, OH										
City of Cincinnati, OH	298,880	2,720	57	249	1,278	1,136	15,382	3,929	10,216	1,237
Total area actually reporting	94.2%	5,377	98	856	2,164	2,259	54,312	10,956	40,542	2,814
Estimated total	100.0%	5,566	101	889	2,213	2,363	56,602	11,377	42,278	2,947
Rate per 100,000 inhabitants		257.3	4.7	41.1	102.3	109.2	2,616.6	525.9	1,954.4	136.2
Clarksville, TN-KY M.S.A.	285,097									
Includes Christian and Trigg Counties, KY and Montgomery County, TN										
City of Clarksville, TN	152,526	935	12	74	131	718	3,853	711	2,960	182
Total area actually reporting	100.0%	1,219	19	115	202	883	6,311	1,283	4,689	339
Rate per 100,000 inhabitants		427.6	6.7	40.3	70.9	309.7	2,213.6	450.0	1,644.7	118.9
Cleveland, TN M.S.A.	121,862									
Includes Bradley and Polk Counties										
City of Cleveland	44,423	384	2	14	50	318	2,704	406	2,044	254
Total area actually reporting	100.0%	624	3	24	64	533	4,102	811	2,867	424
Rate per 100,000 inhabitants		512.1	2.5	19.7	52.5	437.4	3,366.1	665.5	2,352.7	347.9
Cleveland-Elyria, OH M.S.A.	2,055,254									
Includes Cuyahoga, Geauga, Lake, Lorain, and Medina Counties										
City of Cleveland	386,227	6,299	135	488	2,980	2,696	20,533	6,333	10,001	4,199
City of Elyria	53,633	161	4	26	71	60	1,483	344	1,042	97
Total area actually reporting	85.3%	8,691	181	803	3,852	3,855	42,264	10,504	26,216	5,544
Estimated total	100.0%	9,156	189	900	4,009	4,058	48,994	11,617	31,555	5,822
Rate per 100,000 inhabitants		445.5	9.2	43.8	195.1	197.4	2,383.8	565.2	1,535.3	283.3
Coeur d'Alene, ID M.S.A.	153,701									
Includes Kootenai County										
City of Coeur d'Alene	50,155	173	1	48	13	111	1,418	200	1,129	89
Total area actually reporting	100.0%	356	7	74	27	248	3,568	724	2,641	203
Rate per 100,000 inhabitants		231.6	4.6	48.1	17.6	161.4	2,321.4	471.0	1,718.3	132.1
College Station-Bryan, TX M.S.A.	252,572									
Includes Brazos, Burleson, and Robertson Counties										
City of College Station	110,785	245	3	52	50	140	2,290	342	1,840	108
City of Bryan	83,286	420	1	59	96	264	2,552	511	1,899	142
Total area actually reporting	99.5%	833	5	149	162	517	5,969	1,108	4,557	304
Estimated total	100.0%	837	5	150	163	519	6,002	1,113	4,583	306
Rate per 100,000 inhabitants		331.4	2.0	59.4	64.5	205.5	2,376.4	440.7	1,814.5	121.2
Colorado Springs, CO M.S.A.	707,431									
Includes El Paso and Teller Counties										
City of Colorado Springs	464,113	2,301	24	446	437	1,394	16,526	2,677	11,776	2,073
Total area actually reporting	99.9%	2,861	32	575	483	1,771	20,132	3,248	14,421	2,463
Estimated total	100.0%	2,862	32	575	483	1,772	20,150	3,250	14,435	2,465
Rate per 100,000 inhabitants		404.6	4.5	81.3	68.3	250.5	2,848.3	459.4	2,040.5	348.4
Columbia, MO M.S.A.	177,168									
Includes Boone County										
City of Columbia	121,143	517	6	111	127	273	3,245	530	2,469	246
Total area actually reporting	100.0%	674	6	132	138	398	4,230	693	3,217	320
Rate per 100,000 inhabitants		380.4	3.4	74.5	77.9	224.6	2,387.6	391.2	1,815.8	180.6
Columbia, SC M.S.A.	820,037									
Includes Calhoun, Fairfield, Kershaw, Lexington, Richland, and Saluda Counties										
City of Columbia	134,489	1,116	10	99	286	721	7,374	1,114	5,357	903
Total area actually reporting	100.0%	4,834	58	399	849	3,528	28,907	5,013	20,633	3,261
Rate per 100,000 inhabitants		589.5	7.1	48.7	103.5	430.2	3,525.1	611.3	2,516.1	397.7
Columbus, GA-AL M.S.A.	316,990									
Includes Russell County, AL and Chattahoochee, Harris, Marion, and Muscogee Counties, GA										
City of Columbus, GA	202,338	1,218	24	62	523	609	9,625	2,273	6,500	852
Total area actually reporting	99.8%	1,639	33	123	601	882	12,060	2,940	7,996	1,124
Estimated total	100.0%	1,643	33	123	602	885	12,080	2,944	8,011	1,125
Rate per 100,000 inhabitants		518.3	10.4	38.8	189.9	279.2	3,810.8	928.7	2,527.2	354.9
Columbus, IN M.S.A.	81,884									
Includes Bartholomew County										
City of Columbus	47,222	34	0	15	17	2	1,943	180	1,657	106
Total area actually reporting	100.0%	67	0	21	20	26	2,511	326	2,010	175
Rate per 100,000 inhabitants		81.8	0.0	25.6	24.4	31.8	3,066.5	398.1	2,454.7	213.7

Table 4. Crime, by Selected Metropolitan Statistical Area, 2016—Continued

(Number, percent, rate per 100,000 population.)

Area	Population	Violent crime	Murder and nonnegligent manslaughter	Rape[1]	Robbery	Aggravated assault	Property crime	Burglary	Larceny-theft	Motor vehicle theft
Columbus, OH M.S.A.[2]	2,043,036									
Includes Delaware, Fairfield, Franklin, Hocking, Licking, Madison, Morrow, Perry, Pickaway, and Union Counties										
City of Columbus	862,515	4,500	91	867	2,144	1,398	35,106	7,756	23,800	3,550
Total area actually reporting	91.3%	5,585	104	1,166	2,489	1,826	56,162	11,472	40,424	4,266
Estimated total	100.0%	5,820	107	1,219	2,555	1,939	59,476	12,144	42,917	4,415
Rate per 100,000 inhabitants		284.9	5.2	59.7	125.1	94.9	2,911.2	594.4	2,100.6	216.1
Corpus Christi, TX M.S.A.	456,121									
Includes Aransas, Nueces, and San Patricio Counties										
City of Corpus Christi	327,948	2,328	24	259	424	1,621	12,198	2,296	9,246	656
Total area actually reporting	97.9%	2,981	35	306	458	2,182	16,035	3,264	11,933	838
Estimated total	100.0%	3,007	35	310	464	2,198	16,273	3,302	12,116	855
Rate per 100,000 inhabitants		659.3	7.7	68.0	101.7	481.9	3,567.7	723.9	2,656.3	187.5
Corvallis, OR M.S.A.	88,515									
Includes Benton County										
City of Corvallis	56,061	75	1	25	11	38	1,557	207	1,283	67
Total area actually reporting	100.0%	113	1	35	14	63	2,256	287	1,869	100
Rate per 100,000 inhabitants		127.7	1.1	39.5	15.8	71.2	2,548.7	324.2	2,111.5	113.0
Crestview-Fort Walton Beach-Destin, FL M.S.A.	268,298									
Includes Okaloosa and Walton Counties										
City of Crestview	23,749	121	3	20	19	79	897	157	678	62
City of Fort Walton Beach	22,314	67	3	12	10	42	611	72	490	49
Total area actually reporting	99.7%	1,023	14	126	96	787	6,303	1,184	4,759	360
Estimated total	100.0%	1,026	14	126	97	789	6,328	1,188	4,778	362
Rate per 100,000 inhabitants		382.4	5.2	47.0	36.2	294.1	2,358.6	442.8	1,780.9	134.9
Cumberland, MD-WV M.S.A.	98,752									
Includes Allegany County, MD and Mineral County, WV										
City of Cumberland, MD	19,995	177	1	13	53	110	1,218	247	949	22
Total area actually reporting	94.7%	299	6	23	70	200	2,333	457	1,821	55
Estimated total	100.0%	314	6	25	72	211	2,514	487	1,962	65
Rate per 100,000 inhabitants		318.0	6.1	25.3	72.9	213.7	2,545.8	493.2	1,986.8	65.8
Dallas-Fort Worth-Arlington, TX M.S.A.[2]	7,219,989									
Includes the Metropolitan Divisions of Dallas-Plano-Irving and Fort Worth-Arlington										
City of Dallas	1,320,939	10,071	171	767	4,604	4,529	44,910	10,948	26,370	7,592
City of Fort Worth	851,849	4,483	66	499	1,165	2,753	28,124	5,316	20,422	2,386
City of Arlington	392,666	2,188	21	307	557	1,303	12,383	2,115	9,189	1,079
City of Plano	288,242	399	5	77	109	208	5,479	903	4,181	395
City of Irving	240,765	521	5	37	213	266	6,490	1,183	4,674	633
City of Denton	134,054	349	5	95	73	176	3,025	543	2,313	169
City of Richardson	113,216	156	5	16	71	64	2,473	389	1,874	210
Total area actually reporting	99.8%	25,941	368	3,156	8,962	13,455	178,513	34,697	124,766	19,050
Estimated total	100.0%	25,971	368	3,160	8,970	13,473	178,781	34,740	124,971	19,070
Rate per 100,000 inhabitants		359.7	5.1	43.8	124.2	186.6	2,476.2	481.2	1,730.9	264.1
Dallas-Plano-Irving, TX M.D.	4,791,249									
Includes Collin, Dallas, Denton, Ellis, Hunt, Kaufman, and Rockwall Counties										
Total area actually reporting	99.8%	17,064	250	1,922	6,762	8,130	115,705	23,345	78,386	13,974
Estimated total	100.0%	17,092	250	1,926	6,769	8,147	115,952	23,385	78,575	13,992
Rate per 100,000 inhabitants		356.7	5.2	40.2	141.3	170.0	2,420.1	488.1	1,640.0	292.0
Fort Worth-Arlington, TX M.D.[2]	2,428,740									
Includes Hood, Johnson, Parker, Somervell, Tarrant, and Wise Counties										
Total area actually reporting	99.9%	8,877	118	1,234	2,200	5,325	62,808	11,352	46,380	5,076
Estimated total	100.0%	8,879	118	1,234	2,201	5,326	62,829	11,355	46,396	5,078
Rate per 100,000 inhabitants		365.6	4.9	50.8	90.6	219.3	2,586.9	467.5	1,910.3	209.1
Dalton, GA M.S.A.	143,925									
Includes Murray and Whitfield Counties										
City of Dalton	33,989	113	0	17	22	74	1,103	209	834	60
Total area actually reporting	99.6%	988	0	158	67	763	4,880	1,178	3,176	526
Estimated total	100.0%	991	0	158	68	765	4,905	1,182	3,195	528
Rate per 100,000 inhabitants		688.6	0.0	109.8	47.2	531.5	3,408.0	821.3	2,219.9	366.9
Danville, IL M.S.A.	78,439									
Includes Vermilion County										
City of Danville	31,931	502	0	47	88	367	1,894	646	1,185	63
Total area actually reporting	98.4%	631	0	74	98	459	2,720	913	1,711	96
Estimated total	100.0%	634	0	74	99	461	2,741	916	1,728	97
Rate per 100,000 inhabitants		808.3	0.0	94.3	126.2	587.7	3,494.4	1,167.8	2,203.0	123.7
Davenport-Moline-Rock Island, IA-IL M.S.A.[4]	383,016									
Includes Henry, Mercer, and Rock Island Counties, IL and Scott County, IA										
City of Davenport, IA	103,118	750	7	88	155	500	5,001	1,155	3,436	410

Table 4. Crime, by Selected Metropolitan Statistical Area, 2016—Continued

(Number, percent, rate per 100,000 population.)

Area	Population	Violent crime	Murder and nonnegligent manslaughter	Rape[1]	Robbery	Aggravated assault	Property crime	Burglary	Larceny-theft	Motor vehicle theft
City of Moline, IL	42,517	196	0	26	19	151	1,459	227	1,205	27
City of Rock Island, IL	38,543	158	4	6	23	125	1,042	175	782	85
Total area actually reporting	98.6%	1,496	12	185	238	1,061			7,660	602
Estimated total	100.0%	1,506	12	186	240	1,068			7,733	607
Rate per 100,000 inhabitants		393.2	3.1	48.6	62.7	278.8			2,019.0	158.5
Dayton, OH M.S.A.[2]	800,013									
Includes Greene, Miami, and Montgomery Counties										
City of Dayton	140,260	1,402	36	133	496	737	7,235	2,269	4,252	714
Total area actually reporting	96.9%	2,453	62	443	847	1,101	22,891	5,289	15,936	1,666
Estimated total	100.0%	2,491	63	451	860	1,117	23,434	5,379	16,367	1,688
Rate per 100,000 inhabitants		311.4	7.9	56.4	107.5	139.6	2,929.2	672.4	2,045.8	211.0
Decatur, AL M.S.A.	152,077									
Includes Lawrence and Morgan Counties										
City of Decatur	55,374	154	5	9	43	97	2,600	526	1,918	156
Total area actually reporting	99.3%	346	5	29	53	259	3,812	909	2,660	243
Estimated total	100.0%	352	5	29	54	264	3,848	916	2,686	246
Rate per 100,000 inhabitants		231.5	3.3	19.1	35.5	173.6	2,530.3	602.3	1,766.2	161.8
Decatur, IL M.S.A.	106,100									
Includes Macon County										
City of Decatur	72,694	392	3	45	97	247	2,657	859	1,700	98
Total area actually reporting	99.0%	434	3	52	103	276	2,954	926	1,928	100
Estimated total	100.0%	436	3	52	104	277	2,973	929	1,943	101
Rate per 100,000 inhabitants		410.9	2.8	49.0	98.0	261.1	2,802.1	875.6	1,831.3	95.2
Deltona-Daytona Beach-Ormond Beach, FL M.S.A.	631,296									
Includes Flagler and Volusia Counties										
City of Daytona Beach	65,495	814	9	26	94	685	4,197	572	3,234	391
City of Ormond Beach	41,325	202	0	17	40	145	1,602	312	1,158	132
Total area actually reporting	100.0%	2,471	19	168	369	1,915	18,058	3,102	13,650	1,306
Rate per 100,000 inhabitants		391.4	3.0	26.6	58.5	303.3	2,860.5	491.4	2,162.2	206.9
Denver-Aurora-Lakewood, CO M.S.A.	2,868,232									
Includes Adams, Arapahoe, Broomfield, Clear Creek, Denver, Douglas, Elbert, Gilpin, Jefferson, and Park Counties										
City of Denver	699,259	4,597	57	567	1,160	2,813	25,101	4,675	15,638	4,788
City of Aurora	366,477	1,939	22	289	576	1,052	11,213	1,698	7,977	1,538
City of Lakewood	154,553	875	4	144	174	553	8,455	1,014	6,429	1,012
City of Broomfield	66,953	36	0	16	2	18	1,610	216	1,236	158
Total area actually reporting	99.9%	11,149	124	1,919	2,470	6,636	84,650	12,492	58,890	13,268
Estimated total	100.0%	11,156	124	1,921	2,471	6,640	84,729	12,501	58,950	13,278
Rate per 100,000 inhabitants		389.0	4.3	67.0	86.2	231.5	2,954.0	435.8	2,055.3	462.9
Des Moines-West Des Moines, IA M.S.A.[3]	632,763									
Includes Dallas, Guthrie, Madison, Polk, and Warren Counties										
City of Des Moines	211,501	1,497	13	140	318	1,026	8,881	1,944	5,920	1,017
City of West Des Moines	65,631	149	1	24	19	105	1,513	147	1,296	70
Total area actually reporting	100.0%	2,352	25	267	386	1,674		3,458		1,442
Rate per 100,000 inhabitants		371.7	4.0	42.2	61.0	264.6		546.5		227.9
Detroit-Warren-Dearborn, MI M.S.A.	4,302,722									
Includes the Metropolitan Divisions of Detroit-Dearborn-Livonia and Warren-Troy-Farmington Hills										
City of Detroit	669,673	13,705	303	579	2,941	9,882	31,630	8,787	13,938	8,905
City of Warren	135,620	691	6	118	125	442	3,521	927	2,082	512
City of Dearborn	94,646	348	1	30	80	237	2,791	297	2,167	327
City of Livonia	94,226	141	0	18	28	95	1,694	295	1,250	149
City of Troy	83,743	78	1	12	16	49	1,336	94	1,183	59
City of Farmington Hills	81,649	77	0	18	9	50	1,050	145	834	71
City of Southfield	73,438	195	3	44	52	96	2,158	353	1,514	291
City of Taylor	61,290	372	2	37	83	250	1,495	290	1,042	163
City of Pontiac	60,003	749	15	66	121	547	1,425	520	771	134
City of Novi	59,441	32	0	6	2	24	661	56	586	19
Total area actually reporting	99.9%	23,903	389	2,141	4,653	16,720	89,693	18,887	56,067	14,739
Estimated total	100.0%	23,907	389	2,142	4,654	16,722	89,714	18,890	56,083	14,741
Rate per 100,000 inhabitants		555.6	9.0	49.8	108.2	388.6	2,085.1	439.0	1,303.4	342.6
Detroit-Dearborn-Livonia, MI M.D.	1,747,582									
Includes Wayne County										
Total area actually reporting	100.0%	18,073	339	1,104	3,860	12,770	54,744	12,845	30,153	11,746
Rate per 100,000 inhabitants		1,034.2	19.4	63.2	220.9	730.7	3,132.6	735.0	1,725.4	672.1
Warren-Troy-Farmington Hills, MI M.D.	2,555,140									
Includes Lapeer, Livingston, Macomb, Oakland, and St. Clair Counties										
Total area actually reporting	99.9%	5,830	50	1,037	793	3,950	34,949	6,042	25,914	2,993
Estimated total	100.0%	5,834	50	1,038	794	3,952	34,970	6,045	25,930	2,995
Rate per 100,000 inhabitants		228.3	2.0	40.6	31.1	154.7	1,368.6	236.6	1,014.8	117.2

Table 4. Crime, by Selected Metropolitan Statistical Area, 2016—Continued

(Number, percent, rate per 100,000 population.)

Area	Population	Violent crime	Murder and nonnegligent manslaughter	Rape[1]	Robbery	Aggravated assault	Property crime	Burglary	Larceny-theft	Motor vehicle theft
Dothan, AL M.S.A.[4]	148,284									
Includes Geneva, Henry, and Houston Counties										
City of Dothan[4]	67,835		5	35	79		2,758	669	1,928	161
Total area actually reporting	99.4%		10	74	95		4,221	1,072	2,869	280
Estimated total	100.0%		10	74	96		4,248	1,077	2,889	282
Rate per 100,000 inhabitants			6.7	49.9	64.7		2,864.8	726.3	1,948.3	190.2
Dover, DE M.S.A.	175,090									
Includes Kent County										
City of Dover	37,824	307	2	12	57	236	1,880	100	1,699	81
Total area actually reporting	100.0%	829	6	64	156	603	4,399	652	3,579	168
Rate per 100,000 inhabitants		473.5	3.4	36.6	89.1	344.4	2,512.4	372.4	2,044.1	96.0
Dubuque, IA M.S.A.	97,625									
Includes Dubuque County										
City of Dubuque	59,026	210	1	52	26	131	1,832	408	1,349	75
Total area actually reporting	100.0%	237	2	58	28	149	2,054	485	1,477	92
Rate per 100,000 inhabitants		242.8	2.0	59.4	28.7	152.6	2,104.0	496.8	1,512.9	94.2
Duluth, MN-WI M.S.A.	279,220									
Includes Carlton and St. Louis Counties, MN and Douglas County, WI										
City of Duluth, MN	86,090	312	1	51	64	196	3,827	529	3,162	136
Total area actually reporting	100.0%	642	3	126	92	421	8,915	1,374	7,124	417
Rate per 100,000 inhabitants		229.9	1.1	45.1	32.9	150.8	3,192.8	492.1	2,551.4	149.3
East Stroudsburg, PA M.S.A.	165,226									
Includes Monroe County										
Total area actually reporting	100.0%	416	10	73	80	253	3,130	632	2,403	95
Rate per 100,000 inhabitants		251.8	6.1	44.2	48.4	153.1	1,894.4	382.5	1,454.4	57.5
Eau Claire, WI M.S.A.[2]	166,178									
Includes Chippewa and Eau Claire Counties										
City of Eau Claire	68,084	141	1	18	17	105	1,818	277	1,481	60
Total area actually reporting	100.0%	230	5	38	20	167	2,788	493	2,187	108
Rate per 100,000 inhabitants		138.4	3.0	22.9	12.0	100.5	1,677.7	296.7	1,316.1	65.0
El Centro, CA M.S.A.	180,066									
Includes Imperial County										
City of El Centro	44,213	205	1	19	55	130	2,314	506	1,669	139
Total area actually reporting	95.9%	676	3	34	118	521	5,195	1,165	3,483	547
Estimated total	100.0%	701	3	36	126	536	5,372	1,199	3,597	576
Rate per 100,000 inhabitants		389.3	1.7	20.0	70.0	297.7	2,983.4	665.9	1,997.6	319.9
Elizabethtown-Fort Knox, KY M.S.A.	148,206									
Includes Hardin, Larue, and Meade Counties										
City of Elizabethtown	29,821	68	2	15	17	34	476	107	329	40
Total area actually reporting	100.0%	181	3	40	52	86	1,479	406	945	128
Rate per 100,000 inhabitants		122.1	2.0	27.0	35.1	58.0	997.9	273.9	637.6	86.4
Elmira, NY M.S.A.	86,124									
Includes Chemung County										
City of Elmira	27,995	97	2	2	34	59	1,074	172	875	27
Total area actually reporting	100.0%	172	3	28	38	103	1,892	270	1,577	45
Rate per 100,000 inhabitants		199.7	3.5	32.5	44.1	119.6	2,196.8	313.5	1,831.1	52.3
El Paso, TX M.S.A.	843,018									
Includes El Paso and Hudspeth Counties										
City of El Paso	687,193	2,682	17	314	476	1,875	12,357	1,410	10,135	812
Total area actually reporting	99.9%	3,076	23	378	520	2,155	14,413	1,784	11,696	933
Estimated total	100.0%	3,080	23	379	521	2,157	14,442	1,789	11,718	935
Rate per 100,000 inhabitants		365.4	2.7	45.0	61.8	255.9	1,713.1	212.2	1,390.0	110.9
Enid, OK M.S.A.	63,828									
Includes Garfield County										
City of Enid	52,240	214	2	29	27	156	2,041	474	1,489	78
Total area actually reporting	100.0%	233	2	35	27	169	2,220	533	1,590	97
Rate per 100,000 inhabitants		365.0	3.1	54.8	42.3	264.8	3,478.1	835.1	2,491.1	152.0
Erie, PA M.S.A.	276,700									
Includes Erie County										
City of Erie	99,019	353	10	46	115	182	2,278	567	1,607	104
Total area actually reporting	100.0%	594	11	100	157	326	5,307	1,077	4,052	178
Rate per 100,000 inhabitants		214.7	4.0	36.1	56.7	117.8	1,918.0	389.2	1,464.4	64.3
Eugene, OR M.S.A.[2]	367,343									
Includes Lane County										
City of Eugene	164,883	602	6	95	137	364	6,317	1,062	4,622	633
Total area actually reporting	99.1%	1,172	7	174	208	783	12,137	1,994	9,114	1,029
Estimated total	100.0%	1,178	7	175	209	787	12,222	2,004	9,181	1,037
Rate per 100,000 inhabitants		320.7	1.9	47.6	56.9	214.2	3,327.1	545.5	2,499.3	282.3

Table 4. Crime, by Selected Metropolitan Statistical Area, 2016—Continued

(Number, percent, rate per 100,000 population.)

Area	Population	Violent crime	Murder and nonnegligent manslaughter	Rape[1]	Robbery	Aggravated assault	Property crime	Burglary	Larceny-theft	Motor vehicle theft
Evansville, IN-KY M.S.A.	315,875									
Includes Posey, Vanderburgh, and Warrick Counties, IN and Henderson County, KY										
City of Evansville	119,908	762	8	75	210	469	5,881	1,008	4,490	383
Total area actually reporting	97.9%	1,127	11	106	253	757	8,462	1,556	6,375	531
Estimated total	100.0%	1,144	11	107	257	769	8,644	1,577	6,523	544
Rate per 100,000 inhabitants		362.2	3.5	33.9	81.4	243.5	2,736.5	499.2	2,065.1	172.2
Fairbanks, AK M.S.A.	34,657									
Includes Fairbanks North Star Borough										
City of Fairbanks	32,456	223	7	31	31	154	1,350	157	1,069	124
Total area actually reporting	100.0%	232	7	35	32	158	1,517	173	1,207	137
Rate per 100,000 inhabitants		669.4	20.2	101.0	92.3	455.9	4,377.2	499.2	3,482.7	395.3
Fargo, ND-MN M.S.A.	234,910									
Includes Clay County, MN and Cass County, ND										
City of Fargo, ND	121,217	467	3	79	68	317	3,843	566	2,962	315
Total area actually reporting	100.0%	635	5	135	91	404	5,807	974	4,337	496
Rate per 100,000 inhabitants		270.3	2.1	57.5	38.7	172.0	2,472.0	414.6	1,846.2	211.1
Farmington, NM M.S.A.	116,108									
Includes San Juan County										
City of Farmington	42,270	293	1	70	52	170	1,857	332	1,354	171
Total area actually reporting	100.0%	1,100	2	128	68	902	3,174	729	2,168	277
Rate per 100,000 inhabitants		947.4	1.7	110.2	58.6	776.9	2,733.7	627.9	1,867.2	238.6
Fayetteville, NC M.S.A.	378,409									
Includes Cumberland and Hoke Counties										
City of Fayetteville	202,200	1,531	33	99	316	1,083	9,201	1,868	6,942	391
Total area actually reporting	100.0%	1,982	44	123	415	1,400	13,168	3,052	9,577	539
Rate per 100,000 inhabitants		523.8	11.6	32.5	109.7	370.0	3,479.8	806.5	2,530.9	142.4
Flagstaff, AZ M.S.A.	140,312									
Includes Coconino County										
City of Flagstaff	71,179	265	0	26	30	209	2,856	255	2,542	59
Total area actually reporting	100.0%	512	3	72	43	394	4,197	478	3,614	105
Rate per 100,000 inhabitants		364.9	2.1	51.3	30.6	280.8	2,991.2	340.7	2,575.7	74.8
Flint, MI M.S.A.	407,879									
Includes Genesee County										
City of Flint	97,548	1,545	45	96	249	1,155	3,323	1,213	1,867	243
Total area actually reporting	100.0%	2,562	54	299	391	1,818	9,083	2,420	6,047	616
Rate per 100,000 inhabitants		628.1	13.2	73.3	95.9	445.7	2,226.9	593.3	1,482.5	151.0
Florence, SC M.S.A.	207,007									
Includes Darlington and Florence Counties										
City of Florence	38,382	408	1	20	73	314	2,563	407	2,026	130
Total area actually reporting	99.4%	1,320	14	102	222	982	8,787	2,207	6,028	552
Estimated total	100.0%	1,326	14	103	223	986	8,834	2,214	6,065	555
Rate per 100,000 inhabitants		640.6	6.8	49.8	107.7	476.3	4,267.5	1,069.5	2,929.9	268.1
Florence-Muscle Shoals, AL M.S.A.	146,537									
Includes Colbert and Lauderdale Counties										
City of Florence	40,160	196	2	19	46	129	1,400	242	1,052	106
City of Muscle Shoals	13,810	54	0	5	6	43	588	108	443	37
Total area actually reporting	99.8%	428	4	42	72	310	3,197	640	2,275	282
Estimated total	100.0%	429	4	42	72	311	3,207	642	2,282	283
Rate per 100,000 inhabitants		292.8	2.7	28.7	49.1	212.2	2,188.5	438.1	1,557.3	193.1
Fond du Lac, WI M.S.A.	101,860									
Includes Fond du Lac County										
City of Fond du Lac	42,907	136	1	38	12	85	957	75	858	24
Total area actually reporting	100.0%	184	1	52	13	118	1,377	149	1,180	48
Rate per 100,000 inhabitants		180.6	1.0	51.1	12.8	115.8	1,351.9	146.3	1,158.5	47.1
Fort Collins, CO M.S.A.	340,447									
Includes Larimer County										
City of Fort Collins	164,670	342	5	33	40	264	4,036	451	3,384	201
Total area actually reporting	100.0%	712	9	103	71	529	7,524	909	6,229	386
Rate per 100,000 inhabitants		209.1	2.6	30.3	20.9	155.4	2,210.0	267.0	1,829.7	113.4
Fort Smith, AR-OK M.S.A.	279,567									
Includes Crawford and Sebastian Counties, AR and Le Flore and Sequoyah Counties, OK										
City of Fort Smith, AR	88,573	712	4	70	97	541	5,229	888	4,008	333
Total area actually reporting	99.7%	1,388	14	191	117	1,066	9,605	2,150	6,823	632
Estimated total	100.0%	1,391	14	192	117	1,068	9,628	2,155	6,840	633
Rate per 100,000 inhabitants		497.6	5.0	68.7	41.9	382.0	3,443.9	770.8	2,446.6	226.4
Fort Wayne, IN M.S.A.	431,558									
Includes Allen, Wells, and Whitley Counties										
City of Fort Wayne	261,642	1,040	43	95	410	492	8,924	1,698	6,812	414
Total area actually reporting	94.7%	1,257	48	125	446	638	10,858	2,069	8,297	492

Table 4. Crime, by Selected Metropolitan Statistical Area, 2016—Continued

(Number, percent, rate per 100,000 population.)

Area	Population	Violent crime	Murder and nonnegligent manslaughter	Rape[1]	Robbery	Aggravated assault	Property crime	Burglary	Larceny-theft	Motor vehicle theft
Estimated total	100.0%	1,288	49	129	450	660	11,122	2,135	8,468	519
Rate per 100,000 inhabitants		298.5	11.4	29.9	104.3	152.9	2,577.2	494.7	1,962.2	120.3
Fresno, CA M.S.A.	976,874									
Includes Fresno County										
City of Fresno	524,796	3,206	39	158	1,122	1,887	20,523	3,697	13,542	3,284
Total area actually reporting	100.0%	5,983	63	314	1,414	4,192	31,875	6,883	19,806	5,186
Rate per 100,000 inhabitants		612.5	6.4	32.1	144.7	429.1	3,263.0	704.6	2,027.5	530.9
Gadsden, AL M.S.A.	102,537									
Includes Etowah County										
City of Gadsden	35,927	464	4	27	56	377	2,521	401	1,893	227
Total area actually reporting	98.5%	722	6	62	77	577	3,651	700	2,584	367
Estimated total	100.0%	730	6	63	78	583	3,702	710	2,621	371
Rate per 100,000 inhabitants		711.9	5.9	61.4	76.1	568.6	3,610.4	692.4	2,556.2	361.8
Gainesville, FL M.S.A.	280,301									
Includes Alachua and Gilchrist Counties										
City of Gainesville	131,242	870	3	142	189	536	4,908	590	3,951	367
Total area actually reporting	94.6%	1,460	4	216	271	969	7,764	1,258	5,972	534
Estimated total	100.0%	1,513	5	221	280	1,007	8,068	1,320	6,191	557
Rate per 100,000 inhabitants		539.8	1.8	78.8	99.9	359.3	2,878.3	470.9	2,208.7	198.7
Gainesville, GA M.S.A.	196,154									
Includes Hall County										
City of Gainesville	39,425	162	3	14	56	89	1,405	202	1,107	96
Total area actually reporting	100.0%	512	8	39	121	344	5,026	766	3,871	389
Rate per 100,000 inhabitants		261.0	4.1	19.9	61.7	175.4	2,562.3	390.5	1,973.4	198.3
Gettysburg, PA M.S.A.	102,165									
Includes Adams County										
City of Gettysburg	7,608	31	0	4	1	26	106	14	90	2
Total area actually reporting	100.0%	166	2	42	11	111	817	155	636	26
Rate per 100,000 inhabitants		162.5	2.0	41.1	10.8	108.6	799.7	151.7	622.5	25.4
Glens Falls, NY M.S.A.	125,674									
Includes Warren and Washington Counties										
City of Glens Falls	14,212	33	1	5	3	24	220	32	187	1
Total area actually reporting	100.0%	207	2	91	14	100	1,565	227	1,317	21
Rate per 100,000 inhabitants		164.7	1.6	72.4	11.1	79.6	1,245.3	180.6	1,047.9	16.7
Goldsboro, NC M.S.A.	124,396									
Includes Wayne County										
City of Goldsboro	35,871	389	11	3	84	291	1,999	484	1,416	99
Total area actually reporting	97.7%	538	11	7	119	401	3,801	1,212	2,362	227
Estimated total	100.0%	546	11	8	121	406	3,889	1,229	2,430	230
Rate per 100,000 inhabitants		438.9	8.8	6.4	97.3	326.4	3,126.3	988.0	1,953.4	184.9
Grand Forks, ND-MN M.S.A.	101,537									
Includes Polk County, MN and Grand Forks County, ND										
City of Grand Forks, ND	57,853	177	1	36	27	113	1,783	303	1,345	135
Total area actually reporting	100.0%	244	1	60	27	156	2,550	467	1,912	171
Rate per 100,000 inhabitants		240.3	1.0	59.1	26.6	153.6	2,511.4	459.9	1,883.1	168.4
Grand Island, NE M.S.A.	85,552									
Includes Hall, Hamilton, Howard, and Merrick Counties										
City of Grand Island	51,980	173	1	34	20	118	1,620	236	1,297	87
Total area actually reporting	92.5%	236	1	41	20	174	1,893	308	1,467	118
Estimated total	100.0%	245	1	43	21	180	1,973	320	1,527	126
Rate per 100,000 inhabitants		286.4	1.2	50.3	24.5	210.4	2,306.2	374.0	1,784.9	147.3
Grand Junction, CO M.S.A.	148,848									
Includes Mesa County										
City of Grand Junction	60,628	314	4	63	35	212	3,060	362	2,537	161
Total area actually reporting	99.2%	516	9	119	46	342	4,540	656	3,622	262
Estimated total	100.0%	519	9	120	46	344	4,573	660	3,647	266
Rate per 100,000 inhabitants		348.7	6.0	80.6	30.9	231.1	3,072.3	443.4	2,450.2	178.7
Grand Rapids-Wyoming, MI M.S.A.	1,048,249									
Includes Barry, Kent, Montcalm, and Ottawa Counties										
City of Grand Rapids	196,538	1,327	10	142	321	854	4,334	822	3,208	304
City of Wyoming	75,917	352	4	69	62	217	1,758	297	1,273	188
Total area actually reporting	99.8%	3,529	22	825	529	2,153	16,906	2,933	13,028	945
Estimated total	100.0%	3,534	22	826	530	2,156	16,939	2,938	13,053	948
Rate per 100,000 inhabitants		337.1	2.1	78.8	50.6	205.7	1,615.9	280.3	1,245.2	90.4
Grants Pass, OR M.S.A.	85,644									
Includes Josephine County										
City of Grants Pass	37,317	96	0	17	29	50	2,010	249	1,554	207
Total area actually reporting	100.0%	190	2	22	35	131	2,417	385	1,687	345
Rate per 100,000 inhabitants		221.8	2.3	25.7	40.9	153.0	2,822.1	449.5	1,969.8	402.8

Table 4. Crime, by Selected Metropolitan Statistical Area, 2016—Continued

(Number, percent, rate per 100,000 population.)

Area	Population	Violent crime	Murder and nonnegligent manslaughter	Rape[1]	Robbery	Aggravated assault	Property crime	Burglary	Larceny-theft	Motor vehicle theft
Great Falls, MT M.S.A.	82,482									
Includes Cascade County										
City of Great Falls	59,717	162	3	21	15	123	2,944	365	2,364	215
Total area actually reporting	100.0%	189	4	24	16	145	3,149	407	2,508	234
Rate per 100,000 inhabitants		229.1	4.8	29.1	19.4	175.8	3,817.8	493.4	3,040.7	283.7
Greeley, CO M.S.A.	291,675									
Includes Weld County										
City of Greeley	102,491	468	3	85	51	329	3,275	506	2,447	322
Total area actually reporting	99.6%	749	4	123	76	546	5,861	1,001	4,214	646
Estimated total	100.0%	752	4	124	76	548	5,895	1,005	4,240	650
Rate per 100,000 inhabitants		257.8	1.4	42.5	26.1	187.9	2,021.1	344.6	1,453.7	222.9
Green Bay, WI M.S.A.[2]	318,010									
Includes Brown,2 Kewaunee, and Oconto Counties										
City of Green Bay[2]	105,452	505	4	77	73	351	2,306	424	1,795	87
Total area actually reporting	91.0%	662	8	115	80	459	4,418	724	3,506	188
Estimated total	100.0%	681	8	119	81	473	4,618	773	3,645	200
Rate per 100,000 inhabitants		214.1	2.5	37.4	25.5	148.7	1,452.2	243.1	1,146.2	62.9
Hagerstown-Martinsburg, MD-WV M.S.A.	261,805									
Includes Washington County, MD and Berkeley County, WV										
City of Hagerstown, MD	40,567	231	0	19	105	107	1,262	374	775	113
City of Martinsburg, WV	17,789	81	0	13	25	43	882	117	740	25
Total area actually reporting	100.0%	650	7	61	193	389	5,556	1,350	3,871	335
Rate per 100,000 inhabitants		248.3	2.7	23.3	73.7	148.6	2,122.2	515.7	1,478.6	128.0
Hammond, LA M.S.A.	129,819									
Includes Tangipahoa Parish										
City of Hammond	20,576	286	7	12	59	208	2,131	627	1,412	92
Total area actually reporting	96.6%	1,170	17	72	195	886	5,470	1,646	3,459	365
Estimated total	100.0%	1,189	17	73	198	901	5,635	1,674	3,588	373
Rate per 100,000 inhabitants		915.9	13.1	56.2	152.5	694.0	4,340.7	1,289.5	2,763.8	287.3
Hanford-Corcoran, CA M.S.A.	149,661									
Includes Kings County										
City of Hanford	55,973	266	2	21	44	199	1,496	222	1,059	215
City of Corcoran	22,111	68	2	10	7	49	404	114	216	74
Total area actually reporting	100.0%	639	11	72	80	476	3,167	699	1,931	537
Rate per 100,000 inhabitants		427.0	7.3	48.1	53.5	318.1	2,116.1	467.1	1,290.2	358.8
Harrisburg-Carlisle, PA M.S.A.	566,382									
Includes Cumberland, Dauphin, and Perry Counties										
City of Harrisburg	48,996	526	13	54	160	299	1,342	404	803	135
City of Carlisle	19,225	25	1	7	11	6	400	44	345	11
Total area actually reporting	99.4%	1,439	19	214	309	897	8,326	1,536	6,440	350
Estimated total	100.0%	1,445	19	215	310	901	8,379	1,543	6,484	352
Rate per 100,000 inhabitants		255.1	3.4	38.0	54.7	159.1	1,479.4	272.4	1,144.8	62.1
Harrisonburg, VA M.S.A.	131,581									
Includes Rockingham County and Harrisonburg City										
City of Harrisonburg	52,972	117	2	25	29	61	1,099	165	894	40
Total area actually reporting	100.0%	214	3	59	35	117	1,794	328	1,391	75
Rate per 100,000 inhabitants		162.6	2.3	44.8	26.6	88.9	1,363.4	249.3	1,057.1	57.0
Hartford-West Hartford-East Hartford, CT M.S.A.[2]	1,019,846									
Includes Hartford, Middlesex, and Tolland Counties										
City of Hartford	123,736	1,353	14	65	476	798	5,197	808	3,616	773
City of West Hartford	62,979	40	0	2	38	0	1,589	131	1,351	107
City of East Hartford	50,733	147	4	26	51	66	1,312	247	922	143
City of Middletown	46,580	70	0	5	23	42	927	109	731	87
Total area actually reporting	100.0%	2,430	23	257	854	1,296	22,566	3,050	17,098	2,418
Rate per 100,000 inhabitants		238.3	2.3	25.2	83.7	127.1	2,212.7	299.1	1,676.5	237.1
Hattiesburg, MS M.S.A.	149,558									
Includes Forrest, Lamar, and Perry Counties										
City of Hattiesburg	47,006	147	8	10	52	77	2,752	374	2,292	86
Total area actually reporting	90.2%	279	9	23	66	181	3,822	819	2,872	131
Estimated total	100.0%	298	9	25	70	194	4,068	881	3,037	150
Rate per 100,000 inhabitants		199.3	6.0	16.7	46.8	129.7	2,720.0	589.1	2,030.7	100.3
Hilton Head Island-Bluffton-Beaufort, SC M.S.A.	211,983									
Includes Beaufort and Jasper Counties										
City of Bluffton	17,498	25	2	6	5	12	267	39	217	11
City of Beaufort	13,477	85	1	3	21	60	857	100	729	28
Total area actually reporting	100.0%	668	17	76	144	431	4,634	900	3,399	335
Rate per 100,000 inhabitants		315.1	8.0	35.9	67.9	203.3	2,186.0	424.6	1,603.4	158.0
Hinesville, GA M.S.A.	80,776									
Includes Liberty and Long Counties										
City of Hinesville	33,477	215	2	14	49	150	1,252	210	1,011	31
Total area actually reporting	100.0%	344	3	16	65	260	1,850	401	1,372	77
Rate per 100,000 inhabitants		425.9	3.7	19.8	80.5	321.9	2,290.3	496.4	1,698.5	95.3

Table 4. Crime, by Selected Metropolitan Statistical Area, 2016—Continued

(Number, percent, rate per 100,000 population.)

Area	Population	Violent crime	Murder and nonnegligent manslaughter	Rape[1]	Robbery	Aggravated assault	Property crime	Burglary	Larceny-theft	Motor vehicle theft
Homosassa Springs, FL M.S.A.	141,300									
Includes Citrus County										
Total area actually reporting	100.0%	338	4	40	39	255	1,979	426	1,443	110
Rate per 100,000 inhabitants		239.2	2.8	28.3	27.6	180.5	1,400.6	301.5	1,021.2	77.8
Hot Springs, AR M.S.A.	97,312									
Includes Garland County										
City of Hot Springs	35,716	277	4	26	62	185	2,882	1,059	1,586	237
Total area actually reporting	100.0%	634	4	73	82	475	4,605	1,890	2,349	366
Rate per 100,000 inhabitants		651.5	4.1	75.0	84.3	488.1	4,732.2	1,942.2	2,413.9	376.1
Houma-Thibodaux, LA M.S.A.	212,402									
Includes Lafourche and Terrebonne Parishes										
City of Houma	34,410	167	4	17	42	104	1,411	196	1,159	56
City of Thibodaux	14,588	90	0	3	10	77	593	142	443	8
Total area actually reporting	100.0%	954	19	61	114	760	6,693	1,591	4,871	231
Rate per 100,000 inhabitants		449.1	8.9	28.7	53.7	357.8	3,151.1	749.1	2,293.3	108.8
Houston-The Woodlands-Sugar Land, TX M.S.A.	6,789,215									
Includes Austin, Brazoria, Chambers, Fort Bend, Galveston, Harris, Liberty, Montgomery, and Waller Counties										
City of Houston	2,334,348	23,960	301	1,210	9,962	12,487	100,856	18,488	69,630	12,738
City of Sugar Land	90,088	77	0	16	43	18	1,460	250	1,162	48
City of Baytown	77,224	302	9	25	98	170	2,858	525	1,960	373
City of Conroe	71,111	252	1	39	86	126	2,199	376	1,639	184
Total area actually reporting	99.9%	39,255	487	2,710	14,633	21,425	198,490	37,216	138,158	23,116
Estimated total	100.0%	39,256	487	2,710	14,633	21,426	198,500	37,218	138,165	23,117
Rate per 100,000 inhabitants		578.2	7.2	39.9	215.5	315.6	2,923.8	548.2	2,035.1	340.5
Huntington-Ashland, WV-KY-OH M.S.A.[3,4]	359,412									
Includes Boyd and Greenup Counties, KY; Lawrence County OH; and Cabell, Lincoln, Putnam, and Wayne Counties, WV										
City of Huntington, WV[3]	48,540	378	3	33	125	217			1,497	115
City of Ashland, KY	20,987	51	1	16	11	23	885	146	704	35
Total area actually reporting	83.7%	900	6	137	169	588			5,159	
Estimated total	100.0%	1,048	8	158	180	702			5,867	
Rate per 100,000 inhabitants		291.6	2.2	44.0	50.1	195.3			1,632.4	
Huntsville, AL M.S.A.	448,973									
Includes Limestone and Madison Counties										
City of Huntsville	192,587	1,787	18	152	414	1,203	9,398	1,692	6,812	894
Total area actually reporting	100.0%	2,501	22	239	505	1,735	14,340	2,733	10,350	1,257
Rate per 100,000 inhabitants		557.0	4.9	53.2	112.5	386.4	3,194.0	608.7	2,305.3	280.0
Idaho Falls, ID M.S.A.	141,859									
Includes Bonneville, Butte, and Jefferson Counties										
City of Idaho Falls	59,615	253	1	33	13	206	1,367	370	904	93
Total area actually reporting	100.0%	425	1	48	18	358	2,226	599	1,491	136
Rate per 100,000 inhabitants		299.6	0.7	33.8	12.7	252.4	1,569.2	422.3	1,051.0	95.9
Indianapolis-Carmel-Anderson, IN M.S.A.	2,004,800									
Includes Boone, Brown, Hamilton, Hancock, Hendricks, Johnson, Madison, Marion, Morgan, Putnam, and Shelby Counties										
City of Indianapolis	866,351	11,907	148	684	3,976	7,099	41,540	10,209	26,335	4,996
City of Carmel	90,619	25	0	13	7	5	803	58	706	39
City of Anderson	55,134	240	6	63	92	79	2,294	497	1,614	183
Total area actually reporting	82.4%	13,615	173	871	4,261	8,310	57,721	12,253	39,210	6,258
Estimated total	100.0%	14,302	184	939	4,388	8,791	64,291	13,334	44,161	6,796
Rate per 100,000 inhabitants		713.4	9.2	46.8	218.9	438.5	3,206.9	665.1	2,202.8	339.0
Iowa City, IA M.S.A.	169,088									
Includes Johnson and Washington Counties										
City of Iowa City	75,527	197	0	39	43	115	1,551	294	1,169	88
Total area actually reporting	100.0%	493	0	123	71	299	2,921	528	2,261	132
Rate per 100,000 inhabitants		291.6	0.0	72.7	42.0	176.8	1,727.5	312.3	1,337.2	78.1
Jackson, MI M.S.A.	159,287									
Includes Jackson County										
City of Jackson	33,060	409	4	65	49	291	1,504	287	1,159	58
Total area actually reporting	98.7%	843	9	142	74	618	3,489	642	2,678	169
Estimated total	100.0%	849	9	143	75	622	3,528	648	2,708	172
Rate per 100,000 inhabitants		533.0	5.7	89.8	47.1	390.5	2,214.9	406.8	1,700.1	108.0
Jackson, TN M.S.A.	129,606									
Includes Chester, Crockett, and Madison Counties										
City of Jackson	66,990	628	7	36	108	477	2,947	650	2,170	127
Total area actually reporting	100.0%	843	7	45	114	677	3,939	1,028	2,709	202
Rate per 100,000 inhabitants		650.4	5.4	34.7	88.0	522.4	3,039.2	793.2	2,090.2	155.9
Jacksonville, FL M.S.A.	1,473,678									
Includes Baker, Clay, Duval, Nassau, and St. Johns Counties										
City of Jacksonville	880,557	5,504	106	517	1,463	3,418	31,538	5,851	22,660	3,027

Table 4. Crime, by Selected Metropolitan Statistical Area, 2016—Continued

(Number, percent, rate per 100,000 population.)

Area	Population	Violent crime	Murder and nonnegligent manslaughter	Rape[1]	Robbery	Aggravated assault	Property crime	Burglary	Larceny-theft	Motor vehicle theft
Total area actually reporting	100.0%	7,058	125	697	1,681	4,555	42,653	8,196	30,834	3,623
Rate per 100,000 inhabitants		478.9	8.5	47.3	114.1	309.1	2,894.3	556.2	2,092.3	245.8
Janesville-Beloit, WI M.S.A.	161,430									
Includes Rock County										
City of Janesville	64,234	145	0	28	31	86	1,763	238	1,474	51
City of Beloit	36,878	175	2	17	57	99	1,124	149	940	35
Total area actually reporting	100.0%	370	3	57	90	220	3,570	558	2,885	127
Rate per 100,000 inhabitants		229.2	1.9	35.3	55.8	136.3	2,211.5	345.7	1,787.2	78.7
Jefferson City, MO M.S.A.	151,164									
Includes Callaway, Cole, Moniteau, and Osage Counties										
City of Jefferson City	43,171	174	4	9	35	126	1,318	179	1,085	54
Total area actually reporting	100.0%	445	7	33	60	345	2,855	604	2,094	157
Rate per 100,000 inhabitants		294.4	4.6	21.8	39.7	228.2	1,888.7	399.6	1,385.3	103.9
Johnson City, TN M.S.A.	200,977									
Includes Carter, Unicoi, and Washington Counties										
City of Johnson City	66,511	263	4	25	38	196	2,488	392	1,977	119
Total area actually reporting	100.0%	585	5	48	65	467	4,662	846	3,557	259
Rate per 100,000 inhabitants		291.1	2.5	23.9	32.3	232.4	2,319.7	420.9	1,769.9	128.9
Johnstown, PA M.S.A.	134,652									
Includes Cambria County										
City of Johnstown	21,227	100	5	2	20	73	633	198	416	19
Total area actually reporting	98.0%	210	7	15	31	157	1,807	383	1,379	45
Estimated total	100.0%	214	7	15	32	160	1,848	388	1,413	47
Rate per 100,000 inhabitants		158.9	5.2	11.1	23.8	118.8	1,372.4	288.2	1,049.4	34.9
Jonesboro, AR M.S.A.	129,793									
Includes Craighead and Poinsett Counties										
City of Jonesboro	75,230	387	5	35	72	275	3,369	1,528	1,727	114
Total area actually reporting	100.0%	541	7	87	80	367	4,662	1,849	2,626	187
Rate per 100,000 inhabitants		416.8	5.4	67.0	61.6	282.8	3,591.9	1,424.6	2,023.2	144.1
Joplin, MO M.S.A.[4]	177,228									
Includes Jasper and Newton[4] Counties										
City of Joplin	52,001	329	2	52	72	203	3,779	569	2,895	315
Total area actually reporting	100.0%		7	94	100		7,163	1,148	5,400	615
Rate per 100,000 inhabitants			3.9	53.0	56.4		4,041.7	647.8	3,046.9	347.0
Kahului-Wailuku-Lahaina, HI M.S.A.	164,771									
Includes Kalawao and Maui Counties										
Total area actually reporting	100.0%	450	5	77	68	300	5,741	978	4,046	717
Rate per 100,000 inhabitants		273.1	3.0	46.7	41.3	182.1	3,484.2	593.6	2,455.5	435.1
Kalamazoo-Portage, MI M.S.A.	336,919									
Includes Kalamazoo and Van Buren Counties										
City of Kalamazoo	76,389	925	7	125	182	611	3,221	755	2,228	238
City of Portage	48,550	103	0	31	15	57	1,289	149	1,117	23
Total area actually reporting	100.0%	1,776	22	368	264	1,122	9,038	1,966	6,579	493
Rate per 100,000 inhabitants		527.1	6.5	109.2	78.4	333.0	2,682.5	583.5	1,952.7	146.3
Kankakee, IL M.S.A.	109,833									
Includes Kankakee County										
City of Kankakee	26,509	203	5	26	74	98	1,098	251	786	61
Total area actually reporting	86.7%	311	10	33	97	171	2,382	509	1,768	105
Estimated total	100.0%	341	10	37	106	188	2,630	548	1,964	118
Rate per 100,000 inhabitants		310.5	9.1	33.7	96.5	171.2	2,394.5	498.9	1,788.2	107.4
Kennewick-Richland, WA M.S.A.	285,194									
Includes Benton and Franklin Counties										
City of Kennewick	79,837	183	1	31	37	114	2,254	295	1,772	187
City of Richland	55,475	101	1	20	11	69	1,344	174	1,092	78
Total area actually reporting	100.0%	551	5	99	91	356	6,202	1,069	4,602	531
Rate per 100,000 inhabitants		193.2	1.8	34.7	31.9	124.8	2,174.7	374.8	1,613.6	186.2
Killeen-Temple, TX M.S.A.[2]	434,470									
Includes Bell, Coryell, and Lampasas Counties										
City of Killeen	143,248	996	16	129	234	617	3,946	1,124	2,471	351
City of Temple	73,411	226	7	34	89	96	2,298	493	1,620	185
Total area actually reporting	99.3%	1,673	27	242	410	994	10,468	2,458	7,290	720
Estimated total	100.0%	1,681	27	243	412	999	10,542	2,470	7,347	725
Rate per 100,000 inhabitants		386.9	6.2	55.9	94.8	229.9	2,426.4	568.5	1,691.0	166.9
Kingsport-Bristol-Bristol, TN-VA M.S.A.	306,101									
Includes Hawkins and Sullivan Counties, TN and Scott and Washington Counties and Bristol City, VA										
City of Kingsport, TN	53,059	369	1	18	71	279	2,501	374	1,973	154
City of Bristol, TN	26,656	158	1	14	14	129	900	134	670	96
City of Bristol, VA	16,908	37	1	9	7	20	432	56	338	38
Total area actually reporting	100.0%	1,124	8	125	119	872	7,135	1,294	5,236	605
Rate per 100,000 inhabitants		367.2	2.6	40.8	38.9	284.9	2,330.9	422.7	1,710.5	197.6

Table 4. Crime, by Selected Metropolitan Statistical Area, 2016—Continued

(Number, percent, rate per 100,000 population.)

Area	Population	Violent crime	Murder and nonnegligent manslaughter	Rape[1]	Robbery	Aggravated assault	Property crime	Burglary	Larceny-theft	Motor vehicle theft
Kingston, NY M.S.A.	178,502									
Includes Ulster County										
City of Kingston	23,360	76	0	10	23	43	484	57	418	9
Total area actually reporting	100.0%	292	4	72	36	180	2,336	393	1,878	65
Rate per 100,000 inhabitants		163.6	2.2	40.3	20.2	100.8	1,308.7	220.2	1,052.1	36.4
Knoxville, TN M.S.A.	866,010									
Includes Anderson, Blount, Campbell, Grainger, Knox, Loudon, Morgan, Roane, and Union Counties										
City of Knoxville	186,583	1,672	18	157	404	1,093	10,324	1,840	7,620	864
Total area actually reporting	100.0%	3,892	37	296	610	2,949	23,900	5,043	16,881	1,976
Rate per 100,000 inhabitants		449.4	4.3	34.2	70.4	340.5	2,759.8	582.3	1,949.3	228.2
Kokomo, IN M.S.A.	82,350									
Includes Howard County										
City of Kokomo	57,984	441	4	30	84	323	1,760	476	1,196	88
Total area actually reporting	98.7%	519	6	36	92	385	2,046	587	1,350	109
Estimated total	100.0%	522	6	36	93	387	2,077	591	1,375	111
Rate per 100,000 inhabitants		633.9	7.3	43.7	112.9	469.9	2,522.2	717.7	1,669.7	134.8
La Crosse-Onalaska, WI-MN M.S.A.	137,403									
Includes Houston County, MN and La Crosse County, WI										
City of La Crosse, WI	52,498	131	1	32	23	75	2,290	319	1,905	66
City of Onalaska, WI	18,600	13	0	6	0	7	508	60	443	5
Total area actually reporting	100.0%	186	1	41	23	121	3,374	482	2,800	92
Rate per 100,000 inhabitants		135.4	0.7	29.8	16.7	88.1	2,455.6	350.8	2,037.8	67.0
Lafayette, LA M.S.A.[3]	493,575									
Includes Acadia, Iberia,[3] Lafayette, St. Martin, and Vermilion Parishes										
City of Lafayette	128,923	641	11	19	148	463	6,417	1,025	5,013	379
Total area actually reporting	97.4%	1,830	45	58	351	1,376		3,299	10,056	
Estimated total	100.0%	1,887	46	62	360	1,419		3,382	10,432	
Rate per 100,000 inhabitants		382.3	9.3	12.6	72.9	287.5		685.2	2,113.6	
Lafayette-West Lafayette, IN M.S.A.	216,480									
Includes Benton, Carroll, and Tippecanoe Counties										
City of Lafayette	71,562	360	2	35	109	214	3,016	612	2,217	187
City of West Lafayette	46,284	57	0	10	10	37	452	71	360	21
Total area actually reporting	87.1%	491	2	65	127	297	4,401	897	3,253	251
Estimated total	100.0%	536	3	70	134	329	4,799	980	3,532	287
Rate per 100,000 inhabitants		247.6	1.4	32.3	61.9	152.0	2,216.8	452.7	1,631.6	132.6
Lake Charles, LA M.S.A.	206,047									
Includes Calcasieu and Cameron Parishes										
City of Lake Charles	76,864	654	8	40	143	463	3,153	1,626	1,320	207
Total area actually reporting	100.0%	1,357	14	103	192	1,048	8,754	3,142	5,063	549
Rate per 100,000 inhabitants		658.6	6.8	50.0	93.2	508.6	4,248.5	1,524.9	2,457.2	266.4
Lakeland-Winter Haven, FL M.S.A.	661,218									
Includes Polk County										
City of Lakeland	105,766	337	4	89	104	140	5,111	751	4,050	310
City of Winter Haven	38,488	196	2	10	33	151	1,339	238	1,021	80
Total area actually reporting	100.0%	2,199	26	258	350	1,565	15,567	3,214	11,201	1,152
Rate per 100,000 inhabitants		332.6	3.9	39.0	52.9	236.7	2,354.3	486.1	1,694.0	174.2
Lancaster, PA M.S.A.	538,376									
Includes Lancaster County										
City of Lancaster	59,340	487	4	92	164	227	2,164	255	1,828	81
Total area actually reporting	100.0%	944	8	180	270	486	7,411	1,029	6,143	239
Rate per 100,000 inhabitants		175.3	1.5	33.4	50.2	90.3	1,376.5	191.1	1,141.0	44.4
Lansing-East Lansing, MI M.S.A.	473,685									
Includes Clinton, Eaton, and Ingham Counties										
City of Lansing	115,199	1,341	9	142	260	930	3,325	897	2,053	375
City of East Lansing	48,451	115	0	43	24	48	719	124	488	107
Total area actually reporting	100.0%	2,172	16	432	354	1,370	8,730	1,791	6,232	707
Rate per 100,000 inhabitants		458.5	3.4	91.2	74.7	289.2	1,843.0	378.1	1,315.6	149.3
Laredo, TX M.S.A.	272,746									
Includes Webb County										
City of Laredo	259,325	940	12	148	160	620	7,890	1,015	6,646	229
Total area actually reporting	100.0%	986	12	153	165	656	8,188	1,116	6,837	235
Rate per 100,000 inhabitants		361.5	4.4	56.1	60.5	240.5	3,002.1	409.2	2,506.7	86.2
Las Cruces, NM M.S.A.	214,233									
Includes Dona Ana County										
City of Las Cruces	102,349	251	5	41	51	154	4,788	830	3,697	261
Total area actually reporting	95.7%	496	11	92	62	331	6,049	1,226	4,447	376
Estimated total	100.0%	542	11	96	66	369	6,357	1,287	4,652	418
Rate per 100,000 inhabitants		253.0	5.1	44.8	30.8	172.2	2,967.3	600.7	2,171.5	195.1

Table 4. Crime, by Selected Metropolitan Statistical Area, 2016—Continued

(Number, percent, rate per 100,000 population.)

Area	Population	Violent crime	Murder and nonnegligent manslaughter	Rape[1]	Robbery	Aggravated assault	Property crime	Burglary	Larceny-theft	Motor vehicle theft
Las Vegas-Henderson-Paradise, NV M.S.A.	2,155,946									
Includes Clark County										
City of Las Vegas Metropolitan Police Department	1,592,178	13,520	158	1,200	4,974	7,188	46,000	12,500	24,645	8,855
City of Henderson	291,584	617	10	94	235	278	5,484	1,237	3,617	630
Total area actually reporting	100.0%	16,622	194	1,420	5,781	9,227	58,811	15,522	32,417	10,872
Rate per 100,000 inhabitants		771.0	9.0	65.9	268.1	428.0	2,727.9	720.0	1,503.6	504.3
Lawton, OK M.S.A.	129,814									
Includes Comanche and Cotton Counties										
City of Lawton	96,420	781	4	69	110	598	3,691	1,151	2,318	222
Total area actually reporting	99.1%	813	4	75	112	622	4,125	1,303	2,556	266
Estimated total	100.0%	815	4	75	112	624	4,155	1,309	2,577	269
Rate per 100,000 inhabitants		627.8	3.1	57.8	86.3	480.7	3,200.7	1,008.4	1,985.1	207.2
Lebanon, PA M.S.A.	137,357									
Includes Lebanon County										
City of Lebanon	25,549	60	1	3	16	40	619	129	441	49
Total area actually reporting	95.9%	203	3	13	36	151	1,942	307	1,546	89
Estimated total	100.0%	212	3	14	38	157	2,028	318	1,618	92
Rate per 100,000 inhabitants		154.3	2.2	10.2	27.7	114.3	1,476.4	231.5	1,178.0	67.0
Lewiston, ID-WA M.S.A.	62,714									
Includes Nez Perce County, ID and Asotin County, WA										
City of Lewiston, ID	32,665	46	0	14	3	29	1,330	366	883	81
Total area actually reporting	100.0%	95	1	25	6	63	2,189	507	1,562	120
Rate per 100,000 inhabitants		151.5	1.6	39.9	9.6	100.5	3,490.4	808.4	2,490.7	191.3
Lewiston-Auburn, ME M.S.A.	107,279									
Includes Androscoggin County										
City of Lewiston	36,126	64	0	14	18	32	718	140	529	49
City of Auburn	22,836	43	0	14	7	22	730	66	649	15
Total area actually reporting	100.0%	146	0	37	30	79	1,825	308	1,437	80
Rate per 100,000 inhabitants		136.1	0.0	34.5	28.0	73.6	1,701.2	287.1	1,339.5	74.6
Lexington-Fayette, KY M.S.A.	505,664									
Includes Bourbon, Clark, Fayette, Jessamine, Scott, and Woodford Counties										
City of Lexington	317,853	1,079	24	200	575	280	13,058	2,435	9,465	1,158
Total area actually reporting	100.0%	1,335	25	262	667	381	18,168	3,439	13,293	1,436
Rate per 100,000 inhabitants		264.0	4.9	51.8	131.9	75.3	3,592.9	680.1	2,628.8	284.0
Lima, OH M.S.A.	103,900									
Includes Allen County										
City of Lima	37,715	356	8	44	123	181	2,259	602	1,540	117
Total area actually reporting	96.7%	400	8	55	141	196	3,652	894	2,599	159
Estimated total	100.0%	405	8	56	143	198	3,729	907	2,660	162
Rate per 100,000 inhabitants		389.8	7.7	53.9	137.6	190.6	3,589.0	873.0	2,560.2	155.9
Lincoln, NE M.S.A.	327,353									
Includes Lancaster and Seward Counties										
City of Lincoln	281,138	1,006	10	222	191	583	8,730	1,261	7,117	352
Total area actually reporting	99.4%	1,052	10	244	192	606	9,202	1,345	7,477	380
Estimated total	100.0%	1,055	10	245	192	608	9,244	1,349	7,511	384
Rate per 100,000 inhabitants		322.3	3.1	74.8	58.7	185.7	2,823.9	412.1	2,294.5	117.3
Little Rock-North Little Rock-Conway, AR M.S.A.[4]	737,086									
Includes Faulkner, Grant, Lonoke, Perry, Pulaski, and Saline Counties										
City of Little Rock	198,800	3,044	42	159	657	2,186	13,714	2,348	10,223	1,143
City of North Little Rock	67,344	503	11	11	115	366	2,926	523	2,016	387
City of Conway	66,104	335	5	43	84	203	2,970	343	2,429	198
Total area actually reporting	100.0%	5,602	74	437	1,008	4,083			22,971	2,798
Rate per 100,000 inhabitants		760.0	10.0	59.3	136.8	553.9			3,116.5	379.6
Logan, UT-ID M.S.A.	135,889									
Includes Franklin County, ID and Cache County, UT										
City of Logan, UT	50,767	50	1	12	5	32	844	120	685	39
Total area actually reporting	100.0%	90	2	35	8	45	1,481	243	1,155	83
Rate per 100,000 inhabitants		66.2	1.5	25.8	5.9	33.1	1,089.9	178.8	850.0	61.1
Longview, WA M.S.A.	104,085									
Includes Cowlitz County										
City of Longview	36,854	142	0	41	40	61	1,927	409	1,314	204
Total area actually reporting	100.0%	279	2	68	58	151	3,448	712	2,376	360
Rate per 100,000 inhabitants		268.1	1.9	65.3	55.7	145.1	3,312.7	684.1	2,282.7	345.9
Los Angeles-Long Beach-Anaheim, CA M.S.A.	13,350,144									
Includes the Metropolitan Divisions of Anaheim-Santa Ana-Irvine and Los Angeles-Long Beach-Glendale										
City of Los Angeles	4,007,905	28,817	293	2,343	10,307	15,874	99,151	15,821	64,739	18,591
City of Long Beach	476,476	2,846	33	197	1,138	1,478	14,224	2,988	8,377	2,859

Table 4. Crime, by Selected Metropolitan Statistical Area, 2016—Continued

(Number, percent, rate per 100,000 population.)

Area	Population	Violent crime	Murder and nonnegligent manslaughter	Rape[1]	Robbery	Aggravated assault	Property crime	Burglary	Larceny-theft	Motor vehicle theft
City of Anaheim	353,504	1,209	7	123	390	689	9,617	1,469	6,764	1,384
City of Santa Ana	337,419	1,612	23	142	511	936	6,980	1,119	3,913	1,948
City of Irvine	266,663	152	3	41	52	56	3,737	640	2,918	179
City of Glendale	202,903	227	1	38	84	104	3,450	596	2,491	363
City of Torrance	149,078	258	1	28	119	110	3,221	458	2,326	437
City of Pasadena	143,288	477	2	46	164	265	3,446	861	2,261	324
City of Orange	141,841	228	1	25	57	145	2,608	464	1,783	361
City of Costa Mesa	113,816	412	1	60	145	206	4,610	735	3,296	579
City of Burbank	105,720	210	0	24	50	136	2,927	392	2,269	266
City of Carson	93,613	505	10	23	165	307	2,424	439	1,463	522
City of Santa Monica	93,921	475	2	40	189	244	4,039	623	3,180	236
City of Newport Beach	87,482	110	1	34	17	58	2,241	437	1,644	160
City of Tustin	81,642	120	2	13	34	71	1,806	229	1,412	165
City of Monterey Park	61,710	131	1	8	59	63	1,704	460	998	246
City of Gardena	60,770	338	3	24	160	151	1,482	355	772	355
City of Arcadia	58,816	83	2	4	44	33	1,642	520	1,045	77
City of Fountain Valley	57,291	63	0	0	21	42	1,443	246	1,072	125
Total area actually reporting	100.0%	63,646	679	4,968	22,288	35,711	318,559	58,004	204,522	56,033
Rate per 100,000 inhabitants		476.7	5.1	37.2	166.9	267.5	2,386.2	434.5	1,532.0	419.7
Anaheim-Santa Ana-Irvine, CA M.D.	3,179,276									
Includes Orange County										
Total area actually reporting	100.0%	7,275	57	810	2,136	4,272	66,054	11,025	46,507	8,522
Rate per 100,000 inhabitants		228.8	1.8	25.5	67.2	134.4	2,077.6	346.8	1,462.8	268.0
Los Angeles-Long Beach-Glendale, CA M.D.	10,170,868									
Includes Los Angeles County										
Total area actually reporting	100.0%	56,371	622	4,158	20,152	31,439	252,505	46,979	158,015	47,511
Rate per 100,000 inhabitants		554.2	6.1	40.9	198.1	309.1	2,482.6	461.9	1,553.6	467.1
Louisville/Jefferson County, KY-IN M.S.A.	1,285,169									
Includes Clark, Floyd, Harrison, Scott, and Washington Counties, IN and Bullitt, Henry, Jefferson, Oldham, Shelby, Spencer, and Trimble Counties, KY										
City of Louisville Metro, KY	683,825	4,621	119	196	1,514	2,792	30,254	5,907	19,983	4,364
Total area actually reporting	94.2%	5,502	131	291	1,787	3,293	42,026	7,908	28,544	5,574
Estimated total	100.0%	5,627	134	305	1,807	3,381	43,168	8,132	29,361	5,675
Rate per 100,000 inhabitants		437.8	10.4	23.7	140.6	263.1	3,358.9	632.8	2,284.6	441.6
Lubbock, TX M.S.A.[2]	314,167									
Includes Crosby, Lubbock, and Lynn Counties										
City of Lubbock	252,900	2,741	6	177	471	2,087	12,661	2,678	8,933	1,050
Total area actually reporting	98.8%	2,894	9	200	488	2,197	14,117	2,983	9,980	1,154
Estimated total	100.0%	2,904	9	202	490	2,203	14,210	2,998	10,051	1,161
Rate per 100,000 inhabitants		924.3	2.9	64.3	156.0	701.2	4,523.1	954.3	3,199.3	369.5
Lynchburg, VA M.S.A.	259,926									
Includes Amherst, Appomattox, Bedford, and Campbell Counties and Bedford and Lynchburg Cities										
City of Lynchburg	80,215	298	2	33	57	206	1,802	262	1,428	112
Total area actually reporting	100.0%	530	12	83	78	357	3,739	546	2,995	198
Rate per 100,000 inhabitants		203.9	4.6	31.9	30.0	137.3	1,438.5	210.1	1,152.3	76.2
Macon-Bibb County, GA M.S.A.	229,434									
Includes Bibb, Crawford, Jones, Monroe, and Twiggs Counties										
Total area actually reporting	99.6%	872	18	61	279	514	9,457	2,289	6,452	716
Estimated total	100.0%	876	18	61	280	517	9,496	2,295	6,482	719
Rate per 100,000 inhabitants		381.8	7.8	26.6	122.0	225.3	4,138.9	1,000.3	2,825.2	313.4
Madera, CA M.S.A.	154,726									
Includes Madera County										
City of Madera	64,753	505	3	22	98	382	1,859	297	1,262	300
Total area actually reporting	100.0%	1,024	7	51	124	842	3,705	978	2,155	572
Rate per 100,000 inhabitants		661.8	4.5	33.0	80.1	544.2	2,394.6	632.1	1,392.8	369.7
Madison, WI M.S.A.[2]	647,587									
Includes Columbia, Dane, Green, and Iowa Counties										
City of Madison	252,136	832	8	125	235	464	6,932	1,014	5,544	374
Total area actually reporting	98.8%	1,304	13	198	309	784	12,263	1,720	9,959	584
Estimated total	100.0%	1,313	13	199	311	790	12,406	1,736	10,080	590
Rate per 100,000 inhabitants		202.8	2.0	30.7	48.0	122.0	1,915.7	268.1	1,556.5	91.1
Manchester-Nashua, NH M.S.A.	408,233									
Includes Hillsborough County										
City of Manchester	110,353	742	5	69	205	463	3,010	456	2,408	146
City of Nashua	88,252	151	0	48	26	77	1,218	122	1,039	57
Total area actually reporting	98.7%	1,089	5	160	248	676	6,162	846	5,031	285
Estimated total	100.0%	1,096	5	162	249	680	6,228	855	5,085	288
Rate per 100,000 inhabitants		268.5	1.2	39.7	61.0	166.6	1,525.6	209.4	1,245.6	70.5
Manhattan, KS M.S.A.	99,113									
Includes Pottawatomie and Riley Counties										
Total area actually reporting	100.0%	257	1	49	22	185	1,607	250	1,268	89
Rate per 100,000 inhabitants		259.3	1.0	49.4	22.2	186.7	1,621.4	252.2	1,279.3	89.8

Table 4. Crime, by Selected Metropolitan Statistical Area, 2016—Continued

(Number, percent, rate per 100,000 population.)

Area	Population	Violent crime	Murder and nonnegligent manslaughter	Rape[1]	Robbery	Aggravated assault	Property crime	Burglary	Larceny-theft	Motor vehicle theft
Mankato-North Mankato, MN M.S.A.	99,481									
Includes Blue Earth and Nicollet Counties										
City of Mankato	41,300	112	1	27	23	61	1,329	223	1,057	49
City of North Mankato	13,553	7	0	0	0	7	149	30	116	3
Total area actually reporting	100.0%	153	2	37	26	88	1,878	368	1,432	78
Rate per 100,000 inhabitants		153.8	2.0	37.2	26.1	88.5	1,887.8	369.9	1,439.5	78.4
Mansfield, OH M.S.A.	121,064									
Includes Richland County										
City of Mansfield	46,656	209	3	58	63	85	2,605	679	1,805	121
Total area actually reporting	99.3%	290	6	90	73	121	4,437	1,205	3,084	148
Estimated total	100.0%	291	6	90	73	122	4,457	1,208	3,100	149
Rate per 100,000 inhabitants		240.4	5.0	74.3	60.3	100.8	3,681.5	997.8	2,560.6	123.1
McAllen-Edinburg-Mission, TX M.S.A.[2]	853,003									
Includes Hidalgo County										
City of McAllen	142,227	215	3	40	65	107	4,470	331	4,022	117
City of Edinburg	86,535	354	3	61	51	239	4,183	545	3,481	157
City of Mission	84,380	120	0	36	40	44	2,179	358	1,707	114
Total area actually reporting	99.3%	2,505	22	417	444	1,622	24,130	3,939	19,095	1,096
Estimated total	100.0%	2,522	22	420	448	1,632	24,276	3,962	19,207	1,107
Rate per 100,000 inhabitants		295.7	2.6	49.2	52.5	191.3	2,845.9	464.5	2,251.7	129.8
Medford, OR M.S.A.	215,751									
Includes Jackson County										
City of Medford	80,794	407	1	31	115	260	5,688	486	4,793	409
Total area actually reporting	100.0%	772	5	73	150	544	9,339	1,067	7,602	670
Rate per 100,000 inhabitants		357.8	2.3	33.8	69.5	252.1	4,328.6	494.6	3,523.5	310.5
Memphis, TN-MS-AR M.S.A.	1,346,931									
Includes Crittenden County, AR; Benton, DeSoto, Marshall, Tate, and Tunica Counties, MS; and Fayette, Shelby, and Tipton Counties, TN										
City of Memphis, TN	656,434	11,947	196	534	3,188	8,029	36,988	9,150	24,604	3,234
Total area actually reporting	97.3%	14,524	248	730	3,618	9,928	51,468	12,430	34,899	4,139
Estimated total	100.0%	14,575	249	736	3,628	9,962	52,102	12,585	35,333	4,184
Rate per 100,000 inhabitants		1,082.1	18.5	54.6	269.4	739.6	3,868.2	934.3	2,623.2	310.6
Merced, CA M.S.A.	268,999									
Includes Merced County										
City of Merced	83,106	489	1	35	134	319	2,774	558	1,617	599
Total area actually reporting	100.0%	1,488	6	79	238	1,165	7,658	1,830	4,395	1,433
Rate per 100,000 inhabitants		553.2	2.2	29.4	88.5	433.1	2,846.9	680.3	1,633.8	532.7
Miami-Fort Lauderdale-West Palm Beach, FL M.S.A.	6,113,688									
Includes the Metropolitan Divisions of Fort Lauderdale-Pompano Beach-Deerfield Beach, Miami-Miami Beach-Kendall, and West Palm Beach-Boca Raton-Delray Beach										
City of Miami	449,469	3,989	55	90	1,443	2,401	18,974	2,643	14,335	1,996
City of Fort Lauderdale	181,218	1,144	18	71	483	572	10,630	1,856	7,856	918
City of West Palm Beach	108,074	954	10	71	333	540	5,599	946	4,100	553
City of Pompano Beach	109,362	931	7	77	344	503	5,205	903	3,738	564
City of Miami Beach	93,165	940	7	57	345	531	8,419	603	7,251	565
City of Boca Raton	94,931	239	1	22	105	111	2,495	507	1,831	157
City of Deerfield Beach	80,713	277	2	33	93	149	2,193	376	1,597	220
City of Delray Beach	67,400	387	5	31	125	226	2,842	385	2,218	239
City of Jupiter	64,273	147	0	15	40	92	1,261	163	1,038	60
Total area actually reporting	100.0%	29,720	355	1,866	9,299	18,200	196,533	28,357	150,604	17,572
Rate per 100,000 inhabitants		486.1	5.8	30.5	152.1	297.7	3,214.6	463.8	2,463.4	287.4
Fort Lauderdale-Pompano Beach-Deerfield Beach, FL M.D.	1,930,253									
Includes Broward County										
Total area actually reporting	100.0%	7,550	81	559	2,715	4,195	58,871	8,813	44,436	5,622
Rate per 100,000 inhabitants		391.1	4.2	29.0	140.7	217.3	3,049.9	456.6	2,302.1	291.3
Miami-Miami Beach-Kendall, FL M.D.	2,737,194									
Includes Miami-Dade County										
Total area actually reporting	100.0%	15,635	198	796	4,831	9,810	95,584	11,774	75,242	8,568
Rate per 100,000 inhabitants		571.2	7.2	29.1	176.5	358.4	3,492.0	430.1	2,748.9	313.0
West Palm Beach-Boca Raton-Delray Beach, FL M.D.	1,446,241									
Includes Palm Beach County										
Total area actually reporting	100.0%	6,535	76	511	1,753	4,195	42,078	7,770	30,926	3,382
Rate per 100,000 inhabitants		451.9	5.3	35.3	121.2	290.1	2,909.5	537.3	2,138.4	233.8
Michigan City-La Porte, IN M.S.A.	110,541									
Includes La Porte County										
City of Michigan City	31,459	186	2	19	50	115	1,444	213	1,131	100
City of La Porte	21,891	93	0	9	20	64	765	145	576	44
Total area actually reporting	95.8%	320	2	34	76	208	2,814	608	2,021	185
Estimated total	100.0%	333	2	35	79	217	2,943	623	2,126	194
Rate per 100,000 inhabitants		301.2	1.8	31.7	71.5	196.3	2,662.4	563.6	1,923.3	175.5

Table 4. Crime, by Selected Metropolitan Statistical Area, 2016—Continued

(Number, percent, rate per 100,000 population.)

Area	Population	Violent crime	Murder and nonnegligent manslaughter	Rape[1]	Robbery	Aggravated assault	Property crime	Burglary	Larceny-theft	Motor vehicle theft
Midland, MI M.S.A.	83,588									
Includes Midland County										
City of Midland	42,263	48	0	17	5	26	511	77	424	10
Total area actually reporting	100.0%	107	1	44	6	56	887	203	654	30
Rate per 100,000 inhabitants		128.0	1.2	52.6	7.2	67.0	1,061.2	242.9	782.4	35.9
Midland, TX M.S.A.	171,699									
Includes Martin and Midland Counties										
City of Midland	137,780	412	3	24	93	292	3,352	604	2,563	185
Total area actually reporting	100.0%	511	3	29	102	377	4,285	777	3,222	286
Rate per 100,000 inhabitants		297.6	1.7	16.9	59.4	219.6	2,495.6	452.5	1,876.5	166.6
Milwaukee-Waukesha-West Allis, WI M.S.A.[2]	1,577,025									
Includes Milwaukee, Ozaukee, Washington, and Waukesha Counties										
City of Milwaukee	600,193	9,201	141	477	3,283	5,300	24,392	5,862	12,356	6,174
City of Waukesha	72,223	92	0	31	14	47	1,117	182	891	44
City of West Allis[2]	60,558	200	6	20	76	98	2,262	451	1,609	202
Total area actually reporting	100.0%	10,345	156	638	3,661	5,890	42,858	8,074	27,545	7,239
Rate per 100,000 inhabitants		656.0	9.9	40.5	232.1	373.5	2,717.6	512.0	1,746.6	459.0
Minneapolis-St. Paul-Bloomington, MN-WI M.S.A.[2]	3,555,186									
Includes Anoka, Carver,[2] Chisago, Dakota, Hennepin, Isanti, Le Sueur, Mille Lacs, Ramsey, Scott, Sherburne, Sibley, Washington, and Wright Counties, MN and Pierce and St. Croix Counties, WI										
City of Minneapolis, MN	416,751	4,622	35	455	1,844	2,288	17,594	3,424	12,183	1,987
City of St. Paul, MN	303,920	1,970	19	184	700	1,067	9,811	2,278	5,659	1,874
City of Bloomington, MN	87,134	177	0	49	62	66	2,810	181	2,514	115
City of Plymouth, MN	76,996	48	1	12	14	21	1,009	215	759	35
City of Eagan, MN	66,698	40	0	11	13	16	1,144	106	995	43
City of Eden Prairie, MN	64,037	36	2	15	8	11	729	75	627	27
Total area actually reporting	99.8%	10,218	77	1,532	3,372	5,237	82,192	12,585	62,870	6,737
Estimated total	100.0%	10,227	77	1,533	3,374	5,243	82,325	12,600	62,982	6,743
Rate per 100,000 inhabitants		287.7	2.2	43.1	94.9	147.5	2,315.6	354.4	1,771.6	189.7
Missoula, MT M.S.A.	115,226									
Includes Missoula County										
City of Missoula	71,860	377	0	65	60	252	3,761	401	3,156	204
Total area actually reporting	100.0%	476	0	82	64	330	4,087	504	3,356	227
Rate per 100,000 inhabitants		413.1	0.0	71.2	55.5	286.4	3,546.9	437.4	2,912.5	197.0
Mobile, AL M.S.A.[5]	414,817									
Includes Mobile County										
City of Mobile[5]	249,921	1,709	44	89	438	1,138	11,769	2,628	8,261	880
Total area actually reporting	100.0%	2,426	61	137	604	1,624	16,688	4,005	11,299	1,384
Rate per 100,000 inhabitants		584.8	14.7	33.0	145.6	391.5	4,023.0	965.5	2,723.9	333.6
Modesto, CA M.S.A.	539,425									
Includes Stanislaus County										
City of Modesto	212,880	2,104	13	103	481	1,507	9,324	1,421	6,350	1,553
Total area actually reporting	100.0%	3,366	34	199	835	2,298	17,918	3,303	11,119	3,496
Rate per 100,000 inhabitants		624.0	6.3	36.9	154.8	426.0	3,321.7	612.3	2,061.3	648.1
Monroe, LA M.S.A.	179,125									
Includes Ouachita and Union Parishes										
City of Monroe	49,677	1,493	11	52	248	1,182	4,646	1,025	3,397	224
Total area actually reporting	95.6%	2,092	19	64	319	1,690	8,592	2,179	5,965	448
Estimated total	100.0%	2,126	20	66	324	1,716	8,884	2,229	6,193	462
Rate per 100,000 inhabitants		1,186.9	11.2	36.8	180.9	958.0	4,959.7	1,244.4	3,457.4	257.9
Montgomery, AL M.S.A.	372,661									
Includes Autauga, Elmore, Lowndes, and Montgomery Counties										
City of Montgomery	199,565	1,215	30	62	448	675	8,989	2,293	5,824	872
Total area actually reporting	99.3%	1,745	44	136	528	1,037	13,166	3,219	8,761	1,186
Estimated total	100.0%	1,758	44	137	530	1,047	13,248	3,235	8,821	1,192
Rate per 100,000 inhabitants		471.7	11.8	36.8	142.2	281.0	3,555.0	868.1	2,367.0	319.9
Morgantown, WV M.S.A.	138,954									
Includes Monongalia and Preston Counties										
City of Morgantown	31,109	89	2	12	19	56	674	129	517	28
Total area actually reporting	88.4%	318	3	59	27	229	1,684	410	1,186	88
Estimated total	100.0%	366	3	65	34	264	2,245	502	1,623	120
Rate per 100,000 inhabitants		263.4	2.2	46.8	24.5	190.0	1,615.6	361.3	1,168.0	86.4
Mount Vernon-Anacortes, WA M.S.A.	123,317									
Includes Skagit County										
City of Mount Vernon	34,521	88	0	16	28	44	1,324	197	1,014	113
City of Anacortes	16,532	15	0	1	4	10	463	65	369	29
Total area actually reporting	100.0%	230	6	36	54	134	4,424	852	3,263	309
Rate per 100,000 inhabitants		186.5	4.9	29.2	43.8	108.7	3,587.5	690.9	2,646.0	250.6

Table 4. Crime, by Selected Metropolitan Statistical Area, 2016—Continued

(Number, percent, rate per 100,000 population.)

Area	Population	Violent crime	Murder and nonnegligent manslaughter	Rape[1]	Robbery	Aggravated assault	Property crime	Burglary	Larceny-theft	Motor vehicle theft
Muncie, IN M.S.A.	116,443									
Includes Delaware County										
City of Muncie	70,065	252	6	29	95	122	2,755	475	2,083	197
Total area actually reporting	100.0%	304	9	37	99	159	3,429	650	2,533	246
Rate per 100,000 inhabitants		261.1	7.7	31.8	85.0	136.5	2,944.8	558.2	2,175.3	211.3
Muskegon, MI M.S.A.	172,890									
Includes Muskegon County										
City of Muskegon	38,442	273	5	39	62	167	1,468	285	1,094	89
Total area actually reporting	100.0%	754	9	144	142	459	5,211	813	4,148	250
Rate per 100,000 inhabitants		436.1	5.2	83.3	82.1	265.5	3,014.1	470.2	2,399.2	144.6
Myrtle Beach-Conway-North Myrtle Beach, SC-NC M.S.A.	444,122									
Includes Brunswick County, NC and Horry County, SC										
City of Myrtle Beach, SC	31,864	538	5	46	139	348	4,395	469	3,555	371
City of Conway, SC	21,874	174	3	20	24	127	1,016	138	805	73
City of North Myrtle Beach, SC	15,945	121	2	21	28	70	1,227	194	918	115
Total area actually reporting	97.4%	2,015	32	313	336	1,334	15,950	2,824	11,805	1,321
Estimated total	100.0%	2,046	32	315	345	1,354	16,308	2,892	12,082	1,334
Rate per 100,000 inhabitants		460.7	7.2	70.9	77.7	304.9	3,672.0	651.2	2,720.4	300.4
Napa, CA M.S.A.	142,635									
Includes Napa County										
City of Napa	81,115	296	1	38	47	210	1,579	437	1,013	129
Total area actually reporting	100.0%	598	1	62	72	463	2,524	655	1,647	222
Rate per 100,000 inhabitants		419.3	0.7	43.5	50.5	324.6	1,769.6	459.2	1,154.7	155.6
Naples-Immokalee-Marco Island, FL M.S.A.	365,390									
Includes Collier County										
City of Naples	21,917	19	3	4	3	9	408	52	339	17
City of Marco Island	17,947	2	0	1	0	1	94	13	76	5
Total area actually reporting	100.0%	962	10	70	169	713	4,496	807	3,443	246
Rate per 100,000 inhabitants		263.3	2.7	19.2	46.3	195.1	1,230.5	220.9	942.3	67.3
Nashville - Davidson - Murfreesboro - Franklin, TN M.S.A.	1,863,012									
Includes Cannon, Cheatham, Davidson, Dickson, Hickman, Macon, Maury, Robertson, Rutherford, Smith, Sumner, Trousdale, Williamson, and Wilson Counties										
City of Nashville Metropolitan	668,685	7,371	81	464	1,985	4,841	24,719	4,545	18,446	1,728
City of Murfreesboro	129,730	790	6	55	152	577	3,867	627	3,042	198
City of Franklin	74,771	154	0	21	19	114	1,085	84	968	33
Total area actually reporting	100.0%	11,580	115	839	2,435	8,191	46,171	8,320	34,747	3,104
Rate per 100,000 inhabitants		621.6	6.2	45.0	130.7	439.7	2,478.3	446.6	1,865.1	166.6
New Bern, NC M.S.A.	126,088									
Includes Craven, Jones, and Pamlico Counties										
City of New Bern	30,137	124	2	7	41	74	1,046	167	856	23
Total area actually reporting	91.0%	291	3	22	65	201	2,797	823	1,853	121
Estimated total	100.0%	310	3	23	69	215	3,001	885	1,984	132
Rate per 100,000 inhabitants		245.9	2.4	18.2	54.7	170.5	2,380.1	701.9	1,573.5	104.7
New Haven-Milford, CT M.S.A.[2]	804,612									
Includes New Haven County										
City of New Haven	130,425	1,219	13	66	400	740	5,492	832	3,925	735
City of Milford	53,752	34	0	0	27	7	1,215	126	1,001	88
Total area actually reporting	100.0%	2,597	30	185	885	1,497	20,370	3,269	14,656	2,445
Rate per 100,000 inhabitants		322.8	3.7	23.0	110.0	186.1	2,531.7	406.3	1,821.5	303.9
New Orleans-Metairie, LA M.S.A.	1,272,995									
Includes Jefferson, Orleans, Plaquemines, St. Bernard, St. Charles, St. James, St. John the Baptist, and St. Tammany Parishes										
City of New Orleans	397,208	4,249	174	537	1,445	2,093	15,571	2,561	10,583	2,427
Total area actually reporting	99.7%	7,099	240	712	2,060	4,087	38,082	5,940	28,488	3,654
Estimated total	100.0%	7,113	240	713	2,062	4,098	38,206	5,961	28,585	3,660
Rate per 100,000 inhabitants		558.8	18.9	56.0	162.0	321.9	3,001.3	468.3	2,245.5	287.5
New York-Newark-Jersey City, NY-NJ-PA M.S.A.	20,177,990									
Includes the Metropolitan Divisions of Dutchess County-Putnam County, NY; Nassau County-Suffolk County, NY; Newark, NJ-PA; and New York-Jersey City-White Plains, NY-NJ										
City of New York, NY	8,566,917	49,124	335	2,372	15,544	30,873	125,278	12,041	106,868	6,369
City of Newark, NJ	281,450	2,637	100	99	1,334	1,104	6,308	1,138	3,048	2,122
City of Jersey City, NJ	266,179	1,276	24	86	547	619	4,483	953	2,979	551
City of White Plains, NY	58,767	121	0	10	30	81	931	53	854	24
City of New Brunswick, NJ	57,158	392	1	38	211	142	1,252	319	859	74
City of Lakewood Township, NJ	100,269	169	2	12	61	94	949	193	718	38
Total area actually reporting	99.8%	71,541	655	3,940	24,435	42,511	273,117	33,416	221,694	18,007
Estimated total	100.0%	71,614	656	3,949	24,456	42,553	273,749	33,494	222,225	18,030
Rate per 100,000 inhabitants		354.9	3.3	19.6	121.2	210.9	1,356.7	166.0	1,101.3	89.4

Table 4. Crime, by Selected Metropolitan Statistical Area, 2016—Continued

(Number, percent, rate per 100,000 population.)

Area	Population	Violent crime	Murder and nonnegligent manslaughter	Rape[1]	Robbery	Aggravated assault	Property crime	Burglary	Larceny-theft	Motor vehicle theft
Dutchess County-Putnam County, NY M.D.	391,642									
Includes Dutchess and Putnam Counties										
Total area actually reporting	99.1%	601	4	120	119	358	4,079	565	3,414	100
Estimated total	100.0%	607	4	121	121	361	4,130	571	3,457	102
Rate per 100,000 inhabitants		155.0	1.0	30.9	30.9	92.2	1,054.5	145.8	882.7	26.0
Nassau County-Suffolk County, NY M.D.	2,849,237									
Includes Nassau and Suffolk Counties										
Total area actually reporting	98.8%	3,611	53	201	1,294	2,063	33,727	3,530	28,346	1,851
Estimated total	100.0%	3,673	54	208	1,312	2,099	34,264	3,597	28,797	1,870
Rate per 100,000 inhabitants		128.9	1.9	7.3	46.0	73.7	1,202.6	126.2	1,010.7	65.6
Newark, NJ-PA M.D.	2,506,862									
Includes Essex, Hunterdon, Morris, Somerset, Sussex, and Union Counties, NJ and Pike County, PA										
Total area actually reporting	100.0%	7,110	151	423	3,365	3,171	35,082	6,232	23,658	5,192
Rate per 100,000 inhabitants		283.6	6.0	16.9	134.2	126.5	1,399.4	248.6	943.7	207.1
New York-Jersey City-White Plains, NY-NJ M.D.	14,430,249									
Includes Bergen, Hudson, Middlesex, Monmouth, Ocean, and Passaic Counties, NJ and Bronx, Kings, New York, Orange, Queens, Richmond, Rockland, and Westchester Counties, NY										
Total area actually reporting	99.9%	60,219	447	3,196	19,657	36,919	200,229	23,089	166,276	10,864
Estimated total	100.0%	60,224	447	3,197	19,658	36,922	200,273	23,094	166,313	10,866
Rate per 100,000 inhabitants		417.3	3.1	22.2	136.2	255.9	1,387.9	160.0	1,152.5	75.3
Niles-Benton Harbor, MI M.S.A.	154,139									
Includes Berrien County										
City of Niles	11,282	64	0	20	12	32	287	65	191	31
City of Benton Harbor	9,963	179	1	15	41	122	438	137	258	43
Total area actually reporting	100.0%	696	10	151	102	433	3,605	772	2,641	192
Rate per 100,000 inhabitants		451.5	6.5	98.0	66.2	280.9	2,338.8	500.8	1,713.4	124.6
North Port-Sarasota-Bradenton, FL M.S.A.	784,372									
Includes Manatee and Sarasota Counties										
City of North Port	63,386	89	1	21	11	56	861	166	668	27
City of Sarasota	55,732	291	3	19	85	184	2,199	314	1,763	122
City of Bradenton	55,518	328	4	31	72	221	1,713	325	1,323	65
City of Venice	22,514	24	0	5	5	14	374	65	293	16
Total area actually reporting	100.0%	2,678	32	241	428	1,977	15,870	2,822	12,238	810
Rate per 100,000 inhabitants		341.4	4.1	30.7	54.6	252.0	2,023.3	359.8	1,560.2	103.3
Norwich-New London, CT M.S.A.	159,068									
Includes New London County										
City of Norwich	39,771	121	1	15	21	84	621	152	419	50
City of New London	27,092	193	1	11	30	151	743	130	532	81
Total area actually reporting	100.0%	465	3	52	70	340	3,278	513	2,557	208
Rate per 100,000 inhabitants		292.3	1.9	32.7	44.0	213.7	2,060.8	322.5	1,607.5	130.8
Ocala, FL M.S.A.	346,358									
Includes Marion County										
City of Ocala	58,596	463	10	29	111	313	3,174	443	2,600	131
Total area actually reporting	100.0%	1,174	18	90	213	853	7,923	1,926	5,384	613
Rate per 100,000 inhabitants		339.0	5.2	26.0	61.5	246.3	2,287.5	556.1	1,554.5	177.0
Ocean City, NJ M.S.A.	93,755									
Includes Cape May County										
City of Ocean City	11,287	14	0	1	5	8	364	58	306	0
Total area actually reporting	100.0%	217	0	25	54	138	2,830	532	2,249	49
Rate per 100,000 inhabitants		231.5	0.0	26.7	57.6	147.2	3,018.5	567.4	2,398.8	52.3
Odessa, TX M.S.A.	163,843									
Includes Ector County										
City of Odessa	123,209	996	4	75	136	781	4,118	791	2,890	437
Total area actually reporting	100.0%	1,169	7	98	170	894	6,137	1,157	4,300	680
Rate per 100,000 inhabitants		713.5	4.3	59.8	103.8	545.6	3,745.7	706.2	2,624.5	415.0
Ogden-Clearfield, UT M.S.A.[2]	653,748									
Includes Box Elder, Davis, Morgan, and Weber Counties										
City of Ogden	85,930	450	3	65	108	274	3,808	614	2,843	351
City of Clearfield	30,783	29	0	13	3	13	664	120	501	43
Total area actually reporting	98.1%	996	9	267	173	547	14,205	2,418	10,807	980
Estimated total	100.0%	1,017	9	271	178	559	14,508	2,467	11,023	1,018
Rate per 100,000 inhabitants		155.6	1.4	41.5	27.2	85.5	2,219.2	377.4	1,686.1	155.7
Oklahoma City, OK M.S.A.	1,372,721									
Includes Canadian, Cleveland, Grady, Lincoln, Logan, McClain, and Oklahoma Counties										
City of Oklahoma City	641,681	5,027	70	445	1,144	3,368	25,032	5,545	16,582	2,905
Total area actually reporting	100.0%	6,737	92	752	1,433	4,460	42,683	9,427	28,735	4,521
Rate per 100,000 inhabitants		490.8	6.7	54.8	104.4	324.9	3,109.4	686.7	2,093.3	329.3

Table 4. Crime, by Selected Metropolitan Statistical Area, 2016—Continued

(Number, percent, rate per 100,000 population.)

Area	Population	Violent crime	Murder and nonnegligent manslaughter	Rape[1]	Robbery	Aggravated assault	Property crime	Burglary	Larceny-theft	Motor vehicle theft
Olympia-Tumwater, WA M.S.A.	274,020									
Includes Thurston County										
City of Olympia	50,972	200	0	21	47	132	2,491	378	1,889	224
City of Tumwater	19,569	78	0	12	7	59	843	169	585	89
Total area actually reporting	100.0%	668	6	74	108	480	8,060	1,606	5,721	733
Rate per 100,000 inhabitants		243.8	2.2	27.0	39.4	175.2	2,941.4	586.1	2,087.8	267.5
Omaha-Council Bluffs, NE-IA M.S.A.	923,710									
Includes Harrison, Mills, and Pottawattamie Counties, IA and Cass, Douglas, Sarpy, Saunders, and Washington Counties, NE										
City of Omaha, NE	446,163	2,531	29	245	610	1,647	16,807	2,111	11,571	3,125
City of Council Bluffs, IA	62,642	150	4	27	55	64	3,862	387	3,043	432
Total area actually reporting	99.9%	3,242	36	388	722	2,096	25,394	3,334	17,981	4,079
Estimated total	100.0%	3,244	36	389	722	2,097	25,415	3,336	17,998	4,081
Rate per 100,000 inhabitants		351.2	3.9	42.1	78.2	227.0	2,751.4	361.2	1,948.4	441.8
Orlando-Kissimmee-Sanford, FL M.S.A.[6]	2,445,214									
Includes Lake, Orange, Osceola, and Seminole Counties										
City of Orlando[6]	277,719	2,328	84	211	504	1,529	14,498	3,637	9,621	1,240
City of Kissimmee	71,197	508	0	47	114	347	2,670	585	1,955	130
City of Sanford	59,027	542	6	48	138	350	2,812	466	2,165	181
Total area actually reporting	99.4%	12,275	196	1,222	2,412	8,445	72,038	16,639	50,171	5,228
Estimated total	100.0%	12,331	197	1,226	2,428	8,480	72,464	16,703	50,500	5,261
Rate per 100,000 inhabitants		504.3	8.1	50.1	99.3	346.8	2,963.5	683.1	2,065.3	215.2
Oshkosh-Neenah, WI M.S.A.	169,773									
Includes Winnebago County										
City of Oshkosh	66,654	141	0	7	28	106	1,471	194	1,209	68
City of Neenah	25,850	52	0	9	10	33	491	50	420	21
Total area actually reporting	100.0%	281	0	21	45	215	2,857	410	2,313	134
Rate per 100,000 inhabitants		165.5	0.0	12.4	26.5	126.6	1,682.8	241.5	1,362.4	78.9
Owensboro, KY M.S.A.	117,893									
Includes Daviess, Hancock, and McLean Counties										
City of Owensboro	59,359	136	1	34	49	52	2,658	486	1,937	235
Total area actually reporting	100.0%	169	2	46	52	69	3,196	636	2,289	271
Rate per 100,000 inhabitants		143.4	1.7	39.0	44.1	58.5	2,710.9	539.5	1,941.6	229.9
Oxnard-Thousand Oaks-Ventura, CA M.S.A.	849,851									
Includes Ventura County										
City of Oxnard	209,048	948	12	69	429	438	6,073	978	4,309	786
City of Thousand Oaks	129,853	164	0	30	33	101	1,686	272	1,302	112
City of Ventura	110,228	368	8	53	109	198	3,750	628	2,838	284
City of Camarillo	68,072	123	4	21	31	67	1,125	202	824	99
Total area actually reporting	100.0%	2,192	31	269	725	1,167	16,415	2,910	11,855	1,650
Rate per 100,000 inhabitants		257.9	3.6	31.7	85.3	137.3	1,931.5	342.4	1,395.0	194.2
Palm Bay-Melbourne-Titusville, FL M.S.A.	574,187									
Includes Brevard County										
City of Palm Bay	108,823	516	4	57	47	408	1,841	454	1,252	135
City of Melbourne	80,900	667	3	65	126	473	3,308	686	2,439	183
City of Titusville	45,723	355	3	40	61	251	1,868	463	1,183	222
Total area actually reporting	100.0%	2,870	20	255	451	2,144	14,857	3,249	10,454	1,154
Rate per 100,000 inhabitants		499.8	3.5	44.4	78.5	373.4	2,587.5	565.8	1,820.7	201.0
Panama City, FL M.S.A.	200,502									
Includes Bay and Gulf Counties										
City of Panama City	38,847	276	3	17	50	206	2,098	330	1,587	181
Total area actually reporting	100.0%	957	9	90	136	722	6,776	1,208	5,136	432
Rate per 100,000 inhabitants		477.3	4.5	44.9	67.8	360.1	3,379.5	602.5	2,561.6	215.5
Parkersburg-Vienna, WV M.S.A.	91,681									
Includes Wirt and Wood Counties										
City of Parkersburg	30,913	206	4	27	19	156	1,373	371	923	79
City of Vienna	10,537	20	0	4	1	15	447	29	415	3
Total area actually reporting	100.0%	360	4	47	24	285	2,425	596	1,703	126
Rate per 100,000 inhabitants		392.7	4.4	51.3	26.2	310.9	2,645.0	650.1	1,857.5	137.4
Pensacola-Ferry Pass-Brent, FL M.S.A.	484,608									
Includes Escambia and Santa Rosa Counties										
City of Pensacola	53,424	348	7	27	64	250	2,184	341	1,741	102
Total area actually reporting	100.0%	2,219	25	243	396	1,555	12,338	2,441	9,137	760
Rate per 100,000 inhabitants		457.9	5.2	50.1	81.7	320.9	2,546.0	503.7	1,885.4	156.8
Peoria, IL M.S.A.	375,999									
Includes Marshall, Peoria, Stark, Tazewell, and Woodford Counties										
City of Peoria	115,099	875	10	70	305	490	4,429	1,089	3,116	224
Total area actually reporting	95.7%	1,463	14	166	356	927	8,215	1,876	5,981	358
Estimated total	100.0%	1,497	14	171	366	946	8,489	1,919	6,198	372
Rate per 100,000 inhabitants		398.1	3.7	45.5	97.3	251.6	2,257.7	510.4	1,648.4	98.9

Table 4. Crime, by Selected Metropolitan Statistical Area, 2016—Continued

(Number, percent, rate per 100,000 population.)

Area	Population	Violent crime	Murder and nonnegligent manslaughter	Rape[1]	Robbery	Aggravated assault	Property crime	Burglary	Larceny-theft	Motor vehicle theft
Philadelphia-Camden-Wilmington, PA-NJ-DE-MD M.S.A.	6,068,767									
Includes the Metropolitan Divisions of Camden, NJ; Montgomery County-Bucks County-Chester County, PA; Philadelphia, PA; and Wilmington, DE-MD-NJ										
City of Philadelphia, PA	1,570,826	15,534	273	1,259	6,199	7,803	49,334	6,985	36,856	5,493
City of Wilmington, DE	72,183	1,285	26	35	438	786	3,544	812	2,232	500
Total area actually reporting	99.9%	27,091	480	2,046	9,875	14,690	131,765	20,263	101,444	10,058
Estimated total	100.0%	27,098	480	2,046	9,877	14,695	131,822	20,270	101,492	10,060
Rate per 100,000 inhabitants		446.5	7.9	33.7	162.8	242.1	2,172.1	334.0	1,672.4	165.8
Camden, NJ M.D.	1,246,564									
Includes Burlington, Camden, and Gloucester Counties										
Total area actually reporting	100.0%	3,396	83	282	1,112	1,919	24,291	5,135	17,728	1,428
Rate per 100,000 inhabitants		272.4	6.7	22.6	89.2	153.9	1,948.6	411.9	1,422.1	114.6
Montgomery County-Bucks County-Chester County, PA M.D.	1,964,200									
Includes Bucks, Chester, and Montgomery Counties										
Total area actually reporting	99.9%	2,342	33	232	655	1,422	27,761	3,178	23,452	1,131
Estimated total	100.0%	2,345	33	232	656	1,424	27,783	3,181	23,470	1,132
Rate per 100,000 inhabitants		119.4	1.7	11.8	33.4	72.5	1,414.5	161.9	1,194.9	57.6
Philadelphia, PA M.D.	2,134,060									
Includes Delaware and Philadelphia Counties										
Total area actually reporting	99.9%	17,639	311	1,341	6,925	9,062	59,550	8,305	45,163	6,082
Estimated total	100.0%	17,643	311	1,341	6,926	9,065	59,585	8,309	45,193	6,083
Rate per 100,000 inhabitants		826.7	14.6	62.8	324.5	424.8	2,792.1	389.4	2,117.7	285.0
Wilmington, DE-MD-NJ M.D.	723,943									
Includes New Castle County, DE; Cecil County, MD; and Salem County, NJ										
Total area actually reporting	100.0%	3,714	53	191	1,183	2,287	20,163	3,645	15,101	1,417
Rate per 100,000 inhabitants		513.0	7.3	26.4	163.4	315.9	2,785.2	503.5	2,085.9	195.7
Phoenix-Mesa-Scottsdale, AZ M.S.A.	4,662,302									
Includes Maricopa and Pinal Counties										
City of Phoenix	1,586,611	10,700	146	1,019	3,272	6,263	58,552	13,024	37,568	7,960
City of Mesa	478,277	2,051	19	272	450	1,310	11,214	1,950	8,404	860
City of Scottsdale	240,885	369	4	90	112	163	5,698	768	4,681	249
City of Tempe	178,654	902	4	155	237	506	8,144	1,200	6,494	450
Total area actually reporting	99.8%	19,876	256	2,148	5,247	12,225	133,534	25,703	94,366	13,465
Estimated total	100.0%	19,904	256	2,151	5,253	12,244	133,812	25,748	94,580	13,484
Rate per 100,000 inhabitants		426.9	5.5	46.1	112.7	262.6	2,870.1	552.3	2,028.6	289.2
Pine Bluff, AR M.S.A	92,403									
Includes Cleveland, Jefferson, and Lincoln Counties										
City of Pine Bluff	43,976	705	9	38	130	528	2,786	1,062	1,488	236
Total area actually reporting	100.0%	840	10	60	139	631	3,594	1,340	1,944	310
Rate per 100,000 inhabitants		909.1	10.8	64.9	150.4	682.9	3,889.5	1,450.2	2,103.8	335.5
Pittsburgh, PA M.S.A.	2,345,496									
Includes Allegheny, Armstrong, Beaver, Butler, Fayette, Washington, and Westmoreland Counties										
City of Pittsburgh	302,443	2,366	57	100	1,000	1,209	9,868	1,828	7,222	818
Total area actually reporting	97.9%	6,694	118	529	1,924	4,123	40,207	7,165	31,025	2,017
Estimated total	100.0%	6,778	119	536	1,945	4,178	40,964	7,260	31,659	2,045
Rate per 100,000 inhabitants		289.0	5.1	22.9	82.9	178.1	1,746.5	309.5	1,349.8	87.2
Pittsfield, MA M.S.A.	126,594									
Includes Berkshire County										
City of Pittsfield	43,031	340	3	37	39	261	1,016	364	620	32
Total area actually reporting	91.2%	616	3	80	50	483	2,138	649	1,421	68
Estimated total	100.0%	649	3	83	55	508	2,292	676	1,537	79
Rate per 100,000 inhabitants		512.7	2.4	65.6	43.4	401.3	1,810.5	534.0	1,214.1	62.4
Pocatello, ID M.S.A.	84,414									
Includes Bannock County										
City of Pocatello	54,448	207	2	18	14	173	1,630	316	1,184	130
Total area actually reporting	100.0%	241	3	20	18	200	2,218	361	1,712	145
Rate per 100,000 inhabitants		285.5	3.6	23.7	21.3	236.9	2,627.5	427.7	2,028.1	171.8
Portland-South Portland, ME M.S.A.[2]	529,510									
Includes Cumberland, Sagadahoc, and York Counties										
City of Portland	67,041	196	2	36	59	99	1,795	236	1,485	74
City of South Portland	25,674	44	0	6	11	27	596	75	505	16
Total area actually reporting	100.0%	711	8	145	127	431	8,954	1,512	7,148	294
Rate per 100,000 inhabitants		134.3	1.5	27.4	24.0	81.4	1,691.0	285.5	1,349.9	55.5
Portland-Vancouver-Hillsboro, OR-WA M.S.A.	2,435,620									
Includes Clackamas, Columbia, Multnomah, Washington, and Yamhill Counties, OR and Clark and Skamania Counties, WA										
City of Portland, OR	642,129	3,163	14	389	986	1,774	33,087	4,064	24,099	4,924

Table 4. Crime, by Selected Metropolitan Statistical Area, 2016—Continued

(Number, percent, rate per 100,000 population.)

Area	Population	Violent crime	Murder and nonnegligent manslaughter	Rape[1]	Robbery	Aggravated assault	Property crime	Burglary	Larceny-theft	Motor vehicle theft
City of Vancouver, WA	174,912	675	0	117	148	410	5,533	860	3,666	1,007
City of Hillsboro, OR	104,440	298	0	79	64	155	2,010	232	1,613	165
City of Beaverton, OR	97,907	133	0	25	30	78	1,403	124	1,176	103
Total area actually reporting	98.3%	6,635	41	1,181	1,647	3,766	66,937	8,901	48,646	9,390
Estimated total	100.0%	6,725	42	1,199	1,665	3,819	68,056	9,029	49,529	9,498
Rate per 100,000 inhabitants		276.1	1.7	49.2	68.4	156.8	2,794.2	370.7	2,033.5	390.0
Port St. Lucie, FL M.S.A.	461,932									
Includes Martin and St. Lucie Counties										
City of Port St. Lucie	182,365	270	3	22	48	197	2,419	400	1,934	85
Total area actually reporting	100.0%	1,196	19	132	216	829	8,119	1,523	6,224	372
Rate per 100,000 inhabitants		258.9	4.1	28.6	46.8	179.5	1,757.6	329.7	1,347.4	80.5
Prescott, AZ M.S.A.	225,038									
Includes Yavapai County										
City of Prescott	42,321	170	0	10	18	142	924	175	720	29
Total area actually reporting	100.0%	653	6	49	49	549	4,326	841	3,246	239
Rate per 100,000 inhabitants		290.2	2.7	21.8	21.8	244.0	1,922.3	373.7	1,442.4	106.2
Providence-Warwick, RI-MA M.S.A.[3,4]	1,612,295									
Includes Bristol County, MA and Bristol, Kent, Newport, Providence, and Washington Counties, RI										
City of Providence, RI[3]	179,340	1,031	10	112	300	609		1,154	4,132	
City of Warwick, RI	81,481	61	1	17	11	32	1,625	158	1,392	75
Total area actually reporting	100.0%	5,079	39	625	1,059	3,356		5,922		
Rate per 100,000 inhabitants		315.0	2.4	38.8	65.7	208.2		367.3		
Provo-Orem, UT M.S.A.	599,314									
Includes Juab and Utah Counties										
City of Provo	115,739	149	2	57	20	70	2,713	266	2,292	155
City of Orem	95,640	65	0	26	18	21	2,447	209	2,116	122
Total area actually reporting	100.0%	465	5	164	64	232	10,556	1,241	8,766	549
Rate per 100,000 inhabitants		77.6	0.8	27.4	10.7	38.7	1,761.3	207.1	1,462.7	91.6
Pueblo, CO M.S.A.	164,337									
Includes Pueblo County										
City of Pueblo	109,927	1,081	9	171	224	677	7,473	1,797	4,505	1,171
Total area actually reporting	100.0%	1,117	11	172	230	704	8,784	2,089	5,364	1,331
Rate per 100,000 inhabitants		679.7	6.7	104.7	140.0	428.4	5,345.1	1,271.2	3,264.0	809.9
Punta Gorda, FL M.S.A.	176,234									
Includes Charlotte County										
City of Punta Gorda	18,466	12	1	0	1	10	212	24	177	11
Total area actually reporting	100.0%	391	5	35	20	331	2,671	432	2,127	112
Rate per 100,000 inhabitants		221.9	2.8	19.9	11.3	187.8	1,515.6	245.1	1,206.9	63.6
Racine, WI M.S.A.	194,692									
Includes Racine County										
City of Racine	77,536	367	6	16	133	212	2,287	677	1,510	100
Total area actually reporting	100.0%	427	8	29	148	242	3,748	875	2,715	158
Rate per 100,000 inhabitants		219.3	4.1	14.9	76.0	124.3	1,925.1	449.4	1,394.5	81.2
Rapid City, SD M.S.A.	145,700									
Includes Custer, Meade, and Pennington Counties										
City of Rapid City	74,573	536	2	88	80	366	2,966	480	2,236	250
Total area actually reporting	100.0%	721	5	151	87	478	3,806	635	2,861	310
Rate per 100,000 inhabitants		494.9	3.4	103.6	59.7	328.1	2,612.2	435.8	1,963.6	212.8
Reading, PA M.S.A.	414,729									
Includes Berks County										
City of Reading	87,834	597	10	47	233	307	2,292	685	1,417	190
Total area actually reporting	99.1%	1,128	17	110	299	702	6,740	1,416	4,973	351
Estimated total	100.0%	1,135	17	111	301	706	6,795	1,423	5,019	353
Rate per 100,000 inhabitants		273.7	4.1	26.8	72.6	170.2	1,638.4	343.1	1,210.2	85.1
Redding, CA M.S.A.	178,755									
Includes Shasta County										
City of Redding	91,918	720	5	84	143	488	3,837	710	2,608	519
Total area actually reporting	100.0%	1,333	12	150	172	999	5,561	1,217	3,472	872
Rate per 100,000 inhabitants		745.7	6.7	83.9	96.2	558.9	3,111.0	680.8	1,942.3	487.8
Reno, NV M.S.A.	457,558									
Includes Storey and Washoe Counties										
City of Reno	244,554	1,717	9	139	393	1,176	7,933	1,208	5,381	1,344
Total area actually reporting	100.0%	2,354	14	193	491	1,656	11,866	1,919	8,134	1,813
Rate per 100,000 inhabitants		514.5	3.1	42.2	107.3	361.9	2,593.3	419.4	1,777.7	396.2
Riverside-San Bernardino-Ontario, CA M.S.A.	4,509,084									
Includes Riverside and San Bernardino Counties										
City of Riverside	325,896	1,724	10	141	586	987	11,266	1,977	7,355	1,934
City of San Bernardino	217,303	2,878	62	123	903	1,790	9,178	2,353	4,228	2,597
City of Ontario	172,606	602	8	32	227	335	4,718	885	2,764	1,069
City of Corona	166,534	185	3	39	74	69	3,693	741	2,236	716

Table 4. Crime, by Selected Metropolitan Statistical Area, 2016—Continued

(Number, percent, rate per 100,000 population.)

Area	Population	Violent crime	Murder and nonnegligent manslaughter	Rape[1]	Robbery	Aggravated assault	Property crime	Burglary	Larceny-theft	Motor vehicle theft
City of Victorville	123,438	748	7	46	224	471	3,528	953	2,002	573
City of Temecula	114,381	145	2	4	55	84	2,587	341	1,940	306
City of Chino	87,081	207	1	13	52	141	2,151	439	1,407	305
City of Redlands	71,485	225	0	37	76	112	2,913	501	2,014	398
Total area actually reporting	100.0%	17,916	228	1,203	5,186	11,299	120,270	26,204	70,799	23,267
Rate per 100,000 inhabitants		397.3	5.1	26.7	115.0	250.6	2,667.3	581.1	1,570.1	516.0
Roanoke, VA M.S.A.	314,014									
Includes Botetourt, Craig, Franklin, and Roanoke Counties and Roanoke and Salem Cities										
City of Roanoke	99,978	413	13	36	117	247	4,195	423	3,549	223
Total area actually reporting	100.0%	763	16	106	148	493	7,110	771	5,961	378
Rate per 100,000 inhabitants		243.0	5.1	33.8	47.1	157.0	2,264.2	245.5	1,898.3	120.4
Rochester, MN M.S.A.	214,994									
Includes Dodge, Fillmore, Olmsted, and Wabasha Counties										
City of Rochester	113,306	242	0	76	49	117	2,479	375	1,972	132
Total area actually reporting	100.0%	296	0	91	53	152	3,138	526	2,418	194
Rate per 100,000 inhabitants		137.7	0.0	42.3	24.7	70.7	1,459.6	244.7	1,124.7	90.2
Rochester, NY M.S.A.	1,075,149									
Includes Livingston, Monroe, Ontario, Orleans, Wayne, and Yates Counties										
City of Rochester	209,643	1,845	43	161	670	971	7,812	1,475	5,673	664
Total area actually reporting	99.6%	3,012	51	458	913	1,590	21,396	3,539	16,745	1,112
Estimated total	100.0%	3,019	51	459	915	1,594	21,457	3,547	16,796	1,114
Rate per 100,000 inhabitants		280.8	4.7	42.7	85.1	148.3	1,995.7	329.9	1,562.2	103.6
Rockford, IL M.S.A.	337,323									
Includes Boone and Winnebago Counties										
City of Rockford	147,361	2,444	26	137	536	1,745	5,565	1,406	3,696	463
Total area actually reporting	99.0%	2,932	31	234	603	2,064	8,697	2,063	6,047	587
Estimated total	100.0%	2,939	31	235	605	2,068	8,756	2,072	6,094	590
Rate per 100,000 inhabitants		871.3	9.2	69.7	179.4	613.1	2,595.7	614.2	1,806.6	174.9
Rocky Mount, NC M.S.A.[3]	147,228									
Includes Edgecombe and Nash Counties										
City of Rocky Mount[3]	55,431	435	4	12	116	303		593		98
Total area actually reporting	93.9%	635	12	31	148	444		1,062		155
Estimated total	100.0%	660	12	33	155	460		1,114		165
Rate per 100,000 inhabitants		448.3	8.2	22.4	105.3	312.4		756.6		112.1
Rome, GA M.S.A.	96,420									
Includes Floyd County										
City of Rome	36,278	208	4	8	52	144	1,398	239	1,088	71
Total area actually reporting	100.0%	309	5	27	67	210	2,765	624	1,954	187
Rate per 100,000 inhabitants		320.5	5.2	28.0	69.5	217.8	2,867.7	647.2	2,026.6	193.9
Sacramento - Roseville - Arden - Arcade, CA M.S.A.	2,283,312									
Includes El Dorado, Placer, Sacramento, and Yolo Counties										
City of Sacramento	495,471	3,549	41	88	1,136	2,284	15,283	3,070	9,389	2,824
City of Roseville	132,566	199	0	21	95	83	3,316	393	2,596	327
City of Folsom	77,245	76	0	9	34	33	1,384	264	1,006	114
Total area actually reporting	100.0%	9,384	95	595	2,742	5,952	54,595	10,479	35,750	8,366
Rate per 100,000 inhabitants		411.0	4.2	26.1	120.1	260.7	2,391.0	458.9	1,565.7	366.4
Saginaw, MI M.S.A.	191,925									
Includes Saginaw County										
City of Saginaw	48,942	718	10	56	62	590	926	369	503	54
Total area actually reporting	100.0%	1,168	18	128	108	914	3,346	836	2,359	151
Rate per 100,000 inhabitants		608.6	9.4	66.7	56.3	476.2	1,743.4	435.6	1,229.1	78.7
Salem, OR M.S.A.	416,427									
Includes Marion and Polk Counties										
City of Salem	166,508	533	7	38	128	360	6,661	907	5,114	640
Total area actually reporting	100.0%	952	19	94	189	650	11,947	1,769	8,976	1,202
Rate per 100,000 inhabitants		228.6	4.6	22.6	45.4	156.1	2,868.9	424.8	2,155.5	288.6
Salinas, CA M.S.A.	434,506									
Includes Monterey County										
City of Salinas	158,729	1,005	35	86	325	559	4,742	695	2,484	1,563
Total area actually reporting	100.0%	1,822	56	162	506	1,098	10,396	1,666	6,212	2,518
Rate per 100,000 inhabitants		419.3	12.9	37.3	116.5	252.7	2,392.6	383.4	1,429.7	579.5
Salisbury, MD-DE M.S.A.	397,778									
Includes Sussex County, DE and Somerset, Wicomico, and Worcester Counties, MD										
City of Salisbury, MD	33,417	297	2	11	103	181	1,695	234	1,410	51
Total area actually reporting	100.0%	1,609	15	156	352	1,086	10,755	2,533	7,939	283
Rate per 100,000 inhabitants		404.5	3.8	39.2	88.5	273.0	2,703.8	636.8	1,995.8	71.1
Salt Lake City, UT M.S.A.[2]	1,190,065									
Includes Salt Lake and Tooele Counties										

Table 4. Crime, by Selected Metropolitan Statistical Area, 2016—Continued

(Number, percent, rate per 100,000 population.)

Area	Population	Violent crime	Murder and nonnegligent manslaughter	Rape[1]	Robbery	Aggravated assault	Property crime	Burglary	Larceny-theft	Motor vehicle theft
City of Salt Lake City	193,918	1,815	13	264	506	1,032	16,551	1,807	12,814	1,930
Total area actually reporting	99.9%	4,885	47	827	1,236	2,775	54,725	7,286	40,414	7,025
Estimated total	100.0%	4,885	47	827	1,236	2,775	54,736	7,288	40,422	7,026
Rate per 100,000 inhabitants		410.5	3.9	69.5	103.9	233.2	4,599.4	612.4	3,396.6	590.4
San Angelo, TX M.S.A.	120,833									
Includes Irion and Tom Green Counties										
City of San Angelo	101,870	371	6	58	54	253	4,991	875	3,839	277
Total area actually reporting	100.0%	403	6	78	58	261	5,484	1,081	4,095	308
Rate per 100,000 inhabitants		333.5	5.0	64.6	48.0	216.0	4,538.5	894.6	3,389.0	254.9
San Antonio-New Braunfels, TX M.S.A.[2]	2,426,076									
Includes Atascosa, Bandera, Bexar, Comal, Guadalupe, Kendall, Medina, and Wilson Counties										
City of San Antonio	1,498,642	10,754	149	1,190	2,232	7,183	77,786	12,235	58,318	7,233
City of New Braunfels	73,334	207	1	34	25	147	1,721	245	1,295	181
Total area actually reporting	99.9%	12,767	187	1,596	2,544	8,440	99,000	16,088	74,099	8,813
Estimated total	100.0%	12,771	187	1,597	2,545	8,442	99,029	16,093	74,121	8,815
Rate per 100,000 inhabitants		526.4	7.7	65.8	104.9	348.0	4,081.9	663.3	3,055.2	363.3
San Diego-Carlsbad, CA M.S.A.	3,317,259									
Includes San Diego County										
City of San Diego	1,413,414	5,332	50	572	1,387	3,323	28,624	4,743	18,042	5,839
City of Carlsbad	115,040	209	0	37	49	123	2,188	369	1,652	167
Total area actually reporting	100.0%	10,959	101	1,088	2,777	6,993	61,371	10,391	39,955	11,025
Rate per 100,000 inhabitants		330.4	3.0	32.8	83.7	210.8	1,850.1	313.2	1,204.5	332.4
San Francisco-Oakland-Hayward, CA M.S.A.	4,688,840									
Includes the Metropolitan Divisions of Oakland-Hayward-Berkeley, San Francisco-Redwood City-South San Francisco, and San Rafael										
City of San Francisco	871,155	6,190	57	342	3,175	2,616	47,402	4,978	36,991	5,433
City of Oakland	424,998	6,059	85	277	3,076	2,621	23,952	2,900	14,153	6,899
City of Hayward	161,122	631	13	66	348	204	4,641	707	2,308	1,626
City of Berkeley	122,651	602	2	54	361	185	5,420	805	3,965	650
City of San Leandro	91,870	487	3	31	280	173	3,530	499	2,070	961
City of Redwood City	87,046	164	0	43	44	77	1,503	260	1,087	156
City of San Ramon	76,901	39	0	9	12	18	823	140	616	67
City of Pleasanton	81,464	100	0	12	44	44	1,604	208	1,260	136
City of Walnut Creek	69,860	78	1	1	30	46	2,120	275	1,611	234
City of South San Francisco	67,995	149	1	25	43	80	1,416	307	902	207
City of San Rafael	59,435	249	0	28	111	110	1,713	255	1,186	272
Total area actually reporting	100.0%	22,400	239	1,589	10,467	10,105	156,988	21,502	107,276	28,210
Rate per 100,000 inhabitants		477.7	5.1	33.9	223.2	215.5	3,348.1	458.6	2,287.9	601.6
Oakland-Hayward-Berkeley, CA M.D.	2,787,325									
Includes Alameda and Contra Costa Counties										
Total area actually reporting	100.0%	14,022	169	937	6,613	6,303	88,683	12,410	55,717	20,556
Rate per 100,000 inhabitants		503.1	6.1	33.6	237.3	226.1	3,181.7	445.2	1,998.9	737.5
San Francisco-Redwood City-South San Francisco, CA M.D.	1,640,386									
Includes San Francisco and San Mateo Counties										
Total area actually reporting	100.0%	7,903	67	600	3,686	3,550	63,330	8,101	48,115	7,114
Rate per 100,000 inhabitants		481.8	4.1	36.6	224.7	216.4	3,860.7	493.8	2,933.2	433.7
San Rafael, CA M.D.	261,129									
Includes Marin County										
Total area actually reporting	100.0%	475	3	52	168	252	4,975	991	3,444	540
Rate per 100,000 inhabitants		181.9	1.1	19.9	64.3	96.5	1,905.2	379.5	1,318.9	206.8
San Jose-Sunnyvale-Santa Clara, CA M.S.A.	1,991,233									
Includes San Benito and Santa Clara Counties										
City of San Jose	1,041,844	3,887	47	451	1,214	2,175	24,749	4,260	12,786	7,703
City of Sunnyvale	154,108	158	1	21	53	83	2,140	520	1,347	273
City of Santa Clara	128,179	159	3	17	58	81	2,814	362	2,039	413
City of Mountain View	81,726	132	0	9	29	94	1,776	280	1,377	119
City of Milpitas	79,990	96	1	9	52	34	1,791	202	1,320	269
City of Palo Alto	67,317	73	1	9	28	35	1,436	215	1,159	62
City of Cupertino	60,948	71	0	7	16	48	997	268	661	68
Total area actually reporting	100.0%	5,578	58	658	1,645	3,217	43,340	7,661	25,613	10,066
Rate per 100,000 inhabitants		280.1	2.9	33.0	82.6	161.6	2,176.5	384.7	1,286.3	505.5
San Luis Obispo-Paso Robles-Arroyo Grande, CA M.S.A.	281,827									
Includes San Luis Obispo County										
City of San Luis Obispo	47,774	178	0	39	21	118	2,076	251	1,730	95
City of Paso Robles	31,939	67	0	8	20	39	977	144	738	95
City of Arroyo Grande	18,280	35	0	6	9	20	334	53	262	19
Total area actually reporting	100.0%	1,115	4	102	88	921	6,687	1,199	4,987	501
Rate per 100,000 inhabitants		395.6	1.4	36.2	31.2	326.8	2,372.7	425.4	1,769.5	177.8
Santa Cruz-Watsonville, CA M.S.A.	274,494									
Includes Santa Cruz County										
City of Santa Cruz	64,969	521	4	45	106	366	3,610	354	2,874	382

Table 4. Crime, by Selected Metropolitan Statistical Area, 2016—Continued

(Number, percent, rate per 100,000 population.)

Area	Population	Violent crime	Murder and nonnegligent manslaughter	Rape[1]	Robbery	Aggravated assault	Property crime	Burglary	Larceny-theft	Motor vehicle theft
City of Watsonville	54,110	238	0	26	46	166	1,738	214	1,018	506
Total area actually reporting	100.0%	1,101	5	120	209	767	9,485	1,221	6,810	1,454
Rate per 100,000 inhabitants		401.1	1.8	43.7	76.1	279.4	3,455.4	444.8	2,480.9	529.7
Santa Fe, NM M.S.A.	148,925									
Includes Santa Fe County										
City of Santa Fe	84,663	324	1	30	84	209	3,234	1,123	1,870	241
Total area actually reporting	100.0%	555	2	42	107	404	4,267	1,629	2,354	284
Rate per 100,000 inhabitants		372.7	1.3	28.2	71.8	271.3	2,865.2	1,093.8	1,580.7	190.7
Santa Maria-Santa Barbara, CA M.S.A.	445,908									
Includes Santa Barbara County										
City of Santa Maria	106,200	506	9	45	168	284	2,638	521	1,452	665
City of Santa Barbara	92,519	397	0	87	82	228	3,060	433	2,428	199
Total area actually reporting	100.0%	1,527	13	244	325	945	9,779	1,868	6,691	1,220
Rate per 100,000 inhabitants		342.4	2.9	54.7	72.9	211.9	2,193.1	418.9	1,500.5	273.6
Santa Rosa, CA M.S.A.	502,249									
Includes Sonoma County										
City of Santa Rosa	176,383	658	5	94	121	438	3,010	516	2,087	407
Total area actually reporting	100.0%	1,868	10	282	236	1,340	7,794	1,529	5,380	885
Rate per 100,000 inhabitants		371.9	2.0	56.1	47.0	266.8	1,551.8	304.4	1,071.2	176.2
Savannah, GA M.S.A.	385,219									
Includes Bryan, Chatham, and Effingham Counties										
City of Savannah-Chatham Metropolitan	241,296	1,174	50	50	534	540	8,762	1,856	5,946	960
Total area actually reporting	100.0%	1,608	53	79	600	876	11,968	2,564	8,275	1,129
Rate per 100,000 inhabitants		417.4	13.8	20.5	155.8	227.4	3,106.8	665.6	2,148.1	293.1
Seattle-Tacoma-Bellevue, WA M.S.A.	3,808,184									
Includes the Metropolitan Divisions of Seattle-Bellevue-Everett and Tacoma-Lakewood										
City of Seattle	700,313	4,294	19	254	1,547	2,474	38,433	7,666	26,639	4,128
City of Tacoma	209,914	2,000	13	159	540	1,288	13,749	2,420	8,710	2,619
City of Bellevue	142,238	139	0	14	61	64	4,635	877	3,458	300
City of Everett	108,988	490	1	64	148	277	5,608	949	3,701	958
City of Kent	128,604	372	6	66	165	135	7,527	1,060	5,034	1,433
City of Renton	101,908	341	4	36	146	155	5,767	834	3,872	1,061
City of Auburn	78,400	329	6	49	98	176	3,618	732	2,188	698
City of Lakewood	60,153	449	0	47	101	301	2,939	589	1,979	371
City of Redmond	61,893	83	0	15	23	45	1,936	181	1,676	79
Total area actually reporting	100.0%	13,449	101	1,505	4,160	7,683	148,138	27,677	99,143	21,318
Rate per 100,000 inhabitants		353.2	2.7	39.5	109.2	201.7	3,890.0	726.8	2,603.4	559.8
Seattle-Bellevue-Everett, WA M.D.	2,950,845									
Includes King and Snohomish Counties										
Total area actually reporting	100.0%	9,246	71	1,088	3,116	4,971	113,792	20,588	77,667	15,537
Rate per 100,000 inhabitants		313.3	2.4	36.9	105.6	168.5	3,856.3	697.7	2,632.0	526.5
Tacoma-Lakewood, WA M.D.	857,339									
Includes Pierce County										
Total area actually reporting	100.0%	4,203	30	417	1,044	2,712	34,346	7,089	21,476	5,781
Rate per 100,000 inhabitants		490.2	3.5	48.6	121.8	316.3	4,006.1	826.9	2,505.0	674.3
Sebastian-Vero Beach, FL M.S.A.	150,236									
Includes Indian River County										
City of Sebastian	24,441	42	0	4	7	31	467	69	376	22
City of Vero Beach	16,589	69	3	6	12	48	426	88	323	15
Total area actually reporting	100.0%	345	4	21	43	277	2,776	574	2,044	158
Rate per 100,000 inhabitants		229.6	2.7	14.0	28.6	184.4	1,847.8	382.1	1,360.5	105.2
Sebring, FL M.S.A.	99,857									
Includes Highlands County										
City of Sebring	10,516	45	3	4	7	31	499	110	369	20
Total area actually reporting	100.0%	327	7	27	49	244	2,667	674	1,873	120
Rate per 100,000 inhabitants		327.5	7.0	27.0	49.1	244.3	2,670.8	675.0	1,875.7	120.2
Sheboygan, WI M.S.A.	115,401									
Includes Sheboygan County										
City of Sheboygan	48,710	131	1	20	10	100	1,063	119	908	36
Total area actually reporting	100.0%	179	2	29	13	135	1,650	166	1,420	64
Rate per 100,000 inhabitants		155.1	1.7	25.1	11.3	117.0	1,429.8	143.8	1,230.5	55.5
Sherman-Denison, TX M.S.A.	125,998									
Includes Grayson County										
City of Sherman	41,139	127	4	20	23	80	1,251	297	866	88
City of Denison	23,237	110	0	12	12	86	557	135	372	50
Total area actually reporting	97.1%	334	5	49	38	242	2,416	573	1,632	211
Estimated total	100.0%	344	5	51	40	248	2,507	588	1,701	218
Rate per 100,000 inhabitants		273.0	4.0	40.5	31.7	196.8	1,989.7	466.7	1,350.0	173.0
Shreveport-Bossier City, LA M.S.A.	442,787									
Includes Bossier, Caddo, De Soto, and Webster Parishes										

Table 4. Crime, by Selected Metropolitan Statistical Area, 2016—Continued

(Number, percent, rate per 100,000 population.)

Area	Population	Violent crime	Murder and nonnegligent manslaughter	Rape[1]	Robbery	Aggravated assault	Property crime	Burglary	Larceny-theft	Motor vehicle theft
City of Shreveport	196,467	1,865	42	157	492	1,174	10,721	2,318	7,646	757
City of Bossier City	69,384	585	5	33	96	451	3,206	494	2,491	221
Total area actually reporting	99.7%	2,877	52	207	622	1,996	16,786	3,629	12,010	1,147
Estimated total	100.0%	2,882	52	207	623	2,000	16,828	3,636	12,043	1,149
Rate per 100,000 inhabitants		650.9	11.7	46.7	140.7	451.7	3,800.5	821.2	2,719.8	259.5
Sierra Vista-Douglas, AZ M.S.A.	125,652									
Includes Cochise County										
City of Sierra Vista	42,988	85	3	15	18	49	1,278	249	974	55
City of Douglas	16,398	30	0	1	4	25	462	70	377	15
Total area actually reporting	89.6%	392	5	27	28	332	2,547	420	1,986	141
Estimated total	100.0%	428	5	31	36	356	2,906	478	2,262	166
Rate per 100,000 inhabitants		340.6	4.0	24.7	28.7	283.3	2,312.7	380.4	1,800.2	132.1
Sioux City, IA-NE-SD M.S.A.	168,846									
Includes Plymouth and Woodbury Counties, IA; Dakota and Dixon Counties, NE; and Union County, SD										
City of Sioux City, IA	82,819	365	1	40	59	265	3,247	592	2,363	292
Total area actually reporting	98.5%	504	3	57	63	381	4,455	799	3,235	421
Estimated total	100.0%	507	3	57	63	384	4,488	803	3,262	423
Rate per 100,000 inhabitants		300.3	1.8	33.8	37.3	227.4	2,658.0	475.6	1,931.9	250.5
Sioux Falls, SD M.S.A.	256,120									
Includes Lincoln, McCook, Minnehaha, and Turner Counties										
City of Sioux Falls	175,152	897	6	142	121	628	5,563	869	4,076	618
Total area actually reporting	99.7%	993	10	153	124	706	6,429	1,154	4,595	680
Estimated total	100.0%	994	10	153	124	707	6,439	1,155	4,603	681
Rate per 100,000 inhabitants		388.1	3.9	59.7	48.4	276.0	2,514.1	451.0	1,797.2	265.9
South Bend-Mishawaka, IN-MI M.S.A.[2]	319,742									
Includes St. Joseph County, IN and Cass County, MI										
City of South Bend, IN[2]	101,621	1,037	14	70	388	565	5,166	1,241	3,359	566
City of Mishawaka, IN	48,267	165	1	35	69	60	2,523	283	2,034	206
Total area actually reporting	98.0%	1,463	16	172	489	786	9,644	2,214	6,523	907
Estimated total	100.0%	1,481	16	175	492	798	9,767	2,233	6,618	916
Rate per 100,000 inhabitants		463.2	5.0	54.7	153.9	249.6	3,054.7	698.4	2,069.8	286.5
Spokane-Spokane Valley, WA M.S.A.[2]	553,915									
Includes Pend Oreille, Spokane,2 and Stevens Counties										
City of Spokane[2]	214,028	1,279	8	185	306	780	16,455	2,648	11,815	1,992
City of Spokane Valley[2]	95,923	271	5	55	67	144	5,292	912	3,909	471
Total area actually reporting	99.9%	1,859	16	324	411	1,108	27,718	5,011	19,710	2,997
Estimated total	100.0%	1,859	16	324	411	1,108	27,727	5,012	19,717	2,998
Rate per 100,000 inhabitants		335.6	2.9	58.5	74.2	200.0	5,005.6	904.8	3,559.6	541.2
Springfield, IL M.S.A.	210,256									
Includes Menard and Sangamon Counties										
City of Springfield	116,563	1,301	6	99	249	947	5,158	1,250	3,681	227
Total area actually reporting	98.0%	1,547	8	146	276	1,117	6,339	1,575	4,446	318
Estimated total	100.0%	1,556	8	147	279	1,122	6,411	1,586	4,503	322
Rate per 100,000 inhabitants		740.1	3.8	69.9	132.7	533.6	3,049.1	754.3	2,141.7	153.1
Springfield, MA M.S.A.	630,942									
Includes Hampden and Hampshire Counties										
City of Springfield	154,102	1,588	12	81	522	973	5,073	1,486	3,000	587
Total area actually reporting	97.8%	3,351	18	319	775	2,239	14,257	3,313	9,846	1,098
Estimated total	100.0%	3,393	18	323	782	2,270	14,451	3,348	9,991	1,112
Rate per 100,000 inhabitants		537.8	2.9	51.2	123.9	359.8	2,290.4	530.6	1,583.5	176.2
Springfield, MO M.S.A.	459,709									
Includes Christian, Dallas, Greene, Polk, and Webster Counties										
City of Springfield	168,307	2,251	8	293	428	1,522	14,251	2,120	10,483	1,648
Total area actually reporting	100.0%	2,775	12	376	461	1,926	19,475	3,290	14,131	2,054
Rate per 100,000 inhabitants		603.6	2.6	81.8	100.3	419.0	4,236.4	715.7	3,073.9	446.8
Springfield, OH M.S.A.	135,331									
Includes Clark County										
City of Springfield	59,503	411	5	34	184	188	4,040	963	2,817	260
Total area actually reporting	94.4%	460	5	44	193	218	5,259	1,272	3,660	327
Estimated total	100.0%	471	5	46	197	223	5,428	1,300	3,794	334
Rate per 100,000 inhabitants		348.0	3.7	34.0	145.6	164.8	4,010.9	960.6	2,803.5	246.8
State College, PA M.S.A.	161,409									
Includes Centre County										
City of State College	58,119	39	0	8	10	21	491	35	447	9
Total area actually reporting	100.0%	152	2	65	19	66	1,719	238	1,452	29
Rate per 100,000 inhabitants		94.2	1.2	40.3	11.8	40.9	1,065.0	147.5	899.6	18.0
Staunton-Waynesboro, VA M.S.A.	119,934									
Includes Augusta County and Staunton and Waynesboro Cities										
City of Staunton	24,399	41	2	7	7	25	528	34	474	20

Table 4. Crime, by Selected Metropolitan Statistical Area, 2016—Continued

(Number, percent, rate per 100,000 population.)

Area	Population	Violent crime	Murder and nonnegligent manslaughter	Rape[1]	Robbery	Aggravated assault	Property crime	Burglary	Larceny-theft	Motor vehicle theft
City of Waynesboro	21,464	40	1	12	6	21	486	40	424	22
Total area actually reporting	100.0%	159	7	33	16	103	1,746	281	1,377	88
Rate per 100,000 inhabitants		132.6	5.8	27.5	13.3	85.9	1,455.8	234.3	1,148.1	73.4
St. Cloud, MN M.S.A.	195,241									
Includes Benton and Stearns Counties										
City of St. Cloud	67,341	293	1	68	72	152	2,780	329	2,327	124
Total area actually reporting	100.0%	388	1	97	68	222	4,638	532	3,904	202
Rate per 100,000 inhabitants		198.7	0.5	49.7	34.8	113.7	2,375.5	272.5	1,999.6	103.5
St. George, UT M.S.A.	159,745									
Includes Washington County										
City of St. George	81,755	160	0	54	14	92	1,465	350	995	120
Total area actually reporting	98.1%	265	0	78	18	169	2,676	571	1,916	189
Estimated total	100.0%	270	0	79	19	172	2,757	583	1,977	197
Rate per 100,000 inhabitants		169.0	0.0	49.5	11.9	107.7	1,725.9	365.0	1,237.6	123.3
St. Joseph, MO-KS M.S.A.	126,595									
Includes Doniphan County, KS and Andrew, Buchanan, and DeKalb Counties, MO										
City of St. Joseph, MO	76,577	428	7	49	104	268	4,546	749	3,221	576
Total area actually reporting	100.0%	532	10	60	110	352	5,141	920	3,580	641
Rate per 100,000 inhabitants		420.2	7.9	47.4	86.9	278.1	4,061.0	726.7	2,827.9	506.3
St. Louis, MO-IL M.S.A.[2,4]	2,811,156									
Includes Bond, Calhoun, Clinton, Jersey, Macoupin, Madison, Monroe, and St. Clair Counties, IL and Franklin, Jefferson, Lincoln, St. Charles, St. Louis, and Warren Counties and St. Louis City, MO										
City of St. Louis, MO	314,507	6,017	188	289	1,904	3,636	18,653	3,201	12,394	3,058
City of St. Charles, MO	69,364	138	0	22	35	81	1,756	155	1,472	129
Total area actually reporting	98.5%		312	1,058	3,419		69,303	12,322	50,093	6,888
Estimated total	100.0%		313	1,070	3,443		70,004	12,438	50,642	6,924
Rate per 100,000 inhabitants			11.1	38.1	122.5		2,490.2	442.5	1,801.5	246.3
Stockton-Lodi, CA M.S.A.	729,104									
Includes San Joaquin County										
City of Stockton	308,348	4,381	49	128	1,185	3,019	11,634	2,251	7,550	1,833
City of Lodi	65,067	351	5	9	84	253	1,935	438	1,189	308
Total area actually reporting	100.0%	6,005	62	220	1,624	4,099	22,629	4,239	14,848	3,542
Rate per 100,000 inhabitants		823.6	8.5	30.2	222.7	562.2	3,103.7	581.4	2,036.5	485.8
Sumter, SC M.S.A.	107,671									
Includes Sumter County										
City of Sumter	40,864	282	3	9	50	220	1,666	390	1,216	60
Total area actually reporting	100.0%	636	4	31	72	529	3,539	1,014	2,309	216
Rate per 100,000 inhabitants		590.7	3.7	28.8	66.9	491.3	3,286.9	941.8	2,144.5	200.6
Syracuse, NY M.S.A.	655,589									
Includes Madison, Onondaga, and Oswego Counties										
City of Syracuse	143,925	1,063	30	68	329	636	4,651	1,021	3,290	340
Total area actually reporting	100.0%	1,812	35	336	430	1,011	12,838	2,281	9,941	616
Rate per 100,000 inhabitants		276.4	5.3	51.3	65.6	154.2	1,958.2	347.9	1,516.3	94.0
Tallahassee, FL M.S.A.	380,448									
Includes Gadsden, Jefferson, Leon, and Wakulla Counties										
City of Tallahassee	191,564	1,686	11	207	405	1,063	11,073	2,120	7,854	1,099
Total area actually reporting	98.0%	2,373	17	282	476	1,598	15,347	3,279	10,734	1,334
Estimated total	100.0%	2,403	17	284	485	1,617	15,581	3,314	10,915	1,352
Rate per 100,000 inhabitants		631.6	4.5	74.6	127.5	425.0	4,095.4	871.1	2,869.0	355.4
Tampa-St. Petersburg-Clearwater, FL M.S.A.	3,020,266									
Includes Hernando, Hillsborough, Pasco, and Pinellas Counties										
City of Tampa	375,904	1,906	29	80	488	1,309	7,800	1,477	5,695	628
City of St. Petersburg	259,510	1,727	20	122	556	1,029	12,804	1,938	9,771	1,095
City of Clearwater	113,904	636	5	89	145	397	3,755	555	2,968	232
City of Largo	81,402	390	3	60	116	211	2,989	458	2,289	242
Total area actually reporting	100.0%	10,294	118	987	2,283	6,906	70,491	11,898	53,215	5,378
Rate per 100,000 inhabitants		340.8	3.9	32.7	75.6	228.7	2,333.9	393.9	1,761.9	178.1
Texarkana, TX-AR M.S.A.	149,537									
Includes Little River and Miller Counties, AR and Bowie County, TX										
City of Texarkana, TX	37,442	314	4	23	44	243	1,875	338	1,405	132
Total area actually reporting	100.0%	669	11	86	87	485	4,953	1,099	3,511	343
Rate per 100,000 inhabitants		447.4	7.4	57.5	58.2	324.3	3,312.2	734.9	2,347.9	229.4
The Villages, FL M.S.A.	124,785									
Includes Sumter County										
Total area actually reporting	100.0%	292	1	25	12	254	1,093	277	763	53
Rate per 100,000 inhabitants		234.0	0.8	20.0	9.6	203.6	875.9	222.0	611.5	42.5

Table 4. Crime, by Selected Metropolitan Statistical Area, 2016—Continued

(Number, percent, rate per 100,000 population.)

Area	Population	Violent crime	Murder and nonnegligent manslaughter	Rape[1]	Robbery	Aggravated assault	Property crime	Burglary	Larceny-theft	Motor vehicle theft
Toledo, OH M.S.A.	604,373									
Includes Fulton, Lucas, and Wood Counties										
City of Toledo	278,366	3,319	37	316	803	2,163	11,191	3,381	7,081	729
Total area actually reporting	92.8%	3,662	42	419	880	2,321	16,577	4,268	11,358	951
Estimated total	100.0%	3,728	43	433	902	2,350	17,540	4,427	12,122	991
Rate per 100,000 inhabitants		616.8	7.1	71.6	149.2	388.8	2,902.2	732.5	2,005.7	164.0
Topeka, KS M.S.A.	232,459									
Includes Jackson, Jefferson, Osage, Shawnee, and Wabaunsee Counties										
City of Topeka	127,166	711	17	54	248	392	7,148	1,114	5,227	807
Total area actually reporting	97.7%	899	21	74	252	552	8,878	1,497	6,407	974
Estimated total	100.0%	910	21	76	253	560	8,984	1,512	6,489	983
Rate per 100,000 inhabitants		391.5	9.0	32.7	108.8	240.9	3,864.8	650.4	2,791.5	422.9
Trenton, NJ M.S.A.	370,221									
Includes Mercer County										
City of Trenton	83,644	1,127	21	59	427	620	2,186	883	930	373
Total area actually reporting	100.0%	1,490	25	107	587	771	6,585	1,590	4,454	541
Rate per 100,000 inhabitants		402.5	6.8	28.9	158.6	208.3	1,778.7	429.5	1,203.1	146.1
Tucson, AZ M.S.A.	1,017,936									
Includes Pima County										
City of Tucson	533,663	4,245	30	469	1,235	2,511	31,265	4,138	25,185	1,942
Total area actually reporting	99.4%	5,037	49	580	1,432	2,976	43,274	6,080	34,507	2,687
Estimated total	100.0%	5,053	49	582	1,435	2,987	43,432	6,105	34,629	2,698
Rate per 100,000 inhabitants		496.4	4.8	57.2	141.0	293.4	4,266.7	599.7	3,401.9	265.0
Tulsa, OK M.S.A.	984,554									
Includes Creek, Okmulgee, Osage, Pawnee, Rogers, Tulsa, and Wagoner Counties										
City of Tulsa	405,748	4,444	72	439	1,088	2,845	23,956	5,780	14,516	3,660
Total area actually reporting	100.0%	5,798	91	670	1,244	3,793	35,669	8,761	22,107	4,801
Rate per 100,000 inhabitants		588.9	9.2	68.1	126.4	385.3	3,622.9	889.8	2,245.4	487.6
Tuscaloosa, AL M.S.A.	241,294									
Includes Hale, Pickens, and Tuscaloosa Counties										
City of Tuscaloosa	99,925	480	14	54	172	240	3,732	794	2,708	230
Total area actually reporting	100.0%	888	18	92	227	551	6,726	1,560	4,746	420
Rate per 100,000 inhabitants		368.0	7.5	38.1	94.1	228.4	2,787.5	646.5	1,966.9	174.1
Tyler, TX M.S.A.[2,3]	224,848									
Includes Smith County										
City of Tyler[3]	105,044	429	5	64	106	254				159
Total area actually reporting	99.1%	731	7	83	150	491				429
Estimated total	100.0%	736	7	84	151	494				432
Rate per 100,000 inhabitants		327.3	3.1	37.4	67.2	219.7				192.1
Urban Honolulu, HI M.S.A.	995,572									
Includes Honolulu County										
Total area actually reporting	100.0%	3,331	16	382	836	2,097	30,592	3,758	22,488	4,346
Rate per 100,000 inhabitants		334.6	1.6	38.4	84.0	210.6	3,072.8	377.5	2,258.8	436.5
Utica-Rome, NY M.S.A.	292,919									
Includes Herkimer and Oneida Counties										
City of Utica	60,879	382	3	42	115	222	2,265	435	1,751	79
City of Rome	32,345	52	0	13	14	25	619	128	463	28
Total area actually reporting	99.1%	774	4	186	151	433	5,495	1,005	4,316	174
Estimated total	100.0%	779	4	187	152	436	5,534	1,010	4,349	175
Rate per 100,000 inhabitants		265.9	1.4	63.8	51.9	148.8	1,889.3	344.8	1,484.7	59.7
Valdosta, GA M.S.A.	143,315									
Includes Brooks, Echols, Lanier, and Lowndes Counties										
City of Valdosta	55,880	205	6	17	65	117	3,057	581	2,333	143
Total area actually reporting	99.5%	456	7	29	95	325	4,693	1,022	3,424	247
Estimated total	100.0%	459	7	29	96	327	4,719	1,026	3,444	249
Rate per 100,000 inhabitants		320.3	4.9	20.2	67.0	228.2	3,292.7	715.9	2,403.1	173.7
Vallejo-Fairfield, CA M.S.A.	437,638									
Includes Solano County										
City of Vallejo	122,293	1,053	15	111	353	574	4,810	2,366	1,321	1,123
City of Fairfield	114,521	476	7	56	147	266	2,845	420	1,888	537
Total area actually reporting	100.0%	2,022	24	204	647	1,147	11,719	3,397	6,158	2,164
Rate per 100,000 inhabitants		462.0	5.5	46.6	147.8	262.1	2,677.8	776.2	1,407.1	494.5
Vineland-Bridgeton, NJ M.S.A.	154,814									
Includes Cumberland County										
City of Vineland	60,823	297	1	15	128	153	2,412	559	1,779	74
City of Bridgeton	24,982	225	4	13	113	95	952	269	649	34
Total area actually reporting	100.0%	802	11	64	333	394	5,632	1,331	4,118	183
Rate per 100,000 inhabitants		518.0	7.1	41.3	215.1	254.5	3,637.9	859.7	2,660.0	118.2

Table 4. Crime, by Selected Metropolitan Statistical Area, 2016—Continued

(Number, percent, rate per 100,000 population.)

Area	Population	Violent crime	Murder and nonnegligent manslaughter	Rape[1]	Robbery	Aggravated assault	Property crime	Burglary	Larceny-theft	Motor vehicle theft
Virginia Beach-Norfolk-Newport News, VA-NC M.S.A.	1,724,733									
Includes Currituck and Gates Counties, NC and Gloucester, Isle of Wight, James City, Mathews, and York Counties and Chesapeake, Hampton, Newport News, Norfolk, Poquoson, Portsmouth, Suffolk, Virginia Beach, and Williamsburg Cities, VA										
City of Virginia Beach, VA	453,017	700	21	128	266	285	9,858	865	8,485	508
City of Norfolk, VA	245,734	1,616	46	131	489	950	9,617	1,165	7,918	534
City of Newport News, VA	181,676	848	30	71	269	478	5,579	902	4,097	580
City of Hampton, VA	135,504	442	24	40	180	198	4,650	589	3,741	320
City of Portsmouth, VA	95,813	758	14	61	235	448	5,373	1,208	3,707	458
Total area actually reporting	99.3%	6,054	163	642	1,802	3,447	48,315	6,411	38,853	3,051
Estimated total	100.0%	6,072	164	643	1,805	3,460	48,481	6,471	38,949	3,061
Rate per 100,000 inhabitants		352.1	9.5	37.3	104.7	200.6	2,810.9	375.2	2,258.3	177.5
Visalia-Porterville, CA M.S.A.	460,141									
Includes Tulare County										
City of Visalia	131,186	480	8	68	120	284	4,196	998	2,561	637
City of Porterville	56,421	215	0	16	52	147	1,315	280	771	264
Total area actually reporting	100.0%	1,624	33	135	329	1,127	11,608	2,692	6,805	2,111
Rate per 100,000 inhabitants		352.9	7.2	29.3	71.5	244.9	2,522.7	585.0	1,478.9	458.8
Waco, TX M.S.A.	263,878									
Includes Falls and McLennan Counties										
City of Waco	133,790	695	4	126	156	409	4,882	1,087	3,648	147
Total area actually reporting	97.9%	1,104	7	205	185	707	7,216	1,556	5,364	296
Estimated total	100.0%	1,119	7	207	189	716	7,351	1,578	5,467	306
Rate per 100,000 inhabitants		424.1	2.7	78.4	71.6	271.3	2,785.8	598.0	2,071.8	116.0
Walla Walla, WA M.S.A.	64,789									
Includes Columbia and Walla Walla Counties										
City of Walla Walla	32,326	122	2	23	17	80	1,372	233	1,041	98
Total area actually reporting	100.0%	162	2	36	20	104	2,050	365	1,525	160
Rate per 100,000 inhabitants		250.0	3.1	55.6	30.9	160.5	3,164.1	563.4	2,353.8	247.0
Warner Robins, GA M.S.A.	189,578									
Includes Houston, Peach, and Pulaski Counties										
City of Warner Robins	74,419	494	6	31	143	314	4,111	768	3,125	218
Total area actually reporting	100.0%	857	9	45	191	612	6,711	1,315	5,030	366
Rate per 100,000 inhabitants		452.1	4.7	23.7	100.8	322.8	3,540.0	693.6	2,653.3	193.1
Washington-Arlington-Alexandria, DC-VA-MD-WV M.S.A.	6,152,267									
Includes the Metropolitan Divisions of Silver Spring-Frederick-Rockville, MD and Washington-Arlington-Alexandria, DC-VA-MD-WV										
City of Washington, D.C.	681,170	7,711	138	527	3,149	3,897	31,661	2,360	26,402	2,899
City of Alexandria, VA	155,319	286	7	21	134	124	2,798	184	2,343	271
City of Frederick, MD	70,316	343	1	23	70	249	1,411	141	1,222	48
Total area actually reporting	88.6%	16,494	257	1,701	6,074	8,462	100,386	9,239	84,211	6,936
Estimated total	100.0%	18,535	275	1,888	6,663	9,709	113,381	11,316	94,312	7,753
Rate per 100,000 inhabitants		301.3	4.5	30.7	108.3	157.8	1,842.9	183.9	1,533.0	126.0
Silver Spring-Frederick-Rockville, MD M.D.	1,293,480									
Includes Frederick and Montgomery Counties										
Total area actually reporting	100.0%	2,439	17	374	812	1,236	18,777	2,426	15,361	990
Rate per 100,000 inhabitants		188.6	1.3	28.9	62.8	95.6	1,451.7	187.6	1,187.6	76.5
Washington-Arlington-Alexandria, DC-VA-MD-WV M.D.	4,858,787									
Includes District of Columbia; Calvert, Charles, and Prince George's Counties, MD; Arlington, Clarke, Culpeper, Fairfax, Fauquier, Loudoun, Prince William, Rappahannock, Spotsylvania, Stafford, and Warren Counties and Alexandria, Fairfax, Falls Church, Fredericksburg, Manassas, and Manassas Park Cities, VA; and Jefferson County, WV										
Total area actually reporting	85.6%	14,055	240	1,327	5,262	7,226	81,609	6,813	68,850	5,946
Estimated total	100.0%	16,096	258	1,514	5,851	8,473	94,604	8,890	78,951	6,763
Rate per 100,000 inhabitants		331.3	5.3	31.2	120.4	174.4	1,947.1	183.0	1,624.9	139.2
Waterloo-Cedar Falls, IA M.S.A.	170,888									
Includes Black Hawk, Bremer, and Grundy Counties										
City of Waterloo	68,470	507	3	56	61	387	2,120	614	1,368	138
City of Cedar Falls	41,651	66	0	20	9	37	708	118	559	31
Total area actually reporting	100.0%	756	3	92	72	589	3,386	898	2,288	200
Rate per 100,000 inhabitants		442.4	1.8	53.8	42.1	344.7	1,981.4	525.5	1,338.9	117.0
Watertown-Fort Drum, NY M.S.A.	117,080									
Includes Jefferson County										
City of Watertown	26,765	181	1	41	15	124	1,171	194	953	24
Total area actually reporting	100.0%	281	2	92	17	170	2,079	349	1,681	49
Rate per 100,000 inhabitants		240.0	1.7	78.6	14.5	145.2	1,775.7	298.1	1,435.8	41.9

Table 4. Crime, by Selected Metropolitan Statistical Area, 2016—Continued

(Number, percent, rate per 100,000 population.)

Area	Population	Violent crime	Murder and nonnegligent manslaughter	Rape[1]	Robbery	Aggravated assault	Property crime	Burglary	Larceny-theft	Motor vehicle theft
Wausau, WI M.S.A.[2]	136,010									
Includes Marathon County										
City of Wausau	39,091	114	0	29	25	60	959	137	776	46
Total area actually reporting	100.0%	180	1	39	27	113	1,787	296	1,430	61
Rate per 100,000 inhabitants		132.3	0.7	28.7	19.9	83.1	1,313.9	217.6	1,051.4	44.8
Weirton-Steubenville, WV-OH M.S.A.	119,362									
Includes Jefferson County, OH and Brooke and Hancock Counties, WV										
City of Weirton, WV	19,067	22	0	4	7	11	209	41	152	16
City of Steubenville, OH	18,137	60	2	4	22	32	1,085	132	945	8
Total area actually reporting	86.3%	153	2	19	35	97	1,691	276	1,369	46
Estimated total	100.0%	190	2	25	43	120	2,150	351	1,730	69
Rate per 100,000 inhabitants		159.2	1.7	20.9	36.0	100.5	1,801.2	294.1	1,449.4	57.8
Wenatchee, WA M.S.A.	117,637									
Includes Chelan and Douglas Counties										
City of Wenatchee	33,920	88	0	21	14	53	1,128	166	900	62
Total area actually reporting	100.0%	169	1	31	18	119	2,626	502	1,957	167
Rate per 100,000 inhabitants		143.7	0.9	26.4	15.3	101.2	2,232.3	426.7	1,663.6	142.0
Wheeling, WV-OH M.S.A.	142,933									
Includes Belmont County, OH and Marshall and Ohio Counties, WV										
City of Wheeling, WV	27,486	266	1	12	30	223	669	183	453	33
Total area actually reporting	90.0%	475	4	55	36	380	1,878	481	1,295	102
Estimated total	100.0%	500	4	60	43	393	2,223	538	1,568	117
Rate per 100,000 inhabitants		349.8	2.8	42.0	30.1	275.0	1,555.3	376.4	1,097.0	81.9
Wichita, KS M.S.A.[7]	643,764									
Includes Butler, Harvey, Kingman, Sedgwick, and Sumner Counties										
City of Wichita	391,399	4,136	31	309	652	3,144	21,065	3,593	15,284	2,188
Total area actually reporting	99.2%	4,553	42	385	683	3,443			18,728	2,502
Estimated total	100.0%	4,563	42	387	684	3,450			18,806	2,510
Rate per 100,000 inhabitants		708.8	6.5	60.1	106.3	535.9			2,921.3	389.9
Wichita Falls, TX M.S.A.	150,165									
Includes Archer, Clay, and Wichita Counties										
City of Wichita Falls	104,685	445	9	124	123	189	3,734	825	2,646	263
Total area actually reporting	97.7%	535	12	134	127	262	4,493	1,022	3,139	332
Estimated total	100.0%	544	12	135	129	268	4,576	1,035	3,203	338
Rate per 100,000 inhabitants		362.3	8.0	89.9	85.9	178.5	3,047.3	689.2	2,133.0	225.1
Williamsport, PA M.S.A.	115,682									
Includes Lycoming County										
City of Williamsport	29,163	104	5	8	39	52	792	101	668	23
Total area actually reporting	100.0%	238	7	32	58	141	1,752	248	1,452	52
Rate per 100,000 inhabitants		205.7	6.1	27.7	50.1	121.9	1,514.5	214.4	1,255.2	45.0
Wilmington, NC M.S.A.	282,695									
Includes New Hanover and Pender Counties										
City of Wilmington	117,852	759	15	44	204	496	4,771	1,277	3,219	275
Total area actually reporting	99.1%	1,021	17	81	268	655	8,270	2,081	5,771	418
Estimated total	100.0%	1,028	17	82	270	659	8,348	2,096	5,831	421
Rate per 100,000 inhabitants		363.6	6.0	29.0	95.5	233.1	2,953.0	741.4	2,062.6	148.9
Winchester, VA-WV M.S.A.	134,144									
Includes Frederick County and Winchester City, VA and Hampshire County, WV										
City of Winchester, VA	27,363	61	1	27	16	17	776	122	638	16
Total area actually reporting	99.7%	185	7	67	26	85	1,964	341	1,535	88
Estimated total	100.0%	186	7	67	26	86	1,977	343	1,545	89
Rate per 100,000 inhabitants		138.7	5.2	49.9	19.4	64.1	1,473.8	255.7	1,151.7	66.3
Worcester, MA-CT M.S.A.[4]	861,261									
Includes Windham County, CT and Worcester County, MA										
City of Worcester, MA	184,595	1,642	8	63	394	1,177	5,358	1,366	3,473	519
Total area actually reporting	94.7%		12	282	584		13,153	2,815	9,422	916
Estimated total	100.0%		12	295	606		13,782	2,927	9,893	962
Rate per 100,000 inhabitants			1.4	34.3	70.4		1,600.2	339.9	1,148.7	111.7
Yakima, WA M.S.A.	250,717									
Includes Yakima County										
City of Yakima	94,111	496	13	47	126	310	4,943	1,143	3,163	637
Total area actually reporting	100.0%	751	21	82	187	461	9,067	2,060	5,789	1,218
Rate per 100,000 inhabitants		299.5	8.4	32.7	74.6	183.9	3,616.4	821.6	2,309.0	485.8
York-Hanover, PA M.S.A.	443,062									
Includes York County										
City of York	44,017	416	8	12	208	188	1,408	298	917	193
City of Hanover	15,537	23	0	0	9	14	418	43	371	4
Total area actually reporting	100.0%	1,039	19	107	306	607	7,029	948	5,674	407
Rate per 100,000 inhabitants		234.5	4.3	24.2	69.1	137.0	1,586.5	214.0	1,280.6	91.9

Table 4. Crime, by Selected Metropolitan Statistical Area, 2016—Continued

(Number, percent, rate per 100,000 population.)

Area	Population	Violent crime	Murder and nonnegligent manslaughter	Rape[1]	Robbery	Aggravated assault	Property crime	Burglary	Larceny-theft	Motor vehicle theft
Yuba City, CA M.S.A.	170,558									
Includes Sutter and Yuba Counties										
City of Yuba City	67,198	272	8	24	76	164	2,030	406	1,389	235
Total area actually reporting	100.0%	678	13	50	137	478	4,635	1,097	2,800	738
Rate per 100,000 inhabitants		397.5	7.6	29.3	80.3	280.3	2,717.6	643.2	1,641.7	432.7
Aguadilla-Isabela, Puerto Rico M.S.A.	309,696									
Includes Aguada, Aguadilla, Anasco, Isabela, Lares, Moca, Rincon, San Sebastian, and Utuado Municipios										
Total area actually reporting	100.0%	424	22	12	86	304	2,030	703	1,253	74
Rate per 100,000 inhabitants		136.9	7.1	3.9	27.8	98.2	655.5	227.0	404.6	23.9
Arecibo, Puerto Rico M.S.A.	185,250									
Includes Arecibo, Camuy, Hatillo, and Quebradillas Municipios										
Total area actually reporting	100.0%	314	10	4	96	204	1,633	393	1,121	119
Rate per 100,000 inhabitants		169.5	5.4	2.2	51.8	110.1	881.5	212.1	605.1	64.2
Guayama, Puerto Rico M.S.A.	77,771									
Includes Arroyo, Guayama, and Patillas Municipios										
Total area actually reporting	100.0%	182	19	8	39	116	614	222	382	10
Rate per 100,000 inhabitants		234.0	24.4	10.3	50.1	149.2	789.5	285.5	491.2	12.9
Mayaguez, Puerto Rico M.S.A.	94,038									
Includes Hormigueros and Mayaguez Municipios										
Total area actually reporting	100.0%	248	16	4	68	160	1,137	290	811	36
Rate per 100,000 inhabitants		263.7	17.0	4.3	72.3	170.1	1,209.1	308.4	862.4	38.3
Ponce, Puerto Rico M.S.A.	309,512									
Includes Guanica, Guyanilla, Juana Diaz, Penuelas, Ponce, Villalba, and Yauco Municipios										
Total area actually reporting	100.0%	785	70	22	179	514	2,557	611	1,839	107
Rate per 100,000 inhabitants		253.6	22.6	7.1	57.8	166.1	826.1	197.4	594.2	34.6
San German, Puerto Rico M.S.A.	128,279									
Includes Cabo Rojo, Lajas, Sabana Grande, and San German Municipios										
Total area actually reporting	100.0%	117	9	4	34	70	450	173	245	32
Rate per 100,000 inhabitants		91.2	7.0	3.1	26.5	54.6	353.1	134.9	193.3	24.9
San Juan-Carolina-Caguas, Puerto Rico M.S.A.	2,157,729									
Includes Aguas Buenas, Aibonito, Barceloneta, Barranquitas, Bayamon, Caguas, Canovanas, Carolina, Catano, Cayey, Ceiba, Ciales, Cidra, Comerio, Corozal, Dorado, Fajardo, Florida, Guaynabo, Gurabo, Humacao, Juncos, Las Piedras, Loiza, Luquillo, Manati, Maunabo, Morovis, Naguabo, Naranjito, Orocovis, Rio Grande, San Juan, San Lorenzo, Toa Alta, Toa Baja, Trujillo Alto, Vega Alta, Vega Baja, and Yabucoa Municipios										
Total area actually reporting	100.0%	5,292	504	106	2,653	2,029	25,686	5,515	16,802	3,369
Rate per 100,000 inhabitants		245.3	23.4	4.9	123.0	94.0	1,190.4	255.6	778.7	156.1

1 The rape figures in this table are an aggregate total of the data submitted using both the revised and legacy Uniform Crime Reporting (UCR) definitions.   2 Because of changes in the state/local agency's reporting practices, figures are not comparable to previous years' data.   3 The FBI determined that the agency's data were underreported. Consequently, those data are not included in this table.   4 The FBI determined that the agency's data were overreported. Consequently, those data are not included in this table.   5 The population for the city of Mobile, Alabama, includes 55,819 inhabitants from the jurisdiction of the Mobile County Sheriff's Department.   6 The 2016 murder offenses include those victims of the Pulse Nightclub incident; therefore, figures are not comparable to previous years' data.   7 The FBI determined that the agency did not follow national UCR Program guidelines for reporting an offense. Consequently, this figure is not included in this table.

Table 5. Offense Analysis, United States, 2011–2016

(Number.)

Classification	2011	2012	2013 [1]	2014	2015 [1]	2016
Murder	14,661	14,856	14,319	14,164	15,883	17,250
Rape (revised definition)[2]	X	X	113,695	118,027	126,134	130,603
Rape (legacy definition)[3]	84,175	85,141	82,109	84,868	91,261	95,730
Robbery[4]	354,746	355,051	345,093	322,905	328,109	332,198
By location						
Street/highway	155,218	154,289	146,499	132,269	130,724	129,104
Commercial house	46,156	47,151	45,760	45,273	47,229	50,694
Gas or service station	8,539	8,660	8,354	8,072	8,916	9,690
Convenience store	18,108	18,180	17,103	17,380	18,661	20,619
Residence	60,138	59,979	57,372	54,120	54,142	55,002
Bank	7,038	6,666	6,512	5,939	5,691	5,903
Miscellaneous	59,549	60,126	63,495	59,853	62,747	61,185
Burglary[4]	2,185,140	2,109,932	1,932,139	1,713,153	1,587,564	1,515,096
By location						
Residence (dwelling)	1,628,656	1,571,635	1,428,448	1,253,915	1,136,664	1,053,559
Residence, night	442,390	429,662	395,604	349,441	328,736	311,536
Residence, day	859,299	832,944	756,617	669,364	594,668	543,461
Residence, unknown	326,967	309,028	276,227	235,111	213,260	198,563
Nonresidence (store, office, etc.)	556,484	538,297	503,691	459,238	450,900	461,537
Nonresidence, night	227,446	220,784	206,031	188,010	189,167	199,568
Nonresidence, day	196,461	192,963	183,380	167,749	159,177	159,493
Nonresidence, unknown	132,577	124,550	114,280	103,480	102,556	102,476
Larceny-theft (except motor vehicle theft)[4]	6,151,095	6,168,874	6,019,465	5,809,054	5,723,488	5,638,455
By type						
Pocket-picking	26,518	29,550	32,426	31,213	31,208	27,617
Purse-snatching	27,082	26,407	25,867	23,479	23,144	22,645
Shoplifting	1,077,791	1,147,679	1,199,157	1,247,199	1,276,575	1,177,804
From motor vehicles (except accessories)	1,523,950	1,480,790	1,405,858	1,332,924	1,373,720	1,475,917
Motor vehicle accessories	497,980	467,369	439,151	408,545	399,452	415,120
Bicycles	216,987	223,786	212,889	209,762	205,600	184,338
From buildings	728,050	745,238	740,092	712,073	664,381	605,080
From coin-operated machines	19,536	17,240	15,906	13,328	13,020	12,335
All others	2,033,200	2,030,815	1,948,120	1,830,531	1,736,388	1,717,599
By value						
Under $50	2,850,302	2,872,445	2,819,518	2,687,591	2,613,333	2,558,723
$50 to $200	1,399,484	1,398,870	1,342,473	1,306,350	1,278,027	1,219,866
Over $200	1,901,309	1,897,560	1,857,474	1,815,113	1,832,128	1,859,865
Motor vehicle theft	716,508	723,186	700,288	686,803	713,063	765,484

X = Not applicable.
1 The crime figures have been adjusted.   2 The figures shown in this column for the offense of rape were estimated using the revised Uniform Crime Reporting (UCR) definition of rape. See chapter notes for more detail.   3 The figures shown in this column for the offense of rape were estimated using the legacy Uniform Crime Reporting (UCR) definition of rape. See chapter notes for more detail.   4 Because of rounding, the number of offenses may not add to the total.

Table 6. Offenses Known to Law Enforcement, by Selected State and City, 2016

(Number.)

State/city	Population	Violent crime	Murder and nonnegligent manslaughter	Rape (revised definition)[1]	Rape (legacy definition)[2]	Robbery	Aggravated assault	Property crime	Burglary	Larceny-theft	Motor vehicle theft	Arson[3]
ALABAMA												
Abbeville	2608	11	0	1		0	10	51	12	34	5	
Adamsville	4377	19	0	0		10	9	250	33	201	16	
Addison	738	1	0	0		0	1	14	1	11	2	
Alabaster	33040	97	1	2		2	92	488	58	411	19	
Albertville	21525	29	0	5		10	14	721	190	462	69	
Alexander City	14695	277	2	4		14	257	657	123	493	41	
Aliceville	2362	5	0	0		0	5	24	10	14	0	
Andalusia	9071	84	1	6		6	71	477	64	397	16	
Anniston	22205	735	7	39		87	602	1712	712	888	112	
Arab	8334	70	1	11		3	55	511	113	366	32	
Ardmore	1390	2	0	0		0	2	29	8	16	5	
Argo	4220	6	0	1		0	5	44	18	20	6	
Ashford	2161	3	0	0		0	3	32	5	25	2	
Ashland	1974	31	0	1		0	30	51	12	39	0	
Ashville	2264	1	0	1		0	0	36	7	25	4	
Athens	25603	18	1	1		16	0	636	90	538	8	
Atmore	10021	93	0	3		14	76	413	86	315	12	
Attalla	5870	19	0	1		0	18	121	29	92	0	
Auburn	63871	210	4	12		31	163	1125	203	844	78	
Bayou La Batre	2607	36	0	6		3	27	289	81	171	37	
Bear Creek	1043	1	0	0		0	1	25	13	12	0	
Bessemer	26592	763	3	29		127	604	2403	573	1621	209	
Blountsville	1699	6	0	0		0	6	70	14	41	15	
Boaz	9729	146	0	6		3	137	413	74	294	45	
Brent	4890	14	0	2		3	9	113	31	76	6	
Brewton	5441	45	1	7		7	30	202	35	149	18	
Bridgeport	2344	9	0	0		0	9	20	5	14	1	
Brilliant	881	2	0	0		0	2	19	7	7	5	
Brookwood	1821	10	0	2		1	7	109	26	67	16	
Butler	1781	8	0	0		0	8	30	13	14	3	
Camp Hill	975	10	1	0		3	6	18	9	6	3	
Carbon Hill	1965	13	0	0		1	12	56	7	43	6	
Carrollton	982	4	0	0		1	3	14	6	4	4	
Centre	3586	16	0	3		3	10	157	25	116	16	
Chatom	1227	1	0	0		1	0	29	6	21	2	
Chickasaw	5927	28	0	3		2	23	225	70	144	11	
Childersburg	5023	56	1	2		1	52	203	41	159	3	
Citronelle	3884	26	0	4		2	20	167	47	110	10	
Clanton	8888	115	0	4		1	110	458	72	353	33	
Clayton	2910	6	0	0		1	5	29	7	19	3	
Coaling	1646	11	0	2		1	8	68	28	34	6	
Columbiana	4169	41	0	4		2	35	89	19	68	2	
Coosada	1242	3	0	0		0	3	17	8	7	2	
Cordova	2015	4	0	1		0	3	21	7	12	2	
Creola	1961	13	0	0		1	12	53	12	30	11	
Crossville	1845	4	0	0		0	4	27	6	15	6	
Cullman	15459	22	0	4		7	11	575	77	463	35	
Dadeville	3136	23	0	4		9	10	116	27	76	13	
Daleville	5109	11	0	1		2	8	63	10	48	5	
Daphne	25564	35	0	3		8	24	503	70	413	20	
Dauphin Island	1254	8	0	2		0	6	59	7	50	2	
Decatur	55374	154	5	9		43	97	2600	526	1918	156	
Demopolis	7089	39	1	3		4	31	211	39	167	5	
Dora	1947	11	0	1		3	7	114	24	83	7	
Dothan[4]	69071		5	36		80		2808	681	1963	164	
Douglas	761	9	0	1		0	8	65	22	32	11	
East Brewton	2407	13	0	1		0	12	62	8	45	9	
Eclectic	1034	16	0	2		1	13	53	6	45	2	
Elba	3894	5	0	2		0	3	92	33	54	5	
Enterprise	28227	98	1	12		9	76	783	183	552	48	
Eufaula	12503	67	3	4		15	45	455	111	317	27	
Evergreen	3742	31	0	5		4	22	163	38	108	17	
Fairfield	10869	98	4	3		42	49	470	168	261	41	
Fairhope	19470	36	0	4		6	26	649	84	541	24	
Falkville	1266	16	0	2		0	14	43	17	22	4	
Fayette	4465	8	0	2		0	6	94	16	67	11	
Flomaton	1405	23	2	0		3	18	54	18	31	5	
Florala	1971	7	1	2		0	4	17	3	11	3	
Florence	40160	196	2	19		46	129	1400	242	1052	106	
Fort Payne	14156	45	1	6		10	28	459	83	351	25	
Fultondale	9188	50	2	3		15	30	414	68	319	27	
Fyffe	1024	1	0	0		0	1	29	7	17	5	
Gadsden	35927	464	4	27		56	377	2521	401	1893	227	
Gardendale	13675	110	1	2		6	101	430	68	344	18	
Geneva	4460	21	0	5		1	15	144	21	114	9	
Georgiana	1654	4	0	0		1	3	60	20	37	3	
Glencoe	5150	12	0	1		1	10	85	24	51	10	
Goodwater	1318	6	0	0		0	6	20	6	10	4	
Greenville	7788	62	3	3		9	47	354	43	297	14	
Guin	2311	8	0	1		0	7	58	12	42	4	
Gulf Shores	11340	39	0	10		7	22	649	95	524	30	
Guntersville	8421	51	0	3		8	40	458	95	323	40	

Table 6. Offenses Known to Law Enforcement, by Selected State and City, 2016—Continued

(Number.)

State/city	Population	Violent crime	Murder and nonnegligent manslaughter	Rape (revised definition)[1]	Rape (legacy definition)[2]	Robbery	Aggravated assault	Property crime	Burglary	Larceny-theft	Motor vehicle theft	Arson[3]
Gurley	785	2	0	0		0	2	29	5	21	3	
Hackleburg	1480	2	0	1		0	1	28	7	20	1	
Haleyville	4072	18	0	3		1	14	204	41	155	8	
Hamilton	6749	23	1	1		0	21	177	48	113	16	
Hanceville	3314	12	0	2		1	9	112	29	76	7	
Harpersville	1686	7	0	0		3	4	34	13	17	4	
Hartford	2651	17	0	0		2	15	77	21	48	8	
Hartselle	14540	18	0	0		0	18	332	35	277	20	
Headland	4778	11	0	3		3	5	95	24	63	8	
Heflin	3501	8	0	0		1	7	10	3	6	1	
Helena	18525	25	1	6		0	18	115	21	88	6	
Henagar	2346	1	0	0		0	1	63	16	45	2	
Hokes Bluff	4304	2	0	0		1	1	54	13	37	4	
Homewood	25823	84	2	12		38	32	974	137	772	65	
Hoover[5]	85601	104	3	19		40	42		203		81	2
Hueytown	15632	65	1	5		6	53	546	103	425	18	
Huntsville	192587	1787	18	152		414	1203	9398	1692	6812	894	
Irondale	12439	72	1	7		12	52	336	79	224	33	
Jackson	4920	27	0	3		3	21	258	55	195	8	
Jacksonville	12150	123	0	6		16	101	501	140	335	26	
Jasper	14009	160	0	4		18	138	895	120	694	81	
Jemison	2619	26	0	1		2	23	80	14	60	6	
Kimberly	2931	2	0	0		0	2	23	8	14	1	
Lanett	6451	104	0	14		13	77	534	123	345	66	
Leeds	11964	82	0	4		9	69	555	76	443	36	
Leesburg	1012	4	1	1		0	2	57	14	35	8	
Leighton	709	2	0	0		0	2	31	15	14	2	
Level Plains	2012	6	0	1		0	5	39	15	24	0	
Lincoln	6579	46	2	5		5	34	325	87	212	26	
Linden	2008	10	0	1		1	8	50	17	28	5	
Lineville	2306	8	0	1		0	7	25	3	18	4	
Lipscomb	2145	12	0	0		2	10	28	5	20	3	
Luverne	2843	13	0	0		1	12	116	33	75	8	
Madison	47729	209	1	11		24	173	1011	115	826	70	
Maplesville	703	3	0	0		0	3	29	9	19	1	
Margaret	4580	3	0	1		0	2	24	7	15	2	
McIntosh	224	3	0	0		0	3	25	5	17	3	
Midfield	5195	66	1	2		21	42	296	114	164	18	
Midland City	2426	17	0	3		1	13	74	17	48	9	
Mobile[6]	249921	1709	44	89		438	1138	11769	2628	8261	880	
Monroeville	6039	45	1	2		1	41	318	44	259	15	
Montevallo	6716	14	0	3		3	8	149	24	121	4	
Montgomery	199565	1215	30	62		448	675	8989	2293	5824	872	
Moody	12764	43	0	4		1	38	221	31	169	21	
Morris	1950	1	0	1		0	0	23	5	18	0	
Moulton	3312	8	0	1		1	6	52	20	30	2	
Moundville	2465	5	0	1		0	4	89	19	66	4	
Mountain Brook	20737	14	1	1		6	6	289	41	239	9	
Mount Vernon	1508	13	0	1		2	10	59	17	34	8	
Muscle Shoals	13810	54	0	5		6	43	588	108	443	37	
New Brockton	1161	3	0	0		1	2	36	14	20	2	
New Hope	2798	8	0	0		2	6	33	11	19	3	
Newton	1464	4	0	1		1	2	49	7	37	5	
Northport	25045	82	1	16		22	43	878	128	732	18	
Notasulga	835	4	0	0		0	4	29	9	16	4	
Odenville	3715	16	0	2		1	13	39	11	22	6	
Ohatchee	1144	1	0	0		1	0	29	21	8	0	
Oneonta	6624	25	0	2		1	22	207	30	159	18	
Opelika	30180	221	7	18		35	161	1476	233	1158	85	
Opp	6657	38	0	9		2	27	121	31	79	11	
Orange Beach	5932	12	0	0		0	12	187	29	155	3	
Oxford	21234	79	0	0		9	70	949	158	765	26	
Ozark	14679	181	0	12		5	164	691	102	561	28	
Pelham	23162	41	0	6		2	33	509	37	435	37	
Pell City	13835	54	1	4		9	40	451	59	377	15	
Phenix City	38521	327	8	42		78	199	1817	454	1135	228	
Piedmont	4684	44	1	3		3	37	239	74	151	14	
Pine Hill	910	13	0	2		3	8	36	8	23	5	
Pleasant Grove	10293	27	1	0		5	21	199	43	138	18	
Prattville	35698	84	2	17		26	39	1361	171	1099	91	
Prichard	22299	379	8	10		125	236	1227	443	643	141	30
Rainbow City	9573	48	1	4		1	42	182	40	123	19	
Rainsville	5047	8	0	0		0	8	123	29	87	7	
Ranburne	410	0	0	0		0	0	21	3	17	1	
Red Bay	3125	7	0	2		1	4	57	10	42	5	
Reform	1619	10	0	0		1	9	19	7	9	3	
Riverside	2317	2	0	0		1	1	67	21	42	4	
Roanoke	5993	41	0	4		10	27	174	30	130	14	
Robertsdale	6019	26	0	5		2	19	291	33	241	17	
Rogersville	1226	4	0	1		1	2	34	17	12	5	
Russellville	9847	36	0	5		2	29	314	53	237	24	
Samson	1926	27	0	2		0	25	91	18	68	5	
Saraland	13967	34	0	6		4	24	464	51	392	21	

Table 6. Offenses Known to Law Enforcement, by Selected State and City, 2016—Continued

(Number.)

State/city	Population	Violent crime	Murder and nonnegligent manslaughter	Rape (revised definition)[1]	Rape (legacy definition)[2]	Robbery	Aggravated assault	Property crime	Burglary	Larceny-theft	Motor vehicle theft	Arson[3]
Sardis City	1764	1	0	1		0	0	53	8	31	14	
Satsuma	6187	7	0	0		0	7	81	22	51	8	
Scottsboro	14711	229	0	6		6	217	506	80	396	30	
Selma	19283	348	8	21		79	240	1492	399	988	105	44
Sheffield	9121	73	0	9		12	52	375	78	257	40	
Silverhill	772	4	0	0		1	3	30	11	15	4	
Slocomb	1970	4	0	0		0	4	37	12	24	1	
Snead	844	8	0	1		0	7	66	13	49	4	
Southside	8602	17	0	7		3	7	111	29	70	12	
Spanish Fort	8312	15	0	1		3	11	181	26	155	0	
Springville	4221	16	0	0		1	15	86	14	68	4	
Sulligent	1830	4	0	0		0	4	69	24	40	5	
Sumiton	2400	7	0	0		1	6	89	14	70	5	
Summerdale	1181	10	0	3		0	7	59	14	43	2	
Sylacauga	12623	68	0	6		10	52	713	104	574	35	
Talladega	15645	123	0	4		24	95	824	234	544	46	
Tallassee	4769	38	0	3		5	30	285	53	209	23	
Tarrant	6176	71	1	3		20	47	428	148	240	40	
Thomasville	4023	29	0	3		1	25	104	14	83	7	
Town Creek	1058	5	0	0		0	5	22	2	14	6	
Trinity	2170	2	0	0		0	2	37	7	24	6	
Troy	18985	187	0	6		19	162	949	156	740	53	
Tuscaloosa	99925	480	14	54		172	240	3732	794	2708	230	
Tuscumbia	8450	35	1	3		4	27	216	49	146	21	
Tuskegee	8623	103	5	8		7	83	313	117	168	28	
Union Springs	3910	30	1	1		8	20	120	35	75	10	
Uniontown	2364	16	0	0		1	15	46	14	28	4	
Valley	9465	72	0	9		19	44	522	104	371	47	
Vance	1511	16	0	2		4	10	50	26	22	2	
Vestavia Hills	34191	25	0	0		8	17	397	72	292	33	
Warrior	3204	10	0	2		1	7	59	8	48	3	
Weaver	3101	29	0	4		3	22	106	39	59	8	
Wedowee	807	3	0	0		1	2	42	8	27	7	
Wetumpka	8280	32	4	3		6	19	291	37	245	9	
Winfield	4552	20	1	1		5	13	163	41	106	16	
Woodstock	1574	0	0	0		0	0	42	12	26	4	
ALASKA												
Anchorage	299097	3422	28	542		695	2157	14649	2008	10599	2042	69
Bethel	6522	141	0	37		13	91	217	49	116	52	3
Bristol Bay Borough	870	0	0	0		0	0	21	4	11	6	0
Cordova	2186	5	0	0		0	5	26	3	21	2	0
Craig	1256	2	0	0		0	2	16	3	12	1	0
Dillingham	2419	51	0	14		1	36	61	13	42	6	1
Fairbanks	32456	223	7	31		31	154	1350	157	1069	124	4
Haines	2535	4	0	0		0	4	24	7	17	0	0
Homer	5613	10	0	2		0	6	167	16	146	5	0
Juneau	32964	282	0	36		31	215	1595	310	1212	73	4
Kenai	7770	24	0	11		2	11	420	35	361	24	0
Ketchikan	8221	30	0	10		3	17	262	31	220	11	1
Kodiak	6274	62	1	1		5	55	266	36	203	27	1
Kotzebue	3290	111	1	28		4	78	206	41	124	41	3
Nome	3846	49	0	1		0	48	38	5	27	6	0
North Pole	2201	4	0	1		1	2	88	14	67	7	1
North Slope Borough	9710	83	0	11		5	67	106	36	50	20	1
Palmer	6959	26	0	4		3	19	168	10	140	18	0
Petersburg	3162	13	0	3		0	10	69	18	49	2	2
Seward	2813	24	0	1		0	23	68	8	52	8	5
Sitka	8836	12	0	3		0	9	149	12	133	4	0
Skagway	1075	4	0	0		0	4	10	1	9	0	0
Soldotna	4619	34	0	4		5	25	235	14	212	9	2
Unalaska	4517	16	0	1		0	15	29	5	15	9	0
Valdez	3847	7	0	2		0	5	63	7	52	4	1
Wasilla	9585	58	0	2		10	46	487	40	409	38	1
Wrangell	2380	0	0	0		0	0	21	1	17	3	0
ARIZONA												
Apache Junction	38506	107	0	1		15	91	921	251	597	73	9
Avondale	81605	233	2	32		78	121	3262	558	2459	245	8
Buckeye	64563	35	2	2		15	16	1025	115	839	71	2
Bullhead City	39426	99	0	10		16	73	1405	308	999	98	2
Camp Verde	11213	30	1	0		4	25	351	90	235	26	2
Casa Grande	51995	284	1	23		38	222	1744	346	1329	69	12
Chandler	265922	558	4	124		157	273	6152	864	4895	393	21
Chino Valley	11202	74	0	0		2	72	249	55	177	17	0
Clarkdale	4271	11	0	0		1	10	58	13	42	3	1
Coolidge	12387	38	2	3		7	26	597	145	404	48	11
Cottonwood	11932	43	0	1		1	41	496	66	404	26	3
Douglas	16398	30	0	1		4	25	462	70	377	15	3
Eagar	4863	6	0	0		0	6	51	17	32	2	3
El Mirage	34376	74	1	7		16	50	1052	284	667	101	9
Eloy	17110	62	0	3		6	53	460	117	307	36	10
Flagstaff	71179	265	0	26		30	209	2856	255	2542	59	24

Table 6. Offenses Known to Law Enforcement, by Selected State and City, 2016—Continued

(Number.)

State/city	Population	Violent crime	Murder and nonnegligent manslaughter	Rape (revised definition)[1]	Rape (legacy definition)[2]	Robbery	Aggravated assault	Property crime	Burglary	Larceny-theft	Motor vehicle theft	Arson[3]
Florence	31130	22	0	0		0	22	151	36	108	7	0
Fredonia	1320	3	0	0		0	3	20	6	13	1	
Gilbert	255899	200	3	39		37	121	3368	564	2678	126	31
Glendale	242938	1204	23	107		476	598	12805	1981	9690	1134	
Goodyear	82018	310	0	18		28	264	2063	359	1561	143	0
Holbrook	5012	44	0	1		1	42	202	42	145	15	1
Jerome	458	0	0	0		0	0	15	5	10	0	0
Kearny	2055	1	0	0		0	1	27	11	16	0	0
Kingman	29069	101	3	7		21	70	1480	262	1152	66	10
Lake Havasu City	53746	141	2	31		6	102	1218	263	849	106	25
Marana	42808	40	1	8		13	18	1045	66	947	32	2
Maricopa	49627	97	3	10		6	78	648	87	517	44	0
Mesa	478277	2051	19	272		450	1310	11214	1950	8404	860	30
Miami	1776	14	0	0		0	14	101	65	30	6	2
Nogales	20143	62	0	0		2	60	502	80	304	118	0
Oro Valley	44089	29	0	4		7	18	653	70	555	28	1
Page	7516	86	0	13		7	66	500	59	421	20	5
Paradise Valley	14155	9	0	5		1	3	232	57	168	7	0
Patagonia	886	1	0	0		0	1	5	1	0	4	0
Payson	15351	55	0	5		5	45	379	85	265	29	0
Peoria	174797	350	2	37		85	226	3709	645	2804	260	12
Phoenix	1586611	10700	146	1019		3272	6263	58552	13024	37568	7960	216
Pima	2554	0	0	0		0	0	39	7	29	3	0
Pinetop-Lakeside	4354	46	0	0		1	45	172	38	131	3	0
Prescott	42321	170	0	10		18	142	924	175	720	29	5
Prescott Valley	42900	78	1	13		14	50	994	126	836	32	1
Safford	9717	34	0	0		0	34	386	43	313	30	1
Sahuarita	25792	23	0	3		1	19	375	42	320	13	3
San Luis	32227	39	1	1		1	36	427	79	294	54	0
Scottsdale	240885	369	4	90		112	163	5698	768	4681	249	13
Show Low	10892	2	1	0		0	1	439	33	396	10	4
Sierra Vista	42988	85	3	15		18	49	1278	249	974	55	6
Snowflake-Taylor	9835	29	0	0		0	29	169	43	116	10	6
Somerton	15196	26	0	0		0	26	180	47	95	38	0
Springerville	1952	3	0	1		0	2	39	11	26	2	1
Surprise	130679	135	6	12		38	79	2489	353	1980	156	5
Tempe	178654	902	4	155		237	506	8144	1200	6494	450	38
Thatcher	5019	0	0	0		0	0	89	13	76	0	0
Tucson	533663	4245	30	469		1235	2511	31265	4138	25185	1942	119
Wellton	2944	6	0	1		1	4	17	5	11	1	0
Wickenburg	6835	25	0	7		2	16	191	64	108	19	3
Willcox	3511	65	0	1		2	62	201	12	177	12	1
Williams	3140	30	0	2		0	28	116	19	97	0	1
Winslow	9581	75	1	9		3	62	679	67	579	33	4
ARKANSAS												
Alexander	2841	19	0	1		5	13	60	16	35	9	1
Alma	5595	47	0	10		2	35	316	52	251	13	0
Altus	725	2	0	0		0	2	14	5	9	0	0
Amity	698	1	0	0		0	1	2	0	2	0	0
Arkadelphia	10755	45	0	5		4	36	436	100	332	4	1
Ashdown	4434	7	0	1		1	5	144	37	104	3	0
Ash Flat	1060	0	0	0		0	0	7	2	4	1	1
Atkins	3056	10	0	3		0	7	126	34	86	6	0
Augusta	2024	8	0	1		1	6	37	15	22	0	1
Austin[4]	3723	8	0	7		0	1			19	3	0
Bald Knob	2910	15	0	7		0	8	126	40	78	8	1
Barling	4748	18	0	4		0	14	119	17	99	3	0
Batesville	10732	31	0	12		1	18	303	38	249	16	2
Bay	1815	2	0	0		0	2	38	11	26	1	0
Bearden	884	5	0	1		0	4	10	2	8	0	0
Beebe	8269	38	0	11		2	25	303	53	231	19	4
Bella Vista	28274	66	1	26		1	38	193	47	138	8	0
Benton	34920	177	0	20		18	139	1550	269	1177	104	4
Bentonville	46458	85	0	14		3	68	664	83	538	43	1
Berryville	5386	25	2	12		0	11	224	70	145	9	1
Bethel Heights	2512	8	1	0		0	7	37	20	15	2	1
Black Rock	618	1	0	0		1	0	4	1	3	0	0
Blytheville	14523	204	10	13		63	118	876	324	535	17	0
Bono	2257	5	0	2		0	3	28	9	19	0	0
Booneville	3872	14	0	6		0	8	161	24	129	8	0
Bradford	760	1	0	0		0	1	12	4	6	2	1
Brinkley	2837	28	0	0		1	27	138	30	104	4	2
Brookland	3245	3	0	0		1	2	71	6	62	3	0
Bryant	20687	29	0	4		6	19	894	82	760	52	0
Bull Shoals	1929	3	0	0		0	3	47	18	26	3	2
Cabot	25927	62	1	17		9	35	525	99	390	36	2
Caddo Valley	602	4	0	2		0	2	26	8	18	0	0
Camden	11191	113	1	8		14	90	408	129	264	15	0
Cammack Village	744	1	0	1		0	0	11	2	7	2	1
Caraway	1268	1	0	0		0	1	13	5	8	0	0
Carlisle	2176	2	0	0		0	2	78	13	59	6	0
Cave Springs	3369	3	0	1		0	2	50	14	35	1	0

Table 6. Offenses Known to Law Enforcement, by Selected State and City, 2016—Continued

(Number.)

State/city	Population	Violent crime	Murder and nonnegligent manslaughter	Rape (revised definition)[1]	Rape (legacy definition)[2]	Robbery	Aggravated assault	Property crime	Burglary	Larceny-theft	Motor vehicle theft	Arson[3]
Centerton	12584	43	0	26		2	15	134	16	111	7	0
Charleston	2475	19	0	6		0	13	40	9	29	2	0
Cherokee Village	4583	5	0	3		0	2	89	27	59	3	0
Clarendon	1475	4	0	1		0	3	15	4	11	0	0
Clarksville	9482	39	0	16		4	19	435	65	360	10	0
Clinton	2526	1	0	0		0	1	41	1	31	9	0
Conway	66104	335	5	43		84	203	2970	343	2429	198	3
Corning	3122	17	1	2		0	14	37	6	27	4	1
Cotter	947	0	0	0		0	0	24	5	19	0	0
Crossett	5166	29	1	1		5	22	290	77	205	8	3
Damascus	382	0	0	0		0	0	11	0	11	0	0
Danville	2338	4	0	0		0	4	28	11	17	0	0
Dardanelle	4642	33	0	8		7	18	87	26	54	7	1
Decatur	1787	8	0	5		0	3	49	18	28	3	0
Dell	206	0	0	0		0	0	0	0	0	0	0
De Queen	6724	24	2	2		1	19	179	51	124	4	2
Dermott	2688	8	0	0		0	8	49	48	1	0	0
Des Arc	1624	2	0	0		0	2	26	14	11	1	0
De Witt	3162	27	1	9		1	16	151	45	100	6	0
Diaz	1235	4	0	0		0	4	12	3	8	1	0
Dierks	1084	0	0	0		0	0	1	1	0	0	0
Dover	1401	6	0	0		0	6	46	12	33	1	0
Dumas	4253	20	0	0		4	16	105	28	71	6	0
Dyer	857	3	0	2		0	1	17	1	16	0	0
Earle	2256	17	1	2		2	12	37	10	26	1	1
El Dorado	18297	194	5	10		30	149	1037	518	467	52	5
Elkins	3005	7	0	1		0	6	14	2	11	1	0
England	2752	20	0	2		3	15	110	33	74	3	0
Etowah	325	0	0	0		0	0	10	2	6	2	0
Eudora	2070	17	0	0		3	14	78	25	47	6	0
Eureka Springs	2084	18	0	4		2	12	150	33	103	14	0
Fairfield Bay	2254	5	0	2		0	3	57	15	40	2	1
Farmington[4]	6852		0	4		0		112	23	82	7	4
Fayetteville	84726	454	3	59		65	327	3721	485	2895	341	4
Flippin	1331	2	0	2		0	0	48	6	42	0	0
Fordyce	3979	41	0	5		7	29	163	55	105	3	1
Forrest City	14544	171	1	9		37	124	863	180	549	134	9
Fort Smith	88573	712	4	70		97	541	5229	888	4008	333	13
Gassville	2144	6	0	2		0	4	67	13	52	2	0
Gentry	3443	8	0	2		0	6	47	9	36	2	0
Glenwood	2125	3	0	1		0	2	44	23	19	2	0
Gosnell	3261	13	0	0		3	10	49	18	28	3	0
Gravette	3253	5	0	4		0	1	50	7	42	1	1
Greenbrier	5416	0	0	0		0	0	19	1	16	2	0
Green Forest	2769	16	0	8		1	7	54	8	44	2	0
Greenland	1406	11	0	6		0	5	25	6	13	6	0
Greenwood	9372	24	0	6		0	18	36	10	24	2	0
Greers Ferry	867	0	0	0		0	0	7	0	7	0	0
Gurdon	2132	15	1	0		2	12	46	17	27	2	1
Guy	721	1	0	0		0	1	4	1	3	0	0
Hamburg	2772	14	0	1		1	12	34	14	20	0	0
Hampton	1274	7	0	1		1	5	14	5	8	1	0
Hardy	756	8	0	3		0	5	46	11	33	2	0
Harrison	13178	77	2	17		5	53	507	90	369	48	3
Hazen	1392	2	0	0		1	1	14	7	4	3	1
Heber Springs	7144	36	2	11		0	23	229	50	172	7	1
Helena-West Helena	10898	123	0	16		18	89	492	181	282	29	9
Higginson	659	2	0	0		0	2	6	1	5	0	0
Highfill	641	2	0	0		0	2	3	2	0	1	0
Highland	1056	1	0	0		0	1	8	4	4	0	0
Hope	9852	121	2	9		10	100	488	98	371	19	6
Hot Springs	35716	277	4	26		62	185	2882	1059	1586	237	13
Hoxie	2660	4	0	1		0	3	28	8	16	4	0
Hughes	1302	14	0	5		1	8	29	11	17	1	0
Jacksonville	28684	247	3	21		35	188	1307	255	938	114	12
Johnson	3683	7	0	1		1	5	100	52	33	15	2
Jonesboro	75230	387	5	35		72	275	3369	1528	1727	114	11
Judsonia	2028	0	0	0		0	0	42	4	30	8	0
Kensett	1650	5	0	3		0	2	35	2	32	1	0
Lake City	2374	5	0	2		0	3	25	8	16	1	1
Lake Village	2388	7	0	1		1	5	80	29	50	1	0
Lamar	1680	1	0	0		1	0	28	5	23	0	0
Lavaca	2425	5	0	3		0	2	37	12	22	3	0
Leachville	1845	4	0	1		0	3	27	7	20	0	0
Lepanto	1824	1	0	1		0	0	32	4	26	2	0
Lewisville	1161	1	0	0		1	0	22	5	17	0	0
Lincoln	2468	22	0	4		0	18	53	14	35	4	0
Little Flock	2781	4	0	3		0	1	33	3	28	2	0
Little Rock	198800	3044	42	159		657	2186	13714	2348	10223	1143	50
Lonoke	4248	16	0	2		1	13	112	17	92	3	1
Lowell	8812	16	0	9		1	6	104	38	63	3	0
Luxora	1088	2	0	1		0	1	4	1	2	1	0
Magnolia	11642	52	0	4		9	39	382	202	170	10	9

Table 6. Offenses Known to Law Enforcement, by Selected State and City, 2016—Continued

(Number.)

State/city	Population	Violent crime	Murder and nonnegligent manslaughter	Rape (revised definition)[1]	Rape (legacy definition)[2]	Robbery	Aggravated assault	Property crime	Burglary	Larceny-theft	Motor vehicle theft	Arson[3]
Malvern	11016	33	0	3		3	27	408	125	264	19	3
Mammoth Spring	968	1	0	0		0	1	3	2	0	1	0
Marianna	3701	25	0	1		4	20	149	40	95	14	5
Marion	12270	106	1	16		21	68	491	86	383	22	7
Marked Tree	2489	14	1	1		2	10	83	24	56	3	3
Marmaduke	1238	5	0	0		0	5	21	6	14	1	0
Marvell	1022	3	0	0		1	2	7	3	4	0	0
Maumelle	18068	24	0	4		8	12	414	100	302	12	1
Mayflower	2473	13	0	3		2	8	78	25	51	2	0
McCrory	1577	0	0	0		0	0	8	1	7	0	0
McGehee	3866	45	0	7		0	38	152	55	95	2	1
McRae	679	5	0	1		0	4	16	5	11	0	0
Mena	5635	20	0	5		0	15	212	34	176	2	0
Menifee	306	0	0	0		0	0	7	2	3	2	0
Mineral Springs	1152	2	0	1		1	0	7	2	5	0	0
Monette	1533	1	0	1		0	0	33	7	25	1	0
Monticello	9860	44	4	7		7	26	328	77	235	16	1
Morrilton	6733	18	0	7		1	10	397	33	351	13	0
Mountain Home	12305	28	0	21		0	7	494	43	436	15	0
Mountain View	2856	15	0	7		0	8	102	30	68	4	3
Mulberry	1630	14	0	7		0	7	62	20	40	2	0
Murfreesboro	1569	4	0	1		0	3	16	3	13	0	0
Nashville	4450	15	0	3		0	12	167	23	141	3	0
Newport	7733	72	1	12		13	46	452	130	304	18	4
Norfork	497	0	0	0		0	0	1	0	1	0	0
North Little Rock	67344	503	11	11		115	366	2926	523	2016	387	13
Ola	1246	3	0	0		0	3	7	2	4	1	0
Osceola[4]	7138	161	2	12		19	128			227	20	4
Ozark	3572	13	0	4		0	9	128	46	74	8	3
Pangburn	602	3	0	2		0	1	9	2	6	1	0
Paragould	28254	161	0	53		18	90	1380	257	1028	95	5
Paris	3427	22	0	1		0	21	156	60	92	4	1
Parkin	1047	6	0	1		1	4	11	2	7	2	0
Pea Ridge	5331	30	0	7		0	23	92	9	80	3	0
Perryville	1426	7	0	0		1	6	67	17	49	1	2
Piggott	3619	10	0	6		1	3	92	18	72	2	0
Pine Bluff	43976	705	9	38		130	528	2786	1062	1488	236	62
Plainview	596	1	0	1		0	0	14	2	10	2	1
Plumerville	801	2	0	1		0	1	16	2	12	2	0
Pocahontas	6405	27	0	13		1	13	296	37	249	10	0
Pottsville	3131	11	0	0		1	10	43	13	24	6	0
Prairie Grove	5345	16	0	5		0	11	126	19	104	3	0
Quitman	738	4	0	1		0	3	41	6	32	3	0
Ravenden	446	3	0	0		0	3	6	2	4	0	0
Redfield	1593	2	0	1		1	0	27	14	11	2	0
Rison	1270	3	0	0		0	3	29	9	20	0	0
Rogers	64616	336	0	74		20	242	2236	264	1875	97	4
Rose Bud	482	0	0	0		0	0	15	4	9	2	0
Russellville	29366	185	2	21		15	147	1267	183	976	108	1
Salem	1635	6	0	3		0	3	36	9	26	1	0
Shannon Hills	3926	1	0	0		0	1	49	5	42	2	0
Sheridan	4858	15	0	3		2	10	216	27	182	7	0
Sherwood	30676	161	2	19		17	123	1253	258	915	80	1
Siloam Springs	16277	58	0	14		7	37	579	117	436	26	3
Stamps	1525	4	1	0		0	3	26	13	13	0	1
Star City	2163	9	0	3		0	6	76	18	52	6	0
Stuttgart	9002	46	0	8		6	32	396	122	251	23	3
Sulphur Springs	529	2	0	2		0	0	11	3	8	0	0
Swifton	748	1	0	0		0	1	3	1	2	0	2
Texarkana	30429	181	5	20		34	122	1673	336	1238	99	0
Trumann	7118	46	0	15		5	26	429	108	298	23	3
Tuckerman	1739	6	0	5		0	1	47	16	29	2	1
Tyronza	741	1	0	0		0	1	7	2	4	1	0
Van Buren	23133	131	1	15		8	107	868	275	542	51	3
Vilonia	4568	2	0	0		0	2	57	16	36	5	0
Waldron	3406	11	0	0		1	10	128	44	74	10	5
Walnut Ridge	4630	22	0	6		0	16	97	21	72	4	1
Ward	4835	53	1	19		2	31	120	31	80	9	0
Warren	5767	26	2	3		5	16	143	89	50	4	0
Weiner	683	0	0	0		0	0	5	4	1	0	0
West Fork	2587	9	0	3		0	6	32	10	20	2	0
West Memphis	24818	461	14	50		80	317	1200	369	751	80	10
White Hall	5114	12	0	2		0	10	68	14	46	8	1
Wynne	8161	63	1	4		2	56	346	92	237	17	3
CALIFORNIA												
Adelanto	33479	276	1	28		48	199	560	241	218	101	15
Agoura Hills	21032	15	0	2		3	10	253	83	150	20	0
Alameda	79597	151	1	8		68	74	2020	226	1351	443	29
Albany	19975	29	0	0		24	5	533	62	426	45	3
Alhambra	86035	146	0	9		73	64	2107	422	1447	238	4
Aliso Viejo	50604	29	0	4		5	20	411	61	323	27	0
Alturas	2549	22	0	5		1	16	116	34	74	8	0

Table 6. Offenses Known to Law Enforcement, by Selected State and City, 2016—Continued

(Number.)

State/city	Population	Violent crime	Murder and nonnegligent manslaughter	Rape (revised definition)[1]	Rape (legacy definition)[2]	Robbery	Aggravated assault	Property crime	Burglary	Larceny-theft	Motor vehicle theft	Arson[3]
American Canyon	20746	68	0	7		15	46	409	58	295	56	2
Anaheim	353504	1209	7	123		390	689	9617	1469	6764	1384	33
Anderson	10273	92	2	8		6	76	452	51	315	86	7
Angels Camp	3755	9	0	2		0	7	37	8	23	6	0
Antioch	112090	760	9	55		293	403	3690	762	2012	916	56
Apple Valley	72757	314	4	26		74	210	1735	417	1064	254	17
Arcadia	58816	83	2	4		44	33	1642	520	1045	77	5
Arcata	17913	82	0	6		22	54	667	129	461	77	6
Arroyo Grande	18280	35	0	6		9	20	334	53	262	19	3
Artesia	17049	89	2	1		30	56	622	198	350	74	1
Arvin	21195	191	2	3		17	169	634	170	279	185	18
Atascadero	30108	83	1	11		7	64	501	109	345	47	6
Atherton	7218	3	0	1		1	1	104	14	84	6	0
Atwater	29437	203	1	8		27	167	1006	190	670	146	16
Auburn	14078	67	1	5		6	55	305	64	199	42	2
Avalon	3813	10	0	2		0	8	37	2	34	1	0
Avenal	12941	32	3	5		3	21	176	86	72	18	1
Azusa	50393	175	1	18		46	110	1139	261	695	183	6
Bakersfield	378788	1821	32	67		614	1108	17138	3887	10203	3048	332
Baldwin Park	77400	291	5	31		73	182	1514	356	818	340	8
Banning	31191	148	3	13		34	98	676	234	279	163	0
Barstow	23894	361	3	24		106	228	1136	455	465	216	16
Bear Valley	5464	5	0	0		0	5	61	4	56	1	0
Beaumont	45249	144	0	15		29	100	1059	190	696	173	0
Bell	36347	233	5	11		57	160	782	212	414	156	0
Bellflower	78806	392	4	31		160	197	1990	453	1047	490	13
Bell Gardens	43316	155	3	7		64	81	942	103	510	329	4
Belmont	27492	31	0	8		5	18	377	86	266	25	6
Belvedere	2131	1	0	0		0	1	21	5	16	0	0
Benicia	28400	19	0	4		8	7	540	141	299	100	2
Berkeley	122651	602	2	54		361	185	5420	805	3965	650	24
Beverly Hills	35018	106	0	14		49	43	1416	306	1037	73	4
Big Bear	5250	33	1	5		3	24	195	52	127	16	2
Biggs	1703	16	0	2		0	14	29	9	16	4	0
Bishop	3793	29	1	1		5	22	156	31	114	11	0
Blythe	18961	78	1	4		20	53	684	246	413	25	21
Bradbury	1097	0	0	0		0	0	6	4	2	0	0
Brawley	26076	125	0	4		11	110	941	170	692	79	18
Brea	42465	92	0	6		29	57	1431	188	1169	74	6
Brentwood	60512	130	0	17		50	63	1285	146	980	159	6
Brisbane	4807	12	1	0		0	11	99	42	49	8	2
Broadmoor	4411	16	0	2		8	6	77	42	26	9	0
Buellton	5133	5	0	0		3	2	81	16	60	5	0
Buena Park	83768	249	1	16		78	154	2588	322	1891	375	9
Burbank	105720	210	0	24		50	136	2927	392	2269	266	19
Burlingame	30792	62	1	13		18	30	1050	229	688	133	5
Calabasas	24492	15	0	1		3	11	291	90	178	23	2
Calexico	40336	164	0	3		38	123	1267	321	710	236	19
California City	13244	91	1	9		21	60	390	215	152	23	0
Calimesa	8671	15	1	0		8	6	264	67	169	28	0
Calistoga	5364	11	0	5		1	5	76	20	53	3	1
Camarillo	68072	123	4	21		31	67	1125	202	824	99	7
Campbell	41457	108	0	18		33	57	1306	249	908	149	14
Canyon Lake	11176	16	0	2		1	13	136	38	70	28	0
Capitola	10241	28	0	4		11	13	759	35	674	50	3
Carlsbad	115040	209	0	37		49	123	2188	369	1652	167	7
Carmel	3931	7	0	0		1	6	98	18	73	7	0
Carpinteria	13865	26	0	2		8	16	235	50	172	13	0
Carson	93613	505	10	23		165	307	2424	439	1463	522	22
Cathedral City	54317	152	5	18		51	78	1097	275	429	393	5
Central Marin	35265	38	0	4		17	17	656	246	370	40	0
Ceres	48372	186	1	11		66	108	1278	278	616	384	7
Cerritos	50159	111	0	5		48	58	2264	468	1576	220	5
Chico	91122	293	0	66		57	170	3290	499	2336	455	199
Chino	87081	207	1	13		52	141	2151	439	1407	305	2
Chino Hills	78990	59	1	8		12	38	1013	331	595	87	5
Chowchilla	18487	85	0	1		7	77	527	161	281	85	15
Chula Vista	270175	696	1	58		208	429	4254	694	2675	885	39
Citrus Heights	87811	396	3	38		88	267	2676	400	1900	376	16
Claremont	36553	59	0	3		28	28	960	290	607	63	6
Clayton	12057	4	0	0		3	1	146	26	107	13	2
Clearlake	15165	149	1	19		37	92	677	237	336	104	10
Cloverdale	8848	18	0	5		4	9	121	18	90	13	4
Clovis	105865	255	2	35		72	146	2973	434	2337	202	7
Coachella	45402	161	2	9		62	88	1302	232	847	223	6
Coalinga	16282	130	0	10		7	113	293	90	182	21	4
Colma	1534	27	0	1		12	14	297	48	233	16	0
Colton	55100	213	2	10		98	103	1646	304	806	536	12
Colusa	5926	9	0	1		2	6	100	26	57	17	0
Commerce	13128	130	1	7		56	66	1223	119	744	360	10
Compton	98861	1129	35	38		365	691	2528	371	1367	790	46
Concord	129903	447	1	31		159	256	4337	521	2793	1023	17
Corcoran	22111	68	2	10		7	49	404	114	216	74	2

Table 6. Offenses Known to Law Enforcement, by Selected State and City, 2016—Continued

(Number.)

State/city	Population	Violent crime	Murder and nonnegligent manslaughter	Rape (revised definition)[1]	Rape (legacy definition)[2]	Robbery	Aggravated assault	Property crime	Burglary	Larceny-theft	Motor vehicle theft	Arson[3]
Corning	7522	38	0	5		5	28	322	79	202	41	3
Corona	166534	185	3	39		74	69	3693	741	2236	716	14
Coronado	24974	26	0	5		3	18	380	36	312	32	5
Costa Mesa	113816	412	1	60		145	206	4610	735	3296	579	29
Cotati	7479	37	0	3		6	28	82	26	48	8	4
Covina	49222	164	1	23		48	92	1289	309	816	164	5
Crescent City	6622	53	0	2		6	45	147	39	91	17	0
Cudahy	24411	76	3	9		25	39	246	41	127	78	2
Culver City	39880	213	0	3		137	73	2060	304	1599	157	0
Cupertino	60948	71	0	7		16	48	997	268	661	68	15
Cypress	49557	62	1	6		22	33	782	148	525	109	3
Daly City	107640	244	1	22		90	131	1631	246	1152	233	15
Dana Point	34349	64	0	11		17	36	559	121	400	38	0
Danville	44897	9	1	3		0	5	365	68	264	33	2
Davis	68087	108	0	26		31	51	1665	263	1290	112	7
Delano	52656	264	7	9		26	222	1552	305	779	468	26
Del Mar	4388	11	0	4		1	6	167	57	98	12	0
Del Rey Oaks	1700	4	0	0		2	2	78	34	41	3	0
Desert Hot Springs	28573	225	5	14		43	163	926	464	221	241	6
Diamond Bar	57162	66	2	4		22	38	931	364	495	72	3
Dinuba	24156	179	0	6		21	152	655	117	453	85	6
Dixon	19592	63	1	3		21	38	376	62	267	47	5
Dorris	900	5	0	1		0	4	19	10	8	1	0
Dos Palos	5158	34	0	0		1	33	185	75	86	24	1
Downey	114704	373	1	22		188	162	3371	527	2078	766	16
Duarte	22120	72	2	0		19	51	373	77	223	73	3
Dublin	60430	87	0	8		31	48	1097	133	837	127	3
Dunsmuir	1571	6	0	0		0	6	47	15	24	8	0
East Palo Alto	29957	121	3	11		55	52	518	82	344	92	13
Eastvale	60115	71	0	5		24	42	1269	167	935	167	7
El Cajon	104483	395	1	46		146	202	2446	429	1584	433	28
El Centro	44213	205	1	19		55	130	2314	506	1669	139	10
El Cerrito	25222	137	1	6		78	52	1064	126	831	107	3
Elk Grove	169742	547	0	51		94	402	2342	373	1760	209	5
El Monte	117354	448	3	31		167	247	2501	675	1138	688	23
El Segundo	17113	53	0	4		25	24	731	186	472	73	3
Emeryville	12060	132	0	3		97	32	1721	126	1449	146	3
Encinitas	63597	105	0	9		14	82	1037	204	757	76	4
Escalon	7601	34	1	6		3	24	134	28	91	15	2
Escondido	152897	555	4	48		150	353	3286	415	2213	658	12
Etna	712	1	0	0		0	1	7	0	5	2	0
Eureka	26981	255	1	24		76	154	1521	424	854	243	17
Exeter	10589	31	0	1		3	27	269	83	150	36	1
Fairfax	7662	16	0	3		4	9	136	16	113	7	0
Fairfield	114521	476	7	56		147	266	2845	420	1888	537	20
Farmersville	10812	30	0	0		3	27	169	31	103	35	1
Ferndale	1368	7	0	1		1	5	25	7	16	2	0
Fillmore	15653	42	0	4		5	33	100	20	69	11	10
Firebaugh	8484	13	0	7		3	3	111	37	57	17	3
Folsom	77245	76	0	9		34	33	1384	264	1006	114	5
Fontana	209531	870	14	69		218	569	4396	697	2550	1149	17
Fort Bragg	7292	42	1	4		3	34	326	55	261	10	1
Fort Jones	684	1	0	0		0	1	10	2	4	4	0
Fortuna	12013	60	2	5		8	45	458	59	368	31	6
Foster City	34081	32	0	10		5	17	343	60	261	22	2
Fountain Valley	57291	63	0	0		21	42	1443	246	1072	125	3
Fowler	6397	35	0	3		4	28	116	36	55	25	0
Fremont	235881	420	0	59		184	177	4715	923	2997	795	21
Fresno	524796	3206	39	158		1122	1887	20523	3697	13542	3284	260
Fullerton	141968	341	5	55		94	187	3599	456	2740	403	14
Galt	25638	76	0	8		11	57	579	120	404	55	7
Gardena	60770	338	3	24		160	151	1482	355	772	355	7
Garden Grove	176230	545	4	38		186	317	4322	861	2789	672	9
Gilroy	54130	182	0	30		57	95	1742	255	1132	355	19
Glendale	202903	227	1	38		84	104	3450	596	2491	363	5
Glendora	52380	70	0	4		16	50	1361	253	1036	72	11
Goleta	31145	37	0	8		8	21	484	92	364	28	1
Gonzales	8533	35	1	0		9	25	101	18	54	29	0
Grand Terrace	12545	21	0	3		8	10	281	75	161	45	0
Grass Valley	12961	96	0	1		7	88	708	120	521	67	3
Greenfield	17343	56	3	3		21	29	297	55	168	74	7
Gridley	6584	104	0	3		1	100	196	42	132	22	1
Grover Beach	13686	40	1	3		5	31	320	58	241	21	4
Guadalupe	7365	8	0	2		2	4	71	11	47	13	1
Gustine	5801	38	1	2		2	33	113	31	67	15	3
Hanford	55973	266	2	21		44	199	1496	222	1059	215	7
Hawaiian Gardens	14654	73	2	2		27	42	305	54	169	82	1
Hawthorne	89299	654	7	40		298	309	2533	442	1517	574	8
Hayward	161122	631	13	66		348	204	4641	707	2308	1626	20
Healdsburg	11830	14	1	1		3	9	190	35	139	16	0
Hemet	84838	614	5	41		170	398	3391	764	2004	623	12
Hercules	25553	53	1	0		11	41	392	74	266	52	0
Hermosa Beach	19930	47	1	10		14	22	539	85	424	30	1

Table 6. Offenses Known to Law Enforcement, by Selected State and City, 2016—Continued

(Number.)

State/city	Population	Violent crime	Murder and nonnegligent manslaughter	Rape (revised definition)[1]	Rape (legacy definition)[2]	Robbery	Aggravated assault	Property crime	Burglary	Larceny-theft	Motor vehicle theft	Arson[3]
Hesperia	93888	334	3	30		92	209	1799	457	994	348	21
Hidden Hills	1938	1	0	1		0	0	16	8	8	0	0
Highland	55184	239	3	10		79	147	1134	304	532	298	13
Hillsborough	11575	9	0	2		2	5	121	84	36	1	0
Hollister	37953	116	0	12		25	79	396	74	243	79	5
Holtville	6498	12	0	0		1	11	82	28	41	13	2
Hughson	7539	8	0	0		2	6	146	45	86	15	3
Huntington Beach	204071	362	2	55		76	229	4527	650	3466	411	20
Huntington Park	59692	463	2	28		216	217	1988	208	1102	678	20
Huron	6852	54	1	3		8	42	93	43	36	14	7
Imperial	17582	7	0	0		1	6	73	7	60	6	0
Imperial Beach	27616	71	1	7		17	46	372	87	172	113	2
Indian Wells	5352	8	0	1		2	5	110	38	68	4	0
Indio	89201	437	5	26		88	318	1944	400	1165	379	5
Industry	204	96	0	8		40	48	1175	174	783	218	5
Inglewood	112059	830	16	56		406	352	2456	437	1229	790	29
Ione	6860	4	0	1		0	3	49	6	37	6	0
Irvine	266663	152	3	41		52	56	3737	640	2918	179	9
Irwindale	1440	18	0	1		6	11	206	41	127	38	1
Isleton	840	6	0	0		1	5	13	8	5	0	0
Jackson	4649	30	0	1		4	25	156	49	94	13	0
Jurupa Valley	101316	340	7	18		76	239	3078	476	1597	1005	11
Kensington	5364	3	0	0		0	3	56	20	36	0	0
Kerman	14654	35	0	4		7	24	374	74	243	57	0
King City	14111	47	2	4		5	36	236	57	115	64	3
Kingsburg	11905	27	0	3		8	16	346	116	126	104	1
La Canada Flintridge	20659	13	0	0		5	8	303	95	194	14	1
Lafayette	26254	13	0	5		5	3	394	65	288	41	4
Laguna Beach	23486	116	0	15		17	84	646	134	452	60	6
Laguna Hills	32045	34	0	5		9	20	536	107	381	48	0
Laguna Niguel	66352	65	0	9		22	34	751	124	567	60	2
Laguna Woods	16473	12	0	4		2	6	169	21	139	9	0
La Habra	62483	102	1	8		35	58	1352	237	955	160	2
La Habra Heights	5480	4	0	0		2	2	109	37	64	8	1
Lake Elsinore	63907	155	3	10		53	89	1865	274	1224	367	2
Lake Forest	83511	105	0	17		13	75	746	135	533	78	7
Lakeport	4817	47	0	3		14	30	206	50	142	14	0
Lake Shastina	2546	4	0	0		0	4	8	1	5	2	0
Lakewood	81921	223	2	7		113	101	2521	342	1872	307	14
La Mesa	60681	197	0	21		56	120	1669	336	1108	225	11
La Mirada	49715	85	1	9		27	48	889	162	606	121	1
Lancaster	161963	1103	7	73		340	683	3488	1059	1816	613	67
La Palma	15975	37	0	1		10	26	369	141	196	32	1
La Puente	40928	131	1	9		45	76	560	136	260	164	4
La Quinta	41058	86	1	5		34	46	1085	167	852	66	3
Lawndale	33560	194	0	9		71	114	528	93	276	159	1
Lemon Grove	26981	139	0	6		56	77	509	106	311	92	4
Lemoore	25875	98	0	20		10	68	501	111	308	82	7
Lincoln	47206	29	0	5		7	17	541	118	366	57	2
Lindsay	13533	72	0	1		7	64	322	80	151	91	5
Livermore	89553	174	1	26		59	88	2284	255	1739	290	14
Livingston	14076	60	0	5		6	49	372	115	193	64	3
Lodi	65067	351	5	9		84	253	1935	438	1189	308	4
Loma Linda	24190	34	0	3		12	19	649	103	403	143	4
Lomita	20889	69	0	4		27	38	347	73	223	51	0
Lompoc	44541	222	0	27		19	176	977	219	628	130	5
Long Beach	476476	2846	33	197		1138	1478	14224	2988	8377	2859	117
Los Alamitos	11774	13	0	2		4	7	219	73	129	17	0
Los Altos	31000	13	0	3		3	7	343	133	193	17	2
Los Altos Hills	8495	6	0	2		0	4	63	41	22	0	3
Los Angeles	4007905	28817	293	2343		10307	15874	99151	15821	64739	18591	1241
Los Banos	37738	121	1	11		35	74	1161	253	733	175	4
Los Gatos	30947	21	0	2		6	13	616	139	432	45	3
Lynwood	72471	469	9	31		197	232	1713	245	701	767	17
Madera	64753	505	3	22		98	382	1859	297	1262	300	0
Malibu	13030	38	0	6		13	19	402	87	283	32	1
Mammoth Lakes	7891	21	1	5		3	12	109	19	79	11	0
Manhattan Beach	35955	53	0	8		32	13	1030	191	786	53	8
Manteca	77104	244	0	30		91	123	2700	315	2020	365	13
Marina	21539	57	0	12		10	35	499	63	390	46	4
Martinez	38541	51	0	3		21	27	858	112	422	324	0
Marysville	12241	96	1	8		23	64	504	108	295	101	8
Maywood	27985	122	0	9		39	74	441	79	195	167	4
McFarland	14263	33	1	2		4	26	207	76	78	53	21
Menifee	89114	135	0	8		47	80	2119	384	1400	335	0
Mendota	11481	97	4	7		12	74	150	33	85	32	1
Menlo Park	33726	30	0	10		7	13	623	101	493	29	5
Merced	83106	489	1	35		134	319	2774	558	1617	599	82
Mill Valley	14491	9	0	1		2	6	223	45	166	12	1
Milpitas	79990	96	1	9		52	34	1791	202	1320	269	4
Mission Viejo	97950	75	0	7		25	43	983	160	768	55	14
Modesto	212880	2104	13	103		481	1507	9324	1421	6350	1553	65
Monrovia	37637	60	0	8		19	33	832	132	624	76	1

Table 6. Offenses Known to Law Enforcement, by Selected State and City, 2016—Continued

(Number.)

State/city	Population	Violent crime	Murder and nonnegligent manslaughter	Rape (revised definition)[1]	Rape (legacy definition)[2]	Robbery	Aggravated assault	Property crime	Burglary	Larceny-theft	Motor vehicle theft	Arson[3]
Montague	1390	4	0	1		0	3	15	8	6	1	0
Montclair	39085	210	0	32		63	115	1713	326	978	409	27
Montebello	64206	214	0	7		114	93	1978	823	607	548	46
Monterey	28506	100	1	15		29	55	1083	199	816	68	3
Monterey Park	61710	131	1	8		59	63	1704	460	998	246	1
Monte Sereno	3591	0	0	0		0	0	28	14	13	1	0
Moorpark	36423	37	0	12		4	21	296	59	213	24	7
Moraga	17505	10	0	1		2	7	143	24	95	24	0
Moreno Valley	206224	863	9	17		341	496	6118	969	4042	1107	7
Morgan Hill	44015	82	0	3		21	58	642	111	418	113	1
Morro Bay	10719	17	2	0		3	12	204	52	136	16	2
Mountain View	81726	132	0	9		29	94	1776	280	1377	119	5
Mount Shasta	3277	10	0	1		0	9	96	22	63	11	1
Murrieta	111043	49	0	8		17	24	1603	280	1115	208	9
Napa	81115	296	1	38		47	210	1579	437	1013	129	5
National City	61550	267	3	13		108	143	1376	182	734	460	5
Needles	5010	47	0	3		6	38	161	67	77	17	1
Nevada City	3167	9	0	1		1	7	108	21	73	14	4
Newark	45893	108	1	15		45	47	1186	237	710	239	1
Newman	11037	32	0	1		4	27	150	34	74	42	1
Newport Beach	87482	110	1	34		17	58	2241	437	1644	160	4
Norco	26132	51	0	3		16	32	772	164	482	126	1
Norwalk	107453	419	7	18		139	255	1963	372	1125	466	15
Novato	56263	80	0	9		15	56	1038	186	716	136	8
Oakdale	22572	54	0	10		11	33	688	127	482	79	3
Oakland	424998	6059	85	277		3076	2621	23952	2900	14153	6899	191
Oakley	40695	55	0	6		24	25	419	77	221	121	1
Oceanside	177340	639	8	56		172	403	4364	607	3276	481	14
Ojai	7658	10	0	3		1	6	63	14	44	5	0
Ontario	172606	602	8	32		227	335	4718	885	2764	1069	25
Orange	141841	228	1	25		57	145	2608	464	1783	361	9
Orange Cove	9706	39	1	1		3	34	153	30	67	56	3
Orinda	19585	10	0	0		4	6	156	35	110	11	0
Orland	7587	27	0	5		5	17	145	30	96	19	1
Oroville	16322	141	0	15		43	83	1330	282	866	182	10
Oxnard	209048	948	12	69		429	438	6073	978	4309	786	40
Pacifica	39650	65	0	15		11	39	492	89	363	40	3
Pacific Grove	15795	9	0	5		2	2	318	47	249	22	2
Palmdale	159441	697	8	45		222	422	2728	646	1660	422	34
Palm Desert	52528	77	1	2		26	48	2144	380	1586	178	2
Palm Springs	47909	275	2	28		67	178	2754	746	1669	339	7
Palo Alto	67317	73	1	9		28	35	1436	215	1159	62	8
Palos Verdes Estates	13730	4	0	0		1	3	111	28	76	7	1
Paradise	26532	45	1	7		8	29	502	250	178	74	3
Paramount	55673	313	4	18		150	141	1744	226	1125	393	17
Parlier	15262	103	0	11		13	79	256	75	100	81	7
Pasadena	143288	477	2	46		164	265	3446	861	2261	324	66
Paso Robles	31939	67	0	8		20	39	977	144	738	95	6
Patterson	21716	60	1	4		18	37	488	85	297	106	2
Perris	76260	225	2	4		91	128	2158	344	1264	550	1
Petaluma	60933	200	1	29		22	148	1108	194	842	72	4
Pico Rivera	64469	220	2	12		72	134	1621	328	836	457	6
Piedmont	11515	32	0	5		17	10	200	66	109	25	0
Pinole	19451	61	0	4		31	26	892	76	731	85	6
Pismo Beach	8264	12	0	4		6	2	513	80	410	23	0
Pittsburg	70663	278	7	42		116	113	1975	339	961	675	26
Placentia	52800	77	1	2		23	51	790	203	505	82	3
Placerville	10705	27	0	6		9	12	370	76	262	32	3
Pleasant Hill	35140	79	0	3		43	33	1510	146	1179	185	4
Pleasanton	81464	100	0	12		44	44	1604	208	1260	136	2
Pomona	154109	767	13	68		295	391	4676	853	2640	1183	33
Porterville	56421	215	0	16		52	147	1315	280	771	264	0
Port Hueneme	22570	65	1	6		30	28	399	79	264	56	2
Poway	50606	65	0	8		14	43	455	93	329	33	2
Rancho Cordova	72265	245	1	17		74	153	1435	305	998	132	2
Rancho Cucamonga	177089	266	1	43		86	136	3991	974	2563	454	11
Rancho Mirage	18243	23	0	0		3	20	701	174	462	65	0
Rancho Palos Verdes	42947	27	0	7		6	14	417	118	266	33	0
Rancho Santa Margarita	49606	48	0	2		10	36	267	45	206	16	2
Red Bluff	14138	159	0	20		35	104	1097	260	719	118	8
Redding	91918	720	5	84		143	488	3837	710	2608	519	7
Redlands	71485	225	0	37		76	112	2913	501	2014	398	14
Redondo Beach	68447	160	1	8		58	93	1742	428	1154	160	1
Redwood City	87046	164	0	43		44	77	1503	260	1087	156	7
Reedley	25828	190	0	10		19	161	499	154	265	80	6
Rialto	103893	451	4	22		159	266	1887	555	603	729	2
Richmond	110868	1019	21	72		364	562	3785	645	1907	1233	33
Ridgecrest	29003	149	0	24		21	104	565	176	317	72	8
Rio Dell	3390	7	0	0		1	6	40	9	22	9	0
Rio Vista	8554	32	0	1		2	29	99	24	58	17	0
Ripon	15318	12	0	2		9	1	267	22	225	20	0
Riverbank	24401	55	1	3		26	25	615	83	437	95	1
Riverside	325896	1724	10	141		586	987	11266	1977	7355	1934	57

Table 6. Offenses Known to Law Enforcement, by Selected State and City, 2016—Continued

(Number.)

State/city	Population	Violent crime	Murder and nonnegligent manslaughter	Rape (revised definition)[1]	Rape (legacy definition)[2]	Robbery	Aggravated assault	Property crime	Burglary	Larceny-theft	Motor vehicle theft	Arson[3]
Rocklin	62006	65	1	19		14	31	1202	210	895	97	5
Rohnert Park	42723	204	0	31		20	153	743	117	538	88	4
Rolling Hills	1899	0	0	0		0	0	11	3	8	0	1
Rolling Hills Estates	8297	11	0	0		8	3	126	33	88	5	0
Rosemead	55129	167	1	9		73	84	1249	308	714	227	9
Roseville	132566	199	0	21		95	83	3316	393	2596	327	16
Ross	2492	1	0	1		0	0	25	11	13	1	0
Sacramento	495471	3549	41	88		1136	2284	15283	3070	9389	2824	173
Salinas	158729	1005	35	86		325	559	4742	695	2484	1563	11
San Bernardino	217303	2878	62	123		903	1790	9178	2353	4228	2597	70
San Bruno	43613	109	0	16		47	46	1106	141	857	108	1
San Clemente	65915	75	0	10		21	44	799	184	547	68	4
Sand City	391	7	0	0		4	3	140	5	129	6	0
San Diego	1413414	5332	50	572		1387	3323	28624	4743	18042	5839	239
San Dimas	34884	82	0	15		24	43	764	188	491	85	2
San Fernando	25194	132	1	8		38	85	450	90	240	120	3
San Francisco	871155	6190	57	342		3175	2616	47402	4978	36991	5433	255
San Gabriel	40580	98	0	6		38	54	655	224	374	57	3
Sanger	25078	126	3	9		17	97	564	161	315	88	1
San Jacinto	47475	128	4	1		67	56	1673	348	1044	281	5
San Jose	1041844	3887	47	451		1214	2175	24749	4260	12786	7703	137
San Juan Capistrano	36798	87	1	9		15	62	436	108	275	53	7
San Leandro	91870	487	3	31		280	173	3530	499	2070	961	23
San Luis Obispo	47774	178	0	39		21	118	2076	251	1730	95	26
San Marcos	94840	197	0	13		42	142	1145	211	783	151	3
San Marino	13528	15	0	1		7	7	261	106	148	7	0
San Mateo	104802	242	1	18		44	179	2141	732	1194	215	4
San Pablo	30674	213	2	22		90	99	1214	213	576	425	11
San Rafael	59435	249	0	28		111	110	1713	255	1186	272	12
San Ramon	76901	39	0	9		12	18	823	140	616	67	2
Santa Ana	337419	1612	23	142		511	936	6980	1119	3913	1948	42
Santa Barbara	92519	397	0	87		82	228	3060	433	2428	199	20
Santa Clara	128194	159	3	17		58	81	2814	362	2039	413	7
Santa Clarita	219611	331	2	45		122	162	3005	650	1942	413	17
Santa Cruz	64969	521	4	45		106	366	3610	354	2874	382	11
Santa Fe Springs	18401	112	3	8		36	65	1184	168	836	180	4
Santa Maria	106200	506	9	45		168	284	2638	521	1452	665	14
Santa Monica	93921	475	2	40		189	244	4039	623	3180	236	17
Santa Paula	30784	80	2	9		26	43	343	76	218	49	3
Santa Rosa	176383	658	5	94		121	438	3010	516	2087	407	19
Santee	58651	112	2	7		21	82	915	137	681	97	3
Saratoga	31152	28	0	4		6	18	286	159	120	7	3
Sausalito	7198	4	0	0		0	4	247	33	202	12	1
Scotts Valley	12016	16	0	4		1	11	255	84	161	10	2
Seal Beach	24721	28	1	1		4	22	546	80	425	41	1
Seaside	34827	128	2	10		29	87	607	87	421	99	0
Sebastopol	7734	19	0	4		1	14	135	36	83	16	2
Selma	24641	298	1	18		28	251	827	197	447	183	3
Shafter	18608	42	1	7		6	28	567	174	249	144	8
Sierra Madre	11212	25	0	3		3	19	114	47	59	8	0
Signal Hill	11677	69	0	9		29	31	856	103	640	113	2
Simi Valley	127252	174	2	28		39	105	1566	334	1127	105	10
Solana Beach	13561	16	0	1		3	12	224	61	141	22	0
Soledad	24805	76	1	7		14	54	212	40	92	80	0
Solvang	5844	13	0	2		1	10	79	18	61	0	0
Sonoma	11113	37	0	6		4	27	194	36	150	8	4
Sonora	4802	28	0	9		6	13	370	86	263	21	6
South El Monte	21032	109	2	6		44	57	580	152	273	155	6
South Gate	96791	660	5	29		250	376	3435	507	1929	999	8
South Lake Tahoe	21765	71	1	12		23	35	430	90	297	43	0
South Pasadena	26256	27	0	7		10	10	667	162	447	58	4
South San Francisco	67995	149	1	25		43	80	1416	307	902	207	6
Stallion Springs	2628	2	0	0		0	2	17	4	13	0	0
Stanton	39066	131	0	14		56	61	734	120	469	145	6
St. Helena	6142	9	0	2		1	6	116	29	73	14	3
Stockton	308348	4381	49	128		1185	3019	11634	2251	7550	1833	81
Suisun City	29768	80	0	16		23	41	654	79	495	80	5
Sunnyvale	154108	158	1	21		53	83	2140	520	1347	273	16
Susanville	14798	181	0	9		11	161	282	68	193	21	4
Sutter Creek	2484	5	0	0		1	4	55	15	35	5	1
Taft	9543	73	0	3		6	64	355	80	249	26	0
Tehachapi	12770	52	0	6		8	38	273	89	161	23	1
Temecula	114381	145	2	4		55	84	2587	341	1940	306	3
Temple City	36527	49	1	5		15	28	580	264	278	38	2
Thousand Oaks	129853	164	0	30		33	101	1686	272	1302	112	10
Tiburon	9263	4	0	2		0	2	83	18	61	4	0
Torrance	149078	258	1	28		119	110	3221	458	2326	437	5
Tracy	87844	151	0	17		62	72	1899	245	1348	306	12
Truckee	16326	25	0	2		2	21	187	42	121	24	3
Tulare	62902	224	6	13		57	148	1764	292	1110	362	0
Tulelake	990	1	0	0		0	1	10	4	5	1	0
Turlock	73031	384	7	23		93	261	2503	474	1495	534	15
Tustin	81642	120	2	13		34	71	1806	229	1412	165	0

Table 6. Offenses Known to Law Enforcement, by Selected State and City, 2016—Continued

(Number.)

State/city	Population	Violent crime	Murder and nonnegligent manslaughter	Rape (revised definition)[1]	Rape (legacy definition)[2]	Robbery	Aggravated assault	Property crime	Burglary	Larceny-theft	Motor vehicle theft	Arson[3]
Twentynine Palms	26213	92	0	8		15	69	364	148	167	49	5
Ukiah	15897	150	0	15		29	106	431	107	284	40	2
Union City	75501	281	1	12		111	157	1897	298	1258	341	11
Upland	76956	243	1	18		96	128	2301	673	1285	343	11
Vacaville	97671	207	0	11		76	120	2057	189	1690	178	7
Vallejo	122293	1053	15	111		353	574	4810	2366	1321	1123	73
Ventura	110228	368	8	53		109	198	3750	628	2838	284	12
Vernon	114	28	1	1		18	8	376	44	207	125	4
Victorville	123438	748	7	46		224	471	3528	953	2002	573	25
Villa Park	5991	4	0	1		1	2	82	22	57	3	0
Visalia	131186	480	8	68		120	284	4196	998	2561	637	11
Vista	102307	372	2	41		99	230	1615	351	989	275	8
Walnut	30447	25	2	2		7	14	516	285	200	31	3
Walnut Creek	69860	78	1	1		30	46	2120	275	1611	234	4
Waterford	8897	12	0	2		0	10	125	27	75	23	0
Watsonville	54110	238	0	26		46	166	1738	214	1018	506	8
Weed	2479	23	0	1		5	17	99	13	78	8	0
West Covina	108950	265	4	18		110	133	2811	519	1794	498	10
West Hollywood	36594	275	2	26		119	128	1601	241	1217	143	9
Westlake Village	8547	16	0	4		2	10	204	37	161	6	1
Westminster	92582	309	2	31		96	180	2720	529	1854	337	7
Westmorland	2275	2	0	0		0	2	9	4	3	2	0
West Sacramento	53532	233	0	17		95	121	1219	191	856	172	21
Wheatland	3775	12	0	0		0	12	48	13	28	7	1
Whittier	87860	258	2	21		97	138	2790	467	1933	390	7
Wildomar	36310	49	0	5		9	35	655	129	391	135	2
Williams	5208	6	0	2		0	4	61	17	40	4	0
Willits	4856	66	0	3		4	59	54	10	22	22	0
Willows	6053	42	0	2		5	35	222	32	170	20	7
Windsor	27594	84	0	14		7	63	311	49	246	16	1
Winters	7120	12	0	0		3	9	98	18	66	14	3
Woodlake	7727	25	0	2		3	20	99	23	67	9	3
Woodland	59190	218	3	14		54	147	1522	221	1037	264	17
Yorba Linda	68702	41	0	11		6	24	725	150	514	61	0
Yountville	3030	4	0	0		0	4	47	16	28	3	0
Yreka	7559	54	1	2		3	48	268	74	152	42	3
Yuba City	67198	272	8	24		76	164	2030	406	1389	235	7
Yucaipa	53697	113	0	11		20	82	1162	263	730	169	4
Yucca Valley	21774	85	1	2		15	67	417	131	229	57	1
COLORADO												
Aspen	6926	5	0	4		0	1	325	24	289	12	2
Ault	1642	2	0	0		0	2	5	4	0	1	0
Aurora	366477	1939	22	289		576	1052	11213	1698	7977	1538	69
Avon	6532	13	0	8		0	5	147	13	124	10	0
Basalt	3900	2	0	2		0	0	34	2	30	2	0
Bayfield	2611	2	0	1		0	1	45	6	36	3	0
Black Hawk	126	8	0	6		1	1	199	2	184	13	0
Boulder	109189	258	0	52		30	176	3275	559	2497	219	19
Bow Mar	961	0	0	0		0	0	3	1	2	0	0
Breckenridge	4971	12	1	4		0	7	222	25	191	6	0
Brighton	38363	143	1	45		15	82	1328	159	994	175	12
Broomfield	66953	36	0	16		2	18	1610	216	1236	158	4
Brush	5456	5	0	5		0	0	41	22	19	0	1
Buena Vista	2790	1	0	1		0	0	65	4	61	0	0
Burlington	3624	7	1	0		0	6	76	9	62	5	0
Calhan	790	0	0	0		0	0	12	5	7	0	0
Campo	104	0	0	0		0	0	0	0	0	0	0
Carbondale	6728	14	0	2		1	11	74	4	60	10	0
Castle Rock	57109	51	0	22		4	25	882	106	739	37	5
Center	2196	11	1	3		1	6	72	26	43	3	0
Cherry Hills Village	6649	1	0	0		0	1	69	14	51	4	0
Colorado Springs	464113	2301	24	446		437	1394	16526	2677	11776	2073	116
Columbine Valley	1381	0	0	0		0	0	4	2	2	0	0
Commerce City	55341	241	0	52		40	149	1767	230	1127	410	11
Cortez	8761	14	0	0		1	13	209	8	199	2	0
Craig	8724	19	0	6		3	10	238	16	216	6	2
Crested Butte	1599	3	0	0		0	3	19	1	17	1	0
Cripple Creek	1147	19	0	3		0	16	77	12	59	6	1
Dacono	4925	2	0	0		1	1	8	0	4	4	0
Delta	8778	9	0	4		0	5	332	52	257	23	4
Denver	699259	4597	57	567		1160	2813	25101	4675	15638	4788	94
Dillon	972	5	0	2		1	2	42	1	38	3	1
Durango	18248	43	1	5		1	36	718	61	626	31	2
Eagle	6715	4	0	1		0	3	55	5	47	3	1
Eaton	5045	3	0	0		1	2	5	3	1	1	0
Edgewater	5330	10	0	2		3	5	333	24	261	48	0
Erie	22115	12	0	5		1	6	135	24	103	8	1
Estes Park	6335	6	0	0		1	5	72	12	57	3	1
Evans	21975	70	0	4		3	63	409	67	275	67	7
Federal Heights	12563	81	1	11		18	51	718	84	467	167	0
Firestone	12375	6	0	0		2	4	126	24	89	13	0
Florence	3861	7	0	0		0	7	76	16	54	6	0

Table 6. Offenses Known to Law Enforcement, by Selected State and City, 2016—Continued

(Number.)

State/city	Population	Violent crime	Murder and nonnegligent manslaughter	Rape (revised definition)[1]	Rape (legacy definition)[2]	Robbery	Aggravated assault	Property crime	Burglary	Larceny-theft	Motor vehicle theft	Arson[3]
Fort Collins	164670	342	5	33		40	264	4036	451	3384	201	16
Fort Lupton	7903	15	0	2		2	11	101	9	70	22	0
Fort Morgan	11313	36	0	23		1	12	303	54	223	26	3
Fountain	28115	98	1	32		14	51	729	69	563	97	2
Fowler	1141	4	0	1		0	3	5	0	2	3	0
Fraser/Winter Park	2205	3	0	1		0	2	70	3	65	2	0
Frisco	3108	4	0	2		0	2	81	14	63	4	0
Fruita	12825	16	0	4		3	9	184	49	134	1	7
Garden City	269	13	0	0		0	13	29	2	23	4	0
Georgetown	1052	3	0	1		0	2	4	3	0	1	0
Glendale	5396	41	0	4		15	22	759	38	668	53	0
Glenwood Springs	9978	38	1	9		1	27	517	38	454	25	5
Golden	20616	31	0	4		3	24	480	36	402	42	1
Granby	1880	3	0	0		0	3	20	0	20	0	0
Grand Junction	60628	314	4	63		35	212	3060	362	2537	161	15
Greeley	102491	468	3	85		51	329	3275	506	2447	322	19
Greenwood Village	16024	34	0	7		6	21	614	83	480	51	3
Gunnison	6110	19	0	2		1	16	165	20	144	1	1
Gypsum	7012	4	0	1		1	2	71	5	60	6	0
Haxtun	926	1	0	0		0	1	21	2	19	0	0
Holyoke	2237	3	0	1		0	2	23	3	19	1	0
Hotchkiss	895	2	0	2		0	0	16	4	12	0	0
Hugo	737	2	0	0		0	2	12	3	7	2	0
Idaho Springs	1730	33	1	8		1	23	75	10	60	5	1
Ignacio	723	0	0	0		0	0	0	0	0	0	0
Johnstown	16143	13	0	8		0	5	114	7	93	14	0
Kersey	1602	0	0	0		0	0	14	4	10	0	0
Kiowa	753	0	0	0		0	0	2	1	0	1	0
Lafayette	28421	87	0	35		10	42	638	53	545	40	7
Lakeside	8	4	0	0		4	0	319	3	313	3	0
Lakewood	154553	875	4	144		174	553	8455	1014	6429	1012	30
La Salle	2070	3	0	0		0	3	54	11	34	9	1
Leadville	2656	6	1	0		0	5	44	8	32	4	1
Limon	1917	4	0	0		0	4	2	0	1	1	0
Littleton	47288	48	3	12		13	20	1296	240	907	149	2
Lochbuie	5516	7	0	0		2	5	99	13	74	12	0
Lone Tree	13593	33	2	5		7	19	967	56	911	0	3
Longmont	93268	292	0	104		32	156	2300	272	1860	168	41
Louisville	20814	21	0	0		2	19	73	36	27	10	3
Loveland	76936	184	1	41		20	122	1987	193	1719	75	11
Mancos	1388	0	0	0		0	0	19	5	14	0	1
Manitou Springs	5397	17	0	4		4	9	122	20	93	9	2
Mead	4713	11	1	1		1	8	80	16	55	9	1
Meeker	2344	5	0	1		0	4	17	0	15	2	0
Milliken	6551	3	0	0		0	3	41	4	34	3	1
Monte Vista	4262	24	0	3		1	20	224	81	130	13	1
Montrose	19054	29	0	1		2	26	835	87	713	35	2
Monument	6497	2	0	0		1	1	190	24	162	4	0
Morrison	436	0	0	0		0	0	0	0	0	0	0
Mountain View	532	0	0	0		0	0	11	5	4	2	0
Mountain Village	1412	0	0	0		0	0	17	2	15	0	0
Mount Crested Butte	833	2	0	1		0	1	23	4	19	0	0
Nederland	1534	2	0	0		1	1	25	3	19	3	0
New Castle	4706	3	0	1		0	2	43	4	34	5	1
Northglenn	39890	139	0	35		16	88	1353	164	897	292	7
Oak Creek	894	4	0	2		0	2	7	1	6	0	0
Ouray	1008	0	0	0		0	0	21	0	19	2	0
Pagosa Springs	1763	5	0	0		0	5	60	8	50	2	0
Palisade	2654	6	0	1		2	3	38	8	27	3	1
Palmer Lake	2621	0	0	0		0	0	0	0	0	0	0
Parachute	1110	10	0	1		1	8	21	7	12	2	0
Parker	50409	46	0	11		2	33	592	86	461	45	6
Pueblo	109927	1081	9	171		224	677	7473	1797	4505	1171	49
Rangely	2378	1	0	1		0	0	9	0	8	1	1
Rifle	9613	15	1	3		1	10	168	14	148	6	2
Salida	5516	7	0	3		1	3	186	15	157	14	0
Severance	3805	2	0	0		1	1	26	7	15	4	1
Sheridan	6113	20	1	3		5	11	465	48	364	53	2
Silt	3069	3	0	1		1	1	23	3	18	2	0
Simla	635	1	0	1		0	0	3	1	1	1	0
Snowmass Village	2935	1	0	0		0	1	49	0	48	1	0
Springfield	1385	1	0	0		0	1	14	7	6	1	0
Steamboat Springs	12512	31	0	8		2	21	299	40	253	6	1
Sterling	14087	47	0	22		2	23	495	91	375	29	5
Stratton	659	4	0	1		0	3	4	4	0	0	0
Telluride	2434	2	0	0		0	2	54	4	49	1	1
Thornton	136451	477	5	106		73	293	4309	525	3030	754	17
Timnath	3234	3	1	0		0	2	113	14	99	0	0
Trinidad	7990	32	0	3		12	17	490	151	321	18	7
Vail	5496	11	0	3		0	8	283	27	247	9	1
Walsenburg	2871	21	0	4		8	9	196	76	107	13	3
Westminster	114514	269	4	50		71	144	4004	377	2890	737	12
Wheat Ridge	31389	110	0	28		16	66	1490	207	1047	236	12

Table 6. Offenses Known to Law Enforcement, by Selected State and City, 2016—Continued

(Number.)

State/city	Population	Violent crime	Murder and nonnegligent manslaughter	Rape (revised definition)[1]	Rape (legacy definition)[2]	Robbery	Aggravated assault	Property crime	Burglary	Larceny-theft	Motor vehicle theft	Arson[3]
Windsor	22404	3	0	1		1	1	239	36	193	10	0
Woodland Park	7226	17	0	3		1	13	144	12	126	6	0
Wray	2382	0	0	0		0	0	9	2	7	0	0
Yuma	3612	0	0	0		0	0	0	0	0	0	0
CONNECTICUT												
Ansonia	18776	24	0	2		10	12	331	45	245	41	1
Avon	18464	1	0	0		1	0	131	4	119	8	0
Berlin	20695	20	0	3		7	10	323	38	257	28	0
Bethel	19712	1	1	0		0	0	162	26	121	15	0
Bloomfield	20801	52	0	9		11	32	515	54	418	43	4
Branford	28168	10	0	2		5	3	543	32	482	29	0
Bridgeport	148180	1115	10	69		441	595	3258	667	1857	734	9
Bristol	60445	55	0	10		23	22	953	183	660	110	2
Brookfield	17278	10	0	0		1	9	126	22	95	9	0
Canton	10337	0	0	0		0	0	120	4	107	9	0
Cheshire	29259	4	0	2		0	2	244	29	184	31	0
Clinton	13008	20	0	7		1	12	282	26	238	18	0
Coventry	12437	3	0	1		0	2	127	21	99	7	0
Cromwell	14041	7	0	0		4	3	369	18	328	23	0
Danbury	85335	161	0	30		75	56	1363	168	1056	139	5
Darien	21995	1	0	0		0	1	242	39	187	16	2
Derby	12660	39	0	6		21	12	298	65	195	38	0
East Hampton	12839	4	0	0		0	4	107	10	87	10	0
East Hartford	50733	147	4	26		51	66	1312	247	922	143	10
East Haven	28879	32	0	4		14	14	657	101	458	98	1
Easton	7649	1	0	0		0	1	40	7	33	0	0
East Windsor	11443	16	0	3		5	8	197	20	167	10	1
Enfield	44258	75	1	7		20	47	786	161	574	51	8
Fairfield	61889	38	0	3		17	18	1002	121	820	61	0
Farmington	25684	17	0	4		10	3	652	36	595	21	0
Granby	11301	2	0	0		0	2	77	5	71	1	0
Greenwich	62970	14	0	1		6	7	403	50	305	48	1
Groton	9189	17	0	4		1	12	207	29	162	16	2
Groton Long Point	512	0	0	0		0	0	4	2	2	0	0
Groton Town	29910	38	1	5		7	25	475	74	381	20	2
Guilford	22343	8	0	2		2	4	200	31	162	7	0
Hamden	61138	195	1	8		35	151	1507	211	1164	132	1
Hartford	123736	1353	14	65		476	798	5197	808	3616	773	112
Madison	18212	1	0	0		0	1	83	17	57	9	0
Manchester	57957	107	1	14		39	53	1559	152	1297	110	5
Meriden	59812	227	2	28		68	129	1367	292	914	161	9
Middlebury	7645	3	0	1		0	2	61	17	36	8	0
Middletown	46580	70	0	5		23	42	927	109	731	87	0
Milford	53752	34	0	0		27	7	1215	126	1001	88	2
Monroe	19898	2	0	0		2	0	82	16	63	3	0
Naugatuck	31469	37	0	8		13	16	545	86	413	46	1
New Britain	72720	216	1	47		73	95	2121	401	1257	463	2
New Canaan	20509	3	0	1		0	2	131	24	102	5	0
New Haven	130425	1219	13	66		400	740	5492	832	3925	735	21
Newington[7]	30610	22	0	5		10	7	790	60	671	59	1
New London	27092	193	1	11		30	151	743	130	532	81	1
New Milford	27111	29	1	8		2	18	272	3	256	13	4
Newtown	28105	3	0	0		1	2	83	20	58	5	1
North Branford	14234	6	0	1		3	2	125	19	97	9	0
North Haven	23777	22	0	2		6	14	582	100	433	49	0
Norwalk	88989	295	1	18		65	211	1427	239	1034	154	8
Norwich	39771	121	1	15		21	84	621	152	419	50	7
Old Saybrook	10145	1	0	0		0	1	117	2	114	1	0
Orange	13940	9	0	2		6	1	342	39	285	18	1
Plainfield	15015	14	0	7		4	3	61	18	35	8	0
Plainville	17782	31	1	3		6	21	490	45	419	26	2
Plymouth	11731	4	0	2		1	1	131	20	97	14	0
Portland	9369	9	0	0		2	7	79	11	62	6	0
Putnam	9331	25	0	4		3	18	112	19	88	5	0
Redding	9317	1	0	0		0	1	38	11	26	1	0
Ridgefield	25358	2	0	0		0	2	72	7	63	2	0
Rocky Hill	20801	9	0	4		4	1	289	28	239	22	1
Seymour	16462	7	0	2		1	4	178	42	119	17	1
Shelton	41638	28	0	4		15	9	435	134	252	49	0
Simsbury	24519	7	0	2		3	2	166	42	116	8	2
Southington	43948	41	0	15		20	6	942	105	770	67	2
South Windsor	25803	4	0	2		1	1	355	58	271	26	108
Stamford	130116	351	2	29		119	201	2073	268	1613	192	4
Stonington	18337	13	0	2		1	10	252	55	189	8	0
Stratford	52841	67	0	6		34	27	1160	177	867	116	4
Suffield	15641	9	0	2		1	6	96	23	65	8	1
Thomaston	7570	12	0	3		2	7	150	26	116	8	1
Torrington	34626	62	0	5		16	41	576	77	482	17	3
Trumbull	36741	42	0	11		23	8	896	77	796	23	1
Vernon	28915	20	1	1		6	12	339	51	256	32	1
Wallingford	44840	24	2	2		4	16	641	170	446	25	0
Waterbury[7]	108491	550	10	29		216	295	4199	755	2711	733	24

Table 6. Offenses Known to Law Enforcement, by Selected State and City, 2016—Continued

(Number.)

State/city	Population	Violent crime	Murder and nonnegligent manslaughter	Rape (revised definition)[1]	Rape (legacy definition)[2]	Robbery	Aggravated assault	Property crime	Burglary	Larceny-theft	Motor vehicle theft	Arson[3]
Waterford	19236	40	0	9		7	24	438	41	377	20	1
Watertown	21792	21	0	1		12	8	435	75	328	32	0
West Hartford	62979	40	0	2		38	0	1589	131	1351	107	2
West Haven	54800	135	2	15		48	70	1042	128	795	119	4
Weston	10425	0	0	0		0	0	15	1	14	0	0
Westport	28198	7	0	1		1	5	248	39	187	22	1
Willimantic	17766	24	0	5		12	7	232	47	166	19	2
Wilton	18845	1	0	1		0	0	71	15	50	6	0
Winchester	10750	7	0	2		4	1	192	47	138	7	0
Windsor	28998	29	0	7		8	14	543	54	441	48	0
Windsor Locks	12543	12	0	5		2	5	192	32	132	28	0
Wolcott	16666	5	0	0		4	1	288	65	185	38	0
Woodbridge	8864	1	0	0		1	0	132	32	89	11	1
DELAWARE												
Bethany Beach	1193	4	0	0		0	4	67	7	60	0	0
Blades	1377	5	0	0		2	3	29	9	19	1	0
Bridgeville	2297	9	0	0		2	7	59	5	53	1	0
Camden	3512	14	0	1		6	7	196	5	189	2	0
Cheswold	1424	2	0	0		1	1	21	2	19	0	0
Clayton	3165	6	0	0		0	6	37	14	23	0	0
Dagsboro	875	5	0	2		1	2	24	2	22	0	0
Delaware City	1750	4	0	2		1	1	84	18	63	3	0
Delmar	1757	15	0	0		5	10	64	23	39	2	0
Dewey Beach	378	16	0	2		1	13	43	8	34	1	0
Dover	37824	307	2	12		57	236	1880	100	1699	81	5
Ellendale	422	0	0	0		0	0	12	5	7	0	0
Elsmere	6149	28	0	2		5	21	151	29	107	15	0
Felton	1423	4	0	0		2	2	18	3	15	0	0
Fenwick Island	425	0	0	0		0	0	18	7	11	0	0
Frankford	950	2	0	0		0	2	13	5	7	1	0
Georgetown	7177	43	0	5		19	19	408	57	346	5	0
Greenwood	1086	0	0	0		0	0	21	2	19	0	0
Harrington	3719	35	0	4		6	25	110	19	84	7	1
Laurel	4150	47	0	6		6	35	167	42	122	3	0
Lewes	3065	3	0	0		1	2	63	9	53	1	0
Middletown	20666	70	0	8		20	42	500	44	450	6	0
Milford	10392	100	0	8		27	65	548	63	478	7	0
Millsboro	4286	20	0	4		7	9	179	16	161	2	0
Milton	2875	3	0	1		0	2	32	10	22	0	0
Newark	34297	114	0	7		40	67	765	85	654	26	3
New Castle	5392	32	1	3		11	17	189	16	164	9	0
Newport	1059	10	0	0		3	7	28	5	21	2	0
Ocean View	2075	3	0	0		0	3	29	9	20	0	0
Rehoboth Beach	1485	7	0	1		3	3	149	12	137	0	0
Seaford	7725	81	0	6		22	53	398	58	339	1	0
Selbyville	2440	9	0	2		2	5	78	25	49	4	0
Smyrna	11573	70	0	5		19	46	310	50	251	9	0
South Bethany	507	0	0	0		0	0	15	5	10	0	0
Wilmington	72183	1285	26	35		438	786	3544	812	2232	500	5
Wyoming	1497	6	0	0		1	5	22	8	14	0	0
DISTRICT OF COLUMBIA												
Washington	681170	7711	138	527		3149	3897	31661	2360	26402	2899	
FLORIDA												
Alachua	9900	42	0	6		4	32	306	64	219	23	1
Altamonte Springs	43499	152	8	16		35	93	1535	274	1185	76	4
Apalachicola	2291	4	0	0		0	4	26	6	10	10	0
Apopka	49796	224	1	28		39	156	2008	478	1400	130	6
Arcadia	7893	64	1	1		7	55	189	101	81	7	0
Atlantic Beach	13302	46	0	1		16	29	345	64	251	30	0
Atlantis	2126	4	0	0		1	3	48	11	35	2	0
Auburndale	15356	29	1	1		9	18	574	120	428	26	2
Aventura	38009	64	0	0		34	30	1929	99	1789	41	1
Bal Harbour Village	2955	2	0	0		0	2	93	7	84	2	0
Bartow	19322	121	2	13		26	80	869	143	692	34	2
Bay Harbor Islands	6117	1	0	0		0	1	39	4	28	7	0
Belleair	4017	1	0	0		0	1	103	10	75	18	0
Belleair Beach	1619	3	0	0		0	3	26	1	21	4	0
Belleair Bluffs	2108	2	0	0		1	1	49	8	37	4	0
Belle Glade	18405	295	8	12		60	215	966	279	629	58	1
Belle Isle	6835	14	2	0		5	7	107	33	69	5	0
Belleview	4813	26	0	3		8	15	211	57	151	3	1
Biscayne Park	3243	2	0	0		2	0	98	37	54	7	0
Blountstown	2495	13	0	0		1	12	36	4	31	1	0
Boca Raton	94931	239	1	22		105	111	2495	507	1831	157	1
Bowling Green	2916	12	0	0		5	7	68	19	47	2	0
Boynton Beach	75141	495	1	3		167	324	3572	566	2752	254	4
Bradenton	55518	328	4	31		72	221	1713	325	1323	65	5
Bradenton Beach	1257	1	0	0		0	1	23	1	21	1	0
Brooksville	7881	55	0	5		13	37	309	50	241	18	0
Bunnell	2856	24	0	1		2	21	107	13	80	14	0

Table 6. Offenses Known to Law Enforcement, by Selected State and City, 2016—Continued

(Number.)

State/city	Population	Violent crime	Murder and nonnegligent manslaughter	Rape (revised definition)[1]	Rape (legacy definition)[2]	Robbery	Aggravated assault	Property crime	Burglary	Larceny-theft	Motor vehicle theft	Arson[3]
Cape Coral	179631	224	5	16		31	172	3081	632	2286	163	4
Carrabelle	2723	7	0	0		0	7	25	11	12	2	0
Casselberry	27220	153	1	17		32	103	1067	163	862	42	5
Center Hill	1241	3	0	1		0	2	0	0	0	0	0
Chattahoochee	3059	14	1	1		2	10	34	11	16	7	0
Chiefland	2213	9	0	0		3	6	225	110	115	0	0
Chipley	3557	14	0	0		3	11	170	32	133	5	0
Clearwater	113904	636	5	89		145	397	3755	555	2968	232	17
Clermont	33158	53	1	2		10	40	720	108	583	29	2
Clewiston	7579	36	0	1		7	28	240	39	197	4	1
Cocoa	17825	369	3	27		82	257	1210	244	854	112	5
Cocoa Beach	11669	62	1	6		11	44	717	86	597	34	1
Coconut Creek	60633	73	0	12		26	35	1249	136	995	118	0
Cooper City	36900	35	0	9		10	16	438	47	363	28	0
Coral Gables	51980	77	0	8		27	42	1550	197	1285	68	2
Coral Springs	131159	209	1	19		75	114	2411	198	2034	179	3
Crescent City	1533	12	0	0		7	5	48	12	33	3	0
Crestview	23749	121	3	20		19	79	897	157	678	62	3
Cutler Bay	45799	152	0	10		52	90	1531	179	1262	90	0
Dade City	7061	37	0	3		10	24	312	50	251	11	2
Dania	31806	188	3	11		67	107	1104	179	808	117	2
Davenport	3677	11	0	0		1	10	46	12	30	4	0
Davie	102692	228	3	28		74	123	2971	340	2322	309	12
Daytona Beach	65495	814	9	26		94	685	4197	572	3234	391	7
Daytona Beach Shores	4417	25	1	5		5	14	196	26	158	12	3
Deerfield Beach	80713	277	2	33		93	149	2193	376	1597	220	3
De Funiak Springs	5927	49	1	2		2	44	77	9	66	2	0
DeLand	30881	178	3	0		46	129	1447	265	1063	119	4
Delray Beach	67400	387	5	31		125	226	2842	385	2218	239	11
Doral	58309	80	0	6		14	60	1714	157	1408	149	0
Dunedin	36334	54	0	16		8	30	695	84	572	39	1
Dunnellon	1786	4	0	0		1	3	135	21	104	10	0
Eatonville	2293	28	0	3		5	20	104	17	75	12	0
Edgewater	21729	21	0	0		1	20	248	46	187	15	2
Edgewood	2856	5	0	0		2	3	84	17	54	13	0
El Portal	2509	10	0	2		5	3	74	20	47	7	0
Eustis	20292	48	1	7		15	25	669	161	470	38	1
Fellsmere	5572	7	0	0		0	7	89	24	61	4	0
Fernandina Beach	12489	34	2	3		5	24	243	59	183	1	1
Flagler Beach	4946	13	0	3		1	9	91	15	70	6	1
Florida City	12297	344	1	6		112	225	1092	129	917	46	0
Fort Lauderdale	181218	1144	18	71		483	572	10630	1856	7856	918	22
Fort Myers	76579	947	15	55		161	716	2163	354	1589	220	10
Fort Pierce	44987	317	7	23		79	208	1542	360	1088	94	10
Fort Walton Beach	22314	67	3	12		10	42	611	72	490	49	2
Fruitland Park	4548	8	0	2		1	5	123	39	79	5	0
Gainesville	131242	870	3	142		189	536	4908	590	3951	367	8
Golden Beach	982	1	0	0		1	0	7	1	5	1	0
Graceville	2211	3	0	0		0	3	40	22	14	4	0
Greenacres City	40088	145	0	18		48	79	946	171	706	69	2
Green Cove Springs	7352	56	2	11		3	40	172	33	128	11	0
Gretna	1371	9	0	2		3	4	48	28	19	1	1
Gulf Breeze	6435	9	0	0		0	9	102	13	87	2	0
Gulfport	12384	26	0	2		6	18	470	66	375	29	2
Gulf Stream	846	0	0	0		0	0	10	1	8	1	1
Haines City	23278	61	2	5		20	34	434	65	343	26	1
Hallandale	39960	242	3	14		106	119	1561	240	1188	133	2
Havana	1674	5	0	2		0	3	16	6	8	2	0
Hialeah	239451	580	7	39		167	367	5597	465	4503	629	28
Hialeah Gardens	24370	39	0	0		9	30	581	53	460	68	2
Highland Beach	3767	2	0	0		0	2	34	6	22	6	0
High Springs	5932	15	0	1		1	13	104	25	79	0	0
Hillsboro Beach	2030	0	0	0		0	0	24	4	17	3	0
Holly Hill	12002	71	0	3		8	60	698	113	538	47	1
Hollywood	151510	574	7	49		221	297	4990	778	3677	535	4
Holmes Beach	4274	5	0	1		0	4	90	20	67	3	1
Homestead	67700	801	9	55		314	423	2728	481	2087	160	9
Howey-in-the-Hills	1179	2	0	0		0	2	9	5	4	0	0
Hypoluxo	2745	6	0	0		1	5	69	3	53	13	1
Indialantic	2861	6	0	0		1	5	66	24	40	2	0
Indian Creek Village	92	0	0	0		0	0	1	0	1	0	0
Indian Harbour Beach	8523	11	0	1		2	8	121	27	86	8	1
Indian River Shores	4209	1	0	0		0	1	12	3	9	0	0
Indian Rocks Beach	4280	6	0	0		0	6	94	12	75	7	0
Indian Shores	3702	6	0	1		0	5	33	1	30	2	0
Interlachen	1346	5	0	0		1	4	54	18	31	5	0
Jacksonville	880557	5504	106	517		1463	3418	31538	5851	22660	3027	83
Jacksonville Beach	23418	109	0	14		32	63	1237	116	1024	97	1
Jasper	4099	6	0	0		0	6	59	29	24	6	0
Jennings	869	0	0	0		0	0	12	3	9	0	0
Juno Beach	3532	4	0	0		0	4	77	7	66	4	0
Jupiter	64273	147	0	15		40	92	1261	163	1038	60	2
Jupiter Inlet Colony	454	0	0	0		0	0	2	1	0	1	0

Table 6. Offenses Known to Law Enforcement, by Selected State and City, 2016—Continued

(Number.)

State/city	Population	Violent crime	Murder and nonnegligent manslaughter	Rape (revised definition)[1]	Rape (legacy definition)[2]	Robbery	Aggravated assault	Property crime	Burglary	Larceny-theft	Motor vehicle theft	Arson[3]
Jupiter Island	901	0	0	0		0	0	6	1	4	1	0
Kenneth City	5095	19	0	3		4	12	140	13	115	12	0
Key Biscayne	13113	2	0	0		1	1	155	9	124	22	0
Key Colony Beach	862	0	0	0		0	0	12	6	6	0	0
Key West	25976	102	1	12		18	71	1003	110	811	82	0
Kissimmee	71197	508	0	47		114	347	2670	585	1955	130	5
Lady Lake	14877	22	0	0		2	20	223	28	179	16	0
Lake Alfred	5568	3	0	0		2	1	98	32	60	6	0
Lake City	12186	186	2	6		23	155	877	137	707	33	1
Lake Clarke Shores	3586	7	0	0		1	6	66	10	50	6	0
Lake Hamilton	1370	8	0	0		1	7	67	29	33	5	0
Lake Helen	2700	9	0	0		1	8	32	6	24	2	0
Lakeland	105766	337	4	89		104	140	5111	751	4050	310	1
Lake Mary	16506	29	0	5		4	20	311	62	237	12	0
Lake Park	8613	91	2	2		36	51	850	103	662	85	2
Lake Placid	2172	11	0	2		2	7	102	16	84	2	1
Lake Wales	15819	49	1	1		18	29	514	76	412	26	0
Lake Worth	38021	510	10	36		185	279	1878	432	1261	185	7
Lantana	11239	63	0	8		22	33	558	82	417	59	0
Largo	81402	390	3	60		116	211	2989	458	2289	242	7
Lauderdale-by-the-Sea	6541	14	0	3		3	8	124	26	90	8	1
Lauderdale Lakes	35222	265	2	14		102	147	1686	266	1252	168	6
Lauderhill	72504	654	10	22		247	375	2332	541	1452	339	1
Lawtey	717	2	0	0		0	2	12	10	2	0	0
Leesburg	22313	208	1	21		37	149	1110	260	774	76	1
Lighthouse Point	11256	10	0	0		4	6	195	27	156	12	0
Live Oak	6946	84	1	0		25	58	250	124	112	14	0
Longboat Key	7343	0	0	0		0	0	52	8	43	1	0
Longwood	14171	50	0	7		10	33	466	89	337	40	1
Lynn Haven	20496	53	0	4		8	41	439	55	361	23	0
Madeira Beach	4404	18	0	3		3	12	167	17	147	3	0
Madison	2849	47	1	3		3	40	179	60	115	4	0
Maitland	17824	29	0	9		5	15	475	74	369	32	0
Manalapan	458	0	0	0		0	0	16	2	14	0	0
Mangonia Park	1997	38	0	3		5	30	221	24	176	21	0
Marco Island	17947	2	0	1		0	1	94	13	76	5	0
Margate	58030	134	2	8		30	94	962	159	698	105	7
Marianna	9464	56	0	7		1	48	169	53	112	4	3
Mascotte	5549	17	0	3		1	13	86	41	41	4	1
Medley	853	10	0	1		1	8	242	35	159	48	0
Melbourne	80900	667	3	65		126	473	3308	686	2439	183	14
Melbourne Beach	3243	2	0	0		0	2	31	13	17	1	0
Melbourne Village	697	0	0	0		0	0	5	0	5	0	0
Mexico Beach	1187	5	0	0		1	4	46	8	37	1	0
Miami	449469	3989	55	90		1443	2401	18974	2643	14335	1996	56
Miami Beach	93165	940	7	57		345	531	8419	603	7251	565	6
Miami Gardens	114349	743	22	24		265	432	3671	509	2743	419	22
Miami Lakes	31279	31	0	5		10	16	591	58	480	53	1
Miami Shores	10920	53	1	1		31	20	532	103	399	30	0
Miami Springs	14620	37	0	1		15	21	458	48	365	45	0
Midway	3325	5	0	0		3	2	22	11	11	0	0
Milton	9788	28	0	3		7	18	265	101	149	15	0
Minneola	11006	23	0	4		3	16	160	27	126	7	0
Miramar	140288	446	5	28		133	280	2740	344	2117	279	8
Monticello	2393	20	1	0		1	18	35	17	17	1	0
Mount Dora	13796	45	0	9		7	29	356	88	257	11	1
Naples	21917	19	3	4		3	9	408	52	339	17	1
Neptune Beach	7316	15	0	0		6	9	176	27	137	12	0
New Port Richey	16038	166	1	7		29	129	590	105	441	44	10
New Smyrna Beach	24658	103	0	4		7	92	840	166	626	48	7
Niceville	15142	21	0	0		3	18	257	60	184	13	0
North Bay Village	8552	16	0	3		2	11	138	22	88	28	0
North Lauderdale	44229	209	1	24		68	116	941	207	596	138	2
North Miami	62974	454	2	36		171	245	2598	364	1983	251	8
North Miami Beach	44442	301	2	14		107	178	1687	239	1298	150	3
North Palm Beach	13023	11	0	0		2	9	172	44	112	16	0
North Port	63386	89	1	21		11	56	861	166	668	27	0
North Redington Beach	1473	0	0	0		0	0	25	3	21	1	0
Oakland	2890	4	0	1		0	3	55	11	42	2	1
Oakland Park	44903	217	4	18		72	123	2060	370	1516	174	3
Ocala	58596	463	10	29		111	313	3174	443	2600	131	14
Ocean Ridge	1928	3	0	0		1	2	77	5	64	8	0
Ocoee	45330	134	2	11		26	95	1571	307	1197	67	2
Okeechobee	5604	21	0	1		7	13	319	42	259	18	0
Oldsmar	14283	17	1	2		5	9	419	52	355	12	1
Opa Locka	16835	374	5	6		81	282	1082	209	721	152	2
Orange City	11262	48	0	10		12	26	762	76	661	25	2
Orange Park	8763	48	0	12		11	25	178	50	115	13	0
Orlando[8]	277719	2328	84	211		504	1529	14498	3637	9621	1240	15
Ormond Beach	41325	202	0	17		40	145	1602	312	1158	132	8
Oviedo	39636	78	4	14		7	53	361	73	281	7	1
Pahokee	6132	85	1	3		8	73	219	51	155	13	7
Palatka	10362	81	2	2		18	59	587	98	469	20	1

Table 6. Offenses Known to Law Enforcement, by Selected State and City, 2016—Continued

(Number.)

State/city	Population	Violent crime	Murder and nonnegligent manslaughter	Rape (revised definition)[1]	Rape (legacy definition)[2]	Robbery	Aggravated assault	Property crime	Burglary	Larceny-theft	Motor vehicle theft	Arson[3]
Palm Bay	108823	516	4	57		47	408	1841	454	1252	135	13
Palm Beach	8702	4	0	0		0	4	137	31	88	18	0
Palm Beach Gardens	53811	75	1	13		27	34	1421	168	1184	69	2
Palm Beach Shores	1221	7	0	0		0	7	33	11	21	1	0
Palmetto	13371	94	1	13		18	62	412	55	344	13	1
Palmetto Bay	24878	49	0	5		23	21	748	106	607	35	1
Palm Springs	22581	88	1	3		27	57	1086	165	844	77	3
Panama City	38847	276	3	17		50	206	2098	330	1587	181	10
Panama City Beach	12844	118	1	19		25	73	1116	113	993	10	2
Parker	4661	21	1	2		2	16	155	31	115	9	1
Parkland	31571	18	0	4		3	11	170	27	130	13	3
Pembroke Park	6379	35	1	1		17	16	331	53	238	40	2
Pembroke Pines	169156	342	1	26		101	214	3750	346	3141	263	2
Pensacola	53424	348	7	27		64	250	2184	341	1741	102	7
Perry	7063	79	1	5		3	70	188	41	140	7	1
Pinellas Park	52113	211	4	21		56	130	2650	351	2127	172	2
Plantation	94075	217	3	4		104	106	3081	362	2466	253	5
Plant City	37949	157	5	16		35	101	1251	198	970	83	7
Pompano Beach	109362	931	7	77		344	503	5205	903	3738	564	9
Ponce Inlet	3183	5	0	0		0	5	40	6	33	1	0
Port Orange	60546	61	1	1		10	49	1477	182	1216	79	0
Port Richey	2779	5	0	1		1	3	171	14	152	5	1
Port St. Joe	3441	23	0	0		2	21	46	22	24	0	0
Port St. Lucie	182365	270	3	22		48	197	2419	400	1934	85	9
Punta Gorda	18466	12	1	0		1	10	212	24	177	11	0
Redington Beaches	1480	1	0	0		0	1	33	4	26	3	0
Riviera Beach	34304	475	9	23		56	387	1341	309	902	130	6
Rockledge	26967	83	0	10		14	59	512	105	361	46	5
Royal Palm Beach	38353	126	0	10		24	92	789	71	681	37	5
Safety Harbor	17573	20	0	1		3	16	244	39	188	17	0
Sanford	59027	542	6	48		138	350	2812	466	2165	181	3
Sanibel	7395	6	0	1		0	5	86	43	41	2	3
Sarasota	55732	291	3	19		85	184	2199	314	1763	122	2
Satellite Beach	10737	10	0	6		1	3	106	23	73	10	0
Sea Ranch Lakes	739	1	0	0		1	0	15	1	13	1	0
Sebastian	24441	42	0	4		7	31	467	69	376	22	2
Sebring	10516	45	3	4		7	31	499	110	369	20	0
Seminole	18364	34	0	2		13	19	534	59	458	17	0
Sewall's Point	2180	1	0	0		1	0	10	2	8	0	0
South Bay	5147	66	0	0		6	60	123	26	91	6	1
South Daytona	12653	58	1	0		12	45	387	75	272	40	1
South Miami	12354	56	2	6		11	37	541	116	409	16	0
South Palm Beach	1437	0	0	0		0	0	8	2	5	1	0
South Pasadena	5106	7	0	1		3	3	113	7	102	4	0
Southwest Ranches	7953	9	0	1		4	4	144	15	100	29	0
Springfield	9550	49	0	5		6	38	273	54	197	22	0
Starke	5390	53	1	0		7	45	126	7	112	7	0
St. Augustine	14359	110	4	8		14	84	648	75	546	27	7
St. Augustine Beach	6986	4	0	0		0	4	135	16	116	3	0
St. Cloud	47289	134	4	11		12	107	747	189	507	51	3
St. Pete Beach	9654	35	0	6		3	26	386	18	346	22	1
St. Petersburg	259510	1727	20	122		556	1029	12804	1938	9771	1095	37
Stuart	16640	64	0	13		10	41	568	68	491	9	1
Sunny Isles Beach	22374	24	0	3		7	14	350	33	286	31	0
Sunrise	94400	252	0	21		100	131	3076	317	2531	228	3
Surfside	6077	12	0	1		0	11	170	14	148	8	1
Sweetwater	21007	39	0	2		12	25	732	74	594	64	0
Tallahassee	191564	1686	11	207		405	1063	11073	2120	7854	1099	7
Tamarac	65516	133	2	12		54	65	1387	245	1018	124	2
Tampa	375904	1906	29	80		488	1309	7800	1477	5695	628	62
Tarpon Springs	24834	104	1	14		15	74	592	60	506	26	1
Tavares	15741	64	1	5		9	49	310	119	184	7	0
Temple Terrace	25972	97	2	7		25	63	758	163	553	42	2
Tequesta	6003	4	0	1		1	2	65	28	34	3	0
Titusville	45723	355	3	40		61	251	1868	463	1183	222	6
Treasure Island	6925	27	0	3		5	19	259	28	225	6	2
Trenton	2079	3	0	0		0	3	11	2	9	0	0
Umatilla	3751	5	0	0		1	4	79	19	55	5	0
Valparaiso	5023	5	0	0		1	4	93	28	56	9	0
Venice	22514	24	0	5		5	14	374	65	293	16	1
Vero Beach	16589	69	3	6		12	48	426	88	323	15	0
Village of Pinecrest	19692	25	0	0		21	4	571	97	437	37	0
Virginia Gardens	2508	1	0	0		0	1	46	7	34	5	0
Wauchula	4936	19	0	3		0	16	120	34	80	6	0
Welaka	677	5	0	0		0	5	11	6	5	0	0
Wellington	63765	112	2	17		19	74	1020	134	793	93	3
West Melbourne	21156	32	0	1		5	26	574	86	449	39	2
West Miami	7163	8	0	1		3	4	99	18	74	7	0
Weston	70882	36	0	5		13	18	343	43	261	39	3
West Palm Beach	108074	954	10	71		333	540	5599	946	4100	553	23
West Park	15285	121	1	5		29	86	494	104	326	64	2
White Springs	773	1	0	0		0	1	35	11	23	1	1
Wildwood	6788	50	1	3		4	42	200	52	136	12	0

Table 6. Offenses Known to Law Enforcement, by Selected State and City, 2016—Continued

(Number.)

State/city	Population	Violent crime	Murder and nonnegligent manslaughter	Rape (revised definition)[1]	Rape (legacy definition)[2]	Robbery	Aggravated assault	Property crime	Burglary	Larceny-theft	Motor vehicle theft	Arson[3]
Williston	2741	8	0	0		2	6	69	14	52	3	0
Wilton Manors	12535	55	0	6		13	36	504	103	367	34	1
Windermere	3320	6	0	4		0	2	37	9	24	4	0
Winter Garden	41556	134	1	5		19	109	1427	166	1181	80	3
Winter Haven	38488	196	2	10		33	151	1339	238	1021	80	3
Winter Park	30359	100	2	12		21	65	1035	216	766	53	2
Winter Springs	35100	54	0	6		11	37	440	74	347	19	0
Zephyrhills	14833	51	1	7		7	36	879	86	772	21	5
GEORGIA												
Abbeville	2796	4	0		0	0	4	25	12	10	3	0
Acworth	22467	43	0		5	8	30	570	56	480	34	0
Adairsville	4804	12	0		0	3	9	138	23	106	9	0
Adel	5313	48	0		3	19	26	311	71	232	8	0
Alamo	3374	2	0		0	0	2	41	2	39	0	0
Alapaha	653	0	0		0	0	0	8	2	5	1	0
Albany	74330	873	16		28	204	625	3620	888	2585	147	37
Alma	3548	28	1		1	11	15	291	120	156	15	0
Alpharetta	64943	35	1		5	20	9	1308	135	1129	44	1
Alto	1166	1	0		0	0	1	5	1	4	0	0
Americus	15838	174	6		3	45	120	1115	185	911	19	3
Aragon	1241	6	0		0	0	6	9	3	5	1	0
Arcade	1801	7	0		0	1	6	23	8	15	0	0
Arlington	1392	13	0		0	2	11	28	9	18	1	0
Ashburn	3757	40	0		3	7	30	184	45	135	4	0
Athens-Clarke County	123934	533	4		53	163	313	4100	822	3054	224	15
Atlanta	472579	5121	111		136	2070	2804	24804	4411	16400	3993	50
Attapulgus	432	2	0		0	0	2	1	0	1	0	
Auburn	7621	16	0		3	1	12	136	18	106	12	0
Austell	7204	38	0		0	7	31	177	27	117	33	0
Avondale Estates	3175	3	0		0	3	0	72	18	51	3	0
Bainbridge	12473	55	0		4	13	38	464	134	330	0	5
Baldwin	3287	7	0		2	0	5	65	24	40	1	0
Ball Ground	1784	0	0		0	0	0	18	3	15	0	0
Barnesville	6611	36	1		0	3	32	218	30	182	6	5
Baxley	4452	40	0		1	6	33	317	88	218	11	1
Berlin	559	0	0		0	0	0	0	0	0	0	0
Blackshear	3608	41	0		0	3	38	134	15	117	2	0
Blairsville	542	2	0		0	2	0	24	2	20	2	0
Blakely	4839	35	0		2	3	30	97	22	72	3	0
Bloomingdale	2778	7	0		1	1	5	75	24	36	15	0
Blue Ridge	1286	7	0		0	0	7	10	3	6	1	0
Blythe	697	0	0		0	0	0	5	1	3	1	0
Bowdon	2078	6	0		0	0	6	65	12	50	3	0
Braselton	9912	11	2		3	2	4	85	6	59	20	1
Braswell	390	0	0		0	0	0	0	0	0	0	0
Bremen	6380	16	0		0	2	14	269	29	230	10	0
Brookhaven	52442	172	2		5	92	73	1425	276	1018	131	2
Brooklet	1468	3	0		0	2	1	19	3	15	1	0
Brunswick	16309	164	3		5	36	120	775	196	528	51	2
Buchanan	1167	7	0		0	1	6	47	11	35	1	0
Buena Vista	2206	3	0		0	0	3	46	15	29	2	0
Butler	1868	1	0		0	0	1	11	6	5	0	0
Byron	5222	6	0		1	2	3	124	18	98	8	0
Cairo	9772	15	0		0	5	10	274	43	215	16	0
Calhoun	16439	43	0		6	3	34	639	160	464	15	0
Camilla	5080	13	0		0	2	11	237	63	170	4	0
Canon	803	0	0		0	0	0	4	2	2	0	0
Canton	25985	65	3		14	13	35	590	51	523	16	0
Carrollton	26593	138	1		10	27	100	1116	125	957	34	2
Cave Spring	1168	0	0		0	0	0	22	8	14	0	0
Cedartown	9858	50	1		7	4	38	473	117	327	29	0
Centerville	7657	13	0		0	3	10	248	28	203	17	0
Chamblee	28532	189	4		0	86	99	1411	153	1117	141	0
Chatsworth	4362	5	0		0	0	5	29	1	27	1	0
Chattahoochee Hills	2754	3	0		0	1	2	43	13	27	3	0
Chickamauga	3107	2	0		1	1	0	33	12	18	3	0
Clarkston	12335	83	0		2	41	40	461	157	248	56	0
Claxton	2324	13	0		0	7	6	78	32	44	2	1
Clayton	2250	5	0		1	2	2	80	10	69	1	0
Cleveland	3828	16	0		0	1	15	214	47	163	4	0
Cochran	4234	26	2		2	5	17	248	46	197	5	0
College Park	14724	279	6		12	130	131	1405	309	882	214	2
Colquitt	1864	4	0		1	0	3	44	8	36	0	0
Columbus	202338	1218	24		62	523	609	9625	2273	6500	852	19
Commerce	6803	49	0		3	4	42	156	23	124	9	0
Conyers	16004	114	0		4	41	69	701	101	555	45	3
Coolidge	526	4	0		0	4	0	2	0	1	1	0
Cordele	10907	38	2		2	8	26	518	112	390	16	0
Cornelia	4232	15	0		3	0	12	196	23	168	5	1
Covington	14077	71	1		6	24	40	835	141	642	52	0
Cumming	5772	7	0		0	2	5	277	31	233	13	0
Cuthbert	3636	4	0		0	1	3	32	10	22	0	0

Table 6. Offenses Known to Law Enforcement, by Selected State and City, 2016—Continued

(Number.)

State/city	Population	Violent crime	Murder and nonnegligent manslaughter	Rape (revised definition)[1]	Rape (legacy definition)[2]	Robbery	Aggravated assault	Property crime	Burglary	Larceny-theft	Motor vehicle theft	Arson[3]
Dallas	13135	11	0		2	1	8	198	24	160	14	0
Dalton	33989	113	0		17	22	74	1103	209	834	60	6
Danielsville	579	1	0		0	0	1	16	3	13	0	0
Darien	1842	2	0		1	0	1	49	17	31	1	1
Davisboro	1989	0	0		0	0	0	2	2	0	0	0
Dawson	4315	24	0		0	7	17	157	55	101	1	0
Decatur	22449	41	1		2	26	12	525	85	404	36	3
Demorest	2088	3	0		0	0	3	17	6	10	1	0
Dillard	332	1	0		0	1	0	2	1	1	0	0
Doerun	772	1	0		0	0	1	9	2	5	2	0
Donalsonville	2680	12	0		1	5	6	59	9	46	4	2
Doraville	11008	48	0		5	32	11	574	76	449	49	0
Douglasville	33287	234	4		21	49	160	2092	206	1791	95	2
Dublin	16195	122	2		10	46	64	931	224	676	31	0
Duluth	29720	160	0		2	20	138	641	70	527	44	1
Dunwoody	49232	78	0		3	37	38	2067	156	1836	75	0
East Ellijay	558	4	0		0	0	4	114	1	110	3	0
Eastman	5232	47	0		5	7	35	498	63	427	8	0
East Point	35791	422	10		15	224	173	3693	637	2474	582	3
Eatonton	6528	22	1		1	4	16	169	24	140	5	1
Edison	1467	6	0		0	1	5	5	2	3	0	0
Elberton	4432	51	1		2	2	46	275	61	204	10	0
Ellaville	1892	4	0		0	0	4	27	5	22	0	0
Ellijay	1691	5	0		2	0	3	43	7	33	3	0
Emerson	1546	12	0		1	3	8	91	13	77	1	0
Enigma	1285	0	0		0	0	0	9	1	8	0	0
Ephesus	418	0	0		0	0	0	0	0	0	0	0
Eton	902	2	0		1	0	1	15	1	14	0	0
Fairburn	14151	46	0		1	26	19	722	256	407	59	1
Fairmount	739	2	0		0	0	2	12	1	11	0	0
Fayetteville	17157	22	0		2	14	6	523	40	462	21	0
Fitzgerald	9001	41	3		0	10	28	462	130	322	10	5
Flowery Branch	6895	6	1		2	2	1	155	19	131	5	1
Folkston	5349	12	0		0	1	11	103	42	57	4	0
Forest Park	19570	161	4		20	72	65	1066	228	698	140	6
Forsyth	4042	16	0		2	3	11	135	14	114	7	0
Fort Oglethorpe	9911	63	0		3	9	51	635	34	571	30	0
Fort Valley	8374	96	0		0	12	84	331	86	228	17	0
Franklin	964	3	0		1	0	2	46	2	44	0	0
Franklin Springs	1195	1	0		0	0	1	7	1	4	2	0
Gainesville	39425	162	3		14	56	89	1405	202	1107	96	3
Garden City	9040	126	0		4	13	109	457	175	271	11	3
Glennville	5068	10	0		0	2	8	134	26	102	6	1
Glenwood	737	0	0		0	0	0	0	0	0	0	0
Gordon	1946	1	0		0	1	0	11	2	9	0	0
Grantville	3208	2	0		0	1	1	65	15	43	7	0
Gray	3271	7	1		0	2	4	52	3	48	1	0
Greensboro	3411	28	0		0	1	27	104	21	81	2	0
Greenville	860	3	0		1	2	0	13	4	8	1	0
Griffin	23134	228	2		18	43	165	1385	210	1125	50	10
Grovetown	13469	12	1		2	3	6	179	40	131	8	0
Guyton	1891	4	0		1	1	2	36	4	28	4	0
Hagan	962	1	0		0	0	1	5	4	0	1	0
Hahira	2928	5	0		0	3	2	85	16	64	5	0
Hampton	7451	16	0		3	1	12	124	29	88	7	0
Hapeville	6701	58	1		2	38	17	696	43	559	94	0
Harlem	3026	0	0		0	0	0	28	4	22	2	0
Hartwell	4523	15	0		1	2	12	258	26	225	7	0
Hazlehurst	4189	17	0		3	0	14	236	42	191	3	1
Helen	536	9	0		1	4	4	85	13	67	5	0
Hephzibah	3920	16	0		0	0	16	62	15	46	1	0
Hiawassee	911	1	0		0	0	1	34	13	19	2	0
Hinesville	33477	215	2		14	49	150	1252	210	1011	31	6
Hiram	3840	11	0		4	6	1	365	23	325	17	0
Hoboken	531	0	0		0	0	0	2	2	0	0	0
Hogansville	3126	23	0		2	1	20	124	31	86	7	0
Holly Springs	11034	11	0		2	1	8	219	25	187	7	0
Homeland	861	0	0		0	0	0	0	0	0	0	0
Homerville	2487	20	0		0	5	15	155	29	121	5	0
Irwinton	557	0	0		0	0	0	1	1	0	0	0
Jackson	4966	7	0		0	1	6	97	19	73	5	0
Jasper	3777	6	0		0	1	5	195	12	179	4	0
Jefferson	10340	14	0		1	4	9	223	41	171	11	0
Jeffersonville	1055	0	0		0	0	0	6	3	3	0	0
Jesup	9525	53	3		5	9	36	640	82	540	18	0
Johns Creek	84629	27	0		4	12	11	687	120	549	18	4
Jonesboro	4752	18	0		1	5	12	219	30	156	33	0
Kennesaw	34204	66	0		7	16	43	607	103	479	25	1
Kingsland	16597	44	0		1	4	39	377	80	281	16	2
Kingston	657	0	0		0	0	0	1	0	1	0	0
Lafayette	7185	18	0		4	2	12	286	24	251	11	2
LaGrange	30931	154	4		4	63	83	1631	289	1255	87	5
Lake City	2752	13	0		1	6	6	160	17	129	14	0

Table 6. Offenses Known to Law Enforcement, by Selected State and City, 2016—Continued

(Number.)

State/city	Population	Violent crime	Murder and nonnegligent manslaughter	Rape (revised definition)[1]	Rape (legacy definition)[2]	Robbery	Aggravated assault	Property crime	Burglary	Larceny-theft	Motor vehicle theft	Arson[3]
Lakeland	3314	17	1		3	4	9	81	22	46	13	0
Lake Park	729	5	0		0	1	4	21	9	11	1	0
Lavonia	2168	23	1		0	0	22	107	11	92	4	0
Lawrenceville	30913	90	2		10	43	35	979	159	765	55	0
Leary	583	0	0		0	0	0	2	1	1	0	0
Leslie	384	2	0		0	2	0	2	0	2	0	0
Lilburn	12854	35	1		4	14	16	488	58	406	24	0
Lithonia	2042	14	0		0	1	13	105	24	60	21	0
Locust Grove	5862	9	1		2	4	2	392	27	351	14	0
Loganville	11409	11	0		0	3	8	363	44	303	16	0
Lookout Mountain	1574	0	0		0	0	0	10	4	5	1	0
Louisville	2333	12	0		1	3	8	120	28	91	1	0
Ludowici	2160	0	0		0	0	0	25	8	17	0	0
Lumber City	1241	0	0		0	0	0	3	1	2	0	0
Lumpkin	1084	0	0		0	0	0	0	0	0	0	0
Lyons	4372	12	1		1	3	7	180	50	128	2	0
Madison	4034	10	1		0	4	5	163	26	133	4	0
Manchester	4068	21	0		2	3	16	87	17	65	5	3
Marietta	59516	233	1		12	117	103	2282	307	1825	150	2
Marshallville	1313	2	0		0	0	2	8	1	7	0	1
Maysville	1876	0	0		0	0	0	31	4	25	2	1
McDonough	23675	30	0		1	15	14	727	121	568	38	2
McIntyre	615	1	0		0	0	1	11	2	9	0	0
McRae-Helena	8786	13	0		0	4	9	161	35	125	1	0
Metter	4107	23	1		4	5	13	158	34	120	4	2
Midville	262	0	0		0	0	0	0	0	0	0	0
Midway	1992	5	0		0	2	3	44	5	35	4	0
Milledgeville	19072	112	1		8	28	75	774	146	615	13	2
Milton	38551	10	1		3	1	5	338	49	284	5	2
Molena	372	0	0		0	0	0	0	0	0	0	0
Monroe	13716	122	2		5	30	85	835	190	611	34	1
Montezuma	3141	26	0		1	2	23	121	46	70	5	2
Morrow	7501	60	0		3	41	15	709	52	598	59	0
Moultrie	14384	80	3		6	40	31	1010	191	789	30	1
Mountain City	1056	0	0		0	0	0	1	0	0	1	0
Mount Airy	1293	0	0		0	0	0	6	0	5	1	1
Mount Zion	1743	3	0		0	0	3	17	9	7	1	0
Nahunta	1061	0	0		0	0	0	4	3	1	0	0
Nashville	4834	30	0		8	11	11	275	62	210	3	1
Newnan	38137	215	1		6	34	174	1006	155	811	40	3
Norcross	16929	109	0		7	46	56	569	108	408	53	0
Norman Park	961	1	0		1	0	0	20	7	12	1	0
Oak Park	480	4	0		1	0	3	16	5	10	1	0
Oakwood	4218	125	0		0	35	90	1445	130	1250	65	3
Ocilla	3372	16	1		3	1	11	116	16	98	2	0
Oglethorpe	1190	4	0		0	0	4	18	10	7	1	
Omega	1231	7	0		1	2	4	29	5	24	0	0
Oxford	2210	0	0		0	0	0	16	1	13	2	0
Palmetto	4780	24	0		1	12	11	137	40	78	19	0
Patterson	755	0	0		0	0	0	0	0	0	0	0
Peachtree City	35387	19	0		3	7	9	545	44	456	45	0
Pelham	3669	6	1		0	2	3	81	15	62	4	0
Pembroke	2495	8	0		0	0	8	55	17	38	0	0
Pine Lake	770	5	0		0	1	4	32	1	28	3	
Pine Mountain	1368	6	0		0	1	5	48	8	36	4	0
Pooler	24006	52	0		2	20	30	699	65	604	30	0
Porterdale	1494	14	0		0	1	13	59	10	45	4	0
Port Wentworth	8177	13	1		1	2	9	124	21	79	24	0
Powder Springs	15004	52	0		2	12	38	268	43	208	17	0
Quitman	3863	54	0		2	8	44	227	58	159	10	1
Remerton	1127	10	0		0	2	8	52	11	39	2	0
Reynolds	1016	0	0		0	0	0	5	3	1	1	0
Richmond Hill	12520	22	0		2	6	14	225	40	178	7	0
Rincon	10029	28	0		4	2	22	331	24	297	10	0
Ringgold	3722	23	0		2	2	19	171	21	130	20	
Riverdale	16142	77	4		0	31	42	850	141	655	54	0
Rochelle	1109	3	0		0	3	0	54	21	33	0	0
Rockmart	4322	31	1		2	1	27	366	101	249	16	0
Rome	36278	208	4		8	52	144	1398	239	1088	71	10
Roswell	95684	143	2		23	42	76	1702	228	1391	83	12
Sale City	350	0	0		0	0	0	1	0	1	0	0
Sandersville	5724	29	1		1	5	22	276	92	175	9	1
Sandy Springs	107685	117	3		14	66	34	2837	532	2091	214	7
Sardis	957	10	0		0	1	9	31	7	21	3	0
Savannah-Chatham Metropolitan	241296	1174	50		50	534	540	8762	1856	5946	960	12
Screven	767	2	0		0	0	2	46	4	40	2	0
Senoia	4233	2	1		1	0	0	46	3	41	2	0
Sky Valley	264	0	0		0	0	0	1	0	1	0	
Smyrna	57152	196	1		8	57	130	1549	258	1146	145	7
Snellville	20025	70	0		5	10	55	767	61	682	24	0
Social Circle	4414	12	0		1	0	11	84	24	52	8	1
Sparks	1999	12	0		4	2	6	83	24	57	2	0

Table 6. Offenses Known to Law Enforcement, by Selected State and City, 2016—Continued

(Number.)

State/city	Population	Violent crime	Murder and nonnegligent manslaughter	Rape (revised definition)[1]	Rape (legacy definition)[2]	Robbery	Aggravated assault	Property crime	Burglary	Larceny-theft	Motor vehicle theft	Arson[3]
Sparta	1275	9	0		0	3	6	34	13	21	0	0
Springfield	2903	7	0		1	0	6	50	21	29	0	0
Statesboro	31176	99	2		11	47	39	1185	227	919	39	3
Statham	2647	6	0		0	3	3	47	11	34	2	0
Stone Mountain	6171	26	0		0	9	17	268	66	172	30	2
Summerville	4442	1	0		0	1	0	41	2	39	0	0
Suwanee	19432	20	0		5	6	9	658	116	524	18	0
Swainsboro	7512	89	1		4	15	69	376	72	290	14	0
Sylvania	2527	21	1		0	3	17	100	12	81	7	1
Sylvester	6019	61	1		1	7	52	268	123	134	11	0
Talbotton	874	0	0		0	0	0	8	4	4	0	0
Tallapoosa	3170	19	0		1	4	14	135	38	88	9	0
Tallulah Falls	168	0	0		0	0	0	0	0	0	0	0
Temple	4329	11	0		1	0	10	112	23	77	12	0
Tennille	1826	2	0		0	0	2	63	15	44	4	0
Thomasville	18773	34	0		1	16	17	981	212	750	19	3
Thunderbolt	2641	8	0		0	3	5	51	7	37	7	0
Tifton	16799	134	1		6	39	88	956	160	767	29	8
Toccoa	8252	34	1		2	8	23	456	54	390	12	0
Trenton	2226	0	0		0	0	0	38	7	29	2	0
Tunnel Hill	880	2	0		1	0	1	32	2	26	4	0
Tybee Island	3124	4	0		0	1	3	125	6	116	3	0
Tyrone	7243	5	0		1	0	4	72	9	58	5	0
Union City	21065	255	5		11	121	118	2218	234	1617	367	
Union Point	1727	8	0		0	3	5	35	9	23	3	0
Valdosta	55880	205	6		17	65	117	3057	581	2333	143	14
Vidalia	10721	53	1		0	9	43	605	130	447	28	0
Vienna	3735	15	0		1	3	11	94	19	74	1	0
Villa Rica	15095	69	1		6	10	52	562	71	458	33	1
Wadley	2027	9	0		0	2	7	50	11	37	2	
Walthourville	3957	18	0		0	4	14	82	22	56	4	
Warner Robins	74419	494	6		31	143	314	4111	768	3125	218	13
Warwick	404	2	0		0	0	2	10	5	5	0	0
Watkinsville	2877	4	0		0	0	4	55	11	44	0	0
Waverly Hall	842	3	0		0	0	3	4	2	2	0	0
Waycross	13934	102	5		7	23	67	961	125	814	22	5
Waynesboro	5666	77	1		5	14	57	443	88	336	19	0
West Point	3785	36	1		0	7	28	232	47	175	10	0
Whigham	480	0	0		0	0	0	0	0	0	0	0
Whitesburg	597	3	0		0	0	3	12	1	11	0	0
Willacoochee	1395	5	0		0	0	5	31	2	29	0	0
Winder	15652	144	0		6	8	130	603	100	469	34	0
Winterville	1182	1	0		0	0	1	8	1	7	0	0
Woodbury	901	6	1		0	1	4	56	15	40	1	
Woodland	361	1	0		0	1	0	0	0	0	0	
Woodstock	31243	30	1		3	5	21	617	59	541	17	0
Wrens	2026	8	2		1	1	4	113	30	79	4	0
Zebulon	1150	0	0		0	0	0	7	1	4	2	0
HAWAII												
Honolulu	995572	3331	16	382		836	2097	30592	3758	22488	4346	263
IDAHO												
Aberdeen	1915	1	0	0		1	0	21	3	16	2	0
American Falls	4291	10	0	2		0	8	71	18	47	6	0
Bellevue	2296	5	0	2		0	3	18	5	11	2	0
Blackfoot	11700	44	2	9		0	33	361	91	248	22	0
Boise	220749	657	6	143		51	457	5134	732	4066	336	45
Bonners Ferry	2549	7	0	1		0	6	43	15	27	1	0
Buhl	4305	5	0	1		0	4	90	16	72	2	0
Caldwell	52792	131	0	9		7	115	1028	173	722	133	3
Cascade	941	4	0	2		0	2	46	24	20	2	0
Challis	1032	1	0	0		0	1	17	7	10	0	0
Chubbuck	14515	29	0	2		4	23	553	38	503	12	1
Coeur d'Alene	50155	173	1	48		13	111	1418	200	1129	89	18
Cottonwood	925	1	0	1		0	0	2	1	1	0	0
Emmett	6617	25	0	0		2	23	102	19	75	8	4
Filer	2724	0	0	0		0	0	12	3	8	1	0
Fruitland	5170	9	0	2		1	6	45	12	30	3	0
Garden City	11667	76	1	11		5	59	428	74	327	27	1
Gooding	3497	3	1	2		0	0	49	16	25	8	0
Grangeville	3156	2	0	0		0	2	44	21	22	1	0
Hagerman	866	1	0	0		0	1	8	0	5	3	0
Hailey	8175	23	0	1		1	21	40	16	19	5	0
Heyburn	3250	5	0	1		0	4	52	15	32	5	0
Homedale	2554	8	0	1		0	7	53	12	35	6	0
Idaho City	472	1	0	0		1	0	8	3	5	0	0
Idaho Falls	59615	253	1	33		13	206	1367	370	904	93	8
Jerome	11234	42	0	9		6	27	219	46	155	18	1
Kamiah	1269	4	0	0		0	4	31	15	10	6	0
Kellogg	2061	5	0	1		0	4	49	13	33	3	1
Ketchum	2732	10	0	1		0	9	39	7	30	2	0
Kimberly	3680	8	0	0		0	8	38	13	21	4	0

Table 6. Offenses Known to Law Enforcement, by Selected State and City, 2016—Continued

(Number.)

State/city	Population	Violent crime	Murder and nonnegligent manslaughter	Rape (revised definition)[1]	Rape (legacy definition)[2]	Robbery	Aggravated assault	Property crime	Burglary	Larceny-theft	Motor vehicle theft	Arson[3]
Lewiston	32665	46	0	14		3	29	1330	366	883	81	2
McCall	3139	14	0	4		0	10	93	27	66	0	0
Meridian	94113	105	0	24		5	76	1457	225	1166	66	9
Montpelier	2493	3	0	2		0	1	54	3	49	2	0
Moscow	25307	18	0	2		1	15	485	71	398	16	2
Mountain Home	13627	22	0	6		3	13	258	42	211	5	3
Nampa	91520	332	6	89		19	218	2643	541	1840	262	15
Orofino	3056	6	0	1		0	5	99	30	60	9	1
Osburn	1503	3	0	0		2	1	54	33	20	1	0
Parma	2101	6	0	0		1	5	14	4	6	4	0
Payette	7360	27	0	0		0	27	121	24	88	9	2
Pinehurst	1573	1	0	0		0	1	6	2	3	1	0
Pocatello	54462	207	2	18		14	173	1630	316	1184	130	6
Ponderay	1138	2	0	0		0	2	144	6	133	5	0
Post Falls	31026	71	0	6		6	59	759	120	600	39	3
Preston	5214	4	0	1		0	3	77	29	46	2	0
Priest River	1761	2	0	0		0	2	41	2	39	0	0
Rathdrum	7681	8	0	1		2	5	192	52	126	14	0
Rexburg	28112	9	0	3		0	6	189	30	153	6	0
Rigby	4040	4	0	1		0	3	57	6	48	3	0
Rupert	5736	14	1	2		1	10	59	10	47	2	1
Salmon	3019	0	0	0		0	0	12	5	7	0	0
Sandpoint	7931	21	0	2		1	18	217	40	167	10	2
Shelley	4321	16	0	1		1	14	61	14	44	3	0
Shoshone	1492	4	0	0		0	4	15	8	7	0	0
Soda Springs	2921	6	0	2		0	4	27	6	20	1	0
Spirit Lake	2117	1	0	0		0	1	25	6	17	2	0
St. Anthony	3423	5	0	0		0	5	43	3	37	3	0
Sun Valley	1426	1	0	0		0	1	4	1	3	0	0
Twin Falls	48083	157	5	30		10	112	1070	204	778	88	6
Weiser	5281	6	0	3		0	3	70	15	52	3	0
Wendell	2736	6	0	0		0	6	31	8	14	9	0
Wilder	1640	6	0	0		0	6	28	7	16	5	1
ILLINOIS												
Addison	37246	50	0	4		18	28	653	77	536	40	2
Albany	887	0	0	0		0	0	39	23	16	0	0
Aledo	3549	0	0	0		0	0	37	5	32	0	0
Alexis	805	0	0	0		0	0	12	2	9	1	0
Algonquin	30673	12	0	4		1	7	381	30	349	2	1
Alsip	19357	19	0	0		19	0	546	109	407	30	1
Altamont	2306	1	0	0		0	1	33	12	20	1	0
Alton	26829	143	2	28		31	82	1073	266	761	46	5
Amboy	2330	2	0	1		0	1	22	5	17	0	0
Anna	4300	15	0	0		4	11	112	12	97	3	0
Annawan	854	0	0	0		0	0	10	3	7	0	0
Antioch	14302	25	0	10		3	12	201	24	168	9	0
Arlington Heights	76077	58	0	8		14	36	722	79	624	19	3
Arthur	2288	5	0	1		0	4	20	2	17	1	0
Ashland	1241	0	0	0		0	0	5	1	4	0	0
Assumption	1106	3	0	0		0	3	14	8	6	0	0
Athens	1928	2	0	0		0	2	23	3	20	0	0
Auburn	4788	3	0	2		0	1	76	21	53	2	0
Aurora	201159	631	7	57		130	437	2867	441	2259	167	21
Aviston	2108	2	0	0		0	2	4	0	4	0	0
Bannockburn	1569	0	0	0		0	0	14	0	14	0	0
Barrington	10357	3	1	1		0	1	76	7	65	4	0
Barrington Hills	4256	0	0	0		0	0	23	1	22	0	0
Barry	1266	3	0	0		0	3	22	5	15	2	0
Bartlett	41600	32	0	1		8	23	250	17	226	7	3
Bartonville	6367	33	0	3		4	26	176	28	141	7	0
Batavia	26558	26	0	3		3	20	414	15	394	5	6
Beardstown[5]	5664	62	0	2		1	59				0	0
Beecher	4465	3	0	0		2	1	26	1	23	2	1
Belgium	398	0	0	0		0	0	2	0	2	0	0
Belleville	41638	253	1	30		51	171	1659	471	1108	80	9
Bellwood	19353	103	2	14		46	41	406	102	264	40	2
Belvidere	25049	65	0	19		3	43	280	42	227	11	6
Bensenville	18454	21	1	7		8	5	291	56	209	26	0
Berkeley	5201	10	0	1		4	5	87	15	69	3	0
Berwyn	56305	170	2	15		73	80	1235	273	889	73	3
Bethalto	9314	9	0	2		6	1	115	10	101	4	0
Blandinsville	614	0	0	0		0	0	3	0	3	0	0
Bloomington	78604	307	0	42		59	206	1347	224	1064	59	11
Blue Island	23637	115	1	11		49	54	567	127	381	59	1
Bluffs	670	0	0	0		0	0	0	0	0	0	0
Bolingbrook	74471	158	2	23		18	115	944	111	782	51	3
Bourbonnais	18552	20	0	0		1	19	353	33	316	4	0
Bradley	15561	40	0	6		14	20	512	51	447	14	0
Braidwood	6160	6	0	0		2	4	66	10	56	0	0
Breese	4517	5	0	0		0	5	40	0	40	0	0
Bridgeview	16397	48	1	3		17	27	446	44	372	30	5
Brighton	2186	4	0	2		0	2	11	1	8	2	0

Table 6. Offenses Known to Law Enforcement, by Selected State and City, 2016—Continued

(Number.)

State/city	Population	Violent crime	Murder and nonnegligent manslaughter	Rape (revised definition)[1]	Rape (legacy definition)[2]	Robbery	Aggravated assault	Property crime	Burglary	Larceny-theft	Motor vehicle theft	Arson[3]
Broadview	7914	26	1	1		17	7	375	38	305	32	0
Brookfield	18935	15	1	6		2	6	267	67	189	11	3
Buffalo Grove	41511	13	0	2		4	7	208	26	166	16	0
Bunker Hill	1705	3	0	0		0	3	15	4	9	2	0
Burbank	29165	70	0	5		22	43	404	65	299	40	1
Burnham	4209	12	2	0		7	3	97	27	52	18	0
Burr Ridge	10863	2	0	1		0	1	89	7	73	9	0
Byron	3628	2	0	0		0	2	51	6	43	2	0
Cahokia	14242	64	2	5		36	21	668	186	449	33	6
Cairo	2402	69	0	0		4	65	93	25	66	2	2
Calumet City	37022	211	9	16		137	49	1358	307	869	182	12
Cambria	1272	4	0	1		0	3	5	3	2	0	1
Cambridge	2104	3	1	0		0	2	17	5	12	0	0
Camp Point	1123	0	0	0		0	0	1	0	1	0	0
Campton Hills	11390	4	0	3		0	1	35	8	27	0	0
Canton	14116	14	0	2		4	8	194	42	147	5	2
Carbondale	26373	138	3	32		38	65	844	171	649	24	2
Carlinville	5615	19	0	0		0	19	203	43	157	3	0
Carlyle	3211	10	0	0		2	8	59	5	53	1	0
Carol Stream	40473	36	0	3		7	26	306	32	251	23	5
Carpentersville	38664	31	1	14		12	4	668	113	539	16	3
Carrollton	2418	15	0	3		0	12	27	3	24	0	0
Carterville	5881	8	0	1		0	7	55	11	39	5	0
Carthage	2534	1	0	0		0	1	20	12	7	1	0
Cary	17903	20	0	1		1	18	75	17	54	4	1
Caseyville	4003	31	0	4		5	22	106	25	72	9	0
Catlin	2000	3	0	0		0	3	8	6	2	0	0
Centreville	4970	91	1	6		15	69	172	70	83	19	0
Champaign	87071	625	3	41		124	457	2838	728	1979	131	3
Channahon	12597	1	0	0		0	1	34	6	27	1	0
Charleston	21067	79	0	4		12	63	121	40	76	5	1
Chatham	12497	16	0	2		0	14	71	12	56	3	0
Chenoa	3199	4	0	0		1	3	18	3	15	0	0
Cherry Valley	3086	18	0	4		1	13	240	9	227	4	0
Chester	8590	18	1	1		0	16	54	4	49	1	0
Chicago	2725153	30126	765	1589		11957	15815	86960	14258	61229	11473	590
Chicago Heights	30273	175	6	28		74	67	805	126	597	82	37
Chicago Ridge	14383	29	0	2		18	9	575	22	531	22	1
Chillicothe	6253	21	0	5		3	13	106	10	94	2	0
Christopher	2771	2	1	1		0	0	18	5	13	0	0
Cicero	83807	264	1	17		148	98	1713	284	1147	282	28
Clarendon Hills	8724	6	0	0		1	5	32	9	23	0	1
Coal City	5469	5	0	0		1	4	72	6	66	0	0
Coal Valley	3753	4	0	1		0	3	51	18	33	0	0
Cobden	1136	4	0	0		0	4	13	5	7	1	0
Colchester	1325	0	0	0		0	0	0	0	0	0	0
Collinsville	24599	53	0	10		9	34	736	109	586	41	2
Colona	5096	6	0	0		0	6	61	18	42	1	0
Columbia	10288	1	0	0		0	1	79	22	52	5	0
Cortland	4331	2	0	0		0	2	51	2	49	0	0
Country Club Hills	16844	74	1	6		44	23	416	55	332	29	2
Countryside	6015	7	0	0		0	7	200	8	181	11	0
Cowden	577	0	0	0		0	0	5	1	3	1	0
Crest Hill	21211	28	0	5		9	14	212	41	157	14	3
Crete	8171	16	0	0		5	11	140	27	108	5	0
Creve Coeur	5235	45	0	2		4	39	154	20	130	4	0
Crystal Lake	40374	44	0	8		4	32	624	56	561	7	3
Danville	31931	502	0	47		88	367	1894	646	1185	63	7
Darien	22285	6	0	3		2	1	366	47	309	10	1
Davis	635	0	0	0		0	0	0	0	0	0	0
Decatur	72694	392	3	45		97	247	2657	859	1700	98	16
Deer Creek	678	1	0	0		1	0	6	1	5	0	0
Deerfield	19176	5	0	1		1	3	123	17	103	3	0
De Kalb	43034	223	3	53		34	133	1438	203	1203	32	8
Delavan	1622	5	0	0		0	5	50	9	34	7	2
De Pue	1726	0	0	0		0	0	20	4	16	0	0
De Soto	1571	10	0	0		0	10	21	4	16	1	1
Des Plaines	58726	45	0	6		11	28	537	91	423	23	6
Diamond	2480	0	0	0		0	0	5	0	5	0	0
Divernon	1153	3	0	0		2	1	8	3	5	0	0
Dixon	15246	20	0	12		4	4	272	23	243	6	0
Downers Grove	49894	33	0	7		7	19	651	66	555	30	3
Dupo	3881	19	1	1		0	17	95	36	51	8	0
Du Quoin	5919	18	0	0		2	16	62	17	44	1	0
Dwight	4027	7	0	0		1	6	63	16	46	1	0
Earlville	1619	1	0	0		0	1	30	3	27	0	0
East Alton	6152	20	0	9		3	8	163	32	120	11	0
East Carondelet	467	6	0	1		1	4	4	3	0	1	0
East Dubuque	1648	13	0	2		1	10	24	2	19	3	0
East Dundee	3273	1	0	0		1	0	70	15	54	1	0
East Hazel Crest	1545	4	0	0		2	2	49	32	14	3	1
East Moline	21359	91	0	10		22	59	571	120	439	12	1
East Peoria	23008	97	2	12		5	78	625	171	439	15	9

Table 6. Offenses Known to Law Enforcement, by Selected State and City, 2016—Continued

(Number.)

State/city	Population	Violent crime	Murder and nonnegligent manslaughter	Rape (revised definition)[1]	Rape (legacy definition)[2]	Robbery	Aggravated assault	Property crime	Burglary	Larceny-theft	Motor vehicle theft	Arson[3]
East St. Louis	26769	757	27	35		103	592	604	210	266	128	9
Edinburg	1046	0	0	0		0	0	4	2	2	0	0
Edwardsville	25133	33	0	6		7	20	288	33	248	7	0
Effingham	12660	33	0	9		2	22	381	45	330	6	0
Elburn	5776	3	0	0		1	2	30	5	25	0	0
Eldorado	4050	6	0	0		0	6	147	34	98	15	0
Elgin	112886	236	2	34		63	137	1565	218	1279	68	10
Elizabeth	746	1	0	0		0	1	3	2	1	0	0
Elk Grove Village	33255	25	0	4		7	14	510	83	386	41	1
Elmhurst	46318	26	0	1		9	16	536	68	452	16	0
Elmwood	2088	0	0	0		0	0	24	9	14	1	0
Elmwood Park	24829	42	0	3		12	27	328	62	246	20	1
El Paso	2796	7	0	3		0	4	34	3	30	1	0
Energy	1144	2	0	0		0	2	14	6	7	1	0
Erie	1543	3	0	2		0	1	9	2	7	0	0
Eureka	5388	10	1	1		0	8	55	10	43	2	1
Evanston	75716	130	2	6		38	84	1671	329	1269	73	10
Evergreen Park	19836	41	0	5		17	19	600	56	519	25	2
Fairbury	3604	8	0	0		1	7	37	9	28	0	1
Fairfield	5019	21	0	1		3	17	109	29	78	2	1
Fairmont City	2478	1	0	0		0	1	18	7	8	3	0
Fairmount	616	0	0	0		0	0	1	0	1	0	0
Fairview Heights	16773	41	1	6		4	30	870	67	779	24	0
Farmington	2305	3	0	0		0	3	63	19	44	0	2
Findlay	647	0	0	0		0	0	7	2	5	0	0
Fisher	1974	2	0	1		0	1	35	12	23	0	0
Fithian	468	0	0	0		0	0	0	0	0	0	0
Flora	4919	4	0	0		0	4	84	18	63	3	0
Flossmoor	9479	15	0	2		6	7	120	22	95	3	1
Forest Park	14113	46	0	10		23	13	527	75	418	34	0
Forest View	691	3	0	0		0	3	41	11	20	10	8
Fox Lake	10495	17	0	3		1	13	143	28	112	3	0
Fox River Grove	4665	10	0	1		1	8	60	4	54	2	1
Frankfort	18822	8	0	0		5	3	185	14	162	9	0
Franklin Grove	957	0	0	0		0	0	9	4	5	0	0
Franklin Park	18306	27	0	6		5	16	211	40	128	43	6
Freeburg	4218	3	0	0		0	3	35	6	27	2	0
Freeport	24257	48	0	10		11	27	652	166	471	15	4
Fulton	3347	1	0	0		0	1	64	29	34	1	0
Galena	3276	6	0	1		0	5	40	0	38	2	0
Galesburg	31093	124	1	15		23	85	987	203	765	19	1
Geneseo	6522	8	0	2		0	6	83	18	63	2	0
Geneva	21864	11	1	4		1	5	187	23	160	4	4
Georgetown	3341	9	0	2		0	7	89	38	50	1	2
Germantown	1285	1	0	0		0	1	8	2	5	1	0
Gibson City	3408	10	0	2		0	8	33	11	22	0	3
Gifford	1117	0	0	0		0	0	5	0	5	0	0
Gilberts	7792	2	0	0		0	2	23	7	15	1	0
Gillespie	3148	10	0	0		1	9	41	6	35	0	0
Gilman	1743	4	0	0		3	1	99	11	87	1	0
Girard	2012	5	0	2		0	3	14	1	12	1	0
Glasford	1000	2	0	0		0	2	1	1	0	0	0
Glen Carbon	12971	6	0	1		0	5	100	12	87	1	3
Glendale Heights	34472	30	0	0		16	14	571	62	494	15	0
Glen Ellyn	28282	26	1	6		6	13	244	35	202	7	2
Glenview	48008	41	0	5		2	34	611	80	503	28	2
Glenwood	8996	13	0	0		7	6	139	27	105	7	0
Godley	698	0	0	0		0	0	5	2	3	0	0
Golf	505	0	0	0		0	0	1	0	1	0	0
Goodfield	962	1	0	0		0	1	56	5	50	1	0
Grafton	649	0	0	0		0	0	10	1	9	0	0
Grandview	1424	7	0	0		3	4	23	7	15	1	0
Granite City	28899	191	1	24		33	133	600	165	367	68	9
Grantfork	326	0	0	0		0	0	0	0	0	0	0
Grayslake	20916	26	0	4		3	19	342	58	270	14	5
Grayville	1618	5	0	0		1	4	50	16	31	3	0
Greenfield	1010	3	0	1		0	2	15	4	11	0	0
Greenup	1491	3	0	0		0	3	30	10	20	0	0
Greenville	6594	6	0	0		0	6	118	11	102	5	0
Gurnee	31014	23	0	5		8	10	1269	55	1183	31	0
Hampshire	6248	10	0	0		0	10	34	3	24	7	1
Hampton	1835	0	0	0		0	0	29	11	18	0	0
Hanover	808	2	0	0		1	1	4	0	4	0	1
Hanover Park	38402	39	0	4		14	21	256	39	206	11	0
Harrisburg	8863	71	0	3		3	65	178	74	92	12	1
Hartford	1373	5	0	2		3	0	16	0	15	1	0
Harvard	9146	8	0	1		1	6	113	9	103	1	0
Havana	3034	25	0	6		0	19	49	7	42	0	0
Hawthorn Woods	8002	1	0	0		0	1	7	2	5	0	0
Hazel Crest	14119	61	3	3		39	16	488	130	317	41	4
Henning	245	0	0	0		0	0	0	0	0	0	0
Henry	2301	7	0	0		1	6	42	9	33	0	0
Herrin	12985	39	0	6		5	28	450	134	292	24	3

Table 6. Offenses Known to Law Enforcement, by Selected State and City, 2016—Continued

(Number.)

State/city	Population	Violent crime	Murder and nonnegligent manslaughter	Rape (revised definition)[1]	Rape (legacy definition)[2]	Robbery	Aggravated assault	Property crime	Burglary	Larceny-theft	Motor vehicle theft	Arson[3]
Herscher	1547	1	0	0		0	1	9	1	8	0	0
Hickory Hills	14134	17	0	3		6	8	138	13	114	11	1
Highland Park	29737	21	0	7		4	10	265	22	231	12	0
Highwood	5337	3	0	0		1	2	37	2	31	4	0
Hillsboro	5635	14	0	3		0	11	70	15	49	6	0
Hillsdale	509	0	0	0		0	0	2	0	2	0	0
Hinckley	2056	0	0	0		0	0	18	5	13	0	0
Hinsdale	17790	5	0	1		4	0	181	12	154	15	0
Hodgkins	1862	7	0	0		1	6	224	5	217	2	1
Hoffman Estates	52177	55	0	11		15	29	429	52	353	24	0
Homer	1199	0	0	0		0	0	3	0	3	0	0
Homer Glen	24421	6	1	0		2	3	116	20	92	4	0
Hometown	4340	5	0	1		1	3	40	4	31	5	0
Homewood	19379	38	0	4		22	12	569	72	486	11	1
Hoopeston	5194	17	0	1		2	14	169	46	115	8	2
Hopedale	839	0	0	0		0	0	11	5	6	0	0
Hudson	1847	3	0	1		0	2	10	2	8	0	0
Huntley	26345	7	0	0		2	5	213	25	186	2	1
Ina	2365	5	0	0		0	5	3	0	2	1	0
Indian Head Park	3827	0	0	0		0	0	33	1	29	3	0
Indianola	269	0	0	0		0	0	0	0	0	0	0
Island Lake	8079	8	0	3		0	5	60	6	52	2	0
Itasca	8825	2	0	0		2	0	78	8	66	4	0
Jacksonville	19039	61	0	6		4	51	602	102	494	6	1
Jerome	1645	2	0	0		1	1	27	4	22	1	1
Jerseyville	8470	25	0	12		0	13	260	44	207	9	0
Johnsburg	6303	5	0	4		0	1	127	0	126	1	0
Joliet	147886	488	10	51		128	299	2801	517	2143	141	64
Kankakee	26509	203	5	26		74	98	1098	251	786	61	12
Kenilworth	2563	0	0	0		0	0	12	1	11	0	0
Kewanee	12460	38	0	13		2	23	424	43	371	10	0
Kildeer	4066	2	0	1		1	0	19	3	16	0	0
Kincaid	1424	8	0	2		1	5	17	1	15	1	0
Kingston	1154	0	0	0		0	0	3	0	3	0	3
Kirkland	1732	4	0	0		0	4	21	4	17	0	0
Lacon	1805	0	0	0		0	0	10	4	6	0	0
Ladd	1231	1	0	0		0	1	5	4	1	0	0
La Grange	15754	14	0	1		5	8	197	40	153	4	0
La Grange Park	13612	3	0	0		1	2	105	9	91	5	0
La Harpe	1190	1	0	0		0	1	17	5	12	0	0
Lake Bluff	5666	4	0	0		1	3	56	3	50	3	0
Lake Forest	19410	4	0	0		0	4	112	14	98	0	0
Lake in the Hills	29022	24	0	8		0	16	146	31	115	0	1
Lakemoor	6006	2	0	0		0	2	22	6	16	0	0
Lake Villa	8849	11	0	2		1	8	48	8	39	1	0
Lake Zurich	20051	11	0	8		0	3	255	27	227	1	2
Lanark	1357	0	0	0		0	0	7	1	5	1	0
Lansing	28347	113	1	10		70	32	1886	271	1527	88	2
La Salle	9194	3	0	0		0	3	187	31	152	4	0
Lawrenceville	4428	14	0	0		0	14	77	29	42	6	3
Lebanon	4467	9	0	5		3	1	54	17	34	3	0
Lemont	16927	6	0	3		1	2	140	19	113	8	0
Lenzburg	487	0	0	0		0	0	4	2	2	0	0
Le Roy	3585	6	0	1		0	5	29	9	19	1	0
Libertyville	20454	8	1	1		3	3	268	23	239	6	0
Lincoln	13867	38	0	8		3	27	325	61	249	15	2
Lincolnshire	7282	2	0	0		1	1	31	3	26	2	0
Lincolnwood	12655	20	0	0		7	13	454	76	357	21	2
Lindenhurst	14408	3	0	2		1	0	71	8	61	2	1
Lisle	23063	9	0	4		1	4	211	29	173	9	0
Litchfield	6852	5	0	0		1	4	180	19	159	2	1
Loami	756	0	0	0		0	0	17	8	9	0	0
Lockport	25223	22	2	4		5	11	193	20	171	2	2
Lombard	43866	50	0	13		17	20	942	94	830	18	5
Loves Park	23349	79	1	11		17	50	454	98	336	20	2
Lovington	1104	0	0	0		0	0	11	3	7	1	0
Lyons	10719	13	3	0		5	5	120	21	86	13	3
Machesney Park	22816	76	1	14		7	54	566	80	474	12	1
Macomb	18402	72	0	21		3	48	294	65	225	4	1
Mahomet	8216	4	0	0		0	4	32	9	22	1	0
Malta	1150	0	0	0		0	0	0	0	0	0	0
Manhattan	7464	2	0	0		0	2	32	3	29	0	0
Maple Park	1307	0	0	0		0	0	3	0	3	0	0
Marengo	7467	5	0	2		0	3	70	15	54	1	0
Marine	930	0	0	0		0	0	1	0	1	0	0
Marissa	1833	15	0	0		0	15	40	5	33	2	0
Maroa	1727	2	0	1		0	1	20	11	9	0	1
Marquette Heights	2726	6	0	2		0	4	11	4	7	0	0
Marseilles	4934	9	0	1		1	7	104	36	66	2	1
Marshall	3871	8	0	0		2	6	31	2	29	0	2
Martinsville	1129	1	0	0		0	1	14	3	11	0	0
Maryville	7978	7	0	0		1	6	47	11	32	4	0
Mascoutah	8063	5	0	0		2	3	42	7	35	0	0

Table 6. Offenses Known to Law Enforcement, by Selected State and City, 2016—Continued

(Number.)

State/city	Population	Violent crime	Murder and nonnegligent manslaughter	Rape (revised definition)[1]	Rape (legacy definition)[2]	Robbery	Aggravated assault	Property crime	Burglary	Larceny-theft	Motor vehicle theft	Arson[3]
Matteson	19226	71	0	6		18	47	575	54	457	64	0
Mattoon	18026	70	1	10		7	52	371	63	307	1	6
Maywood	23994	165	5	15		68	77	572	144	339	89	2
McCook	230	0	0	0		0	0	21	2	12	7	0
McCullom Lake	1015	0	0	0		0	0	0	0	0	0	0
McHenry	26581	40	1	13		2	24	403	27	372	4	0
McLean	812	2	0	0		1	1	8	3	5	0	0
Melrose Park	25369	51	2	10		17	22	321	42	226	53	0
Mendota	7173	6	0	3		0	3	88	21	67	0	1
Metropolis	6290	36	0	6		2	28	245	50	185	10	0
Midlothian	14850	37	1	0		27	9	373	115	221	37	1
Milan	5082	16	0	3		1	12	121	16	105	0	0
Milledgeville	973	0	0	0		0	0	22	3	17	2	0
Millstadt	3877	1	0	0		0	1	20	5	15	0	0
Minier	1219	0	0	0		0	0	23	3	19	1	0
Mokena	20156	5	0	2		0	3	261	22	232	7	0
Moline	42517	196	0	26		19	151	1459	227	1205	27	4
Monee	5068	2	0	2		0	0	52	7	39	6	0
Monmouth	9261	35	0	9		3	23	193	43	138	12	3
Montgomery	19703	18	1	7		0	10	330	44	270	16	2
Monticello	5501	5	0	0		0	5	46	12	34	0	1
Morris	14507	20	0	4		3	13	303	33	266	4	2
Morrison	4137	6	0	0		0	6	39	5	32	2	0
Morton	16310	14	0	0		0	14	145	47	97	1	2
Morton Grove	23478	11	0	0		3	8	207	57	144	6	1
Mount Carmel	6982	15	0	0		2	13	182	27	153	2	1
Mount Carroll	1602	0	0	0		0	0	30	3	25	2	0
Mount Morris	2854	0	0	0		0	0	20	4	15	1	0
Mount Olive	1995	1	0	0		0	1	4	0	3	1	0
Mount Prospect	54839	26	0	6		10	10	565	53	490	22	5
Mount Pulaski	1505	0	0	0		0	0	6	2	4	0	0
Mount Vernon	15053	194	0	18		24	152	776	183	585	8	15
Mount Zion	5865	3	0	1		1	1	21	2	19	0	0
Moweaqua	1736	1	0	0		0	1	7	5	2	0	0
Mundelein	31685	24	0	1		2	21	292	52	230	10	2
Murphysboro	7726	59	1	13		8	37	433	73	357	3	2
Naperville	148070	92	0	15		34	43	1587	141	1401	45	4
Nashville	3109	12	0	1		0	11	69	8	56	5	0
New Athens	1930	1	0	0		0	1	18	4	14	0	0
New Baden	3304	4	0	1		0	3	27	0	27	0	0
New Lenox	26085	25	0	7		6	12	302	32	265	5	0
Newton	2807	0	0	0		0	0	53	13	40	0	0
Niles	29886	29	0	2		8	19	702	49	639	14	1
Nokomis	2171	8	1	1		0	6	33	9	22	2	1
Normal	54727	144	1	35		29	79	1080	142	912	26	1
Norridge	14629	13	0	1		3	9	414	32	371	11	0
North Aurora	17599	21	0	4		4	13	240	25	208	7	1
Northbrook	33746	11	1	2		5	3	382	42	327	13	0
Northfield	5494	0	0	0		0	0	40	6	33	1	1
Northlake	12308	16	0	2		7	7	252	16	218	18	0
North Riverside	6663	15	0	0		9	6	486	16	459	11	0
Oak Brook	8130	10	0	2		3	5	562	18	536	8	0
Oakbrook Terrace	2169	5	0	1		2	2	108	10	93	5	0
Oak Forest	28088	42	1	5		20	16	300	57	214	29	1
Oak Lawn	56791	79	1	7		38	33	937	99	810	28	3
Oak Park	52365	108	0	2		68	38	1495	359	1057	79	3
Oakwood	1520	4	0	0		0	4	13	8	5	0	0
Oakwood Hills	2059	2	0	2		0	0	19	3	16	0	0
Oblong	1420	7	0	0		0	7	15	8	7	0	0
O'Fallon	29061	45	1	15		7	22	518	65	444	9	0
Oglesby	3619	3	0	2		0	1	43	6	37	0	0
Okawville	1392	3	0	0		0	3	17	7	9	1	0
Olney	8984	49	1	10		0	38	283	32	241	10	4
Olympia Fields	5031	4	0	0		2	2	146	11	134	1	0
Onarga	1313	1	0	0		0	1	5	1	3	1	0
Oregon	3553	6	0	1		0	5	107	12	90	5	0
Orion	1818	0	0	0		0	0	6	3	3	0	0
Orland Hills	7255	4	0	0		0	4	46	5	40	1	0
Orland Park	59009	25	0	2		4	19	1335	53	1263	19	2
Oswego	34681	25	0	7		5	13	389	27	353	9	3
Ottawa	18263	23	0	1		3	19	390	45	333	12	3
Palatine	69447	37	0	14		8	15	600	35	543	22	1
Palestine	1324	9	0	1		0	8	19	1	17	1	0
Palos Heights	12549	2	0	0		0	2	87	7	77	3	1
Palos Hills	17578	16	0	1		5	10	84	6	70	8	0
Palos Park	4894	2	0	0		0	2	32	4	28	0	0
Pana	5562	14	0	6		0	8	91	16	73	2	0
Paris	8356	38	0	1		1	36	116	51	54	11	2
Park City	7357	10	0	4		2	4	103	33	63	7	0
Park Forest	21947	75	2	11		34	28	353	110	209	34	4
Park Ridge	37805	12	0	1		8	3	375	67	294	14	3
Pawnee	2707	1	1	0		0	0	2	1	1	0	0
Paxton	4332	10	0	1		1	8	61	8	51	2	2

Table 6. Offenses Known to Law Enforcement, by Selected State and City, 2016—Continued

(Number.)

State/city	Population	Violent crime	Murder and nonnegligent manslaughter	Rape (revised definition)[1]	Rape (legacy definition)[2]	Robbery	Aggravated assault	Property crime	Burglary	Larceny-theft	Motor vehicle theft	Arson[3]
Pekin	33052	139	0	25		15	99	664	90	562	12	6
Peoria	115099	875	10	70		305	490	4429	1089	3116	224	61
Peoria Heights	5960	30	1	6		1	22	149	27	114	8	0
Peotone	4114	7	0	0		3	4	13	2	10	1	0
Peru	9886	15	0	4		4	7	157	24	132	1	0
Phoenix	1956	14	0	0		2	12	43	23	17	3	0
Pierron	558	0	0	0		0	0	0	0	0	0	0
Pinckneyville	5336	4	0	0		1	3	26	6	20	0	0
Pingree Grove	7162	5	0	5		0	0	20	1	18	1	0
Pittsfield	4468	3	0	0		0	3	66	10	54	2	0
Plainfield	43063	37	0	7		3	27	330	35	280	15	2
Plano	11358	0	0	0		0	0	108	10	96	2	0
Pleasant Hill	937	3	0	3		0	0	9	3	6	0	0
Pleasant Plains	804	0	0	0		0	0	2	0	2	0	0
Pontiac	11771	26	0	0		3	23	222	37	181	4	2
Pontoon Beach	5598	8	0	0		2	6	113	23	84	6	1
Posen	5992	14	1	0		7	6	102	24	65	13	0
Potomac	716	0	0	0		0	0	1	0	1	0	0
Princeton	7534	14	0	2		0	12	103	17	82	4	2
Prophetstown	1999	0	0	0		0	0	0	0	0	0	0
Prospect Heights	16410	19	0	0		5	14	106	19	78	9	1
Quincy	40799	209	0	43		23	143	1323	295	987	41	9
Raleigh	348	0	0	0		0	0	3	2	1	0	0
Rankin	535	0	0	0		0	0	0	0	0	0	0
Rantoul	13018	53	0	14		13	26	339	101	225	13	3
Red Bud	3564	2	0	1		0	1	13	5	8	0	0
Richmond	1904	2	0	0		1	1	19	3	15	1	0
Richton Park	13702	58	0	7		36	15	299	46	220	33	0
Ridge Farm	847	0	0	0		0	0	9	3	6	0	0
River Forest	11203	17	0	0		7	10	291	42	244	5	0
River Grove	10216	11	1	4		3	3	149	37	97	15	0
Riverside	8826	13	0	1		0	12	118	26	90	2	1
Riverton	3463	14	0	2		2	10	70	12	53	5	0
Riverwoods	3639	3	0	1		0	2	26	5	19	2	0
Robinson	7616	31	0	2		0	29	106	13	88	5	1
Rochester	3794	4	0	1		0	3	9	0	8	1	0
Rockdale	1942	2	0	1		0	1	3	0	1	2	0
Rock Falls	9027	35	0	1		4	30	119	60	57	2	0
Rockford	147363	2444	26	137		536	1745	5565	1406	3696	463	78
Rock Island	38543	158	4	6		23	125	1042	175	782	85	6
Rockton	7494	7	0	2		0	5	163	11	150	2	1
Rolling Meadows	24205	16	0	6		2	8	284	12	266	6	0
Romeoville	39727	45	0	8		14	23	623	61	544	18	2
Roscoe	10523	9	0	0		0	9	130	55	73	2	0
Roselle	23037	18	0	11		2	5	190	29	157	4	3
Rosemont	4206	25	0	5		4	16	279	8	263	8	86
Round Lake	18484	19	0	5		5	9	133	24	107	2	0
Round Lake Beach	27796	38	0	10		6	22	581	44	527	10	1
Round Lake Heights	2713	5	0	1		1	3	24	1	23	0	0
Round Lake Park	7415	5	0	0		0	5	83	20	56	7	0
Roxana	1472	6	0	1		1	4	31	9	22	0	0
Royalton	1135	1	0	0		0	1	10	5	4	1	0
Ruma	315	0	0	0		0	0	1	0	1	0	0
Rushville	2927	4	0	2		0	2	30	7	23	0	0
Salem	7249	21	0	1		3	17	379	49	316	14	2
Sandoval	1221	8	0	3		3	2	29	8	20	1	5
Sandwich	7355	8	0	5		0	3	48	10	38	0	0
Sauget	151	4	1	0		1	2	64	0	53	11	0
Sauk Village	10489	54	2	10		11	31	117	38	56	23	3
Savanna	2845	10	0	2		0	8	83	17	63	3	0
Schaumburg	74774	74	0	23		21	30	1685	108	1526	51	4
Schiller Park	11807	19	0	10		6	3	229	41	161	27	0
Shannon	703	0	0	0		0	0	0	0	0	0	0
Shawneetown	1150	4	0	0		1	3	13	3	9	1	0
Sherman	4697	1	0	0		0	1	17	9	8	0	0
Shiloh	13056	29	0	4		7	18	223	38	177	8	1
Shorewood	16968	29	0	10		2	17	174	30	138	6	0
Sidell	587	0	0	0		0	0	0	0	0	0	0
Silvis	7487	24	0	5		2	17	295	38	255	2	0
Skokie	64819	158	1	15		45	97	1557	228	1283	46	5
Sleepy Hollow	3354	0	0	0		0	0	10	1	9	0	0
Smithton	3724	0	0	0		0	0	16	2	14	0	0
South Barrington	4955	2	0	0		0	2	47	10	35	2	0
South Beloit	7639	18	0	1		8	9	117	26	87	4	0
South Chicago Heights	4137	19	0	0		7	12	155	16	128	11	3
South Elgin	22436	27	0	8		3	16	262	18	239	5	0
South Holland	22042	83	2	20		43	18	479	86	332	61	1
South Pekin	1115	2	0	0		0	2	14	3	10	1	0
South Roxana	1986	16	0	5		2	9	49	22	27	0	0
Springfield	116563	1301	6	99		249	947	5158	1250	3681	227	45
Spring Grove	5698	3	0	3		0	0	35	2	30	3	0
Spring Valley	5269	2	0	1		0	1	79	18	58	3	0
Stanford	579	0	0	0		0	0	2	1	1	0	0

Table 6. Offenses Known to Law Enforcement, by Selected State and City, 2016—Continued

(Number.)

State/city	Population	Violent crime	Murder and nonnegligent manslaughter	Rape (revised definition)[1]	Rape (legacy definition)[2]	Robbery	Aggravated assault	Property crime	Burglary	Larceny-theft	Motor vehicle theft	Arson[3]
St. Anne	1213	2	0	0		2	0	43	15	25	3	1
Staunton	4981	11	0	1		1	9	65	11	52	2	0
St. Charles	33556	44	0	6		4	34	432	52	367	13	2
Steger	9502	20	0	1		9	10	288	38	233	17	2
St. Elmo	1402	14	0	1		0	13	44	15	27	2	0
Sterling	14983	39	0	14		5	20	511	48	449	14	3
Stickney	6785	6	1	1		1	3	73	3	58	12	1
Stockton	1778	6	0	1		0	5	41	9	30	2	0
Streator	13082	32	0	17		4	11	357	67	279	11	14
Summit	11457	38	1	1		14	22	216	27	145	44	4
Swansea	13533	19	0	6		5	8	263	47	203	13	0
Sycamore	17750	12	0	3		1	8	257	15	235	7	5
Taylorville	10795	4	0	1		0	3	136	26	107	3	0
Thornton	2513	3	0	1		1	1	38	7	30	1	0
Tilton	2607	10	0	1		0	9	55	19	34	2	0
Tinley Park	57213	48	0	6		11	31	766	86	652	28	2
Tolono	3483	4	0	1		0	3	30	9	21	0	0
Toluca	1314	0	0	0		0	0	13	5	8	0	0
Tonica	732	0	0	0		0	0	7	4	3	0	0
Tower Lakes	1251	0	0	0		0	0	1	0	1	0	0
Troy	10063	15	0	6		0	9	73	14	58	1	0
Tuscola	4437	25	0	2		0	23	72	16	54	2	0
Urbana	42461	162	4	25		54	79	1543	327	1185	31	8
Valmeyer	1260	1	0	0		0	1	8	1	7	0	0
Vernon Hills	26574	19	0	4		7	8	378	20	355	3	1
Vienna	1696	0	0	0		0	0	7	1	5	1	0
Villa Park	21976	23	0	2		7	14	341	34	284	23	0
Virden	3384	15	0	3		1	11	90	26	59	5	0
Walnut	1338	0	0	0		0	0	3	0	2	1	0
Warren	1366	0	0	0		0	0	1	0	1	0	0
Warrensburg	1154	3	0	0		0	3	7	2	5	0	0
Warrenville	13342	11	0	7		3	1	132	14	113	5	0
Warsaw	1541	3	0	0		1	2	14	3	11	0	1
Washington	16965	14	0	0		2	12	178	35	141	2	0
Waterloo	10284	3	0	0		0	3	34	0	34	0	0
Watseka	5027	15	0	4		2	9	153	27	121	5	0
Waukegan	88337	449	1	9		195	244	2287	509	1670	108	7
Waverly	1261	1	0	0		0	1	4	0	4	0	1
Wayne	2450	0	0	0		0	0	12	8	3	1	0
Westchester	16729	23	0	1		14	8	257	35	207	15	1
West Chicago	27490	34	0	6		10	18	293	46	233	14	2
West City	652	0	0	0		0	0	85	5	80	0	0
West Dundee	7406	4	0	2		2	0	103	4	99	0	0
Western Springs	13446	0	0	0		0	0	35	5	28	2	1
West Frankfort	8044	5	0	0		5	0	191	63	110	18	3
Westmont	24992	22	0	4		5	13	292	39	243	10	2
Westville	3087	5	0	1		1	3	31	17	13	1	1
Wheaton	53848	32	0	5		11	16	332	54	276	2	1
Wheeling	38158	47	0	5		5	37	424	60	348	16	1
White Hall	2389	5	0	1		0	4	33	15	18	0	0
Willowbrook	8625	7	0	1		3	3	163	17	141	5	0
Willow Springs	5701	3	0	0		3	0	28	5	20	3	0
Wilmette	27474	11	0	3		3	5	308	51	246	11	3
Wilmington	5683	13	0	6		1	6	52	6	38	8	0
Winfield	9763	3	0	0		0	3	57	9	48	0	1
Winnebago	2995	2	0	0		0	2	49	2	46	1	0
Winnetka	12526	5	0	0		0	5	87	10	69	8	0
Winthrop Harbor	6803	6	0	2		1	3	37	8	29	0	0
Witt	866	0	0	0		0	0	4	4	0	0	0
Wonder Lake	3912	5	0	1		2	2	30	4	24	2	0
Wood Dale	13943	6	0	1		5	0	185	16	161	8	0
Woodridge	33441	37	0	14		15	8	446	48	386	12	3
Wood River	10225	37	0	7		10	20	371	55	289	27	0
Woodstock	25259	34	0	6		8	20	402	29	360	13	3
Worth	10781	24	0	5		5	14	114	18	84	12	1
Yates City	666	0	0	0		0	0	15	1	14	0	0
Yorkville	18752	13	0	4		5	4	170	28	131	11	1
Zeigler	1758	2	0	0		0	2	18	5	12	1	0
Zion	24067	169	2	37		31	99	607	127	449	31	10
INDIANA												
Alexandria	5028	5	0		2	0	3	118	26	85	7	1
Anderson	55134	240	6	63		92	79	2294	497	1614	183	
Auburn	13010	10	1		6	2	1	261	36	212	13	0
Aurora	3691	9	0		0	1	8	170	16	149	5	0
Avon	17076	73	0		0	8	65	670	34	606	30	
Bargersville	7053	6	0		0	4	2	163	16	137	10	0
Batesville	6628	15	0	1		0	14	100	11	81	8	0
Bedford	13335	11	0		2	0	9	344	17	304	23	0
Beech Grove	14618	24	0		6	18	0	432	103	250	79	1
Berne	4100	1	0		1	0	0	15	3	11	1	
Bloomington	84772	378	2	46		70	260	2703	546	2011	146	15
Bluffton	10024	5	0	0		1	4	403	42	350	11	

Table 6. Offenses Known to Law Enforcement, by Selected State and City, 2016—Continued

(Number.)

State/city	Population	Violent crime	Murder and nonnegligent manslaughter	Rape (revised definition)[1]	Rape (legacy definition)[2]	Robbery	Aggravated assault	Property crime	Burglary	Larceny-theft	Motor vehicle theft	Arson[3]
Bremen	4561	8	0		1	2	5	42	6	27	9	0
Brownsburg	25648	29	1		0	4	24	347	36	290	21	1
Brownstown	2953	6	0		0	1	5	100	16	74	10	
Carmel	90619	25	0	13		7	5	803	58	706	39	1
Cedar Lake	12085	13	0		3	1	9	218	44	161	13	
Charlestown	8189	61	0		0	2	59	192	43	133	16	
Clarksville	21888	118	0		1	9	108	1190	55	1019	116	0
Clinton	4799	14	0	0		0	14	154	16	134	4	0
Columbia City	8873	6	0		1	0	5	145	10	129	6	1
Columbus	47222	34	0		15	17	2	1943	180	1657	106	6
Crawfordsville[7]	16047	48	0	4		5	39	422	73	332	17	1
Crown Point	29086	9	0	0		7	2	362	31	320	11	2
Cumberland	5499	25	2		0	7	16	194	40	135	19	0
Danville	9729	38	0		3	2	33	120	12	99	9	0
Decatur	9474	5	0		2	1	2	172	28	136	8	0
Dyer	15983	6	0		0	4	2	175	16	146	13	
East Chicago	28503	192	5		9	79	99	1079	256	707	116	
Edinburgh	4560	15	0	0		1	14	535	43	487	5	0
Elkhart	52505	791	15		38	96	642	2264	485	1540	239	12
Ellettsville	6607	22	0	0		3	19	100	23	66	11	0
Elwood	8427	12	0		6	0	6	175	38	127	10	0
Evansville	119908	762	8	75		210	469	5881	1008	4490	383	
Fairmount	2832	17	0		0	0	17	17	15	1	1	0
Fishers	91100	25	0	4		14	7	940	46	855	39	2
Fort Wayne	261642	1040	43	95		410	492	8924	1698	6812	414	68
Frankfort	15987	18	2	5		8	3	521	92	407	22	
Franklin	24774	115	0	5		11	99	1049	87	947	15	0
Gary	76556	460	46		32	212	170	3617	990	2229	398	32
Gas City	5931	1	0		0	1	0	136	28	105	3	
Goshen	33166	50	3		12	25	10	1272	209	1010	53	0
Greenfield	21653	57	2	6		4	45	464	52	378	34	
Greenwood	56502	261	2		0	21	238	1923	171	1610	142	3
Griffith	16278	22	0	3		14	5	386	41	311	34	0
Hagerstown	1717	3	0	1		0	2	11	2	7	2	0
Hammond	77005	540	8	43		158	331	2756	503	1975	278	22
Hartford City	5949	6	0		1	5	0	80	14	66	0	0
Hobart	28223	82	0		6	16	60	1292	96	1126	70	6
Indianapolis	866351	11907	148	684		3976	7099	41540	10209	26335	4996	251
Jasper	15530	45	0		1	0	44	171	17	147	7	0
Jeffersonville	47327	65	0		11	35	19	1370	186	1035	149	3
Kendallville	9942	72	0		7	1	64	261	39	207	15	
Kokomo	57984	441	4	30		84	323	1760	476	1196	88	5
Lafayette	71562	360	2	35		109	214	3016	612	2217	187	10
Lake Station	11956	35	1		8	14	12	475	37	393	45	0
La Porte	21891	93	0	9		20	64	765	145	576	44	1
Lawrenceburg	4943	9	1	0		4	4	127	20	98	9	
Ligonier	4407	1	0		0	0	1	24	5	18	1	0
Linton	5259	8	0	2		1	5	192	15	160	17	
Logansport	17699	15	1	6		1	7	634	66	523	45	4
Lowell	9476	12	0		0	0	12	73	6	67	0	0
Marion	28926	115	2		13	38	62	1156	176	916	64	3
Merrillville	35276	49	5		3	21	20	1321	105	1089	127	1
Michigan City	31459	186	2		19	50	115	1444	213	1131	100	
Mishawaka	48267	165	1		35	69	60	2523	283	2034	206	
Mooresville	9675	15	0	2		8	5	295	32	234	29	0
Muncie	70065	252	6	29		95	122	2755	475	2083	197	
Munster	22865	10	0		0	9	1	471	32	427	12	
Nappanee	6812	1	0		1	0	0	137	42	91	4	0
New Haven	15886	38	1	3		5	29	353	47	294	12	4
New Whiteland	5991	0	0		0	0	0	71	33	36	2	0
North Vernon	6599	29	0	2		1	26	260	36	224	0	0
Peru	10998	22	0		2	2	18	403	73	313	17	0
Plainfield	31198	89	1	3		16	69	917	81	755	81	2
Plymouth	10037	7	0	1		4	2	222	22	188	12	1
Porter	4882	4	0	1		0	3	47	8	38	1	0
Portland	6183	12	0	4		0	8	81	3	75	3	
Scottsburg	6655	17	0		0	2	15	226	26	197	3	0
Sellersburg	8723	26	0		1	3	22	95	9	79	7	
Seymour	19762	69	1		5	9	54	720	96	573	51	1
Shelbyville	19137	215	0		9	9	197	707	99	569	39	
South Bend[7]	101621	1037	14	70		388	565	5166	1241	3359	566	47
South Whitley	1735	3	0		0	0	3	18	3	10	5	0
Speedway	12189	40	3		4	25	8	632	66	520	46	1
St. John	16822	4	0		2	1	1	124	20	101	3	0
Tell City	7253	1	0	1		0	0	167	26	125	16	2
Terre Haute	60830	157	4	34		96	23	3150	696	2107	347	71
Tipton	5102	2	0		0	0	2	116	23	89	4	1
Union City	3420	13	0	0		0	13	33	17	15	1	0
Vincennes	17937	14	0	3		8	3	850	170	626	54	3
Warsaw	14657	72	0		2	6	64	513	56	440	17	1
Westfield	38186	24	1	2		1	20	411	23	373	15	0
West Lafayette	46284	57	0		10	10	37	452	71	360	21	0
Whitestown	6850	32	0		0	3	29	133	19	111	3	

Table 6. Offenses Known to Law Enforcement, by Selected State and City, 2016—Continued

(Number.)

State/city	Population	Violent crime	Murder and nonnegligent manslaughter	Rape (revised definition)[1]	Rape (legacy definition)[2]	Robbery	Aggravated assault	Property crime	Burglary	Larceny-theft	Motor vehicle theft	Arson[3]
Whiting	4848	23	0		2	13	8	168	10	140	18	
Winchester	4732	2	0		0	0	2	201	29	164	8	0
Zionsville	26877	31	2		2	0	27	108	5	95	8	
IOWA												
Adel	4356	20	0	3		0	17	183	116	62	5	3
Albia	3840	4	0	0		0	4	43	9	29	5	0
Algona	5453	17	0	3		0	14	39	7	28	4	0
Altoona	17503	31	0	1		8	22	523	58	450	15	5
Ames	66333	107	1	39		15	52	1077	164	867	46	1
Anamosa	5454	10	0	0		0	10	73	19	50	4	0
Ankeny	59236	128	2	18		8	100	756	238	468	50	5
Audubon	1988	2	0	0		1	1	19	3	16	0	0
Belmond	2303	0	0	0		0	0	5	2	2	1	0
Bettendorf[4]	35946	59	0	10		5	44			416	23	7
Bloomfield	2611	3	0	0		0	3	4	0	4	0	0
Blue Grass	1724	3	0	3		0	0	4	1	3	0	0
Boone	12702	48	0	1		2	45	169	50	112	7	2
Buffalo	1304	4	0	1		0	2	12	0	12	0	0
Burlington	25376	207	3	14		31	159	1026	247	713	66	10
Camanche	4320	12	0	0		0	12	69	19	42	8	0
Carlisle	4225	28	0	1		1	26	83	23	55	5	0
Carroll	9940	6	0	0		0	6	208	51	149	8	0
Carter Lake	3791	24	0	3		4	17	115	21	72	22	0
Cedar Falls	41651	66	0	20		9	37	708	118	559	31	3
Cedar Rapids	131181	387	4	67		100	216	5019	995	3670	354	19
Centerville	5343	17	0	1		0	16	251	119	122	10	2
Chariton	4194	11	0	0		0	11	114	30	78	6	2
Charles City	7417	21	0	9		0	12	143	26	111	6	0
Cherokee	4983	22	0	0		0	22	69	15	52	2	0
Clarinda	5386	28	0	2		0	26	183	43	128	12	2
Clarion	2752	4	0	1		0	3	13	6	5	2	0
Clear Lake	7555	26	0	0		0	26	189	48	137	4	1
Clinton	25906	229	0	20		28	181	1160	300	795	65	3
Clive[5]	17836	26	2	4		0	20		51		24	4
Coralville	20957	58	0	15		23	20	662	70	582	10	5
Council Bluffs	62642	150	4	27		55	64	3862	387	3043	432	16
Cresco	3826	1	0	1		0	0	29	8	21	0	0
Creston	7860	26	0	0		2	24	160	22	128	10	0
Davenport	103118	750	7	88		155	500	5001	1155	3436	410	8
Decorah	7864	11	0	3		0	8	76	3	70	3	0
Des Moines	211501	1497	13	140		318	1026	8881	1944	5920	1017	44
De Witt	5226	7	0	1		0	6	82	35	44	3	0
Dubuque	59026	210	1	52		26	131	1832	408	1349	75	12
Dyersville	4231	7	0	1		0	6	38	5	32	1	0
Eagle Grove	3389	2	0	1		0	1	48	14	32	2	2
Eldridge	6348	6	0	0		1	5	14	4	8	2	0
Emmetsburg	3795	8	0	4		0	4	22	7	14	1	0
Estherville	5947	21	0	2		1	18	105	40	63	2	0
Evansdale	4824	12	0	3		1	8	101	36	61	4	0
Fairfield	9982	17	0	4		0	13	323	107	196	20	3
Forest City	3994	5	0	2		0	3	20	10	9	1	0
Fort Dodge	24557	144	1	19		22	102	979	96	840	43	8
Fort Madison	10654	53	1	4		7	41	358	25	306	27	6
Glenwood	5250	29	1	1		0	27	82	26	48	8	0
Grinnell	9127	76	0	9		1	66	269	90	173	6	1
Grundy Center	2715	1	0	0		0	1	6	1	4	1	0
Hampton	4256	6	0	2		1	3	14	3	8	3	0
Hawarden	2552	4	0	0		0	4	21	9	12	0	0
Hiawatha	7235	17	1	3		2	11	163	52	96	15	3
Humboldt	4579	3	0	0		0	3	32	4	24	4	0
Indianola	15601	93	1	17		0	75	350	60	278	12	4
Iowa City	75527	197	0	39		43	115	1551	294	1169	88	1
Iowa Falls	5186	2	0	0		1	1	106	13	86	7	0
Jefferson	4176	6	0	0		1	5	140	40	97	3	1
Johnston	21635	26	0	5		3	18	226	40	172	14	0
Keokuk	10577	76	1	2		5	68	536	153	336	47	0
Le Claire	4029	8	0	2		0	6	13	4	9	0	0
Le Mars	9750	10	1	0		0	9	223	61	144	18	4
Leon	1890	6	0	0		0	6	10	3	6	1	1
Manchester	5051	5	0	1		0	4	115	32	80	3	0
Maquoketa	5961	18	0	4		2	12	163	67	91	5	1
Marengo	2511	8	0	0		0	8	6	1	4	1	0
Marion	37845	71	0	14		8	49	604	142	428	34	5
Marshalltown	27628	163	1	15		14	133	813	181	572	60	15
Mason City	27230	37	3	2		5	27	1122	264	837	21	1
Missouri Valley	2668	2	0	0		0	2	57	15	37	5	2
Monticello	3832	30	0	1		2	27	80	14	62	4	0
Mount Pleasant[4]	8389	12	0	1		0	11			128	18	2
Mount Vernon[4]	4482	3	0	2		0	1			24	2	0
Muscatine	24010	158	0	11		8	139	531	114	382	35	17
New Hampton	3430	7	0	2		0	5	20	7	12	1	0
Newton	15102	54	0	10		5	39	461	102	335	24	1

Table 6. Offenses Known to Law Enforcement, by Selected State and City, 2016—Continued

(Number.)

State/city	Population	Violent crime	Murder and nonnegligent manslaughter	Rape (revised definition)[1]	Rape (legacy definition)[2]	Robbery	Aggravated assault	Property crime	Burglary	Larceny-theft	Motor vehicle theft	Arson[3]
North Liberty	16458	52	0	18		2	32	121	32	86	3	0
Norwalk	10371	16	0	2		3	11	87	19	67	1	1
Oelwein	6104	22	0	5		1	16	94	23	67	4	0
Ogden	2041	4	0	0		0	4	13	4	9	0	1
Onawa	2859	14	0	4		0	10	69	23	44	2	1
Orange City	6225	2	0	0		0	2	48	17	30	1	0
Osage	3659	12	0	0		0	12	50	7	40	3	0
Osceola	4976	6	0	0		0	6	94	12	74	8	2
Oskaloosa	11626	49	0	8		7	34	302	70	219	13	1
Ottumwa	24543	101	1	20		8	72	1074	230	753	91	9
Pella	10368	10	0	5		0	5	105	22	73	10	1
Perry	8160	33	3	0		2	28	195	54	122	19	3
Pleasant Hill[5]	9415	26	0	4		1	21		76		20	0
Prairie City	1715	2	1	0		0	1	54	46	7	1	0
Red Oak	5424	21	0	3		1	17	172	54	101	17	3
Rock Valley	3762	0	0	0		0	0	25	15	10	0	0
Sergeant Bluff	4579	13	0	0		0	13	48	10	33	5	0
Sheldon	5067	13	0	2		0	11	53	16	33	4	0
Shenandoah	4996	8	0	1		0	7	43	11	29	3	1
Sigourney	1995	4	0	1		0	3	19	7	12	0	1
Sioux Center	7544	2	0	0		0	2	11	6	5	0	0
Sioux City	82819	365	1	40		59	265	3247	592	2363	292	13
Spencer	11211	9	0	9		0	0	230	49	177	4	1
Spirit Lake	5049	19	0	4		2	13	152	30	120	2	2
State Center	1470	2	0	0		0	2	6	3	3	0	0
Storm Lake	10959	58	0	8		0	50	320	107	207	6	2
Story City	3439	4	0	1		0	3	40	7	28	5	0
Tama	2809	14	0	1		1	12	25	8	13	4	0
Tipton	3196	9	0	0		0	9	21	3	18	0	0
Toledo	2176	7	0	0		0	7	45	12	31	2	0
Urbandale	45012	67	1	9		8	49	700	175	480	45	4
Vinton	5128	9	0	1		0	8	18	5	12	1	0
Walcott	1639	4	0	0		0	4	15	5	10	0	1
Washington	7437	43	0	7		0	36	88	20	61	7	1
Waterloo	68470	507	3	56		61	387	2120	614	1368	138	24
Waukon	3701	7	0	1		0	6	55	9	41	5	1
Waverly	10104	114	0	4		1	109	118	25	91	2	0
Webster City	7768	24	0	3		0	21	126	19	100	7	0
West Branch	2340	7	0	1		0	6	10	2	7	1	0
West Burlington[4]	3055	8	0	0		1	7			288	8	3
West Des Moines	65631	149	1	24		19	105	1513	147	1296	70	7
West Liberty	3723	11	0	6		0	5	28	9	18	1	0
Williamsburg	3221	1	0	0		0	1	23	3	18	2	0
Wilton	2808	2	0	0		0	2	13	2	10	1	0
Windsor Heights	4893	7	0	2		1	4	222	25	195	2	1
Winterset	5170	13	0	1		0	12	83	21	59	3	0
KANSAS												
Abilene	6501	8	0	3		3	2	126	20	101	5	1
Andale	1004	0	0	0		0	0	0	0	0	0	0
Andover	12937	15	0	5		4	6	204	22	173	9	0
Anthony	2224	7	0	3		0	4	80	32	47	1	1
Arkansas City	12085	58	0	11		3	44	439	80	335	24	4
Arma	1445	2	0	1		0	1	41	8	30	3	0
Assaria	410	0	0	0		0	0	0	0	0	0	0
Atchison	10654	38	0	10		7	21	381	73	293	15	2
Atwood	1187	2	0	1		0	1	26	2	23	1	0
Auburn	1216	0	0	0		0	0	0	0	0	0	0
Augusta	9304	29	0	3		4	22	254	63	178	13	1
Basehor	5563	6	0	2		1	3	60	15	44	1	0
Baxter Springs	3989	8	0	0		0	8	86	28	54	4	0
Bel Aire	7574	6	0	1		0	5	58	24	32	2	1
Beloit	3784	4	0	0		0	4	60	18	40	2	0
Benton	875	1	0	0		0	1	36	16	20	0	0
Bronson	308	0	0	0		0	0	0	0	0	0	0
Bucklin	793	0	0	0		0	0	0	0	0	0	0
Burden	533	3	0	0		0	3	6	3	2	1	0
Burlington	2604	4	0	0		0	4	38	11	25	2	0
Clay Center	4140	11	0	2		1	8	55	12	40	3	0
Clearwater	2547	3	0	2		0	1	55	21	33	1	1
Coffeyville[9]	9555	83	0	6		5	72			406	34	5
Colby	5418	5	0	1		0	4	115	24	85	6	1
Columbus	3116	11	0	1		0	10	63	11	47	5	2
Colwich	1388	0	0	0		0	0	4	1	2	1	0
Concordia[9]	5183	21	0	10		0	11			98	10	0
Conway Springs	1231	1	0	0		0	1	22	8	12	2	0
Council Grove	2068	1	0	0		0	1	41	12	26	3	0
Delphos	342	0	0	0		0	0	0	0	0	0	0
Derby	23708	22	0	5		1	16	539	107	409	23	3
Dodge City	27997	99	0	10		9	80	869	127	701	41	4
Eastborough	767	0	0	0		0	0	3	0	3	0	0
Edwardsville	4377	21	0	6		2	13	122	29	80	13	2
El Dorado	12913	23	1	8		2	12	346	82	224	40	2

Table 6. Offenses Known to Law Enforcement, by Selected State and City, 2016—Continued

(Number.)

State/city	Population	Violent crime	Murder and nonnegligent manslaughter	Rape (revised definition)[1]	Rape (legacy definition)[2]	Robbery	Aggravated assault	Property crime	Burglary	Larceny-theft	Motor vehicle theft	Arson[3]
Elkhart	2011	4	0	2		0	2	15	2	12	1	0
Ellinwood	2053	3	0	1		0	2	49	18	29	2	1
Ellis	2065	7	0	0		0	7	11	5	6	0	0
Ellsworth	3043	5	0	2		0	3	36	8	24	4	0
Elwood	1181	3	0	1		0	2	23	12	7	4	0
Emporia	24601	35	0	12		4	19	575	76	482	17	1
Fairway	3987	2	0	0		0	2	27	2	23	2	1
Fort Scott	7792	42	0	6		5	31	316	84	207	25	3
Frontenac	3419	10	0	2		0	8	72	13	52	7	0
Galena	2901	12	0	0		1	11	52	11	37	4	0
Garden City	27038	139	0	20		13	106	837	81	731	25	7
Garnett	3229	10	0	3		1	6	66	9	54	3	0
Girard	2754	8	0	2		0	6	73	21	48	4	0
Goddard	4782	3	0	0		1	2	98	9	85	4	0
Grandview Plaza	1656	15	0	4		0	11	40	9	28	3	0
Great Bend	15661	60	0	7		4	49	601	139	434	28	2
Greensburg	799	0	0	0		0	0	7	2	5	0	0
Halstead	2094	5	0	1		0	4	33	5	26	2	1
Haven	1221	1	0	0		0	1	19	7	11	1	0
Havensville	150	0	0	0		0	0	0	0	0	0	0
Hays	21206	67	1	2		2	62	443	89	328	26	1
Haysville	11288	18	0	5		1	12	295	66	212	17	4
Herington	2371	4	0	0		0	4	74	15	51	8	0
Hesston	3832	0	0	0		0	0	53	13	38	2	0
Hiawatha	3080	11	0	1		0	10	120	20	91	9	0
Highland	1010	0	0	0		0	0	7	1	4	2	0
Hillsboro	2845	3	0	1		0	2	24	6	18	0	0
Holcomb	2167	4	0	0		0	4	24	6	15	3	0
Holton	3250	6	0	0		0	6	71	13	52	6	1
Horton	1711	2	0	0		0	2	46	9	36	1	1
Hugoton	3974	5	0	0		0	5	17	3	14	0	1
Independence	8860	58	0	4		10	44	505	113	375	17	9
Inman	1358	0	0	0		0	0	17	3	13	1	0
Iola	5425	33	0	8		1	24	277	41	224	12	2
Junction City	24780	175	1	16		10	148	513	91	396	26	6
Kanopolis	470	0	0	0		0	0	0	0	0	0	0
Kingman	3070	10	0	1		1	8	78	16	60	2	0
Lake Quivira	941	0	0	0		0	0	1	0	1	0	0
Lansing	11860	21	1	0		4	16	125	25	88	12	0
Larned	3950	17	0	3		1	13	88	33	52	3	3
Leavenworth[9]	36100	234	2	26		44	162			934	102	13
Leawood	35139	30	0	1		6	23	396	62	312	22	1
Lenexa	53376	70	0	8		7	55	921	92	734	95	1
Lindsborg	3369	5	0	2		0	3	79	38	41	0	0
Louisburg	4266	5	0	1		1	3	57	11	43	3	0
Maize	4564	21	0	8		1	12	85	11	62	12	0
Marysville	3329	8	0	0		0	8	75	8	56	11	0
Meade	1605	2	0	0		0	2	13	1	12	0	0
Medicine Lodge	1986	7	0	0		1	6	18	4	13	1	1
Merriam	11337	51	0	8		4	39	555	42	415	98	2
Minneapolis	1996	0	0	0		0	0	31	9	21	1	0
Mission	9523	29	0	8		2	19	414	36	323	55	1
Mission Hills	3621	0	0	0		0	0	41	9	27	5	0
Moran	513	0	0	0		0	0	0	0	0	0	0
Mulvane	6347	6	0	1		1	4	159	10	142	7	0
Neodesha	2333	7	0	0		0	7	27	3	22	2	0
Newton	19226	99	0	16		2	81	611	113	475	23	4
North Newton	1811	4	0	0		0	4	6	1	5	0	0
Norton	2830	4	0	2		0	2	27	5	19	3	0
Nortonville	612	0	0	0		0	0	5	2	3	0	0
Oakley	2104	4	0	2		0	2	20	5	15	0	1
Olathe	135977	222	1	45		31	145	2127	178	1789	160	2
Osage City	2825	5	0	1		0	4	72	10	59	3	1
Osawatomie	4267	22	0	2		0	20	109	34	72	3	1
Osborne	1358	1	0	1		0	0	20	10	7	3	0
Oswego	1755	0	0	0		0	0	21	6	15	0	0
Ottawa	12334	47	0	9		5	33	341	29	293	19	5
Overland Park	189104	376	4	108		58	206	2803	405	2078	320	16
Paola	5509	18	0	7		5	6	171	39	125	7	2
Park City	7671	14	0	4		2	8	212	30	163	19	0
Parsons	10016	72	0	9		10	53	470	100	351	19	4
Peabody	1131	0	0	0		0	0	25	9	11	5	0
Plainville	1893	0	0	0		0	0	1	0	1	0	0
Prairie Village	21958	11	0	1		1	9	222	33	163	26	0
Pratt	6854	10	0	1		0	9	313	96	207	10	0
Russell[9]	4537	18	0	2		0	16			38	7	0
Sabetha	2589	5	0	0		0	5	13	0	12	1	0
Salina	47805	205	2	36		32	135	1827	294	1404	129	19
Scott City	3840	7	0	1		1	5	36	4	30	2	0
Shawnee	65603	133	1	19		10	103	1175	132	897	146	6
Stafford	976	3	1	0		0	2	5	1	4	0	0
Sterling	2285	1	0	0		0	1	16	5	9	2	0
St. Francis	1300	1	0	0		0	1	17	3	12	2	0

Table 6. Offenses Known to Law Enforcement, by Selected State and City, 2016—Continued

(Number.)

State/city	Population	Violent crime	Murder and nonnegligent manslaughter	Rape (revised definition)[1]	Rape (legacy definition)[2]	Robbery	Aggravated assault	Property crime	Burglary	Larceny-theft	Motor vehicle theft	Arson[3]
St. George	991	1	0	0		0	1	6	2	3	1	0
St. John	1212	1	0	0		0	1	12	3	8	1	0
St. Marys	2668	5	0	0		0	5	24	5	15	4	0
Tonganoxie	5295	10	0	2		0	8	100	17	79	4	0
Topeka	127166	711	17	54		248	392	7148	1114	5227	807	1
Ulysses	6084	4	0	2		0	2	55	18	35	2	0
Valley Center	7302	13	0	1		3	9	102	11	87	4	0
Valley Falls	1150	1	0	0		0	1	12	2	9	1	0
Wellington[9]	7954	12	0	1		1	10			290	26	2
Wellsville	1810	0	0	0		0	0	14	4	8	2	0
Westwood	2314	0	0	0		0	0	59	5	52	2	0
Wichita	391399	4136	31	309		652	3144	21065	3593	15284	2188	136
Winfield	12176	38	0	9		1	28	394	57	306	31	1
Yates Center	1315	3	0	1		0	2	24	5	17	2	0
KENTUCKY												
Adairville	888	0	0	0		0	0	4	2	2	0	0
Albany	2008	2	0	0		1	1	7	0	5	2	0
Alexandria	9112	4	0	1		2	1	139	15	112	12	0
Allen	185	0	0	0		0	0	0	0	0	0	0
Anchorage	2434	0	0	0		0	0	18	5	12	1	0
Ashland	20987	51	1	16		11	23	885	146	704	35	9
Auburn	1354	3	0	1		1	1	8	2	6	0	0
Audubon Park	1515	0	0	0		0	0	44	10	23	11	0
Augusta	1157	1	0	0		1	0	14	5	9	0	0
Barbourville	3174	6	0	0		3	3	53	14	29	10	0
Bardstown	13181	20	1	5		7	7	257	62	156	39	1
Bardwell	688	0	0	0		0	0	0	0	0	0	0
Beattyville	1232	0	0	0		0	0	12	6	1	5	0
Beaver Dam	3640	6	0	0		1	5	38	2	30	6	0
Bellefonte	862	0	0	0		0	0	1	0	1	0	0
Bellevue	5879	3	0	1		2	0	100	12	81	7	1
Benham	463	0	0	0		0	0	0	0	0	0	0
Benton	4346	4	0	3		1	0	144	13	120	11	0
Berea	15135	20	0	5		7	8	430	103	277	50	1
Bloomfield	1058	0	0	0		0	0	2	1	1	0	0
Booneville	75	0	0	0		0	0	0	0	0	0	0
Bowling Green	64561	204	4	51		85	64	2773	379	2236	158	6
Brandenburg	2885	0	0	0		0	0	19	5	13	1	0
Brodhead	1204	0	0	0		0	0	0	0	0	0	0
Brooksville	636	0	0	0		0	0	0	0	0	0	0
Brownsville	824	1	0	0		0	1	2	0	0	2	0
Burkesville	1511	1	0	0		0	1	6	1	5	0	0
Burnside	845	0	0	0		0	0	54	14	38	2	0
Butler	583	0	0	0		0	0	0	0	0	0	0
Cadiz	2630	11	0	1		3	7	78	10	65	3	0
Calvert City	2521	4	0	2		0	2	22	5	16	1	0
Campbellsburg	831	0	0	0		0	0	0	0	0	0	0
Campbellsville	11357	31	3	7		9	12	390	93	273	24	0
Caneyville	622	0	0	0		0	0	0	0	0	0	0
Carlisle	2011	4	0	0		1	3	4	0	3	1	0
Carrollton	3877	5	0	0		1	4	66	13	44	9	0
Catlettsburg	1798	0	0	0		0	0	38	9	27	2	0
Cave City	2411	5	0	1		2	2	45	13	27	5	1
Centertown	444	0	0	0		0	0	1	0	1	0	0
Central City	5875	1	0	0		0	1	84	5	77	2	0
Clarkson	899	0	0	0		0	0	0	0	0	0	0
Clay	1134	0	0	0		0	0	0	0	0	0	0
Clay City	1089	2	0	0		0	2	25	8	17	0	0
Clinton	1306	3	0	0		1	2	12	2	10	0	0
Cloverport	1157	1	0	0		0	1	11	3	5	3	0
Coal Run Village	1582	2	0	1		1	0	34	8	26	0	0
Cold Spring	6217	3	0	0		3	0	103	6	89	8	0
Columbia	4685	3	0	0		0	3	13	7	5	1	0
Corbin	7403	9	0	3		3	3	204	48	127	29	3
Covington	41094	204	2	38		103	61	1340	296	921	123	5
Crab Orchard	832	0	0	0		0	0	0	0	0	0	0
Cumberland	2078	2	0	0		1	1	14	1	11	2	1
Cynthiana	6421	20	0	4		6	10	159	33	119	7	0
Danville	16773	22	0	5		7	10	322	113	183	26	3
Dawson Springs	2732	0	0	0		0	0	61	12	43	6	0
Dayton	5450	4	0	0		2	2	119	24	87	8	0
Dry Ridge	2208	4	0	1		2	1	70	3	64	3	1
Eddyville	2582	0	0	0		0	0	29	8	20	1	0
Edgewood	8801	0	0	0		0	0	77	17	56	4	0
Edmonton	1562	1	0	0		1	0	19	7	11	1	0
Elizabethtown	29821	68	2	15		17	34	476	107	329	40	2
Elkhorn City	928	0	0	0		0	0	3	1	2	0	0
Elkton	2181	3	0	0		2	1	37	23	12	2	0
Elsmere	8563	13	2	7		2	2	139	29	98	12	2
Eminence	2544	1	0	0		0	1	26	5	19	2	0
Erlanger	22952	33	0	8		18	7	317	45	250	22	1
Eubank	325	0	0	0		0	0	0	0	0	0	0

Table 6. Offenses Known to Law Enforcement, by Selected State and City, 2016—Continued

(Number.)

State/city	Population	Violent crime	Murder and nonnegligent manslaughter	Rape (revised definition)[1]	Rape (legacy definition)[2]	Robbery	Aggravated assault	Property crime	Burglary	Larceny-theft	Motor vehicle theft	Arson[3]
Evarts	918	0	0	0		0	0	0	0	0	0	0
Falmouth	2109	2	0	0		1	1	28	4	22	2	0
Ferguson	944	0	0	0		0	0	3	1	2	0	0
Flatwoods	7307	1	0	0		0	1	17	4	12	1	0
Fleming-Neon	720	0	0	0		0	0	0	0	0	0	0
Flemingsburg	2902	2	0	1		0	1	43	14	25	4	0
Florence	32671	80	1	13		34	32	1386	92	1235	59	4
Fort Mitchell	8334	7	0	1		4	2	84	12	68	4	2
Fort Thomas	16436	2	0	1		1	0	90	12	70	8	0
Fort Wright	5801	9	0	1		8	0	89	11	74	4	0
Fountain Run	210	0	0	0		0	0	0	0	0	0	0
Frankfort	27926	105	2	12		35	56	1093	256	750	87	4
Franklin	8852	24	0	5		6	13	238	43	181	14	0
Fulton	2195	2	0	1		0	1	76	20	51	5	0
Gamaliel	364	0	0	0		0	0	0	0	0	0	0
Georgetown	33007	57	0	13		21	23	919	136	731	52	2
Glasgow	14560	33	0	6		5	22	466	112	316	38	1
Graymoor-Devondale	2965	3	0	0		3	0	31	9	17	5	0
Grayson	4046	3	0	0		2	1	109	11	92	6	0
Greensburg	2116	1	0	1		0	0	29	8	18	3	0
Greenup	1151	0	0	0		0	0	3	2	0	1	0
Greenville	4378	3	1	0		0	2	24	6	12	6	0
Guthrie	1441	2	0	0		1	1	10	5	5	0	0
Hardinsburg	2332	1	0	0		0	1	14	3	10	1	0
Harlan	1619	2	0	0		2	0	50	9	40	1	0
Harrodsburg	8399	14	0	1		0	13	183	63	102	18	0
Hartford	2765	3	0	1		0	2	6	2	2	2	0
Hawesville	1006	0	0	0		0	0	6	0	6	0	0
Hazard	5310	6	0	3		2	1	272	24	240	8	0
Henderson	28904	56	1	6		24	25	767	171	547	49	1
Heritage Creek	1126	0	0	0		0	0	3	0	3	0	0
Highland Heights	7216	5	0	1		1	3	53	5	47	1	0
Hillview	8177	8	0	5		3	0	126	34	72	20	0
Hodgenville	3259	2	0	0		0	2	19	3	13	3	0
Hopkinsville	32222	94	4	15		44	31	922	202	672	48	1
Horse Cave	2351	0	0	0		0	0	0	0	0	0	0
Hurstbourne Acres	1886	0	0	0		0	0	18	4	14	0	0
Hustonville	398	0	0	0		0	0	0	0	0	0	0
Hyden	348	0	0	0		0	0	0	0	0	0	0
Independence	27227	19	0	10		4	5	154	28	112	14	1
Indian Hills	2977	0	0	0		0	0	41	12	23	6	0
Inez	678	0	0	0		0	0	0	0	0	0	0
Irvine	2404	2	0	0		0	2	2	1	1	0	0
Irvington	1186	2	0	0		0	2	15	6	8	1	0
Jackson	2138	1	0	0		0	1	27	6	19	2	1
Jamestown	1805	1	0	0		0	1	10	1	8	1	0
Jeffersontown	27006	32	1	4		22	5	637	92	459	86	0
Jenkins	2077	0	0	0		0	0	0	0	0	0	0
Junction City	2290	0	0	0		0	0	2	1	1	0	0
La Center	1004	1	0	0		0	1	6	2	4	0	0
La Grange	8728	12	0	0		8	4	182	25	144	13	0
Lakeside Park-Crestview Hills	6159	6	0	1		5	0	118	6	106	6	0
Lancaster	3873	10	0	1		2	7	73	26	43	4	0
Lawrenceburg	11140	14	0	2		5	7	97	18	70	9	0
Lebanon	5710	11	0	3		6	2	100	29	63	8	0
Lebanon Junction	1937	0	0	0		0	0	0	0	0	0	0
Leitchfield	6904	9	0	2		0	7	137	28	97	12	0
Lewisburg	806	0	0	0		0	0	5	2	3	0	0
Lewisport	1704	2	0	0		1	1	6	0	6	0	0
Lexington	317853	1079	24	200		575	280	13058	2435	9465	1158	39
Liberty	2158	1	0	0		0	1	11	6	4	1	0
London	8152	15	1	5		6	3	351	64	263	24	0
Louisa	2452	3	0	0		0	3	27	10	13	4	0
Louisville Metro	683825	4621	119	196		1514	2792	30254	5907	19983	4364	10
Loyall	648	2	0	0		0	2	4	1	3	0	0
Ludlow	4553	13	0	5		3	5	109	21	78	10	2
Lynch	702	0	0	0		0	0	1	1	0	0	0
Lynnview	945	0	0	0		0	0	13	4	8	1	0
Madisonville	19467	30	1	5		8	16	349	75	252	22	2
Manchester	1392	5	0	1		1	3	39	12	21	6	1
Marion	2976	6	0	2		2	2	72	30	37	5	0
Martin	597	1	0	0		0	1	4	0	3	1	0
Mayfield	10086	27	0	6		10	11	326	75	230	21	2
Maysville	8780	19	0	4		9	6	303	53	241	9	0
McKee	786	0	0	0		0	0	1	0	1	0	0
Meadow Vale	762	0	0	0		0	0	1	0	1	0	0
Middlesboro	9615	32	1	2		12	17	525	67	443	15	1
Millersburg	797	0	0	0		0	0	14	6	7	1	0
Monticello	6071	7	0	1		1	5	77	22	51	4	0
Morehead	7085	12	0	7		3	2	139	18	119	2	3
Morganfield	3582	0	0	0		0	0	25	8	17	0	1
Morgantown	2480	2	0	1		0	1	53	13	34	6	0

Table 6. Offenses Known to Law Enforcement, by Selected State and City, 2016—Continued

(Number.)

State/city	Population	Violent crime	Murder and nonnegligent manslaughter	Rape (revised definition)[1]	Rape (legacy definition)[2]	Robbery	Aggravated assault	Property crime	Burglary	Larceny-theft	Motor vehicle theft	Arson[3]
Mortons Gap	850	0	0	0		0	0	0	0	0	0	0
Mount Olivet	342	0	0	0		0	0	0	0	0	0	0
Mount Sterling	7268	24	0	6		13	5	295	37	240	18	2
Mount Vernon	2497	2	0	0		0	2	40	19	16	5	2
Mount Washington	14162	11	0	3		4	4	207	32	156	19	1
Muldraugh	994	1	0	0		1	0	20	3	11	6	0
Munfordville	1645	4	0	0		0	4	16	8	7	1	0
Murray	19182	41	0	11		10	20	611	125	470	16	2
New Haven	893	0	0	0		0	0	0	0	0	0	0
Newport	15330	59	0	9		34	16	715	105	565	45	3
Nicholasville	30093	53	0	11		28	14	1056	199	796	61	3
Northfield	1057	0	0	0		0	0	15	1	14	0	0
Oak Grove	7431	35	0	12		11	12	368	78	266	24	0
Olive Hill	1593	2	0	0		0	2	12	10	2	0	0
Owensboro	59359	136	1	34		49	52	2658	486	1937	235	14
Owenton	1552	0	0	0		0	0	11	4	6	1	0
Owingsville	1595	1	0	0		1	0	9	0	7	2	0
Paducah	24836	87	1	16		31	39	1217	150	999	68	7
Paintsville	4251	6	0	2		0	4	60	9	46	5	0
Paris	9883	15	0	1		5	9	232	65	154	13	1
Park Hills	3011	3	0	1		1	1	33	7	22	4	1
Perryville	763	0	0	0		0	0	0	0	0	0	0
Pewee Valley	1547	0	0	0		0	0	4	2	2	0	0
Pikeville	7037	14	1	6		3	4	404	49	350	5	0
Pineville	1745	0	0	0		0	0	34	12	21	1	1
Pioneer Village	2866	2	0	1		1	0	23	6	11	6	0
Pippa Passes	661	0	0	0		0	0	0	0	0	0	0
Powderly	729	0	0	0		0	0	10	1	9	0	0
Prestonsburg	3326	6	0	0		1	5	51	20	28	3	1
Princeton	6142	21	0	10		3	8	230	85	131	14	1
Prospect	4918	0	0	0		0	0	55	2	49	4	0
Providence	3042	2	0	0		1	1	28	7	17	4	0
Raceland	2383	2	0	0		0	2	9	3	6	0	0
Radcliff	22346	77	0	22		25	30	611	155	418	38	10
Ravenna	587	0	0	0		0	0	7	0	6	1	0
Richmond	33965	75	0	18		37	20	1374	249	1048	77	5
Russell	3245	5	0	2		1	2	60	3	57	0	1
Russell Springs	2525	2	0	1		0	1	67	15	48	4	0
Russellville	7073	25	2	1		7	15	224	54	159	11	2
Sadieville	338	0	0	0		0	0	2	0	2	0	0
Salyersville	1804	0	0	0		0	0	3	0	3	0	0
Science Hill	696	0	0	0		0	0	0	0	0	0	0
Scottsville	4446	12	1	5		2	4	108	28	64	16	0
Sebree	1551	0	0	0		0	0	0	0	0	0	0
Shelbyville	15488	10	0	3		5	2	220	48	163	9	3
Shepherdsville	12098	34	0	8		10	16	521	76	382	63	1
Shively	15800	93	5	10		60	18	654	144	381	129	1
Silver Grove	1123	0	0	0		0	0	0	0	0	0	0
Simpsonville	2744	3	0	0		2	1	97	6	88	3	0
Smiths Grove	740	0	0	0		0	0	4	2	2	0	0
Somerset	11482	22	0	3		8	11	423	79	303	41	4
Southgate	3871	2	0	0		2	0	43	4	31	8	0
South Shore	1097	0	0	0		0	0	0	0	0	0	0
Springfield	3093	3	0	0		1	2	22	4	10	8	0
Stamping Ground	744	0	0	0		0	0	7	1	6	0	0
Stanford	3668	3	0	0		1	2	35	10	17	8	0
Stanton	2651	3	0	0		3	0	63	16	47	0	0
St. Matthews	18127	38	0	1		28	9	803	83	655	65	1
Strathmoor Village	666	0	0	0		0	0	0	0	0	0	0
Sturgis	1914	1	0	0		0	1	16	6	10	0	0
Taylor Mill	6793	5	0	0		1	4	43	9	32	2	0
Taylorsville	1035	0	0	0		0	0	17	6	11	0	0
Tompkinsville	2277	1	0	0		0	1	5	1	2	2	1
Trenton	387	0	0	0		0	0	1	0	1	0	0
Uniontown	960	2	0	0		0	2	15	3	12	0	0
Vanceburg	1445	0	0	0		0	0	5	2	3	0	0
Versailles	25923	15	0	4		4	7	393	105	273	15	0
Villa Hills	7499	2	0	0		0	2	28	2	24	2	0
Vine Grove	5892	7	0	2		2	3	71	26	41	4	0
Warsaw	1697	1	0	0		0	1	20	8	11	1	0
Wayland	406	0	0	0		0	0	1	0	1	0	0
West Buechel	1277	5	0	0		5	0	214	14	186	14	0
West Liberty	3336	0	0	0		0	0	14	0	13	1	0
West Point	856	0	0	0		0	0	10	0	10	0	0
Wheelwright	480	0	0	0		0	0	0	0	0	0	0
Whitesburg	1982	2	0	0		2	0	7	4	3	0	0
Wilder	3099	1	0	0		0	1	48	2	44	2	0
Williamsburg	5324	5	0	2		0	3	70	18	40	12	1
Williamstown	3946	3	0	0		1	2	36	6	27	3	0
Wilmore	6315	1	0	1		0	0	101	29	68	4	0
Winchester	18461	48	1	15		19	13	1018	147	817	54	0
Wingo	641	0	0	0		0	0	0	0	0	0	0
Woodburn	381	0	0	0		0	0	1	0	1	0	0
Worthington	1571	0	0	0		0	0	9	4	5	0	0

Table 6. Offenses Known to Law Enforcement, by Selected State and City, 2016—Continued

(Number.)

State/city	Population	Violent crime	Murder and nonnegligent manslaughter	Rape (revised definition)[1]	Rape (legacy definition)[2]	Robbery	Aggravated assault	Property crime	Burglary	Larceny-theft	Motor vehicle theft	Arson[3]
LOUISIANA												
Abbeville	12471	117	2	5		9	101	474	130	329	15	0
Addis	4808	15	0	0		0	15	0	0	0	0	0
Alexandria	47936	883	11	25		154	693	4091	1057	2765	269	0
Ball	3989	7	0	0		0	7	30	12	13	5	0
Bastrop	10595	153	2	3		29	119	1220	465	717	38	3
Baton Rouge	228389	2143	47	123		824	1149	9934	2364	6907	663	129
Berwick	4732	9	0	0		0	9	89	33	54	2	0
Blanchard	2941	2	0	0		2	0	34	11	22	1	0
Bogalusa	11882	157	1	10		24	122	662	194	424	44	0
Bossier City	69384	585	5	33		96	451	3206	494	2491	221	4
Breaux Bridge	8446	27	0	0		9	18	662	92	551	19	0
Broussard	11998	31	0	1		5	25	288	114	158	16	0
Brusly	2823	0	0	0		0	0	37	2	33	2	0
Bunkie[4]	4044		0	0			16	50	27	23	0	0
Carencro	8763	19	2	0		4	13	180	32	138	10	0
Clarence	486	0	0	0		0	0	0	0	0	0	0
Clinton	1564	9	0	0		3	6	1	0	1	0	0
Cottonport	1943	0	0	0		0	0	45	18	27	0	0
Coushatta	1832	10	0	0		0	10	25	7	18	0	0
Covington	10178	37	1	2		3	31	308	23	278	7	0
Crowley	13119	107	3	1		19	84	431	178	162	91	0
Denham Springs	10107	32	1	2		6	23	652	120	529	3	0
De Quincy	3147	5	0	1		0	4	35	7	27	1	1
De Ridder	10939	20	1	1		2	16	191	37	149	5	1
Epps	834	0	0	0		0	0	0	0	0	0	0
Erath	2106	3	0	0		0	3	11	0	11	0	0
Eunice	10291	65	0	6		7	52	552	123	414	15	0
Farmerville	3849	19	0	1		4	14	218	42	171	5	0
Ferriday	3348	21	0	0		1	20	94	37	52	5	0
Fisher	225	0	0	0		0	0	0	0	0	0	0
Florien	628	2	0	0		0	2	3	0	2	1	0
Folsom	808	2	0	0		0	2	9	2	7	0	0
Franklin	7236	49	1	0		10	38	291	96	191	4	2
Franklinton	3769	17	1	4		2	10	225	38	173	14	1
French Settlement	1132	2	0	0		0	2	4	0	3	1	0
Georgetown	325	0	0	0		0	0	0	0	0	0	0
Golden Meadow	2052	0	0	0		0	0	0	0	0	0	0
Gonzales	10860	53	1	7		17	28	899	64	791	44	1
Gramercy	3430	26	0	0		1	25	80	11	68	1	0
Greenwood	3184	4	0	0		1	3	50	8	37	5	0
Gretna	17908	42	2	2		13	25	679	88	567	24	0
Hammond	20576	286	7	12		59	208	2131	627	1412	92	3
Harahan	9364	9	0	1		0	8	126	23	94	9	1
Haughton	3306	0	0	0		0	0	13	0	13	0	0
Hodge	448	0	0	0		0	0	0	0	0	0	0
Houma	34410	167	4	17		42	104	1411	196	1159	56	4
Ida	214	0	0	0		0	0	0	0	0	0	0
Independence	1820	23	0	1		3	19	73	21	42	10	0
Iowa	3266	22	0	0		3	19	100	32	64	4	0
Jena	3420	1	0	0		0	1	3	3	0	0	0
Jennings	10140	29	1	0		2	26	321	58	252	11	0
Kaplan	4619	9	1	0		1	7	42	8	31	3	0
Kenner	67164	194	6	25		71	92	2235	245	1873	117	4
Kentwood	2368	23	0	3		2	18	170	44	121	5	0
Killian	1324	2	0	0		0	2	15	2	11	2	0
Kinder	2436	7	0	0		1	6	62	4	54	4	0
Krotz Springs	1203	4	0	0		0	4	12	3	5	4	0
Lafayette	128923	641	11	19		148	463	6417	1025	5013	379	22
Lake Charles	76864	654	8	40		143	463	3153	1626	1320	207	0
Lake Providence	3666	51	0	1		5	45	27	11	15	1	0
Leesville	6270	56	1	7		3	45	437	74	356	7	2
Mandeville	12423	26	0	3		4	19	270	31	230	9	0
Mansfield	4937	55	1	0		1	53	204	79	117	8	0
Many	2778	13	0	0		1	12	157	14	143	0	0
Marion	753	1	0	0		0	1	9	2	7	0	0
Marksville	5499	63	0	0		6	57	387	73	312	2	2
Minden	12615	26	0	0		9	17	251	44	193	14	1
Monroe	49677	1493	11	52		248	1182	4646	1025	3397	224	15
Morgan City	11731	93	0	10		13	70	601	167	408	26	1
Natchitoches	18332	188	3	4		33	148	1291	303	963	25	4
New Orleans	397208	4249	174	537		1445	2093	15571	2561	10583	2427	69
Norwood	310	0	0	0		0	0	1	1	0	0	0
Oakdale	7697	18	0	0		2	16	102	9	89	4	0
Oak Grove	1650	15	0	0		0	15	113	20	92	1	0
Oil City	994	2	0	0		0	2	14	5	8	1	0
Olla	1385	0	0	0		0	0	8	4	3	1	0
Opelousas	16557	250	4	13		54	179	1323	423	850	50	7
Patterson	6105	1	0	0		0	1	101	0	99	2	0
Pearl River	2553	24	0	1		2	21	83	17	64	2	0
Pineville	14379	136	0	13		10	113	898	137	715	46	1

Table 6. Offenses Known to Law Enforcement, by Selected State and City, 2016—Continued

(Number.)

State/city	Population	Violent crime	Murder and nonnegligent manslaughter	Rape (revised definition)[1]	Rape (legacy definition)[2]	Robbery	Aggravated assault	Property crime	Burglary	Larceny-theft	Motor vehicle theft	Arson[3]
Plaquemine	6825	43	1	1		0	41	239	40	197	2	1
Pollock	473	4	0	1		0	3	1	0	0	1	0
Ponchatoula	7168	100	1	4		7	88	508	114	378	16	0
Port Allen	5116	19	0	2		2	15	96	22	66	8	0
Port Vincent	750	4	0	0		0	4	32	10	20	2	0
Rayne	8031	39	1	0		4	34	236	51	185	0	0
Ruston	22416	112	2	1		21	88	622	112	491	19	1
Scott	9092	7	0	2		1	4	233	65	150	18	0
Shreveport	196467	1865	42	157		492	1174	10721	2318	7646	757	66
Sibley	1177	1	1	0		0	0	2	2	0	0	0
Slidell	28107	105	0	5		13	87	1224	139	1040	45	1
Springhill	5064	9	0	0		0	9	160	15	145	0	0
St. Gabriel	7183	32	1	3		3	25	96	41	49	6	0
Sulphur	20142	101	0	3		14	84	892	161	678	53	1
Thibodaux	14588	90	0	3		10	77	593	142	443	8	1
Vidalia	4076	26	2	2		1	21	124	23	98	3	0
Ville Platte	7234	21	0	0		5	16	460	96	361	3	0
Vinton	3344	24	0	2		0	22	112	47	60	5	0
Walker	6351	33	0	6		6	21	223	17	198	8	0
Welsh	3226	46	0	0		1	45	116	43	71	2	0
West Monroe	12942	88	3	5		17	63	989	216	721	52	0
Westwego	8543	28	0	4		7	17	229	48	160	21	0
White Castle	1814	7	0	0		0	7	39	8	31	0	0
Wilson	571	0	0	0		0	0	0	0	0	0	0
Winnfield	4514	45	0	5		8	32	224	68	147	9	0
Zachary	16753	75	1	4		6	64	533	67	427	39	0
MAINE												
Ashland[10]	1222	0	0	0		0	0	13	7	5	1	0
Auburn	22836	43	0	14		7	22	730	66	649	15	4
Augusta	18347	76	0	18		13	45	676	112	547	17	0
Baileyville[10]	1444	1	0	0		1	0	10	3	6	1	0
Bangor[10]	32264	75	0	15		30	30	1340	180	1123	37	1
Bar Harbor[7]	5339	2	0	0		0	2	59	3	54	2	0
Bath[10]	8269	7	0	2		0	5	209	22	181	6	1
Belfast[10]	6685	10	0	2		0	8	119	25	88	6	1
Berwick[10]	7567	3	0	0		1	2	74	15	54	5	0
Biddeford[7]	21285	87	1	13		13	60	729	86	626	17	10
Boothbay Harbor[10]	2158	7	0	2		1	4	43	3	37	3	0
Brewer[10]	9185	1	0	0		0	1	205	23	181	1	0
Bridgton[10]	5405	2	0	0		1	1	108	19	86	3	0
Brownville[10]	1189	3	0	0		0	3	20	2	13	5	0
Brunswick[10]	20544	25	0	8		4	13	348	40	304	4	0
Bucksport[10]	4927	4	0	1		2	1	61	8	52	1	0
Buxton[10]	8171	9	0	0		0	9	73	23	49	1	0
Calais[10]	2953	2	0	0		0	2	104	10	93	1	0
Camden[10]	4863	3	0	0		0	3	33	4	29	0	0
Cape Elizabeth[10]	9364	0	0	0		0	0	54	26	28	0	0
Caribou[10]	7747	8	0	0		1	7	126	25	92	9	1
Carrabassett Valley	772	1	0	0		0	1	13	0	13	0	0
Clinton[10]	3291	0	0	0		0	0	40	7	33	0	0
Cumberland[10]	7821	1	0	0		0	1	24	4	20	0	0
Damariscotta[10]	2214	2	0	1		0	1	42	3	39	0	0
Dexter[10]	3775	1	0	0		0	1	69	3	63	3	0
Dixfield[10]	2462	3	0	2		0	1	35	18	17	0	0
Dover-Foxcroft[10]	4004	4	0	1		0	3	73	11	61	1	0
East Millinocket[10]	2986	1	0	1		0	0	38	5	33	0	0
Eastport[10]	1254	4	0	1		0	3	7	3	4	0	0
Eliot[7]	6362	3	0	1		0	2	49	12	35	2	0
Ellsworth[10]	7881	6	0	1		2	3	242	31	204	7	0
Fairfield[10]	6505	7	2	1		1	3	139	23	115	1	0
Falmouth[10]	12154	11	1	1		3	6	144	17	122	5	0
Farmington	7401	6	0	3		0	3	99	18	77	4	0
Fort Fairfield[10]	3330	5	0	0		0	5	26	5	21	0	0
Fort Kent[10]	3940	3	0	0		0	3	22	1	20	1	0
Freeport[10]	8407	3	0	0		1	2	190	13	175	2	0
Fryeburg[10]	3385	3	0	1		0	2	32	9	23	0	2
Gardiner[10]	5558	3	0	0		0	3	130	23	103	4	1
Gorham[10]	17346	12	0	0		0	12	203	44	154	5	0
Gouldsboro[10]	1739	1	0	1		0	0	27	11	15	1	0
Greenville[10]	1582	3	0	0		0	3	22	3	19	0	1
Hallowell[10]	2303	1	0	0		0	1	23	2	18	3	0
Hampden[10]	7414	5	0	1		0	4	67	18	45	4	0
Holden[10]	3077	3	0	0		2	1	32	13	18	1	0
Houlton[10]	5835	25	0	10		1	14	130	20	106	4	0
Islesboro[10]	567	0	0	0		0	0	11	1	10	0	0
Jay[10]	4750	10	0	3		1	6	47	15	28	4	0
Kennebunk[7]	11289	4	0	2		1	1	89	11	77	1	0
Kennebunkport[7]	3586	1	0	0		0	1	24	3	21	0	0
Kittery[10]	9686	15	0	4		3	8	139	6	128	5	0
Lewiston	36126	64	0	14		18	32	718	140	529	49	4
Limestone[10]	2202	1	0	0		0	1	25	3	22	0	0
Lincoln[10]	5020	3	0	1		0	2	105	22	79	4	0

Table 6. Offenses Known to Law Enforcement, by Selected State and City, 2016—Continued

(Number.)

State/city	Population	Violent crime	Murder and nonnegligent manslaughter	Rape (revised definition)[1]	Rape (legacy definition)[2]	Robbery	Aggravated assault	Property crime	Burglary	Larceny-theft	Motor vehicle theft	Arson[3]
Lisbon	8823	5	0	2		0	3	97	15	77	5	0
Livermore Falls[10]	3118	8	0	0		3	5	48	11	34	3	0
Machias[10]	2096	5	0	2		2	1	22	2	20	0	0
Madawaska[10]	3803	1	0	0		0	1	26	1	25	0	0
Mechanic Falls[10]	2990	1	0	0		1	0	27	13	14	0	0
Mexico[10]	2590	14	0	7		2	5	163	44	118	1	0
Milbridge[10]	1283	1	0	0		0	1	12	2	10	0	0
Millinocket[10]	4332	2	0	0		0	2	68	12	54	2	0
Milo[10]	2242	3	0	0		0	3	19	2	17	0	0
Monmouth	4008	2	0	1		0	1	25	13	11	1	0
Mount Desert[10]	2074	0	0	0		0	0	26	0	26	0	0
Newport[10]	3224	5	0	3		0	2	73	14	55	4	0
North Berwick[10]	4672	3	0	1		0	2	29	14	15	0	0
Norway[10]	4911	2	0	2		0	0	91	9	79	3	0
Oakland	6119	1	0	1		0	0	69	10	55	4	0
Ogunquit[10]	916	3	0	0		0	3	17	4	13	0	0
Old Orchard Beach	8807	17	0	5		3	9	224	46	172	6	1
Old Town[10]	7583	6	0	1		2	3	128	23	101	4	0
Orono[10]	10772	4	0	1		1	2	125	22	102	1	1
Oxford[10]	4034	1	0	0		1	0	118	8	110	0	0
Paris[10]	5085	6	0	3		3	0	91	17	71	3	0
Phippsburg[10]	2234	0	0	0		0	0	5	0	5	0	0
Pittsfield[10]	4051	2	0	0		0	2	36	5	31	0	0
Portland[10]	67041	196	2	36		59	99	1795	236	1485	74	11
Presque Isle[10]	9075	33	1	12		4	16	241	29	204	8	1
Rangeley[10]	1149	1	1	0		0	0	6	2	4	0	0
Richmond[10]	3394	2	0	0		0	2	11	5	6	0	0
Rockland[10]	7227	1	0	1		0	0	159	16	140	3	1
Rockport[10]	3392	0	0	0		0	0	27	4	23	0	0
Rumford[10]	5646	7	0	2		0	5	238	43	190	5	0
Sabattus[10]	5038	8	0	1		0	7	34	7	25	2	0
Saco	19197	35	0	11		3	21	345	42	288	15	4
Sanford[10]	20914	58	0	24		4	30	712	89	595	28	3
Scarborough	19851	12	0	1		3	8	396	36	353	7	3
Searsport[10]	2627	1	0	0		0	1	26	5	19	2	0
Skowhegan	8454	24	0	12		5	7	370	44	319	7	1
South Berwick[10]	7454	9	0	4		1	4	50	15	34	1	0
South Portland	25674	44	0	6		11	27	596	75	505	16	1
Southwest Harbor[10]	1774	2	0	0		1	1	42	2	40	0	0
Thomaston[10]	2776	5	0	0		0	5	84	9	73	2	0
Topsham[10]	8748	1	0	0		0	1	101	18	82	1	0
Van Buren[10]	2037	1	0	1		0	0	16	1	15	0	0
Veazie[10]	1855	2	0	0		1	1	23	12	9	2	0
Waldoboro[10]	4954	5	0	1		1	3	70	19	44	7	0
Washburn[10]	1578	0	0	0		0	0	13	3	9	1	0
Waterville	16370	38	0	12		9	17	663	74	577	12	3
Wells	10174	2	0	0		0	2	125	33	91	1	0
Westbrook[10]	18078	40	0	9		7	24	448	60	367	21	0
Willimantic[10]	140	0	0	0		0	0	0	0	0	0	0
Wilton[10]	3922	9	1	3		1	4	32	8	21	3	0
Windham[10]	17983	17	1	1		2	13	267	31	226	10	0
Winslow	7506	2	0	0		0	2	92	21	67	4	0
Winter Harbor[10]	515	0	0	0		0	0	16	7	7	2	0
Winthrop[10]	5888	9	2	5		1	1	56	12	43	1	0
Wiscasset[10]	3638	2	0	0		0	2	36	5	28	3	0
Yarmouth[10]	8584	5	0	0		0	5	68	8	58	2	0
York	12927	8	0	4		0	4	154	27	126	1	0
MARYLAND												
Aberdeen	15704	79	3	8		17	51	251	41	202	8	7
Annapolis	39703	250	10	11		66	163	938	210	684	44	18
Baltimore	618385	11010	318	299		5236	5157	29547	7375	16855	5317	259
Baltimore City Sheriff		0	0	0		0	0	0	0	0	0	0
Bel Air	10200	22	0	1		9	12	255	28	224	3	2
Berwyn Heights	3311	5	0	0		4	1	56	2	52	2	0
Bladensburg	9735	97	4	11		33	49	298	48	203	47	0
Boonsboro	3457	1	0	0		0	1	38	14	24	0	2
Bowie	58631	55	1	4		25	25	756	120	575	61	0
Brentwood	3219	5	0	0		2	3	13	4	6	3	0
Brunswick	6162	26	0	1		11	14	63	22	40	1	0
Cambridge	12524	128	2	12		28	86	632	130	482	20	5
Capitol Heights	4620	17	0	0		8	9	37	3	20	14	0
Centreville	4696	10	0	0		2	8	62	12	49	1	1
Chestertown	5067	28	0	2		10	16	100	28	69	3	0
Cheverly	6546	23	2	0		11	10	128	22	93	13	0
Chevy Chase Village	2080	0	0	0		0	0	55	4	48	3	0
Colmar Manor	1482	11	0	0		3	8	23	3	16	4	0
Cottage City	1383	2	0	0		2	0	20	6	11	3	0
Crisfield	2642	4	0	0		0	4	17	1	16	0	4
Cumberland	19995	177	1	13		53	110	1218	247	949	22	0
Delmar	3068	18	0	1		5	12	104	28	73	3	1
Denton	4337	5	0	2		1	2	213	16	195	2	1
District Heights	6204	23	2	0		13	8	47	13	23	11	0

Table 6. Offenses Known to Law Enforcement, by Selected State and City, 2016—Continued

(Number.)

State/city	Population	Violent crime	Murder and nonnegligent manslaughter	Rape (revised definition)[1]	Rape (legacy definition)[2]	Robbery	Aggravated assault	Property crime	Burglary	Larceny-theft	Motor vehicle theft	Arson[3]
Easton	16689	42	0	6		15	21	462	77	380	5	1
Edmonston	1532	14	0	0		6	8	39	4	29	6	0
Elkton	15837	159	0	13		37	109	1090	144	900	46	14
Fairmount Heights	1585	1	0	0		1	0	11	3	4	4	0
Federalsburg	2646	21	0	1		1	19	76	17	55	4	
Forest Heights	2598	5	0	0		2	3	57	29	26	2	0
Frederick	70316	343	1	23		70	249	1411	141	1222	48	14
Frostburg	8601	17	0	0		2	15	155	23	131	1	2
Fruitland	5287	24	1	1		9	13	290	23	266	1	2
Glenarden	6390	9	1	0		1	7	67	11	49	7	0
Greenbelt	24511	112	1	6		54	51	660	88	500	72	0
Hagerstown	40567	231	1	19		105	107	1262	374	775	113	36
Hampstead	6365	2	0	0		0	2	47	3	43	1	1
Hancock	1548	5	1	1		0	3	18	2	16	0	0
Havre de Grace	13604	37	0	9		9	19	308	37	263	8	3
Hurlock	2036	5	1	0		0	4	83	18	60	5	0
Hyattsville	18666	112	1	3		78	30	1023	80	878	65	
Landover Hills	1828	8	1	0		4	3	34	6	23	5	0
La Plata	9201	32	0	0		13	19	271	52	210	9	9
Laurel	26424	109	0	3		44	62	1011	111	812	88	0
Lonaconing	1135	0	0	0		0	0	0	0	0	0	0
Luke	63	0	0	0		0	0	0	0	0	0	0
Manchester	4820	2	0	0		0	2	17	3	13	1	0
Morningside	2104	7	0	0		2	5	35	9	18	8	0
Mount Rainier	8552	46	0	2		24	20	237	54	143	40	1
New Carrollton	12914	55	0	1		18	36	208	34	156	18	0
North East	3734	10	0	0		5	5	64	11	45	8	5
Oakland	1868	1	0	0		0	1	29	0	29	0	2
Ocean City	7045	89	1	14		28	46	1059	142	901	16	1
Ocean Pines	12207	19	0	0		0	19	106	18	87	1	0
Oxford	615	0	0	0		0	0	1	1	0	0	0
Perryville	4451	21	0	1		2	18	109	16	83	10	1
Pocomoke City	4124	5	0	0		3	2	199	20	178	1	0
Princess Anne	3299	47	1	3		9	34	163	34	128	1	1
Ridgely	1611	2	0	0		0	2	48	9	38	1	3
Rising Sun	2860	11	0	0		2	9	32	8	22	2	6
Riverdale Park	7373	57	0	0		27	30	145	17	110	18	0
Rock Hall	1302	1	0	0		1	0	18	6	11	1	0
Salisbury	33417	297	2	11		103	181	1695	234	1410	51	12
Seat Pleasant	4826	36	0	0		9	27	108	23	72	13	0
Smithsburg	3000	3	0	0		1	2	16	4	11	1	1
St. Michaels	1048	5	0	1		1	3	17	2	14	1	0
Sykesville	4409	14	0	0		0	14	38	12	23	3	1
Takoma Park	17905	60	1	3		28	28	391	95	266	30	0
Taneytown	6749	12	0	0		5	7	62	9	50	3	5
Thurmont	6507	6	0	1		0	5	68	9	55	4	1
Trappe	1015	4	0	0		0	4	8	2	5	1	1
University Park	2688	3	0	0		0	3	42	10	30	2	0
Upper Marlboro	671	0	0	0		0	0	13	3	10	0	0
Westminster	18683	78	0	1		23	54	662	80	570	12	11
MASSACHUSETTS												
Abington	16201	36	0	5		2	29	238	63	164	11	0
Acton	23770	24	1	3		0	20	169	23	141	5	0
Acushnet	10466	19	0	1		1	17	134	61	67	6	0
Adams	8131	24	0	4		1	19	116	29	84	3	1
Agawam	28844	81	0	10		7	64	489	173	284	32	2
Amherst	40063	87	1	20		4	62	240	66	163	11	2
Andover	35558	23	0	3		2	18	216	28	174	14	3
Arlington	45004	54	0	9		7	38	228	42	168	18	3
Ashburnham	6206	10	0	2		0	8	45	11	34	0	1
Ashland	17689	20	0	5		1	14	116	38	74	4	1
Athol	11612	49	0	2		1	46	211	46	158	7	3
Attleboro	44225	93	0	11		14	68	779	139	606	34	4
Auburn	16508	46	1	4		4	37	409	36	355	18	1
Avon	4505	8	0	1		0	7	183	23	154	6	
Ayer	8078	34	0	3		1	30	100	32	65	3	0
Barnstable	43974	199	1	16		15	167	711	133	558	20	2
Becket	1759	2	0	0		0	2	13	10	3	0	
Bedford	14280	6	0	0		2	4	49	4	45	0	0
Belchertown	14985	13	0	1		0	12	81	22	54	5	2
Bellingham	16922	34	0	6		2	26	321	26	278	17	1
Belmont	25637	14	0	5		0	9	177	58	114	5	0
Berkley	6678	7	0	0		0	7	33	13	15	5	0
Berlin	3038	0	0	0		0	0	14	0	14	0	0
Bernardston	2096	2	0	1		0	1	18	4	12	2	0
Beverly	41303	65	1	5		4	55	330	36	277	17	1
Billerica	42965	43	0	3		5	35	201	33	161	7	0
Blackstone	9079	12	0	1		1	10	66	13	47	6	0
Bolton	5210	6	0	1		0	5	45	9	36	0	2
Boston	673880	4767	49	278		1530	2910	14489	1837	11429	1223	
Bourne	19577	49	0	4		6	39	257	83	162	12	1
Boxborough	5223	7	0	0		0	7	21	3	15	3	0

Table 6. Offenses Known to Law Enforcement, by Selected State and City, 2016—Continued

(Number.)

State/city	Population	Violent crime	Murder and nonnegligent manslaughter	Rape (revised definition)[1]	Rape (legacy definition)[2]	Robbery	Aggravated assault	Property crime	Burglary	Larceny-theft	Motor vehicle theft	Arson[3]
Boxford	8271	0	0	0		0	0	15	1	14	0	0
Boylston	4551	6	0	0		0	6	21	14	7	0	0
Braintree	37673	90	0	5		6	79	664	48	569	47	0
Brewster	9888	17	0	2		0	15	99	27	71	1	1
Brimfield	3756	4	0	0		1	3	19	4	13	2	0
Brockton	95189	1029	3	83		169	774	2290	512	1498	280	13
Brookline[4]	59033		0	2		12		610	77	523	10	0
Burlington	26083	52	0	7		8	37	453	23	419	11	3
Cambridge	111030	294	2	28		76	188	2369	326	1924	119	6
Canton	22962	78	0	5		4	69	198	27	156	15	1
Carlisle	5300	1	0	0		1	0	23	1	22	0	0
Carver	11600	28	0	3		2	23	103	17	76	10	1
Charlton	13430	11	0	2		2	7	80	12	63	5	0
Chatham	6119	7	0	2		1	4	75	13	61	1	0
Chelmsford	35251	29	0	2		5	22	422	25	379	18	1
Chelsea	40096	370	1	23		136	210	914	130	671	113	5
Chicopee	56887	265	2	45		50	168	1316	339	882	95	2
Chilmark	926	4	0	0		0	4	7	2	5	0	0
Clinton	13780	8	0	0		2	6	56	7	49	0	0
Cohasset	8538	19	0	3		1	15	66	21	42	3	1
Concord	20189	18	0	2		1	15	132	19	113	0	1
Dalton	6642	12	0	1		0	11	63	17	44	2	1
Danvers	27997	39	1	1		7	30	608	29	559	20	1
Dartmouth	34630	72	0	6		7	59	804	99	678	27	0
Dedham	25402	10	1	0		4	5	504	27	441	36	0
Deerfield	4994	6	0	1		0	5	55	6	47	2	1
Dennis	13905	57	0	9		1	47	320	76	228	16	0
Dighton	7430	8	0	3		1	4	52	16	29	7	
Douglas	8741	12	0	6		0	6	42	5	28	9	0
Dover	6008	2	0	1		0	1	36	8	27	1	0
Dracut	31586	38	1	3		3	31	404	64	316	24	0
Dudley	11558	32	0	8		1	23	56	11	38	7	0
Dunstable	3471	4	0	0		0	4	16	4	12	0	2
Duxbury	15497	14	0	2		0	12	91	16	74	1	0
East Bridgewater	14390	20	0	7		1	12	134	14	112	8	0
East Brookfield	2178	7	0	0		0	7	12	5	6	1	0
Eastham	4886	9	0	1		1	7	56	8	46	2	0
Easthampton	16026	50	0	8		2	40	167	25	137	5	1
East Longmeadow	16267	20	0	7		2	11	193	33	154	6	0
Easton	23918	38	1	9		4	24	223	38	166	19	0
Edgartown	4354	9	0	3		0	6	100	12	87	1	0
Egremont	1207	1	0	0		0	1	4	3	1	0	
Erving	1771	3	0	1		0	2	33	11	22	0	2
Everett	46754	145	1	8		34	102	652	91	489	72	2
Fairhaven	16120	56	0	9		4	43	373	67	294	12	0
Fall River	88371	966	1	67		190	708	1666	485	944	237	49
Falmouth	31382	120	0	7		4	109	625	267	323	35	2
Fitchburg	40391	312	1	27		62	222	846	189	613	44	4
Framingham	71422	211	0	8		18	185	831	122	655	54	0
Franklin	33264	1	0	1		0	0	98	19	73	6	0
Freetown	9199	21	0	3		2	16	105	22	71	12	3
Gardner[4]	20277		1	13		7		509	145	349	15	1
Georgetown	8623	2	0	0		0	2	47	6	39	2	0
Gloucester	29836	73	0	4		4	65	229	21	193	15	2
Goshen	1073	1	0	0		0	1	3	1	1	1	0
Grafton	18613	29	0	7		0	22	80	19	56	5	0
Granby	6375	7	0	0		0	7	49	13	34	2	0
Great Barrington	6870	11	0	4		0	7	67	19	47	1	0
Greenfield	17456	117	3	27		8	79	365	71	280	14	4
Groton	11372	4	0	3		0	1	49	10	38	1	1
Groveland	6776	2	0	0		0	2	11	4	7	0	0
Hadley	5372	24	0	1		3	20	208	16	188	4	0
Halifax	7861	7	0	2		0	5	76	4	65	7	0
Hamilton	8181	6	0	0		0	6	28	4	23	1	0
Hampden	5227	3	0	1		0	2	58	15	33	10	0
Hanover	14466	3	0	0		0	3	115	21	92	2	0
Hanson	10666	29	0	2		2	25	51	13	33	5	2
Hardwick	4019	5	0	1		0	4	35	9	24	2	0
Harvard	6552	9	0	2		0	7	37	14	23	0	1
Harwich	12112	25	0	4		1	20	151	47	97	7	0
Hatfield	3302	2	0	0		0	2	13	1	11	1	0
Haverhill	62851	373	1	20		37	315	982	247	653	82	7
Hingham	23204	24	0	0		0	24	196	34	159	3	0
Holden	18829	13	0	2		0	11	55	15	37	3	1
Holliston	14656	10	0	1		1	8	55	13	39	3	1
Holyoke	40738	436	2	24		97	313	2013	318	1566	129	12
Hopedale	5938	4	0	2		0	2	23	14	7	2	0
Hopkinton	16960	2	0	0		0	2	64	1	63	0	0
Hudson	19931	8	0	0		3	5	227	25	199	3	0
Hull	10482	26	0	1		2	23	80	19	60	1	1
Ipswich	13863	18	0	0		0	18	82	8	73	1	2
Kingston	13378	22	0	3		3	16	142	13	118	11	0
Lakeville	11417	17	0	5		1	11	135	61	68	6	2

Table 6. Offenses Known to Law Enforcement, by Selected State and City, 2016—Continued

(Number.)

State/city	Population	Violent crime	Murder and nonnegligent manslaughter	Rape (revised definition)[1]	Rape (legacy definition)[2]	Robbery	Aggravated assault	Property crime	Burglary	Larceny-theft	Motor vehicle theft	Arson[3]
Lancaster	8150	7	0	2		2	3	56	8	46	2	0
Lawrence	80622	597	5	30		202	360	1509	279	649	581	
Lee	5790	13	0	3		0	10	102	18	81	3	0
Leicester	11355	23	0	4		0	19	149	21	119	9	0
Lenox	4971	8	0	1		0	7	80	11	67	2	0
Leominster	41547	270	0	20		41	209	940	140	764	36	4
Leverett	1843	1	0	0		0	1	19	2	17	0	0
Lexington	33643	23	0	3		1	19	132	22	108	2	0
Lincoln	7550	2	0	1		0	1	45	6	39	0	0
Littleton	10074	11	0	4		0	7	78	10	63	5	0
Longmeadow	15876	11	0	3		2	6	141	39	89	13	0
Lowell	111027	380	0	21		127	232	2199	407	1391	401	13
Ludlow	21484	52	0	8		5	39	287	65	195	27	2
Lunenburg	11438	31	0	5		4	22	210	31	172	7	1
Lynn	92443	714	4	43		175	492	1922	365	1336	221	4
Lynnfield	12946	9	1	0		4	4	90	14	71	5	0
Malden	61102	169	1	10		41	117	717	96	520	101	0
Manchester-by-the-Sea	5387	5	0	2		0	3	15	2	12	1	0
Mansfield	23681	39	0	9		3	27	206	42	148	16	3
Marblehead	20563	22	0	2		1	19	148	20	121	7	0
Marion	5098	6	0	1		0	5	40	7	31	2	0
Marlborough	39899	160	0	15		8	137	561	85	453	23	2
Marshfield	25696	31	0	5		3	23	128	18	100	10	0
Mashpee	14122	33	0	6		2	25	140	26	110	4	4
Mattapoisett	6282	17	0	0		0	17	53	11	39	3	0
Maynard	10745	28	0	6		1	21	61	11	49	1	2
Medford	57367	89	0	4		22	63	670	87	535	48	0
Medway	13289	0	0	0		0	0	59	27	32	0	0
Melrose	28070	19	0	2		4	13	214	17	173	24	0
Mendon	6033	3	0	0		0	3	38	11	21	6	0
Merrimac	6859	7	0	1		1	5	37	11	26	0	1
Methuen	49912	79	1	1		24	53	821	126	616	79	3
Middleboro	24490	101	0	17		5	79	242	32	185	25	2
Middleton	9852	8	0	2		0	6	54	3	50	1	0
Milford	28606	68	0	10		11	47	348	57	269	22	0
Millbury	13532	22	0	4		1	17	224	33	177	14	0
Millville	3228	3	0	0		2	1	14	5	7	2	1
Milton	27317	9	0	1		3	5	223	36	172	15	0
Monson	8812	36	0	5		1	30	58	23	30	5	0
Montague	8242	57	0	3		5	49	178	65	111	2	3
Nahant	3484	4	0	0		0	4	25	3	20	2	0
Nantucket	11036	26	0	4		2	20	306	51	247	8	0
Natick	36777	58	0	5		9	44	495	38	443	14	3
Needham	30733	6	0	2		0	4	177	19	157	1	0
New Bedford	94524	819	3	31		238	547	2924	615	2035	274	22
Newbury	6999	12	0	2		0	10	27	7	17	3	0
Newburyport	18011	17	0	5		1	11	192	23	165	4	0
Newton	89116	46	0	3		11	32	642	80	544	18	0
Norfolk	11991	4	0	1		0	3	21	8	12	1	0
North Adams	13162	181	0	20		9	152	433	122	289	22	1
Northampton	28521	129	0	19		13	97	600	83	506	11	7
North Andover	29853	12	0	0		1	11	179	11	161	7	1
North Attleboro	29013	35	0	5		5	25	433	54	365	14	1
Northborough	15109	3	0	0		2	1	146	20	123	3	0
Northbridge	16638	34	0	5		2	27	196	28	163	5	2
Northfield	2984	7	0	1		1	5	22	5	17	0	0
North Reading	15712	20	0	2		0	18	60	3	53	4	0
Norton	19445	10	1	2		0	7	33	16	15	2	0
Norwell	11030	12	0	2		0	10	69	7	59	3	1
Norwood	29058	31	1	7		9	14	296	44	229	23	3
Oakham	1925	5	0	0		0	5	4	1	2	1	0
Orange	7615	26	1	6		2	17	100	28	66	6	1
Orleans	5810	2	0	1		0	1	116	14	100	2	0
Oxford	13895	26	0	2		0	24	197	37	152	8	0
Palmer	12171	66	0	9		2	55	193	48	139	6	3
Paxton	4874	7	0	2		0	5	16	5	10	1	0
Peabody	52501	206	1	16		22	167	685	56	586	43	0
Pelham	1332	0	0	0		0	0	9	3	2	4	0
Pembroke	18274	17	0	1		0	16	105	25	67	13	1
Pepperell	12242	24	0	5		0	19	88	17	70	1	1
Pittsfield	43031	340	3	37		39	261	1016	364	620	32	9
Plainville	9178	12	0	1		2	9	101	6	91	4	0
Plymouth	59088	93	1	7		13	72	377	74	284	19	1
Plympton	2922	1	0	0		1	0	11	4	6	1	0
Princeton	3465	3	1	0		0	2	18	5	13	0	0
Provincetown	2959	20	0	3		0	17	105	20	81	4	0
Quincy	93437	408	0	30		60	318	1506	295	1113	98	6
Randolph	33807	96	1	14		12	69	471	64	378	29	3
Raynham	13818	28	0	3		4	21	272	26	220	26	0
Reading	25779	11	0	1		5	5	176	34	136	6	0
Rehoboth	12033	17	0	2		1	14	104	35	65	4	1
Revere	53514	262	0	21		44	197	1142	194	835	113	3
Rochester	5522	12	0	0		1	11	33	11	21	1	0

Table 6. Offenses Known to Law Enforcement, by Selected State and City, 2016—Continued

(Number.)

State/city	Population	Violent crime	Murder and nonnegligent manslaughter	Rape (revised definition)[1]	Rape (legacy definition)[2]	Robbery	Aggravated assault	Property crime	Burglary	Larceny-theft	Motor vehicle theft	Arson[3]
Rockport	7222	5	0	3		1	1	15	2	13	0	1
Rowley	6343	7	0	1		1	5	27	10	16	1	0
Rutland	8599	17	0	2		0	15	62	14	44	4	0
Salem	42888	131	2	11		33	85	1033	111	877	45	2
Salisbury	9425	34	0	8		4	22	154	36	111	7	0
Sandwich	20312	33	0	3		0	30	150	29	115	6	0
Saugus	28131	91	0	7		19	65	572	42	499	31	0
Seekonk	15159	30	0	3		2	25	319	34	273	12	0
Sharon	18200	14	0	2		0	12	62	16	43	3	0
Shelburne	1839	1	0	1		0	0	9	4	5	0	0
Sherborn	4317	3	0	1		1	1	13	3	10	0	0
Shirley	7389	17	0	2		0	15	42	6	34	2	0
Shrewsbury	36874	4	0	0		1	3	176	47	115	14	0
Somerset	18223	42	0	12		5	25	218	28	171	19	1
Somerville	80899	206	0	14		48	144	1206	207	897	102	7
Southborough	10048	5	0	0		0	5	53	15	31	7	0
Southbridge	16819	52	0	13		4	35	282	54	214	14	5
South Hadley	17748	23	0	1		5	17	253	123	122	8	1
Southwick	9758	16	0	2		1	13	89	28	54	7	0
Spencer	11782	18	0	3		2	13	122	22	89	11	0
Springfield	154102	1588	12	81		522	973	5073	1486	3000	587	46
Sterling	7993	11	0	3		1	7	54	19	33	2	1
Stockbridge	1936	4	0	2		0	2	24	8	15	1	0
Stoneham	22045	31	1	4		3	23	242	84	140	18	1
Stoughton	28583	83	1	7		9	66	440	66	348	26	2
Stow	7197	10	0	0		0	10	34	14	20	0	0
Sturbridge	9520	34	0	5		3	26	166	19	141	6	2
Sudbury	19035	7	0	0		0	7	41	6	34	1	0
Sunderland	3652	6	0	1		0	5	24	11	11	2	0
Sutton	9292	8	0	1		1	6	88	39	45	4	3
Swampscott	14551	10	0	2		0	8	186	26	154	6	5
Swansea	16418	33	0	3		3	27	246	29	205	12	0
Taunton	56720	203	5	13		36	149	749	262	397	90	7
Templeton	8169	6	0	1		0	5	63	17	41	5	0
Tewksbury	31160	63	0	10		10	43	300	42	246	12	2
Tisbury	4129	27	0	0		0	27	82	12	67	3	0
Topsfield	6590	3	0	1		0	2	11	1	10	0	0
Townsend	9585	15	0	3		0	12	46	11	32	3	0
Truro	1999	6	0	0		0	6	23	3	18	2	1
Tyngsboro	12397	12	0	0		1	11	63	10	50	3	0
Upton	7726	2	0	0		0	2	28	6	22	0	0
Wakefield	27080	60	0	9		7	44	210	27	169	14	2
Wales	1906	2	0	0		1	1	6	2	3	1	0
Walpole	25187	45	0	2		3	40	244	22	215	7	0
Waltham	63613	99	1	12		8	78	688	109	550	29	2
Ware	9891	58	0	4		4	50	169	20	142	7	1
Wareham	22422	123	0	11		15	97	446	90	330	26	4
Watertown	34655	38	0	3		4	31	400	29	360	11	0
Wayland	13760	5	0	0		2	3	6	4	1	1	0
Webster	16842	121	0	14		9	98	292	56	209	27	6
Wellesley	29049	13	0	1		3	9	159	33	125	1	0
Wellfleet	2737	3	0	2		0	1	32	6	23	3	0
Wenham	5198	6	0	1		0	5	11	1	10	0	0
Westborough	18984	15	0	6		0	9	144	16	123	5	0
West Boylston	7895	8	0	0		3	5	89	13	73	3	1
West Bridgewater	7097	14	0	0		2	12	130	19	91	20	0
Westfield	41700	93	0	17		10	66	550	116	414	20	5
Westford	24103	21	0	4		1	16	88	16	69	3	0
Westminster	7595	19	0	0		0	19	71	11	55	5	1
West Newbury	4582	1	0	1		0	0	25	5	18	2	0
Weston	12147	10	0	5		0	5	52	6	42	4	0
Westport	15798	22	0	4		0	18	149	48	92	9	1
West Springfield	28689	188	1	20		38	129	1206	134	1002	70	3
West Tisbury	2927	7	0	0		0	7	19	9	8	2	0
Westwood	16285	22	0	4		4	14	174	11	162	1	0
Weymouth	56149	161	0	11		28	122	527	87	411	29	2
Whately	1523	1	0	0		0	1	16	4	11	1	0
Whitman	14852	33	0	4		4	25	121	26	85	10	0
Wilbraham	14684	18	0	5		1	12	165	48	104	13	3
Williamsburg	2466	2	0	0		0	2	14	8	6	0	0
Williamstown	7591	12	0	6		1	5	130	12	117	1	0
Wilmington	23667	44	0	1		5	38	175	26	136	13	2
Winchendon	10727	38	0	8		2	28	179	18	150	11	2
Winchester	22523	4	0	1		1	2	166	21	140	5	0
Winthrop	18216	75	0	1		3	71	153	58	89	6	0
Woburn	39638	82	0	9		10	63	446	61	365	20	0
Worcester	184595	1642	8	63		394	1177	5358	1366	3473	519	5
Wrentham	11614	5	0	0		1	4	215	9	198	8	0
Yarmouth[4]	23299		0	13		4		468	98	352	18	2
MICHIGAN												
Addison Township	6532	5	0	1		0	4	53	15	36	2	0
Akron	391	3	0	3		0	0	5	2	3	0	0

Table 6. Offenses Known to Law Enforcement, by Selected State and City, 2016—Continued

(Number.)

State/city	Population	Violent crime	Murder and nonnegligent manslaughter	Rape (revised definition)[1]	Rape (legacy definition)[2]	Robbery	Aggravated assault	Property crime	Burglary	Larceny-theft	Motor vehicle theft	Arson[3]
Albion	8155	101	2	18		12	69	280	78	190	12	6
Allegan	5086	16	0	7		1	8	62	4	56	2	0
Allen Park	27284	53	0	6		10	37	500	55	367	78	5
Alma	9159	18	1	6		0	11	147	12	133	2	3
Almont	2734	15	0	1		1	13	53	18	32	3	0
Alpena	10119	29	0	16		2	11	212	26	179	7	2
Ann Arbor	117688	213	1	44		43	125	2051	242	1697	112	10
Argentine Township	6591	15	0	3		0	12	26	12	13	1	1
Armada	1747	0	0	0		0	0	4	0	4	0	1
Auburn Hills	22933	62	0	11		15	36	661	51	578	32	4
Au Gres	853	0	0	0		0	0	5	0	5	0	0
Bad Axe	2989	5	0	4		0	1	83	6	77	0	0
Bancroft	518	0	0	0		0	0	3	1	2	0	0
Bangor	1843	7	0	2		0	5	32	7	25	0	0
Baroda-Lake Township	3774	7	0	0		2	5	24	6	17	1	0
Barryton	357	0	0	0		0	0	4	1	3	0	0
Barry Township	3413	3	0	0		0	3	18	1	16	1	0
Bath Township	12552	11	0	5		3	3	172	49	109	14	0
Battle Creek	60904	594	3	83		64	444	2325	607	1629	89	15
Bay City	33725	205	1	50		25	129	925	291	600	34	10
Beaverton	1044	6	0	1		0	5	18	2	12	4	0
Belding	5772	16	0	5		0	11	48	12	34	2	1
Bellaire	1062	0	0	0		0	0	10	0	10	0	0
Belleville	3860	6	0	5		0	1	90	15	65	10	0
Bellevue	1277	0	0	0		0	0	1	1	0	0	0
Benton Harbor	9963	179	1	15		41	122	438	137	258	43	5
Benton Township	14413	159	1	25		25	108	1094	155	901	38	8
Berkley	15328	12	0	4		2	6	89	11	75	3	0
Berrien Springs-Oronoko Township	9085	17	0	6		0	11	115	26	87	2	0
Beverly Hills	10455	3	1	0		0	2	80	10	65	5	0
Big Rapids	10389	32	0	8		3	21	157	17	133	7	2
Birch Run	1465	2	0	0		0	2	83	0	78	5	0
Birmingham	21012	9	0	1		4	4	242	19	215	8	1
Blackman Township	37522	102	1	23		20	58	1040	140	861	39	5
Blissfield	3239	4	0	1		0	3	25	1	24	0	0
Bloomfield Hills	4031	4	0	0		0	4	35	8	26	1	0
Bloomfield Township	42313	20	0	3		3	14	421	65	338	18	1
Boyne City	3785	6	1	2		1	2	40	5	34	1	0
Brandon Township	15692	18	0	2		0	16	51	16	33	2	1
Breckenridge	1301	2	0	0		0	2	25	1	24	0	0
Bridgeport Township	9993	48	0	6		3	39	179	55	118	6	1
Bridgman	2251	3	0	2		0	1	6	1	5	0	0
Brighton	7643	8	0	1		2	5	131	13	116	2	1
Bronson	2333	8	0	1		1	6	33	5	26	2	0
Brown City	1264	2	0	0		0	2	17	2	15	0	0
Brownstown Township	30864	61	0	18		4	39	342	63	225	54	1
Buchanan	4344	22	0	5		2	15	132	21	110	1	0
Buena Vista Township	8158	89	4	12		5	68	197	78	111	8	2
Burton	28563	105	2	22		19	62	762	120	607	35	5
Cadillac	10372	38	0	6		2	30	322	50	262	10	2
Calumet	698	1	0	0		0	1	4	1	2	1	0
Cambridge Township	5645	4	0	1		0	3	16	6	10	0	0
Canton Township	89861	152	0	21		23	108	1032	79	904	49	6
Capac	1842	7	0	3		0	4	37	6	31	0	0
Carleton	2335	7	0	1		0	6	24	6	17	1	1
Caro	4074	26	0	8		2	16	135	15	118	2	0
Carrollton Township	5781	8	0	1		1	6	53	12	38	3	0
Carson City	1090	3	0	0		1	2	15	1	14	0	0
Caseville	738	2	0	1		0	1	12	1	11	0	1
Caspian-Gaastra	1190	1	0	0		0	1	2	1	1	0	0
Cass City	2343	10	0	2		0	8	66	6	58	2	0
Cassopolis	1721	10	0	3		1	6	31	10	21	0	1
Center Line	8332	40	0	5		11	24	196	30	121	45	0
Central Lake	932	1	0	1		0	0	10	0	10	0	0
Charlevoix	2546	7	0	5		0	2	81	9	69	3	1
Charlotte	9051	29	1	11		0	17	206	26	169	11	0
Cheboygan	4709	13	0	6		1	6	154	10	143	1	1
Chelsea	5254	3	0	1		1	1	56	5	49	2	0
Chesaning	2268	1	0	0		0	1	12	3	9	0	0
Chesterfield Township	44963	93	0	17		5	71	781	100	642	39	6
Chikaming Township	3090	8	0	3		1	4	65	23	40	2	0
Chocolay Township	5952	13	0	3		0	10	37	2	33	2	0
Clare	3071	6	0	3		1	2	48	2	46	0	1
Clarkston	896	0	0	0		0	0	9	4	4	1	0
Clawson	12053	11	0	3		1	7	74	14	58	2	0
Clayton Township	7156	20	0	7		1	12	37	8	24	5	0
Clay Township	8844	26	0	5		1	20	120	33	87	0	1
Clinton	2260	2	0	2		0	0	15	4	9	2	0
Clinton Township	100514	326	3	42		36	245	1686	284	1277	125	9
Clio	2516	5	0	0		1	4	34	7	27	0	0
Coldwater	10827	42	0	16		4	22	328	28	293	7	1
Coleman	1198	1	0	0		0	1	12	3	9	0	1

Table 6. Offenses Known to Law Enforcement, by Selected State and City, 2016—Continued

(Number.)

State/city	Population	Violent crime	Murder and nonnegligent manslaughter	Rape (revised definition)[1]	Rape (legacy definition)[2]	Robbery	Aggravated assault	Property crime	Burglary	Larceny-theft	Motor vehicle theft	Arson[3]
Coloma Township	6388	22	1	5		4	12	145	49	94	2	0
Colon	1156	2	0	0		0	2	26	2	23	1	0
Columbia Township	7424	9	0	1		1	7	43	7	33	3	1
Commerce Township	38218	18	0	2		6	10	358	36	312	10	1
Constantine	2062	6	0	1		0	5	50	8	39	3	0
Corunna	3386	11	0	3		0	8	26	8	17	1	0
Covert Township	2824	16	0	2		0	14	59	19	38	2	1
Croswell	2318	19	0	3		3	13	62	11	48	3	0
Crystal Falls	1404	4	0	3		0	1	17	4	9	4	0
Davison	4927	4	0	2		0	2	64	6	54	4	0
Davison Township	19029	22	1	6		1	14	247	82	159	6	3
Dearborn	94646	348	1	30		80	237	2791	297	2167	327	5
Dearborn Heights	55852	207	5	16		47	139	1080	244	667	169	12
Decatur	1759	13	0	5		0	8	70	17	50	3	0
Denton Township	5358	7	0	2		0	5	101	17	84	0	0
Detroit	669673	13705	303	579		2941	9882	31630	8787	13938	8905	554
DeWitt	4684	6	0	4		0	2	21	4	14	3	2
DeWitt Township	14686	19	0	9		1	9	138	23	110	5	1
Dryden Township	4773	12	0	2		1	9	32	8	22	2	0
Durand	3317	14	0	3		1	10	43	8	34	1	0
East Grand Rapids	11436	2	0	0		0	2	95	14	73	8	0
East Jordan	2376	9	0	2		0	7	73	12	60	1	0
East Lansing	48451	115	0	43		24	48	719	124	488	107	11
Eastpointe	32701	266	1	34		45	186	1062	235	602	225	17
Eaton Rapids	5226	15	0	10		0	5	63	9	53	1	0
Eau Claire	617	0	0	0		0	0	8	3	5	0	0
Ecorse	9213	149	1	13		28	107	343	110	174	59	11
Elk Rapids	1611	0	0	0		0	0	39	2	37	0	0
Elkton	774	0	0	0		0	0	13	1	12	0	0
Elsie	972	0	0	0		0	0	1	1	0	0	0
Emmett Township	11604	56	1	9		6	40	566	75	482	9	1
Escanaba	12278	39	0	7		5	27	505	39	455	11	1
Essexville	3381	8	0	0		2	6	29	6	21	2	2
Evart	1853	6	0	3		0	3	45	6	39	0	0
Fair Haven Township	1051	0	0	0		0	0	2	1	1	0	0
Farmington	10553	5	0	0		0	5	117	10	103	4	0
Farmington Hills	81649	77	0	18		9	50	1050	145	834	71	4
Fennville	1401	1	0	0		0	0	11	0	11	0	0
Fenton	11383	15	0	10		0	5	225	28	184	13	1
Ferndale	20232	45	1	2		8	34	562	86	402	74	0
Flat Rock	9917	20	0	5		4	11	142	16	108	18	0
Flint	97548	1545	45	96		249	1155	3323	1213	1867	243	63
Flint Township	30460	294	0	25		63	206	1656	374	1179	103	5
Flushing	8028	10	0	5		0	5	78	5	69	4	0
Flushing Township	10235	11	0	3		1	7	39	9	29	1	0
Forsyth Township	6196	17	1	2		2	12	81	6	69	6	2
Fowlerville	2898	9	0	7		1	1	114	10	102	2	0
Frankenmuth	5037	7	0	3		1	3	74	7	64	3	0
Frankfort	1283	2	0	0		0	2	44	3	40	1	0
Franklin	3254	2	0	0		0	2	23	9	14	0	0
Fraser	14667	28	0	5		8	15	332	47	258	27	1
Fremont	4027	12	0	6		2	4	116	11	103	2	2
Fruitport Township	13879	25	1	5		8	11	518	22	484	12	3
Gaines Township	6177	1	0	0		0	1	25	10	13	2	1
Galesburg	2050	2	0	0		0	2	22	2	18	2	0
Galien	529	0	0	0		0	0	0	0	0	0	0
Garden City	26781	69	0	13		14	42	491	96	341	54	1
Garfield Township	811	0	0	0		0	0	0	0	0	0	0
Gaylord	3662	12	0	5		1	6	256	8	246	2	2
Genesee Township	20393	70	1	10		9	50	224	76	112	36	1
Gerrish Township	2922	3	0	1		0	2	34	8	22	4	1
Gibraltar	4509	3	0	1		0	2	30	4	26	0	1
Gladstone	4802	5	0	3		0	2	76	10	65	1	1
Gladwin	2869	10	0	5		0	5	54	8	42	4	0
Grand Beach	278	0	0	0		0	0	5	3	2	0	0
Grand Blanc	7940	11	2	3		3	3	85	13	71	1	2
Grand Haven	11196	27	0	20		3	4	212	29	177	6	3
Grand Ledge	7790	15	0	10		1	4	115	9	103	3	0
Grand Rapids	196538	1327	10	142		321	854	4334	822	3208	304	60
Grandville	16070	32	0	8		12	12	683	62	611	10	0
Grant	880	4	0	1		0	3	23	2	21	0	0
Grayling	1836	11	0	4		0	7	79	7	72	0	0
Green Oak Township	18722	16	0	6		1	9	148	16	121	11	1
Greenville	8438	26	0	13		1	12	233	29	204	0	3
Grosse Ile Township	10123	2	0	0		0	2	15	3	12	0	1
Grosse Pointe	5198	4	0	1		1	2	90	8	78	4	0
Grosse Pointe Farms	9188	5	1	1		2	1	157	14	125	18	0
Grosse Pointe Park	11160	13	0	1		3	9	215	20	162	33	0
Grosse Pointe Shores	2920	1	0	0		0	1	28	7	19	2	0
Grosse Pointe Woods	15699	12	0	3		4	5	224	35	178	11	0
Hamburg Township	21714	14	0	9		0	5	80	15	54	11	0
Hampton Township	9401	13	0	4		0	9	139	19	118	2	0
Hamtramck	21929	250	1	11		106	132	684	236	352	96	13

Table 6. Offenses Known to Law Enforcement, by Selected State and City, 2016—Continued

(Number.)

State/city	Population	Violent crime	Murder and nonnegligent manslaughter	Rape (revised definition)[1]	Rape (legacy definition)[2]	Robbery	Aggravated assault	Property crime	Burglary	Larceny-theft	Motor vehicle theft	Arson[3]
Hancock	4537	7	0	5		0	2	33	8	24	1	0
Harbor Beach	1621	2	0	2		0	0	32	9	21	2	1
Harbor Springs	1203	1	0	0		0	1	14	1	13	0	0
Harper Woods	13764	125	0	10		42	73	1013	128	774	111	2
Hart	2093	17	0	4		1	12	185	20	161	4	2
Hartford	2604	4	0	0		1	3	29	3	20	6	1
Hastings	7274	25	0	11		0	14	114	7	99	8	0
Hazel Park	16636	55	1	4		13	37	369	53	243	73	2
Highland Park	10810	188	3	11		39	135	302	81	137	84	14
Highland Township	19801	16	0	6		0	10	112	22	76	14	0
Hillsdale	8139	15	0	3		0	12	55	12	40	3	2
Holland	33867	118	0	41		14	63	848	128	685	35	4
Holly	6186	14	0	2		1	11	101	24	75	2	0
Hopkins	608	0	0	0		0	0	2	1	1	0	0
Houghton	8020	5	0	5		0	0	107	2	104	1	0
Howell	9533	22	0	9		0	13	124	18	105	1	1
Hudson	2229	9	0	3		0	6	28	0	26	2	1
Huntington Woods	6360	2	0	0		1	1	43	2	41	0	0
Huron Township	15622	28	0	7		3	18	198	68	103	27	6
Imlay City	3569	13	0	3		0	10	59	11	42	6	1
Independence Township	36689	23	0	2		3	18	188	42	138	8	2
Inkster	24548	324	7	31		73	213	724	316	322	86	9
Ionia	11370	39	0	21		0	18	150	32	113	5	1
Iron River	2881	10	0	5		0	5	84	22	55	7	0
Ironwood	4929	2	0	0		1	1	66	5	60	1	0
Ishpeming	6485	17	0	9		0	8	85	8	71	6	0
Jackson	33060	409	4	65		49	291	1504	287	1159	58	17
Jonesville	2213	1	0	1		0	0	67	7	57	3	0
Kalamazoo	76389	925	7	125		182	611	3221	755	2228	238	25
Kalamazoo Township	24534	102	1	18		17	66	630	182	410	38	5
Kalkaska	2042	1	0	0		0	1	30	1	29	0	0
Keego Harbor	3040	14	0	4		1	9	33	2	30	1	0
Kentwood	51897	167	1	27		33	106	1469	207	1175	87	4
Kinde	429	0	0	0		0	0	1	0	1	0	0
Kingsford	5057	7	0	5		0	2	42	2	39	1	0
Kinross Township	7536	1	0	1		0	0	13	5	8	0	0
Laingsburg	1276	0	0	0		0	0	34	5	27	2	1
Lake Angelus	298	0	0	0		0	0	0	0	0	0	0
Lake Linden	985	1	0	1		0	0	5	0	5	0	0
Lake Odessa	2032	7	0	4		0	3	10	4	6	0	0
Lake Orion	3065	2	0	1		0	1	30	2	27	1	7
Lakeview	1011	3	0	2		0	1	51	4	47	0	0
Lansing	115199	1341	9	142		260	930	3325	897	2053	375	18
Lansing Township	8148	48	1	7		7	33	310	44	243	23	0
Lapeer	8782	50	0	18		1	31	322	30	285	7	1
Lapeer Township	5066	1	0	1		0	0	25	5	20	0	0
Lathrup Village	4147	9	0	0		1	8	28	8	19	1	0
Laurium	1933	1	1	0		0	0	19	5	13	1	0
Lawton	1860	5	0	1		0	4	52	5	44	3	1
Lennon	499	0	0	0		0	0	3	0	3	0	1
Leslie	1869	2	0	1		0	1	17	1	15	1	0
Lincoln Park	36808	268	0	21		36	211	1111	212	777	122	2
Lincoln Township	14500	10	0	2		0	8	180	25	149	6	0
Linden	3811	0	0	0		0	0	15	2	13	0	0
Litchfield	1343	1	0	1		0	0	15	4	11	0	0
Livonia	94226	141	0	18		28	95	1694	295	1250	149	4
Lowell	3931	15	0	3		1	11	75	12	58	5	3
Ludington	8054	35	0	15		1	19	153	17	130	6	1
Luna Pier	1380	2	0	0		0	2	23	6	17	0	0
Lyon Township	18917	11	0	2		1	8	161	23	127	11	0
Mackinac Island	479	8	0	2		0	6	126	1	125	0	0
Mackinaw City	802	0	0	0		0	0	36	3	32	1	0
Madison Heights	30297	81	0	12		16	53	639	91	468	80	1
Madison Township	8464	10	0	3		1	6	107	6	98	3	0
Mancelona	1361	0	0	0		0	0	23	4	18	1	0
Manistee	6057	21	0	11		0	10	138	19	116	3	0
Manistique	2960	6	0	4		0	2	52	11	41	0	1
Marenisco Township	1681	0	0	0		0	0	1	0	1	0	0
Marine City	4124	14	0	2		2	10	54	9	40	5	0
Marlette	1787	2	0	1		0	1	22	3	17	2	0
Marquette	21283	25	1	11		2	11	310	25	281	4	0
Marshall	7038	14	0	5		1	8	100	14	85	1	1
Marysville	9722	19	0	1		4	14	118	10	105	3	0
Mason	8461	10	0	2		1	7	164	27	133	4	0
Mattawan	1938	5	0	2		1	2	24	3	19	2	1
Mayville	914	1	0	0		0	1	3	1	1	1	1
Melvindale	10348	55	1	1		10	43	239	42	176	21	0
Mendon	859	2	0	0		0	2	11	2	9	0	0
Menominee	8344	31	0	5		0	26	198	28	162	8	3
Meridian Township	42700	86	0	19		10	57	926	96	812	18	5
Metamora Township	4241	9	0	3		0	6	32	6	25	1	0
Michiana	183	0	0	0		0	0	3	0	3	0	0
Midland	42263	48	0	17		5	26	511	77	424	10	0

Table 6. Offenses Known to Law Enforcement, by Selected State and City, 2016—Continued

(Number.)

State/city	Population	Violent crime	Murder and nonnegligent manslaughter	Rape (revised definition)[1]	Rape (legacy definition)[2]	Robbery	Aggravated assault	Property crime	Burglary	Larceny-theft	Motor vehicle theft	Arson[3]
Milan	6012	11	0	1		1	9	100	13	77	10	0
Milford	16707	11	0	7		1	3	85	18	64	3	1
Montague	2362	3	0	1		0	2	28	3	25	0	0
Montrose Township	7524	7	0	1		0	6	62	15	46	1	0
Morenci	2181	8	0	1		1	6	27	8	18	1	0
Morrice	891	3	0	1		0	2	15	5	9	1	0
Mount Morris	2941	26	0	2		4	20	92	23	64	5	2
Mount Morris Township	20502	83	3	14		13	53	443	151	248	44	6
Mount Pleasant	26069	67	0	24		3	40	352	48	287	17	11
Munising	2278	4	0	1		0	3	30	3	27	0	1
Muskegon	38442	273	5	39		62	167	1468	285	1094	89	6
Muskegon Heights	10785	198	1	23		49	125	576	157	360	59	15
Muskegon Township	17791	54	0	15		4	35	787	89	672	26	1
Napoleon Township	6764	4	1	0		0	3	61	22	32	7	0
Nashville	1635	19	0	4		0	15	23	7	14	2	2
Negaunee	4584	9	0	3		2	4	53	7	43	3	0
Newaygo	1951	12	0	5		0	7	85	7	77	1	0
New Baltimore	12409	21	0	6		1	14	96	11	79	6	2
New Buffalo	1875	2	0	0		0	2	28	4	23	1	3
New Era	444	0	0	0		0	0	4	1	3	0	0
New Lothrop	557	0	0	0		0	0	6	2	4	0	0
Niles	11282	64	0	20		12	32	287	65	191	31	4
Northfield Township	8617	13	0	3		0	10	108	36	66	6	1
North Muskegon	3779	4	0	1		0	3	63	1	62	0	0
Northville	6019	2	0	0		0	2	56	7	48	1	2
Northville Township	28890	12	0	6		0	6	343	25	299	19	1
Norton Shores	24256	45	2	6		12	25	695	78	602	15	2
Novi	59441	32	0	6		2	24	661	56	586	19	0
Oakland Township	19659	6	0	2		0	4	52	14	36	2	0
Oak Park	29838	105	2	18		30	55	565	97	391	77	4
Olivet	1611	2	0	0		1	1	13	0	13	0	0
Ontwa Township-Edwardsburg	6481	27	0	6		1	20	116	37	66	13	1
Orchard Lake	2428	4	0	2		0	2	26	2	23	1	0
Orion Township	35550	25	1	3		1	20	220	35	176	9	10
Oscoda Township	6838	22	0	6		0	16	135	34	100	1	1
Otisville	818	2	0	2		0	0	4	0	4	0	0
Otsego	3998	8	0	1		0	7	63	11	50	2	0
Ovid	1614	1	0	0		0	1	10	2	8	0	0
Owendale	230	0	0	0		0	0	2	0	2	0	0
Owosso	14605	69	1	14		7	47	317	64	240	13	8
Oxford	3554	3	0	1		0	2	17	6	7	4	0
Oxford Township	18164	16	0	1		0	15	107	18	86	3	0
Paw Paw	3441	14	0	3		0	11	141	5	133	3	1
Peck	609	1	0	0		0	1	0	0	0	0	0
Pentwater	843	3	0	1		0	2	15	2	13	0	0
Perry	2088	2	0	0		0	2	14	2	10	2	0
Petoskey	5731	9	0	2		0	7	55	10	40	5	1
Pinckney	2439	2	0	0		0	2	15	4	10	1	0
Pinconning	1264	0	0	0		0	0	8	0	7	1	0
Pittsfield Township	38704	79	0	24		10	45	620	62	522	36	9
Plainwell	3826	10	0	2		0	8	69	13	49	7	0
Pleasant Ridge	2562	0	0	0		0	0	16	4	11	1	0
Plymouth	8865	5	0	2		2	1	88	12	65	11	0
Plymouth Township	26870	16	0	2		2	12	280	29	232	19	0
Pontiac	60003	749	15	66		121	547	1425	520	771	134	26
Portage	48550	103	0	31		15	57	1289	149	1117	23	5
Port Austin	638	0	0	0		0	0	11	0	11	0	0
Port Huron	29182	280	1	48		24	207	749	201	510	38	14
Portland	3929	4	0	2		0	2	26	2	22	2	0
Port Sanilac	600	0	0	0		0	0	0	0	0	0	0
Potterville	2619	1	0	1		0	0	7	0	6	1	0
Prairieville Township	3409	0	0	0		0	0	7	3	4	0	0
Quincy	1638	9	0	2		2	5	58	23	35	0	0
Raisin Township	7577	0	0	0		0	0	27	6	21	0	0
Reading	1052	0	0	0		0	0	7	1	6	0	0
Redford Township	47218	334	1	45		65	223	1384	369	752	263	6
Reed City	2383	5	0	1		1	3	38	3	34	1	1
Reese	1398	0	0	0		0	0	9	3	5	1	0
Richfield Township, Genesee County	8315	14	0	6		1	7	88	37	45	6	0
Richfield Township, Roscommon County	3628	8	0	4		0	4	35	5	26	4	0
Richland	793	0	0	0		0	0	12	0	12	0	0
Richland Township, Saginaw County	3961	2	0	0		0	2	16	4	11	1	0
Richmond	5882	16	0	2		0	14	92	15	73	4	1
River Rouge	7480	79	1	12		15	51	186	55	107	24	6
Riverview	12127	37	0	2		8	27	192	24	138	30	1
Rochester	13050	8	0	0		1	7	66	12	53	1	2
Rochester Hills	73913	53	0	8		8	37	545	63	459	23	0
Rockford	6218	23	0	4		1	18	94	7	85	2	0
Rockwood	3183	7	0	1		0	6	35	2	25	8	0

Table 6. Offenses Known to Law Enforcement, by Selected State and City, 2016—Continued

(Number.)

State/city	Population	Violent crime	Murder and nonnegligent manslaughter	Rape (revised definition)[1]	Rape (legacy definition)[2]	Robbery	Aggravated assault	Property crime	Burglary	Larceny-theft	Motor vehicle theft	Arson[3]
Rogers City	2692	0	0	0	.	0	0	50	5	43	2	0
Romeo	3630	1	0	1		0	0	42	1	40	1	0
Romulus	23315	169	4	28		25	112	685	120	418	147	4
Roseville	47704	246	0	32		59	155	1829	193	1482	154	9
Rothbury	422	0	0	0		0	0	11	3	8	0	0
Royal Oak	59367	65	0	14		8	43	612	86	489	37	4
Saginaw	48942	718	10	56		62	590	926	369	503	54	26
Saginaw Township	39421	81	0	10		20	51	916	157	740	19	2
Saline	9158	10	0	0		0	10	53	8	39	6	1
Sand Lake	525	0	0	0		0	0	17	0	17	0	0
Sandusky	2580	7	0	1		0	6	66	12	52	2	0
Saugatuck-Douglas	2262	11	0	0		0	11	37	13	23	1	0
Sault Ste. Marie	13763	54	0	24		3	27	312	41	263	8	1
Schoolcraft	1574	5	0	2		0	3	30	8	21	1	0
Scottville	1213	1	0	1		0	0	43	2	41	0	0
Sebewaing	1679	0	0	0		0	0	5	1	4	0	0
Shelby Township	78427	104	0	34		3	67	720	87	572	61	2
Shepherd	1505	0	0	0		0	0	12	1	11	0	0
Somerset Township	4580	1	0	0		0	1	40	1	38	1	0
Southfield	73438	195	3	44		52	96	2158	353	1514	291	6
Southgate	29158	78	1	12		20	45	864	77	702	85	0
South Lyon	11801	7	0	4		0	3	50	3	43	4	2
South Rockwood	1635	3	0	1		0	2	14	3	9	2	0
Sparta	4346	8	0	3		1	4	116	10	103	3	0
Spaulding Township	2041	2	0	0		0	2	8	3	5	0	0
Spring Arbor Township	8097	7	0	0		0	7	30	7	23	0	1
Springfield Township	14467	7	0	3		0	4	79	18	57	4	1
Standish	1442	0	0	0		0	0	3	0	3	0	0
Stanton	1414	1	0	1		0	0	14	2	12	0	0
St. Charles	1940	10	0	1		1	8	30	3	24	3	3
St. Clair	5368	11	0	1		1	9	71	23	44	4	1
St. Clair Shores	59938	116	0	28		13	75	808	139	606	63	4
Sterling Heights	132523	242	1	32		26	183	1513	177	1221	115	6
St. Ignace	2376	8	0	2		0	6	63	7	55	1	1
St. Johns	7916	11	0	9		0	2	62	4	57	1	0
St. Joseph	8271	18	0	2		0	16	138	12	122	4	0
St. Joseph Township	9850	10	0	1		2	7	170	18	146	6	1
St. Louis	7212	12	0	9		0	3	49	4	44	1	0
Stockbridge	1235	3	0	1		0	2	21	4	16	1	0
Sturgis	10876	32	1	10		2	19	264	25	225	14	3
Sumpter Township	9265	7	1	0		0	6	93	34	49	10	0
Swartz Creek	5531	12	0	3		0	9	103	10	91	2	1
Sylvan Lake	1798	2	0	0		0	2	29	5	20	4	0
Tawas	4515	10	0	3		2	5	104	5	99	0	0
Taylor	61290	372	2	37		83	250	1495	290	1042	163	19
Tecumseh	8353	14	0	2		0	12	78	13	60	5	1
Thetford Township	6696	0	0	0		0	0	8	3	3	2	1
Thomas Township	11505	14	0	5		1	8	158	31	123	4	0
Three Rivers	7738	40	0	12		2	26	307	12	281	14	2
Tittabawassee Township	9782	7	0	3		0	4	64	9	53	2	0
Traverse City	15330	66	0	19		4	43	314	45	257	12	1
Trenton	18294	41	0	8		3	30	153	12	118	23	0
Troy	83743	78	1	12		16	49	1336	94	1183	59	1
Tuscarora Township	2946	3	0	0		0	3	68	2	64	2	0
Ubly	822	3	0	0		0	3	11	4	7	0	0
Unadilla Township	3405	6	0	1		0	5	33	13	19	1	0
Union City	1581	4	0	2		0	2	61	17	44	0	0
Utica	4980	22	0	2		3	17	163	9	145	9	1
Van Buren Township	28090	109	0	17		20	72	657	92	495	70	3
Vassar	2605	11	0	3		0	8	24	3	21	0	2
Vernon	753	0	0	0		0	0	6	0	6	0	2
Vicksburg	3298	13	0	2		1	10	49	3	45	1	0
Walker	24874	41	0	11		8	22	657	46	590	21	2
Walled Lake	7132	6	0	2		0	4	54	7	41	6	1
Warren	135620	691	6	118		125	442	3521	927	2082	512	29
Waterford Township	73308	97	1	25		21	50	793	186	538	69	13
Watervliet	1684	6	0	3		0	3	17	3	12	2	0
Wayland	4184	10	0	4		0	6	96	25	68	3	0
Wayne	16989	163	2	17		32	112	340	86	209	45	6
West Bloomfield Township	66123	45	0	7		2	36	489	59	414	16	2
West Branch	2054	6	0	3		0	3	33	5	25	3	0
Westland	81625	298	0	64		68	166	1709	300	1249	160	18
White Cloud	1378	8	0	3		0	5	27	6	21	0	1
Whitehall	2712	7	0	1		1	5	52	6	46	0	0
White Lake Township	31135	15	0	3		1	11	319	32	276	11	3
White Pigeon	1513	7	0	3		1	3	30	6	23	1	0
Williamston	3888	4	0	0		0	4	18	3	14	1	1
Wixom	13796	22	1	4		2	15	231	19	183	29	0
Wolverine Lake	4397	3	0	1		0	2	16	0	16	0	0
Woodhaven	12478	10	1	2		2	5	259	9	236	14	1
Woodland Township	2065	0	0	0		0	0	3	1	2	0	0
Wyandotte	25029	49	0	7		7	35	384	69	284	31	1
Wyoming	75917	352	4	69		62	217	1758	297	1273	188	18

Table 6. Offenses Known to Law Enforcement, by Selected State and City, 2016—Continued

(Number.)

State/city	Population	Violent crime	Murder and nonnegligent manslaughter	Rape (revised definition)[1]	Rape (legacy definition)[2]	Robbery	Aggravated assault	Property crime	Burglary	Larceny-theft	Motor vehicle theft	Arson[3]
Yale	1896	5	0	1		0	4	26	2	24	0	0
Ypsilanti	20019	151	0	21		42	88	530	108	384	38	5
Zeeland	5650	15	0	7		0	8	98	38	59	1	0
Zilwaukee	1562	0	0	0		0	0	16	2	14	0	0
MINNESOTA												
Aitkin	2031	4	0	1		1	2	74	5	64	5	0
Akeley	431	0	0	0		0	0	20	0	20	0	0
Albany	2661	1	0	0		0	1	11	1	9	1	0
Albert Lea	17604	19	0	0		4	15	331	27	290	14	1
Alexandria	12006	26	1	6		2	17	351	20	294	37	0
Annandale	3317	4	0	2		0	2	45	5	35	5	0
Anoka	17389	36	1	8		10	17	590	65	492	33	4
Appleton	1328	3	0	0		0	3	26	3	23	0	0
Apple Valley	51648	64	1	33		16	14	1149	145	967	37	1
Arlington	2157	0	0	0		0	0	0	0	0	0	0
Ashby	428	0	0	0		0	0	1	0	1	0	0
Atwater	1122	1	0	0		0	1	0	0	0	0	0
Austin	24529	67	0	9		6	52	590	114	449	27	1
Avon	1481	0	0	0		0	0	16	0	16	0	0
Babbitt	1528	0	0	0		0	0	5	0	5	0	0
Barnesville	2581	1	0	0		0	1	0	0	0	0	0
Baudette	1055	0	0	0		0	0	1	1	0	0	0
Baxter	7993	14	0	3		0	11	357	20	330	7	0
Bayport	3763	3	0	2		0	1	30	3	24	3	1
Becker	4730	2	0	0		0	2	42	11	28	3	0
Belgrade/Brooten	1504	0	0	0		0	0	2	1	1	0	0
Belle Plaine	6968	4	0	3		0	1	74	6	65	3	0
Bemidji	14690	72	1	16		11	44	1017	64	911	42	2
Benson	3045	3	0	0		0	3	7	5	1	1	0
Big Lake	10421	15	0	1		1	13	76	10	60	6	0
Blackduck	778	0	0	0		0	0	3	1	2	0	0
Blaine	63115	78	2	28		22	26	1713	198	1474	41	5
Blooming Prairie	1993	2	0	1		0	1	16	3	11	2	0
Bloomington	87134	177	0	49		62	66	2810	181	2514	115	11
Blue Earth	3216	2	0	0		0	2	32	10	18	4	0
Bovey	813	0	0	0		0	0	7	2	5	0	0
Braham	1765	1	0	1		0	0	1	0	1	0	0
Brainerd	13327	86	0	24		2	60	661	90	539	32	4
Breckenridge	3270	2	0	0		0	2	62	13	46	3	0
Breezy Point	2356	2	0	2		0	0	20	4	16	0	0
Breitung Township	607	1	0	0		0	1	12	6	6	0	0
Brooklyn Center	30893	112	1	24		41	46	1084	98	872	114	3
Brooklyn Park	79800	310	1	52		93	164	2428	387	1871	170	16
Brownton	734	2	0	1		0	1	5	3	1	1	0
Buffalo	16134	18	0	7		0	11	319	42	271	6	1
Buffalo Lake	682	1	0	1		0	0	7	3	4	0	0
Burnsville	61697	125	1	27		35	62	1653	202	1374	77	3
Caledonia	2772	1	0	0		0	1	4	0	4	0	0
Cambridge	8515	10	0	0		0	10	305	31	261	13	0
Canby	1693	2	0	1		0	1	9	0	9	0	0
Cannon Falls	4057	6	0	2		0	4	127	10	111	6	1
Centennial Lakes	10937	11	0	5		5	1	128	21	100	7	4
Champlin	24048	24	0	10		3	11	304	49	246	9	1
Chaska	25483	15	0	1		5	9	287	37	238	12	0
Chisholm	4983	4	0	0		0	4	55	5	49	1	0
Clara City	1312	0	0	0		0	0	8	0	8	0	0
Cloquet	12064	33	1	6		3	23	631	59	551	21	1
Cold Spring/Richmond	5547	4	0	0		0	4	41	3	36	2	0
Coleraine	2005	1	0	0		0	1	7	0	7	0	0
Columbia Heights	19754	43	1	11		16	15	426	65	324	37	3
Coon Rapids	62380	104	1	32		24	47	1785	197	1538	50	4
Corcoran	5586	1	0	0		0	1	28	2	25	1	0
Cottage Grove	36164	17	1	2		5	9	568	68	479	21	6
Crookston	7765	19	0	10		0	9	57	13	37	7	2
Crosby	2336	3	0	1		0	2	95	8	87	0	0
Crosslake	2222	2	0	0		0	2	17	2	15	0	0
Crystal	23102	30	0	3		8	19	472	67	374	31	0
Danube	463	0	0	0		0	0	3	0	1	2	0
Dawson/Boyd	1590	0	0	0		0	0	20	4	16	0	0
Dayton	5185	0	0	0		0	0	43	4	34	5	0
Deephaven	3880	0	0	0		0	0	8	2	6	0	1
Deer River	934	0	0	0		0	0	3	0	3	0	0
Detroit Lakes	9075	11	0	5		0	6	171	12	150	9	0
Dilworth	4437	5	0	2		1	2	157	11	134	12	1
Duluth	86090	312	1	51		64	196	3827	529	3162	136	8
Eagan	66698	40	0	11		13	16	1144	106	995	43	5
Eagle Lake	2933	3	0	0		0	3	23	7	13	3	0
East Grand Forks	8649	7	0	2		0	5	190	33	151	6	0
East Range	3665	6	0	2		0	4	15	7	8	0	1
Eden Prairie	64037	36	2	15		8	11	729	75	627	27	2
Eden Valley	1035	0	0	0		0	0	7	3	4	0	0
Edina	50577	26	0	7		13	6	935	94	824	17	2

Table 6. Offenses Known to Law Enforcement, by Selected State and City, 2016—Continued

(Number.)

State/city	Population	Violent crime	Murder and nonnegligent manslaughter	Rape (revised definition)[1]	Rape (legacy definition)[2]	Robbery	Aggravated assault	Property crime	Burglary	Larceny-theft	Motor vehicle theft	Arson[3]
Elbow Lake	1138	0	0	0		0	0	1	0	1	0	0
Elko New Market	4831	0	0	0		0	0	13	0	12	1	0
Elk River	24150	24	0	8		2	14	458	40	399	19	1
Elmore	632	1	0	1		0	0	13	4	7	2	0
Ely	3398	3	0	0		0	3	43	10	33	0	0
Eveleth	3665	4	0	2		1	1	173	41	124	8	1
Fairfax	1160	1	0	0		0	1	30	0	30	0	0
Fairmont	10137	19	0	11		3	5	206	37	160	9	0
Falcon Heights	5619	2	0	1		0	1	88	26	58	4	0
Faribault	23708	67	2	14		9	42	524	64	416	44	1
Farmington	23060	10	0	3		0	7	221	31	174	16	1
Fergus Falls	13312	26	1	3		1	21	490	107	374	9	2
Floodwood	521	1	0	1		0	0	8	0	8	0	0
Forest Lake	19867	41	0	12		4	25	655	92	528	35	6
Fountain	408	1	0	0		0	1	1	1	0	0	0
Franklin	472	0	0	0		0	0	0	0	0	0	0
Fridley	27811	78	0	24		19	35	970	134	762	74	1
Fulda	1229	1	0	1		0	0	17	0	17	0	0
Gaylord	2233	12	0	4		0	8	83	10	73	0	0
Gilbert	1791	2	0	0		0	2	87	15	70	2	0
Glencoe	5495	1	0	1		0	0	68	3	64	1	0
Glenwood	2571	0	0	0		0	0	7	2	5	0	0
Golden Valley	21454	16	0	5		4	7	408	54	323	31	0
Goodview	4168	2	0	0		0	2	64	12	45	7	0
Grand Rapids	11181	16	0	6		1	9	210	27	182	1	0
Granite Falls	2719	9	0	1		1	7	39	9	29	1	0
Hallock	948	0	0	0		0	0	2	0	2	0	0
Hancock	753	0	0	0		0	0	0	0	0	0	0
Hastings	22627	46	1	10		6	29	495	53	412	30	0
Hawley	2203	5	0	0		0	5	1	0	1	0	0
Hector	1062	2	0	0		0	2	28	0	28	0	0
Hermantown	9761	8	0	2		2	4	425	40	372	13	0
Hibbing	16176	20	0	5		0	15	138	12	116	10	1
Hill City	594	0	0	0		0	0	7	0	7	0	0
Hilltop	735	9	0	3		2	4	89	5	79	5	0
Hokah	556	0	0	0		0	0	11	2	9	0	0
Hopkins	18169	44	0	11		11	22	378	58	305	15	4
Houston	964	0	0	0		0	0	0	0	0	0	0
Howard Lake	2052	1	0	0		0	1	12	4	7	1	0
Hutchinson	13867	13	0	4		0	9	281	22	255	4	0
Inver Grove Heights	35049	84	0	28		11	45	795	117	605	73	4
Isanti	5493	1	0	0		0	1	104	23	79	2	0
Isle	790	1	0	1		0	0	15	1	13	1	0
Janesville	2253	4	0	2		0	2	13	3	9	1	0
Jordan	6203	7	0	1		1	5	50	3	46	1	0
Kasson	6157	5	0	0		1	4	65	2	57	6	0
Keewatin	1046	0	0	0		0	0	16	2	13	1	0
Kimball	777	1	0	0		0	1	0	0	0	0	0
La Crescent	4820	2	0	0		0	2	30	2	27	1	0
Lake City	5021	4	0	2		0	2	34	6	21	7	0
Lake Crystal	2522	0	0	0		0	0	26	14	10	2	0
Lakefield	1648	0	0	0		0	0	1	0	1	0	0
Lakes Area	9322	9	0	6		0	3	128	24	96	8	0
Lake Shore	1026	0	0	0		0	0	2	0	2	0	0
Lakeville	61581	42	0	8		7	27	614	77	507	30	1
Lamberton	785	0	0	0		0	0	0	0	0	0	0
Lauderdale	2530	3	0	0		3	0	31	8	20	3	0
Lester Prairie	1678	0	0	0		0	0	15	1	13	1	0
Le Sueur	3988	1	0	0		0	1	63	11	47	5	0
Lewiston	1562	1	0	1		0	0	13	3	10	0	0
Lino Lakes	21212	10	0	5		0	5	209	23	181	5	0
Litchfield	6643	7	0	4		0	3	106	9	91	6	1
Little Falls	8611	4	0	1		1	2	146	15	122	9	1
Long Prairie	3325	5	0	3		0	2	72	7	64	1	1
Lonsdale	3873	1	0	1		0	0	21	1	16	4	0
Madelia	2240	3	0	2		0	1	19	5	13	1	0
Madison Lake	1110	0	0	0		0	0	5	2	2	1	0
Mankato	41300	112	1	27		23	61	1329	223	1057	49	4
Maple Grove	69783	44	0	14		8	22	1187	89	1063	35	4
Mapleton	1726	1	0	0		1	0	13	5	6	2	0
Maplewood	41071	102	0	20		44	38	1752	208	1403	141	1
Marshall	13645	15	1	2		4	8	200	49	142	9	1
Medina	6216	3	0	0		0	3	99	10	87	2	0
Melrose	3620	4	0	0		0	4	16	5	10	1	0
Menahga	1346	0	0	0		0	0	0	0	0	0	0
Mendota Heights	11252	14	0	4		4	6	186	27	153	6	1
Milaca	2871	0	0	0		0	0	32	5	27	0	0
Minneapolis	416751	4622	35	455		1844	2288	17594	3424	12183	1987	85
Minneota	1357	1	0	0		0	1	0	0	0	0	0
Minnesota Lake	654	1	0	1		0	0	6	1	4	1	0
Minnetonka	52055	29	0	5		10	14	769	133	620	16	1
Minnetrista	9675	2	0	0		0	2	84	6	73	5	0
Montevideo	5184	2	0	1		0	1	106	17	81	8	0

Table 6. Offenses Known to Law Enforcement, by Selected State and City, 2016—Continued

(Number.)

State/city	Population	Violent crime	Murder and nonnegligent manslaughter	Rape (revised definition)[1]	Rape (legacy definition)[2]	Robbery	Aggravated assault	Property crime	Burglary	Larceny-theft	Motor vehicle theft	Arson[3]
Montgomery	2907	2	0	1		0	1	75	11	56	8	0
Moorhead	42507	68	1	20		14	33	972	169	712	91	1
Moose Lake	2747	14	0	3		0	11	82	2	78	2	1
Morris	5367	11	0	6		0	5	81	13	63	5	0
Morristown	993	2	0	2		0	0	14	1	13	0	0
Mounds View	13063	21	0	5		6	10	412	47	338	27	0
Mountain Lake	2119	2	0	1		0	1	5	4	1	0	0
Nashwauk	965	0	0	0		0	0	28	3	22	3	0
New Brighton	22521	27	0	3		7	17	514	83	404	27	4
New Hope	21168	27	0	4		10	13	390	56	319	15	1
New Prague	7631	6	0	3		0	3	117	18	98	1	0
New Richland	1185	0	0	0		0	0	0	0	0	0	0
North Branch	10233	7	0	1		0	6	196	25	159	12	1
Northfield	20445	16	0	5		1	10	211	19	187	5	2
North Mankato	13553	7	0	0		0	7	149	30	116	3	3
North St. Paul	12495	15	0	2		3	10	262	30	210	22	2
Oakdale	28211	45	0	15		7	23	851	69	726	56	1
Oak Park Heights	4912	5	0	0		3	2	202	16	181	5	1
Olivia	2333	7	0	3		0	4	70	18	51	1	0
Onamia	861	0	0	0		0	0	5	1	3	1	0
Orono	19799	3	0	1		0	2	166	15	143	8	1
Ortonville	1796	0	0	0		0	0	10	1	9	0	0
Osakis	1715	1	0	0		0	1	31	5	26	0	0
Osseo	2817	0	0	0		0	0	4	1	2	1	0
Ostrander	254	0	0	0		0	0	0	0	0	0	0
Owatonna	25760	38	0	1		9	28	612	81	495	36	2
Park Rapids	3963	9	0	1		1	7	287	32	243	12	1
Paynesville	2434	2	0	0		0	2	11	4	7	0	0
Pequot Lakes	2259	1	0	0		0	1	104	5	99	0	1
Pike Bay	1635	0	0	0		0	0	2	0	2	0	0
Pillager	450	0	0	0		0	0	0	0	0	0	0
Pine River	923	1	0	0		0	1	16	4	11	1	0
Plainview	3217	0	0	0		0	0	13	2	10	1	0
Plymouth	76996	48	1	12		14	21	1009	215	759	35	3
Preston	1294	0	0	0		0	0	1	0	1	0	0
Princeton	4668	6	0	2		1	3	176	19	149	8	0
Proctor	3070	5	0	1		0	4	79	6	67	6	0
Ramsey	26273	16	1	5		1	9	338	33	287	18	0
Red Wing	16442	39	0	8		6	25	486	95	362	29	0
Redwood Falls	5024	16	0	5		1	10	171	21	137	13	1
Renville	1199	2	0	1		0	1	17	2	15	0	0
Richfield	36410	78	0	8		38	32	918	114	742	62	4
Rochester	113306	242	0	76		49	117	2479	375	1972	132	0
Rogers	12847	12	0	3		1	8	185	14	162	9	1
Roseau	2735	0	0	0		0	0	50	5	44	1	0
Rosemount	23717	24	0	9		3	12	192	34	154	4	0
Roseville	35954	71	0	10		33	28	1813	177	1559	77	8
Rushford	1709	0	0	0		0	0	0	0	0	0	0
Sacred Heart	512	0	0	0		0	0	0	0	0	0	0
Sartell	16943	8	0	1		0	7	313	41	265	7	1
Sauk Centre	4367	4	0	0		0	4	82	12	66	4	0
Sauk Rapids	13545	10	0	0		0	10	333	34	287	12	1
Shakopee	40524	67	2	18		16	31	794	96	656	42	0
Silver Bay	1799	0	0	0		0	0	1	0	1	0	0
Silver Lake	807	1	0	1		0	0	21	1	18	2	0
Slayton	2035	3	0	1		0	2	41	2	38	1	0
Sleepy Eye	3414	1	0	1		0	0	9	3	6	0	0
South Lake Minnetonka	12247	10	0	2		0	8	114	18	92	4	3
South St. Paul	20452	127	0	18		21	88	592	87	442	63	6
Springfield	2052	0	0	0		0	0	0	0	0	0	0
Spring Grove	1286	0	0	0		0	0	22	1	20	1	0
Spring Lake Park	6484	14	0	2		5	7	290	58	212	20	1
St. Anthony	9150	7	0	1		2	4	192	40	146	6	0
Staples	2867	3	0	1		0	2	70	13	55	2	0
Starbuck	1258	1	0	0		0	1	19	2	17	0	0
St. Charles	3703	0	0	0		0	0	57	10	45	2	0
St. Cloud	67341	293	1	68		72	152	2780	329	2327	124	7
St. Francis	7442	4	0	0		0	4	66	10	51	5	2
Stillwater	19051	20	1	5		4	10	407	58	331	18	3
St. James	4441	15	0	6		1	8	59	19	39	1	0
St. Joseph	6924	6	0	3		0	3	56	4	47	5	0
St. Louis Park	48770	66	0	12		17	37	1185	99	1042	44	0
St. Paul	303920	1970	19	184		700	1067	9811	2278	5659	1874	109
St. Paul Park	5399	10	0	4		2	4	140	21	102	17	1
St. Peter	11763	10	0	1		2	7	157	20	129	8	1
Thief River Falls	8776	6	0	1		0	5	103	12	86	5	0
Tracy	2108	2	0	0		0	2	44	6	36	2	0
Tri-City	1425	2	0	0		0	2	11	4	6	1	0
Two Harbors	3546	1	0	0		0	1	22	3	16	3	0
Virginia	8564	51	0	6		3	42	510	93	392	25	1
Wabasha	2437	4	0	0		0	4	63	14	48	1	0
Waite Park	7551	18	0	7		1	10	649	15	619	15	0
Walker	925	0	0	0		0	0	17	0	13	4	0

Table 6. Offenses Known to Law Enforcement, by Selected State and City, 2016—Continued

(Number.)

State/city	Population	Violent crime	Murder and nonnegligent manslaughter	Rape (revised definition)[1]	Rape (legacy definition)[2]	Robbery	Aggravated assault	Property crime	Burglary	Larceny-theft	Motor vehicle theft	Arson[3]
Warroad	1804	0	0	0		0	0	43	3	38	2	0
Waseca	9207	12	0	5		0	7	181	19	153	9	0
Wayzata	6627	10	0	2		2	6	116	10	103	3	0
Wells	2231	1	0	1		0	0	1	0	1	0	0
West Concord	772	0	0	0		0	0	18	1	16	1	0
West Hennepin	5575	6	0	1		0	5	46	5	40	1	0
West St. Paul	19762	73	0	9		20	44	1002	116	821	65	3
Wheaton	1351	5	0	0		0	5	38	4	34	0	0
White Bear Lake	25484	33	0	9		6	18	606	131	448	27	6
Willmar	19641	49	0	18		9	22	420	49	353	18	0
Windom	4532	6	0	1		0	5	59	6	48	5	0
Winnebago	1368	1	0	1		0	0	11	4	7	0	0
Winona	27001	46	1	21		8	16	804	92	704	8	2
Winsted	2285	2	0	1		0	1	26	4	22	0	0
Woodbury	69032	46	0	12		11	23	1339	168	1124	47	1
Worthington	13151	21	0	6		4	11	196	41	146	9	0
Wyoming	7816	5	0	0		0	5	78	5	62	11	0
Zumbrota	3385	6	0	2		0	4	60	6	48	6	0
MISSISSIPPI												
Ackerman	1472	3	0		0	0	3	21	6	15	0	0
Amory	7022	10	0		3	3	4	222	47	173	2	0
Batesville	7371	19	1	1		4	13	296	43	249	4	1
Biloxi	45952	181	2	31		80	68	2681	805	1721	155	8
Brandon	23824	15	0	1		3	11	215	41	165	9	2
Byhalia	1247	6	1		0	3	2	64	6	55	3	0
D'Iberville	11795	14	0	5		6	3	829	72	738	19	1
Edwards	1014	12	0		0	0	12	45	24	21	0	0
Flowood	8879	23	0	1		5	17	315	62	246	7	0
Fulton	4101	4	0		0	1	3	110	14	96	0	0
Gautier	18566	52	0		3	12	37	584	133	409	42	1
Greenville	31732	88	7		16	57	8	1969	930	961	78	56
Gulfport	72668	228	10	27		97	94	3818	638	3002	178	26
Hattiesburg	47006	147	8	10		52	77	2752	374	2292	86	3
Hernando	15793	24	0	5		4	15	347	92	251	4	1
Holly Springs	7596	124	1		2	23	98	245	61	165	19	3
Horn Lake	27077	20	0	0		13	7	701	122	557	22	3
Jackson	170070	1451	58		107	681	605	7884	1948	5064	872	95
Laurel	18894	79	1	17		27	34	846	248	569	29	2
Long Beach	15708	11	0		0	3	8	361	62	290	9	0
Madison	26119	14	0		0	4	10	198	14	175	9	0
McComb	12632	64	3		1	32	28	679	163	496	20	0
Meridian	39364	234	8	24		128	74	1813	693	985	135	5
Natchez	15003	64	1		8	18	37	755	123	612	20	16
Ocean Springs	17688	28	0	2		8	18	677	113	523	41	0
Olive Branch	36513	67	2	4		22	39	932	382	510	40	2
Oxford	23052	39	1	10		15	13	646	103	532	11	
Pass Christian	5690	10	3	1		3	3	150	47	101	2	0
Petal	10747	2	0		0	1	1	82	43	35	4	0
Picayune	10631	47	0	7		9	31	512	112	380	20	1
Ridgeland	24406	83	1	6		45	31	729	63	644	22	1
Southaven	53310	59	1	5		27	26	1480	128	1318	34	5
Summit	1677	1	0		0	1	0	54	28	25	1	0
Vicksburg	22986	135	3		7	20	105	1430	240	1126	64	4
Waveland	6382	17	1		1	1	14	298	51	238	9	0
West Point	10935	28	1		4	11	12	315	109	203	3	3
Wiggins	4577	7	0		2	2	3	215	64	148	3	0
MISSOURI												
Adrian	1611	4	0	1		0	3	35	12	21	2	0
Advance	1369	1	0	0		0	1	9	5	4	0	0
Alma	392	0	0	0		0	0	1	0	1	0	0
Anderson	1980	13	0	1		1	11	56	5	42	9	0
Annapolis	343	0	0	0		0	0	3	0	3	0	1
Arcadia	569	0	0	0		0	0	1	0	1	0	0
Archie	1205	2	0	0		0	2	9	1	8	0	0
Arnold	21461	40	3	3		11	23	784	38	710	36	0
Ash Grove	1465	2	0	0		0	2	67	24	43	0	0
Ashland	3895	6	0	0		0	6	58	3	49	6	0
Aurora	7471	55	0	6		3	46	311	68	230	13	1
Auxvasse	985	2	0	0		0	2	27	10	16	1	0
Ava	2924	7	0	0		0	7	83	12	67	4	0
Ballwin	30609	11	0	5		1	5	236	21	206	9	2
Bates City	219	0	0	0		0	0	7	0	4	3	0
Battlefield	6083	3	0	1		1	1	91	26	61	4	0
Bella Villa	739	3	0	0		0	3	6	1	5	0	0
Belle	1524	3	0	0		0	3	11	2	9	0	0
Bellefontaine Neighbors	10788	110	3	6		22	79	329	111	167	51	0
Bellflower	358	0	0	0		0	0	2	2	0	0	0
Bel-Nor	1479	4	0	0		0	4	27	4	21	2	0
Bel-Ridge	2719	46	1	6		3	36	109	43	55	11	0
Belton	23170	71	2	15		19	35	856	127	648	81	3
Bernie	1949	1	0	0		0	1	14	4	8	2	0

Table 6. Offenses Known to Law Enforcement, by Selected State and City, 2016—Continued

(Number.)

State/city	Population	Violent crime	Murder and nonnegligent manslaughter	Rape (revised definition)[1]	Rape (legacy definition)[2]	Robbery	Aggravated assault	Property crime	Burglary	Larceny-theft	Motor vehicle theft	Arson[3]
Bertrand	786	1	0	0		0	1	37	10	26	1	0
Bethany	3122	2	0	0		0	2	93	22	66	5	0
Beverly Hills	564	4	0	0		2	2	36	10	21	5	1
Billings	1092	3	0	1		0	2	13	3	7	3	0
Birch Tree	658	4	0	0		0	4	4	1	2	1	0
Bismarck	1491	4	0	0		0	4	31	10	19	2	0
Blackburn	250	0	0	0		0	0	0	0	0	0	0
Bloomfield	1897	7	0	0		0	7	16	6	10	0	0
Blue Springs	54445	81	1	23		18	39	1500	182	1206	112	1
Bolivar	10790	79	0	10		4	65	642	84	514	44	1
Bonne Terre	7175	16	0	2		0	14	67	6	51	10	0
Boonville	8423	7	0	0		1	6	224	50	162	12	1
Bourbon	1620	8	0	2		0	6	40	9	28	3	0
Branson	11593	84	1	11		25	47	1388	155	1145	88	2
Branson West	434	3	0	0		0	3	86	2	81	3	0
Braymer	842	0	0	0		0	0	1	0	1	0	0
Breckenridge Hills	4709	32	0	2		6	24	140	14	115	11	0
Brentwood	8058	16	0	0		14	2	402	26	360	16	1
Bridgeton	11835	110	4	8		28	70	890	80	761	49	6
Brookfield	4324	18	0	1		0	17	83	20	60	3	2
Bucklin	442	0	0	0		0	0	1	0	1	0	0
Buckner	3065	8	0	1		0	7	56	19	33	4	1
Buffalo	3031	18	0	1		1	16	161	25	125	11	0
Butler	4067	12	0	4		0	8	132	27	95	10	1
Butterfield Village	464	0	0	0		0	0	2	1	1	0	0
Byrnes Mill	2910	2	0	0		0	2	9	2	6	1	0
Cabool	2126	2	0	0		0	2	52	12	39	1	1
California	4415	14	0	0		4	10	65	18	41	6	0
Calverton Park	1287	6	0	0		4	2	22	5	13	4	0
Camden	185	0	0	0		0	0	0	0	0	0	0
Camdenton[7]	3907	13	0	0		1	12	193	15	169	9	4
Cameron	9817	50	0	12		4	34	174	21	142	11	4
Campbell	1908	2	0	0		1	1	43	19	23	1	0
Canton	2391	12	0	0		0	12	43	7	34	2	0
Cape Girardeau	39738	236	5	10		54	167	1628	227	1332	69	6
Cardwell	682	2	0	0		1	1	13	4	8	1	0
Carl Junction	7780	0	0	0		0	0	127	30	87	10	0
Carrollton	3610	7	0	1		0	6	85	24	59	2	0
Carterville	1843	0	0	0		0	0	42	2	36	4	0
Carthage	14300	40	2	6		5	27	570	62	480	28	3
Caruthersville	5887	83	0	4		6	73	260	94	153	13	2
Cassville	3311	16	0	2		0	14	189	22	156	11	1
Center	505	0	0	0		0	0	3	0	2	1	0
Centralia	4226	13	0	0		0	13	85	20	61	4	1
Chaffee	2940	0	0	0		0	0	35	10	20	5	0
Charlack	1372	4	0	0		1	3	46	14	28	4	0
Chesterfield	47939	57	0	7		9	41	868	55	780	33	2
Chillicothe	9495	39	0	4		2	33	156	37	112	7	0
Clarkton	1220	9	0	0		0	9	23	3	16	4	1
Claycomo	1475	8	1	1		0	6	61	8	42	11	0
Clayton	15873	19	0	0		7	12	301	56	222	23	1
Cleveland	663	0	0	0		0	0	0	0	0	0	0
Clever	2592	7	0	0		0	7	14	4	8	2	0
Clinton	8878	26	0	2		4	20	357	63	273	21	0
Cole Camp	1101	0	0	0		0	0	29	11	17	1	0
Columbia	121143	517	6	111		127	273	3245	530	2469	246	13
Concordia	2378	6	0	2		0	4	25	5	19	1	0
Conway	774	1	0	0		0	1	12	7	4	1	0
Cooter	437	0	0	0		0	0	0	0	0	0	0
Corder	395	0	0	0		0	0	0	0	0	0	0
Cottleville	5151	2	0	0		0	2	34	3	30	1	0
Country Club Hills	1271	5	0	0		2	3	46	15	26	5	0
Country Club Village	2465	3	0	0		0	3	20	4	16	0	0
Crane	1337	6	0	0		0	6	25	6	18	1	0
Creighton	343	0	0	0		0	0	0	0	0	0	0
Crestwood	11977	11	0	1		2	8	276	18	247	11	0
Creve Coeur	18367	22	0	5		5	12	281	31	227	23	1
Crocker	1061	3	0	0		0	3	32	10	20	2	1
Crystal City	4845	14	1	0		1	12	178	10	152	16	0
Crystal Lakes	346	0	0	0		0	0	0	0	0	0	0
Cuba	3380	5	0	0		0	5	108	17	85	6	1
Delta	440	0	0	0		0	0	0	0	0	0	0
Desloge	4916	13	2	0		0	11	235	36	197	2	4
De Soto	6512	26	0	2		0	24	199	30	159	10	0
Des Peres	8611	8	0	0		3	5	459	26	423	10	1
Dexter	8014	10	0	0		1	9	238	47	188	3	3
Diamond	930	0	0	0		0	0	6	0	4	2	0
Dixon	1486	4	0	1		0	3	53	8	43	2	1
Doniphan	1990	43	0	3		3	37	157	26	129	2	1
Doolittle	600	0	0	0		0	0	1	0	1	0	0
Drexel	954	2	0	0		0	2	14	4	10	0	0
Duenweg	1300	6	0	1		0	5	41	7	28	6	0
Duquesne	1730	6	0	0		1	5	71	8	61	2	0

Table 6. Offenses Known to Law Enforcement, by Selected State and City, 2016—Continued

(Number.)

State/city	Population	Violent crime	Murder and nonnegligent manslaughter	Rape (revised definition)[1]	Rape (legacy definition)[2]	Robbery	Aggravated assault	Property crime	Burglary	Larceny-theft	Motor vehicle theft	Arson[3]
East Lynne	304	0	0	0		0	0	2	0	1	1	1
East Prairie	3150	6	0	0		0	6	59	7	52	0	0
Edgar Springs	202	0	0	0		0	0	0	0	0	0	0
Edina	1095	0	0	0		0	0	5	1	4	0	0
Edmundson[7]	838	4	0	1		0	3	58	8	43	7	0
Eldon	4646	21	1	0		2	18	117	10	103	4	0
El Dorado Springs	3559	25	0	2		2	23	189	41	140	8	1
Ellisville	9318	8	0	0		2	6	140	8	119	13	1
Elsberry	1996	13	0	0		1	12	55	14	30	11	0
Eureka	10681	6	0	2		1	3	183	14	165	4	1
Everton	300	0	0	0		0	0	0	0	0	0	0
Excelsior Springs	11562	11	0	4		3	4	366	88	257	21	0
Fair Grove	1472	4	0	0		0	4	32	4	25	3	1
Fair Play	464	0	0	0		0	0	7	1	5	1	0
Fairview	380	0	0	0		0	0	0	0	0	0	0
Farmington	18564	77	0	1		3	73	601	53	521	27	0
Fayette	2705	4	0	1		1	2	60	11	45	4	1
Ferguson	21032	170	9	7		68	86	1091	292	684	115	1
Ferrelview	464	1	0	1		0	0	4	0	2	2	0
Festus	12157	72	0	7		5	60	251	33	192	26	1
Fleming	123	0	0	0		0	0	0	0	0	0	0
Flordell Hills	812	17	1	0		3	13	57	19	30	8	1
Florissant	52266	98	2	8		34	54	1172	183	881	108	2
Fordland	818	1	0	0		0	1	28	3	25	0	0
Foristell	523	7	0	0		0	7	26	2	19	5	0
Forsyth	2446	6	1	0		1	4	91	7	80	4	1
Fredericktown	4097	15	0	0		0	15	70	15	51	4	0
Freeman	485	0	0	0		0	0	0	0	0	0	0
Frontenac	3872	6	0	2		2	2	86	7	76	3	0
Fulton	12973	56	0	3		11	42	446	85	342	19	2
Garden City	1621	2	0	0		0	2	29	13	16	0	0
Gerald	1313	12	0	2		0	10	16	12	4	0	0
Gideon	1031	1	0	0		0	1	1	1	0	0	1
Gladstone	27138	85	0	8		9	68	689	128	490	71	5
Glasgow	1103	0	0	0		0	0	0	0	0	0	1
Glendale	5928	2	0	0		0	2	64	7	54	3	0
Goodman	1230	0	0	0		0	0	16	6	5	5	0
Gower	1496	2	0	0		0	2	18	4	14	0	0
Grain Valley	13484	19	0	4		1	14	193	36	135	22	2
Granby	2127	7	0	1		0	6	47	14	27	6	0
Grandview	25412	138	1	5		47	85	867	179	534	154	8
Greenfield	1306	2	0	0		0	2	9	3	6	0	1
Greenwood	5641	1	0	0		1	0	25	6	17	2	0
Hamilton	1692	7	0	0		0	7	29	7	22	0	1
Hannibal	17825	74	1	15		9	49	761	92	637	32	13
Hardin	537	0	0	0		0	0	3	1	2	0	0
Harrisonville	9975	45	1	8		5	31	473	64	380	29	4
Hartville	592	2	0	0		0	2	9	0	8	1	0
Hawk Point	684	0	0	0		0	0	5	1	4	0	0
Hayti	2759	33	1	0		6	26	175	32	129	14	6
Hazelwood[4]	25655		2	5		46		870	178	596	96	1
Henrietta	360	0	0	0		0	0	8	2	6	0	0
Herculaneum	4030	8	0	0		0	8	52	5	45	2	0
Hermann	2365	6	0	3		0	3	31	0	29	2	1
Higginsville	4638	4	0	1		0	3	75	12	56	7	0
Highlandville	967	0	0	0		0	0	5	2	3	0	0
Hillsboro	3121	5	0	3		1	1	100	10	80	10	3
Hillsdale	1520	15	0	1		1	13	25	10	7	8	1
Holcomb	602	0	0	0		0	0	3	1	2	0	0
Holden	2265	3	0	0		0	3	84	10	66	8	0
Hollister	4515	20	0	2		0	18	107	21	80	6	0
Hornersville	630	4	0	0		0	4	10	4	6	0	0
Houston	2081	2	0	0		0	2	146	21	123	2	0
Howardville	364	0	0	0		0	0	1	1	0	0	0
Humansville	1036	1	0	0		1	0	13	7	6	0	1
Huntsville	1516	2	0	0		0	2	20	3	17	0	0
Iberia	745	6	0	1		1	4	13	5	6	2	0
Independence	117335	601	9	49		140	403	6389	891	4542	956	15
Indian Point	511	0	0	0		0	0	1	0	0	1	0
Iron Mountain Lake	713	0	0	0		0	0	1	1	0	0	0
Ironton	1379	3	1	2		0	0	20	3	16	1	0
Jackson	15092	24	0	3		2	19	236	19	205	12	0
Jasper	927	1	0	1		0	0	17	5	11	1	2
Jefferson City	43171	174	4	9		35	126	1318	179	1085	54	1
Jonesburg	722	1	0	0		1	0	23	2	19	2	0
Joplin	52001	329	2	52		72	203	3779	569	2895	315	21
Kahoka	2013	1	0	0		0	1	12	1	11	0	2
Kansas City	478364	7915	129	408		1897	5481	20842	4764	12127	3951	188
Kearney	9629	10	0	0		1	9	107	11	86	10	0
Kennett	10610	67	5	14		17	31	583	153	416	14	0
Kimberling City	2290	7	0	0		0	7	29	1	26	2	0
Kimmswick	158	0	0	0		0	0	0	0	0	0	0
King City	1004	2	0	0		0	2	0	0	0	0	0

Table 6. Offenses Known to Law Enforcement, by Selected State and City, 2016—Continued

(Number.)

State/city	Population	Violent crime	Murder and nonnegligent manslaughter	Rape (revised definition)[1]	Rape (legacy definition)[2]	Robbery	Aggravated assault	Property crime	Burglary	Larceny-theft	Motor vehicle theft	Arson[3]
Kinloch	299	8	2	0		1	5	17	5	8	4	4
Kirksville	17521	41	1	0		4	36	572	93	464	15	2
Kirkwood	27793	29	0	5		9	15	501	41	430	30	0
Knob Noster	2771	3	0	0		0	3	70	7	59	4	1
Laddonia	510	2	0	1		0	1	8	3	3	2	0
Ladue	8612	4	0	0		2	2	92	12	71	9	0
La Grange	941	2	0	0		0	2	3	1	2	0	0
Lake Lotawana	2029	0	0	0		0	0	23	0	20	3	0
Lake Ozark	1795	2	0	0		1	1	70	4	65	1	0
Lakeshire	1427	4	0	0		1	3	14	11	3	0	0
Lake St. Louis	15534	14	1	5		2	6	288	26	257	5	0
Lake Tapawingo	723	3	0	0		0	3	18	3	13	2	0
Lake Waukomis	908	3	0	0		0	3	7	0	4	3	0
Lake Winnebago	1146	0	0	0		0	0	3	0	3	0	0
Lamar	4330	11	0	2		3	6	148	54	91	3	0
Lanagan	410	0	0	0		0	0	2	1	0	1	0
Laurie	929	3	0	0		0	3	19	2	17	0	0
Lawson	2397	9	0	1		0	8	39	12	26	1	0
Leadington	457	3	0	1		0	2	35	11	16	8	0
Leadwood	1227	3	0	0		0	3	21	5	13	3	0
Leasburg	333	0	0	0		0	0	1	0	1	0	0
Lebanon	14721	69	0	5		1	63	443	86	340	17	4
Lee's Summit	95821	104	2	21		35	46	1626	205	1338	83	1
Lexington	4573	16	0	0		1	15	87	17	66	4	0
Liberal	714	2	0	2		0	0	6	4	2	0	0
Liberty	30699	83	0	20		8	55	460	74	328	58	2
Licking	3113	9	1	1		0	7	41	9	29	3	0
Lilbourn	1126	1	0	1		0	0	21	14	6	1	1
Lincoln	1169	1	0	1		0	0	40	15	19	6	0
Linn	1423	2	0	0		0	2	17	5	10	2	0
Linn Creek	244	1	0	0		0	1	6	4	2	0	0
Lone Jack	1139	0	0	0		0	0	5	1	2	2	0
Louisiana	3284	11	0	1		1	9	57	15	39	3	1
Macon	5427	16	1	1		0	14	113	18	88	7	0
Malden	4092	39	2	0		1	36	109	41	60	8	1
Manchester	18256	4	0	0		2	2	325	12	306	7	0
Mansfield	1254	0	0	0		0	0	82	11	69	2	0
Maplewood	7931	50	0	4		16	30	596	44	531	21	3
Marble Hill	1480	4	0	1		0	3	23	3	20	0	0
Marceline	2139	2	0	0		0	2	40	12	25	3	0
Marionville	2181	25	0	1		2	22	76	11	59	6	1
Marshall	13031	41	0	1		2	38	354	64	286	4	2
Marshfield	7230	29	0	2		3	24	231	41	183	7	0
Marthasville	1155	0	0	0		0	0	11	1	9	1	0
Martinsburg	309	0	0	0		0	0	0	0	0	0	0
Maryland Heights	27374	55	0	17		18	20	470	50	385	35	2
Maryville	11855	34	0	6		1	27	138	33	99	6	0
Matthews	628	5	0	1		1	3	18	6	7	5	1
Maysville	1090	0	0	0		0	0	6	0	6	0	0
Memphis	1831	3	0	1		0	2	21	5	14	2	0
Merriam Woods	1764	0	0	0		0	0	7	2	5	0	0
Mexico	11691	9	0	3		4	2	368	45	304	19	1
Milan	1831	4	0	1		0	3	12	4	8	0	0
Miller	684	2	0	0		0	2	7	2	3	2	0
Miner	956	19	0	1		1	17	61	8	49	4	2
Moberly	13900	7	1	4		2	0	356	69	266	21	4
Moline Acres	2428	18	3	1		5	9	102	19	76	7	1
Monett	9006	20	0	1		3	16	300	65	224	11	2
Monroe City	2432	9	0	0		0	9	37	11	26	0	0
Montgomery City	2714	21	0	1		0	20	41	7	32	2	1
Morehouse	916	0	0	0		0	0	5	1	4	0	0
Moscow Mills	2585	11	0	0		1	10	49	9	34	6	1
Mound City	1040	0	0	0		0	0	16	3	9	4	1
Mountain Grove	4662	24	0	1		0	23	118	21	91	6	0
Mountain View	2662	13	0	3		2	8	58	8	46	4	0
Mount Vernon	4531	4	1	0		1	2	106	11	92	3	0
Napoleon	217	0	0	0		0	0	0	0	0	0	0
Neosho	12218	29	1	1		4	23	648	95	504	49	2
Nevada	8230	59	1	6		4	48	554	110	426	18	3
New Bloomfield	677	0	0	0		0	0	0	0	0	0	0
Newburg	448	0	0	0		0	0	0	0	0	0	0
New Florence	720	0	0	0		0	0	8	2	5	1	0
New Franklin	1081	2	0	1		1	0	1	0	1	0	1
New Haven	2097	5	0	0		0	5	23	3	18	2	0
New London	967	4	0	0		0	4	18	0	17	1	0
New Madrid	2988	9	1	1		0	7	32	8	23	1	0
Niangua	412	0	0	0		0	0	0	0	0	0	0
Nixa	21377	21	0	5		1	15	328	38	271	19	0
Noel	1822	1	0	0		0	1	19	0	13	6	1
Normandy	7618	32	0	1		7	24	219	51	147	21	0
North Kansas City[7]	4387	27	1	3		14	9	384	25	275	84	4
Northmoor	327	2	0	0		0	2	19	1	12	6	0
Northwoods	4187	30	0	2		6	22	114	31	65	18	3

Table 6. Offenses Known to Law Enforcement, by Selected State and City, 2016—Continued

(Number.)

State/city	Population	Violent crime	Murder and nonnegligent manslaughter	Rape (revised definition)[1]	Rape (legacy definition)[2]	Robbery	Aggravated assault	Property crime	Burglary	Larceny-theft	Motor vehicle theft	Arson[3]
Oak Grove	7956	21	0	4		7	10	208	35	160	13	0
Oakland	1382	2	0	0		1	1	9	0	9	0	0
Oakview Village	394	2	0	0		0	2	3	1	2	0	0
O'Fallon	86093	71	1	11		9	50	1011	74	901	36	1
Old Monroe	285	0	0	0		0	0	3	1	2	0	0
Olivette	7893	19	0	0		3	16	162	40	118	4	0
Oran	1275	0	0	0		0	0	0	0	0	0	0
Oregon	763	0	0	0		0	0	7	4	2	1	0
Oronogo	2433	4	0	0		0	4	15	3	9	3	0
Orrick	804	6	0	0		0	6	2	2	0	0	0
Osage Beach	4449	26	0	0		0	26	257	24	226	7	1
Osceola	909	3	0	1		0	2	12	3	9	0	1
Overland[7]	15940	68	1	2		21	44	545	106	400	39	1
Owensville	2616	4	1	0		0	3	33	2	28	3	0
Ozark	19366	23	1	2		3	17	471	64	376	31	0
Pacific	7192	10	0	1		0	9	134	18	102	14	0
Pagedale	3312	46	0	1		16	29	117	32	71	14	1
Palmyra	3617	1	0	0		0	1	98	5	90	3	0
Park Hills	8676	12	0	0		2	10	184	15	153	16	0
Parkville	6450	2	0	1		0	1	97	16	75	6	0
Peculiar	4937	2	0	0		1	1	83	14	63	6	0
Perry	696	0	0	0		0	0	4	1	3	0	0
Perryville	8431	41	0	6		1	34	147	17	122	8	0
Pevely	5682	9	0	1		3	5	129	16	106	7	0
Piedmont	1976	0	0	0		0	0	45	8	31	6	0
Pierce City	1277	2	0	0		0	2	28	2	25	1	0
Pilot Grove	760	1	0	0		0	1	5	0	5	0	0
Pilot Knob	707	0	0	0		0	0	10	2	7	1	1
Pine Lawn	3447	58	4	0		10	44	115	52	46	17	0
Pineville	784	0	0	0		0	0	0	0	0	0	0
Platte City	4859	6	0	0		0	6	84	9	65	10	0
Platte Woods	403	0	0	0		0	0	6	0	5	1	0
Plattsburg	2286	6	0	0		0	6	27	7	20	0	0
Pleasant Hill	8320	1	0	1		0	0	127	14	101	12	0
Pleasant Hope	614	0	0	0		0	0	4	2	1	1	0
Pleasant Valley	3074	6	0	0		0	6	41	10	20	11	0
Polo	533	0	0	0		0	0	1	0	1	0	0
Poplar Bluff	17309	132	1	15		25	91	1071	177	824	70	2
Portageville	3131	0	0	0		0	0	14	1	13	0	0
Potosi	2637	5	0	0		0	5	193	37	148	8	0
Purdy	1103	4	0	2		1	1	21	3	17	1	0
Puxico	869	4	0	0		0	4	18	2	16	0	0
Queen City	592	0	0	0		0	0	0	0	0	0	0
Qulin	452	0	0	0		0	0	7	1	6	0	0
Raymore	20600	20	0	2		8	10	410	18	370	22	1
Raytown	29377	180	0	19		55	106	1404	320	916	168	3
Reeds Spring	856	1	0	0		0	1	8	0	8	0	0
Republic	16219	34	0	1		2	31	363	38	306	19	0
Rich Hill	1325	8	0	1		0	7	21	5	16	0	0
Richland	1815	3	0	1		0	2	66	24	39	3	0
Richmond	5558	34	0	2		1	31	236	53	178	5	3
Richmond Heights	8466	24	0	1		9	14	544	24	493	27	0
Risco	325	0	0	0		0	0	0	0	0	0	0
Riverside	3192	14	0	4		2	8	174	18	130	26	0
Riverview	2831	37	3	0		11	23	156	69	64	23	1
Rockaway Beach	871	6	0	0		0	6	5	1	3	1	0
Rock Hill	4648	8	0	0		3	5	61	8	45	8	0
Rock Port	1217	2	0	1		0	1	6	1	4	1	0
Rogersville	3436	6	0	1		0	5	100	7	86	7	0
Rolla	20093	81	0	11		8	62	679	112	534	33	3
Rosebud	407	0	0	0		0	0	0	0	0	0	0
Salem	4998	10	0	1		1	8	177	16	155	6	0
Salisbury	1550	2	0	0		0	2	34	4	27	3	1
Savannah	5115	3	0	0		0	3	38	7	27	4	0
Scott City	4518	6	0	1		0	5	94	29	60	5	0
Sedalia	21536	119	1	5		11	102	1098	176	870	52	6
Seligman	838	2	0	1		1	0	31	2	29	0	0
Senath	1700	16	0	1		6	9	18	6	9	3	0
Seneca	2409	1	0	0		1	0	82	5	76	1	0
Seymour	1975	14	0	1		1	12	45	8	36	1	0
Shelbina	1627	3	0	1		0	2	13	0	13	0	0
Shrewsbury	6197	5	0	1		3	1	179	14	150	15	0
Sikeston	16455	120	3	4		15	98	676	136	521	19	2
Silex	309	0	0	0		0	0	1	0	1	0	0
Slater	1827	4	1	0		0	3	50	13	35	2	0
Smithville	9403	16	0	5		2	9	110	11	90	9	1
Southwest City	956	9	0	0		0	9	9	2	7	0	1
Springfield	168307	2251	8	293		428	1522	14251	2120	10483	1648	70
St. Ann	12925	71	1	1		6	63	264	41	193	30	1
St. Charles	69364	138	0	22		35	81	1756	155	1472	129	12
St. Clair	4701	26	0	1		2	23	360	44	299	17	0
Steele	2091	19	0	1		7	11	76	27	44	5	0
Steelville	1711	4	0	0		0	4	69	22	44	3	0

Table 6. Offenses Known to Law Enforcement, by Selected State and City, 2016—Continued

(Number.)

State/city	Population	Violent crime	Murder and nonnegligent manslaughter	Rape (revised definition)[1]	Rape (legacy definition)[2]	Robbery	Aggravated assault	Property crime	Burglary	Larceny-theft	Motor vehicle theft	Arson[3]
Ste. Genevieve	4486	8	0	1		1	6	70	12	56	2	0
Stewartsville	732	0	0	0		0	0	0	0	0	0	0
St. James	4130	12	0	1		0	11	126	15	107	4	3
St. John	6454	25	0	3		9	13	245	41	185	19	2
St. Joseph	76577	428	7	49		104	268	4546	749	3221	576	13
St. Louis	314507	6017	188	289		1904	3636	18653	3201	12394	3058	269
Stover	1070	11	0	1		0	10	22	1	21	0	1
St. Peters	57835	95	2	18		20	55	1208	101	1059	48	10
Strafford	2366	4	0	0		0	4	84	6	69	9	0
St. Robert	6112	35	0	1		3	31	339	42	288	9	2
Sturgeon	914	2	0	0		0	2	3	0	3	0	0
Sugar Creek	3315	27	0	1		3	23	185	35	119	31	2
Sullivan	7143	18	1	3		5	9	482	78	383	21	0
Summersville	500	1	0	0		0	1	11	2	9	0	0
Sunset Hills	8548	10	0	1		2	7	158	9	141	8	2
Sweet Springs	1463	2	0	0		0	2	8	1	7	0	0
Tarkio	1459	1	0	0		0	1	13	5	5	3	0
Thayer	2248	3	0	0		1	2	43	5	36	2	0
Town and Country	11158	4	0	0		1	3	136	16	108	12	0
Tracy	223	0	0	0		0	0	2	0	0	2	0
Trenton	5874	7	0	2		2	3	134	24	104	6	1
Troy	11730	31	0	2		5	24	264	31	221	12	0
Truesdale	730	2	0	0		1	1	18	4	13	1	1
Union	11092	49	0	1		2	46	528	44	449	35	3
University City	35002	254	3	10		77	164	1386	228	1032	126	7
Urbana	405	0	0	0		0	0	0	0	0	0	0
Van Buren	836	1	0	0		0	1	25	9	16	0	0
Vandalia	4446	10	0	1		0	9	36	8	28	0	0
Velda City	1400	7	0	1		0	6	28	9	12	7	1
Velda Village Hills	1059	3	0	0		0	3	14	6	4	4	0
Verona	601	0	0	0		0	0	8	3	4	1	0
Versailles	2432	3	0	0		0	3	52	6	46	0	0
Viburnum	656	0	0	0		0	0	19	8	11	0	0
Vienna	594	0	0	0		0	0	27	4	22	1	0
Vinita Park	1887	10	0	0		3	7	34	12	16	6	0
Vinita Terrace	278	1	0	0		1	0	6	1	3	2	0
Walnut Grove	787	1	0	1		0	0	5	1	4	0	0
Wardell	397	1	0	0		0	1	2	1	0	1	0
Warrensburg	20136	47	0	12		7	28	561	117	418	26	2
Warrenton	8147	68	0	11		3	54	295	24	260	11	1
Warsaw	2093	12	0	1		0	11	82	17	63	2	0
Warson Woods	1957	0	0	0		0	0	21	1	17	3	0
Washburn	435	0	0	0		0	0	0	0	0	0	0
Washington	14065	28	0	5		5	18	557	46	502	9	0
Waynesville	5467	18	0	2		3	13	85	13	69	3	0
Weatherby Lake	1872	3	0	0		1	2	15	4	10	1	0
Webb City	11192	19	0	1		4	14	431	32	359	40	2
Webster Groves	23216	23	0	4		6	13	275	51	203	21	0
Wellington	785	1	0	0		1	0	0	0	0	0	0
Wellston	2326	70	1	1		16	52	129	28	83	18	0
Wellsville	1138	0	0	0		0	0	10	5	3	2	0
Wentzville	36938	61	1	9		4	47	490	44	419	27	2
Weston	1739	2	0	1		0	1	28	9	18	1	0
West Plains	12334	36	2	7		7	20	578	89	454	35	0
Wheaton	699	0	0	0		0	0	0	0	0	0	0
Willard	5485	9	0	1		0	8	72	6	64	2	0
Willow Springs	2142	21	0	3		1	17	73	9	56	8	0
Winfield	1439	5	0	0		0	5	9	0	9	0	0
Winona	1305	6	0	2		1	3	11	1	9	1	0
Wood Heights	695	1	0	0		1	0	11	3	7	1	0
Woodson Terrace	4074	28	0	0		9	19	144	32	76	36	1
Wright City	3511	3	0	0		0	3	56	16	34	6	0
MONTANA												
Baker	2063	3	0	0		0	3	12	1	10	1	0
Belgrade	8146	24	0	6		1	17	196	15	170	11	7
Billings	111447	514	0	61		81	372	5216	723	3698	795	27
Boulder	1213	7	0	0		0	7	13	0	12	1	0
Bozeman	44739	148	1	44		7	96	1255	124	1061	70	8
Bridger	733	0	0	0		0	0	8	1	7	0	0
Chinook	1233	1	0	0		0	1	7	0	7	0	0
Colstrip	2359	2	0	0		0	2	13	1	12	0	0
Columbia Falls	5175	6	0	1		0	5	118	16	90	12	1
Columbus	2072	8	0	1		0	7	19	1	17	1	0
Conrad	2594	6	0	1		1	4	32	0	28	4	0
Cut Bank	3023	24	0	2		2	20	80	8	70	2	0
Deer Lodge	2938	18	0	1		0	17	121	15	98	8	0
Dillon	4224	3	0	1		0	2	39	6	30	3	0
East Helena	2065	2	0	0		0	2	18	2	16	0	0
Eureka	1078	0	0	0		0	0	4	0	3	1	0
Fort Benton	1459	2	0	1		0	1	16	4	12	0	0
Glasgow	3442	6	0	0		0	6	23	9	13	1	0
Glendive	5608	10	0	0		0	10	108	28	72	8	2

Table 6. Offenses Known to Law Enforcement, by Selected State and City, 2016—Continued

(Number.)

State/city	Population	Violent crime	Murder and nonnegligent manslaughter	Rape (revised definition)[1]	Rape (legacy definition)[2]	Robbery	Aggravated assault	Property crime	Burglary	Larceny-theft	Motor vehicle theft	Arson[3]
Great Falls	59717	162	3	21		15	123	2944	365	2364	215	8
Hamilton	4659	17	0	2		0	15	183	25	153	5	3
Havre	9896	67	0	15		1	51	387	48	314	25	3
Helena	31052	203	3	52		18	130	1203	151	962	90	10
Hot Springs	548	2	0	0		0	2	5	1	4	0	0
Kalispell	22470	91	0	21		11	59	1288	106	1126	56	5
Laurel	6986	10	0	0		1	9	147	13	126	8	0
Lewistown	5863	41	0	5		0	36	76	8	67	1	1
Libby	2646	8	0	0		0	8	99	6	89	4	1
Livingston	7364	17	0	4		1	12	254	20	218	16	1
Manhattan	1656	2	0	0		0	2	16	4	11	1	0
Miles City	8878	18	0	2		1	15	167	11	149	7	1
Missoula	71860	377	0	65		60	252	3761	401	3156	204	13
Plains	1053	5	0	1		0	4	11	1	9	1	0
Polson	4744	39	0	6		3	30	328	35	281	12	4
Red Lodge	2242	9	0	0		0	9	39	5	31	3	0
Ronan City	1998	13	0	1		1	11	83	17	57	9	1
Sidney	7190	29	0	3		0	26	153	35	100	18	4
Stevensville	1940	9	0	1		0	8	28	9	17	2	0
St. Ignatius	820	3	0	0		0	3	8	4	2	2	0
Thompson Falls	1334	4	0	1		0	3	44	5	36	3	0
Troy	876	4	0	2		0	2	20	0	19	1	0
West Yellowstone	1353	3	0	0		0	3	12	3	9	0	0
Whitefish	7226	14	0	4		0	10	189	17	163	9	0
Wolf Point	2901	21	0	2		2	17	71	9	57	5	2
NEBRASKA												
Alliance	8533	22	0	6		1	15	101	32	61	8	0
Ashland	2577	2	0	1		0	1	10	2	8	0	
Aurora	4499	16	0	2		0	14	41	7	29	5	0
Bayard	1136	2	0	2		0	0	17	3	14	0	0
Beatrice	12340	52	0	23		3	26	337	62	260	15	0
Bellevue	56294	74	0	37		14	23	994	114	752	128	7
Bennington	1712	0	0	0		0	0	17	1	10	6	0
Blair	7969	10	0	4		1	5	102	16	81	5	0
Broken Bow	3551	9	0	2		0	7	60	8	46	6	0
Central City	2876	1	0	1		0	0	32	5	24	3	0
Chadron	5761	11	0	3		0	8	125	13	105	7	1
Columbus	22911	25	1	12		0	12	499	52	414	33	1
Cozad	3838	5	0	0		2	3	36	7	28	1	0
Crete	7047	47	0	13		0	34	154	20	125	9	3
Fairbury	3718	29	0	2		0	27	118	19	94	5	0
Falls City	4173	3	0	1		0	2	33	14	18	1	0
Fremont	26490	57	0	23		5	29	597	93	476	28	11
Gering[7]	8297	3	0	1		0	2	122	35	81	6	
Grand Island	51980	173	1	34		20	118	1620	236	1297	87	5
Hastings	24872	61	0	19		9	33	949	166	737	46	4
Holdrege	5575	8	0	2		2	4	128	10	112	6	0
Imperial	2054	0	0	0		0	0	8	2	4	2	0
Kearney	33471	76	0	20		7	49	743	114	594	35	3
Kimball	2388	4	0	0		0	4	0	0	0	0	0
La Vista	16973	21	0	7		9	5	246	14	206	26	1
Lexington	10044	23	0	3		2	18	205	23	170	12	0
Lincoln	281138	1006	10	222		191	583	8730	1261	7117	352	
Madison	2365	2	0	0		0	2	10	0	8	2	0
McCook	7557	10	0	5		0	5	209	40	157	12	0
Minden	3023	1	0	0		0	1	62	10	48	4	1
Mitchell	1658	4	0	0		0	4	27	8	19	0	0
Nebraska City	7341	9	0	4		1	4	294	164	122	8	0
Neligh	1513	0	0	0		0	0	6	0	6	0	0
Norfolk	24389	38	0	14		8	16	558	78	462	18	6
North Platte	24092	82	0	14		4	64	863	142	680	41	8
Ogallala	4538	10	0	2		1	7	190	27	157	6	0
Omaha	446163	2531	29		245	610	1647	16807	2111	11571	3125	
O'Neill	3642	4	1	0		0	3	13	2	10	1	
Ord	2051	1	0	0		0	1	22	9	10	3	0
Papillion	19576	29	0	7		2	20	369	15	333	21	0
Plainview	1216	2	0	0		0	2	5	0	5	0	0
Plattsmouth	6454	4	0	0		0	4	109	11	93	5	1
Ralston	6003	20	0	6		5	9	217	49	134	34	0
Randolph	916	1	0	0		0	1	1	0	1	0	0
Scottsbluff	14747	66	2	5		8	51	641	94	521	26	5
Scribner	844	0	0	0		0	0	5	1	4	0	0
Seward	7204	1	0	1		0	0	57	11	39	7	0
Sidney	6983	17	0	0		1	16	134	20	112	2	0
South Sioux City	13308	44	0	5		1	38	500	28	435	37	0
Superior	1869	2	0	0		0	2	32	6	25	1	0
Tekamah	1727	2	0	0		0	2	12	3	9	0	0
Tilden	936	0	0	0		0	0	2	0	2	0	0
Valentine	2857	18	0	3		1	14	40	7	27	6	0
Valley	2168	4	0	4		0	0	60	16	38	6	0
Wahoo	4508	3	0	1		2	0	54	17	32	5	1
West Point	3367	1	0	0		0	1	1	0	1	0	0

Table 6. Offenses Known to Law Enforcement, by Selected State and City, 2016—Continued

(Number.)

State/city	Population	Violent crime	Murder and nonnegligent manslaughter	Rape (revised definition)[1]	Rape (legacy definition)[2]	Robbery	Aggravated assault	Property crime	Burglary	Larceny-theft	Motor vehicle theft	Arson[3]
Wilber	1873	0	0	0		0	0	7	1	6	0	0
York	7885	0	0	0		0	0	228	21	198	9	0
NEVADA												
Boulder City	15661	19	0	1		6	12	164	60	91	13	4
Carlin	2291	19	0	0		0	19	25	16	6	3	0
Elko	20687	102	2	38		8	54	596	144	395	57	0
Fallon	8433	17	0	0		2	15	230	13	208	9	0
Henderson	291584	617	10	94		235	278	5484	1237	3617	630	19
Las Vegas Metropolitan Police Department	1592178	13520	158	1200		4974	7188	46000	12500	24645	8855	99
Lovelock	1876	25	0	0		1	24	51	23	26	2	0
Mesquite	17969	22	0	7		4	11	336	53	234	49	0
North Las Vegas	238554	2276	26	96		530	1624	5277	1487	2553	1237	17
Reno	244554	1717	9	139		393	1176	7933	1208	5381	1344	10
Sparks	97269	435	3	26		89	317	2450	448	1662	340	12
West Wendover	4271	24	0	5		8	11	145	75	57	13	1
Winnemucca	7978	28	0	6		2	20	148	31	107	10	0
Yerington	3067	2	0	0		0	2	18	1	14	3	0
NEW HAMPSHIRE												
Alexandria	1625	3	0	0		0	3	16	4	10	2	1
Alstead	1911	1	0	0		0	1	6	1	5	0	0
Alton	5338	8	0	6		0	2	38	4	34	0	0
Amherst	11272	3	0	1		0	2	132	16	115	1	0
Antrim	2662	1	0	1		0	0	22	5	14	3	0
Ashland	2055	4	0	2		2	0	30	6	22	2	0
Atkinson	6817	2	0	1		0	1	30	11	19	0	0
Auburn	5368	5	0	2		0	3	52	18	33	1	1
Barnstead	4615	2	0	0		0	2	41	16	24	1	1
Barrington	8894	8	0	2		0	6	76	22	49	5	0
Bedford	22407	13	0	3		3	7	347	18	320	9	0
Belmont	7315	21	0	7		3	11	138	22	112	4	2
Bennington	1471	2	0	1		0	1	15	1	13	1	0
Berlin	9241	24	1	8		3	12	174	44	125	5	1
Bethlehem	2558	3	0	0		0	3	18	6	12	0	0
Boscawen	3950	10	0	2		0	8	52	9	39	4	0
Bow	7779	4	0	0		0	4	28	9	18	1	0
Bradford	1664	3	0	0		0	3	9	6	3	0	0
Brentwood	4786	3	0	0		0	3	23	2	18	3	0
Bristol	3076	3	0	0		1	2	41	4	33	4	0
Brookline	5256	2	0	0		0	2	18	3	14	1	0
Campton	3300	9	0	7		0	2	41	7	32	2	0
Candia	3905	0	0	0		0	0	38	11	27	0	1
Canterbury	2401	1	0	0		1	0	17	5	12	0	0
Carroll	745	0	0	0		0	0	22	4	17	1	0
Center Harbor	1099	5	0	1		0	4	11	6	5	0	0
Charlestown	4969	21	0	2		0	19	39	7	29	3	0
Chester	4962	6	0	2		0	4	27	13	12	2	1
Claremont	12913	29	0	4		5	20	294	32	255	7	1
Colebrook	2167	7	0	1		1	5	35	10	20	5	0
Concord	42610	109	1	34		17	57	889	146	692	51	9
Conway	9915	15	0	6		0	9	275	32	233	10	1
Cornish	1617	0	0	0		0	0	4	2	2	0	0
Dalton	901	0	0	0		0	0	0	0	0	0	0
Danville	4466	3	1	0		0	2	22	1	20	1	0
Deerfield	4436	0	0	0		0	0	29	15	14	0	1
Deering	1924	2	0	0		1	1	26	5	20	1	1
Derry	33249	39	1	12		4	22	500	54	413	33	5
Dover	31054	47	1	28		4	14	415	49	358	8	2
Dublin	1541	2	0	0		0	2	10	6	4	0	0
Dunbarton	2799	1	0	0		0	1	20	8	10	2	0
Durham	17078	18	0	8		0	10	75	14	58	3	0
Effingham	1533	2	1	1		0	0	26	9	17	0	0
Enfield	4544	5	0	2		1	2	30	6	23	1	0
Epping	6927	15	0	2		1	12	147	7	135	5	0
Epsom	4654	4	0	1		0	3	31	5	25	1	0
Exeter	14635	11	0	4		0	7	96	14	80	2	0
Farmington	6841	19	0	2		3	14	112	35	65	12	3
Fitzwilliam	2328	0	0	0		0	0	12	6	5	1	0
Franconia	1120	2	0	0		0	2	18	2	16	0	0
Freedom	1486	1	0	0		0	1	5	1	4	0	0
Fremont	4648	6	0	2		0	4	37	9	28	0	2
Gilford	7182	12	0	6		0	6	142	23	116	3	0
Gilmanton	3780	3	0	0		0	3	29	7	22	0	0
Goffstown	18000	34	0	9		3	22	218	59	156	3	2
Gorham	2622	0	0	0		0	0	48	10	37	1	2
Grantham	2953	0	0	0		0	0	10	5	4	1	2
Greenland	3943	4	0	3		0	1	41	1	39	1	0
Hampstead	8588	4	0	1		1	2	59	10	47	2	0
Hampton	15358	26	0	3		1	22	182	19	151	12	3
Hampton Falls	2303	1	0	0		0	1	26	6	17	3	0
Hancock	1635	2	0	0		0	2	9	1	7	1	0

Table 6. Offenses Known to Law Enforcement, by Selected State and City, 2016—Continued

(Number.)

State/city	Population	Violent crime	Murder and nonnegligent manslaughter	Rape (revised definition)[1]	Rape (legacy definition)[2]	Robbery	Aggravated assault	Property crime	Burglary	Larceny-theft	Motor vehicle theft	Arson[3]
Hanover	11430	11	0	11		0	0	130	12	116	2	3
Haverhill	4641	9	0	2		0	7	134	23	109	2	1
Henniker	4934	6	0	3		0	3	46	16	26	4	0
Hillsborough	5974	17	0	4		1	12	81	16	56	9	1
Hinsdale	3876	19	0	4		1	14	125	18	103	4	1
Holderness	2095	0	0	0		0	0	18	3	15	0	1
Hollis	7814	6	0	1		0	5	39	4	34	1	1
Hooksett	14232	17	0	3		4	10	218	32	177	9	1
Hopkinton	5614	0	0	0		0	0	45	8	36	1	0
Hudson	24997	40	0	5		5	30	306	30	253	23	0
Jackson	814	1	0	1		0	0	10	3	7	0	0
Jaffrey	5270	8	0	1		0	7	49	14	35	0	4
Keene	23244	54	0	12		15	27	675	94	565	16	2
Kensington	2133	0	0	0		0	0	7	2	4	1	0
Kingston	6144	6	0	0		0	6	19	5	8	6	0
Laconia	16300	77	0	8		15	54	665	66	569	30	4
Lancaster	3322	6	0	1		1	4	48	10	34	4	1
Lebanon	13668	38	0	11		4	23	408	26	377	5	2
Lee	4403	1	0	0		0	1	44	9	35	0	0
Lincoln	1721	3	0	2		0	1	46	6	40	0	0
Lisbon	1569	0	0	0		0	0	24	16	6	2	0
Litchfield	8482	3	0	0		0	3	32	9	20	3	0
Littleton	5905	8	1	4		0	3	111	15	93	3	0
Londonderry	25439	22	1	5		5	11	200	23	163	14	4
Loudon	5455	5	0	1		0	4	72	17	51	4	0
Lyndeborough	1706	2	0	1		0	1	14	5	8	1	0
Madison	2521	2	0	0		1	1	15	4	11	0	1
Manchester	110353	742	5	69		205	463	3010	456	2408	146	29
Marlborough	2064	2	0	1		0	1	6	4	2	0	0
Meredith	6396	9	1	2		2	4	116	10	103	3	0
Merrimack	25675	0	0	0		0	0	191	22	166	3	0
Middleton	1788	4	0	0		0	4	21	7	12	2	0
Milford	15317	11	0	2		3	6	147	14	129	4	3
Milton	4583	7	0	2		0	5	79	15	55	9	1
Mont Vernon	2485	1	0	1		0	0	13	1	12	0	1
Moultonborough	4008	5	0	2		0	3	43	8	34	1	0
Nashua	88252	151	0	48		26	77	1218	122	1039	57	12
New Boston	5524	5	0	2		0	3	23	2	21	0	0
Newbury	2184	0	0	0		0	0	8	4	4	0	0
New Durham	2662	4	0	0		0	4	22	5	16	1	0
Newfields	1700	0	0	0		0	0	5	0	5	0	0
New Hampton	2215	8	0	1		0	7	30	5	24	1	0
Newington	777	2	0	0		2	0	93	0	92	1	0
New Ipswich	5212	7	0	3		0	4	30	11	19	0	0
New London	4678	0	0	0		0	0	22	3	18	1	0
Newmarket	8911	12	0	3		1	8	34	4	25	5	0
Newport	6337	12	0	3		1	8	117	22	93	2	2
Newton	4927	5	0	1		0	4	28	6	19	3	1
Northfield	4805	8	0	3		0	5	61	7	51	3	0
North Hampton	4435	2	0	1		0	1	34	8	25	1	2
Northumberland	2145	3	0	2		0	1	19	4	14	1	1
Northwood	4281	8	0	2		1	5	43	9	29	5	1
Nottingham	4977	4	0	3		0	1	28	6	21	1	1
Orford	1246	1	0	1		0	0	1	1	0	0	0
Ossipee	4229	10	0	1		2	7	84	29	52	3	0
Pelham	13384	10	0	2		0	8	108	13	92	3	0
Pembroke	7118	19	0	7		0	12	70	17	50	3	3
Peterborough	6469	7	0	3		0	4	57	7	45	5	1
Pittsfield	4068	10	0	1		0	9	63	10	50	3	2
Plaistow	7612	3	0	1		1	1	99	16	80	3	1
Plymouth	6639	30	0	6		0	24	175	8	161	6	9
Portsmouth	21612	38	0	16		5	17	366	27	313	26	6
Raymond	10324	28	0	9		2	17	86	8	74	4	2
Rindge	5822	3	0	1		1	1	81	9	70	2	0
Rochester	30096	108	1	12		17	78	1003	136	832	35	3
Rollinsford	2527	3	0	1		0	2	30	6	24	0	0
Rye	5396	4	0	3		0	1	49	6	41	2	2
Salem	28949	44	0	3		19	22	607	46	538	23	2
Sanbornton	2979	1	0	0		0	1	39	9	25	5	0
Sandown	6348	1	0	0		0	1	23	8	15	0	0
Sandwich	1307	0	0	0		0	0	26	7	19	0	0
Seabrook	8804	22	0	3		3	16	240	16	213	11	2
Somersworth	11757	34	0	11		7	16	359	25	322	12	8
South Hampton	809	0	0	0		0	0	3	2	1	0	0
Springfield	1313	0	0	0		0	0	0	0	0	0	0
Strafford	4090	1	0	0		0	1	25	6	17	2	0
Stratham	7403	6	0	1		1	4	44	4	40	0	0
Sugar Hill	567	0	0	0		0	0	10	6	4	0	0
Sunapee	3408	0	0	0		0	0	12	4	8	0	0
Thornton	2491	3	0	1		0	2	7	3	4	0	0
Tilton	3588	11	0	3		1	7	210	10	197	3	1
Troy	2075	0	0	0		0	0	35	6	28	1	0
Tuftonboro	2339	5	0	2		0	3	30	10	17	3	0

Table 6. Offenses Known to Law Enforcement, by Selected State and City, 2016—Continued

(Number.)

State/city	Population	Violent crime	Murder and nonnegligent manslaughter	Rape (revised definition)[1]	Rape (legacy definition)[2]	Robbery	Aggravated assault	Property crime	Burglary	Larceny-theft	Motor vehicle theft	Arson[3]
Wakefield	5629	10	0	2		2	6	72	19	49	4	0
Warner	2877	3	0	2		0	1	22	7	12	3	0
Washington	1108	0	0	0		0	0	11	5	6	0	1
Waterville Valley	246	1	0	0		0	1	12	1	11	0	0
Weare	8937	10	0	3		0	7	71	20	43	8	1
Webster	1894	1	0	1		0	0	14	6	8	0	0
Wilton	3692	3	0	1		0	2	29	4	24	1	0
Winchester	4189	9	0	2		0	7	54	10	40	4	0
Windham	14625	4	0	0		1	3	69	13	54	2	0
Wolfeboro	6198	5	0	2		0	3	73	10	60	3	1
Woodstock	1374	2	0	0		1	1	35	10	23	2	0
NEW JERSEY												
Aberdeen Township	18562	18	0	2		5	11	147	33	106	8	0
Absecon	8298	8	0	0		2	6	242	33	203	6	0
Allendale	6849	1	0	0		0	1	37	9	26	2	0
Allenhurst	490	0	0	0		0	0	16	1	15	0	0
Allentown	1824	1	0	0		0	1	9	3	6	0	0
Alpha	2291	1	0	0		0	1	15	3	11	1	1
Alpine	1918	0	0	0		0	0	9	2	6	1	0
Andover Township	5979	6	0	0		0	6	35	2	29	4	0
Asbury Park	15757	223	2	7		101	113	723	145	557	21	4
Atlantic Highlands	4297	3	0	0		1	2	34	4	30	0	0
Audubon	8669	5	0	0		3	2	348	54	290	4	0
Audubon Park	1004	0	0	0		0	0	15	5	10	0	0
Avalon	1273	3	0	0		0	3	191	30	159	2	0
Avon-by-the-Sea	1774	0	0	0		0	0	30	7	22	1	0
Barnegat Light	575	0	0	0		0	0	4	0	4	0	0
Barnegat Township	22272	19	0	2		2	15	129	21	103	5	2
Barrington	6752	5	0	2		2	1	102	21	76	5	0
Bay Head	971	2	0	0		0	2	13	4	6	3	0
Bayonne	66629	147	2	10		56	79	743	93	599	51	3
Beach Haven	1168	1	0	0		0	1	86	4	82	0	0
Beachwood	11219	8	0	1		4	3	126	15	107	4	1
Bedminster Township	8239	0	0	0		0	0	33	7	23	3	0
Belleville	36258	62	0	3		32	27	600	93	419	88	1
Bellmawr	11380	14	0	1		10	3	274	45	222	7	2
Belmar	5694	16	0	1		3	12	176	12	159	5	1
Belvidere	2593	0	0	0		0	0	88	54	30	4	0
Bergenfield	27646	8	1	0		2	5	99	16	79	4	0
Berkeley Heights Township	13548	1	0	1		0	0	89	8	73	8	0
Berkeley Township	41684	58	0	3		13	42	432	99	323	10	1
Berlin	7544	14	0	1		3	10	136	30	100	6	0
Berlin Township	5419	6	0	1		5	0	253	24	226	3	1
Bernards Township	27024	0	0	0		0	0	94	7	79	8	0
Bernardsville	7802	2	0	0		0	2	61	7	48	6	0
Beverly	2555	21	1	0		11	9	52	17	31	4	1
Blairstown Township	5791	1	0	0		0	1	26	12	13	1	0
Bloomfield	48215	64	0	0		31	33	805	78	625	102	0
Bloomingdale	8290	6	0	1		3	2	36	7	28	1	0
Bogota	8397	1	0	0		0	1	47	3	37	7	0
Boonton	8414	7	0	1		2	4	78	8	66	4	0
Boonton Township	4359	7	0	3		0	4	12	5	6	1	0
Bordentown City	3873	2	0	0		1	1	13	3	10	0	0
Bordentown Township	12049	12	0	5		4	3	107	26	77	4	0
Bound Brook	10494	12	0	0		8	4	127	33	88	6	0
Bradley Beach	4261	6	0	0		3	3	79	7	72	0	0
Branchburg Township	14676	8	2	0		0	6	65	6	58	1	0
Brick Township	74818	71	0	11		18	42	1059	180	861	18	1
Bridgeton	24982	225	4	13		113	95	952	269	649	34	5
Bridgewater Township	45251	15	0	1		9	5	412	53	348	11	0
Brielle	4753	0	0	0		0	0	22	3	19	0	0
Brigantine	9156	1	0	1		0	0	161	35	126	0	1
Brooklawn	1919	20	0	4		8	8	209	34	167	8	0
Buena	4520	19	0	4		7	8	77	21	54	2	1
Burlington City	9785	52	2	1		23	26	220	55	153	12	1
Burlington Township	22867	25	2	6		7	10	343	50	277	16	1
Butler	7691	14	0	1		1	12	67	21	45	1	0
Byram Township	7969	1	0	0		0	1	26	5	21	0	0
Caldwell	7933	6	0	1		1	4	33	7	23	3	0
Califon	1081	0	0	0		0	0	2	0	2	0	0
Cape May	3496	6	0	6		0	0	107	13	94	0	0
Cape May Point	279	0	0	0		0	0	0	0	0	0	0
Carlstadt	6277	10	1	0		3	6	129	4	99	26	0
Carney's Point Township	7809	27	0	7		12	8	175	42	123	10	2
Carteret	24316	38	3	2		17	16	243	39	175	29	0
Cedar Grove Township	12603	3	0	0		3	0	100	18	75	7	0
Chatham	8954	3	0	0		1	2	43	6	33	4	0
Chatham Township	10555	3	0	0		1	2	42	4	35	3	0
Cherry Hill Township	71079	92	1	2		49	40	1949	216	1678	55	1
Chesilhurst	1626	8	0	0		1	7	42	19	19	4	0
Chester	1671	0	0	0		0	0	16	1	12	3	0
Chesterfield Township	7534	2	0	0		0	2	23	2	20	1	0

Table 6. Offenses Known to Law Enforcement, by Selected State and City, 2016—Continued

(Number.)

State/city	Population	Violent crime	Murder and nonnegligent manslaughter	Rape (revised definition)[1]	Rape (legacy definition)[2]	Robbery	Aggravated assault	Property crime	Burglary	Larceny-theft	Motor vehicle theft	Arson[3]
Chester Township	7940	4	0	3		0	1	31	9	21	1	0
Cinnaminson Township	16871	25	0	3		7	15	305	38	258	9	0
Clark Township	15609	4	0	0		1	3	177	2	169	6	0
Clayton	8511	7	0	1		4	2	159	35	121	3	1
Clementon	4913	14	0	1		9	4	169	59	104	6	1
Cliffside Park	24977	27	0	1		2	24	183	21	155	7	1
Clifton	86324	202	0	7		83	112	1308	202	991	115	1
Clinton	2645	4	0	1		0	3	27	4	21	2	0
Clinton Township	12933	1	0	0		0	1	42	9	32	1	0
Closter	8674	2	1	1		0	0	34	6	27	1	0
Collingswood	13943	26	1	3		10	12	391	103	265	23	2
Colts Neck Township	10018	5	0	1		0	4	62	14	45	3	0
Cranbury Township	3958	2	0	0		0	2	34	3	30	1	0
Cranford Township	24324	7	0	0		3	4	174	20	149	5	2
Cresskill	8815	2	0	0		1	1	29	7	22	0	0
Deal	735	1	0	0		0	1	32	9	23	0	0
Delanco Township	4592	5	0	0		4	1	97	22	68	7	0
Delaware Township	4478	1	0	0		0	1	12	7	5	0	1
Delran Township	16739	16	1	6		3	6	262	38	214	10	0
Demarest	5051	1	0	0		0	1	21	4	15	2	0
Denville Township	16759	3	0	0		2	1	81	14	62	5	0
Deptford Township	30400	61	0	7		30	24	1170	193	943	34	5
Dover	18290	34	0	3		16	15	226	43	168	15	0
Dumont	18010	3	0	0		0	3	95	13	80	2	0
Dunellen	7434	0	0	0		0	0	55	5	44	6	0
Eastampton Township	6005	6	0	3		2	1	65	12	49	4	0
East Brunswick Township	49016	23	0	1		11	11	725	71	646	8	5
East Greenwich Township	10473	4	0	1		0	3	47	16	31	0	0
East Hanover Township	11233	2	0	0		2	0	132	5	116	11	0
East Newark	2707	0	0	0		0	0	34	2	31	1	0
East Orange	64787	437	6	22		179	230	898	205	462	231	10
East Rutherford	9166	7	0	0		0	7	107	8	87	12	0
East Windsor Township	27537	17	1	3		3	10	227	32	190	5	1
Eatontown	12264	39	0	3		17	19	401	34	363	4	0
Edgewater	12079	4	0	1		1	2	141	12	128	1	0
Edgewater Park Township	8769	21	0	1		9	11	165	38	114	13	0
Edison Township	102679	104	0	7		37	60	1088	165	844	79	1
Egg Harbor City	4238	13	0	0		4	9	131	41	86	4	0
Egg Harbor Township	43971	86	1	13		21	51	746	166	555	25	5
Elizabeth	129096	1054	5	33		528	488	4134	730	2536	868	5
Elk Township	4122	2	0	0		1	1	65	22	40	3	0
Elmer	1334	0	0	0		0	0	8	1	5	2	0
Elmwood Park	20348	45	0	0		23	22	328	37	278	13	0
Elsinboro Township	990	2	0	1		0	1	13	4	9	0	0
Emerson	7716	2	0	0		0	2	44	1	43	0	0
Englewood	28677	61	0	8		19	34	325	47	267	11	0
Englewood Cliffs	5397	1	0	0		0	1	44	26	16	2	0
Englishtown	1979	2	0	0		0	2	43	6	35	2	0
Essex Fells	2157	0	0	0		0	0	12	0	9	3	0
Evesham Township	45581	32	0	3		13	16	661	79	559	23	3
Ewing Township	36435	72	2	13		36	21	660	121	511	28	3
Fairfield Township, Essex County	7561	5	0	0		0	5	172	10	146	16	1
Fair Haven	6010	1	0	0		1	0	40	2	38	0	1
Fair Lawn	33646	25	3	3		9	10	437	63	353	21	3
Fairview	14497	15	0	1		10	4	118	26	83	9	0
Fanwood	7677	3	0	0		3	0	54	12	41	1	0
Far Hills	930	0	0	0		0	0	9	4	3	2	0
Fieldsboro	531	0	0	0		0	0	8	3	5	0	0
Flemington	4654	8	0	1		1	6	65	10	55	0	0
Florence Township	12805	19	1	5		4	9	83	29	47	7	0
Florham Park	11794	7	0	4		0	3	100	12	80	8	0
Fort Lee	36739	37	0	5		7	25	259	50	199	10	1
Franklin	4814	6	0	0		0	6	67	3	63	1	0
Franklin Lakes	10902	5	0	0		3	2	75	13	56	6	0
Franklin Township, Gloucester County	16551	10	1	0		4	5	193	75	106	12	0
Franklin Township, Hunterdon County	3237	1	0	0		0	1	16	0	16	0	0
Franklin Township, Somerset County	66791	62	1	10		37	14	791	190	570	31	2
Freehold Borough	11941	22	0	0		8	14	118	26	90	2	0
Freehold Township	35736	45	0	2		8	35	610	54	550	6	0
Frenchtown	1389	0	0	0		0	0	11	0	11	0	0
Galloway Township	37280	90	0	5		14	71	591	168	408	15	3
Garfield	31895	89	0	8		41	40	580	82	462	36	0
Garwood	4352	1	0	0		0	1	65	11	54	0	0
Gibbsboro	2228	1	0	1		0	0	32	8	23	1	0
Glassboro	19245	34	0	0		22	12	385	96	272	17	0
Glen Ridge	7647	4	0	0		3	1	158	46	110	2	0
Glen Rock	12014	1	0	0		0	1	74	2	70	2	0
Gloucester City	11247	16	1	0		4	11	278	54	204	20	1
Gloucester Township	63484	87	1	8		23	55	1036	171	822	43	0

Table 6. Offenses Known to Law Enforcement, by Selected State and City, 2016—Continued

(Number.)

State/city	Population	Violent crime	Murder and nonnegligent manslaughter	Rape (revised definition)[1]	Rape (legacy definition)[2]	Robbery	Aggravated assault	Property crime	Burglary	Larceny-theft	Motor vehicle theft	Arson[3]
Green Brook Township	7266	3	0	0		1	2	73	15	51	7	1
Greenwich Township, Gloucester County	4824	3	0	0		1	2	82	5	76	1	0
Greenwich Township, Warren County	5527	1	0	0		0	1	72	5	65	2	1
Guttenberg	11701	14	0	1		0	13	87	18	62	7	1
Hackensack	44968	88	0	8		21	59	693	50	593	50	0
Hackettstown	9549	8	0	0		2	6	94	14	77	3	0
Haddonfield	11323	2	0	0		0	2	191	28	161	2	0
Haddon Heights	7482	5	0	0		1	4	72	18	50	4	2
Haddon Township	14439	18	0	0		8	10	391	85	286	20	0
Haledon	8432	29	0	0		13	16	171	33	126	12	0
Hamburg	3131	2	0	0		0	2	17	3	14	0	2
Hamilton Township, Atlantic County	26824	38	2	1		8	27	935	128	780	27	5
Hamilton Township, Mercer County	88665	162	1	10		85	66	1516	320	1108	88	5
Hammonton	14585	16	0	1		1	14	170	59	104	7	1
Hanover Township	14468	12	0	3		7	2	176	19	151	6	0
Harding Township	3900	0	0	0		0	0	28	13	12	3	0
Hardyston Township	7991	5	0	1		0	4	63	17	42	4	0
Harrington Park	4830	1	0	0		0	1	9	1	8	0	0
Harrison	15788	41	0	0		23	18	355	55	252	48	0
Harrison Township	13023	7	0	2		1	4	92	34	56	2	2
Harvey Cedars	340	0	0	0		0	0	14	0	14	0	0
Hasbrouck Heights	12239	7	0	0		2	5	72	5	67	0	0
Haworth	3469	2	0	0		0	2	15	2	13	0	0
Hawthorne	19031	10	0	0		7	3	229	24	196	9	0
Hazlet Township	20050	11	0	1		6	4	206	43	157	6	0
Helmetta	2231	0	0	0		0	0	11	4	7	0	0
High Bridge	3538	2	0	0		0	2	29	13	15	1	1
Highland Park	14346	1	0	0		1	0	179	27	147	5	1
Highlands	4838	8	0	0		2	6	22	4	17	1	0
Hightstown	5491	6	0	1		4	1	41	3	37	1	0
Hillsborough Township	40037	15	0	10		2	3	263	50	206	7	7
Hillsdale	10569	3	0	0		1	2	35	5	30	0	0
Hillside Township	21981	79	1	2		34	42	466	79	291	96	1
Hi-Nella	854	5	0	0		1	4	14	5	9	0	0
Hoboken	54095	121	0	2		22	97	943	104	809	30	1
Ho-Ho-Kus	4161	0	0	0		0	0	14	3	11	0	0
Holland Township	5137	1	0	1		0	0	20	6	14	0	0
Holmdel Township	16651	4	0	1		0	3	166	30	133	3	0
Hopatcong	14388	7	0	0		0	7	104	25	79	0	1
Hopewell Borough	1919	1	0	1		0	0	5	0	5	0	0
Hopewell Township	18570	3	0	1		0	2	100	21	78	1	0
Howell Township	52306	45	0	3		9	33	384	77	299	8	1
Independence Township	5502	2	0	0		0	2	28	10	16	2	0
Interlaken	806	0	0	0		0	0	11	4	7	0	0
Irvington	54430	509	4	25		284	196	1258	332	559	367	17
Island Heights	1664	0	0	0		0	0	8	2	6	0	0
Jackson Township	56563	13	1	0		4	8	473	89	368	16	9
Jamesburg	6028	6	0	2		3	1	51	16	32	3	0
Jefferson Township	21418	15	0	0		2	13	80	13	59	8	0
Jersey City	266179	1276	24	86		547	619	4483	953	2979	551	40
Keansburg	9828	30	0	1		13	16	183	21	154	8	2
Kearny	42208	85	0	2		49	34	773	61	603	109	3
Kenilworth	8229	6	0	1		1	4	162	19	130	13	0
Keyport	7126	23	0	0		7	16	93	17	73	3	1
Kinnelon	10367	4	0	0		0	4	45	8	37	0	0
Lacey Township	28540	19	0	2		2	15	376	49	322	5	0
Lake Como	1718	5	0	1		0	4	34	4	30	0	0
Lakehurst	2696	2	0	0		1	1	31	3	26	2	0
Lakewood Township	100269	169	2	12		61	94	949	193	718	38	7
Lambertville	3817	4	0	3		1	0	62	5	55	2	0
Laurel Springs	1870	1	0	0		0	1	43	8	35	0	0
Lavallette	1789	1	0	0		0	1	29	7	22	0	1
Lawnside	2898	19	0	0		9	10	115	14	93	8	0
Lawrence Township, Mercer County	33023	43	0	5		17	21	666	60	592	14	1
Lebanon Township	6356	1	0	1		0	0	29	7	20	2	0
Leonia	9224	2	0	0		0	2	47	14	27	6	0
Lincoln Park	10327	4	0	2		1	1	75	17	54	4	0
Linden	42100	136	0	19		39	78	982	123	785	74	1
Lindenwold	17340	111	0	11		49	51	491	130	328	33	2
Linwood	6950	0	0	0		0	0	86	20	63	3	0
Little Egg Harbor Township	20686	33	0	11		1	21	279	54	221	4	0
Little Falls Township	14478	10	0	0		1	9	151	11	125	15	1
Little Ferry	10970	10	0	0		0	10	75	7	59	9	0
Little Silver	5901	2	0	0		1	1	45	3	42	0	0
Livingston Township	29788	14	2	3		5	4	340	29	299	12	0
Loch Arbour	186	0	0	0		0	0	9	3	6	0	0
Lodi	24841	32	0	2		13	17	317	55	241	21	0
Logan Township	5939	4	0	0		1	3	92	14	71	7	0

Table 6. Offenses Known to Law Enforcement, by Selected State and City, 2016—Continued

(Number.)

State/city	Population	Violent crime	Murder and nonnegligent manslaughter	Rape (revised definition)[1]	Rape (legacy definition)[2]	Robbery	Aggravated assault	Property crime	Burglary	Larceny-theft	Motor vehicle theft	Arson[3]
Long Beach Township	3015	2	0	0		0	2	70	10	59	1	0
Long Branch	30959	107	1	13		37	56	752	107	628	17	0
Long Hill Township	8749	0	0	0		0	0	39	1	36	2	0
Longport	884	2	0	0		0	2	8	0	8	0	0
Lopatcong Township	8281	1	0	0		1	0	50	18	27	5	0
Lower Alloways Creek Township	1702	2	0	1		0	1	7	3	4	0	0
Lower Township	21982	20	0	1		6	13	387	89	292	6	0
Lumberton Township	12400	17	2	1		6	8	217	16	193	8	1
Lyndhurst Township	22530	19	0	3		7	9	237	14	202	21	0
Madison	16098	3	0	1		1	1	96	14	81	1	1
Magnolia	4267	10	0	0		3	7	73	13	52	8	0
Mahwah Township	26588	4	0	0		2	2	150	7	135	8	1
Manalapan Township	40407	27	0	4		4	19	241	39	195	7	0
Manasquan	5798	0	0	0		0	0	119	15	103	1	0
Manchester Township	43525	25	0	3		6	16	216	84	128	4	2
Mansfield Township, Burlington County	8578	5	1	3		0	1	83	14	57	12	1
Mansfield Township, Warren County	7461	2	0	0		1	1	125	12	111	2	0
Mantoloking	244	0	0	0		0	0	7	1	6	0	0
Mantua Township	14939	4	0	0		2	2	273	52	215	6	2
Manville	10424	11	0	2		2	7	265	34	214	17	1
Maple Shade Township	18927	43	0	10		19	14	313	71	218	24	0
Maplewood Township	24743	25	0	1		23	1	331	43	257	31	0
Margate City	6214	10	0	6		1	3	123	25	94	4	0
Marlboro Township	40764	10	0	1		2	7	243	25	202	16	0
Matawan	8851	2	0	0		1	1	35	5	25	5	0
Maywood	9804	5	0	0		2	3	77	13	64	0	0
Medford Lakes	4072	3	0	1		0	2	35	4	30	1	0
Medford Township	23481	21	0	5		4	12	182	25	154	3	2
Mendham	4979	2	0	0		0	2	17	2	15	0	0
Mendham Township	5846	0	0	0		0	0	20	7	11	2	0
Merchantville	3751	1	1	0		0	0	38	8	27	3	3
Metuchen	13879	4	0	0		3	1	177	38	131	8	0
Middlesex Borough	13923	5	0	2		1	2	91	20	69	2	0
Middle Township	18555	49	0	4		9	36	483	72	390	21	4
Middletown Township	65919	17	0	3		4	10	436	62	364	10	1
Midland Park	7330	4	0	2		1	1	34	1	33	0	0
Millburn Township	20310	7	0	0		6	1	347	17	311	19	0
Milltown	7044	5	1	2		1	1	87	10	77	0	1
Millville	28177	223	4	22		82	115	1714	304	1352	58	3
Mine Hill Township	3547	1	0	0		1	0	30	8	21	1	0
Monmouth Beach	3233	8	0	1		2	5	46	5	41	0	0
Monroe Township, Gloucester County	36805	34	0	1		20	13	549	139	394	16	2
Monroe Township, Middlesex County	44923	5	0	0		0	5	162	30	123	9	0
Montclair	38108	49	0	4		24	21	572	124	417	31	0
Montgomery Township	23160	4	0	0		0	4	93	16	76	1	1
Montvale	8519	1	0	0		0	1	34	3	29	2	0
Montville Township	21801	10	0	1		0	9	253	146	102	5	1
Moonachie	2790	0	0	0		0	0	44	8	28	8	0
Moorestown Township	20530	8	0	2		3	3	299	48	245	6	0
Morris Plains	5615	5	0	0		2	3	73	6	57	10	1
Morristown	18544	62	0	5		33	24	314	26	275	13	0
Morris Township	22555	8	0	0		1	7	131	20	106	5	0
Mountain Lakes	4291	0	0	0		0	0	47	8	33	6	0
Mountainside	6887	0	0	0		0	0	35	20	14	1	0
Mount Arlington	5324	1	0	0		0	1	32	6	25	1	0
Mount Ephraim	4609	9	0	0		7	2	166	15	147	4	1
Mount Holly Township	9483	44	1	11		7	25	303	35	262	6	1
Mount Laurel Township	41828	33	0	9		8	16	630	79	529	22	0
Mount Olive Township	29095	10	0	5		3	2	155	36	115	4	1
Mullica Township	6089	6	0	0		0	6	81	24	52	5	1
National Park	2975	5	0	0		2	3	43	17	25	1	1
Neptune City	4790	12	0	0		6	6	142	23	117	2	0
Neptune Township	27505	158	3	5		64	86	917	132	774	11	3
Netcong	3240	7	0	0		4	3	34	5	26	3	0
Newark	281450	2637	100	99		1334	1104	6308	1138	3048	2122	41
New Brunswick	57158	392	1	38		211	142	1252	319	859	74	15
Newfield	1522	1	0	0		1	0	15	3	12	0	0
New Hanover Township	8218	2	0	0		1	1	4	3	1	0	0
New Milford	16804	2	0	0		2	0	41	7	34	0	0
New Providence	12461	1	0	0		1	0	56	7	46	3	0
Newton	7950	13	0	0		3	10	138	25	107	6	2
North Arlington	15921	9	1	0		2	6	156	20	130	6	4
North Bergen Township	63113	107	1	17		35	54	602	81	444	77	3
North Brunswick Township	42777	64	0	8		18	38	602	107	469	26	1
North Caldwell	6732	0	0	0		0	0	29	7	20	2	0
Northfield	8502	3	0	0		0	3	71	18	53	0	0
North Haledon	8529	2	0	1		1	0	44	13	28	3	0
North Hanover Township	7594	0	0	0		0	0	32	8	22	2	0

Table 6. Offenses Known to Law Enforcement, by Selected State and City, 2016—Continued

(Number.)

State/city	Population	Violent crime	Murder and nonnegligent manslaughter	Rape (revised definition)[1]	Rape (legacy definition)[2]	Robbery	Aggravated assault	Property crime	Burglary	Larceny-theft	Motor vehicle theft	Arson[3]
North Plainfield	22135	55	0	6		29	20	385	90	272	23	0
Northvale	4876	0	0	0		0	0	5	0	5	0	0
North Wildwood	3874	7	0	2		2	3	188	20	168	0	0
Norwood	5869	1	0	0		1	0	13	0	13	0	0
Nutley Township	28673	34	0	4		12	18	255	40	205	10	0
Oakland	13176	8	0	0		1	7	71	15	54	2	0
Oaklyn	3963	5	0	2		3	0	140	32	99	9	1
Ocean City	11287	14	0	1		5	8	364	58	306	0	1
Ocean Gate	2004	1	0	0		0	1	28	7	20	1	0
Oceanport	5718	6	0	0		3	3	45	6	38	1	0
Ocean Township, Monmouth County	27070	35	0	1		18	16	615	94	514	7	3
Ocean Township, Ocean County	8927	0	0	0		0	0	63	6	56	1	0
Ogdensburg	2266	0	0	0		0	0	11	3	8	0	0
Old Bridge Township	67238	28	1	1		5	21	665	68	567	30	2
Old Tappan	6039	0	0	0		0	0	27	5	22	0	0
Oradell	8222	0	0	0		0	0	31	4	27	0	0
Orange	30470	342	11	11		210	110	843	198	417	228	5
Oxford Township	2449	0	0	0		0	0	16	3	12	1	0
Palisades Park	20861	18	0	0		8	10	113	28	74	11	0
Palmyra	7296	13	0	1		2	10	198	22	173	3	0
Paramus	26958	33	0	1		21	11	1147	37	1097	13	0
Park Ridge	8927	4	0	0		1	3	19	11	8	0	0
Parsippany-Troy Hills Township	53447	34	0	7		11	16	363	82	260	21	0
Passaic	70972	398	0	5		178	215	1106	198	754	154	3
Paterson	147265	1126	19	56		551	500	3154	957	1526	671	12
Paulsboro	5937	22	2	1		14	5	168	56	109	3	1
Peapack and Gladstone	2603	0	0	0		0	0	27	13	12	2	1
Pemberton Borough	1378	2	0	1		0	1	49	5	38	6	1
Pemberton Township	27739	97	3	13		31	50	643	240	381	22	9
Pennington	2586	0	0	0		0	0	8	1	7	0	0
Pennsauken Township	35402	103	3	3		39	58	928	344	517	67	9
Penns Grove	4908	41	1	2		17	21	177	41	124	12	4
Pennsville Township	12720	5	1	0		2	2	207	30	175	2	0
Pequannock Township	15425	3	0	0		1	2	107	17	90	0	0
Perth Amboy	52767	210	0	7		68	135	806	185	534	87	4
Phillipsburg	14435	29	0	4		14	11	300	68	218	14	1
Pine Beach	2149	0	0	0		0	0	8	0	8	0	0
Pine Hill	10514	21	0	2		8	11	192	52	125	15	2
Pine Valley	12	0	0	0		0	0	0	0	0	0	0
Piscataway Township	58181	36	1	4		10	21	467	84	358	25	0
Pitman	8830	2	0	0		0	2	55	10	42	3	0
Plainfield	51221	346	12	17		147	170	958	283	599	76	6
Plainsboro Township	23621	9	0	0		0	9	140	22	105	13	0
Pleasantville	20855	114	3	1		42	68	368	141	186	41	1
Plumsted Township	8511	7	0	3		1	3	29	8	19	2	0
Pohatcong Township	3224	1	0	0		1	0	129	4	124	1	0
Point Pleasant	18502	4	0	0		0	4	158	34	121	3	0
Point Pleasant Beach	4519	3	0	0		2	1	106	10	92	4	1
Pompton Lakes	11164	10	0	0		1	9	94	14	78	2	0
Princeton	29660	15	0	2		0	13	233	34	194	5	0
Prospect Park	5940	14	0	0		3	11	101	4	85	12	0
Rahway	29797	37	1	3		14	19	348	49	253	46	2
Ramsey	15145	12	0	0		6	6	127	5	116	6	0
Randolph Township	25877	5	0	0		2	3	127	21	100	6	0
Raritan	8268	4	0	0		0	4	159	17	135	7	0
Raritan Township	22011	2	0	0		0	2	112	26	81	5	0
Readington Township	15893	8	0	1		2	5	93	29	63	1	0
Red Bank	12187	25	0	2		13	10	205	20	180	5	0
Ridgefield	11380	3	1	0		1	1	58	13	39	6	0
Ridgefield Park	13107	17	0	0		7	10	130	20	105	5	0
Ridgewood	25617	7	0	0		3	4	205	32	171	2	0
Ringwood	12427	3	0	0		1	2	60	13	46	1	0
Riverdale	4409	5	0	1		1	3	131	4	123	4	0
River Edge	11671	5	0	1		1	3	59	23	36	0	1
Riverside Township	7980	11	1	1		2	7	11	4	6	1	0
Riverton	2741	1	0	0		0	1	53	5	47	1	0
River Vale Township	10053	0	0	0		0	0	26	2	24	0	0
Robbinsville Township	14209	7	0	3		3	1	62	14	48	0	0
Rochelle Park Township	5683	4	0	0		3	1	98	16	80	2	0
Rockaway	6471	4	0	0		4	0	86	12	71	3	0
Rockaway Township	24655	12	0	0		8	4	381	22	352	7	0
Rockleigh	530	0	0	0		0	0	1	0	1	0	0
Roseland	5857	1	0	0		0	1	41	1	37	3	0
Roselle	21669	36	0	0		26	10	327	76	207	44	1
Roselle Park	13669	5	0	3		1	1	146	34	102	10	1
Roxbury Township	23425	8	0	0		1	7	213	34	177	2	0
Rumson	6886	2	0	0		2	0	38	2	28	8	0
Runnemede	8322	10	0	1		4	5	358	145	199	14	0
Rutherford	18717	13	0	0		2	11	204	29	168	7	1
Saddle Brook Township	14108	2	0	1		1	0	250	17	218	15	0

Table 6. Offenses Known to Law Enforcement, by Selected State and City, 2016—Continued

(Number.)

State/city	Population	Violent crime	Murder and nonnegligent manslaughter	Rape (revised definition)[1]	Rape (legacy definition)[2]	Robbery	Aggravated assault	Property crime	Burglary	Larceny-theft	Motor vehicle theft	Arson[3]
Saddle River	3256	1	0	0		0	1	20	5	13	2	0
Salem	4849	53	3	3		16	31	178	74	95	9	2
Sayreville	45141	30	1	4		7	18	373	48	292	33	0
Scotch Plains Township	24144	9	0	3		0	6	153	31	119	3	0
Sea Bright	1331	2	0	0		0	2	2	0	2	0	0
Sea Girt	1807	4	0	0		0	4	28	3	24	1	0
Sea Isle City	2080	3	0	0		2	1	244	61	181	2	0
Seaside Heights	2886	26	0	0		5	21	173	29	139	5	0
Seaside Park	1541	0	0	0		0	0	31	3	26	2	0
Secaucus	19528	39	0	3		10	26	391	32	333	26	0
Ship Bottom	1128	0	0	0		0	0	16	6	10	0	0
Shrewsbury	4199	1	0	0		1	0	58	3	54	1	0
Somerdale	5496	10	0	1		3	6	239	24	211	4	0
Somers Point	10667	35	0	3		7	25	260	77	173	10	0
Somerville	12198	23	0	3		9	11	180	28	143	9	0
South Amboy	8843	4	0	1		1	2	94	31	53	10	0
South Bound Brook	4624	6	0	0		4	2	38	5	31	2	0
South Brunswick Township	45862	18	0	3		8	7	382	79	274	29	2
South Hackensack Township	2469	10	0	1		3	6	59	8	44	7	1
South Harrison Township	3116	0	0	0		0	0	11	4	6	1	0
South Orange	16332	43	0	1		31	11	333	60	237	36	0
South Plainfield	24349	33	0	0		15	18	407	34	349	24	1
South River	16391	14	0	1		1	12	138	27	107	4	5
South Toms River	3737	12	0	1		3	8	64	14	45	5	0
Sparta Township	19049	2	0	1		0	1	78	10	65	3	1
Spotswood	8477	8	0	0		1	7	59	7	52	0	0
Springfield	17764	15	2	6		6	1	171	28	131	12	0
Springfield Township	3343	3	0	0		1	2	26	10	13	3	0
Spring Lake	2959	1	0	0		0	1	53	7	45	1	0
Spring Lake Heights	4648	1	0	0		0	1	15	2	13	0	0
Stafford Township	26972	21	0	2		2	17	196	15	174	7	1
Stanhope	3372	4	0	3		0	1	33	6	24	3	0
Stone Harbor	830	2	0	0		0	2	99	18	81	0	0
Stratford	6974	15	1	0		8	6	142	32	104	6	0
Summit	22078	10	0	2		5	3	181	18	153	10	0
Surf City	1201	0	0	0		0	0	18	0	18	0	0
Swedesboro	2602	1	1	0		0	0	26	8	15	3	0
Tavistock	5	0	0	0		0	0	4	0	4	0	0
Teaneck Township	40988	72	0	10		23	39	424	80	330	14	0
Tenafly	14877	4	0	2		1	1	68	20	42	6	0
Teterboro	69	2	0	0		1	1	108	1	103	4	0
Tewksbury Township	5862	0	0	0		0	0	27	6	19	2	0
Tinton Falls	17747	9	0	1		4	4	269	27	237	5	0
Toms River Township	90504	67	1	2		31	33	1836	254	1546	36	5
Totowa	10948	12	0	0		5	7	278	23	241	14	1
Trenton	83644	1127	21	59		427	620	2186	883	930	373	17
Tuckerton	3374	3	0	0		0	3	44	12	32	0	0
Union Beach	5476	2	0	0		0	2	40	8	30	2	0
Union City	69345	211	1	1		71	138	1134	116	914	104	2
Union Township	58109	62	2	4		35	21	879	99	698	82	2
Upper Saddle River	8369	5	0	2		1	2	32	2	21	9	0
Ventnor City	10455	18	3	2		9	4	305	73	226	6	0
Vernon Township	22359	6	0	0		2	4	206	16	184	6	2
Verona	13523	3	0	0		0	3	82	13	65	4	0
Vineland	60823	297	1	15		128	153	2412	559	1779	74	4
Voorhees Township	29235	53	0	9		11	33	444	70	358	16	0
Waldwick	10134	2	0	1		0	1	59	7	49	3	0
Wallington	11731	8	0	0		4	4	148	22	118	8	0
Wall Township	26033	16	0	1		4	11	256	33	221	2	1
Wanaque	11937	7	0	0		0	7	83	7	73	3	0
Warren Township	16051	1	0	0		1	0	55	14	37	4	0
Washington	6508	6	0	0		1	5	94	22	68	4	0
Washington Township, Bergen County	9381	0	0	0		0	0	17	7	10	0	0
Washington Township, Gloucester County	47477	53	0	2		15	36	865	176	655	34	0
Washington Township, Morris County	18696	16	0	2		0	14	37	5	32	0	0
Washington Township, Warren County	6430	2	0	0		0	2	57	9	48	0	0
Watchung	5925	1	0	0		1	0	411	12	392	7	0
Waterford Township	10720	3	0	0		0	3	76	10	60	6	0
Wayne Township	55023	17	0	2		7	8	1119	85	990	44	0
Weehawken Township	14284	15	0	1		3	11	285	35	229	21	0
Wenonah	2237	0	0	0		0	0	17	7	9	1	0
Westampton Township	8707	23	0	7		6	10	139	16	113	10	1
West Amwell Township	2767	2	0	0		0	2	33	3	30	0	0
West Caldwell Township	11057	4	0	0		0	4	78	11	65	2	0
West Cape May	1015	0	0	0		0	0	14	3	11	0	0
West Deptford Township	21257	16	2	0		7	7	271	65	193	13	1
Westfield	30427	5	0	1		2	2	255	58	192	5	0
West Long Branch	7975	3	0	0		2	1	139	18	118	3	0
West Milford Township	26734	23	0	6		3	14	216	72	138	6	0

Table 6. Offenses Known to Law Enforcement, by Selected State and City, 2016—Continued

(Number.)

State/city	Population	Violent crime	Murder and nonnegligent manslaughter	Rape (revised definition)[1]	Rape (legacy definition)[2]	Robbery	Aggravated assault	Property crime	Burglary	Larceny-theft	Motor vehicle theft	Arson[3]
West New York	53813	131	2	12		46	71	549	106	401	42	0
West Orange	47374	106	0	17		37	52	843	119	650	74	2
Westville	4189	7	0	0		6	1	101	17	76	8	0
West Wildwood	566	2	0	0		0	2	18	8	9	1	0
West Windsor Township	28482	15	0	1		5	9	455	40	411	4	1
Westwood	11252	2	0	0		0	2	49	6	41	2	0
Wharton	6593	2	0	0		1	1	89	16	69	4	1
Wildwood	5115	67	0	6		26	35	403	63	334	6	2
Wildwood Crest	3162	15	0	2		1	12	108	32	74	2	0
Willingboro Township	31195	101	4	7		33	57	633	220	374	39	5
Winfield Township	1509	0	0	0		0	0	17	6	9	2	0
Winslow Township	38724	40	0	8		10	22	139	55	79	5	7
Woodbridge Township	102124	104	0	10		46	48	1715	226	1389	100	7
Woodbury	9937	35	0	0		24	11	401	76	301	24	1
Woodbury Heights	2985	3	0	0		3	0	64	8	53	3	0
Woodcliff Lake	5925	3	0	0		0	3	21	3	18	0	0
Woodland Park	12594	7	0	1		3	3	184	22	149	13	0
Woodlynne	2922	9	0	0		2	7	51	3	37	11	0
Wood-Ridge	8335	4	0	0		0	4	58	9	46	3	0
Woodstown	3529	3	0	1		1	1	48	20	27	1	0
Woolwich Township	12675	3	0	0		2	1	49	8	37	4	0
Wyckoff Township	17242	5	0	2		2	1	104	15	85	4	1
NEW MEXICO												
Alamogordo	30768	115	1		5	7	102	1010	106	861	43	
Albuquerque	561560	6245	61		381	1957	3846	38528	6236	24582	7710	
Angel Fire	1104	7	0		0	0	7	39	18	13	8	
Artesia	12180	109	2		5	6	96	540	171	337	32	
Aztec	6031	35	0		4	1	30	182	66	101	15	
Belen	7127	122	0		0	9	113	537	126	341	70	
Bernalillo	8946	86	2		3	11	70	393	155	173	65	
Bloomfield	7163	40	0		10	2	28	185	53	119	13	
Bosque Farms	3823	20	0		0	1	19	58	8	41	9	
Capitan	1373	11	0		0	0	11	20	8	12	0	
Carlsbad	29538	133	1		15	19	98	1157	169	862	126	
Carrizozo	931	0	0		0	0	0	17	6	11	0	
Clayton	2735	4	0		0	0	4	19	4	15	0	
Cloudcroft	683	0	0		0	0	0	4	0	4	0	
Clovis	39725	223	2		23	46	152	2385	529	1689	167	
Corrales	8530	7	0		0	0	7	94	31	56	7	
Cuba	736	22	0		0	0	22	9	6	3	0	
Deming	14457	87	0		9	6	72	623	120	474	29	
Dexter	1273	0	0		0	0	0	3	2	0	1	
Edgewood	3819	5	0		2	0	3	96	29	49	18	
Espanola	10030	268	0		4	26	238	557	211	303	43	
Estancia	1586	1	0		0	0	1	21	12	8	1	
Eunice	3182	6	2		0	0	4	70	35	28	7	
Farmington	42270	293	1		70	52	170	1857	332	1354	171	
Gallup	23528	406	1		22	80	303	1648	282	1231	135	
Grants	9245	39	0		4	4	31	241	72	120	49	
Hatch	1596	10	0		0	0	10	23	4	19	0	
Hobbs	39349	221	3		28	20	170	1895	382	1421	92	
Hope	107	0	0		0	0	0	0	0	0	0	
Hurley	1249	0	0		0	0	0	4	2	2	0	
Jal	2234	4	0		1	0	3	35	8	26	1	
Las Cruces	102349	251	5		41	51	154	4788	830	3697	261	
Las Vegas	13256	117	2		11	13	91	419	87	317	15	
Logan	951	2	0		0	0	2	21	9	9	3	
Lordsburg	2485	17	0		0	1	16	15	6	7	2	
Los Alamos	17667	18	0		3	1	14	139	16	117	6	
Los Lunas	15398	129	0		4	9	116	756	123	498	135	
Lovington	11970	18	0		2	0	16	319	110	188	21	
Magdalena	906	6	0		0	1	5	40	10	30	0	
Mesilla	1869	3	0		0	0	3	13	7	4	2	
Milan	3248	22	0		1	1	20	86	19	62	5	
Moriarty	1786	3	0		0	1	2	77	32	36	9	
Portales	11921	50	2		11	5	32	472	286	165	21	
Questa	1750	0	0		0	0	0	4	0	4	0	
Raton	6058	13	3		0	5	5	191	77	93	21	
Rio Rancho	95454	215	1		42	33	139	2250	355	1585	310	
Roswell	48556	311	12		41	31	227	2132	363	1666	103	31
Ruidoso	7683	21	0		3	1	17	211	78	117	16	
Ruidoso Downs	2548	30	0		0	0	30	141	20	117	4	
Santa Clara	1629	2	0		0	0	2	28	14	9	5	
Santa Fe	84663	324	1		30	84	209	3234	1123	1870	241	
Santa Rosa	2641	11	0		0	0	11	60	14	42	4	
San Ysidro	195	1	0		0	1	0	10	4	3	3	
Socorro	8665	64	2		1	4	57	476	134	314	28	
Springer	924	2	0		1	0	1	10	0	9	1	
Sunland Park	16301	24	0		3	2	19	124	43	67	14	
Taos	5746	57	0		1	10	46	452	96	333	23	
Texico	1114	0	0		0	0	0	6	2	4	0	
Truth or Consequences	6000	22	1		0	0	21	208	63	134	11	
Tularosa	2863	9	0		0	0	9	49	19	28	2	

Table 6. Offenses Known to Law Enforcement, by Selected State and City, 2016—Continued

(Number.)

State/city	Population	Violent crime	Murder and nonnegligent manslaughter	Rape (revised definition)[1]	Rape (legacy definition)[2]	Robbery	Aggravated assault	Property crime	Burglary	Larceny-theft	Motor vehicle theft	Arson[3]
NEW YORK												
Adams Village	1837	0	0	0		0	0	4	0	3	1	0
Addison Town and Village	2541	5	0		0	0	5	17	1	16	0	0
Akron Village	2840	0	0		0	0	0	8	1	6	1	0
Albany	98617	848	2	59		250	537	3461	491	2858	112	5
Albion Village	5984	28	0	2		5	21	199	35	153	11	0
Alexandria Bay Village	1102	1	0	0		0	1	10	0	10	0	0
Alfred Village	4039	3	0	2		0	1	22	3	18	1	0
Allegany Village	1726	0	0		0	0	0	10	0	10	0	0
Altamont Village	1721	0	0	0		0	0	10	2	8	0	0
Amherst Town	120436	99	1	9		38	51	2066	183	1842	41	5
Amity Town and Belmont Village	2210	0	0	0		0	0	0	0	0	0	0
Amityville Village	9477	17	0		2	6	9	112	13	96	3	0
Amsterdam	17891	23	1	9		9	4	324	68	247	9	7
Andover Village	1001	0	0	0		0	0	3	1	1	1	0
Angelica Village	832	0	0	0		0	0	6	4	2	0	0
Arcade Village	1971	1	0		0	0	1	15	2	13	0	0
Ardsley Village	4674	1	0		0	1	0	29	2	27	0	0
Asharoken Village	653	0	0		0	0	0	4	0	4	0	0
Attica Village	2457	1	0		0	0	1	6	1	5	0	0
Auburn	26854	128	0	34		15	79	805	132	657	16	1
Avon Village	3308	4	0	0		0	4	8	0	8	0	0
Bainbridge Village	1320	0	0	0		0	0	7	2	5	0	0
Baldwinsville Village	7805	1	0	0		0	1	91	13	78	0	0
Ballston Spa Village	5366	7	0	1		4	2	57	6	50	1	0
Batavia	14931	69	0	11		14	44	508	86	410	12	4
Bath Village	5605	26	0	4		6	16	136	20	115	1	1
Beacon	14291	44	1	5		13	25	242	23	213	6	0
Bedford Town	18063	8	0	2		1	5	66	13	49	4	0
Bethlehem Town	35148	22	0	11		2	9	468	53	409	6	0
Binghamton	45780	353	4	41		93	215	1844	436	1306	102	5
Black River	1328	0	0		0	0	0	5	3	2	0	0
Blooming Grove Town	11907	3	0	0		0	3	117	29	80	8	0
Bolton Town	2284	1	0		0	0	1	10	4	5	1	0
Boonville Village	2034	1	0		0	0	1	3	1	2	0	0
Brant Town	2064	1	0		0	0	1	17	4	11	2	0
Brewster	2321	1	0		0	0	1	12	2	9	1	0
Briarcliff Manor Village	8066	0	0		0	0	0	23	5	18	0	0
Brighton Town	36889	29	0	14		8	7	742	82	642	18	1
Brockport Village	8355	10	0	1		5	4	121	29	89	3	0
Brownville Village	1162	0	0		0	0	0	1	0	1	0	0
Buffalo	257446	2857	44	153		1049	1611	10599	2631	7133	835	228
Cairo Town	6437	2	0	0		0	2	14	2	12	0	0
Caledonia Village	2136	0	0	0		0	0	2	0	2	0	0
Cambridge Village	1822	2	0	1		0	1	21	7	14	0	0
Camden Village	2196	1	0		0	0	1	43	6	37	0	0
Camillus Town and Village	24622	12	0	6		1	5	419	20	391	8	0
Canajoharie Village	2149	7	0	3		1	3	21	5	14	2	0
Canandaigua	10407	50	0	19		6	25	214	30	179	5	0
Canastota Village	4638	9	0	4		1	4	71	7	59	5	0
Canisteo Village	2191	3	0		0	0	3	7	1	6	0	0
Canton Village	6619	2	0	0		0	2	29	5	24	0	0
Cape Vincent Village	744	1	0		0	0	1	5	0	5	0	0
Carmel Town	34355	5	0	0		1	4	107	16	81	10	0
Carroll Town	3391	0	0		0	0	0	0	0	0	0	0
Carthage Village	3575	2	0	1		0	1	42	2	40	0	1
Cattaraugus Village	931	0	0		0	0	0	3	1	2	0	0
Cayuga Heights Village	3840	2	0	0		0	2	46	6	40	0	0
Cazenovia Village	2861	5	0	1		0	4	22	5	17	0	0
Central Square Village	1806	1	0		0	0	1	45	1	44	0	0
Centre Island Village	409	0	0	0		0	0	1	0	0	1	0
Cheektowaga Town	78100	181	2	22		68	89	2523	280	2128	115	7
Chester Town	7941	5	0	0		0	5	14	3	10	1	0
Chester Village	3907	1	0	1		0	0	86	4	79	3	0
Chittenango Village	4855	2	0	0		1	1	11	3	8	0	0
Cicero Town	29482	9	0	0		2	7	290	38	248	4	0
Clarkstown Town	82171	81	0	16		26	39	1264	60	1171	33	0
Clayton Village	1950	0	0	0		0	0	6	0	6	0	0
Clyde Village	1990	2	0	0		1	1	23	3	20	0	0
Cobleskill Village	4545	4	0	2		1	1	144	11	131	2	0
Coeymans Town	7420	9	0		0	0	9	58	8	46	4	0
Cohocton Town	2508	1	0		0	1	0	1	1	0	0	0
Cohoes	16615	26	0	3		6	17	224	39	167	18	1
Colonie Town	80075	91	0	5		25	61	1966	141	1787	38	5
Cooperstown Village	1780	0	0	0		0	0	13	1	12	0	0
Corning	10841	54	0	16		3	35	326	65	257	4	4
Cornwall-on-Hudson Village	2955	1	0	0		0	1	23	1	22	0	0
Cornwall Town	9589	4	0	1		0	3	29	3	25	1	0
Cortland	18856	17	0	4		0	13	347	78	264	5	0
Coxsackie Village	2681	5	0	1		0	4	6	1	5	0	0

Table 6. Offenses Known to Law Enforcement, by Selected State and City, 2016—Continued

(Number.)

State/city	Population	Violent crime	Murder and nonnegligent manslaughter	Rape (revised definition)[1]	Rape (legacy definition)[2]	Robbery	Aggravated assault	Property crime	Burglary	Larceny-theft	Motor vehicle theft	Arson[3]
Crawford Town	9202	7	0	1		3	3	65	9	54	2	0
Croton-on-Hudson Village	8308	0	0	0		0	0	31	5	26	0	0
Cuba Town	3153	8	0		1	0	7	66	8	58	0	0
Dansville Village	4525	6	0		1	3	2	95	10	84	1	0
Deerpark Town	7749	6	0	0		2	4	75	20	52	3	1
Delhi Village	3173	2	0	0		0	2	33	12	20	1	0
Depew Village	15116	16	0	1		1	14	312	52	254	6	1
DeWitt Town	25616	40	0	5		13	22	802	72	697	33	3
Dexter Village	1093	0	0		0	0	0	6	1	5	0	0
Dobbs Ferry Village	11180	7	0	1		3	3	92	20	71	1	0
Dolgeville Village	2119	2	0	0		0	2	19	2	17	0	0
Dryden Village	2137	5	0	2		0	3	55	9	46	0	0
Dunkirk	11991	33	0	3		5	25	277	70	193	14	1
Durham Town	2661	0	0	0		0	0	6	3	3	0	0
East Aurora-Aurora Town	13823	2	0	1		0	1	118	11	105	2	0
Eastchester Town	20150	5	0		0	2	3	173	16	154	3	0
East Fishkill Town	29316	13	0	3		0	10	170	11	149	10	0
East Greenbush Town	16483	18	0		2	2	14	329	48	274	7	1
East Hampton Town	19950	12	0	0		0	12	278	41	233	4	0
East Hampton Village	1130	0	0		0	0	0	48	4	42	2	0
East Rochester Village	6679	9	0	1		5	3	116	28	86	2	1
Eden Town	7670	0	0	0		0	0	43	8	33	2	0
Ellenville Village	4070	15	1		2	2	10	114	23	90	1	0
Ellicott Town	5140	9	0	4		2	3	234	44	186	4	2
Ellicottville	1598	0	0	0		0	0	6	0	6	0	0
Elmira	27995	97	2		2	34	59	1074	172	875	27	6
Elmira Heights Village	3959	4	0		0	1	3	71	6	65	0	1
Elmira Town	5786	0	0		0	0	0	3	2	0	1	0
Elmsford Village	4838	6	0	1		2	3	20	4	14	2	0
Endicott Village	12944	61	1	8		15	37	491	113	364	14	1
Evans Town	16234	36	0	10		5	21	218	30	180	8	2
Fairport Village	5350	4	0	0		0	4	47	4	43	0	0
Fallsburg Town	11966	15	0	1		2	12	100	36	62	2	0
Fishkill Town	21620	10	0		0	5	5	194	21	167	6	2
Fishkill Village	2125	1	0	0		0	1	49	0	49	0	0
Floral Park Village	15986	12	0		0	5	7	59	13	42	4	1
Florida Village	2912	0	0	0		0	0	13	5	8	0	0
Fort Edward Village	3258	1	0	0		0	1	5	2	3	0	0
Fort Plain Village	2232	16	0	4		0	12	67	9	57	1	0
Frankfort Town	4925	2	0	0		0	2	22	5	16	1	0
Frankfort Village	2490	1	0	0		1	0	12	2	10	0	0
Fredonia Village	10604	11	0	3		3	5	232	38	192	2	0
Freeport Village	43419	106	1	2		43	60	697	70	592	35	1
Friendship Town	1914	3	0	0		0	3	4	0	4	0	0
Fulton City	11483	10	0		3	3	4	362	69	291	2	1
Garden City Village	22656	8	0		0	5	3	193	19	168	6	0
Gates Town	28669	73	0	10		22	41	912	99	764	49	0
Geddes Town	10349	6	0		0	3	3	218	18	195	5	0
Geneseo Village	8199	7	2		1	3	1	171	33	138	0	0
Geneva	13033	24	1	9		5	9	290	77	212	1	0
Germantown Town	1876	0	0		0	0	0	1	0	1	0	0
Glen Cove[10]	27480	17	1	3		8	5	108	15	85	8	1
Glen Park Village	510	0	0		0	0	0	1	0	1	0	0
Glens Falls	14212	33	1	5		3	24	220	32	187	1	1
Glenville Town	21754	14	0	4		4	6	480	34	439	7	0
Gloversville	14908	93	1	32		11	49	444	77	358	9	3
Goshen Town	8515	4	0	1		0	3	69	8	55	6	2
Goshen Village	5384	1	0		0	0	1	76	8	67	1	1
Gowanda Village	2622	3	0		0	0	3	78	12	63	3	0
Granville Village	2451	3	0	0		3	0	26	8	18	0	0
Great Neck Estates Village	2839	0	0		0	0	0	5	1	4	0	0
Greece Town	96975	190	0	20		58	112	2105	253	1775	77	8
Greenburgh Town	45745	57	0	12		15	30	764	36	706	22	0
Greene Village	1488	0	0		0	0	0	15	1	14	0	0
Green Island Village	2611	1	0	0		0	1	47	15	28	4	0
Greenport Town	4060	0	0	0		0	0	122	3	119	0	0
Greenwich Village	1738	2	0	2		0	0	14	1	13	0	0
Greenwood Lake Village	3104	4	0	0		0	4	23	6	12	5	0
Groton Village	2402	3	0	1		0	2	42	1	40	1	1
Guilderland Town	34405	15	0	5		2	8	674	40	633	1	0
Hamburg Town	46028	34	0	0		11	23	928	90	814	24	6
Hamburg Village	9608	17	0	5		1	11	101	17	82	2	0
Hamilton Village	4166	1	0	0		0	1	13	1	12	0	0
Hammondsport Village	641	0	0		0	0	0	12	1	11	0	0
Hancock Village	966	0	0	0		0	0	15	4	11	0	0
Harriman Village	2486	2	0	0		0	2	29	5	24	0	0
Harrison Town	28518	1	0	0		0	1	126	7	118	1	0
Hastings-on-Hudson Village	8044	2	0		0	2	0	55	2	50	3	0
Haverstraw Town	37756	38	0		2	13	23	335	41	274	20	0
Hempstead Village	55870	400	6	5		149	240	725	131	459	135	5
Herkimer Village[10]	7478	54	0	11		5	38	331	29	302	0	0
Highlands Town	8237	1	0	0		0	1	10	0	10	0	0
Holley Village	1721	0	0	0		0	0	47	7	37	3	0

Table 6. Offenses Known to Law Enforcement, by Selected State and City, 2016—Continued

(Number.)

State/city	Population	Violent crime	Murder and nonnegligent manslaughter	Rape (revised definition)[1]	Rape (legacy definition)[2]	Robbery	Aggravated assault	Property crime	Burglary	Larceny-theft	Motor vehicle theft	Arson[3]
Homer Village	3163	5	1	1		0	3	23	9	14	0	0
Hoosick Falls Village	3419	2	0	0		0	2	23	5	17	1	0
Hornell	8289	4	0	3		1	0	137	7	130	0	0
Horseheads Village	6653	0	0		0	0	0	102	8	94	0	0
Hudson	6381	20	0	7		2	11	144	9	131	4	1
Hudson Falls Village	7170	22	0	9		2	11	90	14	74	2	0
Hunter Town	2634	0	0		0	0	0	15	3	12	0	0
Huntington Bay Village	1431	0	0		0	0	0	7	0	7	0	0
Hyde Park Town	21140	9	0		1	3	5	113	18	94	1	1
Ilion Village	7877	14	0	1		3	10	161	14	145	2	0
Independence Town	1166	0	0	0		0	0	6	2	4	0	0
Inlet Town	322	0	0	0		0	0	8	1	7	0	0
Irvington Village	6643	2	0		0	1	1	21	8	13	0	0
Ithaca	30937	72	2	10		19	41	894	88	787	19	1
Jamestown	29879	225	4	40		47	134	1063	323	687	53	15
Johnson City Village	14699	74	0	10		17	47	715	125	568	22	2
Jordan Village	1326	0	0		0	0	0	1	0	1	0	0
Kenmore Village	15110	29	0	0		11	18	247	40	202	5	2
Kensington Village	1189	0	0		0	0	0	3	0	2	1	0
Kent Town	13274	2	0	2		0	0	55	6	47	2	0
Kings Point Village	5147	3	0		0	0	3	11	1	8	2	0
Kingston	23360	76	0	10		23	43	484	57	418	9	0
Kirkland Town	8279	2	0	0		0	2	25	2	23	0	0
Lackawanna	17932	98	1	18		18	61	445	99	316	30	3
Lake Placid Village	2453	4	0	2		0	2	28	9	15	4	0
Lake Success Village	3072	2	0	0		2	0	14	7	7	0	0
Lakewood-Busti	4509	2	0	0		0	2	374	30	342	2	0
Lancaster Town	37418	19	0	8		2	9	442	48	383	11	0
Larchmont Village	6186	2	0	0		1	1	104	10	91	3	0
Le Roy Village	4269	4	0	1		0	3	57	18	39	0	1
Lewisboro Town	12862	0	0	0		0	0	2	0	2	0	0
Lewiston Town and Village	16009	6	0	2		0	4	155	24	119	12	2
Liberty Village	4090	22	0	6		5	11	155	26	123	6	1
Little Falls	4757	17	0	4		1	12	131	16	112	3	1
Liverpool Village	2284	0	0	0		0	0	12	3	9	0	0
Lloyd Harbor Village	3695	0	0		0	0	0	18	3	14	1	0
Lloyd Town	10568	7	0		1	0	6	95	8	81	6	0
Lockport	20519	95	0	1		25	69	659	129	508	22	4
Long Beach	33591	23	0	0		3	20	282	22	246	14	1
Lowville Village	3406	6	0	3		0	3	32	7	23	2	0
Lynbrook Village	19579	24	0	2		10	12	120	13	99	8	0
Macedon Town and Village	8911	7	0	1		1	5	102	14	85	3	0
Malone Village	5726	30	0	12		1	17	166	23	143	0	1
Malverne Village	8579	4	0		0	3	1	28	8	20	0	0
Mamaroneck Town	12292	4	0		0	1	3	84	14	67	3	0
Mamaroneck Village	19460	17	0		1	2	14	96	11	82	3	0
Manchester Village	1656	0	0		0	0	0	0	0	0	0	0
Manlius Town	24687	18	0	4		2	12	359	44	304	11	0
Marcellus Village	1765	0	0	0		0	0	36	1	35	0	0
Marlborough Town	8682	7	0	0		3	4	72	18	51	3	0
Massena Village	10571	29	1	6		8	14	491	67	418	6	0
Maybrook Village	3356	0	0	0		0	0	14	1	12	1	0
Mechanicville	5160	5	0	0		0	5	72	10	58	4	0
Medina Village	5781	15	0	3		1	11	158	29	122	7	3
Menands Village	4000	16	0	1		4	11	144	11	128	5	1
Middleport Village	1778	0	0		0	0	0	25	1	24	0	0
Middletown	27752	149	1	9		43	96	665	105	539	21	3
Monroe Village	8680	5	0	0		3	2	164	17	144	3	1
Montgomery Village	4782	1	0		0	0	1	20	1	17	2	0
Monticello Village	6438	30	2	4		9	15	185	53	125	7	1
Moravia Village	1227	0	0		0	0	0	17	1	16	0	0
Moriah Town	3585	6	0		0	0	6	2	0	2	0	0
Mount Hope Town	6899	1	0	1		0	0	16	3	11	2	0
Mount Morris Village	2883	12	0	2		1	9	75	11	61	3	1
Mount Pleasant Town	26903	14	0		3	6	5	210	28	182	0	1
Mount Vernon	68881	457	11	31		156	259	1231	196	918	117	14
Nassau Village	1122	1	0	0		0	1	7	1	6	0	0
Newark Village	8786	28	0	6		3	19	296	36	255	5	0
New Berlin Town	1548	1	0	0		0	1	21	2	19	0	0
Newburgh	28171	403	6	22		125	250	885	206	626	53	9
Newburgh Town	30933	36	0	1		16	19	1183	68	1103	12	4
New Castle Town	18167	2	0		0	1	1	56	5	50	1	0
New Hartford Town and Village	20441	15	0	2		5	8	652	53	594	5	1
New Paltz Town and Village	14214	26	0		2	1	23	173	16	156	1	0
New Rochelle	80389	174	3	14		66	91	1173	118	994	61	1
New Windsor Town	26835	25	1		1	1	22	387	45	335	7	1
New York	8566917	49124	335	2372		15544	30873	125278	12041	106868	6369	
New York Mills Village	3303	1	0		0	0	1	35	4	30	1	0
Niagara Falls	48675	565	3	14		199	349	2402	551	1665	186	22
Niagara Town	8080	18	0	1		11	6	395	32	355	8	0
Niskayuna Town	22171	21	0	5		3	13	319	42	266	11	0
Nissequogue Village	1762	0	0		0	0	0	11	1	9	1	0

Table 6. Offenses Known to Law Enforcement, by Selected State and City, 2016—Continued

(Number.)

State/city	Population	Violent crime	Murder and nonnegligent manslaughter	Rape (revised definition)[1]	Rape (legacy definition)[2]	Robbery	Aggravated assault	Property crime	Burglary	Larceny-theft	Motor vehicle theft	Arson[3]
Norfolk Town	4494	0	0	0		0	0	5	1	3	1	0
North Castle Town	12390	1	0		0	0	1	77	6	69	2	0
North Greenbush Town	12232	9	0	2		1	6	181	16	156	9	0
Northport Village	7387	6	0		0	0	6	57	7	47	3	0
North Syracuse Village	6861	2	0		0	2	0	72	9	60	3	0
North Tonawanda	30634	55	1	17		12	25	554	115	403	36	2
Northville Village	1058	0	0		0	0	0	4	0	4	0	0
Norwich	6929	24	0	13		6	5	251	30	220	1	0
Nunda Town and Village	2977	6	0	2		0	4	15	2	13	0	0
Ocean Beach Village	81	0	0	0		0	0	19	0	17	2	0
Ogdensburg	10840	27	0	2		8	17	356	87	267	2	2
Ogden Town	20257	10	0	1		0	9	282	37	239	6	0
Old Brookville Village	2230	1	0		0	0	1	29	2	25	2	0
Old Westbury Village	4678	0	0		0	0	0	25	4	20	1	0
Olean	13765	44	0	4		5	35	428	38	380	10	1
Olive Town	4331	1	0	0		0	1	18	3	14	1	0
Oneida	11081	44	1	12		7	24	435	52	374	9	0
Oneonta City	13857	31	0	8		7	16	269	57	208	4	5
Orangetown Town	37962	41	0	2		14	25	282	26	248	8	0
Orchard Park Town	29721	20	1	7		1	11	343	41	297	5	2
Oriskany Village	1369	0	0		0	0	0	10	3	7	0	0
Ossining Village	25516	17	0		1	6	10	155	32	117	6	0
Oswego City	17717	80	0	16		8	56	494	80	398	16	1
Owego Village	3705	18	0	5		1	12	127	15	107	5	2
Oxford Village	1404	0	0	0		0	0	30	3	27	0	0
Oyster Bay Cove Village	4313	1	0		0	0	1	10	3	6	1	0
Palmyra Village	3390	0	0	0		0	0	22	5	17	0	1
Peekskill	24129	27	0	1		9	17	173	19	146	8	1
Pelham Manor Village	5614	3	0	0		2	1	163	20	130	13	0
Pelham Village	7074	6	0	0		1	5	83	6	73	4	0
Penn Yan Village	4988	0	0		0	0	0	70	16	54	0	0
Perry Village	3487	9	1	6		0	2	52	11	40	1	1
Phoenix Village	2298	1	0	0		1	0	24	4	19	1	0
Piermont Village	2585	0	0	0		0	0	16	4	12	0	0
Pine Plains Town	2436	0	0		0	0	0	0	0	0	0	0
Plattekill Town	10264	15	0	1		1	13	47	12	31	4	0
Plattsburgh City	19765	36	0	10		2	24	379	44	332	3	1
Pleasantville Village	7205	1	0		0	0	1	70	7	61	2	0
Port Byron Village	1234	1	0		0	0	1	3	0	3	0	0
Port Chester Village	29750	44	0	2		21	21	506	47	441	18	0
Port Dickinson Village	1585	0	0		0	0	0	21	1	18	2	0
Port Jervis	8565	21	0		2	2	17	193	43	148	2	2
Port Washington	19272	7	0		0	6	1	95	9	85	1	0
Potsdam Village	9744	8	0	4		0	4	106	5	101	0	0
Poughkeepsie	30262	234	3	23		60	148	599	129	442	28	6
Poughkeepsie Town	39222	40	0	9		18	13	1045	59	980	6	0
Pound Ridge Town	5275	1	0	1		0	0	37	2	34	1	0
Pulaski Village	2299	0	0		0	0	0	33	3	29	1	0
Quogue Village	995	0	0		0	0	0	20	6	12	2	0
Ramapo Town	92620	77	1	11		10	55	660	62	564	34	0
Red Hook Village	1996	3	0		0	0	3	42	5	37	0	0
Rensselaer City	9441	16	0	3		4	9	101	18	78	5	3
Rhinebeck Village	2601	6	0		0	1	5	34	3	31	0	0
Rochester	209643	1845	43	161		670	971	7812	1475	5673	664	101
Rockville Centre Village	24229	25	0		0	13	12	224	14	202	8	1
Rome	32345	52	0	13		14	25	619	128	463	28	2
Rosendale Town	5927	0	0	0		0	0	25	2	23	0	0
Rotterdam Town	29352	44	1	6		11	26	886	86	777	23	2
Rouses Point Village	2161	2	0		0	0	2	12	4	8	0	0
Rye	16108	1	0	0		0	1	62	8	50	4	0
Rye Brook Village[10]	9658	3	0	2		0	1	64	7	52	5	0
Sackets Harbor Village	1497	0	0	0		0	0	1	0	1	0	0
Sag Harbor Village	2305	0	0		0	0	0	2	0	2	0	0
Salamanca	5545	14	0	3		1	10	75	9	61	5	2
Sands Point Village	2767	0	0		0	0	0	16	2	14	0	0
Saranac Lake Village	5248	13	0	1		0	12	75	7	67	1	0
Saratoga Springs	28005	64	0	9		8	47	527	54	441	32	2
Saugerties Town	19128	23	2	6		3	12	200	62	132	6	2
Scarsdale Village	18026	4	1	1		0	2	153	38	112	3	0
Schenectady	65138	595	6	58		146	385	2100	378	1525	197	19
Schodack Town	11730	10	0	5		2	3	45	14	30	1	0
Schoharie Village	823	0	0		0	0	0	0	0	0	0	0
Scotia Village	7725	8	0	1		1	6	112	21	86	5	0
Seneca Falls Town	8808	26	0	5		1	20	279	36	238	5	1
Shandaken Town	2986	0	0	0		0	0	31	5	26	0	0
Shawangunk Town	14098	5	0	1		0	4	54	9	42	3	0
Shelter Island Town	2423	1	0	0		0	1	27	3	24	0	0
Sherburne Village	1326	0	0		0	0	0	21	3	18	0	0
Sherrill	3066	2	0	0		0	2	6	1	4	1	0
Shortsville Village	1430	0	0		0	0	0	0	0	0	0	0
Sidney Village	3729	13	0	1		0	12	96	13	81	2	0
Skaneateles Village	2479	1	0		0	1	0	39	2	37	0	1
Sleepy Hollow Village	10315	6	0		0	2	4	17	6	10	1	1

Table 6. Offenses Known to Law Enforcement, by Selected State and City, 2016—Continued

(Number.)

State/city	Population	Violent crime	Murder and nonnegligent manslaughter	Rape (revised definition)[1]	Rape (legacy definition)[2]	Robbery	Aggravated assault	Property crime	Burglary	Larceny-theft	Motor vehicle theft	Arson[3]
Sodus Point Village	874	0	0	0		0	0	0	0	0	0	0
Sodus Village	1743	1	0	1		0	0	30	5	25	0	0
Solvay Village[10]	6394	22	0	3		6	13	114	30	75	9	2
Southampton Town	51191	54	0	13		9	32	698	137	513	48	1
Southampton Village	3296	2	0		0	0	2	96	12	81	3	0
South Glens Falls Village	3593	8	0	3		1	4	93	16	73	4	0
South Nyack Village	3539	0	0	0		0	0	13	3	10	0	0
Southold Town	20114	17	0	2		4	11	244	48	191	5	0
Spring Valley Village	32844	125	1	14		39	71	385	37	335	13	1
Stillwater Town	6753	0	0		0	0	0	24	5	19	0	0
St. Johnsville Village	1687	3	0	1		1	1	22	5	16	1	0
Stockport Town	2709	0	0		0	0	0	0	0	0	0	0
Stony Point Town	15599	5	0	0		0	5	80	8	67	5	0
Suffern Village	11053	2	0		0	0	2	71	11	57	3	0
Syracuse	143925	1063	30	68		329	636	4651	1021	3290	340	58
Tarrytown Village	11620	5	0		0	0	5	59	8	50	1	0
Ticonderoga Town	4965	7	0	0		0	7	58	17	41	0	0
Tonawanda	14864	41	0	10		14	17	355	51	300	4	2
Tonawanda Town	57698	133	1	9		37	86	1108	238	832	38	2
Troy	49876	362	3	25		102	232	1792	394	1308	90	8
Trumansburg Village	1836	0	0	0		0	0	47	7	40	0	0
Tuckahoe Village	6673	1	0	0		0	1	49	4	40	5	0
Tupper Lake Village	3560	6	0	3		1	2	79	8	68	3	1
Ulster Town	12264	6	0	2		0	4	309	23	279	7	2
Utica	60879	382	3	42		115	222	2265	435	1751	79	4
Vernon Village	1154	2	0	1		0	1	16	2	14	0	0
Vestal Town	28253	16	0	4		6	6	485	34	444	7	0
Walden Village	6810	1	0	0		0	1	79	4	72	3	0
Wallkill Town	28540	66	0	7		21	38	661	60	580	21	0
Walton Village	2901	9	0	3		0	6	64	14	49	1	2
Wappingers Falls Village	5566	2	0		0	1	1	59	5	54	0	0
Warsaw Village	3357	4	0	1		0	3	33	1	32	0	0
Warwick Town	18345	15	0	4		3	8	158	25	127	6	1
Washingtonville Village	5765	4	0		0	1	3	46	0	45	1	0
Waterford Town and Village[10]	8439	3	0	1		1	1	52	7	42	3	0
Waterloo Village	5012	7	0	4		0	3	118	21	95	2	0
Watertown	26765	181	1	41		15	124	1171	194	953	24	11
Watervliet	10208	25	1	3		2	19	200	52	137	11	0
Watkins Glen Village	1860	3	0	0		0	3	59	8	51	0	0
Waverly Village	4231	5	0	0		1	4	7	0	7	0	0
Wayland Village	1804	0	0	0		0	0	10	0	10	0	0
Webb Town	1817	0	0	0		0	0	5	1	4	0	0
Webster Town and Village	44487	25	0	2		8	15	445	52	381	12	0
Weedsport Village	1751	1	0		0	0	1	13	3	10	0	0
Wellsville Village	4506	12	0		0	0	12	75	14	58	3	0
West Carthage Village	2075	0	0	0		0	0	6	1	4	1	0
Westfield Village	3066	1	0	0		0	1	7	1	5	1	0
Westhampton Beach Village	1790	5	0		2	2	1	41	3	38	0	0
West Seneca Town	45752	63	0	11		14	38	592	114	463	15	0
White Plains	58767	121	0	10		30	81	931	53	854	24	2
Whitesboro Village	3680	1	0		0	1	0	35	8	27	0	0
Whitestown Town	9275	0	0		0	0	0	27	4	23	0	1
Windham Town	1674	0	0	0		0	0	7	1	6	0	0
Woodbury Town	10917	4	0	1		1	2	500	4	492	4	0
Woodridge Village	789	7	0		0	2	5	21	5	16	0	0
Woodstock Town	5865	4	0	0		0	4	60	9	51	0	0
Yonkers	202075	942	8	34		408	492	2190	422	1518	250	15
Yorktown Town	37287	14	0	4		6	4	342	39	299	4	2
Yorkville Village	2625	5	0		0	1	4	24	3	21	0	0
Youngstown Village	1912	0	0	0		0	0	10	2	7	1	0
NORTH CAROLINA												
Aberdeen	7549	25	0		3	10	12	289	52	226	11	1
Ahoskie	4883	43	2		3	8	30	291	81	201	9	0
Albemarle	16024	107	1		6	24	76	771	201	538	32	4
Angier	5097	14	0		2	2	10	129	62	59	8	3
Apex	47324	40	1		2	13	24	601	83	501	17	1
Asheboro	26230	104	1		11	39	53	1501	300	1161	40	10
Asheville	89546	537	10		48	144	335	4357	752	3345	260	7
Atlantic Beach	1503	14	0		4	1	9	130	42	84	4	0
Ayden	5078	29	0		0	5	24	195	49	137	9	0
Bailey	564	1	0		0	0	1	21	3	17	1	0
Banner Elk	1163	2	0		0	0	2	16	3	12	1	0
Beaufort	4244	10	0		0	0	10	90	19	67	4	1
Beech Mountain	320	1	0		0	1	0	15	3	11	1	0
Belhaven	1586	3	0		1	0	2	35	12	22	1	0
Belmont	10593	35	0		2	12	21	513	58	445	10	0
Benson	3648	20	0		0	13	7	235	71	148	16	0
Bessemer City	5591	10	0		1	3	6	87	38	47	2	1
Biltmore Forest	1461	1	0		0	0	1	14	3	11	0	0
Biscoe	1689	3	0		0	1	2	150	13	136	1	4
Black Mountain	8368	12	0		1	1	10	124	21	96	7	0
Blowing Rock	1303	2	0		0	0	2	35	9	26	0	0

Table 6. Offenses Known to Law Enforcement, by Selected State and City, 2016—Continued

(Number.)

State/city	Population	Violent crime	Murder and nonnegligent manslaughter	Rape (revised definition)[1]	Rape (legacy definition)[2]	Robbery	Aggravated assault	Property crime	Burglary	Larceny-theft	Motor vehicle theft	Arson[3]
Boiling Spring Lakes	5873	11	0		2	2	7	173	29	138	6	7
Boone	18374	35	0		13	2	20	393	74	307	12	1
Brevard	7747	16	0		4	4	8	206	33	168	5	0
Burgaw	4147	5	0		1	2	2	145	7	132	6	0
Burlington	52760	392	6		15	71	300	1833	430	1309	94	1
Butner	7781	26	0		0	3	23	166	52	104	10	2
Cape Carteret	2080	4	0		0	0	4	22	3	19	0	0
Carrboro	21478	35	0		3	7	25	434	88	334	12	3
Carthage	2416	3	0		1	0	2	63	9	52	2	0
Cary	164835	151	1		20	68	62	1656	234	1363	59	7
Chapel Hill	60004	113	2		15	33	63	1363	280	1017	66	3
Charlotte-Mecklenburg	896379	6560	67		219	2121	4153	36732	6691	27280	2761	220
Cherryville	6018	20	0		1	2	17	171	61	105	5	0
Claremont	1368	8	0		2	0	6	28	6	21	1	0
Clayton	19968	28	1		1	9	17	380	86	285	9	0
Clinton	8789	52	0		1	16	35	471	123	332	16	3
Clyde	1247	5	0		0	1	4	38	11	27	0	0
Columbus	994	1	0		0	0	1	28	2	22	4	0
Concord	89446	124	5		13	45	61	2205	346	1759	100	8
Conover	8261	17	0		3	1	13	271	46	216	9	0
Creedmoor	4487	7	0		1	0	6	127	53	70	4	0
Davidson	12469	9	0		1	1	7	137	19	114	4	1
Dobson	1570	1	0		0	0	1	38	8	29	1	0
Drexel	1864	0	0		0	0	0	22	8	12	2	0
Duck	386	0	0		0	0	0	35	12	23	0	0
Eden	15343	81	2		3	27	49	567	126	419	22	4
Edenton	4822	70	0		2	3	65	157	53	101	3	0
Elizabeth City	17852	127	2		6	35	84	835	213	602	20	1
Elkin	4067	24	1		1	4	18	378	40	337	1	0
Elon	10150	3	0		0	0	3	81	28	53	0	0
Emerald Isle	3731	9	0		2	3	4	198	85	110	3	1
Erwin	4730	20	2		1	6	11	193	57	129	7	1
Fairmont	2703	31	3		1	15	12	123	43	77	3	5
Farmville	4776	33	1		1	5	26	168	53	112	3	0
Fayetteville	202200	1531	33		99	316	1083	9201	1868	6942	391	60
Fletcher	7660	7	2		1	0	4	161	71	84	6	1
Forest City	7246	56	0		2	3	51	514	133	350	31	2
Fuquay-Varina	25249	28	1		6	7	14	479	84	383	12	2
Garner	28508	86	0		6	28	52	993	172	782	39	1
Gibsonville	6843	16	0		0	4	12	85	43	36	6	0
Goldsboro	35871	389	11		3	84	291	1999	484	1416	99	5
Graham	14712	77	2		2	15	58	475	118	338	19	2
Granite Falls	4651	5	0		0	5	0	283	11	257	15	0
Hamlet	6430	51	1		3	13	34	224	103	109	12	4
Haw River	2420	13	0		1	2	10	83	27	49	7	0
Henderson	15249	160	3		6	32	119	873	210	638	25	6
Hendersonville	13954	50	0		9	23	18	844	119	680	45	2
Hickory	40437	165	6		19	56	84	1953	362	1482	109	8
Highlands	939	1	0		0	0	1	66	23	42	1	0
High Point	111435	721	7		36	220	458	3983	781	2992	210	9
Holly Ridge	2300	1	0		1	0	0	76	26	47	3	0
Holly Springs	32862	9	0		1	2	6	295	45	245	5	0
Hope Mills	16268	63	1		3	28	31	789	163	603	23	2
Hudson	3710	6	0		3	1	2	105	22	80	3	0
Huntersville	53932	63	0		7	19	37	1157	148	959	50	3
Jefferson	1605	0	0		0	0	0	16	2	14	0	0
Kannapolis	46867	118	1		15	32	70	936	228	636	72	3
Kenansville	872	5	0		0	2	3	10	3	7	0	0
Kernersville	23943	102	1		7	23	71	1143	151	956	36	3
Kill Devil Hills	7132	41	0		7	1	33	344	150	188	6	1
King	7091	28	1		4	1	22	233	23	208	2	1
Kings Mountain	10785	20	0		1	8	11	293	68	224	1	1
Kinston	21268	257	2		8	37	210	1296	326	938	32	6
Kitty Hawk	3482	12	0		2	2	8	132	31	98	3	1
Knightdale	14875	21	0		1	7	13	316	31	273	12	0
Lake Royale	2670	3	1		1	0	1	47	10	37	0	0
Laurel Park	2341	0	0		0	0	0	9	0	7	2	0
Laurinburg	15423	201	3		4	43	151	901	521	358	22	4
Leland	18842	26	0		1	3	22	427	85	323	19	1
Lenoir	17822	56	0		0	13	43	843	161	630	52	4
Long View	4901	47	1		2	6	38	243	88	131	24	3
Louisburg	3582	11	0		0	4	7	89	24	63	2	0
Lumberton	21683	393	9		5	132	247	2998	920	1917	161	21
Maiden	3379	4	0		0	1	3	109	23	79	7	0
Manteo	1401	0	0		0	0	0	60	6	50	4	0
Marion	7827	35	2		0	6	27	612	179	403	30	1
Marshville	2684	20	0		2	2	16	95	25	67	3	0
Matthews	31401	46	0		5	22	19	1075	110	909	56	4
Maxton	2454	7	0		1	5	1	143	68	71	4	2
Mayodan	2469	11	0		1	4	6	182	34	145	3	0
Maysville	1003	4	0		1	1	2	21	6	15	0	0
Mebane	14201	47	0		2	5	40	578	46	516	16	3
Mint Hill	26221	36	5		5	13	13	632	114	491	27	5

Table 6. Offenses Known to Law Enforcement, by Selected State and City, 2016—Continued

(Number.)

State/city	Population	Violent crime	Murder and nonnegligent manslaughter	Rape (revised definition)[1]	Rape (legacy definition)[2]	Robbery	Aggravated assault	Property crime	Burglary	Larceny-theft	Motor vehicle theft	Arson[3]
Monroe	34978	227	1		5	68	153	1964	348	1534	82	7
Mooresville	36482	100	0		10	27	63	1443	178	1232	33	8
Morehead City	9477	38	1		2	4	31	382	56	322	4	0
Mount Airy	10345	46	1		1	10	34	511	94	378	39	4
Mount Holly	14284	27	1		2	7	17	305	85	199	21	3
Mount Olive	4752	16	0		0	6	10	213	53	152	8	1
Murphy	1613	15	1		2	3	9	117	24	85	8	0
Nags Head	2938	14	0		1	1	12	247	123	119	5	1
New Bern	30137	124	2		7	41	74	1046	167	856	23	5
Newland	684	0	0		0	0	0	23	5	17	1	0
Newport	4841	7	0		1	2	4	85	14	67	4	0
Newton	13049	34	0		2	5	27	446	103	325	18	2
North Wilkesboro	4215	22	0		1	3	18	144	3	135	6	1
Oxford	8794	100	0		2	24	74	536	122	388	26	4
Pilot Mountain	1462	2	0		0	0	2	57	13	43	1	1
Pinebluff	1467	1	0		0	1	0	15	11	3	1	0
Pinehurst	15948	6	2		0	2	2	84	0	82	2	0
Pine Knoll Shores	1368	1	0		0	1	0	21	2	19	0	0
Pine Level	1893	1	0		0	1	0	37	9	26	2	0
Pineville	8626	53	1		5	24	23	1221	127	1055	39	6
Pittsboro	4287	14	0		0	1	13	133	16	113	4	2
Plymouth	3618	34	0		2	1	31	161	23	130	8	6
Raeford	4907	13	0		0	5	8	194	25	165	4	1
Randleman	4160	14	0		0	9	5	394	94	295	5	1
Reidsville	13991	102	1		3	25	73	766	167	573	26	1
Richlands	1720	0	0		0	0	0	14	7	7	0	0
Roanoke Rapids	15273	108	2		9	25	72	1045	265	747	33	4
Robersonville	1412	11	0		0	2	9	58	19	37	2	0
Rockingham	9155	50	2		2	13	33	707	163	528	16	3
Rockwell	2148	2	0		0	1	1	58	8	43	7	0
Rocky Mount[5]	55431	435	4		12	116	303		593		98	12
Rolesville	6962	6	1		1	1	3	121	15	103	3	0
Rose Hill	1672	2	0		1	0	1	23	5	17	1	0
Rowland	1052	16	0		0	7	9	59	22	37	0	0
Rutherfordton	4173	0	0		0	0	0	139	0	136	3	0
Salisbury	34121	332	14		9	74	235	1662	416	1169	77	15
Selma	6351	36	0		4	15	17	329	130	185	14	1
Shallotte	4066	7	0		0	3	4	156	27	122	7	0
Shelby	20168	123	5		6	30	82	728	203	475	50	6
Siler City	8498	39	0		1	13	25	350	71	266	13	0
Snow Hill	1570	3	0		0	2	1	53	8	44	1	0
Southern Pines	13778	69	3		3	16	47	360	76	272	12	0
Spencer	3296	19	0		0	3	16	139	46	85	8	1
Stallings	15569	14	0		0	6	8	207	48	140	19	1
Stanley	3712	11	0		0	1	10	85	26	57	2	0
Star	874	1	0		0	1	0	16	4	12	0	0
St. Pauls	2422	6	1		0	3	2	126	29	97	0	0
Surf City	2256	3	0		1	0	2	170	14	149	7	0
Swansboro	3250	6	0		0	1	5	81	4	73	4	0
Sylva	2623	10	0		0	0	10	237	53	168	16	0
Tabor City	3910	17	1		1	4	11	132	36	89	7	0
Tarboro	11113	59	1		2	14	42	370	68	297	5	0
Thomasville	27117	87	1		3	25	58	1101	221	842	38	7
Trent Woods	4192	0	0		0	0	0	30	23	7	0	0
Troutman	2576	6	0		1	1	4	80	14	64	2	1
Troy	3411	11	2		1	2	6	78	26	49	3	0
Wadesboro	5541	62	0		2	7	53	331	89	230	12	0
Wake Forest	39996	54	0		3	11	40	954	77	866	11	2
Wallace	3979	8	0		1	3	4	168	32	127	9	0
Warrenton	861	2	0		1	0	1	36	3	32	1	0
Warsaw	3191	19	0		0	2	17	102	25	68	9	0
Washington	9796	66	1		7	16	42	509	98	403	8	1
Waxhaw	14367	20	0		1	3	16	145	35	109	1	0
Waynesville	9801	26	2		4	3	17	450	171	233	46	0
Weaverville[5]	3988	4	0		0	1	3			80	5	0
Weldon	1574	20	0		0	2	18	54	12	36	6	0
Wendell	6368	16	0		2	2	12	109	28	76	5	0
West Jefferson	1309	5	0		1	0	4	85	2	80	3	0
Whispering Pines	3187	0	0		0	0	0	12	2	10	0	0
White Lake	778	3	0		1	0	2	87	17	67	3	0
Wilkesboro	3527	8	0		0	1	7	267	7	254	6	1
Wilmington	117852	759	15		44	204	496	4771	1277	3219	275	11
Windsor	3819	13	0		2	3	8	42	12	24	6	0
Winterville	9502	16	0		0	4	12	147	46	99	2	0
Woodfin	6411	8	0		0	4	4	90	39	42	9	0
Wrightsville Beach	2581	13	0		2	3	8	179	35	136	8	1
Yadkinville	2918	16	0		2	2	12	116	27	88	1	1
Youngsville	1228	1	0		0	0	1	40	10	25	5	0
NORTH DAKOTA												
Arnegard	129	0	0	0		0	0	5	1	3	1	0
Belfield	1115	0	0	0		0	0	12	2	7	3	0
Berthold	510	0	0	0		0	0	6	1	4	1	0

Table 6. Offenses Known to Law Enforcement, by Selected State and City, 2016—Continued

(Number.)

State/city	Population	Violent crime	Murder and nonnegligent manslaughter	Rape (revised definition)[1]	Rape (legacy definition)[2]	Robbery	Aggravated assault	Property crime	Burglary	Larceny-theft	Motor vehicle theft	Arson[3]
Beulah	3450	6	0	0		0	6	36	4	29	3	0
Bismarck	73248	212	2	35		29	146	2472	468	1715	289	6
Bowman	1764	5	1	0		0	4	20	1	17	2	1
Burlington	1208	0	0	0		0	0	2	0	1	1	0
Carrington	2073	0	0	0		0	0	7	2	4	1	0
Cavalier	1233	0	0	0		0	0	24	7	17	0	1
Devils Lake	7394	7	0	3		1	3	314	37	245	32	0
Dickinson	25130	34	0	1		1	32	495	43	398	54	2
Ellendale	1281	2	0	0		0	2	5	2	3	0	0
Emerado	434	2	0	1		0	1	10	1	9	0	0
Fargo	121217	467	3	79		68	317	3843	566	2962	315	21
Fessenden	471	0	0	0		0	0	4	1	3	0	0
Grafton	4237	13	0	3		0	10	113	13	96	4	1
Grand Forks	57853	177	1	36		27	113	1783	303	1345	135	1
Harvey	1779	7	0	1		0	6	22	6	14	2	0
Hazen	2504	0	0	0		0	0	2	0	2	0	0
Hillsboro	1576	1	0	0		0	1	17	1	11	5	0
Jamestown	15417	63	0	10		1	52	471	98	344	29	0
Kenmare	1080	2	0	1		0	1	5	2	1	2	0
Killdeer	1392	4	0	3		0	1	8	3	3	2	0
Lamoure	920	0	0	0		0	0	1	0	1	0	0
Lincoln	3776	3	0	1		0	2	11	0	10	1	0
Lisbon	2146	2	0	0		0	2	25	9	12	4	0
Mandan	22011	48	1	7		4	36	803	116	589	98	6
Medora	138	0	0	0		0	0	0	0	0	0	0
Minot	51265	138	1	24		23	90	1373	305	854	214	7
Napoleon	785	1	0	0		0	1	1	1	0	0	0
New Town	2656	1	0	0		0	1	23	5	15	3	0
Northwood	924	0	0	0		0	0	2	1	1	0	0
Powers Lake	313	0	0	0		0	0	3	0	3	0	0
Ray	761	1	0	0		0	1	3	0	2	1	0
Rolla	1333	2	0	0		0	2	37	1	35	1	0
Rugby	2841	5	0	1		0	4	54	6	44	4	0
Sherwood	253	0	0	0		0	0	1	1	0	0	0
Stanley	3079	1	0	0		0	1	12	4	6	2	0
Steele	707	0	0	0		0	0	8	2	5	1	0
Surrey	1462	3	0	2		1	0	6	2	3	1	0
Thompson	1009	1	0	0		0	1	8	2	6	0	0
Tioga	1738	1	0	0		0	1	19	0	17	2	0
Valley City	6680	13	0	1		1	11	187	32	136	19	3
Wahpeton	7927	10	0	0		0	10	208	26	176	6	1
Watford City	8819	20	0	3		1	16	114	21	84	9	0
West Fargo	35389	66	1	23		6	36	489	138	305	46	6
Williston	29929	75	2	18		6	49	694	91	517	86	3
Wishek	986	0	0	0		0	0	4	0	4	0	0
OHIO												
Ada	5782	1	0	0		0	1	38	7	27	4	0
Akron	197257	1216	34	212		415	555	8646	2483	5483	680	94
Albany	918	0	0	0		0	0	20	6	13	1	0
Alliance[7]	22012	99	0	13		11	75	770	149	602	19	8
Amberley Village	3592	1	0		0	1	0	43	0	42	1	0
Amelia	4957	0	0	0		0	0	25	5	20	0	0
American Township	12254	6	0	0		3	3	167	10	152	5	0
Amherst	12156	7	0	1		3	3	188	21	164	3	0
Archbold	4342	4	0	0		0	4	58	12	46	0	1
Ashland	20278	24	2	14		1	7	405	73	325	7	1
Ashville	4207	1	0	1		0	0	67	15	49	3	0
Athens	25203	27	0	6		8	13	462	47	404	11	1
Aurora	15897	11	0	2		5	4	168	9	157	2	0
Austintown	35680	52	0	9		13	30	818	114	674	30	0
Baltimore	2970	1	0	0		0	1	25	7	16	2	0
Barberton	26172	75	0	17		10	48	799	145	614	40	3
Barnesville	4112	1	0	0		0	1	14	6	8	0	0
Batavia	1654	6	0	1		2	3	55	11	42	2	2
Bath Township, Summit County	9896	4	0	1		0	3	156	13	141	2	0
Bazetta Township	5683	2	0	0		0	2	207	14	190	3	0
Beavercreek	46490	32	0	14		13	5	1065	64	969	32	2
Beaver Township	6492	4	0	0		0	4	95	31	56	8	0
Bedford	12678	30	0		1	18	11	255	29	187	39	0
Bedford Heights	10594	28	0		4	9	15	290	71	176	43	0
Bellaire	4172	9	0	0		1	8	46	5	38	3	1
Bellbrook	7074	3	0	2		0	1	57	4	51	2	0
Bellefontaine	13073	23	0	8		2	13	404	59	342	3	1
Bellville	1863	1	0	1		0	0	29	3	25	1	0
Belpre	6484	11	0	3		2	6	107	13	85	9	1
Berea	18805	11	0	2		5	4	181	19	154	8	1
Bethel	2782	6	0	1		0	5	95	9	84	2	0
Bexley	13775	26	0	12		13	1	359	99	242	18	0
Blanchester	4249	6	1	0		1	4	75	6	65	4	1
Blue Ash	12169	11	0	4		4	3	320	41	273	6	3
Bluffton	4127	1	0		0	1	0	82	16	62	4	0

Table 6. Offenses Known to Law Enforcement, by Selected State and City, 2016—Continued

(Number.)

State/city	Population	Violent crime	Murder and nonnegligent manslaughter	Rape (revised definition)[1]	Rape (legacy definition)[2]	Robbery	Aggravated assault	Property crime	Burglary	Larceny-theft	Motor vehicle theft	Arson[3]
Bowling Green	31404	42	0	19		8	15	560	64	486	10	1
Brady Lake	464	1	0	0		0	1	5	2	3	0	0
Brecksville	13390	4	0	0		2	2	54	5	47	2	1
Brewster	2169	0	0	0		0	0	20	2	17	1	0
Bridgeport	1786	3	1	1		0	1	18	5	12	1	0
Brimfield Township	10406	9	0		5	3	1	243	16	221	1	0
Brooklyn	10841	29	2		5	15	7	673	44	585	44	0
Brookville	5902	7	0		5	1	1	59	15	43	1	0
Brunswick	34774	25	0	1		0	24	224	28	182	14	1
Brunswick Hills Township	10402	5	0	0		0	5	38	9	29	0	0
Bucyrus	11830	24	0	4		9	11	491	90	394	7	2
Butler Township	7856	36	0	10		18	8	458	51	382	25	0
Cadiz	3256	7	0	2		2	3	60	16	42	2	0
Cambridge	10341	14	1	0		3	10	484	83	388	13	0
Campbell	7936	4	0	3		1	0	41	15	21	5	1
Canal Fulton	5489	2	0	2		0	0	73	14	56	3	0
Canfield	7323	1	0	1		0	0	60	8	52	0	0
Canton	71652	677	8	77		171	421	3664	951	2474	239	18
Carey	3570	0	0	0		0	0	5	2	3	0	0
Carlisle	5323	4	0	0		2	2	25	6	17	2	0
Carroll Township	2109	1	0	1		0	0	31	3	26	2	0
Centerville	23853	13	0	0		3	10	352	41	290	21	0
Chagrin Falls	4003	4	2	1		0	1	27	3	24	0	0
Chardon	5162	7	0		0	0	7	66	3	63	0	0
Chester Township	10371	0	0	0		0	0	18	3	15	0	0
Cheviot	8281	30	0	4		10	16	254	46	198	10	0
Chillicothe	21692	94	0	8		34	52	1747	350	1355	42	2
Cincinnati	298880	2720	57	249		1278	1136	15382	3929	10216	1237	485
Circleville	13390	37	0	5		12	20	674	97	569	8	0
Clayton	13129	6	0	0		3	3	135	27	97	11	0
Clay Township, Montgomery County	4217	2	0	2		0	0	20	6	14	0	0
Clearcreek Township	15322	4	1	2		0	1	92	18	73	1	0
Cleveland	386227	6299	135	488		2980	2696	20533	6333	10001	4199	315
Cleveland Heights	44696	145	3		9	80	53	997	118	781	98	3
Clyde	6233	3	0	0		2	1	148	39	108	1	1
Coitsville Township	1344	3	0	0		0	3	35	14	18	3	0
Colerain Township	58907	111	2	19		59	31	2135	310	1760	65	3
Columbiana	6269	3	0	2		0	1	88	22	66	0	2
Columbus	862515	4500	91	867		2144	1398	35106	7756	23800	3550	405
Commercial Point	1616	2	0	2		0	0	10	0	9	1	0
Cortland	6894	1	0	0		0	1	77	15	59	3	0
Covington	2633	3	0	0		2	1	29	2	27	0	0
Crestline	4402	9	0	3		2	4	98	35	56	7	0
Cuyahoga Falls	49064	67	0	24		14	29	1143	116	977	50	5
Dayton	140260	1402	36	133		496	737	7235	2269	4252	714	80
Deer Park	5672	9	0		1	4	4	74	9	63	2	0
Defiance	16697	25	0	16		1	8	341	42	291	8	3
Delaware	38658	73	0	35		14	24	890	154	714	22	7
Delhi Township	29573	20	0	10		1	9	514	84	409	21	1
Delphos	7011	2	0		1	0	1	151	24	125	2	0
Dennison	2638	2	0	0		0	2	12	0	12	0	0
Dover	12906	12	1	4		1	6	96	15	80	1	1
Dublin[7]	45860	22	0	9		5	8	517	97	406	14	2
East Cleveland	17240	111	7		4	66	34	342	94	131	117	4
Eastlake	18166	10	1		0	3	6	443	54	375	14	1
East Palestine	4548	6	0	1		2	3	62	21	39	2	0
Elmwood Place	2160	10	2	2		3	3	35	10	21	4	0
Elyria	53633	161	4	26		71	60	1483	344	1042	97	8
Englewood	13455	13	0	2		5	6	409	30	367	12	0
Evendale	2766	6	0	0		1	5	238	7	231	0	0
Fairborn	33587	84	3	32		21	28	908	189	664	55	8
Fairfax	1704	3	0	0		2	1	261	12	249	0	0
Fairfield	42810	110	1	17		21	71	1045	144	866	35	2
Fairfield Township	22417	28	1	9		4	14	598	56	534	8	1
Fairport Harbor	3093	5	0		0	1	4	102	19	77	6	0
Fairview Park	16318	32	0	0		6	26	227	35	183	9	0
Felicity	830	2	0	0		0	2	42	6	36	0	0
Forest Park	18669	47	0	9		21	17	633	157	449	27	2
Franklin	11782	23	1	4		10	8	542	136	390	16	0
Frazeysburg	1321	1	0	1		0	0	16	1	12	3	0
Fredericktown	2486	6	0	2		0	4	41	11	29	1	0
Fremont	16215	32	2		0	11	19	842	155	668	19	0
Gahanna	34859	20	0	10		6	4	789	99	660	30	2
Galion	10053	17	0	5		4	8	341	73	264	4	3
Gallipolis	3435	10	0	1		3	6	442	46	382	14	2
Geneva-on-the-Lake	1207	7	1	2		0	4	27	9	17	1	0
Georgetown	4436	5	0	3		1	1	102	21	78	3	0
Germantown	5495	6	0	0		0	6	40	5	34	1	0
German Township, Montgomery County	2893	1	0	0		0	1	42	13	26	3	0
Glouster	1798	3	0	2		0	1	39	15	23	1	2

Table 6. Offenses Known to Law Enforcement, by Selected State and City, 2016—Continued

(Number.)

State/city	Population	Violent crime	Murder and nonnegligent manslaughter	Rape (revised definition)[1]	Rape (legacy definition)[2]	Robbery	Aggravated assault	Property crime	Burglary	Larceny-theft	Motor vehicle theft	Arson[3]
Goshen Township, Clermont County	15787	6	0	3		1	2	166	33	126	7	1
Goshen Township, Mahoning County	3106	5	0	0		0	5	76	17	57	2	0
Grafton	6105	4	1		0	2	1	38	10	28	0	0
Grandview Heights	7502	1	0	0		1	0	144	43	95	6	0
Granville	5762	0	0	0		0	0	41	5	35	1	0
Greenfield	4559	6	0	1		1	4	102	20	72	10	1
Greenhills	3589	1	0	1		0	0	36	8	27	1	1
Green Township	58764	39	0	10		22	7	1215	176	989	50	3
Greenville	12962	44	0	13		8	23	315	74	217	24	14
Grove City	40161	43	2	7		26	8	1678	144	1476	58	4
Groveport	5813	5	0	2		1	2	178	19	149	10	2
Hamilton	62423	320	9	64		131	116	3316	942	2365	9	26
Harrison	10819	0	0		0	0	0	306	15	282	9	0
Hartford Township	1999	0	0	0		0	0	8	0	8	0	0
Hartville	2974	1	0	0		1	0	53	8	45	0	0
Heath	10528	23	0	10		2	11	664	155	488	21	1
Highland Heights	8402	1	0		0	1	0	99	5	93	1	0
Hilliard[7]	34832	33	0	11		9	13	344	67	253	24	4
Hillsboro	6547	8	1	2		1	4	203	33	166	4	0
Hinckley Township	8041	6	2	0		0	4	28	15	13	0	0
Holland	1698	6	0	1		5	0	288	21	266	1	0
Howland Township	16759	13	0	1		2	10	384	73	295	16	0
Hubbard	7609	10	0	0		0	10	133	21	107	5	1
Huber Heights	38180	84	1	19		30	34	1270	176	1003	91	10
Hudson	22470	4	0	1		0	3	92	27	62	3	0
Independence	7132	11	0	0		1	10	120	6	111	3	0
Indian Hill	5801	1	0	0		0	1	44	8	36	0	0
Ironton	10856	21	0	3		7	11	270	70	190	10	1
Jackson	6211	10	1	3		1	5	151	18	127	6	1
Jackson Township, Mahoning County	2042	1	0	0		0	1	16	4	10	2	0
Jackson Township, Stark County	40780	72	0	14		31	27	1234	126	1087	21	3
Jamestown	2034	1	0	0		0	1	72	28	42	2	0
Johnstown	4973	6	0	1		0	5	79	9	69	1	0
Kent	29995	67	1	0		13	53	496	95	385	16	2
Kenton	8199	19	0	7		5	7	415	96	311	8	1
Kettering	55384	73	0	26		26	21	1008	223	732	53	10
Kirtland	6780	3	0	2		0	1	27	4	23	0	0
Kirtland Hills	640	1	0		0	0	1	0	0	0	0	0
Lakewood	50349	63	3	8		32	20	876	144	665	67	4
Lancaster	39959	141	0	30		46	65	1826	271	1499	56	6
Lawrence Township	8265	2	0	0		0	2	71	23	45	3	0
Lebanon	20726	22	1		7	5	9	361	40	313	8	4
Lexington	4715	0	0	0		0	0	5	0	5	0	0
Liberty Township	11655	32	1	1		7	23	188	42	132	14	0
Lima	37715	356	8		44	123	181	2259	602	1540	117	22
Lisbon	2709	0	0	0		0	0	39	5	33	1	0
Lithopolis	1401	0	0	0		0	0	13	3	10	0	0
Lockland	3422	20	0	3		10	7	121	22	92	7	1
Logan	7106	15	0	6		1	8	243	38	200	5	2
London	10092	7	0	2		2	3	284	48	221	15	0
Loudonville	2621	14	0	7		0	7	47	4	42	1	0
Louisville	9115	14	0	2		2	10	114	24	84	6	0
Loveland	12691	6	0	2		3	1	132	21	101	10	1
Lynchburg	1484	4	0	3		0	1	20	8	12	0	0
Lyndhurst	13624	14	0	5		6	3	194	19	169	6	2
Macedonia	11794	8	0	1		4	3	197	11	183	3	0
Madison Township, Franklin County	18466	22	0	1		12	9	210	59	137	14	0
Magnolia	972	2	0	0		0	2	44	13	27	4	0
Mansfield	46656	209	3	58		63	85	2605	679	1805	121	26
Mariemont	3431	1	0		0	1	0	45	3	40	2	0
Marion	36278	107	1	22		37	47	1320	517	772	31	9
Martins Ferry	6761	12	0	2		0	10	110	33	72	5	0
Marysville	22952	7	0	2		1	4	144	15	123	6	1
Mason	33026	6	0	3		2	1	330	17	305	8	1
Maumee	13875	15	0	8		3	4	380	37	336	7	0
McArthur	1656	2	0	2		0	0	27	8	18	1	0
McConnelsville	1790	4	0	2		0	2	29	5	22	2	0
Mechanicsburg	1591	3	0	1		0	2	45	10	32	3	0
Medina Township	9015	5	0	2		0	3	141	13	126	2	0
Mentor	46852	51	0	10		11	30	1034	105	899	30	6
Mentor-on-the-Lake	7375	10	0	1		0	9	91	19	67	5	1
Miamisburg	20000	20	0	4		12	4	228	40	178	10	1
Miami Township, Clermont County	42109	26	0	11		4	11	569	84	459	26	4
Miami Township, Montgomery County	29140	39	0	16		11	12	1159	130	985	44	3
Middlefield	2694	0	0		0	0	0	44	1	43	0	0
Middleport	2464	4	0	0		1	3	17	4	13	0	1

Table 6. Offenses Known to Law Enforcement, by Selected State and City, 2016—Continued

(Number.)

State/city	Population	Violent crime	Murder and nonnegligent manslaughter	Rape (revised definition)[1]	Rape (legacy definition)[2]	Robbery	Aggravated assault	Property crime	Burglary	Larceny-theft	Motor vehicle theft	Arson[3]
Middletown	48768	255	5		43	71	136	3296	778	2384	134	0
Milan	1343	1	0	1		0	0	25	5	20	0	0
Milford	6910	9	0	1		5	3	231	25	202	4	0
Millersburg	3174	3	0	0		3	0	91	4	86	1	0
Milton Township	2470	1	0	1		0	0	33	9	23	1	0
Minerva[10]	3670	5	1	0		0	4	46	0	44	2	0
Mingo Junction	3299	15	0		0	3	12	44	14	28	2	10
Mogadore	3919	1	0		0	0	1	41	8	31	2	0
Monroe	15933	24	0	3		3	18	436	26	406	4	1
Montgomery	10558	4	0	0		0	4	148	14	130	4	0
Montpelier	3980	14	1	5		3	5	146	18	113	15	2
Montville Township	11815	2	0	1		0	1	46	8	38	0	0
Moraine	6385	34	1	14		10	9	684	82	565	37	3
Moreland Hills	3303	1	0		0	1	0	10	3	7	0	0
Mount Healthy	6028	31	4	3		16	8	259	45	196	18	1
Mount Orab	3649	5	0	0		2	3	94	4	89	1	0
Mount Vernon	16685	17	0	6		2	9	680	87	592	1	1
Munroe Falls	5012	2	0	1		0	1	40	5	35	0	2
Napoleon	8566	11	0	3		1	7	197	25	171	1	0
Navarre	1916	0	0	0		0	0	19	4	15	0	0
Nelsonville	5159	11	0	1		7	3	195	34	148	13	1
New Albany	10340	5	0	2		1	2	170	16	144	10	0
Newcomerstown	3789	5	1		1	0	3	82	15	62	5	
New Concord	2317	0	0	0		0	0	15	1	14	0	0
New Franklin	14285	9	0	1		2	6	110	30	74	6	2
New Lebanon	4001	9	0	0		2	7	116	26	79	11	0
New Lexington	4721	12	0	5		1	6	188	34	149	5	0
New Middletown	1568	1	0	0		0	1	10	2	8	0	0
New Philadelphia	17526	3	0	1		0	2	188	9	177	2	0
New Richmond	2651	12	0	3		2	7	74	22	47	5	1
Newton Falls	4628	9	0	3		2	4	92	17	72	3	0
Newtown	2663	3	0	0		1	2	31	6	22	3	0
Niles	18538	53	1	8		21	23	524	79	431	14	1
North Baltimore	3568	9	0	2		2	5	67	21	45	1	0
North Canton	17435	9	0	3		2	4	271	44	219	8	1
North College Hill	9320	30	1	4		13	12	311	38	247	26	0
Northfield	3630	2	0	0		1	1	46	4	40	2	0
North Ridgeville	33095	12	1	4		3	4	193	37	154	2	0
Northwood	5376	6	0	2		3	1	133	21	110	2	0
Norton	12026	5	0	1		1	3	135	37	84	14	1
Norwalk	16792	10	0	3		2	5	440	68	365	7	1
Norwood	20065	52	0	12		28	12	1013	166	798	49	2
Oak Harbor	2705	1	0	1		0	0	42	5	37	0	0
Oak Hill	1490	2	0	0		0	2	30	4	25	1	0
Oberlin	8342	38	0	27		4	7	212	27	184	1	0
Olmsted Falls	8859	3	0		0	0	3	30	11	17	2	0
Olmsted Township	13228	1	0		0	1	0	43	15	25	3	0
Ontario	6091	5	0	1		1	3	370	16	352	2	0
Oregon	20055	37	0	5		6	26	665	85	553	27	1
Orrville[7]	8514	16	3	4		1	8	111	30	80	1	1
Ottawa Hills	4429	1	0	0		0	1	37	10	24	3	1
Oxford Township	2175	4	0	1		0	3	32	11	21	0	0
Parma	79576	108	0	26		43	39	1102	271	712	119	11
Peninsula	572	1	0	0		1	0	27	3	24	0	0
Pepper Pike	6247	1	0	0		1	0	32	6	25	1	0
Perkins Township	11844	16	0	0		7	9	308	5	303	0	0
Perrysburg	21548	8	0	3		3	2	244	16	223	5	0
Perrysburg Township	12813	6	0	1		2	3	162	28	129	5	0
Perry Township, Columbiana County	4420	0	0	0		0	0	0	0	0	0	0
Perry Township, Franklin County	3799	0	0	0		0	0	53	5	48	0	0
Perry Township, Montgomery County	3346	1	0	0		0	1	9	4	5	0	0
Pickerington	20040	16	0	0		10	6	430	42	382	6	0
Pierce Township	11559	3	0	1		1	1	182	33	148	1	0
Pioneer	1406	2	0	1		0	1	23	7	16	0	0
Piqua	20845	39	1	19		13	6	882	135	728	19	7
Poland Township	12052	3	0	1		0	2	66	16	48	2	0
Poland Village	2471	1	0	1		0	0	11	1	10	0	0
Port Clinton	5939	13	0	8		2	3	170	38	129	3	1
Powell	13273	0	0	0		0	0	106	24	80	2	0
Reminderville	4097	0	0		0	0	0	30	1	28	1	0
Reynoldsburg	37406	82	6	8		35	33	1345	157	1135	53	7
Richmond Heights	10445	27	0	2		15	10	249	56	165	28	0
Rio Grande	839	3	0	2		0	1	16	7	9	0	1
Rittman	6598	4	0		1	1	2	137	37	86	14	2
Riverside	24920	51	1	15		16	19	618	133	429	56	3
Rocky River	20400	7	0	1		0	6	81	15	62	4	0
Roseville	1851	8	0	0		0	8	34	9	23	2	0
Ross Township	8720	6	0	2		1	3	83	19	60	4	0
Russells Point	1355	0	0	0		0	0	26	6	19	1	0
Russell Township	5250	1	0	0		0	1	15	0	15	0	0

Table 6. Offenses Known to Law Enforcement, by Selected State and City, 2016—Continued

(Number.)

State/city	Population	Violent crime	Murder and nonnegligent manslaughter	Rape (revised definition)[1]	Rape (legacy definition)[2]	Robbery	Aggravated assault	Property crime	Burglary	Larceny-theft	Motor vehicle theft	Arson[3]
Sabina	2530	2	0	1		0	1	63	14	46	3	0
Sagamore Hills[7]	11184	4	0	3		1	0	46	8	37	1	0
Salem	11943	9	0	1		1	7	310	18	286	6	1
Salineville	1266	1	0	0		0	1	23	1	22	0	1
Sandusky	25078	45	1	6		19	19	911	199	680	32	3
Sebring	4240	4	0	1		1	2	149	25	121	3	0
Seven Hills	11661	4	0	1		1	2	64	16	46	2	0
Shadyside	3701	0	0	0		0	0	6	3	2	1	0
Sharon Township	2451	0	0	0		0	0	33	3	29	1	0
Shawnee Township	12173	7	0	4		0	3	144	40	99	5	0
Shelby	9012	17	0	5		2	10	258	58	199	1	0
Sidney	20797	45	0	16		16	13	926	206	699	21	3
Solon	22971	11	1	5		1	4	175	15	154	6	1
South Bloomfield	1873	1	0	0		0	1	35	5	28	2	0
South Charleston	1655	2	0	0		0	2	23	3	18	2	0
South Euclid	21686	35	0	4		23	8	570	57	474	39	0
South Russell	3827	2	0		1	1	0	4	0	4	0	0
South Zanesville	1974	1	0	0		1	0	22	6	15	1	0
Spencerville	2195	1	0	0		0	1	28	5	23	0	1
Springboro	18379	11	0	6		1	4	103	9	88	6	0
Springfield	59503	411	5	34		184	188	4040	963	2817	260	58
Springfield Township, Hamilton County	36527	60	1	6		33	20	794	172	565	57	5
Springfield Township, Mahoning County	6446	3	0	2		0	1	76	32	40	4	0
Springfield Township, Summit County	17813	34	0	10		4	20	895	119	748	28	3
St. Clairsville	5090	4	0	0		0	4	9	1	8	0	0
St. Clair Township	7704	0	0	0		0	0	40	0	40	0	0
Steubenville	18137	60	2		4	22	32	1085	132	945	8	2
St. Marys	8256	5	0	0		2	3	130	29	98	3	1
Stow	34792	30	0	11		5	14	642	66	569	7	2
St. Paris	2014	0	0	0		0	0	16	0	15	1	0
Strasburg	2693	0	0	0		0	0	21	1	19	1	0
Streetsboro	16364	6	0	0		1	5	244	28	207	9	1
Strongsville	44626	19	0	0		14	5	882	65	797	20	1
Struthers	10314	27	0	1		8	18	244	75	161	8	0
Sugarcreek Township	8283	3	0	1		2	0	159	9	146	4	0
Sunbury	5242	0	0	0		0	0	56	9	46	1	0
Swanton	3889	3	0	2		0	1	28	4	24	0	0
Sylvania Township	29416	18	0	2		7	9	632	99	507	26	0
Tallmadge	17502	23	0		4	9	10	403	73	315	15	0
Tiffin	17637	13	0		5	3	5	418	76	328	14	0
Tipp City	9941	7	0	1		1	5	181	23	148	10	1
Toledo[11]	278366	3319	37	316		803	2163	11191	3381	7081	729	
Toronto	4843	6	0	3		0	3	16	4	12	0	0
Trotwood	24024	90	11	20		37	22	962	341	506	115	11
Troy	25745	22	0	13		3	6	724	145	567	12	6
Twinsburg	18888	20	1	1		5	13	131	19	109	3	1
Uhrichsville	5403	3	0	1		0	2	45	3	41	1	0
Uniontown	3330	2	0	1		0	1	81	21	58	2	0
Union Township, Clermont County	47933	43	0	17		12	14	962	87	854	21	2
University Heights	13131	45	0		7	27	11	305	29	260	16	4
Upper Arlington	35150	16	1	4		8	3	535	67	449	19	1
Upper Sandusky	6515	12	2	4		0	6	153	25	123	5	1
Urbana	11482	14	0	3		5	6	420	78	323	19	7
Utica	2206	5	1	1		0	3	16	4	11	1	0
Valley View, Cuyahoga County	2007	0	0		0	0	0	35	8	23	4	0
Vandalia	15073	14	0	2		9	3	328	63	232	33	3
Van Wert	10794	29	0	10		1	18	353	86	262	5	0
Vermilion	10404	3	0	0		0	3	107	14	90	3	0
Vienna Township	3817	5	0	1		0	4	65	15	49	1	0
Village of Leesburg	1289	0	0	0		0	0	46	9	37	0	0
Wadsworth	21910	24	0	7		2	15	479	40	436	3	4
Walton Hills	2236	0	0		0	0	0	29	3	24	2	0
Wapakoneta	9815	10	0	3		0	7	144	20	121	3	0
Warren	40005	228	2	27		90	109	1509	511	905	93	6
Warren Township	5320	16	0	3		2	11	126	53	65	8	0
Washington Court House	13986	37	0	9		9	19	612	137	459	16	2
Waterville	5511	2	0	0		1	1	29	4	24	1	0
Wauseon	7311	7	0	3		1	3	197	13	183	1	0
Waverly	4248	3	0	0		1	2	93	8	83	2	0
Wellston	5459	18	0	2		6	10	161	40	115	6	1
West Alexandria	1334	1	0	0		0	1	23	7	15	1	0
West Carrollton	12944	22	0	8		6	8	358	87	235	36	4
West Chester Township	61080	43	0	15		14	14	1340	155	1161	24	4
Westerville	38808	21	0	7		9	5	935	75	844	16	5
West Jefferson	4291	3	0	0		1	2	101	14	84	3	0
West Lafayette	2279	3	0	2		0	1	8	1	7	0	0
Westlake	32353	14	0	0		5	9	461	37	403	21	3
West Liberty	1769	3	0	0		0	3	21	8	13	0	0

Table 6. Offenses Known to Law Enforcement, by Selected State and City, 2016—Continued

(Number.)

State/city	Population	Violent crime	Murder and nonnegligent manslaughter	Rape (revised definition)[1]	Rape (legacy definition)[2]	Robbery	Aggravated assault	Property crime	Burglary	Larceny-theft	Motor vehicle theft	Arson[3]
West Union	3167	5	0	0		0	5	44	15	23	6	0
Whitehall	18804	153	2	25		74	52	1163	299	794	70	9
Whitehouse	4528	1	0	0		0	1	30	4	23	3	0
Wickliffe	12506	17	0	0		9	8	233	41	178	14	0
Willard	6031	4	0	1		2	1	302	68	222	12	2
Williamsburg	2560	3	0	0		1	2	63	9	54	0	0
Willoughby	22701	45	1	8		21	15	478	62	394	22	1
Wilmington	12443	18	0	9		2	7	578	59	499	20	2
Windham	2201	3	0	0		1	2	32	6	26	0	0
Wintersville	3770	1	0	0		0	1	57	3	54	0	0
Woodlawn	3292	6	0	1		1	4	115	11	98	6	0
Woodmere Village	859	2	0		1	0	1	56	1	38	17	0
Wooster	26883	73	0	24		14	35	776	127	633	16	10
Worthington	14689	5	0	0		4	1	233	28	195	10	2
Wyoming	8407	5	0	0		4	1	159	17	139	3	1
Xenia	26037	53	1	13		11	28	821	134	665	22	6
Yellow Springs[7]	3857	2	0	0		1	1	79	18	59	2	0
Youngstown	64181	415	12	28		151	224	2426	921	1264	241	137
Zanesville	25494	93	0	18		28	47	1288	230	1036	22	10
OKLAHOMA												
Ada	17390	57	1	3		7	46	633	198	399	36	4
Allen	935	0	0	0		0	0	9	4	4	1	0
Altus	19093	58	1	10		3	44	621	189	416	16	4
Alva	5227	3	0	1		0	2	62	20	35	7	0
Anadarko	6702	50	2	5		6	37	282	89	172	21	7
Antlers	2336	9	0	1		2	6	35	13	18	4	0
Apache	1426	3	0	0		0	3	20	7	13	0	0
Ardmore	25315	148	6	13		35	94	1287	303	929	55	9
Arkoma	1912	0	0	0		0	0	12	2	8	2	0
Atoka	3055	8	0	0		1	7	121	25	88	8	1
Barnsdall	1203	5	0	2		2	1	19	9	9	1	3
Bartlesville	36753	109	2	11		21	75	1132	231	821	80	3
Beaver	1442	1	0	1		0	0	6	2	3	1	0
Beggs	1242	3	0	1		0	2	16	7	5	4	0
Bethany	19690	61	0	8		22	31	685	190	419	76	2
Big Cabin	261	0	0	0		0	0	6	0	6	0	0
Bixby	25453	25	0	9		3	13	384	74	271	39	1
Blackwell	6837	21	0	4		1	16	115	37	71	7	6
Blanchard	8461	6	0	1		0	5	87	24	55	8	0
Boise City	1103	3	0	1		0	2	8	5	1	2	0
Bristow	4251	13	1	4		1	7	149	56	85	8	0
Broken Arrow	108088	166	3	26		46	91	2296	413	1712	171	4
Broken Bow	4133	31	0	3		1	27	328	74	231	23	2
Cache	2944	7	0	3		0	4	53	18	30	5	1
Caddo	1055	1	0	0		0	1	15	8	5	2	0
Calera	2262	22	0	0		0	22	26	8	18	0	0
Caney	197	0	0	0		0	0	8	2	5	1	0
Carnegie	1695	0	0	0		0	0	12	5	7	0	0
Carney	664	1	0	1		0	0	13	9	4	0	0
Cashion	857	3	0	0		0	3	11	2	9	0	0
Catoosa	7145	65	0	7		7	51	340	45	222	73	0
Chandler	3189	8	0	3		0	5	63	12	48	3	1
Checotah	3246	9	0	0		0	9	126	37	78	11	1
Chelsea	1970	3	0	3		0	4	42	9	30	3	1
Cherokee	1574	5	0	1		0	4	20	5	15	0	0
Chickasha	16579	110	0	22		7	81	502	166	302	34	4
Choctaw	12382	10	0	1		2	7	164	62	89	13	1
Claremore	19076	38	0	12		3	23	562	101	436	25	0
Clayton	790	8	0	0		0	8	11	2	7	2	2
Cleveland	3209	3	0	0		0	3	31	0	30	1	0
Clinton	9675	24	0	4		5	15	202	73	110	19	3
Coalgate	1849	2	0	1		0	1	6	1	2	3	0
Colbert	1191	1	0	1		0	0	17	7	10	0	0
Collinsville	6678	8	1	1		1	5	111	23	77	11	1
Comanche	1618	5	0	2		0	3	32	13	17	2	1
Cordell	2917	20	1	0		1	18	60	20	39	1	0
Coweta	9589	27	2	2		1	22	239	41	188	10	2
Crescent	1550	0	0	0		0	0	33	12	18	3	0
Cushing	7874	33	0	4		2	27	324	88	211	25	2
Davenport	822	4	0	2		0	2	12	6	6	0	1
Davis	2816	18	0	10		0	8	78	20	47	11	1
Del City	22152	142	6	12		41	83	1047	186	761	100	4
Depew	483	0	0	0		0	0	1	0	1	0	0
Dewar	866	1	0	0		0	1	4	0	4	0	0
Dewey	3511	12	1	1		0	10	98	23	68	7	0
Dibble	830	0	0	0		0	0	4	2	2	0	0
Drumright	2874	7	0	0		1	6	76	18	55	3	0
Duncan	23188	61	0	11		10	40	950	290	621	39	7
Durant	17566	64	0	6		5	53	923	168	722	33	3
Edmond	91869	133	1	23		21	88	1396	258	1073	65	4
Elgin	3146	2	0	0		0	2	4	1	3	0	0
Elk City	12939	13	1	1		4	7	302	60	224	18	0

Table 6. Offenses Known to Law Enforcement, by Selected State and City, 2016—Continued

(Number.)

State/city	Population	Violent crime	Murder and nonnegligent manslaughter	Rape (revised definition)[1]	Rape (legacy definition)[2]	Robbery	Aggravated assault	Property crime	Burglary	Larceny-theft	Motor vehicle theft	Arson[3]
El Reno	18872	99	0	9		4	86	337	69	254	14	6
Enid	52240	214	2	29		27	156	2041	474	1489	78	1
Eufaula	2960	7	0	1		0	6	87	15	62	10	0
Fairfax	1344	2	0	1		0	1	20	7	12	1	0
Fairview	2672	1	0	0		0	1	23	12	11	0	0
Forest Park	1089	1	0	1		0	0	12	4	7	1	0
Fort Gibson	4068	9	0	0		1	8	42	20	16	6	0
Frederick	3645	14	0	2		1	11	133	54	74	5	1
Geary	1309	3	0	0		1	2	39	13	23	3	0
Glenpool	13717	52	0	8		4	40	290	67	212	11	0
Goodwell	1331	1	0	0		0	1	8	1	6	1	0
Grandfield	959	1	0	0		0	1	29	10	16	3	0
Grove	6773	21	0	2		1	18	186	20	157	9	3
Guthrie	11486	47	0	9		7	31	408	153	221	34	1
Guymon	12001	26	0	5		0	21	203	46	140	17	0
Harrah	6061	12	0	1		2	9	122	33	81	8	1
Hartshorne	1997	7	0	3		0	4	30	14	13	3	0
Haskell	1974	1	0	0		0	1	3	0	3	0	0
Healdton	2774	11	0	0		0	11	44	9	31	4	1
Heavener	3321	8	0	1		0	7	73	25	48	0	1
Hennessey	2212	2	0	1		0	1	17	1	15	1	0
Henryetta	5732	13	0	0		2	11	192	68	110	14	1
Hinton	3252	0	0	0		0	0	18	2	14	2	0
Hobart	3596	2	0	1		0	1	61	21	33	7	0
Holdenville	5743	8	0	3		1	4	118	40	58	20	6
Hollis	1950	10	0	0		0	10	67	34	28	5	0
Hominy	3499	8	0	0		0	8	67	25	33	9	1
Hooker	2009	1	0	0		0	1	16	1	12	3	0
Howe	787	1	0	0		0	1	9	0	7	2	0
Hulbert	605	1	0	0		0	1	0	0	0	0	0
Hydro	958	4	0	0		0	4	16	6	9	1	1
Idabel	7006	28	1	8		5	14	362	90	265	7	1
Jay	2479	1	0	0		0	1	49	12	34	3	2
Jenks	21535	24	0	2		1	21	287	51	209	27	0
Jones	3000	8	0	4		0	4	60	21	30	9	2
Kellyville	1147	4	0	1		0	3	12	1	10	1	0
Kiefer	1960	7	0	1		0	6	39	10	27	2	0
Kingfisher	4912	8	0	2		0	6	72	11	56	5	1
Kingston	1638	1	0	0		0	1	2	0	2	0	0
Krebs	1958	7	2	1		0	4	54	22	27	5	1
Lamont	410	1	0	0		0	1	17	9	8	0	0
Lawton	96420	781	4	69		110	598	3691	1151	2318	222	13
Lexington	2161	4	0	1		0	3	54	18	30	6	0
Lindsay	2829	8	0	0		0	8	89	31	52	6	0
Locust Grove	1403	3	0	1		0	2	14	6	8	0	0
Lone Grove	5243	19	0	2		2	15	138	26	98	14	0
Luther	1611	5	0	0		1	4	26	8	16	2	0
Madill	3957	4	0	0		0	4	153	27	119	7	0
Mangum	2894	5	0	1		0	4	30	16	14	0	0
Mannford	3131	5	0	1		0	4	37	8	23	6	1
Marietta	2750	6	0	1		0	5	61	18	36	7	2
Marlow	4580	8	0	0		0	8	99	41	57	1	0
McAlester	18300	55	1	11		8	35	810	186	582	42	2
McLoud	4633	11	0	1		1	9	104	20	71	13	0
Medicine Park	456	0	0	0		0	0	6	3	3	0	0
Meeker	1177	14	0	1		1	12	30	7	18	5	0
Miami	13620	26	1	2		1	22	155	56	86	13	3
Midwest City	57797	126	2	26		37	61	2225	412	1611	202	9
Moore	61511	82	1	24		28	29	1436	282	1005	149	6
Mooreland	1298	0	0	0		0	0	4	1	3	0	0
Morris	1458	2	0	0		0	2	17	2	15	0	0
Mounds	1182	0	0	0		0	0	22	6	9	7	0
Mountain View	764	0	0	0		0	0	7	4	3	0	0
Muldrow	3248	17	0	4		0	13	124	49	65	10	0
Muskogee	38293	394	1	17		60	316	1480	576	810	94	17
Mustang	20813	21	0	1		1	19	246	34	189	23	0
Newcastle	9816	5	0	0		2	3	197	50	123	24	1
Newkirk	2242	1	0	1		0	0	24	5	14	5	0
Nichols Hills	3921	0	0	0		0	0	66	23	39	4	0
Nicoma Park	2483	6	0	1		0	5	93	47	39	7	0
Noble	6699	7	1	3		0	3	110	30	62	18	4
Norman	122143	329	0	69		57	203	3948	713	2804	431	6
North Enid	938	0	0	0		0	0	11	4	7	0	0
Nowata	3747	16	0	3		0	13	82	37	41	4	1
Oilton	1015	1	0	0		0	1	21	6	12	3	1
Okemah	3249	9	0	1		0	8	148	57	88	3	0
Oklahoma City	641681	5027	70	445		1144	3368	25032	5545	16582	2905	93
Okmulgee	12177	86	2	25		11	48	486	104	359	23	3
Owasso	35551	60	1	11		6	42	686	75	562	49	1
Pauls Valley	6163	25	0	7		0	18	302	82	191	29	2
Pawhuska	3590	19	0	6		0	13	98	36	56	6	0
Pawnee	2153	10	0	4		1	5	42	16	21	5	1
Perkins	2862	4	0	3		0	1	70	13	51	6	0

Table 6. Offenses Known to Law Enforcement, by Selected State and City, 2016—Continued

(Number.)

State/city	Population	Violent crime	Murder and nonnegligent manslaughter	Rape (revised definition)[1]	Rape (legacy definition)[2]	Robbery	Aggravated assault	Property crime	Burglary	Larceny-theft	Motor vehicle theft	Arson[3]
Perry	5091	10	0	0		2	8	104	37	62	5	2
Piedmont	7420	5	0	2		0	3	35	7	23	5	1
Pocola	4026	10	2	1		1	6	63	24	30	9	0
Ponca City	24647	215	0	43		30	142	966	241	676	49	14
Porum	711	0	0	0		0	0	3	1	2	0	0
Poteau	8770	52	1	6		2	43	560	171	365	24	3
Prague	2466	8	0	4		1	3	46	10	29	7	0
Pryor Creek	9455	59	0	4		2	53	259	69	162	28	1
Purcell	6405	25	1	3		4	17	305	58	227	20	1
Ringling	996	3	0	0		0	3	20	6	14	0	0
Roland	3604	14	1	2		1	10	74	12	55	7	1
Rush Springs	1283	5	0	0		0	5	31	8	23	0	0
Salina	1381	2	0	0		1	1	19	3	12	4	0
Sallisaw	8530	23	0	8		0	15	421	55	352	14	1
Sand Springs	19961	27	0	5		7	15	663	88	508	67	2
Sapulpa	20667	59	1	11		12	35	484	101	315	68	2
Sawyer	316	1	0	0		0	1	4	2	2	0	0
Sayre	4858	13	0	0		0	13	51	17	30	4	0
Seiling	887	0	0	0		0	0	2	0	2	0	0
Seminole	7531	49	0	5		3	41	263	60	191	12	2
Shawnee	31560	265	1	27		20	217	1419	296	991	132	7
Skiatook	8005	8	0	2		0	6	179	44	129	6	2
Snyder	1336	3	0	0		0	3	17	6	11	0	0
South Coffeyville	771	1	0	0		0	1	11	3	7	1	0
Sparks	174	0	0	0		0	0	1	0	1	0	0
Spencer	4049	17	0	3		8	6	80	23	40	17	1
Sperry	1281	4	0	1		0	3	49	12	32	5	0
Spiro	2167	1	0	0		0	1	18	3	13	2	0
Stigler	2783	11	0	2		0	9	107	42	56	9	1
Stillwater	49637	143	1	26		18	98	1577	285	1215	77	4
Stilwell	4026	16	2	4		1	9	203	55	131	17	0
Stonewall	475	0	0	0		0	0	4	1	3	0	0
Stratford	1537	1	0	0		0	1	33	14	15	4	0
Stringtown	400	0	0	0		0	0	3	1	2	0	0
Stroud	2782	6	0	1		1	4	74	27	39	8	0
Sulphur	5130	9	0	1		0	8	121	28	87	6	1
Talala	277	0	0	0		0	0	3	3	0	0	0
Talihina	1091	2	0	0		0	2	24	11	12	1	1
Tecumseh	6662	17	1	6		1	9	176	45	106	25	0
The Village	9493	18	0	1		4	13	232	51	165	16	1
Tishomingo	3080	4	0	3		0	1	56	12	39	5	2
Tonkawa	3111	4	0	0		0	4	41	11	29	1	0
Tryon	504	3	0	1		0	2	2	0	1	1	0
Tulsa	405748	4444	72	439		1088	2845	23956	5780	14516	3660	171
Tushka	300	2	0	0		1	1	7	1	4	2	0
Tuttle	6974	29	0	2		0	27	111	30	69	12	1
Union City	2004	2	1	1		0	0	21	8	10	3	0
Valley Brook	784	4	0	0		1	3	32	14	11	7	0
Valliant	744	1	0	0		0	1	16	4	11	1	0
Verdigris	4428	4	0	1		0	3	42	9	30	3	0
Vian	1383	15	0	2		1	12	26	10	15	1	1
Vici	731	1	0	0		0	1	6	1	4	1	0
Vinita	5621	8	0	4		0	4	68	17	46	5	0
Wagoner	8787	18	0	2		3	13	262	81	170	11	1
Walters	2486	0	0	0		0	0	37	9	25	3	1
Warner	1619	0	0	0		0	0	5	2	2	1	0
Warr Acres	10505	54	0	2		16	36	405	97	271	37	0
Washington	637	0	0	0		0	0	3	0	2	1	0
Watonga	3002	3	0	2		0	1	25	5	20	0	0
Watts	308	1	0	0		0	1	2	1	0	1	0
Waukomis	1381	1	0	0		0	1	14	1	12	1	0
Waurika	1974	3	0	2		0	1	6	0	5	1	0
Waynoka	974	0	0	0		0	0	7	6	0	1	0
Weatherford	12399	11	0	1		1	9	189	28	144	17	2
Webbers Falls	597	0	0	0		0	0	13	3	7	3	0
Weleetka	984	5	0	0		0	5	19	2	14	3	1
West Siloam Springs	839	4	0	1		1	2	61	13	37	11	1
Westville	1554	3	0	1		0	2	48	16	29	3	1
Wetumka	1238	2	0	0		0	2	20	8	11	1	1
Wewoka	3449	9	0	0		0	9	61	26	34	1	3
Wilburton	2653	5	0	0		0	5	42	10	29	3	0
Wilson	1731	0	0	0		0	0	31	10	19	2	0
Woodward	13223	26	0	3		2	21	374	116	238	20	0
Wright City	741	1	0	0		0	1	4	1	3	0	0
Wyandotte	333	3	0	0		0	3	9	0	9	0	0
Wynnewood	2226	3	0	1		0	2	21	8	10	3	0
Yale	1222	2	0	0		0	2	29	6	20	3	1
Yukon	26546	44	0	8		4	32	519	65	436	18	1
OREGON												
Albany	52544	43	0		12	21	10	1512	146	1256	110	8
Amity	1646	1	0	0		0	1	17	2	14	1	0
Ashland	21017	48	1	2		10	35	828	74	727	27	5

Table 6. Offenses Known to Law Enforcement, by Selected State and City, 2016—Continued

(Number.)

State/city	Population	Violent crime	Murder and nonnegligent manslaughter	Rape (revised definition)[1]	Rape (legacy definition)[2]	Robbery	Aggravated assault	Property crime	Burglary	Larceny-theft	Motor vehicle theft	Arson[3]
Astoria	9655	16	0		0	5	11	450	62	370	18	3
Aumsville	4101	7	0	0		0	7	51	10	38	3	2
Banks	1965	2	0	1		0	1	19	4	14	1	0
Beaverton	97907	133	0	25		30	78	1403	124	1176	103	22
Bend	89244	96	0	17		20	59	2010	178	1740	92	8
Black Butte		0	0	0		0	0	6	1	5	0	0
Boardman	3378	18	1	4		1	12	43	4	34	5	1
Brookings	6506	3	0		0	2	1	50	6	40	4	0
Burns[7]	2748	13	0	2		1	10	85	35	44	6	0
Canby	17395	21	0	6		1	14	179	31	138	10	0
Cannon Beach[7]	1704	1	0	0		1	0	47	16	31	0	0
Carlton	2080	1	0	0		0	1	10	1	8	1	0
Central Point	18161	33	0	3		4	26	516	56	436	24	4
Coburg	1059	0	0		0	0	0	33	3	21	9	0
Coquille	3857	5	0		1	3	4	76	12	57	7	1
Cornelius	12402	35	0	7		3	25	244	25	200	19	3
Corvallis	56061	75	1	25		11	38	1557	207	1283	67	15
Cottage Grove[7]	10025	24	0	1		4	19	546	43	465	38	5
Dallas	15411	27	1	3		2	21	304	36	253	15	1
Eagle Point	8987	21	0	5		1	15	353	44	291	18	0
Estacada	3249	6	0	3		1	2	83	14	65	4	1
Eugene	164883	602	6	95		137	364	6317	1062	4622	633	72
Fairview	9350	20	0	5		3	12	289	22	190	77	3
Florence	8685	10	0		3	4	3	417	46	358	13	9
Forest Grove	24433	49	0	19		4	26	520	87	398	35	9
Gaston	698	1	0	1		0	0	4	0	3	1	0
Gearhart	1536	0	0	0		0	0	6	0	6	0	0
Gervais	2663	12	0	1		0	11	31	9	17	5	0
Gladstone	12083	17	1	9		1	6	308	36	229	43	8
Grants Pass	37317	96	0	17		29	50	2010	249	1554	207	10
Gresham	111491	424	5	71		113	235	3065	415	1837	813	20
Hermiston	17280	32	1	5		3	23	455	57	368	30	3
Hillsboro	104440	298	0	79		64	155	2010	232	1613	165	17
Hines	1517	7	0	0		0	7	47	10	34	3	0
Independence	9355	22	0	6		2	14	180	16	152	12	3
Jacksonville	2903	1	0	0		0	1	53	13	38	2	0
John Day	1667	4	0		0	0	4	96	9	79	8	0
Junction City	5935	3	0		0	2	1	29	2	25	2	0
Keizer	38165	66	2	4		12	48	771	89	630	52	4
King City	3804	2	1	0		0	1	37	7	27	3	0
Klamath Falls	22296	73	5		9	24	35	785	159	555	71	9
La Grande	13071	21	0	9		2	10	361	82	257	22	4
Lake Oswego	38860	31	0	9		5	17	446	62	370	14	5
Lebanon	16487	40	0	9		6	25	574	49	477	48	8
Lincoln City	8588	51	1	5		3	42	435	84	323	28	1
Madras	6735	22	0	2		3	17	240	43	173	24	0
Manzanita	627	1	0	0		0	1	10	0	7	3	0
McMinnville	34242	56	0	15		10	31	827	90	687	50	2
Medford	80794	407	1	31		115	260	5688	486	4793	409	48
Milwaukie	20935	29	0	5		11	13	445	48	311	86	3
Molalla	9064	22	0	5		4	13	285	68	206	11	9
Monmouth	10131	14	0	1		2	11	199	33	158	8	0
Mount Angel	3448	8	0	0		1	7	41	9	29	3	0
Myrtle Creek	3466	9	0	1		0	8	105	9	87	9	0
Newberg-Dundee	26105	33	0	16		5	12	443	64	355	24	1
North Plains	2131	1	0	1		0	0	27	4	23	0	0
Ontario	10925	22	0		0	6	16	739	115	587	37	5
Oregon City	36485	72	1	22		10	39	735	86	592	57	6
Pendleton	16927	46	0	11		4	31	492	63	403	26	3
Philomath	4602	2	0		2	0	0	70	6	62	2	0
Phoenix	4578	8	0	1		4	3	172	16	142	14	0
Pilot Rock	1514	3	0	1		0	2	16	5	10	1	0
Portland	642129	3163	14	389		986	1774	33087	4064	24099	4924	234
Prineville	9595	55	0	12		2	41	298	42	227	29	2
Rainier	1921	0	0		0	0	0	58	11	38	9	0
Redmond	29164	80	1	13		9	57	973	84	801	88	7
Reedsport	4098	7	0	0		0	7	141	18	116	7	4
Rockaway Beach	1354	5	0	0		0	5	64	19	39	6	0
Rogue River	2246	3	0	1		1	1	80	8	67	5	0
Roseburg	22159	43	0	8		9	26	1348	123	1122	103	13
Salem	166508	533	7	38		128	360	6661	907	5114	640	28
Sandy	10855	8	0	2		1	5	190	43	135	12	3
Scappoose	7005	12	0	5		3	4	61	5	48	8	1
Seaside	6556	12	1		1	5	5	491	60	421	10	0
Sherwood	19486	13	0	6		1	6	220	20	185	15	3
Silverton	9860	10	1	3		1	5	192	25	151	16	2
Springfield	61164	183	1	35		47	100	2958	315	2477	166	17
Stayton	8028	19	0	2		1	16	276	20	232	24	0
St. Helens	13184	38	0	9		3	26	327	40	260	27	2
Sunriver		4	0	1		0	3	65	17	46	2	0
Sutherlin	7932	15	0	3		0	12	179	22	132	25	0
Sweet Home	9337	9	0		3	2	4	431	53	365	13	2
Talent	6483	27	0	4		1	22	109	21	81	7	1

Table 6. Offenses Known to Law Enforcement, by Selected State and City, 2016—Continued

(Number.)

State/city	Population	Violent crime	Murder and nonnegligent manslaughter	Rape (revised definition)[1]	Rape (legacy definition)[2]	Robbery	Aggravated assault	Property crime	Burglary	Larceny-theft	Motor vehicle theft	Arson[3]
The Dalles	15413	20	0		5	8	7	486	82	375	29	5
Tigard	51885	125	0	23		38	64	1495	114	1298	83	12
Tillamook	5003	4	0	1		1	2	151	26	118	7	1
Toledo	3521	5	0	3		0	2	59	21	35	3	0
Tualatin	27370	52	0	7		13	32	723	64	614	45	4
Umatilla	7026	11	0	4		0	7	47	9	28	10	0
Vernonia	2139	5	0	0		0	5	10	1	8	1	0
Warrenton	5340	1	0		0	1	0	155	18	126	11	0
Winston	5396	16	0	1		2	13	177	36	130	11	2
Woodburn	25395	76	0	6		21	49	663	86	478	99	8
Yamhill	1109	1	0	0		0	1	21	5	15	1	0
PENNSYLVANIA												
Abington Township, Montgomery County	55623	49	0	5		28	16	1089	84	977	28	3
Adamstown	1848	1	0	0		0	1	17	6	11	0	0
Adams Township, Butler County	13531	5	0	1		0	4	46	2	44	0	0
Akron	4014	5	0	1		0	4	29	6	23	0	1
Albion	1459	7	0	1		0	6	25	12	13	0	1
Aldan	4168	7	0	1		1	5	80	7	72	1	1
Aleppo Township	1903	0	0	0		0	0	4	0	4	0	0
Allegheny Township, Blair County	6652	29	0	1		1	27	158	1	153	4	2
Allegheny Township, Westmoreland County	8213	7	0	0		2	5	75	17	58	0	0
Allentown	120615	552	10	55		274	213	3337	668	2387	282	18
Altoona	45158	156	1	23		37	95	821	169	619	33	7
Ambler	6517	10	2	3		1	4	67	3	61	3	0
Ambridge	6822	94	0	0		17	77	240	64	169	7	1
Amity Township	12884	9	1	2		4	2	99	23	75	1	0
Annville Township	4835	15	0	0		1	14	48	4	42	2	1
Apollo	1577	1	0	1		0	0	11	2	9	0	0
Archbald	6951	12	0	0		1	11	61	12	49	0	0
Armagh Township	3813	2	0	1		0	1	20	5	14	1	0
Ashley	2714	4	0	1		1	2	68	10	56	2	0
Aspinwall	2756	1	0	0		0	1	38	4	33	1	0
Aston Township	16828	7	0	1		5	1	184	21	154	9	1
Athens	3234	5	0	3		0	2	42	0	41	1	0
Athens Township	5058	5	0	2		3	0	185	9	175	1	0
Avalon	4630	21	0	0		2	19	72	4	62	6	0
Avis	1513	0	0	0		0	0	4	0	4	0	0
Avoca	2661	2	0	0		1	1	26	3	22	1	0
Avonmore Boro	976	0	0	0		0	0	0	0	0	0	0
Baden	4018	5	0	1		0	4	33	2	31	0	0
Baldwin Borough	19828	13	0	1		6	6	165	48	102	15	0
Bally	1105	1	0	0		0	1	0	0	0	0	0
Bangor	5189	37	0	1		3	33	80	11	64	5	1
Beaver	4399	8	0	1		2	5	85	5	76	4	1
Beaver Falls	8598	29	1	0		10	18	318	34	266	18	2
Bedford	2724	7	0	0		2	5	30	2	27	1	1
Bedminster Township	7123	2	0	0		0	2	29	8	20	1	0
Bell Acres	1396	0	0	0		0	0	5	1	4	0	0
Bellevue	8229	24	2	2		10	10	183	31	141	11	0
Bellwood	1779	2	0	0		0	2	39	3	35	1	0
Ben Avon	1776	0	0	0		0	0	26	2	24	0	0
Ben Avon Heights	377	0	0	0		0	0	9	1	8	0	0
Bensalem Township	60362	71	1	4		34	32	1626	122	1436	68	8
Berlin	2003	1	0	0		0	1	4	1	3	0	0
Bern Township	6967	5	0	0		2	3	66	4	59	3	0
Berwick	10170	25	0	6		2	17	240	23	211	6	1
Bethel Park	32077	22	0	0		7	15	308	23	282	3	1
Bethel Township, Berks County	4136	0	0	0		0	0	14	1	10	3	0
Bethlehem[5]	74869		4	21		58		1487	213	1226	48	7
Bethlehem Township	23869	31	0	6		4	21	384	29	345	10	4
Biglerville	1211	0	0	0		0	0	12	0	12	0	0
Birdsboro	5158	7	0	1		0	6	64	13	50	1	1
Birmingham Township	4272	0	0	0		0	0	16	2	13	1	0
Blairsville	3304	9	0	0		0	9	87	13	73	1	0
Blair Township	4564	0	0	0		0	0	36	5	30	1	0
Blakely	6289	5	0	0		1	4	68	8	59	1	0
Blawnox	1413	3	0	0		0	3	1	0	1	0	0
Blossburg	1512	1	0	0		0	1	4	1	3	0	0
Boyertown	4043	9	0	1		1	7	139	16	119	4	0
Brackenridge	3201	14	1	1		4	8	67	6	59	2	1
Braddock	2122	11	0	0		1	10	4	0	4	0	0
Braddock Hills	1857	3	0	0		0	3	22	4	18	0	0
Bradford	8459	81	0	4		2	75	239	27	205	7	4
Bradford Township	4814	9	0	0		0	9	15	2	13	0	1
Brecknock Township, Berks County	4636	1	0	0		0	1	31	10	20	1	1
Brentwood	9486	22	0	0		2	20	208	38	162	8	0

Table 6. Offenses Known to Law Enforcement, by Selected State and City, 2016—Continued

(Number.)

State/city	Population	Violent crime	Murder and nonnegligent manslaughter	Rape (revised definition)[1]	Rape (legacy definition)[2]	Robbery	Aggravated assault	Property crime	Burglary	Larceny-theft	Motor vehicle theft	Arson[3]
Briar Creek Township	3005	1	0	0		0	1	27	6	21	0	0
Bridgeville	5081	6	0	1		4	1	118	11	106	1	0
Bridgewater	690	3	0	0		0	3	16	3	13	0	0
Brighton Township	8434	6	0	0		0	6	22	4	18	0	0
Bristol	9539	17	1	1		6	9	210	26	172	12	0
Bristol Township	53978	103	1	14		50	38	1176	157	943	76	8
Brockway	2034	4	0	0		0	4	22	5	16	1	0
Brookhaven	8090	15	0	0		8	7	80	8	71	1	0
Brookville	3855	6	0	0		0	6	38	3	34	1	0
Brownsville	2285	9	0	1		3	5	31	5	22	4	0
Bryn Athyn	1397	0	0	0		0	0	10	0	10	0	0
Buckingham Township	20440	3	0	2		0	1	91	5	81	5	0
Buffalo Township	7258	8	1	1		0	6	86	11	72	3	0
Buffalo Valley Regional	12284	3	0	0		1	2	104	18	86	0	1
Burgettstown	1345	4	1	1		1	1	36	11	23	2	0
Bushkill Township	8430	15	0	0		1	14	31	1	29	1	0
Butler Township, Butler County	16713	25	0	1		5	19	374	26	342	6	1
Butler Township, Luzerne County	9713	19	0	1		0	18	72	18	53	1	0
Butler Township, Schuylkill County	5657	3	0	0		2	1	18	5	13	0	0
Caernarvon Township, Berks County	4074	4	0	0		1	3	82	10	68	4	0
California	7004	11	0	2		1	8	87	6	80	1	1
Callery	389	0	0	0		0	0	0	0	0	0	0
Caln Township	14167	53	0	4		7	42	356	17	329	10	0
Cambria Township	5885	5	0	2		0	3	81	2	76	3	0
Cambridge Springs	2528	2	0	0		0	2	3	1	2	0	0
Camp Hill	7929	4	0	0		3	1	57	7	49	1	0
Canonsburg	8909	10	0	0		2	8	49	4	45	0	0
Canton	1910	3	0	0		0	3	14	3	11	0	0
Carbondale	8503	4	0	1		1	2	90	12	73	5	0
Carlisle	19225	25	1	7		11	6	400	44	345	11	2
Carnegie	7923	7	0	0		1	6	135	22	98	15	0
Carrolltown	810	4	0	0		0	4	8	0	8	0	0
Carroll Township, Washington County	5539	9	0	0		0	9	50	9	36	5	0
Carroll Township, York County	6309	4	0	1		0	3	63	8	55	0	0
Carroll Valley	3954	2	0	2		0	0	35	0	35	0	0
Cass Township	1900	1	0	0		0	1	4	1	1	2	0
Castle Shannon	8219	12	0	1		4	7	62	14	44	4	0
Catasauqua	6543	6	0	0		3	3	71	9	57	5	0
Catawissa	1506	3	0	0		0	3	16	2	14	0	0
Cecil Township	12059	3	1	0		0	2	69	11	56	2	0
Center Township	11750	33	0	0		5	28	346	19	321	6	1
Central Berks Regional	9458	12	0	4		3	5	202	26	161	15	3
Central Bucks Regional	15380	12	0	4		2	6	145	8	128	9	0
Chambersburg	20770	87	2	14		27	44	630	83	527	20	5
Charleroi Regional	6630	35	0	2		15	18	222	21	198	3	0
Chartiers Township	7960	6	0	1		0	5	57	12	42	3	2
Cheltenham Township	37064	61	2	2		41	16	944	121	789	34	5
Cherry Tree	350	0	0	0		0	0	0	0	0	0	0
Chester	34109	536	23	30		210	273	1049	300	649	100	21
Chester Township	4130	41	0	1		10	30	95	25	55	15	0
Cheswick	1727	0	0	0		0	0	18	3	14	1	0
Chippewa Township	8192	4	0	0		3	1	198	6	188	4	0
Christiana	1171	6	0	0		0	6	15	0	14	1	0
Churchill	2973	26	0	0		0	26	22	5	15	2	0
Clarion	6284	3	0	1		1	1	46	6	38	2	1
Clarks Summit	6336	6	0	0		3	3	22	2	20	0	0
Clearfield	5996	56	0	0		3	53	173	14	156	3	0
Cleona	2146	0	0	0		0	0	10	2	7	1	0
Clifton Heights	6691	27	0	0		2	25	103	14	82	7	0
Coaldale	2181	4	0	0		0	4	7	0	7	0	0
Coal Township	10480	9	0	1		0	8	168	25	140	3	1
Coatesville	13157	111	8	1		38	64	329	52	251	26	2
Cochranton	1104	0	0	0		0	0	1	0	1	0	0
Colebrookdale District	6007	5	0	2		1	2	120	7	109	4	1
Collegeville	5327	5	0	1		2	2	45	11	33	1	2
Collier Township	8096	7	0	1		4	2	159	25	133	1	0
Collingdale	8794	89	0	1		15	73	219	36	159	24	0
Colonial Regional	20361	3	0	1		2	0	506	41	458	7	2
Columbia	10385	23	1	7		7	8	218	32	174	12	0
Conemaugh Township, Cambria County	1910	3	0	1		0	2	11	3	7	1	0
Conemaugh Township, Somerset County	6961	9	0	0		2	7	40	13	27	0	0
Conewago Township, Adams County	7200	5	1	1		0	3	48	5	43	0	0
Conewango Township	3422	11	0	0		0	11	86	6	79	1	1
Conneaut Lake Regional	3505	1	0	0		0	1	44	15	28	1	0

Table 6. Offenses Known to Law Enforcement, by Selected State and City, 2016—Continued

(Number.)

State/city	Population	Violent crime	Murder and nonnegligent manslaughter	Rape (revised definition)[1]	Rape (legacy definition)[2]	Robbery	Aggravated assault	Property crime	Burglary	Larceny-theft	Motor vehicle theft	Arson[3]
Connellsville	7492	25	0	5		11	9	299	53	239	7	4
Conoy Township	3472	1	0	0		0	1	40	5	35	0	0
Conshohocken	7979	2	1	0		1	0	102	5	84	13	2
Conway	2145	1	0	0		0	1	15	1	12	2	0
Conyngham	1874	0	0	0		0	0	17	2	15	0	0
Coopersburg	2428	1	0	0		0	1	26	6	16	4	0
Coplay	3236	2	0	0		0	2	49	9	39	1	0
Coraopolis	5573	41	0	3		5	33	141	28	106	7	0
Cornwall	4249	1	0	1		0	0	2	1	1	0	0
Corry	6384	35	0	3		0	32	198	21	173	4	0
Coudersport	2469	15	0	0		0	15	6	0	6	0	0
Courtdale	736	0	0	0		0	0	2	1	1	0	0
Covington Township	2265	3	0	0		0	3	53	14	38	1	2
Crafton	6316	19	0	0		5	14	234	17	212	5	0
Cranberry Township	30940	15	0	2		4	9	391	23	363	5	2
Crescent Township	2601	4	0	0		0	4	21	5	14	2	1
Cresson	1619	1	0	0		1	0	22	0	22	0	0
Cresson Township	2562	0	0	0		0	0	6	0	6	0	0
Croyle Township	2274	0	0	0		0	0	10	1	8	1	0
Cumberland Township, Adams County	6243	5	0	1		0	4	38	11	27	0	0
Cumru Township	15385	15	0	1		4	10	254	36	208	10	0
Curwensville	2461	15	0	3		0	12	29	6	22	1	1
Dallas	2779	6	0	1		0	5	21	1	20	0	0
Dalton	1204	1	0	0		0	1	32	7	24	1	0
Danville	4686	23	0	1		2	20	84	4	79	1	0
Darby	10687	228	3	5		69	151	398	110	248	40	0
Darby Township	9329	38	0	1		14	23	148	12	129	7	0
Darlington Township	1921	1	0	0		0	1	33	10	23	0	0
Delano Township	423	0	0	0		0	0	0	0	0	0	0
Delaware Water Gap	707	0	0	0		0	0	0	0	0	0	0
Delmont	2631	2	0	0		0	2	18	2	16	0	0
Denver	3877	6	0	3		3	0	28	2	25	1	0
Derry Township, Dauphin County	25044	26	0	3		3	20	349	49	293	7	4
Dickson City	5839	16	0	1		0	15	304	11	291	2	0
Dormont	8440	9	0	0		4	5	103	11	84	8	0
Douglass Township, Berks County	3554	0	0	0		0	0	21	2	16	3	0
Douglass Township, Montgomery County	10475	13	0	1		2	10	125	10	112	3	0
Downingtown	7957	16	0	0		3	13	189	13	166	10	0
Doylestown Township	17539	9	0	2		1	6	187	11	168	8	0
Dublin Borough	2171	4	0	0		0	4	12	0	12	0	0
Du Bois	7561	30	0	10		0	20	218	29	187	2	1
Duboistown	1208	0	0	0		0	0	0	0	0	0	0
Dunbar	1014	1	0	0		0	1	0	0	0	0	0
Duncansville	1198	0	0	0		0	0	14	3	11	0	0
Dunmore	13247	40	0	3		5	32	237	46	182	9	3
Dunnstable Township	1019	0	0	0		0	0	1	0	1	0	0
Dupont	2714	10	0	1		1	8	28	12	16	0	0
Duquesne	5528	69	0	10		21	38	230	94	114	22	8
Duryea	4935	20	0	2		2	16	67	8	55	4	1
Earl Township	7191	0	0	0		0	0	43	10	31	2	0
East Bangor	1655	0	0	0		0	0	15	3	12	0	0
East Bethlehem Township	2288	12	0	2		0	10	22	2	19	1	0
East Brandywine Township	8642	13	0	2		0	11	29	7	21	1	0
East Cocalico Township	10502	7	0	2		2	3	71	16	49	6	0
East Conemaugh	1448	5	0	0		0	5	21	9	12	0	0
East Coventry Township	6767	2	0	0		0	2	50	6	43	1	0
East Earl Township	6848	1	0	0		1	0	70	9	60	1	1
Eastern Adams Regional	7403	19	0	1		2	16	65	12	53	0	0
Eastern Pike Regional	4614	16	1	5		1	9	155	9	142	4	0
East Fallowfield Township	7590	2	0	0		0	2	39	9	30	0	0
East Franklin Township	3949	0	0	0		0	0	18	1	17	0	0
East Hempfield Township	24462	13	0	4		6	3	316	36	278	2	0
East Lampeter Township	17090	37	0	0		12	25	614	37	565	12	1
East Lansdowne	2665	12	0	0		6	6	88	12	72	4	3
East Marlborough Township	7334	0	0	0		0	0	38	3	35	0	0
East Norriton Township	14171	18	0	0		3	15	280	11	256	13	1
Easton	26938	74	1	7		34	32	445	47	366	32	5
East Pennsboro Township	21712	13	0	3		4	6	158	34	122	2	2
East Petersburg	4528	3	0	2		1	0	16	3	13	0	0
East Pikeland Township	7411	5	0	1		0	4	49	7	41	1	2
East Rochester	547	0	0	0		0	0	19	0	19	0	0
East Taylor Township	2577	3	0	1		2	0	8	3	4	1	0
Easttown Township	10644	1	0	0		0	1	98	9	84	5	0
East Union Township	1591	1	0	0		0	1	2	0	2	0	1
East Vincent Township	6938	2	0	1		0	1	43	9	34	0	1
East Washington	1959	8	0	0		0	8	24	4	20	0	0
East Whiteland Township	10711	6	0	0		1	5	120	12	106	2	0
Ebensburg	3175	7	0	0		0	7	21	1	18	2	0
Economy	9389	0	0	0		0	0	134	3	130	1	0

Table 6. Offenses Known to Law Enforcement, by Selected State and City, 2016—Continued

(Number.)

State/city	Population	Violent crime	Murder and nonnegligent manslaughter	Rape (revised definition)[1]	Rape (legacy definition)[2]	Robbery	Aggravated assault	Property crime	Burglary	Larceny-theft	Motor vehicle theft	Arson[3]
Eddystone	2407	13	0	0		7	6	277	11	264	2	0
Edgewood	3059	5	0	0		5	0	148	9	138	1	0
Edinboro	6316	6	0	1		0	5	60	13	45	2	0
Edwardsville	4716	16	0	2		0	14	156	7	149	0	0
Elderton	346	0	0	0		0	0	0	0	0	0	0
Elizabethtown	11592	12	0	7		1	4	192	16	176	0	1
Elizabeth Township	13216	4	0	0		1	3	124	44	78	2	0
Elkland	1771	8	0	0		3	5	55	13	42	0	0
Elk Lick Township	2143	0	0	0		0	0	0	0	0	0	0
Ellwood City	7561	26	0	0		3	23	147	15	125	7	1
Emlenton Borough	595	2	0	0		0	2	12	1	11	0	0
Emmaus	11398	6	1	0		4	1	156	21	130	5	0
Emporium	1908	5	0	0		0	5	39	2	37	0	1
Emsworth	2413	1	0	0		0	1	20	2	18	0	0
Ephrata	13955	30	0	3		6	21	172	20	147	5	0
Ephrata Township	10309	9	0	1		3	5	151	13	136	2	2
Erie	99019	353	10	46		115	182	2278	567	1607	104	29
Etna	3391	13	2	0		0	11	48	5	40	3	0
Everett	1745	1	0	1		0	0	18	0	14	4	0
Exeter Township, Berks County	25930	21	0	4		3	14	404	21	379	4	0
Fairfield	509	0	0	0		0	0	9	2	6	1	0
Fairview Township, Luzerne County	4486	0	0	0		0	0	36	6	28	2	0
Fairview Township, York County	17312	25	0	4		3	18	191	28	157	6	0
Falls Township, Bucks County	33823	68	3	9		21	35	722	85	596	41	0
Fawn Township	2348	0	0	0		0	0	14	3	7	4	0
Ferguson Township	19222	5	1	2		1	1	138	26	110	2	1
Findlay Township	5637	2	0	0		0	2	55	15	38	2	0
Fleetwood	4085	14	0	1		2	11	112	47	61	4	3
Ford City	2857	11	0	0		1	10	29	6	22	1	1
Forest City	1789	5	0	0		1	4	39	6	32	1	0
Forks Township	15390	6	0	3		2	1	92	11	79	2	0
Forty Fort	4109	7	0	0		1	6	50	4	44	2	0
Foster Township, McKean County	4191	2	0	0		0	2	54	3	51	0	0
Foster Township, Schuykill County	253	1	0	0		0	1	4	0	4	0	0
Fountain Hill	4635	13	0	4		2	7	106	13	89	4	0
Fox Chapel	5381	1	0	0		0	1	34	5	27	2	0
Frackville	3715	4	0	0		1	3	22	3	16	3	0
Franconia Township	13272	6	0	0		0	6	90	11	78	1	0
Franklin	6255	17	0	1		1	15	129	22	102	5	1
Franklin Park	14600	1	0	0		1	0	76	27	48	1	0
Franklin Township, Beaver County	3970	4	0	0		1	3	47	4	43	0	1
Franklin Township, Carbon County	4134	15	0	0		0	15	38	11	25	2	1
Franklin Township, Columbia County	588	0	0	0		0	0	0	0	0	0	0
Frazer Township	1159	2	0	1		1	0	228	3	224	1	0
Freedom	1521	8	0	1		1	6	26	6	19	1	0
Freedom Township	3418	1	0	0		0	1	69	4	64	1	1
Freemansburg	2611	2	0	0		0	2	17	3	13	1	0
Freeport	1730	1	0	1		0	0	4	0	4	0	0
Gaines Township	547	0	0	0		0	0	6	1	5	0	0
Galeton	1119	5	0	1		2	2	21	8	13	0	0
Gallitzin	1828	1	0	0		0	1	12	2	10	0	0
Gallitzin Township	1281	0	0	0		0	0	0	0	0	0	0
Garrett	432	0	0	0		0	0	2	0	2	0	0
Geistown	2353	0	0	0		0	0	2	0	2	0	0
Gettysburg	7608	31	0	4		1	26	106	14	90	2	3
Girard	3007	2	0	0		0	2	33	4	28	1	0
Girardville	1480	4	0	0		0	4	9	4	5	0	0
Glassport	4408	23	0	0		8	15	150	18	123	9	1
Glenolden	7177	8	0	1		4	3	163	16	143	4	1
Granville Township	5046	3	0	0		0	3	104	4	98	2	1
Great Bend	686	1	0	0		0	1	2	0	2	0	0
Greencastle	4051	5	0	0		1	4	30	4	26	0	0
Greenfield Township, Blair County	4075	4	0	0		0	4	24	2	22	0	1
Greensburg	14419	47	0	8		10	29	355	47	300	8	3
Green Tree	5089	7	1	0		0	6	50	14	36	0	0
Greenville	5794	15	0	1		0	14	100	18	77	5	1
Grove City	8169	4	0	0		2	2	105	15	88	2	0
Halifax	831	0	0	0		0	0	11	2	8	1	0
Hamburg	4420	20	0	0		0	20	77	16	56	5	1
Hampden Township	29684	11	0	2		6	3	235	30	202	3	0
Hanover	15537	23	0	0		9	14	418	43	371	4	2
Hanover Township, Luzerne County	10901	27	0	1		6	20	242	55	184	3	1

Table 6. Offenses Known to Law Enforcement, by Selected State and City, 2016—Continued

(Number.)

State/city	Population	Violent crime	Murder and nonnegligent manslaughter	Rape (revised definition)[1]	Rape (legacy definition)[2]	Robbery	Aggravated assault	Property crime	Burglary	Larceny-theft	Motor vehicle theft	Arson[3]
Harmar Township	3100	7	0	1		2	4	95	6	86	3	0
Harrisburg	48996	526	13	54		160	299	1342	404	803	135	27
Harrisville	876	0	0	0		0	0	2	0	2	0	0
Hartleton	285	0	0	0		0	0	0	0	0	0	0
Harveys Lake	2763	3	0	0		0	3	13	1	12	0	0
Hatfield Township	20925	16	0	2		8	6	259	59	184	16	0
Haverford Township	49168	25	0	5		10	10	696	62	605	29	0
Hawley	1140	1	0	0		1	0	4	0	4	0	0
Hazleton	24725	93	1	8		45	39	360	125	208	27	3
Hegins Township	3457	2	0	0		1	1	15	4	10	1	0
Heidelberg	1228	4	0	0		0	4	5	2	2	1	0
Heidelberg Township, Berks County	1740	3	0	0		0	3	3	1	2	0	0
Hellam Township	8666	15	0	2		1	12	51	11	37	3	0
Hellertown	5809	8	0	0		1	7	59	9	47	3	0
Hemlock Township	2266	0	0	0		0	0	113	6	106	1	0
Hempfield Township, Mercer County	3705	10	0	0		1	9	124	15	106	3	0
Hermitage	15958	30	1	0		6	23	487	45	429	13	0
Highspire	2374	9	0	0		3	6	85	10	75	0	0
Hilltown Township	15308	10	0	3		2	5	231	20	204	7	0
Hollidaysburg	5782	7	0	1		0	6	28	1	26	1	1
Homestead	3104	54	2	3		23	26	371	42	311	18	0
Honesdale	4185	7	0	2		3	2	84	22	61	1	1
Honey Brook	1766	2	0	0		0	2	0	0	0	0	0
Hopewell Township	12466	21	0	1		2	18	144	25	116	3	1
Horsham Township	26669	10	0	2		2	6	230	15	194	21	3
Houston	1260	1	0	0		1	0	20	2	17	1	0
Hughestown	1398	4	0	0		1	3	14	2	12	0	0
Hughesville	2093	3	0	0		1	2	15	0	15	0	0
Hulmeville	995	0	0	0		0	0	6	4	1	1	0
Hummelstown	4565	10	0	1		1	8	76	10	60	6	1
Huntingdon	7017	16	0	0		0	16	80	5	74	1	0
Independence Township, Beaver County	2442	1	0	0		1	0	9	3	6	0	0
Independence Township, Washington County	1513	0	0	0		0	0	5	0	5	0	0
Indiana Township	7267	0	0	0		0	0	35	9	22	4	0
Indian Lake	388	0	0	0		0	0	2	2	0	0	0
Ingram	3271	3	0	0		3	0	38	3	35	0	0
Irwin	3838	8	0	0		0	8	48	9	35	4	0
Jackson Township, Butler County	3708	3	0	0		0	3	21	13	8	0	0
Jackson Township, Cambria County	4180	3	0	0		0	3	2	0	2	0	0
Jackson Township, Luzerne County	4648	1	0	0		0	1	13	4	7	2	0
Jamestown	591	1	0	0		0	1	3	0	3	0	0
Jeannette	9274	10	0	0		3	7	78	16	62	0	0
Jefferson Hills Borough	11505	9	2	0		0	7	88	12	68	8	0
Jefferson Township, Lackawanna County	3675	0	0	0		0	0	6	0	6	0	0
Jefferson Township, Mercer County	1875	0	0	0		0	0	9	5	4	0	0
Jefferson Township, Washington County	1161	0	0	0		0	0	0	0	0	0	0
Jenkins Township	4453	2	0	0		1	1	64	16	42	6	0
Jennerstown	664	1	0	0		0	1	4	2	2	0	0
Jermyn	2082	10	0	0		0	10	34	10	23	1	0
Jessup	4460	10	0	0		0	10	18	3	15	0	3
Jim Thorpe	4614	18	0	2		1	15	99	18	79	2	0
Johnsonburg	2351	0	0	0		0	0	43	14	29	0	0
Johnstown	21227	100	5	2		20	73	633	198	416	19	4
Kane	3588	0	0	0		0	0	58	22	35	1	0
Kenhorst	2865	2	1	1		0	0	59	6	50	3	0
Kennett Square	6188	8	0	2		3	3	69	15	47	7	0
Kennett Township	8294	2	0	0		2	0	63	13	49	1	1
Kidder Township	1935	7	0	1		1	5	47	4	41	2	0
Kilbuck Township	689	0	0	0		0	0	8	0	8	0	0
Kingston	12894	34	0	2		15	17	232	30	196	6	3
Kingston Township	6963	12	1	0		0	11	45	4	40	1	0
Kiskiminetas Township	4611	3	0	0		2	1	18	3	15	0	0
Knox	1091	4	0	1		0	3	7	0	7	0	0
Kutztown	5032	14	0	2		1	11	93	15	73	5	0
Lake City	2952	8	1	0		0	7	39	6	33	0	0
Lancaster	59340	487	4	92		164	227	2164	255	1828	81	17
Lancaster Township, Butler County	2520	4	0	0		0	4	15	2	13	0	0
Lancaster Township, Lancaster County	17244	18	0	0		10	8	342	33	298	11	0
Lanesboro	474	0	0	0		0	0	0	0	0	0	0
Langhorne Manor	1429	0	0	0		0	0	7	2	5	0	0
Lansdale	16558	18	0	3		3	12	196	18	173	5	2

Table 6. Offenses Known to Law Enforcement, by Selected State and City, 2016—Continued

(Number.)

State/city	Population	Violent crime	Murder and nonnegligent manslaughter	Rape (revised definition)[1]	Rape (legacy definition)[2]	Robbery	Aggravated assault	Property crime	Burglary	Larceny-theft	Motor vehicle theft	Arson[3]
Lansdowne	10643	20	0	3		10	7	280	58	206	16	0
Lansford	3771	33	0	1		2	30	47	4	41	2	1
Latrobe	8032	26	1	3		2	20	132	16	112	4	0
Laureldale	3882	6	0	1		1	4	34	7	25	2	0
Lawrence Park Township	3830	4	0	0		0	4	7	0	6	1	0
Lawrence Township, Clearfield County	7489	61	0	1		0	60	150	10	137	3	5
Lawrence Township, Tioga County	1697	6	0	0		0	6	0	0	0	0	0
Lebanon	25549	60	1	3		16	40	619	129	441	49	6
Leetsdale	1195	2	0	1		1	0	47	12	32	3	0
Leet Township	1616	0	0	0		0	0	14	0	14	0	0
Lehigh Township, Northampton County	10344	11	0	0		0	11	83	17	64	2	0
Lehigh Township, Wayne County	1776	1	0	0		0	1	4	1	3	0	0
Lehman Township	3474	9	0	0		1	8	25	9	15	1	0
Lewistown	8260	25	0	2		0	23	288	36	247	5	0
Liberty	2514	2	0	0		0	2	4	1	2	1	0
Ligonier	1534	0	0	0		0	0	1	0	0	1	0
Limerick Township	18939	5	0	0		1	4	319	25	285	9	0
Linesville	990	1	0	0		0	1	4	1	3	0	0
Lititz	9232	2	0	1		1	0	37	3	33	1	2
Little Beaver Township	1357	0	0	0		0	0	0	0	0	0	0
Littlestown	4486	6	1	3		1	1	55	5	49	1	1
Lock Haven	9572	15	0	3		3	9	152	17	134	1	2
Locust Township	1414	2	0	2		0	0	18	6	12	0	1
Logan Township	12313	8	0	3		1	4	189	1	182	6	1
Loretto	1392	0	0	0		0	0	4	0	4	0	0
Lower Allen Township	19206	19	0	3		6	10	343	21	315	7	8
Lower Burrell	11408	20	0	1		0	19	146	14	128	4	0
Lower Frederick Township	4901	1	0	0		0	1	35	11	21	3	0
Lower Gwynedd Township	11574	17	0	0		1	16	144	16	119	9	0
Lower Heidelberg Township	6059	15	0	0		1	14	25	1	23	1	0
Lower Merion Township	58234	28	0	0		18	10	1068	136	882	50	0
Lower Moreland Township	13261	8	0	2		1	5	179	26	147	6	0
Lower Paxton Township	48582	74	0	22		12	40	643	79	545	19	9
Lower Pottsgrove Township	12194	12	0	1		1	10	193	21	164	8	0
Lower Providence Township	26333	57	0	4		7	46	265	38	214	13	1
Lower Salford Township	15415	10	0	0		2	8	63	6	57	0	0
Lower Saucon Township	10764	8	0	0		0	8	74	10	63	1	0
Lower Southampton Township	19185	60	0	2		12	46	325	38	281	6	1
Lower Swatara Township	8881	1	0	1		0	0	106	16	90	0	0
Lower Windsor Township	7486	3	0	0		1	2	57	6	43	8	0
Macungie	3146	0	0	0		0	0	11	4	5	2	0
Madison Township	1607	1	0	0		0	1	2	0	1	1	0
Mahoning Township, Carbon County[4]	4211	18	0	1		0	17		11		3	0
Mahoning Township, Montour County	4275	17	0	1		0	16	37	0	36	1	0
Malvern	3527	6	0	0		1	5	29	2	27	0	0
Manheim	4871	19	0	2		4	13	135	25	106	4	1
Manheim Township	39930	20	0	4		8	8	546	54	474	18	1
Manor	3310	3	0	0		1	2	17	2	14	1	0
Manor Township, Lancaster County	20778	33	0	4		1	28	153	13	134	6	1
Mansfield	3395	4	0	0		1	3	8	0	8	0	0
Marcus Hook	2397	25	0	1		3	21	58	8	47	3	0
Marietta	2612	2	0	1		0	1	36	9	27	0	0
Marion Township, Beaver County	899	0	0	0		0	0	0	0	0	0	0
Marion Township, Berks County	1843	1	0	0		0	1	9	2	7	0	0
Marlborough Township	3332	3	0	0		0	3	13	3	10	0	0
Marple Township	23805	9	0	0		4	5	298	23	270	5	0
Martinsburg	1903	2	0	1		1	0	7	1	6	0	0
Marysville	2535	4	0	0		0	4	16	0	16	0	0
Masontown	3389	7	0	1		2	4	57	8	48	1	0
Mayfield	1723	0	0	0		0	0	0	0	0	0	0
McAdoo	2187	0	0	0		0	0	34	1	31	2	0
McCandless	28902	13	0	0		1	12	227	13	211	3	0
McDonald Borough	2085	1	0	0		0	1	43	4	38	1	0
McSherrystown	3072	3	0	0		0	3	23	2	21	0	0
Meadville	12999	26	0	1		12	13	233	35	191	7	1
Mechanicsburg	9003	6	0	0		2	4	140	15	124	1	3
Media	5370	34	0	2		5	27	58	3	54	1	1
Mercersburg	1557	2	0	1		0	1	22	6	16	0	0
Meshoppen	1452	16	0	0		0	16	46	8	35	3	0
Middleburg	1313	2	0	1		1	0	30	8	20	2	1
Middlesex Township, Butler County	5640	0	0	0		0	0	32	2	27	3	0

Table 6. Offenses Known to Law Enforcement, by Selected State and City, 2016—Continued

(Number.)

State/city	Population	Violent crime	Murder and nonnegligent manslaughter	Rape (revised definition)[1]	Rape (legacy definition)[2]	Robbery	Aggravated assault	Property crime	Burglary	Larceny-theft	Motor vehicle theft	Arson[3]
Middlesex Township, Cumberland County	7364	14	0	5		4	5	125	17	107	1	0
Middletown	9153	28	0	1		3	24	125	55	70	0	0
Middletown Township	45408	37	0	0		11	26	901	92	780	29	3
Midway	890	1	0	0		0	1	10	1	8	1	0
Mifflinburg	3516	6	0	0		0	6	12	3	9	0	0
Mifflin County Regional	16889	20	0	2		3	15	160	21	132	7	0
Milford	972	4	0	1		1	2	30	13	17	0	0
Millbourne	1162	11	0	0		6	5	28	9	19	0	0
Millcreek Township, Lebanon County	5600	1	0	0		0	1	13	3	9	1	0
Millersburg	2532	7	0	0		0	7	36	16	20	0	0
Millersville	8471	9	0	2		5	2	79	13	66	0	0
Mill Hall	1615	0	0	0		0	0	0	0	0	0	0
Millvale	3678	2	0	1		0	1	79	1	77	1	0
Millville	953	0	0	0		0	0	0	0	0	0	0
Minersville	4232	17	0	0		0	17	26	6	17	3	0
Mohnton	3034	2	0	0		0	2	27	8	19	0	0
Monaca	5631	14	0	0		5	9	75	22	46	7	0
Monessen	7438	64	0	1		8	55	148	29	110	9	1
Monongahela	4172	17	0	1		3	13	116	15	95	6	0
Monroeville	28142	71	0	5		11	55	524	25	478	21	1
Montgomery	1553	0	0	0		0	0	0	0	0	0	0
Montgomery Township	26272	13	0	0		6	7	386	15	368	3	2
Montoursville	4536	8	0	1		3	4	86	3	81	2	0
Montour Township	1314	3	0	0		1	2	8	0	7	1	0
Moon Township	25845	19	0	4		2	13	253	45	204	4	0
Moore Township	9235	8	0	1		0	7	67	7	56	4	0
Moosic	5758	22	0	0		3	19	198	25	162	11	0
Morrisville	8581	10	0	1		7	2	205	34	161	10	1
Morton	2700	4	0	0		2	2	86	7	79	0	0
Moscow	1947	3	0	1		0	2	8	2	6	0	0
Mount Carmel	5698	29	0	7		3	19	122	34	85	3	2
Mount Carmel Township	3057	8	0	0		1	7	19	1	18	0	0
Mount Gretna Borough	197	0	0	0		0	0	0	0	0	0	0
Mount Holly Springs	2038	4	0	0		1	3	27	3	23	1	0
Mount Joy	8204	30	0	6		1	23	110	15	92	3	5
Mount Lebanon	32692	27	0	4		8	15	343	37	297	9	0
Mount Oliver	3344	54	0	2		25	27	135	46	87	2	1
Mount Pleasant Township	3510	2	0	0		0	2	18	7	10	1	0
Mountville	2862	4	0	1		2	1	23	4	19	0	0
Muhlenberg Township	20181	24	0	0		9	15	515	83	424	8	0
Muncy Township	1091	0	0	0		0	0	95	2	93	0	0
Murrysville	20142	9	0	2		3	4	148	6	141	1	0
Nanticoke	10218	20	0	6		5	9	205	35	165	5	0
Nanty Glo	2575	0	0	0		0	0	5	2	3	0	0
Narberth	4314	5	0	1		2	2	25	0	23	2	0
Neshannock Township	9319	5	0	0		3	2	39	9	29	1	0
Neville Township	1065	1	0	0		0	1	29	1	28	0	0
New Beaver	1441	1	0	0		0	1	0	0	0	0	0
New Berlin	866	1	0	0		0	1	3	1	2	0	0
Newberry Township	15470	20	0	3		4	13	251	38	203	10	0
New Bethlehem	2741	2	0	1		0	1	1	0	1	0	0
New Brighton	8991	29	0	3		6	20	393	53	335	5	0
New Castle	22211	124	3	6		53	62	676	236	401	39	6
New Castle Township	390	0	0	0		0	0	2	0	2	0	0
New Cumberland	7297	3	0	2		0	1	63	6	55	2	0
New Garden Township	12113	10	0	0		2	8	88	15	66	7	0
New Hanover Township	12814	3	0	0		0	3	53	6	43	4	2
New Holland	5439	1	0	0		1	0	80	5	69	6	0
New Hope	2507	8	0	1		1	6	29	3	24	2	0
New Sewickley Township	7454	3	0	0		1	2	114	23	85	6	0
Newtown Township, Bucks County	22914	8	0	2		0	6	183	21	158	4	0
Newtown Township, Delaware County	12864	11	0	4		3	4	94	12	78	4	0
New Wilmington	2190	1	0	0		0	1	22	0	22	0	0
Norristown	34425	148	2	2		83	61	618	95	465	58	0
Northampton	9846	7	1	0		1	5	109	12	92	5	1
Northampton Township	39559	6	0	1		0	5	222	16	192	14	0
North Beaver	3993	0	0	0		0	0	5	1	3	1	0
North Belle Vernon	1892	10	0	0		1	9	60	5	52	3	0
North Braddock	4773	7	0	0		0	7	7	4	2	1	0
North Catasauqua	2824	5	0	1		0	4	40	5	32	3	1
North Cornwall Township	7811	19	0	0		2	17	160	10	148	2	0
North Coventry Township	8054	2	0	0		0	2	204	22	177	5	2
Northeast, Bradford County	414	0	0	0		0	0	1	1	0	0	0
North East, Erie County	4148	7	0	3		0	4	111	9	99	3	0
Northeastern Regional	11655	23	0	5		0	18	133	11	120	2	10
Northern Berks Regional	13228	4	0	1		2	1	137	35	93	9	1
Northern Cambria Borough	3625	8	0	0		0	8	28	9	18	1	1
Northern Lancaster County Regional	34756	7	0	0		1	6	233	30	192	11	0

Table 6. Offenses Known to Law Enforcement, by Selected State and City, 2016—Continued

(Number.)

State/city	Population	Violent crime	Murder and nonnegligent manslaughter	Rape (revised definition)[1]	Rape (legacy definition)[2]	Robbery	Aggravated assault	Property crime	Burglary	Larceny-theft	Motor vehicle theft	Arson[3]
Northern Regional	34787	2	0	0		0	2	194	0	192	2	0
Northern York Regional	68894	50	2	3		8	37	737	85	615	37	7
North Franklin Township	4601	10	0	2		2	6	131	12	118	1	0
North Hopewell Township	2798	2	0	1		0	1	11	2	9	0	0
North Huntingdon Township	30787	14	0	4		0	10	541	42	472	27	0
North Lebanon Township	11839	15	0	0		3	12	261	32	224	5	0
North Londonderry Township	8420	0	0	0		0	0	190	12	178	0	0
North Middleton Township	11542	9	0	1		0	8	107	6	100	1	1
North Sewickley Township	5513	10	0	0		0	10	66	11	51	4	0
North Strabane Township	14523	10	0	1		1	8	127	20	100	7	3
Northumberland	3715	1	0	0		0	1	43	8	34	1	0
North Versailles Township	12322	41	0	2		6	33	260	25	228	7	1
North Wales	3254	8	1	0		0	7	54	7	47	0	0
Northwest Lancaster County Regional	19732	7	0	4		1	2	146	0	144	2	0
Norwood	5899	6	0	0		2	4	63	4	57	2	0
Oakdale	1472	0	0	0		0	0	0	0	0	0	0
Oakland	574	0	0	0		0	0	3	3	0	0	0
Oakmont	6472	9	1	2		0	6	90	32	55	3	0
O'Hara Township	8591	2	0	0		0	2	34	6	24	4	0
Ohio Township	6401	0	0	0		0	0	92	4	88	0	0
Ohioville	3461	10	0	0		0	10	19	3	16	0	0
Oil City	10057	30	0	4		0	26	164	5	158	1	3
Old Forge	7996	13	0	0		5	8	106	21	82	3	0
Old Lycoming Township	5059	4	0	0		1	3	123	13	109	1	0
Oley Township	3736	2	0	1		0	1	18	4	13	1	0
Orwigsburg	2983	5	0	0		0	5	27	1	25	1	0
Otto Eldred Regional	2327	0	0	0		0	0	6	0	6	0	0
Oxford	5449	20	0	2		2	16	99	15	81	3	0
Palmerton	5282	6	0	1		2	3	93	24	68	1	0
Palmer Township	21492	26	1	7		4	14	256	30	218	8	0
Palmyra	7476	21	1	0		1	19	102	15	83	4	0
Patterson Township	2962	2	0	0		1	1	81	14	64	3	0
Patton	1665	4	0	0		0	4	7	1	6	0	1
Patton Township	16027	4	0	4		0	0	164	14	150	0	0
Penbrook	2968	10	0	1		3	6	73	16	52	5	2
Penn	474	3	0	0		0	3	0	0	0	0	0
Penndel	2200	3	0	0		0	3	23	2	21	0	0
Penn Hills	41841	167	4	17		40	106	926	168	682	76	16
Pennridge Regional	11029	9	0	1		0	8	52	6	46	0	0
Penn Township, Butler County	4941	3	0	0		0	3	41	6	32	3	0
Penn Township, Westmoreland County	19632	24	0	0		2	22	49	6	42	1	0
Penn Township, York County	16243	20	0	1		1	18	128	16	108	4	0
Pequea Township	4778	7	0	0		0	7	34	14	19	1	0
Perkasie	8464	7	2	0		0	5	120	7	112	1	0
Peters Township	22274	4	0	0		1	3	156	13	143	0	3
Philadelphia	1570826	15534	273	1259		6199	7803	49334	6985	36856	5493	416
Phoenixville	16695	40	0	1		0	39	203	8	187	8	0
Pine Creek Township	3302	1	0	0		0	1	9	1	7	1	0
Pitcairn	3236	42	0	2		5	35	90	23	65	2	0
Pittsburgh	302443	2366	57	100		1000	1209	9868	1828	7222	818	153
Pittston Township	3395	11	0	0		2	9	133	13	116	4	0
Plains Township	9743	12	0	1		7	4	191	26	160	5	0
Pleasant Hills	8248	3	0	0		3	0	99	6	92	1	0
Plumstead Township	13735	8	0	1		1	6	104	22	73	9	0
Plymouth Township, Montgomery County	17887	27	0	3		18	6	536	51	463	22	2
Pocono Mountain Regional	42284	112	0	22		23	67	688	174	492	22	11
Pocono Township	10723	25	0	1		5	19	282	34	238	10	0
Polk	790	0	0	0		0	0	0	0	0	0	0
Portage	2484	4	0	0		0	4	28	9	19	0	0
Port Carbon	1803	0	0	0		0	0	1	0	1	0	0
Portersville	236	0	0	0		0	0	0	0	0	0	0
Portland	508	0	0	0		0	0	5	1	4	0	0
Port Vue	3733	10	0	0		0	10	35	4	30	1	0
Pottstown	22719	154	0	22		48	84	930	122	753	55	4
Pottsville	13703	46	0	14		8	24	315	31	266	18	2
Pringle	967	1	0	0		1	0	39	4	34	1	0
Prospect	1128	0	0	0		0	0	0	0	0	0	0
Pulaski Township, Lawrence County	3323	6	0	1		1	4	14	5	7	2	0
Punxsutawney	5841	4	0	3		1	0	39	3	35	1	0
Pymatuning Township	3158	34	0	3		1	30	54	7	46	1	0
Quakertown	8831	30	0	3		1	26	181	17	161	3	2
Quarryville	2762	6	0	0		0	6	85	8	76	1	0
Raccoon Township	2992	1	0	0		1	0	14	4	10	0	0
Radnor Township	31625	22	0	1		0	21	291	30	251	10	0
Rankin	2084	8	0	0		0	8	25	7	12	6	0
Reading	87834	597	10	47		233	307	2292	685	1417	190	12
Redstone Township	5425	0	0	0		0	0	10	3	7	0	0

Table 6. Offenses Known to Law Enforcement, by Selected State and City, 2016—Continued

(Number.)

State/city	Population	Violent crime	Murder and nonnegligent manslaughter	Rape (revised definition)[1]	Rape (legacy definition)[2]	Robbery	Aggravated assault	Property crime	Burglary	Larceny-theft	Motor vehicle theft	Arson[3]
Reserve Township	3285	4	0	1		1	2	47	9	36	2	0
Rice Township	3544	9	0	0		0	9	17	5	12	0	0
Richland Township, Bucks County	13176	7	0	1		2	4	260	16	232	12	1
Richland Township, Cambria County	12140	10	0	2		4	4	517	33	482	2	0
Ridgway	3863	6	0	1		1	4	95	7	86	2	0
Ridley Park	7041	7	0	0		2	5	52	4	44	4	0
Ridley Township	31110	47	0	2		22	23	372	35	320	17	1
Ringtown	791	0	0	0		0	0	2	0	2	0	0
Riverside	1909	0	0	0		0	0	8	0	7	1	0
Roaring Brook Township	1936	0	0	0		0	0	13	2	8	3	0
Roaring Creek Township	539	6	0	0		0	6	1	1	0	0	1
Roaring Spring	2528	0	0	0		0	0	16	1	15	0	1
Robinson Township, Allegheny County	13813	22	0	3		1	18	319	14	295	10	0
Robinson Township, Washington County	1901	1	0	0		0	1	15	4	11	0	0
Rochester	3551	13	1	7		1	4	203	45	153	5	0
Rochester Township	2726	5	0	0		0	5	23	3	17	3	0
Rockledge	2540	5	0	0		2	3	31	8	23	0	0
Roseto	1545	0	0	0		0	0	14	0	12	2	0
Ross Township	30858	22	0	2		6	14	650	46	595	9	0
Rostraver Township	11130	27	1	1		10	15	417	21	388	8	1
Royersford	4771	6	0	0		1	5	62	8	53	1	0
Rural Valley	844	0	0	0		0	0	0	0	0	0	0
Rush Township	3310	2	0	1		0	1	145	7	137	1	0
Ryan Township	2541	0	0	0		0	0	7	1	5	1	0
Salem Township, Luzerne County	4197	3	0	0		1	2	49	6	43	0	0
Salisbury Township	13762	9	0	0		6	3	258	43	202	13	0
Saltsburg	832	0	0	0		0	0	4	0	4	0	0
Sandy Township	10699	9	0	4		1	4	198	26	168	4	0
Saxton	701	0	0	0		0	0	0	0	0	0	0
Sayre	6418	22	0	4		1	17	139	20	118	1	1
Schuylkill Haven	5189	10	0	0		0	10	71	1	69	1	0
Schuylkill Township, Chester County	8587	8	1	0		0	7	68	4	60	4	0
Scottdale	4226	11	1	0		2	8	103	10	91	2	0
Scott Township, Allegheny County	16848	23	0	2		2	19	215	31	181	3	3
Scott Township, Columbia County	5081	3	0	1		0	2	55	1	54	0	0
Scott Township, Lackawanna County	4812	0	0	0		0	0	0	0	0	0	0
Scranton	77332	216	2	35		63	116	1696	360	1228	108	9
Selinsgrove	5820	56	1	4		0	51	173	23	149	1	1
Seward	473	0	0	0		0	0	0	0	0	0	0
Sewickley Heights	821	0	0	0		0	0	5	4	1	0	0
Shaler Township	28467	16	0	0		8	8	253	37	210	6	1
Shamokin	7124	22	0	1		6	15	156	31	118	7	3
Shamokin Dam	1710	4	0	0		0	4	11	0	11	0	0
Sharon	13472	54	3	10		20	21	422	116	285	21	7
Sharon Hill	5703	48	1	0		9	38	241	19	207	15	0
Sharpsville	4244	7	1	0		0	6	73	12	60	1	0
Shenandoah	4835	10	0	3		0	7	101	25	73	3	7
Shenango Township, Lawrence County	7323	10	0	0		1	9	51	14	31	6	2
Shenango Township, Mercer County	3810	13	0	1		2	10	48	8	39	1	0
Shillington	5263	7	0	0		0	7	64	9	52	3	0
Shinglehouse	1086	3	0	0		0	3	1	0	1	0	0
Shippensburg	5568	2	0	0		0	2	69	6	61	2	0
Shippingport	210	1	0	0		0	1	2	0	2	0	0
Shiremanstown	1582	1	0	0		0	1	1	1	0	0	0
Shohola Township	2332	1	0	0		0	1	12	3	9	0	0
Silver Spring Township	16884	3	0	1		0	2	152	11	139	2	0
Sinking Spring	4121	5	4	1		0	0	55	11	42	2	0
Slate Belt Regional	12358	26	0	5		1	20	167	30	134	3	1
Slatington	4285	4	0	0		0	4	76	9	65	2	1
Slippery Rock	3605	7	0	1		1	5	42	4	38	0	0
Smethport	1584	0	0	0		0	0	7	2	5	0	0
Solebury Township	8628	3	0	1		0	2	43	4	37	2	0
Somerset	5985	5	0	0		1	4	111	14	94	3	2
Souderton	6771	19	0	3		1	15	56	8	46	2	0
South Abington Township	9010	13	0	1		1	11	84	10	72	2	0
South Annville Township	2939	0	0	0		0	0	8	1	7	0	0
South Beaver Township	2656	3	0	0		0	3	10	0	10	0	0
South Buffalo Township	2593	0	0	0		0	0	14	1	13	0	0
South Centre Township	4197	4	0	0		0	4	14	5	9	0	0
South Coatesville	1461	6	0	1		3	2	20	8	10	2	0
Southern Regional Lancaster County	3863	5	0	0		1	4	10	1	7	2	0

Table 6. Offenses Known to Law Enforcement, by Selected State and City, 2016—Continued

(Number.)

State/city	Population	Violent crime	Murder and nonnegligent manslaughter	Rape (revised definition)[1]	Rape (legacy definition)[2]	Robbery	Aggravated assault	Property crime	Burglary	Larceny-theft	Motor vehicle theft	Arson[3]
Southern Regional York County	13766	25	0	9		3	13	92	15	76	1	0
South Fayette Township	15723	2	0	0		2	0	65	6	59	0	0
South Fork	866	0	0	0		0	0	0	0	0	0	0
South Greensburg	2042	5	0	0		0	5	19	2	17	0	0
South Heights	457	0	0	0		0	0	0	0	0	0	0
South Londonderry Township	7807	12	1	2		1	8	50	8	42	0	0
South Pymatuning Township	2615	0	0	0		0	0	2	1	1	0	0
South Strabane Township	9561	13	0	1		6	6	543	12	525	6	0
Southwestern Regional	17774	23	0	17		0	6	99	13	82	4	0
Southwest Regional, Fayette County	7688	5	0	0		0	5	62	17	42	3	0
Southwest Regional, Greene County	2639	0	0	0		0	0	14	1	13	0	0
South Whitehall Township	19797	9	0	1		4	4	660	45	596	19	1
South Williamsport	6261	9	0	2		1	6	93	5	88	0	0
Springdale	3369	11	0	1		0	10	37	4	32	1	1
Springettsbury Township	26931	36	0	7		12	17	963	35	907	21	0
Springfield Township, Delaware County	24438	15	0	1		5	9	690	43	638	9	2
Springfield Township, Montgomery County	19603	22	0	2		3	17	148	13	129	6	0
Spring Garden Township	12977	43	1	2		17	23	481	77	368	36	1
Spring Township, Berks County	27517	15	0	1		5	9	291	31	254	6	0
Spring Township, Centre County	7693	2	0	0		0	2	36	1	35	0	0
State College	58119	39	0	8		10	21	491	35	447	9	3
St. Clair Township	1464	0	0	0		0	0	3	0	2	1	0
Steelton	5921	78	0	5		10	63	206	31	149	26	2
Stockertown	914	0	0	0		0	0	0	0	0	0	0
Stoneboro	1008	0	0	0		0	0	0	0	0	0	0
Stowe Township	6247	16	0	0		3	13	209	28	168	13	0
Strasburg	2925	3	0	1		0	2	18	2	15	1	0
Stroud Area Regional	34242	84	9	7		28	40	979	93	855	31	3
Sugarcreek	5085	5	0	0		0	5	45	19	25	1	0
Sugarloaf Township, Luzerne County	4111	3	0	0		0	3	48	6	40	2	0
Summerhill Township	2354	0	0	0		0	0	29	9	20	0	2
Summit Township	2184	0	0	0		0	0	0	0	0	0	0
Sunbury	9607	78	0	11		3	64	266	56	194	16	3
Susquehanna	1543	2	0	0		0	2	0	0	0	0	0
Susquehanna Regional	8334	8	0	1		1	6	109	8	99	2	4
Susquehanna Township, Dauphin County	24846	48	0	3		15	30	320	50	258	12	3
Swarthmore	6214	5	0	0		0	5	56	8	48	0	0
Swatara Township	24916	77	2	6		21	48	894	76	805	13	9
Swissvale	8829	30	0	0		12	18	220	65	141	14	0
Swoyersville	4969	4	0	0		0	4	90	18	71	1	0
Sykesville	1131	0	0	0		0	0	0	0	0	0	0
Tamaqua	6777	10	0	1		0	9	188	38	143	7	1
Tarentum	4449	30	0	0		6	24	107	14	88	5	0
Tatamy	1128	0	0	0		0	0	2	0	2	0	0
Taylor	5979	55	1	1		2	51	150	31	116	3	1
Terre Hill	1399	1	0	0		0	1	5	2	3	0	0
Throop	3934	8	0	1		0	7	55	10	43	2	0
Tiadaghton Valley Regional	6554	12	0	4		1	7	90	7	83	0	0
Tidioute	670	2	0	0		0	2	0	0	0	0	0
Tinicum Township, Bucks County	3957	0	0	0		0	0	13	5	8	0	0
Tinicum Township, Delaware County	4113	17	0	0		6	11	136	8	114	14	0
Tioga	661	2	0	1		0	1	2	0	2	0	0
Titusville	5349	10	0	1		1	8	97	17	80	0	0
Towamencin Township	18409	6	0	0		1	5	139	18	121	0	1
Towanda	2792	12	0	2		0	10	89	6	83	0	1
Trainer	1847	9	0	0		3	6	51	5	46	0	0
Tredyffrin Township	29601	22	1	2		6	13	220	25	185	10	1
Troy	1259	5	0	1		1	3	29	4	25	0	0
Tullytown	1856	1	0	0		0	1	25	0	25	0	0
Tulpehocken Township	3309	1	0	0		0	1	4	1	3	0	0
Tunkhannock Township, Wyoming County	6254	7	0	0		1	6	44	10	34	0	0
Turtle Creek	5257	7	0	0		1	6	10	1	7	2	0
Tyrone	5330	21	0	1		2	18	100	7	93	0	0
Union City	3197	0	0	0		0	0	68	22	45	1	0
Uniontown	9919	32	2	2		17	11	292	47	235	10	0
Union Township, Lawrence County	4985	12	0	0		0	12	134	5	129	0	0
Upland	3254	47	0	0		4	43	113	22	85	6	0
Upper Allen Township	19815	0	0	0		0	0	139	20	117	2	2
Upper Burrell Township	2260	0	0	0		0	0	22	4	16	2	0

Table 6. Offenses Known to Law Enforcement, by Selected State and City, 2016—Continued

(Number.)

State/city	Population	Violent crime	Murder and nonnegligent manslaughter	Rape (revised definition)[1]	Rape (legacy definition)[2]	Robbery	Aggravated assault	Property crime	Burglary	Larceny-theft	Motor vehicle theft	Arson[3]
Upper Chichester Township	17054	50	1	2		20	27	337	29	290	18	2
Upper Darby Township	82896	386	6	9		207	164	1354	140	1094	120	6
Upper Dublin Township	26333	11	0	3		5	3	222	18	191	13	1
Upper Gwynedd Township	15999	13	0	1		0	12	64	3	60	1	0
Upper Leacock Township	8902	7	0	0		2	5	67	11	51	5	0
Upper Macungie Township	23396	11	0	1		4	6	226	23	191	12	0
Upper Makefield Township	8267	2	0	2		0	0	79	8	71	0	0
Upper Merion Township	28661	15	0	2		10	3	1147	54	1073	20	0
Upper Moreland Township	24270	15	0	1		6	8	377	24	334	19	3
Upper Nazareth Township	6795	5	0	1		0	4	24	3	20	1	0
Upper Perkiomen	6869	9	0	2		2	5	93	16	70	7	2
Upper Pottsgrove Township	5511	5	0	0		1	4	44	6	37	1	0
Upper Providence Township, Delaware County	10510	0	0	0		0	0	73	6	66	1	0
Upper Providence Township, Montgomery County	23927	5	0	0		4	1	290	18	263	9	0
Upper Saucon Township	16451	10	0	1		0	9	109	20	85	4	0
Upper Southampton Township	15114	9	0	1		3	5	115	27	81	7	1
Upper St. Clair Township	19726	3	0	0		0	3	126	8	117	1	0
Upper Uwchlan Township	11603	2	0	0		2	0	56	10	45	1	0
Uwchlan Township	19274	14	2	0		5	7	159	28	128	3	0
Valley Township	7803	8	0	0		0	8	88	14	71	3	0
Vandergrift	4999	16	0	0		2	14	7	1	6	0	0
Vandling	716	2	0	0		0	2	3	1	0	2	0
Vernon Township	5449	1	0	1		0	0	42	0	42	0	0
Verona	2436	17	0	3		1	13	64	18	42	4	0
Vintondale	387	0	0	0		0	0	0	0	0	0	0
Walker Township	1018	0	0	0		0	0	0	0	0	0	0
Wampum	683	0	0	0		0	0	4	2	2	0	0
Warminster Township	32577	25	0	8		10	7	380	29	339	12	2
Warren	9264	30	0	3		0	27	206	6	200	0	1
Warrington Township	24044	7	0	1		4	2	275	34	235	6	6
Warwick Township, Bucks County	14741	13	1	0		0	12	77	5	67	5	0
Washington, Washington County	13421	92	1	9		29	53	437	86	333	18	2
Washington Township, Fayette County	3740	11	0	0		1	10	49	10	38	1	1
Washington Township, Franklin County	14631	11	0	2		6	3	286	26	258	2	3
Washington Township, Northampton County	5180	0	0	0		0	0	56	7	49	0	0
Washington Township, Westmoreland County	7216	3	0	0		0	3	56	4	50	2	0
Watsontown	2315	5	0	0		2	3	23	4	19	0	1
Waverly Township	1708	1	0	0		0	1	15	7	8	0	0
Waymart	1267	0	0	0		0	0	5	1	4	0	0
Waynesboro	10902	29	6	6		6	11	266	43	211	12	2
Waynesburg	4021	9	0	0		2	7	77	10	66	1	0
Wayne Township, Lawrence County	2509	3	0	0		0	3	1	1	0	0	1
Weatherly	2450	18	0	0		0	18	66	11	55	0	0
West Brandywine Township	7482	11	1	1		0	9	85	20	58	7	1
West Caln Township	9097	23	0	0		1	22	69	21	42	6	0
West Carroll Township	1234	2	0	0		0	2	5	2	3	0	1
West Chester	20129	59	0	16		19	24	403	68	320	15	18
West Cocalico Township	7439	7	0	0		0	7	31	8	23	0	1
West Conshohocken	1393	4	0	0		0	4	26	1	22	3	0
West Cornwall Township	1997	4	0	0		1	3	1	0	1	0	1
West Deer Township	11975	2	0	0		1	1	86	19	65	2	0
West Earl Township	8195	10	0	3		7	0	56	18	38	0	0
Western Berks Regional	2549	4	0	1		1	2	14	10	3	1	0
West Fallowfield Township	2602	0	0	0		0	0	13	2	11	0	0
West Goshen Township	23398	22	0	1		2	19	315	24	282	9	0
West Hempfield Township	16538	16	0	2		2	12	139	13	122	4	4
West Hills Regional	10302	11	0	0		1	10	95	19	72	4	0
West Homestead	1917	8	0	1		1	6	30	1	29	0	0
West Kittanning	1126	1	0	0		0	1	1	1	0	0	0
West Lebanon Township	805	2	0	0		1	1	63	6	57	0	0
West Leechburg	1260	0	0	0		0	0	4	0	4	0	0
West Manchester Township	18880	40	3	3		13	21	626	44	572	10	0
West Manheim Township	8371	5	0	2		0	3	123	7	113	3	0
West Mead Township	5121	5	0	0		0	5	57	8	48	1	0
West Mifflin	20028	24	0	2		4	18	180	13	158	9	0
West Newton	2527	9	0	4		0	5	42	2	38	2	0
West Norriton Township	15799	24	0	1		4	19	328	35	280	13	0
West Nottingham Township	2703	0	0	0		0	0	0	0	0	0	0
West Penn Township	4327	0	0	0		0	0	13	6	7	0	0
West Pittston	4753	16	0	0		1	15	72	5	63	4	0
West Pottsgrove Township	3885	6	0	0		4	2	128	8	115	5	0
West Reading	4186	15	0	2		4	9	173	14	151	8	0
West Sadsbury Township	2481	3	0	0		1	2	95	5	89	1	0

Table 6. Offenses Known to Law Enforcement, by Selected State and City, 2016—Continued

(Number.)

State/city	Population	Violent crime	Murder and nonnegligent manslaughter	Rape (revised definition)[1]	Rape (legacy definition)[2]	Robbery	Aggravated assault	Property crime	Burglary	Larceny-theft	Motor vehicle theft	Arson[3]
West Salem Township	3463	18	0	1		0	17	63	12	48	3	1
West Shore Regional	7734	8	0	0		6	2	44	8	31	5	0
Westtown-East Goshen Regional	32687	35	0	6		1	28	264	16	238	10	0
West View	6668	11	0	1		0	10	114	9	105	0	0
West Vincent Township	5133	0	0	0		0	0	18	3	14	1	0
Whitaker Borough	1250	2	0	1		0	1	22	4	18	0	0
Whitehall	13812	7	0	1		2	4	62	16	45	1	2
Whitehall Township	27426	28	1	1		17	9	1098	60	1009	29	4
Whitemarsh Township	17721	6	0	1		0	5	240	24	196	20	0
White Oak	7758	8	0	1		4	3	129	12	107	10	0
Whitpain Township	19237	15	0	0		2	13	153	24	118	11	0
Wilkes-Barre Township	2921	16	0	1		6	9	668	18	649	1	0
Wilkinsburg	15692	167	2	3		60	102	532	168	304	60	9
Wilkins Township	6283	7	0	3		0	4	165	15	138	12	0
Williamsburg	1216	0	0	0		0	0	5	0	4	1	0
Williamsport	29163	104	5	8		39	52	792	101	668	23	2
Wilson	7758	53	0	7		11	35	296	49	240	7	2
Windber	3938	23	0	0		3	20	26	3	22	1	1
Womelsdorf	2860	2	0	1		0	1	19	5	13	1	0
Worthington	609	0	0	0		0	0	0	0	0	0	0
Wright Township	5659	0	0	0		0	0	53	4	46	3	0
Wyoming	3038	5	0	1		2	2	118	13	100	5	0
Wyomissing	10473	9	0	1		2	6	378	14	361	3	1
Yardley	2442	17	0	0		0	17	28	3	24	1	0
Yeadon	11537	40	3	0		17	20	337	48	265	24	0
York	44017	416	8	12		208	188	1408	298	917	193	11
York Area Regional	55292	67	1	13		6	47	465	78	371	16	2
Youngsville	1653	1	0	0		0	1	13	3	10	0	0
RHODE ISLAND												
Barrington	16218	4	0	1		2	1	117	19	96	2	2
Bristol	22229	18	0	8		1	9	150	16	127	7	0
Burrillville	16357	15	0	9		0	6	110	22	82	6	1
Central Falls	19277	126	1	16		29	80	451	122	281	48	5
Charlestown	7762	7	0	2		1	4	84	31	50	3	0
Cranston	81162	124	1	31		22	70	1509	231	1142	136	8
Cumberland	34708	35	0	5		6	24	333	70	245	18	1
East Greenwich	13120	8	0	3		2	3	86	14	69	3	0
East Providence	47456	69	2	9		10	48	550	86	424	40	6
Foster	4713	5	0	0		0	5	40	17	23	0	0
Glocester	10037	1	0	0		0	1	32	9	21	2	0
Hopkinton	8093	6	0	1		1	4	91	16	72	3	0
Jamestown	5494	1	0	1		0	0	36	4	32	0	0
Johnston	29322	43	1	7		7	28	451	64	340	47	2
Lincoln	21770	20	0	3		5	12	430	56	344	30	2
Little Compton	3505	0	0	0		0	0	27	4	23	0	0
Middletown	16035	14	1	7		2	4	172	21	143	8	5
Narragansett	15600	11	0	7		1	3	127	19	105	3	0
Newport	24077	62	1	14		7	40	695	105	554	36	9
New Shoreham[5]	1046	0	0		0	0	0		4		0	0
North Kingstown	26120	22	0	7		2	13	268	55	203	10	1
North Providence	32540	43	1	12		6	24	398	79	275	44	3
North Smithfield	12377	10	0	3		1	6	209	16	185	8	1
Pawtucket[4]	71640	305	4	40		60	201		484	1350		15
Portsmouth	17362	18	1	3		0	14	106	30	70	6	1
Providence[5]	179340	1031	10	112		300	609		1154	4132		26
Richmond	7621	5	0	1		0	4	44	14	28	2	2
Scituate	10587	4	0	1		0	3	63	14	46	3	1
Smithfield	21660	12	0	1		1	10	206	29	164	13	2
South Kingstown	30872	13	0	2		1	10	249	63	170	16	2
Tiverton	15768	22	1	5		2	14	205	57	139	9	3
Warren	10460	12	0	4		1	7	177	46	126	5	2
Warwick	81481	61	1	17		11	32	1625	158	1392	75	19
Westerly	22675	19	0	6		4	9	411	91	305	15	3
West Greenwich	6132	5	1	1		0	3	39	5	31	3	1
West Warwick	28777	60	0	16		10	34	332	80	225	27	3
Woonsocket	41511	212	1	39		41	131	972	296	606	70	7
SOUTH CAROLINA												
Abbeville	5177	30	0	6		2	22	199	59	131	9	1
Aiken	30800	241	1	23		43	174	1785	287	1401	97	6
Allendale	3064	40	2	0		7	31	116	55	57	4	1
Andrews	2894	21	0	3		5	13	160	59	95	6	0
Atlantic Beach	394	0	0	0		0	0	0	0	0	0	0
Aynor	689	3	0	0		0	3	32	3	24	5	0
Bamberg	3341	17	0	0		5	12	136	42	89	5	0
Barnwell	4561	51	0	1		6	43	278	107	160	11	2
Batesburg-Leesville	5457	79	0	4		11	64	275	40	226	9	3
Beaufort	13477	85	1	3		21	60	857	100	729	28	1
Belton	4374	12	2	1		3	6	216	42	147	27	0
Bennettsville	8514	83	1	2		19	61	321	60	244	17	0
Bishopville	3237	38	1	4		1	32	166	27	132	7	0

Table 6. Offenses Known to Law Enforcement, by Selected State and City, 2016—Continued

(Number.)

State/city	Population	Violent crime	Murder and nonnegligent manslaughter	Rape (revised definition)[1]	Rape (legacy definition)[2]	Robbery	Aggravated assault	Property crime	Burglary	Larceny-theft	Motor vehicle theft	Arson[3]
Blacksburg	1889	13	0	2		2	9	92	15	68	9	0
Blackville	2273	23	2	1		1	19	92	40	50	2	0
Bluffton	17498	25	2	6		5	12	267	39	217	11	0
Branchville	983	1	0	0		0	1	17	3	11	3	0
Briarcliffe Acres	544	0	0	0		0	0	0	0	0	0	0
Burnettown	2795	5	0	0		1	4	48	8	34	6	1
Camden	7132	112	1	4		21	86	569	67	485	17	0
Cameron	414	0	0	0		0	0	2	1	1	0	0
Campobello	532	1	0	0		0	1	13	2	9	2	0
Cayce	13729	149	0	8		22	119	662	104	462	96	2
Chapin	1578	4	0	0		2	2	47	4	43	0	0
Charleston	135153	408	11	44		107	246	3359	417	2681	261	8
Cheraw	5766	49	0	3		8	38	395	59	325	11	0
Chesnee	907	1	0	0		0	1	38	5	31	2	1
Chester	5462	52	0	0		12	40	291	92	188	11	1
Chesterfield	1450	3	0	0		0	3	45	8	36	1	0
Clemson	15767	26	0	6		7	13	463	57	309	97	1
Clinton	8664	101	1	7		12	81	353	82	252	19	1
Clover	5874	10	0	2		4	4	128	16	106	6	0
Columbia	134489	1116	10	99		286	721	7374	1114	5357	903	18
Conway	21874	174	3	20		24	127	1016	138	805	73	0
Cottageville	733	3	0	0		1	2	22	6	16	0	0
Coward	749	0	0	0		0	0	9	1	7	1	0
Cowpens	2288	4	0	0		0	4	27	5	18	4	1
Darlington	6130	68	0	2		9	57	530	60	455	15	0
Denmark	3274	19	0	0		7	12	146	56	79	11	1
Dillon	6648	127	8	2		22	95	725	119	584	22	1
Due West	1238	0	0	0		0	0	26	1	25	0	0
Duncan	3350	6	0	3		1	2	97	9	83	5	0
Easley	20911	131	1	5		13	112	1165	114	992	59	2
Edgefield	4762	6	0	0		2	4	39	12	24	3	0
Edisto Beach	415	0	0	0		0	0	39	15	24	0	0
Ehrhardt	499	4	0	0		2	2	15	7	8	0	0
Elgin	1510	9	0	1		2	6	75	5	69	1	1
Elloree	677	1	0	0		0	1	11	5	6	0	0
Estill	1933	60	2	0		6	52	80	26	53	1	0
Eutawville	305	0	0	0		0	0	4	0	4	0	0
Florence	38382	408	1	20		73	314	2563	407	2026	130	5
Forest Acres	10654	77	0	3		13	61	562	89	420	53	1
Fort Lawn	862	3	0	0		0	3	34	12	20	2	2
Fort Mill	14150	34	0	2		10	22	304	27	267	10	2
Fountain Inn	8450	16	0	2		3	11	159	20	126	13	1
Gaffney	12568	104	1	14		28	61	622	117	479	26	1
Gaston	1662	4	0	0		2	2	48	14	30	4	0
Georgetown	9044	81	0	7		10	64	322	50	257	15	0
Gifford	270	0	0	0		0	0	1	1	0	0	0
Goose Creek	41540	158	4	13		22	119	915	159	710	46	6
Great Falls	1923	10	0	1		0	9	119	16	100	3	1
Greeleyville	405	3	0	0		2	1	8	3	5	0	0
Greenville	65686	399	2	33		98	266	2823	366	2259	198	10
Greer	28927	97	0	19		22	56	733	102	575	56	1
Hampton	2637	24	0	6		5	13	165	51	107	7	1
Hanahan	22357	44	2	6		16	20	419	124	258	37	4
Hardeeville	5893	48	0	3		20	25	224	58	148	18	1
Harleyville	699	3	0	0		2	1	15	3	12	0	0
Hartsville	7837	154	2	9		13	130	817	116	674	27	3
Hemingway	427	1	0	1		0	0	29	5	23	1	0
Holly Hill	1230	7	0	1		0	6	59	9	49	1	0
Honea Path	3737	19	0	4		1	14	254	27	200	27	3
Inman	2294	6	0	1		3	2	68	8	58	2	0
Irmo	12240	66	0	3		5	58	414	62	332	20	0
Isle of Palms	4419	0	0	0		0	0	118	28	83	7	0
Iva	1288	9	0	0		0	9	55	10	42	3	1
Jackson	1774	3	0	1		1	1	29	7	18	4	0
Jamestown	82	0	0	0		0	0	0	0	0	0	0
Johnsonville	1509	2	0	0		0	2	28	9	18	1	0
Johnston	2345	9	0	0		1	8	40	12	25	3	0
Jonesville	856	18	1	1		5	11	27	8	18	1	0
Kingstree	3155	29	0	6		7	16	248	57	177	14	0
Lake City	6809	128	0	8		25	95	439	100	307	32	3
Lamar	968	5	0	0		0	5	25	7	17	1	0
Landrum	2517	10	0	3		1	6	82	25	52	5	0
Lane	471	2	0	0		0	2	3	1	2	0	0
Latta	1345	20	0	0		3	17	104	19	77	8	1
Lexington	20597	71	1	8		3	59	614	64	529	21	1
Liberty	3242	8	0	5		0	3	155	37	112	6	0
Loris	2630	32	1	4		3	24	160	28	117	15	0
Lyman	3456	15	0	1		2	12	71	11	57	3	0
Manning	4023	46	0	4		6	36	360	59	291	10	3
Marion	6674	61	4	6		8	43	598	157	411	30	5
Mauldin	25540	54	2	5		9	38	507	56	405	46	4
McBee	853	11	0	0		1	10	21	5	16	0	0
McColl	2049	23	1	0		5	17	92	28	61	3	1

Table 6. Offenses Known to Law Enforcement, by Selected State and City, 2016—Continued

(Number.)

State/city	Population	Violent crime	Murder and nonnegligent manslaughter	Rape (revised definition)[1]	Rape (legacy definition)[2]	Robbery	Aggravated assault	Property crime	Burglary	Larceny-theft	Motor vehicle theft	Arson[3]
McCormick	2540	14	0	0		1	13	74	23	47	4	3
Moncks Corner	10298	50	1	4		11	34	530	51	464	15	0
Mount Pleasant	84277	127	0	6		20	101	1433	169	1200	64	2
Mullins	4491	49	0	4		14	31	268	82	168	18	1
Myrtle Beach	31864	538	5	46		139	348	4395	469	3555	371	10
Newberry	10338	65	0	3		12	50	438	52	380	6	2
New Ellenton	2134	23	0	2		8	13	37	10	20	7	0
Nichols	356	4	0	0		4	0	32	20	12	0	0
Ninety Six	2050	9	0	0		0	9	60	9	47	4	0
North	737	6	0	0		4	2	40	8	30	2	0
North Augusta	22755	49	0	8		25	16	989	124	821	44	2
North Charleston	110490	993	32	89		293	579	6218	918	4655	645	16
North Myrtle Beach	15945	121	2	21		28	70	1227	194	918	115	4
Olanta	571	0	0	0		0	0	12	1	11	0	0
Orangeburg	13365	80	0	10		19	51	980	173	748	59	2
Pacolet	2373	2	0	0		1	1	55	9	42	4	1
Pageland	2745	25	1	1		3	20	143	46	91	6	2
Pelion	708	1	0	1		0	0	20	8	8	4	0
Perry	236	0	0	0		0	0	0	0	0	0	0
Pickens	3183	26	0	5		4	17	239	31	199	9	0
Pine Ridge	2263	5	0	1		1	3	19	4	13	2	0
Port Royal	12417	32	0	2		11	19	281	56	202	23	1
Prosperity	1204	0	0	0		0	0	15	5	10	0	0
Quinby	947	0	0	0		0	0	2	0	2	0	0
Ridgeland	3991	14	2	0		9	3	129	12	108	9	0
Ridge Spring	748	2	1	0		1	0	4	1	3	0	0
Rock Hill	72589	447	5	61		60	321	2544	336	2054	154	10
Salem	148	0	0	0		0	0	0	0	0	0	0
Saluda	3603	22	0	0		2	20	50	10	35	5	0
Santee	930	8	0	1		0	7	103	22	78	3	0
Scranton	864	0	0	0		0	0	4	1	3	0	0
Seneca	8308	35	0	7		5	23	227	48	167	12	0
Simpsonville	21223	70	0	15		14	41	766	69	650	47	1
Society Hill	545	0	0	0		0	0	4	2	2	0	0
South Congaree	2404	4	0	1		1	2	33	1	27	5	1
Springdale	2814	22	0	4		9	9	123	20	84	19	0
Springfield	499	2	0	0		1	1	10	5	4	1	0
St. George	2197	10	0	1		3	6	130	41	80	9	0
St. Matthews	1978	12	0	1		4	7	81	19	60	2	0
St. Stephen	1829	17	0	0		5	12	49	13	30	6	0
Sullivans Island	1940	2	0	0		2	0	28	6	22	0	0
Summerton	959	7	0	1		1	5	53	14	34	5	0
Summerville	50154	160	5	14		29	112	1802	188	1509	105	0
Sumter	40864	282	3	9		50	220	1666	390	1216	60	10
Surfside Beach	4372	5	0	1		2	2	211	45	143	23	1
Swansea	904	6	0	0		1	5	43	8	32	3	0
Tega Cay	10032	8	0	4		2	2	193	8	184	1	0
Travelers Rest	5074	10	1	1		6	2	228	10	207	11	1
Turbeville	798	2	0	0		0	2	19	3	13	3	1
Union	7981	89	0	4		11	74	473	89	374	10	2
Wagener	827	4	0	0		3	1	25	10	13	2	0
Walhalla	4254	14	0	1		2	11	102	19	78	5	0
Walterboro	5253	59	2	4		5	48	449	35	393	21	5
Ware Shoals	2175	19	0	1		2	16	106	22	81	3	0
Wellford	2549	4	0	1		2	1	53	14	36	3	0
Westminster	2493	8	0	1		0	7	97	21	72	4	0
West Pelzer	914	7	0	1		0	6	36	1	28	7	0
West Union	313	3	0	1		1	1	27	1	26	0	0
Whitmire	1466	1	0	0		0	1	50	13	35	2	0
Williamston	4161	19	0	1		1	17	144	34	95	15	4
Williston	3007	9	1	1		2	5	93	15	69	9	2
Winnsboro	3316	32	0	2		3	27	200	37	155	8	0
Woodruff	4137	24	1	1		4	18	105	22	73	10	2
York	8058	82	2	8		14	58	350	48	291	11	3
SOUTH DAKOTA												
Aberdeen	28498	134	0	29		5	100	621	117	467	37	4
Alcester	752	5	0	1		0	4	8	4	4	0	0
Avon	567	0	0	0		0	0	0	0	0	0	0
Belle Fourche	5714	13	0	1		0	12	76	19	57	0	0
Beresford	1969	4	0	1		0	3	13	1	12	0	0
Box Elder	9607	30	0	6		2	22	168	30	127	11	1
Brandon	10042	0	0	0		0	0	38	4	33	1	0
Brookings	23971	35	0	12		1	22	374	44	294	36	2
Burke	586	0	0	0		0	0	0	0	0	0	0
Canton	3380	7	0	1		0	6	27	11	14	2	0
Chamberlain	2383	18	0	2		1	15	71	10	61	0	0
Clark	1033	2	0	0		0	2	23	5	16	2	0
Deadwood	1255	5	0	0		0	5	6	0	6	0	0
Eagle Butte	1355	0	0	0		0	0	2	0	2	0	0
Flandreau	2296	14	0	1		2	11	57	10	41	6	0
Freeman	1284	0	0	0		0	0	0	0	0	0	0
Hermosa	390	0	0	0		0	0	0	0	0	0	0

Table 6. Offenses Known to Law Enforcement, by Selected State and City, 2016—Continued

(Number.)

State/city	Population	Violent crime	Murder and nonnegligent manslaughter	Rape (revised definition)[1]	Rape (legacy definition)[2]	Robbery	Aggravated assault	Property crime	Burglary	Larceny-theft	Motor vehicle theft	Arson[3]
Hot Springs	3507	9	0	1		0	8	40	11	29	0	0
Huron	13459	35	0	10		0	25	257	39	201	17	1
Kadoka	718	1	0	0		0	1	5	1	4	0	0
Lead	2974	1	0	0		0	1	15	0	15	0	0
Lennox	2304	2	0	1		0	1	9	1	7	1	0
Leola	437	0	0	0		0	0	0	0	0	0	0
Madison	7411	4	0	0		0	4	76	15	57	4	0
Martin	1059	17	1	1		2	13	65	16	46	3	1
Menno	593	0	0	0		0	0	0	0	0	0	0
Miller	1427	0	0	0		0	0	14	8	6	0	0
Mitchell	15749	90	0	8		5	77	579	88	443	48	2
Mobridge	3465	15	0	2		0	13	45	2	35	8	0
North Sioux City	2772	0	0	0		0	0	52	0	49	3	0
Parkston	1483	3	0	1		0	2	0	0	0	0	0
Philip	747	0	0	0		0	0	0	0	0	0	0
Pierre	14068	63	0	7		1	55	642	85	529	28	0
Rapid City	74573	536	2	88		80	366	2966	480	2236	250	2
Rosholt	428	0	0	0		0	0	1	1	0	0	0
Scotland	816	0	0	0		0	0	0	0	0	0	0
Sioux Falls	175152	897	6	142		121	628	5563	869	4076	618	45
Sisseton	2451	3	0	0		0	3	10	3	7	0	0
Spearfish	11429	28	0	9		2	17	377	43	321	13	0
Springfield	1947	0	0	0		0	0	0	0	0	0	0
Sturgis	6699	10	0	0		0	10	124	12	105	7	1
Summerset	2329	0	0	0		0	0	20	2	17	1	1
Tea	5064	9	0	1		1	7	67	16	48	3	0
Tripp	627	0	0	0		0	0	3	3	0	0	0
Tyndall	1046	0	0	0		0	0	0	0	0	0	0
Vermillion	10774	20	0	4		0	16	212	25	170	17	0
Viborg	758	2	0	0		0	2	1	0	1	0	0
Wagner	1593	10	0	2		0	8	19	0	18	1	0
Watertown	22186	89	0	13		8	68	596	73	489	34	2
Whitewood	916	1	0	0		0	1	3	0	2	1	0
Winner	2805	9	0	1		1	7	18	2	13	3	0
Worthing	955	0	0	0		0	0	0	0	0	0	0
Yankton	14575	48	0	10		4	34	453	57	384	12	0
TENNESSEE												
Adamsville	2245	5	0	0		0	5	56	20	33	3	0
Alamo	2486	7	0	0		0	7	13	3	9	1	0
Alcoa	9503	77	1	3		12	61	531	48	442	41	5
Alexandria	978	11	0	0		4	7	26	8	16	2	2
Algood	3770	8	0	0		0	8	128	10	116	2	0
Ardmore	1213	2	0	0		0	2	21	8	13	0	0
Ashland City	4650	13	0	1		1	11	198	29	160	9	2
Athens	13717	137	2	6		19	110	1068	183	803	82	3
Atoka	9176	19	0	3		3	13	101	28	70	3	1
Baileyton	431	3	0	1		0	2	19	7	11	1	0
Baneberry	526	1	0	0		0	1	9	2	6	1	0
Bartlett	58897	189	0	13		15	161	956	117	788	51	2
Baxter	1388	7	0	0		1	6	78	6	69	3	0
Bean Station	3085	12	1	0		3	8	53	15	36	2	0
Belle Meade	3021	0	0	0		0	0	31	6	25	0	0
Bells	2449	4	0	0		1	3	25	6	15	4	0
Benton	1275	1	0	0		0	1	32	1	30	1	0
Berry Hill	549	9	0	1		2	6	79	10	66	3	0
Big Sandy	540	1	0	0		0	1	11	4	7	0	0
Blaine	1869	0	0	0		0	0	12	3	8	1	1
Bluff City	1719	1	0	0		1	0	33	5	26	2	0
Bolivar	5032	60	2	2		15	41	191	58	120	13	1
Bradford	1004	15	0	1		0	14	16	2	14	0	0
Brentwood	42739	25	1	2		5	17	397	53	325	19	0
Brighton	3018	14	0	0		1	13	42	11	30	1	0
Bristol	26656	158	1	14		14	129	900	134	670	96	6
Brownsville	9795	165	1	6		16	142	460	120	323	17	2
Bruceton	1426	6	0	0		0	6	44	8	35	1	0
Burns	1475	1	0	0		0	1	21	1	16	4	0
Calhoun	496	0	0	0		0	0	1	0	0	1	0
Camden	3574	7	0	1		1	5	126	16	103	7	0
Carthage	2273	4	0	0		1	3	42	9	32	1	0
Caryville	2182	12	0	0		2	10	79	29	36	14	0
Celina	1494	7	0	0		0	7	23	2	17	4	0
Centerville	3574	14	0	0		1	13	110	41	59	10	0
Chapel Hill	1471	3	0	1		1	1	27	3	22	2	1
Charleston	681	0	0	0		0	0	5	3	2	0	0
Chattanooga	177801	1819	26	111		375	1307	9752	1570	7122	1060	23
Church Hill	6714	12	0	0		1	11	28	6	21	1	1
Clarksburg	378	0	0	0		0	0	1	0	1	0	0
Clarksville	152526	935	12	74		131	718	3853	711	2960	182	10
Cleveland	44423	384	2	14		50	318	2704	406	2044	254	3
Clifton	2657	2	0	1		0	1	7	1	6	0	0
Clinton	10091	65	0	2		13	50	440	58	356	26	3
Collegedale	11245	8	0	3		1	4	137	19	111	7	0

Table 6. Offenses Known to Law Enforcement, by Selected State and City, 2016—Continued

(Number.)

State/city	Population	Violent crime	Murder and nonnegligent manslaughter	Rape (revised definition)[1]	Rape (legacy definition)[2]	Robbery	Aggravated assault	Property crime	Burglary	Larceny-theft	Motor vehicle theft	Arson[3]
Collierville	49531	80	0	6		10	64	740	89	623	28	0
Collinwood	972	0	0	0		0	0	10	2	5	3	0
Columbia	37219	254	0	30		35	189	1079	205	807	67	5
Cookeville	32292	165	0	27		21	117	1395	295	999	101	4
Coopertown	4426	8	0	0		1	7	24	9	13	2	0
Cornersville	1227	5	0	0		0	5	29	0	25	4	0
Cowan	1698	5	0	1		0	4	26	7	17	2	0
Cross Plains	1725	2	0	0		1	1	23	10	13	0	0
Crossville	11514	95	0	7		6	82	584	67	473	44	2
Crump	1394	1	0	1		0	0	24	3	18	3	0
Cumberland City	300	1	1	0		0	0	2	1	1	0	0
Dandridge	2949	9	0	3		0	6	58	11	43	4	0
Dayton	7421	35	1	0		1	33	271	49	213	9	0
Decatur	1571	16	0	0		1	15	44	12	28	4	0
Decaturville	869	1	0	0		0	1	18	12	5	1	0
Decherd	2439	12	0	0		0	12	112	12	97	3	0
Dickson	15501	150	1	18		5	126	922	104	759	59	0
Dover	1465	3	0	1		0	2	39	13	23	3	1
Dresden	2879	1	0	0		0	1	30	12	15	3	0
Dunlap	5167	21	0	1		2	18	229	33	170	26	2
Dyer	2262	8	0	2		1	5	57	4	48	5	0
Dyersburg	16711	231	2	6		21	202	1128	263	828	37	9
Eagleville	661	0	0	0		0	0	0	0	0	0	0
East Ridge	21311	195	0	13		33	149	982	194	670	118	4
Elizabethton	13672	46	0	1		10	35	651	78	555	18	0
Elkton	563	0	0	0		0	0	2	1	1	0	0
Englewood	1529	5	1	0		0	4	51	19	28	4	0
Erin	1288	5	0	1		0	4	19	6	12	1	0
Erwin	5959	7	0	0		0	7	62	5	48	9	1
Estill Springs	2043	13	0	1		0	12	22	2	19	1	0
Ethridge	476	2	0	0		0	2	9	6	3	0	0
Etowah	3503	16	0	0		0	16	98	20	70	8	2
Fairview	8440	29	0	5		2	22	160	7	146	7	0
Fayetteville	7182	78	0	4		6	68	394	59	323	12	4
Franklin	74771	154	0	21		19	114	1085	84	968	33	1
Friendship	668	1	0	0		0	1	9	5	3	1	0
Gadsden	469	3	0	1		0	2	7	5	2	0	0
Gainesboro	954	1	0	0		0	1	8	1	7	0	0
Gallatin	35154	139	2	3		16	118	452	49	393	10	2
Gallaway	654	7	0	0		3	4	18	13	4	1	0
Gates	623	1	0	0		1	0	10	5	4	1	0
Gatlinburg	4229	51	0	4		4	43	298	90	190	18	1
Germantown	39311	46	0	2		8	36	503	82	411	10	2
Gibson	370	2	0	0		0	2	12	2	9	1	0
Gleason	1399	0	0	0		0	0	32	11	19	2	0
Goodlettsville	23358	54	0	1		9	44	518	61	430	27	0
Gordonsville	1203	3	0	0		0	3	17	4	11	2	0
Grand Junction	299	1	1	0		0	0	9	3	6	0	0
Graysville	1517	9	0	0		0	9	16	6	9	1	0
Greenbrier	6807	27	0	3		1	23	59	9	44	6	0
Greeneville	15101	49	1	0		5	43	556	65	450	41	1
Greenfield	2108	4	0	0		0	4	39	11	27	1	0
Halls	2164	10	0	0		0	10	64	2	61	1	0
Harriman	6195	45	2	3		2	38	247	61	175	11	1
Henderson	6597	25	0	0		1	24	93	41	48	4	0
Hendersonville	56965	75	2	2		9	62	874	81	765	28	2
Henry	467	2	0	0		0	2	5	2	3	0	0
Hohenwald	3650	40	0	1		1	38	190	47	133	10	4
Hollow Rock	693	1	0	0		0	1	16	2	11	3	0
Hornbeak	406	0	0	0		0	0	1	0	1	0	0
Humboldt	8287	62	0	5		3	54	293	66	217	10	0
Huntingdon	3912	9	0	1		2	6	87	10	75	2	0
Huntland	852	0	0	0		0	0	3	1	2	0	0
Jacksboro	1935	6	0	0		1	5	169	3	160	6	0
Jackson	66990	628	7	36		108	477	2947	650	2170	127	14
Jamestown	1945	3	0	0		1	2	77	1	73	3	0
Jasper	3323	12	0	1		0	11	68	12	42	14	3
Jefferson City	8549	29	0	0		1	28	258	29	224	5	0
Jellico	2244	3	0	0		3	0	32	9	20	3	0
Johnson City	66511	263	4	25		38	196	2488	392	1977	119	9
Jonesborough	5338	10	0	3		0	7	79	13	61	5	2
Kenton	1213	1	0	0		0	1	23	5	17	1	0
Kimball	1398	3	0	0		1	2	128	5	117	6	0
Kingsport	53059	369	1	18		71	279	2501	374	1973	154	10
Kingston	5823	19	0	1		2	16	96	21	68	7	0
Kingston Springs	2773	0	0	0		0	0	5	0	5	0	0
Knoxville	186583	1672	18	157		404	1093	10324	1840	7620	864	19
Lafayette	5088	19	0	1		1	17	193	44	130	19	2
La Follette	6977	55	0	1		7	47	477	130	318	29	0
La Vergne	35228	241	0	19		16	206	646	132	449	65	11
Lawrenceburg	10595	79	0	5		5	69	562	87	456	19	2
Lebanon	31125	200	0	18		35	147	951	150	735	66	12
Lenoir City	9175	15	0	0		5	10	280	29	236	15	2

Table 6. Offenses Known to Law Enforcement, by Selected State and City, 2016—Continued

(Number.)

State/city	Population	Violent crime	Murder and nonnegligent manslaughter	Rape (revised definition)[1]	Rape (legacy definition)[2]	Robbery	Aggravated assault	Property crime	Burglary	Larceny-theft	Motor vehicle theft	Arson[3]
Lewisburg	11552	110	0	2		6	102	230	41	175	14	0
Lexington	7859	59	0	2		6	51	258	33	207	18	1
Livingston	4073	20	0	1		1	18	74	12	57	5	0
Lookout Mountain	1887	0	0	0		0	0	16	3	12	1	0
Loretto	1752	4	0	1		0	3	31	17	13	1	0
Loudon	5800	7	0	1		0	6	73	6	66	1	0
Madisonville	4823	24	0	0		2	22	309	63	224	22	0
Manchester	10596	76	0	1		5	70	478	85	375	18	0
Martin	10859	32	0	2		7	23	266	33	227	6	2
Maryville	28661	55	0	4		7	44	680	102	552	26	3
Maury City	675	2	0	0		0	2	13	3	8	2	0
Maynardville	2343	11	0	1		0	10	76	17	55	4	0
McEwen	1693	6	0	2		0	4	18	1	17	0	0
McKenzie	5294	9	0	0		0	9	147	39	101	7	0
McMinnville	13789	135	2	21		5	107	523	98	390	35	1
Medina	4238	8	0	1		2	5	59	6	52	1	0
Memphis	656434	11947	196	534		3188	8029	36988	9150	24604	3234	387
Middleton	652	1	0	0		0	1	13	8	5	0	0
Milan	7803	84	1	6		9	68	269	59	204	6	2
Millersville	6748	28	0	1		2	25	60	13	40	7	0
Millington	11002	76	0	6		11	59	418	71	322	25	1
Minor Hill	525	0	0	0		0	0	1	1	0	0	0
Monteagle	1174	4	0	0		0	4	49	11	34	4	2
Monterey	2858	16	0	0		0	16	35	11	19	5	1
Moscow	528	1	0	0		0	1	11	1	6	4	0
Mountain City	2463	4	0	0		0	4	19	4	13	2	0
Mount Carmel	5424	10	0	3		0	7	37	16	18	3	0
Mount Juliet	33048	54	0	6		3	45	490	57	419	14	0
Mount Pleasant	4835	21	0	3		4	14	95	12	69	14	0
Munford	6140	16	0	1		1	14	95	17	74	4	0
Murfreesboro	129730	790	6	55		152	577	3867	627	3042	198	8
Nashville Metropolitan	668685	7371	81	464		1985	4841	24719	4545	18446	1728	77
Newbern	3341	26	0	0		2	24	90	18	68	4	0
New Johnsonville	1884	3	0	1		0	2	22	11	10	1	0
New Market	1371	0	0	0		0	0	4	0	4	0	0
Newport	6812	99	0	5		6	88	636	71	526	39	3
New Tazewell	2943	5	0	0		0	5	89	9	77	3	1
Niota	718	5	0	0		1	4	37	5	29	3	1
Nolensville	7164	12	0	0		0	12	105	22	80	3	0
Norris	1655	3	0	1		0	2	16	3	12	1	0
Oakland	7670	4	0	0		1	3	75	7	67	1	0
Oak Ridge	29296	196	1	20		18	157	863	175	624	64	4
Obion	1065	1	0	0		0	1	20	1	17	2	0
Oliver Springs	3238	10	0	1		2	7	116	10	89	17	2
Oneida	3701	13	0	1		0	12	130	22	101	7	0
Paris	10143	49	1	2		8	38	556	107	434	15	3
Parsons	2331	8	0	2		0	6	44	9	31	4	0
Petersburg	549	2	0	1		0	1	6	1	5	0	0
Pigeon Forge	6230	47	0	12		7	28	496	93	335	68	3
Pikeville	1642	0	0	0		0	0	46	13	29	4	0
Piperton	1667	1	0	0		0	1	19	5	13	1	0
Pittman Center	578	0	0	0		0	0	5	0	5	0	0
Plainview	2049	4	0	1		1	2	24	15	9	0	0
Pleasant View	4327	2	0	0		0	1	33	5	24	4	0
Portland	12502	45	0	1		9	35	278	68	194	16	0
Pulaski	7572	50	0	7		4	39	347	69	269	9	5
Puryear	668	1	0	0		0	1	11	3	7	1	0
Red Bank	11789	85	0	14		10	61	320	63	226	31	0
Red Boiling Springs	1146	8	0	0		0	8	16	9	6	1	0
Ridgely	1690	10	0	0		1	9	41	4	36	1	0
Ridgetop	2021	1	0	0		0	1	9	1	8	0	0
Ripley	8129	97	2	6		12	77	362	145	201	16	0
Rockwood	5400	24	0	1		4	19	300	46	229	25	1
Rocky Top	1764	8	0	1		0	7	102	17	74	11	0
Rogersville	4374	23	0	2		1	20	233	42	181	10	1
Rossville	790	1	0	0		0	1	15	3	9	3	0
Rutherford	1101	1	0	0		0	1	9	0	8	1	0
Rutledge	1200	0	0	0		0	0	25	4	21	0	0
Saltillo	502	2	0	0		0	2	17	1	15	1	0
Savannah	7035	100	2	10		5	83	526	104	397	25	0
Scotts Hill	985	2	0	0		0	2	10	1	9	0	0
Selmer	4507	29	0	1		0	28	175	39	121	15	0
Sevierville	16843	56	1	8		7	40	938	83	783	72	0
Sharon	911	2	0	1		0	1	20	8	10	2	0
Shelbyville	21511	157	0	18		13	126	694	130	512	52	2
Signal Mountain	8577	4	0	0		1	3	37	3	31	3	0
Smithville	4662	24	0	3		2	19	139	26	104	9	2
Smyrna	48016	250	2	41		32	175	1260	166	1034	60	4
Sneedville	1338	0	0	0		0	0	56	2	46	8	0
Soddy-Daisy	13215	35	0	1		1	33	298	56	214	28	1
Somerville	3095	24	0	1		2	21	112	24	82	6	0
South Carthage	1337	1	0	0		0	1	22	7	11	4	0
South Fulton	2243	13	0	0		3	10	53	23	28	2	0

Table 6. Offenses Known to Law Enforcement, by Selected State and City, 2016—Continued

(Number.)

State/city	Population	Violent crime	Murder and nonnegligent manslaughter	Rape (revised definition)[1]	Rape (legacy definition)[2]	Robbery	Aggravated assault	Property crime	Burglary	Larceny-theft	Motor vehicle theft	Arson[3]
South Pittsburg	3115	14	1	2		0	11	51	7	34	10	0
Sparta	5131	9	0	1		3	5	268	49	209	10	3
Spencer	1640	8	0	0		0	8	11	1	9	1	0
Spring City	1998	0	0	0		0	0	44	15	26	3	0
Springfield	16873	123	0	5		19	99	551	53	482	16	3
Spring Hill	37599	72	0	7		3	62	313	31	273	9	6
St. Joseph	791	2	0	0		0	2	6	1	5	0	0
Sunbright	544	0	0	0		0	0	0	0	0	0	0
Surgoinsville	1785	0	0	0		0	0	20	1	19	0	0
Sweetwater	5957	68	1	0		3	64	384	102	248	34	3
Tazewell	2301	14	0	1		0	13	53	11	37	5	0
Tellico Plains	955	3	0	0		0	3	18	5	10	3	1
Tiptonville	4331	7	0	2		1	4	38	15	22	1	1
Toone	339	0	0	0		0	0	2	1	0	1	0
Townsend	453	0	0	0		0	0	10	1	7	2	0
Tracy City	1433	5	0	0		1	4	27	7	18	2	1
Trenton	4108	28	1	0		5	22	96	22	74	0	0
Trezevant	838	5	0	0		0	5	26	1	23	2	0
Trimble	620	0	0	0		0	0	0	0	0	0	0
Troy	1307	1	0	0		0	1	16	1	13	2	0
Tullahoma	19229	106	1	9		2	94	701	97	581	23	2
Tusculum	2667	0	0	0		0	0	10	1	8	1	0
Union City	10506	91	0	6		14	71	656	153	476	27	3
Vonore	1496	8	0	0		1	7	76	20	51	5	0
Wartburg	901	0	0	0		0	0	13	1	12	0	0
Wartrace	661	0	0	0		0	0	3	2	1	0	0
Watertown	1524	3	0	0		0	3	23	7	13	3	0
Waverly	4089	10	0	1		0	9	119	13	101	5	0
Waynesboro	2380	14	0	0		1	13	9	5	3	1	1
Westmoreland	2308	9	0	0		0	9	39	2	32	5	0
White Bluff	3442	9	0	0		1	8	64	14	45	5	0
White House	11419	41	0	4		5	32	196	24	165	7	1
White Pine	2250	4	0	0		3	1	74	6	60	8	0
Whiteville	4502	6	0	0		3	3	38	11	22	5	0
Whitwell	1731	5	1	0		0	4	20	4	14	2	1
Winchester	8545	62	0	6		6	50	355	49	298	8	7
Winfield	948	3	1	0		0	2	9	4	4	1	0
Woodbury	2779	9	0	0		1	8	58	19	35	4	0
TEXAS												
Abernathy	2728	3	0	0		0	3	57	23	29	5	0
Abilene	122523	546	8	70		133	335	4269	905	3113	251	21
Addison	16067	101	1	12		28	60	840	100	650	90	6
Alamo	19409	166	0	8		26	132	1013	108	833	72	3
Alamo Heights	8248	8	1	1		2	4	268	37	227	4	1
Alice	19464	109	0	7		5	97	1270	371	859	40	10
Allen	101020	80	0	25		11	44	1143	153	937	53	0
Alpine	5939	3	1	0		0	2	46	18	27	1	3
Alton	16137	11	0	1		5	5	280	50	212	18	1
Alvarado	4058	10	0	2		2	6	117	20	87	10	0
Alvin	26100	56	0	17		10	29	645	86	495	64	2
Amarillo	200141	1414	11	162		260	981	9472	1797	6756	919	32
Andrews	14428	71	0	15		2	54	284	47	219	18	4
Angleton	19546	58	0	14		16	28	372	69	287	16	1
Anna	12233	9	0	0		0	9	134	23	104	7	0
Anson	2315	5	0	0		0	5	35	9	22	4	0
Anthony	5618	7	0	1		2	4	158	9	144	5	0
Aransas Pass	8603	58	2	0		8	48	469	120	327	22	3
Arcola	1679	1	0	0		0	1	4	1	1	2	0
Argyle	4047	3	0	0		0	3	21	8	12	1	0
Arlington	392666	2188	21	307		557	1303	12383	2115	9189	1079	15
Arp	1001	0	0	0		0	0	0	0	0	0	0
Athens	12802	43	1	11		7	24	421	140	251	30	0
Atlanta	5594	35	1	7		4	23	242	54	178	10	0
Aubrey	3527	8	0	0		0	8	20	8	11	1	0
Austin	956911	3903	39	751		1048	2065	33545	5232	26125	2188	74
Azle	11854	17	1	0		2	14	331	65	245	21	8
Baird	1481	1	0	1		0	0	28	8	17	3	1
Balch Springs	25474	146	2	12		59	73	889	176	573	140	0
Balcones Heights	3366	32	0	1		13	18	409	21	346	42	0
Ballinger	3767	16	0	1		0	15	109	46	58	5	1
Bangs	1575	1	0	0		0	1	15	1	14	0	0
Bartonville	1702	0	0	0		0	0	15	1	14	0	0
Bastrop	8447	40	3	7		7	23	547	40	473	34	1
Bay City	17595	57	1	9		12	35	749	152	593	4	3
Bayou Vista	1603	0	0	0		0	0	15	4	10	1	0
Baytown	77224	302	9	25		98	170	2858	525	1960	373	7
Beaumont	118283	1316	14	86		379	837	5065	1460	3299	306	49
Bedford	49803	129	0	21		42	66	1077	166	837	74	2
Bee Cave	6891	11	0	4		1	6	142	25	110	7	0
Beeville	13362	81	2	5		4	70	343	82	259	2	1
Bellaire	18859	28	1	0		22	5	277	84	178	15	1
Bellmead	10212	152	1	26		12	113	742	82	628	32	3

Table 6. Offenses Known to Law Enforcement, by Selected State and City, 2016—Continued

(Number.)

State/city	Population	Violent crime	Murder and nonnegligent manslaughter	Rape (revised definition)[1]	Rape (legacy definition)[2]	Robbery	Aggravated assault	Property crime	Burglary	Larceny-theft	Motor vehicle theft	Arson[3]
Bellville	4296	9	0	3		2	4	71	10	59	2	0
Belton	20988	40	2	3		12	23	591	103	482	6	2
Benbrook	22906	36	2	7		10	17	457	80	353	24	0
Beverly Hills	2034	10	0	1		0	9	61	10	46	5	0
Big Sandy	1380	0	0	0		0	0	0	0	0	0	0
Big Spring	29189	174	3	6		15	150	1406	305	1022	79	8
Bishop	3154	4	0	0		0	4	54	8	43	3	1
Blanco	1913	8	1	0		1	6	20	7	12	1	0
Boerne[7]	14368	25	0	9		3	13	374	39	309	26	1
Bogata	1103	3	0	0		0	3	22	4	18	0	2
Bonham	10070	19	0	2		5	12	223	45	167	11	0
Borger	12894	40	0	15		3	22	502	167	301	34	1
Bovina	1750	6	0	1		0	5	7	2	4	1	1
Bowie	5108	11	0	2		4	5	343	67	255	21	0
Boyd	1362	7	0	1		0	6	14	10	4	0	0
Brady	5560	2	0	0		0	2	122	21	95	6	1
Brazoria	3082	5	0	3		0	2	51	11	34	6	0
Breckenridge	5556	15	0	9		0	6	131	30	97	4	0
Bremond	919	2	0	0		0	2	5	3	1	1	0
Brenham	16736	44	1	13		9	21	390	92	264	34	0
Bridge City	7959	16	1	1		0	14	116	26	75	15	0
Bridgeport	6466	15	0	2		0	13	79	18	60	1	0
Brookshire	5203	23	0	1		6	16	77	34	28	15	0
Brookside Village	1577	0	0	0		0	0	0	0	0	0	0
Brownfield	9750	28	1	3		2	22	181	63	108	10	1
Brownsville	185583	448	4	50		130	264	6028	917	4960	151	9
Brownwood	18983	82	0	16		3	63	607	99	474	34	1
Bryan	83286	420	1	59		96	264	2552	511	1899	142	7
Buda	15449	13	0	0		6	7	273	14	236	23	0
Bullard	2906	8	0	1		1	7	66	11	53	2	0
Bulverde	4999	6	0	0		1	5	126	14	112	0	0
Burkburnett	11088	46	0	4		3	39	331	64	244	23	1
Burleson	45116	84	0	16		13	55	843	114	680	49	3
Burnet	6288	22	0	0		2	20	103	30	69	4	0
Cactus	3198	6	0	0		0	6	44	17	23	4	0
Caddo Mills	1497	10	0	0		0	10	17	14	1	2	0
Caldwell	4318	8	0	3		1	4	17	1	16	0	0
Calvert	1144	4	0	0		1	3	20	8	11	1	0
Cameron	5445	28	0	4		2	22	179	39	134	6	0
Canton	3790	0	0	0		0	0	92	0	86	6	0
Canyon[7]	15212	24	0	7		1	16	151	20	119	12	0
Carrollton	136095	220	4	51		65	100	2659	500	1901	258	2
Carthage	6858	24	0	0		5	19	315	39	264	12	0
Castle Hills	4485	5	0	0		3	2	358	49	299	10	0
Castroville	2960	0	0	0		0	0	50	7	41	2	0
Cedar Hill	49215	116	2	10		50	54	1541	207	1240	94	2
Cedar Park	69051	116	0	41		17	58	964	152	777	35	7
Celina	8074	13	0	4		1	8	58	11	46	1	3
Center[7]	5218	32	0	7		1	24	253	35	212	6	1
Chillicothe	650	0	0	0		0	0	3	2	1	0	0
Cibolo	28077	24	0	3		4	17	302	31	253	18	1
Cisco	3769	2	0	0		0	2	56	23	27	6	0
Cleburne	30069	87	0	15		13	59	765	153	570	42	1
Cleveland	7893	71	1	3		16	51	445	57	340	48	1
Clifton	3344	3	0	0		1	2	42	12	30	0	0
Clute	11490	16	1	1		5	9	195	47	138	10	0
Clyde	3784	3	0	0		1	2	64	18	46	0	0
Cockrell Hill	4340	31	0	5		13	13	108	21	75	12	0
Coleman	4334	7	0	0		0	7	69	44	21	4	0
College Station	110785	245	3	52		50	140	2290	342	1840	108	1
Colleyville	26038	6	0	1		2	3	149	45	100	4	0
Collinsville	1700	0	0	0		0	0	9	1	8	0	0
Colorado City	4111	8	0	1		1	6	95	38	52	5	0
Columbus	3625	6	0	2		0	4	52	9	38	5	0
Comanche	4171	16	0	5		4	7	159	57	101	1	0
Combes	3089	0	0	0		0	0	39	8	31	0	0
Commerce	9062	43	0	2		6	35	176	37	136	3	0
Conroe	71111	252	1	39		86	126	2199	376	1639	184	3
Converse[7]	22782	123	1	6		11	105	481	92	338	51	0
Coppell	41654	27	0	8		4	15	516	74	416	26	0
Copperas Cove	33237	178	1	7		39	131	942	173	741	28	3
Corinth	21243	36	0	1		1	34	189	31	148	10	0
Corpus Christi	327948	2328	24	259		424	1621	12198	2296	9246	656	53
Corrigan	1529	13	0	3		0	10	36	16	17	3	1
Corsicana	23974	158	0	31		36	91	879	222	608	49	2
Crandall	3318	13	0	0		1	12	39	16	20	3	0
Crane	4013	2	0	1		0	1	8	1	6	1	1
Crockett	6480	41	0	0		0	41	233	41	180	12	0
Crosbyton[7]	1692	0	0	0		0	0	24	11	12	1	0
Crowell	850	0	0	0		0	0	0	0	0	0	0
Crowley	15272	16	2	0		2	12	323	34	275	14	0
Crystal City	7566	17	0	0		2	15	72	36	35	1	0
Cumby	792	1	0	0		0	1	1	0	0	1	0

Table 6. Offenses Known to Law Enforcement, by Selected State and City, 2016—Continued

(Number.)

State/city	Population	Violent crime	Murder and nonnegligent manslaughter	Rape (revised definition)[1]	Rape (legacy definition)[2]	Robbery	Aggravated assault	Property crime	Burglary	Larceny-theft	Motor vehicle theft	Arson[3]
Daingerfield	2432	14	0	2		2	10	115	24	82	9	1
Dalhart	8455	71	0	7		1	63	306	91	196	19	0
Dallas	1320939	10071	171	767		4604	4529	44910	10948	26370	7592	369
Dalworthington Gardens	2395	3	0	0		2	1	37	15	21	1	0
Danbury	1788	2	0	1		0	1	2	2	0	0	1
Dayton	7638	32	1	6		3	22	240	32	178	30	0
Decatur	6621	13	0	1		1	11	286	13	258	15	0
Deer Park	34156	65	0	16		15	34	592	48	509	35	0
De Kalb	1653	1	0	0		1	0	17	11	6	0	0
De Leon	2132	4	0	2		0	2	34	12	18	4	0
Del Rio	36177	58	1	3		11	43	844	156	664	24	2
Denison	23237	110	0	12		12	86	557	135	372	50	0
Denton	134054	349	5	95		73	176	3025	543	2313	169	1
Denver City	4949	7	0	3		0	4	68	17	48	3	0
DeSoto	53143	174	4	19		61	90	1675	396	1103	176	4
Devine	4775	16	0	3		1	12	105	19	80	6	0
Diboll	5399	7	0	2		1	4	47	19	24	4	0
Dickinson	20131	71	0	24		16	31	430	77	307	46	1
Dilley	4290	12	0	1		2	9	94	39	51	4	1
Dimmitt	4153	6	0	0		1	5	112	37	74	1	0
Donna	16672	179	0	35		14	130	806	165	604	37	0
Double Oak	3118	0	0	0		0	0	13	2	11	0	0
Driscoll	754	2	0	0		0	2	5	2	3	0	0
Dublin	3667	7	0	3		0	4	44	25	18	1	0
Dumas	15051	23	0	3		1	19	232	44	177	11	2
Duncanville	40075	203	0	21		121	61	1249	240	821	188	1
Eagle Lake	3652	6	0	0		3	3	14	6	8	0	0
Eagle Pass	29257	43	1	0		10	32	689	145	533	11	1
Early	2842	19	0	0		0	19	69	19	47	3	1
Eastland	3799	8	0	0		0	8	126	20	100	6	0
East Mountain	818	1	0	0		0	1	6	3	3	0	0
Edcouch	3344	0	0	0		0	0	0	0	0	0	0
Edgewood	1452	3	0	0		0	3	2	2	0	0	0
Edinburg	86535	354	3	61		51	239	4183	545	3481	157	9
Edna	5855	12	0	1		1	10	130	27	101	2	2
El Campo	11604	50	1	4		6	39	339	48	279	12	1
Electra	2695	5	0	0		0	5	61	21	37	3	0
Elgin	9229	32	1	2		17	12	182	29	132	21	0
El Paso	687193	2682	17	314		476	1875	12357	1410	10135	812	49
Elsa[7]	6861	46	0	1		1	44	257	31	226	0	0
Encinal	599	0	0	0		0	0	0	0	0	0	0
Ennis	19096	67	1	23		13	30	526	99	389	38	0
Estelline	134	0	0	0		0	0	0	0	0	0	0
Euless	54791	112	2	12		47	51	1215	212	890	113	5
Everman	6399	22	1	1		4	16	193	36	138	19	0
Fairfield	2905	4	0	0		1	3	34	4	26	4	0
Fair Oaks Ranch	7723	3	0	0		1	2	45	34	11	0	0
Fairview	8685	2	0	0		0	2	53	8	41	4	0
Falfurrias	4962	14	0	1		0	13	149	54	95	0	5
Farmers Branch	33571	55	0	10		29	16	875	165	625	85	2
Farmersville	3474	9	0	3		3	3	57	12	43	2	0
Farwell	1301	0	0	0		0	0	17	5	11	1	0
Ferris	2552	8	0	2		1	5	54	14	35	5	0
Flatonia	1404	1	0	0		0	1	11	4	7	0	0
Florence	1249	0	0	0		0	0	3	1	1	1	0
Floresville	7499	25	0	4		3	18	249	19	210	20	0
Flower Mound	72600	33	0	7		4	22	601	64	507	30	2
Floydada	2729	17	1	2		0	14	59	19	37	3	1
Forest Hill	12984	60	3	2		33	22	427	84	290	53	0
Forney	19252	24	0	5		3	16	324	58	240	26	1
Fort Stockton	8721	45	0	5		1	39	221	43	168	10	1
Fort Worth	851849	4483	66	499		1165	2753	28124	5316	20422	2386	140
Frankston	1163	12	0	1		0	11	37	12	19	6	0
Fredericksburg	11205	9	0	0		1	8	196	28	163	5	1
Freeport	12175	30	0	2		6	22	328	75	238	15	1
Freer	2718	16	0	1		2	13	75	13	57	5	0
Friendswood	39402	27	0	11		6	10	302	36	250	16	0
Friona	3849	1	0	1		0	0	33	12	16	5	0
Frisco	162917	126	0	21		27	78	2392	314	2018	60	9
Fulshear	8237	2	0	0		0	2	55	16	38	1	0
Fulton	1580	1	0	0		0	1	37	22	15	0	0
Gainesville	16349	98	0	25		8	65	563	97	427	39	9
Galena Park	11209	41	0	5		11	25	162	43	98	21	0
Galveston	50667	244	6	60		77	101	1771	331	1244	196	3
Ganado	2116	6	0	2		1	3	17	6	11	0	0
Garden Ridge	3971	7	0	3		0	4	83	10	70	3	0
Garland	238859	767	7	117		345	298	7663	1477	5348	838	23
Gatesville[7]	15717	25	1	12		1	11	169	32	119	18	0
Georgetown	67436	85	0	22		11	52	707	124	544	39	2
George West	2670	10	0	0		1	9	25	4	21	0	0
Giddings	5102	18	0	1		4	13	110	0	104	6	0
Gilmer	5246	40	0	3		1	36	194	32	142	20	0
Gladewater	6427	40	2	2		3	33	199	39	141	19	3

Table 6. Offenses Known to Law Enforcement, by Selected State and City, 2016—Continued

(Number.)

State/city	Population	Violent crime	Murder and nonnegligent manslaughter	Rape (revised definition)[1]	Rape (legacy definition)[2]	Robbery	Aggravated assault	Property crime	Burglary	Larceny-theft	Motor vehicle theft	Arson[3]
Glenn Heights	12185	48	0	3		13	32	291	68	199	24	4
Godley	1082	1	0	0		0	1	11	1	9	1	1
Gonzales	7609	91	0	14		1	76	192	32	153	7	1
Gorman	1045	6	0	2		0	4	19	8	11	0	0
Graham[7]	8857	18	0	3		2	13	128	23	98	7	0
Granbury	9683	15	0	3		2	10	466	47	407	12	1
Grand Prairie	190270	587	9	139		185	254	4527	704	3320	503	8
Grand Saline	3130	5	0	4		0	1	51	9	38	4	0
Granger	1536	1	0	0		0	1	16	1	15	0	0
Granite Shoals	5104	7	0	0		0	7	49	4	40	5	0
Grapeland	1404	4	0	0		0	4	36	21	15	0	0
Grapevine	52423	87	0	7		20	60	1256	139	1052	65	2
Greenville	26689	128	4	22		33	69	804	140	602	62	12
Gregory	2012	4	0	0		0	4	7	3	3	1	0
Groesbeck	4299	8	0	3		1	4	102	43	57	2	0
Groves	15680	82	0	8		12	62	387	85	281	21	1
Gun Barrel City	6048	16	0	1		2	13	175	50	91	34	1
Hallettsville	2601	4	0	1		0	3	50	6	43	1	0
Haltom City	44558	117	0	30		30	57	1059	222	738	99	5
Hamilton	2908	13	0	1		0	12	102	36	58	8	1
Hamlin	2026	6	0	0		2	4	24	9	11	4	0
Happy	651	0	0	0		0	0	0	0	0	0	0
Harker Heights	29600	72	0	14		24	34	944	146	759	39	2
Harlingen	65913	281	2	35		58	186	2590	503	2018	69	35
Haskell	3209	7	0	0		1	6	14	3	7	4	0
Hawkins	1296	0	0	0		0	0	9	4	5	0	0
Hawley	610	0	0	0		0	0	5	0	4	1	0
Hearne	4459	28	0	6		6	16	79	26	51	2	0
Heath	8400	7	0	4		0	3	47	13	33	1	0
Hedwig Village	2724	3	0	0		3	0	183	13	166	4	0
Helotes	8855	7	0	4		3	0	211	27	180	4	1
Hemphill	1209	0	0	0		0	0	16	2	12	2	0
Hempstead	7403	78	0	10		9	59	163	37	122	4	1
Henderson	13491	103	1	4		6	92	571	85	458	28	2
Hereford	14941	56	0	1		7	48	378	97	258	23	1
Hewitt	14384	23	0	3		3	17	133	29	98	6	1
Hickory Creek	4348	3	0	0		1	2	77	6	67	4	1
Hidalgo	13943	22	0	5		3	14	291	30	244	17	1
Highland Park	9316	5	0	0		1	4	199	32	148	19	0
Highland Village	16357	8	0	2		1	5	109	17	89	3	0
Hill Country Village	1083	0	0	0		0	0	52	8	40	4	0
Hillsboro	8297	20	0	4		9	7	278	44	218	16	0
Hitchcock	7753	27	1	3		5	18	206	59	136	11	1
Hollywood Park	3338	2	0	0		1	1	78	10	61	7	0
Hondo	9178	66	0	13		2	51	306	49	248	9	0
Hooks	2739	0	0	0		0	0	39	13	24	2	0
Horizon City	19808	10	0	0		4	6	153	19	115	19	2
Horseshoe Bay	3585	10	0	1		0	9	37	7	23	7	0
Houston	2334348	23960	301	1210		9962	12487	100856	18488	69530	12738	668
Howe	2840	7	0	0		0	7	16	4	12	0	0
Hubbard	1359	0	0	0		0	0	3	1	2	0	0
Hudson	4837	10	0	0		1	9	23	14	8	1	0
Hudson Oaks	2262	4	0	2		1	1	117	11	105	1	0
Hughes Springs	1780	1	0	0		0	1	8	2	5	1	1
Humble	15770	121	0	16		64	41	1567	158	1238	171	1
Huntington	2145	6	0	3		0	3	44	17	26	1	0
Huntsville[7]	41390	174	1	27		26	120	745	139	556	50	1
Hurst	39345	96	1	17		39	39	1627	156	1403	68	5
Hutchins	5809	23	0	0		12	11	191	44	133	14	0
Hutto	24160	19	0	4		2	13	178	28	142	8	1
Idalou	2343	2	0	0		0	2	18	4	11	3	0
Indian Lake	642	0	0	0		0	0	1	0	1	0	0
Ingram	1828	5	0	0		0	5	40	7	32	1	0
Iowa Park	6338	5	0	1		0	4	75	20	53	2	1
Irving	240765	521	5	37		213	266	6490	1183	4674	633	23
Italy	1904	8	0	1		0	7	14	7	6	1	0
Itasca	1621	5	0	1		0	4	26	11	14	1	1
Jacinto City	10825	27	0	0		15	12	270	48	191	31	0
Jacksboro	4410	12	0	5		0	7	83	20	53	10	1
Jacksonville	14950	116	0	11		17	88	513	118	380	15	2
Jamaica Beach	1059	1	0	0		1	0	15	2	10	3	0
Jarrell	1209	0	0	0		0	0	14	3	10	1	0
Jasper	7617	38	0	0		6	32	403	123	274	6	3
Jefferson	2038	15	0	2		2	11	42	14	28	0	0
Jersey Village	7954	16	0	2		5	9	208	33	147	28	0
Johnson City	2021	1	0	0		0	1	6	0	6	0	0
Jones Creek	2076	0	0	0		0	0	23	5	17	1	0
Jonestown	2074	3	0	2		0	1	31	9	18	4	1
Josephine	1139	1	0	0		1	0	0	0	0	0	0
Joshua	6101	26	0	5		0	21	69	15	49	5	0
Jourdanton	4355	3	0	0		0	3	3	1	2	0	0
Junction	2421	3	0	0		0	3	14	1	13	0	0
Karnes City	3437	18	0	3		1	14	87	22	63	2	0

Table 6. Offenses Known to Law Enforcement, by Selected State and City, 2016—Continued

(Number.)

State/city	Population	Violent crime	Murder and nonnegligent manslaughter	Rape (revised definition)[1]	Rape (legacy definition)[2]	Robbery	Aggravated assault	Property crime	Burglary	Larceny-theft	Motor vehicle theft	Arson[3]
Keene[7]	6206	26	0	3		1	22	96	24	68	4	0
Keller	47047	30	0	8		3	19	265	48	210	7	0
Kemah	2028	7	0	1		4	2	159	11	141	7	0
Kenedy	3444	14	1	0		2	11	185	41	139	5	0
Kennedale	7910	12	1	3		3	5	155	56	91	8	0
Kermit	6596	2	0	0		1	1	36	13	21	2	0
Kerrville	23287	72	2	9		6	55	597	92	477	28	5
Kilgore	15258	64	0	12		11	41	523	86	406	31	1
Killeen	143248	996	16	129		234	617	3946	1124	2471	351	42
Kingsville	26227	65	2	3		8	52	919	193	704	22	3
Kirby	8658	32	0	0		7	25	193	53	118	22	0
Kirbyville	2128	8	0	1		1	6	33	8	25	0	1
Knox City	1194	9	0	1		0	8	29	11	18	0	0
Kountze	2074	5	0	0		0	5	31	9	16	6	0
Kress	681	3	0	1		0	2	2	1	0	1	0
Kyle	37407	77	3	8		7	59	612	75	483	54	1
Lacy-Lakeview	6629	31	0	5		5	21	235	40	181	14	2
La Feria	7349	19	0	2		1	16	174	40	132	2	5
Lago Vista	6643	35	0	6		2	27	68	18	45	5	0
La Grange	4728	30	0	6		3	21	73	18	53	2	0
La Grulla	1709	4	0	0		0	4	16	3	13	0	0
Laguna Vista	3223	7	0	0		0	7	27	8	19	0	0
Lake City	520	0	0	0		0	0	0	0	0	0	0
Lake Dallas	8053	24	0	6		2	16	75	19	46	10	1
Lake Jackson	27676	54	1	15		15	23	443	63	350	30	0
Lakeside	1401	1	0	0		0	1	7	1	4	2	0
Lakeway	14771	18	0	2		0	16	203	22	169	12	0
Lake Worth	4870	15	0	0		10	5	451	101	339	11	0
La Marque	16191	123	4	10		21	88	845	172	619	54	1
Lamesa	9429	60	1	9		3	47	371	88	266	17	3
Lancaster	39219	224	4	21		88	111	1257	288	762	207	3
La Porte	35410	73	1	11		13	48	602	97	432	73	0
Laredo	259325	940	12	148		160	620	7890	1015	6646	229	53
La Vernia	1312	3	0	0		1	2	25	5	19	1	0
La Villa	2632	3	0	0		0	3	9	2	6	1	0
Lavon	3045	1	0	0		0	1	13	2	11	0	0
League City	101436	82	5	35		22	20	1937	256	1589	92	10
Leander	40650	46	0	19		4	23	455	57	377	21	3
Leon Valley	11376	36	0	2		6	28	779	94	622	63	0
Levelland	13997	84	0	25		4	55	526	148	359	19	5
Lewisville	105762	211	0	45		49	117	2558	449	1839	270	9
Lexington	1183	6	0	1		1	4	27	4	23	0	1
Liberty	9169	37	0	6		1	30	329	36	274	19	0
Lindale	5883	26	0	3		1	22	208	47	155	6	1
Linden	1978	16	0	0		2	14	36	20	13	3	1
Little Elm	41421	41	0	12		1	28	397	55	322	20	1
Littlefield	6033	49	0	5		1	43	151	40	94	17	0
Live Oak	15809	25	1	3		9	12	714	76	586	52	3
Livingston	5140	26	0	6		4	16	210	22	173	15	2
Lockhart	13590	36	0	7		6	23	318	79	229	10	0
Lone Star	1514	9	0	0		2	7	57	16	41	0	0
Lorena	1745	3	0	1		1	1	30	2	25	3	0
Los Fresnos	6716	43	0	2		1	40	203	27	174	2	0
Lubbock	252900	2741	6	177		471	2087	12661	2678	8933	1050	47
Lufkin	36581	139	1	4		32	102	1542	293	1164	85	5
Luling	5838	25	0	4		2	19	111	21	85	5	0
Lumberton	12500	22	1	2		0	19	207	32	156	19	0
Lyford	2605	11	0	2		1	8	50	13	33	4	1
Lytle	2946	2	0	0		0	2	174	20	148	6	0
Madisonville[7]	4681	38	0	1		5	32	175	41	122	12	0
Magnolia	1932	5	0	0		4	1	38	17	17	4	0
Malakoff	2292	16	0	1		1	14	13	8	4	1	0
Manor	8200	36	1	2		4	29	279	22	252	5	0
Mansfield	65882	67	1	16		19	31	777	118	610	49	4
Manvel	8645	4	0	0		1	3	108	41	63	4	1
Marble Falls	6323	23	0	6		0	17	298	60	228	10	0
Marlin	5626	14	0	0		0	14	26	9	11	6	0
Marshall	23876	137	3	5		31	98	982	298	625	59	10
Martindale	1237	0	0	0		0	0	1	1	0	0	0
Mathis	5062	51	0	0		2	49	146	43	97	6	5
McAllen	142227	215	3	40		65	107	4470	331	4022	117	13
McKinney	169689	243	5	49		65	124	2231	288	1793	150	14
Meadows Place	4781	8	2	1		3	2	115	22	82	11	0
Melissa	8132	7	1	0		1	5	84	13	68	3	0
Memorial Villages	12282	6	0	0		5	1	114	26	85	3	2
Memphis	2109	9	0	0		1	8	23	10	13	0	0
Mercedes	16830	84	0	13		6	65	668	106	528	34	5
Merkel	2619	7	0	0		0	7	36	10	25	1	0
Mesquite	145786	603	2	66		250	285	5534	957	3843	734	9
Mexia	7393	61	1	7		10	43	233	47	174	12	3
Midland	137780	412	3	24		93	292	3352	604	2563	185	11
Midlothian	23085	32	1	10		3	18	287	43	226	18	0
Milford	741	0	0	0		0	0	5	2	2	1	0

Table 6. Offenses Known to Law Enforcement, by Selected State and City, 2016—Continued

(Number.)

State/city	Population	Violent crime	Murder and nonnegligent manslaughter	Rape (revised definition)[1]	Rape (legacy definition)[2]	Robbery	Aggravated assault	Property crime	Burglary	Larceny-theft	Motor vehicle theft	Arson[3]
Mineola	4649	9	0	3		0	6	107	19	83	5	1
Mineral Wells	14391	56	0	1		3	52	649	138	459	52	1
Mission	84380	120	0	36		40	44	2179	358	1707	114	40
Missouri City	75607	144	3	22		56	63	1263	216	953	94	3
Monahans	7854	24	0	5		1	18	144	32	100	12	0
Mont Belvieu	5482	15	0	2		6	7	114	12	73	29	0
Montgomery	849	4	0	1		0	3	22	8	14	0	0
Morgans Point Resort	4257	6	0	0		0	6	14	3	11	0	0
Moulton	911	1	0	0		0	1	0	0	0	0	0
Mount Pleasant	16058	73	0	16		13	44	585	117	451	17	0
Muleshoe	5193	1	0	0		0	1	77	10	64	3	0
Munday	1347	1	0	0		0	1	25	11	14	0	0
Murphy	21175	6	0	0		0	6	153	7	143	3	1
Mustang Ridge	990	1	0	0		0	1	10	5	2	3	2
Nacogdoches	34079	116	1	29		27	59	865	185	642	38	0
Naples	1333	3	1	1		1	0	45	13	29	3	1
Nash	3177	10	0	1		0	9	59	10	46	3	0
Nassau Bay	4118	4	0	1		2	1	140	20	101	19	0
Natalia	1504	2	0	0		0	2	51	21	29	1	0
Navasota	7545	57	1	5		6	45	215	57	136	22	1
Nederland	17240	45	0	9		2	34	409	62	319	28	0
Needville	3088	3	0	1		0	2	20	8	12	0	0
New Boston	4666	7	0	0		0	7	141	14	122	5	0
New Braunfels	73334	207	1	34		25	147	1721	245	1295	181	1
Nixon	2482	2	0	0		1	1	52	22	29	1	0
Nocona	2921	11	0	1		1	9	13	7	4	2	0
Normangee	695	4	0	0		0	4	19	7	8	4	0
Northeast	2535	2	0	0		1	1	74	6	67	1	0
Northlake	2329	6	0	0		0	6	57	13	37	7	0
North Richland Hills	70409	129	2	35		39	53	1370	198	1090	82	3
Oak Ridge	180	1	0	0		0	1	0	0	0	0	0
Oak Ridge North	3181	4	0	0		1	3	76	7	66	3	0
Odessa	123209	996	4	75		136	781	4118	791	2890	437	14
Olmos Park	2420	0	0	0		0	0	41	2	35	4	0
Olney	3159	2	0	0		2	0	54	20	31	3	1
Olton	2121	4	0	0		0	4	8	3	4	1	1
Omaha	986	1	0	0		0	1	9	3	5	1	0
Onalaska	1770	8	0	0		0	8	14	10	1	3	0
Orange	19493	126	3	0		39	84	530	177	301	52	12
Orange Grove	1337	7	0	0		1	6	30	6	20	4	0
Overton	2532	27	1	1		0	25	40	12	26	2	0
Ovilla	3933	0	0	0		0	0	31	8	20	3	0
Oyster Creek	1136	19	0	1		0	18	34	9	22	3	0
Paducah	1109	1	0	0		0	1	10	4	5	1	0
Palacios	4617	13	0	4		0	9	136	39	88	9	0
Palestine	18194	240	2	37		17	184	471	114	309	48	1
Palmer	2064	3	0	0		1	2	46	13	33	0	0
Palmhurst	2714	7	0	1		1	5	86	6	75	5	0
Palm Valley	1291	1	0	1		0	0	0	0	0	0	0
Palmview	5763	83	3	4		7	69	300	59	223	18	0
Pampa	18228	101	3	0		11	87	837	178	615	44	0
Panhandle	2321	10	0	0		0	10	13	4	9	0	0
Paris	24706	169	1	3		28	137	990	276	668	46	0
Parker	4488	5	0	2		0	3	22	10	12	0	0
Pasadena	154648	691	3	105		211	372	4008	683	2912	413	20
Patton Village	1632	3	0	0		0	3	12	3	6	3	0
Pearland	112814	197	1	37		62	97	2046	254	1683	109	5
Pearsall	10151	16	0	1		3	12	182	56	121	5	0
Pecos	9669	58	1	6		2	49	191	31	158	2	0
Pelican Bay	1653	2	1	0		1	0	7	4	2	1	1
Penitas	4785	22	0	2		1	19	103	15	79	9	1
Pflugerville	58975	144	2	21		28	93	948	119	789	40	1
Pharr	77744	228	1	25		35	167	1807	292	1431	84	18
Pilot Point	4140	12	1	3		2	6	39	14	21	4	0
Pinehurst	2078	8	0	0		1	7	56	4	48	4	0
Pittsburg	4622	25	0	2		2	21	127	24	99	4	0
Plainview	20667	59	0	9		6	44	770	130	602	38	4
Plano	288242	399	5	77		109	208	5479	903	4181	395	15
Pleasanton	10013	34	2	5		8	19	499	97	378	24	0
Ponder	1559	4	0	3		0	1	19	2	16	1	0
Port Aransas	4055	17	1	3		3	10	430	36	362	32	1
Port Arthur	55510	362	5	18		105	234	1829	580	1123	126	8
Port Isabel	5015	40	0	2		1	37	237	26	199	12	0
Portland	16340	21	1	5		3	12	539	55	458	26	1
Port Lavaca	12458	112	2	19		6	85	429	144	266	19	2
Port Neches[7]	12741	51	0	5		4	42	174	34	122	18	1
Poteet	3450	5	0	1		1	3	140	24	107	9	0
Poth	2220	1	0	0		0	1	13	7	6	0	0
Pottsboro	2267	2	0	1		1	0	8	1	6	1	0
Prairie View	6538	7	0	0		1	6	34	16	17	1	0
Presidio	3802	1	0	0		0	1	16	4	11	1	0
Primera	4748	2	0	0		0	2	20	9	10	1	0
Princeton	9426	19	0	1		1	17	188	20	163	5	0

Table 6. Offenses Known to Law Enforcement, by Selected State and City, 2016—Continued

(Number.)

State/city	Population	Violent crime	Murder and nonnegligent manslaughter	Rape (revised definition)[1]	Rape (legacy definition)[2]	Robbery	Aggravated assault	Property crime	Burglary	Larceny-theft	Motor vehicle theft	Arson[3]
Prosper	17634	11	0	3		4	4	227	37	188	2	0
Queen City	1466	16	0	1		0	15	23	4	15	4	0
Quitman	1830	7	0	1		1	5	37	12	23	2	0
Ralls	1890	2	0	0		0	2	0	0	0	0	0
Rancho Viejo	2502	0	0	0		0	0	12	6	5	1	0
Ranger	2463	20	1	1		0	18	47	14	30	3	0
Raymondville	11104	80	0	7		4	69	374	92	277	5	4
Red Oak	12278	23	0	0		15	8	382	140	212	30	1
Refugio	2850	23	0	0		1	22	22	6	14	2	0
Reno	3302	2	0	0		0	2	63	12	51	0	0
Richardson	113216	156	5	16		71	64	2473	389	1874	210	1
Richland Hills	8159	19	0	7		5	7	256	38	197	21	0
Richmond	12245	43	2	0		10	31	267	59	193	15	3
Richwood	3895	3	0	0		0	3	34	5	27	2	0
Riesel	1021	1	0	0		0	1	9	5	4	0	0
Rio Bravo	4819	0	0	0		0	0	0	0	0	0	0
Rio Grande City	14518	17	0	0		4	13	227	30	162	35	0
Rio Hondo	2453	4	0	1		0	3	32	10	22	0	1
River Oaks	7782	13	0	0		3	10	126	32	85	9	1
Roanoke	7707	8	0	2		2	4	146	10	125	11	0
Robinson	11674	29	0	3		1	25	98	20	75	3	0
Robstown	11596	202	2	0		7	193	397	147	235	15	4
Rockdale	5619	13	0	4		0	9	155	55	95	5	0
Rockport	10725	38	1	5		6	26	591	165	409	17	0
Rockwall	43542	40	0	14		5	21	800	63	660	77	0
Rollingwood	1570	0	0	0		0	0	6	2	4	0	0
Roma[7]	10310	19	0	3		0	16	144	29	94	21	0
Roman Forest	1910	0	0	0		0	0	13	2	9	2	0
Rosenberg	36360	107	2	19		21	65	618	160	396	62	1
Round Rock	119308	173	0	31		44	98	2653	303	2270	80	6
Rowlett	61047	91	0	18		16	57	915	172	711	32	3
Royse City	11914	17	1	2		3	11	120	18	92	10	0
Runaway Bay	1433	1	0	1		0	0	2	0	2	0	0
Sabinal	1721	2	0	0		1	1	37	2	35	0	0
Sachse	25467	12	0	6		1	5	323	40	267	16	0
Saginaw	22540	39	1	16		6	16	476	68	361	47	1
Salado	2140	3	0	1		0	2	26	8	15	3	0
San Angelo	101870	371	6	58		54	253	4991	875	3839	277	13
San Antonio	1498642	10754	149	1190		2232	7183	77786	12235	58318	7233	254
San Augustine	1989	3	0	0		1	2	10	6	4	0	0
San Benito	24535	81	0	39		12	30	979	194	762	23	2
San Diego	4350	11	0	0		0	11	3	3	0	0	0
Sanger	7913	10	0	3		1	6	113	21	83	9	1
San Marcos	64380	227	1	58		56	112	2004	321	1466	217	3
San Saba	3004	2	0	0		0	2	1	0	1	0	1
Santa Anna	1022	5	0	4		0	1	8	4	4	0	0
Santa Fe	13172	23	0	10		3	10	196	42	134	20	2
Santa Rosa	2875	2	0	1		0	1	22	2	19	1	0
Schertz	39225	85	0	19		6	60	729	105	570	54	0
Schulenburg	2941	23	0	1		3	19	67	15	50	2	0
Seabrook	14091	21	0	5		5	11	211	24	160	27	0
Seagoville	16085	17	0	0		12	5	466	93	276	97	0
Seagraves	2836	9	0	0		0	9	46	24	20	2	0
Sealy	6469	21	0	0		6	15	181	68	107	6	0
Seguin	28319	111	4	26		15	66	1076	173	869	34	3
Selma	10027	31	1	5		7	18	361	38	312	11	0
Seminole	7656	0	0	0		0	0	121	13	105	3	0
Seven Points	1447	7	0	0		0	7	34	9	14	11	0
Seymour	2636	8	0	1		0	7	40	7	32	1	0
Shallowater	2568	1	0	0		1	0	28	15	9	4	0
Shamrock	2007	5	0	0		1	4	17	6	10	1	0
Shavano Park	3631	0	0	0		0	0	81	17	62	2	0
Shenandoah	2914	6	1	0		5	0	277	14	250	13	0
Sherman	41139	127	4	20		23	80	1251	297	866	88	4
Shiner	2152	2	0	0		1	1	16	2	14	0	0
Shoreacres	1624	3	0	0		0	3	12	5	7	0	0
Silsbee	6693	14	0	0		1	13	170	29	138	3	0
Sinton	5756	53	0	3		0	50	184	39	140	5	1
Slaton	6061	23	1	2		6	14	109	20	84	5	0
Smithville	4159	19	0	4		4	11	137	22	104	11	1
Snyder	11882	9	0	2		0	7	305	74	227	4	0
Socorro	33447	44	0	5		7	32	303	42	237	24	0
Somerset	1814	3	0	0		0	3	29	7	16	6	0
Sonora	2841	2	0	2		0	0	43	14	29	0	1
Sour Lake	1765	1	0	0		0	1	35	8	20	7	0
South Houston	17650	89	1	5		34	49	496	70	286	140	0
Southlake	30644	19	2	0		4	13	396	52	330	14	0
South Padre Island	2895	49	0	16		5	28	486	39	421	26	0
Southside Place	1859	1	0	0		1	0	27	1	25	1	0
Spearman	3378	0	0	0		0	0	0	0	0	0	0
Splendora	1697	3	0	0		0	3	28	9	14	5	0
Springtown	2841	4	0	2		0	2	52	10	40	2	0
Spring Valley	4289	6	0	0		0	6	145	21	119	5	0

Table 6. Offenses Known to Law Enforcement, by Selected State and City, 2016—Continued

(Number.)

State/city	Population	Violent crime	Murder and nonnegligent manslaughter	Rape (revised definition)[1]	Rape (legacy definition)[2]	Robbery	Aggravated assault	Property crime	Burglary	Larceny-theft	Motor vehicle theft	Arson[3]
Spur	1183	11	0	0		1	10	13	6	2	5	1
Stafford	18602	96	2	13		35	46	713	113	548	52	1
Stagecoach	589	0	0	0		0	0	0	0	0	0	0
Stamford	2944	7	1	0		0	6	59	21	29	9	2
Stanton	3032	7	0	3		1	3	44	2	41	1	0
Stephenville	20787	29	0	8		3	18	458	69	367	22	1
Stratford	2085	5	0	0		1	4	4	2	2	0	0
Sugar Land	90088	77	0	16		43	18	1460	250	1162	48	1
Sullivan City	4223	17	0	0		2	15	58	15	43	0	0
Sulphur Springs	16227	29	0	5		6	18	252	36	196	20	2
Sunrise Beach Village	734	1	0	0		0	1	8	4	4	0	0
Surfside Beach	557	3	0	0		0	3	20	9	9	2	0
Sweeny	3780	11	0	5		2	4	118	21	91	6	2
Sweetwater	10785	49	1	3		11	34	581	200	354	27	0
Taft	3104	9	0	0		0	9	63	9	54	0	0
Tahoka	2551	6	0	2		0	4	38	10	23	5	0
Tatum	1378	2	0	0		1	1	26	7	18	1	0
Taylor	16979	32	0	3		5	24	432	100	312	20	1
Teague	3575	13	0	5		1	7	71	26	37	8	1
Temple	73411	226	7	34		89	96	2298	493	1620	185	4
Terrell	17211	103	0	14		21	68	841	158	621	62	1
Terrell Hills	5369	4	0	1		2	1	123	29	90	4	0
Texarkana	37442	314	4	23		44	243	1875	338	1405	132	16
Texas City	48095	249	2	33		63	151	1759	324	1349	86	1
The Colony	42925	64	1	28		6	29	482	79	376	27	1
Thorndale	1313	3	0	0		0	3	17	5	12	0	0
Thrall	936	6	0	3		0	3	8	1	7	0	0
Three Rivers	1996	10	0	1		0	9	33	6	26	1	0
Tioga	874	3	0	1		0	2	14	6	6	2	1
Tomball	11700	46	0	9		13	24	394	59	288	47	1
Tool	2274	2	0	1		0	1	23	8	8	7	0
Trophy Club	12645	11	0	1		0	10	80	8	69	3	0
Troy	1883	0	0	0		0	0	36	9	27	0	1
Tulia	4716	45	0	8		3	34	95	16	78	1	0
Tye	1263	1	0	0		1	0	31	5	26	0	0
Tyler[5]	105044	429	5	64		106	254				159	2
Universal City	20275	34	0	5		14	15	522	98	373	51	1
University Park	25103	16	0	1		13	2	303	33	253	17	0
Uvalde	16619	47	0	9		5	33	640	82	543	15	1
Van	2695	2	0	1		0	1	48	11	31	6	0
Van Alstyne	3406	8	0	1		0	7	35	6	23	6	0
Venus	3366	5	0	1		0	4	29	5	21	3	2
Vernon	10495	60	0	11		4	45	330	69	249	12	3
Vidor	10991	36	0	0		4	32	370	81	258	31	0
Waco	133790	695	4	126		156	409	4882	1087	3648	147	12
Wake Village	5466	7	0	0		4	3	130	18	106	6	0
Waller	2559	8	0	0		1	7	65	19	40	6	0
Wallis	1303	4	0	0		0	4	11	6	4	1	0
Watauga	24725	46	1	17		8	20	426	55	353	18	1
Waxahachie	34152	52	0	0		14	38	874	110	712	52	1
Weatherford	29422	52	0	14		9	29	615	82	502	31	1
Webster	11213	61	0	16		26	19	842	72	699	71	0
Weimar	2163	8	0	2		3	3	20	4	15	1	0
Weslaco	39987	172	1	24		41	106	1937	267	1607	63	2
West	2898	5	0	0		0	5	50	12	34	4	0
West Columbia	3941	16	0	4		1	11	82	23	58	1	0
West Lake Hills	3364	1	0	0		1	0	76	11	61	4	0
West Orange	3459	11	0	0		6	5	181	25	137	19	0
Westover Hills	729	1	0	0		0	1	6	2	4	0	0
West University Place	15932	9	0	0		7	2	133	79	48	6	0
Westworth	2687	6	0	2		2	2	216	5	208	3	0
Wharton	8706	49	0	3		9	37	440	44	377	19	2
Whitehouse[7]	8286	35	0	12		1	22	91	18	71	2	0
White Oak	6317	7	0	1		1	5	120	23	87	10	0
Whitesboro	3931	6	0	1		1	4	34	7	26	1	1
White Settlement	17267	30	1	0		17	12	433	108	257	68	0
Whitney	2103	1	0	0		1	0	46	10	36	0	0
Wichita Falls	104685	445	9	124		123	189	3734	825	2646	263	0
Willis	6401	51	0	7		13	31	180	42	124	14	2
Willow Park	5130	2	0	0		0	2	42	9	29	4	0
Wills Point	3551	14	1	4		1	8	62	15	43	4	0
Wilmer	3978	10	0	1		2	7	109	35	68	6	0
Windcrest	5877	19	0	2		9	8	351	18	306	27	0
Wink	1087	0	0	0		0	0	10	1	8	1	0
Winnsboro	3354	12	0	2		1	9	70	18	50	2	0
Winters	2563	3	0	1		1	1	82	34	44	4	0
Wolfforth[7]	4371	0	0	0		0	0	51	11	38	2	0
Woodbranch	1396	0	0	0		0	0	4	1	3	0	0
Woodville	2457	3	0	2		1	0	11	6	5	0	1
Woodway	8836	15	0	4		1	10	113	5	102	6	0
Wortham	1019	2	0	0		0	2	15	9	6	0	0
Wylie	47772	50	0	7		6	37	411	60	330	21	2
Yoakum	6059	14	0	1		3	10	94	44	49	1	1
Yorktown	2157	5	0	1		0	4	34	17	16	1	0

Table 6. Offenses Known to Law Enforcement, by Selected State and City, 2016—Continued

(Number.)

State/city	Population	Violent crime	Murder and nonnegligent manslaughter	Rape (revised definition)[1]	Rape (legacy definition)[2]	Robbery	Aggravated assault	Property crime	Burglary	Larceny-theft	Motor vehicle theft	Arson[3]
UTAH												
American Fork/Cedar Hills	39028	24	1	8		7	8	858	101	715	42	0
Big Water	465	0	0	0		0	0	2	1	1	0	0
Blanding	3876	4	0	1		0	3	57	11	43	3	0
Bluffdale	11765	5	0	0		0	5	120	28	74	18	1
Bountiful	44003	46	1	19		2	24	744	83	602	59	0
Brigham City	18914	38	0	11		5	22	472	121	325	26	8
Cedar City	30441	67	1	13		3	50	635	116	484	35	0
Centerfield	1389	0	0	0		0	0	6	0	6	0	0
Centerville	17204	34	1	11		3	19	594	102	465	27	6
Clearfield	30783	29	0	13		3	13	664	120	501	43	3
Clinton	21567	8	0	4		0	4	367	66	289	12	0
Cottonwood Heights	34493	40	0	5		13	22	918	150	725	43	0
Draper	47696	75	0	28		5	42	1417	201	1032	184	7
East Carbon	1548	3	0	0		0	3	20	5	14	1	0
Enoch	6348	32	0	3		0	29	58	16	33	9	0
Fairview	1265	3	0	1		0	2	6	0	5	1	0
Farmington	23505	14	0	6		3	5	468	45	405	18	8
Garland	2449	0	0	0		0	0	45	9	32	4	0
Grantsville	10253	24	0	7		1	16	175	40	113	22	0
Harrisville[7]	6347	6	0	1		3	2	240	50	181	9	0
Heber	14954	16	0	4		2	10	181	27	131	23	2
Helper	2094	1	0	0		0	1	36	8	25	3	0
Hurricane	15869	23	0	6		2	15	326	58	256	12	0
Kanab	4406	15	0	0		0	15	58	4	47	7	0
Kaysville	31055	18	0	7		4	7	273	54	211	8	1
La Verkin	4220	5	0	0		0	5	84	16	57	11	0
Layton	75482	118	0	43		15	60	1639	233	1309	97	10
Lehi	60806	77	0	36		8	33	769	130	599	40	1
Lindon	10958	5	0	2		2	1	293	37	230	26	0
Logan	50767	50	1	12		5	32	844	120	685	39	5
Lone Peak	28862	4	0	0		0	4	180	38	124	18	0
Mapleton	9479	2	0	1		0	1	69	10	58	1	0
Moab	5262	26	0	5		0	21	73	15	48	10	1
Monticello	2085	2	0	0		0	2	23	3	20	0	0
Mount Pleasant	3306	0	0	0		0	0	40	12	25	3	0
Murray	49758	276	0	66		68	142	3521	470	2636	415	6
Naples	2320	1	0	0		0	1	36	8	21	7	0
Nephi	5594	4	0	1		0	3	148	25	114	9	1
North Ogden	18654	5	0	2		2	1	222	41	168	13	1
North Park	15088	6	0	6		0	0	210	26	169	15	2
North Salt Lake	20572	14	0	3		2	9	391	84	274	33	0
Ogden	85930	450	3	65		108	274	3808	614	2843	351	17
Orem	95640	65	0	26		18	21	2447	209	2116	122	3
Payson	19738	13	0	2		1	10	445	44	386	15	0
Perry	4739	6	0	0		3	3	118	13	100	5	0
Pleasant Grove	38984	12	1	1		0	10	252	41	203	8	0
Pleasant View[7]	9548	10	0	2		2	6	116	29	76	11	1
Price	8310	10	0	4		2	4	356	58	296	2	1
Provo	115739	149	2	57		20	70	2713	266	2292	155	4
Richfield	7597	7	0	3		1	3	282	22	252	8	0
Riverdale	8699	17	1	9		0	7	607	40	546	21	1
Roosevelt	7179	48	0	31		7	10	330	46	254	30	1
Roy	38167	43	2	10		5	26	701	178	466	57	2
Salem	7696	0	0	0		0	0	58	1	56	1	0
Salina	2527	2	0	1		0	1	100	15	82	3	0
Salt Lake City	193918	1815	13	264		506	1032	16551	1807	12814	1930	45
Sandy	94601	161	0	57		48	56	3140	577	2322	241	12
Santa Clara/Ivins	15107	3	0	0		0	3	119	33	78	8	0
Santaquin/Genola	12289	5	0	3		0	2	136	27	104	5	0
Saratoga Springs	27211	13	0	2		0	11	199	51	141	7	1
Smithfield	11015	7	1	5		1	0	36	5	26	5	0
South Jordan	70226	53	0	19		7	27	1546	197	1247	102	1
South Ogden	17026	21	0	9		4	8	329	65	229	35	0
South Salt Lake	25022	204	3	37		58	106	1963	323	1268	372	4
Spanish Fork	38529	10	0	3		4	3	541	75	445	21	1
Spring City	1004	0	0	0		0	0	36	2	34	0	0
Springdale	561	4	0	2		0	2	28	8	19	1	0
Springville	32825	28	0	7		2	19	667	86	544	37	4
St. George	81755	160	0	54		14	92	1465	350	995	120	5
Stockton	644	1	0	0		0	1	5	4	0	1	0
Sunset	5191	2	0	2		0	0	97	18	78	1	0
Syracuse	28011	12	0	5		1	6	306	43	257	6	0
Tremonton	8333	10	0	4		1	5	186	42	129	15	1
Vernal	11687	25	0	4		1	20	349	45	291	13	1
Washington	25564	41	0	8		1	32	517	63	430	24	1
West Bountiful	5559	13	0	10		1	2	143	16	109	18	2
West Jordan	113595	309	1	39		58	211	3644	413	2866	365	6
West Valley	137558	823	10	122		186	505	6425	888	4285	1252	8
Willard	1789	2	0	0		0	2	45	21	23	1	0
Woods Cross	11600	5	0	2		2	1	200	32	157	11	0

Table 6. Offenses Known to Law Enforcement, by Selected State and City, 2016—Continued

(Number.)

State/city	Population	Violent crime	Murder and nonnegligent manslaughter	Rape (revised definition)[1]	Rape (legacy definition)[2]	Robbery	Aggravated assault	Property crime	Burglary	Larceny-theft	Motor vehicle theft	Arson[3]
VERMONT												
Barre Town	7791	7	0	4		0	3	103	29	74	0	0
Bellows Falls	3030	6	0	2		0	4	51	6	45	0	1
Bennington	15265	37	1	2		9	25	369	62	289	18	0
Berlin	2802	6	0	1		2	3	115	12	99	4	0
Brandon	3801	4	0	2		0	2	35	5	30	0	0
Brattleboro	11607	38	0	3		17	18	455	60	380	15	1
Bristol	3955	1	0	0		0	1	12	1	11	0	1
Chester	3069	1	0	0		0	1	18	5	13	0	0
Colchester	17437	20	0	11		2	7	323	55	268	0	2
Essex	21217	8	1	0		0	7	335	49	282	4	1
Fair Haven	2614	1	0	0		1	0	37	4	32	1	0
Hardwick	2925	4	0	2		1	1	62	13	49	0	0
Hartford	9747	20	0	5		2	13	126	23	99	4	1
Lyndonville	1187	0	0	0		0	0	8	4	4	0	0
Manchester	4310	7	0	0		0	7	78	19	59	0	0
Middlebury	8570	2	0	1		0	1	114	13	101	0	0
Milton	10921	7	0	2		0	5	98	13	85	0	0
Montpelier	7542	15	0	8		0	7	226	34	192	0	1
Morristown	5452	4	0	0		0	4	50	3	47	0	0
Newport	4415	22	0	6		0	16	44	5	39	0	1
Randolph	4788	3	0	1		0	2	35	7	28	0	0
Richmond	4134	2	0	1		0	1	33	6	26	1	0
Royalton	2741	5	0	0		0	5	25	5	18	2	0
Rutland Town	4009	2	0	0		0	2	28	2	26	0	0
Shelburne	7887	2	0	0		0	2	56	7	44	5	0
South Burlington	18962	14	0	4		1	9	577	37	540	0	0
Springfield	9132	9	0	2		2	5	162	36	123	3	0
St. Albans	6799	39	0	3		2	34	449	52	397	0	1
St. Johnsbury	7414	12	0	3		0	9	147	16	131	0	0
Stowe	4474	4	0	2		0	2	79	9	70	0	1
Wilmington	1825	1	0	0		0	1	29	5	21	3	0
Winooski	7178	33	0	3		4	26	178	24	154	0	0
VIRGINIA												
Abingdon	8105	11	0	3		1	7	179	13	158	8	0
Alexandria	155319	286	7	21		134	124	2798	184	2343	271	9
Altavista	3478	4	1	1		1	1	102	5	97	0	0
Amherst	2206	1	0	0		0	1	9	2	7	0	0
Appalachia	1655	7	0	3		1	3	18	5	12	1	0
Ashland	7559	24	0	5		5	14	215	11	197	7	0
Bedford	6556	11	0	4		0	7	284	9	271	4	5
Berryville	4323	4	0	0		1	3	44	10	32	2	0
Big Stone Gap	5378	5	0	0		1	4	154	19	133	2	0
Blacksburg	44528	43	0	19		3	21	409	62	333	14	1
Blackstone	3467	5	0	2		1	2	121	10	103	8	0
Bluefield	5247	12	0	5		0	7	265	19	240	6	3
Bowling Green	1169	0	0	0		0	0	0	0	0	0	0
Boykins	539	0	0	0		0	0	8	1	6	1	0
Bridgewater	5939	1	0	1		0	0	17	4	13	0	0
Bristol	16908	37	1	9		7	20	432	56	338	38	2
Broadway	3831	1	0	0		0	1	49	18	31	0	0
Brookneal	1120	1	0	0		0	1	30	4	26	0	0
Buena Vista	6576	3	0	1		0	2	55	7	47	1	0
Burkeville	408	0	0	0		0	0	12	1	11	0	0
Cape Charles	1019	0	0	0		0	0	7	2	4	1	0
Charlottesville	46979	245	1	36		43	165	1228	170	983	75	1
Chase City	2285	4	1	1		1	1	39	8	31	0	0
Chatham	1482	0	0	0		0	0	17	0	17	0	0
Chesapeake	236570	969	14	78		215	662	6001	743	4938	320	21
Chilhowie	1733	0	0	0		0	0	18	3	15	0	0
Chincoteague	2909	10	0	3		0	7	63	14	46	3	0
Christiansburg	22134	35	0	12		3	20	575	62	505	8	0
Clarksville	1199	2	0	0		2	0	9	3	6	0	0
Clifton Forge	3713	9	0	1		0	8	56	3	51	2	1
Clintwood	1309	2	0	0		0	2	29	1	28	0	0
Coeburn	1982	5	0	2		1	2	29	3	25	1	0
Colonial Beach	3589	7	0	3		0	4	77	11	56	10	0
Colonial Heights	17814	58	0	22		19	17	816	45	751	20	2
Covington	5570	8	0	0		0	8	121	10	110	1	2
Crewe	2225	8	0	0		1	7	44	7	35	2	0
Culpeper	17733	43	1	6		11	25	338	17	311	10	1
Damascus	799	2	0	0		0	2	29	1	27	1	0
Danville	41686	335	16	31		76	212	1529	259	1197	73	8
Dayton	1598	0	0	0		0	0	14	2	11	1	0
Dublin	2719	5	0	0		1	4	36	9	27	0	0
Dumfries	5263	0	0	0		0	0	75	7	62	6	0
Elkton	2826	5	0	1		0	4	19	4	13	2	0
Emporia	5382	34	0	5		10	19	263	30	228	5	0
Exmore	1443	5	0	1		0	4	19	1	17	1	0
Fairfax City	24173	23	0	7		8	8	407	33	354	20	8
Falls Church	14124	27	0	4		14	9	219	10	190	19	0
Farmville	8159	19	0	4		4	11	232	14	217	1	0

Table 6. Offenses Known to Law Enforcement, by Selected State and City, 2016—Continued

(Number.)

State/city	Population	Violent crime	Murder and nonnegligent manslaughter	Rape (revised definition)[1]	Rape (legacy definition)[2]	Robbery	Aggravated assault	Property crime	Burglary	Larceny-theft	Motor vehicle theft	Arson[3]
Franklin	8423	24	1	5		8	10	310	28	274	8	2
Fredericksburg	28823	104	2	8		19	75	1040	60	941	39	6
Front Royal	15193	44	0	20		8	16	330	25	293	12	2
Galax	6858	21	2	6		1	12	220	30	185	5	0
Gate City	1937	0	0	0		0	0	31	3	26	2	2
Glasgow	1116	0	0	0		0	0	2	0	2	0	0
Glen Lyn	116	0	0	0		0	0	6	1	5	0	0
Gordonsville	1595	1	0	1		0	0	16	3	10	3	0
Gretna	1243	1	0	1		0	0	9	2	4	3	0
Grottoes	2776	2	0	1		0	1	26	2	24	0	0
Grundy	970	0	0	0		0	0	29	3	26	0	0
Halifax	1243	1	0	1		0	0	4	1	3	0	0
Hampton	135504	442	24	40		180	198	4650	589	3741	320	14
Harrisonburg	52972	117	2	25		29	61	1099	165	894	40	3
Haymarket	2019	0	0	0		0	0	8	1	6	1	0
Haysi	470	0	0	0		0	0	4	3	1	0	0
Herndon	24806	51	0	9		15	27	381	34	335	12	0
Hillsville	2666	2	0	1		0	1	80	12	60	8	0
Honaker	1382	9	0	0		2	7	17	6	11	0	1
Hopewell	22204	103	4	2		44	53	641	153	442	46	1
Hurt	1269	1	0	0		0	1	3	0	3	0	0
Independence	923	1	0	1		0	0	9	1	8	0	0
Jonesville	968	0	0	0		0	0	2	0	2	0	0
Kenbridge	1220	3	1	0		0	2	1	0	0	1	0
Kilmarnock	1428	2	0	0		0	2	32	12	20	0	0
La Crosse	586	0	0	0		0	0	1	0	1	0	0
Lawrenceville	1019	1	0	0		0	1	12	7	5	0	0
Lebanon	3323	7	0	2		0	5	132	3	127	2	0
Leesburg	53016	109	3	29		12	65	820	18	770	32	0
Lexington	7264	10	0	2		0	8	77	10	66	1	0
Louisa	1633	1	0	0		0	1	45	1	42	2	0
Luray	4817	4	0	1		0	3	108	12	93	3	0
Lynchburg	80215	298	2	33		57	206	1802	262	1428	112	5
Manassas	42267	123	1	21		27	74	815	92	677	46	9
Manassas Park	15912	24	0	8		6	10	160	14	135	11	0
Marion	5956	46	0	7		2	37	261	33	212	16	2
Martinsville	13553	28	0	0		2	26	366	50	286	30	4
Middleburg	835	0	0	0		0	0	18	0	18	0	0
Middletown	1324	0	0	0		0	0	12	2	9	1	0
Mount Jackson	2051	3	0	2		0	1	28	4	23	1	0
Narrows	1940	1	0	0		0	1	2	0	2	0	0
New Market	2220	1	0	0		0	1	25	1	22	2	1
Newport News	181676	848	30	71		269	478	5579	902	4097	580	51
Norfolk	245734	1616	46	131		489	950	9617	1165	7918	534	20
Norton	3911	16	0	7		0	9	144	6	136	2	3
Occoquan	1042	0	0	0		0	0	0	0	0	0	0
Onancock	1260	5	0	2		2	1	25	5	17	3	0
Onley	516	0	0	0		0	0	12	1	11	0	0
Orange	4992	10	0	5		2	3	87	11	72	4	1
Parksley	840	4	0	0		1	3	11	2	9	0	0
Pearisburg	2655	3	0	1		2	0	76	8	66	2	1
Pembroke	1073	0	0	0		0	0	21	3	15	3	0
Pennington Gap	1793	2	0	0		0	2	33	8	25	0	0
Petersburg	32293	239	11	6		67	155	1072	230	742	100	1
Pocahontas	376	0	0	0		0	0	2	1	1	0	0
Poquoson	11975	20	0	3		1	16	171	38	129	4	0
Portsmouth	95813	758	14	61		235	448	5373	1208	3707	458	9
Pound	957	2	0	0		0	2	13	3	10	0	0
Pulaski	8855	32	0	17		2	13	251	36	204	11	0
Purcellville	9547	3	0	0		0	3	54	7	47	0	0
Quantico	548	0	0	0		0	0	3	1	2	0	0
Radford	17504	83	1	22		8	52	316	60	244	12	6
Remington	634	1	0	0		0	1	0	0	0	0	0
Rich Creek	744	4	0	2		1	1	26	5	20	1	0
Richlands	5443	8	0	3		3	2	111	21	86	4	1
Roanoke	99978	413	13	36		117	247	4195	423	3549	223	29
Rocky Mount	4803	14	0	2		2	10	184	7	172	5	3
Salem	25396	24	0	5		6	13	527	26	466	35	1
Saltville	2022	0	0	0		0	0	29	3	23	3	0
Shenandoah	2334	1	0	1		0	0	42	4	32	6	0
Smithfield	8418	7	0	1		2	4	151	14	128	9	0
South Boston	7944	37	1	4		8	24	315	79	229	7	2
South Hill	4503	13	0	4		3	6	125	7	115	3	1
Stanley	1649	1	0	1		0	0	25	3	22	0	0
Staunton	24399	41	2	7		7	25	528	34	474	20	4
Stephens City	1962	3	0	1		2	0	26	9	17	0	0
St. Paul	910	5	0	2		1	2	37	4	31	2	0
Strasburg	6622	10	0	5		1	4	79	13	64	2	0
Suffolk	88342	246	4	33		59	150	2141	302	1746	93	8
Tappahannock	2387	15	0	1		2	12	79	4	70	5	0
Tazewell	4378	12	0	4		0	8	80	28	51	1	1
Timberville	2618	2	0	0		0	2	33	3	30	0	1
Victoria	1668	6	0	1		1	4	21	6	15	0	0

Table 6. Offenses Known to Law Enforcement, by Selected State and City, 2016—Continued

(Number.)

State/city	Population	Violent crime	Murder and nonnegligent manslaughter	Rape (revised definition)[1]	Rape (legacy definition)[2]	Robbery	Aggravated assault	Property crime	Burglary	Larceny-theft	Motor vehicle theft	Arson[3]
Vienna	16679	7	0	5		0	2	169	15	145	9	1
Vinton	8266	18	0	2		5	11	214	15	185	14	2
Virginia Beach	453017	700	21	128		266	285	9858	865	8485	508	70
Warrenton	9953	12	0	6		0	6	215	7	206	2	0
Warsaw	1492	1	0	0		0	1	12	2	10	0	0
Waverly	2057	5	0	0		0	5	35	13	17	5	1
Waynesboro	21464	40	1	12		6	21	486	40	424	22	3
Weber City	1251	1	0	1		0	0	21	1	19	1	0
West Point	3336	3	0	0		1	2	21	4	14	3	0
White Stone	339	0	0	0		0	0	2	0	2	0	0
Williamsburg	15256	25	0	9		9	7	230	10	211	9	0
Winchester	27363	61	1	27		16	17	776	122	638	16	1
Windsor	2681	8	0	1		0	7	25	2	23	0	0
Wise	3093	7	0	2		0	5	32	8	24	0	0
Woodstock	5277	9	0	5		0	4	123	9	111	3	2
Wytheville	8097	16	1	1		2	12	224	9	209	6	1
WASHINGTON												
Aberdeen	16155	74	1	8		19	46	711	160	501	50	5
Algona	3166	2	0	1		0	1	49	16	31	2	0
Anacortes	16532	15	0	1		4	10	463	65	369	29	2
Arlington	19142	51	0	5		10	36	871	127	635	109	3
Asotin	1287	0	0	0		0	0	23	6	16	1	0
Auburn	78400	329	6	49		98	176	3618	732	2188	698	23
Bainbridge Island	23998	26	0	8		1	17	320	64	243	13	1
Battle Ground	19734	26	2	9		1	14	372	40	291	41	1
Bellevue	142238	139	0	14		61	64	4635	877	3458	300	13
Bellingham	86005	224	0	61		47	116	4743	751	3709	283	18
Bingen	722	0	0	0		0	0	15	1	11	3	0
Black Diamond	4420	3	0	2		0	1	53	19	31	3	0
Blaine	5130	8	0	1		1	6	142	26	113	3	0
Bonney Lake	20449	30	0	5		5	20	563	120	401	42	0
Bothell	43828	50	0	11		15	24	1214	227	889	98	7
Bremerton	39862	198	0	29		38	131	1576	257	1159	160	9
Brewster	2350	11	0	2		1	8	28	9	15	4	0
Brier	6753	4	0	0		0	4	65	18	38	9	0
Buckley	5077	5	0	2		0	3	69	9	56	4	0
Burien	50934	249	3		43	77	126	2581	551	1364	666	19
Burlington	8680	27	5	3		12	7	1041	103	894	44	0
Camas	22350	15	0	7		2	6	309	67	219	23	2
Carnation	1890	1	0		0	0	1	40	14	21	5	2
Castle Rock	2197	5	0	0		0	5	65	4	56	5	0
Centralia	16785	68	1	10		22	35	1022	177	729	116	7
Chehalis	7417	15	0	2		4	9	619	68	514	37	0
Cheney	11703	31	0	13		3	15	348	57	243	48	0
Chewelah	2607	5	0	0		0	5	68	22	42	4	0
Clarkston	7330	27	1	6		2	18	556	69	474	13	1
Cle Elum	2812	5	0	1		1	3	88	25	58	5	0
Clyde Hill	3279	0	0	0		0	0	56	20	36	0	0
College Place	9114	11	0	6		1	4	283	26	233	24	0
Colville	4728	3	0	0		1	2	116	13	100	3	0
Connell	5747	1	0	0		0	1	32	8	24	0	1
Cosmopolis	1583	0	0	0		0	0	13	1	12	0	1
Coulee Dam	1092	0	0	0		0	0	47	5	34	8	0
Covington	19529	29	0		4	11	14	660	100	497	63	2
Darrington	1381	7	0	4		0	3	38	13	19	6	0
Des Moines	31523	118	3	25		42	48	1294	161	817	316	11
Dupont	9593	16	0	1		1	14	53	4	38	11	3
Duvall	7876	0	0	0		0	0	50	9	41	0	0
East Wenatchee	13746	20	0	4		1	15	507	57	423	27	0
Eatonville	2930	8	0	0		0	8	60	17	33	10	1
Edgewood	9918	19	0	0		5	14	253	66	162	25	1
Edmonds	41705	71	1	15		13	42	1154	169	899	86	4
Ellensburg	19148	32	0	9		6	17	661	87	534	40	2
Elma	3020	9	0	1		1	7	131	38	87	6	0
Enumclaw	11709	16	0	3		4	9	292	39	210	43	1
Ephrata	8116	19	0	3		3	13	411	97	299	15	0
Everett	108988	490	1	64		148	277	5608	949	3701	958	24
Everson	4128	0	0	0		0	0	40	2	34	4	0
Federal Way	96338	454	9	49		192	204	6015	681	4246	1088	18
Ferndale	13338	16	0	6		3	7	314	51	242	21	2
Fife	10134	73	0	7		16	50	714	91	479	144	2
Fircrest	6728	6	0	0		2	4	177	37	120	20	0
Gig Harbor	9124	24	0	4		9	11	524	69	427	28	2
Gold Bar	2119	1	0	0		1	0	26	7	14	5	0
Goldendale	3439	12	0	3		2	7	120	15	100	5	0
Grand Coulee	2064	3	0	0		1	2	154	57	77	20	0
Grandview	11230	17	0	4		1	12	235	38	169	28	0
Granger	3792	3	0	1		0	2	108	23	69	16	1
Granite Falls	3516	12	0	1		2	9	72	18	37	17	0
Hoquiam	8342	18	1	3		4	10	296	52	223	21	3
Ilwaco	914	0	0	0		0	0	8	1	5	2	0
Issaquah	37308	37	0	12		12	13	1149	160	917	72	2

Table 6. Offenses Known to Law Enforcement, by Selected State and City, 2016—Continued

(Number.)

State/city	Population	Violent crime	Murder and nonnegligent manslaughter	Rape (revised definition)[1]	Rape (legacy definition)[2]	Robbery	Aggravated assault	Property crime	Burglary	Larceny-theft	Motor vehicle theft	Arson[3]
Kalama	2410	7	0	0		3	4	37	6	27	4	0
Kelso	11897	54	0	8		11	35	755	115	574	66	4
Kenmore	22340	22	0		3	6	13	305	102	178	25	1
Kennewick	79837	183	1	31		37	114	2254	295	1772	187	31
Kent	128604	372	6	66		165	135	7527	1060	5034	1433	16
Kettle Falls	1596	6	0	0		1	5	21	11	9	1	0
Kirkland	88627	81	1	26		21	33	2004	293	1545	166	4
Kittitas	1439	0	0	0		0	0	19	2	12	5	0
La Center	3159	7	0	0		0	7	51	14	30	7	0
Lacey	47215	108	0	14		29	65	1722	242	1347	133	3
Lake Forest Park	13369	10	0	4		4	2	253	50	186	17	0
Lake Stevens	31440	67	0	21		12	34	498	99	338	61	5
Lakewood	60153	449	0	47		101	301	2939	589	1979	371	15
Liberty Lake	9187	7	0	4		1	2	183	25	146	12	0
Long Beach	1359	1	0	0		0	1	39	7	31	1	0
Longview	36854	142	0	41		40	61	1927	409	1314	204	22
Lynden	13834	9	0	2		0	7	134	18	110	6	2
Lynnwood	37217	143	0	25		46	72	2624	246	2145	233	8
Mabton	2300	2	0	0		0	2	19	11	7	1	0
Maple Valley	26304	21	0		5	10	6	361	87	216	58	6
Marysville	68172	157	4	37		44	72	1916	325	1345	246	11
Mattawa	4568	4	0	0		2	2	34	5	20	9	1
Medina	3278	2	0	0		0	2	78	12	62	4	0
Mercer Island	25527	6	0	2		3	1	531	105	415	11	1
Mill Creek	20419	16	0	3		5	8	425	88	302	35	2
Milton	7785	11	0	2		0	9	304	41	204	59	1
Monroe	18247	60	0	10		6	44	636	73	516	47	2
Montesano	3875	3	0	0		1	2	70	8	60	2	0
Morton	1129	1	0	0		0	1	22	5	16	1	0
Moses Lake	22372	111	1	10		12	88	1365	262	1000	103	4
Mossyrock	749	0	0	0		0	0	13	3	7	3	0
Mountlake Terrace	21212	28	0	8		7	13	513	120	320	73	4
Mount Vernon	34521	88	0	16		28	44	1324	197	1014	113	1
Moxee	3911	8	0	1		1	6	35	11	21	3	0
Mukilteo	21416	24	3	3		4	14	441	85	320	36	1
Napavine	1794	0	0	0		0	0	13	2	9	2	0
Newcastle	11576	5	0		2	2	1	264	62	165	37	0
Normandy Park	6733	3	0	1		1	1	172	25	134	13	0
North Bend	6863	6	0	1		1	4	149	10	123	16	1
Oak Harbor	22795	49	0	16		3	30	322	64	228	30	1
Oakville	659	3	0	0		0	3	19	7	11	1	0
Ocean Shores	5721	11	0	2		0	9	118	40	75	3	1
Odessa	864	3	0	0		0	3	10	1	8	1	0
Olympia	50972	200	0	21		47	132	2491	378	1889	224	7
Omak	4854	26	0	5		8	13	190	44	128	18	2
Oroville	1674	3	0	1		1	1	66	16	50	0	0
Orting	7594	12	0	1		2	9	152	26	110	16	1
Othello	7893	17	0	3		5	9	244	40	163	41	1
Pacific	7228	7	0	2		2	3	146	22	90	34	0
Pasco	71077	148	2	26		34	86	1651	304	1148	199	17
Port Angeles	19525	111	1	26		5	79	982	209	716	57	4
Port Orchard	13897	59	0	7		13	39	790	131	609	50	0
Port Townsend	9378	24	1	3		1	19	306	70	230	6	1
Poulsbo	10199	19	0	5		3	11	294	37	242	15	2
Prosser	5895	15	0	1		0	14	108	24	79	5	2
Pullman	33456	50	0	15		7	28	672	265	388	19	1
Puyallup	40167	135	2	18		58	57	2773	386	2060	327	23
Quincy	7482	21	0	2		5	14	293	102	142	49	0
Raymond	2804	3	0	3		0	0	27	6	19	2	0
Reardan	551	0	0	0		0	0	2	1	0	1	0
Redmond	61893	83	0	15		23	45	1936	181	1676	79	3
Renton	101908	341	4	36		146	155	5767	834	3872	1061	27
Richland	55475	101	1	20		11	69	1344	174	1092	78	6
Ridgefield	6852	6	0	1		0	5	84	21	57	6	5
Ritzville	1663	0	0	0		0	0	103	21	77	5	0
Roy	809	4	0	1		0	3	19	5	13	1	0
Royal City	2234	1	0	1		0	0	30	6	15	9	0
Ruston	808	0	0	0		0	0	40	7	30	3	0
Sammamish	53387	19	0		9	2	8	443	84	327	32	1
SeaTac	28466	151	2		20	69	60	1598	280	866	452	9
Seattle	700313	4294	19	254		1547	2474	38433	7666	26639	4128	101
Sedro Woolley	10860	8	0	1		2	5	402	60	312	30	0
Selah	7753	0	0	0		0	0	71	5	58	8	0
Sequim	6868	17	1	5		2	9	261	32	220	9	0
Shelton	9830	27	0	7		5	15	598	76	454	68	1
Shoreline	55905	92	1		25	26	40	1374	323	861	190	9
Snohomish	9773	21	0	0		4	17	314	52	225	37	2
Snoqualmie	13713	3	0	1		0	2	234	24	191	19	1
Soap Lake	1586	5	0	1		1	3	72	36	27	9	0
South Bend	1609	4	0	1		0	3	6	3	3	0	0
Spokane[7]	214028	1279	8	185		306	780	16455	2648	11815	1992	36
Spokane Valley[7]	95923	271	5	55		67	144	5292	912	3909	471	12
Stanwood	6888	7	0	3		2	2	237	33	194	10	1

Table 6. Offenses Known to Law Enforcement, by Selected State and City, 2016—Continued

(Number.)

State/city	Population	Violent crime	Murder and nonnegligent manslaughter	Rape (revised definition)[1]	Rape (legacy definition)[2]	Robbery	Aggravated assault	Property crime	Burglary	Larceny-theft	Motor vehicle theft	Arson[3]
Steilacoom	6257	12	0	6		1	5	69	18	45	6	0
Sultan	4826	22	0	3		1	18	75	24	46	5	0
Sumas	1386	0	0	0		0	0	13	2	11	0	0
Sumner	9753	22	1	1		4	16	578	82	392	104	2
Sunnyside	16387	22	1	1		6	14	442	63	321	58	1
Tacoma	209914	2000	13	159		540	1288	13749	2420	8710	2619	78
Tenino	1761	5	0	3		0	2	53	20	30	3	0
Tieton	1264	0	0	0		0	0	18	3	12	3	0
Toledo	727	0	0	0		0	0	10	0	10	0	0
Tonasket	1012	4	0	0		0	4	29	11	17	1	0
Toppenish	8997	34	0	5		12	17	486	97	307	82	1
Tukwila	20195	168	2	27		83	56	3128	203	2391	534	3
Tumwater	19569	78	0	12		7	59	843	169	585	89	1
Twisp	946	0	0	0		0	0	16	3	13	0	0
Union Gap	6031	22	1	3		12	6	717	45	635	37	0
University Place	33196	73	1	13		19	40	847	175	564	108	5
Vancouver	174912	675	0	117		148	410	5533	860	3666	1007	50
Walla Walla	32326	122	2	23		17	80	1372	233	1041	98	17
Wapato	5067	12	0	1		4	7	182	30	94	58	0
Warden	2743	2	0	1		1	0	37	4	28	5	0
Washougal	15527	29	0	6		1	22	199	38	141	20	1
Wenatchee	33920	88	0	21		14	53	1128	166	900	62	6
Westport	2011	2	0	1		0	1	116	23	88	5	3
West Richland	14127	12	0	4		0	8	133	30	100	3	0
White Salmon	2364	2	0	1		0	1	24	3	18	3	0
Winlock	1317	3	0	2		1	0	30	3	25	2	0
Winthrop	425	1	0	0		0	1	7	1	6	0	0
Woodinville	11953	17	0		3	8	6	371	78	257	36	4
Woodland	5902	19	1	4		0	14	245	25	204	16	1
Woodway	1375	0	0	0		0	0	12	4	8	0	0
Yakima	94111	496	13	47		126	310	4943	1143	3163	637	29
Yarrow Point	1097	0	0	0		0	0	11	1	7	3	0
Yelm	8780	20	0	0		3	17	544	43	475	26	0
Zillah	3157	3	0	2		1	0	49	8	40	1	0
WEST VIRGINIA												
Alderson	1181	1	0	0		0	1	18	1	16	1	1
Barboursville	4091	3	0	1		2	0	313	15	292	6	0
Beckley	16940	214	3	14		38	159	1278	246	984	48	2
Beech Bottom	496	0	0	0		0	0	3	2	1	0	0
Belington	1935	8	0	0		0	8	10	4	6	0	0
Benwood	1350	1	0	0		0	1	0	0	0	0	0
Bethlehem	2410	1	0	0		0	1	8	3	5	0	0
Bluefield	10298	113	1	2		5	105	208	51	136	21	3
Bridgeport	8402	16	0	3		4	9	219	23	191	5	0
Buckhannon	5662	10	0	3		2	5	219	21	192	6	2
Ceredo	1377	0	0	0		0	0	8	0	7	1	0
Charleston	49429	767	13	36		152	566	3939	947	2694	298	28
Charles Town	6030	16	0	5		7	4	141	61	74	6	1
Dunbar	7612	30	0	3		6	21	234	68	147	19	6
Fairmont	18733	79	0	13		17	49	329	77	224	28	6
Fayetteville	2885	4	0	1		0	3	81	9	68	4	0
Glen Dale	1452	0	0	0		0	0	14	5	9	0	0
Grafton	5145	3	0	1		0	2	5	2	3	0	0
Huntington[5]	48540	378	3	33		125	217			1497	115	20
Kenova	3058	2	0	1		1	0	96	6	85	5	1
Lewisburg	3971	2	0	0		0	2	107	0	106	1	0
Marmet	1440	0	0	0		0	0	36	7	25	4	1
Martinsburg	17789	81	0	13		25	43	882	117	740	25	3
Mason	937	1	0	1		0	0	65	8	57	0	0
McMechen	1826	0	0	0		0	0	0	0	0	0	0
Milton	2683	6	0	1		0	5	104	19	80	5	0
Monongah	1100	2	0	0		0	2	0	0	0	0	0
Moorefield	2467	30	0	1		0	29	56	6	48	2	0
Morgantown	31109	89	2	12		19	56	674	129	517	28	3
Moundsville	8644	30	0	5		3	22	308	45	244	19	3
Mount Hope	1371	2	0	0		1	1	15	4	11	0	0
New Martinsville	5190	6	0	0		0	6	24	3	15	6	0
Nitro	6729	17	0	2		6	9	293	31	235	27	0
Oak Hill	8104	17	0	3		3	11	289	68	214	7	1
Parkersburg	30913	206	4	27		19	156	1373	371	923	79	6
Pennsboro	1068	0	0	0		0	0	1	0	1	0	0
Philippi	3320	19	0	0		0	19	29	9	20	0	0
Point Pleasant	4262	8	0	0		2	6	72	15	55	2	0
Princeton	6017	42	1	2		1	38	215	59	146	10	0
Ravenswood	3837	3	0	0		0	3	9	1	7	1	0
Ripley	3255	1	0	0		0	1	18	2	16	0	0
Romney	1759	0	0	0		0	0	1	1	0	0	0
Ronceverte	1749	4	0	0		0	4	18	1	15	2	1
Shinnston	2164	8	0	0		0	8	19	4	14	1	0
South Charleston	12957	91	1	9		6	75	914	113	754	47	5
St. Albans	10635	37	0	1		6	30	486	100	340	46	0
St. Marys	1859	0	0	0		0	0	2	0	2	0	0

Table 6. Offenses Known to Law Enforcement, by Selected State and City, 2016—Continued

(Number.)

State/city	Population	Violent crime	Murder and nonnegligent manslaughter	Rape (revised definition)[1]	Rape (legacy definition)[2]	Robbery	Aggravated assault	Property crime	Burglary	Larceny-theft	Motor vehicle theft	Arson[3]
Summersville	3459	8	0	0		1	7	128	7	117	4	1
Vienna	10537	20	0	4		1	15	447	29	415	3	0
Weirton	19067	22	0	4		7	11	209	41	152	16	5
Wellsburg	2685	3	0	0		1	2	44	8	36	0	0
West Liberty	1561	1	0	0		0	1	0	0	0	0	0
Weston	4078	2	0	0		1	1	8	1	7	0	0
Wheeling	27486	266	1	12		30	223	669	183	453	33	1
White Hall	665	3	0	0		0	3	5	1	4	0	0
Williamson	2968	16	0	1		1	14	38	4	32	2	0
Williamstown	2977	11	0	0		0	11	17	5	8	4	0
Winfield	2364	1	0	0		1	0	18	2	15	1	1
WISCONSIN												
Adams	1879	23	0	9		0	14	105	12	93	0	0
Albany	1018	3	0		0	0	3	18	1	16	1	0
Algoma	3079	9	0	1		0	8	29	5	23	1	0
Alma	742	0	0		0	0	0	0	0	0	0	0
Altoona	7446	4	0		2	0	2	38	7	30	1	0
Amery	2816	15	0		2	0	13	50	7	42	1	0
Antigo	7801	8	0		0	0	8	466	47	405	14	0
Appleton	74439	208	2	30		20	156	1294	175	1080	39	6
Arcadia	3004	1	0		1	0	0	15	2	12	1	0
Ashland	8005	22	0		0	2	20	400	45	340	15	1
Ashwaubenon[7]	17219	20	0	6		2	12	558	39	506	13	0
Athens	1094	0	0		0	0	0	3	1	2	0	0
Avoca	625	1	0		0	0	1	2	0	2	0	0
Balsam Lake	988	5	0		1	0	4	31	5	24	2	0
Bangor	1498	0	0	0		0	0	15	5	10	0	0
Baraboo	12174	24	0		6	2	16	391	40	345	6	1
Barneveld	1233	0	0		0	0	0	3	0	3	0	0
Barron	3303	2	0		0	0	2	3	1	1	1	0
Bayfield	478	0	0		0	0	0	32	11	19	2	0
Bayside	4417	0	0		0	0	0	22	1	18	3	0
Beaver Dam	16640	19	0		1	3	15	389	59	329	1	2
Beaver Dam Township	3887	0	0		0	0	0	6	1	5	0	0
Belleville	2433	1	0	0		0	1	11	0	11	0	0
Beloit	36878	175	2		17	57	99	1124	149	940	35	8
Beloit Town	7672	3	0		0	0	3	92	26	61	5	0
Berlin	5400	3	0		0	0	3	83	13	66	4	0
Big Bend	1318	1	0		0	0	1	15	2	12	1	0
Black River Falls	3557	3	0		0	0	3	87	7	76	4	0
Blair	1348	0	0		0	0	0	15	5	7	3	0
Blanchardville	817	1	0		0	0	1	2	0	2	0	0
Bloomer	3515	4	0		0	0	3	30	4	24	2	0
Bloomfield	6253	8	0		4	0	4	77	9	67	1	1
Blue Mounds	955	1	0		0	0	1	7	0	7	0	0
Boscobel	3181	5	1		1	0	3	24	7	15	2	0
Boyceville	1106	3	0		0	0	3	8	2	6	0	0
Brandon-Fairwater	1221	1	0		0	0	1	0	0	0	0	0
Brillion	3138	7	0	1		1	5	28	5	22	1	1
Brodhead	3291	1	0		0	0	1	47	9	38	0	0
Brookfield	38043	25	0		0	13	12	870	84	769	17	1
Brookfield Township	6093	4	0		0	2	2	108	5	99	4	0
Brooklyn	1458	0	0		0	0	0	0	0	0	0	0
Brown Deer	12101	48	1	5		20	22	555	41	457	57	0
Brownsville	582	0	0		0	0	0	6	0	6	0	0
Burlington	10669	4	0		2	1	1	201	15	184	2	1
Butler	1822	3	0		0	0	3	36	6	23	7	0
Caledonia	24681	21	0		3	2	16	253	52	191	10	0
Campbellsport	1970	0	0		0	0	0	3	1	2	0	0
Campbell Township	4419	5	0	0		0	5	68	9	57	2	0
Cashton	1095	1	0		0	1	0	1	1	0	0	0
Cedarburg	11488	2	1		1	0	0	81	2	78	1	0
Chenequa	606	0	0		0	0	0	6	0	6	0	0
Chetek	2185	1	0		0	0	1	30	13	17	0	0
Chilton	3886	2	0	0		0	2	22	0	21	1	0
Chippewa Falls[7]	14109	32	0	10		0	22	164	27	128	9	0
Cleveland	1464	0	0		0	0	0	4	1	3	0	0
Clinton	2138	1	0		0	0	1	26	5	18	3	0
Clintonville	4434	5	0		2	1	2	252	33	217	2	0
Colby-Abbotsford	4078	4	0		0	1	3	33	1	31	1	0
Colfax	1161	0	0		0	0	0	10	2	5	3	0
Columbus[7]	4996	2	0	0		0	2	81	1	79	1	0
Cornell	1435	5	0		0	0	5	13	5	8	0	1
Cottage Grove	6954	4	0	0		0	4	61	15	46	0	0
Crandon	1852	0	0		0	0	0	17	2	14	1	0
Cross Plains	4072	4	0	0		1	3	32	3	26	3	0
Cuba City[7]	2049	4	0	2		0	2	16	3	13	0	0
Cudahy	18338	37	3		5	11	18	340	63	248	29	2
Cumberland	2142	1	0		0	0	1	0	0	0	0	0
Dane	1146	0	0		0	0	0	0	0	0	0	0
Darlington	2397	11	0		0	0	11	42	4	38	0	0
Deforest	9674	19	0	5		1	13	76	3	69	4	0

Table 6. Offenses Known to Law Enforcement, by Selected State and City, 2016—Continued

(Number.)

State/city	Population	Violent crime	Murder and nonnegligent manslaughter	Rape (revised definition)[1]	Rape (legacy definition)[2]	Robbery	Aggravated assault	Property crime	Burglary	Larceny-theft	Motor vehicle theft	Arson[3]
Delafield	7194	2	0		0	1	1	167	6	159	2	0
Delavan	9992	22	0		3	3	16	300	21	274	5	0
Delavan Town	5337	4	0		0	0	4	44	10	28	6	1
De Pere[7]	24896	25	0	2		0	23	243	34	204	5	0
Dodgeville	4645	10	0		0	0	10	59	9	48	2	0
Durand	1831	0	0		0	0	0	4	1	3	0	0
Eagle River	1356	2	0		1	0	1	91	6	82	3	0
Eagle Village	1978	1	0		0	1	0	19	2	17	0	0
East Troy	4298	8	0		2	0	6	37	2	35	0	0
Eau Claire	68084	141	1		18	17	105	1818	277	1481	60	4
Edgar	1459	1	0		0	0	1	0	0	0	0	0
Edgerton	5554	6	0		0	0	6	92	6	82	4	2
Elkhart Lake	962	0	0		0	0	0	13	0	10	3	0
Elkhorn	9859	7	0		1	1	5	127	14	108	5	1
Elk Mound	874	0	0		0	0	0	2	0	2	0	0
Ellsworth	3180	10	0		3	0	7	46	9	36	1	0
Elm Grove	6222	1	0		0	1	0	80	10	64	6	0
Elroy	1359	0	0		0	0	0	13	8	5	0	0
Endeavor	458	0	0	0		0	0	2	2	0	0	0
Evansville	5268	3	0		0	0	3	57	8	45	4	0
Everest Metropolitan	17318	26	0		2	1	23	261	42	218	1	0
Fall Creek	1315	2	0		0	1	1	9	4	5	0	0
Fall River	1675	0	0		0	0	0	14	1	13	0	0
Fennimore	2485	2	0	1		0	1	15	3	8	4	0
Fitchburg	28588	72	0		11	21	40	426	79	323	24	3
Fond du Lac	42907	136	1	38		12	85	957	75	858	24	3
Fontana	1702	0	0		0	0	0	14	2	11	1	0
Fort Atkinson	12433	25	0		0	3	22	212	22	184	6	1
Fox Lake	1470	0	0		0	0	0	6	1	4	1	0
Fox Point	6754	0	0	0		0	0	53	6	45	2	0
Fox Valley Metro[7]	21515	15	0	2		1	12	180	28	150	2	0
Franklin[7]	36313	21	0	3		10	8	684	65	602	17	2
Frederic	1099	0	0	0		0	0	2	0	2	0	0
Freedom	6098	0	0	0		0	0	9	1	6	2	0
Galesville	1565	2	0		0	0	2	24	7	16	1	0
Geneva Town	5050	1	0		0	0	1	62	8	53	1	0
Genoa City	3026	7	0		0	0	7	36	2	33	1	0
Germantown[7]	20042	10	0	4		1	5	234	20	209	5	1
Gillett[7]	1346	0	0	0		0	0	47	22	22	3	0
Gilman	395	0	0		0	0	0	5	0	5	0	0
Glendale[7]	12846	26	1	2		21	2	929	49	828	52	0
Grafton	11532	12	0		1	2	9	225	9	216	0	1
Grand Chute	22463	47	0	16		7	24	889	26	842	21	0
Grand Rapids	7466	1	0		1	0	0	74	13	54	7	0
Grantsburg	1279	1	0		0	0	1	30	5	25	0	0
Green Bay	105452	505	4	77		73	351	2306	424	1795	87	9
Greendale[7]	14367	8	0	1		2	5	564	7	549	8	2
Greenfield[7]	37405	86	0	9		30	47	1044	138	827	79	2
Green Lake	989	0	0		0	0	0	14	1	13	0	0
Hales Corners	7758	7	1		0	4	2	118	8	106	4	0
Hancock	397	0	0		0	0	0	0	0	0	0	0
Hartford	14377	7	0		4	1	2	284	24	249	11	0
Hartland	9239	1	0		0	0	1	55	7	48	0	0
Hayward	2287	11	0	0		0	11	104	14	86	4	1
Hazel Green	1245	1	0		0	0	1	16	5	11	0	0
Highland	843	0	0		0	0	0	5	2	3	0	0
Hillsboro	1422	1	0		0	0	1	3	1	2	0	0
Hobart-Lawrence	13793	2	2		0	0	0	61	11	47	3	0
Holmen	9760	9	0	0		0	9	72	22	46	4	1
Horicon	3697	0	0		0	0	0	30	1	29	0	0
Hortonville	2714	1	0		0	0	1	19	1	18	0	0
Hudson	13740	11	0	2		0	9	398	26	358	14	0
Hurley	1484	0	0		0	0	0	28	1	26	1	0
Independence	1342	0	0		0	0	0	13	9	3	1	0
Iron Ridge	899	0	0		0	0	0	7	1	5	1	0
Iron River	1128	0	0		0	0	0	11	4	5	2	0
Jackson	6877	2	0		0	0	2	28	1	23	4	0
Janesville	64234	145	0		28	31	86	1763	238	1474	51	4
Jefferson[7]	7935	20	0	9		3	8	246	4	237	5	0
Juneau	2669	1	0		0	0	1	28	1	26	1	1
Kaukauna	15928	14	0	1		1	12	125	17	98	10	0
Kendall	476	0	0		0	0	0	0	0	0	0	3
Kenosha	99954	357	3		26	115	213	2189	393	1702	94	4
Kewaskum	4117	1	0		0	0	1	38	2	34	2	0
Kewaunee	2862	2	0	2		0	0	22	0	22	0	0
Kiel	3720	15	0		0	0	15	41	3	37	1	0
Kohler	2108	0	0		0	0	0	97	1	95	1	0
Kronenwetter	7714	3	0		0	0	3	43	26	14	3	1
La Crosse	52498	131	1	32		23	75	2290	319	1905	66	6
Ladysmith	3147	10	1		1	0	8	62	8	54	0	0
Lake Delton	2975	14	0		4	1	9	484	25	449	10	0
Lake Geneva	7803	3	0		0	1	2	241	16	222	3	0
Lake Hallie	6546	5	0		1	0	4	139	11	124	4	1

Table 6. Offenses Known to Law Enforcement, by Selected State and City, 2016—Continued

(Number.)

State/city	Population	Violent crime	Murder and nonnegligent manslaughter	Rape (revised definition)[1]	Rape (legacy definition)[2]	Robbery	Aggravated assault	Property crime	Burglary	Larceny-theft	Motor vehicle theft	Arson[3]
Lake Mills[7]	5816	7	0	2		0	5	30	2	27	1	0
Lancaster[7]	3760	13	0	3		0	10	65	2	55	8	0
Linn Township	2404	1	0		1	0	0	6	3	3	0	0
Lodi[7]	3052	5	0	0		1	4	35	3	30	2	0
Lomira	2376	2	0	1		0	1	15	3	11	1	0
Luxemburg	2562	2	0	1		0	1	9	1	8	0	0
Madison	252136	832	8	125		235	464	6932	1014	5544	374	19
Manawa	1306	2	0		0	0	2	23	3	20	0	1
Manitowoc	32877	106	1	8		7	90	927	162	749	16	1
Maple Bluff	1344	1	0	0		0	1	30	2	28	0	0
Marathon City[7]	1513	0	0	0		0	0	5	0	5	0	0
Marinette	10771	5	0		2	0	3	354	57	293	4	0
Marion	1213	3	0		0	0	3	10	2	6	2	0
Markesan	1406	2	0		1	0	1	22	2	20	0	0
Marshall Village	3940	7	0	1		0	6	23	6	16	1	0
Marshfield	18530	8	0		4	0	4	423	48	370	5	1
Mauston	4365	18	0		0	4	14	84	8	71	5	1
Mayville[7]	4958	5	0	1		0	4	64	8	56	0	0
McFarland	8290	8	0	1		2	5	91	9	78	4	0
Medford	4335	4	1		0	0	3	141	4	134	3	1
Menasha	17609	38	0		4	2	32	362	34	304	24	0
Menomonee Falls	36218	16	0		0	8	8	436	25	382	29	0
Menomonie	16308	32	1		7	0	24	380	41	328	11	0
Mequon	24114	6	0		0	2	4	197	35	149	13	0
Merrill[7]	9150	25	1	7		0	17	292	32	255	5	0
Middleton	19263	8	0		0	4	4	255	28	221	6	0
Milton	5601	7	0		0	1	6	91	17	68	6	2
Milwaukee	600193	9201	141	477		3283	5300	24392	5862	12356	6174	311
Mineral Point	2496	3	0		0	0	3	24	3	19	2	0
Minocqua	4438	4	0	1		0	3	103	16	87	0	0
Mishicot	1401	1	0		0	0	1	10	0	9	1	0
Mondovi	2631	3	0		1	0	2	34	2	31	1	0
Monona	8288	7	0		4	1	2	654	28	616	10	0
Monroe	10794	19	0		4	0	15	201	25	166	10	0
Montello	1449	1	0	0		0	1	25	3	21	1	0
Mosinee	4038	4	0		0	0	4	45	9	33	3	0
Mount Pleasant	26286	16	0		5	7	4	705	85	593	27	1
Mukwonago[7]	7795	10	0	2		2	6	150	15	131	4	0
Mukwonago Town	8147	7	0		0	0	7	29	10	19	0	0
Muscoda	1259	6	0	2		0	4	32	3	28	1	0
Muskego	24876	5	0	1		1	3	186	25	157	4	0
Neenah	25850	52	0		9	10	33	491	50	420	21	2
Neillsville	2399	0	0		0	0	0	38	1	36	1	0
Neshkoro	421	0	0	0		0	0	3	0	3	0	1
New Berlin	39873	12	0	4		4	4	420	55	356	9	1
New Glarus	2170	1	0		0	0	1	26	2	24	0	0
New Holstein	3213	3	0	1		0	2	43	0	42	1	0
New Lisbon	2473	5	0		1	0	4	30	1	28	1	0
New London	7148	12	0	4		0	8	108	5	102	1	0
New Richmond	8913	14	0	0		0	14	174	22	142	10	0
Niagara	1580	0	0		0	0	0	10	1	9	0	0
North Fond du Lac	5003	7	0	2		0	5	71	5	64	2	0
North Hudson	3832	2	0		1	0	1	9	3	6	0	0
North Prairie	2163	1	0		0	0	1	10	1	9	0	0
Norwalk	635	0	0		0	0	0	0	0	0	0	0
Oak Creek[7]	35337	31	0	4		7	20	897	91	772	34	1
Oconomowoc[7]	16480	11	1	0		1	9	141	7	129	5	0
Oconomowoc Lake	615	0	0		0	0	0	15	0	15	0	0
Oconomowoc Town	8662	2	0		0	1	1	14	3	6	5	0
Oconto	4468	3	0		0	1	2	119	10	100	9	1
Oconto Falls	2823	6	0	3		0	3	38	3	30	5	0
Omro	3560	6	0		0	0	6	54	6	47	1	0
Onalaska	18600	13	0	6		0	7	508	60	443	5	0
Oregon	10189	17	0	1		1	15	47	7	39	1	0
Osceola	2502	14	0		1	0	13	13	1	10	2	0
Oshkosh	66654	141	0		7	28	106	1471	194	1209	68	2
Osseo	1703	5	0		1	0	4	35	5	26	4	0
Owen	929	4	0		0	0	4	15	0	15	0	0
Oxford	587	1	0	0		0	1	5	2	3	0	0
Palmyra[7]	1775	4	0	0		0	4	41	4	37	0	0
Park Falls	2311	3	0		2	0	1	30	1	28	1	0
Pepin	787	6	0		1	0	5	34	2	30	2	0
Peshtigo	3416	1	0		0	0	1	71	11	59	1	0
Pewaukee Village	8207	7	0	6		0	1	95	6	84	5	0
Phillips	1371	1	0	0		0	1	28	4	24	0	0
Plainfield	829	1	0		0	0	1	6	3	3	0	0
Platteville[7]	12859	26	0	4		1	21	261	16	238	7	0
Pleasant Prairie	20928	19	0		10	5	4	390	22	354	14	0
Plover	12360	19	0	6		3	10	165	15	148	2	1
Plymouth	8518	16	0		1	2	13	132	13	116	3	0
Portage	10394	22	2		1	3	16	229	40	184	5	2
Port Washington	11633	21	0		0	2	19	86	6	79	1	1
Poynette[7]	2485	3	0	0		0	3	21	5	16	0	1

Table 6. Offenses Known to Law Enforcement, by Selected State and City, 2016—Continued

(Number.)

State/city	Population	Violent crime	Murder and nonnegligent manslaughter	Rape (revised definition)[1]	Rape (legacy definition)[2]	Robbery	Aggravated assault	Property crime	Burglary	Larceny-theft	Motor vehicle theft	Arson[3]
Prairie du Chien	5731	5	0		1	0	4	96	7	88	1	0
Princeton	1180	0	0		0	0	0	21	1	20	0	0
Pulaski	3552	4	0		0	0	4	39	5	34	0	0
Racine	77536	367	6		16	133	212	2287	677	1510	100	11
Reedsburg	9605	14	0		6	1	7	131	6	123	2	0
Rhinelander	7477	17	0	4		1	12	184	34	145	5	0
Rib Lake	891	0	0		0	0	0	0	0	0	0	0
Rice Lake[7]	8391	22	0	5		1	16	298	31	261	6	0
Richland Center	4980	1	0		0	0	1	64	8	56	0	1
Rio	1041	2	1		1	0	0	4	2	2	0	0
Ripon	7694	9	0	0		0	9	108	12	92	4	0
Ripon Town	1392	0	0		0	0	0	5	2	3	0	0
River Falls	15314	53	0	9		2	42	285	51	220	14	0
River Hills	1606	1	0	0		0	1	12	0	9	3	0
Rome Town	2692	2	0	0		0	2	16	4	12	0	0
Rosendale	1038	0	0		0	0	0	0	0	0	0	0
Rothschild	5342	7	0		1	0	6	103	6	95	2	0
Sauk Prairie	4640	0	0		0	0	0	73	7	65	1	0
Saukville	4465	2	0		0	0	2	69	5	59	5	0
Seymour	3437	8	0	0		0	8	31	5	25	1	0
Sharon	1582	1	0		0	0	1	13	7	4	2	1
Shawano	9095	16	0		1	0	15	318	30	279	9	1
Sheboygan	48710	131	1		20	10	100	1063	119	908	36	5
Sheboygan Falls	7849	2	1		1	0	0	35	1	32	2	0
Shiocton	921	0	0	0		0	0	15	0	13	2	0
Shorewood	13319	13	0		1	8	4	259	26	207	26	0
Shorewood Hills	2149	0	0	0		0	0	34	0	33	1	0
Siren	773	1	0	0		0	1	45	7	35	3	1
Slinger	5232	1	0		0	0	1	71	3	66	2	0
South Milwaukee	21212	43	0		7	16	20	504	79	398	27	0
Sparta	9708	30	1		7	1	21	176	29	136	11	0
Spencer[7]	1920	4	0	2		0	2	8	0	8	0	0
Spooner	2565	12	0		0	0	12	61	8	52	1	0
Spring Green	1655	0	0		0	0	0	28	1	26	1	0
Stanley	3560	8	0		1	1	6	37	7	28	2	1
St. Croix Falls	2048	2	0		0	0	2	116	6	110	0	0
Stevens Point	26587	50	1	8		2	39	426	48	375	3	1
St. Francis	9580	13	0		4	6	3	186	25	148	13	1
Stoughton	13148	26	0	0		5	21	157	15	136	6	0
Strum	1127	0	0		0	0	0	8	1	7	0	0
Sturgeon Bay	8925	4	0		2	0	2	80	9	71	0	0
Sturtevant	6958	2	0		0	0	2	45	7	36	2	0
Summit	4828	2	0		0	0	2	46	9	34	3	0
Sun Prairie	32943	35	0		5	6	24	586	36	528	22	1
Superior	26451	60	0		12	12	36	1255	131	1066	58	6
Theresa	1204	0	0		0	0	0	14	1	13	0	0
Thiensville	3167	0	0		0	0	0	31	2	29	0	0
Three Lakes	2124	0	0	0		0	0	38	13	24	1	0
Tomah	9398	21	0		3	1	17	223	20	198	5	0
Tomahawk[7]	3189	7	0	3		1	3	73	10	60	3	0
Town of East Troy	4094	6	0		1	0	5	23	7	15	1	0
Town of Madison	6878	32	1	2		13	16	181	43	123	15	0
Town of Menasha	19083	19	0		0	4	15	209	54	147	8	1
Trempealeau	1632	1	0		0	1	0	12	6	5	1	0
Twin Lakes	6119	8	0		2	3	3	62	11	51	0	0
Two Rivers	11259	26	0	2		2	22	185	44	132	9	1
Verona	12942	10	0		3	0	7	178	18	151	9	0
Viroqua	4364	3	0		0	0	3	85	3	79	3	0
Walworth	2843	0	0		0	0	0	5	2	3	0	0
Washburn	2043	8	0		0	0	8	13	1	11	1	0
Waterloo	3345	2	0	0		0	2	29	3	26	0	0
Watertown	23816	64	0		8	7	49	375	55	315	5	2
Waukesha	72223	92	0		31	14	47	1117	182	891	44	3
Waunakee	13556	12	0		0	0	12	74	19	55	0	0
Waupaca	6001	21	0		4	0	17	216	14	194	8	1
Waupun	11342	20	0	6		1	13	107	19	85	3	0
Wausau	39091	114	0		29	25	60	959	137	776	46	2
Wautoma	2120	3	0		0	0	3	101	6	95	0	0
Wauwatosa	47771	77	1		0	65	11	1856	233	1478	145	0
West Allis[7]	60558	200	6	20		76	98	2262	451	1609	202	15
West Bend	31791	58	0		25	4	29	683	52	616	15	0
Westby	2276	1	0		1	0	0	35	4	30	1	1
Westfield	1221	0	0	0		0	0	33	6	27	0	0
West Milwaukee	4206	47	0		3	26	18	501	46	406	49	0
West Salem	5055	5	0	0		0	5	62	5	55	2	0
Whitefish Bay	14087	7	0	0		1	6	164	19	138	7	0
Whitehall	1570	1	0		0	0	1	14	1	13	0	0
Whitewater	14752	28	1		11	4	12	201	34	157	10	1
Wild Rose	694	0	0		0	0	0	6	0	6	0	0
Williams Bay	2605	0	0		0	0	0	22	3	19	0	0
Wilton	504	0	0		0	0	0	2	1	1	0	0
Winneconne	2458	2	0		0	0	2	5	0	5	0	0
Wisconsin Dells	2702	17	0		4	0	13	168	16	143	9	0

Table 6. Offenses Known to Law Enforcement, by Selected State and City, 2016—Continued

(Number.)

State/city	Population	Violent crime	Murder and nonnegligent manslaughter	Rape (revised definition)[1]	Rape (legacy definition)[2]	Robbery	Aggravated assault	Property crime	Burglary	Larceny-theft	Motor vehicle theft	Arson[3]
Wisconsin Rapids	17802	9	2		3	0	4	729	114	603	12	1
Woodruff	1979	1	0	0		0	1	5	0	5	0	0
WYOMING												
Afton	1983	0	0	0		0	0	27	3	24	0	0
Buffalo	4640	7	0	1		0	6	87	11	69	7	0
Casper	61343	70	0	2		7	61	1669	255	1297	117	6
Cheyenne	64046	172	5	26		15	126	2427	356	1873	198	6
Cody	9842	11	0	2		0	9	221	35	181	5	1
Diamondville	738	0	0	0		0	0	0	0	0	0	0
Douglas	6617	40	0	0		1	39	118	22	91	5	0
Evanston	12087	15	2	2		2	9	347	24	311	12	0
Evansville	2999	34	0	2		1	31	67	17	46	4	0
Gillette	33218	62	2	3		7	50	708	99	571	38	1
Glenrock	2603	7	0	1		0	6	36	5	31	0	0
Green River	12477	32	0	1		0	31	119	24	90	5	2
Greybull	1886	4	0	0		0	4	14	4	9	1	0
Hanna	809	0	0	0		0	0	4	3	1	0	0
Jackson	10713	30	0	11		1	18	195	17	160	18	0
Kemmerer	2757	7	0	1		1	5	16	1	13	2	1
Lander	7699	0	0	0		0	0	242	3	231	8	0
Laramie	32411	38	0	12		2	24	410	57	336	17	1
Mills	3854	8	0	0		1	7	97	33	56	8	0
Moorcroft	1072	3	0	2		0	1	32	10	20	2	0
Newcastle	3537	7	0	2		0	5	54	5	47	2	0
Pine Bluffs	1149	3	0	0		0	3	17	4	12	1	0
Powell	6491	13	0	5		0	8	152	26	124	2	1
Rawlins	9004	17	0	6		1	10	280	34	228	18	2
Riverton	10905	47	1	8		4	34	610	52	521	37	1
Rock Springs	24161	79	2	35		2	40	491	58	406	27	0
Saratoga	1675	0	0	0		0	0	19	6	11	2	0
Sheridan	17956	17	2	0		1	14	362	54	295	13	2
Sundance	1289	1	0	1		0	0	14	0	14	0	0
Thermopolis	2967	7	1	0		3	3	32	3	28	1	0
Torrington	6676	25	0	0		0	25	99	19	77	3	0
Wheatland	3665	8	0	0		0	8	63	13	47	3	0
Worland	5348	6	0	3		0	3	62	18	43	1	0

1 The figures shown in this column for the offense of rape were reported using the revised Uniform Crime Reporting (UCR) definition of rape. 2 The figures shown in this column for the offense of rape were reported using the legacy UCR definition of rape. 3 The FBI does not publish arson data unless it receives data from either the agency or the state for all 12 months of the calendar year. 4 The FBI determined that the agency's data were overreported. Consequently, those data are not included in this table. 5 The FBI determined that the agency's data were underreported. Consequently, those data are not included in this table. 6 The population for the city of Mobile, Alabama, includes 55,819 inhabitants from the jurisdiction of the Mobile County Sheriff's Department. 7 Because of changes in the state/local agency's reporting practices, figures are not comparable to previous years' data. 8 The 2016 murder offenses include those victims of the Pulse Nightclub incident; therefore, figures are not comparable to previous years' data. 9 The FBI determined that the agency did not follow national UCR Program guidelines for reporting an offense. Consequently, this figure is not included in this table. 10 This agency began the year submitting rape data classified according to the legacy UCR definition. However, at some point during the calendar year, the agency modified its reporting methods and began classifying and submitting rape offenses according to the revised UCR definition of rape. See the data declaration for further explanation. 11 Arson offenses are reported by the Toledo Fire Department; therefore, those figures are not included in this report.

Table 7. Offenses Known to Law Enforcement, by Selected State and University or College, 2016

(Number.)

State and university/college	Student enrollment[1]	Violent crime	Murder and nonnegligent manslaughter	Rape (revised definition)[2]	Rape (legacy definition)[3]	Robbery	Aggravated assault	Property crime	Burglary	Larceny-theft	Motor vehicle theft	Arson[4]
ALABAMA												
Jacksonville State University	8,314	5	0	0		1	4	72	12	60	0	
Samford University	5,206	0	0	0		0	0	57	7	50	0	
Troy University	17,765	4	0	2		1	1	116	11	102	3	
Tuskegee University	2,996	4	0	0		0	4	84	0	81	3	
University of Alabama												
Birmingham	18,333	32	0	5		4	23	353	4	340	9	
Tuscaloosa	37,098	20	0	4		1	15	306	33	269	4	
University of South Alabama	16,211	22	0	3		1	18	119	13	104	2	
ALASKA												
University of Alaska												
Anchorage	16,762	4	0	0		0	4	139	7	120	12	1
Fairbanks	8,638	4	0	2		0	2	66	1	62	3	0
ARIZONA												
Arizona State University, Main Campus	90,906	45	0	10		13	22	902	82	803	17	3
Central Arizona College	5,849	2	0	0		0	2	13	7	4	2	0
Northern Arizona University	29,021	26	0	15		2	9	232	15	214	3	1
Pima Community College	26,880	2	0	1		1	0	87	9	75	3	0
University of Arizona	42,595	24	0	17		1	6	612	47	548	17	0
ARKANSAS												
Arkansas State University												
Beebe	3,935	1	0	1		0	0	6	0	4	2	0
Jonesboro	13,410	6	0	4		0	2	113	8	103	2	0
Arkansas Tech University	12,054	6	0	0		2	4	83	20	60	3	0
University of Arkansas												
Fayetteville	26,754	9	0	3		1	5	233	16	185	32	1
Little Rock	11,891	1	0	0		0	1	82	2	76	4	0
Medical Sciences	3,021	4	0	0		0	4	85	2	77	6	0
Pine Bluff	2,658	1	0	0		1	0	56	5	51	0	1
University of Central Arkansas	11,754	4	0	3		0	1	112	9	99	4	0
CALIFORNIA												
Allan Hancock College	10,949	0	0	0		0	0	15	5	10	0	0
California State Polytechnic University												
Pomona	23,717	7	0	4		2	1	175	20	142	13	0
San Luis Obispo	20,944	12	0	10		1	1	136	10	125	1	1
California State University												
Bakersfield	9,228	1	0	0		0	1	59	4	53	2	0
Channel Islands	6,167	5	0	5		0	0	72	6	64	2	0
Chico	17,220	8	0	6		1	1	256	12	233	11	0
Dominguez Hills	14,635	4	0	0		1	3	45	6	34	5	0
East Bay	15,528	3	0	2		1	0	75	11	62	2	0
Fresno	24,136	15	0	5		5	5	337	62	245	30	1
Fullerton	38,948	4	0	0		1	3	213	28	177	8	0
Long Beach	37,446	9	0	3		2	4	193	8	165	20	1
Los Angeles	27,680	8	0	4		0	4	145	9	124	12	0
Monterey Bay	7,102	4	0	2		1	1	48	3	45	0	1
Northridge	41,548	21	0	10		7	4	258	17	225	16	0
Sacramento	30,284	4	0	1		2	1	198	10	181	7	0
San Bernardino	20,024	10	0	4		3	3	99	5	69	25	2
San Jose	32,773	30	0	6		4	20	424	34	356	34	6
San Marcos	12,793	4	0	2		1	1	49	5	44	0	0
Stanislaus	9,282	1	0	0		0	1	72	3	65	4	0
College of the Sequoias	11,266	2	0	0		1	1	77	14	57	6	0
Contra Costa Community College	34,910	7	0	0		5	2	230	20	181	29	1
Cuesta College	9,600	0	0	0		0	0	11	0	10	1	0
El Camino College	24,001	3	0	0		3	0	103	11	84	8	1
Foothill-De Anza College	37,960	1	0	0		1	0	46	1	42	3	0
Humboldt State University	8,790	6	0	4		2	0	112	5	107	0	2
Irvine Valley College	13,183	0	0	0		0	0	31	5	26	0	0
Marin Community College	5,490	1	0	0		0	1	17	2	15	0	0
Mt. San Jacinto College	15,010	2	0	1		0	1	33	12	17	4	0
Pasadena Community College	27,050	4	0	0		1	3	83	1	81	1	1
Riverside Community College	37,594	0	0	0		0	0	88	7	69	12	0
San Bernardino Community College	19,121	4	0	0		3	1	86	23	55	8	1
San Diego State University	34,254	19	0	8		9	2	593	65	515	13	3
San Francisco State University	30,256	9	0	4		4	1	260	33	212	15	0
San Jose/Evergreen Community College	17,136	1	0	0		0	1	39	0	36	3	0
Santa Rosa Junior College	22,411	5	0	0		0	5	51	2	49	0	0
Sonoma State University	9,408	5	0	4		0	1	91	5	74	12	0
State Center Community College District	32,533	6	0	0		3	3	139	18	113	8	0
University of California												
Berkeley	38,189	44	0	16		13	15	699	41	621	37	5
Davis	35,186	12	0	7		1	4	555	29	517	9	0
Hastings College of Law	950	8	0	0		5	3	27	1	26	0	0
Irvine	30,836	21	0	12		2	7	442	39	391	12	6
Los Angeles	41,908	84	0	26		8	50	768	127	612	29	1
Medical Center, Sacramento[5]		13	0	1		1	11	145	3	135	7	1
Merced	6,685	1	0	0		0	1	52	7	45	0	0
Riverside	21,385	8	0	2		4	2	289	23	249	17	1

Table 7. Offenses Known to Law Enforcement, by Selected State and University or College, 2016—Continued

(Number.)

State and university/college	Student enrollment[1]	Violent crime	Murder and nonnegligent manslaughter	Rape (revised definition)[2]	Rape (legacy definition)[3]	Robbery	Aggravated assault	Property crime	Burglary	Larceny-theft	Motor vehicle theft	Arson[4]
San Diego	32,906	13	0	4		4	5	418	26	378	14	5
San Francisco	3,107	12	1	0		3	8	464	72	382	10	1
Santa Barbara	23,497	48	0	22		2	24	288	27	259	2	1
Santa Cruz	17,868	12	0	5		1	6	344	48	282	14	0
Ventura County Community College District	34,022	3	0	0		0	3	77	16	61	0	1
West Valley-Mission College	17,375	3	0	1		0	2	39	9	27	3	0
COLORADO												
Adams State University	3,404	2	0	1		0	1	44	10	33	1	0
Aims Community College	5,298	0	0	0		0	0	2	0	1	1	1
Colorado School of Mines	6,054	2	0	2		0	0	50	0	48	2	1
Colorado State University, Fort Collins	30,614	6	0	3		0	3	322	22	293	7	7
Fort Lewis College	3,707	1	0	1		0	0	49	19	30	0	1
Pikes Peak Community College	13,311	0	0	0		0	0	10	1	8	1	0
Red Rocks Community College	7,789	0	0	0		0	0	7	0	7	0	1
University of Colorado												
Boulder	33,056	18	0	9		1	8	545	33	495	17	4
Colorado Springs	11,988	11	0	6		1	4	46	3	42	1	0
Denver	23,671	1	0	0		1	0	56	0	51	5	0
University of Northern Colorado	12,216	7	0	6		1	0	152	2	147	3	0
CONNECTICUT												
Central Connecticut State University	12,086	2	0	1		1	0	25	3	22	0	0
Eastern Connecticut State University	5,261	0	0	0		0	0	18	1	16	1	0
Southern Connecticut State University	10,473	4	0	3		0	1	24	2	22	0	0
University of Connecticut												
Health Center[5]		0	0	0		0	0	17	2	15	0	0
Storrs, Avery Point, and Hartford[5]		5	0	3		1	1	189	22	156	11	3
Western Connecticut State University	5,826	1	0	1		0	0	34	9	25	0	0
Yale University	12,385	1	0	0		1	0	274	33	238	3	1
DELAWARE												
Delaware State University	4,288	4	0	1		0	3	119	7	111	1	0
University of Delaware	22,852	3	0	0		0	3	143	6	137	0	1
FLORIDA												
Florida A&M University	9,928	6	0	1		3	2	97	4	85	8	0
Florida Atlantic University	30,380	6	0	1		3	2	160	20	127	13	0
Florida Gulf Coast University	14,833	3	0	2		1	0	53	1	52	0	0
Florida International University	49,782	15	0	5		7	3	355	28	309	18	0
Florida Polytechnic University[5]		1	0	0		1	0	6	0	6	0	0
Florida SouthWestern State College	15,709	0	0	0		0	0	14	2	12	0	0
Florida State University												
Panama City[5]		0	0	0		0	0	4	0	4	0	0
Tallahassee	40,830	20	0	10		6	4	523	38	452	33	1
New College of Florida	861	1	0	0		0	1	28	0	27	1	1
Pensacola State College	9,840	0	0	0		0	0	31	8	23	0	0
Santa Fe College	14,767	0	0	0		0	0	24	0	22	2	0
Tallahassee Community College	12,445	2	0	1		0	1	52	0	50	2	0
University of Central Florida	62,953	14	0	5		4	5	297	27	260	10	0
University of Florida	50,645	10	0	5		2	3	367	32	315	20	0
University of North Florida	15,675	3	0	0		1	2	89	21	63	5	0
University of South Florida												
St. Petersburg	4,739	0	0	0		0	0	40	3	37	0	0
Tampa	42,067	8	0	3		3	2	323	54	262	7	0
University of West Florida	12,763	10	0	6		1	3	55	11	44	0	0
GEORGIA												
Abraham Baldwin Agricultural College	3,393	0	0		0	0	0	26	2	23	1	0
Agnes Scott College	902	0	0		0	0	0	13	3	10	0	0
Albany State University	3,492	1	0		1	0	0	39	0	39	0	0
Andrew College	311	0	0		0	0	0	16	5	11	0	0
Armstrong State University	7,103	1	0		1	0	0	46	8	38	0	0
Atlanta Metropolitan State College	3,129	0	0		0	0	0	24	0	24	0	0
Augusta Technical College	4,490	0	0		0	0	0	16	0	16	0	0
Augusta University	8,333	2	0		1	1	0	136	1	130	5	0
Bainbridge State College	2,401	0	0		0	0	0	0	0	0	0	0
Berry College	2,245	1	0		1	0	0	48	5	42	1	0
Chattahoochee Technical College	9,817	1	0		0	0	1	3	0	3	0	0
Clark Atlanta University	3,661	12	0		0	11	1	75	12	59	4	0
Clayton State University	7,012	2	0		1	0	1	19	2	17	0	0
College of Coastal Georgia	3,131	0	0		0	0	0	25	3	22	0	1
Columbus State University	8,440	7	0		3	1	3	74	5	67	2	0
Dalton State College	5,044	2	0		1	0	1	12	1	11	0	0
Emory University	13,788	10	0		1	3	6	419	29	388	2	0
Fort Valley State University	2,696	3	1		0	1	1	25	8	17	0	0
Georgia College and State University	6,889	1	0		1	0	0	43	6	29	8	1
Georgia Gwinnett College	11,468	0	0		0	0	0	20	1	19	0	0
Georgia Institute of Technology	25,034	17	0		3	9	5	243	21	217	5	0
Georgia Military College	7,876	0	0		0	0	0	1	0	0	1	0
Georgia Southern University	20,459	3	0		2	0	1	121	1	118	2	0
Georgia Southwestern State University	2,755	0	0		0	0	0	56	2	54	0	0
Georgia State University	32,058	25	0		3	20	2	242	5	234	3	0

Table 7. Offenses Known to Law Enforcement, by Selected State and University or College, 2016—Continued

(Number.)

State and university/college	Student enrollment[1]	Violent crime	Murder and nonnegligent manslaughter	Rape (revised definition)[2]	Rape (legacy definition)[3]	Robbery	Aggravated assault	Property crime	Burglary	Larceny-theft	Motor vehicle theft	Arson[4]
Gordon State College	4,084	1	0		0	1	0	25	13	12	0	0
Gwinnett Technical College	6,959	0	0		0	0	0	0	0	0	0	0
Kennesaw State University	33,252	11	0		10	1	0	209	14	184	11	0
Mercer University	8,600	4	0		0	3	1	88	7	71	10	1
Middle Georgia State University	7,676	3	0		1	1	1	22	3	18	1	0
Morehouse College	2,167	3	0		0	2	1	127	19	105	3	0
Piedmont College	2,264	0	0		0	0	0	0	0	0	0	
Savannah State University	4,800	12	0		0	4	8	114	20	92	2	0
Savannah Technical College	4,196	0	0		0	0	0	22	0	20	2	
Southern Crescent Technical College	4,867	0	0		0	0	0	12	0	11	1	0
South Georgia State College	2,648	1	0		0	0	1	7	0	7	0	0
Spelman College	2,144	0	0		0	0	0	23	9	14	0	0
University of Georgia	36,130	18	0		14	2	2	342	38	295	9	0
University of North Georgia	17,289	0	0		0	0	0	18	1	17	0	0
University of West Georgia	12,834	7	0		7	0	0	49	7	40	2	0
Valdosta State University	11,302	3	0		0	2	1	122	11	109	2	0
Wesleyan College	708	0	0		0	0	0	5	0	5	0	0
West Georgia Technical College	6,431	0	0		0	0	0	22	1	21	0	0
Young Harris College	1,204	0	0		0	0	0	13	0	13	0	0
ILLINOIS												
Black Hawk College												
Kewanee[5]		0	0	0		0	0	3	1	2	0	0
Moline	5,271	0	0	0		0	0	6	0	6	0	0
Chicago State University	4,767	3	0	0		2	1	22	0	22	0	0
College of Lake County	14,964	0	0	0		0	0	26	3	23	0	0
Eastern Illinois University	8,520	0	0	0		0	0	59	2	56	1	0
Elgin Community College	10,336	0	0	0		0	0	10	0	10	0	0
Illinois Central College	9,704	0	0	0		0	0	35	7	28	0	0
John Wood Community College	2,016	0	0	0		0	0	2	0	2	0	0
Joliet Junior College	14,944	0	0	0		0	0	13	0	13	0	0
Kankakee Community College	3,306	0	0	0		0	0	1	0	1	0	0
Lake Land College	5,241	0	0	0		0	0	4	0	4	0	0
Lewis University	6,679	2	0	1		0	1	20	2	18	0	0
Lincoln Land Community College	6,447	1	0	0		0	1	7	0	7	0	0
Loyola University of Chicago	16,437	26	0	15		10	1	112	10	101	1	0
McHenry County College	6,561	0	0	0		0	0	15	0	15	0	0
Millikin University	2,152	0	0	0		0	0	17	0	17	0	0
Moraine Valley Community College	15,016	0	0	0		0	0	43	0	43	0	0
Morton College	4,592	0	0	0		0	0	5	1	3	1	0
Northeastern Illinois University	9,891	0	0	0		0	0	21	0	20	1	0
Northern Illinois University	20,130	13	0	6		2	5	141	8	131	2	1
Oakton Community College	9,864	0	0	0		0	0	12	1	11	0	0
Parkland College	8,147	0	0	0		0	0	15	1	14	0	0
Prairie State College	4,699	1	0	0		0	1	10	0	10	0	0
Rend Lake College	2,303	0	0	0		0	0	1	0	1	0	0
Southern Illinois University												
Carbondale	17,292	11	0	2		0	9	149	16	131	2	1
Edwardsville	14,265	5	0	2		0	3	81	8	73	0	1
School of Medicine[5]	4,205	0	0	0		0	0	17	6	11	0	0
South Suburban College	9,943	4	0	0		2	2	32	2	28	2	0
Southwestern Illinois College	11,684	1	0	0		0	1	32	2	28	2	0
University of Chicago, Cook County	15,391	14	0	0		7	7	215	3	211	1	0
University of Illinois												
Springfield	5,402	2	0	1		0	1	34	4	30	0	0
Urbana	45,842	20	1	11		8	0	269	26	234	9	1
Western Illinois University	11,094	9	0	8		0	1	68	3	64	1	1
INDIANA												
Ball State University	21,196	7	0	5		2	0	237	26	205	6	2
Indiana State University	13,584	19	0		0	1	18	162	2	160	0	
Indiana University	48,514	14	0	9		1	4	338	33	300	5	
Bloomington												
Indianapolis	30,105	9	0	3		2	4	318	21	279	18	1
Northwest	5,848	0	0	0		0	0	18	2	16	0	
Southeast	6,173	2	0	1		0	1	15	3	12	0	1
Marian University	2,897	0	0	0		0	0	23	1	22	0	0
Purdue University	40,472	8	0	3		2	3	256	15	238	3	0
IOWA												
Iowa State University	35,714	14	0	7		1	6	255	12	238	5	0
University of Iowa	30,844	18	0	11		0	7	256	32	215	9	2
University of Northern Iowa	11,981	7	0	3		0	4	81	4	72	5	0
KANSAS												
Emporia State University	6,094	0	0	0		0	0	45	16	29	0	1
Fort Hays State University	14,210	4	0	2		0	2	44	9	35	0	0
Kansas City Kansas Community College	5,625	1	0	1		0	0	17	1	16	0	0
Kansas State University	24,146	7	0	2		0	5	77	4	72	1	0
Pittsburg State University	7,244	2	0	1		1	0	60	6	50	4	0
University of Kansas												
Main Campus	27,259	5	0	3		1	1	205	27	173	5	0
Medical Center[6]		17	0	0		2	15	133	3	126	4	0

Table 7. Offenses Known to Law Enforcement, by Selected State and University or College, 2016—Continued

(Number.)

State and university/college	Student enrollment[1]	Violent crime	Murder and nonnegligent manslaughter	Rape (revised definition)[2]	Rape (legacy definition)[3]	Robbery	Aggravated assault	Property crime	Burglary	Larceny-theft	Motor vehicle theft	Arson[4]
Washburn University	6,615	2	0	0		1	1	73	6	64	3	0
Wichita State University	14,240	1	0	0		0	1	93	8	80	5	1
KENTUCKY												
Eastern Kentucky University	16,844	7	0	6		1	0	193	41	147	5	0
Kentucky State University	1,586	0	0	0		0	0	8	2	6	0	0
Morehead State University	10,872	0	0	0		0	0	50	14	36	0	0
Murray State University	10,998	4	0	4		0	0	79	7	66	6	0
Northern Kentucky University	14,699	0	0	0		0	0	50	4	46	0	0
Transylvania University	1,053	0	0	0		0	0	3	0	3	0	0
University of Kentucky	29,727	17	0	3		6	8	499	20	452	27	1
University of Louisville	21,294	10	0	1		6	3	321	25	282	14	1
Western Kentucky University	20,063	3	0	2		1	0	95	19	74	2	1
LOUISIANA												
Delgado Community College	16,131	1	0	0		0	1	14	1	12	1	0
Dillard University	1,185	1	0	1		0	0	39	12	26	1	0
Grambling State University	4,541	20	0	3		5	12	113	34	77	2	0
Louisiana State University												
Baton Rouge	31,524	11	0	3		3	5	366	46	297	23	0
Health Sciences Center, New Orleans	2,791	0	0	0		0	0	0	0	0	0	0
Health Sciences Center, Shreveport	891	0	0	0		0	0	52	1	49	2	0
Shreveport	4,428	0	0	0		0	0	25	10	15	0	0
Louisiana Tech University	12,371	2	0	0		2	0	56	3	52	1	0
Nicholls State University	6,158	1	0	0		0	1	7	1	6	0	0
Northwestern State University	9,179	8	0	3		3	2	68	14	54	0	0
Southern University and A&M College												
Baton Rouge	6,401	14	0	0		9	5	98	14	84	0	1
New Orleans	2,792	0	0	0		0	0	0	0	0	0	0
Shreveport	3,174	0	0	0		0	0	0	0	0	0	0
Tulane University	12,485	7	0	2		4	1	243	20	221	2	3
University of Louisiana												
Lafayette	17,508	20	0	3		3	14	221	34	183	4	0
Monroe	8,804	7	0	0		2	5	58	7	50	1	0
University of New Orleans	8,423	6	0	4		0	2	69	11	58	0	0
MAINE												
University of Maine												
Farmington[6]	2,016	1	0	1		0	0	18	2	16	0	0
Orono[6]	10,922	20	0	19		1	0	138	2	136	0	4
University of Southern Maine[6]	7,739	1	0	1		0	0	29	3	25	1	0
MARYLAND												
Bowie State University	5,430	3	0	0		2	1	46	23	22	1	0
Coppin State University	3,108	6	0	0		3	3	77	16	55	6	0
Frostburg State University	5,756	10	0	0		3	7	44	4	39	1	0
Hagerstown Community College	4,276	0	0	0		0	0	0	0	0	0	0
Morgan State University	7,725	6	0	0		3	3	105	3	102	0	0
Salisbury University	8,671	2	0	2		0	0	70	3	67	0	0
St. Mary's College	1,735	3	0	2		0	1	69	8	59	2	7
Towson University	22,284	2	0	1		1	0	76	8	68	0	0
University of Baltimore	6,229	0	0	0		0	0	36	1	35	0	0
University of Maryland												
Baltimore City	6,329	6	0	0		2	4	77	1	74	2	0
Baltimore County	13,839	0	0	0		0	0	79	5	73	1	
College Park	38,140	18	0	4		4	10	341	26	297	18	0
Eastern Shore	4,465	9	0	6		1	2	62	29	33	0	0
MASSACHUSETTS												
Amherst College	1,795	9	0	8		0	1	59	10	46	3	
Assumption College	2,675	10	0	4		0	6	27	1	26	0	0
Babson College	3,057	9	0	6		0	3	33	0	33	0	
Becker College	2,153	3	0	2		0	1	14	0	14	0	0
Bentley University	5,552	3	0	2		0	1	42	8	34	0	
Boston College	14,354	10	0	7		0	3	122	15	106	1	
Boston University	32,158	19	0	7		5	7	364	23	338	3	1
Brandeis University	5,752	0	0	0		0	0	39	3	35	1	
Bridgewater State University	11,089	12	0	3		1	8	31	6	25	0	0
Bristol Community College	8,761	1	0	0		0	1	4	0	4	0	
Bunker Hill Community College	13,142	0	0	0		0	0	46	0	46	0	
Cape Cod Community College	3,627	0	0	0		0	0	1	0	1	0	
Clark University	3,485	3	0	1		0	2	45	10	34	1	
College of the Holy Cross	2,729	3	0	2		0	1	37	4	33	0	
Curry College	2,950	0	0	0		0	0	2	0	2	0	
Dean College	1,363	2	0	2		0	0	31	13	18	0	0
Emerson College	4,479	14	0	8		2	4	40	6	34	0	
Endicott College	4,695	0	0	0		0	0	0	0	0	0	
Fitchburg State University	6,598	9	0	4		0	5	19	2	17	0	
Framingham State University	6,398	0	0	0		0	0	21	1	20	0	
Gordon College	2,045	0	0	0		0	0	47	0	47	0	
Greenfield Community College	2,050	0	0	0		0	0	8	0	8	0	
Hampshire College	1,410	2	0	1		0	1	33	4	29	0	0
Harvard University	29,652	3	0	1		0	2	574	74	499	1	

Table 7. Offenses Known to Law Enforcement, by Selected State and University or College, 2016—Continued

(Number.)

State and university/college	Student enrollment[1]	Violent crime	Murder and nonnegligent manslaughter	Rape (revised definition)[2]	Rape (legacy definition)[3]	Robbery	Aggravated assault	Property crime	Burglary	Larceny-theft	Motor vehicle theft	Arson[4]
Lasell College	2,160	8	0	0		0	8	14	3	11	0	
Massachusetts Bay Community College	4,859	1	0	0		0	1	6	0	6	0	
Massachusetts College of Art	1,990	1	0	0		0	1	27	0	27	0	
Massachusetts College of Liberal Arts	1,641	4	0	1		0	3	28	5	23	0	
Massachusetts Institute of Technology	11,331	4	0	0		0	4	334	19	313	2	0
Massasoit Community College	7,637	3	0	0		0	3	15	1	14	0	0
MCPHS University	7,074	1	0	0		1	0	9	0	9	0	0
Merrimack College	3,620	2	0	1		1	0	38	6	32	0	
Mount Holyoke College	2,215	3	0	3		0	0	56	13	42	1	1
Mount Ida College	1,345	2	0	0		0	2	12	1	11	0	
Mount Wachusett Community College	4,074	0	0	0		0	0	30	0	30	0	
Northeastern University	19,940	25	0	11		6	8	253	13	240	0	
North Shore Community College	6,961	4	0	0		1	3	17	0	17	0	0
Regis College	1,954	1	0	1		0	0	3	0	3	0	
Salem State University	9,215	7	0	5		0	2	53	12	41	0	0
Smith College	2,874	2	0	2		0	0	43	3	40	0	0
Springfield College	3,241	6	0	5		0	1	34	1	30	3	
Springfield Technical Community College	6,286	0	0	0		0	0	18	0	18	0	0
Stonehill College	2,400	7	0	1		0	6	10	1	9	0	
Tufts University												
Medford	11,137	7	0	4		2	1	74	19	55	0	1
Suffolk[5]		1	0	1		0	0	23	2	21	0	0
Worcester[5]		0	0	0		0	0	5	3	2	0	0
University of Massachusetts												
Amherst	29,269	14	0	2		2	10	229	13	215	1	4
Dartmouth	8,916	17	0	8		0	9	77	5	68	4	
Harbor Campus, Boston	17,030	2	0	0		0	2	75	2	72	1	0
Medical Center, Worcester	1,079	21	0	0		0	21	64	1	60	3	1
Wellesley College	2,510	1	0	0		0	1	28	4	24	0	
Wentworth Institute of Technology	4,576	4	0	0		1	3	56	6	50	0	
Western New England University	3,912	5	0	5		0	0	52	1	50	1	
Westfield State University	6,496	2	0	2		0	0	25	1	24	0	1
Worcester Polytechnic Institute	6,573	0	0	0		0	0	35	4	31	0	0
MICHIGAN												
Central Michigan University	26,825	5	0	5		0	0	83	0	82	1	0
Delta College	9,291	0	0	0		0	0	11	0	11	0	0
Eastern Michigan University	21,824	19	0	11		3	5	150	5	139	6	4
Ferris State University	14,715	5	0	1		0	4	38	6	32	0	0
Grand Rapids Community College	14,926	0	0	0		0	0	71	2	69	0	0
Grand Valley State University	25,325	8	0	5		1	2	134	6	126	2	0
Kalamazoo Valley Community College	8,836	2	0	1		1	0	27	0	27	0	0
Kellogg Community College	5,081	0	0	0		0	0	10	0	10	0	0
Lansing Community College	14,851	1	0	0		0	1	37	0	36	1	0
Macomb Community College	22,182	0	0	0		0	0	21	1	20	0	0
Michigan State University	50,538	38	0	15		10	13	578	65	487	26	0
Michigan Technological University	7,218	1	0	1		0	0	50	0	50	0	0
Mott Community College	8,617	2	0	1		0	1	36	3	33	0	0
Northern Michigan University	8,303	4	0	3		0	1	85	3	82	0	0
Oakland Community College	21,061	0	0	0		0	0	27	1	26	0	0
Oakland University	20,261	0	0	0		0	0	37	3	33	1	0
Saginaw Valley State University	9,633	4	0	3		0	1	48	0	48	0	0
Schoolcraft College	11,687	0	0	0		0	0	14	0	14	0	0
University of Michigan												
Ann Arbor	43,651	13	0	5		2	6	534	12	518	4	3
Dearborn	9,066	0	0	0		0	0	31	1	19	11	0
Flint	8,470	1	0	1		0	0	59	0	58	1	0
Western Michigan University	23,529	16	0	7		3	6	150	2	148	0	2
MINNESOTA												
University of Minnesota												
Duluth	10,878	5	0	3		1	1	55	6	48	1	0
Morris	1,856	0	0	0		0	0	8	2	6	0	0
Twin Cities	50,678	8	0	2		4	2	485	23	452	10	0
MISSISSIPPI												
Coahoma Community College	2,148	1	0	0		1	0	16	12	3	1	0
Jackson State University	9,802	17	0	3		8	6	221	36	179	6	0
Mississippi State University	20,873	7	0	4		0	3	165	14	149	2	0
Northeast Mississippi Community College	3,569	1	0	0		0	1	29	0	29	0	0
University of Mississippi												
Medical Center[6]		1	0		0	0	1	112	0	109	3	0
Oxford	23,212	6	0		5	0	1	160	11	148	1	0
MISSOURI												
Jefferson College	4,705	0	0	0		0	0	2	0	2	0	0
Lincoln University	2,944	10	0	3		0	7	60	14	46	0	0
Metropolitan Community College	17,821	1	0	0		0	1	30	2	24	4	0
Mineral Area College	4,388	0	0	0		0	0	1	1	0	0	0
Missouri Southern State University	5,783	2	0	2		0	0	29	10	18	1	0
Missouri University of Science and Technology	8,886	3	0	1		0	2	56	7	47	2	1
Missouri Western State University	5,513	2	0	2		0	0	15	2	11	2	0
Northwest Missouri State University	6,593	4	0	3		1	0	36	3	33	0	0

Table 7. Offenses Known to Law Enforcement, by Selected State and University or College, 2016—Continued

(Number.)

State and university/college	Student enrollment[1]	Violent crime	Murder and nonnegligent manslaughter	Rape (revised definition)[2]	Rape (legacy definition)[3]	Robbery	Aggravated assault	Property crime	Burglary	Larceny-theft	Motor vehicle theft	Arson[4]
Southeast Missouri State University	11,987	7	0	4		0	3	36	4	31	1	0
St. Charles Community College	6,865	0	0	0		0	0	11	0	11	0	0
St. Louis Community College												
Florissant Valley[5]		2	0	0		0	2	18	0	18	0	0
Meramec	18,902	0	0	0		0	0	22	1	21	0	0
Truman State University	6,208	2	0	1		0	1	51	3	48	0	0
University of Central Missouri	14,395	25	0	12		2	11	146	10	135	1	0
University of Missouri												
Columbia	35,424	9	0	7		0	2	228	4	218	6	0
Kansas City	16,685	5	0	1		3	1	64	15	45	4	0
St. Louis	16,738	5	0	3		2	0	80	3	76	1	0
Washington University	14,688	4	0	0		1	3	90	1	88	1	0
MONTANA												
Montana State University	15,236	12	0	8		0	4	212	13	193	6	5
University of Montana	13,044	6	0	1		1	4	127	3	122	2	1
NEBRASKA												
Metropolitan Community College, Douglas County	14,812	2	0	0		0	2	32	0	32	0	0
University of Nebraska												
Kearney	6,747	4	0	4		0	0	29	2	27	0	0
Lincoln	25,260	15	0	11		1	3	187	6	175	6	1
NEVADA												
College of Southern Nevada	33,313	0	0	0		0	0	25	9	7	9	0
University of Nevada												
Las Vegas	28,600	11	0	2		4	5	279	12	214	53	1
Reno	20,898	1	0	1		0	0	179	11	161	7	0
NEW HAMPSHIRE												
University of New Hampshire	15,351	26	0	25		0	1	105	4	101	0	0
NEW JERSEY												
Brookdale Community College	13,835	0	0	0		0	0	23	1	22	0	0
Essex County College	10,954	1	0	0		1	0	48	1	47	0	0
Kean University	14,112	1	0	0		1	0	128	6	119	3	0
Middlesex County College	11,662	0	0	0		0	0	17	0	17	0	0
Monmouth University	6,394	1	0	0		1	0	45	0	42	3	0
Montclair State University	20,465	3	0	0		0	3	84	1	82	1	0
New Jersey Institute of Technology	11,325	6	0	3		3	0	101	8	89	4	0
Princeton University	8,138	8	0	3		5	0	274	28	232	14	0
Rowan University	16,155	8	0	6		0	2	210	65	144	1	0
Rutgers University												
Camden	6,408	7	0	0		3	4	80	4	74	2	0
Newark	11,720	10	0	1		7	2	256	9	242	5	0
New Brunswick	49,428	29	0	11		2	16	542	60	482	0	1
Stevens Institute of Technology	6,359	0	0	0		0	0	17	1	16	0	0
Stockton University	8,674	2	0	2		0	0	39	0	39	0	0
The College of New Jersey	7,406	1	0	1		0	0	91	23	62	6	1
William Paterson University	10,862	0	0	0		0	0	63	4	59	0	0
NEW MEXICO												
Eastern New Mexico University	5,725	5	0		3	0	2	46	9	37	0	
New Mexico Institute of Mining and Technology	2,150	0	0		0	0	0	92	3	88	1	
New Mexico Military Institute	428	2	0		1	0	1	32	2	29	1	
New Mexico State University	15,490	20	0		6	3	11	267	34	223	10	
University of New Mexico	27,285	23	0		5	5	13	736	35	577	124	
Western New Mexico University	3,354	1	0		0	0	1	22	3	18	1	
NEW YORK												
Cornell University	21,904	7	0	4		1	2	217	19	196	2	1
Ithaca College	6,769	10	0	10		0	0	90	11	78	1	0
State University of New York												
Binghamton	16,913	9	0	4		2	3	166	10	156	0	2
Buffalo	29,796	10	0	3		3	4	268	23	243	2	1
Downstate Medical Center	1,858	1	0	0		1	0	69	0	69	0	0
Maritime College	1,860	0	0	0		0	0	25	5	20	0	0
Stony Brook	25,272	14	0	3		1	10	250	17	232	1	3
Upstate Medical Center	1,480	2	0	0		1	1	80	1	78	1	0
State University of New York Agricultural and Technical College												
Alfred	3,699	3	0	3		0	0	47	5	41	1	0
Canton	3,140	3	0	2		0	1	39	2	37	0	0
Cobleskill	2,441	2	0	1		1	0	23	3	20	0	0
Farmingdale	8,648	1	0	1		0	0	41	1	39	1	0
Morrisville	2,940	5	0	3		0	2	26	3	23	0	0
State University of New York College												
Brockport	8,161	2	0	1		1	0	51	7	44	0	0
Buffalo	10,330	18	0	15		2	1	155	12	143	0	4
Cortland	6,926	1	0	1		0	0	64	7	57	0	0
Environmental Science and Forestry	2,222	0	0	0		0	0	20	1	19	0	0
Fredonia	4,842	0	0	0		0	0	34	4	30	0	0

Table 7. Offenses Known to Law Enforcement, by Selected State and University or College, 2016—Continued

(Number.)

State and university/college	Student enrollment[1]	Violent crime	Murder and nonnegligent manslaughter	Rape (revised definition)[2]	Rape (legacy definition)[3]	Robbery	Aggravated assault	Property crime	Burglary	Larceny-theft	Motor vehicle theft	Arson[4]
Geneseo	5,699	1	0	1		0	0	80	9	71	0	0
New Paltz	7,751	2	0	2		0	0	26	3	23	0	0
Oneonta	6,119	6	0	6		0	0	38	1	37	0	0
Optometry	381	0	0	0		0	0	5	0	5	0	0
Oswego	7,937	6	0	5		0	1	89	15	72	2	0
Potsdam	3,904	6	0	3		0	3	66	7	59	0	0
Purchase	4,169	1	0	1		0	0	43	7	36	0	1
Technology	3,457	1	0		0	1	0	59	9	50	0	0
Utica-Rome	2,779	2	0	1		0	1	7	0	7	0	0
NORTH CAROLINA												
Appalachian State University	17,932	4	0		4	0	0	70	17	52	1	1
Duke University	15,984	10	0		3	5	2	466	26	430	10	0
East Carolina University	28,289	13	0		6	4	3	144	12	132	0	1
Elizabeth City State University	1,585	4	0		3	0	1	44	15	27	2	1
Elon University	6,631	2	0		2	0	0	12	0	11	1	0
Fayetteville State University	6,104	9	0		3	3	3	53	13	39	1	0
Methodist University	2,474	1	0		0	0	1	57	6	51	0	0
North Carolina Agricultural and Technical State University	10,852	8	0		4	2	2	189	51	136	2	1
North Carolina Central University	8,011	17	0		7	2	8	133	31	100	2	0
North Carolina State University, Raleigh	34,015	17	0		7	5	5	264	32	226	6	0
University of North Carolina												
Asheville	3,891	1	0		1	0	0	19	0	19	0	0
Chapel Hill	29,084	12	0		4	7	1	204	14	187	3	0
Charlotte	27,983	2	0		1	0	1	128	14	110	4	1
Greensboro	19,393	12	0		6	2	4	159	23	135	1	1
Wilmington	14,918	4	0		4	0	0	208	2	203	3	1
Wake Forest University	7,837	1	0		0	0	1	170	38	132	0	0
Western Carolina University	10,340	5	0		2	0	3	79	14	65	0	1
Winston-Salem State University	5,107	6	0		4	1	1	53	17	34	2	0
NORTH DAKOTA												
Bismarck State College	4,078	0	0	0		0	0	1	0	1	0	0
North Dakota State College of Science	3,123	1	0	0		1	0	8	0	8	0	0
North Dakota State University	14,516	1	0	0		1	0	109	4	103	2	0
University of North Dakota	14,951	4	0	1		0	3	159	7	148	4	0
OHIO												
Bowling Green State University	16,908	0	0	0		0	0	135	4	130	1	2
Capital University	3,465	0	0	0		0	0	51	20	30	1	1
Central State University	1,804	2	0	1		0	1	77	13	60	4	0
Cleveland State University	16,915	8	0	4		3	1	187	3	178	6	0
Columbus State Community College	25,983	0	0	0		0	0	52	1	51	0	0
Cuyahoga Community College	25,449	3	0	1		1	1	66	4	58	4	0
Kent State University	30,067	7	0		2	2	3	159	4	155	0	1
Lakeland Community College	7,941	0	0	0		0	0	11	0	11	0	0
Miami University	19,076	26	0	15		0	11	232	57	170	5	2
Notre Dame College	2,094	1	0	1		0	0	39	6	32	1	0
Ohio State University	58,663	33	0	14		8	11	820	23	783	14	2
Ohio University, Columbus	29,157	15	0	13		0	2	172	10	157	5	1
Otterbein University	2,808	0	0	0		0	0	34	2	32	0	0
Shawnee State University	3,881	1	0		1	0	0	28	2	26	0	1
Sinclair Community College	18,136	0	0		0	0	0	40	11	29	0	0
University of Akron	23,101	10	0	3		5	2	191	10	172	9	0
University of Cincinnati	36,042	45	0		40	2	3	254	18	233	3	0
University of Toledo	20,377	10	0	6		3	1	207	14	192	1	2
Wright State University	17,070	5	0	2		2	1	88	13	72	3	0
OKLAHOMA												
Cameron University	5,177	0	0	0		0	0	21	3	18	0	0
East Central University	4,444	0	0	0		0	0	21	2	19	0	0
Langston University	2,543	9	0	2		3	4	50	30	19	1	0
Northeastern Oklahoma A&M College	2,107	4	0	2		0	2	41	19	18	4	0
Northeastern State University, Tahlequah	8,251	1	0	1		0	0	12	1	11	0	0
Oklahoma City University	2,991	1	0	0		1	0	39	6	30	3	0
Oklahoma State University												
Main Campus	25,930	6	0	3		2	1	178	44	131	3	0
Okmulgee	2,617	2	0	1		1	0	14	0	14	0	0
Tulsa	787	0	0	0		0	0	16	1	15	0	0
Rogers State University	4,081	0	0	0		0	0	7	1	6	0	0
Seminole State College	1,839	0	0	0		0	0	4	0	4	0	0
Southeastern Oklahoma State University	3,754	0	0	0		0	0	14	1	11	2	0
Southwestern Oklahoma State University	5,113	0	0	0		0	0	4	1	3	0	0
Tulsa Community College	17,160	0	0	0		0	0	6	0	5	1	0
University of Central Oklahoma	16,910	3	0	0		1	2	61	9	51	1	0
University of Oklahoma												
Health Sciences Center	3,389	4	0	0		3	1	172	11	155	6	0
Norman	27,428	5	0	2		0	3	334	7	318	9	0
OREGON												
Portland State University	27,488	6	0	1		4	1	244	20	224	0	0
University of Oregon	24,032	20	0	10		1	9	359	27	325	7	5

Table 7. Offenses Known to Law Enforcement, by Selected State and University or College, 2016—Continued

(Number.)

State and university/college	Student enrollment[1]	Violent crime	Murder and nonnegligent manslaughter	Rape (revised definition)[2]	Rape (legacy definition)[3]	Robbery	Aggravated assault	Property crime	Burglary	Larceny-theft	Motor vehicle theft	Arson[4]
PENNSYLVANIA												
Bloomsburg University	9,737	1	0	0		0	1	34	1	33	0	0
California University	7,854	7	0	4		0	3	28	0	28	0	0
Cheyney University	711	5	0	2		0	3	37	7	30	0	0
Clarion University	5,368	1	0	0		1	0	30	0	30	0	0
Dickinson College	2,420	1	0	1		0	0	98	11	87	0	0
East Stroudsburg University	6,828	3	0	2		0	1	37	0	37	0	0
Edinboro University	6,548	5	0	2		0	3	36	3	33	0	0
Elizabethtown College	1,820	3	0	3		0	0	16	0	16	0	0
Indiana University	13,835	2	0	1		1	0	52	0	52	0	0
Kutztown University	8,995	8	0	7		0	1	72	6	66	0	0
Lehigh University	7,054	0	0	0		0	0	28	0	28	0	0
Lock Haven University	4,607	5	0	2		0	3	21	2	19	0	0
Mansfield University	2,352	0	0	0		0	0	10	0	10	0	0
Millersville University	7,959	0	0	0		0	0	29	3	26	0	0
Moravian College	2,261	6	0	2		1	3	37	15	22	0	0
Pennsylvania State University												
Altoona	3,839	5	0	4		0	1	29	0	28	1	0
Beaver	705	1	0	1		0	0	12	0	12	0	3
Behrend	4,327	0	0	0		0	0	12	2	10	0	0
Berks	2,906	1	0	0		1	0	17	0	17	0	0
Brandywine	1,457	0	0	0		0	0	5	1	4	0	0
Greater Allegheny	577	0	0	0		0	0	10	1	9	0	0
Harrisburg	4,678	0	0	0		0	0	21	0	21	0	0
Hazleton	831	0	0	0		0	0	7	1	6	0	0
Mont Alto	893	0	0	0		0	0	2	0	2	0	0
Schuylkill	783	1	0	1		0	0	3	2	1	0	0
University Park	47,307	50	0	33		6	11	502	79	423	0	7
Wilkes-Barre	501	2	0	0		0	2	2	0	2	0	0
Worthington Scranton	1,034	0	0	0		0	0	0	0	0	0	0
Shippensburg University	7,048	2	0	2		0	0	24	4	20	0	0
Slippery Rock University	8,611	1	0	0		0	1	16	2	14	0	0
University of Pittsburgh												
Bradford	1,453	2	0	0		0	2	18	5	13	0	0
Greensburg	1,562	1	0	1		0	0	7	0	7	0	0
Johnstown	2,816	7	0	2		1	4	31	2	29	0	0
Pittsburgh	28,649	15	0	5		3	7	242	9	233	0	0
Titusville	346	2	0	1		0	1	10	0	10	0	0
West Chester University	16,597	5	0	3		0	2	68	5	61	2	0
RHODE ISLAND												
Brown University	9,458	1	0	1		0	0	110	7	102	1	0
University of Rhode Island	16,613	2	0	0		0	2	70	7	62	1	2
SOUTH CAROLINA												
Benedict College	2,465	44	1	1		32	10	105	23	78	4	3
Bob Jones University	3,005	0	0	0		0	0	18	6	12	0	0
Clemson University	22,698	4	0	2		1	1	209	21	147	41	2
Coastal Carolina University	10,263	13	0	6		1	6	236	12	222	2	0
College of Charleston	11,531	0	0	0		0	0	56	0	54	2	0
Columbia College	1,484	0	0	0		0	0	9	0	9	0	0
Denmark Technical College	1,043	0	0	0		0	0	0	0	0	0	0
Erskine College	761	0	0	0		0	0	19	0	19	0	0
Francis Marion University	3,947	0	0	0		0	0	38	1	37	0	0
Greenville Technical College	12,280	0	0	0		0	0	29	4	25	0	0
Lander University	2,701	3	0	3		0	0	16	3	13	0	0
Medical University of South Carolina	2,992	2	0	1		0	1	102	1	96	5	0
Midlands Technical College	10,946	0	0	0		0	0	17	0	15	2	0
Orangeburg-Calhoun Technical College	2,774	0	0	0		0	0	3	1	2	0	0
Presbyterian College	1,379	1	0	1		0	0	22	7	15	0	0
South Carolina State University	3,054	9	0	3		2	4	96	15	72	9	0
Spartanburg Methodist College	771	3	0	2		1	0	6	0	6	0	0
The Citadel	3,506	1	0	0		1	0	19	7	11	1	0
Tri-County Technical College	6,128	0	0	0		0	0	11	0	11	0	0
Trident Technical College	15,043	0	0	0		0	0	21	0	21	0	0
University of South Carolina												
Aiken	3,448	1	0	0		1	0	21	0	21	0	0
Beaufort	1,980	1	0	0		0	1	8	0	7	1	0
Columbia	33,724	3	0	0		1	2	314	9	240	65	0
Upstate	5,996	2	0	1		0	1	18	4	14	0	0
Winthrop University	6,031	1	0	0		1	0	29	7	21	1	0
SOUTH DAKOTA												
South Dakota State University	12,576	3	0	1		0	2	59	2	56	1	0
TENNESSEE												
Austin Peay State University	10,099	5	0	1		3	1	62	4	58	0	0
Chattanooga State Community College	9,374	1	0	0		0	1	13	1	12	0	0
Christian Brothers University	1,842	1	0	0		0	1	27	1	26	0	0
Cleveland State Community College	3,509	0	0	0		0	0	0	0	0	0	0
East Tennessee State University	14,334	9	0	2		4	3	76	5	70	1	0
Jackson State Community College	4,746	0	0	0		0	0	0	0	0	0	0
Lincoln Memorial University	3,983	0	0	0		0	0	0	0	0	0	0

Table 7. Offenses Known to Law Enforcement, by Selected State and University or College, 2016—Continued

(Number.)

State and university/college	Student enrollment[1]	Violent crime	Murder and nonnegligent manslaughter	Rape (revised definition)[2]	Rape (legacy definition)[3]	Robbery	Aggravated assault	Property crime	Burglary	Larceny-theft	Motor vehicle theft	Arson[4]
Middle Tennessee State University	22,511	10	0	2		2	6	134	10	121	3	0
Northeast State Community College	6,084	0	0	0		0	0	11	1	10	0	0
Pellissippi State Community College	10,325	0	0	0		0	0	23	3	19	1	0
Roane State Community College	5,861	0	0	0		0	0	2	0	2	0	0
Southwest Tennessee Community College	9,135	2	0	0		0	2	18	0	18	0	0
Tennessee State University	9,167	6	0	0		2	4	56	15	39	2	0
Tennessee Technological University	10,900	4	0	2		0	2	80	10	70	0	0
University of Memphis	20,585	15	0	6		1	8	155	25	121	9	0
University of Tennessee												
Chattanooga	11,387	4	0	2		1	1	74	5	64	5	0
Health Science Center[6]	3,075	2	0	0		2	0	34	4	30	0	0
Knoxville	27,845	5	0	3		1	1	270	14	246	10	0
Martin	6,827	3	0	1		0	2	39	5	33	1	0
University of the South	1,797	13	0	12		0	1	72	29	43	0	1
Volunteer State Community College	8,098	0	0	0		0	0	9	0	9	0	0
Walters State Community College	5,947	0	0	0		0	0	7	2	4	1	0
TEXAS												
Abilene Christian University	4,544	4	0	2		0	2	73	12	61	0	0
Alamo Community College District	57,165	2	0	0		2	0	159	10	143	6	0
Alvin Community College	5,114	0	0	0		0	0	23	1	22	0	0
Amarillo College	9,936	0	0	0		0	0	28	0	27	1	0
Angelo State University	8,483	2	0	2		0	0	61	7	53	1	0
Austin College	1,255	0	0	0		0	0	29	2	26	1	0
Baylor Health Care System[5]		4	0	2		0	2	449	1	430	18	0
Baylor University, Waco	16,787	11	0	5		0	6	143	13	127	3	0
Brookhaven College	10,553	0	0	0		0	0	16	0	16	0	0
Central Texas College	19,562	1	0	0		0	1	10	0	10	0	0
College of the Mainland	4,013	0	0	0		0	0	19	2	16	1	0
El Paso Community College	28,764	1	0	0		0	1	38	3	35	0	0
Grayson College	4,591	1	0	0		0	1	13	9	4	0	0
Hardin-Simmons University	2,112	0	0	0		0	0	20	0	20	0	0
Houston Baptist University	3,160	5	0	2		2	1	76	16	58	2	3
Houston Community College	56,522	1	0	0		0	1	138	2	132	4	0
Lamar University, Beaumont	14,965	10	0	6		4	0	76	5	70	1	0
Laredo Community College	8,749	0	0	0		0	0	10	0	10	0	0
McLennan Community College	8,305	0	0	0		0	0	8	0	8	0	0
Midwestern State University	6,043	2	0	1		0	1	58	21	37	0	0
Mountain View College	8,539	2	0	0		0	2	12	0	12	0	0
Paris Junior College	4,999	0	0	0		0	0	15	1	13	1	0
Rice University	6,719	9	0	3		5	1	147	5	140	2	0
Richland College	16,687	0	0	0		0	0	20	0	20	0	0
Southern Methodist University	11,643	13	0	5		3	5	160	5	149	6	1
South Plains College	9,126	2	0	1		0	1	7	1	6	0	0
Southwestern University	1,515	0	0	0		0	0	24	1	23	0	0
Stephen F. Austin State University	12,606	4	0	4		0	0	50	4	46	0	0
St. Thomas University	3,359	2	0	0		1	1	18	5	13	0	0
Sul Ross State University	2,967	4	0	3		0	1	36	6	30	0	0
Tarleton State University	12,330	6	0	2		0	4	107	8	98	1	0
Texas A&M International University	7,192	6	0	5		0	1	33	12	21	0	0
Texas A&M University												
Central Texas	2,466	0	0	0		0	0	0	0	0	0	0
College Station	63,813	14	0	8		3	3	452	29	409	14	0
Commerce	12,928	3	0	3		0	0	81	15	65	1	0
Corpus Christi	11,661	5	0	4		1	0	80	8	65	7	0
Galveston[5]		3	0	3		0	0	14	1	11	2	0
Kingsville	9,207	4	0	2		1	1	107	35	70	2	0
San Antonio	4,564	0	0	0		0	0	4	0	4	0	0
Texas Christian University	10,323	4	0	3		0	1	129	16	111	2	0
Texas Southern University	8,965	8	0	1		4	3	150	22	127	1	0
Texas State Technical College												
Harlingen[5]		0	0	0		0	0	14	0	13	1	0
Waco[5]		5	0	4		0	1	71	19	51	1	0
West Texas[5]		0	0	0		0	0	2	0	2	0	0
Texas State University, San Marcos	37,979	3	0	0		1	2	169	23	137	9	1
Texas Tech University, Lubbock	35,859	6	0	4		1	1	458	13	438	7	4
Texas Woman's University	15,286	4	0	3		0	1	55	5	48	2	0
Tyler Junior College	10,934	2	0	0		1	1	61	5	54	2	0
University of Houston												
Central Campus	42,704	18	0	0		12	6	517	31	469	17	0
Clearlake	8,906	1	0	1		0	0	31	4	26	1	0
Downtown Campus	14,262	1	0	0		0	1	37	0	36	1	0
University of Mary Hardin-Baylor	3,898	0	0	0		0	0	44	2	42	0	0
University of North Texas, Denton	37,299	9	0	5		2	2	154	9	143	2	0
University of Texas												
Arlington	41,988	11	0	4		3	4	115	12	100	3	0
Austin	50,950	13	1	5		3	4	337	10	325	2	1
Dallas	24,554	5	0	1		1	3	113	7	105	1	0
El Paso	23,397	10	0	5		0	5	138	25	110	3	1
Health Science Center, San Antonio	3,130	2	0	1		1	0	40	4	33	3	0
Health Science Center, Tyler[5]		3	0	0		0	3	9	0	9	0	0
Houston	5,115	1	0	1		0	0	295	23	267	5	0
Medical Branch	3,169	4	0	0		1	3	111	4	106	1	0

Table 7. Offenses Known to Law Enforcement, by Selected State and University or College, 2016—Continued

(Number.)

State and university/college	Student enrollment[1]	Violent crime	Murder and nonnegligent manslaughter	Rape (revised definition)[2]	Rape (legacy definition)[3]	Robbery	Aggravated assault	Property crime	Burglary	Larceny-theft	Motor vehicle theft	Arson[4]
Permian Basin	6,077	0	0	0		0	0	9	2	7	0	0
Rio Grande Valley	28,584	0	0	0		0	0	100	1	99	0	2
San Antonio	28,787	10	0	5		3	2	112	8	87	17	0
Southwestern Medical School	2,295	7	0	0		4	3	177	0	169	8	0
Tyler	8,785	0	0	0		0	0	26	4	21	1	0
West Texas A&M University	9,489	2	0	2		0	0	54	6	46	2	0
UTAH												
Brigham Young University	33,469	1	0	1		0	0	185	0	183	2	0
Southern Utah University	8,881	0	0	0		0	0	24	2	22	0	0
University of Utah	31,592	12	1	2		0	9	437	59	357	21	1
Utah State University												
Eastern[5]		1	0	1		0	0	12	1	11	0	0
Logan	28,622	4	0	4		0	0	28	3	25	0	3
Utah Valley University	33,211	4	0	1		2	1	80	4	76	0	0
VERMONT												
University of Vermont	12,815	6	0	5		0	1	94	7	87	0	0
VIRGINIA												
Bridgewater College	1,834	0	0	0		0	0	9	0	9	0	0
Christopher Newport University	5,172	3	0	2		0	1	72	2	70	0	0
College of William and Mary	8,484	4	0	1		2	1	136	9	127	0	0
Eastern Virginia Medical School	1,096	0	0	0		0	0	21	0	20	1	0
Emory and Henry College	1,117	0	0	0		0	0	3	2	1	0	0
Ferrum College	1,334	1	0	1		0	0	24	3	21	0	0
George Mason University	33,929	12	0	9		2	1	115	6	109	0	0
James Madison University	21,227	6	0	4		1	1	124	12	112	0	3
J. Sargeant Reynolds Community College	10,889	0	0	0		0	0	17	0	17	0	0
Longwood University	5,087	5	0	5		0	0	34	2	31	1	0
Lord Fairfax Community College	7,002	0	0	0		0	0	3	0	3	0	0
Norfolk State University	5,107	6	0	3		1	2	87	3	81	3	0
Northern Virginia Community College	52,078	4	0	3		1	0	65	0	65	0	0
Old Dominion University	24,672	31	0	2		11	18	368	24	340	4	1
Radford University	9,743	7	0	6		1	0	64	6	52	6	3
Richard Bland College	2,255	0	0	0		0	0	40	6	33	1	0
Thomas Nelson Community College	9,316	2	0	1		1	0	12	0	12	0	0
University of Richmond	4,181	5	0	4		0	1	129	9	117	3	0
University of Virginia	23,883	16	0	8		1	7	189	25	161	3	0
University of Virginia's College at Wise	2,027	1	0	1		0	0	23	11	12	0	0
Virginia Commonwealth University	30,918	33	0	9		8	16	512	19	489	4	1
Virginia Military Institute	1,717	0	0	0		0	0	20	8	12	0	0
Virginia Polytechnic Institute and State University	32,663	10	0	5		1	4	175	26	147	2	0
Virginia State University	4,696	4	0	0		3	1	73	7	66	0	0
Virginia Western Community College	7,932	0	0	0		0	0	9	0	9	0	0
WASHINGTON												
Central Washington University	11,993	4	0	4		0	0	108	5	103	0	0
Eastern Washington University	12,361	11	0	7		1	3	52	11	36	5	0
Evergreen State College	4,190	2	0	1		1	0	82	6	74	2	0
University of Washington	45,408	13	0	4		5	4	712	50	656	6	1
Washington State University												
Pullman	29,686	15	0	4		2	9	142	31	109	2	1
Vancouver[5]		0	0	0		0	0	4	1	3	0	0
Western Washington University	15,332	3	0	1		2	0	120	13	105	2	0
WEST VIRGINIA												
Concord University	2,507	0	0	0		0	0	1	0	1	0	0
Fairmont State University	4,041	1	0	1		0	0	20	1	18	1	0
Glenville State College	1,732	0	0	0		0	0	10	5	5	0	0
Marshall University	13,621	25	0	2		2	21	22	4	18	0	0
Potomac State College	1,475	9	0	0		1	8	6	2	4	0	0
Shepherd University	3,861	0	0	0		0	0	5	1	4	0	0
West Virginia State University	3,166	2	0	0		0	2	29	5	24	0	0
West Virginia Tech	1,263	0	0	0		0	0	3	0	3	0	0
West Virginia University	28,776	5	0	2		0	3	81	13	67	1	1
WISCONSIN												
Marquette University	11,491	19	0		5	4	10	267	22	225	20	0
University of Wisconsin												
Eau Claire	10,592	1	0		1	0	0	58	2	56	0	0
Green Bay	6,784	0	0		0	0	0	16	0	15	1	0
La Crosse	10,490	0	0		0	0	0	119	1	118	0	0
Madison	42,716	13	0		6	2	5	287	33	249	5	1
Milwaukee	26,726	7	0		5	0	2	153	13	137	3	1
Oshkosh	14,051	3	0		0	0	3	42	7	35	0	0
Parkside	4,412	2	0		2	0	0	32	2	30	0	0
Platteville	8,945	0	0	0		0	0	58	2	55	1	2
River Falls	5,949	4	0		2	0	2	35	0	35	0	0
Stevens Point	9,265	4	0		4	0	0	58	0	58	0	0
Stout	9,554	3	0		3	0	0	83	3	80	0	0
Superior	2,497	0	0		0	0	0	19	0	19	0	0

Table 7. Offenses Known to Law Enforcement, by Selected State and University or College, 2016—Continued

(Number.)

State and university/college	Student enrollment[1]	Violent crime	Murder and nonnegligent manslaughter	Rape (revised definition)[2]	Rape (legacy definition)[3]	Robbery	Aggravated assault	Property crime	Burglary	Larceny-theft	Motor vehicle theft	Arson[4]
WYOMING												
University of Wyoming	12,648	0	0	0		0	0	102	3	98	1	0

Note: Caution should be exercised in making any intercampus comparisons or ranking schools because university/college crime statistics are affected by a variety of factors. These include demographic characteristics of the surrounding community, ratio of male to female students, number of on-campus residents, accessibility of the campus to outside visitors, size of enrollment, etc.
1 The student enrollment figures provided by the United States Department of Education are for the 2015 school year, the most recent available. The enrollment figures include full-time and part-time students.   2 The figures shown in this column for the offense of rape were reported using the revised Uniform Crime Reporting (UCR) definition of rape. See chapter notes for more detail.   3 The figures shown in this column for the offense of rape were estimated using the legacy Uniform Crime Reporting (UCR) definition of rape. See chapter notes for more detail.   4 The FBI does not publish arson data unless it receives data from either the agency or the state for all 12 months of the calendar year.   5 Student enrollment figures were not available.   6 This agency began the year submitting rape data classified according to the legacy UCR definition. However, at some point during the calendar year, the agency modified its reporting methods and began classifying and submitting rape offenses according to the revised UCR definition of rape.

Table 8. Offenses Known to Law Enforcement, by Selected State Metropolitan and Nonmetropolitan Counties, 2016

(Number.)

State/county	Violent crime	Murder and nonnegligent manslaughter	Rape (revised definition)[1]	Rape (legacy definition)[2]	Robbery	Aggravated assault	Property crime	Burglary	Larceny-theft	Motor vehicle theft	Arson[3]
ALABAMA											
Metropolitan Counties											
Autauga	73	1	12		8	52	429	146	233	50	
Baldwin	127	1	5		23	98	613	229	342	42	
Bibb	0	0	0		0	0	37	20	14	3	
Blount	394	1	17		9	367	867	261	501	105	
Calhoun	23	0	7		5	11	319	137	181	1	
Chilton	151	0	10		3	138	592	247	295	50	
Elmore	88	4	22		7	55	677	223	408	46	
Etowah	135	1	20		7	107	480	149	255	76	
Geneva	46	1	9		2	34	205	71	106	28	
Hale	33	0	2		2	29	139	73	55	11	
Henry	13	0	1		1	11	86	34	44	8	
Houston	114	4	18		7	85	616	179	395	42	
Jefferson	693	5	48		173	467	2,659	1,589	919	151	31
Lauderdale	30	1	2		0	27	285	54	190	41	
Lawrence	70	0	7		6	57	326	105	189	32	
Lee	443	10	21		18	394	1,296	389	807	100	
Limestone	120	0	29		9	82	829	202	565	62	
Lowndes	51	2	5		9	35	224	96	108	20	
Madison	341	2	44		39	256	2,257	576	1,474	207	
Mobile	151	9	13		26	103	2,149	612	1,299	238	
Montgomery	117	1	4		8	104	360	121	198	41	
Morgan	71	0	10		2	59	373	192	165	16	
Russell	66	2	20		5	39	372	124	206	42	
Shelby	111	3	25		8	75	886	251	537	98	
St. Clair	236	0	20		4	212	541	214	303	24	
Tuscaloosa	185	1	6		22	156	1,234	387	726	121	
Walker	121	2	18		10	91	908	262	526	120	
Nonmetropolitan Counties											
Barbour	32	0	4		2	26	124	50	65	9	
Butler	51	2	3		6	40	140	47	87	6	
Chambers	1	0	0		0	1	89	36	53	0	
Cherokee	72	2	9		4	57	387	147	192	48	
Clarke	54	3	5		2	44	105	47	47	11	
Clay	2	0	0		0	2	38	9	27	2	
Cleburne	7	0	1		0	6	145	40	96	9	
Coffee	28	0	6		0	22	153	68	73	12	
Coosa	23	0	1		1	21	174	54	102	18	
Covington	19	0	3		1	15	151	52	84	15	
Cullman	58	2	24		1	31	910	245	574	91	
Dale	38	1	12		1	24	248	64	161	23	
Dallas	76	1	8		4	63	428	173	229	26	
DeKalb	162	2	18		2	140	736	225	403	108	
Escambia	3	0	0		0	3	36	10	20	6	
Franklin	45	1	5		4	35	300	85	182	33	
Greene	42	0	0		5	37	126	71	49	6	
Marengo	35	1	1		4	29	183	72	105	6	
Marion	31	3	3		0	25	217	91	115	11	
Marshall	45	1	9		1	34	454	189	227	38	
Monroe	41	1	0		3	37	116	51	62	3	
Pike	21	1	0		2	18	100	27	69	4	
Talladega	120	2	9		12	97	708	210	430	68	
Tallapoosa	25	1	3		0	21	131	56	68	7	
Washington	42	2	4		1	35	137	44	65	28	
Wilcox	52	2	2		1	47	137	64	59	14	
ARIZONA											
Metropolitan Counties											
Cochise	212	2	10		4	196	606	89	458	59	0
Coconino	99	3	15		4	77	419	113	288	18	20
Maricopa	1,146	22	100		110	914	5,365	1,250	3,455	660	77
Pima	652	18	77		172	385	8,936	1,674	6,660	602	69
Pinal	263	4	44		13	202	1,640	442	987	211	10
Yavapai	226	4	22		9	191	1,028	280	653	95	12
Yuma	131	6	20		6	99	1,004	387	535	82	5
Nonmetropolitan Counties											
Graham	5	0	1		0	4	129	30	95	4	13
Greenlee	0	0	0		0	0	60	30	16	14	0
La Paz	38	3	2		3	30	407	155	222	30	0
Navajo	73	6	8		4	55	409	159	214	36	6
ARKANSAS											
Metropolitan Counties											
Benton	95	2	26		2	65	663	328	300	35	3
Cleveland	10	0	2		1	7	71	30	38	3	2
Craighead	46	1	17		0	28	343	102	205	36	6
Crawford	89	2	14		0	73	422	99	268	55	0
Crittenden	128	7	8		20	93	338	129	180	29	2

Table 8. Offenses Known to Law Enforcement, by Selected State Metropolitan and Nonmetropolitan Counties, 2016—Continued

(Number.)

State/county	Violent crime	Murder and nonnegligent manslaughter	Rape (revised definition)[1]	Rape (legacy definition)[2]	Robbery	Aggravated assault	Property crime	Burglary	Larceny-theft	Motor vehicle theft	Arson[3]
Faulkner	122	1	27		3	91	1,040	285	609	146	10
Garland	357	0	47		20	290	1,723	831	763	129	0
Grant	47	0	4		0	43	206	65	123	18	0
Jefferson	82	1	13		6	62	405	159	200	46	6
Lincoln	16	0	1		0	15	76	29	38	9	0
Little River	11	0	3		0	8	71	27	36	8	0
Lonoke	104	1	13		8	82	456	87	274	95	2
Madison	22	0	4		1	17	73	35	32	6	2
Miller	27	1	11		1	14	315	118	159	38	0
Perry	46	0	2		1	43	150	36	114	0	0
Poinsett	6	0	4		0	2	1	1	0	0	0
Pulaski	375	5	24		27	319	1,831	411	1,190	230	9
Saline	158	2	28		4	124	837	255	467	115	6
Sebastian	62	0	15		2	45	313	104	190	19	5
Washington	188	3	18		0	167	564	185	329	50	5
Nonmetropolitan Counties											
Arkansas	10	0	0		3	7	129	42	73	14	2
Ashley	22	0	6		1	15	184	71	100	13	1
Baxter	57	0	13		1	43	682	84	551	47	2
Boone	179	0	36		2	141	310	97	184	29	1
Bradley	8	0	2		0	6	29	24	2	3	0
Calhoun	4	0	1		0	3	53	20	30	3	1
Carroll	41	2	7		0	32	17	1	11	5	1
Chicot	3	0	1		0	2	76	26	50	0	0
Clark	22	0	0		1	21	86	18	58	10	1
Clay	6	0	2		0	4	41	17	21	3	0
Cleburne	78	2	22		0	54	330	97	199	34	2
Columbia	27	2	1		0	24	53	28	23	2	2
Conway	21	0	10		0	11	285	53	203	29	7
Cross	26	0	3		1	22	121	35	74	12	9
Dallas	4	0	0		0	4	21	10	11	0	0
Drew	18	0	2		0	16	131	42	77	12	2
Franklin	52	0	8		0	44	267	100	149	18	3
Fulton	13	0	2		0	11	66	0	61	5	0
Greene	25	0	7		0	18	216	71	135	10	1
Hempstead	31	1	3		1	26	214	66	121	27	2
Hot Spring	44	1	6		2	35	226	75	116	35	3
Howard	10	0	0		0	10	44	32	12	0	0
Independence	152	2	15		1	134	479	160	269	50	20
Izard	34	0	12		0	22	245	69	158	18	7
Jackson	25	0	4		0	21	172	46	98	28	1
Johnson	29	2	6		2	19	180	110	50	20	3
Lawrence	10	0	1		1	8	71	26	40	5	2
Lee	9	0	0		0	9	73	26	39	8	0
Logan	46	2	7		2	35	280	100	156	24	3
Marion	51	0	9		1	41	288	77	198	13	7
Mississippi	42	1	10		2	29	303	98	173	32	3
Monroe	3	0	1		0	2	44	10	22	12	0
Newton	26	1	3		0	22	90	35	49	6	3
Ouachita	30	0	2		0	28	98	33	51	14	3
Pike	4	0	0		1	3	49	20	26	3	0
Polk	38	0	10		0	28	99	31	63	5	4
Pope	78	1	11		4	62	416	173	183	60	10
Prairie	4	0	1		0	3	42	11	28	3	0
Randolph	29	0	11		1	17	171	38	126	7	1
Scott	18	0	4		1	13	75	22	43	10	2
Searcy	11	0	3		0	8	56	21	32	3	0
Sevier	27	2	5		0	20	75	37	36	2	3
St. Francis	17	0	5		1	11	281	87	192	2	1
Stone	26	0	4		0	22	84	40	41	3	4
Union	49	0	2		6	41	298	113	165	20	0
Van Buren	39	1	3		0	35	219	29	162	28	1
White	158	1	39		2	116	827	230	493	104	3
Woodruff	0	0	0		0	0	45	9	28	8	0
Yell	32	3	3		1	25	225	77	120	28	3
CALIFORNIA											
Metropolitan Counties											
Alameda	589	8	30		204	347	2,195	490	1,104	601	20
Butte	183	3	34		28	118	1,344	656	666	22	0
Contra Costa	347	9	25		108	205	1,485	505	957	23	20
El Dorado	291	1	53		37	200	2,085	512	1,534	39	5
Fresno	1,177	12	29		82	1,054	3,798	1,625	1,468	705	170
Imperial	161	2	8		12	139	453	129	298	26	9
Kern	2,403	44	177		443	1,739	10,440	3,161	5,109	2,170	281
Kings	157	4	16		16	121	426	164	236	26	4
Los Angeles	6,124	94	307		1,474	4,249	17,498	3,816	9,328	4,354	227
Madera	434	4	28		19	383	1,102	517	568	17	2
Marin	72	3	4		19	46	730	172	554	4	1
Merced	542	2	18		33	489	1,541	601	886	54	8

Table 8. Offenses Known to Law Enforcement, by Selected State Metropolitan and Nonmetropolitan Counties, 2016—Continued

(Number.)

State/county	Violent crime	Murder and nonnegligent manslaughter	Rape (revised definition)[1]	Rape (legacy definition)[2]	Robbery	Aggravated assault	Property crime	Burglary	Larceny-theft	Motor vehicle theft	Arson[3]
Monterey	286	11	18		54	203	1,377	303	1,041	33	11
Napa	61	0	7		8	46	270	93	175	2	0
Orange	229	0	20		30	179	1,123	213	765	145	11
Placer	261	1	33		34	193	1,539	471	1,040	28	8
Riverside	841	28	56		177	580	7,651	1,695	4,630	1,326	22
Sacramento	2,797	42	155		880	1,720	10,142	3,062	6,943	137	68
San Benito	39	1	6		4	28	126	64	52	10	1
San Bernardino	924	12	88		151	673	5,235	1,525	2,513	1,197	54
San Diego	1,422	29	115		206	1,072	4,617	1,131	2,656	830	26
San Joaquin	793	7	26		174	586	3,072	826	2,106	140	19
San Luis Obispo	356	0	21		16	319	1,384	441	920	23	10
San Mateo	298	1	57		64	176	2,843	454	2,089	300	9
Santa Barbara	265	4	49		32	180	1,639	476	1,146	17	7
Santa Clara	316	4	46		15	251	1,312	260	826	226	5
Santa Cruz	285	1	36		44	204	2,050	485	1,533	32	14
Shasta	519	5	58		22	434	962	451	471	40	23
Solano	92	1	2		17	72	312	115	139	58	9
Sonoma	583	3	91		48	441	1,450	494	937	19	12
Stanislaus	470	11	42		134	283	1,821	726	1,034	61	14
Sutter	88	1	7		6	74	618	235	329	54	2
Tulare[4]	350	19	28		62	241	2,074	756	1,318	0	1
Ventura	171	2	29		19	121	767	224	467	76	11
Yolo	56	0	8		7	41	248	69	158	21	4
Yuba	210	3	11		32	164	1,086	335	744	7	18
Nonmetropolitan Counties											
Alpine	6	0	0		0	6	34	7	26	1	0
Amador	53	0	6		8	39	371	142	225	4	3
Calaveras	169	3	26		16	124	535	183	341	11	0
Colusa	31	0	2		6	23	186	78	108	0	0
Del Norte	115	0	30		11	74	355	251	96	8	7
Glenn	34	1	0		1	32	159	60	96	3	1
Humboldt	265	9	22		57	177	773	366	385	22	4
Inyo	85	0	7		5	73	158	67	84	7	1
Lake	179	2	17		15	145	635	337	283	15	11
Lassen	43	1	4		2	36	202	87	114	1	0
Mariposa	80	0	12		1	67	217	53	161	3	0
Mendocino	346	7	42		19	278	477	246	228	3	5
Modoc	19	1	3		0	15	44	9	35	0	0
Mono	16	1	2		1	12	51	20	31	0	0
Nevada	80	5	4		5	66	697	285	395	17	3
Plumas	120	2	10		6	102	335	120	207	8	1
Sierra	14	0	0		0	14	26	8	18	0	1
Siskiyou	52	2	5		2	43	225	118	102	5	1
Tehama	163	3	6		12	142	371	235	130	6	2
Trinity	65	3	3		6	53	234	101	133	0	0
Tuolumne	159	1	45		9	104	737	350	377	10	6
COLORADO											
Metropolitan Counties											
Adams	523	11	94		93	325	2,954	437	1,582	935	33
Arapahoe	269	4	74		46	145	1,381	269	904	208	25
Boulder	83	1	20		6	56	586	161	388	37	10
Clear Creek	15	0	1		0	14	64	10	48	6	18
Douglas	326	2	133		7	184	1,939	380	1,366	193	29
El Paso	390	7	80		25	278	2,186	402	1,526	258	30
Gilpin	4	0	1		0	3	47	12	32	3	1
Jefferson	224	2	66		15	141	2,889	454	2,167	268	13
Larimer	171	2	26		10	133	930	208	625	97	7
Mesa	180	5	51		6	118	1,258	237	924	97	8
Park	16	1	2		0	13	67	28	29	10	2
Pueblo	35	2	1		6	26	1,309	291	858	160	3
Teller	6	0	1		0	5	90	23	59	8	1
Weld	102	0	12		6	84	847	259	472	116	4
Nonmetropolitan Counties											
Alamosa	6	0	2		0	4	73	9	59	5	0
Archuleta	19	0	3		1	15	106	32	71	3	0
Baca	1	0	0		0	1	1	0	1	0	0
Bent	7	0	2		1	4	139	63	71	5	1
Chaffee	0	0	0		0	0	70	12	52	6	0
Cheyenne	1	0	0		0	1	3	2	1	0	0
Conejos	6	0	1		0	5	62	59	1	2	0
Crowley	5	1	1		0	3	58	31	20	7	0
Custer	7	0	1		0	6	99	22	70	7	5
Delta	16	0	13		1	2	149	49	79	21	0
Dolores	5	0	0		1	4	17	7	8	2	0
Eagle[5]	33	0	14		0	19		37		15	3
Fremont	28	0	1		3	24	208	60	123	25	2
Garfield	39	1	15		2	21	231	57	156	18	3
Gunnison	3	0	0		1	2	25	1	23	1	0

Table 8. Offenses Known to Law Enforcement, by Selected State Metropolitan and Nonmetropolitan Counties, 2016—Continued

(Number.)

State/county	Violent crime	Murder and nonnegligent manslaughter	Rape (revised definition)[1]	Rape (legacy definition)[2]	Robbery	Aggravated assault	Property crime	Burglary	Larceny-theft	Motor vehicle theft	Arson[3]
Hinsdale	4	0	1		0	3	6	2	4	0	0
Jackson	0	0	0		0	0	5	0	4	1	0
Kit Carson	5	0	0		0	5	36	11	21	4	0
La Plata	49	0	22		1	26	265	75	164	26	0
Lake	6	0	3		0	3	41	5	34	2	1
Lincoln	1	0	0		0	1	23	13	7	3	0
Logan	15	0	11		0	4	125	39	58	28	0
Moffat	3	0	1		0	2	45	10	31	4	1
Montezuma	21	0	1		2	18	174	47	117	10	1
Montrose	12	0	6		1	5	229	93	118	18	2
Morgan	10	0	0		1	9	116	35	71	10	4
Otero	8	0	0		0	8	78	34	36	8	0
Phillips	3	0	0		0	3	4	1	3	0	0
Pitkin	5	0	3		0	2	55	6	41	8	2
Prowers	3	0	1		0	2	23	6	12	5	0
Rio Blanco	0	0	0		0	0	25	2	22	1	0
Rio Grande	2	0	0		0	2	12	6	4	2	0
Routt	7	0	6		0	1	37	6	28	3	1
Saguache	4	0	0		0	4	25	7	14	4	0
San Juan	0	0	0		0	0	10	1	8	1	0
San Miguel	7	0	1		0	6	3	2	1	0	0
Summit	30	0	20		2	8	241	49	183	9	2
Washington	7	0	5		0	2	88	24	61	3	1
DELAWARE											
Metropolitan Counties											
New Castle County Police Department	969	14	44		212	699	5,485	1,318	3,667	500	1
FLORIDA											
Metropolitan Counties											
Alachua	519	1	62		75	381	2,044	545	1,377	122	14
Baker	118	1	4		8	105	316	103	194	19	0
Bay	375	4	40		41	290	2,433	536	1,716	181	6
Brevard	756	6	42		101	607	4,494	1,038	3,096	360	19
Broward	380	3	20		92	265	768	160	529	79	4
Charlotte	379	4	35		19	321	2,456	408	1,948	100	5
Citrus	338	4	40		39	255	1,979	426	1,443	110	8
Clay	450	3	87		81	279	3,256	618	2,475	163	13
Collier	941	7	65		166	703	3,994	742	3,028	224	16
Escambia	1,614	12	153		308	1,141	8,129	1,618	5,958	553	29
Flagler	221	0	16		29	176	1,646	306	1,255	85	7
Gadsden	69	2	6		5	56	379	173	193	13	2
Gulf	37	0	3		1	33	163	59	99	5	2
Hernando	412	4	62		60	286	3,113	620	2,283	210	18
Highlands	271	4	21		40	206	2,066	548	1,420	98	10
Hillsborough	1,926	27	173		352	1,374	13,758	2,600	9,972	1,186	75
Indian River	226	1	11		24	190	1,782	390	1,275	117	1
Jefferson	87	0	10		2	75	152	65	72	15	0
Lake	472	2	52		36	382	2,686	711	1,747	228	12
Lee	1,379	21	175		252	931	6,196	1,427	4,336	433	50
Leon	394	1	39		42	312	2,397	670	1,594	133	12
Manatee	1,349	18	120		169	1,042	5,491	1,070	4,086	335	21
Marion	679	8	58		93	520	4,403	1,405	2,529	469	5
Martin	304	6	45		48	205	1,909	323	1,509	77	8
Miami-Dade	6,278	84	409		1,537	4,248	36,318	4,605	28,416	3,297	25
Nassau	137	3	19		4	111	956	474	433	49	4
Okaloosa	585	4	76		51	454	3,057	525	2,384	148	4
Orange	5,106	61	498		1,159	3,388	25,493	6,091	17,208	2,194	0
Osceola	835	7	79		83	666	4,671	1,240	3,173	258	5
Palm Beach	2,005	25	216		436	1,328	13,158	2,968	9,080	1,110	55
Pasco	1,391	10	165		169	1,047	8,594	1,786	6,140	668	41
Pinellas	727	5	111		149	462	5,839	907	4,511	421	22
Polk	1,374	14	139		135	1,086	6,506	1,748	4,124	634	26
Santa Rosa	201	6	52		16	127	1,571	349	1,134	88	6
Sarasota	494	5	31		68	390	4,586	797	3,598	191	1
Seminole	637	6	81		55	495	3,224	735	2,350	139	2
St. Johns	346	4	13		32	297	2,896	602	2,177	117	4
St. Lucie	237	3	29		30	175	1,659	369	1,186	104	9
Sumter	237	0	21		8	208	891	225	627	39	1
Volusia	609	4	81		100	424	4,088	922	2,881	285	15
Wakulla	52	1	3		4	44	504	134	350	20	2
Walton	175	3	16		10	146	1,311	333	901	77	3
Nonmetropolitan Counties											
Bradford	75	1	4		1	69	211	96	102	13	1
Calhoun	17	0	1		0	16	48	16	29	3	0
Columbia	186	1	14		13	158	995	425	505	65	0
DeSoto	99	1	12		8	78	622	167	411	44	6
Dixie	80	1	13		1	65	329	128	191	10	3
Franklin	17	0	1		0	16	85	20	61	4	0
Glades	29	0	2		2	25	128	33	85	10	0

Table 8. Offenses Known to Law Enforcement, by Selected State Metropolitan and Nonmetropolitan Counties, 2016—Continued

(Number.)

State/county	Violent crime	Murder and nonnegligent manslaughter	Rape (revised definition)[1]	Rape (legacy definition)[2]	Robbery	Aggravated assault	Property crime	Burglary	Larceny-theft	Motor vehicle theft	Arson[3]
Hamilton	26	0	3		1	22	169	58	99	12	1
Hardee	50	0	8		6	36	333	105	209	19	0
Hendry	118	5	13		22	78	675	281	371	23	15
Holmes	64	0	6		6	52	241	86	137	18	0
Jackson	94	0	16		6	72	681	167	474	40	2
Lafayette	13	0	0		0	13	60	27	31	2	1
Levy	403	1	8		2	392	461	139	294	28	1
Liberty	2	1	0		0	1	7	1	4	2	0
Madison	126	1	6		2	117	240	108	132	0	2
Monroe	179	1	21		15	142	1,061	205	807	49	0
Okeechobee	132	5	18		10	99	953	204	680	69	0
Putnam	265	4	33		28	200	1,201	396	743	62	11
Suwannee	155	3	11		8	133	404	123	243	38	0
Taylor	182	2	9		1	170	267	116	135	16	2
Union	37	2	0		2	33	60	25	34	1	1
Washington	30	0	3		3	24	167	60	92	15	1
GEORGIA											
Metropolitan Counties											
Augusta-Richmond	845	18		66	323	438	8,643	1,637	6,560	446	
Bartow	338	0		27	33	278	2,181	508	1,451	222	0
Bibb	756	15		53	261	427	7,934	1,939	5,395	600	67
Brantley	40	0		7	5	28	478	119	344	15	0
Brooks	35	0		0	4	31	179	50	118	11	1
Bryan	93	2		5	1	85	269	74	188	7	2
Burke	55	3		0	0	52	447	103	325	19	0
Butts	90	1		2	7	80	368	71	276	21	0
Carroll	165	1		19	21	124	1,398	484	786	128	16
Catoosa	74	2		5	8	59	904	165	584	155	7
Cherokee	123	4		25	15	79	1,568	286	1,256	26	5
Clarke	0	0		0	0	0	0	0	0	0	0
Clayton	6	0		0	1	5	27	5	19	3	0
Clayton County Police Department	1,504	39		162	603	700	8,686	2,348	5,081	1,257	16
Cobb	79	0		5	8	66	39	8	31	0	0
Cobb County Police Department	1,262	16		88	461	697	11,609	2,184	8,490	935	33
Columbia	65	8		9	17	31	1,952	202	1,680	70	4
Coweta	116	0		16	25	75	1,372	336	940	96	6
Crawford	23	0		2	2	19	252	62	167	23	0
Dawson	24	0		6	2	16	442	73	331	38	1
DeKalb	0	0		0	0	0	0	0	0	0	0
DeKalb County Police Department	3,452	76		138	1,595	1,643	23,887	6,024	14,072	3,791	141
Dougherty	1	0		0	0	1	171	0	171	0	0
Dougherty County Police Department	44	0		3	8	33	308	107	183	18	0
Douglas	235	7		13	60	155	2,636	488	2,015	133	6
Echols	3	0		1	0	2	27	12	14	1	0
Effingham	41	0		6	7	28	435	192	199	44	0
Fayette	33	1		4	11	17	405	104	276	25	0
Floyd	16	0		1	4	11	81	21	56	4	0
Floyd County Police Department	84	1		17	11	55	1,216	351	754	111	10
Fulton	11	0		2	1	8	11	0	11	0	0
Fulton County Police Department	1,067	18		52	333	664	6,005	1,146	3,863	996	4
Glynn	0	0		0	0	0	0	0	0	0	0
Glynn County Police Department	201	2		10	36	153	1,852	422	1,316	114	5
Gwinnett County Police Department	1,738	24		152	745	817	14,726	3,182	10,384	1,160	53
Hall	215	3		22	27	163	1,999	413	1,368	218	24
Haralson	125	1		1	3	120	456	146	271	39	1
Harris	41	0		1	1	39	227	90	119	18	2
Heard	20	0		0	1	19	122	40	60	22	0
Henry	0	0		0	0	0	135	0	135	0	0
Henry County Police Department	334	7		39	120	168	4,136	994	2,697	445	12
Houston	127	0		9	11	107	1,087	206	828	53	0
Jasper	56	0		0	2	54	166	56	98	12	0
Jones	21	0		1	6	14	418	130	254	34	0
Lamar	18	1		1	2	14	135	25	89	21	0
Lanier	28	0		3	0	25	122	23	91	8	
Lee	40	0		4	8	28	576	112	452	12	
Liberty	99	0		1	8	90	276	79	176	21	
Lincoln	25	2		2	1	20	178	31	140	7	0
Long	7	1		1	2	3	171	77	77	17	0
Lowndes	91	0		3	6	82	720	229	440	51	
Madison	58	0		7	8	43	436	125	270	41	5
Marion	2	0		0	0	2	30	17	10	3	0
McDuffie	31	0		4	7	20	235	103	117	15	2
McIntosh	23	0		4	7	12	285	83	183	19	2
Meriwether	43	0		2	3	38	254	72	173	9	2
Monroe	22	0		1	0	21	355	90	236	29	1
Newton	364	7		14	43	300	1,412	377	862	173	
Oconee	39	2		0	0	37	507	84	404	19	0
Oglethorpe	46	0		4	3	39	293	61	214	18	0
Paulding	185	1		10	17	157	2,230	418	1,540	272	40
Peach	26	2		4	3	17	257	83	151	23	0

Table 8. Offenses Known to Law Enforcement, by Selected State Metropolitan and Nonmetropolitan Counties, 2016—Continued

(Number.)

State/county	Violent crime	Murder and nonnegligent manslaughter	Rape (revised definition)[1]	Rape (legacy definition)[2]	Robbery	Aggravated assault	Property crime	Burglary	Larceny-theft	Motor vehicle theft	Arson[3]
Pickens	64	0		5	0	59	345	77	226	42	
Pike	12	0		1	0	11	228	41	178	9	
Rockdale	171	4		15	30	122	1,628	320	1,187	121	0
Spalding	147	0		13	18	116	1,220	289	809	121	9
Terrell	10	1		0	1	8	69	25	42	2	2
Walton	73	0		8	10	55	795	171	542	82	0
Whitfield	204	0		27	9	168	1,424	349	953	122	0
Worth	36	0		4	0	32	238	79	147	12	11
Nonmetropolitan Counties											
Baldwin	259	5		3	12	239	638	154	453	31	2
Banks	57	0		5	5	47	445	134	290	21	1
Ben Hill	29	1		1	3	24	223	81	133	9	0
Berrien	14	0		5	1	8	181	49	126	6	0
Bleckley	12	0		0	1	11	151	34	109	8	0
Bulloch	28	1		3	7	17	526	154	341	31	2
Calhoun	4	0		0	0	4	9	1	7	1	0
Camden	25	0		0	5	20	257	84	163	10	
Charlton	12	0		0	1	11	96	38	40	18	0
Chattooga	26	0		2	3	21	346	101	233	12	0
Clay	4	0		0	0	4	3	1	2	0	0
Clinch	8	0		0	0	8	56	19	30	7	1
Coffee	65	1		7	3	54	780	190	528	62	10
Cook	12	0		1	4	7	112	31	72	9	0
Crisp	13	0		0	2	11	363	52	304	7	0
Decatur	48	1		4	2	41	254	81	163	10	0
Dodge	22	0		1	2	19	284	86	187	11	0
Dooly	6	0		0	1	5	81	11	56	14	1
Early	15	0		1	0	14	84	21	55	8	0
Elbert	27	0		1	0	26	295	99	166	30	0
Emanuel	10	1		0	0	9	260	94	149	17	0
Evans	7	0		0	2	5	26	17	6	3	0
Fannin	19	0		0	1	18	289	103	161	25	4
Franklin	9	1		2	1	5	234	58	161	15	1
Gilmer	65	1		7	3	54	349	119	209	21	0
Glascock	4	0		0	0	4	18	8	7	3	0
Gordon	106	3		6	5	92	711	175	480	56	0
Grady	30	0		1	1	28	181	79	91	11	0
Greene	15	0		0	0	15	157	27	124	6	0
Habersham	50	1		9	5	35	348	141	186	21	0
Hancock	19	0		0	2	17	113	28	75	10	0
Hart	51	0		3	1	47	294	87	200	7	0
Irwin	6	0		0	0	6	100	40	54	6	0
Jackson	105	0		6	7	92	756	120	601	35	
Jeff Davis	25	1		2	0	22	150	45	99	6	0
Jefferson	28	0		3	1	24	100	49	45	6	0
Laurens	84	0		5	2	77	504	162	297	45	1
Lumpkin	12	1		7	3	1	443	101	321	21	3
Miller	2	0		0	0	2	28	9	19	0	
Mitchell	36	0		2	1	33	258	65	184	9	0
Pierce	50	2		5	4	39	247	82	162	3	0
Polk	0	0		0	0	0	0	0	0	0	0
Polk County Police Department	39	1		4	5	29	590	167	340	83	
Putnam	34	0		1	0	33	358	94	258	6	
Quitman	5	0		0	0	5	36	15	21	0	
Rabun	14	0		0	0	14	260	62	189	9	
Randolph	15	0		0	1	14	53	24	27	2	0
Schley	2	0		1	0	1	20	6	13	1	0
Screven	13	0		1	2	10	146	65	62	19	0
Seminole	21	0		0	0	21	70	17	49	4	0
Stephens	35	1		7	3	24	312	77	229	6	0
Stewart	0	0		0	0	0	3	0	2	1	
Sumter	33	0		6	4	23	212	60	137	15	0
Talbot	6	0		0	0	6	67	30	31	6	0
Taliaferro	2	0		0	1	1	30	11	17	2	0
Tattnall	29	1		4	4	20	244	72	163	9	0
Taylor	9	0		0	0	9	80	32	39	9	1
Thomas	63	0		7	12	44	484	147	289	48	6
Tift	95	3		4	13	75	711	183	500	28	0
Towns	39	1		0	0	38	128	52	70	6	0
Treutlen	2	0		0	0	2	54	16	33	5	
Troup	42	0		10	7	25	665	159	455	51	0
Turner	7	0		1	0	6	43	12	27	4	
Union	21	0		4	1	16	243	60	160	23	0
Upson	30	0		3	8	19	262	58	181	23	0
Ware	82	0		4	12	66	604	143	440	21	9
Warren	10	0		1	1	8	62	21	36	5	
Washington	14	0		0	1	13	131	35	84	12	0
Wayne	149	1		6	4	138	731	169	528	34	2
Webster	1	0		0	0	1	7	3	4	0	0
White	30	0		2	0	28	287	80	177	30	0

Table 8. Offenses Known to Law Enforcement, by Selected State Metropolitan and Nonmetropolitan Counties, 2016—Continued

(Number.)

State/county	Violent crime	Murder and nonnegligent manslaughter	Rape (revised definition)[1]	Rape (legacy definition)[2]	Robbery	Aggravated assault	Property crime	Burglary	Larceny-theft	Motor vehicle theft	Arson[3]
Wilcox	12	0		1	0	11	61	34	27	0	0
Wilkes	30	1		2	4	23	21	7	13	1	1
Wilkinson	13	2		0	0	11	40	12	20	8	3
HAWAII											
Metropolitan Counties											
Maui Police Department	450	5	77		68	300	5,741	978	4,046	717	150
Nonmetropolitan Counties											
Hawaii Police Department	467	9	115		69	274	4,928	823	3,580	525	41
Kauai Police Department	169	5	45		21	98	1,492	458	968	66	31
IDAHO											
Metropolitan Counties											
Ada	202	1	53		12	136	700	154	502	44	9
Bannock	5	1	0		0	4	35	7	25	3	2
Boise	14	1	1		0	12	63	12	46	5	0
Bonneville	151	0	11		5	135	682	191	455	36	6
Butte	0	0	0		0	0	3	0	3	0	0
Canyon	93	1	14		0	78	528	212	271	45	6
Franklin	2	0	0		0	2	49	4	42	3	0
Gem	19	0	3		0	16	31	10	19	2	2
Jefferson	17	0	3		0	14	117	32	81	4	0
Kootenai	103	6	19		6	72	1,174	346	769	59	11
Nez Perce	8	0	1		1	6	108	31	72	5	0
Owyhee	18	1	1		0	16	65	15	43	7	1
Nonmetropolitan Counties											
Adams	4	0	0		0	4	33	3	27	3	0
Bear Lake	2	0	0		0	2	26	12	14	0	0
Benewah	18	2	1		0	15	71	22	43	6	0
Bingham	41	0	15		0	26	203	52	111	40	2
Blaine	5	0	1		0	4	42	14	24	4	1
Bonner	63	1	13		2	47	376	150	198	28	3
Boundary	6	0	2		0	4	85	40	39	6	1
Camas	0	0	0		0	0	8	3	5	0	0
Caribou	1	0	0		0	1	11	4	4	3	0
Cassia	49	0	8		3	38	363	133	207	23	1
Clark	3	0	1		0	2	8	1	6	1	0
Clearwater	14	1	0		0	13	57	20	30	7	4
Custer	2	0	1		0	1	27	4	21	2	0
Elmore	14	0	1		1	12	58	14	39	5	0
Fremont	6	0	3		0	3	62	9	50	3	0
Gooding	12	0	1		0	11	64	23	32	9	0
Idaho	24	0	5		0	19	99	41	52	6	0
Jerome	31	0	2		0	29	116	56	48	12	2
Latah	32	0	5		0	27	163	66	90	7	1
Lemhi	7	1	0		1	5	31	17	10	4	0
Lewis	2	0	0		0	2	16	3	12	1	0
Lincoln	2	0	0		0	2	2	0	2	0	0
Madison	15	0	9		0	6	85	40	39	6	1
Minidoka	18	0	3		0	15	141	34	93	14	0
Oneida	5	0	1		0	4	34	14	18	2	0
Payette	13	0	3		0	10	77	21	50	6	1
Power	0	0	0		0	0	28	5	18	5	2
Shoshone	47	0	4		2	41	158	49	90	19	0
Teton	6	1	0		0	5	74	14	53	7	0
Twin Falls	34	0	4		2	28	236	120	86	30	1
Valley	11	0	4		0	7	67	19	47	1	0
Washington	8	0	7		0	1	46	13	33	0	0
ILLINOIS											
Metropolitan Counties											
Alexander	9	0	0		0	9	39	11	24	4	1
Bond	0	0	0		0	0	63	24	38	1	0
Boone	28	0	12		2	14	167	25	135	7	3
Champaign	110	3	21		12	74	655	202	419	34	7
Clinton	9	0	1		0	8	64	11	50	3	0
Cook	167	7	29		22	109	689	162	447	80	16
De Kalb	34	2	11		3	18	148	25	118	5	2
De Witt	9	0	5		1	3	25	10	15	0	1
DuPage	73	1	8		20	44	764	140	586	38	0
Ford	19	0	6		2	11	84	25	50	9	5
Grundy	11	0	5		0	6	146	38	99	9	1
Henry	4	0	0		2	2	46	14	31	1	0
Jackson	21	0	1		0	20	242	79	152	11	1
Jersey	11	0	6		0	5	107	45	59	3	0
Kane	80	0	15		5	60	511	135	349	27	5
Kankakee	45	5	1		6	33	366	158	185	23	17
Kendall	36	0	8		4	24	222	71	140	11	4
Lake	90	0	20		18	52	1,055	270	733	52	7

Table 8. Offenses Known to Law Enforcement, by Selected State Metropolitan and Nonmetropolitan Counties, 2016—Continued

(Number.)

State/county	Violent crime	Murder and nonnegligent manslaughter	Rape (revised definition)[1]	Rape (legacy definition)[2]	Robbery	Aggravated assault	Property crime	Burglary	Larceny-theft	Motor vehicle theft	Arson[3]
Macon	28	0	5		4	19	217	48	167	2	1
Macoupin	10	1	0		0	9	150	30	113	7	0
Madison	119	0	17		16	86	1,023	239	731	53	6
Marshall	7	0	3		0	4	41	21	16	4	0
McHenry	74	0	17		2	55	275	53	208	14	0
McLean	20	2	5		0	13	99	34	58	7	0
Menard	4	0	2		1	1	31	8	23	0	0
Mercer	15	0	2		1	12	64	29	32	3	1
Monroe	3	0	1		0	2	42	13	28	1	0
Peoria	101	0	15		15	71	833	166	615	52	15
Piatt	22	0	1		0	21	105	31	69	5	1
Rock Island	41	0	6		4	31	304	64	239	1	3
Sangamon	151	1	36		17	97	602	211	343	48	7
Stark	0	0	0		0	0	41	10	28	3	0
St. Clair	99	2	20		24	53	632	356	238	38	6
Tazewell	40	0	15		0	25	171	55	114	2	1
Vermilion	81	0	22		7	52	448	130	297	21	1
Will	128	5	19		25	79	896	309	513	74	14
Williamson	9	0	4		0	5	297	87	195	15	1
Winnebago	134	3	34		20	77	874	285	530	59	7
Woodford	4	0	2		0	2	106	26	72	8	2
Nonmetropolitan Counties											
Adams	26	1	12		0	13	169	55	108	6	0
Brown	10	0	0		0	10	14	1	13	0	0
Bureau	25	0	2		1	22	130	56	71	3	1
Carroll	0	0	0		0	0	62	16	46	0	0
Cass	4	0	0		0	4	6	1	4	1	0
Clark	5	1	0		0	4	39	11	23	5	1
Clay	6	0	0		1	5	54	23	30	1	0
Coles	25	0	2		2	21	93	33	54	6	1
Crawford	4	0	0		0	4	45	18	25	2	2
Cumberland	3	0	1		0	2	22	9	12	1	0
Douglas	4	0	0		0	4	29	7	20	2	0
Effingham	18	0	2		1	15	161	48	106	7	2
Fayette	8	0	4		0	4	88	20	63	5	1
Franklin	30	0	0		0	30	262	93	167	2	0
Fulton	14	1	2		3	8	102	40	57	5	1
Gallatin	4	0	0		0	4	26	5	20	1	0
Greene	4	0	1		0	3	32	13	19	0	2
Hamilton	4	0	0		0	4	29	7	19	3	1
Hancock	7	0	1		1	5	102	39	59	4	0
Hardin	6	0	0		0	6	36	6	25	5	0
Iroquois	18	1	4		1	12	167	67	87	13	3
Jefferson	42	0	5		0	37	211	83	117	11	2
Jo Daviess	5	0	2		0	3	74	25	40	9	1
Johnson	34	0	0		0	34	68	16	48	4	0
Knox	38	0	3		3	32	150	50	96	4	0
La Salle	41	0	18		5	18	302	101	188	13	0
Lee	42	1	0		0	41	130	60	62	8	2
Livingston	22	0	12		4	6	180	46	129	5	1
Logan	7	0	1		0	6	58	28	23	7	0
Marion	22	0	5		0	17	86	47	35	4	0
Mason	16	0	6		1	9	76	23	47	6	3
Massac	9	1	1		1	6	54	20	32	2	2
McDonough	5	0	0		0	5	45	12	33	0	0
Montgomery	1	0	0		1	0	122	42	80	0	1
Morgan	19	0	5		2	12	106	39	62	5	1
Ogle	13	0	3		2	8	181	27	147	7	0
Perry	10	0	1		0	9	51	12	34	5	0
Pike	6	0	4		0	2	81	31	49	1	0
Putnam	1	0	0		0	1	14	6	7	1	0
Randolph	0	0	0		0	0	27	15	10	2	0
Richland	13	0	1		0	12	67	30	28	9	1
Schuyler	6	0	0		0	6	2	1	1	0	0
Scott	0	0	0		0	0	25	11	14	0	0
Stephenson	9	0	5		1	3	163	47	104	12	7
Union	24	0	15		0	9	84	25	56	3	0
Wabash	0	0	0		0	0	17	5	10	2	0
Warren	9	0	1		0	8	68	22	46	0	0
Washington	18	0	0		0	18	44	12	29	3	0
White	21	0	0		0	21	149	50	94	5	1
Whiteside	28	0	5		0	23	70	15	53	2	0
INDIANA **Metropolitan Counties**											
Allen	156	4		20	30	102	866	225	603	38	0
Bartholemew	32	0		6	3	23	508	141	303	64	0
Brown	45	0		1	1	43	232	38	171	23	1
Clark	99	0		7	2	90	546	200	295	51	
Delaware	43	3		2	2	36	417	149	232	36	2

Table 8. Offenses Known to Law Enforcement, by Selected State Metropolitan and Nonmetropolitan Counties, 2016—Continued

(Number.)

State/county	Violent crime	Murder and nonnegligent manslaughter	Rape (revised definition)[1]	Rape (legacy definition)[2]	Robbery	Aggravated assault	Property crime	Burglary	Larceny-theft	Motor vehicle theft	Arson[3]
Floyd	33	1		3	7	22	389	80	274	35	
Howard	72	1		4	7	60	277	108	149	20	0
La Porte	29	0		5	4	20	525	238	257	30	
Lake	62	4	5		36	17	639	104	453	82	1
Madison	46	1	29		8	8	467	104	334	29	0
Shelby	36	1	2		0	33	200	72	104	24	0
St. Joseph	148	1	28		27	92	1,162	375	695	92	3
Sullivan	6	0		0	1	5	174	44	105	25	
Tippecanoe	45	0		8	6	31	571	181	355	35	
Vanderburgh	55	0	9		9	37	627	113	482	32	2
Wells	1	0	0		0	1	123	40	80	3	
Nonmetropolitan Counties											
Blackford	1	0		0	0	1	30	7	22	1	0
Clinton	14	0		6	6	2	208	44	148	16	0
Crawford	21	0		1	0	20	105	92	0	13	0
Daviess	0	0	0		0	0	109	31	64	14	
De Kalb	7	0	4		0	3	195	54	124	17	
Franklin	2	0		0	1	1	145	64	74	7	
Gibson	12	0		3	0	9	151	24	102	25	1
Grant	35	0		5	3	27	276	84	181	11	0
Greene	1	0	1		0	0	226	52	156	18	1
Huntington	6	0	1		0	5	103	25	69	9	
Jackson	24	1	4		1	18	349	63	270	16	
Jay	5	0		1	0	4	57	5	43	9	
Jennings	17	0		3	0	14	266	153	102	11	
Knox	9	1	0		1	7	37	12	22	3	
Kosciusko	62	1		7	3	51	497	155	315	27	3
LaGrange	40	2	5		1	32	147	43	83	21	
Lawrence	129	0		5	2	122	221	71	120	30	6
Miami	10	0		2	2	6	252	73	173	6	0
Noble	17	0		1	0	16	234	93	126	15	0
Steuben	22	1	8		1	12	439	123	287	29	0
Wabash	3	0		0	0	3	135	35	95	5	0
Wayne	12	1	5		1	5	275	104	162	9	
White	0	0	0		0	0	0	0	0	0	0
IOWA											
Metropolitan Counties											
Black Hawk	29	0	4		0	25	144	64	65	15	1
Bremer	11	0	2		0	9	42	15	24	3	0
Dallas	43	0	7		1	35	126	26	89	11	0
Dubuque	20	1	5		2	12	186	72	98	16	0
Grundy	9	0	0		0	9	66	21	44	1	1
Guthrie	0	0	0		0	0	35	10	23	2	0
Harrison	4	0	0		0	4	53	10	37	6	1
Johnson	91	0	24		2	65	168	55	100	13	0
Linn	23	0	6		2	15	318	156	127	35	1
Madison	4	0	0		0	4	60	23	33	4	0
Mills	18	0	1		0	17	108	63	34	11	0
Plymouth	8	0	4		0	4	28	7	12	9	0
Polk	91	2	21		11	57	714	247	365	102	5
Pottawattamie	65	0	10		2	53	271	90	141	40	4
Scott	58	0	7		0	51	195	89	83	23	1
Story	16	0	4		0	12	145	52	70	23	2
Warren	42	0	8		2	32	166	47	98	21	2
Washington	34	0	9		1	24	75	25	48	2	0
Woodbury	25	0	0		0	25	174	63	71	40	1
Nonmetropolitan Counties											
Adair	10	0	4		0	6	46	18	19	9	2
Adams	0	0	0		0	0	30	6	22	2	0
Allamakee	4	0	0		0	4	53	14	36	3	0
Appanoose	10	0	1		0	9	101	57	37	7	1
Audubon	2	0	0		0	2	36	1	34	1	0
Boone	13	0	0		0	13	32	17	9	6	0
Buchanan	8	0	5		1	2	112	44	54	14	3
Buena Vista	8	0	3		0	5	21	7	13	1	0
Butler	2	0	1		0	1	4	1	3	0	0
Calhoun	5	0	0		0	5	76	33	34	9	0
Carroll	2	0	0		0	2	35	16	16	3	0
Cass	17	0	1		0	16	30	6	21	3	0
Cedar	6	0	3		0	3	54	15	34	5	0
Cerro Gordo	1	0	0		1	0	97	46	44	7	0
Cherokee	2	0	1		1	0	22	7	15	0	1
Chickasaw	11	0	3		0	8	35	11	20	4	0
Clarke	8	0	1		0	7	64	19	28	17	0
Clay	12	0	0		1	11	40	11	26	3	0
Clayton	7	0	1		0	6	40	14	24	2	0
Clinton	12	0	0		0	12	133	41	85	7	0
Crawford	1	0	0		0	1	6	1	4	1	0

Table 8. Offenses Known to Law Enforcement, by Selected State Metropolitan and Nonmetropolitan Counties, 2016—Continued

(Number.)

State/county	Violent crime	Murder and nonnegligent manslaughter	Rape (revised definition)[1]	Rape (legacy definition)[2]	Robbery	Aggravated assault	Property crime	Burglary	Larceny-theft	Motor vehicle theft	Arson[3]
Delaware	18	0	0		1	17	65	28	34	3	0
Dickinson	12	0	3		0	9	16	3	7	6	0
Emmet	17	0	0		0	17	29	10	14	5	0
Fayette	12	0	0		0	12	49	12	30	7	0
Floyd	6	0	3		0	3	28	12	13	3	0
Fremont	27	0	4		0	23	64	31	26	7	1
Hancock	19	0	5		0	14	51	35	13	3	0
Hardin	10	0	1		0	9	102	52	37	13	1
Henry	19	0	3		0	16	57	18	34	5	1
Howard	2	0	1		0	1	68	25	36	7	0
Humboldt	0	0	0		0	0	47	19	25	3	0
Ida	11	0	3		0	8	34	12	18	4	0
Iowa	8	0	0		1	7	60	22	33	5	1
Jackson	2	1	1		0	0	11	4	7	0	0
Jasper	24	0	3		0	21	159	92	54	13	5
Jefferson	3	1	0		0	2	50	18	26	6	0
Keokuk	9	0	0		0	9	36	25	9	2	0
Kossuth	6	0	1		0	5	31	13	14	4	0
Lee	28	0	1		0	27	155	76	66	13	0
Louisa	23	0	5		0	18	76	32	34	10	2
Lucas	6	0	0		1	5	73	31	36	6	0
Lyon	14	0	3		0	11	66	25	35	6	0
Mahaska	11	0	1		0	10	84	42	33	9	1
Marshall	34	0	2		0	32	125	58	51	16	1
Mitchell	0	0	0		0	0	13	10	2	1	0
Monroe	3	0	1		0	2	54	35	15	4	0
Muscatine	24	0	6		0	18	80	36	34	10	0
O'Brien	13	0	2		0	11	54	13	38	3	0
Osceola	7	0	2		1	4	57	18	36	3	1
Page	5	0	2		0	3	37	20	11	6	1
Palo Alto	13	0	2		0	11	49	21	26	2	0
Pocahontas	9	0	1		0	8	47	11	31	5	1
Ringgold	2	0	1		0	1	31	21	10	0	1
Sac	3	0	1		0	2	32	16	14	2	0
Sioux	7	0	0		1	6	45	16	29	0	1
Tama	30	0	2		0	28	113	67	34	12	2
Taylor	3	0	1		0	2	25	5	15	5	0
Union	7	0	0		0	7	46	5	36	5	0
Van Buren	7	0	0		0	7	30	11	16	3	0
Wapello	18	1	0		0	17	122	46	58	18	2
Wayne	5	0	0		0	5	57	30	21	6	0
Webster	19	1	1		2	15	105	37	52	16	0
Winneshiek	5	1	0		0	4	34	3	26	5	0
Worth	3	0	0		0	3	22	7	15	0	0
Wright	4	0	1		0	3	31	17	11	3	0
KANSAS											
Metropolitan Counties											
Butler	46	0	8		5	33	486	150	293	43	7
Doniphan	2	0	0		0	2	29	13	14	2	0
Harvey	13	6	0		0	7	59	30	24	5	0
Jackson	13	0	4		0	9	96	31	55	10	1
Jefferson	30	1	3		0	26	163	39	103	21	0
Johnson	40	0	9		2	29	225	52	149	24	3
Kingman	2	0	1		0	1	71	31	37	3	1
Leavenworth	36	0	4		2	30	177	60	96	21	6
Linn	6	0	1		0	5	77	28	37	12	1
Miami	29	0	5		2	22	225	94	104	27	3
Osage	15	0	1		0	14	67	31	34	2	1
Pottawatomie	43	0	2		1	40	226	69	145	12	5
Riley County Police Department	193	1	44		20	128	1,223	164	993	66	9
Sedgwick	24	4	1		1	18	89	37	31	21	1
Shawnee	78	0	7		3	68	981	188	692	101	0
Sumner	20	0	1		1	18	142	23	99	20	2
Wabaunsee	10	0	0		0	10	73	24	37	12	2
Wyandotte	27	0	2		8	17	53	5	43	5	3
Nonmetropolitan Counties											
Allen	15	0	1		0	14	45	20	22	3	0
Anderson	2	0	0		0	2	30	17	12	1	1
Barber	2	0	0		0	2	19	7	11	1	0
Bourbon	25	0	4		1	20	94	32	49	13	0
Brown	5	0	1		0	4	32	3	26	3	0
Chautauqua	0	0	0		0	0	21	6	14	1	0
Cherokee[6]	32	0	3		4	25			102	21	4
Clay	1	0	0		0	1	27	15	11	1	0
Cloud	9	0	4		0	5	56	16	33	7	2
Coffey	7	0	1		0	6	51	9	38	4	1
Cowley	20	0	0		0	20	140	58	68	14	0
Crawford	24	0	4		2	18	175	57	99	19	4
Dickinson	17	1	5		0	11	107	38	55	14	2

Table 8. Offenses Known to Law Enforcement, by Selected State Metropolitan and Nonmetropolitan Counties, 2016—Continued

(Number.)

State/county	Violent crime	Murder and nonnegligent manslaughter	Rape (revised definition)[1]	Rape (legacy definition)[2]	Robbery	Aggravated assault	Property crime	Burglary	Larceny-theft	Motor vehicle theft	Arson[3]
Edwards	2	0	0		1	1	19	5	14	0	0
Ellis	9	0	2		0	7	70	32	33	5	2
Ellsworth	0	0	0		0	0	22	11	9	2	0
Finney	34	1	5		3	25	113	39	68	6	3
Ford[6]	14	0	1		0	13			41	14	0
Franklin	37	0	5		2	30	158	65	72	21	5
Geary	14	0	1		1	12	50	19	31	0	0
Gove	0	0	0		0	0	10	1	7	2	0
Grant	5	1	0		0	4	22	6	15	1	0
Gray	6	0	0		0	6	85	39	39	7	2
Greenwood	19	1	1		0	17	78	21	54	3	1
Hamilton	3	0	0		0	3	4	1	1	2	0
Harper	6	0	1		0	5	36	15	19	2	0
Haskell	3	0	1		0	2	25	3	19	3	0
Kiowa	1	0	0		0	1	12	4	8	0	1
Labette[6]	15	1	0		0	14			20	1	0
Logan	1	0	0		0	1	4	1	3	0	0
Lyon	28	0	2		1	25	80	23	51	6	16
Marion	4	0	0		1	3	56	24	27	5	2
Marshall	5	0	2		0	3	25	8	16	1	0
Montgomery	13	1	2		2	8	114	52	49	13	1
Morris	2	0	0		0	2	36	15	18	3	0
Morton	9	0	1		0	8	32	11	17	4	0
Nemaha	6	0	0		1	5	55	18	31	6	2
Neosho	25	1	1		0	23	59	19	33	7	1
Ness	2	0	1		0	1	30	7	15	8	0
Norton	0	0	0		0	0	11	4	4	3	0
Osborne	4	0	1		0	3	42	15	21	6	0
Ottawa	1	0	0		0	1	68	19	46	3	0
Pawnee[6]	2	0	0		0	2			11	4	2
Phillips	11	0	0		0	11	20	9	11	0	1
Pratt	4	0	0		1	3	56	28	23	5	2
Rawlins	2	0	1		0	1	11	1	9	1	0
Republic	1	0	0		0	1	19	5	12	2	1
Rice	10	0	0		0	10	60	21	35	4	0
Rooks	1	0	1		0	0	11	6	5	0	0
Rush	3	0	1		0	2	67	27	37	3	1
Russell	8	0	1		0	7	39	13	24	2	0
Saline	25	1	4		0	20	128	39	74	15	9
Scott	4	0	1		0	3	9	2	6	1	0
Sherman	0	0	0		0	0	0	0	0	0	0
Smith	1	0	0		0	1	13	4	8	1	0
Thomas	0	0	0		0	0	15	4	6	5	0
Trego	7	0	0		0	7	8	4	4	0	0
Washington	4	0	0		0	4	23	7	12	4	0
Wichita	1	0	0		0	1	29	15	14	0	0
Wilson	5	0	0		0	5	52	24	22	6	0
Woodson	5	0	1		0	4	24	8	12	4	5
KENTUCKY											
Metropolitan Counties											
Allen	14	1	4		0	9	127	56	57	14	1
Boone	62	1	18		19	24	967	204	682	81	4
Bourbon	4	0	0		0	4	82	35	44	3	0
Boyd	12	0	3		2	7	129	38	82	9	0
Bracken	0	0	0		0	0	37	15	19	3	0
Bullitt	33	2	9		7	15	489	158	265	66	5
Butler	3	0	0		0	3	45	19	19	7	1
Campbell	0	0	0		0	0	1	0	1	0	0
Campbell County Police Department	15	0	10		0	5	220	47	152	21	2
Christian	21	1	6		6	8	327	101	190	36	4
Clark	14	0	5		1	8	201	94	94	13	0
Daviess	26	1	12		2	11	471	125	317	29	2
Edmonson	5	0	1		0	4	24	14	9	1	1
Fayette	0	0	0		0	0	0	0	0	0	0
Gallatin	2	0	0		0	2	44	12	28	4	1
Grant	5	0	2		1	2	92	29	55	8	0
Greenup	2	0	0		0	2	44	19	18	7	1
Hancock	1	0	0		0	1	9	5	3	1	0
Hardin	13	1	1		7	4	106	35	58	13	1
Henderson	11	0	4		1	6	151	63	71	17	0
Henry	0	0	0		0	0	17	7	8	2	0
Jefferson	0	0	0		0	0	2	1	1	0	0
Jessamine	8	0	3		1	4	211	94	106	11	0
Kenton	10	0	0		2	8	6	0	6	0	0
Kenton County Police Department	8	0	4		1	3	128	48	75	5	3
Larue	2	0	0		0	2	31	9	15	7	1
McLean	4	0	0		0	4	46	20	20	6	0
Meade	11	0	0		0	11	114	62	36	16	0
Oldham	3	0	0		0	3	5	3	2	0	0
Oldham County Police Department	30	0	7		5	18	421	118	277	26	1

Table 8. Offenses Known to Law Enforcement, by Selected State Metropolitan and Nonmetropolitan Counties, 2016—Continued

(Number.)

State/county	Violent crime	Murder and nonnegligent manslaughter	Rape (revised definition)[1]	Rape (legacy definition)[2]	Robbery	Aggravated assault	Property crime	Burglary	Larceny-theft	Motor vehicle theft	Arson[3]
Pendleton	5	0	1		0	4	55	17	32	6	1
Scott	11	0	5		4	2	196	64	113	19	2
Shelby	23	0	8		4	11	376	86	269	21	0
Spencer	3	0	1		0	2	61	23	33	5	1
Trigg	5	0	1		0	4	85	25	52	8	0
Trimble	2	0	0		0	2	10	5	5	0	0
Warren	36	0	10		3	23	432	161	244	27	0
Woodford	0	0	0		0	0	33	5	27	1	0
Nonmetropolitan Counties											
Adair	0	0	0		0	0	20	11	5	4	0
Anderson	2	0	0		2	0	50	24	22	4	0
Ballard	4	0	1		1	2	51	24	22	5	1
Barren	12	0	3		0	9	119	57	42	20	0
Bath	1	0	1		0	0	34	16	17	1	0
Bell	12	0	1		1	10	149	41	95	13	2
Boyle	7	0	2		1	4	29	13	9	7	0
Breathitt	0	0	0		0	0	0	0	0	0	0
Breckinridge	7	1	1		0	5	33	7	18	8	0
Caldwell	3	0	0		0	3	62	31	24	7	0
Calloway	15	1	3		1	10	202	90	101	11	1
Carlisle	1	0	0		0	1	23	8	14	1	0
Carroll	2	0	0		1	1	11	5	6	0	0
Carter	5	0	0		4	1	31	13	12	6	0
Clay	11	1	0		1	9	108	31	48	29	2
Clinton	4	1	1		1	1	21	5	6	10	0
Crittenden	0	0	0		0	0	13	4	8	1	0
Cumberland	0	0	0		0	0	9	2	5	2	0
Elliott	0	0	0		0	0	0	0	0	0	0
Estill	1	0	0		1	0	16	5	9	2	0
Fleming	5	0	0		0	5	20	11	5	4	0
Floyd	4	0	1		1	2	59	18	34	7	0
Franklin	16	2	3		4	7	261	70	170	21	0
Fulton	0	0	0		0	0	16	7	9	0	0
Garrard	2	0	0		0	2	32	11	17	4	0
Graves	21	1	7		1	12	243	96	130	17	0
Grayson	8	0	2		0	6	77	34	30	13	1
Green	0	0	0		0	0	13	6	5	2	0
Harlan	4	0	3		0	1	16	3	13	0	0
Harrison	2	0	0		1	1	106	54	44	8	0
Hart	2	0	0		0	2	40	18	17	5	0
Hopkins	17	0	0		2	15	250	89	133	28	1
Jackson	3	0	0		1	2	68	36	24	8	1
Johnson	5	0	1		0	4	55	10	36	9	1
Knott	0	0	0		0	0	10	2	6	2	0
Knox	9	0	1		2	6	124	50	48	26	1
Laurel	34	2	4		11	17	400	137	201	62	3
Lawrence	2	0	0		1	1	53	25	13	15	0
Leslie	3	0	0		0	3	12	4	5	3	0
Letcher	6	0	2		1	3	22	7	12	3	1
Lewis	0	0	0		0	0	12	8	4	0	0
Lincoln	3	0	0		1	2	60	29	16	15	1
Livingston	1	0	0		1	0	63	27	28	8	0
Logan	16	0	4		2	10	160	64	86	10	1
Lyon	1	0	0		0	1	28	13	14	1	0
Madison	22	0	9		6	7	484	155	294	35	1
Magoffin	3	0	0		2	1	13	3	6	4	0
Marion	5	0	0		2	3	74	26	44	4	0
Marshall	13	0	4		1	8	199	81	91	27	0
Martin	4	0	1		0	3	56	10	40	6	0
Mason	9	0	2		2	5	85	29	53	3	0
McCracken	61	1	26		4	30	451	149	255	47	3
McCreary	2	0	0		0	2	66	26	29	11	0
Menifee	1	0	0		0	1	20	12	5	3	0
Mercer	1	0	1		0	0	21	9	7	5	0
Metcalfe	7	0	0		1	6	87	41	33	13	0
Monroe	1	0	0		1	0	1	0	1	0	1
Montgomery	10	0	1		6	3	325	133	165	27	0
Morgan	0	0	0		0	0	1	0	1	0	0
Muhlenberg	12	0	1		2	9	53	22	27	4	0
Muhlenberg County Police Department	0	0	0		0	0	0	0	0	0	0
Nelson	19	2	7		1	9	175	62	89	24	2
Nicholas	1	0	0		0	1	11	4	6	1	0
Ohio	18	0	5		1	12	81	37	34	10	0
Owen	0	0	0		0	0	40	20	19	1	0
Owsley	6	0	0		2	4	49	19	26	4	0
Perry	1	0	0		1	0	24	5	13	6	0
Pike	4	0	3		1	0	126	16	107	3	0
Powell	0	0	0		0	0	34	10	18	6	0
Pulaski	25	0	4		6	15	449	188	202	59	4
Robertson	0	0	0		0	0	3	0	3	0	0

Table 8. Offenses Known to Law Enforcement, by Selected State Metropolitan and Nonmetropolitan Counties, 2016—Continued

(Number.)

State/county	Violent crime	Murder and nonnegligent manslaughter	Rape (revised definition)[1]	Rape (legacy definition)[2]	Robbery	Aggravated assault	Property crime	Burglary	Larceny-theft	Motor vehicle theft	Arson[3]
Rockcastle	4	0	0		2	2	35	15	9	11	0
Rowan	8	0	1		1	6	61	13	43	5	1
Russell	5	0	1		0	4	22	10	9	3	0
Simpson	7	0	1		2	4	71	31	37	3	0
Taylor	6	0	2		1	3	148	61	77	10	0
Todd	5	0	0		1	4	47	20	19	8	0
Union	2	1	0		1	0	44	9	30	5	1
Washington	3	0	0		1	2	36	17	19	0	0
Wayne	5	0	0		2	3	59	23	24	12	1
Webster	1	0	0		0	1	19	6	9	4	0
Whitley	7	0	0		3	4	150	50	68	32	2
Wolfe	2	0	0		0	2	12	6	2	4	0
LOUISIANA											
Metropolitan Counties											
Acadia	107	7	0		20	80	854	373	399	82	0
Ascension	360	4	24		33	299	2,898	578	2,125	195	4
Bossier	85	0	5		10	70	654	193	425	36	1
Caddo	81	2	2		6	71	796	225	509	62	2
Calcasieu	523	6	52		31	434	4,216	1,227	2,714	275	5
Cameron	19	0	2		0	17	123	9	110	4	0
De Soto	68	0	6		4	58	387	124	242	21	0
East Baton Rouge	397	14	47		194	142	7,252	1,263	5,705	284	14
East Feliciana	95	0	5		1	89	144	32	96	16	0
Grant	5	0	2		0	3	144	62	78	4	0
Iberia[5]	136	0	4		64	68		437	1,083		2
Iberville	285	1	7		15	262	553	114	429	10	0
Jefferson	1,590	44	66		399	1,081	11,217	1,503	9,009	705	59
Lafayette	309	10	9		31	259	1,629	351	1,134	144	6
Lafourche	320	9	22		28	261	1,868	628	1,168	72	7
Livingston	297	2	22		12	261	2,941	933	1,993	15	0
Ouachita	457	5	6		48	398	2,642	875	1,601	166	5
Plaquemines	38	1	5		3	29	226	53	168	5	1
Pointe Coupee	89	3	4		8	74	267	107	136	24	0
Rapides	379	1	35		15	328	2,004	678	1,169	157	5
St. Bernard	135	0	11		32	92	1,507	264	1,173	70	7
St. Charles	175	3	4		23	145	837	188	612	37	8
St. John the Baptist	70	3	4		11	52	989	243	713	33	2
St. Martin	129	4	13		16	96	362	112	234	16	0
St. Tammany	242	4	31		23	184	1,749	366	1,264	119	7
Tangipahoa	738	9	52		124	553	2,585	840	1,503	242	9
Terrebonne	376	6	19		34	317	2,814	624	2,095	95	11
Union	27	0	0		0	27	30	12	18	0	0
Vermilion	89	4	1		17	67	736	285	265	186	0
Webster	94	1	4		1	88	217	100	98	19	0
West Baton Rouge	53	0	6		9	38	404	48	331	25	0
West Feliciana	38	1	5		2	30	80	7	72	1	0
Nonmetropolitan Counties											
Allen	18	0	6		1	11	73	9	53	11	0
Assumption	85	0	3		6	76	240	38	192	10	1
Avoyelles	121	3	11		3	104	500	186	290	24	3
Beauregard	18	0	1		0	17	128	11	105	12	4
Bienville	63	1	10		8	44	254	92	147	15	0
Caldwell	21	0	0		1	20	248	58	180	10	0
Concordia	77	3	2		6	66	276	76	182	18	2
Evangeline	31	1	1		1	28	472	119	352	1	0
Franklin	38	1	2		0	35	126	34	80	12	0
Jackson	6	0	2		0	4	52	19	31	2	2
La Salle	40	2	1		2	35	36	10	24	2	0
Lincoln	62	1	5		4	52	202	59	133	10	0
Madison	25	4	0		0	21	32	9	19	4	1
Natchitoches	60	2	5		4	49	426	103	293	30	0
Red River	33	0	3		3	27	141	33	102	6	0
Richland	76	2	1		1	72	258	66	173	19	0
Sabine	8	0	0		2	6	150	35	115	0	1
St. Landry	228	5	3		14	206	992	477	422	93	0
St. Mary	148	2	5		17	124	711	169	502	40	1
Tensas	7	0	1		0	6	8	2	6	0	0
Vernon	87	4	5		2	76	552	96	419	37	3
Washington	187	1	24		7	155	696	224	414	58	3
West Carroll	48	1	0		0	47	181	59	99	23	0
Winn	18	0	0		0	18	61	27	29	5	0
MAINE											
Metropolitan Counties											
Androscoggin[7]	14	0	6		1	7	122	38	80	4	0
Cumberland[7]	21	0	5		3	13	536	190	312	34	0
Penobscot[7]	5	0	1		2	2	340	117	212	11	1
Sagadahoc[7]	6	0	1		0	5	81	24	57	0	2
York[7]	26	0	4		2	20	326	142	176	8	0

Table 8. Offenses Known to Law Enforcement, by Selected State Metropolitan and Nonmetropolitan Counties, 2016—Continued

(Number.)

State/county	Violent crime	Murder and nonnegligent manslaughter	Rape (revised definition)[1]	Rape (legacy definition)[2]	Robbery	Aggravated assault	Property crime	Burglary	Larceny-theft	Motor vehicle theft	Arson[3]
Nonmetropolitan Counties											
Aroostook[7]	2	0	0		0	2	53	19	27	7	
Franklin	7	0	5		0	2	75	23	44	8	0
Hancock[7]	1	0	0		0	1	165	53	108	4	0
Kennebec	26	2	8		4	12	177	60	99	18	0
Knox[7]	17	0	0		1	16	170	38	120	12	0
Lincoln[7]	31	0	13		0	18	221	57	155	9	0
Oxford[7]	18	0	8		1	9	343	82	245	16	0
Piscataquis[7]	6	0	2		0	4	41	5	34	2	0
Somerset	29	0	12		4	13	328	90	216	22	0
Waldo[7]	11	0	2		1	8	170	46	118	6	2
Washington[7]	17	0	4		1	12	136	46	83	7	1
MARYLAND											
Metropolitan Counties											
Allegany	23	1	3		7	12	336	52	276	8	0
Anne Arundel	0	0	0		0	0	0	0	0	0	0
Anne Arundel County Police Department	2,053	14	143		492	1,404	11,642	1,767	9,302	573	33
Baltimore County	0	0	0		0	0	0	0	0	0	0
Baltimore County Police Department	4,397	35	318		1,497	2,547	23,344	3,681	17,599	2,064	163
Calvert	121	1	14		12	94	1,070	223	810	37	9
Carroll	100	2	20		9	69	807	190	584	33	0
Cecil	90	2	10		16	62	619	179	395	45	1
Charles	527	6	38		126	357	2,305	344	1,803	158	31
Frederick	185	1	13		30	141	1,485	251	1,180	54	
Harford	384	6	24		81	273	2,430	453	1,915	62	0
Howard	0	0	0		0	0	0	0	0	0	0
Howard County Police Department	712	6	66		201	439	5,522	840	4,379	303	3
Montgomery	0	0	0		0	0	0	0	0	0	0
Montgomery County Police Department	1,749	14	331		659	745	15,066	1,855	12,374	837	62
Prince George's	10	0	0		0	10	1	0	1	0	0
Queen Anne's	72	0	6		11	55	472	106	355	11	4
Somerset	24	0	2		1	21	52	15	35	2	0
St. Mary's	202	2	21		28	151	1,814	378	1,372	64	2
Washington	193	0	7		35	151	1,721	416	1,201	104	4
Wicomico	105	1	6		24	74	644	172	442	30	2
Worcester	13	2	2		5	4	249	63	178	8	0
Nonmetropolitan Counties											
Caroline	17	0	2		1	14	200	67	124	9	0
Dorchester	10	1	0		1	8	203	55	132	16	0
Garrett	45	0	1		0	44	239	46	187	6	1
Kent	8	0	1		3	4	130	53	75	2	0
Talbot	22	0	11		0	11	175	55	119	1	1
MICHIGAN											
Metropolitan Counties											
Barry	34	1	11		0	22	255	54	193	8	0
Bay	44	0	14		2	28	593	113	462	18	1
Berrien	122	2	47		10	63	587	168	379	40	5
Calhoun	121	1	28		4	88	501	137	341	23	1
Cass	50	0	20		0	30	551	234	294	23	4
Clinton	23	0	4		1	18	172	51	108	13	0
Eaton	164	2	61		26	75	986	183	750	53	2
Genesee	67	0	7		4	56	326	39	269	18	0
Ingham	146	2	36		9	99	504	128	348	28	2
Jackson	218	1	23		4	190	631	111	478	42	6
Kalamazoo	297	4	102		37	154	2,236	514	1,608	114	7
Kent	386	1	105		38	242	2,264	441	1,701	122	15
Lapeer	60	2	15		4	39	351	112	213	26	2
Livingston	70	1	28		4	37	552	97	427	28	7
Macomb	322	2	55		36	229	1,436	196	1,168	72	12
Midland	50	1	22		1	26	356	120	217	19	8
Monroe	167	5	56		19	87	1,521	344	1,065	112	23
Montcalm	54	0	21		2	31	226	51	164	11	0
Muskegon	66	0	25		1	40	555	95	437	23	5
Oakland	33	0	10		0	23	52	7	37	8	6
Ottawa	559	3	204		29	323	2,492	467	1,942	83	19
Saginaw	98	2	10		11	75	494	80	382	32	4
St. Clair	189	2	34		3	150	974	190	730	54	14
Van Buren	120	0	29		4	87	437	194	210	33	5
Washtenaw	588	1	69		80	438	1,667	391	1,067	209	16
Wayne	6	0	4		1	1	0	0	0	0	0
Nonmetropolitan Counties											
Alcona	10	0	2		0	8	94	40	53	1	1
Alger	0	0	0		0	0	5	0	4	1	0
Allegan	131	0	28		2	101	558	147	369	42	5
Alpena	10	0	3		1	6	36	10	23	3	0
Antrim	15	0	6		0	9	279	118	153	8	0

Table 8. Offenses Known to Law Enforcement, by Selected State Metropolitan and Nonmetropolitan Counties, 2016—Continued

(Number.)

State/county	Violent crime	Murder and nonnegligent manslaughter	Rape (revised definition)[1]	Rape (legacy definition)[2]	Robbery	Aggravated assault	Property crime	Burglary	Larceny-theft	Motor vehicle theft	Arson[3]
Arenac	29	1	16		0	12	100	33	57	10	2
Baraga	3	0	0		0	3	26	9	17	0	0
Benzie	18	0	6		0	12	100	11	86	3	0
Branch	10	0	5		0	5	61	11	45	5	0
Charlevoix	21	0	12		1	8	121	20	96	5	0
Cheboygan	7	0	6		0	1	70	27	41	2	1
Chippewa	6	0	1		0	5	55	16	37	2	0
Clare	90	1	21		1	67	412	101	291	20	8
Crawford	18	0	9		0	9	104	39	58	7	2
Delta	9	0	5		0	4	52	14	36	2	0
Emmet	28	0	10		0	18	176	54	121	1	2
Gladwin	27	0	5		1	21	126	58	64	4	0
Gogebic	6	0	4		0	2	52	10	39	3	0
Grand Traverse	125	2	34		5	84	593	100	460	33	5
Gratiot	21	0	9		2	10	279	45	221	13	2
Hillsdale	30	1	11		0	18	132	43	83	6	1
Houghton	13	0	9		1	3	77	19	51	7	1
Huron	24	0	7		1	16	103	32	66	5	0
Ionia	45	1	30		1	13	267	54	204	9	1
Iosco	0	0	0		0	0	0	0	0	0	0
Iron	8	1	3		1	3	19	8	11	0	0
Isabella	48	0	16		6	26	301	92	201	8	3
Kalkaska	60	0	2		1	57	195	38	145	12	2
Keweenaw	3	0	2		0	1	26	11	15	0	0
Lake	20	0	2		1	17	156	68	82	6	0
Leelanau	12	0	2		2	8	77	16	55	6	1
Lenawee	30	0	7		2	21	230	85	132	13	0
Luce	20	0	1		0	19	73	19	51	3	0
Mackinac	6	0	4		0	2	69	11	54	4	1
Manistee	36	0	17		0	19	261	48	206	7	2
Marquette	13	0	3		3	7	142	17	120	5	0
Mason	28	0	8		0	20	191	39	144	8	1
Mecosta	241	0	18		2	221	378	62	302	14	3
Menominee	16	0	9		0	7	49	19	28	2	0
Missaukee	21	0	6		1	14	139	26	110	3	0
Montmorency	4	0	0		0	4	19	7	5	7	0
Newaygo	45	1	13		0	31	257	67	184	6	2
Oceana	32	0	4		2	26	245	66	170	9	1
Ogemaw	22	0	3		1	18	163	57	99	7	1
Ontonagon	13	0	0		0	13	20	6	10	4	0
Osceola	45	0	17		2	26	205	31	143	31	0
Oscoda	27	0	4		0	23	158	43	109	6	0
Otsego	13	0	8		0	5	49	16	33	0	0
Presque Isle	5	0	3		0	2	21	7	13	1	0
Roscommon	19	1	7		0	11	148	40	103	5	1
Sanilac	45	0	8		2	35	192	84	94	14	1
Shiawassee	23	0	13		2	8	134	39	93	2	1
St. Joseph	54	0	10		0	44	131	43	76	12	2
Tuscola	43	0	8		0	35	205	58	123	24	0
Wexford	41	0	18		0	23	260	47	209	4	3
MINNESOTA											
Metropolitan Counties											
Anoka	44	1	15		5	23	977	157	767	53	7
Blue Earth	15	1	7		0	7	103	42	52	9	1
Carlton	19	0	8		2	9	166	49	99	18	3
Carver[3]	49	0	5		4	40	542	83	432	27	1
Chisago	12	0	2		0	10	213	51	145	17	0
Clay	5	0	0		1	4	65	27	29	9	0
Dakota	32	0	1		0	31	90	31	56	3	0
Dodge	4	0	0		0	4	71	12	47	12	0
Fillmore	7	0	0		1	6	73	23	46	4	1
Hennepin	19	0	0		3	16	61	2	54	5	0
Houston	4	0	2		0	2	42	7	32	3	0
Isanti	28	0	10		0	18	328	88	216	24	1
Le Sueur	5	0	1		0	4	109	31	78	0	0
Mille Lacs	23	1	5		3	14	455	79	321	55	0
Nicollet	3	0	2		0	1	62	21	41	0	0
Olmsted	23	0	13		2	8	280	85	170	25	7
Polk	30	0	9		0	21	228	72	146	10	3
Ramsey	63	0	23		16	24	1,096	140	876	80	1
Sherburne	35	0	12		3	20	405	68	319	18	0
Sibley	4	0	3		0	1	2	0	2	0	0
Stearns	47	0	15		2	30	454	79	345	30	1
St. Louis	51	1	13		1	36	717	244	397	76	9
Wabasha	6	0	0		0	6	45	6	33	6	0
Washington	75	0	19		4	52	848	180	603	65	0
Wright	97	2	41		5	49	1,737	126	1,545	66	11
Nonmetropolitan Counties											
Aitkin	11	1	4		2	4	263	104	143	16	0

Table 8. Offenses Known to Law Enforcement, by Selected State Metropolitan and Nonmetropolitan Counties, 2016—Continued

(Number.)

State/county	Violent crime	Murder and nonnegligent manslaughter	Rape (revised definition)[1]	Rape (legacy definition)[2]	Robbery	Aggravated assault	Property crime	Burglary	Larceny-theft	Motor vehicle theft	Arson[3]
Becker	17	0	4		0	13	118	51	48	19	0
Beltrami	52	0	9		2	41	387	94	251	42	2
Big Stone	1	0	1		0	0	23	11	12	0	0
Brown	4	0	0		0	4	20	2	17	1	0
Cass	54	1	30		3	20	401	122	235	44	0
Chippewa	1	0	0		0	1	30	11	17	2	0
Clearwater	16	0	3		0	13	93	36	53	4	2
Cook	5	0	3		0	2	115	29	83	3	0
Cottonwood	2	0	0		0	2	15	4	11	0	0
Crow Wing	24	0	6		1	17	321	116	190	15	1
Douglas	14	0	5		2	7	162	55	97	10	0
Faribault	2	0	2		0	0	62	29	24	9	0
Freeborn	3	1	2		0	0	79	27	43	9	1
Goodhue	19	0	8		2	9	161	46	95	20	1
Grant	1	0	0		0	1	13	5	8	0	0
Hubbard	20	0	6		1	13	209	74	126	9	1
Itasca	37	1	13		0	23	135	40	89	6	1
Jackson	2	0	1		1	0	40	7	31	2	0
Kanabec	22	0	0		0	22	237	68	140	29	0
Kandiyohi	22	0	3		2	17	166	26	126	14	0
Kittson	1	0	0		0	1	20	2	18	0	0
Lac qui Parle	1	0	1		0	0	26	11	15	0	1
Lake	1	0	0		0	1	14	4	5	5	0
Lake of the Woods	1	0	1		0	0	5	2	2	1	0
Lincoln	12	0	0		0	12	0	0	0	0	0
Lyon	3	0	0		0	3	56	20	32	4	0
Marshall	5	0	1		0	4	44	8	29	7	1
Martin	2	0	1		0	1	15	5	9	1	0
McLeod	14	0	6		0	8	81	28	51	2	0
Meeker	17	1	11		0	5	113	25	73	15	0
Mower	10	0	2		0	8	91	35	47	9	0
Murray	1	0	0		0	1	37	4	31	2	0
Nobles	4	0	1		0	3	24	15	8	1	0
Norman	0	0	0		0	0	2	0	2	0	1
Otter Tail	20	0	6		0	14	379	155	206	18	3
Pennington	2	0	0		0	2	15	5	7	3	0
Pine	78	0	20		6	52	864	164	597	103	6
Pope	4	0	0		0	4	33	6	22	5	0
Red Lake	0	0	0		0	0	8	0	7	1	0
Redwood	6	0	1		0	5	58	13	40	5	0
Renville	7	0	0		0	7	87	20	61	6	0
Rice	16	0	4		1	11	153	41	92	20	2
Rock	36	0	0		0	36	70	11	53	6	0
Roseau	1	0	1		0	0	75	18	50	7	0
Steele	13	1	1		1	10	80	21	49	10	1
Stevens	5	0	4		0	1	36	17	19	0	0
Swift	2	0	0		0	2	6	5	0	1	0
Todd	22	0	13		0	9	153	51	96	6	3
Traverse	1	0	0		0	1	20	4	15	1	1
Wadena	1	0	0		0	1	3	3	0	0	1
Waseca	3	0	2		0	1	54	19	29	6	0
Watonwan	4	0	2		0	2	30	18	8	4	0
Wilkin	3	0	1		1	1	20	1	18	1	0
Winona	12	1	0		0	11	47	7	34	6	0
Yellow Medicine	4	0	1		0	3	35	18	14	3	0
MISSISSIPPI											
Metropolitan Counties											
DeSoto	36	1	2		6	27	454	200	238	16	0
Hancock	42	2		0	2	38	590	129	396	65	2
Harrison	59	1	8		10	40	1,016	216	671	129	9
Hinds8	89	2	11		8	68	406	158	181	67	
Jackson	114	4		38	15	57	1,426	381	874	171	7
Lamar	96	1		7	9	79	692	270	415	7	0
Madison	24	0		5	4	15	277	95	152	30	4
Marshall	3	0	1		0	2	158	3	145	10	1
Rankin	36	2	3		3	28	622	147	432	43	4
Tunica	34	0		9	7	18	417	93	292	32	
Nonmetropolitan Counties											
Choctaw	3	0		0	0	3	72	29	42	1	1
Claiborne	22	3	4		1	14	73	50	14	9	0
Grenada	9	0		0	3	6	136	54	80	2	
Jones	142	1	50		9	82	768	363	405	0	0
Kemper	10	0		0	3	7	58	31	26	1	1
Lauderdale	53	5		15	18	15	604	300	264	40	7
Lincoln	16	0		4	0	12	280	112	150	18	4
Marion	41	2	7		6	26	296	141	128	27	2
Oktibbeha	40	0		7	7	26	385	210	163	12	5
Panola	102	5		0	5	92	790	389	386	15	0
Scott	34	1	1		3	29	188	95	72	21	0

Table 8. Offenses Known to Law Enforcement, by Selected State Metropolitan and Nonmetropolitan Counties, 2016—Continued

(Number.)

State/county	Violent crime	Murder and nonnegligent manslaughter	Rape (revised definition)[1]	Rape (legacy definition)[2]	Robbery	Aggravated assault	Property crime	Burglary	Larceny-theft	Motor vehicle theft	Arson[3]
Stone	34	0	6		2	26	168	60	92	16	2
Sunflower	24	0		0	12	12	12	12	0	0	0
Warren	17	1	5		1	10	263	51	182	30	2
Washington	20	0	3		6	11	323	88	223	12	0
MISSOURI											
Metropolitan Counties											
Andrew	33	2	2		1	28	107	38	63	6	0
Bates	50	0	1		0	49	125	49	64	12	0
Bollinger	87	1	3		7	76	91	34	51	6	0
Boone	125	0	14		11	100	601	130	413	58	10
Buchanan	28	1	0		2	25	188	62	95	31	9
Caldwell	17	0	0		0	17	68	28	36	4	1
Callaway	117	3	16		8	90	502	160	303	39	0
Cape Girardeau	33	0	0		5	28	196	73	112	11	0
Cass	60	1	5		2	52	406	120	249	37	5
Christian	95	0	7		2	86	327	116	196	15	3
Clay	50	1	1		11	37	236	86	131	19	3
Clinton	24	0	0		0	24	105	37	52	16	3
Cole	42	0	1		2	39	278	77	179	22	3
Dallas	22	0	3		1	18	138	47	73	18	0
DeKalb	5	0	0		1	4	44	14	24	6	1
Franklin	71	2	0		1	68	548	171	325	52	2
Greene	83	2	35		10	36	1,318	394	782	142	7
Jackson	85	2	10		9	64	383	125	220	38	3
Jasper	123	2	16		6	99	507	143	302	62	0
Jefferson	196	2	14		15	165	2,284	449	1,565	270	15
Lafayette	10	0	1		0	9	131	38	82	11	2
Lincoln	132	0	4		1	127	189	64	99	26	3
McDonald	101	0	2		3	96	387	85	262	40	0
Moniteau	1	0	0		0	1	40	29	5	6	0
Newton[9]		0	13		7		719	159	475	85	21
Osage	3	0	1		0	2	42	21	17	4	0
Platte	41	4	13		4	20	262	66	168	28	2
Polk	50	0	7		2	41	333	133	174	26	3
Ray	102	0	3		0	99	111	47	53	11	0
St. Charles	0	0	0		0	0	1	0	1	0	0
St. Charles County Police Department	114	3	18		9	84	789	198	522	69	8
St. Louis County Police Department	1,784	25	195		399	1,165	8,291	1,729	5,728	834	63
Warren	68	0	11		2	55	219	58	141	20	3
Webster	11	1	3		1	6	256	80	155	21	0
Nonmetropolitan Counties											
Adair	8	0	1		0	7	116	46	63	7	0
Atchison	1	0	0		0	1	8	1	4	3	0
Audrain	22	0	7		2	13	76	22	48	6	0
Barry	40	0	6		0	34	345	124	190	31	1
Barton	27	0	0		0	27	97	41	50	6	7
Benton	80	1	2		4	73	232	81	133	18	0
Butler	86	2	1		6	77	497	110	338	49	0
Camden[5]		4			0	79	457	205	229	23	7
Carroll	3	0	0		1	3	26	6	19	1	0
Carter	36	0	5		0	30	60	25	33	2	0
Cedar	37	0	1		0	36	101	43	54	4	1
Chariton	13	0	0		0	13	50	22	26	2	0
Clark	12	0	1		1	10	40	5	30	5	0
Cooper	7	0	0		1	6	83	29	44	10	1
Crawford	20	0	1		0	19	223	87	108	28	0
Dade	28	0	0		0	28	84	38	43	3	1
Daviess	9	1	1		0	7	49	20	24	5	0
Dent	7	2	2		1	2	60	29	22	9	0
Douglas	17	0	0		0	17	51	19	28	4	3
Dunklin	22	0	0		1	21	165	40	110	15	1
Gasconade	18	0	0		0	18	116	46	60	10	0
Gentry	4	0	0		0	4	37	9	23	5	0
Grundy	2	0	0		0	2	18	12	5	1	0
Harrison	2	0	1		0	1	61	27	28	6	1
Henry	54	1	1		2	50	228	94	115	19	3
Hickory	0	0	0		0	0	90	43	45	2	0
Holt	5	0	0		0	5	44	20	23	1	0
Howard	9	0	0		1	8	67	19	41	7	0
Howell	53	0	0		4	49	191	67	102	22	0
Iron	16	0	0		1	15	67	32	32	3	1
Johnson	38	1	4		1	32	253	67	164	22	0
Knox	0	0	0		0	0	15	8	7	0	0
Laclede	45	0	6		0	39	268	82	144	42	2
Lawrence	60	2	7		1	50	220	94	122	4	1
Lewis	3	0	1		0	2	39	15	22	2	1
Linn	10	0	2		1	7	45	16	19	10	2
Livingston	1	0	0		0	1	37	10	23	4	0
Macon	14	0	0		1	13	94	32	57	5	6

Table 8. Offenses Known to Law Enforcement, by Selected State Metropolitan and Nonmetropolitan Counties, 2016—Continued

(Number.)

State/county	Violent crime	Murder and nonnegligent manslaughter	Rape (revised definition)[1]	Rape (legacy definition)[2]	Robbery	Aggravated assault	Property crime	Burglary	Larceny-theft	Motor vehicle theft	Arson[3]
Madison	17	0	5		1	11	61	11	48	2	1
Maries	10	0	0		0	10	38	16	16	6	0
Marion	8	0	0		0	8	90	21	63	6	0
Mercer	0	0	0		0	0	30	16	8	6	0
Miller	61	0	3		1	57	219	67	131	21	3
Mississippi	9	0	1		0	8	46	19	23	4	0
Monroe	5	0	0		1	4	50	30	15	5	1
Montgomery	12	0	0		1	11	83	40	42	1	0
Morgan	36	0	7		1	28	202	92	83	27	0
Nodaway	7	0	4		0	3	60	25	31	4	0
Oregon	12	0	1		0	11	42	18	20	4	1
Ozark	15	0	0		2	13	79	23	50	6	4
Pemiscot	23	0	1		0	22	100	28	65	7	0
Perry	36	1	0		0	35	72	23	39	10	0
Pettis	29	0	1		1	27	194	54	126	14	0
Phelps	19	0	4		0	15	243	61	171	11	0
Pike	2	0	0		1	1	38	17	16	5	2
Pulaski	65	1	3		3	58	236	79	138	19	0
Putnam	0	0	0		0	0	8	3	3	2	1
Ralls	19	0	0		0	19	76	23	42	11	0
Randolph	10	0	0		0	10	107	38	61	8	1
Reynolds	11	2	1		0	8	41	11	22	8	2
Ripley	15	0	1		1	13	193	72	104	17	0
Saline	5	1	0		0	4	57	26	27	4	1
Schuyler	7	0	4		0	3	29	4	25	0	0
Scotland	6	0	2		0	4	24	8	12	4	1
Scott	178	0	1		0	177	206	73	120	13	1
Shannon	24	0	3		2	19	56	6	41	9	1
Shelby	3	0	3		0	0	22	9	11	2	0
St. Clair	22	1	3		0	18	148	67	70	11	4
Ste. Genevieve	31	0	8		0	23	116	28	71	17	1
St. Francois	70	2	3		3	62	390	111	222	57	2
Stoddard	15	0	0		1	14	148	39	96	13	0
Stone	130	0	3		1	126	378	124	235	19	1
Sullivan	9	0	2		0	7	51	24	18	9	0
Taney	93	0	6		0	87	337	81	206	50	1
Texas	21	2	2		1	16	156	62	79	15	1
Vernon	68	0	6		1	61	300	112	165	23	1
Washington	106	0	14		4	88	297	98	170	29	5
Wayne	20	2	5		0	13	215	80	104	31	1
Worth	1	0	0		0	1	8	1	7	0	0
Wright	26	0	0		0	26	98	39	43	16	0
MONTANA											
Metropolitan Counties											
Carbon	15	3	0		0	12	57	21	31	5	1
Cascade	27	1	3		1	22	205	42	144	19	2
Golden Valley	2	0	0		0	2	6	3	2	1	0
Missoula	93	0	16		3	74	199	100	78	21	4
Yellowstone	91	0	18		10	63	668	146	421	101	8
Nonmetropolitan Counties											
Beaverhead	3	0	0		0	3	9	2	7	0	0
Big Horn	71	2	3		0	66	411	13	332	66	1
Blaine	10	0	1		0	9	3	1	2	0	0
Broadwater	28	0	0		0	28	37	10	22	5	0
Carter	0	0	0		0	0	0	0	0	0	0
Custer	9	0	2		1	6	37	9	22	6	1
Daniels	0	0	0		0	0	2	0	1	1	0
Dawson	18	0	1		0	17	63	25	31	7	0
Deer Lodge	37	1	2		1	33	335	84	217	34	0
Fallon	2	0	0		0	2	4	2	1	1	0
Fergus	32	0	11		1	20	58	21	34	3	1
Flathead	191	2	23		4	162	1,372	225	991	156	5
Gallatin	73	2	24		1	46	420	58	324	38	1
Garfield	1	0	0		0	1	8	2	5	1	0
Glacier	15	0	0		0	15	43	6	25	12	1
Granite	5	0	1		0	4	59	11	43	5	0
Hill	23	0	2		0	21	143	28	103	12	1
Jefferson	34	0	0		0	34	124	20	93	11	1
Judith Basin	2	0	0		0	2	12	3	7	2	0
Lake	72	1	5		5	61	316	106	166	44	7
Lewis and Clark	104	1	25		5	73	440	111	286	43	9
Liberty	9	1	0		0	8	0	0	0	0	0
Lincoln	28	1	2		0	25	162	34	118	10	0
Madison	8	0	0		0	8	42	12	28	2	1
McCone	2	0	0		0	2	11	3	4	4	0
Meagher	2	0	0		0	2	13	1	10	2	0
Mineral	4	0	0		0	4	0	0	0	0	0
Musselshell	31	1	1		1	28	90	14	66	10	2
Park	16	0	2		0	14	80	8	65	7	0

Table 8. Offenses Known to Law Enforcement, by Selected State Metropolitan and Nonmetropolitan Counties, 2016—Continued

(Number.)

State/county	Violent crime	Murder and nonnegligent manslaughter	Rape (revised definition)[1]	Rape (legacy definition)[2]	Robbery	Aggravated assault	Property crime	Burglary	Larceny-theft	Motor vehicle theft	Arson[3]
Phillips	11	0	1		0	10	39	5	31	3	0
Pondera	1	0	1		0	0	10	0	9	1	0
Powder River	0	0	0		0	0	9	0	8	1	0
Powell	8	0	2		0	6	17	5	10	2	0
Prairie	3	0	0		0	3	12	1	6	5	0
Ravalli	61	0	7		2	52	246	33	207	6	1
Richland	15	0	4		0	11	70	10	50	10	0
Roosevelt	53	2	0		0	51	43	12	25	6	0
Rosebud	5	0	1		0	4	27	6	15	6	0
Sanders	14	0	4		1	9	58	11	44	3	2
Sheridan	6	0	0		0	6	57	5	52	0	1
Silver Bow	98	0	10		3	85	1,738	210	1,372	156	1
Stillwater	17	0	7		0	10	46	17	22	7	1
Sweet Grass	5	3	0		0	2	12	0	10	2	0
Teton	19	0	2		1	16	50	23	22	5	0
Toole	22	0	3		0	19	72	8	60	4	1
Treasure	0	0	0		0	0	1	0	0	1	0
Valley	8	1	2		0	5	9	4	5	0	0
Wheatland	10	0	1		0	9	6	1	4	1	0
Wibaux	0	0	0		0	0	2	0	2	0	0
NEBRASKA											
Metropolitan Counties											
Cass	23	0	9		0	14	202	39	146	17	0
Dakota	18	1	1		3	13	69	17	43	9	0
Dixon	3	0	2		0	1	47	12	30	5	1
Douglas	159	2	12		9	136	663	193	402	68	3
Hall	33	0	1		0	32	144	42	88	14	2
Hamilton	8	0	2		0	6	40	15	17	8	0
Lancaster	22	0	7		0	15	200	59	129	12	1
Merrick	4	0	1		0	3	10	3	6	1	0
Sarpy	52	0	9		8	35	826	90	649	87	0
Saunders	10	0	3		0	7	72	28	33	11	1
Seward	8	0	3		0	5	27	8	16	3	1
Washington	4	0	1		0	3	60	6	47	7	0
Nonmetropolitan Counties											
Adams	6	0	3		0	3	87	29	48	10	3
Antelope	9	0	2		0	7	19	2	16	1	0
Arthur	0	0	0		0	0	0	0	0	0	0
Box Butte	1	0	0		0	1	14	5	7	2	0
Brown	0	0	0		0	0	25	11	12	2	0
Buffalo	10	0	6		0	4	109	16	84	9	1
Burt	2	0	1		0	1	21	5	16	0	0
Butler	5	0	2		0	3	14	4	9	1	0
Cedar	2	0	1		0	1	23	0	20	3	0
Chase	2	0	0		0	2	7	0	6	1	0
Cherry	0	0	0		0	0	13	3	10	0	0
Cheyenne	4	0	2		0	2	15	4	8	3	0
Clay	6	0	0		0	6	15	10	1	4	0
Colfax	5	0	4		1	0	26	1	21	4	0
Cuming	1	0	0		0	1	14	5	7	2	0
Custer	6	0	2		0	4	68	21	42	5	0
Dawes	2	0	0		0	2	11	3	8	0	0
Dawson	8	1	2		0	5	50	9	37	4	0
Dodge	19	0	7		2	10	98	20	68	10	0
Fillmore	1	0	0		0	1	15	6	7	2	0
Franklin	2	0	0		0	2	7	3	2	2	0
Furnas	3	0	0		0	3	60	19	39	2	0
Gage	25	0	5		0	20	108	67	39	2	1
Garfield	0	0	0		0	0	0	0	0	0	0
Gosper	2	0	0		0	2	11	4	6	1	0
Hayes	3	0	1		0	2	4	0	4	0	0
Hitchcock	4	1	3		0	0	20	8	11	1	1
Holt	2	0	1		0	1	11	1	8	2	0
Hooker	0	0	0		0	0	2	0	2	0	0
Kearney	3	0	0		0	3	39	12	25	2	0
Keith	2	0	1		0	1	20	7	11	2	0
Keya Paha	0	0	0		0	0	1	0	0	1	0
Kimball	0	0	0		0	0	14	3	9	2	0
Knox	2	0	0		0	2	25	4	13	8	0
Lincoln	19	0	2		0	17	116	27	77	12	2
Madison	10	0	2		0	8	51	11	32	8	0
Morrill	2	0	0		0	2	39	6	29	4	0
Nemaha	9	0	2		0	7	61	17	40	4	0
Otoe	3	0	0		1	2	44	6	32	6	0
Pawnee	1	0	0		0	1	44	10	33	1	0
Perkins	0	0	0		0	0	21	7	10	4	0
Phelps	2	0	1		0	1	25	6	16	3	0
Pierce	2	0	0		0	2	11	5	5	1	0
Platte	15	0	2		0	13	82	12	63	7	0

Table 8. Offenses Known to Law Enforcement, by Selected State Metropolitan and Nonmetropolitan Counties, 2016—Continued

(Number.)

State/county	Violent crime	Murder and nonnegligent manslaughter	Rape (revised definition)[1]	Rape (legacy definition)[2]	Robbery	Aggravated assault	Property crime	Burglary	Larceny-theft	Motor vehicle theft	Arson[3]
Red Willow	2	0	0		0	2	18	7	9	2	0
Richardson	0	0	0		0	0	27	6	21	0	0
Rock	0	0	0		0	0	0	0	0	0	0
Saline	5	0	1		0	4	33	9	19	5	1
Scotts Bluff	12	0	3		1	8	128	62	58	8	0
Sheridan	14	0	1		1	12	33	7	21	5	0
Sherman	1	0	0		0	1	14	3	9	2	0
Stanton	6	0	4		0	2	41	5	36	0	1
Thayer	1	0	0		0	1	55	2	51	2	0
Thurston	6	0	0		1	5	16	3	7	6	1
Webster	2	0	0		0	2	11	2	5	4	0
Wheeler	3	0	0		0	3	0	0	0	0	0
York	2	0	2		0	0	34	6	22	6	0
NEVADA											
Metropolitan Counties											
Carson City	154	1	3		18	132	971	206	681	84	6
Storey	43	1	1		0	41	73	21	46	6	1
Washoe	132	1	24		7	100	770	202	465	103	7
Nonmetropolitan Counties											
Churchill	28	0	5		0	23	185	63	108	14	2
Douglas	67	0	11		2	54	795	117	633	45	3
Elko	48	2	0		0	46	193	38	127	28	4
Esmeralda	1	0	0		0	1	5	1	4	0	0
Eureka	7	0	1		1	5	38	19	17	2	0
Humboldt	29	0	4		0	25	67	32	30	5	2
Lander	40	3	12		1	24	112	57	45	10	1
Lincoln	3	0	1		0	2	37	9	27	1	2
Lyon	137	3	15		8	111	567	138	367	62	7
Mineral	6	0	1		0	5	21	12	1	8	0
Nye	80	0	13		12	55	915	338	465	112	1
Pershing	29	2	4		0	23	46	20	25	1	0
White Pine	13	0	1		3	9	82	25	42	15	3
NEW HAMPSHIRE											
Metropolitan Counties											
Rockingham	7	0	3		0	4	2	0	1	1	0
Strafford	4	0	2		0	2	1	0	1	0	0
Nonmetropolitan Counties											
Carroll	13	0	1		2	10	78	19	52	7	0
Cheshire	0	0	0		0	0	10	4	6	0	0
Grafton	3	0	2		0	1	5	0	5	0	0
Merrimack	2	0	1		0	1	0	0	0	0	0
NEW JERSEY											
Metropolitan Counties											
Atlantic	0	0	0		0	0	0	0	0	0	0
Bergen	8	0	0		0	8	56	3	51	2	2
Burlington	0	0	0		0	0	0	0	0	0	0
Camden	9	0	0		1	8	32	2	30	0	0
Camden County Police Department	1,574	47	88		427	1,012	2,644	648	1,492	504	94
Cape May	0	0	0		0	0	2	0	2	0	0
Cumberland	0	0	0		0	0	1	0	1	0	0
Essex	95	1	0		46	48	79	19	59	1	0
Gloucester	6	0	0		0	6	0	0	0	0	0
Hudson	0	0	0		0	0	0	0	0	0	0
Hunterdon	0	0	0		0	0	0	0	0	0	0
Mercer	2	0	0		1	1	8	2	6	0	0
Middlesex	0	0	0		0	0	0	0	0	0	0
Monmouth	2	0	0		0	2	1	0	1	0	0
Morris	0	0	0		0	0	0	0	0	0	0
Ocean	0	0	0		0	0	5	3	2	0	0
Passaic	0	0	0		0	0	0	0	0	0	0
Salem	0	0	0		0	0	4	0	4	0	0
Somerset	0	0	0		0	0	0	0	0	0	0
Sussex	0	0	0		0	0	0	0	0	0	0
Union	0	0	0		0	0	0	0	0	0	0
Warren	0	0	0		0	0	0	0	0	0	0
NEW MEXICO											
Metropolitan Counties											
Bernalillo	763	9		52	122	580	2,820	909	1,452	459	103
Dona Ana	188	6		42	6	134	834	308	437	89	
Sandoval	25	0		3	1	21	166	47	111	8	
Santa Fe	111	1		8	13	89	656	397	257	2	
Torrance	66	1		11	4	50	193	106	59	28	
Valencia	386	0		19	11	356	1,196	414	516	266	

Table 8. Offenses Known to Law Enforcement, by Selected State Metropolitan and Nonmetropolitan Counties, 2016—Continued

(Number.)

State/county	Violent crime	Murder and nonnegligent manslaughter	Rape (revised definition)[1]	Rape (legacy definition)[2]	Robbery	Aggravated assault	Property crime	Burglary	Larceny-theft	Motor vehicle theft	Arson[3]
Nonmetropolitan Counties											
Catron	7	0		0	0	7	17	3	12	2	
Chaves	62	1		12	1	48	207	89	89	29	
Cibola	78	0		3	0	75	91	44	33	14	
Colfax	12	0		0	2	10	23	13	7	3	
Curry	18	2		2	1	13	158	74	68	16	
De Baca	2	0		0	1	1	31	16	11	4	
Eddy	39	2		0	1	36	328	63	202	63	
Hidalgo	4	0		0	1	3	18	11	6	1	
Lea	22	1		5	2	14	384	135	215	34	
Lincoln	23	0		4	0	19	102	48	49	5	
Luna	44	0		0	1	43	242	91	123	28	
McKinley	85	1		8	5	71	265	87	157	21	
Mora	5	0		0	0	5	25	12	8	5	
Otero	124	0		10	0	114	272	115	139	18	
Quay	3	0		0	0	3	29	12	15	2	
San Miguel	8	0		0	0	8	4	1	1	2	
Sierra	35	2		8	0	25	76	27	41	8	
Socorro	18	0		3	0	15	47	11	30	6	
Union	2	0		0	0	2	11	8	3	0	
NEW YORK											
Metropolitan Counties											
Albany	19	0	7		0	12	157	24	124	9	0
Broome	45	0	13		5	27	528	141	362	25	0
Chemung	20	1	5		2	12	390	40	342	8	1
Dutchess	35	0	17		2	16	496	112	378	6	0
Erie	71	0	0		12	59	762	141	600	21	5
Herkimer	2	0		0	0	2	0	0	0	0	0
Jefferson	38	0	15		1	22	272	48	218	6	0
Livingston	31	1	10		0	20	312	48	249	15	0
Madison	16	0	9		0	7	116	24	81	11	1
Nassau	1,157	12	38		478	629	10,660	1,144	9,054	462	68
Niagara	70	0	17		20	33	822	166	609	47	3
Oneida	71	0	45		1	25	342	96	229	17	1
Onondaga	187	4	42		34	107	1,783	306	1,409	68	9
Ontario	61	0	28		7	26	904	157	730	17	0
Orange	14	0	0		1	13	17	0	17	0	1
Orleans	20	0	8		1	11	200	56	140	4	0
Oswego	56	0	26		3	27	304	68	218	18	0
Putnam	16	0	3		4	9	291	44	243	4	0
Rensselaer	15	1	2		3	9	249	39	201	9	2
Rockland	7	0	0		0	7	33	2	30	1	0
Saratoga	85	2	14		2	67	1,102	167	892	43	0
Schenectady	1	0		0	1	0	16	6	9	1	0
Schoharie	2	0	2		0	0	49	15	34	0	2
Suffolk	63	0		0	0	63	0	0	0	0	0
Suffolk County Police Department	1,577	33	109		541	894	18,254	1,743	15,432	1,079	109
Tioga	16	1	2		1	12	181	51	119	11	1
Ulster	30	1	4		1	24	212	44	150	18	0
Warren	44	0	17		5	22	620	77	541	2	1
Washington	27	0	20		0	7	169	31	133	5	0
Westchester Public Safety	72	0		2	7	63	305	19	270	16	5
Yates	16	0	5		1	10	216	58	156	2	0
Nonmetropolitan Counties											
Allegany	1	0	0		0	1	1	0	1	0	0
Cattaraugus	34	0	19		1	14	282	80	180	22	4
Cayuga	22	1	15		2	4	166	49	113	4	1
Chautauqua	51	0	17		6	28	571	181	368	22	2
Chenango	22	0	8		0	14	319	69	248	2	0
Clinton	8	0	0		0	8	13	2	11	0	0
Columbia	19	0	4		1	14	285	77	203	5	0
Cortland	7	0	4		2	1	246	43	203	0	0
Delaware	29	0	22		3	4	110	31	73	6	0
Essex	0	0	0		0	0	6	0	6	0	0
Franklin	0	0		0	0	0	0	0	0	0	0
Fulton[7]	22	0	6		0	16	345	51	283	11	2
Genesee	39	0	16		5	18	430	74	322	34	0
Greene	7	0		0	0	7	22	6	16	0	0
Hamilton	3	0		1	0	2	2	0	2	0	0
Lewis	4	1	1		0	2	65	26	38	1	0
Montgomery	22	0	5		3	14	392	47	343	2	0
Otsego	19	0	0		3	16	59	23	33	3	0
Schuyler	7	0	1		0	6	25	10	14	1	0
Seneca	4	0	0		0	4	51	14	35	2	0
Steuben	13	0	7		0	6	118	29	85	4	1
St. Lawrence	14	0	2		0	12	50	7	42	1	0
Sullivan	29	1	0		3	25	294	56	233	5	3
Wyoming	14	0	3		1	10	152	35	115	2	0

Table 8. Offenses Known to Law Enforcement, by Selected State Metropolitan and Nonmetropolitan Counties, 2016—Continued

(Number.)

State/county	Violent crime	Murder and nonnegligent manslaughter	Rape (revised definition)[1]	Rape (legacy definition)[2]	Robbery	Aggravated assault	Property crime	Burglary	Larceny-theft	Motor vehicle theft	Arson[3]
NORTH CAROLINA											
Metropolitan Counties											
Alamance	95	3		6	6	80	752	328	372	52	2
Alexander	83	4		10	2	67	546	213	312	21	5
Buncombe	155	5		9	28	113	1,826	666	1,019	141	8
Burke	91	5		2	16	68	1,143	459	575	109	2
Cabarrus	38	1		3	19	15	730	231	461	38	4
Caldwell	95	1		11	12	71	1,271	492	686	93	6
Catawba	165	3		21	16	125	1,261	476	712	73	14
Chatham	55	2		6	9	38	602	258	323	21	1
Currituck	37	0		5	2	30	356	129	215	12	1
Davidson	105	5		5	21	74	1,621	938	562	121	5
Davie	58	0		5	3	50	589	190	375	24	1
Durham	80	5		5	22	48	566	231	295	40	0
Edgecombe	65	5		6	13	41	461	202	233	26	7
Forsyth	276	2		13	40	221	2,168	551	1,508	109	19
Franklin	69	4		7	9	49	889	376	451	62	6
Gaston	15	0		0	0	15	0	0	0	0	0
Haywood	148	1		13	10	124	975	454	457	64	7
Iredell	205	3		11	17	174	1,449	457	874	118	4
Johnston	160	3		16	39	102	1,874	776	1,000	98	7
Lincoln	85	0		12	4	69	1,024	305	655	64	6
Madison	7	1		0	1	5	182	86	91	5	1
Nash	70	2		11	5	52	425	183	218	24	2
New Hanover	155	2		15	44	94	1,779	468	1,249	62	19
Orange	43	2		5	6	30	505	213	273	19	1
Pamlico	6	0		1	2	3	207	33	158	16	1
Pender	57	0		11	8	38	867	208	607	52	2
Person	49	6		3	3	37	294	133	149	12	2
Pitt	157	5		6	28	118	1,066	423	573	70	1
Rockingham	66	6		2	14	44	916	406	466	44	4
Rowan	151	7		12	14	118	905	293	562	50	4
Stokes	45	1		0	0	44	772	216	514	42	1
Union	182	6		21	38	117	2,102	618	1,387	97	16
Wake	173	5		15	25	128	1,678	582	967	129	14
Wayne	133	0		4	29	100	1,592	676	796	120	4
Yadkin	57	1		4	6	46	485	179	268	38	1
Nonmetropolitan Counties											
Anson	33	0		0	5	28	274	184	85	5	2
Ashe	24	0		3	0	21	197	73	110	14	0
Beaufort	68	1		5	9	53	496	190	285	21	1
Camden	10	0		1	2	7	64	17	46	1	0
Caswell	73	4		1	6	62	381	98	267	16	0
Cherokee	36	0		6	5	25	611	172	404	35	9
Chowan	16	0		1	1	14	127	60	64	3	4
Clay	26	1		1	1	23	278	117	138	23	0
Columbus	72	2		4	13	53	1,004	523	416	65	2
Dare	13	0		1	0	12	523	128	389	6	0
Duplin	93	5		5	7	76	750	284	415	51	8
Halifax[5]	69	3		1	13	52			504	18	6
Harnett	233	4		14	33	182	1,868	734	1,032	102	19
Hertford	21	5		0	2	14	227	124	93	10	0
Lee	47	2		4	10	31	515	136	346	33	3
Lenoir	122	3		10	24	85	663	285	348	30	5
Martin	49	0		1	6	42	234	100	115	19	5
McDowell	37	1		8	9	19	706	247	383	76	22
Montgomery	43	2		4	4	33	284	149	120	15	3
Northampton	34	2		4	4	24	276	163	97	16	3
Pasquotank	35	1		2	3	29	259	92	160	7	0
Perquimans	4	0		0	0	4	86	59	24	3	2
Polk	16	1		3	1	11	255	78	161	16	1
Richmond[5]	156	3		6	23	124		440		66	5
Rutherford	103	0		0	5	98	1,010	542	391	77	9
Sampson[5]	100	3		9	22	66			359	75	5
Scotland[5]	57	3		7	7	40			167	44	11
Stanly	29	1		1	2	25	440	183	244	13	7
Surry	51	1		13	9	28	1,089	466	567	56	13
Swain	20	0		4	2	14	205	101	89	15	0
Transylvania	24	0		5	6	13	309	137	156	16	3
Tyrrell	8	0		2	0	6	40	5	35	0	0
Vance	69	5		1	13	50	707	309	362	36	6
Watauga	26	0		0	3	23	293	28	257	8	0
Wilkes	115	2		8	12	93	740	330	373	37	12
Wilson	57	6		2	4	45	731	201	501	29	2
Yancey	7	0		2	0	5	66	36	28	2	0
NORTH DAKOTA											
Metropolitan Counties											
Burleigh	20	0	5		0	15	246	82	128	36	1
Cass	17	0	11		0	6	171	59	91	21	3
Grand Forks	4	0	1		0	3	113	35	69	9	0

Table 8. Offenses Known to Law Enforcement, by Selected State Metropolitan and Nonmetropolitan Counties, 2016—Continued

(Number.)

State/county	Violent crime	Murder and nonnegligent manslaughter	Rape (revised definition)[1]	Rape (legacy definition)[2]	Robbery	Aggravated assault	Property crime	Burglary	Larceny-theft	Motor vehicle theft	Arson[3]
Morton	10	0	4		1	5	115	26	74	15	4
Oliver	0	0	0		0	0	7	3	3	1	0
Sioux	0	0	0		0	0	2	2	0	0	0
Nonmetropolitan Counties											
Adams	1	0	0		0	1	5	1	4	0	0
Barnes	0	0	0		0	0	57	30	21	6	0
Benson	3	0	0		0	3	41	4	31	6	1
Billings	1	0	0		0	1	10	3	7	0	0
Bottineau	4	0	0		0	4	70	19	37	14	0
Bowman	0	0	0		0	0	7	1	1	5	0
Burke	0	0	0		0	0	5	1	4	0	0
Cavalier	3	0	2		0	1	30	9	19	2	0
Dickey	0	0	0		0	0	10	3	7	0	1
Divide	0	0	0		0	0	2	0	1	1	0
Dunn	1	0	0		0	1	30	5	21	4	1
Eddy	7	0	4		0	3	27	5	19	3	0
Emmons	3	0	1		0	2	36	9	21	6	1
Foster	0	0	0		0	0	6	4	2	0	0
Golden Valley	1	1	0		0	0	2	0	1	1	0
Grant	2	0	1		0	1	7	4	3	0	0
Griggs	0	0	0		0	0	13	6	6	1	0
Hettinger	2	0	0		0	2	23	4	16	3	1
Kidder	0	0	0		0	0	14	2	5	7	0
Lamoure	1	0	0		0	1	1	0	0	1	0
Logan	0	0	0		0	0	6	2	4	0	0
McHenry	2	0	0		0	2	46	12	28	6	0
McIntosh	0	0	0		0	0	3	2	1	0	0
McKenzie	25	0	5		0	20	205	40	122	43	0
McLean	12	0	3		0	9	132	24	88	20	1
Mercer	9	0	0		1	8	22	5	14	3	0
Mountrail	6	0	1		0	5	77	5	61	11	2
Nelson	3	0	1		0	2	47	7	36	4	0
Pembina	3	0	1		0	2	69	16	37	16	1
Pierce	3	0	1		0	2	20	8	8	4	0
Ramsey	4	0	0		0	4	34	5	18	11	0
Ransom	6	1	0		0	5	24	10	8	6	0
Renville	2	0	0		0	2	11	1	6	4	0
Richland	7	0	3		0	4	100	19	70	11	0
Rolette	6	0	0		1	5	46	14	27	5	1
Sargent	5	0	1		0	4	13	2	8	3	0
Sheridan	1	0	0		0	1	21	4	16	1	0
Slope	0	0	0		0	0	1	0	0	1	0
Stark	3	0	0		0	3	48	7	29	12	0
Steele	1	0	0		0	1	1	0	1	0	0
Stutsman	4	0	4		0	0	68	18	44	6	0
Traill	3	0	1		1	1	56	16	36	4	1
Walsh	7	0	1		0	6	87	12	70	5	1
Ward	30	0	7		6	17	227	88	91	48	0
Wells	2	0	0		0	2	4	0	2	2	0
Williams	18	0	4		0	14	224	54	129	41	0
OHIO											
Metropolitan Counties											
Allen	27	0	6		14	7	870	205	639	26	3
Belmont	45	1	21		1	22	374	77	274	23	1
Brown	17	1	5		2	9	309	103	191	15	1
Butler	45	0	17		6	22	1,035	276	748	11	2
Clark	46	0	10		9	27	1,174	303	807	64	4
Clermont	98	1	27		7	63	1,366	501	814	51	3
Delaware	63	1	23		14	25	1,107	246	847	14	5
Fairfield	40	0	14		1	25	946	143	791	12	4
Fulton	15	2	7		1	5	250	82	156	12	4
Geauga	20	2	7		2	9	210	49	144	17	2
Greene	15	0	7		2	6	384	101	262	21	4
Hamilton	183	2	41		38	102	2,743	436	2,163	144	12
Hocking	14	0	5		1	8	358	120	218	20	3
Jefferson	2	0	0		0	2	55	19	33	3	0
Lake	240	0		15	10	215	341	93	244	4	1
Lawrence	75	1	19		8	47	663	191	443	29	2
Lorain	50	0	17		8	25	686	260	385	41	4
Lucas	128	3	26		31	68	852	240	518	94	5
Madison	20	0	8		4	8	444	148	274	22	7
Mahoning	1	0		0	0	1	94	30	53	11	0
Medina	2	0	0		0	2	106	36	70	0	0
Miami	24	0	12		2	10	372	107	252	13	2
Montgomery	234	7	50		89	88	1,440	527	723	190	23
Perry	15	0	10		2	3	150	42	105	3	2
Pickaway	29	0	3		3	23	700	173	497	30	2
Portage	48	4		10	13	21	1,109	294	778	37	7
Richland	57	3	24		7	23	1,164	447	694	23	5

Table 8. Offenses Known to Law Enforcement, by Selected State Metropolitan and Nonmetropolitan Counties, 2016—Continued

(Number.)

State/county	Violent crime	Murder and nonnegligent manslaughter	Rape (revised definition)[1]	Rape (legacy definition)[2]	Robbery	Aggravated assault	Property crime	Burglary	Larceny-theft	Motor vehicle theft	Arson[3]
Stark	89	1	22		17	49	1,659	379	1,146	134	10
Summit	63	1	22		13	27	1,050	214	791	45	7
Trumbull	19	1	4		3	11	332	130	174	28	2
Union	17	0	7		1	9	173	48	113	12	1
Warren	58	0	11		13	34	912	150	703	59	2
Wood	13	0	7		1	5	358	85	251	22	4
Nonmetropolitan Counties											
Adams	6	0	3		0	3	157	57	83	17	1
Ashland	31	1	15		4	11	190	63	116	11	0
Ashtabula	54	1	10		14	29	640	172	438	30	4
Athens	19	0	5		3	11	458	145	284	29	1
Champaign	17	1	4		0	12	330	108	191	31	3
Clinton	2	0	0		0	2	28	9	19	0	0
Columbiana	19	1	9		0	9	5	3	2	0	0
Coshocton	39	0	9		5	25	514	184	307	23	7
Crawford	6	0	5		0	1	138	61	70	7	0
Defiance	22	1	13		3	5	141	38	102	1	0
Erie	3	0	0		1	2	378	84	289	5	0
Fayette	24	2	10		5	7	513	157	346	10	2
Gallia	21	1	4		2	14	302	98	188	16	1
Hancock	12	1	3		2	6	227	80	142	5	0
Hardin	8	0	2		1	5	147	43	97	7	2
Harrison	6	0	1		2	3	94	34	56	4	1
Henry	20	2	1		1	16	164	43	120	1	0
Highland	26	4	6		1	15	385	130	237	18	7
Holmes	5	1	4		0	0	204	50	139	15	1
Jackson	26	1	12		7	6	234	73	148	13	4
Knox	33	0	18		0	15	487	99	388	0	2
Logan	14	1	3		0	10	368	148	210	10	2
Marion	38	0	19		12	7	1,175	166	1,001	8	4
Meigs	36	2	4		6	24	232	71	146	15	5
Mercer	11	0	3		1	7	138	18	111	9	1
Monroe	11	0	5		0	6	56	19	31	6	1
Morgan	24	0	5		1	18	172	57	101	14	3
Muskingum	48	0	27		9	12	1,029	310	653	66	5
Noble	0	0	0		0	0	88	24	59	5	1
Ottawa	8	0		5	2	1	231	50	178	3	0
Paulding	14	1	7		1	5	138	39	99	0	0
Pike	22	1	7		2	12	335	100	202	33	0
Preble	14	2	6		3	3	307	125	169	13	0
Putnam	13	1	8		0	4	91	21	68	2	0
Ross	120	1	31		12	76	1,316	405	844	67	11
Sandusky	54	0		0	1	53	211	41	166	4	
Scioto	40	0	13		11	16	1,026	344	620	62	9
Seneca	70	0		4	64	2	319	91	228	0	0
Shelby	15	0	2		1	12	245	59	177	9	2
Tuscarawas	10	0	4		1	5	346	107	215	24	2
Van Wert	9	1	7		0	1	138	46	88	4	1
Vinton	20	0	8		2	10	108	50	54	4	0
Washington	31	1	6		1	23	305	94	190	21	2
Wayne	32	0	12		2	18	497	202	270	25	0
Wyandot	2	0	0		0	2	17	8	9	0	0
OKLAHOMA											
Metropolitan Counties											
Canadian	15	0	3		1	11	144	29	97	18	0
Cleveland	58	1	14		3	40	286	102	144	40	6
Comanche	21	0	3		2	16	273	109	129	35	2
Cotton	2	0	0		0	2	40	9	30	1	1
Creek	57	2	11		3	41	431	139	233	59	6
Garfield	17	0	6		0	11	152	52	82	18	6
Grady	34	0	7		0	27	334	114	187	33	6
Le Flore	68	3	8		2	55	376	139	207	30	5
Lincoln	25	1	5		2	17	149	50	81	18	4
Logan	34	1	12		1	20	327	145	152	30	3
McClain	26	1	8		2	15	251	89	135	27	3
Oklahoma	32	5	3		0	24	183	52	97	34	0
Okmulgee	36	1	5		3	27	309	145	127	37	4
Osage	47	0	13		4	30	370	131	199	40	4
Pawnee	36	0	0		9	27	93	47	28	18	2
Rogers	89	2	14		6	67	626	260	296	70	8
Sequoyah	72	0	13		1	58	406	171	186	49	6
Tulsa	241	2	26		12	201	929	403	341	185	6
Wagoner	68	1	12		6	49	601	231	313	57	10
Nonmetropolitan Counties											
Adair	73	0	1		1	71	191	75	95	21	3
Alfalfa	3	0	1		0	2	16	5	9	2	1
Atoka	3	0	1		1	1	55	20	28	7	2
Beaver	0	0	0		0	0	27	9	17	1	0

Table 8. Offenses Known to Law Enforcement, by Selected State Metropolitan and Nonmetropolitan Counties, 2016—Continued

(Number.)

State/county	Violent crime	Murder and nonnegligent manslaughter	Rape (revised definition)[1]	Rape (legacy definition)[2]	Robbery	Aggravated assault	Property crime	Burglary	Larceny-theft	Motor vehicle theft	Arson[3]
Beckham	21	0	2		1	18	148	60	76	12	8
Blaine	2	0	0		1	1	41	24	15	2	0
Caddo	21	0	3		0	18	184	55	114	15	3
Carter	20	1	6		0	13	205	96	101	8	2
Cherokee	88	0	10		5	73	436	173	211	52	10
Choctaw	16	0	0		0	16	102	75	17	10	2
Cimarron	0	0	0		0	0	0	0	0	0	0
Coal	4	0	1		0	3	51	14	29	8	1
Craig	7	0	2		1	4	82	37	41	4	2
Custer	8	0	3		0	5	73	25	42	6	2
Delaware	47	0	7		3	37	237	103	107	27	4
Dewey	2	0	0		0	2	31	17	14	0	0
Ellis	4	0	0		0	4	44	20	22	2	0
Garvin	49	1	8		0	40	295	87	167	41	5
Grant	2	0	2		0	0	27	14	12	1	2
Harmon	0	0	0		0	0	20	8	12	0	0
Harper	0	0	0		0	0	9	2	7	0	0
Haskell	11	0	1		1	9	52	20	28	4	2
Hughes	12	0	2		2	8	104	34	54	16	2
Jackson	16	1	2		0	13	58	25	26	7	1
Jefferson	3	0	2		0	1	51	10	36	5	3
Johnston	12	0	3		0	9	118	48	54	16	4
Kay	36	0	1		1	34	76	43	23	10	1
Kingfisher	3	0	2		0	1	34	7	24	3	1
Kiowa	1	0	0		0	1	44	12	29	3	0
Latimer	8	0	0		0	8	65	27	29	9	3
Love	5	0	1		1	3	35	7	21	7	1
Major	3	0	0		0	3	55	27	25	3	0
Marshall	19	0	1		0	18	184	81	91	12	0
Mayes	28	1	7		0	20	287	124	129	34	4
McCurtain	25	0	1		3	21	308	118	169	21	4
McIntosh	47	2	2		1	42	210	89	94	27	5
Murray	10	0	1		0	9	27	9	14	4	0
Muskogee	66	0	5		1	60	261	96	120	45	15
Noble	6	2	1		0	3	90	37	47	6	1
Nowata	2	0	0		0	2	52	17	30	5	2
Okfuskee	19	0	1		0	18	93	41	30	22	1
Payne	46	2	10		1	33	308	118	160	30	7
Pittsburg	45	2	9		0	34	368	167	171	30	15
Pontotoc	24	0	6		0	18	184	78	85	21	2
Pottawatomie	56	1	5		0	50	426	143	205	78	5
Pushmataha	2	0	0		0	2	48	28	11	9	3
Roger Mills	8	0	0		0	8	49	13	28	8	2
Seminole	22	2	4		1	15	237	79	129	29	5
Stephens	10	0	3		0	7	222	71	127	24	1
Texas	9	0	2		0	7	51	20	28	3	0
Tillman	3	0	0		0	3	37	15	20	2	0
Washita	19	0	4		0	15	93	29	53	11	3
Woods	4	0	0		0	4	36	14	19	3	0
Woodward	14	0	2		0	12	71	18	48	5	0
OREGON											
Metropolitan Counties											
Benton	27	0	4		0	23	183	49	120	14	4
Clackamas	365	8	100		80	177	5,083	683	3,815	585	20
Columbia	18	0	4		0	14	102	53	35	14	2
Deschutes	76	1	16		1	58	842	157	627	58	3
Josephine	35	0	1		5	29	372	127	118	127	5
Lane	307	0	29		12	266	1,424	489	778	157	10
Linn	36	0		12	7	17	958	234	628	96	9
Marion	65	5		19	19	22	2,176	415	1,498	263	5
Multnomah	119	1	16		23	79	1,352	130	1,073	149	7
Polk	43	1	7		0	35	278	99	147	32	2
Washington	287	4	78		26	179	1,921	325	1,418	178	39
Yamhill	35	0	10		3	22	487	117	326	44	2
Nonmetropolitan Counties											
Baker	2	0		0	0	2	67	15	49	3	0
Clatsop	12	2		0	2	8	214	64	125	25	1
Coos	21	2		1	4	14	652	168	401	83	1
Crook	51	1	7		0	43	180	50	106	24	4
Harney	5	0	0		0	5	65	15	13	37	1
Hood River	17	0	5		1	11	149	28	108	13	1
Jefferson	28	2	2		1	23	159	28	103	28	2
Morrow	33	0	5		2	26	209	43	141	25	4
Tillamook	10	0	1		0	9	181	63	92	26	3
Umatilla	51	5	9		1	36	433	147	235	51	7
Union	11	1	1		0	9	237	39	187	11	1
Wasco	27	0	4		1	22	96	36	56	4	2
Wheeler	2	0	0		0	2	5	3	1	1	0

Table 8. Offenses Known to Law Enforcement, by Selected State Metropolitan and Nonmetropolitan Counties, 2016—Continued

(Number.)

State/county	Violent crime	Murder and nonnegligent manslaughter	Rape (revised definition)[1]	Rape (legacy definition)[2]	Robbery	Aggravated assault	Property crime	Burglary	Larceny-theft	Motor vehicle theft	Arson[3]
PENNSYLVANIA											
Metropolitan Counties											
Allegheny	12	0	3		1	8	0	0	0	0	0
Berks	3	0	0		0	3	0	0	0	0	0
Blair	0	0	0		0	0	0	0	0	0	0
Bucks	0	0	0		0	0	0	0	0	0	0
Butler	0	0	0		0	0	0	0	0	0	0
Cumberland	1	0	0		0	1	0	0	0	0	0
Erie	0	0	0		0	0	4	0	4	0	0
Franklin	0	0	0		0	0	0	0	0	0	0
Lancaster	2	0	0		0	2	0	0	0	0	0
Lycoming	0	0	0		0	0	0	0	0	0	0
Mercer	5	0	0		0	5	0	0	0	0	0
Montgomery	0	0	0		0	0	0	0	0	0	0
Northampton	0	0	0		0	0	0	0	0	0	0
Pike	0	0	0		0	0	0	0	0	0	0
Washington	2	0	1		1	0	0	0	0	0	0
Wyoming	0	0	0		0	0	0	0	0	0	0
York	7	0	0		0	7	0	0	0	0	0
Nonmetropolitan Counties											
Bedford	0	0	0		0	0	0	0	0	0	0
Clarion	0	0	0		0	0	0	0	0	0	0
Elk	0	0	0		0	0	0	0	0	0	0
Greene	0	0	0		0	0	0	0	0	0	0
Indiana	0	0	0		0	0	0	0	0	0	0
Jefferson	4	0	0		0	4	2	0	2	0	0
Lawrence	0	0	0		0	0	0	0	0	0	0
Schuylkill	1	0	0		0	1	1	1	0	0	0
Snyder	0	0	0		0	0	0	0	0	0	0
Tioga	0	0	0		0	0	0	0	0	0	0
Union	0	0	0		0	0	0	0	0	0	0
Warren	0	0	0		0	0	0	0	0	0	0
Wayne	0	0	0		0	0	0	0	0	0	0
SOUTH CAROLINA											
Metropolitan Counties											
Aiken	549	10	90		50	399	3,105	902	1,791	412	6
Anderson	918	16	66		91	745	6,334	1,560	4,042	732	22
Beaufort	421	8	58		63	292	2,360	501	1,672	187	11
Berkeley	444	8	44		63	329	2,847	735	1,750	362	12
Calhoun	30	2	2		3	23	213	77	115	21	3
Chester	151	1	11		13	126	555	149	357	49	6
Darlington	224	4	25		28	167	1,780	706	948	126	17
Fairfield	142	1	3		8	130	544	147	341	56	7
Florence	324	7	38		74	205	2,507	784	1,507	216	6
Greenville	1,800	24	184		277	1,315	9,352	2,281	6,072	999	61
Horry	6	0	1		0	5	2	0	2	0	0
Horry County Police Department	994	21	201		120	652	6,888	1,412	4,833	643	48
Jasper	40	4	4		14	18	503	134	311	58	2
Lancaster	254	5	25		29	195	1,715	468	1,173	74	8
Laurens	142	4	12		11	115	920	280	536	104	9
Lexington	514	11	65		78	360	4,506	860	3,115	531	17
Pickens	281	5	37		17	222	1,587	545	853	189	4
Richland	1,959	26	137		300	1,496	9,684	1,832	6,649	1,203	36
Saluda	46	1	5		2	38	179	46	117	16	4
Spartanburg	749	14	70		94	571	5,532	1,287	3,751	494	20
Sumter	354	1	22		22	309	1,872	624	1,093	155	11
Union	120	1	11		14	94	607	156	418	33	8
York	365	2	51		38	274	2,235	598	1,516	121	11
Nonmetropolitan Counties											
Abbeville	44	1	4		6	33	289	103	171	15	2
Bamberg	26	0	4		0	22	144	58	76	10	1
Barnwell	79	0	5		7	67	247	67	159	21	6
Cherokee	115	1	14		25	75	1,236	358	807	71	4
Chesterfield	131	0	7		8	116	862	268	453	141	5
Clarendon	78	2	6		9	61	595	193	355	47	2
Colleton	209	3	17		17	172	806	225	505	76	15
Dillon	142	7	10		13	112	769	249	474	46	13
Georgetown	164	2	28		17	117	1,184	320	748	116	7
Greenwood	165	0	25		15	125	1,172	270	848	54	0
Hampton	51	0	3		8	40	233	76	145	12	0
Lee	66	1	4		7	54	307	98	173	36	7
Marion[9]	130	2	11		14	103		270	299		1
Marlboro	116	2	5		13	96	561	196	312	53	4
McCormick	21	0	0		3	18	90	35	44	11	0
Newberry	43	1	1		6	35	293	87	189	17	1
Oconee	146	1	36		9	100	1,501	376	1,032	93	5
Williamsburg	136	3	11		20	102	689	234	379	76	9

Table 8. Offenses Known to Law Enforcement, by Selected State Metropolitan and Nonmetropolitan Counties, 2016—Continued

(Number.)

State/county	Violent crime	Murder and nonnegligent manslaughter	Rape (revised definition)[1]	Rape (legacy definition)[2]	Robbery	Aggravated assault	Property crime	Burglary	Larceny-theft	Motor vehicle theft	Arson[3]
SOUTH DAKOTA											
Metropolitan Counties											
Custer	4	0	1		0	3	42	8	30	4	0
Lincoln	14	0	1		1	12	216	65	139	12	1
McCook	3	0	0		0	3	32	7	22	3	0
Meade	23	2	4		0	17	104	25	66	13	1
Minnehaha	47	4	6		1	36	424	171	222	31	3
Pennington	118	1	52		5	60	382	78	280	24	1
Turner	11	0	1		0	10	50	10	31	9	0
Union	10	0	3		0	7	46	4	39	3	0
Nonmetropolitan Counties											
Aurora	0	0	0		0	0	5	1	4	0	0
Beadle	5	1	0		0	4	14	4	6	4	0
Bennett	3	0	0		0	3	5	1	1	3	0
Bon Homme	1	0	0		0	1	0	0	0	0	0
Brookings	6	0	0		0	6	53	12	37	4	0
Brown	9	0	1		0	8	41	11	25	5	0
Butte	1	0	0		0	1	6	4	2	0	0
Campbell	1	0	0		0	1					
Charles Mix	6	0	1		1	4	36	20	10	6	1
Clark	3	0	2		0	1	8	3	5	0	0
Clay	9	0	1		0	8	67	30	35	2	0
Codington	9	0	2		0	7	40	3	33	4	0
Corson	1	0	0		1	0	32	7	22	3	0
Davison	3	0	2		0	1	18	5	8	5	0
Deuel	1	0	0		0	1	27	4	20	3	0
Dewey	0	0	0		0	0	0	0	0	0	0
Douglas	2	0	0		0	2	4	2	1	1	0
Edmunds	2	0	0		0	2	2	0	2	0	0
Faulk	0	0	0		0	0	14	5	9	0	1
Hamlin	6	0	1		0	5	17	4	12	1	0
Harding	2	0	0		0	2	0	0	0	0	0
Hughes	7	0	1		0	6	21	11	7	3	0
Hutchinson	0	0	0		0	0	11	9	1	1	0
Jerauld	0	0	0		0	0	0	0	0	0	0
Lawrence	8	0	0		2	6	168	14	152	2	0
Marshall	9	0	5		0	4	47	14	26	7	0
McPherson	1	0	1		0	0	14	7	4	3	0
Miner	0	0	0		0	0	6	5	1	0	0
Moody	4	0	0		0	4	12	3	9	0	0
Oglala Lakota	0	0	0		0	0	0	0	0	0	0
Potter	1	0	1		0	0	0	0	0	0	0
Roberts	10	0	0		0	10	13	4	5	4	0
Sanborn	8	1	1		0	6	29	12	16	1	1
Spink	2	0	1		0	1	38	10	28	0	0
Stanley	4	0	1		0	3	11	6	1	4	0
Sully	1	0	0		0	1	1	1	0	0	0
Tripp	0	0	0		0	0	16	0	15	1	0
Walworth	4	0	1		1	2	4	0	4	0	0
Yankton	16	0	4		0	12	38	15	16	7	0
Ziebach	0	0	0		0	0	0	0	0	0	0
TENNESSEE											
Metropolitan Counties											
Anderson	99	0	2		6	91	550	188	303	59	5
Blount	412	3	20		27	362	1,281	410	773	98	13
Bradley	204	1	9		13	181	966	263	584	119	1
Campbell	108	0	22		4	82	601	221	325	55	3
Cannon	15	0	0		1	14	107	42	52	13	2
Carter	57	1	2		4	50	385	107	242	36	0
Cheatham	84	2	9		6	67	535	139	345	51	3
Chester	18	0	1		0	17	108	38	59	11	1
Crockett	25	0	0		0	25	147	49	87	11	1
Dickson	116	2	12		4	98	478	201	232	45	4
Fayette	60	1	1		7	51	347	116	189	42	0
Grainger	43	0	5		0	38	211	75	118	18	3
Hamblen	111	0	7		5	99	458	148	251	59	5
Hamilton	283	2	38		17	226	1,673	419	1,088	166	3
Hartsville/Trousdale	41	0	4		0	37	197	33	150	14	0
Hawkins	74	2	7		1	64	573	176	337	60	3
Hickman	81	0	7		1	73	430	137	251	42	1
Jefferson	71	1	5		3	62	469	146	277	46	4
Knox	698	8	30		72	588	4,318	954	2,962	402	24
Loudon	80	1	2		2	75	445	120	274	51	2
Macon	55	1	3		0	51	207	73	112	22	1
Madison	130	0	7		4	119	572	227	304	41	2
Marion	53	0	1		1	51	270	83	136	51	0
Maury	136	2	19		9	106	441	100	292	49	4
Montgomery	113	2	5		4	102	599	149	413	37	3
Morgan	49	2	3		4	40	334	121	170	43	2

Table 8. Offenses Known to Law Enforcement, by Selected State Metropolitan and Nonmetropolitan Counties, 2016—Continued

(Number.)

State/county	Violent crime	Murder and nonnegligent manslaughter	Rape (revised definition)[1]	Rape (legacy definition)[2]	Robbery	Aggravated assault	Property crime	Burglary	Larceny-theft	Motor vehicle theft	Arson[3]
Polk	34	0	1		1	32	393	138	205	50	2
Roane	57	0	2		5	50	447	179	232	36	1
Robertson	64	1	5		3	55	211	69	123	19	2
Rutherford	261	0	18		9	234	750	178	510	62	11
Sequatchie	41	0	3		0	38	121	29	61	31	2
Shelby	607	18	28		105	456	2,490	667	1,631	192	15
Smith	32	0	3		4	25	176	61	100	15	2
Sullivan	324	0	46		19	259	1,152	276	721	155	16
Sumner	113	4	20		3	86	531	121	371	39	8
Tipton	161	2	16		12	131	567	147	351	69	4
Unicoi	30	0	1		2	27	199	30	155	14	2
Union	39	0	9		3	27	345	114	202	29	6
Washington	164	0	14		7	143	736	218	460	58	6
Williamson	70	2	9		2	57	346	93	234	19	0
Wilson	113	1	6		3	103	725	243	413	69	0
Nonmetropolitan Counties											
Bedford	76	1	7		0	68	283	84	168	31	3
Benton	7	1	0		0	6	180	60	111	9	0
Bledsoe	18	1	2		0	15	109	17	63	29	0
Carroll	42	1	5		1	35	142	63	58	21	0
Claiborne	55	0	3		10	42	431	184	200	47	2
Clay	16	0	0		0	16	47	11	26	10	1
Cocke	144	3	6		8	127	530	193	282	55	9
Coffee	70	1	3		1	65	275	103	151	21	2
Cumberland	50	0	1		2	47	746	224	426	96	5
Decatur	22	0	1		3	18	189	86	80	23	1
DeKalb	28	0	2		2	24	155	38	97	20	0
Dyer	47	0	8		3	36	342	71	244	27	1
Fentress	21	0	6		0	15	217	24	172	21	0
Franklin	51	0	2		1	48	161	36	107	18	3
Gibson	60	0	3		2	55	241	58	156	27	2
Giles	46	0	6		3	37	195	70	105	20	2
Greene	156	1	5		15	135	1,015	293	567	155	11
Grundy	54	0	4		0	50	192	92	72	28	3
Hancock	3	0	1		0	2	73	17	45	11	1
Hardeman	57	2	5		8	42	283	127	123	33	6
Hardin	59	1	1		5	52	303	116	150	37	0
Haywood	34	1	5		5	23	148	61	76	11	0
Henderson	66	0	4		3	59	289	120	141	28	1
Henry	60	2	5		3	50	452	181	233	38	0
Houston	11	0	0		0	11	57	18	37	2	0
Humphreys	35	0	8		2	25	195	87	100	8	1
Jackson	14	0	1		0	13	132	44	72	16	0
Johnson	116	0	0		2	114	221	88	112	21	5
Lake	1	0	0		0	1	5	1	4	0	0
Lauderdale	37	0	0		2	35	309	102	180	27	5
Lawrence	86	1	15		4	66	429	147	238	44	3
Lewis	29	0	0		0	29	159	57	84	18	0
Lincoln	101	0	8		4	89	348	122	198	28	3
Marshall	25	0	0		2	23	70	19	44	7	0
McMinn	117	0	8		5	104	671	198	362	111	8
McNairy	56	0	7		0	49	327	52	230	45	4
Meigs	40	1	2		2	35	272	84	148	40	2
Monroe	160	0	6		5	149	881	264	501	116	1
Moore	7	0	1		1	5	67	5	61	1	1
Obion	40	0	5		0	35	209	48	149	12	4
Overton	19	0	2		0	17	214	32	171	11	3
Perry	19	0	2		1	16	107	37	60	10	1
Pickett	17	0	3		0	14	54	10	36	8	2
Putnam	112	0	20		1	91	494	66	378	50	6
Rhea	46	0	5		2	39	276	80	185	11	3
Scott	37	1	2		0	34	174	76	74	24	2
Sevier	155	2	10		10	133	1,146	344	671	131	11
Stewart	57	2	6		0	49	133	73	49	11	1
Van Buren	10	1	2		0	7	56	11	33	12	0
Warren	60	0	4		1	55	377	100	237	40	6
Wayne	37	2	2		0	33	68	32	28	8	2
Weakley	21	1	2		0	18	136	74	51	11	1
White	62	0	3		1	58	320	50	235	35	5
TEXAS											
Metropolitan Counties											
Aransas	91	0	18		2	71	314	110	188	16	0
Archer	11	0	1		1	9	43	9	28	6	1
Armstrong	3	0	0		0	3	10	4	5	1	0
Atascosa	65	1	2		8	54	510	177	280	53	0
Austin	26	0	3		3	20	139	52	65	22	0
Bandera	38	0	11		1	26	246	75	146	25	1
Bastrop	225	5	45		24	151	822	268	472	82	3
Bell	103	0	42		9	52	753	199	489	65	27

Table 8. Offenses Known to Law Enforcement, by Selected State Metropolitan and Nonmetropolitan Counties, 2016—Continued

(Number.)

State/county	Violent crime	Murder and nonnegligent manslaughter	Rape (revised definition)[1]	Rape (legacy definition)[2]	Robbery	Aggravated assault	Property crime	Burglary	Larceny-theft	Motor vehicle theft	Arson[3]
Bexar	611	20	143		118	330	6,784	1,370	4,898	516	53
Bowie	104	1	27		2	74	489	177	265	47	5
Brazoria	174	6	8		36	124	1,079	270	679	130	8
Brazos	80	1	10		2	67	320	90	206	24	3
Burleson	25	0	6		3	16	139	64	67	8	1
Caldwell	35	2	0		6	27	141	60	65	16	2
Callahan	5	0	0		0	5	64	19	31	14	2
Cameron	195	2	51		16	126	1,068	321	705	42	4
Carson	19	0	0		0	19	40	9	27	4	1
Chambers	134	3	17		12	102	706	137	523	46	5
Clay	14	3	3		0	8	100	24	63	13	0
Collin	66	3	18		2	43	365	107	229	29	1
Comal	146	1	37		8	100	688	201	432	55	1
Coryell	9	0	0		1	8	98	41	52	5	0
Crosby	1	0	0		0	1	3	3	0	0	0
Dallas	45	1	13		3	28	303	78	187	38	1
Denton	70	1	15		8	46	630	143	427	60	3
Ector	135	3	24		35	73	1,962	361	1,354	247	1
Ellis	72	3	13		6	50	458	132	284	42	1
El Paso	267	6	50		25	186	847	231	556	60	11
Falls	5	1	0		1	3	84	28	47	9	0
Fort Bend	758	18	83		141	516	4,419	1,149	3,006	264	32
Galveston	141	1	23		22	95	1,007	292	620	95	16
Goliad	16	0	2		2	12	92	38	51	3	1
Grayson	70	1	13		1	55	450	105	283	62	0
Gregg	55	1	7		10	37	451	149	253	49	2
Guadalupe	60	1	31		10	18	584	174	347	63	4
Hardin	41	2	11		0	28	301	108	144	49	3
Harris	8,854	92	537		3,044	5,181	45,228	9,162	29,962	6,104	292
Hays	157	1	28		22	106	882	262	545	75	1
Hidalgo	586	10	133		130	313	4,528	1,417	2,813	298	29
Hood	85	0	11		7	67	389	121	240	28	6
Hudspeth	4	0	0		0	4	12	0	11	1	0
Hunt	104	2	9		9	84	660	259	300	101	3
Irion	1	0	0		0	1	29	9	20	0	0
Jefferson	70	1	11		9	49	366	95	231	40	6
Johnson	129	2	25		5	97	740	220	433	87	9
Kaufman	136	1	28		11	96	551	196	275	80	0
Lampasas	1	0	0		0	1	120	33	83	4	0
Liberty	166	2	36		4	124	685	256	348	81	6
Lubbock	109	0	15		9	85	686	192	420	74	1
Lynn	2	2	0		0	0	25	20	3	2	0
Martin	2	0	0		0	2	67	32	33	2	0
McLennan	96	1	25		5	65	503	183	265	55	6
Medina	48	2	20		1	25	372	121	219	32	0
Midland	61	0	1		6	54	727	125	511	91	0
Montgomery	531	10	52		90	379	4,982	1,011	3,480	491	15
Nueces	65	2	9		2	52	216	92	118	6	1
Oldham	3	0	0		0	3	8	5	3	0	0
Orange	90	0	10		7	73	645	196	361	88	9
Parker	110	1	23		3	83	747	258	428	61	4
Potter	42	3	3		7	29	235	65	134	36	1
Randall	43	0	14		1	28	339	94	193	52	2
Robertson	7	0	5		0	2	95	34	57	4	0
Rockwall	21	0	5		3	13	70	19	40	11	0
Rusk	92	2	11		1	78	565	196	310	59	1
San Patricio	31	2	0		0	29	303	108	169	26	0
Smith	226	2	3		41	180	2,259	750	1,252	257	17
Somervell	13	0	0		1	12	70	33	32	5	0
Tarrant	113	3	40		14	56	823	249	481	93	22
Taylor	27	0	6		0	21	155	74	72	9	0
Tom Green	29	0	18		4	7	403	190	183	30	4
Travis	684	10	53		64	557	3,339	856	2,234	249	32
Upshur	49	0	3		4	42	358	162	161	35	0
Victoria	112	0	34		6	72	501	173	289	39	2
Waller	46	1	22		1	22	341	114	205	22	0
Webb	35	0	0		3	32	226	84	138	4	1
Wichita	7	0	0		0	7	91	38	31	22	0
Williamson	175	1	44		15	115	1,366	308	956	102	6
Wilson	29	1	1		1	26	220	79	111	30	2
Wise	74	1	10		2	61	273	88	147	38	8
Nonmetropolitan Counties											
Anderson	55	0	6		7	42	330	133	157	40	0
Andrews	14	1	6		0	7	116	31	67	18	0
Angelina	88	0	23		2	63	539	189	301	49	1
Bailey	10	0	0		0	10	41	18	21	2	0
Baylor	0	0	0		0	0	20	12	7	1	0
Bee	25	0	0		1	24	127	42	78	7	2
Blanco	11	0	4		0	7	49	13	28	8	0
Borden	4	0	0		0	4	7	3	3	1	0

Table 8. Offenses Known to Law Enforcement, by Selected State Metropolitan and Nonmetropolitan Counties, 2016—Continued

(Number.)

State/county	Violent crime	Murder and nonnegligent manslaughter	Rape (revised definition)[1]	Rape (legacy definition)[2]	Robbery	Aggravated assault	Property crime	Burglary	Larceny-theft	Motor vehicle theft	Arson[3]
Bosque[9]	4	0	0		0	4			42	2	0
Brewster	6	0	2		0	4	35	15	19	1	0
Briscoe	0	0	0		0	0	13	5	7	1	1
Brooks	1	0	0		0	1	2	2	0	0	0
Brown	22	3	0		0	19	144	54	85	5	4
Burnet	51	0	21		1	29	276	87	158	31	0
Calhoun	16	0	2		0	14	156	47	102	7	0
Camp	6	1	1		2	2	99	31	55	13	0
Cass	44	0	10		1	33	326	152	146	28	1
Castro	1	0	0		0	1	52	22	26	4	0
Cherokee	72	3	16		2	51	534	201	284	49	1
Childress	0	0	0		0	0	10	6	3	1	0
Cochran	7	0	4		0	3	76	20	50	6	0
Coke	1	0	0		0	1	29	14	12	3	0
Collingsworth	9	0	0		0	9	12	6	5	1	0
Colorado	33	0	3		2	28	140	44	73	23	0
Comanche	6	0	0		0	6	88	24	62	2	0
Concho	1	0	0		0	1	14	8	4	2	0
Cooke	33	0	5		2	26	149	64	72	13	2
Cottle	0	0	0		0	0	0	0	0	0	0
Crane	2	0	0		0	2	26	9	16	1	0
Crockett	3	0	0		0	3	37	14	20	3	0
Culberson	0	0	0		0	0	0	0	0	0	0
Dallam	0	0	0		0	0	8	5	2	1	0
Dawson	2	0	1		0	1	45	18	21	6	0
Deaf Smith	4	0	1		0	3	73	27	41	5	1
Delta	0	0	0		0	0	28	18	9	1	4
DeWitt	25	0	6		1	18	123	49	66	8	0
Dickens	1	0	0		0	1	12	6	6	0	0
Dimmit	3	0	1		0	2	182	39	135	8	2
Donley	3	0	1		1	1	45	8	31	6	1
Duval	41	1	0		1	39	143	55	67	21	4
Eastland	3	0	3		0	0	57	31	26	0	0
Edwards	4	0	0		0	4	18	4	11	3	0
Erath	21	0	9		0	12	105	42	59	4	1
Fannin	25	0	4		2	19	112	43	52	17	3
Fayette	11	1	2		2	6	137	54	74	9	4
Fisher	13	0	0		0	13	53	19	29	5	1
Floyd	10	0	3		0	7	42	16	23	3	0
Foard	0	0	0		0	0	0	0	0	0	0
Franklin	27	1	9		0	17	92	46	40	6	0
Freestone	9	0	0		0	9	113	52	57	4	0
Frio	6	0	0		2	4	66	25	36	5	0
Gaines	11	0	4		1	6	68	27	34	7	1
Garza	10	0	4		1	5	53	13	37	3	0
Gillespie	4	0	0		0	4	75	25	42	8	0
Glasscock	0	0	0		0	0	17	7	8	2	0
Gonzales	19	0	5		1	13	107	33	67	7	0
Gray	16	0	2		4	10	114	38	67	9	0
Grimes	23	4	0		4	15	246	89	141	16	3
Hale	18	0	0		0	18	91	37	53	1	0
Hall	2	0	0		1	1	8	5	3	0	0
Hansford	8	0	0		0	8	11	0	11	0	0
Hardeman	2	0	0		0	2	39	12	22	5	1
Harrison	53	0	19		2	32	269	115	141	13	0
Hartley	1	0	0		0	1	29	12	13	4	0
Haskell	1	0	0		0	1	38	12	16	10	0
Hemphill	12	0	2		1	9	37	7	25	5	1
Henderson	206	2	52		4	148	1,062	424	543	95	0
Hill	38	0	5		5	28	268	124	140	4	0
Hockley	25	0	0		1	24	93	34	54	5	0
Hopkins	22	0	4		0	18	87	35	45	7	6
Houston	9	1	1		0	7	144	70	64	10	0
Howard	25	0	4		1	20	237	66	157	14	6
Hutchinson	21	0	4		0	17	86	35	41	10	4
Jack	11	0	1		0	10	41	17	19	5	1
Jackson	18	0	4		1	13	56	20	29	7	0
Jasper	80	0	27		3	50	296	135	123	38	3
Jeff Davis	2	0	1		0	1	8	8	0	0	1
Jim Hogg	2	0	0		0	2	9	4	5	0	0
Karnes	13	0	1		3	9	80	17	57	6	0
Kenedy	6	0	3		0	3	7	3	2	2	0
Kent	3	0	0		0	3	10	5	5	0	0
Kerr	47	6	19		1	21	305	82	206	17	2
Kimble	1	0	0		0	1	14	9	3	2	0
King	0	0	0		0	0	0	0	0	0	0
Kinney	1	0	0		0	1	11	10	0	1	0
Kleberg	26	0	7		1	18	85	17	59	9	0
Knox	4	0	3		1	0	20	8	11	1	0
Lamar	29	0	10		3	16	238	69	159	10	2
Lamb	2	0	0		1	1	73	25	41	7	7

Table 8. Offenses Known to Law Enforcement, by Selected State Metropolitan and Nonmetropolitan Counties, 2016—Continued

(Number.)

State/county	Violent crime	Murder and nonnegligent manslaughter	Rape (revised definition)[1]	Rape (legacy definition)[2]	Robbery	Aggravated assault	Property crime	Burglary	Larceny-theft	Motor vehicle theft	Arson[3]
La Salle	7	0	1		0	6	55	5	49	1	0
Lavaca[9]	13	0	2		0	11			30	4	0
Lee	16	0	4		3	9	104	38	62	4	1
Leon	24	0	2		0	22	211	79	120	12	0
Limestone	19	0	2		2	15	156	47	99	10	2
Lipscomb	4	0	0		0	4	12	2	10	0	0
Live Oak	15	2	1		1	11	147	59	75	13	0
Llano	11	1	2		0	8	132	50	80	2	0
Loving	0	0	0		0	0	11	0	10	1	0
Madison	9	0	4		3	2	102	52	48	2	0
Mason	2	0	0		0	2	43	19	20	4	0
Matagorda	65	1	9		6	49	336	126	192	18	1
Maverick	62	0	9		0	53	482	127	322	33	0
McCulloch	2	1	0		0	1	6	1	5	0	0
McMullen	1	0	0		0	1	26	12	14	0	0
Menard	0	0	0		0	0	4	2	2	0	0
Milam	11	0	0		0	11	96	32	58	6	0
Mills	2	0	0		0	2	26	10	14	2	1
Mitchell	1	0	0		0	1	13	8	5	0	0
Montague	9	0	0		0	9	49	12	31	6	0
Moore	10	0	0		0	10	69	24	40	5	0
Morris	11	0	4		0	7	81	31	39	11	0
Motley	0	0	0		0	0	14	0	13	1	0
Nacogdoches	70	0	12		2	56	275	89	162	24	2
Nolan	5	0	0		1	4	39	13	23	3	0
Ochiltree	7	0	1		0	6	30	11	16	3	0
Palo Pinto	2	0	0		1	1	95	55	33	7	0
Panola	27	0	3		1	23	291	94	163	34	0
Parmer	1	0	0		0	1	34	16	18	0	0
Pecos	9	1	1		1	6	60	45	14	1	1
Polk	66	1	29		8	28	523	185	296	42	0
Presidio	3	0	0		0	3	28	13	9	6	0
Rains	14	0	0		0	14	117	34	70	13	0
Reagan	4	0	0		0	4	67	12	53	2	1
Real	6	0	0		0	6	39	17	20	2	0
Red River	8	0	2		0	6	87	41	44	2	0
Reeves	5	1	1		0	3	107	15	88	4	0
Refugio	8	0	1		0	7	44	8	28	8	0
Roberts	0	0	0		0	0	8	1	6	1	0
Runnels	3	0	0		0	3	33	9	23	1	0
Sabine	29	0	4		0	25	150	63	73	14	1
San Augustine	36	1	5		0	30	81	39	33	9	0
San Jacinto	47	1	13		4	29	362	144	170	48	0
San Saba	2	0	1		0	1	26	11	10	5	0
Schleicher	0	0	0		0	0	54	13	40	1	0
Scurry	11	0	1		1	9	67	30	34	3	0
Shackelford	2	0	1		0	1	32	9	18	5	0
Shelby	27	1	3		2	21	176	81	86	9	0
Sherman	1	0	0		0	1	4	0	3	1	0
Starr	115	4	20		9	82	298	100	155	43	3
Stephens	4	0	2		0	2	30	15	13	2	3
Sterling	0	0	0		0	0	1	0	0	1	0
Stonewall	2	0	0		0	2	5	4	0	1	0
Sutton	0	0	0		0	0	1	1	0	0	0
Terrell	2	2	0		0	0	12	3	8	1	0
Terry	4	0	0		0	4	49	13	34	2	0
Throckmorton	0	0	0		0	0	0	0	0	0	0
Titus	45	1	11		1	32	179	87	84	8	0
Trinity[9]	20	0	4		0	16				9	0
Tyler	75	2	13		5	55	238	122	92	24	3
Upton	5	0	2		0	3	15	4	11	0	0
Uvalde	11	3	0		1	7	103	40	61	2	1
Val Verde	12	0	3		2	7	188	84	97	7	5
Van Zandt	3	0	0		1	2	312	157	154	1	0
Walker	91	1	20		6	64	276	99	130	47	0
Ward	49	0	6		1	42	140	54	72	14	1
Washington	26	0	5		2	19	131	68	59	4	1
Wharton	74	0	16		2	56	315	123	159	33	2
Wheeler	5	0	0		0	5	55	14	39	2	2
Wilbarger	1	0	0		0	1	38	22	15	1	0
Willacy	52	0	10		5	37	151	46	102	3	1
Winkler	2	0	0		0	2	37	11	21	5	0
Wood	43	1	16		2	24	292	143	129	20	0
Yoakum	10	0	1		0	9	40	14	22	4	0
Young	5	0	0		0	5	49	19	28	2	0
Zavala	17	0	1		0	16	91	31	56	4	0
UTAH											
Metropolitan Counties											
Box Elder	18	0	7		0	11	228	61	148	19	0
Cache	17	0	7		2	8	237	56	162	19	0

Table 8. Offenses Known to Law Enforcement, by Selected State Metropolitan and Nonmetropolitan Counties, 2016—Continued

(Number.)

State/county	Violent crime	Murder and nonnegligent manslaughter	Rape (revised definition)[1]	Rape (legacy definition)[2]	Robbery	Aggravated assault	Property crime	Burglary	Larceny-theft	Motor vehicle theft	Arson[3]
Davis	20	0	11		0	9	238	41	190	7	1
Juab	6	0	0		0	6	88	14	65	9	0
Salt Lake County Unified Police Department	861	17	126		246	472	12,091	1,845	8,594	1,652	22
Utah	40	1	12		0	27	363	73	268	22	1
Washington	29	0	8		1	20	137	43	81	13	0
Weber	36	1	11		4	20	936	197	666	73	1
Nonmetropolitan Counties											
Beaver	1	1	0		0	0	119	29	81	9	4
Carbon	11	0	2		1	8	86	22	62	2	2
Duchesne	38	1	12		0	25	331	79	195	57	2
Emery	16	3	2		0	11	106	22	71	13	1
Iron	25	0	3		1	21	146	57	70	19	2
Kane	10	0	3		0	7	19	1	10	8	0
Millard	38	0	5		2	31	203	29	149	25	3
Rich	2	0	0		0	2	32	14	18	0	0
San Juan	7	1	0		1	5	73	16	52	5	1
Sanpete	22	0	7		0	15	145	33	102	10	0
Sevier	15	1	3		0	11	149	29	108	12	0
Summit	25	0	6		4	15	472	55	390	27	2
Uintah	19	0	5		1	13	260	68	158	34	0
Wasatch	12	0	2		0	10	78	14	56	8	1
VERMONT											
Metropolitan Counties											
Chittenden	0	0	0		0	0	2	0	2	0	0
Franklin	5	0	2		0	3	60	17	43	0	0
Grand Isle	1	0	1		0	0	42	18	23	1	0
Nonmetropolitan Counties											
Lamoille	8	0	1		0	7	44	11	33	0	1
Windham	0	0	0		0	0	25	10	15	0	0
VIRGINIA											
Metropolitan Counties											
Albemarle County Police Department	88	1	29		21	37	1,271	145	1,061	65	8
Amelia	18	2	6		2	8	125	28	87	10	0
Amherst	32	1	13		6	12	279	35	222	22	2
Appomattox	14	0	5		2	7	129	18	107	4	0
Arlington County Police Department	363	1	56		103	203	3,252	170	2,912	170	5
Augusta	65	4	11		3	47	715	206	467	42	5
Bedford	40	1	11		4	24	478	107	347	24	2
Botetourt	36	0	14		1	21	234	34	187	13	0
Buckingham	18	0	4		2	12	145	26	108	11	1
Campbell	112	6	15		8	83	612	104	479	29	0
Caroline	37	1	15		3	18	303	65	238	0	1
Charles City	3	0	0		0	3	29	11	15	3	1
Chesterfield County Police Department	469	9	94		194	172	6,546	1,096	5,096	354	55
Clarke	11	1	3		0	7	93	26	62	5	0
Craig	2	0	1		0	1	23	4	18	1	0
Culpeper	27	0	2		7	18	163	26	122	15	2
Dinwiddie	56	0	4		7	45	303	57	215	31	0
Fairfax County Police Department	1,052	20	173		461	398	14,511	822	12,876	813	30
Fauquier	38	0	8		2	28	434	53	351	30	1
Floyd	22	0	11		0	11	106	32	68	6	0
Fluvanna	30	0	3		3	24	184	32	140	12	4
Franklin	74	0	17		4	53	508	88	380	40	4
Frederick	68	2	33		8	25	1,005	161	782	62	2
Giles	9	0	1		0	8	72	16	53	3	1
Gloucester	37	1	13		6	17	501	61	403	37	4
Goochland	18	0	1		0	17	169	21	138	10	1
Greene	22	0	2		8	12	180	17	156	7	2
Hanover	98	4	20		10	64	1,052	69	921	62	9
Henrico County Police Department	606	16	39		203	348	8,072	1,147	6,439	486	22
Isle of Wight	31	0	6		3	22	300	63	223	14	6
James City County Police Department	90	1	17		12	60	1,143	123	995	25	2
King William	11	1	1		1	8	79	9	68	2	0
Loudoun	336	2	114		46	174	2,647	196	2,315	136	33
Mathews	4	1	0		0	3	73	24	46	3	0
Montgomery	45	1	13		2	29	303	63	212	28	2
Nelson	24	1	7		1	15	158	30	119	9	3
New Kent	13	0	6		0	7	265	45	208	12	2
Powhatan	18	1	7		2	8	210	31	160	19	2
Prince George County Police Department	40	0	7		13	20	381	68	292	21	1
Prince William County Police Department	843	22	83		230	508	5,159	549	4,280	330	10
Pulaski	48	2	6		3	37	607	80	516	11	4
Rappahannock	1	0	1		0	0	27	9	18	0	0
Roanoke County Police Department	167	1	25		12	129	1,168	169	958	41	1
Rockingham	70	1	27		5	37	362	116	239	7	5
Scott	16	1	7		0	8	177	33	126	18	2
Spotsylvania	227	3	35		54	135	1,693	193	1,416	84	1

Table 8. Offenses Known to Law Enforcement, by Selected State Metropolitan and Nonmetropolitan Counties, 2016—Continued

(Number.)

State/county	Violent crime	Murder and nonnegligent manslaughter	Rape (revised definition)[1]	Rape (legacy definition)[2]	Robbery	Aggravated assault	Property crime	Burglary	Larceny-theft	Motor vehicle theft	Arson[3]
Stafford	308	5	46		37	220	1,814	165	1,572	77	12
Sussex	9	0	1		2	6	77	19	55	3	1
Warren	20	0	11		0	9	221	24	179	18	1
Washington	67	1	15		3	48	717	148	519	50	2
York	123	4	34		34	51	1,269	125	1,100	44	7
Nonmetropolitan Counties											
Accomack	43	5	16		5	17	379	112	241	26	1
Alleghany	12	0	3		1	8	69	28	34	7	1
Bath	7	0	0		0	7	18	3	15	0	0
Bland	1	0	1		0	0	48	7	39	2	0
Brunswick	16	0	11		1	4	82	20	57	5	0
Buchanan	53	2	21		0	30	301	85	196	20	3
Carroll	18	0	5		1	12	339	85	212	42	4
Charlotte	26	1	4		1	20	107	26	73	8	0
Cumberland	19	0	5		0	14	47	16	27	4	2
Dickenson	26	0	16		0	10	107	24	76	7	0
Essex	5	0	1		0	4	63	33	26	4	1
Grayson	17	2	6		1	8	154	21	122	11	1
Greensville	9	0	2		5	2	98	26	64	8	1
Halifax	37	1	11		3	22	295	102	168	25	3
Henry	114	3	21		29	61	1,302	271	956	75	15
Highland	4	0	0		0	4	24	6	17	1	0
King and Queen	18	1	3		2	12	50	19	27	4	0
King George	25	0	10		2	13	263	27	220	16	0
Lancaster	13	0	8		0	5	108	27	73	8	2
Lee	15	0	5		0	10	295	18	276	1	2
Louisa	57	2	11		4	40	355	39	293	23	2
Lunenburg	5	0	2		0	3	54	16	33	5	1
Madison	11	0	3		1	7	99	8	83	8	0
Mecklenburg	32	2	11		4	15	219	84	122	13	1
Middlesex	13	0	8		1	4	124	23	91	10	2
Northampton	8	3	0		2	3	89	31	54	4	0
Northumberland	22	0	6		2	14	101	34	64	3	1
Nottoway	6	2	1		0	3	67	12	51	4	1
Orange	21	0	6		2	13	210	43	156	11	0
Page	26	5	11		1	9	150	39	101	10	5
Patrick	33	1	9		6	17	228	34	177	17	2
Pittsylvania	46	2	17		2	25	367	117	230	20	12
Prince Edward	12	0	4		1	7	87	21	61	5	1
Richmond	9	0	1		0	8	43	12	26	5	0
Rockbridge	23	0	6		0	17	237	45	177	15	2
Russell	35	1	12		1	21	197	77	109	11	4
Shenandoah	41	1	16		0	24	229	61	163	5	1
Smyth	30	1	9		1	19	259	57	188	14	5
Southampton	23	4	6		4	9	171	48	111	12	5
Surry	16	0	1		2	13	51	18	29	4	0
Tazewell	42	1	17		2	22	377	76	283	18	8
Westmoreland	10	0	0		0	10	108	27	79	2	0
Wise	48	1	34		0	13	284	50	216	18	4
Wythe	16	0	3		1	12	149	22	107	20	0
WASHINGTON											
Metropolitan Counties											
Asotin	14	0	4		0	10	172	35	117	20	1
Benton	68	1	14		6	47	522	172	300	50	7
Chelan	35	0	2		2	31	655	187	428	40	1
Clark	323	4	80		44	195	2,706	673	1,455	578	22
Columbia	3	0	0		0	3	134	20	111	3	1
Cowlitz	52	1	15		4	32	422	153	204	65	6
Douglas	26	1	4		1	20	328	91	200	37	3
Franklin	23	0	3		3	17	158	62	87	9	7
King	385	3		67	98	217	4,397	1,352	2,166	879	44
Kitsap	376	1	63		38	274	3,985	965	2,723	297	17
Pend Oreille	26	0	8		1	17	282	71	189	22	2
Pierce	1,193	12	142		243	796	9,191	2,649	5,001	1,541	40
Skagit	90	1	15		8	66	1,135	417	626	92	4
Skamania	8	0	1		0	7	70	21	43	6	0
Snohomish	566	4	106		89	367	5,748	1,692	3,082	974	29
Spokane[8]	184	2	47		28	107	3,885	936	2,611	338	15
Stevens	32	1	5		1	25	547	259	253	35	2
Thurston	255	6	23		21	205	2,314	748	1,310	256	9
Walla Walla	26	0	7		2	17	261	86	140	35	1
Whatcom	166	4	41		14	107	1,216	427	705	84	9
Yakima	132	6	17		24	85	1,761	583	892	286	19
Nonmetropolitan Counties											
Adams	23	1	4		3	15	189	80	87	22	0
Clallam	89	2	15		2	70	605	192	376	37	6
Ferry	7	0	4		0	3	21	8	12	1	1
Garfield	2	0	0		0	2	64	31	32	1	1

Table 8. Offenses Known to Law Enforcement, by Selected State Metropolitan and Nonmetropolitan Counties, 2016—Continued

(Number.)

State/county	Violent crime	Murder and nonnegligent manslaughter	Rape (revised definition)[1]	Rape (legacy definition)[2]	Robbery	Aggravated assault	Property crime	Burglary	Larceny-theft	Motor vehicle theft	Arson[3]
Grant	83	2	11		8	62	1,307	365	766	176	7
Grays Harbor	26	1	4		0	21	390	100	255	35	6
Island	32	1	2		1	28	524	194	312	18	2
Jefferson	17	0	2		1	14	189	65	103	21	2
Kittitas	8	0	3		0	5	131	36	80	15	1
Klickitat	8	2	2		0	4	82	47	25	10	0
Lewis	48	0	9		1	38	504	184	273	47	3
Lincoln	9	0	2		2	5	152	52	83	17	2
Mason	99	5	15		9	70	1,022	347	557	118	3
Okanogan	29	0	3		0	26	242	99	120	23	1
Pacific	25	1	4		1	19	201	74	117	10	0
San Juan	10	1	1		1	7	177	35	136	6	3
Wahkiakum	9	0	2		0	7	42	14	26	2	0
Whitman	19	0	8		1	10	94	55	28	11	1
WEST VIRGINIA											
Metropolitan Counties											
Berkeley	78	2	14		16	46	952	248	667	37	5
Boone	4	0	1		0	3	83	22	42	19	0
Brooke	5	0	1		1	3	61	20	36	5	0
Cabell	26	0	2		2	22	591	133	428	30	2
Fayette	73	2	2		5	64	284	108	157	19	2
Hancock	10	0	3		1	6	50	18	27	5	2
Jefferson	46	3	8		6	29	474	168	291	15	3
Marshall	42	0	3		0	39	117	65	43	9	0
Mineral	17	0	1		1	15	60	16	42	2	3
Monongalia	73	0	3		1	69	277	74	192	11	1
Ohio	46	0	9		0	37	148	39	104	5	1
Preston	56	0	5		0	51	81	36	35	10	0
Putnam	131	0	12		2	117	337	89	199	49	2
Raleigh	109	5	0		10	94	730	288	407	35	7
Wirt	7	0	0		0	7	23	6	16	1	0
Wood	101	0	11		4	86	296	83	192	21	2
Nonmetropolitan Counties											
Barbour	31	0	2		0	29	38	9	26	3	0
Calhoun	0	0	0		0	0	0	0	0	0	0
Doddridge	2	0	1		0	1	19	8	10	1	1
Gilmer	0	0	0		0	0	7	1	5	1	0
Grant	4	0	0		0	4	10	3	7	0	0
Greenbrier	3	0	1		0	2	50	12	32	6	0
Hardy	16	1	0		0	15	6	0	5	1	0
Harrison	56	0	8		5	43	181	66	96	19	6
Jackson	95	1	1		0	93	70	24	38	8	0
Lewis	0	0	0		0	0	57	13	44	0	2
Logan	97	1	2		1	93	49	12	32	5	2
Mason	12	0	3		3	6	173	81	76	16	5
McDowell	15	2	0		2	11	33	16	16	1	0
Mercer	80	4	5		13	58	376	119	231	26	1
Mingo	1	0	0		0	1	4	1	3	0	0
Monroe	3	0	0		0	3	41	14	24	3	1
Morgan	50	0	5		0	45	70	20	48	2	0
Nicholas	123	1	5		2	115	110	32	77	1	0
Pleasants	5	0	0		0	5	12	5	7	0	0
Pocahontas	8	0	0		0	8	9	2	7	0	0
Randolph	74	2	1		0	71	127	28	99	0	2
Ritchie	0	0	0		0	0	30	6	23	1	0
Roane	21	0	3		1	17	63	1	51	11	0
Summers	15	0	3		1	11	28	15	13	0	0
Tyler	10	0	0		0	10	19	9	10	0	0
Upshur	5	1	0		0	4	72	10	46	16	0
Wetzel	3	0	1		0	2	26	15	11	0	0
Wyoming	39	0	1		1	37	67	22	43	2	2
WASHINGTON											
Metropolitan Counties											
Brown[8]	67	2	17		3	45	866	156	653	57	2
Calumet	12	0	3		0	9	124	39	83	2	0
Chippewa	15	1	2		0	12	270	68	187	15	0
Columbia	30	1	8		0	21	213	43	164	6	1
Dane	57	0	15		11	31	747	155	539	53	1
Douglas	16	0		6	1	9	203	70	114	19	0
Eau Claire	13	3		3	0	7	212	81	116	15	0
Fond du Lac	25	0	10		1	14	200	48	135	17	0
Green	5	0		1	0	4	76	28	47	1	0
Iowa	13	0	0		0	13	67	14	46	7	0
Kenosha	52	0		6	3	43	427	86	320	21	2
Kewaunee	17	0	6		1	10	67	14	49	4	0
La Crosse	16	0	1		1	15	131	49	74	8	0
Marathon	20	1		5	1	13	331	73	252	6	0
Milwaukee	41	0	1		5	35	125	5	80	40	0

Table 8. Offenses Known to Law Enforcement, by Selected State Metropolitan and Nonmetropolitan Counties, 2016—Continued

(Number.)

State/county	Violent crime	Murder and nonnegligent manslaughter	Rape (revised definition)[1]	Rape (legacy definition)[2]	Robbery	Aggravated assault	Property crime	Burglary	Larceny-theft	Motor vehicle theft	Arson[3]
Outagamie	32	2	5		1	24	285	106	162	17	3
Ozaukee	12	0		4	0	8	111	18	88	5	0
Pierce	20	0		0	0	20	125	55	62	8	0
Racine	17	2		3	3	9	257	39	201	17	0
Rock	30	1		12	1	16	325	109	197	19	6
Sheboygan	29	0		7	1	21	310	32	259	19	2
St. Croix	18	0	2		2	14	297	111	169	17	1
Washington	3	0		2	1	0	327	103	206	18	2
Waukesha	71	0		1	4	66	451	82	352	17	1
Winnebago	21	0		1	1	19	242	65	163	14	0
Nonmetropolitan Counties											
Adams	15	0		0	0	15	355	171	179	5	0
Ashland	16	0		0	0	16	28	3	21	4	0
Barron	0	0	0		0	0	201	84	110	7	1
Bayfield	28	1		2	1	24	121	51	63	7	0
Buffalo	2	0		0	0	2	19	4	11	4	0
Burnett	33	1	3		0	29	298	90	187	21	2
Clark	18	0	0		0	18	86	19	59	8	0
Crawford	14	1		0	0	13	119	25	92	2	0
Dodge	26	1	5		2	18	177	68	100	9	0
Door	8	0	3		0	5	122	18	102	2	0
Dunn	35	1		4	1	29	138	38	89	11	1
Florence	5	0		0	0	5	100	27	72	1	0
Forest	26	0		5	0	21	104	32	67	5	1
Grant	32	0	5		0	27	147	46	91	10	1
Green Lake	1	0			1	0	70	23	45	2	1
Iron	1	1			0	0	83	17	60	6	4
Jackson	17	0		5	3	9	175	72	76	27	1
Jefferson	43	0		8	4	31	259	66	183	10	0
Juneau	46	0	7		0	39	240	107	120	13	1
Lafayette	6	0		5	0	1	94	40	52	2	0
Langlade	4	0		0	0	4	150	42	103	5	1
Lincoln	23	0	10		0	13	87	31	45	11	0
Manitowoc	27	0	4		0	23	164	53	102	9	0
Marinette	10	0		3	2	5	205	78	111	16	0
Marquette	6	0	2		1	3	86	31	53	2	0
Menominee	0	0		0	0	0	45	19	24	2	0
Monroe	16	0	3		0	13	148	51	87	10	1
Oneida	24	0	4		0	20	163	51	106	6	0
Pepin	3	0		1	0	2	38	15	20	3	1
Polk	99	0		7	0	92	233	53	161	19	1
Portage	15	0	4		1	10	135	41	87	7	1
Price	1	0	0		0	1	101	35	62	4	1
Richland	0	0		0	0	0	57	12	39	6	0
Rusk	23	1	2		0	20	71	30	38	3	1
Sauk	27	0	4		4	19	363	76	259	28	0
Sawyer	19	1	4		3	11	161	52	99	10	1
Shawano	26	1		8	4	13	344	110	213	21	1
Taylor	17	0		2	2	15	83	10	63	10	0
Trempealeau	9	0		6	0	3	99	28	65	6	1
Vernon	7	0		0	1	6	91	30	54	7	0
Vilas	8	0	2		0	6	202	58	136	8	1
Walworth	10	0		0	2	8	197	64	128	5	0
Washburn	17	0	4		1	12	178	60	108	10	1
Waupaca	82	1		8	1	72	436	117	300	19	3
Waushara[8]	23	0	17		0	6	171	47	123	1	2
Wood	5	0		2	1	2	192	71	113	8	2
WYOMING											
Metropolitan Counties											
Laramie	70	3	10		3	54	495	117	319	59	1
Natrona	56	0	19		3	34	248	84	136	28	3
Nonmetropolitan Counties											
Albany	9	0	0		0	9	36	5	29	2	1
Big Horn	2	0	2		0	0	24	7	15	2	1
Campbell	126	2	5		0	119	121	33	82	6	3
Carbon	8	0	1		0	7	25	6	17	2	0
Crook	1	0	0		0	1	47	12	30	5	0
Fremont	25	0	4		0	21	169	13	144	12	0
Goshen	27	0	1		0	26	42	12	27	3	0
Hot Springs	1	0	0		0	1	16	0	11	5	0
Johnson	5	0	1		0	4	29	10	18	1	2
Lincoln	19	0	4		0	15	58	15	39	4	0
Park	30	0	1		1	28	82	24	58	0	0
Platte	1	0	0		0	1	24	13	10	1	0
Sheridan	27	0	0		0	27	36	7	25	4	0
Sublette	3	0	0		1	2	79	5	69	5	0
Sweetwater	25	0	7		0	18	124	33	69	22	5
Uinta	4	0	0		0	4	60	5	50	5	0

Table 8. Offenses Known to Law Enforcement, by Selected State Metropolitan and Nonmetropolitan Counties, 2016—Continued

(Number.)

State/county	Violent crime	Murder and nonnegligent manslaughter	Rape (revised definition)[1]	Rape (legacy definition)[2]	Robbery	Aggravated assault	Property crime	Burglary	Larceny-theft	Motor vehicle theft	Arson[3]
Washakie	0	0	0		0	0	14	4	7	3	0
Weston	1	0	0		0	1	3	0	3	0	0

1 The figures shown in this column for the offense of rape were reported using the revised Uniform Crime Reporting (UCR) definition of rape.   2 The figures shown in this column for the offense of rape were reported using the legacy UCR definition of rape.   3 The FBI does not publish arson data unless it receives data from either the agency or the state for all 12 months of the calendar year.   4 The Tulare County Highway Patrol collects the motor vehicle thefts for this county. These data can be found in Table 9.   5 The FBI determined that the agency's data were underreported. Consequently, those data are not included in this table.   6 The FBI determined that the agency did not follow national UCR Program guidelines for reporting an offense. Consequently, this figure is not included in this table.   7 This agency began the year submitting rape data classified according to the legacy UCR definition. However, at some point during the calendar year, the agency modified its reporting methods and began classifying and submitting rape offenses according to the revised UCR definition of rape. See the data declaration for further explanation.   8 Because of changes in the state/local agency's reporting practices, figures are not comparable to previous years' data.   9 The FBI determined that the agency's data were overreported. Consequently, those data are not included in this table.

Table 9. Offenses Known to Law Enforcement, by Selected State, Tribal, and Other Agencies, 2016

(Number.)

State/other agency unit/office	Violent crime	Murder and nonnegligent manslaughter	Rape (revised definition)[1]	Rape (legacy definition)[2]	Robbery	Aggravated assault	Property crime	Burglary	Larceny-theft	Motor vehicle theft	Arson[3]
ALABAMA											
Tribal Agencies											
Poarch Creek Tribal	13	0	0		4	9	365	5	347	13	
ALASKA											
State Agencies											
Alaska State Troopers	1,226	15	301		36	874	3,556	1,138	1,962	456	43
Other Agencies											
Fairbanks International Airport	1	0	1		0	0	13	1	9	3	1
Ted Stevens Anchorage International Airport	9	0	0		1	8	183	5	145	33	0
ARIZONA											
State Agencies											
Arizona Department of Public Safety	67	0	0		1	66	11	3	8	0	1
Tribal Agencies											
Cocopah Tribal	7	0	0		0	7	9	3	5	1	0
Fort Apache Agency	42	1	18		1	22	0	0	0	0	
Fort McDowell Tribal	17	0	0		3	14	22	2	16	4	
Gila River Indian Community	232	8	21		29	174	479	86	324	69	
Hopi Tribal	30	1	1		1	27	171	72	89	10	
Hualapai Tribal	45	0	5		1	39	81	23	45	13	0
Navajo Nation	2,069	24	170		15	1,860	719	204	298	217	
Pascua Yaqui Tribal	21	0	1		2	18	217	31	183	3	0
Salt River Tribal	399	0	7		3	389	596	53	492	51	
San Carlos Agency	0	0	0		0	0	0	0	0	0	0
Truxton Canon Agency	8	0	0		0	8	2	2	0	0	0
Yavapai-Apache Nation	6	0	0		0	6	4	0	4	0	
Yavapai-Prescott Tribal	6	0	0		0	6	47	1	45	1	
Other Agencies											
Tucson Airport Authority	1	0	0		0	1	84	3	34	47	0
ARKANSAS											
State Agencies											
Camp Robinson	1	0	0		0	1	5	1	4	0	0
State Capitol Police	0	0	0		0	0	38	0	38	0	0
CALIFORNIA											
State Agencies											
Atascadero State Hospital	309	0	0		0	309	4	0	4	0	0
California State Fair	2	0	0		0	2	90	20	66	4	0
Coalinga State Hospital	173	0	1		0	172	4	1	3	0	0
Department of Parks and Recreation											
Angeles	2	0	0		0	2	10	0	10	0	0
Bay Area	0	0	0		0	0	0	0	0	0	0
Calaveras County	0	0	0		0	0	0	0	0	0	0
Capital	0	0	0		0	0	6	1	5	0	0
Channel Coast	1	0	0		0	1	36	2	33	1	0
Colorado	0	0	0		0	0	0	0	0	0	0
Four Rivers District	0	0	0		0	0	1	0	1	0	0
Gold Fields District	2	0	0		0	2	78	1	75	2	0
Hollister Hills	0	0	0		0	0	0	0	0	0	0
Hungry Valley	0	0	0		0	0	0	0	0	0	0
Inland Empire	0	0	0		0	0	4	3	1	0	0
Marin County	0	0	0		0	0	11	2	9	0	0
Mendocino Headquarters	1	0	0		1	0	10	0	10	0	0
Monterey County	1	0	0		0	1	90	33	53	4	0
North Coast Redwoods	0	0	0		0	0	33	5	27	1	1
Northern Buttes	0	0	0		0	0	15	1	13	1	0
Oceano Dunes	5	0	0		0	5	41	0	39	2	1
Ocotillo Wells	1	0	0		0	1	3	0	3	0	0
Orange Coast	0	0	0		0	0	57	19	37	1	0
Russian River	0	0	0		0	0	16	0	16	0	0
San Diego Coast	7	0	0		1	6	9	2	7	0	0
San Joaquin	2	0	0		0	2	1	0	1	0	0
San Luis Obispo Coast	1	0	0		0	1	26	1	24	1	0
Santa Cruz Mountains	1	0	0		0	1	109	1	107	1	0
Sierra	0	0	0		0	0	6	0	6	0	0
Silverado	0	0	0		0	0	4	0	4	0	0
Tehachapi District	0	0	0		0	0	18	10	6	2	0
Twin Cities	0	0	0		0	0	0	0	0	0	0
Fairview Developmental Center	4	0	0		0	4	2	1	1	0	0
Highway Patrol											
Alameda County	1	0	0		0	1	275	0	74	201	0
Alpine County	0	0	0		0	0	0	0	0	0	0
Amador County	0	0	0		0	0	38	0	5	33	0
Butte County	0	0	0		0	0	339	2	87	250	0
Calaveras County	0	0	0		0	0	84	0	4	80	0
Colusa County	0	0	0		0	0	10	0	5	5	0
Contra Costa County	3	0	0		0	3	679	0	2	677	0
Del Norte County	0	0	0		0	0	106	0	1	105	0
El Dorado County	0	0	0		0	0	157	2	64	91	0
Fresno County	0	0	0		0	0	225	0	27	198	0
Glenn County	0	0	0		0	0	33	0	5	28	0

Table 9. Offenses Known to Law Enforcement, by Selected State, Tribal, and Other Agencies, 2016—Continued

(Number.)

State/other agency unit/office	Violent crime	Murder and nonnegligent manslaughter	Rape (revised definition)[1]	Rape (legacy definition)[2]	Robbery	Aggravated assault	Property crime	Burglary	Larceny-theft	Motor vehicle theft	Arson[3]
Humboldt County	0	0	0		0	0	372	0	53	319	0
Imperial County	0	0	0		0	0	50	0	4	46	0
Inyo County	0	0	0		0	0	20	0	5	15	0
Kern County	1	0	0		0	1	291	1	28	262	0
Kings County	0	0	0		0	0	156	0	34	122	0
Lake County	4	0	0		0	4	228	3	18	207	0
Lassen County	1	0	0		0	1	29	0	8	21	0
Los Angeles County	29	0	1		3	25	926	5	71	850	0
Madera County	0	0	0		0	0	217	3	44	170	0
Marin County	0	0	0		0	0	75	0	23	52	0
Mariposa County	0	0	0		0	0	24	0	5	19	0
Mendocino County	1	0	0		0	1	146	1	21	124	0
Merced County	0	0	0		0	0	453	0	97	356	0
Modoc County	0	0	0		0	0	3	0	0	3	0
Mono County	0	0	0		0	0	2	0	1	1	0
Monterey County	0	0	0		0	0	454	0	37	417	0
Napa County	0	0	0		0	0	19	0	4	15	0
Nevada County	2	1	0		0	1	106	0	10	96	0
Orange County	8	0	0		0	8	53	0	32	21	0
Placer County	1	0	0		0	1	156	0	65	91	0
Plumas County	0	0	0		0	0	24	0	12	12	0
Riverside County	15	0	0		1	14	121	8	27	86	0
Sacramento County	7	0	0		0	7	4,571	7	1,564	3,000	4
San Benito County	0	0	0		0	0	21	0	0	21	0
San Bernardino County	19	0	0		1	18	66	6	21	39	0
San Diego County	10	0	0		0	10	118	1	17	100	0
San Francisco County	1	0	0		0	1	30	0	1	29	0
San Joaquin County	1	0	0		0	1	705	0	153	552	0
San Luis Obispo County	0	0	0		0	0	158	0	1	157	0
San Mateo County	0	0	0		0	0	12	0	4	8	0
Santa Barbara County	0	0	0		0	0	210	0	62	148	0
Santa Clara County	0	0	0		0	0	86	0	24	62	0
Santa Cruz County	0	0	0		0	0	620	0	161	459	0
Shasta County	1	0	0		1	0	308	5	76	227	0
Sierra County	0	0	0		0	0	0	0	0	0	0
Siskiyou County	0	0	0		0	0	69	0	12	57	0
Solano County	0	0	0		0	0	24	0	0	24	0
Sonoma County	0	0	0		0	0	284	1	73	210	0
Stanislaus County	0	0	0		0	0	705	0	105	600	0
Sutter County	0	0	0		0	0	42	0	0	42	0
Tehama County	0	0	0		0	0	146	0	27	119	0
Trinity County	1	0	0		0	1	65	0	5	60	0
Tulare County	0	0	0		0	0	621	0	38	583	0
Tuolumne County	0	0	0		0	0	165	0	81	84	0
Ventura County	0	0	0		0	0	50	0	10	40	0
Yolo County	0	0	0		0	0	60	0	6	54	0
Yuba County	0	0	0		0	0	303	0	11	292	0
Napa State Hospital	149	0	3		0	146	8	2	6	0	0
Patton State Hospital	504	0	1		1	502	7	0	7	0	0
Porterville Developmental Center	18	0	0		0	18	8	2	6	0	0
Sonoma Developmental Center	4	0	0		0	4	4	0	4	0	0
Tribal Agencies											
Sycuan Tribal	11	0	0		3	8	63	11	29	23	
Other Agencies											
East Bay Municipal Utility	0	0	0		0	0	27	0	25	2	1
East Bay Regional Parks											
Alameda County	13	0	3		1	9	110	0	103	7	0
Contra Costa County	10	0	0		3	7	146	0	143	3	0
Fontana Unified School District	17	0	0		1	16	77	30	41	6	5
Los Angeles County Metropolitan Transportation Authority	3	0	1		1	1	22	0	22	0	1
Los Angeles Transportation Services Bureau	734	3	6		410	315	975	12	854	109	7
Monterey Peninsula Airport	0	0	0		0	0	16	9	4	3	0
Port of San Diego Harbor	79	0	7		10	62	523	34	478	11	0
San Bernardino Unified School District	70	0	4		58	8	289	127	144	18	10
San Francisco Bay Area Rapid Transit											
Alameda County	184	1	1		148	34	1,560	5	1,206	349	0
Contra Costa County	79	0	4		49	26	774	2	598	174	1
San Francisco County	49	0	0		34	15	254	0	254	0	0
San Mateo County	20	0	0		9	11	140	0	121	19	0
Santa Clara Transit District	56	0	2		20	34	119	9	79	31	0
Shasta County Marshal	0	0	0		0	0	0	0	0	0	0
Stockton Unified School District	38	0	2		16	20	239	90	146	3	1
Twin Rivers Unified School District	14	0	1		5	8	153	102	45	6	0
Union Pacific Railroad											
Alameda County	0	0	0		0	0	3	1	2	0	0
Amador County	0	0	0		0	0	0	0	0	0	0
Butte County	0	0	0		0	0	6	2	4	0	0
Calaveras County	0	0	0		0	0	0	0	0	0	0
Colusa County	0	0	0		0	0	0	0	0	0	0
Contra Costa County	0	0	0		0	0	1	0	1	0	0
El Dorado County	0	0	0		0	0	0	0	0	0	0
Fresno County	0	0	0		0	0	2	0	2	0	0

Table 9. Offenses Known to Law Enforcement, by Selected State, Tribal, and Other Agencies, 2016—Continued

(Number.)

State/other agency unit/office	Violent crime	Murder and nonnegligent manslaughter	Rape (revised definition)[1]	Rape (legacy definition)[2]	Robbery	Aggravated assault	Property crime	Burglary	Larceny-theft	Motor vehicle theft	Arson[3]
Glenn County	0	0	0		0	0	0	0	0	0	0
Humboldt County	0	0	0		0	0	0	0	0	0	0
Imperial County	0	0	0		0	0	6	0	6	0	0
Inyo County	0	0	0		0	0	0	0	0	0	0
Kern County	0	0	0		0	0	21	5	16	0	0
Kings County	0	0	0		0	0	0	0	0	0	0
Lassen County	0	0	0		0	0	0	0	0	0	0
Los Angeles County	1	0	0		0	1	229	178	51	0	0
Madera County	0	0	0		0	0	0	0	0	0	0
Marin County	0	0	0		0	0	0	0	0	0	0
Mendocino County	0	0	0		0	0	0	0	0	0	0
Merced County	0	0	0		0	0	0	0	0	0	0
Modoc County	0	0	0		0	0	0	0	0	0	0
Monterey County	0	0	0		0	0	0	0	0	0	0
Napa County	0	0	0		0	0	0	0	0	0	0
Nevada County	0	0	0		0	0	0	0	0	0	0
Orange County	0	0	0		0	0	2	1	1	0	0
Placer County	0	0	0		0	0	15	2	13	0	0
Plumas County	0	0	0		0	0	0	0	0	0	0
Riverside County	2	0	0		0	2	18	7	11	0	0
Sacramento County	0	0	0		0	0	10	4	6	0	0
San Benito County	0	0	0		0	0	0	0	0	0	0
San Bernardino County	0	0	0		0	0	32	10	22	0	0
San Francisco County	0	0	0		0	0	0	0	0	0	0
San Joaquin County	0	0	0		0	0	44	24	20	0	0
San Luis Obispo County	0	0	0		0	0	2	0	2	0	0
San Mateo County	0	0	0		0	0	0	0	0	0	0
Santa Barbara County	0	0	0		0	0	2	0	2	0	0
Santa Clara County	0	0	0		0	0	3	2	1	0	0
Santa Cruz County	0	0	0		0	0	0	0	0	0	0
Shasta County	1	0	0		0	1	2	0	2	0	0
Sierra County	0	0	0		0	0	0	0	0	0	0
Siskiyou County	0	0	0		0	0	3	0	3	0	0
Solano County	0	0	0		0	0	2	1	1	0	0
Sonoma County	0	0	0		0	0	0	0	0	0	0
Stanislaus County	0	0	0		0	0	3	0	3	0	0
Sutter County	0	0	0		0	0	1	0	1	0	0
Tehama County	0	0	0		0	0	1	0	1	0	0
Trinity County	0	0	0		0	0	0	0	0	0	0
Tulare County	0	0	0		0	0	2	0	2	0	0
Ventura County	0	0	0		0	0	2	0	2	0	0
Yolo County	0	0	0		0	0	1	0	1	0	0
Yuba County	0	0	0		0	0	3	0	3	0	0
COLORADO											
State Agencies											
Colorado Bureau of Investigation	0	0	0		0	0	0	0	0	0	0
Colorado Mental Health Institute	1	0	0		0	1	2	1	1	0	0
Colorado State Patrol	9	0	0		0	9	29	1	7	21	0
Tribal Agencies											
Southern Ute Tribal	9	0	4		0	5	63	9	44	10	1
Other Agencies											
All Crimes Enforcement Team	0	0	0		0	0	0	0	0	0	0
Southwest Drug Task Force	0	0	0		0	0	0	0	0	0	0
CONNECTICUT											
State Agencies											
Connecticut State Police	282	7	57		37	181	2,848	743	1,793	312	17
Department of Motor Vehicles	0	0	0		0	0	0	0	0	0	0
State Capitol Police	0	0	0		0	0	7	1	6	0	0
Tribal Agencies											
Mashantucket Pequot Tribal	20	0	3		1	16	146	3	140	3	1
Mohegan Tribal	14	0	2		2	10	307	3	298	6	0
Other Agencies											
Metropolitan Transportation Authority	7	0	0		1	6	62	0	62	0	0
DELAWARE											
State Agencies											
Alcohol and Tobacco Enforcement	0	0	0		0	0	0	0	0	0	0
Animal Welfare											
Kent County	0	0	0		0	0	1	0	1	0	0
New Castle County	0	0	0		0	0	1	0	1	0	0
Sussex County	0	0	0		0	0	1	0	1	0	0
Attorney General, New Castle County	1	0	0		0	1	0	0	0	0	0
Environmental Control	0	0	0		0	0	1	0	1	0	0
Fish and Wildlife	1	0	0		0	1	19	1	18	0	0
Park Rangers	3	0	1		1	1	81	22	59	0	0
River and Bay Authority	4	0	0		1	3	11	2	8	1	0
State Capitol Police	3	0	0		0	3	15	0	14	1	0
State Fire Marshal	9	0	0		0	9	8	6	2	0	155
State Police	1	0	1		0	0	1	0	1	0	0
State Police											
Kent County	324	4	37		52	231	1,332	387	882	63	1

Table 9. Offenses Known to Law Enforcement, by Selected State, Tribal, and Other Agencies, 2016—Continued

(Number.)

State/other agency unit/office	Violent crime	Murder and nonnegligent manslaughter	Rape (revised definition)[1]	Rape (legacy definition)[2]	Robbery	Aggravated assault	Property crime	Burglary	Larceny-theft	Motor vehicle theft	Arson[3]
New Castle County	652	4	45		323	280	5,606	479	4,978	149	0
Sussex County	510	5	63		62	380	3,222	1,203	1,905	114	1
Other Agencies											
Amtrak Police	0	0	0		0	0	3	0	2	1	1
Dover Fire Marshal	0	0	0		0	0	0	0	0	0	6
DISTRICT OF COLUMBIA											
Other Agencies											
District of Columbia Fire and Emergency Medical Services, Arson Investigation Unit	0	0	0		0	0	0	0	0	0	203
Metro Transit Police	503	1	5		331	166	1,055	1	980	74	3
FLORIDA											
State Agencies											
Capitol Police	1	0	0		0	1	11	2	9	0	0
Department of Corrections, Office of the Inspector General											
Alachua County	0	0	0		0	0	0	0	0	0	0
Baker County	0	0	0		0	0	0	0	0	0	0
Bay County	0	0	0		0	0	0	0	0	0	0
Bradford County	0	0	0		0	0	0	0	0	0	0
Brevard County	0	0	0		0	0	0	0	0	0	0
Broward County	0	0	0		0	0	0	0	0	0	0
Calhoun County	0	0	0		0	0	0	0	0	0	0
Charlotte County	0	0	0		0	0	0	0	0	0	0
Citrus County	0	0	0		0	0	0	0	0	0	0
Clay County	0	0	0		0	0	0	0	0	0	0
Collier County	0	0	0		0	0	0	0	0	0	0
Columbia County	0	0	0		0	0	0	0	0	0	0
DeSoto County	0	0	0		0	0	0	0	0	0	0
Dixie County	0	0	0		0	0	0	0	0	0	0
Duval County	0	0	0		0	0	0	0	0	0	0
Escambia County	0	0	0		0	0	0	0	0	0	0
Flagler County	0	0	0		0	0	0	0	0	0	0
Franklin County	0	0	0		0	0	0	0	0	0	0
Gadsden County	0	0	0		0	0	0	0	0	0	0
Gilchrist County	0	0	0		0	0	0	0	0	0	0
Glades County	0	0	0		0	0	0	0	0	0	0
Gulf County	0	0	0		0	0	0	0	0	0	0
Hamilton County	0	0	0		0	0	0	0	0	0	0
Hardee County	0	0	0		0	0	0	0	0	0	0
Hendry County	0	0	0		0	0	0	0	0	0	0
Hernando County	0	0	0		0	0	0	0	0	0	0
Highlands County	0	0	0		0	0	0	0	0	0	0
Hillsborough County	0	0	0		0	0	0	0	0	0	0
Holmes County	0	0	0		0	0	0	0	0	0	0
Indian River County	0	0	0		0	0	0	0	0	0	0
Jackson County	0	0	0		0	0	0	0	0	0	0
Jefferson County	0	0	0		0	0	0	0	0	0	0
Lafayette County	0	0	0		0	0	0	0	0	0	0
Lake County	0	0	0		0	0	0	0	0	0	0
Lee County	0	0	0		0	0	0	0	0	0	0
Leon County	0	0	0		0	0	0	0	0	0	0
Levy County	0	0	0		0	0	0	0	0	0	0
Liberty County	0	0	0		0	0	0	0	0	0	0
Madison County	0	0	0		0	0	0	0	0	0	0
Manatee County	0	0	0		0	0	0	0	0	0	0
Marion County	0	0	0		0	0	0	0	0	0	0
Martin County	0	0	0		0	0	0	0	0	0	0
Miami-Dade County	0	0	0		0	0	0	0	0	0	0
Monroe County	0	0	0		0	0	0	0	0	0	0
Nassau County	0	0	0		0	0	0	0	0	0	0
Okaloosa County	0	0	0		0	0	0	0	0	0	0
Okeechobee County	0	0	0		0	0	0	0	0	0	0
Orange County	0	0	0		0	0	0	0	0	0	0
Osceola County	0	0	0		0	0	0	0	0	0	0
Palm Beach County	0	0	0		0	0	0	0	0	0	0
Pasco County	0	0	0		0	0	0	0	0	0	0
Pinellas County	0	0	0		0	0	0	0	0	0	0
Polk County	0	0	0		0	0	0	0	0	0	0
Putnam County	0	0	0		0	0	0	0	0	0	0
Santa Rosa County	0	0	0		0	0	0	0	0	0	0
Sarasota County	0	0	0		0	0	0	0	0	0	0
Seminole County	0	0	0		0	0	0	0	0	0	0
St. Johns County	0	0	0		0	0	0	0	0	0	0
St. Lucie County	0	0	0		0	0	0	0	0	0	0
Sumter County	0	0	0		0	0	0	0	0	0	0
Suwannee County	0	0	0		0	0	0	0	0	0	0
Taylor County	0	0	0		0	0	0	0	0	0	0
Union County	0	0	0		0	0	0	0	0	0	0
Volusia County	0	0	0		0	0	0	0	0	0	0
Wakulla County	0	0	0		0	0	0	0	0	0	0
Walton County	0	0	0		0	0	0	0	0	0	0

Table 9. Offenses Known to Law Enforcement, by Selected State, Tribal, and Other Agencies, 2016—Continued

(Number.)

State/other agency unit/office	Violent crime	Murder and nonnegligent manslaughter	Rape (revised definition)[1]	Rape (legacy definition)[2]	Robbery	Aggravated assault	Property crime	Burglary	Larceny-theft	Motor vehicle theft	Arson[3]
Washington County	0	0	0		0	0	0	0	0	0	0
Department of Insurance											
Broward County	0	0	0		0	0	0	0	0	0	0
Duval County	0	0	0		0	0	0	0	0	0	0
Escambia County	0	0	0		0	0	0	0	0	0	0
Hillsborough County	0	0	0		0	0	0	0	0	0	0
Lee County	0	0	0		0	0	0	0	0	0	0
Miami-Dade County	0	0	0		0	0	0	0	0	0	0
Orange County	0	0	0		0	0	0	0	0	0	0
Palm Beach County	0	0	0		0	0	0	0	0	0	0
Pinellas County	0	0	0		0	0	0	0	0	0	0
Department of Law Enforcement											
Duval County, Jacksonville	0	0	0		0	0	0	0	0	0	0
Escambia County, Pensacola	2	0	2		0	0	1	0	1	0	0
Hillsborough County, Tampa	2	0	1		0	1	0	0	0	0	0
Lee County, Fort Myers	0	0	0		0	0	0	0	0	0	0
Leon County, Tallahassee	0	0	0		0	0	1	0	1	0	0
Miami-Dade County, Miami	0	0	0		0	0	0	0	0	0	0
Orange County, Orlando	1	0	0		0	1	4	0	4	0	0
Division of Alcoholic Beverages and Tobacco											
Alachua County	0	0	0		0	0	0	0	0	0	0
Baker County	0	0	0		0	0	0	0	0	0	0
Bay County	0	0	0		0	0	0	0	0	0	0
Bradford County	0	0	0		0	0	0	0	0	0	0
Brevard County	0	0	0		0	0	0	0	0	0	0
Broward County	0	0	0		0	0	0	0	0	0	0
Calhoun County	0	0	0		0	0	0	0	0	0	0
Charlotte County	0	0	0		0	0	0	0	0	0	0
Citrus County	0	0	0		0	0	0	0	0	0	0
Clay County	0	0	0		0	0	0	0	0	0	0
Collier County	0	0	0		0	0	0	0	0	0	0
Columbia County	0	0	0		0	0	0	0	0	0	0
DeSoto County	0	0	0		0	0	0	0	0	0	0
Dixie County	0	0	0		0	0	0	0	0	0	0
Duval County	0	0	0		0	0	0	0	0	0	0
Escambia County	0	0	0		0	0	0	0	0	0	0
Flagler County	0	0	0		0	0	0	0	0	0	0
Franklin County	0	0	0		0	0	0	0	0	0	0
Gadsden County	0	0	0		0	0	0	0	0	0	0
Gilchrist County	0	0	0		0	0	0	0	0	0	0
Glades County	0	0	0		0	0	0	0	0	0	0
Gulf County	0	0	0		0	0	0	0	0	0	0
Hamilton County	0	0	0		0	0	0	0	0	0	0
Hardee County	0	0	0		0	0	0	0	0	0	0
Hendry County	0	0	0		0	0	0	0	0	0	0
Hernando County	0	0	0		0	0	0	0	0	0	0
Highlands County	0	0	0		0	0	0	0	0	0	0
Hillsborough County	0	0	0		0	0	0	0	0	0	0
Holmes County	0	0	0		0	0	0	0	0	0	0
Indian River County	0	0	0		0	0	0	0	0	0	0
Jackson County	0	0	0		0	0	0	0	0	0	0
Jefferson County	0	0	0		0	0	0	0	0	0	0
Lafayette County	0	0	0		0	0	0	0	0	0	0
Lake County	0	0	0		0	0	0	0	0	0	0
Lee County	0	0	0		0	0	0	0	0	0	0
Leon County	0	0	0		0	0	0	0	0	0	0
Levy County	0	0	0		0	0	0	0	0	0	0
Liberty County	0	0	0		0	0	0	0	0	0	0
Madison County	0	0	0		0	0	0	0	0	0	0
Manatee County	0	0	0		0	0	0	0	0	0	0
Marion County	0	0	0		0	0	0	0	0	0	0
Martin County	0	0	0		0	0	0	0	0	0	0
Miami-Dade County	0	0	0		0	0	0	0	0	0	0
Monroe County	0	0	0		0	0	0	0	0	0	0
Nassau County	0	0	0		0	0	0	0	0	0	0
Okaloosa County	0	0	0		0	0	0	0	0	0	0
Okeechobee County	0	0	0		0	0	0	0	0	0	0
Orange County	0	0	0		0	0	0	0	0	0	0
Osceola County	0	0	0		0	0	0	0	0	0	0
Palm Beach County	0	0	0		0	0	0	0	0	0	0
Pasco County	0	0	0		0	0	0	0	0	0	0
Pinellas County	0	0	0		0	0	0	0	0	0	0
Polk County	0	0	0		0	0	0	0	0	0	0
Putnam County	0	0	0		0	0	0	0	0	0	0
Santa Rosa County	0	0	0		0	0	0	0	0	0	0
Sarasota County	0	0	0		0	0	0	0	0	0	0
Seminole County	0	0	0		0	0	0	0	0	0	0
St. Johns County	0	0	0		0	0	0	0	0	0	0
St. Lucie County	0	0	0		0	0	0	0	0	0	0
Sumter County	0	0	0		0	0	0	0	0	0	0
Suwannee County	0	0	0		0	0	0	0	0	0	0
Taylor County	0	0	0		0	0	0	0	0	0	0
Union County	0	0	0		0	0	0	0	0	0	0

Table 9. Offenses Known to Law Enforcement, by Selected State, Tribal, and Other Agencies, 2016—Continued

(Number.)

State/other agency unit/office	Violent crime	Murder and nonnegligent manslaughter	Rape (revised definition)[1]	Rape (legacy definition)[2]	Robbery	Aggravated assault	Property crime	Burglary	Larceny-theft	Motor vehicle theft	Arson[3]
Volusia County	0	0	0		0	0	0	0	0	0	
Wakulla County	0	0	0		0	0	0	0	0	0	0
Walton County	0	0	0		0	0	0	0	0	0	0
Washington County	0	0	0		0	0	0	0	0	0	0
Florida Game Commission											
Alachua County	0	0	0		0	0	0	0	0	0	0
Baker County	0	0	0		0	0	0	0	0	0	0
Bay County	0	0	0		0	0	0	0	0	0	0
Bradford County	0	0	0		0	0	0	0	0	0	0
Brevard County	0	0	0		0	0	0	0	0	0	0
Broward County	0	0	0		0	0	0	0	0	0	0
Calhoun County	0	0	0		0	0	0	0	0	0	0
Charlotte County	0	0	0		0	0	0	0	0	0	0
Citrus County	0	0	0		0	0	0	0	0	0	0
Clay County	0	0	0		0	0	0	0	0	0	0
Collier County	0	0	0		0	0	0	0	0	0	0
Columbia County	0	0	0		0	0	0	0	0	0	0
DeSoto County	0	0	0		0	0	0	0	0	0	0
Dixie County	0	0	0		0	0	0	0	0	0	0
Duval County	0	0	0		0	0	0	0	0	0	0
Escambia County	0	0	0		0	0	0	0	0	0	0
Flagler County	0	0	0		0	0	0	0	0	0	0
Franklin County	0	0	0		0	0	0	0	0	0	0
Gadsden County	0	0	0		0	0	0	0	0	0	0
Gilchrist County	0	0	0		0	0	0	0	0	0	0
Glades County	0	0	0		0	0	0	0	0	0	0
Gulf County	0	0	0		0	0	0	0	0	0	0
Hamilton County	0	0	0		0	0	0	0	0	0	0
Hardee County	0	0	0		0	0	0	0	0	0	0
Hendry County	0	0	0		0	0	0	0	0	0	0
Hernando County	0	0	0		0	0	0	0	0	0	0
Highlands County	0	0	0		0	0	0	0	0	0	0
Hillsborough County	0	0	0		0	0	0	0	0	0	0
Holmes County	0	0	0		0	0	0	0	0	0	0
Indian River County	0	0	0		0	0	0	0	0	0	0
Jackson County	0	0	0		0	0	0	0	0	0	0
Jefferson County	0	0	0		0	0	0	0	0	0	0
Lafayette County	0	0	0		0	0	0	0	0	0	0
Lake County	0	0	0		0	0	0	0	0	0	0
Lee County	0	0	0		0	0	0	0	0	0	0
Leon County	0	0	0		0	0	0	0	0	0	0
Levy County	0	0	0		0	0	0	0	0	0	0
Liberty County	0	0	0		0	0	0	0	0	0	0
Madison County	0	0	0		0	0	0	0	0	0	0
Manatee County	0	0	0		0	0	0	0	0	0	0
Marion County	0	0	0		0	0	0	0	0	0	0
Martin County	0	0	0		0	0	0	0	0	0	0
Miami-Dade County	0	0	0		0	0	0	0	0	0	0
Monroe County	0	0	0		0	0	0	0	0	0	0
Nassau County	0	0	0		0	0	0	0	0	0	0
Okaloosa County	0	0	0		0	0	0	0	0	0	0
Okeechobee County	0	0	0		0	0	0	0	0	0	0
Orange County	0	0	0		0	0	0	0	0	0	0
Osceola County	0	0	0		0	0	0	0	0	0	0
Palm Beach County	0	0	0		0	0	0	0	0	0	0
Pasco County	0	0	0		0	0	0	0	0	0	0
Pinellas County	0	0	0		0	0	0	0	0	0	0
Polk County	0	0	0		0	0	0	0	0	0	0
Putnam County	0	0	0		0	0	0	0	0	0	0
Santa Rosa County	0	0	0		0	0	0	0	0	0	0
Sarasota County	0	0	0		0	0	0	0	0	0	0
Seminole County	0	0	0		0	0	0	0	0	0	0
St. Johns County	0	0	0		0	0	0	0	0	0	0
St. Lucie County	0	0	0		0	0	0	0	0	0	0
Sumter County	0	0	0		0	0	0	0	0	0	0
Suwannee County	0	0	0		0	0	0	0	0	0	0
Taylor County	0	0	0		0	0	0	0	0	0	0
Union County	0	0	0		0	0	0	0	0	0	0
Volusia County	0	0	0		0	0	0	0	0	0	0
Wakulla County	0	0	0		0	0	0	0	0	0	0
Walton County	0	0	0		0	0	0	0	0	0	0
Washington County	0	0	0		0	0	0	0	0	0	0
Highway Patrol											
Alachua County	1	0	0		0	1	0	0	0	0	0
Baker County	0	0	0		0	0	0	0	0	0	0
Bay County	0	0	0		0	0	0	0	0	0	0
Bradford County	0	0	0		0	0	0	0	0	0	0
Brevard County	1	0	0		0	1	1	0	0	1	0
Broward County	3	0	0		0	3	5	0	2	3	0
Calhoun County	0	0	0		0	0	0	0	0	0	0
Charlotte County	0	0	0		0	0	3	0	2	1	0
Citrus County	0	0	0		0	0	0	0	0	0	0
Clay County	0	0	0		0	0	0	0	0	0	0

Table 9. Offenses Known to Law Enforcement, by Selected State, Tribal, and Other Agencies, 2016—Continued

(Number.)

State/other agency unit/office	Violent crime	Murder and nonnegligent manslaughter	Rape (revised definition)[1]	Rape (legacy definition)[2]	Robbery	Aggravated assault	Property crime	Burglary	Larceny-theft	Motor vehicle theft	Arson[3]
Collier County	0	0	0		0	0	0	0	0	0	0
Columbia County	1	0	0		0	1	0	0	0	0	0
DeSoto County	0	0	0		0	0	0	0	0	0	0
Dixie County	0	0	0		0	0	0	0	0	0	0
Duval County	7	0	0		0	7	8	0	0	8	0
Escambia County	6	0	0		0	6	0	0	0	0	0
Flagler County	0	0	0		0	0	0	0	0	0	0
Franklin County	0	0	0		0	0	0	0	0	0	0
Gadsden County	0	0	0		0	0	0	0	0	0	0
Gilchrist County	0	0	0		0	0	0	0	0	0	0
Glades County	0	0	0		0	0	0	0	0	0	0
Gulf County	0	0	0		0	0	0	0	0	0	0
Hamilton County	3	0	0		0	3	0	0	0	0	0
Hardee County	0	0	0		0	0	0	0	0	0	0
Hendry County	0	0	0		0	0	0	0	0	0	0
Hernando County	0	0	0		0	0	0	0	0	0	0
Highlands County	0	0	0		0	0	0	0	0	0	0
Hillsborough County	3	0	0		0	3	2	0	1	1	0
Holmes County	0	0	0		0	0	0	0	0	0	0
Indian River County	0	0	0		0	0	0	0	0	0	0
Jackson County	0	0	0		0	0	0	0	0	0	0
Jefferson County	0	0	0		0	0	0	0	0	0	0
Lafayette County	0	0	0		0	0	0	0	0	0	0
Lake County	2	0	0		0	2	0	0	0	0	0
Lee County	3	0	0		0	3	1	0	1	0	0
Leon County	3	0	0		0	3	3	0	3	0	0
Levy County	0	0	0		0	0	0	0	0	0	0
Liberty County	0	0	0		0	0	0	0	0	0	0
Madison County	0	0	0		0	0	4	0	0	4	0
Manatee County	0	0	0		0	0	3	0	0	3	0
Marion County	2	0	0		0	2	0	0	0	0	0
Martin County	2	0	0		0	2	1	0	1	0	0
Miami-Dade County	20	0	0		0	20	8	0	4	4	0
Monroe County	0	0	0		0	0	3	0	0	3	0
Nassau County	0	0	0		0	0	1	0	0	1	0
Okaloosa County	0	0	0		0	0	0	0	0	0	0
Okeechobee County	3	0	0		0	3	0	0	0	0	0
Orange County	6	0	0		0	6	1	0	0	1	0
Osceola County	1	0	0		0	1	7	0	3	4	0
Palm Beach County	8	0	0		0	8	6	0	2	4	0
Pasco County	3	0	0		0	3	5	0	2	3	0
Pinellas County	0	0	0		0	0	0	0	0	0	0
Polk County	9	0	0		0	9	3	0	2	1	0
Putnam County	0	0	0		0	0	3	0	3	0	0
Santa Rosa County	1	0	0		0	1	0	0	0	0	0
Sarasota County	2	0	0		0	2	0	0	0	0	0
Seminole County	0	0	0		0	0	0	0	0	0	0
St. Johns County	0	0	0		0	0	2	0	1	1	0
St. Lucie County	1	0	0		0	1	5	0	3	2	0
Sumter County	2	0	0		0	2	2	0	0	2	0
Suwannee County	2	0	0		0	2	0	0	0	0	0
Taylor County	0	0	0		0	0	0	0	0	0	0
Union County	0	0	0		0	0	0	0	0	0	0
Volusia County	0	0	0		0	0	4	0	0	4	0
Wakulla County	0	0	0		0	0	0	0	0	0	0
Walton County	0	0	0		0	0	0	0	0	0	0
Washington County	0	0	0		0	0	0	0	0	0	0
State Treasurer's Office, Division of Insurance Fraud	0	0	0		0	0	0	0	0	0	0
Tribal Agencies											
Miccosukee Tribal	5	1	0		1	3	65	5	48	12	0
Seminole Tribal	82	2	9		26	45	638	34	566	38	2
Other Agencies											
Duval County Schools	71	0	8		5	58	415	87	311	17	5
Florida School for the Deaf and Blind	0	0	0		0	0	0	0	0	0	0
Fort Lauderdale Airport	4	0	0		0	4	277	3	211	63	0
Jacksonville Aviation Authority	0	0	0		0	0	42	0	20	22	0
Lee County Port Authority	0	0	0		0	0	43	0	42	1	0
Melbourne International Airport	0	0	0		0	0	3	0	2	1	0
Northwest Florida Beaches International Airport	0	0	0		0	0	3	0	3	0	0
Palm Beach County School District	73	0	3		14	56	753	38	705	10	3
Port Everglades	12	0	5		0	7	72	3	65	4	0
Sarasota-Manatee Airport Authority	0	0	0		0	0	38	1	5	32	0
St. Petersburg-Clearwater International Airport	0	0	0		0	0	6	0	4	2	0
Tampa International Airport	4	0	0		0	4	161	1	99	61	0
Volusia County Beach Management	9	0	1		1	7	196	1	194	1	0
GEORGIA											
State Agencies											
Georgia Department of Transportation, Office of Investigations	0	0		0	0	0	0	0	0	0	0
Georgia Forestry Commission	0	0		0	0	0	0	0	0	0	91

Table 9. Offenses Known to Law Enforcement, by Selected State, Tribal, and Other Agencies, 2016—Continued

(Number.)

State/other agency unit/office	Violent crime	Murder and nonnegligent manslaughter	Rape (revised definition)[1]	Rape (legacy definition)[2]	Robbery	Aggravated assault	Property crime	Burglary	Larceny-theft	Motor vehicle theft	Arson[3]
Georgia Public Safety Training Center	0	0			0	0	0	0	0	0	0
Georgia World Congress	4	0			1	3	191	1	186	0	0
Ports Authority, Savannah	0	0			0	0	7	1	5	4	0
State Board of Workers Compensation, Fraud Investigation Division	0	0			0	0	0	0	0	0	
Other Agencies											
Appling County Board of Education	0	0			0	0	5	0	5	0	0
Atlanta Public Schools	41	0			2	13	26	298	33	243	22	0
Augusta Board of Education	1	0			1	0	0	155	4	151	0	
Chatham County Board of Education	8	0			1	5	2	85	9	74	2	0
Cherokee County Board of Education	1	0			1	0	0	69	1	68	0	0
Cherokee County Marshal	0	0			0	0	0	0	0	0	0	0
Cobb County Board of Education	93	0			1	4	88	526	17	507	2	0
Decatur County Schools	1	0			1	0	0	1	0	1	0	0
DeKalb County School System	61	0			7	24	30	485	62	402	21	6
Dougherty County Board of Education	2	0			0	2	0	41	3	38	0	0
Fayette County Marshal	0	0			0	0	0	0	0	0	0	0
Forsyth County Fire Investigation Unit	0	0			0	0	0	0	0	0	0	8
Fulton County Marshal	14	1			0	0	13	39	0	39	0	0
Fulton County School System	16	0			3	1	12	135	33	95	7	1
Glynn County School System	4	0			0	1	3	50	5	45	0	0
Gwinnett County Public Schools	16	0			1	5	10	332	10	318	4	0
Hall County Marshal	0	0			0	0	0	0	0	0	0	0
Hartsfield-Jackson Atlanta International Airport	19	0			0	4	15	374	3	261	110	0
Metropolitan Atlanta Rapid Transit Authority	169	2			0	45	122	294	2	267	25	7
Muscogee City Marshal	0	0			0	0	0	0	0	0	0	0
Richmond County Marshal	0	0			0	0	0	0	0	0	0	0
Stone Mountain Park	0	0			0	0	0	0	0	0	0	0
Twiggs County Board of Education	1	1			0	0	0	41	0	40	1	0
Washington County Board of Education	0	0			0	0	0	27	1	26	0	0
IDAHO											
State Agencies											
Idaho State Police	14	4	1		0	9	7	2	5	0	0
ILLINOIS											
State Agencies											
Illinois Department of Natural Resources	3	0	0		0	3	20	4	16	0	0
Illinois State Police	215	15	65		13	122	181	37	98	46	3
Secretary of State Police	1	0	0		0	1	10	1	9	0	0
State Fire Marshal	0	0	0		0	0	0	0	0	0	333
Other Agencies											
Alton & Southern Railway	0	0	0		0	0	0	0	0	0	340
Belt Railway	0	0	0		0	0	2	0	2	0	1
Canadian National Railway	0	0	0		0	0	6	2	4	0	0
Canton Park District	0	0	0		0	0	68	0	68	0	0
Capitol Airport Authority	0	0	0		0	0	0	0	0	0	0
Chicago Fire Department, Arson Investigations	0	0	0		0	0	0	0	0	0	505
Cook County Forest Preserve	21	0	5		8	8	93	0	68	25	0
Crystal Lake Park District	4	0	0		0	4	4	1	3	0	0
Decatur Park District	6	0	0		1	5	11	3	8	0	2
DuPage County Forest Preserve	0	0	0		0	0	29	1	28	0	0
Fon du Lac Park District	0	0	0		0	0	1	0	1	0	0
Fox Valley Park District	3	0	0		3	0	45	0	45	0	0
Indiana Harbor Belt Railroad	0	0	0		0	0	3	2	1	0	0
Kane County Forest Preserve	1	0	0		0	1	3	0	3	0	0
Lake County Forest Preserve	2	0	0		0	2	13	0	13	0	0
McHenry County Conservation District	0	0	0		0	0	4	0	4	0	0
Naperville Park District	0	0	0		0	0	13	0	13	0	1
Norfolk Southern Railway											
Cook County	0	0	0		0	0	648	542	106	0	0
Macon County	0	0	0		0	0	4	1	3	0	0
Madison County	0	0	0		0	0	2	1	1	0	0
Pekin Park District	0	0	0		0	0	2	0	2	0	0
Rockford Park District	52	0	0		9	43	90	24	64	2	0
Springfield Park District	27	0	1		1	25	25	10	12	3	0
Terminal Railroad Association	0	0	0		0	0	2	0	2	0	0
Tri-County Drug Enforcement Narcotics Team	1	0	0		0	1	0	0	0	0	0
Union Pacific Railroad, Cook County	0	0	0		0	0	292	93	199	0	0
INDIANA											
State Agencies											
Indiana State Excise Police	0	0	0		0	0	3	0	3	0	0
Northern Indiana Commuter Transportation District	2	0		0	2	0	26	0	24	2	0
State Police											
Allen County	3	0	1		0	2	16	0	13	3	0
Bartholomew County	0	0	0		0	0	14	1	8	5	0
Brown County	1	0	1		0	0	6	1	3	2	0
Cass County	2	0	1		0	1	7	1	6	0	0
Clark County	1	0	0		0	1	41	3	27	11	0
Clay County	3	0	0		0	3	8	2	6	0	0
Crawford County	4	1	1		0	2	14	3	7	4	0

Table 9. Offenses Known to Law Enforcement, by Selected State, Tribal, and Other Agencies, 2016—Continued

(Number.)

State/other agency unit/office	Violent crime	Murder and nonnegligent manslaughter	Rape (revised definition)[1]	Rape (legacy definition)[2]	Robbery	Aggravated assault	Property crime	Burglary	Larceny-theft	Motor vehicle theft	Arson[3]
Daviess County	3	0	0		0	3	11	0	10	1	0
Dearborn County	2	0	0		1	1	12	4	7	1	0
Decatur County	3	0	3		0	0	9	0	4	5	0
De Kalb County	6	1	3		0	2	6	2	4	0	0
Delaware County	2	0	1		0	1	20	0	13	7	0
Dubois County	3	0	1		0	2	27	3	21	3	0
Elkhart County	3	1	1		0	1	13	0	8	5	0
Floyd County	0	0	0		0	0	11	1	7	3	0
Franklin County	3	1	0		0	2	11	5	4	2	1
Fulton County	2	0	1		0	1	9	1	4	4	0
Gibson County	6	0	0		0	6	12	1	9	2	0
Greene County	3	0	2		0	1	21	1	19	1	0
Hancock County	1	0	0		0	1	5	0	3	2	0
Harrison County	3	0	0		0	3	17	4	11	2	0
Hendricks County	2	0	0		1	1	11	1	8	2	0
Henry County	2	0	0		0	2	8	1	6	1	0
Howard County	6	1	2		1	2	9	3	5	1	0
Huntington County	0	0	0		0	0	3	1	2	0	1
Jackson County	6	1	2		0	3	14	1	9	4	0
Jasper County	5	0	0		0	5	10	0	7	3	0
Jay County	2	0	1		0	1	4	0	4	0	0
Jefferson County	8	0	1		0	7	13	5	7	1	0
Jennings County	10	0	1		0	9	11	2	6	3	0
Johnson County	2	0	0		0	2	9	0	5	4	0
Knox County	7	0	0		0	7	15	1	13	1	0
Kosciusko County	4	0	1		0	3	14	8	5	1	0
LaGrange County	3	0	1		2	0	6	2	4	0	1
Lake County	13	0	1		0	12	62	0	34	28	0
La Porte County	1	0	1		0	0	15	0	9	6	0
Lawrence County	6	1	3		0	2	13	4	6	3	0
Madison County	4	0	1		1	2	17	2	12	3	0
Marion County	25	0	5		5	15	335	1	162	172	1
Marshall County	9	0	1		1	7	18	1	16	1	0
Martin County	3	0	0		0	3	10	2	7	1	0
Miami County	14	0	3		1	10	14	3	11	0	0
Monroe County	10	0	3		1	6	37	7	25	5	0
Montgomery County	4	0	3		0	1	4	0	4	0	0
Morgan County	4	0	1		0	3	13	0	6	7	0
Noble County	2	0	1		0	1	8	4	3	1	1
Orange County	14	1	9		0	4	11	2	9	0	0
Perry County	4	1	0		0	3	12	3	8	1	0
Pike County	11	0	1		0	10	12	2	9	1	0
Porter County	0	0	0		0	0	12	0	8	4	0
Posey County	9	0	0		1	8	9	1	7	1	1
Putnam County	6	2	2		0	2	12	3	7	2	0
Ripley County	9	0	3		0	6	47	16	24	7	0
Scott County	6	0	1		1	4	15	1	13	1	1
Shelby County	3	0	0		0	3	4	1	2	1	0
Spencer County	3	0	0		0	3	12	1	11	0	0
St. Joseph County	3	0	1		0	2	22	1	16	5	0
Sullivan County	12	1	5		1	5	8	1	4	3	0
Switzerland County	0	0	0		0	0	0	0	0	0	0
Tippecanoe County	9	0	2		0	7	26	2	19	5	0
Vanderburgh County	1	0	0		0	1	11	3	8	0	0
Vermillion County	1	0	0		0	1	8	0	8	0	0
Vigo County	2	0	0		0	2	25	2	17	6	0
Wabash County	2	1	1		0	0	2	0	1	1	0
Warren County	3	1	1		0	1	3	1	2	0	1
Washington County	6	2	1		0	3	3	0	3	0	0
Wayne County	5	0	0		0	5	5	0	4	1	0
White County	2	0	1		1	0	11	2	6	3	0
Whitley County	5	0	5		0	0	6	2	4	0	1
Other Agencies											
Indianapolis International Airport	6	0	0		0	6	65	1	58	6	0
KANSAS											
State Agencies											
Kansas Alcoholic Beverage Control	0	0	0		0	0	0	0	0	0	0
Kansas Bureau of Investigation	18	3	4		0	11	3	0	3	0	0
Kansas Department of Wildlife and Parks	5	0	0		0	5	27	3	22	2	0
Kansas Highway Patrol	31	4	1		2	24	59	4	40	15	2
Kansas Lottery Security Division	0	0	0		0	0	0	0	0	0	0
Kansas Racing Commission, Security Division	0	0	0		0	0	2	0	2	0	0
Tribal Agencies											
Iowa Tribal	0	0	0		0	0	0	0	0	0	0
Kickapoo Tribal	2	0	0		0	2	14	10	3	1	0
Sac and Fox Tribal	0	0	0		0	0	7	0	7	0	0
Other Agencies											
El Dorado School District	0	0	0		0	0	1	0	1	0	0
Johnson County Park	1	0	0		0	1	32	3	29	0	2
Salina Drug Unit	0	0	0		0	0	2	1	1	0	0
Shawnee Mission Public Schools	1	0	0		0	1	9	0	9	0	1
Topeka Fire Department, Arson Investigation	1	0	0		0	1	11	10	1	0	59

Table 9. Offenses Known to Law Enforcement, by Selected State, Tribal, and Other Agencies, 2016—Continued

(Number.)

State/other agency unit/office	Violent crime	Murder and nonnegligent manslaughter	Rape (revised definition)[1]	Rape (legacy definition)[2]	Robbery	Aggravated assault	Property crime	Burglary	Larceny-theft	Motor vehicle theft	Arson[3]
Unified School District											
Kansas City	0	0	0		0	0	50	1	49	0	0
Shawnee Heights	0	0	0		0	0	0	0	0	0	0
KENTUCKY											
State Agencies											
Alcohol Beverage Control											
Enforcement Division	0	0	0		0	0	0	0	0	0	0
Investigative Division	0	0	0		0	0	1	0	1	0	0
Fish and Wildlife Enforcement	0	0	0		0	0	9	1	8	0	0
Kentucky Fairgrounds Security	0	0	0		0	0	0	0	0	0	0
Kentucky Horse Park	0	0	0		0	0	29	0	27	2	0
Motor Vehicle Enforcement	1	0	0		1	0	8	3	5	0	0
Park Security	0	0	0		0	0	18	1	17	0	0
State Police											
Ashland	38	3	18		3	14	162	43	96	23	2
Bowling Green	46	6	21		3	16	120	54	58	8	7
Campbellsburg	56	0	32		4	20	175	70	82	23	5
Cannabis Suppression Section	0	0	0		0	0	0	0	0	0	0
Columbia	69	9	43		1	16	105	46	48	11	10
Drug Enforcement Area	1	0	0		1	0	1	0	1	0	0
Dry Ridge	41	0	28		1	12	142	58	69	15	1
Electronic Crimes	0	0	0		0	0	0	0	0	0	0
Elizabethtown	52	2	33		3	14	127	50	57	20	1
Frankfort	31	1	14		1	15	134	35	82	17	12
Harlan	65	5	34		2	24	272	113	112	47	1
Hazard	103	3	16		10	74	272	139	98	35	8
Henderson	24	2	13		3	6	113	38	62	13	6
London	83	2	43		4	34	290	121	122	47	7
Madisonville	41	1	26		3	11	120	59	48	13	4
Mayfield	64	5	28		2	29	165	60	92	13	2
Morehead	64	8	33		3	20	227	107	101	19	9
Pikeville	111	2	45		14	50	280	126	106	48	7
Richmond	60	8	29		5	18	327	128	166	33	9
Vehicle Investigations	0	0	0		0	0	1	0	1	0	0
West Drug Enforcement Branch	0	0	0		0	0	10	2	8	0	0
Unlawful Narcotics Investigation, Treatment and Education	0	0	0		0	0	0	0	0	0	0
Other Agencies											
Barren County Drug Task Force	0	0	0		0	0	1	0	1	0	1
Cincinnati-Northern Kentucky International Airport	0	0	0		0	0	48	0	42	6	0
Clark County School System	0	0	0		0	0	4	1	3	0	0
Cumberland River Drug Task Force	0	0	0		0	0	0	0	0	0	0
Daniel Boone National Forest	0	0	0		0	0	0	0	0	0	0
Estill County Constable, District 1	0	0	0		0	0	0	0	0	0	0
Fayette County Schools	13	0	1		3	9	104	3	99	2	3
FIVCO Area Drug Task Force	0	0	0		0	0	0	0	0	0	0
Graves County Schools	0	0	0		0	0	0	0	0	0	0
Greater Hardin County Narcotics Task Force	0	0	0		0	0	2	1	1	0	0
Hardin County Constable, District 5	0	0	0		0	0	0	0	0	0	0
Jefferson County School District	16	0	0		1	15	58	22	36	0	1
Lake Cumberland Area Drug Enforcement Task Force	0	0	0		0	0	0	0	0	0	0
Laurel County Constable, District 1	0	0	0		0	0	0	0	0	0	0
Lee County Constable, District 3	0	0	0		0	0	0	0	0	0	0
Lexington Bluegrass Airport	0	0	0		0	0	6	0	6	0	0
Louisville Regional Airport Authority	0	0	0		0	0	24	2	7	15	0
McCracken County Public Schools	1	0	0		0	1	1	0	1	0	0
Montgomery County School District	0	0	0		0	0	7	0	7	0	0
Northern Kentucky Drug Strike Force	0	0	0		0	0	1	0	1	0	0
Ohio County School System	0	0	0		0	0	0	0	0	0	0
Pennyrile Narcotics Task Force	0	0	0		0	0	6	0	6	0	0
Pulaski County Constable, District 5	6	0	0		1	5	0	0	0	0	0
South Central Kentucky Drug Task Force	0	0	0		0	0	1	0	1	0	0
Tennessee Valley Authority	0	0	0		0	0	0	0	0	0	0
Warren County Constable, District 4	0	0	0		0	0	0	0	0	0	0
LOUISIANA											
State Agencies											
Tensas Basin Levee District	0	0	0		0	0	0	0	0	0	0
Tribal Agencies											
Chitimacha Tribal	9	0	0		1	8	45	1	42	2	0
Coushatta Tribal	1	0	0		1	0	49	2	46	1	0
Tunica-Biloxi Tribal	2	0	1		0	1	115	4	105	6	0
MAINE											
State Agencies											
Bureau of Capitol Police	2	0	0		0	2	13	0	13	0	0
Drug Enforcement Agency											
Androscoggin County	0	0	0		0	0	0	0	0	0	0
Aroostook County	0	0	0		0	0	0	0	0	0	0

Table 9. Offenses Known to Law Enforcement, by Selected State, Tribal, and Other Agencies, 2016—Continued

(Number.)

State/other agency unit/office	Violent crime	Murder and nonnegligent manslaughter	Rape (revised definition)[1]	Rape (legacy definition)[2]	Robbery	Aggravated assault	Property crime	Burglary	Larceny-theft	Motor vehicle theft	Arson[3]
Cumberland County	0	0	0		0	0	0	0	0	0	0
Franklin County	0	0	0		0	0	0	0	0	0	0
Hancock County	0	0	0		0	0	0	0	0	0	0
Kennebec County	0	0	0		0	0	0	0	0	0	0
Knox County	0	0	0		0	0	0	0	0	0	0
Lincoln County	0	0	0		0	0	0	0	0	0	0
Oxford County	0	0	0		0	0	0	0	0	0	0
Penobscot County	0	0	0		0	0	0	0	0	0	0
Piscataquis County	0	0	0		0	0	0	0	0	0	0
Sagadahoc County	0	0	0		0	0	0	0	0	0	0
Somerset County	0	0	0		0	0	0	0	0	0	0
Waldo County	0	0	0		0	0	0	0	0	0	0
Washington County	0	0	0		0	0	0	0	0	0	0
York County	0	0	0		0	0	0	0	0	0	0
State Fire Marshal											
Androscoggin County	0	0	0		0	0	0	0	0	0	5
Aroostook County	0	0	0		0	0	0	0	0	0	8
Cumberland County	0	0	0		0	0	0	0	0	0	9
Franklin County	0	0	0		0	0	0	0	0	0	6
Hancock County	0	0	0		0	0	0	0	0	0	9
Kennebec County	0	0	0		0	0	0	0	0	0	23
Knox County	0	0	0		0	0	0	0	0	0	6
Lincoln County	0	0	0		0	0	0	0	0	0	3
Oxford County	0	0	0		0	0	0	0	0	0	12
Penobscot County	0	0	0		0	0	0	0	0	0	17
Piscataquis County	0	0	0		0	0	0	0	0	0	5
Sagadahoc County	0	0	0		0	0	0	0	0	0	8
Somerset County	0	0	0		0	0	1	1	0	0	6
Waldo County	0	0	0		0	0	0	0	0	0	8
Washington County	0	0	0		0	0	0	0	0	0	4
York County	0	0	0		0	0	0	0	0	0	19
State Police Computer Crimes Task Force											
Androscoggin County	0	0	0		0	0	0	0	0	0	0
Aroostook County	0	0	0		0	0	0	0	0	0	0
Cumberland County	0	0	0		0	0	0	0	0	0	0
Franklin County	0	0	0		0	0	0	0	0	0	0
Hancock County	0	0	0		0	0	0	0	0	0	0
Kennebec County	0	0	0		0	0	0	0	0	0	0
Knox County	0	0	0		0	0	0	0	0	0	0
Lincoln County	0	0	0		0	0	0	0	0	0	0
Oxford County	0	0	0		0	0	0	0	0	0	0
Penobscot County	0	0	0		0	0	0	0	0	0	0
Piscataquis County	0	0	0		0	0	0	0	0	0	0
Sagadahoc County	0	0	0		0	0	0	0	0	0	0
Somerset County	0	0	0		0	0	0	0	0	0	0
Waldo County	0	0	0		0	0	0	0	0	0	0
Washington County	0	0	0		0	0	0	0	0	0	0
York County	0	0	0		0	0	0	0	0	0	0
State Police											
Androscoggin County	3	0	0		0	3	49	18	29	2	0
Aroostook County	14	1	3		0	10	145	36	98	11	0
Cumberland County	5	2	0		0	3	19	4	13	2	0
Franklin County	4	0	0		0	4	35	13	20	2	0
Hancock County	14	0	4		1	9	126	55	66	5	0
Kennebec County	22	0	5		2	15	229	57	151	21	0
Knox County	3	0	1		0	2	2	1	1	0	0
Lincoln County	1	0	0		0	1	5	1	4	0	0
Oxford County	2	1	1		0	0	37	12	22	3	0
Penobscot County	13	0	0		2	11	213	118	85	10	0
Piscataquis County	0	0	0		0	0	1	0	1	0	0
Sagadahoc County	0	0	0		0	0	1	0	1	0	0
Somerset County	11	1	1		0	9	87	14	70	3	0
Waldo County	3	0	1		0	2	85	24	56	5	0
Washington County	8	0	0		0	8	102	25	73	4	0
York County	17	1	1		2	13	162	69	83	10	0
Tribal Agencies											
Passamaquoddy Pleasant Point Tribal	10	0	2		0	8	17	6	10	1	0
MARYLAND											
State Agencies											
Comptroller of the Treasury, Field Enforcement Division	0	0	0		0	0	0	0	0	0	0
Department of Public Safety and Correctional Services, Internal Investigations Unit	355	0	1		0	354	2	0	2	0	
General Services, Annapolis, Anne Arundel County	1	0	0		0	1	10	0	10	0	0
Maryland State Police Statewide	3	0	0		3	0	1	0	1	0	0
Natural Resources Police	12	0	0		0	12	160	17	140	3	26
Springfield Hospital	0	0	0		0	0	5	0	5	0	0
State Fire Marshal	4	0	0		0	4	0	0	0	0	0
State Police											
Allegany County	20	3	0		2	15	321	62	247	12	9
Anne Arundel County	8	1	0		0	7	36	2	29	5	0

Table 9. Offenses Known to Law Enforcement, by Selected State, Tribal, and Other Agencies, 2016—Continued

(Number.)

State/other agency unit/office	Violent crime	Murder and nonnegligent manslaughter	Rape (revised definition)[1]	Rape (legacy definition)[2]	Robbery	Aggravated assault	Property crime	Burglary	Larceny-theft	Motor vehicle theft	Arson[3]
Baltimore City	0	0	0		0	0	0	0	0	0	0
Baltimore County	17	0	0		0	17	31	1	22	8	1
Calvert County	18	0	0		2	16	114	15	95	4	9
Caroline County	13	0	1		1	11	67	26	34	7	4
Carroll County	49	0	0		19	30	362	55	296	11	5
Cecil County	81	1	1		8	71	688	168	477	43	5
Charles County	5	0	0		0	5	5	0	5	0	0
Dorchester County	11	0	0		1	10	32	11	21	0	1
Frederick County	49	0	1		4	44	141	42	88	11	1
Garrett County	14	0	5		2	7	107	38	61	8	5
Harford County	30	0	0		5	25	228	10	209	9	21
Howard County	9	0	0		1	8	15	0	12	3	0
Kent County	4	0	0		0	4	5	2	3	0	1
Montgomery County	2	0	0		0	2	2	0	2	0	0
Prince George's County	3	0	0		0	3	38	0	25	13	0
Queen Anne's County	36	0	1		2	33	74	15	53	6	10
Somerset County	31	1	6		5	19	198	66	120	12	4
St. Mary's County	22	0	5		3	14	192	27	160	5	25
Talbot County	7	0	0		0	7	45	13	26	6	0
Wicomico County	53	1	4		7	41	201	82	108	11	5
Worcester County	12	0	1		1	10	123	31	87	5	2
Transit Administration	84	0	0		43	41	151	3	138	10	0
Transportation Authority	8	0	0		2	6	127	2	96	29	0
Other Agencies											
Maryland-National Capital Park Police, Montgomery County	19	0	1		10	8	95	7	86	2	1
MASSACHUSETTS											
State Agencies											
Division of Law Enforcement, Environmental Polic	9	0	0		1	8	24	7	11	6	2
Massachusetts Bay Transportation Authority											
Bristol County	0	0	0		0	0	12	0	5	7	
Essex County	6	0	0		5	1	11	0	9	2	
Middlesex County	22	0	0		10	12	147	4	141	2	
Norfolk County	12	0	0		4	8	53	1	46	6	
Plymouth County	0	0	0		0	0	9	0	8	1	
Suffolk County	216	0	1		128	87	286	16	265	5	
Worcester County	0	0	0		0	0	2	0	2	0	
State Police											
Barnstable County	0	0	0		0	0	0	0	0	0	
Berkshire County	3	0	0		0	3	54	28	26	0	
Bristol County	7	0	0		0	7	6	0	3	3	
Dukes County	0	0	0		0	0	0	0	0	0	
Franklin County	5	0	1		0	4	0	0	0	0	
Hampden County	22	0	0		0	22	9	0	2	7	
Hampshire County	6	0	0		0	6	0	0	0	0	
Norfolk County	22	0	0		0	22	12	0	3	9	
Plymouth County	0	0	0		0	0	0	0	0	0	
Worcester County	4	0	0		0	4	6	0	4	2	
MICHIGAN											
State Agencies											
State Police											
Alcona County	4	0	3		0	1	1	1	0	0	0
Alger County	11	0	4		0	7	26	7	17	2	0
Allegan County	112	2	50		3	57	314	99	203	12	3
Alpena County	60	3	30		0	27	146	33	107	6	1
Antrim County	5	0	5		0	0	24	7	16	1	0
Arenac County	11	0	11		0	0	9	3	5	1	0
Baraga County	13	0	4		0	9	18	4	14	0	0
Barry County	37	1	12		0	24	101	34	65	2	1
Bay County	119	2	41		3	73	243	76	137	30	3
Benzie County	4	0	4		0	0	8	2	6	0	0
Berrien County	47	5	15		3	24	163	53	97	13	2
Branch County	45	1	20		0	24	176	99	57	20	2
Calhoun County	107	0	35		0	72	321	143	153	25	4
Cass County	19	0	7		1	11	44	23	19	2	0
Charlevoix County	4	0	2		0	2	11	0	10	1	2
Cheboygan County	14	0	10		0	4	23	12	11	0	0
Chippewa County	52	0	18		0	34	68	26	39	3	0
Clare County	25	0	13		0	12	23	11	11	1	1
Clinton County	6	0	4		0	2	13	5	8	0	0
Crawford County	7	0	2		0	5	21	9	11	1	1
Delta County	25	0	16		1	8	67	24	36	7	0
Dickinson County	8	0	6		0	2	51	13	32	6	1
Eaton County	22	0	13		0	9	40	12	23	5	0
Emmet County	10	0	3		0	7	48	6	37	5	0
Genesee County	115	0	51		2	62	305	93	186	26	4
Gladwin County	13	0	8		0	5	12	6	6	0	0
Gogebic County	9	0	4		0	5	39	13	22	4	0
Grand Traverse County	18	0	13		0	5	70	13	56	1	0
Gratiot County	25	0	8		0	17	42	11	27	4	0

Table 9. Offenses Known to Law Enforcement, by Selected State, Tribal, and Other Agencies, 2016—Continued

(Number.)

State/other agency unit/office	Violent crime	Murder and nonnegligent manslaughter	Rape (revised definition)[1]	Rape (legacy definition)[2]	Robbery	Aggravated assault	Property crime	Burglary	Larceny-theft	Motor vehicle theft	Arson[3]
Hillsdale County	37	0	11		0	26	113	51	47	15	2
Houghton County	41	0	18		1	22	104	33	64	7	0
Huron County	1	0	1		0	0	6	3	2	1	0
Ingham County	53	1	25		0	27	86	23	53	10	0
Ionia County	50	0	24		0	26	117	21	90	6	3
Iosco County	45	1	23		1	20	121	49	65	7	2
Iron County	3	0	2		0	1	18	5	11	2	1
Isabella County	104	1	65		0	38	191	43	139	9	3
Jackson County	94	2	30		0	62	180	68	92	20	3
Kalamazoo County	23	5	5		0	13	40	9	30	1	0
Kalkaska County	10	0	4		0	6	39	12	25	2	0
Kent County	98	0	44		2	52	236	58	158	20	1
Keweenaw County	0	0	0		0	0	1	0	1	0	1
Lake County	12	0	9		0	3	16	8	8	0	0
Lapeer County	34	0	21		1	12	85	37	45	3	0
Leelanau County	3	0	1		0	2	2	2	0	0	0
Lenawee County	46	0	21		0	25	87	37	43	7	0
Livingston County	98	1	31		7	59	329	115	188	26	3
Luce County	9	0	4		0	5	29	9	16	4	0
Mackinac County	14	0	9		0	5	54	11	43	0	0
Macomb County	40	0	10		1	29	70	22	37	11	3
Manistee County	14	0	6		1	7	59	22	35	2	0
Marquette County	57	1	12		0	44	134	32	93	9	1
Mason County	10	0	3		0	7	45	13	30	2	0
Mecosta County	9	0	8		0	1	47	5	41	1	0
Menominee County	9	0	7		0	2	28	17	11	0	0
Midland County	8	0	5		0	3	10	3	6	1	0
Missaukee County	8	0	5		0	3	7	1	5	1	0
Monroe County	94	1	43		2	48	196	66	113	17	2
Montcalm County	164	1	65		1	97	359	120	220	19	7
Montmorency County	3	0	1		0	2	9	6	2	1	0
Muskegon County	73	0	28		1	44	249	63	167	19	0
Newaygo County	58	0	20		0	38	125	38	85	2	0
Oakland County	152	3	36		12	101	267	63	157	47	7
Oceana County	114	1	47		2	64	227	78	140	9	2
Ogemaw County	82	1	47		2	32	167	66	96	5	2
Ontonagon County	6	0	4		0	2	16	8	6	2	0
Osceola County	24	0	11		0	13	24	7	16	1	1
Oscoda County	1	0	1		0	0	4	3	1	0	1
Otsego County	59	1	38		0	20	190	51	130	9	2
Ottawa County	7	0	1		1	5	3	0	3	0	0
Presque Isle County	4	1	3		0	0	0	0	0	0	1
Roscommon County	41	0	21		0	20	123	42	78	3	1
Saginaw County	77	2	18		3	54	72	23	38	11	3
Sanilac County	29	0	6		2	21	44	10	33	1	0
Schoolcraft County	19	0	12		0	7	27	8	19	0	2
Shiawassee County	72	0	32		2	38	257	68	175	14	0
St. Clair County	7	0	4		0	3	32	13	18	1	0
St. Joseph County	32	0	10		0	22	142	69	67	6	1
Tuscola County	69	0	29		2	38	123	46	72	5	1
Van Buren County	76	5	25		0	46	190	60	113	17	2
Washtenaw County	50	0	11		4	35	119	43	64	12	3
Wayne County	87	3	15		8	61	105	4	79	22	0
Wexford County	80	0	40		1	39	242	67	169	6	1
Tribal Agencies											
Little River Band of Ottawa Indians	1	0	0		0	1	17	0	17	0	0
Nottawaseppi Huron Band of Potawatomi	7	0	0		2	5	101	11	88	2	0
Other Agencies											
Bishop International Airport	0	0	0		0	0	19	0	3	16	0
Capitol Region Airport Authority	0	0	0		0	0	5	0	3	2	0
Genesee County Parks and Recreation	11	0	0		6	5	17	4	10	3	2
Gerald R. Ford International Airport											
Huron-Clinton Metropolitan Authority	0	0	0		0	0	9	0	5	4	0
Hudson Mills Metropark	0	0	0		0	0	1	0	1	0	0
Kensington Metropark	0	0	0		0	0	3	0	3	0	0
Lower Huron Metropark	0	0	0		0	0	18	0	18	0	0
Stony Creek Metropark	1	0	0		0	1	13	0	13	0	0
Wayne County Airport	4	0	0		1	3	240	1	135	104	1
MINNESOTA											
State Agencies											
Bureau of Criminal Apprehension	0	0	0		0	0	0	0	0	0	0
Capitol Security, St. Paul	0	0	0		0	0	31	1	28	2	0
Department of Natural Resources Enforcement Division	0	0	0		0	0	0	0	0	0	0
Minnesota State Patrol	0	0	0		0	0	0	0	0	0	0
State Patrol											
Brainerd	0	0	0		0	0	0	0	0	0	0
Detroit Lakes	0	0	0		0	0	0	0	0	0	0
Duluth	0	0	0		0	0	0	0	0	0	0
Golden Valley	0	0	0		0	0	0	0	0	0	0
Mankato	0	0	0		0	0	0	0	0	0	0
Marshall	0	0	0		0	0	0	0	0	0	0

Table 9. Offenses Known to Law Enforcement, by Selected State, Tribal, and Other Agencies, 2016—Continued

(Number.)

State/other agency unit/office	Violent crime	Murder and nonnegligent manslaughter	Rape (revised definition)[1]	Rape (legacy definition)[2]	Robbery	Aggravated assault	Property crime	Burglary	Larceny-theft	Motor vehicle theft	Arson[3]
Oakdale	0	0	0		0	0	0	0	0	0	0
Rochester	0	0	0		0	0	0	0	0	0	0
St. Cloud	0	0	0		0	0	0	0	0	0	0
Thief River Falls	0	0	0		0	0	0	0	0	0	0
Virginia	0	0	0		0	0	0	0	0	0	0
Tribal Agencies											
Fond du Lac Tribal	27	0	5		2	20	410	49	340	21	2
Mille Lacs Tribal	11	1	0		4	6	115	28	79	8	2
Upper Sioux Community	0	0	0		0	0	2	0	2	0	0
Other Agencies											
Minneapolis-St. Paul International Airport	5	0	2		1	2	318	0	260	58	0
Three Rivers Park District	5	0	1		2	2	64	2	62	0	1
MISSISSIPPI											
State Agencies											
Department of Marine Resources	2	0		0	0	2	1	0	1	0	0
Tribal Agencies											
Choctaw Tribal	153	0	5		0	148	223	33	190	0	3
Other Agencies											
Singing River Health System	0	0		0	0	0	0	0	0	0	0
MISSOURI											
State Agencies											
Capitol Police	1	0	0		0	1	14	0	14	0	0
Department of Conservation	1	0	0		0	1	0	0	0	0	0
Department of Revenue, Compliance and Investigation Bureau	0	0	0		0	0	0	0	0	0	0
Department of Social Services, State Technical Assistance Team	2	0	2		0	0	0	0	0	0	0
Division of Alcohol and Tobacco Control	0	0	0		0	0	0	0	0	0	0
Gaming Commission, Enforcement Division	7	0	0		2	5	214	0	211	3	1
State Fire Marshal	0	0	0		0	0	0	0	0	0	234
State Highway Patrol											
Jefferson City	18	3	1		2	12	65	0	55	10	0
Kirkwood	5	0	0		0	5	14	0	1	13	0
Lee's Summit	14	0	0		0	14	21	4	6	11	0
Macon	13	1	1		0	11	7	2	3	2	0
Poplar Bluff	5	0	0		0	5	10	0	2	8	0
Rolla	4	1	0		0	3	4	1	0	3	0
Springfield	8	0	0		0	8	45	1	29	15	1
St. Joseph	10	0	1		1	8	2	0	0	2	0
Willow Springs	3	0	0		0	3	6	1	1	4	0
State Park Rangers	3	0	0		0	3	85	5	79	1	2
Other Agencies											
Clay County Drug Task Force	0	0	0		0	0	0	0	0	0	0
Clay County Park Authority	1	0	0		0	1	6	0	6	0	0
Jackson County Drug Task Force	0	0	0		0	0	0	0	0	0	0
Jackson County Park Rangers	0	0	0		0	0	0	0	0	0	0
Kansas City International Airport	0	0	0		0	0	72	2	60	10	0
Lambert-St. Louis International Airport	2	0	0		0	2	147	0	143	4	0
Platte County Multi-Jurisdictional Enforcement Group	0	0	0		0	0	0	0	0	0	0
Springfield-Branson Airport	0	0	0		0	0	30	0	15	15	0
Springfield-Greene County Park Rangers	0	0	0		0	0	13	2	10	1	0
St. Charles County Park Rangers	0	0	0		0	0	0	0	0	0	0
Terminal Railroad	0	0	0		0	0	0	0	0	0	0
Western Missouri Cyber Crimes Task Force	0	0	0		0	0	0	0	0	0	0
MONTANA											
Tribal Agencies											
Blackfeet Agency	120	0	18		13	89	79	52	0	27	0
Crow Agency	61	1	6		2	52	387	57	156	174	6
Fort Belknap Tribal	29	0	2		0	27	42	5	36	1	1
Fort Peck Assiniboine and Sioux Tribes	58	3	8		2	45	94	26	40	28	2
Northern Cheyenne Agency	55	2	8		0	45	24	6	10	8	1
Rocky Boy's Tribal	120	1	12		2	105	157	34	97	26	6
NEBRASKA											
State Agencies											
Nebraska State Patrol	5	0	0		0	5	10	1	9	0	0
State Patrol											
Adams County	0	0	0		0	0	0	0	0	0	0
Antelope County	0	0	0		0	0	0	0	0	0	0
Arthur County	0	0	0		0	0	0	0	0	0	0
Banner County	0	0	0		0	0	0	0	0	0	0
Blaine County	0	0	0		0	0	0	0	0	0	0
Boone County	0	0	0		0	0	0	0	0	0	0
Box Butte County	0	0	0		0	0	2	1	1	0	0
Boyd County	0	0	0		0	0	0	0	0	0	0
Brown County	0	0	0		0	0	0	0	0	0	0
Buffalo County	0	0	0		0	0	1	0	1	0	0
Burt County	0	0	0		0	0	0	0	0	0	0
Butler County	0	0	0		0	0	0	0	0	0	0

Table 9. Offenses Known to Law Enforcement, by Selected State, Tribal, and Other Agencies, 2016—Continued

(Number.)

State/other agency unit/office	Violent crime	Murder and nonnegligent manslaughter	Rape (revised definition)[1]	Rape (legacy definition)[2]	Robbery	Aggravated assault	Property crime	Burglary	Larceny-theft	Motor vehicle theft	Arson[3]
Cass County	1	0	0		1	0	0	0	0	0	0
Cedar County	0	0	0		0	0	0	0	0	0	0
Chase County	0	0	0		0	0	0	0	0	0	0
Cherry County	0	0	0		0	0	0	0	0	0	0
Cheyenne County	0	0	0		0	0	1	1	0	0	0
Clay County	0	0	0		0	0	0	0	0	0	0
Colfax County	0	0	0		0	0	0	0	0	0	0
Cuming County	0	0	0		0	0	0	0	0	0	0
Custer County	0	0	0		0	0	0	0	0	0	0
Dakota County	0	0	0		0	0	0	0	0	0	0
Dawes County	0	0	0		0	0	2	1	1	0	0
Dawson County	0	0	0		0	0	0	0	0	0	0
Deuel County	0	0	0		0	0	0	0	0	0	0
Dixon County	0	0	0		0	0	0	0	0	0	0
Dodge County	0	0	0		0	0	1	0	1	0	0
Douglas County	0	0	0		0	0	4	0	1	3	0
Dundy County	0	0	0		0	0	0	0	0	0	0
Fillmore County	0	0	0		0	0	0	0	0	0	0
Franklin County	0	0	0		0	0	0	0	0	0	0
Frontier County	0	0	0		0	0	1	0	1	0	0
Furnas County	0	0	0		0	0	0	0	0	0	0
Gage County	0	0	0		0	0	0	0	0	0	0
Garden County	0	0	0		0	0	0	0	0	0	0
Garfield County	1	0	0		1	0	1	0	1	0	0
Gosper County	0	0	0		0	0	0	0	0	0	0
Grant County	0	0	0		0	0	0	0	0	0	0
Greeley County	0	0	0		0	0	0	0	0	0	0
Hall County	1	0	0		0	1	6	0	6	0	0
Hamilton County	0	0	0		0	0	0	0	0	0	0
Harlan County	0	0	0		0	0	0	0	0	0	0
Hayes County	0	0	0		0	0	0	0	0	0	0
Hitchcock County	1	0	0		0	1	0	0	0	1	0
Holt County	0	0	0		0	0	1	0	0	0	0
Hooker County	0	0	0		0	0	0	0	0	0	0
Howard County	0	0	0		0	0	0	0	0	0	0
Jefferson County	0	0	0		0	0	0	0	0	0	0
Johnson County	0	0	0		0	0	0	0	0	0	0
Kearney County	0	0	0		0	0	0	0	0	0	0
Keith County	1	0	0		0	1	1	0	0	1	0
Keya Paha County	0	0	0		0	0	0	0	0	0	0
Kimball County	0	0	0		0	0	1	0	1	0	0
Knox County	0	0	0		0	0	1	1	0	0	0
Lancaster County	0	0	0		0	0	1	0	1	0	0
Lincoln County	2	0	0		0	2	2	0	1	1	0
Logan County	0	0	0		0	0	0	0	0	0	0
Loup County	0	0	0		0	0	0	0	0	0	0
Madison County	0	0	0		0	0	2	0	2	0	0
McPherson County	0	0	0		0	0	0	0	0	0	0
Merrick County	0	0	0		0	0	0	0	0	0	0
Morrill County	0	0	0		0	0	1	0	1	0	0
Nance County	0	0	0		0	0	0	0	0	0	0
Nemaha County	1	0	0		0	1	0	0	0	0	0
Nuckolls County	0	0	0		0	0	0	0	0	0	0
Otoe County	0	0	0		0	0	1	0	1	0	0
Pawnee County	0	0	0		0	0	0	0	0	0	0
Perkins County	0	0	0		0	0	1	0	0	1	0
Phelps County	0	0	0		0	0	0	0	0	0	0
Pierce County	0	0	0		0	0	0	0	0	0	0
Platte County	0	0	0		0	0	0	0	0	0	0
Polk County	0	0	0		0	0	0	0	0	0	0
Red Willow County	1	0	0		0	1	0	0	0	0	0
Richardson County	0	0	0		0	0	0	0	0	0	0
Rock County	0	0	0		0	0	0	0	0	0	0
Saline County	0	0	0		0	0	0	0	0	0	0
Sarpy County	1	0	0		0	1	1	0	1	0	0
Saunders County	0	0	0		0	0	1	0	0	1	0
Scotts Bluff County	1	0	0		0	1	5	1	4	0	0
Seward County	0	0	0		0	0	0	0	0	0	0
Sheridan County	0	0	0		0	0	1	0	1	0	0
Sherman County	0	0	0		0	0	0	0	0	0	0
Sioux County	0	0	0		0	0	0	0	0	0	0
Stanton County	0	0	0		0	0	0	0	0	0	0
Thayer County	0	0	0		0	0	0	0	0	0	0
Thomas County	0	0	0		0	0	0	0	0	0	0
Thurston County	0	0	0		0	0	1	0	1	0	0
Valley County	0	0	0		0	0	0	0	0	0	0
Washington County	0	0	0		0	0	0	0	0	0	0
Wayne County	1	0	0		0	1	1	1	0	0	0
Webster County	0	0	0		0	0	0	0	0	0	0
Wheeler County	0	0	0		0	0	0	0	0	0	0
York County	1	0	0		0	1	1	0	1	0	0

Table 9. Offenses Known to Law Enforcement, by Selected State, Tribal, and Other Agencies, 2016—Continued

(Number.)

State/other agency unit/office	Violent crime	Murder and nonnegligent manslaughter	Rape (revised definition)[1]	Rape (legacy definition)[2]	Robbery	Aggravated assault	Property crime	Burglary	Larceny-theft	Motor vehicle theft	Arson[3]
NEVADA											
State Agencies											
Capitol Police	3	0	0		2	1	24	5	17	2	0
Department of Public Safety, Investigative Division	0	0	0		0	0	0	0	0	0	0
Highway Patrol											
Northeastern Division	0	0	0		0	0	0	0	0	0	0
Northwestern Division	1	0	0		0	1	3	2	1	0	0
Southern Division	3	0	0		0	3	1	0	1	0	0
Secretary of State Securities Division, Enforcement Section	0	0	0		0	0	0	0	0	0	0
State Fire Marshal	0	0	0		0	0	0	0	0	0	6
Tribal Agencies											
Fallon Tribal	8	0	0		0	8	15	1	11	3	0
Las Vegas Paiute Tribal	1	0	0		0	1	18	0	18	0	
Lovelock Paiute Tribal	2	1	0		0	1	3	1	2	0	
Moapa Tribal	10	0	0		0	10	88	6	75	7	
Pyramid Lake Tribal	15	0	2		1	12	41	7	28	6	
Other Agencies											
Clark County School District	146	0	20		28	98	1,140	158	963	19	29
Humboldt County School District	0	0	0		0	0	3	1	2	0	0
Las Vegas Fire and Rescue, Arson Bomb Unit	0	0	0		0	0	0	0	0	0	63
North Las Vegas Fire Department Arson Investigations	0	0	0		0	0	0	0	0	0	62
Reno Municipal Court Marshal	0	0	0		0	0	0	0	0	0	0
Reno Tahoe Airport Authority	0	0	0		0	0	38	4	27	7	0
Washoe County School District	11	0	0		1	10	132	18	114	0	1
NEW HAMPSHIRE											
State Agencies											
Liquor Commission	0	0	0		0	0	4	0	4	0	0
State Police											
Belknap County	0	0	0		0	0	1	0	1	0	0
Carroll County	0	0	0		0	0	2	0	1	1	0
Cheshire County	8	0	2		0	6	25	9	13	3	1
Coos County	7	0	3		0	4	79	33	42	4	1
Grafton County	8	1	1		0	6	53	26	21	6	0
Hillsborough County	15	0	0		1	14	6	2	3	1	0
Merrimack County	11	0	2		1	8	40	14	21	5	2
Rockingham County	4	0	1		0	3	3	0	2	1	0
Strafford County	1	0	0		0	1	3	1	1	1	0
Sullivan County	9	0	2		0	7	16	6	7	3	0
NEW JERSEY											
State Agencies											
New Jersey Transit Police	52	0	0		34	18	371	5	363	3	2
Palisades Interstate Parkway	0	0	0		0	0	1	0	1	0	0
Port Authority of New York and New Jersey	41	0	1		10	30	441	4	417	20	1
State Police	0	0	0		0	0	0	0	0	0	0
Atlantic County	41	0	2		12	27	663	62	587	14	1
Bergen County	16	1	0		2	13	46	1	41	4	0
Burlington County	37	1	7		16	13	309	105	186	18	3
Camden County	7	1	0		1	5	16	3	11	2	
Cape May County	29	0	3		3	23	222	65	148	9	1
Cumberland County	57	2	14		10	31	553	199	337	17	6
Essex County	10	0	0		3	7	7	1	5	1	0
Hunterdon County	14	0	3		3	8	119	44	69	6	1
Mercer County	11	0	4		1	6	53	8	43	2	1
Middlesex County	10	0	0		1	9	29	0	27	2	0
Monmouth County	11	0	2		2	7	141	49	87	5	0
Morris County	7	0	1		2	4	25	8	14	3	0
Ocean County	5	0	2		1	2	38	7	31	0	0
Salem County	37	0	5		11	21	237	90	132	15	0
Sussex County	28	0	7		2	19	385	115	255	15	1
Union County	4	0	0		1	3	14	1	7	6	1
Warren County	19	1	3		2	13	115	36	72	7	0
Other Agencies											
Prosecutor											
Atlantic County	0	0	0		0	0	0	0	0	0	0
Bergen County	0	0	0		0	0	0	0	0	0	0
Burlington County	0	0	0		0	0	0	0	0	0	0
Camden County	0	0	0		0	0	0	0	0	0	0
Cape May County	0	0	0		0	0	0	0	0	0	0
Cumberland County	0	0	0		0	0	0	0	0	0	0
Essex County	0	0	0		0	0	0	0	0	0	0
Gloucester County	0	0	0		0	0	0	0	0	0	0
Hudson County	0	0	0		0	0	0	0	0	0	0
Hunterdon County	0	0	0		0	0	0	0	0	0	0
Mercer County	0	0	0		0	0	0	0	0	0	0
Middlesex County	0	0	0		0	0	0	0	0	0	0
Monmouth County	0	0	0		0	0	0	0	0	0	0
Morris County	0	0	0		0	0	0	0	0	0	0
Ocean County	0	0	0		0	0	0	0	0	0	0

Table 9. Offenses Known to Law Enforcement, by Selected State, Tribal, and Other Agencies, 2016—Continued

(Number.)

State/other agency unit/office	Violent crime	Murder and nonnegligent manslaughter	Rape (revised definition)[1]	Rape (legacy definition)[2]	Robbery	Aggravated assault	Property crime	Burglary	Larceny-theft	Motor vehicle theft	Arson[3]
Passaic County	0	0	0		0	0	0	0	0	0	0
Salem County	0	0	0		0	0	0	0	0	0	0
Somerset County	0	0	0		0	0	0	0	0	0	0
Sussex County	0	0	0		0	0	0	0	0	0	0
Union County	0	0	0		0	0	0	0	0	0	0
Warren County	0	0	0		0	0	0	0	0	0	0
Park Police											
Morris County	0	0	0		0	0	10	0	10	0	0
Union County	47	0	1		4	42	48	3	43	2	0
NEW MEXICO											
State Agencies											
Motor Transportation Police	11	0		0	0	11	10	0	8	2	
New Mexico State Police	396	3		49	9	335	527	136	297	94	
Tribal Agencies											
Acoma Tribal	6	0	0		0	6	7	1	4	2	0
Jicarilla Apache Tribal	21	0	0		1	20	0	0	0	0	0
Laguna Tribal	36	0	5		5	26	96	10	65	21	2
Mescalero Tribal	10	0	1		0	9	7	2	5	0	0
Northern Pueblos Agency	6	0	0		0	6	9	4	4	1	1
Pojoaque Tribal	14	0	1		1	12	83	11	65	7	0
Ramah Navajo Tribal	6	0	0		0	6	4	4	0	0	2
Santa Ana Tribal	12	1	0		0	11	62	7	44	11	0
Taos Pueblo	2	0	1		0	1	8	4	3	1	0
Tesuque Pueblo	2	0	0		0	2	6	0	6	0	0
Zuni Tribal	16	0	1		0	15	0	0	0	0	0
NEW YORK											
State Agencies											
State Park											
Allegany Region	0	0	0		0	0	12	3	9	0	0
Central Region	0	0	0		0	0	23	2	21	0	0
Finger Lakes Region	0	0	0		0	0	30	5	25	0	0
Genesee Region	2	2	0		0	0	7	2	5	0	
Long Island Region	13	0	1		3	9	116	2	113	1	
New York City Region	6	0	2		2	2	89	2	84	3	0
Niagara Region	7	0	0		7	0	43	1	42	0	0
Palisades Region	2	0	0		0	2	18	3	15	0	0
Taconic Region	1	0	0		0	1	22	2	20	0	0
Thousand Island Region	0	0	0		0	0	26	1	24	1	0
State Police											
Albany County	15	2	9		2	2	122	9	110	3	3
Allegany County	50	0	30		0	20	259	82	161	16	2
Broome County	82	0	48		4	30	516	127	371	18	1
Cattaraugus County	42	0	30		1	11	248	71	169	8	2
Cayuga County	32	0	15		0	17	235	56	168	11	0
Chautauqua County	24	0	17		2	5	154	33	114	7	0
Chemung County	51	0	21		1	29	252	42	201	9	0
Chenango County	52	0	30		1	21	199	61	131	7	1
Clinton County	84	0	53		2	29	803	148	639	16	7
Columbia County	58	0	29		3	26	143	36	105	2	1
Cortland County	13	0	9		0	4	97	17	78	2	1
Delaware County	33	0	13		1	19	174	53	120	1	0
Duchess County	166	0	52		9	105	469	83	372	14	2
Erie County	44	1	23		1	19	293	28	257	8	
Essex County	39	0	20		1	18	243	73	166	4	8
Franklin County	59	0	43		1	15	278	59	211	8	6
Fulton County	29	0	20		2	7	72	12	59	1	0
Genesee County	14	0	9		1	4	137	25	107	5	0
Greene County	82	0	29		2	51	288	90	187	11	9
Hamilton County	2	0	1		0	1	39	15	23	1	0
Herkimer County	28	0	15		1	12	257	82	160	15	2
Jefferson County	58	1	35		1	21	549	100	432	17	7
Lewis County	20	0	16		0	4	106	37	68	1	0
Livingston County	24	1	8		1	14	32	7	22	3	0
Madison County	40	0	30		2	8	200	43	147	10	3
Monroe County	16	0	10		1	5	58	1	52	5	0
Montgomery County	12	0	7		0	5	113	19	91	3	0
Nassau County	6	0	0		0	6	5	0	3	2	1
New York County	3	0	1		0	2	11	0	11	0	0
Niagara County	29	0	16		4	9	228	39	180	9	0
Oneida County	117	1	51		3	62	449	108	319	22	3
Onondaga County	52	0	28		4	20	672	104	538	30	3
Ontario County	29	0	22		0	7	293	39	244	10	4
Orange County	138	3	82		12	41	700	76	596	28	7
Orleans County	15	0	10		1	4	65	15	46	4	0
Oswego County	111	0	71		6	34	683	218	436	29	4
Otsego County	34	0	21		0	13	308	30	273	5	0
Putnam County	13	0	5		1	7	89	18	66	5	1
Rensselaer County	38	0	23		0	15	407	76	300	31	5
Rockland County	5	0	3		1	1	16	1	14	1	0
Saratoga County	80	0	45		8	27	628	60	556	12	0
Schenectady County	10	0	5		0	5	59	4	54	1	1

Table 9. Offenses Known to Law Enforcement, by Selected State, Tribal, and Other Agencies, 2016—Continued

(Number.)

State/other agency unit/office	Violent crime	Murder and nonnegligent manslaughter	Rape (revised definition)[1]	Rape (legacy definition)[2]	Robbery	Aggravated assault	Property crime	Burglary	Larceny-theft	Motor vehicle theft	Arson[3]
Schoharie County	28	0	20		1	7	133	37	86	10	2
Schuyler County	3	0	3		0	0	17	5	10	2	0
Seneca County	29	0	18		0	11	120	23	94	3	1
Steuben County	79	1	43		3	32	485	84	367	34	6
St. Lawrence County	84	0	47		6	31	414	95	300	19	
Suffolk County	30	0	16		3	11	44	10	30	4	0
Sullivan County	95	1	57		2	35	269	87	168	14	2
Tioga County	24	0	18		1	5	84	13	68	3	0
Tompkins County	47	0	26		1	20	242	64	168	10	0
Ulster County	75	0	41		2	32	416	99	311	6	1
Warren County	33	1	19		1	12	234	19	210	5	1
Washington County	36	0	18		0	18	124	25	94	5	3
Wayne County	74	1	40		7	26	527	120	382	25	3
Westchester County	63	0	20		8	35	443	58	372	13	1
Wyoming County	17	0	4		0	13	19	2	16	1	0
Yates County	1	0	1		0	0	17	4	13	0	0
Tribal Agencies											
Oneida Indian Nation	10	0	0		0	10	192	2	190	0	1
St. Regis Tribal	11	0	0		0	11	31	4	18	9	0
Other Agencies											
New York City Department of Environmental Protection Police											
Delaware County	0	0		0	0	0	8	0	8	0	0
Schoharie County	0	0		0	0	0	0	0	0	0	0
Sullivan County	0	0		0	0	0	3	0	3	0	0
Ulster County	0	0		0	0	0	0	0	0	0	0
Westchester County, Croton-Kensico	0	0		0	0	0	3	0	3	0	0
Westchester County, Hillview	0	0		0	0	0	0	0	0	0	0
New York City Metropolitan Transportation Authority	82	0	1		40	41	632	35	593	4	0
Onondaga County Parks	0	0		0	0	0	59	0	59	0	0
NORTH CAROLINA											
State Agencies											
Department of Health and Human Resources	0	0		0	0	0	2	0	2	0	0
North Carolina Highway Patrol	0	0		0	0	0	0	0	0	0	0
State Park Rangers											
Crowders Mountain	0	0		0	0	0	3	0	3	0	0
Hanging Rock	0	0		0	0	0	0	0	0	0	0
Lake Norman	0	0		0	0	0	11	1	10	0	0
Morrow Mountain	0	0		0	0	0	4	0	4	0	0
New River-Mount Jefferson	0	0		0	0	0	0	0	0	0	0
Other Agencies											
Raleigh-Durham International Airport	2	0		0	0	2	126	0	90	36	1
WakeMed Campus Police	19	0		0	2	17	78	0	78	0	0
NORTH DAKOTA											
State Agencies											
North Dakota Highway Patrol	1	0	1		0	0	9	0	1	8	1
Tribal Agencies											
Standing Rock Agency	87	0	10		0	77	20	7	4	9	0
OHIO											
State Agencies											
Ohio Department of Natural Resources	2	0	0		1	1	17	2	15	0	1
Ohio State Highway Patrol	291	1	35		4	251	233	12	179	42	2
Other Agencies											
Cleveland Metropolitan Park District	12	0	5		5	2	164	3	159	2	3
Hamilton County Park District	0	0	0		0	0	66	1	62	3	0
Lake Metroparks	3	0		0	2	1	11	0	11	0	0
Toledo Fire Department, Fire Investigation Unit	0	0	0		0	0	0	0	0	0	152
University Hospitals Portage Medical Center	1	0		0	0	1	2	0	2	0	0
OKLAHOMA											
State Agencies											
Capitol Park Police	0	0	0		0	0	1	0	1	0	0
Oklahoma Highway Patrol	8	4	0		0	4	11	0	3	8	0
Tribal Agencies											
Absentee Shawnee Tribal	3	0	1		0	2	29	9	19	1	0
Anadarko Agency	7	0	0		0	7	47	7	35	5	1
Cherokee Nation	17	0	0		1	16	25	7	8	10	2
Chickasaw Nation	34	0	2		15	17	954	45	842	67	0
Choctaw Nation	33	0	0		0	33	307	21	261	25	0
Citizen Potawatomi Nation	4	0	0		0	4	136	34	92	10	0
Comanche Nation	12	0	1		5	6	86	7	72	7	2
Concho Agency	10	0	0		0	10	20	1	14	5	1
Eastern Shawnee Tribal	0	0	0		0	0	62	0	55	7	0
Iowa Tribal	1	0	0		0	1	17	2	14	1	0
Kickapoo Tribal	1	0	0		0	1	18	2	14	2	0
Miami Agency	0	0	0		0	0	41	2	34	5	0
Miami Tribal	2	0	0		0	2	9	1	6	2	0
Muscogee Nation Tribal	7	1	0		1	5	102	14	64	24	0
Osage Nation	10	1	0		3	6	95	20	59	16	6

Table 9. Offenses Known to Law Enforcement, by Selected State, Tribal, and Other Agencies, 2016—Continued

(Number.)

State/other agency unit/office	Violent crime	Murder and nonnegligent manslaughter	Rape (revised definition)[1]	Rape (legacy definition)[2]	Robbery	Aggravated assault	Property crime	Burglary	Larceny-theft	Motor vehicle theft	Arson[3]
Otoe-Missouria Tribal	7	0	0		0	7	15	3	9	3	0
Pawnee Tribal	0	0	0		0	0	4	0	4	0	
Ponca Tribal	5	0	0		0	5	30	8	17	5	4
Quapaw Tribal	3	0	1		2	0	78	6	67	5	2
Sac and Fox Tribal	3	0	0		0	3	19	3	10	6	0
Seminole Nation Lighthorse	3	0	0		2	1	21	6	14	1	0
Tonkawa Tribal	0	0	0		0	0	12	1	11	0	2
Wyandotte Nation	6	0	0		1	5	46	2	40	4	0
Other Agencies											
Jenks Public Schools	1	0	0		0	1	21	0	20	1	0
McAlester Public Schools	0	0	0		0	0	0	0	0	0	0
Putnam City Campus	1	0	0		0	1	13	2	11	0	0
OREGON											
State Agencies											
Liquor Commission											
Baker County	0	0	0		0	0	0	0	0	0	0
Benton County	0	0	0		0	0	0	0	0	0	0
Clackamas County	0	0	0		0	0	0	0	0	0	0
Clatsop County	0	0	0		0	0	0	0	0	0	0
Coos County	0	0	0		0	0	0	0	0	0	0
Crook County	0	0	0		0	0	0	0	0	0	0
Deschutes County	0	0	0		0	0	0	0	0	0	0
Douglas County	0	0	0		0	0	0	0	0	0	0
Hood River County	0	0	0		0	0	0	0	0	0	0
Jackson County	0	0	0		0	0	0	0	0	0	0
Klamath County	0	0	0		0	0	0	0	0	0	0
Lane County	0	0	0		0	0	0	0	0	0	0
Lincoln County	0	0	0		0	0	0	0	0	0	0
Marion County	0	0	0		0	0	0	0	0	0	0
Multnomah County	0	0	0		0	0	0	0	0	0	0
Polk County	0	0	0		0	0	0	0	0	0	0
Umatilla County	0	0	0		0	0	0	0	0	0	0
Washington County	0	0	0		0	0	0	0	0	0	0
State Police											
Baker County	1	0	1		0	0	0	0	0	0	0
Benton County	3	0	2		0	1	236	5	229	2	2
Clackamas County	11	0	0		2	9	24	0	13	11	1
Clatsop County	12	0	0		0	12	6	0	5	1	0
Columbia County	3	0	0		0	3	6	0	5	1	1
Coos County	14	0	0		0	14	33	1	30	2	1
Crook County	1	0	0		0	1	1	0	1	0	0
Curry County	3	0	0		0	3	17	0	15	2	1
Deschutes County	17	0	0		0	17	13	1	10	2	1
Douglas County	12	0	0		0	12	19	1	17	1	0
Gilliam County	1	0	0		0	1	3	0	3	0	0
Grant County	3	0	0		0	3	4	0	3	1	0
Harney County	3	0	2		0	1	3	1	2	0	0
Hood River County	4	0	0		0	4	3	0	3	0	1
Jackson County	20	1	1		0	18	24	1	11	12	3
Jefferson County	6	0	0		0	6	2	0	1	1	0
Josephine County	59	2	4		1	52	35	9	15	11	12
Klamath County	26	4	2		0	20	30	2	19	9	1
Lake County	1	0	0		0	1	1	0	1	0	0
Lane County	23	0	1		1	21	54	7	43	4	1
Lincoln County	4	0	0		0	4	17	0	16	1	0
Linn County	17	0	0		0	17	18	0	13	5	0
Malheur County	13	1	0		0	12	4	0	3	1	0
Marion County	41	0	1		0	40	83	5	56	22	0
Morrow County	2	0	0		0	2	2	0	2	0	0
Multnomah County	5	0	0		0	5	14	1	10	3	0
Polk County	3	2	0		0	1	3	0	2	1	0
Sherman County	6	0	0		1	5	3	0	2	1	0
Tillamook County	1	0	0		0	1	21	1	16	4	2
Umatilla County	19	0	2		1	16	10	0	10	0	0
Union County	3	0	0		0	3	3	0	2	1	0
Wallowa County	1	0	0		0	1	1	0	1	0	0
Wasco County	2	0	1		0	1	7	0	3	4	1
Washington County	1	0	0		0	1	4	0	3	1	0
Wheeler County	0	0	0		0	0	0	0	0	0	0
Yamhill County	5	0	1		1	3	2	0	2	0	0
Tribal Agencies											
Grand Ronde Tribal	6	0	1		3	2	71	6	62	3	0
Other Agencies											
Port of Portland	3	0	1		0	2	484	1	425	58	1
PENNSYLVANIA											
State Agencies											
Bureau of Forestry											
Adams County	0	0	0		0	0	0	0	0	0	0
Allegheny County	0	0	0		0	0	0	0	0	0	0
Armstrong County	0	0	0		0	0	0	0	0	0	0
Beaver County	0	0	0		0	0	0	0	0	0	1

Table 9. Offenses Known to Law Enforcement, by Selected State, Tribal, and Other Agencies, 2016—Continued

(Number.)

State/other agency unit/office	Violent crime	Murder and nonnegligent manslaughter	Rape (revised definition)[1]	Rape (legacy definition)[2]	Robbery	Aggravated assault	Property crime	Burglary	Larceny-theft	Motor vehicle theft	Arson[3]
Bedford County	0	0	0		0	0	0	0	0	0	3
Berks County	0	0	0		0	0	0	0	0	0	6
Blair County	0	0	0		0	0	0	0	0	0	1
Bradford County	0	0	0		0	0	0	0	0	0	0
Bucks County	0	0	0		0	0	0	0	0	0	0
Butler County	0	0	0		0	0	0	0	0	0	0
Cambria County	0	0	0		0	0	0	0	0	0	1
Cameron County	0	0	0		0	0	0	0	0	0	0
Carbon County	0	0	0		0	0	0	0	0	0	7
Centre County	0	0	0		0	0	0	0	0	0	4
Chester County	0	0	0		0	0	0	0	0	0	0
Clarion County	0	0	0		0	0	0	0	0	0	0
Clearfield County	0	0	0		0	0	0	0	0	0	8
Clinton County	0	0	0		0	0	0	0	0	0	3
Columbia County	0	0	0		0	0	0	0	0	0	4
Crawford County	0	0	0		0	0	0	0	0	0	1
Cumberland County	0	0	0		0	0	0	0	0	0	4
Dauphin County	6	1	1		2	2	5	1	1	3	1
Delaware County	0	0	0		0	0	0	0	0	0	0
Elk County	0	0	0		0	0	0	0	0	0	0
Erie County	0	0	0		0	0	0	0	0	0	1
Fayette County	0	0	0		0	0	0	0	0	0	3
Forest County	0	0	0		0	0	0	0	0	0	5
Franklin County	0	0	0		0	0	0	0	0	0	1
Fulton County	0	0	0		0	0	0	0	0	0	2
Greene County	0	0	0		0	0	0	0	0	0	0
Huntingdon County	0	0	0		0	0	0	0	0	0	1
Indiana County	0	0	0		0	0	0	0	0	0	13
Jefferson County	0	0	0		0	0	0	0	0	0	3
Juniata County	0	0	0		0	0	0	0	0	0	0
Lackawanna County	0	0	0		0	0	0	0	0	0	0
Lancaster County	0	0	0		0	0	0	0	0	0	8
Lawrence County	0	0	0		0	0	0	0	0	0	0
Lebanon County	0	0	0		0	0	0	0	0	0	3
Lehigh County	0	0	0		0	0	0	0	0	0	0
Luzerne County	0	0	0		0	0	0	0	0	0	1
Lycoming County	0	0	0		0	0	0	0	0	0	35
McKean County	0	0	0		0	0	0	0	0	0	0
Mercer County	0	0	0		0	0	0	0	0	0	0
Mifflin County	0	0	0		0	0	0	0	0	0	1
Monroe County	0	0	0		0	0	0	0	0	0	3
Montgomery County	0	0	0		0	0	0	0	0	0	0
Montour County	0	0	0		0	0	0	0	0	0	2
Northampton County	0	0	0		0	0	0	0	0	0	0
Northumberland County	0	0	0		0	0	0	0	0	0	5
Perry County	0	0	0		0	0	0	0	0	0	1
Philadelphia County	0	0	0		0	0	0	0	0	0	0
Pike County	0	0	0		0	0	0	0	0	0	5
Potter County	0	0	0		0	0	0	0	0	0	1
Schuylkill County	0	0	0		0	0	0	0	0	0	18
Snyder County	0	0	0		0	0	0	0	0	0	1
Somerset County	0	0	0		0	0	0	0	0	0	0
Sullivan County	0	0	0		0	0	0	0	0	0	0
Susquehanna County	0	0	0		0	0	0	0	0	0	0
Tioga County	0	0	0		0	0	0	0	0	0	0
Union County	0	0	0		0	0	0	0	0	0	2
Venango County	0	0	0		0	0	0	0	0	0	0
Warren County	0	0	0		0	0	0	0	0	0	3
Washington County	0	0	0		0	0	0	0	0	0	0
Wayne County	0	0	0		0	0	0	0	0	0	2
Westmoreland County	0	0	0		0	0	0	0	0	0	18
Wyoming County	0	0	0		0	0	0	0	0	0	1
York County	0	0	0		0	0	0	0	0	0	0
Bureau of Narcotics											
Allegheny County	0	0	0		0	0	0	0	0	0	0
Armstrong County	0	0	0		0	0	0	0	0	0	0
Beaver County	0	0	0		0	0	0	0	0	0	0
Bedford County	0	0	0		0	0	0	0	0	0	0
Berks County	0	0	0		0	0	0	0	0	0	0
Blair County	0	0	0		0	0	0	0	0	0	0
Bradford County	0	0	0		0	0	0	0	0	0	0
Bucks County	0	0	0		0	0	0	0	0	0	0
Butler County	0	0	0		0	0	0	0	0	0	0
Cambria County	1	0	0		0	1	0	0	0	0	0
Cameron County	0	0	0		0	0	0	0	0	0	0
Carbon County	0	0	0		0	0	0	0	0	0	0
Centre County	0	0	0		0	0	0	0	0	0	0
Chester County	0	0	0		0	0	0	0	0	0	0
Clarion County	0	0	0		0	0	0	0	0	0	0
Clearfield County	0	0	0		0	0	0	0	0	0	0
Clinton County	0	0	0		0	0	0	0	0	0	0
Columbia County	0	0	0		0	0	0	0	0	0	0
Crawford County	0	0	0		0	0	0	0	0	0	0

Table 9. Offenses Known to Law Enforcement, by Selected State, Tribal, and Other Agencies, 2016—Continued

(Number.)

State/other agency unit/office	Violent crime	Murder and nonnegligent manslaughter	Rape (revised definition)[1]	Rape (legacy definition)[2]	Robbery	Aggravated assault	Property crime	Burglary	Larceny-theft	Motor vehicle theft	Arson[3]
Delaware County	0	0	0		0	0	0	0	0	0	0
Elk County	0	0	0		0	0	0	0	0	0	0
Erie County	0	0	0		0	0	0	0	0	0	0
Fayette County	0	0	0		0	0	0	0	0	0	0
Forest County	0	0	0		0	0	0	0	0	0	0
Greene County	0	0	0		0	0	0	0	0	0	0
Huntingdon County	0	0	0		0	0	0	0	0	0	0
Indiana County	0	0	0		0	0	0	0	0	0	0
Jefferson County	0	0	0		0	0	0	0	0	0	0
Juniata County	0	0	0		0	0	0	0	0	0	0
Lackawanna County	0	0	0		0	0	0	0	0	0	0
Lawrence County	0	0	0		0	0	0	0	0	0	0
Lehigh County	0	0	0		0	0	0	0	0	0	0
Luzerne County	0	0	0		0	0	0	0	0	0	0
Lycoming County	0	0	0		0	0	0	0	0	0	0
McKean County	0	0	0		0	0	0	0	0	0	0
Mercer County	0	0	0		0	0	0	0	0	0	0
Mifflin County	0	0	0		0	0	0	0	0	0	0
Monroe County	0	0	0		0	0	0	0	0	0	0
Montgomery County	0	0	0		0	0	0	0	0	0	0
Montour County	0	0	0		0	0	0	0	0	0	0
Northampton County	0	0	0		0	0	0	0	0	0	0
Northumberland County	0	0	0		0	0	0	0	0	0	0
Philadelphia County	0	0	0		0	0	0	0	0	0	0
Pike County	0	0	0		0	0	0	0	0	0	0
Potter County	0	0	0		0	0	0	0	0	0	0
Schuylkill County	0	0	0		0	0	0	0	0	0	0
Snyder County	0	0	0		0	0	0	0	0	0	0
Somerset County	0	0	0		0	0	0	0	0	0	0
Sullivan County	0	0	0		0	0	0	0	0	0	0
Susquehanna County	0	0	0		0	0	0	0	0	0	0
Tioga County	0	0	0		0	0	0	0	0	0	0
Union County	0	0	0		0	0	0	0	0	0	0
Venango County	0	0	0		0	0	0	0	0	0	0
Warren County	0	0	0		0	0	0	0	0	0	0
Washington County	0	0	0		0	0	0	0	0	0	0
Wayne County	0	0	0		0	0	0	0	0	0	0
Westmoreland County	1	0	0		0	1	0	0	0	0	0
Wyoming County	0	0	0		0	0	0	0	0	0	0
State Park Rangers											
Bald Eagle	0	0	0		0	0	5	0	5	0	0
Beltzville	0	0	0		0	0	5	0	5	0	0
Ben Rush	0	0	0		0	0	0	0	0	0	0
Bendigo	0	0	0		0	0	0	0	0	0	0
Blue Knob	0	0	0		0	0	0	0	0	0	0
Caledonia	0	0	0		0	0	1	0	1	0	0
Clear Creek	0	0	0		0	0	0	0	0	0	0
Codorus	1	0	0		1	0	13	1	12	0	0
Colonel Denning	0	0	0		0	0	0	0	0	0	0
Cook Forest	0	0	0		0	0	0	0	0	0	0
Cowans Gap	1	0	0		0	1	6	3	3	0	0
Delaware Canal	1	0	0		1	0	8	0	8	0	0
Fort Washington	0	0	0		0	0	0	0	0	0	0
Frances Slocum	1	0	0		1	0	6	0	6	0	0
Gifford Pinchot	0	0	0		0	0	5	0	5	0	0
Greenwood Furnace	0	0	0		0	0	0	0	0	0	0
Hills Creek	0	0	0		0	0	0	0	0	0	0
Jacobsburg Environmental Education Center	0	0	0		0	0	0	0	0	0	0
Jennings Environmental Education Center	0	0	0		0	0	0	0	0	0	0
Keystone	1	0	0		0	1	4	0	4	0	1
Kings Gap Environmental Education Center	0	0	0		0	0	0	0	0	0	0
Kooser	0	0	0		0	0	1	0	1	0	0
Laurel Hill	0	0	0		0	0	3	0	3	0	0
Laurel Ridge	0	0	0		0	0	2	1	1	0	0
Leonard Harrison	0	0	0		0	0	2	0	2	0	0
Linn Run	0	0	0		0	0	0	0	0	0	0
Little Buffalo	0	0	0		0	0	0	0	0	0	0
Little Pine	0	0	0		0	0	0	0	0	0	0
Lyman Run	0	0	0		0	0	1	0	1	0	0
Maurice K. Goddard	0	0	0		0	0	0	0	0	0	0
Memorial Lake	0	0	0		0	0	0	0	0	0	0
Moraine	0	0	0		0	0	11	1	10	0	0
Mount Pisgah	0	0	0		0	0	0	0	0	0	0
Neshaminy	0	0	0		0	0	0	0	0	0	0
Nockamixon	0	0	0		0	0	5	0	5	0	0
Ohiopyle	0	0	0		0	0	11	2	9	0	0
Oil Creek	0	0	0		0	0	0	0	0	0	0
Pine Grove Furnace	0	0	0		0	0	2	0	2	0	0
Point	1	0	0		0	1	0	0	0	0	0
Presque Isle	0	0	0		0	0	18	0	18	0	0
Prince Gallitzin	0	0	0		0	0	2	0	1	1	0
Promised Land	0	0	0		0	0	2	1	1	0	0
Pymatuning	0	0	0		0	0	0	0	0	0	0

Table 9. Offenses Known to Law Enforcement, by Selected State, Tribal, and Other Agencies, 2016—Continued

(Number.)

State/other agency unit/office	Violent crime	Murder and nonnegligent manslaughter	Rape (revised definition)[1]	Rape (legacy definition)[2]	Robbery	Aggravated assault	Property crime	Burglary	Larceny-theft	Motor vehicle theft	Arson[3]
Reeds Gap	0	0	0		0	0	0	0	0	0	
Ricketts Glen	0	0	0		0	0	0	0	0	0	0
Ridley Creek	0	0	0		0	0	0	0	0	0	0
Samuel S. Lewis	0	0	0		0	0	5	1	4	0	0
Shawnee	0	0	0		0	0	0	0	0	0	0
Shikellamy	0	0	0		0	0	0	0	0	0	0
Sinnemahoning	0	0	0		0	0	8	1	6	1	0
Sizerville	0	0	0		0	0	0	0	0	0	0
Susquehannock	0	0	0		0	0	0	0	0	0	0
Tobyhanna	0	0	0		0	0	0	0	0	0	0
Tyler	0	0	0		0	0	0	0	0	0	0
White Clay	0	0	0		0	0	0	0	0	0	0
Worlds End	0	0	0		0	0	0	0	0	0	0
Yellow Creek	0	0	0		0	0	2	0	2	0	0
State Police, Bureau of Criminal Investigation											
Adams County	1	0	1		0	0	1	0	1	0	0
Allegheny County	0	0	0		0	0	6	6	0	0	0
Armstrong County	0	0	0		0	0	0	0	0	0	0
Beaver County	0	0	0		0	0	1	0	1	0	0
Bedford County	0	0	0		0	0	0	0	0	0	0
Berks County	0	0	0		0	0	0	0	0	0	0
Blair County	0	0	0		0	0	0	0	0	0	0
Bradford County	0	0	0		0	0	0	0	0	0	0
Bucks County	0	0	0		0	0	0	0	0	0	0
Butler County	0	0	0		0	0	0	0	0	0	0
Cambria County	0	0	0		0	0	1	1	0	0	0
Cameron County	0	0	0		0	0	0	0	0	0	0
Carbon County	0	0	0		0	0	0	0	0	0	0
Centre County	0	0	0		0	0	0	0	0	0	0
Chester County	0	0	0		0	0	0	0	0	0	0
Clarion County	0	0	0		0	0	0	0	0	0	0
Clearfield County	0	0	0		0	0	0	0	0	0	0
Clinton County	0	0	0		0	0	0	0	0	0	0
Columbia County	0	0	0		0	0	0	0	0	0	0
Crawford County	0	0	0		0	0	1	0	1	0	0
Cumberland County	0	0	0		0	0	0	0	0	0	0
Dauphin County	0	0	0		0	0	3	0	3	0	0
Delaware County	0	0	0		0	0	0	0	0	0	0
Elk County	0	0	0		0	0	0	0	0	0	0
Erie County	0	0	0		0	0	0	0	0	0	0
Fayette County	0	0	0		0	0	3	1	1	1	0
Forest County	0	0	0		0	0	0	0	0	0	0
Franklin County	1	0	1		0	0	0	0	0	0	0
Fulton County	0	0	0		0	0	0	0	0	0	0
Greene County	0	0	0		0	0	0	0	0	0	0
Huntingdon County	0	0	0		0	0	0	0	0	0	0
Indiana County	0	0	0		0	0	0	0	0	0	0
Jefferson County	0	0	0		0	0	0	0	0	0	0
Juniata County	0	0	0		0	0	0	0	0	0	0
Lackawanna County	0	0	0		0	0	0	0	0	0	0
Lancaster County	0	0	0		0	0	2	0	2	0	0
Lawrence County	0	0	0		0	0	0	0	0	0	0
Lebanon County	0	0	0		0	0	0	0	0	0	0
Lehigh County	0	0	0		0	0	0	0	0	0	0
Luzerne County	0	0	0		0	0	0	0	0	0	0
Lycoming County	0	0	0		0	0	0	0	0	0	0
McKean County	0	0	0		0	0	0	0	0	0	0
Mercer County	0	0	0		0	0	1	0	1	0	0
Mifflin County	0	0	0		0	0	1	0	1	0	0
Monroe County	0	0	0		0	0	0	0	0	0	0
Montgomery County	0	0	0		0	0	0	0	0	0	0
Montour County	0	0	0		0	0	0	0	0	0	0
Northampton County	0	0	0		0	0	0	0	0	0	0
Northumberland County	0	0	0		0	0	0	0	0	0	0
Perry County	1	0	1		0	0	0	0	0	0	0
Philadelphia County	0	0	0		0	0	0	0	0	0	0
Pike County	0	0	0		0	0	0	0	0	0	0
Potter County	0	0	0		0	0	0	0	0	0	0
Schuylkill County	0	0	0		0	0	0	0	0	0	0
Snyder County	0	0	0		0	0	0	0	0	0	0
Somerset County	0	0	0		0	0	0	0	0	0	0
Sullivan County	0	0	0		0	0	0	0	0	0	0
Susquehanna County	0	0	0		0	0	0	0	0	0	0
Tioga County	0	0	0		0	0	0	0	0	0	0
Union County	0	0	0		0	0	0	0	0	0	0
Venango County	0	0	0		0	0	0	0	0	0	0
Warren County	0	0	0		0	0	0	0	0	0	0
Washington County	0	0	0		0	0	1	0	1	0	0
Wayne County	0	0	0		0	0	0	0	0	0	0
Westmoreland County	0	0	0		0	0	0	0	0	0	0
Wyoming County	0	0	0		0	0	0	0	0	0	0
York County	0	0	0		0	0	0	0	0	0	0

Table 9. Offenses Known to Law Enforcement, by Selected State, Tribal, and Other Agencies, 2016—Continued

(Number.)

State/other agency unit/office	Violent crime	Murder and nonnegligent manslaughter	Rape (revised definition)[1]	Rape (legacy definition)[2]	Robbery	Aggravated assault	Property crime	Burglary	Larceny-theft	Motor vehicle theft	Arson[3]
State Police											
Adams County	91	0	29		7	55	379	102	260	17	7
Allegheny County	22	0	0		2	20	144	0	140	4	0
Armstrong County	34	0	9		5	20	198	60	131	7	2
Beaver County	29	2	4		2	21	141	57	78	6	0
Berks County	100	1	25		17	57	676	216	430	30	14
Blair County	30	0	6		4	20	143	39	98	6	1
Bradford County	57	2	31		7	17	416	127	265	24	3
Bucks County	34	0	9		6	19	338	53	277	8	1
Butler County	53	0	14		2	37	451	114	317	20	2
Cambria County	23	2	2		1	18	141	57	74	10	7
Cameron County	2	1	1		0	0	32	7	24	1	0
Carbon County	32	0	10		5	17	306	123	164	19	1
Centre County	52	1	18		2	31	320	71	231	18	6
Chester County	130	1	27		27	75	1,427	307	1,079	41	11
Clarion County	34	0	14		1	19	356	48	299	9	0
Clearfield County	44	1	25		5	13	395	91	286	18	3
Clinton County	33	0	6		3	24	226	46	174	6	0
Columbia County	6	0	5		0	1	118	34	83	1	1
Crawford County	33	0	7		5	21	619	292	295	32	4
Cumberland County	57	0	25		10	22	581	190	366	25	3
Delaware County	59	0	8		8	43	773	80	655	38	0
Elizabethville	266	2	43		14	207	802	171	598	33	10
Elk County	23	0	6		0	17	152	37	107	8	8
Erie County	115	0	39		24	52	1,475	253	1,182	40	3
Fayette County	205	4	53		44	104	1,828	523	1,234	71	21
Franklin County	86	5	28		16	37	1,030	281	709	40	6
Fulton County	24	2	9		1	12	150	41	107	2	1
Greene County	28	0	7		10	11	306	74	208	24	2
Huntingdon County	50	1	13		2	34	336	109	219	8	7
Indiana County	68	3	22		15	28	744	138	574	32	4
Jefferson County	46	0	17		0	29	203	45	145	13	3
Juniata County	20	0	5		2	13	176	48	120	8	2
Lackawanna County	23	0	12		3	8	96	35	52	9	10
Lancaster County	65	3	22		13	27	634	256	342	36	4
Lawrence County	20	2	3		1	14	206	72	117	17	7
Lebanon County	49	0	7		8	34	329	76	228	25	2
Lehigh County	42	2	6		8	26	785	133	615	37	13
Luzerne County	92	7	20		13	52	630	136	479	15	12
Lycoming County	98	2	17		12	67	447	115	306	26	0
McKean County	17	0	7		0	10	108	31	74	3	1
Mercer County	34	1	10		4	19	309	89	212	8	2
Mifflin County	8	0	3		2	3	108	34	74	0	0
Monroe County	131	1	41		24	65	1,132	331	769	32	4
Montour County	7	0	2		0	5	81	15	63	3	0
Northampton County	13	0	3		1	9	279	63	206	10	0
Northumberland County	22	1	9		2	10	194	68	114	12	1
Perry County	64	0	18		8	38	356	103	232	21	3
Philadelphia County	22	0	0		0	22	20	0	15	5	0
Pike County	62	0	28		8	26	396	148	239	9	11
Potter County	20	0	9		0	11	131	42	77	12	0
Schuylkill County[6]		4			21	64	669	164	475	30	13
Skippack	90	0	8		5	77	475	109	348	18	13
Snyder County	19	3	2		3	11	291	48	232	11	0
Somerset County	47	1	12		2	32	536	143	372	21	3
Sullivan County	5	0	1		0	4	52	27	23	2	0
Susquehanna County	50	1	12		6	31	385	148	222	15	5
Tioga County	34	0	9		10	15	291	76	201	14	0
Tionesta	35	0	5		5	25	62	18	40	4	1
Union County	17	0	7		0	10	214	31	171	12	0
Venango County	22	1	11		2	8	246	45	195	6	0
Warren County	40	1	15		2	22	263	87	164	12	3
Washington County	90	3	23		20	44	729	191	507	31	15
Wayne County	50	0	24		11	15	463	126	327	10	6
Westmoreland County	179	3	48		32	96	1,313	339	930	44	12
Wyoming County	27	0	10		5	12	189	38	139	12	0
York County	178	4	21		17	136	504	108	361	35	0
State Capitol Police	0	0	0		0	0	28	3	25	0	0
Other Agencies											
Allegheny County District Attorney, Criminal Investigation Division	0	0	0		0	0	53	0	53	0	1
Allegheny County Housing Authority	14	2	0		3	9	21	2	18	1	0
Allegheny County Port Authority	88	0	2		9	77	57	1	51	5	0
County Detective											
Adams County	0	0	0		0	0	1	0	1	0	0
Beaver County	0	0	0		0	0	1	0	1	0	0
Berks County	156	0	1		0	155	6	1	1	4	0
Bucks County	2	0	0		1	6	5	0	5	0	0
Chester County	9	1	1		0	6	6	0	6	0	0
Clarion County	2	0	0		0	2	3	1	2	0	0
Cumberland County	0	0	0		0	0	0	0	0	0	0
Lackawanna County	11	0	1		0	10	0	0	0	0	0
Lebanon County	0	0	0		0	0	0	0	0	0	0

Table 9. Offenses Known to Law Enforcement, by Selected State, Tribal, and Other Agencies, 2016—Continued

(Number.)

State/other agency unit/office	Violent crime	Murder and nonnegligent manslaughter	Rape (revised definition)[1]	Rape (legacy definition)[2]	Robbery	Aggravated assault	Property crime	Burglary	Larceny-theft	Motor vehicle theft	Arson[3]
Lehigh County	3	0	0		3	0	77	11	0	66	0
Luzerne County	5	1	0		0	4	0	0	0	0	0
McKean County	0	0	0		0	0	8	0	8	0	0
Monroe County	61	0	0		0	61	12	0	12	0	0
Montgomery County	4	0	1		1	2	6	0	6	0	1
Montour County	0	0	0		0	0	0	0	0	0	0
Pike County	0	0	0		0	0	0	0	0	0	0
Schuylkill County	0	0	0		0	0	3	0	3	0	0
Wayne County	2	0	0		0	2	10	0	10	0	0
Westmoreland County	14	0	2		0	12	68	0	68	0	0
Wyoming County	2	0	0		0	2	8	0	8	0	0
York County	1	0	0		0	1	7	0	3	4	0
Delaware County Park	26	0	0		0	26	91	2	89	0	0
Erie Municipal Airport Authority	0	0	0		0	0	0	0	0	0	0
Franklin County Drug Task Force	0	0	0		0	0	1	0	1	0	0
Harrisburg International Airport	0	0	0		0	0	7	0	6	1	0
Lehigh Valley International Airport	0	0	0		0	0	14	0	6	8	0
Westmoreland County Park	13	0	0		0	13	10	0	10	0	0
Wyoming Area School District	0	0	0		0	0	0	0	0	0	0
RHODE ISLAND											
State Agencies											
Department of Environmental Management	2	0	1		0	1	27	3	24	0	0
Rhode Island State Airport	0	0	0		0	0	27	0	21	6	0
Rhode Island State Police Headquarters	35	1	22		1	11	80	1	63	16	1
State Police											
Chepachet	8	0	8		0	0	17	0	12	5	0
Hope Valley	5	1	1		0	3	36	7	25	4	1
Lincoln	13	0	4		2	7	58	0	28	30	0
Portsmouth	0	0	0		0	0	0	0	0	0	0
Wickford	5	0	3		1	1	36	9	23	4	0
SOUTH CAROLINA											
State Agencies											
Bureau of Protective Services	1	0	0		0	1	10	1	7	2	0
Department of Mental Health	5	0	1		0	4	15	0	15	0	0
Department of Natural Resources											
Abbeville County	0	0	0		0	0	0	0	0	0	0
Aiken County	0	0	0		0	0	0	0	0	0	0
Allendale County	0	0	0		0	0	0	0	0	0	0
Anderson County	0	0	0		0	0	0	0	0	0	0
Bamberg County	0	0	0		0	0	0	0	0	0	0
Barnwell County	0	0	0		0	0	0	0	0	0	0
Beaufort County	0	0	0		0	0	0	0	0	0	0
Berkeley County	0	0	0		0	0	0	0	0	0	0
Calhoun County	0	0	0		0	0	0	0	0	0	0
Charleston County	0	0	0		0	0	0	0	0	0	0
Cherokee County	0	0	0		0	0	0	0	0	0	0
Chester County	0	0	0		0	0	0	0	0	0	0
Chesterfield County	0	0	0		0	0	0	0	0	0	0
Clarendon County	0	0	0		0	0	0	0	0	0	0
Colleton County	0	0	0		0	0	0	0	0	0	0
Darlington County	0	0	0		0	0	0	0	0	0	0
Dillon County	0	0	0		0	0	0	0	0	0	0
Dorchester County	0	0	0		0	0	0	0	0	0	0
Edgefield County	0	0	0		0	0	0	0	0	0	0
Fairfield County	0	0	0		0	0	0	0	0	0	0
Florence County	0	0	0		0	0	0	0	0	0	0
Georgetown County	0	0	0		0	0	0	0	0	0	0
Greenville County	0	0	0		0	0	0	0	0	0	0
Greenwood County	0	0	0		0	0	0	0	0	0	0
Hampton County	0	0	0		0	0	0	0	0	0	0
Horry County	0	0	0		0	0	0	0	0	0	0
Jasper County	0	0	0		0	0	0	0	0	0	0
Kershaw County	0	0	0		0	0	0	0	0	0	0
Lancaster County	0	0	0		0	0	0	0	0	0	0
Laurens County	0	0	0		0	0	0	0	0	0	0
Lee County	0	0	0		0	0	0	0	0	0	0
Lexington County	0	0	0		0	0	0	0	0	0	0
Marion County	0	0	0		0	0	0	0	0	0	0
Marlboro County	0	0	0		0	0	0	0	0	0	0
McCormick County	0	0	0		0	0	0	0	0	0	0
Newberry County	0	0	0		0	0	0	0	0	0	0
Oconee County	0	0	0		0	0	0	0	0	0	0
Orangeburg County	0	0	0		0	0	0	0	0	0	0
Pickens County	0	0	0		0	0	0	0	0	0	0
Richland County	0	0	0		0	0	0	0	0	0	0
Saluda County	0	0	0		0	0	0	0	0	0	0
Spartanburg County	0	0	0		0	0	0	0	0	0	0
Sumter County	0	0	0		0	0	0	0	0	0	0
Union County	0	0	0		0	0	0	0	0	0	0
Williamsburg County	0	0	0		0	0	0	0	0	0	0
York County	0	0	0		0	0	0	0	0	0	0

Table 9. Offenses Known to Law Enforcement, by Selected State, Tribal, and Other Agencies, 2016—Continued

(Number.)

State/other agency unit/office	Violent crime	Murder and nonnegligent manslaughter	Rape (revised definition)[1]	Rape (legacy definition)[2]	Robbery	Aggravated assault	Property crime	Burglary	Larceny-theft	Motor vehicle theft	Arson[3]
Department of Public Safety, Illegal Immigration Enforcement Unit	0	0	0		0	0	0	0	0	0	0
Forestry Commission											
Abbeville County	0	0	0		0	0	0	0	0	0	6
Aiken County	0	0	0		0	0	0	0	0	0	0
Allendale County	0	0	0		0	0	0	0	0	0	0
Anderson County	0	0	0		0	0	0	0	0	0	0
Bamberg County	0	0	0		0	0	1	0	1	0	0
Barnwell County	0	0	0		0	0	0	0	0	0	0
Beaufort County	0	0	0		0	0	0	0	0	0	0
Berkeley County	0	0	0		0	0	0	0	0	0	0
Calhoun County	0	0	0		0	0	0	0	0	0	0
Charleston County	0	0	0		0	0	0	0	0	0	0
Cherokee County	0	0	0		0	0	0	0	0	0	0
Chester County	0	0	0		0	0	1	0	1	0	0
Chesterfield County	0	0	0		0	0	0	0	0	0	0
Clarendon County	0	0	0		0	0	0	0	0	0	0
Colleton County	0	0	0		0	0	1	0	1	0	0
Darlington County	0	0	0		0	0	0	0	0	0	0
Dillon County	0	0	0		0	0	0	0	0	0	0
Dorchester County	0	0	0		0	0	0	0	0	0	0
Edgefield County	0	0	0		0	0	0	0	0	0	0
Fairfield County	0	0	0		0	0	0	0	0	0	0
Florence County	0	0	0		0	0	0	0	0	0	2
Georgetown County	0	0	0		0	0	0	0	0	0	0
Greenville County	0	0	0		0	0	0	0	0	0	0
Greenwood County	0	0	0		0	0	0	0	0	0	0
Hampton County	0	0	0		0	0	0	0	0	0	0
Horry County	0	0	0		0	0	0	0	0	0	0
Jasper County	0	0	0		0	0	0	0	0	0	0
Kershaw County	0	0	0		0	0	0	0	0	0	1
Lancaster County	0	0	0		0	0	0	0	0	0	0
Laurens County	0	0	0		0	0	0	0	0	0	1
Lee County	0	0	0		0	0	0	0	0	0	0
Lexington County	0	0	0		0	0	1	0	1	0	0
Marion County	0	0	0		0	0	0	0	0	0	0
Marlboro County	0	0	0		0	0	1	0	1	0	0
McCormick County	0	0	0		0	0	0	0	0	0	0
Newberry County	0	0	0		0	0	0	0	0	0	0
Oconee County	0	0	0		0	0	0	0	0	0	0
Orangeburg County	0	0	0		0	0	0	0	0	0	0
Pickens County	0	0	0		0	0	0	0	0	0	0
Richland County	0	0	0		0	0	0	0	0	0	0
Saluda County	0	0	0		0	0	0	0	0	0	0
Spartanburg County	0	0	0		0	0	0	0	0	0	0
Sumter County	0	0	0		0	0	0	0	0	0	1
Union County	0	0	0		0	0	0	0	0	0	0
Williamsburg County	0	0	0		0	0	0	0	0	0	1
York County	0	0	0		0	0	0	0	0	0	0
Highway Patrol											
Abbeville County	0	0	0		0	0	0	0	0	0	0
Aiken County	0	0	0		0	0	1	0	0	1	0
Allendale County	0	0	0		0	0	0	0	0	0	0
Anderson County	0	0	0		0	0	0	0	0	0	0
Bamberg County	0	0	0		0	0	0	0	0	0	0
Barnwell County	0	0	0		0	0	0	0	0	0	0
Beaufort County	0	0	0		0	0	0	0	0	0	0
Berkeley County	0	0	0		0	0	0	0	0	0	0
Calhoun County	0	0	0		0	0	0	0	0	0	0
Charleston County	0	0	0		0	0	1	0	0	1	0
Cherokee County	0	0	0		0	0	0	0	0	0	0
Chester County	0	0	0		0	0	0	0	0	0	0
Chesterfield County	0	0	0		0	0	0	0	0	0	0
Clarendon County	0	0	0		0	0	0	0	0	0	0
Colleton County	0	0	0		0	0	0	0	0	0	0
Darlington County	0	0	0		0	0	0	0	0	0	0
Dillon County	0	0	0		0	0	0	0	0	0	0
Dorchester County	1	0	0		0	1	0	0	0	0	0
Edgefield County	0	0	0		0	0	0	0	0	0	0
Fairfield County	0	0	0		0	0	0	0	0	0	0
Florence County	0	0	0		0	0	1	0	0	1	0
Georgetown County	0	0	0		0	0	1	0	1	0	0
Greenville County	0	0	0		0	0	2	0	0	2	0
Greenwood County	0	0	0		0	0	0	0	0	0	0
Hampton County	0	0	0		0	0	0	0	0	0	0
Horry County	0	0	0		0	0	0	0	0	0	0
Jasper County	0	0	0		0	0	0	0	0	0	0
Kershaw County	0	0	0		0	0	0	0	0	0	0
Lancaster County	0	0	0		0	0	0	0	0	0	0
Laurens County	0	0	0		0	0	0	0	0	0	0
Lee County	0	0	0		0	0	0	0	0	0	0
Lexington County	0	0	0		0	0	1	0	0	1	0
Marion County	0	0	0		0	0	0	0	0	0	0

Table 9. Offenses Known to Law Enforcement, by Selected State, Tribal, and Other Agencies, 2016—Continued

(Number.)

State/other agency unit/office	Violent crime	Murder and nonnegligent manslaughter	Rape (revised definition)[1]	Rape (legacy definition)[2]	Robbery	Aggravated assault	Property crime	Burglary	Larceny-theft	Motor vehicle theft	Arson[3]
Marlboro County	0	0	0		0	0	0	0	0	0	
McCormick County	0	0	0		0	0	0	0	0	0	0
Newberry County	0	0	0		0	0	0	0	0	0	0
Oconee County	0	0	0		0	0	0	0	0	0	0
Orangeburg County	0	0	0		0	0	0	0	0	0	0
Pickens County	0	0	0		0	0	0	0	0	0	0
Richland County	0	0	0		0	0	0	0	0	0	0
Saluda County	0	0	0		0	0	0	0	0	0	0
Spartanburg County	0	0	0		0	0	2	0	2	0	0
Sumter County	0	0	0		0	0	1	0	0	1	0
Union County	0	0	0		0	0	0	0	0	0	0
Williamsburg County	0	0	0		0	0	0	0	0	0	0
York County	0	0	0		0	0	0	0	0	0	0
South Carolina Division of Public Railways	0	0	0		0	0	0	0	0	0	0
South Carolina School for the Deaf and Blind	0	0	0		0	0	0	0	0	0	0
State Museum	0	0	0		0	0	0	0	0	0	0
State Ports Authority	2	0	0		0	2	3	1	2	0	0
State Transport Police											
Abbeville County	0	0	0		0	0	0	0	0	0	0
Aiken County	0	0	0		0	0	0	0	0	0	0
Allendale County	0	0	0		0	0	0	0	0	0	0
Anderson County	0	0	0		0	0	0	0	0	0	0
Bamberg County	0	0	0		0	0	0	0	0	0	0
Barnwell County	0	0	0		0	0	0	0	0	0	0
Beaufort County	0	0	0		0	0	0	0	0	0	0
Berkeley County	0	0	0		0	0	0	0	0	0	0
Calhoun County	0	0	0		0	0	0	0	0	0	0
Charleston County	0	0	0		0	0	0	0	0	0	0
Cherokee County	0	0	0		0	0	0	0	0	0	0
Chester County	0	0	0		0	0	0	0	0	0	0
Chesterfield County	0	0	0		0	0	0	0	0	0	0
Clarendon County	0	0	0		0	0	0	0	0	0	0
Colleton County	0	0	0		0	0	0	0	0	0	0
Darlington County	0	0	0		0	0	0	0	0	0	0
Dillon County	0	0	0		0	0	0	0	0	0	0
Dorchester County	0	0	0		0	0	0	0	0	0	0
Edgefield County	0	0	0		0	0	0	0	0	0	0
Fairfield County	0	0	0		0	0	0	0	0	0	0
Florence County	0	0	0		0	0	0	0	0	0	0
Georgetown County	0	0	0		0	0	0	0	0	0	0
Greenville County	0	0	0		0	0	0	0	0	0	0
Greenwood County	0	0	0		0	0	0	0	0	0	0
Hampton County	0	0	0		0	0	0	0	0	0	0
Horry County	0	0	0		0	0	0	0	0	0	0
Jasper County	0	0	0		0	0	0	0	0	0	0
Kershaw County	0	0	0		0	0	0	0	0	0	0
Lancaster County	0	0	0		0	0	0	0	0	0	0
Laurens County	0	0	0		0	0	0	0	0	0	0
Lee County	0	0	0		0	0	0	0	0	0	0
Lexington County	0	0	0		0	0	0	0	0	0	0
Marion County	0	0	0		0	0	0	0	0	0	0
Marlboro County	0	0	0		0	0	0	0	0	0	0
McCormick County	0	0	0		0	0	0	0	0	0	0
Newberry County	0	0	0		0	0	0	0	0	0	0
Oconee County	0	0	0		0	0	0	0	0	0	0
Orangeburg County	0	0	0		0	0	0	0	0	0	0
Pickens County	0	0	0		0	0	0	0	0	0	0
Richland County	0	0	0		0	0	0	0	0	0	0
Saluda County	0	0	0		0	0	0	0	0	0	0
Spartanburg County	0	0	0		0	0	0	0	0	0	0
Sumter County	0	0	0		0	0	0	0	0	0	0
Union County	0	0	0		0	0	0	0	0	0	0
Williamsburg County	0	0	0		0	0	0	0	0	0	0
York County	0	0	0		0	0	0	0	0	0	0
United States Department of Energy, Savannah River Plant	0	0	0		0	0	20	1	19	0	0
Other Agencies											
16th Circuit Drug Enforcement Unit	0	0	0		0	0	0	0	0	0	0
Charleston County Aviation Authority	0	0	0		0	0	39	0	24	15	0
Columbia Metropolitan Airport	0	0	0		0	0	7	0	3	4	0
Greenville Hospital											
Greenville	9	0	0		0	9	107	0	101	6	0
Oconee	0	0	0		0	0	17	1	16	0	0
Greenville-Spartanburg International Airport	0	0	0		0	0	10	1	5	4	0
Lexington County Medical Center	1	0	1		0	0	57	2	54	1	0
SOUTH DAKOTA											
State Agencies											
Division of Criminal Investigation	13	3	7		0	3	1	0	1	0	1
South Dakota Highway Patrol	8	0	0		0	8	12	0	6	6	0
Tribal Agencies											
Cheyenne River Tribal	229	0	4		2	223	89	40	28	21	2
Crow Creek Tribal	67	0	4		2	61	50	10	28	12	2

Table 9. Offenses Known to Law Enforcement, by Selected State, Tribal, and Other Agencies, 2016—Continued

(Number.)

State/other agency unit/office	Violent crime	Murder and nonnegligent manslaughter	Rape (revised definition)[1]	Rape (legacy definition)[2]	Robbery	Aggravated assault	Property crime	Burglary	Larceny-theft	Motor vehicle theft	Arson[3]
Lower Brule Tribal	36	0	5		0	31	49	18	23	8	42
Sisseton-Wahpeton Tribal	21	0	2		0	19	25	6	11	8	1
TENNESSEE											
State Agencies											
Alcoholic Beverage Commission	0	0	0		0	0	0	0	0	0	0
Department of Correction, Internal Affairs	15	0	1		0	14	0	0	0	0	0
Department of Safety	46	3	0		0	43	100	0	25	75	0
State Fire Marshal	0	0	0		0	0	0	0	0	0	4
State Park Rangers											
Bicentennial Capitol Mall	0	0	0		0	0	0	0	0	0	0
Big Hill Pond	0	0	0		0	0	0	0	0	0	0
Big Ridge	0	0	0		0	0	0	0	0	0	0
Bledsoe Creek	0	0	0		0	0	1	0	1	0	0
Booker T. Washington	0	0	0		0	0	1	0	1	0	0
Burgess Falls Natural Area	0	0	0		0	0	1	0	1	0	0
Cedars of Lebanon	0	0	0		0	0	8	0	8	0	0
Chickasaw	0	0	0		0	0	1	0	1	0	0
Cordell Hull Birthplace	0	0	0		0	0	0	0	0	0	0
Cove Lake	0	0	0		0	0	1	0	1	0	0
Cumberland Mountain	0	0	0		0	0	0	0	0	0	0
Cumberland Trail	1	0	0		0	1	3	0	3	0	0
Cummins Falls	0	0	0		0	0	0	0	0	0	0
David Crockett	0	0	0		0	0	3	0	3	0	0
Davy Crockett Birthplace	0	0	0		0	0	0	0	0	0	0
Dunbar Cave Natural Area	0	0	0		0	0	2	1	1	0	0
Edgar Evins	0	0	0		0	0	14	2	12	0	0
Fall Creek Falls	0	0	0		0	0	2	0	2	0	0
Fort Loudon State Historic Park	0	0	0		0	0	0	0	0	0	0
Fort Pillow State Historic Park	0	0	0		0	0	1	0	1	0	0
Frozen Head Natural Area	0	0	0		0	0	5	0	5	0	0
Harpeth Scenic Rivers	0	0	0		0	1	6	0	6	0	0
Harrison Bay	1	0	0		0	0	6	0	6	0	0
Henry Horton	0	0	0		0	0	2	0	2	0	0
Hiwassee/Ocoee State Scenic Rivers	0	0	0		0	0	1	0	1	0	0
Indian Mountain	0	0	0		0	0	0	0	0	0	0
Johnsonville State Historic Park	0	0	0		0	0	5	0	5	0	0
Long Hunter	0	0	0		0	0	2	1	1	0	1
Meeman-Shelby Forest	0	0	0		0	0	4	0	4	0	0
Montgomery Bell	0	0	0		0	0	0	0	0	0	0
Mousetail Landing	0	0	0		0	0	4	2	1	1	0
Natchez Trace	0	0	0		0	0	0	0	0	0	0
Nathan Bedford Forrest	0	0	0		0	0	8	1	7	0	1
Norris Dam	0	0	0		0	0	2	0	2	0	0
Old Stone Fort State Archaeological Park	0	0	0		1	0	3	0	3	0	0
Panther Creek	1	0	0		0	0	2	0	2	0	0
Paris Landing	0	0	0		0	0	0	0	0	0	0
Pickett	0	0	0		0	0	4	0	3	1	0
Pickwick Landing	0	0	0		0	0	1	0	1	0	0
Pinson Mounds State Archaeological Park	0	0	0		0	0	0	0	0	0	0
Radnor Lake Natural Area	0	0	0		0	1	0	0	0	0	0
Red Clay State Historic Park	1	0	0		0	0	0	0	0	0	0
Reelfoot Lake	0	0	0		0	0	1	0	1	0	0
Roan Mountain	0	0	0		0	0	7	1	6	0	0
Rock Island	0	0	0		0	0	0	0	0	0	0
Rocky Fork	0	0	0		0	0	1	0	1	0	0
Seven Islands Birding Park	0	0	0		0	0	0	0	0	0	0
Sgt. Alvin C. York	0	0	0		0	0	1	0	1	0	1
South Cumberland Recreation Area	0	0	0		0	0	3	1	2	0	0
Standing Stone	0	0	0		0	0	0	0	0	0	0
Sycamore Shoals State Historic Park	0	0	0		0	0	0	0	0	0	0
Tim's Ford	0	0	0		0	0	0	0	0	0	0
T.O. Fuller	0	0	0		0	0	0	0	0	0	0
Warrior's Path	0	0	0		0	0	6	0	6	0	0
TennCare Office of Inspector General	0	0	0		0	0	0	0	0	0	0
Tennessee Bureau of Investigation	7	2	2		1	2	8	0	8	0	2
Tennessee Department of Revenue, Special Investigations Unit	0	0	0		0	0	0	0	0	0	0
Wildlife Resources Agency											
Region 1	0	0	0		0	0	0	0	0	0	0
Region 2	0	0	0		0	0	0	0	0	0	0
Region 3	0	0	0		0	0	0	0	0	0	0
Region 4	0	0	0		0	0	0	0	0	0	0
Other Agencies											
8th Judicial District Crime Task Force	0	0	0		0	0	0	0	0	0	0
Chattanooga Housing Authority	0	0	0		0	0	0	0	0	0	0
Chattanooga Metropolitan Airport	0	0	0		0	0	1	1	0	0	0
Dickson City Park Ranger Division	0	0	0		0	0	0	0	0	0	0
Drug Task Force											
1st Judicial District	0	0	0		0	0	0	0	0	0	0
2nd Judicial District	0	0	0		0	0	0	0	0	0	0
3rd Judicial District	0	0	0		0	0	0	0	0	0	0
4th Judicial District	0	0	0		0	0	0	0	0	0	0

Table 9. Offenses Known to Law Enforcement, by Selected State, Tribal, and Other Agencies, 2016—Continued

(Number.)

State/other agency unit/office	Violent crime	Murder and nonnegligent manslaughter	Rape (revised definition)[1]	Rape (legacy definition)[2]	Robbery	Aggravated assault	Property crime	Burglary	Larceny-theft	Motor vehicle theft	Arson[3]
5th Judicial District	0	0	0		0	0	0	0	0	0	0
8th Judicial District	0	0	0		0	0	0	0	0	0	0
9th Judicial District	0	0	0		0	0	0	0	0	0	0
10th Judicial District	0	0	0		0	0	6	0	6	0	0
12th Judicial District	0	0	0		0	0	0	0	0	0	0
14th Judicial District	0	0	0		0	0	0	0	0	0	0
15th Judicial District	0	0	0		0	0	1	0	1	0	0
17th Judicial District	0	0	0		0	0	0	0	0	0	0
18th Judicial District	1	0	0		0	1	0	0	0	0	0
19th Judicial District	0	0	0		0	0	1	0	0	1	0
21st Judicial District	0	0	0		0	0	1	0	0	1	0
22nd Judicial District	0	0	0		0	0	0	0	0	0	0
23rd Judicial District	0	0	0		0	0	1	0	1	0	0
24th Judicial District	0	0	0		0	0	0	0	0	0	0
25th Judicial District	0	0	0		0	0	0	0	0	0	0
27th Judicial District	1	0	0		0	1	0	0	0	0	0
31st Judicial District	0	0	0		0	0	0	0	0	0	0
Knoxville Metropolitan Airport	2	0	0		0	2	14	0	10	4	0
Memphis-Shelby County Airport Authority	0	0	0		0	0	223	1	102	120	0
Metropolitan Nashville Park Police	13	0	2		3	8	97	7	89	1	1
Nashville International Airport	2	0	0		0	2	98	2	73	23	0
Tri-Cities Regional Airport	0	0	0		0	0	0	0	0	0	0
West Tennessee Violent Crime Task Force	0	0	0		0	0	0	0	0	0	0
TEXAS											
State Agencies											
Department of Public Safety	0	0	0		0	0	0	0	0	0	0
Tribal Agencies											
Ysleta del Sur Pueblo Tribal	17	0	0		0	17	36	2	30	4	0
Other Agencies											
Amarillo International Airport	0	0	0		0	0	2	0	2	0	0
Dallas-Fort Worth International Airport	7	0	3		0	4	361	6	323	32	0
Hospital District											
Dallas County	14	0	0		5	9	254	2	244	8	0
Tarrant County	9	0	1		1	7	178	0	177	1	0
Houston Metropolitan Transit Authority	0	0	0		0	0	34	0	29	5	0
Independent School District											
Aldine	8	0	0		8	0	102	43	56	3	0
Alief	45	0	1		6	38	51	9	36	6	0
Alvin	10	0	0		0	10	132	3	129	0	1
Angleton	7	0	0		0	7	61	0	60	1	0
Austin	17	0	2		4	11	409	35	368	6	7
Barbers Hill	0	0	0		0	0	26	0	25	1	0
Bastrop	88	0	0		0	88	31	1	29	1	0
Bay City	0	0	0		0	0	7	2	5	0	0
Brownsville	434	0	0		0	434	151	4	147	0	0
Calhoun County	1	0	0		0	1	12	10	2	0	2
Columbia-Brazoria	1	0	0		0	1	13	0	13	0	0
Conroe	15	0	5		0	10	133	15	118	0	0
East Central	1	0	0		0	1	15	0	15	0	0
Ector County	54	0	0		1	53	117	16	98	3	0
Edinburg	26	0	0		0	26	141	5	135	1	4
El Paso	26	0	3		6	17	315	35	276	4	3
Floresville	1	0	0		0	1	9	2	4	3	0
Galveston	2	0	0		0	2	34	2	31	1	1
Hallsville	0	0	0		0	0	6	1	5	0	0
Houston	84	0	2		20	62	401	169	215	17	3
Humble	12	0	2		3	7	167	1	162	4	0
Idalou	0	0	0		0	0	1	0	1	0	0
Judson	1	0	0		1	0	178	2	174	2	0
Killeen	4	0	0		1	3	85	7	78	0	0
Klein	12	0	1		6	5	131	7	119	5	0
Lyford	0	0	0		0	0	1	0	1	0	0
Madisonville	3	0	1		1	1	2	0	2	0	0
Malakoff	0	0	0		0	0	0	0	0	0	0
Mexia	0	0	0		0	0	6	2	4	0	0
Midland	13	0	0		0	13	26	1	25	0	0
Pasadena	9	0	4		2	3	94	14	76	4	0
Pflugerville	14	0	2		0	12	41	4	36	1	0
Raymondville	0	0	0		0	0	12	0	12	0	0
Rio Grande City	8	0	0		0	8	51	8	43	0	0
Santa Fe	1	0	1		0	0	19	2	17	0	0
Santa Rosa	1	0	1		0	0	2	0	2	0	0
Sealy	0	0	0		0	0	4	0	4	0	0
Socorro	8	0	0		0	8	56	8	47	1	0
Spring	55	0	1		10	44	97	2	89	6	0
Spring Branch	3	0	0		2	1	46	7	38	1	0
Taft	1	0	0		0	1	2	1	1	0	0
United	5	0	0		2	3	29	5	22	2	0
Port of Brownsville	0	0	0		0	0	16	2	14	0	0
Port of Houston Authority	0	0	0		0	0	21	0	12	9	0

Table 9. Offenses Known to Law Enforcement, by Selected State, Tribal, and Other Agencies, 2016—Continued

(Number.)

State/other agency unit/office	Violent crime	Murder and nonnegligent manslaughter	Rape (revised definition)[1]	Rape (legacy definition)[2]	Robbery	Aggravated assault	Property crime	Burglary	Larceny-theft	Motor vehicle theft	Arson[3]
UTAH											
State Agencies											
Parks and Recreation	3	0	1		1	1	31	2	26	3	1
Utah Highway Patrol	63	0	2		1	60	177	5	126	46	0
Wildlife Resources	0	0	0		0	0	8	0	6	2	0
Tribal Agencies											
Cache-Rich Drug Task Force	0	0	0		0	0	1	0	1	0	0
Davis Metropolitan Narcotics Strike Force	0	0	0		0	0	0	0	0	0	0
Granite School District	12	0	0		2	10	166	18	146	2	12
Utah County Major Crimes Task Force	0	0	0		0	0	4	0	3	1	0
Utah Transit Authority	26	1	3		16	6	925	5	864	56	2
VERMONT											
State Agencies											
Department of Motor Vehicles	0	0	0		0	0	0	0	0	0	0
State Police											
Derby	28	0	4		0	24	241	114	115	12	1
New Haven	18	0	1		1	16	192	57	129	6	0
Shaftsbury	18	3	3		1	11	112	29	75	8	0
St. Johnsbury	19	0	5		2	12	308	144	150	14	3
Williston	9	1	2		1	5	172	50	117	5	2
Vermont State Police	2	2	0		0	0	2	0	2	0	0
Vermont State Police Headquarters, Bureau of Criminal Investigations	0	0	0		0	0	0	0	0	0	0
VIRGINIA											
State Agencies											
Alcoholic Beverage Control Commission	0	0	0		0	0	99	4	95	0	0
Department of Game and Inland Fisheries, Enforcement Division	1	0	0		0	1	10	1	9	0	0
Department of Motor Vehicles	0	0	0		0	0	50	0	3	47	1
State Police											
Accomack County	4	0	0		0	4	11	2	8	1	7
Albemarle County	2	0	0		0	2	1	0	1	0	0
Alexandria	2	0	0		1	1	0	0	0	0	0
Alleghany County	21	1	0		0	20	2	0	2	0	0
Amelia County	3	0	0		0	3	3	1	2	0	0
Amherst County	8	0	1		0	7	3	0	2	1	0
Appomattox County	4	0	0		0	4	1	0	0	0	0
Arlington County	2	0	0		0	2	0	0	0	0	0
Augusta County	6	0	1		0	5	15	1	10	4	4
Bath County	3	0	0		0	3	1	0	1	0	0
Bedford	0	0	0		0	0	0	0	0	0	0
Bedford County	1	1	0		0	0	5	0	3	2	0
Bland County	1	0	0		0	1	7	4	2	1	0
Botetourt County	2	0	0		0	2	3	0	3	0	1
Bristol	0	0	0		0	0	1	0	1	0	0
Brunswick County	3	0	0		0	3	0	0	0	0	0
Buchanan County	4	2	1		0	1	11	3	8	0	7
Buckingham County	2	0	0		1	1	1	0	0	1	1
Buena Vista	1	0	1		0	0	1	0	1	0	0
Campbell County	4	0	0		0	4	3	0	3	0	2
Caroline County	6	0	0		0	6	17	3	9	5	1
Carroll County	5	0	1		0	4	12	1	8	3	3
Charles City County	0	0	0		0	0	0	0	0	0	0
Charlotte County	2	0	0		0	2	1	0	1	0	1
Charlottesville	0	0	0		0	0	1	0	1	0	0
Chesapeake	7	1	1		0	5	14	0	2	12	2
Chesterfield County	9	0	0		0	9	9	0	7	2	0
Clarke County	1	0	0		0	1	1	0	1	0	0
Clifton Forge	0	0	0		0	0	0	0	0	0	0
Colonial Heights	4	0	0		0	4	2	0	1	1	0
Covington	10	0	0		0	10	1	1	0	0	0
Craig County	1	0	1		0	0	1	0	0	1	0
Culpeper County	14	3	3		0	8	1	0	1	0	0
Cumberland County	1	0	0		0	1	1	0	0	1	0
Danville	0	0	0		0	0	4	0	2	2	0
Dickenson County	5	0	0		0	5	4	0	4	1	9
Dinwiddie County	2	0	0		0	2	2	0	1	1	0
Emporia	2	0	0		0	2	0	0	0	0	0
Essex County	3	0	0		0	3	1	0	1	0	0
Fairfax City	0	0	0		0	0	0	0	0	0	0
Fairfax County	9	0	0		1	8	24	0	18	6	1
Falls Church	0	0	0		0	0	0	0	0	0	0
Fauquier County	0	0	0		0	0	5	0	4	1	1
Floyd County	5	0	0		0	5	0	0	0	0	1
Fluvanna County	1	0	0		0	1	2	0	2	0	0
Franklin	0	0	0		0	0	0	0	0	0	1
Franklin County	4	1	0		0	3	3	1	2	0	0
Frederick County	13	3	1		0	9	10	0	9	1	2
Fredericksburg	4	1	0		0	3	4	2	2	0	1
Galax	0	0	0		0	0	1	0	1	0	0
Giles County	1	0	0		0	1	0	0	0	0	0

Table 9. Offenses Known to Law Enforcement, by Selected State, Tribal, and Other Agencies, 2016—Continued

(Number.)

State/other agency unit/office	Violent crime	Murder and nonnegligent manslaughter	Rape (revised definition)[1]	Rape (legacy definition)[2]	Robbery	Aggravated assault	Property crime	Burglary	Larceny-theft	Motor vehicle theft	Arson[3]
Gloucester County	4	0	0		0	4	2	0	2	0	0
Goochland County	5	2	0		0	3	2	0	2	0	0
Grayson County	1	1	0		0	0	3	2	1	0	1
Greene County	1	0	0		0	1	2	0	1	1	2
Greensville County	1	0	0		0	1	1	0	1	0	1
Halifax County	1	0	1		0	0	3	0	2	1	0
Hampton	7	1	0		0	6	8	0	1	7	0
Hanover County	8	0	0		0	8	3	0	3	0	0
Harrisonburg	2	0	0		0	2	3	0	0	3	0
Henrico County	13	0	0		0	13	7	0	5	2	0
Henry County	0	0	0		0	0	4	0	1	3	2
Highland County	0	0	0		0	0	0	0	0	0	0
Hopewell	1	0	0		0	1	0	0	0	0	0
Isle of Wight County	1	0	1		0	0	0	0	0	0	2
James City County	1	0	0		1	0	0	0	0	0	0
King and Queen County	1	1	0		0	0	2	0	1	1	0
King George County	0	0	0		0	0	1	0	1	0	0
King William County	1	0	1		0	0	1	0	1	0	0
Lancaster County	3	0	0		0	3	2	1	1	0	1
Lee County	2	0	1		0	1	10	0	7	3	11
Lexington	0	0	0		0	0	0	0	0	0	0
Loudoun County	1	0	0		0	1	5	0	2	3	1
Louisa County	5	1	0		0	4	2	1	1	0	3
Lunenburg County	4	0	0		0	4	0	0	0	0	0
Lynchburg	0	0	0		0	0	2	0	2	0	1
Madison County	3	0	0		0	3	1	0	1	0	0
Manassas	0	0	0		0	0	1	0	1	0	0
Manassas Park	0	0	0		0	0	0	0	0	0	0
Martinsville	0	0	0		0	0	0	0	0	0	0
Mathews County	2	0	0		0	2	0	0	0	0	0
Mecklenburg County	8	1	0		0	7	13	1	10	2	0
Middlesex County	1	0	0		0	1	1	0	1	0	0
Montgomery County	2	1	0		0	1	2	0	2	0	0
Nelson County	8	0	0		0	8	7	1	5	1	1
New Kent County	6	0	0		0	6	5	0	3	2	0
Newport News	7	0	0		0	7	15	0	1	14	1
Norfolk	7	0	0		0	7	12	0	1	11	0
Northampton County	2	1	1		0	0	1	0	0	1	2
Northumberland County	8	0	0		0	8	1	0	1	0	0
Norton	1	0	0		0	1	0	0	0	0	0
Nottoway County	0	0	0		0	0	4	0	3	1	0
Orange County	4	1	1		0	2	3	1	2	0	1
Page County	1	1	0		0	0	33	0	32	1	0
Patrick County	0	0	0		0	0	2	0	1	1	0
Petersburg	7	0	0		0	7	3	0	1	2	1
Pittsylvania County	3	0	0		0	3	13	0	2	11	1
Poquoson	0	0	0		0	0	0	0	0	0	0
Portsmouth	1	1	0		0	0	8	0	1	7	0
Powhatan County	2	0	0		0	2	1	0	1	0	0
Prince Edward County	2	0	0		1	1	3	0	3	0	2
Prince George County	1	0	0		0	1	3	0	2	1	0
Prince William County	9	0	0		0	9	11	0	8	3	0
Pulaski County	3	0	0		0	3	4	1	3	0	0
Radford	1	0	0		0	1	0	0	0	0	0
Rappahannock County	0	0	0		0	0	0	0	0	0	0
Richmond	21	1	1		1	18	23	0	4	19	0
Richmond County	0	0	0		0	0	0	0	0	0	0
Roanoke	3	1	1		0	1	8	0	6	2	1
Roanoke County	4	0	1		1	2	5	1	3	1	0
Rockbridge County	5	1	0		0	4	4	0	3	1	1
Rockingham County	8	0	0		0	8	39	2	15	22	1
Russell County	6	0	1		1	4	9	1	8	0	3
Salem	0	0	0		0	0	4	0	2	2	0
Scott County	6	1	0		0	5	5	0	5	0	2
Shenandoah County	11	0	0		0	11	3	0	2	1	0
Smyth County	3	2	1		0	0	14	2	9	3	4
South Boston	0	0	0		0	0	0	0	0	0	0
Southampton County	0	0	0		0	0	2	1	1	0	0
Spotsylvania County	2	1	0		0	1	4	1	3	0	2
Stafford County	1	1	0		0	0	6	0	3	3	1
Staunton	3	0	2		0	1	0	0	0	0	0
Suffolk	0	0	0		0	0	3	0	0	3	1
Surry County	0	0	0		0	0	1	0	1	0	2
Sussex County	0	0	0		0	0	1	0	1	0	0
Tazewell County	11	0	1		1	9	22	5	16	1	6
Virginia Beach	6	0	0		0	6	18	0	4	14	0
Warren County	0	0	0		0	0	2	0	1	1	0
Washington County	10	0	0		0	10	9	1	5	3	4
Waynesboro	4	0	0		0	4	2	0	2	0	1
Westmoreland County	6	0	0		0	6	2	0	2	0	0
Williamsburg	1	0	0		1	0	0	0	0	0	0
Winchester	1	1	0		0	0	2	0	2	0	0
Wise County	3	1	2		0	0	3	0	3	0	4

Table 9. Offenses Known to Law Enforcement, by Selected State, Tribal, and Other Agencies, 2016—Continued

(Number.)

State/other agency unit/office	Violent crime	Murder and nonnegligent manslaughter	Rape (revised definition)[1]	Rape (legacy definition)[2]	Robbery	Aggravated assault	Property crime	Burglary	Larceny-theft	Motor vehicle theft	Arson[3]
Wythe County	7	0	0		0	7	12	2	9	1	3
York County	0	0	0		0	0	1	0	0	1	0
State Police	0	0	0		0	0	0	0	0	0	0
Virginia State Capitol	1	0	0		0	1	21	1	20	0	0
Other Agencies											
Norfolk Airport Authority	0	0	0		0	0	52	0	48	4	0
Port Authority, Norfolk	0	0	0		0	0	4	0	4	0	0
Reagan National Airport	4	0	0		1	3	427	0	426	1	0
Richmond International Airport	0	0	0		0	0	65	0	22	43	0
WASHINGTON											
State Agencies											
State Gambling Commission, Enforcement Unit	0	0	0		0	0	11	0	11	0	0
State Insurance Commissioner, Special Investigations Unit	0	0	0		0	0	0	0	0	0	0
Washington State Patrol	0	0	0		0	0	0	0	0	0	0
Tribal Agencies											
Lummi Tribal	52	0	12		2	38	260	88	148	24	1
Swinomish Tribal	2	0	0		0	2	59	10	48	1	0
Other Agencies											
Law Enforcement Against Drugs Task Force	0	0	0		0	0	1	0	1	0	0
Port of Seattle	10	0	0		0	10	1,027	22	926	79	1
Skagit County Interlocal Drug Enforcement Unit	0	0	0		0	0	0	0	0	0	0
WEST VIRGINIA											
State Agencies											
Department of Natural Resources											
Barbour County	0	0	0		0	0	0	0	0	0	0
Berkeley County	0	0	0		0	0	0	0	0	0	0
Boone County	0	0	0		0	0	0	0	0	0	0
Braxton County	0	0	0		0	0	0	0	0	0	0
Brooke County	0	0	0		0	0	0	0	0	0	0
Cabell County	0	0	0		0	0	0	0	0	0	0
Calhoun County	0	0	0		0	0	0	0	0	0	0
Clay County	0	0	0		0	0	0	0	0	0	0
Doddridge County	0	0	0		0	0	0	0	0	0	0
Fayette County	0	0	0		0	0	0	0	0	0	0
Gilmer County	0	0	0		0	0	0	0	0	0	0
Grant County	0	0	0		0	0	0	0	0	0	0
Greenbrier County	0	0	0		0	0	0	0	0	0	0
Hampshire County	0	0	0		0	0	0	0	0	0	0
Hancock County	0	0	0		0	0	0	0	0	0	0
Hardy County	0	0	0		0	0	0	0	0	0	0
Harrison County	0	0	0		0	0	0	0	0	0	0
Jackson County	0	0	0		0	0	0	0	0	0	0
Jefferson County	0	0	0		0	0	0	0	0	0	0
Kanawha County	0	0	0		0	0	0	0	0	0	0
Lewis County	0	0	0		0	0	0	0	0	0	0
Lincoln County	0	0	0		0	0	0	0	0	0	0
Logan County	0	0	0		0	0	0	0	0	0	0
Marion County	0	0	0		0	0	0	0	0	0	0
Marshall County	0	0	0		0	0	0	0	0	0	0
Mason County	0	0	0		0	0	0	0	0	0	0
McDowell County	0	0	0		0	0	0	0	0	0	0
Mercer County	0	0	0		0	0	1	0	1	0	0
Mineral County	0	0	0		0	0	0	0	0	0	0
Mingo County	0	0	0		0	0	0	0	0	0	0
Monongalia County	0	0	0		0	0	0	0	0	0	0
Monroe County	0	0	0		0	0	0	0	0	0	0
Morgan County	0	0	0		0	0	0	0	0	0	0
Nicholas County	0	0	0		0	0	0	0	0	0	0
Ohio County	1	0	0		0	1	0	0	0	0	0
Pendleton County	0	0	0		0	0	0	0	0	0	0
Pleasants County	0	0	0		0	0	0	0	0	0	0
Pocahontas County	0	0	0		0	0	0	0	0	0	0
Preston County	0	0	0		0	0	0	0	0	0	0
Putnam County	0	0	0		0	0	0	0	0	0	0
Raleigh County	0	0	0		0	0	0	0	0	0	0
Randolph County	0	0	0		0	0	0	0	0	0	0
Ritchie County	0	0	0		0	0	0	0	0	0	0
Roane County	0	0	0		0	0	0	0	0	0	0
Summers County	0	0	0		0	0	0	0	0	0	0
Taylor County	0	0	0		0	0	0	0	0	0	0
Tucker County	0	0	0		0	0	0	0	0	0	0
Tyler County	0	0	0		0	0	0	0	0	0	0
Upshur County	0	0	0		0	0	0	0	0	0	0
Wayne County	0	0	0		0	0	0	0	0	0	0
Webster County	0	0	0		0	0	0	0	0	0	0
Wetzel County	0	0	0		0	0	0	0	0	0	0
Wirt County	0	0	0		0	0	0	0	0	0	0
Wood County	0	0	0		0	0	0	0	0	0	0

Table 9. Offenses Known to Law Enforcement, by Selected State, Tribal, and Other Agencies, 2016—Continued

(Number.)

State/other agency unit/office	Violent crime	Murder and nonnegligent manslaughter	Rape (revised definition)[1]	Rape (legacy definition)[2]	Robbery	Aggravated assault	Property crime	Burglary	Larceny-theft	Motor vehicle theft	Arson[3]
Wyoming County	0	0	0		0	0	0	0	0	0	0
State Fire Marshal											
Barbour County	0	0	0		0	0	0	0	0	0	0
Berkeley County	0	0	0		0	0	0	0	0	0	9
Boone County	0	0	0		0	0	0	0	0	0	0
Braxton County	0	0	0		0	0	0	0	0	0	0
Brooke County	0	0	0		0	0	0	0	0	0	0
Cabell County	0	0	0		0	0	0	0	0	0	0
Calhoun County	0	0	0		0	0	0	0	0	0	0
Clay County	0	0	0		0	0	0	0	0	0	0
Doddridge County	0	0	0		0	0	0	0	0	0	0
Fayette County	0	0	0		0	0	0	0	0	0	0
Gilmer County	0	0	0		0	0	0	0	0	0	0
Grant County	0	0	0		0	0	0	0	0	0	0
Greenbrier County	0	0	0		0	0	0	0	0	0	2
Hampshire County	0	0	0		0	0	0	0	0	0	0
Hancock County	0	0	0		0	0	0	0	0	0	4
Hardy County	0	0	0		0	0	0	0	0	0	0
Harrison County	0	0	0		0	0	0	0	0	0	0
Jackson County	0	0	0		0	0	0	0	0	0	0
Jefferson County	0	0	0		0	0	0	0	0	0	2
Kanawha County	0	0	0		0	0	0	0	0	0	0
Lewis County	0	0	0		0	0	0	0	0	0	0
Lincoln County	0	0	0		0	0	0	0	0	0	0
Logan County	0	0	0		0	0	0	0	0	0	0
Marion County	0	0	0		0	0	0	0	0	0	0
Marshall County	0	0	0		0	0	0	0	0	0	0
Mason County	0	0	0		0	0	0	0	0	0	0
McDowell County	0	0	0		0	0	0	0	0	0	0
Mercer County	0	0	0		0	0	0	0	0	0	0
Mineral County	0	0	0		0	0	0	0	0	0	0
Mingo County	0	0	0		0	0	0	0	0	0	5
Monongalia County	0	0	0		0	0	0	0	0	0	0
Monroe County	0	0	0		0	0	0	0	0	0	0
Nicholas County	0	0	0		0	0	0	0	0	0	0
Ohio County	0	0	0		0	0	0	0	0	0	0
Pendleton County	0	0	0		0	0	0	0	0	0	0
Pleasants County	0	0	0		0	0	0	0	0	0	0
Pocahontas County	0	0	0		0	0	0	0	0	0	0
Preston County	0	0	0		0	0	0	0	0	0	0
Putnam County	0	0	0		0	0	0	0	0	0	0
Raleigh County	0	0	0		0	0	0	0	0	0	0
Randolph County	0	0	0		0	0	0	0	0	0	1
Ritchie County	0	0	0		0	0	0	0	0	0	0
Roane County	0	0	0		0	0	0	0	0	0	0
Summers County	0	0	0		0	0	0	0	0	0	0
Taylor County	0	0	0		0	0	0	0	0	0	0
Tucker County	0	0	0		0	0	0	0	0	0	0
Tyler County	0	0	0		0	0	0	0	0	0	0
Upshur County	0	0	0		0	0	0	0	0	0	0
Wayne County	0	0	0		0	0	0	0	0	0	0
Webster County	0	0	0		0	0	0	0	0	0	0
Wetzel County	0	0	0		0	0	0	0	0	0	0
Wirt County	0	0	0		0	0	0	0	0	0	0
Wood County	0	0	0		0	0	0	0	0	0	0
Wyoming County	0	0	0		0	0	0	0	0	0	0
State Police, Bureau of Criminal Investigations											
Beckley	0	0	0		0	0	1	0	1	0	0
Bluefield	0	0	0		0	0	0	0	0	0	0
Buckhannon	0	0	0		0	0	0	0	0	0	0
Charleston	0	0	0		0	0	0	0	0	0	0
Fairmont	0	0	0		0	0	0	0	0	0	2
Martinsburg	0	0	0		0	0	0	0	0	0	0
State Police, Parkway Authority											
Fayette County	0	0	0		0	0	0	0	0	0	0
Kanawha County	0	0	0		0	0	0	0	0	0	0
Mercer County	0	0	0		0	0	2	1	1	0	0
Raleigh County	0	0	0		0	0	3	0	2	1	0
State Police											
Beckley	56	0	12		0	44	309	87	205	17	0
Berkeley Springs	7	0	3		0	3	84	9	67	8	0
Bridgeport	10	0	2		1	7	132	33	87	12	0
Clay	25	0	2		1	22	120	41	55	24	1
Elizabeth	6	0	1		0	5	47	11	34	2	0
Elkins	40	1	13		2	24	217	50	151	16	1
Fairmont	13	0	4		0	9	76	19	47	10	0
Franklin	13	0	1		0	12	20	6	9	5	0
Gilbert	0	0	0		0	0	0	0	0	0	0
Glenville	19	1	3		0	15	31	5	23	3	0
Grafton	1	0	0		0	1	18	4	13	1	0
Grantsville	15	0	3		0	12	36	14	17	5	0
Hamlin[6]	39	0	11		2	26		92	148		2
Hinton	4	0	0		0	4	35	14	19	2	0

Table 9. Offenses Known to Law Enforcement, by Selected State, Tribal, and Other Agencies, 2016—Continued

(Number.)

State/other agency unit/office	Violent crime	Murder and nonnegligent manslaughter	Rape (revised definition)[1]	Rape (legacy definition)[2]	Robbery	Aggravated assault	Property crime	Burglary	Larceny-theft	Motor vehicle theft	Arson[3]
Hundred	4	0	2		0	2	16	7	8	1	0
Huntington	33	1	15		1	16	375	94	262	19	1
Internet Crimes Against Children Unit	29	0	23		0	6	1	0	1	0	0
Jesse	17	0	4		1	12	55	22	26	7	0
Kearneysville	12	0	2		2	8	142	28	110	4	0
Keyser	24	1	6		1	16	170	51	110	9	0
Kingwood	22	0	2		1	19	131	39	79	13	2
Lewisburg	11	0	8		0	3	88	16	67	5	0
Logan	74	1	13		10	50	282	75	184	23	3
Madison	30	1	4		0	25	156	25	106	25	0
Marlinton	15	0	2		0	13	49	18	28	3	0
Martinsburg	38	2	6		4	26	528	149	334	45	5
Moorefield	17	0	6		1	10	32	9	22	1	0
Morgantown	44	1	12		6	25	439	119	295	25	0
Moundsville	8	1	1		1	5	18	9	6	3	0
New Cumberland	4	0	2		0	2	2	0	2	0	0
Oak Hill	15	1	2		0	12	118	17	91	10	2
Paden City	9	0	4		0	5	29	14	12	3	1
Parkersburg	9	0	4		0	5	221	91	114	16	0
Parsons	9	0	0		2	7	42	13	27	2	0
Petersburg	18	2	7		0	9	33	15	15	3	0
Philippi	13	1	2		1	9	86	34	44	8	2
Point Pleasant	7	0	1		0	6	59	18	33	8	0
Princeton	28	1	4		4	19	218	39	169	10	1
Quincy	38	1	3		0	34	192	20	157	15	2
Rainelle	11	0	0		0	11	81	43	33	5	0
Richwood	9	0	0		0	9	106	38	56	12	0
Ripley	13	0	3		0	10	77	17	52	8	1
Romney	23	0	5		0	18	61	12	45	4	0
South Charleston	16	0	5		0	11	252	9	223	20	0
Spencer	23	0	0		1	22	36	10	20	6	1
St. Marys	6	0	0		0	6	11	3	6	2	0
Summersville	17	1	0		1	15	66	11	48	7	1
Sutton	22	0	5		2	15	128	31	87	10	4
Union	11	0	3		0	8	34	16	17	1	1
Upperglade	43	0	0		0	43	38	12	20	6	0
Wayne	63	0	11		0	52	445	117	284	44	5
Welch	44	0	4		4	36	89	32	44	13	3
Wellsburg	16	0	2		0	14	12	1	10	1	0
West Union	15	0	3		0	12	23	3	19	1	0
Weston	11	0	1		0	10	66	12	51	3	0
Wheeling	3	0	1		0	2	16	2	14	0	0
Whitesville	11	0	1		0	10	86	38	41	7	0
Williamson	37	3	5		0	29	95	27	60	8	3
Winfield	16	0	2		0	14	127	25	92	10	2
Other Agencies											
Central West Virginia Drug Task Force	0	0	0		0	0	0	0	0	0	0
Eastern Panhandle Drug and Violent Crime Task Force	0	0	0		0	0	0	0	0	0	0
Greenbrier County Drug and Violent Crime Task Force	0	0	0		0	0	0	0	0	0	0
Hancock/Brooke/Weirton Drug Task Force	0	0	0		0	0	0	0	0	0	0
Harrison County Drug and Violent Crime Task Force	0	0	0		0	0	0	0	0	0	0
Huntington Drug and Violent Crime Task Force	0	0	0		0	0	0	0	0	0	0
Kanawha County Parks and Recreation	0	0	0		0	0	5	2	3	0	0
Logan County Drug and Violent Crime Task Force	0	0	0		0	0	0	0	0	0	0
Metropolitan Drug Enforcement Network Team	0	0	0		0	0	0	0	0	0	0
Mon Metro Drug Task Force	0	0	0		0	0	0	0	0	0	0
Ohio Valley Drug and Violent Crime Task Force	0	0	0		0	0	0	0	0	0	0
Parkersburg Narcotics and Violent Crime Task Force	0	0	0		0	0	1	0	1	0	0
Potomac Highlands Drug and Violent Crime Task Force	0	0	0		0	0	0	0	0	0	0
Three Rivers Drug and Violent Crime Task Force	0	0	0		0	0	0	0	0	0	0
WISCONSIN											
State Agencies											
Capitol Police	2	0		0	2	0	97	4	92	1	0
Department of Natural Resources	0	0		0	0	0	0	0	0	0	0
State Fair Park Police	1	0		0	0	1	42	0	41	1	1
Wisconsin State Patrol	0	0		0	0	0	0	0	0	0	0
Tribal Agencies											
Bad River Tribal	14	0		0	1	13	23	12	9	2	0
Lac du Flambeau Tribal	53	0	9		1	43	227	56	167	4	0
Menominee Tribal	27	0	2		1	24	96	9	70	17	0
Oneida Tribal	23	2	2		0	19	100	10	84	6	1
St. Croix Tribal	7	1	0		0	6	43	3	30	10	0

Table 9. Offenses Known to Law Enforcement, by Selected State, Tribal, and Other Agencies, 2016—Continued

(Number.)

State/other agency unit/office	Violent crime	Murder and nonnegligent manslaughter	Rape (revised definition)[1]	Rape (legacy definition)[2]	Robbery	Aggravated assault	Property crime	Burglary	Larceny-theft	Motor vehicle theft	Arson[3]
WYOMING											
Tribal Agencies											
Wind River Agency	152	0	16		1	135	175	36	90	49	3
PUERTO RICO											
Puerto Rico	7,643	679	169		3,201	3,594	35,201	8,251	23,163	3,787	

1 The figures shown in this column for the offense of rape were reported using the revised Uniform Crime Reporting (UCR) definition of rape.   2 The figures shown in this column for the offense of rape were reported using the legacy UCR definition of rape.   3 The FBI does not publish arson data unless it receives data from either the agency or the state for all 12 months of the calendar year.

Table 10. Crime Trends, by Population Group, 2015–2016

(Number, percent change.)

Population group	Violent crime	Murder and nonnegligent manslaughter	Rape (revised definition)[1]	Rape (legacy definition)[2]	Robbery	Aggravated assault	Property crime	Burglary	Larceny-theft	Motor vehicle theft	Arson	Number of agencies	Estimated population, 2016
Total, All Agencies													
2015	1,173,095	15,181	108,930	6,310	315,137	727,537	7,538,827	1,482,228	5,375,095	681,504	42,259	15,623	305,431,251
2016	1,217,400	16,459	112,470	6,616	319,826	762,029	7,440,034	1,413,294	5,296,630	730,110	43,249		
Percent change	+3.8	+8.4	+3.2	+4.8	+1.5	+4.7	-1.3	-4.7	-1.5	+7.1	+2.3		
Total, Cities													
2015	938,136	11,826	81,231	4,191	276,513	564,375	5,983,208	1,087,800	4,347,725	547,683	32,487	11,158	208,061,722
2016	978,267	12,863	84,460	4,272	282,000	594,672	5,923,615	1,042,326	4,292,416	588,873	33,104		
Percent change	+4.3	+8.8	+4.0	+1.9	+2.0	+5.4	-1.0	-4.2	-1.3	+7.5	+1.9		
Group I (250,000 and over)													
2015	445,645	6,177	30,970	936	156,058	251,504	2,034,720	384,817	1,398,652	251,251	12,645	83	61,199,316
2016	473,049	6,973	32,986	892	159,314	272,884	2,045,407	368,854	1,408,114	268,439	12,914		
Percent change	+6.1	+12.9	+6.5	-4.7	+2.1	+8.5	+0.5	-4.1	+0.7	+6.8	+2.1		
1,000,000 and over (Group I subset)													
2015	188,327	2,234	13,138	-	69,293	103,662	727,139	131,821	501,813	93,505	3,923	11	27,658,777
2016	201,825	2,688	13,972	-	71,652	113,513	742,200	125,303	517,051	99,846	4,229		
Percent change	+7.2	+20.3	+6.3	-	+3.4	+9.5	+2.1	-4.9	+3.0	+6.8	+7.8		
500,000 to 999,999 (Group I subset)													
2015	139,003	2,092	9,109	620	46,953	80,229	703,775	133,644	487,061	83,070	4,125	23	16,781,999
2016	147,007	2,228	9,603	600	47,395	87,181	699,498	128,981	482,417	88,100	4,116		
Percent change	+5.8	+6.5	+5.4	-3.2	+0.9	+8.7	-0.6	-3.5	-1.0	+6.1	-0.2		
250,000 to 499,999 (Group I subset)													
2015	118,315	1,851	8,723	316	39,812	67,613	603,806	119,352	409,778	74,676	4,597	49	16,758,540
2016	124,217	2,057	9,411	292	40,267	72,190	603,709	114,570	408,646	80,493	4,569		
Percent change	+5.0	+11.1	+7.9	-7.6	+1.1	+6.8	*	-4.0	-0.3	+7.8	-0.6		
Group II (100,000 to 249,999)													
2015	151,098	1,992	13,776	627	44,621	90,082	1,053,444	198,316	745,157	109,971	4,997	219	32,521,418
2016	157,638	2,118	14,186	624	45,659	95,051	1,044,575	188,685	737,743	118,147	5,165		
Percent change	+4.3	+6.3	+3.0	-0.5	+2.3	+5.5	-0.8	-4.9	-1.0	+7.4	+3.4		
Group III (50,000 to 99,999)													
2015	109,770	1,201	10,405	551	29,904	67,709	868,445	153,641	640,351	74,453	4,268	477	33,071,956
2016	112,649	1,210	11,041	603	30,509	69,286	866,392	148,627	637,330	80,435	4,228		
Percent change	+2.6	+0.7	+6.1	+9.4	+2.0	+2.3	-0.2	-3.3	-0.5	+8.0	-0.9		
Group IV (25,000 to 49,999)													
2015	84,736	983	9,235	775	20,836	52,907	735,602	128,058	560,829	46,715	3,301	853	29,586,018
2016	87,565	1,007	9,482	864	21,127	55,085	721,325	123,562	547,145	50,618	3,376		
Percent change	+3.3	+2.4	+2.7	+11.5	+1.4	+4.1	-1.9	-3.5	-2.4	+8.4	+2.3		
Group V (10,000 to 24,999)													
2015	76,897	833	8,553	601	15,603	51,307	694,375	121,359	535,782	37,234	2,974	1,793	28,626,434
2016	77,258	861	8,486	616	15,795	51,500	671,568	115,873	515,328	40,367	2,874		
Percent change	+0.5	+3.4	-0.8	+2.5	+1.2	+0.4	-3.3	-4.5	-3.8	+8.4	-3.4		
Group VI (under 10,000)													
2015	69,990	640	8,292	701	9,491	50,866	596,622	101,609	466,954	28,059	4,302	7,733	23,056,580
2016	70,108	694	8,279	673	9,596	50,866	574,348	96,725	446,756	30,867	4,547		
Percent change	+0.2	+8.4	-0.2	-4.0	+1.1	0.0	-3.7	-4.8	-4.3	+10.0	+5.7		
Metropolitan Counties													
2015	187,976	2,453	19,865	1,606	35,981	128,071	1,250,091	297,579	842,845	109,667	7,305	2,010	73,068,087
2016	191,384	2,754	20,068	1,828	35,054	131,680	1,226,478	280,397	828,604	117,477	7,637		
Percent change	+1.8	+12.3	+1.0	+13.8	-2.6	+2.8	-1.9	-5.8	-1.7	+7.1	+4.5		
Nonmetropolitan Counties[3]													
2015	46,983	902	7,834	513	2,643	35,091	305,528	96,849	184,525	24,154	2,467	2,455	24,301,442
2016	47,749	842	7,942	516	2,772	35,677	289,941	90,571	175,610	23,760	2,508		
Percent change	+1.6	-6.7	+1.4	+0.6	+4.9	+1.7	-5.1	-6.5	-4.8	-1.6	+1.7		
Suburban Areas[4]													
2015	327,013	3,865	35,735	2,592	67,586	217,235	2,569,624	510,961	1,869,364	189,299	13,482	8,552	132,442,308
2016	334,222	4,245	36,342	2,870	67,524	223,241	2,516,026	483,816	1,828,325	203,885	14,220		
Percent change	+2.2	+9.8	+1.7	+10.7	-0.1	+2.8	-2.1	-5.3	-2.2	+7.7	+5.5		

Note: No agencies over 1,000,000 in population submitted rape data using the legacy UCR definition in 2016; therefore, the UCR Program could not provide a 2-year comparison for this agency group size.
* = Less than one-tenth of one percent.
1 The figures shown in the rape (revised definition) column include only those reported by law enforcement agencies that used the revised Uniform Crime Reporting (UCR) definition of rape.   2 The figures shown in the rape (legacy definition) column include only those reported by law enforcement agencies that used the legacy UCR definition of rape.   3 Includes state police agencies that report aggregately for the entire state.   4 Suburban areas include law enforcement agencies in cities with less than 50,000 inhabitants and county law enforcement agencies that are within a Metropolitan Statistical Area. Suburban areas exclude all metropolitan agencies associated with a principal city. The agencies associated with suburban areas also appear in other groups within this table.

Table 11. Rate: Number of Crimes Per 100,000 Population, by Population Group, 2016

(Number, rate.)

Population group	Violent crime		Murder and nonnegligent manslaughter		Rape (revised definition)[1]		Rape (legacy definition)[2]		Robbery		Aggravated assault	
	Number of offenses known	Rate	Number of offenses known	Rate	Number of offenses known	Rate	Number of offenses known	Rate	Number of offenses known	Rate	Number of offenses known	Rate
Total, All Agencies	1,223,265	401.3	16,470	5.4	114,730	41.2	6,607	25.1	321,464	105.5	763,994	250.6
Total, Cities	979,579	471.6	12,802	6.2	86,015	44.4	4,268	31.0	282,459	136.0	594,035	286.0
Group I (250,000 and over)	472,814	771.4	6,928	11.3	33,385	56.7	981	41.3	159,106	259.6	272,414	444.5
1,000,000 and over (Group I subset)	201,825	729.7	2,688	9.7	13,972	50.5	0	0.0	71,652	259.1	113,513	410.4
500,000 to 999,999 (Group I subset)	150,170	861.9	2,242	12.9	9,992	62.6	600	41.2	48,381	277.7	88,955	510.5
250,000 to 499,999 (Group I subset)	120,819	745.5	1,998	12.3	9,421	61.6	381	41.5	39,073	241.1	69,946	431.6
Group II (100,000 to 249,999)	156,588	485.3	2,098	6.5	14,459	47.1	526	34.1	45,431	140.8	94,074	291.6
Group III (50,000 to 99,999)	114,031	342.2	1,214	3.6	11,438	36.5	588	29.5	30,879	92.7	69,912	209.8
Group IV (25,000 to 49,999)	88,973	299.1	1,012	3.4	9,619	35.5	871	32.8	21,403	72.0	56,068	188.5
Group V (10,000 to 24,999)	78,120	272.6	880	3.1	8,723	33.7	632	22.9	16,079	56.1	51,806	180.8
Group VI (under 10,000)	69,053	307.9	670	3.0	8,391	42.0	670	27.3	9,561	42.6	49,761	221.9
Metropolitan Counties	195,630	267.3	2,807	3.8	20,618	32.3	1,819	19.6	36,227	49.5	134,159	183.3
Nonmetropolitan Counties[3]	48,056	200.6	861	3.6	8,097	39.1	520	16.1	2,778	11.6	35,800	149.5
Suburban Areas[4]	339,130	256.2	4,300	3.2	37,237	31.5	2,890	20.5	68,951	52.1	225,752	170.5

Table 11. Rate: Number of Crimes Per 100,000 Population, by Population Group, 2016—Continued

(Number, rate.)

Population group	Property crime		Burglary		Larceny-theft		Motor vehicle theft		Number of agencies	Estimated population, 2016
	Number of offenses known	Rate	Number of offenses known	Rate	Number of offenses known	Rate	Number of offenses known	Rate		
Total, All Agencies	7,514,851	2,465.2	1,421,596	466.3	5,353,887	1,756.3	739,368	242.5	15,310	304,839,823
Total, Cities	5,969,716	2,874.1	1,045,176	503.2	4,328,750	2,084.1	595,790	286.8	10,831	207,707,230
Group I (250,000 and over)	2,061,132	3,363.0	368,632	601.5	1,420,247	2,317.3	272,253	444.2	82	61,289,111
1,000,000 and over (Group I subset)	742,200	2,683.4	125,303	453.0	517,051	1,869.4	99,846	361.0	11	27,658,777
500,000 to 999,999 (Group I subset)	732,585	4,204.4	133,045	763.6	506,516	2,907.0	93,024	533.9	24	17,424,128
250,000 to 499,999 (Group I subset)	586,347	3,618.0	110,284	680.5	396,680	2,447.7	79,383	489.8	47	16,206,206
Group II (100,000 to 249,999)	1,036,660	3,212.9	186,189	577.1	731,555	2,267.3	118,916	368.6	218	32,265,177
Group III (50,000 to 99,999)	881,257	2,644.6	151,264	453.9	648,625	1,946.5	81,368	244.2	480	33,323,383
Group IV (25,000 to 49,999)	730,697	2,456.7	124,824	419.7	554,893	1,865.7	50,980	171.4	857	29,742,465
Group V (10,000 to 24,999)	685,091	2,390.3	118,082	412.0	525,509	1,833.5	41,500	144.8	1,794	28,661,210
Group VI (under 10,000)	574,879	2,563.5	96,185	428.9	447,921	1,997.3	30,773	137.2	7,400	22,425,884
Metropolitan Counties	1,254,279	1,713.9	285,709	390.4	848,805	1,159.9	119,765	163.7	2,010	73,181,004
Nonmetropolitan Counties[3]	290,856	1,214.3	90,711	378.7	176,332	736.2	23,813	99.4	2,469	23,951,589
Suburban Areas[4]	2,559,769	1,933.8	490,432	370.5	1,862,114	1,406.7	207,223	156.5	8,400	132,369,940

1 The figures shown in the rape (revised definition) column include only those reported by law enforcement agencies that used the revised Uniform Crime Reporting (UCR) definition of rape.   2 The figures shown in the rape (legacy definition) column include only those reported by law enforcement agencies that used the legacy UCR definition of rape.   3 Includes state police agencies that report aggregately for the entire state.   4 Suburban areas include law enforcement agencies in cities with less than 50,000 inhabitants and county law enforcement agencies that are within a Metropolitan Statistical Area. Suburban areas exclude all metropolitan agencies associated with a principal city. The agencies associated with suburban areas also appear in other groups within this table.

Table 12. Murder, by Selected State, Territory, and Type of Weapon, 2016

(Number.)

State/territory	Total murders[1]	Total firearms	Handguns	Rifles	Shotguns	Firearms (type unknown)	Knives or cutting instruments	Other weapons	Hands, fists, feet, etc.[2]
Alabama[3]	3	1	0	0	0	1	0	2	0
Alaska	52	43	12	4	1	26	3	6	0
Arizona	336	227	156	16	10	45	40	63	6
Arkansas	209	151	72	11	3	65	25	25	8
California	1,930	1,368	930	37	36	365	280	193	89
Colorado	202	136	87	4	4	41	27	28	11
Connecticut	76	48	24	0	1	23	12	13	3
Delaware	56	41	17	0	0	24	7	8	0
District of Columbia	136	105	105	0	0	0	19	6	6
Georgia	646	522	421	20	14	67	48	71	5
Hawaii	35	19	12	3	2	2	8	5	3
Idaho	47	17	13	1	0	3	5	21	4
Illinois[3]	941	799	728	14	5	52	61	62	19
Indiana	348	287	169	12	2	104	19	32	10
Iowa	71	43	25	2	1	15	12	10	6
Kansas	96	61	43	5	1	12	8	19	8
Kentucky	260	207	143	7	8	49	20	22	11
Louisiana	543	445	219	26	7	193	33	52	13
Maine	20	11	2	1	3	5	5	2	2
Maryland	430	328	309	2	3	14	52	29	21
Massachusetts	132	85	34	0	0	51	25	11	11
Michigan	597	443	191	15	12	225	45	89	20
Minnesota	99	60	42	2	1	15	12	19	8
Mississippi	154	128	101	4	6	17	4	14	8
Missouri	535	437	211	23	6	197	37	50	11
Montana	34	17	6	4	3	4	9	5	3
Nebraska	41	30	30	0	0	0	9	2	0
Nevada	209	141	21	2	0	118	20	42	6
New Hampshire	16	8	4	1	1	2	2	0	6
New Jersey	372	278	212	1	3	62	29	42	23
New Mexico	99	60	13	1	0	46	17	19	3
New York	628	367	305	2	9	51	130	99	32
North Carolina	595	421	262	20	22	117	50	80	44
North Dakota	14	8	5	2	0	1	3	1	2
Ohio	627	452	197	7	8	240	39	104	32
Oklahoma	243	171	135	9	9	18	31	23	18
Oregon	100	51	32	6	1	12	24	24	1
Pennsylvania	655	486	395	10	12	69	68	78	23
Rhode Island	29	12	5	0	0	7	9	6	2
South Carolina	363	281	172	7	9	93	29	36	17
South Dakota	21	7	7	0	0	0	5	4	5
Tennessee	486	356	202	10	7	137	49	69	12
Texas	1,459	1,066	630	51	31	354	175	136	82
Utah	71	42	31	1	0	10	6	20	3
Vermont	14	6	2	2	1	1	2	6	0
Virginia	482	352	151	10	10	181	33	67	30
Washington	195	127	69	11	5	42	19	38	11
West Virginia	76	47	30	2	0	15	4	21	4
Wisconsin	226	166	119	6	4	37	27	21	12
Wyoming	19	6	1	0	1	4	8	3	2
U.S. Virgin Islands	42	34	3	0	0	31	0	8	0

1 Total number of murders for which supplemental homicide data were received.   2 Pushed is included in hands, fists, feet, etc.   3 Limited supplemental homicide data were received.

Table 13. Robbery, by State and Type of Weapon, 2016

(Number.)

State	Total robberies[1]	Firearms	Knives or cutting instruments	Other weapons	Strong-arm	Agency count	Population
Alabama	4,415	2,876	143	369	1,027	264	4,392,449
Alaska	848	242	81	116	409	32	738,566
Arizona	6,882	3,002	802	716	2,362	90	6,514,042
Arkansas	2,045	1,096	120	176	653	272	2,827,056
California	54,762	15,489	5,207	6,063	28,003	732	39,209,622
Colorado	3,432	1,357	349	433	1,293	197	5,109,023
Connecticut	2,696	896	294	227	1,279	103	3,500,401
Delaware	1,359	648	99	101	511	56	950,787
District of Columbia	3,480	1,430	273	225	1,552	3	681,170
Florida	20,132	8,717	1,299	1,914	8,202	668	20,566,240
Georgia	11,935	7,409	425	931	3,170	504	9,639,636
Hawaii	994	162	93	135	604	4	1,428,557
Idaho	209	56	36	32	85	108	1,680,830
Illinois[2]	536	307	24	48	157	1	147,363
Indiana	6,883	3,420	360	586	2,517	217	4,663,407
Iowa	1,131	482	87	115	447	207	2,867,132
Kansas	1,248	607	98	97	446	227	2,211,329
Kentucky	3,369	1,664	238	330	1,137	420	4,424,357
Louisiana	5,514	2,976	238	419	1,881	187	4,553,790
Maine	266	59	40	34	133	197	1,331,479
Maryland	9,660	4,008	1,029	732	3,891	148	5,312,551
Massachusetts	5,247	1,357	977	930	1,983	346	6,477,104
Michigan	7,067	3,286	400	579	2,802	613	9,757,748
Minnesota	3,725	1,193	288	588	1,656	377	5,519,952
Mississippi	1,570	1,043	74	134	319	71	1,565,661
Missouri	6,481	3,508	323	440	2,210	576	5,939,159
Montana	266	70	32	49	115	106	1,036,405
Nebraska	940	477	68	70	325	224	1,820,419
Nevada	6,340	2,433	551	651	2,705	52	2,940,058
New Hampshire	415	83	75	41	216	174	1,275,170
New Jersey	8,934	3,157	782	579	4,416	569	8,944,469
New Mexico	2,697	1,171	379	304	843	104	1,906,995
New York	22,247	4,648	2,387	2,122	13,090	549	19,508,097
North Carolina	5,543	2,993	370	420	1,760	275	6,638,699
North Dakota	181	34	29	28	90	106	753,138
Ohio	11,576	3,497	517	766	6,796	472	9,736,188
Oklahoma	3,150	1,513	275	235	1,127	341	3,833,107
Oregon	2,194	521	220	251	1,202	180	3,681,279
Pennsylvania	11,764	5,077	786	780	5,121	1,241	11,691,589
Rhode Island	480	128	79	53	220	46	983,740
South Carolina	3,871	2,147	254	286	1,184	434	4,794,988
South Dakota	252	71	27	34	120	108	791,627
Tennessee	7,770	4,410	460	927	1,973	462	6,610,985
Texas	33,015	18,312	2,275	2,733	9,695	984	27,340,228
Utah	1,505	463	199	167	676	116	2,937,596
Vermont	48	16	6	4	22	46	348,314
Virginia	4,765	2,593	314	433	1,425	413	8,406,696
Washington	5,596	1,431	546	601	3,018	236	7,263,284
West Virginia	497	176	69	76	176	301	1,380,643
Wisconsin	4,698	2,557	222	393	1,526	413	5,730,771
Wyoming	58	21	2	13	22	55	556,446

1 The number of robberies from agencies that submitted 12 months of data in 2015 for which breakdowns by type of weapon were included.   2 Limited data were received.

Table 14. Aggravated Assault, by State and Type of Weapon, 2016

(Number.)

State	Total aggravated assaults[1]	Firearms	Knives or cutting instruments	Other weapons	Personal weapons	Agency count	Population
Alabama	17,364	3,994	1,762	10,068	1,540	264	4,392,449
Alaska	3,992	883	750	1,224	1,135	32	738,566
Arizona	19,232	5,024	2,822	4,559	6,827	90	6,514,042
Arkansas	11,385	3,884	1,662	2,564	3,275	272	2,827,056
California	104,295	20,633	17,156	36,031	30,475	732	39,209,622
Colorado	11,271	3,590	2,651	2,778	2,252	197	5,109,023
Connecticut	4,558	746	1,053	1,579	1,180	103	3,500,401
Delaware	3,120	1,054	596	1,095	375	56	950,787
District of Columbia	4,063	1,057	1,181	1,341	484	3	681,170
Florida	59,678	17,506	10,874	21,084	10,214	668	20,566,240
Georgia	22,896	8,329	3,204	5,867	5,496	504	9,639,636
Hawaii	2,769	180	424	1,074	1,091	4	1,428,557
Idaho	2,866	613	464	838	951	108	1,680,830
Illinois[2]	1,745	955	184	278	328	1	147,363
Indiana	14,225	3,233	1,506	3,876	5,610	217	4,663,407
Iowa	6,321	920	978	1,260	3,163	207	2,867,132
Kansas	6,441	2,223	1,282	1,652	1,284	227	2,211,329
Kentucky	5,035	1,714	662	1,829	830	420	4,424,357
Louisiana	18,173	5,284	2,803	4,958	5,128	187	4,553,790
Maine	948	74	160	218	496	197	1,331,479
Maryland	14,595	2,474	3,420	5,387	3,314	148	5,312,551
Massachusetts	17,289	1,940	3,935	7,504	3,910	346	6,477,104
Michigan	30,387	8,401	5,521	10,177	6,288	613	9,757,748
Minnesota	7,028	1,635	1,239	1,739	2,415	377	5,519,952
Mississippi	2,469	902	340	593	634	71	1,565,661
Missouri	21,610	7,914	2,563	5,792	5,341	576	5,939,159
Montana	2,948	477	399	964	1,108	106	1,036,405
Nebraska	3,409	763	641	1,077	928	224	1,820,419
Nevada	11,557	2,445	2,122	4,806	2,184	52	2,940,058
New Hampshire	1,546	302	375	323	546	174	1,275,170
New Jersey	11,075	2,196	2,313	3,741	2,825	569	8,944,469
New Mexico	9,104	2,092	1,627	2,775	2,610	104	1,906,995
New York	44,896	4,943	11,305	13,527	15,121	549	19,508,097
North Carolina	15,209	6,878	2,355	3,118	2,858	275	6,638,699
North Dakota	1,207	60	143	285	719	106	753,138
Ohio	14,648	5,339	2,608	4,218	2,483	472	9,736,188
Oklahoma	12,086	2,827	2,080	3,970	3,209	341	3,833,107
Oregon	6,061	904	1,095	1,981	2,081	180	3,681,279
Pennsylvania	20,817	4,731	3,033	4,977	8,076	1,241	11,691,589
Rhode Island	1,312	268	399	385	260	46	983,740
South Carolina	17,360	7,186	2,831	4,198	3,145	434	4,794,988
South Dakota	2,176	235	451	551	939	108	791,627
Tennessee	30,777	10,924	5,361	11,120	3,372	462	6,610,985
Texas	71,583	21,222	14,482	22,677	13,202	984	27,340,228
Utah	4,057	849	1,027	1,210	971	116	2,937,596
Vermont	302	39	59	53	151	46	348,314
Virginia	10,239	3,229	1,787	2,701	2,522	413	8,406,696
Washington	12,907	2,708	1,987	4,012	4,200	236	7,263,284
West Virginia	4,004	1,025	536	929	1,514	301	1,380,643
Wisconsin	10,729	2,824	1,175	2,324	4,406	413	5,730,771
Wyoming	1,087	90	159	257	581	55	556,446

1 The number of aggravated assaults from agencies that submitted 12 months of data in 2015 for which breakdowns by type of weapon were included.   2 Limited data were received.

Table 15. Offense Analysis, Number and Percent Change, 2015–2016

(Number, percent, dollars; 14,554 agencies; 2016 estimated population 282,238,499.)

Classification	Number of offenses, 2016	Percent change from 2015	Percent distribution[1]	Average value (dollars)
Murder	14,774	+7.8	NA	X
Rape[2]	100,373	NA	NA	X
Robbery	280,357	+1.7	100.0	$1,400
By location				
Street/highway	108,957	-1.8	38.9	1,191
Commercial house	42,783	+4.6	15.3	1,689
Gas or service station	8,178	+2.1	2.9	970
Convenience store	17,401	+6.7	6.2	732
Residence	46,419	+2.3	16.6	1,758
Bank	4,982	+0.8	1.8	3,531
Miscellaneous	51,637	+5.0	18.4	1,367
Burglary	1,354,920	-4.4	100.0	2,361
By location				
Residence (dwelling)	942,177	-7.1	69.5	2,273
Residence, night	278,600	-4.5	20.6	1,913
Residence, day	486,006	-8.6	35.9	2,258
Residence, unknown	177,571	-7.1	13.1	2,879
Nonresidence (store, office, etc.)	412,743	+2.6	30.5	2,562
Nonresidence, night	178,470	+6.0	13.2	2,585
Nonresidence, day	142,631	-0.1	10.5	2,182
Nonresidence, unknown	91,642	+0.7	6.8	3,109
Larceny-theft (except motor vehicle theft)	4,971,925	-1.3	100.0	999
By type				
Pocket-picking	24,352	-0.4	0.5	646
Purse-snatching	19,968	-1.6	0.4	475
Shoplifting	1,038,574	-6.7	20.9	250
From motor vehicles (except accessories)	1,301,447	+6.5	26.2	869
Motor vehicle accessories	366,048	+2.0	7.4	541
Bicycles	162,547	-10.8	3.3	483
From buildings	533,553	-6.3	10.7	1,449
From coin-operated machines	10,877	-6.8	0.2	607
All others	1,514,559	-1.4	30.5	1,649
By value				
Over $200	2,256,253	-1.5	45.4	2,140
$50 to $200	1,075,664	-4.3	21.6	108
Under $50	1,640,008	+0.9	33.0	14
Motor Vehicle Theft	700,143	+6.9	NA	7,680

NA = Not available.
X = Not applicable.
* = Less than one-tenth of one percent.
1 Because of rounding, the percentages may not add to 100.0.   2 The rape figure in this table is an aggregate total of the data submitted using both the revised and legacy Uniform Crime Reporting definitions.

Table 16. Property Stolen and Recovered, by Type and Value, 2016

(Dollars, percent; 13,981 agencies; 2016 estimated population 273,294,030.)

Type of property	Value of property (dollars)		Percent recovered
	Stolen	Recovered	
Total	$13,667,503,625	$3,776,517,466	27.6
Currency, notes, etc.	1,429,781,653	33,375,702	2.3
Jewelry and precious metals	1,362,002,838	55,751,909	4.1
Clothing and furs	362,025,765	38,980,936	10.8
Locally stolen motor vehicles	5,527,133,714	3,228,597,961	58.4
Office equipment	483,550,405	25,750,989	5.3
Televisions, radios, stereos, etc.	455,215,103	22,319,049	4.9
Firearms	155,186,427	14,794,219	9.5
Household goods	228,961,414	10,003,415	4.4
Consumable goods	139,167,892	15,512,495	11.1
Livestock	22,666,215	2,570,359	11.3
Miscellaneous	3,501,812,199	328,860,432	9.4

SECTION III

OFFENSES CLEARED

SECTION III: OFFENSES CLEARED

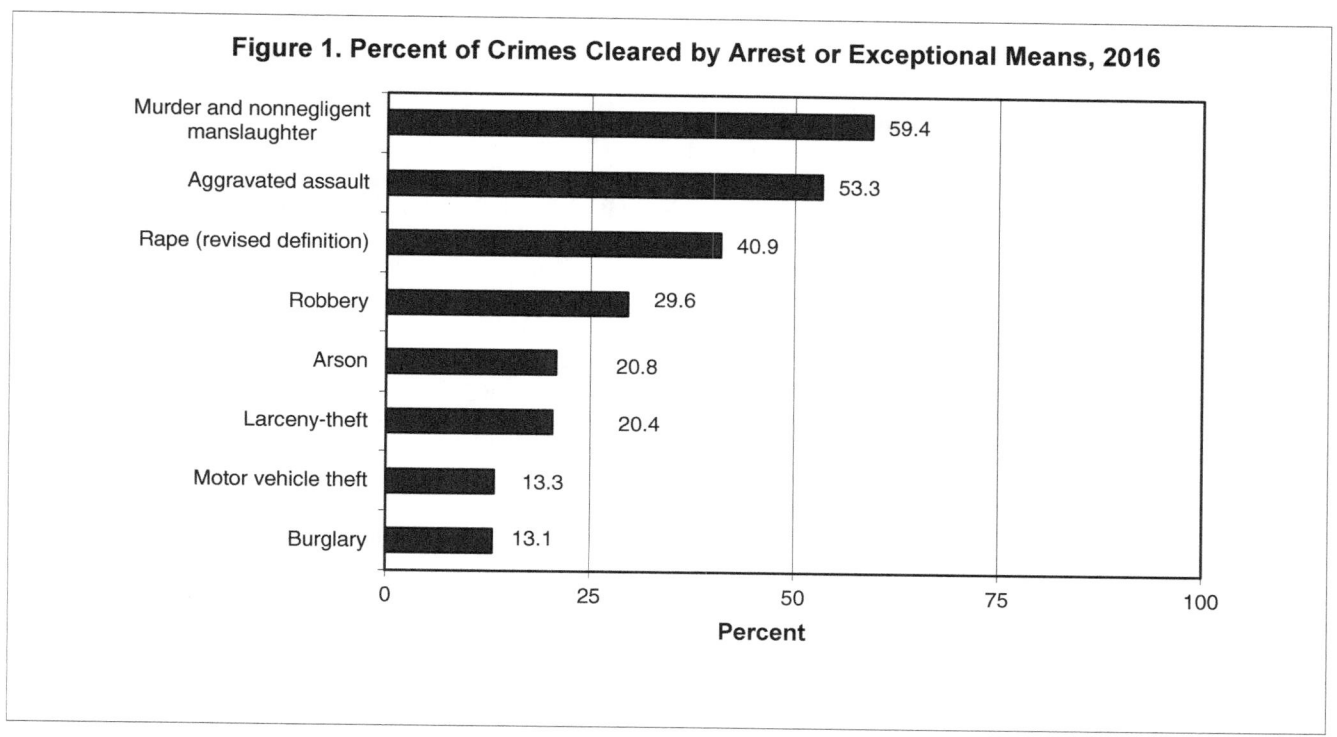

Figure 1. Percent of Crimes Cleared by Arrest or Exceptional Means, 2016

Offense	Percent
Murder and nonnegligent manslaughter	59.4
Aggravated assault	53.3
Rape (revised definition)	40.9
Robbery	29.6
Arson	20.8
Larceny-theft	20.4
Motor vehicle theft	13.3
Burglary	13.1

Law enforcement agencies that report crime to the Federal Bureau of Investigation (FBI) can clear, or "close," offenses in one of two ways: by arrest or by exceptional means. However, the administrative closing of a case by a local law enforcement agency does not necessarily mean that the agency can clear an offense for Uniform Crime Reporting (UCR) purposes. To clear an offense within the program's guidelines, the reporting agency must adhere to certain criteria, which are outlined in this section. (*Note:* The UCR program does not distinguish between offenses cleared by arrest and those cleared by exceptional means in its data presentations. The distinction is made solely for the purpose of a definition and not for data collection and publication.) See Appendix I for information on the UCR program's statistical methodology.

Important Note: Rape Data

In 2013, the FBI UCR Program initiated the collection of rape data within the Summary Reporting System under a revised definition. The changes bring uniformity to the offense in both the Summary Reporting System (SRS) and the National Incident-Based Reporting System (NIBRS) by capturing data (1) without regard to gender, (2) including penetration of any bodily orifice by any object or body part, and (3) including offenses where physical force is not involved. The term "forcible" was

removed, and the definition changed to the revised UCR definition below.

- Legacy UCR definition of rape: The carnal knowledge of a female forcibly and against her will.

- Revised UCR definition of rape: Penetration, no matter how slight, of the vagina or anus with any body part or object, or oral penetration by a sex organ of another person, without the consent of the victim.

For more information, please see <https://www.fbi.gov/about-us/cjis/ucr/crime-in-the-u.s/2013/crime-in-the-u.s.-2013/resource-pages/rape-addendum>.

Beginning January 1, 2017, the UCR Program will discontinue collecting rape data via the SRS according to the historical, legacy definition. Only rape data submitted under the revised definition will be published for 2017 and subsequent years. This change will not affect agencies that submit rape data via NIBRS.

Cleared by Arrest

In the UCR program, a law enforcement agency reports that an offense is cleared by arrest, or solved for crime reporting purposes, when at least one person is arrested, charged with the commission of the offense, and turned over to the court for prosecution (whether following arrest, court summons, or police notice). To qualify as a clearance, *all* of these conditions must be met.

In its calculations, the UCR program counts the number of offenses that are cleared, not the number of arrestees. Therefore, the arrest of one person may clear several crimes, and the arrest of many persons may clear only one offense. In addition, some clearances recorded by an agency during a particular calendar year, such as 2016, may pertain to offenses that occurred in previous years.

Cleared by Exceptional Means

In certain situations, elements beyond law enforcement's control prevent the agency from arresting and formally charging the offender. When this occurs, the agency can clear the offense *exceptionally*. There are four UCR program requirements that law enforcement must meet in order to clear an offense by exceptional means. The agency must have:

- Identified the offender

- Gathered enough evidence to support an arrest, make a charge, and turn over the offender to the court for prosecution

- Identified the offender's exact location so that the suspect could be taken into custody immediately

- Encountered a circumstance outside the control of law enforcement that prohibits the agency from arresting, charging, and prosecuting the offender

Examples of exceptional clearances include, but are not limited to, the death of the offender (e.g., suicide or justifiably killed by a law enforcement officer or a citizen), the victim's refusal to cooperate with the prosecution after the offender has been identified, or the denial of extradition because the offender committed a crime in another jurisdiction and is being prosecuted for that offense. In the UCR program, the recovery of property does not clear an offense.

National Clearances

A review of the data for 2016 revealed law enforcement agencies in the United States cleared 46.0 percent of violent crimes (murder, rape, robbery, and aggravated assault) and 19.4 percent of property crimes (burglary, larceny-theft, and motor vehicle theft) brought to their attention. In addition, law enforcement cleared 20.4 percent of arson offenses, which are reported in a slightly different manner than the other property crimes. (Table 25) More details concerning this offense are furnished in the arson text in this section.

As in most years, law enforcement agencies cleared a higher percentage of violent crimes than property crimes in 2016. As a rule, clearance rates generally rise due to the more vigorous investigative efforts put forth for violent crimes. In addition, violent crimes more often involve victims and/ or witnesses who are able to identify the perpetrators.

A breakdown of the clearances for violent crimes for 2016 revealed that the nation's law enforcement agencies cleared 59.4 percent of murder offenses (a decrease from 2015), 53.3 percent of aggravated assault offenses, 36.5 percent of rape offenses (revised definition), and 29.6 percent of robbery offenses. (Table 25)

For property crime offenses in 2016, law enforcement agencies throughout the nation collectively 13.1 percent of burglary offenses, 20.4 percent of larceny-theft offenses, and 13.3 percent of motor vehicle theft offenses. (Table 17)

Regional Clearances

The UCR program divides the nation into four regions: the Northeast, the Midwest, the South, and the West. (See Appendix III for further details.) A review of clearance data for 2015 by region showed that agencies in the Northeast cleared the greatest proportion of their violent crime offenses (54.3 percent) and was the only region to clear more than half of these types of offenses by arrest. Law enforcement agencies in the West cleared 45.5 percent of their violent crimes, agencies in the South cleared 45.0 percent of their violent crimes, and agencies in the Midwest cleared 41.3 percent of their violent crimes, respectively. (Table 18)

For murder and nonnegligent manslaughter in 2015, the West cleared 64.7 percent of offenses, closely followed by the South (62.5 percent). The Northeast cleared 61.7 percent and the Midwest cleared 54.9 percent of these offenses. Rape (revised definition) offenses were cleared 42.1 percent of the time in the South and in the Northeast, 34.5 percent of the time in the West, and 31.4 percent of the time in the Midwest. For robbery, the Northeast had the highest clearance rate, at 36.2 percent. The Northeast also had the highest proportion of clearances for aggravated assault (65.6 percent). (Table 18)

Clearance data for 2015 showed that, among the regions, law enforcement agencies in the Northeast cleared the highest percentage of their property crimes (23.7 percent). Agencies in the South and Midwest cleared 20.5 percent and 19.6 percent, respectively. Agencies in the West cleared 15.4 percent of their property crimes. (Table 18)

Agencies in the Northeast cleared the highest percentage of burglary offenses at 17.3 percent, followed by the South at 13.8 percent, the Midwest at 10.9 percent, and the West at 10.8 percent. For larceny-theft, the Northeast (25.7 percent) was followed by the South at 22.9 percent, the Midwest at 22.7 percent, and the West at 17.9 percent. The South and Northeast cleared the highest proportion of motor vehicle thefts at 16.1 and 15.7 percent, respectively, followed by the Midwest at 13.7 percent and the West at 9.7 percent. The Northeast cleared the greatest percentage of arson offenses (26.6 percent), followed by the South (20.9 percent). (Table 18)

Clearances by Population Groups

The UCR program uses the following population group designations in its data presentations: cities (grouped according to population size) and counties (classified as either metropolitan or nonmetropolitan counties). A breakdown of these classifications is furnished in Appendix III.

CITIES

In 2015, the clearance data collected showed that law enforcement agencies in the nation's cities cleared 43.7 percent of their violent crime offenses. Among the city population groups, agencies in the smallest cities, those with fewer than 10,000 inhabitants, cleared the greatest proportion of their violent crime offenses (54.0 percent), and law enforcement in cities with 500,000 to 999,999 inhabitants cleared the smallest proportion of their violent crime offenses (34.9 percent). (Table 17)

The clearance data for murder showed that among the city population groups, cities with populations of 10,000 to 24,999 cleared the greatest percentage of their murders (65.3 percent). Law enforcement agencies in cities with 500,000 to 999,999 inhabitants cleared the lowest percentage of their murders (49.3 percent). For rape (revised definition), cities with 500,000 to 999,999 inhabitants cleared the largest percentage of offenses at 40.8 percent, while cities with 10,000 to 24,999 inhabitants cleared the lowest percentage of offenses at 32.1 percent. Cities with under 10,000 inhabitants cleared the greatest percentage of their robbery offenses at 36.2 percent, and cities with 500,000 to 999,999 inhabitants cleared the lowest proportion of their robbery offenses at 23.2 percent. For aggravated assault, cities with less than 10,000 inhabitants cleared the highest proportion of offenses (60.6 percent); cities with 500,000 to 999,999 inhabitants cleared the lowest percentage of offenses (40.5 percent). (Table 17)

In 2015, agencies in the nation's cities collectively cleared 18.2 percent of their property crime offenses. Law enforcement in cities with 10,000 to 24,999 inhabitants cleared the highest proportion of the property crimes (25.4 percent) brought to their attention; cities with 500,000 to 999,999 inhabitants cleared the smallest proportion of their property crimes (11.3 percent). (Table 17)

Law enforcement agencies in cities cleared 12.4 percent of burglaries, 20.5 percent of larceny-thefts, 13.1 percent of motor vehicle thefts, and 12.2 percent of arsons in 2015. For burglaries, cities with fewer than 10,000 inhabitants cleared the largest percentage of their offenses at 17.7 percent, while cities with 500,000 to 999,999 inhabitants cleared the smallest percentage of their offenses at 9.0 percent. Cities with 10,000 to 24,999 inhabitants cleared the greatest percentage of their larceny-theft offenses (28.0 percent), and cities with 500,000 to 999,999 inhabitants cleared the lowest proportion of larceny-theft offenses (12.3 percent). For motor vehicle theft, cities with fewer than 10,000 inhabitants cleared the highest percentages of their offenses at 24.0 percent. Cities with 10,000 to 24,999 inhabitants cleared the greatest percentage of their arson offenses, at 29.1 percent. (Table 17)

METROPOLITAN AND NONMETROPOLITAN COUNTIES

In 2016, law enforcement agencies in metropolitan counties cleared 51.9 percent of their violent crime offenses. Of the violent crimes made known to law enforcement agencies in metropolitan counties, murder offenses had the highest proportion of clearance (66.1 percent), followed by aggravated assaults (58.7 percent), robberies (34.4 percent), and rapes (revised definition, 42.8 percent). Law enforcement agencies in metropolitan counties cleared 18.3 percent of their total property crimes, 14.7 percent of burglaries, 19.7 percent of larceny-thefts, 16.8 percent of motor vehicle thefts, and 21.6 percent of their arsons. (Table 17)

Like their counterparts in metropolitan counties, nonmetropolitan counties collectively cleared a greater proportion of their violent crimes than did the nation as a whole in 2016. Nonmetropolitan counties cleared 57.3 percent of their violent crime offenses and 18.7 percent of property crimes. Of the violent crimes known to them, law enforcement in nonmetropolitan counties had the highest number of clearances for murder (69.4 percent), with 41.3 percent of rapes (revised definition), 44.1 percent of robberies, and 61.7 percent of aggravated assaults being cleared. Agencies in nonmetropolitan counties reported clearing 19.1 percent of their total property crimes, 16.5 percent of burglaries, 19.8 percent of larceny-thefts, 24.8 percent of motor vehicle thefts, and 25.8 percent of their arsons. (Table 17)

Clearances by Classification Group and Type

For rape (revised definition), by classification group and type, law enforcement agencies cleared 38.7 percent of assault-to-rape attempts and 37.1 percent of rapes by force in 2015. Cleared robbery offenses included 33.8 percent of offenses involving strong-arm tactics, 33.2 percent of offenses involving knives or other cutting instruments,

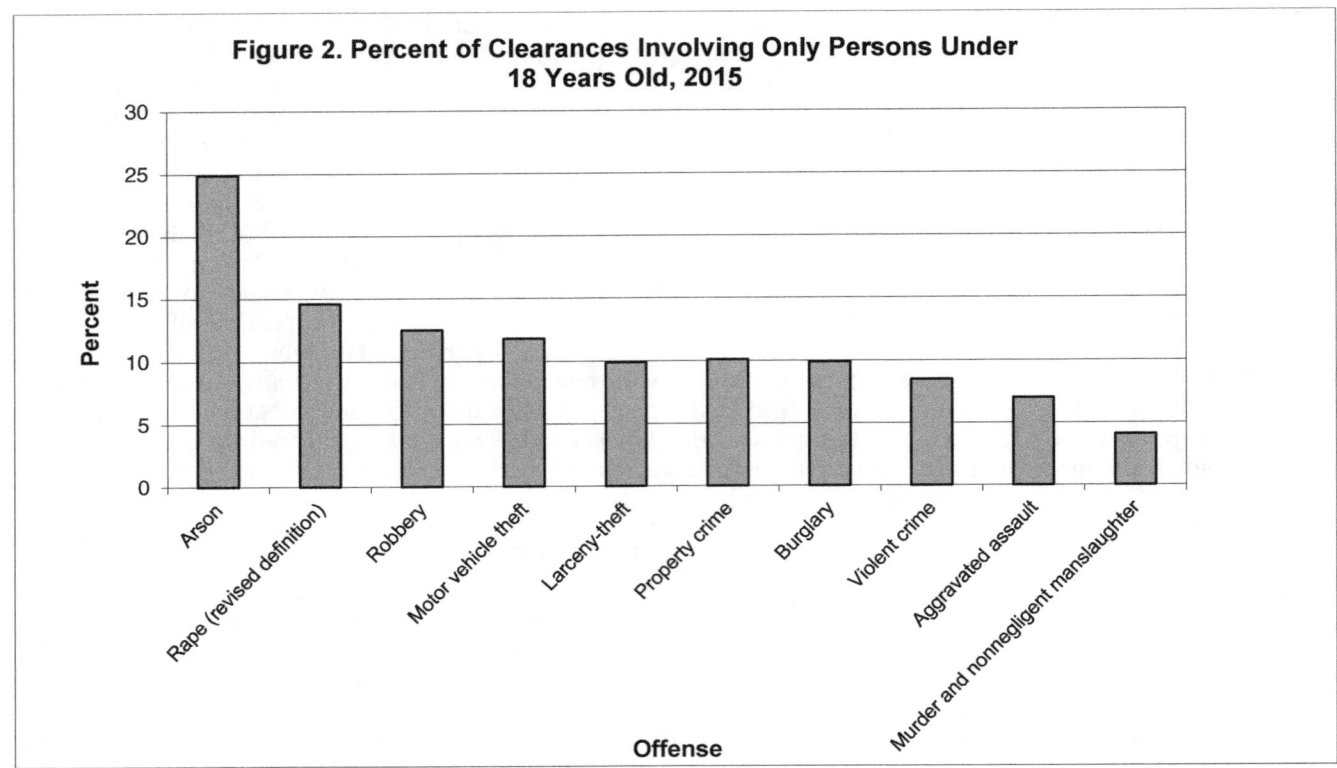

Figure 2. Percent of Clearances Involving Only Persons Under 18 Years Old, 2015

31.2 percent of offenses involving other weapons, and 22.7 percent of offenses involving firearms. For aggravated assaults, agencies cleared 37.3 percent of offenses involving knives or other cutting instruments; 61.8 percent of offenses involving hands, feet, fists, etc.; 54.5 percent of offenses involving other weapons; and 37.3 percent of offenses involving firearms. (Table 19)

For property crime clearances grouped by classification and type, data showed that the highest percentage of burglary clearances in the nation in 2015 (14.1 percent) were of offenses that involved unlawful entry. Law enforcement agencies cleared 11.7 percent of burglaries involving forcible entry and 11.6 percent of attempted forcible entry offenses. For motor vehicle theft, agencies cleared 13.3 percent of motor vehicle theft offenses involving automobiles and 10.4 percent of motor vehicle theft offenses involving trucks and buses. (Table 19)

In 2015, 24.9 percent of structural arson offenses were cleared by arrest or exceptional means, while 9.5 percent of mobile arson offenses and 21.7 percent of other arson crimes were cleared. (Table 19)

CLEARANCES AND JUVENILES

When an offender under 18 years of age is cited to appear in juvenile court or before other juvenile authorities, the UCR program considers the incident for which the juvenile is being held responsible to be cleared by arrest, although a physical arrest may not have occurred. In addition, according to program definitions, clearances that include both adult and juvenile offenders are classified as clearances for crimes committed by adults. Therefore, the juvenile clearance data are limited to those clearances involving juveniles only, and the figures in this publication should not be used to present a definitive picture of juvenile involvement in crime.

Of the clearances for violent crimes that were reported in the nation in 2015, 8.5 percent involved only juveniles, down from 9.5 percent in 2011. In the nation's cities, collectively, 8.7 percent of violent crime clearances involved only juveniles (unchanged from 2014), with juveniles in cities exclusively involved in 4.4 percent of murder clearances, 13.9 percent of rape (revised definition) clearances, 12.8 percent of robbery clearances, and 7.1 percent of aggravated assault clearances. Of the nation's city population groups, cities with under 10,000 inhabitants had the highest percentage of overall clearances for violent crime only involving juveniles (9.0 percent); cities with 1,000,000 or more inhabitants had the lowest percentage, 8.4 percent. (Table 20)

Law enforcement agencies in metropolitan counties reported that 8.1 percent of their violent crime clearances—including 3.3 percent of their murder clearances, 16.9 percent of their rape (revised definition) clearances, 10.8 percent of their robbery clearances, and 6.8 percent of their aggravated assault clearances— involved only juveniles. Agencies in nonmetropolitan counties reported that 6.8 percent of their clearances for violent crime involved only juveniles, including 2.8 percent of their murder clearances, 16.1 percent of their rape (revised definition) clearances, 4.3 percent of their robbery clearances, and 5.6 percent of their aggravated assault clearances. (Table 20)

In 2015, 10.1 percent of clearances for property crime involved only juveniles. In cities collectively, 10.4 percent of the clearances for property crime, 10.8 percent of clearances for burglary, 10.2 percent of clearances for larceny-theft, 12.4 percent of clearances for motor vehicle theft, and 26.3 percent of clearances for arson involved juveniles only. Among the population groups labeled *city*,

the percentages of clearances involving only juveniles for overall property crime ranged from a low of 8.7 percent in cities with fewer than 10,000 inhabitants to a high of 11.5 percent in cities with populations of 500,000 to 999,999 inhabitants and cities with 50,000 to 99,999 inhabitants. (Table 20)

Metropolitan counties reported that 9.4 percent of all property crime clearances, 8.7 percent of burglary clearances, 9.5 percent of larceny-theft clearances, 10.1 percent of motor vehicle theft clearances, and 23.2 percent of arson clearances involved persons under 18 years of age. In nonmetropolitan counties, 6.6 percent of property crime clearances, 6.3 percent of burglary clearances, 6.5 percent of larceny-theft clearances, 8.5 percent of motor vehicle theft clearances, and 15.5 percent of arson clearances involved juveniles exclusively. In suburban areas, 27.2 percent of arson clearances involved only juveniles. (Table 20)

Table 17. Number and Percent of Offenses Cleared by Arrest or Exceptional Means, by Population Group, 2016

(Number, percent.)

Population group	Violent crime	Murder and nonnegligent manslaughter	Rape (revised definition)[1]	Rape (legacy definition)[2]	Robbery	Aggravated assault	Property crime	Burglary	Larceny-theft	Motor vehicle theft	Arson[3]	Number of agencies	Estimated population, 2016
Total, All Agencies													
Offenses known	1,183,933	15,566	111,241	6,822	306,172	744,132	7,319,177	1,393,570	5,211,566	714,041	42,131	15,336	297,593,825
Percent cleared by arrest	45.6	59.4	36.5	40.9	29.6	53.3	18.3	13.1	20.4	13.3	20.8		
Total Cities													
Offenses known	944,676	11,978	82,764	4,534	268,367	577,033	5,818,143	1,025,177	4,213,156	579,810	31,622	10,953	201,336,755
Percent cleared by arrest	43.7	57.1	34.7	43.3	29.1	51.6	18.2	12.4	20.5	12.2	20.1		
Group I (250,000 and over)													
Offenses known	446,513	6,229	31,796	1,137	148,440	258,911	1,992,102	358,785	1,371,236	262,081	12,563	83	59,116,292
Percent cleared by arrest	39.1	52.9	36.4	43.7	26.8	46.2	12.7	9.6	14.2	9.2	15.3		
1,000,000 and over (Group I subset)													
Offenses known	171,699	1,923	12,383	0	59,695	97,698	655,240	111,045	455,822	88,373	3,639	10	24,933,624
Percent cleared by arrest	44.4	60.2	37.6	0.0	31.1	53.0	12.4	9.6	13.9	8.3	14.1		
500,000 to 999,999 (Group I subset)													
Offenses known	150,170	2,242	9,992	600	48,381	88,955	732,585	133,045	506,516	93,024	4,350	24	17,424,128
Percent cleared by arrest	34.9	49.3	38.4	35.3	23.2	40.5	11.3	9.0	12.3	9.0	16.6		
250,000 to 499,999 (Group I subset)													
Offenses known	124,644	2,064	9,421	537	40,364	72,258	604,277	114,695	408,898	80,684	4,574	49	16,758,540
Percent cleared by arrest	37.1	50.1	32.6	53.1	24.6	44.2	14.8	10.3	16.9	10.5	14.9		
Group II (100,000 to 249,999)													
Offenses known	154,137	2,067	14,154	624	44,621	92,671	1,029,742	185,432	726,965	117,345	4,968	214	31,784,818
Percent cleared by arrest	42.0	59.5	33.2	42.1	27.7	49.8	16.6	11.6	18.7	11.8	20.2		
Group III (50,000 to 99,999)													
Offenses known	112,984	1,188	11,254	601	30,104	69,837	868,828	149,523	639,214	80,091	4,265	468	32,549,603
Percent cleared by arrest	49.2	63.5	35.5	43.1	33.7	57.9	19.9	13.0	22.4	12.5	21.3		
Group IV (25,000 to 49,999)													
Offenses known	84,913	949	9,055	856	20,613	53,440	703,177	120,839	532,352	49,986	3,232	813	28,308,217
Percent cleared by arrest	47.5	61.7	32.1	35.4	33.9	55.3	22.8	13.6	25.7	14.9	24.1		
Group V (10,000 to 24,999)													
Offenses known	75,496	848	8,180	632	15,109	50,727	654,670	113,344	501,960	39,366	2,839	1,702	27,155,943
Percent cleared by arrest	52.4	65.3	34.4	42.9	36.1	60.1	25.4	15.8	28.0	19.6	29.1		
Group VI (under 10,000)													
Offenses known	70,633	697	8,325	684	9,480	51,447	569,624	97,254	441,429	30,941	3,755	7,673	22,421,882
Percent cleared by arrest	54.0	60.4	32.5	54.2	36.2	60.6	24.1	17.7	25.6	24.0	24.8		
Metropolitan Counties													
Offenses known	191,881	2,736	20,192	1,716	35,096	132,141	1,214,788	278,245	825,554	110,989	7,842	1,997	72,365,974
Percent cleared by arrest	51.9	66.1	41.3	34.2	32.0	58.7	18.3	14.7	19.7	16.9	21.6		
Nonmetropolitan Counties													
Offenses known	47,376	852	8,285	572	2,709	34,958	286,246	90,148	172,856	23,242	2,667	2,386	23,891,096
Percent cleared by arrest	57.3	69.4	42.8	41.3	44.1	61.7	19.1	16.5	19.8	24.8	25.8		
Suburban Areas[4]													
Offenses known	329,716	4,147	35,781	2,790	66,051	220,947	2,461,511	475,833	1,790,558	195,120	13,728	8,314	128,677,778
Percent cleared by arrest	51.7	63.9	38.0	39.7	33.3	59.3	20.9	15.0	22.9	16.8	23.7		

1 The figures shown in this column for the offense of rape were reported using the revised Uniform Crime Reporting (UCR) definition of rape. See chapter notes for more detail.   2 The figures shown in this column for the offense of rape were reported using the legacy Uniform Crime Reporting (UCR) definition of rape. See chapter notes for more detail.   3 Not all agencies submit reports for arson to the FBI. As a result, the number of reports the FBI uses to compute the percent of offenses cleared for arson is less than the number it uses to compute the percent of offenses cleared for all other offenses.   4 Suburban area includes law enforcement agencies in cities with less than 50,000 inhabitants and county law enforcement agencies that are within a Metropolitan Statistical Area. Suburban area excludes all metropolitan agencies associated with a principal city. The agencies associated with suburban areas also appear in other groups within this table.

Table 18. Number and Percent of Offenses Cleared by Arrest or Exceptional Means, by Region and Geographic Division, 2015

(Number, percent.)

Geographic region/division	Violent crime	Murder and nonnegligent manslaughter	Rape (revised definition)[1]	Rape (legacy definition)[2]	Robbery	Aggravated assault	Property crime	Burglary	Larceny-theft	Motor vehicle theft	Arson[3]	Number of agencies	Estimated population, 2015
Total, All Agencies													
Offenses known	1,131,223	14,392	103,064	7,518	299,232	707,017	7,332,702	1,450,074	5,225,538	657,090	40,260	15,239	294,548,721
Percent cleared by arrest	46.0	61.5	37.8	36.2	29.3	54.0	19.4	12.9	21.9	13.1	20.4		
Northeast													
Offenses known	175,431	1,914	15,531	286	54,964	102,736	926,067	153,688	717,792	54,587	4,435	3,440	55,131,257
Percent cleared by arrest	54.3	61.7	42.1	52.1	36.2	65.6	23.7	17.3	25.7	15.7	26.6		
New England													
Offenses known	38,959	297	3,981	240	8,798	25,643	243,282	43,776	183,453	16,053	1,058	923	14,206,163
Percent cleared by arrest	48.2	64.3	25.7	48.3	26.9	58.8	18.6	13.7	20.3	12.6	22.5		
Middle Atlantic													
Offenses known	136,472	1,617	11,550	46	46,166	77,093	682,785	109,912	534,339	38,534	3,377	2,517	40,925,094
Percent cleared by arrest	56.0	61.2	47.7	71.7	37.9	67.9	25.5	18.7	27.6	16.9	27.9		
Midwest													
Offenses known	181,411	2,461	21,557	1,523	43,059	112,811	1,196,340	240,489	862,296	93,555	8,705	3,828	51,109,670
Percent cleared by arrest	41.3	54.9	31.4	36.6	24.4	49.4	19.6	10.9	22.7	13.7	16.2		
East North Central													
Offenses known	108,747	1,523	12,733	1,261	28,877	64,353	693,940	146,544	496,048	51,348	5,336	1,836	30,534,385
Percent cleared by arrest	36.7	47.5	27.6	39.3	22.6	44.6	17.6	9.9	20.6	11.2	14.6		
West North Central													
Offenses known	72,664	938	8,824	262	14,182	48,458	502,400	93,945	366,248	42,207	3,369	1,992	20,575,285
Percent cleared by arrest	48.2	67.0	36.9	23.7	28.0	55.9	22.4	12.4	25.6	16.8	18.8		
South													
Offenses known	480,571	6,914	38,414	3,893	120,795	310,555	3,182,039	666,963	2,275,629	239,447	14,020	5,871	114,964,068
Percent cleared by arrest	45.0	62.5	42.1	39.5	27.5	51.9	20.5	13.8	22.9	16.1	20.9		
South Atlantic													
Offenses known	236,534	3,635	14,739	3,650	61,789	152,721	1,587,176	321,823	1,150,675	114,678	6,486	2,790	59,461,566
Percent cleared by arrest	46.9	61.7	47.4	41.0	29.3	53.8	21.8	16.2	23.9	17.0	23.9		
East South Central													
Offenses known	76,392	1,102	6,330	243	16,760	51,957	474,490	110,904	330,362	33,224	2,238	1,272	17,181,649
Percent cleared by arrest	45.6	59.5	41.8	16.9	28.5	51.4	22.6	14.0	25.5	22.2	19.4		
West South Central													
Offenses known	167,645	2,177	17,345	0	42,246	105,877	1,120,373	234,236	794,592	91,545	5,296	1,809	38,320,853
Percent cleared by arrest	42.1	65.2	37.8	0.0	24.3	49.4	17.7	10.5	20.4	12.7	17.9		
West													
Offenses known	293,810	3,103	27,562	1,816	80,414	180,915	2,028,256	388,934	1,369,821	269,501	13,100	2,100	73,343,726
Percent cleared by arrest	45.5	64.7	34.5	26.5	30.1	53.8	15.4	10.8	17.9	9.7	20.4		
Mountain													
Offenses known	94,953	906	10,775	1,292	20,116	61,864	646,043	123,510	457,245	65,288	3,506	903	23,119,372
Percent cleared by arrest	42.8	67.1	26.4	30.3	26.0	51.0	19.4	10.4	22.9	11.5	24.8		
Pacific													
Offenses known	198,857	2,197	16,787	524	60,298	119,051	1,382,213	265,424	912,576	204,213	9,594	1,197	50,224,354
Percent cleared by arrest	46.7	63.7	39.7	17.2	31.4	55.3	13.6	11.0	15.4	9.1	18.8		

1 The figures shown in this column for the offense of rape were reported using the revised Uniform Crime Reporting (UCR) definition of rape. See chapter notes for more detail. 2 The figures shown in this column for the offense of rape were reported using the legacy Uniform Crime Reporting (UCR) definition of rape. See chapter notes for more detail. 3 Not all agencies submit reports for arson to the FBI. As a result, the number of reports the FBI uses to compute the percent of offenses cleared for arson is less than the number it uses to compute the percent of offenses cleared for all other offenses.

Table 19. Number and Percent of Offenses Cleared by Arrest or Exceptional Means, Additional Information About Selected Offenses, by Population Group, 2016

(Number, percent.)

Population group	Rape (revised definition)[1] Rape by force	Rape (revised definition)[1] Assault to rape-attempts	Rape (legacy definition)[2] Rape by force	Rape (legacy definition)[2] Assault to rape-attempts	Robbery Firearm	Robbery Knife or cutting instrument	Robbery Other weapon	Robbery Strong-arm	Aggravated assault Firearm	Aggravated assault Knife or cutting instrument	Aggravated assault Other weapon	Aggravated assault Hands, fists, feet, etc.
Total, All Agencies												
Offenses known	90,823	4,795	7,072	446	113,375	22,428	25,306	117,130	153,226	116,180	199,849	174,739
Percent cleared by arrest	37.1	38.7	36.4	34.1	22.7	33.2	31.2	33.8	37.3	62.3	54.5	61.8
Total Cities												
Offenses known	69,091	3,903	4,689	295	98,192	20,063	22,071	105,964	124,009	95,944	158,454	131,290
Percent cleared by arrest	35.7	39.0	36.5	38.3	22.7	32.9	30.7	33.6	34.0	61.7	53.3	62.2
Group I (250,000 and over)												
Offenses known	25,802	1,865	1,067	62	57,610	10,718	11,622	58,836	65,397	43,332	73,321	42,641
Percent cleared by arrest	37.8	39.1	32.1	40.3	20.3	30.7	28.3	31.1	29.3	59.5	49.6	59.8
1,000,000 and over (Group I subset)												
Offenses known	10,743	913	0	0	21,504	5,053	5,262	27,833	20,164	19,501	29,960	20,942
Percent cleared by arrest	40.4	45.0	0.0	0.0	22.0	35.0	31.2	36.9	32.8	62.8	54.7	67.8
500,000 to 999,999 (Group I subset)												
Offenses known	7,924	536	599	21	20,714	3,365	4,060	17,384	24,772	13,663	26,066	12,153
Percent cleared by arrest	34.7	35.3	30.6	61.9	17.1	24.3	22.6	23.7	28.0	54.2	41.9	50.9
250,000 to 499,999 (Group I subset)												
Offenses known	7,135	416	468	41	15,392	2,300	2,300	13,619	20,461	10,168	17,295	9,546
Percent cleared by arrest	37.2	31.3	34.2	29.3	22.4	30.7	31.8	28.5	27.4	60.1	52.5	53.7
Group II (100,000 to 249,999)												
Offenses known	11,798	515	602	36	16,045	3,385	3,525	16,286	20,831	15,870	25,092	17,437
Percent cleared by arrest	34.3	43.3	26.1	47.2	22.5	29.7	30.2	33.8	32.5	60.1	52.1	59.9
Group III (50,000 to 99,999)												
Offenses known	9,141	428	698	29	9,172	2,450	2,780	12,264	12,897	11,915	19,251	17,205
Percent cleared by arrest	36.4	36.7	42.1	51.7	27.9	35.8	33.6	37.3	39.3	65.8	59.6	67.0
Group IV (25,000 to 49,999)												
Offenses known	7,885	358	795	40	6,711	1,559	1,897	8,340	9,606	9,325	14,608	14,428
Percent cleared by arrest	33.3	36.3	35.0	32.5	26.7	38.2	32.6	37.0	40.7	63.5	56.6	63.6
Group V (10,000 to 24,999)												
Offenses known	7,171	319	735	28	5,329	1,167	1,379	5,958	8,750	7,916	13,751	16,109
Percent cleared by arrest	35.7	37.6	43.1	17.9	29.6	42.8	38.2	40.4	45.5	66.1	60.1	66.6
Group VI (under 10,000)												
Offenses known	7,294	418	792	100	3,325	784	868	4,280	6,528	7,586	12,431	23,470
Percent cleared by arrest	32.7	38.5	40.7	38.0	30.6	41.7	40.1	41.0	49.4	64.1	56.1	61.0
Metropolitan Counties												
Offenses known	14,891	598	1,762	111	14,092	2,144	2,899	10,305	22,793	16,031	32,170	30,917
Percent cleared by arrest	40.4	43.8	35.1	24.3	21.6	35.2	33.3	35.1	49.5	65.4	58.7	61.8
Nonmetropolitan Counties												
Offenses known	6,841	294	621	40	1,091	221	336	861	6,424	4,205	9,225	12,532
Percent cleared by arrest	43.3	25.2	39.0	30.0	36.1	49.3	40.2	42.9	59.6	66.2	60.8	57.8
Suburban Areas[4]												
Offenses known	27,997	1,219	2,910	181	24,357	4,425	5,670	22,701	35,837	29,631	55,883	59,772
Percent cleared by arrest	37.8	39.6	38.8	27.1	24.1	38.9	35.4	38.0	48.2	65.8	58.9	64.3

Table 19. Number and Percent of Offenses Cleared by Arrest or Exceptional Means, Additional Information About Selected Offenses, by Population Group, 2016—Continued

(Number, percent.)

Population group	Burglary			Motor vehicle theft			Arson[3]			Number of agencies	Estimated population, 2015
	Forcible entry	Unlawful entry	Attempted forcible entry	Autos	Trucks and buses	Other vehicles	Structure	Mobile	Other		
Total, All Agencies											
Offenses known	779,097	476,326	86,874	467,079	87,996	61,719	17,177	9,288	11,404	14,593	274,604,622
Percent cleared by arrest	11.7	14.1	11.6	13.3	10.4	10.4	24.9	9.5	21.7		
Total Cities											
Offenses known	576,506	351,202	68,356	389,270	68,984	43,485	13,209	6,940	8,786	10,596	188,057,806
Percent cleared by arrest	11.1	13.7	11.7	12.3	9.3	9.6	24.2	8.7	21.5		
Group I (250,000 and over)											
Offenses known	224,383	98,315	25,282	172,672	37,107	16,811	4,900	3,195	3,100	74	54,786,571
Percent cleared by arrest	8.6	11.2	11.0	9.2	6.6	7.1	20.8	5.3	18.2		
1,000,000 and over (Group I subset)											
Offenses known	78,837	31,548	8,267	60,697	16,586	5,991	1,375	1,041	971	10	24,675,984
Percent cleared by arrest	8.5	10.7	15.8	8.6	4.5	7.1	23.0	6.0	11.2		
500,000 to 999,999 (Group I subset)											
Offenses known	82,646	35,024	9,701	59,089	11,801	6,851	1,705	1,052	1,006	22	15,742,712
Percent cleared by arrest	7.5	10.4	7.8	8.9	7.3	6.8	17.9	4.8	21.7		
250,000 to 499,999 (Group I subset)											
Offenses known	62,900	31,743	7,314	52,886	8,720	3,969	1,820	1,102	1,123	42	14,367,875
Percent cleared by arrest	10.4	12.7	9.9	10.2	9.5	7.6	21.8	5.2	21.2		
Group II (100,000 to 249,999)											
Offenses known	102,432	62,039	11,460	78,777	12,955	8,009	2,044	1,120	1,270	189	28,281,300
Percent cleared by arrest	10.2	12.5	9.9	11.8	11.2	9.5	23.3	10.0	24.2		
Group III (50,000 to 99,999)											
Offenses known	77,346	56,095	9,430	55,150	8,556	6,167	1,646	847	1,491	435	30,343,562
Percent cleared by arrest	11.9	13.7	12.8	12.8	10.5	8.6	24.6	9.1	20.9		
Group IV (25,000 to 49,999)											
Offenses known	62,754	46,500	8,166	34,524	3,985	4,868	1,336	541	1,090	769	26,625,101
Percent cleared by arrest	12.9	14.3	11.2	15.1	13.6	10.4	28.4	12.8	22.5		
Group V (10,000 to 24,999)											
Offenses known	58,034	46,431	6,958	26,832	3,662	3,937	1,315	551	886	1,630	25,941,688
Percent cleared by arrest	14.7	16.0	13.8	19.5	15.2	13.9	30.2	12.5	24.7		
Group VI (under 10,000)											
Offenses known	51,557	41,822	7,060	21,315	2,719	3,693	1,968	686	949	7,499	22,079,584
Percent cleared by arrest	16.5	18.0	14.2	25.2	20.1	16.8	26.8	15.9	25.4		
Metropolitan Counties											
Offenses known	146,693	91,059	14,608	64,186	15,414	13,886	2,785	1,817	2,022	1,726	62,778,487
Percent cleared by arrest	12.7	15.1	10.3	15.9	13.0	11.6	25.6	10.4	21.6		
Nonmetropolitan Counties											
Offenses known	55,898	34,065	3,910	13,623	3,598	4,348	1,183	531	596	2,271	23,768,329
Percent cleared by arrest	15.4	16.0	13.3	27.5	19.9	14.8	30.6	16.0	24.3		
Suburban Areas[4]											
Offenses known	248,041	169,076	29,185	122,110	22,729	21,987	5,265	2,914	3,771	7,799	115,973,258
Percent cleared by arrest	13.3	15.5	11.1	16.2	13.0	11.9	27.0	11.1	22.7		

1 The figures shown in this column for the offense of rape were reported using the revised Uniform Crime Reporting (UCR) definition of rape. See chapter notes for more detail.   2 The figures shown in this column for the offense of rape were reported using the legacy Uniform Crime Reporting (UCR) definition of rape. See chapter notes for more detail.   3 Not all agencies submit reports for arson to the FBI. As a result, the number of reports the FBI uses to compute the percent of offenses cleared for arson is less than the number it uses to compute the percent of offenses cleared for all other offenses.   4 Suburban area includes law enforcement agencies in cities with less than 50,000 inhabitants and county law enforcement agencies that are within a Metropolitan Statistical Area. Suburban area excludes all metropolitan agencies associated with a principal city. The agencies associated with suburban areas also appear in other groups within this table.

Table 20. Number of Offenses Cleared by Arrest or Exceptional Means and Percent Involving Persons Under 18 Years of Age, by Population Group, 2015

(Number, percent.)

Population group	Violent crime	Murder and nonnegligent manslaughter	Rape (revised definition)[1]	Rape (legacy definition)[2]	Robbery	Aggravated assault	Property crime	Burglary	Larceny-theft	Motor vehicle theft	Arson[3]	Number of agencies	Estimated population, 2015
Total, All Agencies													
Offenses known	473,793	8,232	35,521	2,723	80,641	346,676	1,296,532	168,516	1,050,449	77,567	7,847	14,592	274,604,622
Percent under 18 years	8.5	4.1	14.6	11.1	12.5	7.0	10.1	10.0	9.9	11.8	24.9		
Total Cities													
Offenses known	373,044	6,309	26,213	1,824	71,253	267,445	1,059,235	120,141	880,450	58,644	5,845	10,595	188,057,806
Percent under 18 years	8.7	4.4	13.9	10.9	12.8	7.1	10.4	10.8	10.2	12.4	26.3		
Group I (250,000 and over)													
Offenses known	157,297	3,057	10,478	368	36,569	106,825	256,304	33,198	203,623	19,483	1,777	74	54,786,571
Percent under 18 years	8.5	4.6	12.9	7.9	14.7	6.1	10.8	11.8	10.3	13.7	23.5		
1,000,000 and over (Group I subset)													
Offenses known	73,768	1,165	4,751	0	18,425	49,427	89,891	11,349	72,147	6,395	487	10	24,675,984
Percent under 18 years	8.4	4.1	13.0	0.0	15.8	5.4	9.7	9.1	9.6	11.9	18.9		
500,000 to 999,999 (Group I subset)													
Offenses known	44,997	1,000	2,941	196	9,390	31,470	81,320	10,578	64,170	6,572	594	22	15,742,712
Percent under 18 years	8.6	5.4	12.4	11.2	14.1	6.7	11.5	14.0	10.6	16.4	27.4		
250,000 to 499,999 (Group I subset)													
Offenses known	38,532	892	2,786	172	8,754	25,928	85,093	11,271	67,306	6,516	696	42	14,367,875
Percent under 18 years	8.6	4.4	13.2	4.1	13.0	6.8	11.3	12.6	10.9	12.9	23.3		
Group II (100,000 to 249,999)													
Offenses known	56,565	1,101	4,271	174	11,184	39,835	162,451	19,323	131,579	11,549	916	189	28,281,300
Percent under 18 years	8.5	4.5	15.8	9.8	11.2	7.1	11.3	11.9	11.0	12.9	22.2		
Group III (50,000 to 99,999)													
Offenses known	49,353	696	3,486	309	8,950	35,912	171,173	18,073	144,621	8,479	820	435	30,343,562
Percent under 18 years	8.9	4.5	13.5	12.6	11.7	7.8	11.5	10.4	11.6	11.3	27.7		
Group IV (25,000 to 49,999)													
Offenses known	36,994	573	2,752	291	6,095	27,283	159,435	15,630	137,548	6,257	716	769	26,625,101
Percent under 18 years	8.9	3.8	14.4	13.7	10.3	8.1	9.9	9.9	9.8	11.9	33.7		
Group V (10,000 to 24,999)													
Offenses known	36,678	467	2,679	322	5,010	28,200	168,427	16,887	145,213	6,327	705	1,630	25,941,688
Percent under 18 years	8.9	3.2	15.0	11.2	10.0	8.2	9.5	10.1	9.4	11.1	31.2		
Group VI (under 10,000)													
Offenses known	36,157	415	2,547	360	3,445	29,390	141,445	17,030	117,866	6,549	911	7,498	22,079,584
Percent under 18 years	9.0	4.6	13.6	10.3	10.5	8.4	8.7	9.8	8.4	10.9	25.0		
Metropolitan Counties													
Offenses known	76,409	1,346	6,272	645	8,381	59,765	184,115	33,808	136,484	13,823	1,370	1,726	62,778,487
Percent under 18 years	8.1	3.3	16.9	13.3	10.8	6.8	9.4	8.7	9.5	10.1	23.2		
Nonmetropolitan Counties													
Offenses known	24,340	577	3,036	254	1,007	19,466	53,182	14,567	33,515	5,100	632	2,271	23,768,329
Percent under 18 years	6.8	2.8	16.1	7.1	4.3	5.6	6.6	6.3	6.5	8.5	15.5		
Suburban Areas[4]													
Offenses known	140,676	2,111	11,070	1,178	18,229	108,088	470,020	62,506	382,135	25,379	2,673	7,799	115,973,258
Percent under 18 years	8.8	3.4	16.0	12.7	10.9	7.7	9.3	9.3	9.2	10.3	27.2		

1 The figures shown in this column for the offense of rape were reported using the revised Uniform Crime Reporting (UCR) definition of rape. See chapter notes for more detail.   2 The figures shown in this column for the offense of rape were reported using the legacy Uniform Crime Reporting (UCR) definition of rape. See chapter notes for more detail.   3 Not all agencies submit reports for arson to the FBI. As a result, the number of reports the FBI uses to compute the percent of offenses cleared for arson is less than the number it uses to compute the percent of offenses cleared for all other offenses.   4 Suburban area includes law enforcement agencies in cities with less than 50,000 inhabitants and county law enforcement agencies that are within a Metropolitan Statistical Area. Suburban area excludes all metropolitan agencies associated with a principal city. The agencies associated with suburban areas also appear in other groups within this table.

SECTION IV

PERSONS ARRESTED

SECTION IV: PERSONS ARRESTED

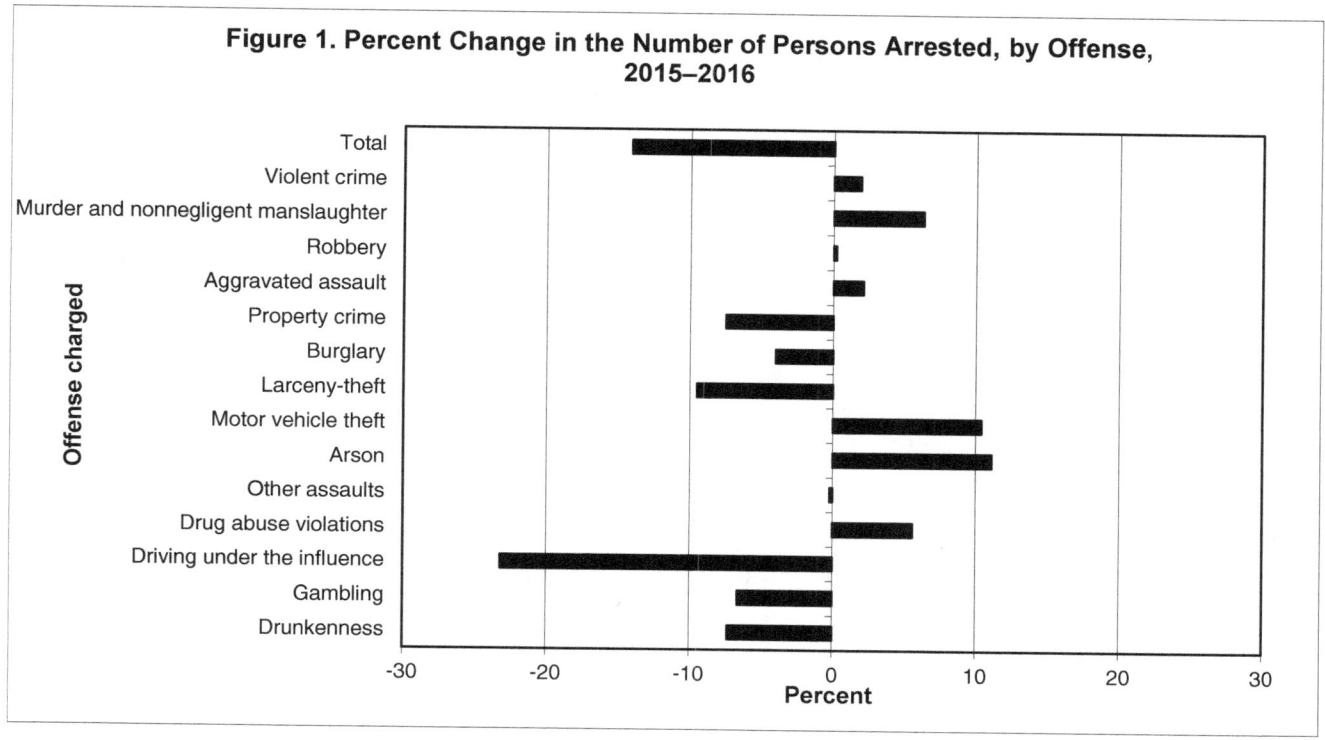

Figure 1. Percent Change in the Number of Persons Arrested, by Offense, 2015–2016

In the Uniform Crime Reporting (UCR) program, one arrest is counted for each separate instance in which an individual is arrested, cited, or summoned for criminal acts in Part I and Part II crimes. (See Appendix I for additional information concerning Part I and Part II crimes.) One person may be arrested multiple times during the year; as a result, the arrest figures in this section should not be taken as the total number of individuals arrested. Instead, it provides the number of *arrest occurrences* reported by law enforcement. Information regarding the UCR program's statistical methodology and table construction can be found in Appendix I.

Important Note: Rape Data

In 2013, the FBI UCR Program initiated the collection of rape data within the Summary Reporting System under a revised definition. The changes bring uniformity to the offense in both the Summary Reporting System (SRS) and the National Incident-Based Reporting System (NIBRS) by capturing data (1) without regard to

gender, (2) including penetration of any bodily orifice by any object or body part, and (3) including offenses where physical force is not involved. The term "forcible" was removed, and the definition changed to the revised UCR definition below.

- Legacy UCR definition of rape: The carnal knowledge of a female forcibly and against her will.

- Revised UCR definition of rape: Penetration, no matter how slight, of the vagina or anus with any body part or object, or oral penetration by a sex organ of another person, without the consent of the victim.

Beginning January 1, 2017, the UCR Program discontinued collecting rape data via the SRS according to the historical, legacy definition. Only rape data submitted under the revised definition will be published for 2017 and subsequent years. This change will not affect agencies that submit rape data via NIBRS.

Data Collection: Juveniles

The UCR Program considers a juvenile to be an individual under 18 years of age regardless of state definition. The program does not collect data regarding police contact with a juvenile who has not committed an offense, nor does it collect data on situations in which police take a juvenile into custody for his or her protection, e.g., neglect cases.

National Volume, Trends, and Rates

VOLUME

The FBI estimated that an estimated 10,662,252 arrests occurred in 2016 for all offenses (except traffic violations). Of these arrests, 515,151 were for violent crimes, and 1,353,283 were for property crimes. UCR does not collect data for traffic violations. Of the total violent crimes in 2016, aggravated assaults accounted for 74.5 percent of the violent crime total, or 383,977 incidents. Robbery had the next highest proportion with 18.6 percent, or 95,754 incidents; followed by rape at 4.6 percent (23,632 incidents) and murder and non-negligent manslaughter, at 2.3 percent (11,788 incidents). Of the estimated arrests for property crimes in 2015, 1,050,058 (77.6 percent) were for larceny-theft, 207,325 (15.3 percent) were for burglary, 86,088 (6.4 percent) were for motor vehicle theft, and 9,812 (0.7 percent) were for arson. Outside of these categories, the most frequent identifiable arrests made in 2015 were for drug abuse violations (estimated at 1,572,579 arrests). These arrests comprised 14.7 percent of the total number of all arrests. (Table 21)

A comparison of arrest figures from 2014 to 2015 revealed a 3.5 percent decrease. However, arrests for violent crimes increased 1.5 percent during this period; arrests for property crimes decreased 4.9 percent. An examination of the 5-year and 10-year arrest trends showed that the total number of arrests in 2015 fell 12.3 percent from the 2011 total. Arrests for violent crimes showed a 5.3 percent decrease from 2011 to 2015 and property crimes showed a 9.4 percent decrease. In the 10-year trend data (2006 to 2015), the number of arrests decreased 19.7 percent. For violent crimes, the number of arrests fell 15.3 percent, while arrests for property crimes decreased 0.9 percent. (Tables 32, 34, and 36)

TRENDS

The number of adults arrested for violent crime (arrestees age 18 years and over) increased 22.0 percent from 2015 to 2016, decreased 2.6 percent from 2011 to 2015, and increased 21.3 percent from 2006 to 2015. The number of juveniles arrested for violent crime (arrestees under 18 years of age) increased 24.1 percent from 2014 to 2016, decreased 5.9 percent from 2011 to 2016, and decreased 27.4 percent from 2006 to 2016. Arrests for all violent crimes increased from 2015 to 2016, both for juveniles and adults. From 2006 to 2016, arrests rose for adults and adults/juveniles combined in all violent crime categories, while declining for juveniles in the categories of robbery, aggravated assault, and violent crime in general. Arrests from 2011 to 2016 increased in every category, with the exception of overall violent crime and aggravated assault arrests for juveniles. (Tables 24, 25, and 26)

The trend data for murder and nonnegligent manslaughter showed that the number of arrests for this offense increased 18.6 percent from 2014 to 2015, increased 0.5 percent from 2011 to 2015, and decreased 12.7 percent from 2006 to 2015. The number of adults arrested for murder decreased 6.7 percent from 2014 to 2015, increased 1.3 percent from 2011 to 2015, and fell 10.6 percent from 2006 to 2015. The number of juveniles arrested for murder increased 6.8 percent from 2014 to 2015, decreased 8.5 percent from 2011 to 2015, and fell 34.4 percent from 2006 to 2015. (Tables 24, 25, and 26)

The trend data showed that the number of arrests for property crime increased 8.0 percent from 2014 to 2015, decreased 2.2 percent from 2011 to 2015, and increased 13.8 percent from 2006 to 2015. The number of adults arrested for property crime offenses (arrestees age 18 years and over) increased 1.8 percent from 2014 to 2015, increased 6.7 percent from 2011 to 2015, and increased 34.4 percent from 2006 to 2015. The number of juveniles arrested for property crime (arrestees under 18 years of age) increased 9.0 percent from 2014 to 2015, decreased 35.8 percent from 2011 to 2015, and increased 34.4 percent from 2006 to 2015. (Tables 24, 25, and 26)

RATES

The rate of arrests was estimated at 3,298.5 arrests per 100,000 inhabitants in 2016. The arrest rate for violent crime was 159.7 arrests per 100,000 inhabitants, and the arrest rate for property crime was 420.6 arrests per 100,000 inhabitants. Law enforcement agencies throughout the nation reported 3.7 murder arrests, 7.3 rape arrests, 29.8 robbery arrests, and 119.0 aggravated assault arrests per 100,000 inhabitants in 2016. Agencies throughout the nation reported 64.3 burglary arrests, 326.5 larceny-theft arrests, 36.7 motor vehicle theft arrests, and 3.0 arson arrests per 100,000 inhabitants in 2015. (Table 22)

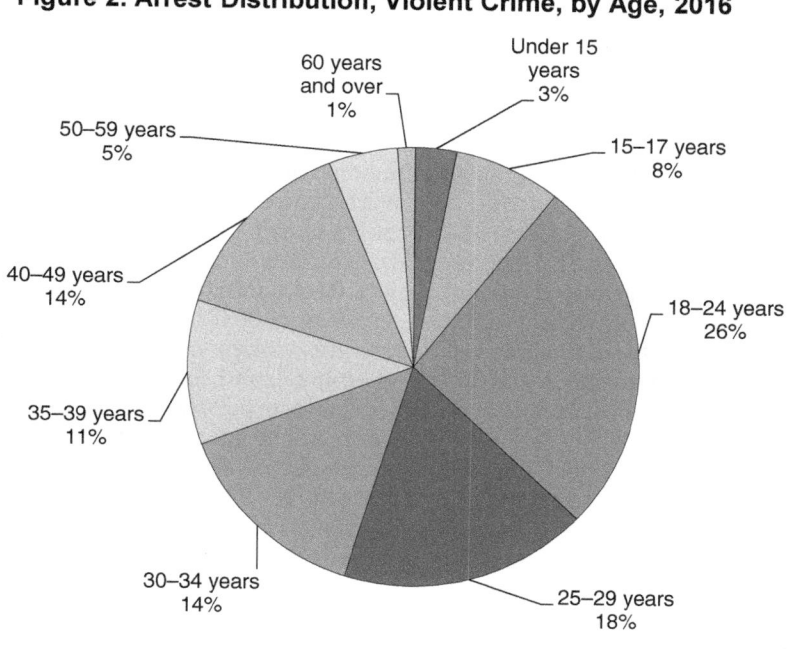

Figure 2. Arrest Distribution, Violent Crime, by Age, 2016

Figure 3. Arrest Distribution, Property Crime, by Age, 2016

By Sex and Race

Law enforcement agencies that contributed arrest data to the UCR program reported information on the sex and race of the persons they arrested.

By sex, males accounted for 73.1 percent of all persons arrested in 2015. Males represented 79.7 percent of arrestees for violent crime, 88.5 percent of arrestees for murder, 97.1 percent of arrestees for rape, 85.6 percent for robbery, and 76.9 percent for aggravated assault. Females accounted for 20.3 percent of violent crime arrestees, 11.5 percent of murder arrestees, 2.9 percent of rape arrestees, 14.4 percent of robbery arrestees, and 23.1 percent of aggravated assault arrestees. (Table 31)

Most arrestees for property crime in 2015 (85.7 percent) were over 18 years of age. By sex, males accounted for 61.7 percent of arrestees for property crime, 81.1 percent of arrestees for burglary, 56.8 percent of arrestees for larceny-theft, 78.8 percent of arrestees for motor vehicle theft, and 80.3 percent of arrestees for arson. Females accounted for 38.3 percent of property crime arrestees. Of the four property crimes, larceny-theft had the highest proportion of female arrestees at 43.2 percent. (Tables 28, 29, and 31)

In 2016, 69.6 percent of all persons arrested were White, 26.9 percent were Black, and the remaining arrestees were of other races (American Indian or Alaskan Native, Asian, and Native Hawaiian or Pacific Islander). Of all arrestees for violent crimes, 59.0 percent were White, 37.5 percent were Black, and 3.5 percent were of other races. For murder, 44.7 percent of arrestees were White, 52.6 percent were Black, and 2.7 percent were of other races. For rape (an aggregate total of the revised and legacy definitions), 67.6 percent of arrestees were White, 29.1 percent were Black, and 2.7 percent of arrestees were of other races. For robbery, 43.4 percent of arrestees were White, 54.5 percent of arrestees were Black, and 3.2 percent of arrestees were of other races. For aggravated assault, 62.8 percent of arrestees were White, 33.3 percent of arrestees were Black, and 3.9 percent were of other races. (Table 32)

Of all arrestees for property crimes in 2015, 68.7 percent were White, 28.1 percent were Black, and 3.2 percent were of other races. For burglary, 68.4 percent of arrestees were White, 29.1 percent were Black, and 2.5 percent were of other races. For larceny-theft, 69.0 percent of arrestees were White, 27.7 percent were Black, and 3.2 percent were of other races. For motor vehicle theft, 66.0 percent of arrestees were White, 30.7 percent of arrestees were Black, and 2.2 percent were of other races. For arson, 72.0 percent of arrestees were White, 23.3 percent of arrestees were Black, and 4.6 percent were of other races. (Table 32)

Regional Arrest Rates

The UCR program divides the United States into four regions: the Northeast, the Midwest, the South, and the West. (Appendix III provides more information about the regions.) Law enforcement agencies in the Northeast in 2016 had an overall arrest rate of 2,797.2 arrests per 100,000 inhabitants, below the national rate (3,298.5 arrests per 100,000 inhabitants). In this region, the arrest rate for violent crimes was 128.2 arrests per 100,000 inhabitants, and for property crime, the arrest rate was 376.8 arrests per 100,000 inhabitants. In the Midwest, law enforcement agencies reported an arrest rate of 3,219.7 arrests per 100,000 inhabitants. The arrest rate for violent crimes was 127.6 and the arrest rate for property crime was 434.5. Law enforcement agencies in the South, the nation's most populous region, reported an arrest rate of 3,610.9 per 100,000 inhabitants. Arrests for violent crime occurred at a rate of 148.0 arrests per 100,000 residents, and for property crime, the arrest rate was 454.1 arrests per 100,000 inhabitants. In the West, law enforcement agencies reported an overall arrest rate of 3,283.3 arrests per 100,000 inhabitants. The region's violent crime arrest rate was 215.7, the highest of the regions, while its property crime arrest rate was 397.4. (Table 22)

The regional murder arrest rates were 2.2 in the Northeast, 3.3 in the Midwest, 4.9 in the South, and 3.3 in the West. For rape (the aggregate of the revised and legacy definitions), the regional arrest rates were 7.2 in the Northeast, 8.4 in the Midwest, 7.1 in the South, and 6.9 in the West. Regional arrest rates for robbery were 30.7 in the Northeast, 23.8 in the Midwest, 29.5 in the South, and 33.6 in the West. For aggravated assault, the regional arrest rates were 88.1 in the Northeast, 92.1 in the Midwest, 106.5 in the South, and 171.9 in the West. (Table 22)

The regional burglary arrest rates were 48.9 in the Northeast, 45.2 in the Midwest, 67.4 in the South, and 83.3 in the West. For larceny-theft, the regional arrest rates were 310.7 in the Northeast, 358.7 in the Midwest, 362.6 in the South, and 270.3 in the West. Regional arrest rates for motor vehicle theft were 14.6 in the Northeast, 27.7 in the Midwest, 21.6 in the South, and 39.6 in the West. For arson, the regional arrest rates were 2.5 in the Northeast, 2.9 in the Midwest, 2.5 in the South, and 4.2 in the West. (Table 22)

Population Groups: Trends and Rates

The national UCR program aggregates data by various population groups, which include cities, metropolitan counties, and nonmetropolitan counties. Definitions of these groups can be found in Appendix III.

In 2015, law enforcement agencies in cities collectively recorded an arrest rate of 3,576.2 arrests per 100,000 inhabitants. The nation's smallest cities, those with fewer than 10,000 inhabitants, had the highest arrest rate among the city population groups with 4,912.8 arrests per 100,000 inhabitants. Law enforcement agencies in cities with 250,000 or more inhabitants recorded the lowest rate, 3,253.1. In the nation's metropolitan counties, law enforcement agencies reported an arrest rate of 2,801.2 per 100,000 inhabitants. Agencies in nonmetropolitan counties reported an arrest rate of 3,175.6. (Table 23)

By population group, law enforcement agencies in the nation's cities collectively reported 177.8 violent crime arrests per 100,000 inhabitants in 2015. In the city population groups, cities with 250,000 or more inhabitants reported the highest violent crime arrest rate (243.4) and cities with 10,000 to 24,999 inhabitants reported the lowest violent crime arrest rate (128.6). Cities reported an overall murder arrest rate of 3.7 per 100,000 inhabitants; cities with 250,000 or more inhabitants had the highest murder arrest rate (6.2) and cities with under 10,000 inhabitants had the lowest murder arrest rate (1.9). The collective city rape arrest rate (an aggregate derived from the revised and legacy definitions) was 7.4 per 100,000 inhabitants, with the highest rate in cities with 250,000 or more inhabitants (9.3) and the lowest rate in cities with 25,000 to 49,999 inhabitants (6.1). The overall robbery arrest rate for cities was 36.9 per 100,000 inhabitants; cities with 250,000 or more inhabitants had the highest robbery arrest rate (60.9) and cities with fewer than 10,000 inhabitants had the lowest robbery arrest rate (17.1). For aggravated assault, the collective city arrest rate was 129.8 per 100,000 inhabitants, with the greatest arrest rate in cities with 250,000 or more inhabitants (167.0) and the lowest arrest rate in cities with 25,000 to 49,999 inhabitants (97.7). (Table 23)

Agencies in metropolitan counties reported a violent crime arrest rate of 118.3 per 100,000 inhabitants, with arrest rates of 2.9 for murder, 6.0 for rape, 17.0 for robbery, and 92.4 for aggravated assault. Agencies in nonmetropolitan counties reported arrest rates of 97.4 for violent crime, 2.8 for murder, 7.3 for rape, 6.1 for robbery, and 81.2 for aggravated assault. (Table 23)

By population group, law enforcement agencies in the nation's cities collectively reported 550.8 property crime arrests per 100,000 inhabitants in 2015. In the city population groups, cities with 10,000 to 24,999 inhabitants reported the highest property crime arrest rate (628.0) and cities with 250,000 or more inhabitants reported the lowest property crime arrest rate (465.4). Cities reported an overall burglary arrest rate of 73.1 per 100,000 inhabitants; cities with 100,000 to 249,999 inhabitants had the highest burglary arrest rate (85.4) and cities with 10,000 to 24,999 inhabitants and 25,000 to 49,999 inhabitants each had the lowest burglary arrest rate (65.0). The collective city larceny-theft arrest rate was 448.2 per 100,000 inhabitants, with the highest rate in cities with 10,000 to 24,999 inhabitants (542.80) and the lowest rate in cities with 250,000 or more inhabitants (353.2). The overall motor vehicle theft arrest rate for cities was 26.4 per 100,000 inhabitants; cities with 250,000 or more inhabitants had the highest motor vehicle theft arrest rate (35.7), and cities with 10,000 to 24,999 inhabitants had the lowest motor vehicle theft arrest rate (17.2). For arson, the collective city arrest rate was 3.0 per 100,000 inhabitants, with the greatest arrest rate in cities with less than 10,000 inhabitants (4.0) and the lowest arrest rate in cities with 50,000 to 99,999 inhabitants and 25,000 to 49,999 inhabitants (2.5). (Table 23)

Agencies in metropolitan counties reported a property crime arrest rate of 280.4 per 100,000 inhabitants, with arrest rates of 53.8 for burglary, 204.5 for larceny-theft, 20.1 for motor vehicle theft, and 2.0 for arson. Agencies in nonmetropolitan counties reported arrest rates of 208.5 for property crime, 59.2 for burglary, 128.6 for larceny-theft, 17.9 for motor vehicle theft, and 2.7 for arson. (Table 23)

In suburban areas, the rates per 100,000 inhabitants for violent crime and property crime were 120.0 and 412.3, respectively. The rate for murder was 2.4; for rape, 6.0; for robbery, 19.7; and for aggravated assault, 91.9. Specific property crime rates included 57.1 for burglary, 334.3 for larceny-theft, 18.6 for motor vehicle theft, and 2.3 for arson. (Table 23)

Table 21. Estimated Number of Arrests, 2016

(Number.)

Offense	Arrests
Total[1]	10,662,252
Violent crime[2]	515,151
Murder and nonnegligent manslaughter	11,788
Rape[3]	23,632
Robbery	95,754
Aggravated assault	383,977
Property crime[2]	1,353,283
Burglary	207,325
Larceny-theft	1,050,058
Motor vehicle theft	86,088
Arson	9,812
Other assaults	1,078,808
Forgery and counterfeiting	56,661
Fraud	128,531
Embezzlement	15,937
Stolen property; buying, receiving, possessing	93,981
Vandalism	195,951
Weapons; carrying, possessing, etc.	156,777
Prostitution and commercialized vice	38,306
Sex offenses (except forcible rape and prostitution)	51,063
Drug abuse violations	1,572,579
Gambling	3,705
Offenses against the family and children	88,748
Driving under the influence	1,017,808
Liquor laws	234,899
Drunkenness	376,433
Disorderly conduct	369,733
Vagrancy	24,851
All other offenses	3,254,871
Suspicion	576
Curfew and loitering law violations	34,176

1 Does not include suspicion. 2 Violent crimes are offenses of murder and nonnegligent manslaughter, rape, robbery, and aggravated assault. Property crimes are offenses of burglary, larceny-theft, motor vehicle theft, and arson. 3 The rape figures in this table are an aggregate total of the data submitted using both the revised and legacy Uniform Crime Reporting definitions.

Table 22. Number and Rate of Arrests, by Geographic Region, 2016

(Number, rate per 100,000 inhabitants.)

Offense charged	United States total (13,055 agencies; population 257,118,573)		Northeast (3,130 agencies; population 45,162,860)		Midwest (3,222 agencies; population 50,287,054)		South (4,892 agencies; population 88,748,151)		West (1,811 agencies; population 72,920,508)	
	Total	Rate	Total	Rate	Total	Rate	Total	Rate	Total	Rate
Total[1]	8,481,162	3,298.5	1,263,318	2,797.2	1,619,069	3,219.7	3,204,603	3,610.9	2,394,172	3,283.3
Violent crime[2]	410,717	159.7	57,910	128.2	64,152	127.6	131,356	148.0	157,299	215.7
Murder and nonnegligent manslaughter	9,427	3.7	993	2.2	1,670	3.3	4,354	4.9	2,410	3.3
Rape[3]	18,802	7.3	3,247	7.2	4,200	8.4	6,303	7.1	5,052	6.9
Robbery	76,503	29.8	13,863	30.7	11,951	23.8	26,180	29.5	24,509	33.6
Aggravated assault	305,985	119.0	39,807	88.1	46,331	92.1	94,519	106.5	125,328	171.9
Property crime[2]	1,081,387	420.6	170,160	376.8	218,504	434.5	402,962	454.1	289,761	397.4
Burglary	165,376	64.3	22,105	48.9	22,747	45.2	59,811	67.4	60,713	83.3
Larceny-theft	839,617	326.5	140,326	310.7	180,355	358.7	321,813	362.6	197,123	270.3
Motor vehicle theft	68,567	26.7	6,584	14.6	13,951	27.7	19,158	21.6	28,874	39.6
Arson	7,827	3.0	1,145	2.5	1,451	2.9	2,180	2.5	3,051	4.2
Other assaults	859,316	334.2	143,394	317.5	166,385	330.9	340,331	383.5	209,206	286.9
Forgery and counterfeiting	45,067	17.5	7,719	17.1	7,783	15.5	19,319	21.8	10,246	14.1
Fraud	101,980	39.7	20,528	45.5	18,692	37.2	44,814	50.5	17,946	24.6
Embezzlement	12,688	4.9	1,494	3.3	2,302	4.6	6,617	7.5	2,275	3.1
Stolen property; buying, receiving, possessing	74,895	29.1	10,890	24.1	13,796	27.4	23,355	26.3	26,854	36.8
Vandalism	156,186	60.7	33,731	74.7	30,437	60.5	41,286	46.5	50,732	69.6
Weapons; carrying, possessing, etc.	124,741	48.5	15,560	34.5	25,195	50.1	43,243	48.7	40,743	55.9
Prostitution and commercialized vice	30,509	11.9	4,313	9.5	3,865	7.7	9,635	10.9	12,696	17.4
Sex offenses (except forcible rape and prostitution)	40,546	15.8	6,259	13.9	7,541	15.0	12,203	13.8	14,543	19.9
Drug abuse violations	1,250,650	486.4	215,838	477.9	229,151	455.7	462,354	521.0	343,307	470.8
Gambling	2,916	1.1	659	1.5	691	1.4	1,180	1.3	386	0.5
Offenses against the family and children	70,072	27.3	12,751	28.2	14,835	29.5	31,418	35.4	11,068	15.2
Driving under the influence	806,369	313.6	128,536	284.6	158,400	315.0	257,142	289.7	262,291	359.7
Liquor laws	186,047	72.4	21,718	48.1	63,418	126.1	50,259	56.6	50,652	69.5
Drunkenness	300,473	116.9	28,794	63.8	16,864	33.5	164,418	185.3	90,397	124.0
Disorderly conduct	294,345	114.5	73,545	162.8	91,602	182.2	80,286	90.5	48,912	67.1
Vagrancy	19,873	7.7	1,205	2.7	2,977	5.9	6,338	7.1	9,353	12.8
All other offenses (except traffic)	2,585,233	1,005.5	299,603	663.4	476,644	947.8	1,069,304	1,204.9	739,682	1,014.4
Suspicion	440	0.2	2	*	28	0.1	248	0.3	162	0.2
Curfew and loitering law violations	27,152	10.6	8,711	19.3	5,835	11.6	6,783	7.6	5,823	8.0

1 Does not include suspicion.   2 Violent crimes are offenses of murder and nonnegligent manslaughter, rape, robbery, and aggravated assault. Property crimes are offenses of burglary, larceny-theft, motor vehicle theft, and arson.   3 The rape figures in this table are an aggregate total of the data submitted using both the revised and legacy Uniform Crime Reporting definitions.

Table 22A. Arrests, by State, 2016

(Number.)

State	Total, all classes[1]	Violent crime[2]	Property crime[2]	Murder and nonnegligent manslaughter	Rape[3]	Robbery	Aggravated assault	Burglary	Larceny-theft	Motor vehicle theft	Arson
Alabama											
Under 18	4,800	321	1,229	15	32	109	165	318	833	72	6
Total, all ages	154,482	6,187	18,479	312	384	1,177	4,314	3,004	14,495	880	100
Alaska											
Under 18	1,893	216	494	8	21	35	152	104	300	62	28
Total, all ages	29,462	2,298	3,495	41	130	282	1,845	538	2,401	505	51
Arizona											
Under 18	22,997	1,020	5,113	15	53	336	616	759	3,968	341	45
Total, all ages	263,699	11,145	37,592	242	344	1,849	8,710	3,957	31,907	1,551	177
Arkansas											
Under 18	8,045	424	1,801	10	44	91	279	414	1,308	74	5
Total, all ages	132,165	4,860	13,791	143	289	561	3,867	2,174	11,084	488	45
California											
Under 18	58,758	7,015	12,519	92	275	2,601	4,047	4,583	6,169	1,508	259
Total, all ages	1,118,712	106,828	115,354	1,437	2,560	15,866	86,965	40,808	54,720	18,521	1,305
Colorado											
Under 18	21,548	636	4,753	6	52	126	452	432	3,794	450	77
Total, all ages	225,710	6,691	29,879	150	414	941	5,186	2,571	24,495	2,585	228
Connecticut											
Under 18	8,264	416	1,902	5	28	161	222	261	1,330	275	36
Total, all ages	100,280	3,741	14,845	62	222	1,016	2,441	1,935	11,971	842	97
Delaware											
Under 18	3,704	348	712	5	12	119	212	137	537	34	4
Total, all ages	33,553	2,224	7,165	29	58	526	1,611	1,053	5,964	122	26
District of Columbia[5]											
Under 18	671	83	47	0	0	58	25	0	44	3	0
Total, all ages	10,271	161	132	1	2	94	64	0	122	10	0
Florida[6,7]											
Under 18	57,843	3,861	17,688	45	248	1,541	2,027	4,817	10,005	2,810	56
Total, all ages	726,396	35,807	102,639	642	1,747	6,521	26,897	18,037	76,139	8,211	252
Georgia											
Under 18	22,646	1,282	5,599	60	42	514	666	1,043	4,145	382	29
Total, all ages	238,684	11,105	32,573	403	274	2,018	8,410	4,506	26,601	1,328	138
Hawaii											
Under 18	3,597	175	688	1	23	72	79	85	545	50	8
Total, all ages	42,301	1,341	4,426	35	154	294	858	636	3,365	389	36
Idaho											
Under 18	5,298	117	1,028	0	23	8	86	163	788	57	20
Total, all ages	46,962	1,279	4,955	23	99	79	1,078	808	3,909	196	42
Illinois[6]											
Under 18	10,186	1,003	2,964	45	35	665	258	301	1,161	1,489	13
Total, all ages	67,983	4,030	12,623	287	276	1,631	1,836	992	8,060	3,505	66
Indiana											
Under 18	12,420	758	3,074	12	19	298	429	317	2,400	316	41
Total, all ages	143,554	7,323	19,954	160	193	1,325	5,645	2,208	16,014	1,625	107
Iowa											
Under 18	10,671	558	2,556	3	34	110	411	391	1,978	152	35
Total, all ages	95,962	4,876	13,033	55	154	396	4,271	1,585	10,839	525	84
Kansas											
Under 18	4,081	170	910	6	25	33	106	84	738	69	19
Total, all ages	53,823	1,948	4,899	50	126	205	1,567	579	3,907	363	50
Kentucky											
Under 18	5,639	402	1,466	17	32	223	130	340	853	263	10
Total, all ages	210,586	3,487	18,219	185	236	1,122	1,944	2,994	14,286	886	53
Louisiana											
Under 18	19,018	1,328	4,669	28	112	333	855	1,211	3,085	353	20
Total, all ages	191,920	11,372	32,355	339	499	1,646	8,888	5,422	25,436	1,388	109
Maine											
Under 18	3,160	45	814	1	13	7	24	136	604	57	17
Total, all ages	43,473	774	5,668	16	61	139	558	681	4,704	206	77
Maryland											
Under 18	19,506	1,935	4,862	11	74	1,067	783	932	3,169	620	141
Total, all ages	182,631	9,737	25,715	270	403	3,223	5,841	4,777	19,083	1,502	353
Massachusetts											
Under 18	6,939	849	1,285	6	28	185	630	213	928	111	33
Total, all ages	119,180	9,656	14,973	58	303	1,263	8,032	2,135	12,140	618	80
Michigan											
Under 18	17,629	1,160	4,802	14	117	276	753	715	3,695	325	67
Total, all ages	255,900	12,163	26,295	166	760	1,467	9,770	3,284	21,366	1,412	233
Minnesota											
Under 18	19,648	900	4,993	6	101	359	434	426	4,221	316	30
Total, all ages	135,455	5,404	25,116	103	565	1,155	3,581	2,109	21,652	1,264	91
Mississippi											
Under 18	3,812	131	817	6	8	87	30	191	594	26	6
Total, all ages	76,489	1,588	8,209	117	84	450	937	1,309	6,505	342	53
Missouri											
Under 18	19,416	966	4,265	18	101	339	508	493	3,439	270	63
Total, all ages	240,878	10,223	34,373	339	516	1,926	7,442	4,153	27,668	2,344	208

Table 22A. Arrests, by State, 2016—Continued

(Number.)

State	Total, all classes[1]	Violent crime[2]	Property crime[2]	Murder and nonnegligent manslaughter	Rape[3]	Robbery	Aggravated assault	Burglary	Larceny-theft	Motor vehicle theft	Arson
Montana											
Under 18	4,263	78	859	0	9	8	61	83	704	56	16
Total, all ages	30,550	1,114	4,883	14	48	69	983	326	4,229	293	35
Nebraska											
Under 18	8,921	168	2,377	5	59	54	50	102	2,133	115	27
Total, all ages	68,310	1,912	10,124	40	259	296	1,317	582	9,070	416	56
Nevada											
Under 18	8,441	1,047	1,408	5	52	372	618	264	995	137	12
Total, all ages	125,932	8,351	10,450	166	257	1,905	6,023	2,519	6,978	900	53
New Hampshire											
Under 18	3,564	78	404	0	12	24	42	33	343	15	13
Total, all ages	47,282	874	3,975	5	58	179	632	336	3,499	114	26
New Jersey											
Under 18	17,784	1,409	2,794	13	69	637	690	615	2,029	88	62
Total, all ages	294,972	10,001	26,736	198	396	3,000	6,407	4,334	21,723	499	180
New Mexico											
Under 18	4,254	248	1,070	9	8	20	211	79	813	54	124
Total, all ages	77,509	4,007	10,421	66	118	360	3,463	918	8,419	447	637
New York[6]											
Under 18	20,322	1,692	5,312	16	193	693	790	851	3,998	392	71
Total, all ages	271,780	13,238	49,196	255	1,091	3,280	8,612	5,780	41,354	1,820	242
North Carolina											
Under 18	16,027	923	4,413	26	14	504	379	1,189	3,003	178	43
Total, all ages	231,449	11,607	36,802	497	273	2,610	8,227	7,909	27,736	969	188
North Dakota											
Under 18	3,788	53	626	0	4	6	43	31	540	48	7
Total, all ages	34,817	743	3,563	14	45	76	608	281	2,894	234	154
Ohio											
Under 18	22,552	732	4,174	12	88	307	325	696	3,241	172	65
Total, all ages	213,801	6,683	33,524	189	481	1,847	4,166	3,851	28,735	681	257
Oklahoma											
Under 18	9,236	449	2,272	17	30	118	284	356	1,772	102	42
Total, all ages	112,401	4,653	15,856	183	207	649	3,614	2,056	12,965	623	212
Oregon											
Under 18	10,407	307	2,198	3	25	72	207	234	1,804	111	49
Total, all ages	131,085	3,715	19,456	66	146	767	2,736	1,618	16,190	1,439	209
Pennsylvania											
Under 18	40,826	2,678	5,563	22	202	1,045	1,409	868	4,120	450	125
Total, all ages	350,797	18,416	50,837	377	1,003	4,820	12,216	6,158	41,938	2,340	401
Rhode Island											
Under 18	2,489	109	494	0	17	38	54	92	365	20	17
Total, all ages	27,494	896	2,881	18	85	143	650	592	2,126	127	36
South Carolina											
Under 18	12,987	682	3,308	35	63	258	326	614	2,527	145	22
Total, all ages	158,298	6,929	24,138	293	411	1,200	5,025	3,385	19,664	968	121
South Dakota											
Under 18	5,016	106	1,000	0	3	11	92	103	770	122	5
Total, all ages	47,214	1,291	3,554	23	44	57	1,167	352	2,897	289	16
Tennessee											
Under 18	22,110	1,401	4,060	21	42	364	974	815	2,766	421	58
Total, all ages	339,280	16,142	37,897	301	291	1,936	13,614	5,322	29,785	2,606	184
Texas											
Under 18	65,539	3,938	14,953	62	375	1,422	2,079	2,590	11,155	1,101	107
Total, all ages	820,979	31,989	95,012	889	2,311	7,056	21,733	12,201	76,604	5,795	412
Utah											
Under 18	13,187	268	2,740	2	75	51	140	165	2,463	82	30
Total, all ages	102,988	2,252	16,044	50	258	413	1,531	935	14,617	421	71
Vermont											
Under 18	425	13	60	0	4	0	9	13	40	6	1
Total, all ages	8,062	314	1,049	4	28	23	259	154	871	18	6
Virginia											
Under 18	16,838	735	3,907	20	69	385	261	504	3,162	211	30
Total, all ages	271,921	7,410	30,793	351	480	1,755	4,824	2,928	26,706	1,013	146
Washington											
Under 18	12,184	782	3,151	15	79	295	393	442	2,432	247	30
Total, all ages	171,211	7,778	30,229	107	491	1,665	5,515	4,847	23,705	1,518	159
West Virginia											
Under 18	1,050	48	152	2	5	6	35	24	110	13	5
Total, all ages	39,742	1,905	5,826	41	101	157	1,606	771	4,777	238	40
Wisconsin											
Under 18	41,813	1,111	6,135	7	149	434	521	655	4,900	532	48
Total, all ages	261,400	7,556	31,446	244	781	1,570	4,961	2,771	27,253	1,293	129
Wyoming											
Under 18	3,332	22	558	0	2	3	17	46	476	27	9
Total, all ages	28,213	500	2,577	13	33	19	435	232	2,188	109	48

Table 22A. Arrests, by State, 2016—Continued

(Number.)

State	Other assaults	Forgery and counterfeiting	Fraud	Embezzlement	Stolen property; buying, receiving, possessing	Vandalism	Weapons; carrying, possessing, etc.	Prostitution and commercialized vice	Sex offenses (except forcible rape and prostitution)	Drug abuse violations
Alabama										
Under 18	777	20	24	1	121	190	93	0	29	191
Total, all ages	18,151	1,382	3,774	190	2,020	1,583	1,681	1	706	10,193
Alaska										
Under 18	297	1	10	8	5	135	24	0	33	207
Total, all ages	4,300	96	236	81	82	1,024	311	13	281	1,006
Arizona										
Under 18	3,667	13	80	19	126	1,761	221	2	259	3,090
Total, all ages	26,150	1,098	2,005	352	1,341	10,031	2,878	387	1,388	30,309
Arkansas										
Under 18	1,433	8	31	1	163	298	123	0	35	770
Total, all ages	11,849	813	1,114	64	1,437	1,460	1,040	277	119	15,736
California										
Under 18	8,977	62	180	15	982	3,050	3,379	112	1,123	6,291
Total, all ages	80,835	5,000	6,324	955	16,500	17,202	27,707	7,601	9,222	219,016
Colorado										
Under 18	1,697	6	63	7	32	833	294	1	102	2,440
Total, all ages	17,079	679	2,512	101	456	5,354	2,363	510	437	14,790
Connecticut										
Under 18	1,974	13	35	5	54	432	178	1	71	581
Total, all ages	17,935	553	893	161	366	2,063	1,185	212	348	9,349
Delaware										
Under 18	1,008	3	70	2	119	207	98	0	33	340
Total, all ages	6,630	290	1,769	198	468	886	388	89	128	4,289
District of Columbia[5]										
Under 18	75	0	0	0	14	20	35	0	0	19
Total, all ages	360	1	9	0	22	43	83	0	5	328
Florida[6,7]										
Under 18	8,670	45	388	26	157	1,166	801	7	293	5,584
Total, all ages	76,450	2,247	11,954	1,041	1,774	6,192	5,152	2,397	2,728	114,550
Georgia										
Under 18	3,636	65	112	8	373	620	551	12	418	2,402
Total, all ages	22,486	2,379	3,323	223	2,819	3,643	3,141	455	2,783	39,593
Hawaii										
Under 18	470	2	8	0	21	121	15	3	42	454
Total, all ages	4,621	140	265	32	130	570	297	159	218	2,574
Idaho										
Under 18	668	1	33	1	30	247	77	0	60	730
Total, all ages	4,270	111	252	40	243	761	306	11	209	8,031
Illinois[6]										
Under 18	1,576	9	4	0	39	294	738	0	17	1,343
Total, all ages	13,371	128	183	0	87	2,072	3,234	187	302	12,958
Indiana										
Under 18	2,161	18	68	3	83	447	255	2	105	1,100
Total, all ages	12,547	1,351	1,670	204	547	1,419	2,386	309	776	18,041
Iowa										
Under 18	1,560	21	39	8	47	766	120	1	64	935
Total, all ages	7,790	584	752	79	177	2,283	844	104	186	9,550
Kansas										
Under 18	643	5	10	8	47	226	54	1	42	668
Total, all ages	7,741	189	403	107	577	1,458	541	56	138	7,519
Kentucky										
Under 18	1,039	20	13	7	464	184	95	0	33	501
Total, all ages	11,703	1,021	1,003	441	2,628	1,132	891	252	297	23,308
Louisiana										
Under 18	3,061	10	38	4	372	600	452	11	172	1,475
Total, all ages	23,075	731	1,473	172	2,283	3,739	3,777	521	1,355	27,529
Maine										
Under 18	442	10	11	2	11	232	14	1	30	383
Total, all ages	4,719	229	552	66	90	1,052	149	105	187	5,430
Maryland										
Under 18	4,630	26	42	1	22	929	636	8	144	2,167
Total, all ages	21,522	582	896	115	144	2,721	3,181	584	687	30,692
Massachusetts										
Under 18	1,485	20	29	3	153	415	158	1	47	228
Total, all ages	19,027	469	1,263	136	1,084	2,692	1,238	553	418	9,770
Michigan										
Under 18	2,601	32	208	30	249	548	348	4	150	2,207
Total, all ages	27,475	652	3,909	1,009	1,645	2,828	4,128	528	687	38,780
Minnesota										
Under 18	2,120	17	147	8	285	895	392	2	147	1,525
Total, all ages	13,688	985	2,187	29	1,684	3,057	1,786	344	1,047	15,397
Mississippi										
Under 18	559	0	21	1	44	109	131	2	13	273
Total, all ages	6,680	378	980	395	670	751	1,016	38	204	10,414
Missouri										
Under 18	3,253	21	98	18	370	816	294	7	254	2,452
Total, all ages	23,578	1,351	2,454	369	3,195	4,076	3,706	415	1,289	41,674

Table 22A. Arrests, by State, 2016—Continued

(Number.)

State	Other assaults	Forgery and counterfeiting	Fraud	Embezzlement	Stolen property; buying, receiving, possessing	Vandalism	Weapons; carrying, possessing, etc.	Prostitution and commercialized vice	Sex offenses (except forcible rape and prostitution)	Drug abuse violations
Montana										
Under 18	504	2	12	2	4	245	6	0	38	360
Total, all ages	4,092	112	258	32	62	952	112	3	126	2,638
Nebraska										
Under 18	1,351	7	77	15	80	654	93	0	95	1,304
Total, all ages	8,242	274	1,374	98	619	2,210	1,103	131	453	11,878
Nevada										
Under 18	1,444	10	37	3	144	282	167	70	42	837
Total, all ages	14,022	605	1,635	331	1,584	1,482	1,893	2,892	714	13,770
New Hampshire										
Under 18	568	4	18	3	43	223	1	0	26	637
Total, all ages	5,115	236	843	122	547	1,178	171	91	128	8,346
New Jersey										
Under 18	1,633	40	64	10	415	693	667	9	107	3,574
Total, all ages	22,348	1,047	3,896	320	2,693	3,858	4,054	849	963	61,579
New Mexico										
Under 18	681	2	15	7	55	154	66	1	16	512
Total, all ages	8,482	237	631	214	1,449	1,214	576	36	83	6,924
New York[6]										
Under 18	2,767	102	159	1	485	2,075	395	16	296	3,331
Total, all ages	29,532	2,801	4,419	62	3,441	14,798	3,624	627	1,970	65,379
North Carolina										
Under 18	3,195	24	171	30	343	570	592	7	73	1,227
Total, all ages	32,067	1,167	7,337	983	2,836	3,989	4,485	182	823	18,247
North Dakota										
Under 18	391	3	7	8	44	156	22	0	25	442
Total, all ages	2,789	124	351	59	320	506	340	20	89	5,093
Ohio										
Under 18	4,295	30	134	0	521	1,034	318	10	157	1,811
Total, all ages	28,812	1,002	2,086	21	3,202	3,599	3,211	1,308	558	32,324
Oklahoma										
Under 18	964	3	38	20	287	277	166	0	48	1,328
Total, all ages	8,195	673	1,621	376	2,737	1,229	2,183	5	408	22,107
Oregon										
Under 18	1,093	9	54	1	27	1,040	106	0	67	1,854
Total, all ages	10,241	558	1,752	44	558	4,012	1,660	284	519	13,639
Pennsylvania										
Under 18	4,811	55	653	29	342	1,501	789	6	493	3,177
Total, all ages	39,904	2,253	7,954	485	2,268	6,858	4,660	1,792	2,125	53,633
Rhode Island										
Under 18	411	2	17	3	71	189	135	0	16	80
Total, all ages	4,002	111	586	87	342	1,035	465	80	91	1,759
South Carolina										
Under 18	2,116	11	74	9	162	456	434	7	63	2,080
Total, all ages	16,445	1,130	3,452	325	1,996	2,794	2,251	578	319	30,020
South Dakota										
Under 18	492	2	44	8	35	135	49	1	13	847
Total, all ages	4,447	96	664	38	177	466	255	26	53	7,912
Tennessee										
Under 18	4,106	45	142	4	117	1,036	391	0	116	2,501
Total, all ages	29,825	1,876	5,797	707	1,038	4,563	2,741	1,161	568	44,185
Texas										
Under 18	12,047	135	275	153	181	1,779	843	53	431	10,612
Total, all ages	94,190	4,659	6,515	918	1,057	8,120	12,375	4,506	3,005	140,314
Utah										
Under 18	1,305	7	30	0	94	694	205	16	214	1,786
Total, all ages	8,780	680	886	21	1,053	2,631	844	191	600	15,111
Vermont										
Under 18	96	0	2	2	4	37	7	0	10	23
Total, all ages	812	20	122	55	59	197	14	4	29	593
Virginia										
Under 18	2,735	36	129	37	177	753	328	3	122	2,068
Total, all ages	32,469	1,905	5,240	1,405	917	4,021	3,562	913	692	39,132
Washington										
Under 18	2,642	10	28	1	210	756	237	9	133	1,360
Total, all ages	24,266	881	994	60	3,354	4,973	1,711	553	637	11,017
West Virginia										
Under 18	249	1	3	1	5	40	24	0	12	110
Total, all ages	4,684	332	511	105	283	612	448	73	104	6,267
Wisconsin										
Under 18	2,570	22	116	31	605	1,873	598	14	674	3,154
Total, all ages	15,905	1,047	2,659	289	1,566	6,463	3,661	437	1,963	28,025
Wyoming										
Under 18	419	2	7	2	2	154	38	3	13	543
Total, all ages	2,068	49	196	12	42	526	85	56	109	4,482

Table 22A. Arrests, by State, 2016—Continued

(Number.)

State	Gambling	Offenses against the family and children	Driving under the influence	Liquor laws	Drunkenness[4]	Disorderly conduct	Vagrancy	All other offenses (except traffic)	Suspicion	Curfew and loitering law violations	Number of agencies	Estimated population, 2016
Alabama											240	3,800,629
Under 18	0	44	28	225	31	378	2	1,096	0	0		
Total, all ages	0	982	8,126	2,496	7,283	2,129	67	69,052	0	0		
Alaska											32	738,566
Under 18	0	1	31	121	18	11	0	269	0	12		
Total, all ages	0	195	3,063	775	112	738	4	11,340	0	12		
Arizona											90	6,391,343
Under 18	0	177	211	1,668	84	1,436	65	2,924	0	1,061		
Total, all ages	3	2,520	23,498	9,745	14,100	15,874	351	71,741	130	1,061		
Arkansas											271	2,786,173
Under 18	0	10	44	219	87	470	0	1,765	0	363		
Total, all ages	8	354	6,703	1,769	6,589	2,425	890	60,504	0	363		
California											613	39,012,007
Under 18	3	3	493	1,210	880	1,264	101	9,645	0	1,454		
Total, all ages	266	236	129,752	8,857	69,869	3,906	6,597	285,231	0	1,454		
Colorado											193	5,008,754
Under 18	0	52	217	1,389	47	1,727	0	6,099	0	1,153		
Total, all ages	3	2,849	23,364	9,025	249	7,486	453	100,277	0	1,153		
Connecticut											104	3,526,707
Under 18	0	45	41	49	0	1,485	0	978	0	4		
Total, all ages	19	1,450	8,533	225	8	11,640	36	26,714	0	4		
Delaware											56	950,787
Under 18	0	0	0	84	1	287	0	345	0	47		
Total, all ages	1	195	355	884	345	1,312	332	5,558	0	47		
District of Columbia[5]											2	0
Under 18	0	0	0	0	0	39	0	338	0	1		
Total, all ages	0	2	11	1,024	89	172	30	7,798	0	1		
Florida[6,7]											668	20,566,240
Under 18	4	0	109	496	0	0	0	18,548	0	0		
Total, all ages	149	0	35,042	14,280	0	0	0	313,994	0	0		
Georgia											402	8,150,300
Under 18	7	133	89	326	20	2,184	99	4,380	0	330		
Total, all ages	76	2,944	18,939	4,262	1,442	14,886	1,574	69,708	0	330		
Hawaii											4	1,428,557
Under 18	0	1	23	92	4	95	3	1,201	7	172		
Total, all ages	76	17	5,929	575	4	1,074	3	19,671	7	172		
Idaho											101	1,324,720
Under 18	0	40	61	324	30	237	0	1,557	0	57		
Total, all ages	0	724	6,195	1,324	254	1,458	10	16,472	0	57		
Illinois[6]											2	2,872,516
Under 18	44	6	7	32	0	877	0	1,154	0	79		
Total, all ages	456	254	2,929	165	0	3,756	4	11,165	0	79		
Indiana											204	4,305,899
Under 18	1	171	61	745	38	697	33	2,374	8	218		
Total, all ages	21	1,042	13,492	3,665	4,316	3,517	81	50,656	19	218		
Iowa											206	2,810,823
Under 18	0	3	71	689	99	1,211	0	1,519	0	404		
Total, all ages	5	1,242	9,836	3,943	6,983	4,104	9	29,178	0	404		
Kansas											228	1,732,223
Under 18	0	8	58	408	0	204	0	619	0	0		
Total, all ages	0	182	5,923	2,593	134	1,558	0	17,857	0	0		
Kentucky											419	4,424,357
Under 18	0	5	66	26	57	230	0	1,028	0	3		
Total, all ages	9	4,547	16,901	94	14,259	4,095	137	106,159	0	3		
Louisiana											168	4,183,659
Under 18	14	42	32	233	25	2,537	51	3,584	9	299		
Total, all ages	79	1,538	7,587	3,596	3,567	10,435	250	56,154	33	299		
Maine											195	1,328,762
Under 18	0	0	28	459	4	105	0	561	0	8		
Total, all ages	1	122	5,834	2,218	17	1,309	0	14,943	0	8		
Maryland											143	5,197,665
Under 18	19	10	60	512	8	873	23	2,522	30	47		
Total, all ages	133	1,972	17,809	5,398	14	4,639	139	55,773	131	47		
Massachusetts											342	6,436,240
Under 18	0	33	46	291	38	394	0	1,464	0	0		
Total, all ages	14	1,231	9,008	2,000	5,600	4,329	11	35,706	2	0		
Michigan											606	9,696,514
Under 18	3	4	194	1,371	4	666	0	2,723	0	325		
Total, all ages	37	2,799	27,571	10,690	367	6,536	241	87,235	0	325		
Minnesota											365	5,237,709
Under 18	0	10	144	1,795	0	2,039	2	3,280	0	947		
Total, all ages	12	507	19,196	8,054	1	8,679	38	27,297	0	947		
Mississippi											63	1,383,530
Under 18	1	263	66	29	23	511	15	709	4	90		
Total, all ages	63	2,407	7,160	983	3,721	3,790	41	26,836	75	90		
Missouri											375	5,768,437
Under 18	3	45	182	877	16	1,325	6	3,333	0	815		
Total, all ages	75	2,596	19,729	5,280	330	8,158	1,222	75,970	0	815		

Table 22A. Arrests, by State, 2016—Continued

(Number.)

State	Gambling	Offenses against the family and children	Driving under the influence	Liquor laws	Drunkenness[4]	Disorderly conduct	Vagrancy	All other offenses (except traffic)	Suspicion	Curfew and loitering law violations	Number of agencies	Estimated population, 2016
Montana												
Under 18	0	271	42	454	0	467	0	619	0	300		
Total, all ages	0	442	4,392	1,871	0	2,878	21	6,262	0	300	100	1,036,405
Nebraska												
Under 18	0	27	109	682	0	427	0	1,311	0	144		
Total, all ages	0	1,257	6,948	4,862	0	2,714	16	13,951	0	144	153	1,721,852
Nevada												
Under 18	2	29	58	521	6	167	8	1,682	5	472		
Total, all ages	33	963	10,660	3,383	214	1,292	1,512	49,669	5	472	51	2,940,058
New Hampshire												
Under 18	1	8	42	389	233	99	0	774	0	13		
Total, all ages	7	160	4,874	2,907	3,683	954	65	12,993	0	13	174	1,275,170
New Jersey												
Under 18	31	37	129	778	0	1,413	11	2,574	0	1,396		
Total, all ages	421	7,426	22,745	3,044	0	12,723	274	108,599	0	1,396	494	8,747,889
New Mexico												
Under 18	0	14	62	163	19	178	0	986	1	4		
Total, all ages	0	850	6,178	1,977	445	1,602	247	31,924	8	4	57	1,498,550
New York[6]												
Under 18	1	29	113	201	0	592	10	2,745	0	0		
Total, all ages	74	595	29,238	1,599	0	6,355	565	44,267	0	0	544	10,621,114
North Carolina												
Under 18	0	34	201	457	0	1,305	0	2,447	0	15		
Total, all ages	43	4,412	30,380	2,286	0	4,497	12	69,279	0	15	235	6,270,620
North Dakota												
Under 18	0	129	26	469	0	662	0	617	0	108		
Total, all ages	0	313	5,725	2,922	309	2,202	6	9,234	1	108	106	753,138
Ohio												
Under 18	1	184	84	672	28	1,811	4	6,010	5	537		
Total, all ages	41	1,622	15,060	5,973	1,886	14,608	99	57,640	5	537	461	8,954,617
Oklahoma												
Under 18	4	32	107	105	293	505	2	1,267	0	1,069		
Total, all ages	35	609	12,200	1,433	13,507	1,996	34	21,466	9	1,069	336	3,744,169
Oregon												
Under 18	0	6	108	916	0	509	0	1,600	0	512		
Total, all ages	0	335	14,282	4,844	0	6,555	4	48,115	0	512	185	3,707,053
Pennsylvania												
Under 18	2	31	365	2,134	170	7,352	26	3,371	0	7,278		
Total, all ages	105	1,581	44,111	9,179	19,475	33,487	254	44,142	0	7,278	1,183	11,822,238
Rhode Island												
Under 18	0	30	11	48	1	452	0	408	0	12		
Total, all ages	18	68	2,719	486	10	2,239	0	9,607	0	12	48	1,056,426
South Carolina												
Under 18	3	8	90	286	71	1,447	0	1,649	0	31		
Total, all ages	51	1,237	15,947	5,014	6,956	8,738	425	29,522	0	31	434	4,794,988
South Dakota												
Under 18	0	388	77	569	14	330	0	786	0	120		
Total, all ages	0	766	7,196	2,596	2,538	2,454	436	12,126	3	120	107	789,651
Tennessee												
Under 18	39	55	143	586	141	1,912	0	4,080	0	1,235		
Total, all ages	170	4,036	22,563	4,278	14,029	7,079	25	139,365	0	1,235	455	6,454,266
Texas												
Under 18	15	95	421	1,596	1,104	1,836	61	12,532	0	2,479		
Total, all ages	490	4,264	67,950	10,928	71,819	10,520	2,194	247,675	0	2,479	973	27,089,093
Utah												
Under 18	0	36	196	675	80	807	27	3,538	2	467		
Total, all ages	4	1,297	8,713	3,860	2,909	2,809	40	33,791	5	467	109	2,801,231
Vermont												
Under 18	0	8	8	23	1	67	0	64	0	0		
Total, all ages	0	118	1,474	60	1	509	0	2,632	0	0	46	348,314
Virginia												
Under 18	0	55	97	620	112	490	0	3,667	0	767		
Total, all ages	20	1,780	20,084	5,223	20,125	2,965	157	92,341	0	767	404	8,266,632
Washington												
Under 18	0	9	121	776	3	178	0	1,775	0	3		
Total, all ages	0	280	23,209	2,487	22	2,415	81	56,261	0	3	223	6,483,494
West Virginia												
Under 18	0	2	11	52	3	27	0	303	0	7		
Total, all ages	2	139	4,427	591	673	608	31	12,114	0	7	291	1,251,283
Wisconsin												
Under 18	8	105	235	2,266	0	7,876	61	12,221	0	2,138		
Total, all ages	44	2,255	24,795	12,675	0	33,316	825	84,335	0	2,138	409	5,643,675
Wyoming												
Under 18	1	10	26	461	12	124	12	764	3	156		
Total, all ages	1	360	3,056	1,929	2,219	825	30	8,928	7	156	53	549,770

Note: Because the number of agencies submitting arrest data varies from year to year, users are cautioned about making direct comparisons between 2013 arrest totals and those published in previous years' editions of Crime in the United States. Further, arrest figures may vary widely from state to state because some Part II crimes are not considered crimes in some states.
1 Does not include traffic arrests.   2 Violent crimes are offenses of murder and nonnegligent manslaughter, rape, robbery, and aggravated assault. Property crimes are offenses of burglary, larceny-theft, motor vehicle theft, and arson.   3 The rape figures in this table are an aggregate total of the data submitted using both the revised and legacy Uniform Crime Reporting definitions.   4 Drunkenness is not considered a crime in some states; therefore, the figures vary widely from state to state.   5 Includes arrests reported by the Metro Transit Police. This agency has no population associated with it.   6 See 2016 Arrest Data for details.   7 The arrest category "All other offenses" for Florida also includes the arrest counts for offenses against the family and children, drunkenness, disorderly conduct, vagrancy, suspicion, curfew and loitering law violations, and runaways.

Table 23. Number and Rate of Arrests, by Population Group, 2015

(Number, rate per 100,000 inhabitants.)

Offense charged	Total (12,706 agencies; population 246,947,242)		Total cities (9,115 cities; population 168,734,653)		Group I (66 cities, 250,000 and over; population 44,563,106)		Group II (180 cities, 100,000 to 249,999; population 27,033,841)		Group III (404 cities, 50,000 to 99,999; population 28,217,031)	
	Total	Rate	Total	Rate	Total	Rate	Total	Rate	Total	Rate
Total[2]	8,304,874	3,363.0	6,034,206	3,576.2	1,449,692	3,253.1	933,850	3,454.4	949,975	3,366.7
Violent crime[3]	388,082	157.2	299,984	177.8	108,478	243.4	53,861	199.2	46,308	164.1
Murder and nonnegligent manslaughter	8,533	3.5	6,258	3.7	2,771	6.2	1,169	4.3	767	2.7
Rape[4]	17,504	7.1	12,521	7.4	4,128	9.3	1,879	7.0	1,863	6.6
Robbery	73,230	29.7	62,265	36.9	27,161	60.9	10,792	39.9	9,219	32.7
Aggravated assault	288,815	117.0	218,940	129.8	74,418	167.0	40,021	148.0	34,459	122.1
Property crime[3]	1,133,319	458.9	929,358	550.8	207,416	465.4	152,576	564.4	158,016	560.0
Burglary	166,609	67.5	123,383	73.1	32,908	73.8	23,084	85.4	21,426	75.9
Larceny-theft	900,077	364.5	756,295	448.2	157,390	353.2	119,421	441.7	129,062	457.4
Motor vehicle theft	59,831	24.2	44,572	26.4	15,895	35.7	9,028	33.4	6,828	24.2
Arson	6,802	2.8	5,108	3.0	1,223	2.7	1,043	3.9	700	2.5
Other assaults	831,684	336.8	624,009	369.8	171,099	383.9	99,791	369.1	99,999	354.4
Forgery and counterfeiting	42,681	17.3	31,437	18.6	6,200	13.9	5,015	18.6	5,248	18.6
Fraud	102,339	41.4	70,891	42.0	13,350	30.0	9,435	34.9	11,223	39.8
Embezzlement	12,247	5.0	9,562	5.7	2,358	5.3	1,408	5.2	1,708	6.1
Stolen property; buying, receiving, possessing	68,341	27.7	50,592	30.0	12,910	29.0	8,704	32.2	9,691	34.3
Vandalism	147,191	59.6	113,543	67.3	27,794	62.4	17,112	63.3	18,762	66.5
Weapons; carrying, possessing, etc.	111,316	45.1	85,618	50.7	31,535	70.8	14,199	52.5	12,194	43.2
Prostitution and commercialized vice	31,534	12.8	28,450	16.9	19,017	42.7	4,138	15.3	2,353	8.3
Sex offenses (except forcible rape and prostitution)	39,393	16.0	27,417	16.2	7,777	17.5	4,282	15.8	4,460	15.8
Drug abuse violations	1,144,021	463.3	810,262	480.2	204,753	459.5	129,009	477.2	131,689	466.7
Gambling	3,607	1.5	2,848	1.7	1,645	3.7	216	0.8	295	1.0
Offenses against the family and children	72,418	29.3	37,512	22.2	5,975	13.4	6,420	23.7	5,585	19.8
Driving under the influence	833,833	337.7	468,701	277.8	94,408	211.9	62,531	231.3	70,006	248.1
Liquor laws	204,665	82.9	160,696	95.2	25,348	56.9	19,435	71.9	20,421	72.4
Drunkenness	314,856	127.5	271,597	161.0	44,198	99.2	43,997	162.7	46,923	166.3
Disorderly conduct	298,253	120.8	247,467	146.7	41,893	94.0	30,411	112.5	36,229	128.4
Vagrancy	19,414	7.9	16,892	10.0	5,574	12.5	3,400	12.6	3,861	13.7
All other offenses (except traffic)	2,471,772	1,000.9	1,715,484	1,016.7	400,810	899.4	265,232	981.1	261,665	927.3
Suspicion	1,045	0.4	842	0.5	4	*	0	0.0	139	0.5
Curfew and loitering law violations	33,908	13.7	31,886	18.9	17,154	38.5	2,678	9.9	3,339	11.8

Table 23. Number and Rate of Arrests, by Population Group, 2015—Continued

(Number, rate per 100,000 inhabitants.)

Offense charged	Group IV (726 cities, 25,000 to 49,999; population 25,112,170)		Group V (1,501 cities, 10,000 to 24,999; population 23,998,482)		Group VI (6,238 cities, under 10,000; population 19,810,023)		Metropolitan counties (1,536 agencies; population 56,900,141)		Nonmetropolitan counties (2,055 agencies; population 21,312,448)		Suburban areas[1] (7,022 agencies; population 111,227,944)	
	Total	Rate	Total	Rate	Total	Rate	Total	Rate	Total	Rate	Total	Rate
Total[2]	839,653	3,343.6	887,804	3,699.4	973,232	4,912.8	1,593,867	2,801.2	676,801	3,175.6	3,484,480	3,132.7
Violent crime[3]	32,819	130.7	30,874	128.6	27,644	139.5	67,337	118.3	20,761	97.4	133,451	120.0
Murder and nonnegligent manslaughter	632	2.5	538	2.2	381	1.9	1,675	2.9	600	2.8	2,713	2.4
Rape[4]	1,536	6.1	1,589	6.6	1,526	7.7	3,427	6.0	1,556	7.3	6,639	6.0
Robbery	6,407	25.5	5,297	22.1	3,389	17.1	9,667	17.0	1,298	6.1	21,909	19.7
Aggravated assault	24,244	96.5	23,450	97.7	22,348	112.8	52,568	92.4	17,307	81.2	102,190	91.9
Property crime[3]	143,723	572.3	150,713	628.0	116,914	590.2	159,526	280.4	44,435	208.5	458,610	412.3
Burglary	16,311	65.0	15,604	65.0	14,050	70.9	30,602	53.8	12,624	59.2	63,491	57.1
Larceny-theft	122,330	487.1	130,263	542.8	97,829	493.8	116,364	204.5	27,418	128.6	371,823	334.3
Motor vehicle theft	4,455	17.7	4,127	17.2	4,239	21.4	11,442	20.1	3,817	17.9	20,720	18.6
Arson	627	2.5	719	3.0	796	4.0	1,118	2.0	576	2.7	2,576	2.3
Other assaults	85,694	341.2	84,879	353.7	82,547	416.7	151,543	266.3	56,132	263.4	327,735	294.7
Forgery and counterfeiting	4,790	19.1	5,139	21.4	5,045	25.5	8,719	15.3	2,525	11.8	19,346	17.4
Fraud	11,324	45.1	11,027	45.9	14,532	73.4	21,816	38.3	9,632	45.2	47,639	42.8
Embezzlement	1,477	5.9	1,445	6.0	1,166	5.9	2,154	3.8	531	2.5	5,050	4.5
Stolen property; buying, receiving, possessing	7,352	29.3	6,675	27.8	5,260	26.6	13,606	23.9	4,143	19.4	28,868	26.0
Vandalism	17,244	68.7	16,088	67.0	16,543	83.5	25,194	44.3	8,454	39.7	59,966	53.9
Weapons; carrying, possessing, etc.	9,027	35.9	8,673	36.1	9,990	50.4	18,786	33.0	6,912	32.4	39,175	35.2
Prostitution and commercialized vice	1,246	5.0	1,082	4.5	614	3.1	2,860	5.0	224	1.1	5,413	4.9
Sex offenses (except forcible rape and prostitution)	3,586	14.3	3,637	15.2	3,675	18.6	8,775	15.4	3,201	15.0	16,661	15.0
Drug abuse violations	108,677	432.8	111,099	462.9	125,035	631.2	234,082	411.4	99,677	467.7	488,748	439.4
Gambling	97	0.4	266	1.1	329	1.7	601	1.1	158	0.7	982	0.9
Offenses against the family and children	5,576	22.2	5,822	24.3	8,134	41.1	25,945	45.6	8,961	42.0	37,718	33.9
Driving under the influence	68,851	274.2	79,161	329.9	93,744	473.2	213,047	374.4	152,085	713.6	387,181	348.1
Liquor laws	21,446	85.4	26,020	108.4	48,026	242.4	28,369	49.9	15,600	73.2	90,670	81.5
Drunkenness	35,479	141.3	39,409	164.2	61,591	310.9	29,836	52.4	13,423	63.0	109,959	98.9
Disorderly conduct	36,844	146.7	45,801	190.8	56,289	284.1	34,508	60.6	16,278	76.4	127,083	114.3
Vagrancy	1,549	6.2	964	4.0	1,544	7.8	2,191	3.9	331	1.6	5,324	4.8
All other offenses (except traffic)	240,097	956.1	255,954	1,066.5	291,726	1,472.6	543,199	954.7	213,089	999.8	1,086,779	977.1
Suspicion	56	0.2	30	0.1	613	3.1	42	0.1	161	0.8	277	0.2
Curfew and loitering law violations	2,755	11.0	3,076	12.8	2,884	14.6	1,773	3.1	249	1.2	8,122	7.3

* = Less than one-tenth of one percent.
1 Suburban areas include law enforcement agencies in cities with less than 50,000 inhabitants and county law enforcement agencies that are within a Metropolitan Statistical Area. Suburban areas exclude all metropolitan agencies associated with a principal city. The agencies associated with suburban areas also appear in other groups within this table. 2 Does not include suspicion. 3 Violent crimes are offenses of murder and nonnegligent manslaughter, forcible rape, robbery, and aggravated assault. Property crimes are offenses of burglary, larceny-theft, motor vehicle theft, and arson. 4 The rape figures in this table are an aggregate total of the data submitted using both the revised and legacy Uniform Crime Reporting definitions.

Table 24. Long-Term Arrest Trends, 2006 and 2016

(Number, percent change; 13,055 agencies; 2016 estimated population 257,118,573; 2006 estimated population 186,371,331.)

	Number of persons arrested								
	Total, all ages			Under 18 years of age			18 years of age and over		
Offense charged	2006	2016	Percent change	2006	2016	Percent change	2006	2016	Percent change
Total[1]	8,676,456	8,481,602	-2.2	1,280,195	681,701	-46.8	7,396,261	7,799,901	+5.5
Violent crime[2]	361,401	410,717	+13.6	56,938	41,335	-27.4	304,463	369,382	+21.3
Murder and nonnegligent manslaughter	7,104	9,427	+32.7	642	682	+6.2	6,462	8,745	+35.3
Rape[3]	14,120	18,802	NA	2,111	2,952	NA	12,009	15,850	NA
Robbery	68,437	76,503	+11.8	18,201	15,339	-15.7	50,236	61,164	+21.8
Aggravated assault	271,740	305,985	+12.6	35,984	22,362	-37.9	235,756	283,623	+20.3
Property crime[2]	950,507	1,081,387	+13.8	255,450	147,350	-42.3	695,057	934,037	+34.4
Burglary	188,122	165,376	-12.1	51,953	25,513	-50.9	136,169	139,863	+2.7
Larceny-theft	679,290	839,617	+23.6	180,623	107,287	-40.6	498,667	732,330	+46.9
Motor vehicle theft	72,650	68,567	-5.6	17,651	12,520	-29.1	54,999	56,047	+1.9
Arson	10,445	7,827	-25.1	5,223	2,030	-61.1	5,222	5,797	+11.0
Other assaults	792,178	859,316	+8.5	152,396	102,694	-32.6	639,782	756,622	+18.3
Forgery and counterfeiting	68,319	45,067	-34.0	2,288	967	-57.7	66,031	44,100	-33.2
Fraud	181,863	101,980	-43.9	5,090	3,680	-27.7	176,773	98,300	-44.4
Embezzlement	13,008	12,688	-2.5	949	540	-43.1	12,059	12,148	+0.7
Stolen property; buying, receiving, possessing	79,077	74,895	-5.3	14,032	8,679	-38.1	65,045	66,216	+1.8
Vandalism	189,867	156,186	-17.7	76,202	31,181	-59.1	113,665	125,005	+10.0
Weapons; carrying, possessing, etc.	114,104	124,741	+9.3	27,707	15,452	-44.2	86,397	109,289	+26.5
Prostitution and commercialized vice	33,402	30,509	-8.7	733	396	-46.0	32,669	30,113	-7.8
Sex offenses (except forcible rape and prostitution)	50,656	40,546	-20.0	9,948	6,723	-32.4	40,708	33,823	-16.9
Drug abuse violations	1,078,156	1,250,650	+16.0	113,132	78,330	-30.8	965,024	1,172,320	+21.5
Gambling	2,807	2,916	+3.9	292	203	-30.5	2,515	2,713	+7.9
Offenses against the family and children	79,568	70,072	-11.9	3,348	2,738	-18.2	76,220	67,334	-11.7
Driving under the influence	925,818	806,369	-12.9	12,947	5,135	-60.3	912,871	801,234	-12.2
Liquor laws	408,511	186,047	-54.5	94,729	29,073	-69.3	313,782	156,974	-50.0
Drunkenness	368,271	300,473	-18.4	11,093	3,805	-65.7	357,178	296,668	-16.9
Disorderly conduct	422,187	294,345	-30.3	129,948	52,315	-59.7	292,239	242,030	-17.2
Vagrancy	18,106	19,873	+9.8	3,475	622	-82.1	14,631	19,251	+31.6
All other offenses (except traffic)	2,477,981	2,585,233	+4.3	248,829	123,257	-50.5	2,229,152	2,461,976	+10.4
Suspicion	1,125	440	-60.9	203	74	-63.5	922	366	-60.3
Curfew and loitering law violations	60,669	27,152	-55.2	60,669	27,152	-55.2	NA	NA	NA

NA = Not available.

1 Does not include suspicion.   2 Violent crimes are offenses of murder and nonnegligent manslaughter, rape, robbery, and aggravated assault. Property crimes are offenses of burglary, larceny-theft, motor vehicle theft, and arson.   3 The 2006 rape figures are based on the legacy definition, and the 2016 rape figures are aggregate totals based on both the legacy and revised Uniform Crime Reporting definitions. For this reason, a percent change is not provided.

Table 25. Half-Decade Arrest Trends, by Age, 2011 and 2016

(Number, percent change; 13,055 agencies; 2016 estimated population 257,118,573; 2011 estimated population 211,166,146.)

Offense charged	Number of persons arrested								
	Total, all ages			Under 18 years of age			18 years of age and over		
	2011	2016	Percent change	2011	2016	Percent change	2011	2016	Percent change
Total[1]	8,225,888	8,481,602	+3.1	991,398	681,701	-31.2	7,234,490	7,799,901	+7.8
Violent crime[2]	346,801	410,717	+18.4	43,914	41,335	-5.9	302,887	369,382	+22.0
Murder and nonnegligent manslaughter	6,968	9,427	+35.3	539	682	+26.5	6,429	8,745	+36.0
Rape[3]	13,168	18,802	NA	1,917	2,952	NA	11,251	15,850	NA
Robbery	67,650	76,503	+13.1	15,037	15,339	+2.0	52,613	61,164	+16.3
Aggravated assault	259,015	305,985	+18.1	26,421	22,362	-15.4	232,594	283,623	+21.9
Property crime[2]	1,105,151	1,081,387	-2.2	229,384	147,350	-35.8	875,767	934,037	+6.7
Burglary	197,756	165,376	-16.4	41,018	25,513	-37.8	156,738	139,863	-10.8
Larceny-theft	855,183	839,617	-1.8	175,433	107,287	-38.8	679,750	732,330	+7.7
Motor vehicle theft	44,336	68,567	+54.7	9,581	12,520	+30.7	34,755	56,047	+61.3
Arson	7,876	7,827	-0.6	3,352	2,030	-39.4	4,524	5,797	+28.1
Other assaults	827,577	859,316	+3.8	127,310	102,694	-19.3	700,267	756,622	+8.0
Forgery and counterfeiting	46,264	45,067	-2.6	1,065	967	-9.2	45,199	44,100	-2.4
Fraud	110,363	101,980	-7.6	3,583	3,680	+2.7	106,780	98,300	-7.9
Embezzlement	10,931	12,688	+16.1	301	540	+79.4	10,630	12,148	+14.3
Stolen property; buying, receiving, possessing	63,792	74,895	+17.4	9,127	8,679	-4.9	54,665	66,216	+21.1
Vandalism	160,380	156,186	-2.6	46,688	31,181	-33.2	113,692	125,005	+10.0
Weapons; carrying, possessing, etc.	99,115	124,741	+25.9	18,665	15,452	-17.2	80,450	109,289	+35.8
Prostitution and commercialized vice	26,777	30,509	+13.9	461	396	-14.1	26,316	30,113	+14.4
Sex offenses (except forcible rape and prostitution)	44,870	40,546	-9.6	8,482	6,723	-20.7	36,388	33,823	-7.0
Drug abuse violations	1,020,875	1,250,650	+22.5	101,191	78,330	-22.6	919,684	1,172,320	+27.5
Gambling	4,929	2,916	-40.8	618	203	-67.2	4,311	2,713	-37.1
Offenses against the family and children	76,387	70,072	-8.3	2,378	2,738	+15.1	74,009	67,334	-9.0
Driving under the influence	825,909	806,369	-2.4	7,013	5,135	-26.8	818,896	801,234	-2.2
Liquor laws	323,529	186,047	-42.5	63,622	29,073	-54.3	259,907	156,974	-39.6
Drunkenness	361,587	300,473	-16.9	8,185	3,805	-53.5	353,402	296,668	-16.1
Disorderly conduct	382,589	294,345	-23.1	91,752	52,315	-43.0	290,837	242,030	-16.8
Vagrancy	14,587	19,873	+36.2	641	622	-3.0	13,946	19,251	+38.0
All other offenses (except traffic)	2,325,288	2,585,233	+11.2	178,831	123,257	-31.1	2,146,457	2,461,976	+14.7
Suspicion	732	440	-39.9	78	74	-5.1	654	366	-44.0
Curfew and loitering law violations	48,187	27,152	-43.7	48,187	27,152	-43.7	NA	NA	NA

NA = Not available.

1 Does not include suspicion.   2 Violent crimes are offenses of murder and nonnegligent manslaughter, rape, robbery, and aggravated assault. Property crimes are offenses of burglary, larceny-theft, motor vehicle theft, and arson. 3 The 2011 rape figures are based on the legacy definition, and the 2016 rape figures are aggregate totals based on both the legacy and revised Uniform Crime Reporting definitions. For this reason, a percent change is not provided.

Table 26. Year-to-Year Arrest Trends, by Age, 2015 and 2016

(Number, percent change; 13,055 agencies; 2016 estimated population 257,118,573; 2015 estimated population 217,039,923.)

Offense charged	Number of persons arrested								
	Total, all ages			Under 18 years of age			18 years of age and over		
	2015	2016	Percent change	2015	2016	Percent change	2015	2016	Percent change
Total[1]	7,213,389	8,481,602	+17.6	634,718	681,701	+7.4	6,578,671	7,799,901	+18.6
Violent crime[2]	328,454	410,717	+25.0	33,306	41,335	+24.1	295,148	369,382	+25.2
Murder and nonnegligent manslaughter	7,005	9,427	+34.6	493	682	+38.3	6,512	8,745	+34.3
Rape	15,126	18,802	+24.3	2,401	2,952	+22.9	12,725	15,850	+24.6
Robbery	60,085	76,503	+27.3	11,404	15,339	+34.5	48,681	61,164	+25.6
Aggravated assault	246,238	305,985	+24.3	19,008	22,362	+17.6	227,230	283,623	+24.8
Property crime[2]	1,001,386	1,081,387	+8.0	144,781	147,350	+1.8	856,605	934,037	+9.0
Burglary	145,163	165,376	+13.9	23,887	25,513	+6.8	121,276	139,863	+15.3
Larceny-theft	799,643	839,617	+5.0	109,356	107,287	-1.9	690,287	732,330	+6.1
Motor vehicle theft	50,447	68,567	+35.9	9,624	12,520	+30.1	40,823	56,047	+37.3
Arson	6,133	7,827	+27.6	1,914	2,030	+6.1	4,219	5,797	+37.4
Other assaults	727,435	859,316	+18.1	89,835	102,694	+14.3	637,600	756,622	+18.7
Forgery and counterfeiting	36,642	45,067	+23.0	694	967	+39.3	35,948	44,100	+22.7
Fraud	90,590	101,980	+12.6	3,246	3,680	+13.4	87,344	98,300	+12.5
Embezzlement	11,011	12,688	+15.2	426	540	+26.8	10,585	12,148	+14.8
Stolen property; buying, receiving, possessing	59,223	74,895	+26.5	6,715	8,679	+29.2	52,508	66,216	+26.1
Vandalism	130,154	156,186	+20.0	29,227	31,181	+6.7	100,927	125,005	+23.9
Weapons; carrying, possessing, etc.	95,803	124,741	+30.2	13,078	15,452	+18.2	82,725	109,289	+32.1
Prostitution and commercialized vice	19,797	30,509	+54.1	292	396	+35.6	19,505	30,113	+54.4
Sex offenses (except forcible rape and prostitution)	34,420	40,546	+17.8	6,048	6,723	+11.2	28,372	33,823	+19.2
Drug abuse violations	1,016,402	1,250,650	+23.0	69,355	78,330	+12.9	947,047	1,172,320	+23.8
Gambling	3,055	2,916	-4.5	294	203	-31.0	2,761	2,713	-1.7
Offenses against the family and children	65,357	70,072	+7.2	2,335	2,738	+17.3	63,022	67,334	+6.8
Driving under the influence	676,560	806,369	+19.2	4,432	5,135	+15.9	672,128	801,234	+19.2
Liquor laws	181,462	186,047	+2.5	30,876	29,073	-5.8	150,586	156,974	+4.2
Drunkenness	268,115	300,473	+12.1	3,836	3,805	-0.8	264,279	296,668	+12.3
Disorderly conduct	264,528	294,345	+11.3	49,315	52,315	+6.1	215,213	242,030	+12.5
Vagrancy	15,495	19,873	+28.3	648	622	-4.0	14,847	19,251	+29.7
All other offenses (except traffic)	2,157,131	2,585,233	+19.8	115,610	123,257	+6.6	2,041,521	2,461,976	+20.6
Suspicion	573	440	-23.2	132	74	-43.9	441	366	-17.0
Curfew and loitering law violations	30,369	27,152	-10.6	30,369	27,152	-10.6	NA	NA	NA

NA = Not available.
1 Does not include suspicion.   2 Violent crimes are offenses of murder and nonnegligent manslaughter, rape, robbery, and aggravated assault. Property crimes are offenses of burglary, larceny-theft, motor vehicle theft, and arson.

Table 27. Arrests, Distribution by Age, 2016

(Number, percent; 13,055 agencies; 2016 estimated population 257,118,573.)

Offense charged	Total, all ages	Ages under 15	Ages under 18	Ages 18 and over	Under 10	10–12	13–14	15	16	17	18	19	20
Total	8,481,602	190,575	681,701	7,799,901	4,902	42,347	143,326	127,828	164,010	199,288	269,618	294,446	295,134
Total percent distribution[1]	100.0	2.2	8.0	92.0	0.1	0.5	1.7	1.5	1.9	2.3	3.2	3.5	3.5
Violent crime[2]	410,717	11,306	41,335	369,382	198	2,543	8,565	7,860	10,175	11,994	14,062	14,219	14,040
Violent crime percent distribution[1]	100.0	2.8	10.1	89.9	*	0.6	2.1	1.9	2.5	2.9	3.4	3.5	3.4
Murder and nonnegligent manslaughter	9,427	60	682	8,745	0	5	55	93	198	331	503	511	493
Rape[3]	18,802	1,190	2,952	15,850	30	331	829	514	561	687	794	736	652
Robbery	76,503	2,898	15,339	61,164	20	368	2,510	3,123	4,367	4,951	5,448	4,726	4,052
Aggravated assault	305,985	7,158	22,362	283,623	148	1,839	5,171	4,130	5,049	6,025	7,317	8,246	8,843
Property crime[2]	1,081,387	40,956	147,350	934,037	783	8,512	31,661	29,385	36,501	40,508	46,090	41,888	37,463
Property crime percent distribution[1]	100.0	3.8	13.6	86.4	0.1	0.8	2.9	2.7	3.4	3.7	4.3	3.9	3.5
Burglary	165,376	7,646	25,513	139,863	193	1,596	5,857	5,243	6,117	6,507	7,889	7,320	6,411
Larceny-theft	839,617	29,321	107,287	732,330	476	6,207	22,638	20,954	26,589	30,423	34,793	31,534	28,229
Motor vehicle theft	68,567	2,824	12,520	56,047	15	295	2,514	2,837	3,519	3,340	3,221	2,827	2,623
Arson	7,827	1,165	2,030	5,797	99	414	652	351	276	238	187	207	200
Other assaults	859,316	39,768	102,694	756,622	1,321	10,824	27,623	19,949	21,673	21,304	20,131	21,251	22,747
Forgery and counterfeiting	45,067	105	967	44,100	1	11	93	107	237	518	1,239	1,936	2,124
Fraud	101,980	771	3,680	98,300	4	119	648	660	964	1,285	2,147	2,807	3,224
Embezzlement	12,688	49	540	12,148	0	6	43	49	157	285	593	753	640
Stolen property; buying, receiving, possessing	74,895	1,866	8,679	66,216	8	272	1,586	1,857	2,354	2,602	3,224	3,173	3,003
Vandalism	156,186	12,524	31,181	125,005	534	3,253	8,737	5,663	6,457	6,537	6,573	6,281	5,727
Weapons; carrying, possessing, etc.	124,741	4,800	15,452	109,289	203	1,377	3,220	2,734	3,551	4,367	5,407	5,502	5,251
Prostitution and commercialized vice	30,509	48	396	30,113	1	4	43	54	95	199	772	1,032	1,251
Sex offenses (except forcible rape and prostitution)	40,546	3,237	6,723	33,823	107	876	2,254	1,267	1,074	1,145	1,214	1,149	1,123
Drug abuse violations	1,250,650	12,067	78,330	1,172,320	91	1,737	10,239	12,096	20,639	33,528	57,653	61,810	58,365
Gambling	2,916	23	203	2,713	2	0	21	33	65	82	113	132	120
Offenses against the family and children	70,072	1,048	2,738	67,334	96	255	697	581	533	576	805	918	1,165
Driving under the influence	806,369	87	5,135	801,234	8	9	70	225	1,243	3,580	10,260	15,436	19,384
Liquor laws	186,047	3,058	29,073	156,974	9	267	2,782	4,404	8,044	13,567	27,689	29,826	24,901
Drunkenness	300,473	455	3,805	296,668	14	35	406	521	907	1,922	5,137	6,405	6,913
Disorderly conduct	294,345	19,949	52,315	242,030	498	4,964	14,487	10,521	11,221	10,624	9,678	8,961	8,896
Vagrancy	19,873	151	622	19,251	3	23	125	119	166	186	532	496	520
All other offenses (except traffic)	2,585,233	30,487	123,257	2,461,976	886	5,639	23,962	23,543	30,647	38,580	56,283	70,462	78,265
Suspicion	440	24	74	366	0	6	18	14	19	17	16	9	12
Curfew and loitering law violations	27,152	7,796	27,152	NA	135	1,615	6,046	6,186	7,288	5,882	NA	NA	NA

Table 27. Arrests, Distribution by Age, 2016—Continued

(Number, percent; 13,055 agencies; 2016 estimated population 257,118,573.)

Offense charged	21	22	23	24	25–29	30–34	35–39	40–44	45–49	50–54	55–59	60–64	65 and over
Total	297,815	304,569	310,118	316,603	1,446,803	1,178,723	917,096	633,112	550,673	454,140	293,893	140,568	96,590
Total percent distribution[1]	3.5	3.6	3.7	3.7	17.1	13.9	10.8	7.5	6.5	5.4	3.5	1.7	1.1
Violent crime[2]	14,623	15,061	14,992	15,390	69,214	55,774	42,961	29,494	25,056	20,228	13,016	6,229	5,023
Violent crime percent distribution[1]	3.6	3.7	3.7	3.7	16.9	13.6	10.5	7.2	6.1	4.9	3.2	1.5	1.2
Murder and nonnegligent manslaughter	467	475	433	469	1,745	1,152	788	515	412	323	195	136	128
Rape[3]	664	608	522	532	2,360	2,266	1,907	1,409	1,187	886	586	369	372
Robbery	3,517	3,303	3,034	3,044	11,787	7,911	5,229	3,158	2,585	1,911	984	325	150
Aggravated assault	9,975	10,675	11,003	11,345	53,322	44,445	35,037	24,412	20,872	17,108	11,251	5,399	4,373
Property crime[2]	35,346	35,341	35,609	36,910	173,238	143,464	108,311	72,708	63,702	50,094	30,696	13,960	9,217
Property crime percent distribution[1]	3.3	3.3	3.3	3.4	16.0	13.3	10.0	6.7	5.9	4.6	2.8	1.3	0.9
Burglary	5,971	5,857	5,862	5,952	27,290	21,721	15,852	9,789	8,327	6,110	3,448	1,360	704
Larceny-theft	26,698	26,858	27,111	28,192	133,335	111,662	85,045	58,510	52,166	41,687	26,092	12,164	8,254
Motor vehicle theft	2,481	2,440	2,455	2,555	11,648	9,221	6,692	3,908	2,801	1,871	869	284	151
Arson	196	186	181	211	965	860	722	501	408	426	287	152	108
Other assaults	26,351	27,986	29,328	30,162	139,697	117,671	94,570	67,678	58,012	46,809	28,940	14,115	11,174
Forgery and counterfeiting	1,527	1,659	1,718	1,772	8,806	7,379	5,927	3,597	2,741	1,902	1,027	460	286
Fraud	3,135	3,323	3,557	3,665	18,800	16,411	13,101	9,169	7,475	5,480	3,296	1,533	1,177
Embezzlement	587	587	555	532	2,235	1,625	1,217	921	761	565	332	146	99
Stolen property; buying, receiving, possessing	2,843	2,885	2,842	2,934	13,500	10,945	8,072	4,901	3,666	2,341	1,202	456	229
Vandalism	6,137	5,955	5,737	5,717	24,087	18,506	13,316	8,433	6,933	5,400	3,353	1,606	1,244
Weapons; carrying, possessing, etc.	5,623	5,828	5,576	5,519	22,344	15,765	11,263	6,858	5,324	3,946	2,694	1,313	1,076
Prostitution and commercialized vice	1,357	1,419	1,320	1,361	5,855	4,477	3,303	2,427	2,181	1,565	960	456	377
Sex offenses (except forcible rape and prostitution)	1,095	987	1,013	896	4,459	4,373	3,892	3,021	2,827	2,734	2,172	1,316	1,552
Drug abuse violations	55,548	54,681	53,861	53,677	231,196	174,620	127,217	80,183	65,702	50,589	29,799	12,136	5,283
Gambling	92	97	89	88	396	311	241	215	231	226	132	112	118
Offenses against the family and children	1,300	1,560	1,955	2,288	12,741	13,608	11,416	7,369	5,389	3,647	1,865	789	519
Driving under the influence	29,998	32,006	33,203	34,106	149,864	114,804	91,267	69,029	63,734	57,107	41,309	22,607	17,120
Liquor laws	4,392	3,324	2,687	2,533	10,395	8,803	8,060	6,837	7,662	8,288	6,460	3,274	1,843
Drunkenness	10,524	9,897	9,949	9,591	44,260	39,462	33,807	27,676	29,718	28,417	19,950	9,716	5,246
Disorderly conduct	10,766	10,199	9,906	9,524	41,020	33,043	26,114	19,078	17,910	16,060	11,224	5,470	4,181
Vagrancy	437	514	460	522	2,637	2,284	2,260	1,721	1,968	2,070	1,650	791	389
All other offenses (except traffic)	86,121	91,249	95,745	99,396	471,985	395,354	310,741	211,764	179,652	146,649	93,794	44,082	30,434
Suspicion	13	11	16	20	74	44	40	33	29	23	22	1	3
Curfew and loitering law violations	NA	NA	NA	NA	NA	NA	NA	NA	NA	NA	NA	NA	NA

NA = Not available.
* = Less than one-tenth of one percent. 1 Because of rounding, the percentages may not sum to 100 percent. 2 Violent crimes are offenses of murder and nonnegligent manslaughter, rape, robbery, and aggravated assault. Property crimes are offenses of burglary, larceny-theft, motor vehicle theft, and arson. 3 The rape figures in this table are aggregate totals of the data submitted based on both the legacy and revised Uniform Crime Reporting definitions.

Table 28. Male Arrests, Distribution by Age, 2015

(Number, percent; 12,706 agencies; 2015 estimated population 246,947,242.)

Offense charged	Total, all ages	Ages under 15	Ages under 18	Ages 18 and over	Under 10	10–12	13–14	15	16	17	18	19	20
Total	6,067,584	137,176	501,480	5,566,104	4,236	31,012	101,928	92,982	121,649	149,673	200,805	220,673	222,937
Total percent distribution[1]	100.0	2.3	8.3	91.7	0.1	0.5	1.7	1.5	2.0	2.5	3.3	3.6	3.7
Violent crime[2]	309,253	8,766	32,233	277,020	213	1,966	6,587	6,328	7,925	9,214	11,177	11,191	11,221
Violent crime percent distribution[1]	100.0	2.8	10.4	89.6	0.1	0.6	2.1	2.0	2.6	3.0	3.6	3.6	3.6
Murder and nonnegligent manslaughter	7,549	46	566	6,983	0	4	42	84	168	268	410	426	437
Rape[3]	16,990	1,040	2,637	14,353	23	293	724	492	514	591	744	702	673
Robbery	62,721	2,414	12,675	50,046	14	293	2,107	2,691	3,478	4,092	4,587	3,946	3,436
Aggravated assault	221,993	5,266	16,355	205,638	176	1,376	3,714	3,061	3,765	4,263	5,436	6,117	6,675
Property crime[2]	699,250	31,135	106,863	592,387	726	6,682	23,727	21,152	25,950	28,626	32,321	29,560	26,606
Property crime percent distribution[1]	100.0	4.5	15.3	84.7	0.1	1.0	3.4	3.0	3.7	4.1	4.6	4.2	3.8
Burglary	135,064	7,034	23,801	111,263	185	1,419	5,430	4,967	5,787	6,013	7,206	6,443	5,678
Larceny-theft	511,557	21,184	72,136	439,421	422	4,632	16,130	13,759	17,334	19,859	22,548	20,901	18,887
Motor vehicle theft	47,169	1,858	9,175	37,994	19	215	1,624	2,136	2,595	2,586	2,400	2,067	1,904
Arson	5,460	1,059	1,751	3,709	100	416	543	290	234	168	167	149	137
Other assaults	598,000	24,154	63,935	534,065	980	6,930	16,244	11,929	13,754	14,098	13,259	14,270	15,770
Forgery and counterfeiting	27,596	71	584	27,012	5	14	52	55	135	323	761	1,064	1,204
Fraud	62,721	460	2,313	60,408	8	67	385	391	559	903	1,450	1,864	2,186
Embezzlement	6,093	17	259	5,834	0	3	14	11	75	156	309	336	356
Stolen property; buying, receiving, possessing	53,621	1,386	6,673	46,948	20	212	1,154	1,392	1,843	2,052	2,570	2,362	2,205
Vandalism	115,695	10,346	26,731	88,964	494	2,718	7,134	4,950	5,678	5,757	5,377	4,838	4,383
Weapons; carrying, possessing, etc.	101,366	3,981	13,177	88,189	150	1,005	2,826	2,274	3,093	3,829	4,464	4,670	4,536
Prostitution and commercialized vice	11,355	21	108	11,247	0	4	17	18	23	46	132	182	224
Sex offenses (except forcible rape and prostitution)	36,361	2,764	5,848	30,513	95	722	1,947	1,040	1,014	1,030	1,138	1,130	1,068
Drug abuse violations	886,022	8,862	59,999	826,027	62	1,174	7,626	9,267	15,851	26,015	43,259	46,390	43,932
Gambling	2,883	44	325	2,558	1	10	33	62	104	115	180	144	146
Offenses against the family and children	51,598	624	1,648	49,950	72	123	429	333	305	386	610	689	798
Driving under the influence	625,927	82	3,813	622,114	17	4	61	159	831	2,741	8,160	12,365	15,624
Liquor laws	145,238	1,807	19,927	125,311	9	142	1,656	2,858	5,506	9,756	20,201	22,913	19,606
Drunkenness	253,565	322	3,033	250,532	16	24	282	442	689	1,580	4,272	5,535	5,855
Disorderly conduct	214,118	13,432	35,684	178,434	438	3,565	9,429	7,169	7,585	7,498	7,228	6,624	6,699
Vagrancy	15,080	156	618	14,462	3	29	124	139	157	166	334	303	307
All other offenses (except traffic)	1,826,711	21,679	93,273	1,733,438	714	3,936	17,029	17,720	24,056	29,818	43,571	54,211	60,185
Suspicion	802	41	111	691	4	10	27	22	26	22	32	32	26
Curfew and loitering law violations	24,329	7,026	24,329	NA	209	1,672	5,145	5,271	6,490	5,542	NA	NA	NA

Table 28. Male Arrests, Distribution by Age, 2015—Continued

(Number, percent; 12,706 agencies; 2015 estimated population 246,947,242.)

Offense charged	21	22	23	24	25–29	30–34	35–39	40–44	45–49	50–54	55–59	60–64	65 and over
Total	228,956	230,870	232,860	229,337	995,408	803,968	605,453	453,236	400,223	344,582	220,377	104,688	71,731
Total percent distribution[1]	3.8	3.8	3.8	3.8	16.4	13.3	10.0	7.5	6.6	5.7	3.6	1.7	1.2
Violent crime[2]	11,926	11,885	12,005	11,582	50,475	40,595	30,433	22,331	18,825	15,400	9,645	4,512	3,817
Violent crime percent distribution[1]	3.9	3.8	3.9	3.7	16.3	13.1	9.8	7.2	6.1	5.0	3.1	1.5	1.2
Murder and nonnegligent manslaughter	436	417	408	368	1,291	901	601	384	292	251	174	92	95
Rape[3]	625	557	485	532	2,128	2,018	1,610	1,303	1,000	879	507	279	311
Robbery	3,201	2,864	2,776	2,386	9,365	6,172	3,985	2,505	2,133	1,500	795	271	124
Aggravated assault	7,664	8,047	8,336	8,296	37,691	31,504	24,237	18,139	15,400	12,770	8,169	3,870	3,287
Property crime[2]	25,414	24,675	24,949	24,045	107,017	85,551	62,098	44,491	40,323	32,748	19,011	8,284	5,294
Property crime percent distribution[1]	3.6	3.5	3.6	3.4	15.3	12.2	8.9	6.4	5.8	4.7	2.7	1.2	0.8
Burglary	5,495	5,213	4,984	4,773	20,964	16,336	11,330	7,226	6,599	4,965	2,590	995	466
Larceny-theft	18,030	17,644	18,026	17,487	78,051	62,619	46,147	34,252	31,430	26,161	15,615	6,976	4,647
Motor vehicle theft	1,759	1,669	1,790	1,639	7,438	6,030	4,254	2,743	2,024	1,326	627	210	114
Arson	130	149	149	146	564	566	367	270	270	296	179	103	67
Other assaults	18,950	20,198	20,963	21,213	96,534	82,109	64,769	49,801	42,203	34,931	21,223	9,881	7,991
Forgery and counterfeiting	953	1,057	1,136	1,194	5,279	4,449	3,253	2,256	1,817	1,375	754	293	167
Fraud	2,054	2,230	2,237	2,376	11,259	9,460	7,442	5,721	4,683	3,504	2,135	1,006	801
Embezzlement	309	290	298	246	1,085	753	569	413	342	258	149	83	38
Stolen property; buying, receiving, possessing	2,288	2,077	2,153	2,162	9,079	7,353	5,191	3,432	2,730	1,800	969	372	205
Vandalism	4,699	4,547	4,449	4,008	16,559	12,370	8,733	5,944	4,903	3,905	2,360	1,053	836
Weapons; carrying, possessing, etc.	4,830	4,818	4,702	4,595	17,568	12,452	8,361	5,502	4,201	3,273	2,124	1,107	986
Prostitution and commercialized vice	316	325	328	337	1,778	1,733	1,496	1,250	960	839	635	374	338
Sex offenses (except forcible rape and prostitution)	1,040	927	923	842	4,007	3,776	3,302	2,766	2,594	2,525	1,829	1,151	1,495
Drug abuse violations	42,100	41,521	40,553	38,407	157,321	118,291	82,269	55,305	45,816	36,538	21,588	8,928	3,809
Gambling	125	126	122	90	431	270	212	184	164	113	119	71	61
Offenses against the family and children	951	1,165	1,332	1,518	8,677	9,237	8,600	6,166	4,438	3,157	1,613	621	378
Driving under the influence	23,835	25,661	26,992	26,804	114,340	89,293	67,972	54,611	48,865	44,675	31,916	17,399	13,602
Liquor laws	3,775	2,701	2,358	2,056	8,234	7,244	6,293	5,892	6,677	7,383	5,528	2,815	1,635
Drunkenness	9,255	8,739	8,535	8,432	36,530	32,154	26,611	23,321	25,174	25,770	17,555	8,385	4,409
Disorderly conduct	9,062	8,389	7,804	7,355	29,511	23,154	17,765	14,071	13,364	12,237	8,230	4,042	2,899
Vagrancy	362	368	364	361	1,842	1,819	1,467	1,170	1,612	1,723	1,389	708	333
All other offenses (except traffic)	66,684	69,151	70,629	71,685	317,746	261,808	198,531	148,553	130,495	112,382	71,588	33,593	22,626
Suspicion	28	20	28	29	136	97	86	56	37	46	17	10	11
Curfew and loitering law violations	NA	NA	NA	NA	NA	NA	NA	NA	NA	NA	NA	NA	NA

NA = Not available.

1 Because of rounding, the percentages may not sum to 100 percent.   2 Violent crimes are offenses of murder and nonnegligent manslaughter, rape, robbery, and aggravated assault. Property crimes are offenses of burglary, larceny-theft, motor vehicle theft, and arson.   3 The rape figures in this table are an aggregate total of the data submitted using both the revised and legacy Uniform Crime Reporting definitions.

Table 29. Female Arrests, Distribution by Age, 2015

(Number, percent; 12,706 agencies; 2015 estimated population 246,947,242.)

Offense charged	Total, all ages	Ages under 15	Ages under 18	Ages 18 and over	Under 10	10–12	13–14	15	16	17	18	19	20
Total	2,238,335	59,947	207,853	2,030,482	908	11,846	47,193	41,096	50,315	56,495	72,355	78,315	79,147
Total percent distribution[1]	100.0	2.7	9.3	90.7	*	0.5	2.1	1.8	2.2	2.5	3.2	3.5	3.5
Violent crime[2]	78,829	2,270	7,286	71,543	37	499	1,734	1,462	1,647	1,907	2,195	2,427	2,546
Violent crime percent distribution[1]	100.0	2.9	9.2	90.8	*	0.6	2.2	1.9	2.1	2.4	2.8	3.1	3.2
Murder and nonnegligent manslaughter	984	6	39	945	0	1	5	6	7	20	44	43	29
Rape[3]	514	58	108	406	1	13	44	19	15	16	17	22	10
Robbery	10,509	338	1,501	9,008	1	35	302	344	395	424	568	537	491
Aggravated assault	66,822	1,868	5,638	61,184	35	450	1,383	1,093	1,230	1,447	1,566	1,825	2,016
Property crime[2]	434,069	13,709	54,829	379,240	168	2,712	10,829	10,503	14,209	16,408	19,072	17,809	16,011
Property crime percent distribution[1]	100.0	3.2	12.6	87.4	*	0.6	2.5	2.4	3.3	3.8	4.4	4.1	3.7
Burglary	31,545	1,138	3,672	27,873	40	237	861	763	830	941	1,091	1,160	1,070
Larceny-theft	388,520	11,826	48,831	339,689	115	2,357	9,354	9,173	12,844	14,988	17,514	16,183	14,426
Motor vehicle theft	12,662	559	1,994	10,668	4	50	505	497	494	444	446	441	472
Arson	1,342	186	332	1,010	9	68	109	70	41	35	21	25	43
Other assaults	233,684	14,248	37,045	196,639	182	3,274	10,792	7,578	7,993	7,226	6,418	6,567	7,196
Forgery and counterfeiting	15,085	27	207	14,878	2	2	23	27	46	107	310	454	636
Fraud	39,618	210	1,161	38,457	1	34	175	215	308	428	696	930	1,146
Embezzlement	6,154	10	191	5,963	0	2	8	7	56	118	288	391	337
Stolen property; buying, receiving, possessing	14,720	376	1,317	13,403	2	43	331	280	294	367	451	534	518
Vandalism	31,496	2,094	5,414	26,082	62	494	1,538	1,022	1,087	1,211	1,112	1,122	1,168
Weapons; carrying, possessing, etc.	9,950	629	1,602	8,348	13	177	439	279	335	359	338	323	339
Prostitution and commercialized vice	20,179	30	334	19,845	0	6	24	53	93	158	717	1,035	1,100
Sex offenses (except forcible rape and prostitution)	3,032	416	851	2,181	15	100	301	160	160	115	97	93	94
Drug abuse violations	257,999	3,241	16,177	241,822	17	422	2,802	2,730	4,084	6,122	10,641	11,457	11,348
Gambling	724	1	32	692	0	0	1	4	10	17	14	24	19
Offenses against the family and children	20,820	366	980	19,840	62	63	241	167	212	235	287	325	395
Driving under the influence	207,906	38	1,251	206,655	3	0	35	64	319	830	2,433	3,875	4,738
Liquor laws	59,427	1,682	13,228	46,199	6	132	1,544	2,175	3,714	5,657	10,438	10,555	8,394
Drunkenness	61,291	216	1,210	60,081	4	18	194	208	307	479	1,334	1,467	1,490
Disorderly conduct	84,135	7,758	19,418	64,717	80	1,646	6,032	4,342	3,956	3,362	2,622	2,487	2,495
Vagrancy	4,334	56	207	4,127	2	11	43	55	52	44	102	124	134
All other offenses (except traffic)	645,061	9,719	35,497	609,564	204	1,664	7,851	7,436	8,784	9,558	12,780	16,312	19,036
Suspicion	243	10	37	206	1	2	7	7	11	9	10	4	7
Curfew and loitering law violations	9,579	2,841	9,579	NA	47	545	2,249	2,322	2,638	1,778	NA	NA	NA

Table 29. Female Arrests, Distribution by Age, 2015—Continued

(Number, percent; 12,706 agencies; 2015 estimated population 246,947,242.)

Offense charged	21	22	23	24	25–29	30–34	35–39	40–44	45–49	50–54	55–59	60–64	65 and over
Total	80,774	83,464	85,502	86,629	384,567	317,727	235,566	172,973	140,846	108,616	59,405	26,168	18,428
Total percent distribution[1]	3.6	3.7	3.8	3.9	17.2	14.2	10.5	7.7	6.3	4.9	2.7	1.2	0.8
Violent crime[2]	2,913	3,087	3,095	3,175	13,912	11,177	8,209	6,086	5,032	4,009	2,168	890	622
Violent crime percent distribution[1]	3.7	3.9	3.9	4.0	17.6	14.2	10.4	7.7	6.4	5.1	2.8	1.1	0.8
Murder and nonnegligent manslaughter	36	48	50	46	181	154	89	62	55	59	25	11	13
Rape[3]	16	11	12	20	59	78	58	46	25	11	16	4	1
Robbery	505	469	477	484	1,855	1,343	890	561	404	270	116	22	16
Aggravated assault	2,356	2,559	2,556	2,625	11,817	9,602	7,172	5,417	4,548	3,669	2,011	853	592
Property crime[2]	15,435	15,503	15,272	15,375	69,496	58,624	42,222	30,367	24,829	19,036	10,908	5,363	3,918
Property crime percent distribution[1]	3.6	3.6	3.5	3.5	16.0	13.5	9.7	7.0	5.7	4.4	2.5	1.2	0.9
Burglary	1,219	1,187	1,251	1,205	5,568	4,691	3,279	2,214	1,694	1,215	622	251	156
Larceny-theft	13,674	13,767	13,480	13,629	61,302	51,844	37,602	27,318	22,559	17,469	10,129	5,070	3,723
Motor vehicle theft	510	527	509	515	2,457	1,937	1,216	734	494	260	105	25	20
Arson	32	22	32	26	169	152	125	101	82	92	52	17	19
Other assaults	8,230	8,386	8,622	8,504	36,429	29,919	22,729	17,349	14,192	11,341	6,069	2,701	1,987
Forgery and counterfeiting	501	571	601	641	3,156	2,660	1,991	1,365	956	613	266	99	58
Fraud	1,156	1,218	1,372	1,418	7,153	6,905	5,440	3,983	2,914	2,009	1,155	528	434
Embezzlement	304	300	294	252	1,033	814	603	481	350	262	151	69	34
Stolen property; buying, receiving, possessing	607	634	633	625	3,030	2,444	1,656	949	605	418	189	72	38
Vandalism	1,333	1,251	1,286	1,234	5,221	3,876	2,645	1,881	1,577	1,239	632	283	222
Weapons; carrying, possessing, etc.	370	392	411	404	1,690	1,368	911	644	450	343	223	69	73
Prostitution and commercialized vice	1,215	1,205	1,192	1,049	4,277	2,574	1,806	1,355	1,112	789	303	88	28
Sex offenses (except forcible rape and prostitution)	88	99	105	81	349	314	271	180	177	118	65	29	21
Drug abuse violations	11,168	11,286	11,359	11,539	48,570	38,570	26,965	18,024	14,103	10,019	4,605	1,576	592
Gambling	9	13	11	14	73	84	69	64	87	71	66	44	30
Offenses against the family and children	566	698	773	845	4,367	4,309	2,991	1,789	1,156	729	338	166	106
Driving under the influence	8,493	8,982	9,396	9,371	37,851	29,149	22,850	19,299	17,623	15,266	9,504	4,621	3,204
Liquor laws	1,294	922	760	672	2,609	2,136	1,911	1,809	1,729	1,482	896	378	214
Drunkenness	2,175	2,016	2,052	2,136	9,077	8,451	7,167	6,435	6,282	5,420	2,958	1,083	538
Disorderly conduct	3,007	2,925	2,780	2,728	11,497	8,897	6,920	5,452	4,843	4,092	2,249	948	775
Vagrancy	85	104	154	114	573	481	539	498	413	388	257	105	56
All other offenses (except traffic)	21,811	23,864	25,318	26,448	124,165	104,945	77,654	54,941	42,406	30,963	16,399	7,055	5,467
Suspicion	14	8	16	4	39	30	17	22	10	9	4	1	11
Curfew and loitering law violations	NA	NA	NA	NA	NA	NA	NA	NA	NA	NA	NA	NA	NA

NA = Not available.
* = Less than one-tenth of one percent.
1 Because of rounding, the percentages may not sum to 100 percent.   2 Violent crimes are offenses of murder and nonnegligent manslaughter, rape, robbery, and aggravated assault. Property crimes are offenses of burglary, larceny-theft, motor vehicle theft, and arson.   3 The rape figures in this table are an aggregate total of the data submitted using both the revised and legacy Uniform Crime Reporting definitions.

Table 30. Arrests of Persons Under 15, 18, 21, and 25 Years of Age, 2015

(Number, percent; 12,706 agencies; 2015 estimated population 246,947,242.)

Offense charged	Total, all ages	Number of persons arrested				Percent of total all ages			
		Under 15	Under 18	Under 21	Under 25	Under 15	Under 18	Under 21	Under 25
Total	8,305,919	197,123	709,333	1,583,565	2,841,957	2.4	8.5	19.1	34.2
Violent crime[1]	388,082	11,036	39,519	80,276	139,944	2.8	10.2	20.7	36.1
Murder and nonnegligent manslaughter	8,533	52	605	1,994	3,803	0.6	7.1	23.4	44.6
Rape[2]	17,504	1,098	2,745	4,913	7,171	6.3	15.7	28.1	41.0
Robbery	73,230	2,752	14,176	27,741	40,903	3.8	19.4	37.9	55.9
Aggravated assault	288,815	7,134	21,993	45,628	88,067	2.5	7.6	15.8	30.5
Property crime[1]	1,133,319	44,844	161,692	303,071	463,739	4.0	14.3	26.7	40.9
Burglary	166,609	8,172	27,473	50,121	75,448	4.9	16.5	30.1	45.3
Larceny-theft	900,077	33,010	120,967	231,426	357,163	3.7	13.4	25.7	39.7
Motor vehicle theft	59,831	2,417	11,169	18,899	27,817	4.0	18.7	31.6	46.5
Arson	6,802	1,245	2,083	2,625	3,311	18.3	30.6	38.6	48.7
Other assaults	831,684	38,402	100,980	164,460	279,526	4.6	12.1	19.8	33.6
Forgery and counterfeiting	42,681	98	791	5,220	11,874	0.2	1.9	12.2	27.8
Fraud	102,339	670	3,474	11,746	25,807	0.7	3.4	11.5	25.2
Embezzlement	12,247	27	450	2,467	4,760	0.2	3.7	20.1	38.9
Stolen property; buying, receiving, possessing	68,341	1,762	7,990	16,630	27,809	2.6	11.7	24.3	40.7
Vandalism	147,191	12,440	32,145	50,145	72,952	8.5	21.8	34.1	49.6
Weapons; carrying, possessing, etc.	111,316	4,610	14,779	29,449	49,971	4.1	13.3	26.5	44.9
Prostitution and commercialized vice	31,534	51	442	3,832	9,799	0.2	1.4	12.2	31.1
Sex offenses (except forcible rape and prostitution)	39,393	3,180	6,699	10,319	14,424	8.1	17.0	26.2	36.6
Drug abuse violations	1,144,021	12,103	76,172	243,199	451,132	1.1	6.7	21.3	39.4
Gambling	3,607	45	357	884	1,394	1.2	9.9	24.5	38.6
Offenses against the family and children	72,418	990	2,628	5,732	13,580	1.4	3.6	7.9	18.8
Driving under the influence	833,833	120	5,064	52,259	191,793	*	0.6	6.3	23.0
Liquor laws	204,665	3,489	33,155	125,262	139,800	1.7	16.2	61.2	68.3
Drunkenness	314,856	538	4,243	24,196	67,536	0.2	1.3	7.7	21.4
Disorderly conduct	298,253	21,190	55,102	83,257	127,307	7.1	18.5	27.9	42.7
Vagrancy	19,414	212	825	2,129	4,041	1.1	4.2	11.0	20.8
All other offenses (except traffic)	2,471,772	31,398	128,770	334,865	710,455	1.3	5.2	13.5	28.7
Suspicion	1,045	51	148	259	406	4.9	14.2	24.8	38.9
Curfew and loitering law violations	33,908	9,867	33,908	33,908	33,908	29.1	100.0	100.0	100.0

* = Less than one-tenth of one percent.
1 Violent crimes in this table are offenses of murder and nonnegligent manslaughter, rape, robbery, and aggravated assault. Property crimes are offenses of burglary, larceny-theft, motor vehicle theft, and arson.   2 The rape figures in this table are an aggregate total of the data submitted using both the revised and legacy Uniform Crime Reporting definitions.

Table 31. Arrests, Distribution by Sex, 2015

(Number, percent; 12,706 agencies; 2015 estimated population 246,947,242.)

Offense charged	Number of persons arrested			Percent male	Percent female	Percent distribution[1]		
	Total	Male	Female			Total	Male	Female
Total	8,305,919	6,067,584	2,238,335	73.1	26.9	100.0	100.0	100.0
Violent crime[2]	388,082	309,253	78,829	79.7	20.3	4.7	5.1	3.5
Murder and nonnegligent manslaughter	8,533	7,549	984	88.5	11.5	0.1	0.1	*
Rape[3]	17,504	16,990	514	97.1	2.9	0.2	0.3	*
Robbery	73,230	62,721	10,509	85.6	14.4	0.9	1.0	0.5
Aggravated assault	288,815	221,993	66,822	76.9	23.1	3.5	3.7	3.0
Property crime[2]	1,133,319	699,250	434,069	61.7	38.3	13.6	11.5	19.4
Burglary	166,609	135,064	31,545	81.1	18.9	2.0	2.2	1.4
Larceny-theft	900,077	511,557	388,520	56.8	43.2	10.8	8.4	17.4
Motor vehicle theft	59,831	47,169	12,662	78.8	21.2	0.7	0.8	0.6
Arson	6,802	5,460	1,342	80.3	19.7	0.1	0.1	0.1
Other assaults	831,684	598,000	233,684	71.9	28.1	10.0	9.9	10.4
Forgery and counterfeiting	42,681	27,596	15,085	64.7	35.3	0.5	0.5	0.7
Fraud	102,339	62,721	39,618	61.3	38.7	1.2	1.0	1.8
Embezzlement	12,247	6,093	6,154	49.8	50.2	0.1	0.1	0.3
Stolen property; buying, receiving, possessing	68,341	53,621	14,720	78.5	21.5	0.8	0.9	0.7
Vandalism	147,191	115,695	31,496	78.6	21.4	1.8	1.9	1.4
Weapons; carrying, possessing, etc.	111,316	101,366	9,950	91.1	8.9	1.3	1.7	0.4
Prostitution and commercialized vice	31,534	11,355	20,179	36.0	64.0	0.4	0.2	0.9
Sex offenses (except forcible rape and prostitution)	39,393	36,361	3,032	92.3	7.7	0.5	0.6	0.1
Drug abuse violations	1,144,021	886,022	257,999	77.4	22.6	13.8	14.6	11.5
Gambling	3,607	2,883	724	79.9	20.1	*	*	*
Offenses against the family and children	72,418	51,598	20,820	71.3	28.7	0.9	0.9	0.9
Driving under the influence	833,833	625,927	207,906	75.1	24.9	10.0	10.3	9.3
Liquor laws	204,665	145,238	59,427	71.0	29.0	2.5	2.4	2.7
Drunkenness	314,856	253,565	61,291	80.5	19.5	3.8	4.2	2.7
Disorderly conduct	298,253	214,118	84,135	71.8	28.2	3.6	3.5	3.8
Vagrancy	19,414	15,080	4,334	77.7	22.3	0.2	0.2	0.2
All other offenses (except traffic)	2,471,772	1,826,711	645,061	73.9	26.1	29.8	30.1	28.8
Suspicion	1,045	802	243	76.7	23.3	*	*	*
Curfew and loitering law violations	33,908	24,329	9,579	71.8	28.2	0.4	0.4	0.4

* = Less than one-tenth of 1 percent.
1 Because of rounding, the percentages may not sum to 100. 2 Violent crimes in this table are offenses of murder and nonnegligent manslaughter, rape, robbery, and aggravated assault. Property crimes are offenses of burglary, larceny-theft, motor vehicle theft, and arson. 3 The rape figures in this table are an aggregate total of the data submitted using both the revised and legacy Uniform Crime Reporting definitions.

Table 32. Arrests, Distribution by Race, 2016

(Number, percent; 13,049 agencies; 2016 estimated population 257,112,535.)

Offense charged	Total arrests						Percent distribution[1]					
	Total	White	Black	American Indian or Alaskan Native	Asian	Native Hawaiian or Other Pacific Islander	Total	White	Black	American Indian or Alaskan Native	Asian	Native Hawaiian or Other Pacific Islander
Total	8,421,481	5,858,330	2,263,112	171,185	103,244	25,610	100.0	69.6	26.9	2.0	1.2	0.3
Violent crime[2]	408,873	241,063	153,341	7,378	5,755	1,336	100.0	59.0	37.5	1.8	1.4	0.3
Murder and nonnegligent manslaughter	9,374	4,192	4,935	108	109	30	100.0	44.7	52.6	1.2	1.2	0.3
Rape[3]	18,606	12,571	5,412	233	309	81	100.0	67.6	29.1	1.3	1.7	0.4
Robbery	76,267	33,095	41,562	663	659	288	100.0	43.4	54.5	0.9	0.9	0.4
Aggravated assault	304,626	191,205	101,432	6,374	4,678	937	100.0	62.8	33.3	2.1	1.5	0.3
Property crime[2]	1,074,136	738,319	301,958	17,782	13,217	2,860	100.0	68.7	28.1	1.7	1.2	0.3
Burglary	164,641	112,651	47,991	1,613	1,925	461	100.0	68.4	29.1	1.0	1.2	0.3
Larceny-theft	833,558	575,105	231,199	14,933	10,277	2,044	100.0	69.0	27.7	1.8	1.2	0.2
Motor vehicle theft	68,170	44,970	20,955	1,018	895	332	100.0	66.0	30.7	1.5	1.3	0.5
Arson	7,767	5,593	1,813	218	120	23	100.0	72.0	23.3	2.8	1.5	0.3
Other assaults	853,493	556,871	267,764	15,505	10,511	2,842	100.0	65.2	31.4	1.8	1.2	0.3
Forgery and counterfeiting	44,831	29,375	14,308	290	752	106	100.0	65.5	31.9	0.6	1.7	0.2
Fraud	101,301	67,860	30,888	1,248	1,164	141	100.0	67.0	30.5	1.2	1.1	0.1
Embezzlement	12,592	7,732	4,512	104	209	35	100.0	61.4	35.8	0.8	1.7	0.3
Stolen property; buying, receiving, possessing	74,492	47,818	24,851	876	812	135	100.0	64.2	33.4	1.2	1.1	0.2
Vandalism	154,958	105,933	43,499	3,370	1,768	388	100.0	68.4	28.1	2.2	1.1	0.3
Weapons; carrying, possessing, etc.	124,150	69,414	51,898	1,135	1,401	302	100.0	55.9	41.8	0.9	1.1	0.2
Prostitution and commercialized vice	30,322	16,819	11,495	121	1,821	66	100.0	55.5	37.9	0.4	6.0	0.2
Sex offenses (except forcible rape and prostitution)	40,292	28,837	9,949	633	749	124	100.0	71.6	24.7	1.6	1.9	0.3
Drug abuse violations	1,242,630	881,885	332,131	12,746	13,593	2,275	100.0	71.0	26.7	1.0	1.1	0.2
Gambling	2,905	1,308	1,405	8	167	17	100.0	45.0	48.4	0.3	5.7	0.6
Offenses against the family and children	69,546	46,661	20,265	2,065	519	36	100.0	67.1	29.1	3.0	0.7	0.1
Driving under the influence	798,012	655,648	108,881	14,700	15,969	2,814	100.0	82.2	13.6	1.8	2.0	0.4
Liquor laws	183,514	145,328	26,545	8,413	2,792	436	100.0	79.2	14.5	4.6	1.5	0.2
Drunkenness	299,248	228,784	43,948	23,043	3,046	427	100.0	76.5	14.7	7.7	1.0	0.1
Disorderly conduct	291,951	184,903	94,004	10,121	2,320	603	100.0	63.3	32.2	3.5	0.8	0.2
Vagrancy	19,755	13,033	6,063	412	234	13	100.0	66.0	30.7	2.1	1.2	0.1
All other offenses (except traffic)	2,567,092	1,775,423	704,293	50,666	26,136	10,574	100.0	69.2	27.4	2.0	1.0	0.4
Suspicion	440	154	135	143	5	3	100.0	35.0	30.7	32.5	1.1	0.7
Curfew and loitering law violations	26,948	15,162	10,979	426	304	77	100.0	56.3	40.7	1.6	1.1	0.3

Table 32. Arrests, Distribution by Race, 2016—Continued

(Number, percent; 13,049 agencies; 2016 estimated population 257,112,535.)

Offense charged	Arrests under 18						Percent distribution[1]					
	Total	White	Black	American Indian or Alaskan Native	Asian	Native Hawaiian or Other Pacific Islander	Total	White	Black	American Indian or Alaskan Native	Asian	Native Hawaiian or Other Pacific Islander
Total	674,820	419,393	234,092	11,509	7,424	2,402	100.0	62.1	34.7	1.7	1.1	0.4
Violent crime[2]	41,089	18,675	21,375	476	404	159	100.0	45.5	52.0	1.2	1.0	0.4
Murder and nonnegligent manslaughter	679	244	413	9	11	2	100.0	35.9	60.8	1.3	1.6	0.3
Rape[3]	2,900	1,877	956	23	31	13	100.0	64.7	33.0	0.8	1.1	0.4
Robbery	15,293	4,468	10,520	94	139	72	100.0	29.2	68.8	0.6	0.9	0.5
Aggravated assault	22,217	12,086	9,486	350	223	72	100.0	54.4	42.7	1.6	1.0	0.3
Property crime[2]	145,751	85,097	55,711	2,343	2,111	489	100.0	58.4	38.2	1.6	1.4	0.3
Burglary	25,360	14,036	10,606	351	302	65	100.0	55.3	41.8	1.4	1.2	0.3
Larceny-theft	106,014	63,842	38,364	1,754	1,672	382	100.0	60.2	36.2	1.7	1.6	0.4
Motor vehicle theft	12,394	5,810	6,255	190	106	33	100.0	46.9	50.5	1.5	0.9	0.3
Arson	1,983	1,409	486	48	31	9	100.0	71.1	24.5	2.4	1.6	0.5
Other assaults	101,852	58,674	40,635	1,425	782	336	100.0	57.6	39.9	1.4	0.8	0.3
Forgery and counterfeiting	961	534	405	6	14	2	100.0	55.6	42.1	0.6	1.5	0.2
Fraud	3,646	1,818	1,745	49	29	5	100.0	49.9	47.9	1.3	0.8	0.1
Embezzlement	537	316	202	7	12	0	100.0	58.8	37.6	1.3	2.2	0.0
Stolen property; buying, receiving, possessing	8,614	3,390	5,035	87	81	21	100.0	39.4	58.5	1.0	0.9	0.2
Vandalism	30,863	21,355	8,536	620	260	92	100.0	69.2	27.7	2.0	0.8	0.3
Weapons; carrying, possessing, etc.	15,342	8,249	6,698	162	211	22	100.0	53.8	43.7	1.1	1.4	0.1
Prostitution and commercialized vice	395	157	227	2	5	4	100.0	39.7	57.5	0.5	1.3	1.0
Sex offenses (except forcible rape and prostitution)	6,659	4,786	1,707	62	85	19	100.0	71.9	25.6	0.9	1.3	0.3
Drug abuse violations	77,527	58,017	17,107	1,242	917	244	100.0	74.8	22.1	1.6	1.2	0.3
Gambling	203	50	150	0	3	0	100.0	24.6	73.9	0.0	1.5	0.0
Offenses against the family and children	2,703	1,596	646	443	17	1	100.0	59.0	23.9	16.4	0.6	*
Driving under the influence	5,059	4,499	338	132	73	17	100.0	88.9	6.7	2.6	1.4	0.3
Liquor laws	28,598	25,203	1,923	1,055	352	65	100.0	88.1	6.7	3.7	1.2	0.2
Drunkenness	3,753	3,132	373	194	46	8	100.0	83.5	9.9	5.2	1.2	0.2
Disorderly conduct	51,928	27,777	22,915	829	332	75	100.0	53.5	44.1	1.6	0.6	0.1
Vagrancy	608	368	220	11	7	2	100.0	60.5	36.2	1.8	1.2	0.3
All other offenses (except traffic)	121,710	80,504	37,132	1,938	1,375	761	100.0	66.1	30.5	1.6	1.1	0.6
Suspicion	74	34	33	0	4	3	100.0	45.9	44.6	0.0	5.4	4.1
Curfew and loitering law violations	26,948	15,162	10,979	426	304	77	100.0	56.3	40.7	1.6	1.1	0.3

Table 32. Arrests, Distribution by Race, 2016—Continued

(Number, percent; 13,049 agencies; 2016 estimated population 257,112,535.)

Offense charged	Arrests 18 and over						Percent distribution[1]					
	Total	White	Black	American Indian or Alaskan Native	Asian	Native Hawaiian or Other Pacific Islander	Total	White	Black	American Indian or Alaskan Native	Asian	Native Hawaiian or Other Pacific Islander
Total	7,746,661	5,438,937	2,029,020	159,676	95,820	23,208	100.0	70.2	26.2	2.1	1.2	0.3
Violent crime[2]	367,784	222,388	131,966	6,902	5,351	1,177	100.0	60.5	35.9	1.9	1.5	0.3
Murder and nonnegligent manslaughter	8,695	3,948	4,522	99	98	28	100.0	45.4	52.0	1.1	1.1	0.3
Rape[3]	15,706	10,694	4,456	210	278	68	100.0	68.1	28.4	1.3	1.8	0.4
Robbery	60,974	28,627	31,042	569	520	216	100.0	46.9	50.9	0.9	0.9	0.4
Aggravated assault	282,409	179,119	91,946	6,024	4,455	865	100.0	63.4	32.6	2.1	1.6	0.3
Property crime[2]	928,385	653,222	246,247	15,439	11,106	2,371	100.0	70.4	26.5	1.7	1.2	0.3
Burglary	139,281	98,615	37,385	1,262	1,623	396	100.0	70.8	26.8	0.9	1.2	0.3
Larceny-theft	727,544	511,263	192,835	13,179	8,605	1,662	100.0	70.3	26.5	1.8	1.2	0.2
Motor vehicle theft	55,776	39,160	14,700	828	789	299	100.0	70.2	26.4	1.5	1.4	0.5
Arson	5,784	4,184	1,327	170	89	14	100.0	72.3	22.9	2.9	1.5	0.2
Other assaults	751,641	498,197	227,129	14,080	9,729	2,506	100.0	66.3	30.2	1.9	1.3	0.3
Forgery and counterfeiting	43,870	28,841	13,903	284	738	104	100.0	65.7	31.7	0.6	1.7	0.2
Fraud	97,655	66,042	29,143	1,199	1,135	136	100.0	67.6	29.8	1.2	1.2	0.1
Embezzlement	12,055	7,416	4,310	97	197	35	100.0	61.5	35.8	0.8	1.6	0.3
Stolen property; buying, receiving, possessing	65,878	44,428	19,816	789	731	114	100.0	67.4	30.1	1.2	1.1	0.2
Vandalism	124,095	84,578	34,963	2,750	1,508	296	100.0	68.2	28.2	2.2	1.2	0.2
Weapons; carrying, possessing, etc.	108,808	61,165	45,200	973	1,190	280	100.0	56.2	41.5	0.9	1.1	0.3
Prostitution and commercialized vice	29,927	16,662	11,268	119	1,816	62	100.0	55.7	37.7	0.4	6.1	0.2
Sex offenses (except forcible rape and prostitution)	33,633	24,051	8,242	571	664	105	100.0	71.5	24.5	1.7	2.0	0.3
Drug abuse violations	1,165,103	823,868	315,024	11,504	12,676	2,031	100.0	70.7	27.0	1.0	1.1	0.2
Gambling	2,702	1,258	1,255	8	164	17	100.0	46.6	46.4	0.3	6.1	0.6
Offenses against the family and children	66,843	45,065	19,619	1,622	502	35	100.0	67.4	29.4	2.4	0.8	0.1
Driving under the influence	792,953	651,149	108,543	14,568	15,896	2,797	100.0	82.1	13.7	1.8	2.0	0.4
Liquor laws	154,916	120,125	24,622	7,358	2,440	371	100.0	77.5	15.9	4.7	1.6	0.2
Drunkenness	295,495	225,652	43,575	22,849	3,000	419	100.0	76.4	14.7	7.7	1.0	0.1
Disorderly conduct	240,023	157,126	71,089	9,292	1,988	528	100.0	65.5	29.6	3.9	0.8	0.2
Vagrancy	19,147	12,665	5,843	401	227	11	100.0	66.1	30.5	2.1	1.2	0.1
All other offenses (except traffic)	2,445,382	1,694,919	667,161	48,728	24,761	9,813	100.0	69.3	27.3	2.0	1.0	0.4
Suspicion	366	120	102	143	1	0	100.0	32.8	27.9	39.1	0.3	0.0
Curfew and loitering law violations	NA	NA	NA	NA	NA	NA	NA	NA	NA	NA	NA	NA

NA = Not available.
* = Less than one-tenth of one percent.
1 Because of rounding, the percentages may not sum to 100.   2 Violent crimes are offenses of murder and nonnegligent manslaughter, rape, robbery, and aggravated assault. Property crimes are offenses of burglary, larceny-theft, motor vehicle theft, and arson.   3 The rape figures in this table are an aggregate total of the data submitted using both the revised and legacy Uniform Crime Reporting definitions.

Table 33. Arrests, Distribution by Ethnicity, 2016

(Number, percent; 13,049 agencies; 2016 estimated population 257,112,535.)

Offense charged	Total arrests			Percent distribution[1]			Arrests under 18		
	Total[2]	Hispanic or Latino	Not Hispanic or Latino	Total[2]	Hispanic or Latino	Not Hispanic or Latino	Total[2]	Hispanic or Latino	Not Hispanic or Latino
Total	6,647,012	1,221,066	5,425,946	100.0	18.4	81.6	496,233	113,244	382,989
Violent crime[3]	331,656	78,862	252,794	100.0	23.8	76.2	31,245	7,620	23,625
Murder and nonnegligent manslaughter	6,882	1,374	5,508	100.0	20.0	80.0	416	103	313
Rape[4]	13,896	3,758	10,138	100.0	27.0	73.0	2,137	455	1,682
Robbery	60,116	12,657	47,459	100.0	21.1	78.9	11,254	2,462	8,792
Aggravated assault	250,762	61,073	189,689	100.0	24.4	75.6	17,438	4,600	12,838
Property crime[3]	813,260	133,393	679,867	100.0	16.4	83.6	99,685	22,450	77,235
Burglary	130,179	27,113	103,066	100.0	20.8	79.2	17,560	4,874	12,686
Larceny-theft	624,800	91,210	533,590	100.0	14.6	85.4	72,692	15,155	57,537
Motor vehicle theft	52,786	14,160	38,626	100.0	26.8	73.2	7,979	2,123	5,856
Arson	5,495	910	4,585	100.0	16.6	83.4	1,454	298	1,156
Other assaults	665,711	121,329	544,382	100.0	18.2	81.8	78,351	17,144	61,207
Forgery and counterfeiting	35,180	5,580	29,600	100.0	15.9	84.1	715	126	589
Fraud	79,089	9,084	70,005	100.0	11.5	88.5	2,788	384	2,404
Embezzlement	10,178	1,225	8,953	100.0	12.0	88.0	443	144	299
Stolen property; buying, receiving, possessing	56,243	11,067	45,176	100.0	19.7	80.3	5,849	1,228	4,621
Vandalism	121,519	22,425	99,094	100.0	18.5	81.5	22,603	5,175	17,428
Weapons; carrying, possessing, etc.	97,279	22,753	74,526	100.0	23.4	76.6	11,505	3,644	7,861
Prostitution and commercialized vice	25,718	5,123	20,595	100.0	19.9	80.1	331	52	279
Sex offenses (except forcible rape and prostitution)	32,402	8,134	24,268	100.0	25.1	74.9	5,169	1,278	3,891
Drug abuse violations	991,426	201,110	790,316	100.0	20.3	79.7	57,833	16,358	41,475
Gambling	1,958	502	1,456	100.0	25.6	74.4	102	21	81
Offenses against the family and children	55,805	6,345	49,460	100.0	11.4	88.6	2,205	306	1,899
Driving under the influence	657,336	148,548	508,788	100.0	22.6	77.4	4,074	977	3,097
Liquor laws	134,376	19,488	114,888	100.0	14.5	85.5	21,892	3,540	18,352
Drunkenness	266,894	64,347	202,547	100.0	24.1	75.9	3,326	1,405	1,921
Disorderly conduct	207,010	26,664	180,346	100.0	12.9	87.1	35,870	6,040	29,830
Vagrancy	16,265	2,624	13,641	100.0	16.1	83.9	383	102	281
All other offenses (except traffic)	2,024,802	327,510	1,697,292	100.0	16.2	83.8	89,152	20,306	68,846
Suspicion	239	17	222	100.0	7.1	92.9	46	8	38
Curfew and loitering law violations	22,666	4,936	17,730	100.0	21.8	78.2	22,666	4,936	17,730

Table 33. Arrests, Distribution by Ethnicity, 2016—Continued

(Number, percent; 13,049 agencies; 2016 estimated population 257,112,535.)

Offense charged	Percent distribution[1]				Arrests 18 and over			Percent distribution[1]	
	Total[2]	Hispanic or Latino	Not Hispanic or Latino	Total[2]	Hispanic or Latino	Not Hispanic or Latino	Total[2]	Hispanic or Latino	Not Hispanic or Latino
Total	100.0	22.8	77.2	6,150,779	1,107,822	5,042,957	100.0	18.0	82.0
Violent crime[3]	100.0	24.4	75.6	300,411	71,242	229,169	100.0	23.7	76.3
Murder and nonnegligent manslaughter	100.0	24.8	75.2	6,466	1,271	5,195	100.0	19.7	80.3
Rape[4]	100.0	21.3	78.7	11,759	3,303	8,456	100.0	28.1	71.9
Robbery	100.0	21.9	78.1	48,862	10,195	38,667	100.0	20.9	79.1
Aggravated assault	100.0	26.4	73.6	233,324	56,473	176,851	100.0	24.2	75.8
Property crime[3]	100.0	22.5	77.5	713,575	110,943	602,632	100.0	15.5	84.5
Burglary	100.0	27.8	72.2	112,619	22,239	90,380	100.0	19.7	80.3
Larceny-theft	100.0	20.8	79.2	552,108	76,055	476,053	100.0	13.8	86.2
Motor vehicle theft	100.0	26.6	73.4	44,807	12,037	32,770	100.0	26.9	73.1
Arson	100.0	20.5	79.5	4,041	612	3,429	100.0	15.1	84.9
Other assaults	100.0	21.9	78.1	587,360	104,185	483,175	100.0	17.7	82.3
Forgery and counterfeiting	100.0	17.6	82.4	34,465	5,454	29,011	100.0	15.8	84.2
Fraud	100.0	13.8	86.2	76,301	8,700	67,601	100.0	11.4	88.6
Embezzlement	100.0	32.5	67.5	9,735	1,081	8,654	100.0	11.1	88.9
Stolen property; buying, receiving, possessing	100.0	21.0	79.0	50,394	9,839	40,555	100.0	19.5	80.5
Vandalism	100.0	22.9	77.1	98,916	17,250	81,666	100.0	17.4	82.6
Weapons; carrying, possessing, etc.	100.0	31.7	68.3	85,774	19,109	66,665	100.0	22.3	77.7
Prostitution and commercialized vice	100.0	15.7	84.3	25,387	5,071	20,316	100.0	20.0	80.0
Sex offenses (except forcible rape and prostitution)	100.0	24.7	75.3	27,233	6,856	20,377	100.0	25.2	74.8
Drug abuse violations	100.0	28.3	71.7	933,593	184,752	748,841	100.0	19.8	80.2
Gambling	100.0	20.6	79.4	1,856	481	1,375	100.0	25.9	74.1
Offenses against the family and children	100.0	13.9	86.1	53,600	6,039	47,561	100.0	11.3	88.7
Driving under the influence	100.0	24.0	76.0	653,262	147,571	505,691	100.0	22.6	77.4
Liquor laws	100.0	16.2	83.8	112,484	15,948	96,536	100.0	14.2	85.8
Drunkenness	100.0	42.2	57.8	263,568	62,942	200,626	100.0	23.9	76.1
Disorderly conduct	100.0	16.8	83.2	171,140	20,624	150,516	100.0	12.1	87.9
Vagrancy	100.0	26.6	73.4	15,882	2,522	13,360	100.0	15.9	84.1
All other offenses (except traffic)	100.0	22.8	77.2	1,935,650	307,204	1,628,446	100.0	15.9	84.1
Suspicion	100.0	17.4	82.6	193	9	184	100.0	4.7	95.3
Curfew and loitering law violations	100.0	21.8	78.2	NA	NA	NA	NA	NA	NA

NA = Not available.

1 Because of rounding, the percentages may not sum to 100.   2 The ethnicity totals are representative of those agencies that provided ethnicity breakdowns. Not all agencies provide ethnicity data; therefore, the race and ethnicity totals will not be equal.   3 Violent crimes are offenses of murder and nonnegligent manslaughter, rape, robbery, and aggravated assault. Property crimes are offenses of burglary, larceny-theft, motor vehicle theft, and arson.   4 The rape figures in this table are an aggregate total of the data submitted using both the revised and legacy Uniform Crime Reporting definitions.

Table 34. Arrest Trends, Cities, 2014–2015

(Number, percent change; 8,198 agencies; 2015 estimated population 157,654,489; 2015 estimated population 155,864,591.)

Offense charged	Number of persons arrested								
	Total, all ages			Under 18 years of age			18 years of age and over		
	2014	2015	Percent change	2014	2015	Percent change	2014	2015	Percent change
Total[1]	5,796,997	5,580,654	-3.7	574,963	525,831	-8.5	5,222,034	5,054,823	-3.2
Violent crime[2]	275,237	278,854	+1.3	30,411	29,272	-3.7	244,826	249,582	+1.9
Murder and nonnegligent manslaughter	5,022	5,478	+9.1	377	431	+14.3	4,645	5,047	+8.7
Rape[3]	10,642	11,300	+6.2	1,648	1,730	+5.0	8,994	9,570	+6.4
Robbery	54,622	56,073	+2.7	11,186	10,862	-2.9	43,436	45,211	+4.1
Aggravated assault	204,951	206,003	+0.5	17,200	16,249	-5.5	187,751	189,754	+1.1
Property crime[2]	916,275	868,028	-5.3	142,753	128,622	-9.9	773,522	739,406	-4.4
Burglary	125,702	116,201	-7.6	22,814	20,361	-10.8	102,888	95,840	-6.9
Larceny-theft	751,358	708,313	-5.7	111,534	99,287	-11.0	639,824	609,026	-4.8
Motor vehicle theft	34,112	39,013	+14.4	6,540	7,433	+13.7	27,572	31,580	+14.5
Arson	5,103	4,501	-11.8	1,865	1,541	-17.4	3,238	2,960	-8.6
Other assaults	580,633	575,863	-0.8	74,136	71,305	-3.8	506,497	504,558	-0.4
Forgery and counterfeiting	30,089	29,659	-1.4	657	575	-12.5	29,432	29,084	-1.2
Fraud	69,150	66,042	-4.5	2,507	2,402	-4.2	66,643	63,640	-4.5
Embezzlement	8,991	9,101	+1.2	270	379	+40.4	8,721	8,722	+0.0
Stolen property; buying, receiving, possessing	47,774	47,333	-0.9	6,173	6,216	+0.7	41,601	41,117	-1.2
Vandalism	108,090	107,051	-1.0	25,475	24,038	-5.6	82,615	83,013	+0.5
Weapons; carrying, possessing, etc.	75,402	77,960	+3.4	11,601	11,013	-5.1	63,801	66,947	+4.9
Prostitution and commercialized vice	29,676	26,643	-10.2	470	377	-19.8	29,206	26,266	-10.1
Sex offenses (except forcible rape and prostitution)	27,154	25,904	-4.6	4,841	4,615	-4.7	22,313	21,289	-4.6
Drug abuse violations	778,019	743,722	-4.4	62,000	54,219	-12.6	716,019	689,503	-3.7
Gambling	1,878	1,860	-1.0	186	179	-3.8	1,692	1,681	-0.7
Offenses against the family and children	35,303	35,283	-0.1	1,980	1,857	-6.2	33,323	33,426	+0.3
Driving under the influence	461,589	437,686	-5.2	3,192	2,996	-6.1	458,397	434,690	-5.2
Liquor laws	181,406	152,545	-15.9	28,060	22,917	-18.3	153,346	129,628	-15.5
Drunkenness	268,680	248,405	-7.5	4,264	3,447	-19.2	264,416	244,958	-7.4
Disorderly conduct	247,339	225,762	-8.7	46,509	42,969	-7.6	200,830	182,793	-9.0
Vagrancy	18,251	16,355	-10.4	579	649	+12.1	17,672	15,706	-11.1
All other offenses (except traffic)	1,612,964	1,585,583	-1.7	105,802	96,769	-8.5	1,507,162	1,488,814	-1.2
Suspicion	551	641	+16.3	90	54	-40.0	461	587	+27.3
Curfew and loitering law violations	23,097	21,015	-9.0	23,097	21,015	-9.0	NA	NA	NA

NA = Not available.
1 Does not include suspicion.   2 Violent crimes are offenses of murder and nonnegligent manslaughter, rape, robbery, and aggravated assault. Property crimes are offenses of burglary, larceny-theft, motor vehicle theft, and arson.   3 The rape figures in this table are aggregate totals of the data submitted based on both the legacy and revised Uniform Crime Reporting definitions.

Table 35. Arrests, Cities, Distribution by Age, 2015

(Number, percent; 9,115 agencies; 2015 estimated population 168,734,653.)

Offense charged	Total, all ages	Ages under 15	Ages under 18	Ages 18 and over	Under 10	10–12	13–14	15	16	17	18	19	20
Total	6,035,048	162,640	574,162	5,460,886	3,912	35,272	123,456	110,055	138,904	162,563	208,976	225,300	224,118
Total percent distribution[1]	100.0	2.7	9.5	90.5	0.1	0.6	2.0	1.8	2.3	2.7	3.5	3.7	3.7
Violent crime[2]	299,984	8,962	32,380	267,604	178	1,994	6,790	6,460	7,870	9,088	10,638	10,805	10,879
Violent crime percent distribution[1]	100.0	3.0	10.8	89.2	0.1	0.7	2.3	2.2	2.6	3.0	3.5	3.6	3.6
Murder and nonnegligent manslaughter	6,258	41	502	5,756	0	5	36	80	145	236	348	363	369
Rape[3]	12,521	762	1,915	10,606	12	213	537	361	381	411	540	500	483
Robbery	62,265	2,486	12,527	49,738	13	312	2,161	2,700	3,410	3,931	4,354	3,780	3,305
Aggravated assault	218,940	5,673	17,436	201,504	153	1,464	4,056	3,319	3,934	4,510	5,396	6,162	6,722
Property crime[2]	929,358	38,670	138,053	791,305	733	8,014	29,923	27,110	34,246	38,027	42,548	38,865	34,785
Property crime percent distribution[1]	100.0	4.2	14.9	85.1	0.1	0.9	3.2	2.9	3.7	4.1	4.6	4.2	3.7
Burglary	123,383	6,624	21,895	101,488	166	1,331	5,127	4,623	5,253	5,395	6,219	5,625	4,903
Larceny-theft	756,295	29,023	105,239	651,056	464	6,061	22,498	19,992	26,222	30,002	33,955	31,197	27,966
Motor vehicle theft	44,572	1,994	9,229	35,343	12	226	1,756	2,201	2,551	2,483	2,243	1,922	1,786
Arson	5,108	1,029	1,690	3,418	91	396	542	294	220	147	131	121	130
Other assaults	624,009	29,622	76,469	547,540	847	7,965	20,810	14,730	16,243	15,874	14,905	16,157	17,868
Forgery and counterfeiting	31,437	85	603	30,834	5	15	65	65	125	328	840	1,177	1,448
Fraud	70,891	530	2,847	68,044	3	87	440	503	743	1,071	1,707	2,127	2,598
Embezzlement	9,562	19	389	9,173	0	2	17	13	113	244	513	605	563
Stolen property; buying, receiving, possessing	50,592	1,524	6,653	43,939	20	221	1,283	1,397	1,772	1,960	2,358	2,258	2,092
Vandalism	113,543	10,109	25,302	88,241	452	2,623	7,034	4,718	5,147	5,328	4,868	4,562	4,278
Weapons; carrying, possessing, etc.	85,618	3,730	12,330	73,288	116	926	2,688	2,115	2,913	3,572	4,006	4,076	3,972
Prostitution and commercialized vice	28,450	42	388	28,062	0	7	35	60	105	181	785	1,124	1,206
Sex offenses (except forcible rape and prostitution)	27,417	2,309	4,831	22,586	67	602	1,640	868	843	811	849	821	787
Drug abuse violations	810,262	9,857	59,277	750,985	52	1,292	8,513	9,671	15,705	24,044	39,206	41,130	38,726
Gambling	2,848	42	310	2,538	1	9	32	58	96	114	180	149	148
Offenses against the family and children	37,512	732	1,943	35,569	66	135	531	383	394	434	659	717	830
Driving under the influence	468,701	74	3,172	465,529	12	3	59	155	742	2,201	6,075	9,397	11,571
Liquor laws	160,696	2,729	23,939	136,757	8	217	2,504	3,815	6,556	10,839	23,891	26,390	21,718
Drunkenness	271,597	470	3,649	267,948	18	37	415	565	838	1,776	4,800	6,028	6,223
Disorderly conduct	247,467	17,975	46,302	201,165	413	4,368	13,194	9,685	9,605	9,037	8,343	7,797	7,896
Vagrancy	16,892	159	682	16,210	3	24	132	164	174	185	394	379	392
All other offenses (except traffic)	1,715,484	25,637	102,690	1,612,794	670	4,581	20,386	20,380	26,198	30,475	41,373	50,702	56,107
Suspicion	842	17	67	775	0	6	11	9	21	20	38	34	31
Curfew and loitering law violations	31,886	9,346	31,886	NA	248	2,144	6,954	7,131	8,455	6,954	NA	NA	NA

Table 35. Arrests, Cities, Distribution by Age, 2015—Continued

(Number, percent; 9,115 agencies; 2015 estimated population 168,734,653.)

Offense charged	21	22	23	24	25–29	30–34	35–39	40–44	45–49	50–54	55–59	60–64	65 and over
Total	228,372	229,788	231,275	227,876	986,640	792,482	589,402	439,319	386,375	328,143	204,141	95,229	63,450
Total percent distribution[1]	3.8	3.8	3.8	3.8	16.3	13.1	9.8	7.3	6.4	5.4	3.4	1.6	1.1
Violent crime[2]	11,660	11,955	11,987	11,558	49,977	39,613	29,189	21,204	17,854	14,553	8,819	3,908	3,005
Violent crime percent distribution[1]	3.9	4.0	4.0	3.9	16.7	13.2	9.7	7.1	6.0	4.9	2.9	1.3	1.0
Murder and nonnegligent manslaughter	370	352	363	319	1,077	758	463	305	218	205	123	63	60
Rape[3]	443	408	372	383	1,646	1,520	1,199	953	741	670	364	187	197
Robbery	3,069	2,823	2,738	2,392	9,344	6,354	4,146	2,603	2,162	1,523	778	247	120
Aggravated assault	7,778	8,372	8,514	8,464	37,910	30,981	23,381	17,343	14,733	12,155	7,554	3,411	2,628
Property crime[2]	33,246	32,690	32,658	31,964	142,510	116,286	84,354	60,804	53,483	42,976	25,016	11,447	7,673
Property crime percent distribution[1]	3.6	3.5	3.5	3.4	15.3	12.5	9.1	6.5	5.8	4.6	2.7	1.2	0.8
Burglary	4,918	4,674	4,548	4,325	18,933	14,930	10,429	6,899	6,231	4,801	2,569	992	492
Larceny-theft	26,508	26,262	26,250	25,936	115,878	95,139	69,709	51,221	45,229	36,808	21,769	10,199	7,030
Motor vehicle theft	1,708	1,632	1,724	1,561	7,188	5,679	3,863	2,409	1,772	1,088	513	162	93
Arson	112	122	136	142	511	538	353	275	251	279	165	94	58
Other assaults	21,282	22,314	23,005	23,173	102,243	84,121	64,399	48,708	40,795	33,348	19,645	8,903	6,674
Forgery and counterfeiting	1,133	1,236	1,325	1,319	6,193	5,181	3,841	2,610	1,939	1,452	711	264	165
Fraud	2,454	2,626	2,642	2,748	13,144	11,080	8,514	6,281	4,832	3,529	2,071	985	706
Embezzlement	493	486	489	392	1,695	1,180	866	662	485	363	210	125	46
Stolen property; buying, receiving, possessing	2,212	2,079	2,104	2,089	8,749	7,046	4,822	3,040	2,290	1,525	821	307	147
Vandalism	4,757	4,544	4,520	4,093	16,974	12,406	8,657	5,919	4,877	3,820	2,247	973	746
Weapons; carrying, possessing, etc.	4,189	4,142	4,072	3,894	14,801	10,260	6,777	4,325	3,305	2,466	1,569	751	683
Prostitution and commercialized vice	1,400	1,397	1,379	1,266	5,507	3,859	2,995	2,320	1,838	1,443	828	387	328
Sex offenses (except forcible rape and prostitution)	792	689	701	621	3,027	2,854	2,453	2,058	1,928	1,853	1,354	813	986
Drug abuse violations	37,270	36,888	36,317	35,139	144,487	109,932	76,275	51,402	42,387	33,029	18,527	7,372	2,898
Gambling	127	124	121	97	428	260	205	175	160	120	104	72	68
Offenses against the family and children	1,035	1,174	1,365	1,422	7,136	6,640	5,108	3,445	2,460	1,832	1,008	444	294
Driving under the influence	18,973	20,083	20,750	20,536	86,270	66,581	50,479	40,681	36,819	32,743	22,833	12,268	9,470
Liquor laws	4,003	2,836	2,477	2,113	8,399	7,381	6,528	6,335	7,114	7,699	5,594	2,741	1,538
Drunkenness	9,893	9,298	9,146	9,120	39,042	34,615	28,968	25,645	27,303	27,189	17,939	8,341	4,398
Disorderly conduct	10,469	9,693	9,010	8,518	34,160	26,251	20,053	15,734	14,591	13,191	8,533	4,050	2,876
Vagrancy	389	402	441	401	1,994	1,970	1,783	1,446	1,796	1,869	1,484	729	341
All other offenses (except traffic)	62,558	65,107	66,729	67,386	299,756	244,860	183,051	136,457	120,079	103,095	64,808	30,340	20,386
Suspicion	37	25	37	27	148	106	85	68	40	48	20	9	22
Curfew and loitering law violations	NA	NA	NA	NA	NA	NA	NA	NA	NA	NA	NA	NA	NA

NA = Not available.

1 Because of rounding, the percentages may not sum to 100.   2 Violent crimes are offenses of murder and nonnegligent manslaughter, rape, robbery, and aggravated assault. Property crimes are offenses of burglary, larceny-theft, motor vehicle theft, and arson.   3 The rape figures in this table are an aggregate total of the data submitted using both the revised and legacy Uniform Crime Reporting definitions.

Table 36. Arrests, Cities, Persons Under 15, 18, 21, and 25 Years of Age, 2015

(9,115 agencies; 2015 estimated population 168,734,653.)

Offense charged	Total, all ages	Number of persons arrested				Percent of total of all ages			
		Under 15	Under 18	Under 21	Under 25	Under 15	Under 18	Under 21	Under 25
Total	6,035,048	162,640	574,162	1,232,556	2,149,867	2.7	9.5	20.4	35.6
Violent crime[1]	299,984	8,962	32,380	64,702	111,862	3.0	10.8	21.6	37.3
Murder and nonnegligent manslaughter	6,258	41	502	1,582	2,986	0.7	8.0	25.3	47.7
Rape[2]	12,521	762	1,915	3,438	5,044	6.1	15.3	27.5	40.3
Robbery	62,265	2,486	12,527	23,966	34,988	4.0	20.1	38.5	56.2
Aggravated assault	218,940	5,673	17,436	35,716	68,844	2.6	8.0	16.3	31.4
Property crime[1]	929,358	38,670	138,053	254,251	384,809	4.2	14.9	27.4	41.4
Burglary	123,383	6,624	21,895	38,642	57,107	5.4	17.7	31.3	46.3
Larceny-theft	756,295	29,023	105,239	198,357	303,313	3.8	13.9	26.2	40.1
Motor vehicle theft	44,572	1,994	9,229	15,180	21,805	4.5	20.7	34.1	48.9
Arson	5,108	1,029	1,690	2,072	2,584	20.1	33.1	40.6	50.6
Other assaults	624,009	29,622	76,469	125,399	215,173	4.7	12.3	20.1	34.5
Forgery and counterfeiting	31,437	85	603	4,068	9,081	0.3	1.9	12.9	28.9
Fraud	70,891	530	2,847	9,279	19,749	0.7	4.0	13.1	27.9
Embezzlement	9,562	19	389	2,070	3,930	0.2	4.1	21.6	41.1
Stolen property; buying, receiving, possessing	50,592	1,524	6,653	13,361	21,845	3.0	13.2	26.4	43.2
Vandalism	113,543	10,109	25,302	39,010	56,924	8.9	22.3	34.4	50.1
Weapons; carrying, possessing, etc.	85,618	3,730	12,330	24,384	40,681	4.4	14.4	28.5	47.5
Prostitution and commercialized vice	28,450	42	388	3,503	8,945	0.1	1.4	12.3	31.4
Sex offenses (except forcible rape and prostitution)	27,417	2,309	4,831	7,288	10,091	8.4	17.6	26.6	36.8
Drug abuse violations	810,262	9,857	59,277	178,339	323,953	1.2	7.3	22.0	40.0
Gambling	2,848	42	310	787	1,256	1.5	10.9	27.6	44.1
Offenses against the family and children	37,512	732	1,943	4,149	9,145	2.0	5.2	11.1	24.4
Driving under the influence	468,701	74	3,172	30,215	110,557	*	0.7	6.4	23.6
Liquor laws	160,696	2,729	23,939	95,938	107,367	1.7	14.9	59.7	66.8
Drunkenness	271,597	470	3,649	20,700	58,157	0.2	1.3	7.6	21.4
Disorderly conduct	247,467	17,975	46,302	70,338	108,028	7.3	18.7	28.4	43.7
Vagrancy	16,892	159	682	1,847	3,480	0.9	4.0	10.9	20.6
All other offenses (except traffic)	1,715,484	25,637	102,690	250,872	512,652	1.5	6.0	14.6	29.9
Suspicion	842	17	67	170	296	2.0	8.0	20.2	35.2
Curfew and loitering law violations	31,886	9,346	31,886	31,886	31,886	29.3	100.0	100.0	100.0

* = Less than one-tenth of one percent.

1 Violent crimes are offenses of murder and nonnegligent manslaughter, rape, robbery, and aggravated assault. Property crimes are offenses of burglary, larceny-theft, motor vehicle theft, and arson.   2 The rape figures in this table are an aggregate total of the data submitted using both the revised and legacy Uniform Crime Reporting definitions.

Table 37. Arrests, Cities, Distribution by Sex, 2015

(Number, percent; 9,115 agencies; 2015 estimated population 168,734,653.)

Offense charged	Number of persons arrested			Percent male	Percent female	Percent distribution[1]		
	Total	Male	Female			Total	Male	Female
Total	6,035,048	4,389,502	1,645,546	72.7	27.3	100.0	100.0	100.0
Violent crime[2]	299,984	237,841	62,143	79.3	20.7	5.0	5.4	3.8
Murder and nonnegligent manslaughter	6,258	5,581	677	89.2	10.8	0.1	0.1	*
Rape[3]	12,521	12,153	368	97.1	2.9	0.2	0.3	*
Robbery	62,265	53,310	8,955	85.6	14.4	1.0	1.2	0.5
Aggravated assault	218,940	166,797	52,143	76.2	23.8	3.6	3.8	3.2
Property crime[2]	929,358	563,418	365,940	60.6	39.4	15.4	12.8	22.2
Burglary	123,383	99,446	23,937	80.6	19.4	2.0	2.3	1.5
Larceny-theft	756,295	424,635	331,660	56.1	43.9	12.5	9.7	20.2
Motor vehicle theft	44,572	35,249	9,323	79.1	20.9	0.7	0.8	0.6
Arson	5,108	4,088	1,020	80.0	20.0	0.1	0.1	0.1
Other assaults	624,009	447,677	176,332	71.7	28.3	10.3	10.2	10.7
Forgery and counterfeiting	31,437	20,312	11,125	64.6	35.4	0.5	0.5	0.7
Fraud	70,891	44,217	26,674	62.4	37.6	1.2	1.0	1.6
Embezzlement	9,562	4,680	4,882	48.9	51.1	0.2	0.1	0.3
Stolen property; buying, receiving, possessing	50,592	39,634	10,958	78.3	21.7	0.8	0.9	0.7
Vandalism	113,543	88,870	24,673	78.3	21.7	1.9	2.0	1.5
Weapons; carrying, possessing, etc.	85,618	78,148	7,470	91.3	8.7	1.4	1.8	0.5
Prostitution and commercialized vice	28,450	10,008	18,442	35.2	64.8	0.5	0.2	1.1
Sex offenses (except forcible rape and prostitution)	27,417	25,250	2,167	92.1	7.9	0.5	0.6	0.1
Drug abuse violations	810,262	632,793	177,469	78.1	21.9	13.4	14.4	10.8
Gambling	2,848	2,454	394	86.2	13.8	*	0.1	*
Offenses against the family and children	37,512	24,363	13,149	64.9	35.1	0.6	0.6	0.8
Driving under the influence	468,701	349,900	118,801	74.7	25.3	7.8	8.0	7.2
Liquor laws	160,696	114,830	45,866	71.5	28.5	2.7	2.6	2.8
Drunkenness	271,597	219,473	52,124	80.8	19.2	4.5	5.0	3.2
Disorderly conduct	247,467	177,808	69,659	71.9	28.1	4.1	4.1	4.2
Vagrancy	16,892	13,172	3,720	78.0	22.0	0.3	0.3	0.2
All other offenses (except traffic)	1,715,484	1,270,980	444,504	74.1	25.9	28.4	29.0	27.0
Suspicion	842	654	188	77.7	22.3	*	*	*
Curfew and loitering law violations	31,886	23,020	8,866	72.2	27.8	0.5	0.5	0.5

* = Less than one-tenth of 1 percent.
1 Because of rounding, the percentages may not sum to 100.   2 Violent crimes are offenses of murder and nonnegligent manslaughter, rape, robbery, and aggravated assault. Property crimes are offenses of burglary, larceny-theft, motor vehicle theft, and arson.   3 The rape figures in this table are an aggregate total of the data submitted using both the revised and legacy Uniform Crime Reporting definitions.

Table 38. Arrests, Cities, Distribution by Race, 2015

(Number, percent; 9,102 agencies; 2015 estimated population 168,717,865.)

Offense charged	Total arrests						Percent distribution[1]					
	Total	White	Black	American Indian or Alaskan Native	Asian	Native Hawaiian or Other Pacific Islander	Total	White	Black	American Indian or Alaskan Native	Asian	Native Hawaiian or Other Pacific Islander
Total	5,996,307	4,038,898	1,716,106	143,628	79,162	18,513	100.0	67.4	28.6	2.4	1.3	0.3
Violent crime[2]	298,747	169,437	117,997	5,380	4,937	996	100.0	56.7	39.5	1.8	1.7	0.3
Murder and nonnegligent manslaughter	6,238	2,505	3,521	85	108	19	100.0	40.2	56.4	1.4	1.7	0.3
Rape[3]	12,420	7,848	4,055	214	233	70	100.0	63.2	32.6	1.7	1.9	0.6
Robbery	62,086	26,918	33,822	487	600	259	100.0	43.4	54.5	0.8	1.0	0.4
Aggravated assault	218,003	132,166	76,599	4,594	3,996	648	100.0	60.6	35.1	2.1	1.8	0.3
Property crime[2]	922,952	630,326	262,929	15,396	12,059	2,242	100.0	68.3	28.5	1.7	1.3	0.2
Burglary	122,876	79,551	40,060	1,270	1,703	292	100.0	64.7	32.6	1.0	1.4	0.2
Larceny-theft	750,656	519,257	206,764	13,309	9,654	1,672	100.0	69.2	27.5	1.8	1.3	0.2
Motor vehicle theft	44,339	27,947	14,828	674	631	259	100.0	63.0	33.4	1.5	1.4	0.6
Arson	5,081	3,571	1,277	143	71	19	100.0	70.3	25.1	2.8	1.4	0.4
Other assaults	620,307	387,601	210,072	12,081	8,387	2,166	100.0	62.5	33.9	1.9	1.4	0.3
Forgery and counterfeiting	31,269	19,968	10,477	236	518	70	100.0	63.9	33.5	0.8	1.7	0.2
Fraud	70,394	44,635	23,784	924	933	118	100.0	63.4	33.8	1.3	1.3	0.2
Embezzlement	9,493	5,611	3,612	72	176	22	100.0	59.1	38.0	0.8	1.9	0.2
Stolen property; buying, receiving, possessing	50,379	31,597	17,378	576	712	116	100.0	62.7	34.5	1.1	1.4	0.2
Vandalism	112,645	75,534	33,069	2,312	1,412	318	100.0	67.1	29.4	2.1	1.3	0.3
Weapons; carrying, possessing, etc.	85,280	46,382	36,855	842	1,027	174	100.0	54.4	43.2	1.0	1.2	0.2
Prostitution and commercialized vice	28,295	15,301	11,470	101	1,371	52	100.0	54.1	40.5	0.4	4.8	0.2
Sex offenses (except forcible rape and prostitution)	27,269	18,982	7,053	503	611	120	100.0	69.6	25.9	1.8	2.2	0.4
Drug abuse violations	806,290	554,237	232,736	8,646	9,420	1,251	100.0	68.7	28.9	1.1	1.2	0.2
Gambling	2,840	905	1,764	12	157	2	100.0	31.9	62.1	0.4	5.5	0.1
Offenses against the family and children	37,119	23,787	10,628	2,295	388	21	100.0	64.1	28.6	6.2	1.0	0.1
Driving under the influence	465,075	380,102	62,362	10,716	9,843	2,052	100.0	81.7	13.4	2.3	2.1	0.4
Liquor laws	158,561	123,687	23,276	8,849	2,300	449	100.0	78.0	14.7	5.6	1.5	0.3
Drunkenness	270,264	202,159	40,151	24,896	2,657	401	100.0	74.8	14.9	9.2	1.0	0.1
Disorderly conduct	245,451	153,185	79,155	10,604	1,991	516	100.0	62.4	32.2	4.3	0.8	0.2
Vagrancy	16,757	11,363	4,534	664	181	15	100.0	67.8	27.1	4.0	1.1	0.1
All other offenses (except traffic)	1,704,346	1,127,532	511,879	37,849	19,763	7,323	100.0	66.2	30.0	2.2	1.2	0.4
Suspicion	882	321	254	292	11	4	100.0	36.4	28.8	33.1	1.2	0.5
Curfew and loitering law violations	31,692	16,246	14,671	382	308	85	100.0	51.3	46.3	1.2	1.0	0.3

Table 38. Arrests, Cities, Distribution by Race, 2015—Continued

(Number, percent; 9,102 agencies; 2015 estimated population 168,717,865.)

Offense charged	Arrests under 18						Percent distribution[1]					
	Total	White	Black	American Indian or Alaskan Native	Asian	Native Hawaiian or Other Pacific Islander	Total	White	Black	American Indian or Alaskan Native	Asian	Native Hawaiian or Other Pacific Islander
Total	569,025	349,333	200,840	10,133	6,356	2,363	100.0	61.4	35.3	1.8	1.1	0.4
Violent crime[2]	32,224	14,316	17,104	352	300	152	100.0	44.4	53.1	1.1	0.9	0.5
Murder and nonnegligent manslaughter	498	178	315	4	1	0	100.0	35.7	63.3	0.8	0.2	0.0
Rape[3]	1,890	1,149	681	28	23	9	100.0	60.8	36.0	1.5	1.2	0.5
Robbery	12,500	3,644	8,630	55	88	83	100.0	29.2	69.0	0.4	0.7	0.7
Aggravated assault	17,336	9,345	7,478	265	188	60	100.0	53.9	43.1	1.5	1.1	0.3
Property crime[2]	136,759	80,158	52,079	2,086	1,915	521	100.0	58.6	38.1	1.5	1.4	0.4
Burglary	21,803	11,731	9,540	247	223	62	100.0	53.8	43.8	1.1	1.0	0.3
Larceny-theft	104,088	63,074	37,324	1,649	1,616	425	100.0	60.6	35.9	1.6	1.6	0.4
Motor vehicle theft	9,185	4,160	4,795	139	61	30	100.0	45.3	52.2	1.5	0.7	0.3
Arson	1,683	1,193	420	51	15	4	100.0	70.9	25.0	3.0	0.9	0.2
Other assaults	75,911	43,303	30,598	1,041	628	341	100.0	57.0	40.3	1.4	0.8	0.4
Forgery and counterfeiting	598	353	236	3	5	1	100.0	59.0	39.5	0.5	0.8	0.2
Fraud	2,824	1,342	1,387	52	38	5	100.0	47.5	49.1	1.8	1.3	0.2
Embezzlement	383	224	147	5	6	1	100.0	58.5	38.4	1.3	1.6	0.3
Stolen property; buying, receiving, possessing	6,615	2,750	3,708	63	77	17	100.0	41.6	56.1	1.0	1.2	0.3
Vandalism	25,052	17,282	7,003	412	254	101	100.0	69.0	28.0	1.6	1.0	0.4
Weapons; carrying, possessing, etc.	12,248	6,780	5,129	116	190	33	100.0	55.4	41.9	0.9	1.6	0.3
Prostitution and commercialized vice	388	123	254	1	6	4	100.0	31.7	65.5	0.3	1.5	1.0
Sex offenses (except forcible rape and prostitution)	4,782	3,289	1,324	57	72	40	100.0	68.8	27.7	1.2	1.5	0.8
Drug abuse violations	58,770	43,388	13,427	1,095	674	186	100.0	73.8	22.8	1.9	1.1	0.3
Gambling	308	55	244	6	3	0	100.0	17.9	79.2	1.9	1.0	0.0
Offenses against the family and children	1,921	1,185	593	123	20	0	100.0	61.7	30.9	6.4	1.0	0.0
Driving under the influence	3,130	2,727	186	141	59	17	100.0	87.1	5.9	4.5	1.9	0.5
Liquor laws	23,632	20,368	1,760	1,127	315	62	100.0	86.2	7.4	4.8	1.3	0.3
Drunkenness	3,623	2,959	347	266	42	9	100.0	81.7	9.6	7.3	1.2	0.2
Disorderly conduct	45,930	25,172	19,407	921	330	100	100.0	54.8	42.3	2.0	0.7	0.2
Vagrancy	677	423	221	25	8	0	100.0	62.5	32.6	3.7	1.2	0.0
All other offenses (except traffic)	101,495	66,868	30,985	1,848	1,106	688	100.0	65.9	30.5	1.8	1.1	0.7
Suspicion	63	22	30	11	0	0	100.0	34.9	47.6	17.5	0.0	0.0
Curfew and loitering law violations	31,692	16,246	14,671	382	308	85	100.0	51.3	46.3	1.2	1.0	0.3

Table 38. Arrests, Cities, Distribution by Race, 2015—Continued

(Number, percent; 9,102 agencies; 2015 estimated population 168,717,865.)

Offense charged	Arrests 18 and over						Percent distribution[1]					
	Total	White	Black	American Indian or Alaskan Native	Asian	Native Hawaiian or Other Pacific Islander	Total	White	Black	American Indian or Alaskan Native	Asian	Native Hawaiian or Other Pacific Islander
Total	5,427,282	3,689,565	1,515,266	133,495	72,806	16,150	100.0	68.0	27.9	2.5	1.3	0.3
Violent crime[2]	266,523	155,121	100,893	5,028	4,637	844	100.0	58.2	37.9	1.9	1.7	0.3
Murder and nonnegligent manslaughter	5,740	2,327	3,206	81	107	19	100.0	40.5	55.9	1.4	1.9	0.3
Rape[3]	10,530	6,699	3,374	186	210	61	100.0	63.6	32.0	1.8	2.0	0.6
Robbery	49,586	23,274	25,192	432	512	176	100.0	46.9	50.8	0.9	1.0	0.4
Aggravated assault	200,667	122,821	69,121	4,329	3,808	588	100.0	61.2	34.4	2.2	1.9	0.3
Property crime[2]	786,193	550,168	210,850	13,310	10,144	1,721	100.0	70.0	26.8	1.7	1.3	0.2
Burglary	101,073	67,820	30,520	1,023	1,480	230	100.0	67.1	30.2	1.0	1.5	0.2
Larceny-theft	646,568	456,183	169,440	11,660	8,038	1,247	100.0	70.6	26.2	1.8	1.2	0.2
Motor vehicle theft	35,154	23,787	10,033	535	570	229	100.0	67.7	28.5	1.5	1.6	0.7
Arson	3,398	2,378	857	92	56	15	100.0	70.0	25.2	2.7	1.6	0.4
Other assaults	544,396	344,298	179,474	11,040	7,759	1,825	100.0	63.2	33.0	2.0	1.4	0.3
Forgery and counterfeiting	30,671	19,615	10,241	233	513	69	100.0	64.0	33.4	0.8	1.7	0.2
Fraud	67,570	43,293	22,397	872	895	113	100.0	64.1	33.1	1.3	1.3	0.2
Embezzlement	9,110	5,387	3,465	67	170	21	100.0	59.1	38.0	0.7	1.9	0.2
Stolen property; buying, receiving, possessing	43,764	28,847	13,670	513	635	99	100.0	65.9	31.2	1.2	1.5	0.2
Vandalism	87,593	58,252	26,066	1,900	1,158	217	100.0	66.5	29.8	2.2	1.3	0.2
Weapons; carrying, possessing, etc.	73,032	39,602	31,726	726	837	141	100.0	54.2	43.4	1.0	1.1	0.2
Prostitution and commercialized vice	27,907	15,178	11,216	100	1,365	48	100.0	54.4	40.2	0.4	4.9	0.2
Sex offenses (except forcible rape and prostitution)	22,487	15,693	5,729	446	539	80	100.0	69.8	25.5	2.0	2.4	0.4
Drug abuse violations	747,520	510,849	219,309	7,551	8,746	1,065	100.0	68.3	29.3	1.0	1.2	0.1
Gambling	2,532	850	1,520	6	154	2	100.0	33.6	60.0	0.2	6.1	0.1
Offenses against the family and children	35,198	22,602	10,035	2,172	368	21	100.0	64.2	28.5	6.2	1.0	0.1
Driving under the influence	461,945	377,375	62,176	10,575	9,784	2,035	100.0	81.7	13.5	2.3	2.1	0.4
Liquor laws	134,929	103,319	21,516	7,722	1,985	387	100.0	76.6	15.9	5.7	1.5	0.3
Drunkenness	266,641	199,200	39,804	24,630	2,615	392	100.0	74.7	14.9	9.2	1.0	0.1
Disorderly conduct	199,521	128,013	59,748	9,683	1,661	416	100.0	64.2	29.9	4.9	0.8	0.2
Vagrancy	16,080	10,940	4,313	639	173	15	100.0	68.0	26.8	4.0	1.1	0.1
All other offenses (except traffic)	1,602,851	1,060,664	480,894	36,001	18,657	6,635	100.0	66.2	30.0	2.2	1.2	0.4
Suspicion	819	299	224	281	11	4	100.0	36.5	27.4	34.3	1.3	0.5
Curfew and loitering law violations	NA	NA	NA	NA	NA	NA	NA	NA	NA	NA	NA	NA

NA = Not available.
1 Because of rounding, the percentages may not sum to 100.   2 Violent crimes are offenses of murder and nonnegligent manslaughter, rape, robbery, and aggravated assault.   Property crimes are offenses of burglary, larceny-theft, motor vehicle theft, and arson.   3 The rape figures in this table are an aggregate total of the data submitted using both the revised and legacy Uniform Crime Reporting definitions.

Table 39. Arrests, Cities, Distribution by Ethnicity, 2015

(Number, percent; 9,102 agencies; 2015 estimated population 168,717,865.)

Offense charged	Total arrests			Percent distribution[1]			Arrests under 18		
	Total[2]	Hispanic or Latino	Not Hispanic or Latino	Total[2]	Hispanic or Latino	Not Hispanic or Latino	Total[2]	Hispanic or Latino	Not Hispanic or Latino
Total	4,817,478	938,061	3,879,417	100.0	19.5	80.5	445,762	107,998	337,764
Violent crime[3]	255,552	64,074	191,478	100.0	25.1	74.9	26,700	6,638	20,062
Murder and nonnegligent manslaughter	4,935	996	3,939	100.0	20.2	79.8	395	91	304
Rape[4]	9,612	2,734	6,878	100.0	28.4	71.6	1,429	314	1,115
Robbery	52,818	11,222	41,596	100.0	21.2	78.8	10,423	2,266	8,157
Aggravated assault	188,187	49,122	139,065	100.0	26.1	73.9	14,453	3,967	10,486
Property crime[3]	736,833	128,808	608,025	100.0	17.5	82.5	107,195	24,658	82,537
Burglary	106,305	24,411	81,894	100.0	23.0	77.0	18,305	5,060	13,245
Larceny-theft	591,097	93,358	497,739	100.0	15.8	84.2	80,901	17,512	63,389
Motor vehicle theft	35,400	10,287	25,113	100.0	29.1	70.9	6,608	1,792	4,816
Arson	4,031	752	3,279	100.0	18.7	81.3	1,381	294	1,087
Other assaults	494,276	98,402	395,874	100.0	19.9	80.1	60,381	14,397	45,984
Forgery and counterfeiting	25,641	4,176	21,465	100.0	16.3	83.7	483	126	357
Fraud	57,512	6,792	50,720	100.0	11.8	88.2	2,276	314	1,962
Embezzlement	7,818	917	6,901	100.0	11.7	88.3	318	57	261
Stolen property; buying, receiving, possessing	40,920	8,456	32,464	100.0	20.7	79.3	5,441	1,154	4,287
Vandalism	92,487	17,966	74,521	100.0	19.4	80.6	20,955	5,110	15,845
Weapons; carrying, possessing, etc.	69,104	16,895	52,209	100.0	24.4	75.6	9,663	3,247	6,416
Prostitution and commercialized vice	25,755	4,879	20,876	100.0	18.9	81.1	350	50	300
Sex offenses (except forcible rape and prostitution)	22,534	6,013	16,521	100.0	26.7	73.3	3,689	1,000	2,689
Drug abuse violations	667,017	144,695	522,322	100.0	21.7	78.3	46,603	13,922	32,681
Gambling	1,656	376	1,280	100.0	22.7	77.3	167	23	144
Offenses against the family and children	28,353	3,859	24,494	100.0	13.6	86.4	1,421	271	1,150
Driving under the influence	376,047	90,011	286,036	100.0	23.9	76.1	2,449	695	1,754
Liquor laws	117,273	17,881	99,392	100.0	15.2	84.8	18,292	3,388	14,904
Drunkenness	251,757	57,387	194,370	100.0	22.8	77.2	3,396	1,450	1,946
Disorderly conduct	172,677	22,373	150,304	100.0	13.0	87.0	32,053	6,213	25,840
Vagrancy	13,335	1,999	11,336	100.0	15.0	85.0	538	199	339
All other offenses (except traffic)	1,332,286	236,287	1,095,999	100.0	17.7	82.3	75,373	19,303	56,070
Suspicion	677	36	641	100.0	5.3	94.7	51	4	47
Curfew and loitering law violations	27,968	5,779	22,189	100.0	20.7	79.3	27,968	5,779	22,189

Table 39. Arrests, Cities, Distribution by Ethnicity, 2015—Continued

(Number, percent; 9,102 agencies; 2015 estimated population 168,717,865.)

Offense charged	Percent distribution[1]				Arrests 18 and over			Percent distribution[1]	
	Total[2]	Hispanic or Latino	Not Hispanic or Latino	Total[2]	Hispanic or Latino	Not Hispanic or Latino	Total[2]	Hispanic or Latino	Not Hispanic or Latino
Total	100.0	24.2	75.8	4,371,716	830,063	3,541,653	100.0	19.0	81.0
Violent crime[3]	100.0	24.9	75.1	228,852	57,436	171,416	100.0	25.1	74.9
Murder and nonnegligent manslaughter	100.0	23.0	77.0	4,540	905	3,635	100.0	19.9	80.1
Rape[4]	100.0	22.0	78.0	8,183	2,420	5,763	100.0	29.6	70.4
Robbery	100.0	21.7	78.3	42,395	8,956	33,439	100.0	21.1	78.9
Aggravated assault	100.0	27.4	72.6	173,734	45,155	128,579	100.0	26.0	74.0
Property crime[3]	100.0	23.0	77.0	629,638	104,150	525,488	100.0	16.5	83.5
Burglary	100.0	27.6	72.4	88,000	19,351	68,649	100.0	22.0	78.0
Larceny-theft	100.0	21.6	78.4	510,196	75,846	434,350	100.0	14.9	85.1
Motor vehicle theft	100.0	27.1	72.9	28,792	8,495	20,297	100.0	29.5	70.5
Arson	100.0	21.3	78.7	2,650	458	2,192	100.0	17.3	82.7
Other assaults	100.0	23.8	76.2	433,895	84,005	349,890	100.0	19.4	80.6
Forgery and counterfeiting	100.0	26.1	73.9	25,158	4,050	21,108	100.0	16.1	83.9
Fraud	100.0	13.8	86.2	55,236	6,478	48,758	100.0	11.7	88.3
Embezzlement	100.0	17.9	82.1	7,500	860	6,640	100.0	11.5	88.5
Stolen property; buying, receiving, possessing	100.0	21.2	78.8	35,479	7,302	28,177	100.0	20.6	79.4
Vandalism	100.0	24.4	75.6	71,532	12,856	58,676	100.0	18.0	82.0
Weapons; carrying, possessing, etc.	100.0	33.6	66.4	59,441	13,648	45,793	100.0	23.0	77.0
Prostitution and commercialized vice	100.0	14.3	85.7	25,405	4,829	20,576	100.0	19.0	81.0
Sex offenses (except forcible rape and prostitution)	100.0	27.1	72.9	18,845	5,013	13,832	100.0	26.6	73.4
Drug abuse violations	100.0	29.9	70.1	620,414	130,773	489,641	100.0	21.1	78.9
Gambling	100.0	13.8	86.2	1,489	353	1,136	100.0	23.7	76.3
Offenses against the family and children	100.0	19.1	80.9	26,932	3,588	23,344	100.0	13.3	86.7
Driving under the influence	100.0	28.4	71.6	373,598	89,316	284,282	100.0	23.9	76.1
Liquor laws	100.0	18.5	81.5	98,981	14,493	84,488	100.0	14.6	85.4
Drunkenness	100.0	42.7	57.3	248,361	55,937	192,424	100.0	22.5	77.5
Disorderly conduct	100.0	19.4	80.6	140,624	16,160	124,464	100.0	11.5	88.5
Vagrancy	100.0	37.0	63.0	12,797	1,800	10,997	100.0	14.1	85.9
All other offenses (except traffic)	100.0	25.6	74.4	1,256,913	216,984	1,039,929	100.0	17.3	82.7
Suspicion	100.0	7.8	92.2	626	32	594	100.0	5.1	94.9
Curfew and loitering law violations	100.0	20.7	79.3	NA	NA	NA	NA	NA	NA

NA = Not available.

1 Because of rounding, the percentages may not sum to 100.   2 The ethnicity totals are representative of those agencies that provided ethnicity breakdowns. Not all agencies provide ethnicity data; therefore, the race and ethnicity totals will not be equal.   3 Violent crimes are offenses of murder and nonnegligent manslaughter, rape, robbery, and aggravated assault. Property crimes are offenses of burglary, larceny-theft, motor vehicle theft, and arson.   4 The rape figures in this table are an aggregate total of the data submitted using both the revised and legacy Uniform Crime Reporting definitions.

Table 40. Arrest Trends, Metropolitan Counties, 2014–2015

(Number, percent change; 1,389 agencies; 2015 estimated population 52,022,397; 2014 estimated population 52,398,432.)

	Number of persons arrested								
	Total, all ages			Under 18 years of age			18 years of age and over		
Offense charged	2014	2015	Percent change	2014	2015	Percent change	2014	2015	Percent change
Total[1]	1,531,861	1,469,661	-4.1	104,672	95,651	-8.6	1,427,189	1,374,010	-3.7
Violent crime[2]	62,168	63,175	+1.6	5,497	5,427	-1.3	56,671	57,748	+1.9
Murder and nonnegligent manslaughter	1,487	1,507	+1.3	94	69	-26.6	1,393	1,438	+3.2
Rape[3]	3,007	3,213	+6.9	491	559	+13.8	2,516	2,654	+5.5
Robbery	8,790	8,899	+1.2	1,343	1,395	+3.9	7,447	7,504	+0.8
Aggravated assault	48,884	49,556	+1.4	3,569	3,404	-4.6	45,315	46,152	+1.8
Property crime[2]	154,599	144,679	-6.4	18,520	17,263	-6.8	136,079	127,416	-6.4
Burglary	32,488	28,558	-12.1	4,093	3,903	-4.6	28,395	24,655	-13.2
Larceny-theft	111,389	104,291	-6.4	12,914	11,751	-9.0	98,475	92,540	-6.0
Motor vehicle theft	9,561	10,795	+12.9	1,191	1,347	+13.1	8,370	9,448	+12.9
Arson	1,161	1,035	-10.9	322	262	-18.6	839	773	-7.9
Other assaults	143,777	140,440	-2.3	19,252	18,278	-5.1	124,525	122,162	-1.9
Forgery and counterfeiting	8,132	7,878	-3.1	156	141	-9.6	7,976	7,737	-3.0
Fraud	22,162	19,775	-10.8	483	469	-2.9	21,679	19,306	-10.9
Embezzlement	2,232	2,060	-7.7	49	48	-2.0	2,183	2,012	-7.8
Stolen property; buying, receiving, possessing	13,073	12,532	-4.1	945	929	-1.7	12,128	11,603	-4.3
Vandalism	24,559	23,322	-5.0	5,307	4,972	-6.3	19,252	18,350	-4.7
Weapons; carrying, possessing, etc.	16,577	17,438	+5.2	2,039	1,968	-3.5	14,538	15,470	+6.4
Prostitution and commercialized vice	2,920	2,413	-17.4	45	31	-31.1	2,875	2,382	-17.1
Sex offenses (except forcible rape and prostitution)	8,599	8,161	-5.1	1,427	1,298	-9.0	7,172	6,863	-4.3
Drug abuse violations	232,400	218,931	-5.8	13,916	12,168	-12.6	218,484	206,763	-5.4
Gambling	660	562	-14.8	54	40	-25.9	606	522	-13.9
Offenses against the family and children	25,791	24,848	-3.7	326	355	+8.9	25,465	24,493	-3.8
Driving under the influence	210,218	198,854	-5.4	1,015	961	-5.3	209,203	197,893	-5.4
Liquor laws	33,224	26,270	-20.9	6,985	5,396	-22.7	26,239	20,874	-20.4
Drunkenness	31,687	28,434	-10.3	478	412	-13.8	31,209	28,022	-10.2
Disorderly conduct	35,217	31,436	-10.7	6,571	5,850	-11.0	28,646	25,586	-10.7
Vagrancy	1,832	2,173	+18.6	103	128	+24.3	1,729	2,045	+18.3
All other offenses (except traffic)	500,211	494,706	-1.1	19,681	17,943	-8.8	480,530	476,763	-0.8
Suspicion	7	34	+385.7	1	5	+400.0	6	29	+383.3
Curfew and loitering law violations	1,823	1,574	-13.7	1,823	1,574	-13.7	NA	NA	NA

NA = Not available.

1 Does not include suspicion.   2 Violent crimes in this table are offenses of murder and nonnegligent manslaughter, rape, robbery, and aggravated assault. Property crimes are offenses of burglary, larceny-theft, motor vehicle theft, and arson.   3 The rape figures in this table are aggregate totals of the data submitted based on both the legacy and revised Uniform Crime Reporting definitions.

Table 41. Arrests, Metropolitan Counties, Distribution by Age, 2015

(Number, percent; 1,536 agencies; 2015 estimated population 56,900,141.)

Offense charged	Total, all ages	Ages under 15	Ages under 18	Ages 18 and over	Under 10	10–12	13–14	15	16	17	18	19	20
Total	1,593,909	27,327	105,281	1,488,628	888	5,928	20,511	19,093	26,028	32,833	46,177	52,775	55,533
Total percent distribution[1]	100.0	1.7	6.6	93.4	0.1	0.4	1.3	1.2	1.6	2.1	2.9	3.3	3.5
Violent crime[2]	67,337	1,658	5,874	61,463	57	364	1,237	1,101	1,450	1,665	2,212	2,256	2,309
Violent crime percent distribution[1]	100.0	2.5	8.7	91.3	0.1	0.5	1.8	1.6	2.2	2.5	3.3	3.4	3.4
Murder and nonnegligent manslaughter	1,675	9	80	1,595	0	0	9	7	24	40	85	88	79
Rape[3]	3,427	250	591	2,836	7	74	169	97	103	141	146	151	138
Robbery	9,667	257	1,553	8,114	2	16	239	320	446	530	722	625	549
Aggravated assault	52,568	1,142	3,650	48,918	48	274	820	677	877	954	1,259	1,392	1,543
Property crime[2]	159,526	5,040	19,515	140,011	115	1,081	3,844	3,782	4,958	5,735	7,147	6,785	6,270
Property crime percent distribution[1]	100.0	3.2	12.2	87.8	0.1	0.7	2.4	2.4	3.1	3.6	4.5	4.3	3.9
Burglary	30,602	1,168	4,192	26,410	40	238	890	829	1,048	1,147	1,511	1,448	1,336
Larceny-theft	116,364	3,416	13,579	102,785	54	762	2,600	2,583	3,448	4,132	5,124	4,863	4,450
Motor vehicle theft	11,442	301	1,458	9,984	8	24	269	323	422	412	474	446	455
Arson	1,118	155	286	832	13	57	85	47	40	44	38	28	29
Other assaults	151,543	7,145	19,733	131,810	240	1,814	5,091	3,898	4,442	4,248	3,545	3,536	3,732
Forgery and counterfeiting	8,719	6	149	8,570	0	1	5	15	47	81	195	288	323
Fraud	21,816	119	519	21,297	6	12	101	89	104	207	342	501	558
Embezzlement	2,154	7	52	2,102	0	3	4	3	15	27	71	112	117
Stolen property; buying, receiving, possessing	13,606	205	1,070	12,536	2	29	174	225	288	352	512	495	498
Vandalism	25,194	1,771	5,282	19,912	61	443	1,267	970	1,254	1,287	1,174	1,076	965
Weapons; carrying, possessing, etc.	18,786	767	2,099	16,687	42	222	503	378	448	506	645	746	732
Prostitution and commercialized vice	2,860	4	36	2,824	0	0	4	8	6	18	62	86	111
Sex offenses (except forcible rape and prostitution)	8,775	660	1,377	7,398	36	159	465	244	230	243	265	287	262
Drug abuse violations	234,082	1,848	13,205	220,877	19	258	1,571	1,898	3,345	6,114	10,484	11,937	11,726
Gambling	601	3	42	559	0	1	2	6	18	15	12	12	17
Offenses against the family and children	25,945	199	511	25,434	63	38	98	79	80	153	154	194	240
Driving under the influence	213,047	28	1,057	211,990	6	1	21	36	213	780	2,528	3,950	5,106
Liquor laws	28,369	484	5,873	22,496	2	36	446	760	1,731	2,898	4,251	4,391	3,896
Drunkenness	29,836	55	420	29,416	0	4	51	51	107	207	570	669	817
Disorderly conduct	34,508	2,500	6,710	27,798	65	657	1,778	1,432	1,471	1,307	1,069	940	903
Vagrancy	2,191	50	128	2,063	1	16	33	27	32	19	39	46	39
All other offenses (except traffic)	543,199	4,347	19,851	523,348	166	738	3,443	3,688	5,176	6,640	10,900	14,468	16,911
Suspicion	42	0	5	37	0	0	0	1	2	2	0	0	1
Curfew and loitering law violations	1,773	431	1,773	NA	7	51	373	402	611	329	NA	NA	NA

Table 41. Arrests, Metropolitan Counties, Distribution by Age, 2015—Continued

(Number, percent; 1,536 agencies; 2015 estimated population 56,900,141.)

Offense charged	21	22	23	24	25–29	30–34	35–39	40–44	45–49	50–54	55–59	60–64	65 and over
Total	58,618	60,716	62,346	62,903	278,508	228,912	173,025	127,563	106,559	84,715	50,481	23,189	16,608
Total percent distribution[1]	3.7	3.8	3.9	3.9	17.5	14.4	10.9	8.0	6.7	5.3	3.2	1.5	1.0
Violent crime[2]	2,519	2,403	2,458	2,475	11,081	9,137	7,063	5,290	4,528	3,534	2,150	1,050	998
Violent crime percent distribution[1]	3.7	3.6	3.7	3.7	16.5	13.6	10.5	7.9	6.7	5.2	3.2	1.6	1.5
Murder and nonnegligent manslaughter	82	86	74	75	303	215	153	86	89	72	50	26	32
Rape[3]	123	114	82	111	366	411	314	263	204	161	102	69	81
Robbery	571	452	438	416	1,592	1,014	605	413	328	218	115	38	18
Aggravated assault	1,743	1,751	1,864	1,873	8,820	7,497	5,991	4,528	3,907	3,083	1,883	917	867
Property crime[2]	6,034	5,896	5,985	5,738	26,168	21,189	15,100	10,722	9,154	6,967	3,918	1,749	1,189
Property crime percent distribution[1]	3.8	3.7	3.8	3.6	16.4	13.3	9.5	6.7	5.7	4.4	2.5	1.1	0.7
Burglary	1,267	1,192	1,229	1,122	5,284	4,246	2,884	1,701	1,481	1,001	446	172	90
Larceny-theft	4,294	4,236	4,307	4,158	18,712	15,147	10,902	8,152	7,049	5,547	3,276	1,510	1,058
Motor vehicle theft	440	436	420	437	2,030	1,664	1,227	806	561	355	157	49	27
Arson	33	32	29	21	142	132	87	63	63	64	39	18	14
Other assaults	4,414	4,701	4,754	4,805	22,450	20,055	16,446	13,117	11,091	9,021	5,362	2,560	2,221
Forgery and counterfeiting	260	305	339	414	1,730	1,438	1,070	766	635	420	239	100	48
Fraud	565	630	720	745	3,783	3,459	2,936	2,349	1,904	1,344	818	348	295
Embezzlement	104	90	93	86	350	298	236	164	158	122	62	18	21
Stolen property; buying, receiving, possessing	531	525	541	552	2,623	2,096	1,514	986	732	504	256	101	70
Vandalism	947	956	920	847	3,560	2,847	2,013	1,400	1,180	993	568	261	205
Weapons; carrying, possessing, etc.	784	802	781	823	3,268	2,528	1,720	1,234	925	738	485	269	207
Prostitution and commercialized vice	125	129	130	112	513	426	293	264	217	162	96	67	31
Sex offenses (except forcible rape and prostitution)	257	227	243	223	943	887	829	649	649	603	397	276	401
Drug abuse violations	11,452	11,297	11,017	10,647	43,229	32,601	22,518	14,835	12,105	9,103	5,037	2,000	889
Gambling	4	11	7	3	47	79	61	62	76	57	64	32	15
Offenses against the family and children	337	484	530	684	4,366	5,086	4,810	3,434	2,463	1,586	703	242	121
Driving under the influence	8,077	9,020	9,677	9,803	40,624	31,208	23,299	18,725	16,547	14,736	9,892	5,087	3,711
Liquor laws	654	487	410	402	1,665	1,440	1,188	917	883	820	584	306	202
Drunkenness	1,136	1,042	1,030	1,043	4,664	4,107	3,161	2,690	2,819	2,717	1,783	815	353
Disorderly conduct	1,095	1,076	1,070	1,078	4,644	3,781	3,058	2,418	2,338	1,988	1,221	609	510
Vagrancy	44	57	68	65	353	270	194	191	212	219	149	77	40
All other offenses (except traffic)	19,277	20,578	21,571	22,356	102,438	85,973	65,510	47,346	37,940	29,080	16,697	7,222	5,081
Suspicion	2	0	2	2	9	7	6	4	3	1	0	0	0
Curfew and loitering law violations	NA	NA	NA	NA	NA	NA	NA	NA	NA	NA	NA	NA	NA

NA = Not available.

1 Because of rounding, the percentages may not sum to 100.   2 Violent crimes are offenses of murder and nonnegligent manslaughter, rape, robbery, and aggravated assault. Property crimes are offenses of burglary, larceny-theft, motor vehicle theft, and arson.   3 The rape figures in this table are an aggregate total of the data submitted using both the revised and legacy Uniform Crime Reporting definitions.

Table 42. Arrests, Metropolitan Counties, Persons Under 15, 18, 21, and 25 Years of Age, 2015

(Number, percent; 1,536 agencies; 2015 estimated population 56,900,141.)

Offense charged	Total, all ages	Number of persons arrested				Percent of total all ages			
		Under 15	Under 18	Under 21	Under 25	Under 15	Under 18	Under 21	Under 25
Total	1,593,909	27,327	105,281	259,766	504,349	1.7	6.6	16.3	31.6
Violent crime[1]	67,337	1,658	5,874	12,651	22,506	2.5	8.7	18.8	33.4
Murder and nonnegligent manslaughter	1,675	9	80	332	649	0.5	4.8	19.8	38.7
Rape[2]	3,427	250	591	1,026	1,456	7.3	17.2	29.9	42.5
Robbery	9,667	257	1,553	3,449	5,326	2.7	16.1	35.7	55.1
Aggravated assault	52,568	1,142	3,650	7,844	15,075	2.2	6.9	14.9	28.7
Property crime[1]	159,526	5,040	19,515	39,717	63,370	3.2	12.2	24.9	39.7
Burglary	30,602	1,168	4,192	8,487	13,297	3.8	13.7	27.7	43.5
Larceny-theft	116,364	3,416	13,579	28,016	45,011	2.9	11.7	24.1	38.7
Motor vehicle theft	11,442	301	1,458	2,833	4,566	2.6	12.7	24.8	39.9
Arson	1,118	155	286	381	496	13.9	25.6	34.1	44.4
Other assaults	151,543	7,145	19,733	30,546	49,220	4.7	13.0	20.2	32.5
Forgery and counterfeiting	8,719	6	149	955	2,273	0.1	1.7	11.0	26.1
Fraud	21,816	119	519	1,920	4,580	0.5	2.4	8.8	21.0
Embezzlement	2,154	7	52	352	725	0.3	2.4	16.3	33.7
Stolen property; buying, receiving, possessing	13,606	205	1,070	2,575	4,724	1.5	7.9	18.9	34.7
Vandalism	25,194	1,771	5,282	8,497	12,167	7.0	21.0	33.7	48.3
Weapons; carrying, possessing, etc.	18,786	767	2,099	4,222	7,412	4.1	11.2	22.5	39.5
Prostitution and commercialized vice	2,860	4	36	295	791	0.1	1.3	10.3	27.7
Sex offenses (except forcible rape and prostitution)	8,775	660	1,377	2,191	3,141	7.5	15.7	25.0	35.8
Drug abuse violations	234,082	1,848	13,205	47,352	91,765	0.8	5.6	20.2	39.2
Gambling	601	3	42	83	108	0.5	7.0	13.8	18.0
Offenses against the family and children	25,945	199	511	1,099	3,134	0.8	2.0	4.2	12.1
Driving under the influence	213,047	28	1,057	12,641	49,218	*	0.5	5.9	23.1
Liquor laws	28,369	484	5,873	18,411	20,364	1.7	20.7	64.9	71.8
Drunkenness	29,836	55	420	2,476	6,727	0.2	1.4	8.3	22.5
Disorderly conduct	34,508	2,500	6,710	9,622	13,941	7.2	19.4	27.9	40.4
Vagrancy	2,191	50	128	252	486	2.3	5.8	11.5	22.2
All other offenses (except traffic)	543,199	4,347	19,851	62,130	145,912	0.8	3.7	11.4	26.9
Suspicion	42	0	5	6	12	0.0	11.9	14.3	28.6
Curfew and loitering law violations	1,773	431	1,773	1,773	1,773	24.3	100.0	100.0	100.0

* = Less than one-tenth of one percent.
1 Violent crimes are offenses of murder and nonnegligent manslaughter, rape, robbery, and aggravated assault. Property crimes are offenses of burglary, larceny-theft, motor vehicle theft, and arson.   2 The rape figures in this table are an aggregate total of the data submitted using both the revised and legacy Uniform Crime Reporting definitions.

Table 43. Arrests, Metropolitan Counties, Distribution by Sex, 2015

(Number, percent; 1,536 agencies; 2015 estimated population 56,900,141.)

Offense charged	Number of persons arrested			Percent male	Percent female	Percent distribution[1]		
	Total	Male	Female			Total	Male	Female
Total	1,593,909	1,175,645	418,264	73.8	26.2	100.0	100.0	100.0
Violent crime[2]	67,337	54,359	12,978	80.7	19.3	4.2	4.6	3.1
Murder and nonnegligent manslaughter	1,675	1,464	211	87.4	12.6	0.1	0.1	0.1
Rape[3]	3,427	3,335	92	97.3	2.7	0.2	0.3	*
Robbery	9,667	8,293	1,374	85.8	14.2	0.6	0.7	0.3
Aggravated assault	52,568	41,267	11,301	78.5	21.5	3.3	3.5	2.7
Property crime[2]	159,526	104,441	55,085	65.5	34.5	10.0	8.9	13.2
Burglary	30,602	25,341	5,261	82.8	17.2	1.9	2.2	1.3
Larceny-theft	116,364	69,246	47,118	59.5	40.5	7.3	5.9	11.3
Motor vehicle theft	11,442	8,953	2,489	78.2	21.8	0.7	0.8	0.6
Arson	1,118	901	217	80.6	19.4	0.1	0.1	0.1
Other assaults	151,543	109,203	42,340	72.1	27.9	9.5	9.3	10.1
Forgery and counterfeiting	8,719	5,770	2,949	66.2	33.8	0.5	0.5	0.7
Fraud	21,816	13,282	8,534	60.9	39.1	1.4	1.1	2.0
Embezzlement	2,154	1,148	1,006	53.3	46.7	0.1	0.1	0.2
Stolen property; buying, receiving, possessing	13,606	10,717	2,889	78.8	21.2	0.9	0.9	0.7
Vandalism	25,194	20,022	5,172	79.5	20.5	1.6	1.7	1.2
Weapons; carrying, possessing, etc.	18,786	16,953	1,833	90.2	9.8	1.2	1.4	0.4
Prostitution and commercialized vice	2,860	1,196	1,664	41.8	58.2	0.2	0.1	0.4
Sex offenses (except forcible rape and prostitution)	8,775	8,121	654	92.5	7.5	0.6	0.7	0.2
Drug abuse violations	234,082	179,212	54,870	76.6	23.4	14.7	15.2	13.1
Gambling	601	326	275	54.2	45.8	*	*	0.1
Offenses against the family and children	25,945	20,602	5,343	79.4	20.6	1.6	1.8	1.3
Driving under the influence	213,047	160,069	52,978	75.1	24.9	13.4	13.6	12.7
Liquor laws	28,369	19,617	8,752	69.1	30.9	1.8	1.7	2.1
Drunkenness	29,836	23,927	5,909	80.2	19.8	1.9	2.0	1.4
Disorderly conduct	34,508	24,690	9,818	71.5	28.5	2.2	2.1	2.3
Vagrancy	2,191	1,649	542	75.3	24.7	0.1	0.1	0.1
All other offenses (except traffic)	543,199	399,148	144,051	73.5	26.5	34.1	34.0	34.4
Suspicion	42	34	8	81.0	19.0	*	*	*
Curfew and loitering law violations	1,773	1,159	614	65.4	34.6	0.1	0.1	0.1

* = Less than one-tenth of one percent.
1 Because of rounding, the percentages may not sum to 100.   2 Violent crimes are offenses of murder and nonnegligent manslaughter, rape, robbery, and aggravated assault. Property crimes are offenses of burglary, larceny-theft, motor vehicle theft, and arson.   3 The rape figures in this table are an aggregate total of the data submitted using both the revised and legacy Uniform Crime Reporting definitions.

Table 44. Arrests, Metropolitan Counties, Distribution by Race, 2015

(Number, percent; 1,536 agencies; 2015 estimated population 56,900,141.)

Offense charged	Total arrests						Percent distribution[1]					
	Total	White	Black	American Indian or Alaskan Native	Asian	Native Hawaiian or Other Pacific Islander	Total	White	Black	American Indian or Alaskan Native	Asian	Native Hawaiian or Other Pacific Islander
Total	1,585,353	1,154,488	395,800	12,613	17,909	4,543	100.0	72.8	25.0	0.8	1.1	0.3
Violent crime[2]	67,113	46,080	19,513	582	699	239	100.0	68.7	29.1	0.9	1.0	0.4
Murder and nonnegligent manslaughter	1,672	977	669	7	14	5	100.0	58.4	40.0	0.4	0.8	0.3
Rape[3]	3,407	2,655	687	23	32	10	100.0	77.9	20.2	0.7	0.9	0.3
Robbery	9,643	4,695	4,795	43	67	43	100.0	48.7	49.7	0.4	0.7	0.4
Aggravated assault	52,391	37,753	13,362	509	586	181	100.0	72.1	25.5	1.0	1.1	0.3
Property crime[2]	158,896	111,339	44,574	738	1,703	542	100.0	70.1	28.1	0.5	1.1	0.3
Burglary	30,523	22,770	7,279	124	243	107	100.0	74.6	23.8	0.4	0.8	0.4
Larceny-theft	115,849	78,888	34,778	519	1,331	333	100.0	68.1	30.0	0.4	1.1	0.3
Motor vehicle theft	11,412	8,792	2,326	85	114	95	100.0	77.0	20.4	0.7	1.0	0.8
Arson	1,112	889	191	10	15	7	100.0	79.9	17.2	0.9	1.3	0.6
Other assaults	150,894	110,302	37,698	1,191	1,394	309	100.0	73.1	25.0	0.8	0.9	0.2
Forgery and counterfeiting	8,671	5,419	3,109	21	115	7	100.0	62.5	35.9	0.2	1.3	0.1
Fraud	21,652	15,040	6,274	116	210	12	100.0	69.5	29.0	0.5	1.0	0.1
Embezzlement	2,148	1,298	817	6	26	1	100.0	60.4	38.0	0.3	1.2	*
Stolen property; buying, receiving, possessing	13,571	9,679	3,692	76	110	14	100.0	71.3	27.2	0.6	0.8	0.1
Vandalism	25,055	18,844	5,739	225	219	28	100.0	75.2	22.9	0.9	0.9	0.1
Weapons; carrying, possessing, etc.	18,709	12,242	6,132	100	182	53	100.0	65.4	32.8	0.5	1.0	0.3
Prostitution and commercialized vice	2,847	1,606	1,014	6	218	3	100.0	56.4	35.6	0.2	7.7	0.1
Sex offenses (except forcible rape and prostitution)	8,738	6,896	1,671	53	106	12	100.0	78.9	19.1	0.6	1.2	0.1
Drug abuse violations	232,847	168,929	59,662	1,221	2,466	569	100.0	72.5	25.6	0.5	1.1	0.2
Gambling	601	289	237	5	59	11	100.0	48.1	39.4	0.8	9.8	1.8
Offenses against the family and children	25,838	16,161	9,426	115	128	8	100.0	62.5	36.5	0.4	0.5	*
Driving under the influence	211,691	175,760	29,581	1,276	4,627	447	100.0	83.0	14.0	0.6	2.2	0.2
Liquor laws	28,006	23,439	3,743	420	355	49	100.0	83.7	13.4	1.5	1.3	0.2
Drunkenness	29,763	25,436	3,682	252	343	50	100.0	85.5	12.4	0.8	1.2	0.2
Disorderly conduct	34,306	23,092	10,434	471	254	55	100.0	67.3	30.4	1.4	0.7	0.2
Vagrancy	2,182	1,625	544	0	13	0	100.0	74.5	24.9	0.0	0.6	0.0
All other offenses (except traffic)	540,021	379,658	147,886	5,736	4,639	2,102	100.0	70.3	27.4	1.1	0.9	0.4
Suspicion	42	36	6	0	0	0	100.0	85.7	14.3	0.0	0.0	0.0
Curfew and loitering law violations	1,762	1,318	366	3	43	32	100.0	74.8	20.8	0.2	2.4	1.8

Table 44. Arrests, Metropolitan Counties, Distribution by Race, 2015—Continued

(Number, percent; 1,536 agencies; 2015 estimated population 56,900,141.)

Offense charged	Arrests under 18						Percent distribution[1]					
	Total	White	Black	American Indian or Alaskan Native	Asian	Native Hawaiian or Other Pacific Islander	Total	White	Black	American Indian or Alaskan Native	Asian	Native Hawaiian or Other Pacific Islander
Total	104,577	68,725	33,708	905	953	286	100.0	65.7	32.2	0.9	0.9	0.3
Violent crime[2]	5,851	3,131	2,625	31	47	17	100.0	53.5	44.9	0.5	0.8	0.3
Murder and nonnegligent manslaughter	80	42	37	1	0	0	100.0	52.5	46.3	1.3	0.0	0.0
Rape[3]	588	438	140	6	3	1	100.0	74.5	23.8	1.0	0.5	0.2
Robbery	1,547	495	1,031	2	12	7	100.0	32.0	66.6	0.1	0.8	0.5
Aggravated assault	3,636	2,156	1,417	22	32	9	100.0	59.3	39.0	0.6	0.9	0.2
Property crime[2]	19,413	11,348	7,657	97	236	75	100.0	58.5	39.4	0.5	1.2	0.4
Burglary	4,169	2,483	1,610	23	38	15	100.0	59.6	38.6	0.6	0.9	0.4
Larceny-theft	13,512	7,649	5,556	62	190	55	100.0	56.6	41.1	0.5	1.4	0.4
Motor vehicle theft	1,450	985	445	10	7	3	100.0	67.9	30.7	0.7	0.5	0.2
Arson	282	231	46	2	1	2	100.0	81.9	16.3	0.7	0.4	0.7
Other assaults	19,629	11,690	7,612	156	137	34	100.0	59.6	38.8	0.8	0.7	0.2
Forgery and counterfeiting	149	100	45	2	1	1	100.0	67.1	30.2	1.3	0.7	0.7
Fraud	498	303	179	7	9	0	100.0	60.8	35.9	1.4	1.8	0.0
Embezzlement	51	23	28	0	0	0	100.0	45.1	54.9	0.0	0.0	0.0
Stolen property; buying, receiving, possessing	1,065	515	533	6	11	0	100.0	48.4	50.0	0.6	1.0	0.0
Vandalism	5,247	3,786	1,371	48	40	2	100.0	72.2	26.1	0.9	0.8	*
Weapons; carrying, possessing, etc.	2,094	1,255	804	10	23	2	100.0	59.9	38.4	0.5	1.1	0.1
Prostitution and commercialized vice	36	22	12	1	0	1	100.0	61.1	33.3	2.8	0.0	2.8
Sex offenses (except forcible rape and prostitution)	1,368	1,035	316	7	10	0	100.0	75.7	23.1	0.5	0.7	0.0
Drug abuse violations	13,102	10,117	2,636	145	149	55	100.0	77.2	20.1	1.1	1.1	0.4
Gambling	42	21	19	0	2	0	100.0	50.0	45.2	0.0	4.8	0.0
Offenses against the family and children	505	320	177	6	2	0	100.0	63.4	35.0	1.2	0.4	0.0
Driving under the influence	1,043	951	77	7	7	1	100.0	91.2	7.4	0.7	0.7	0.1
Liquor laws	5,805	5,286	347	89	63	20	100.0	91.1	6.0	1.5	1.1	0.3
Drunkenness	413	375	30	2	5	1	100.0	90.8	7.3	0.5	1.2	0.2
Disorderly conduct	6,678	3,385	3,191	68	34	0	100.0	50.7	47.8	1.0	0.5	0.0
Vagrancy	128	35	92	0	1	0	100.0	27.3	71.9	0.0	0.8	0.0
All other offenses (except traffic)	19,693	13,706	5,589	220	133	45	100.0	69.6	28.4	1.1	0.7	0.2
Suspicion	5	3	2	0	0	0	100.0	60.0	40.0	0.0	0.0	0.0
Curfew and loitering law violations	1,762	1,318	366	3	43	32	100.0	74.8	20.8	0.2	2.4	1.8

Table 44. Arrests, Metropolitan Counties, Distribution by Race, 2015—Continued

(Number, percent; 1,536 agencies; 2015 estimated population 56,900,141.)

Offense charged	Arrests 18 and over						Percent distribution[1]					
	Total	White	Black	American Indian or Alaskan Native	Asian	Native Hawaiian or Other Pacific Islander	Total	White	Black	American Indian or Alaskan Native	Asian	Native Hawaiian or Other Pacific Islander
Total	1,480,776	1,085,763	362,092	11,708	16,956	4,257	100.0	73.3	24.5	0.8	1.1	0.3
Violent crime[2]	61,262	42,949	16,888	551	652	222	100.0	70.1	27.6	0.9	1.1	0.4
Murder and nonnegligent manslaughter	1,592	935	632	6	14	5	100.0	58.7	39.7	0.4	0.9	0.3
Rape[3]	2,819	2,217	547	17	29	9	100.0	78.6	19.4	0.6	1.0	0.3
Robbery	8,096	4,200	3,764	41	55	36	100.0	51.9	46.5	0.5	0.7	0.4
Aggravated assault	48,755	35,597	11,945	487	554	172	100.0	73.0	24.5	1.0	1.1	0.4
Property crime[2]	139,483	99,991	36,917	641	1,467	467	100.0	71.7	26.5	0.5	1.1	0.3
Burglary	26,354	20,287	5,669	101	205	92	100.0	77.0	21.5	0.4	0.8	0.3
Larceny-theft	102,337	71,239	29,222	457	1,141	278	100.0	69.6	28.6	0.4	1.1	0.3
Motor vehicle theft	9,962	7,807	1,881	75	107	92	100.0	78.4	18.9	0.8	1.1	0.9
Arson	830	658	145	8	14	5	100.0	79.3	17.5	1.0	1.7	0.6
Other assaults	131,265	98,612	30,086	1,035	1,257	275	100.0	75.1	22.9	0.8	1.0	0.2
Forgery and counterfeiting	8,522	5,319	3,064	19	114	6	100.0	62.4	36.0	0.2	1.3	0.1
Fraud	21,154	14,737	6,095	109	201	12	100.0	69.7	28.8	0.5	1.0	0.1
Embezzlement	2,097	1,275	789	6	26	1	100.0	60.8	37.6	0.3	1.2	*
Stolen property; buying, receiving, possessing	12,506	9,164	3,159	70	99	14	100.0	73.3	25.3	0.6	0.8	0.1
Vandalism	19,808	15,058	4,368	177	179	26	100.0	76.0	22.1	0.9	0.9	0.1
Weapons; carrying, possessing, etc.	16,615	10,987	5,328	90	159	51	100.0	66.1	32.1	0.5	1.0	0.3
Prostitution and commercialized vice	2,811	1,584	1,002	5	218	2	100.0	56.4	35.6	0.2	7.8	0.1
Sex offenses (except forcible rape and prostitution)	7,370	5,861	1,355	46	96	12	100.0	79.5	18.4	0.6	1.3	0.2
Drug abuse violations	219,745	158,812	57,026	1,076	2,317	514	100.0	72.3	26.0	0.5	1.1	0.2
Gambling	559	268	218	5	57	11	100.0	47.9	39.0	0.9	10.2	2.0
Offenses against the family and children	25,333	15,841	9,249	109	126	8	100.0	62.5	36.5	0.4	0.5	*
Driving under the influence	210,648	174,809	29,504	1,269	4,620	446	100.0	83.0	14.0	0.6	2.2	0.2
Liquor laws	22,201	18,153	3,396	331	292	29	100.0	81.8	15.3	1.5	1.3	0.1
Drunkenness	29,350	25,061	3,652	250	338	49	100.0	85.4	12.4	0.9	1.2	0.2
Disorderly conduct	27,628	19,707	7,243	403	220	55	100.0	71.3	26.2	1.5	0.8	0.2
Vagrancy	2,054	1,590	452	0	12	0	100.0	77.4	22.0	0.0	0.6	0.0
All other offenses (except traffic)	520,328	365,952	142,297	5,516	4,506	2,057	100.0	70.3	27.3	1.1	0.9	0.4
Suspicion	37	33	4	0	0	0	100.0	89.2	10.8	0.0	0.0	0.0
Curfew and loitering law violations	NA	NA	NA	NA	NA	NA	NA	NA	NA	NA	NA	NA

NA = Not available.
* = Less than one-tenth of one percent.
1 Because of rounding, the percentages may not sum to 100.   2 Violent crimes are offenses of murder and nonnegligent manslaughter, rape, robbery, and aggravated assault.   Property crimes are offenses of burglary, larceny-theft, motor vehicle theft, and arson.   3 The rape figures in this table are an aggregate total of the data submitted using both the revised and legacy Uniform Crime Reporting definitions.

Table 45. Arrests, Metropolitan Counties, Distribution by Ethnicity, 2015

(Number, percent; 1,536 agencies; 2015 estimated population 56,900,141.)

Offense charged	Total arrests			Percent distribution[1]			Arrests under 18		
	Total[2]	Hispanic or Latino	Not Hispanic or Latino	Total[2]	Hispanic or Latino	Not Hispanic or Latino	Total[2]	Hispanic or Latino	Not Hispanic or Latino
Total	1,253,230	228,371	1,024,859	100.0	18.2	81.8	77,863	13,444	64,419
Violent crime[3]	54,064	12,198	41,866	100.0	22.6	77.4	4,468	904	3,564
Murder and nonnegligent manslaughter	1,253	342	911	100.0	27.3	72.7	55	25	30
Rape[4]	2,484	673	1,811	100.0	27.1	72.9	403	75	328
Robbery	7,729	1,507	6,222	100.0	19.5	80.5	1,236	251	985
Aggravated assault	42,598	9,676	32,922	100.0	22.7	77.3	2,774	553	2,221
Property crime[3]	124,637	16,244	108,393	100.0	13.0	87.0	14,681	2,377	12,304
Burglary	24,850	3,318	21,532	100.0	13.4	86.6	3,219	545	2,674
Larceny-theft	89,368	10,188	79,180	100.0	11.4	88.6	10,120	1,513	8,607
Motor vehicle theft	9,508	2,615	6,893	100.0	27.5	72.5	1,094	289	805
Arson	911	123	788	100.0	13.5	86.5	248	30	218
Other assaults	117,070	17,079	99,991	100.0	14.6	85.4	14,929	2,336	12,593
Forgery and counterfeiting	6,497	1,171	5,326	100.0	18.0	82.0	131	19	112
Fraud	16,868	1,633	15,235	100.0	9.7	90.3	359	43	316
Embezzlement	1,714	155	1,559	100.0	9.0	91.0	42	8	34
Stolen property; buying, receiving, possessing	9,800	2,014	7,786	100.0	20.6	79.4	726	166	560
Vandalism	20,920	3,167	17,753	100.0	15.1	84.9	4,387	674	3,713
Weapons; carrying, possessing, etc.	14,832	3,388	11,444	100.0	22.8	77.2	1,590	323	1,267
Prostitution and commercialized vice	2,310	381	1,929	100.0	16.5	83.5	25	3	22
Sex offenses (except forcible rape and prostitution)	6,620	1,569	5,051	100.0	23.7	76.3	923	156	767
Drug abuse violations	184,773	35,265	149,508	100.0	19.1	80.9	10,034	2,103	7,931
Gambling	482	72	410	100.0	14.9	85.1	40	11	29
Offenses against the family and children	19,208	2,266	16,942	100.0	11.8	88.2	237	36	201
Driving under the influence	182,786	50,360	132,426	100.0	27.6	72.4	838	176	662
Liquor laws	21,510	3,476	18,034	100.0	16.2	83.8	4,402	524	3,878
Drunkenness	27,831	7,322	20,509	100.0	26.3	73.7	391	142	249
Disorderly conduct	23,174	2,962	20,212	100.0	12.8	87.2	4,249	486	3,763
Vagrancy	1,862	279	1,583	100.0	15.0	85.0	29	7	22
All other offenses (except traffic)	415,323	67,195	348,128	100.0	16.2	83.8	14,445	2,775	11,670
Suspicion	13	0	13	100.0	0.0	100.0	1	0	1
Curfew and loitering law violations	936	175	761	100.0	18.7	81.3	936	175	761

Table 45. Arrests, Metropolitan Counties, Distribution by Ethnicity, 2015—Continued

(Number, percent; 1,536 agencies; 2015 estimated population 56,900,141.)

Offense charged	Percent distribution[1]			Arrests 18 and over			Percent distribution[1]		
	Total[2]	Hispanic or Latino	Not Hispanic or Latino	Total[2]	Hispanic or Latino	Not Hispanic or Latino	Total[2]	Hispanic or Latino	Not Hispanic or Latino
Total	100.0	17.3	82.7	1,175,367	214,927	960,440	100.0	18.3	81.7
Violent crime[3]	100.0	20.2	79.8	49,596	11,294	38,302	100.0	22.8	77.2
Murder and nonnegligent manslaughter	100.0	45.5	54.5	1,198	317	881	100.0	26.5	73.5
Rape[4]	100.0	18.6	81.4	2,081	598	1,483	100.0	28.7	71.3
Robbery	100.0	20.3	79.7	6,493	1,256	5,237	100.0	19.3	80.7
Aggravated assault	100.0	19.9	80.1	39,824	9,123	30,701	100.0	22.9	77.1
Property crime[3]	100.0	16.2	83.8	109,956	13,867	96,089	100.0	12.6	87.4
Burglary	100.0	16.9	83.1	21,631	2,773	18,858	100.0	12.8	87.2
Larceny-theft	100.0	15.0	85.0	79,248	8,675	70,573	100.0	10.9	89.1
Motor vehicle theft	100.0	26.4	73.6	8,414	2,326	6,088	100.0	27.6	72.4
Arson	100.0	12.1	87.9	663	93	570	100.0	14.0	86.0
Other assaults	100.0	15.6	84.4	102,141	14,743	87,398	100.0	14.4	85.6
Forgery and counterfeiting	100.0	14.5	85.5	6,366	1,152	5,214	100.0	18.1	81.9
Fraud	100.0	12.0	88.0	16,509	1,590	14,919	100.0	9.6	90.4
Embezzlement	100.0	19.0	81.0	1,672	147	1,525	100.0	8.8	91.2
Stolen property; buying, receiving, possessing	100.0	22.9	77.1	9,074	1,848	7,226	100.0	20.4	79.6
Vandalism	100.0	15.4	84.6	16,533	2,493	14,040	100.0	15.1	84.9
Weapons; carrying, possessing, etc.	100.0	20.3	79.7	13,242	3,065	10,177	100.0	23.1	76.9
Prostitution and commercialized vice	100.0	12.0	88.0	2,285	378	1,907	100.0	16.5	83.5
Sex offenses (except forcible rape and prostitution)	100.0	16.9	83.1	5,697	1,413	4,284	100.0	24.8	75.2
Drug abuse violations	100.0	21.0	79.0	174,739	33,162	141,577	100.0	19.0	81.0
Gambling	100.0	27.5	72.5	442	61	381	100.0	13.8	86.2
Offenses against the family and children	100.0	15.2	84.8	18,971	2,230	16,741	100.0	11.8	88.2
Driving under the influence	100.0	21.0	79.0	181,948	50,184	131,764	100.0	27.6	72.4
Liquor laws	100.0	11.9	88.1	17,108	2,952	14,156	100.0	17.3	82.7
Drunkenness	100.0	36.3	63.7	27,440	7,180	20,260	100.0	26.2	73.8
Disorderly conduct	100.0	11.4	88.6	18,925	2,476	16,449	100.0	13.1	86.9
Vagrancy	100.0	24.1	75.9	1,833	272	1,561	100.0	14.8	85.2
All other offenses (except traffic)	100.0	19.2	80.8	400,878	64,420	336,458	100.0	16.1	83.9
Suspicion	100.0	0.0	100.0	12	0	12	100.0	0.0	100.0
Curfew and loitering law violations	100.0	18.7	81.3	NA	NA	NA	NA	NA	NA

NA = Not available.

1 Because of rounding, the percentages may not sum to 100.   2 The ethnicity totals are representative of those agencies that provided ethnicity breakdowns. Not all agencies provide ethnicity data; therefore, the race and ethnicity totals will not be equal.   3 Violent crimes are offenses of murder and nonnegligent manslaughter, rape, robbery, and aggravated assault. Property crimes are offenses of burglary, larceny-theft, motor vehicle theft, and arson.   4 The rape figures in this table are an aggregate total of the data submitted using both the revised and legacy Uniform Crime Reporting definitions.

Table 46. Arrest Trends, Nonmetropolitan Counties, 2014–2015

(Number, percent change; 1,850 agencies; 2015 estimated population 19,769,186; 2014 estimated population 19,890,479.)

	Number of persons arrested								
	Total, all ages			Under 18 years of age			18 years of age and over		
Offense charged	2014	2015	Percent change	2014	2015	Percent change	2014	2015	Percent change
Total[1]	639,076	639,440	+0.1	29,682	28,488	-4.0	609,394	610,952	+0.3
Violent crime[2]	18,356	19,212	+4.7	1,112	1,187	+6.7	17,244	18,025	+4.5
Murder and nonnegligent manslaughter	535	534	-0.2	17	21	+23.5	518	513	-1.0
Rape[3]	1,342	1,421	+5.9	217	226	+4.1	1,125	1,195	+6.2
Robbery	1,200	1,166	-2.8	68	90	+32.4	1,132	1,076	-4.9
Aggravated assault	15,279	16,091	+5.3	810	850	+4.9	14,469	15,241	+5.3
Property crime[2]	45,933	41,965	-8.6	4,466	3,889	-12.9	41,467	38,076	-8.2
Burglary	13,247	11,660	-12.0	1,479	1,263	-14.6	11,768	10,397	-11.7
Larceny-theft	28,794	26,270	-8.8	2,441	2,076	-15.0	26,353	24,194	-8.2
Motor vehicle theft	3,354	3,507	+4.6	451	456	+1.1	2,903	3,051	+5.1
Arson	538	528	-1.9	95	94	-1.1	443	434	-2.0
Other assaults	51,319	51,811	+1.0	4,605	4,496	-2.4	46,714	47,315	+1.3
Forgery and counterfeiting	2,617	2,381	-9.0	31	36	+16.1	2,586	2,345	-9.3
Fraud	9,814	8,384	-14.6	148	106	-28.4	9,666	8,278	-14.4
Embezzlement	614	496	-19.2	11	9	-18.2	603	487	-19.2
Stolen property; buying, receiving, possessing	3,708	3,837	+3.5	215	262	+21.9	3,493	3,575	+2.3
Vandalism	8,214	8,042	-2.1	1,647	1,524	-7.5	6,567	6,518	-0.7
Weapons; carrying, possessing, etc.	5,830	6,497	+11.4	354	336	-5.1	5,476	6,161	+12.5
Prostitution and commercialized vice	171	218	+27.5	18	18	0.0	153	200	+30.7
Sex offenses (except forcible rape and prostitution)	3,177	3,058	-3.7	518	477	-7.9	2,659	2,581	-2.9
Drug abuse violations	91,861	95,644	+4.1	3,588	3,577	-0.3	88,273	92,067	+4.3
Gambling	148	158	+6.8	4	5	+25.0	144	153	+6.3
Offenses against the family and children	8,948	8,497	-5.0	207	172	-16.9	8,741	8,325	-4.8
Driving under the influence	147,589	146,933	-0.4	792	796	+0.5	146,797	146,137	-0.4
Liquor laws	16,512	14,828	-10.2	3,363	3,236	-3.8	13,149	11,592	-11.8
Drunkenness	14,152	12,895	-8.9	207	167	-19.3	13,945	12,728	-8.7
Disorderly conduct	16,075	15,611	-2.9	2,065	2,069	+0.2	14,010	13,542	-3.3
Vagrancy	171	328	+91.8	25	15	-40.0	146	313	+114.4
All other offenses (except traffic)	193,580	198,396	+2.5	6,019	5,862	-2.6	187,561	192,534	+2.7
Suspicion	192	161	-16.1	73	76	+4.1	119	85	-28.6
Curfew and loitering law violations	287	249	-13.2	287	249	-13.2	NA	NA	NA

NA = Not available.

1 Does not include suspicion.   2 Violent crimes are offenses of murder and nonnegligent manslaughter, rape, robbery, and aggravated assault. Property crimes are offenses of burglary, larceny-theft, motor vehicle theft, and arson.   3 The rape figures in this table are aggregate totals of the data submitted based on both the legacy and revised Uniform Crime Reporting definitions.

Table 47. Arrests, Nonmetropolitan Counties, Distribution by Age, 2015

(Number, percent; 2,055 agencies; 2015 estimated population 21,312,448.)

Offense charged	Total, all ages	Ages under 15	Ages under 18	Ages 18 and over	Under 10	10–12	13–14	15	16	17	18	19	20
Total	676,962	7,156	29,890	647,072	344	1,658	5,154	4,930	7,032	10,772	18,007	20,913	22,433
Total percent distribution[1]	100.0	1.1	4.4	95.6	0.1	0.2	0.8	0.7	1.0	1.6	2.7	3.1	3.3
Violent crime[2]	20,761	416	1,265	19,496	15	107	294	229	252	368	522	557	579
Violent crime percent distribution[1]	100.0	2.0	6.1	93.9	0.1	0.5	1.4	1.1	1.2	1.8	2.5	2.7	2.8
Murder and nonnegligent manslaughter	600	2	23	577	0	0	2	3	6	12	21	18	18
Rape[3]	1,556	86	239	1,317	5	19	62	53	45	55	75	73	62
Robbery	1,298	9	96	1,202	0	0	9	15	17	55	79	78	73
Aggravated assault	17,307	319	907	16,400	10	88	221	158	184	246	347	388	426
Property crime[2]	44,435	1,134	4,124	40,311	46	299	789	763	955	1,272	1,698	1,719	1,562
Property crime percent distribution[1]	100.0	2.6	9.3	90.7	0.1	0.7	1.8	1.7	2.1	2.9	3.8	3.9	3.5
Burglary	12,624	380	1,386	11,238	19	87	274	278	316	412	567	530	509
Larceny-theft	27,418	571	2,149	25,269	19	166	386	357	508	713	983	1,024	897
Motor vehicle theft	3,817	122	482	3,335	3	15	104	109	116	135	129	140	135
Arson	576	61	107	469	5	31	25	19	15	12	19	25	21
Other assaults	56,132	1,635	4,778	51,354	75	425	1,135	879	1,062	1,202	1,227	1,144	1,366
Forgery and counterfeiting	2,525	7	39	2,486	2	0	5	2	9	21	36	53	69
Fraud	9,632	21	108	9,524	0	2	19	14	20	53	97	166	176
Embezzlement	531	1	9	522	0	0	1	2	3	3	13	10	13
Stolen property; buying, receiving, possessing	4,143	33	267	3,876	0	5	28	50	77	107	151	143	133
Vandalism	8,454	560	1,561	6,893	43	146	371	284	364	353	447	322	308
Weapons; carrying, possessing, etc.	6,912	113	350	6,562	5	34	74	60	67	110	151	171	171
Prostitution and commercialized vice	224	5	18	206	0	3	2	3	5	5	2	7	7
Sex offenses (except forcible rape and prostitution)	3,201	211	491	2,710	7	61	143	88	101	91	121	115	113
Drug abuse violations	99,677	398	3,690	95,987	8	46	344	428	885	1,979	4,210	4,780	4,828
Gambling	158	0	5	153	0	0	0	2	0	3	2	7	0
Offenses against the family and children	8,961	59	174	8,787	5	13	41	38	43	34	84	103	123
Driving under the influence	152,085	18	835	151,250	2	0	16	32	195	590	1,990	2,893	3,685
Liquor laws	15,600	276	3,343	12,257	5	21	250	458	933	1,676	2,497	2,687	2,386
Drunkenness	13,423	13	174	13,249	2	1	10	34	51	76	236	305	305
Disorderly conduct	16,278	715	2,090	14,188	40	186	489	394	465	516	438	374	395
Vagrancy	331	3	15	316	1	0	2	3	3	6	3	2	10
All other offenses (except traffic)	213,089	1,414	6,229	206,860	82	281	1,051	1,088	1,466	2,261	4,078	5,353	6,203
Suspicion	161	34	76	85	5	6	23	19	14	9	4	2	1
Curfew and loitering law violations	249	90	249	NA	1	22	67	60	62	37	NA	NA	NA

Table 47. Arrests, Nonmetropolitan Counties, Distribution by Age, 2015—Continued

(Number, percent; 2,055 agencies; 2015 estimated population 21,312,448.)

Offense charged	21	22	23	24	25–29	30–34	35–39	40–44	45–49	50–54	55–59	60–64	65 and over
Total	22,740	23,830	24,741	25,187	114,827	100,301	78,592	59,327	48,135	40,340	25,160	12,438	10,101
Total percent distribution[1]	3.4	3.5	3.7	3.7	17.0	14.8	11.6	8.8	7.1	6.0	3.7	1.8	1.5
Violent crime[2]	660	614	655	724	3,329	3,022	2,390	1,923	1,475	1,322	844	444	436
Violent crime percent distribution[1]	3.2	3.0	3.2	3.5	16.0	14.6	11.5	9.3	7.1	6.4	4.1	2.1	2.1
Murder and nonnegligent manslaughter	20	27	21	20	92	82	74	55	40	33	26	14	16
Rape[3]	75	46	43	58	175	165	155	133	80	59	57	27	34
Robbery	66	58	77	62	284	147	124	50	47	29	18	8	2
Aggravated assault	499	483	514	584	2,778	2,628	2,037	1,685	1,308	1,201	743	395	384
Property crime[2]	1,569	1,592	1,578	1,718	7,835	6,700	4,866	3,332	2,515	1,841	985	451	350
Property crime percent distribution[1]	3.5	3.6	3.6	3.9	17.6	15.1	11.0	7.5	5.7	4.1	2.2	1.0	0.8
Burglary	529	534	458	531	2,315	1,851	1,296	840	581	378	197	82	40
Larceny-theft	902	913	949	1,022	4,763	4,177	3,138	2,197	1,711	1,275	699	337	282
Motor vehicle theft	121	128	155	156	677	624	380	262	185	143	62	24	14
Arson	17	17	16	9	80	48	52	33	38	45	27	8	14
Other assaults	1,484	1,569	1,826	1,739	8,270	7,852	6,653	5,325	4,509	3,903	2,285	1,119	1,083
Forgery and counterfeiting	61	87	73	102	512	490	333	245	199	116	70	28	12
Fraud	191	192	247	301	1,485	1,826	1,432	1,074	861	640	401	201	234
Embezzlement	16	14	10	20	73	89	70	68	49	35	28	9	5
Stolen property; buying, receiving, possessing	152	107	141	146	737	655	511	355	313	189	81	36	26
Vandalism	328	298	295	302	1,246	993	708	506	423	331	177	102	107
Weapons; carrying, possessing, etc.	227	266	260	282	1,189	1,032	775	587	421	412	293	156	169
Prostitution and commercialized vice	6	4	11	8	35	22	14	21	17	23	14	8	7
Sex offenses (except forcible rape and prostitution)	79	110	84	79	386	349	291	239	194	187	143	91	129
Drug abuse violations	4,546	4,622	4,578	4,160	18,175	14,328	10,441	7,092	5,427	4,425	2,629	1,132	614
Gambling	3	4	5	4	29	15	15	11	15	7	17	11	8
Offenses against the family and children	145	205	210	257	1,542	1,820	1,673	1,076	671	468	240	101	69
Driving under the influence	5,278	5,540	5,961	5,836	25,297	20,653	17,044	14,504	13,122	12,462	8,695	4,665	3,625
Liquor laws	412	300	231	213	779	559	488	449	409	346	246	146	109
Drunkenness	401	415	411	405	1,901	1,883	1,649	1,421	1,334	1,284	791	312	196
Disorderly conduct	505	545	504	487	2,204	2,019	1,574	1,371	1,278	1,150	725	331	288
Vagrancy	14	13	9	9	68	60	29	31	17	23	13	7	8
All other offenses (except traffic)	6,660	7,330	7,647	8,391	39,717	35,920	27,624	19,691	14,882	11,170	6,482	3,086	2,626
Suspicion	3	3	5	4	18	14	12	6	4	6	1	2	0
Curfew and loitering law violations	NA	NA	NA	NA	NA	NA	NA	NA	NA	NA	NA	NA	NA

NA = Not available.

1 Because of rounding, the percentages may not sum to 100.   2 Violent crimes are offenses of murder and nonnegligent manslaughter, rape, robbery, and aggravated assault.   Property crimes are offenses of burglary, larceny-theft, motor vehicle theft, and arson.   3 The rape figures in this table are an aggregate total of the data submitted using both the revised and legacy Uniform Crime Reporting definitions.

Table 48. Arrests, Nonmetropolitan Counties, Persons Under 15, 18, 21, and 25 Years of Age, 2015

(Number, percent; 2,055 agencies; 2015 estimated population 21,312,448.)

Offense charged	Total, all ages	Number of persons arrested				Percent of total all ages			
		Under 15	Under 18	Under 21	Under 25	Under 15	Under 18	Under 21	Under 25
Total	676,962	7,156	29,890	91,243	187,741	1.1	4.4	13.5	27.7
Violent crime[1]	20,761	416	1,265	2,923	5,576	2.0	6.1	14.1	26.9
Murder and nonnegligent manslaughter	600	2	23	80	168	0.3	3.8	13.3	28.0
Rape[2]	1,556	86	239	449	671	5.5	15.4	28.9	43.1
Robbery	1,298	9	96	326	589	0.7	7.4	25.1	45.4
Aggravated assault	17,307	319	907	2,068	4,148	1.8	5.2	11.9	24.0
Property crime[1]	44,435	1,134	4,124	9,103	15,560	2.6	9.3	20.5	35.0
Burglary	12,624	380	1,386	2,992	5,044	3.0	11.0	23.7	40.0
Larceny-theft	27,418	571	2,149	5,053	8,839	2.1	7.8	18.4	32.2
Motor vehicle theft	3,817	122	482	886	1,446	3.2	12.6	23.2	37.9
Arson	576	61	107	172	231	10.6	18.6	29.9	40.1
Other assaults	56,132	1,635	4,778	8,515	15,133	2.9	8.5	15.2	27.0
Forgery and counterfeiting	2,525	7	39	197	520	0.3	1.5	7.8	20.6
Fraud	9,632	21	108	547	1,478	0.2	1.1	5.7	15.3
Embezzlement	531	1	9	45	105	0.2	1.7	8.5	19.8
Stolen property; buying, receiving, possessing	4,143	33	267	694	1,240	0.8	6.4	16.8	29.9
Vandalism	8,454	560	1,561	2,638	3,861	6.6	18.5	31.2	45.7
Weapons; carrying, possessing, etc.	6,912	113	350	843	1,878	1.6	5.1	12.2	27.2
Prostitution and commercialized vice	224	5	18	34	63	2.2	8.0	15.2	28.1
Sex offenses (except forcible rape and prostitution)	3,201	211	491	840	1,192	6.6	15.3	26.2	37.2
Drug abuse violations	99,677	398	3,690	17,508	35,414	0.4	3.7	17.6	35.5
Gambling	158	0	5	14	30	0.0	3.2	8.9	19.0
Offenses against the family and children	8,961	59	174	484	1,301	0.7	1.9	5.4	14.5
Driving under the influence	152,085	18	835	9,403	32,018	*	0.5	6.2	21.1
Liquor laws	15,600	276	3,343	10,913	12,069	1.8	21.4	70.0	77.4
Drunkenness	13,423	13	174	1,020	2,652	0.1	1.3	7.6	19.8
Disorderly conduct	16,278	715	2,090	3,297	5,338	4.4	12.8	20.3	32.8
Vagrancy	331	3	15	30	75	0.9	4.5	9.1	22.7
All other offenses (except traffic)	213,089	1,414	6,229	21,863	51,891	0.7	2.9	10.3	24.4
Suspicion	161	34	76	83	98	21.1	47.2	51.6	60.9
Curfew and loitering law violations	249	90	249	249	249	36.1	100.0	100.0	100.0

* = Less than one-tenth of one percent.

1 Violent crimes are offenses of murder and nonnegligent manslaughter, rape, robbery, and aggravated assault. Property crimes are offenses of burglary, larceny-theft, motor vehicle theft, and arson.   2 The rape figures in this table are an aggregate total of the data submitted using both the revised and legacy Uniform Crime Reporting definitions.

Table 49. Arrests, Nonmetropolitan Counties, Distribution by Sex, 2015

(Number, percent; 2,055 agencies; 2015 estimated population 21,312,448.)

Offense charged	Number of persons arrested			Percent male	Percent female	Percent distribution[1]		
	Total	Male	Female			Total	Male	Female
Total	676,962	502,437	174,525	74.2	25.8	100.0	100.0	100.0
Violent crime[2]	20,761	17,053	3,708	82.1	17.9	3.1	3.4	2.1
Murder and nonnegligent manslaughter	600	504	96	84.0	16.0	0.1	0.1	0.1
Rape[3]	1556	1502	54	96.5	3.5	0.2	0.3	*
Robbery	1,298	1,118	180	86.1	13.9	0.2	0.2	0.1
Aggravated assault	17,307	13,929	3,378	80.5	19.5	2.6	2.8	1.9
Property crime[2]	44,435	31,391	13,044	70.6	29.4	6.6	6.2	7.5
Burglary	12,624	10,277	2,347	81.4	18.6	1.9	2.0	1.3
Larceny-theft	27,418	17,676	9,742	64.5	35.5	4.1	3.5	5.6
Motor vehicle theft	3,817	2,967	850	77.7	22.3	0.6	0.6	0.5
Arson	576	471	105	81.8	18.2	0.1	0.1	0.1
Other assaults	56,132	41,120	15,012	73.3	26.7	8.3	8.2	8.6
Forgery and counterfeiting	2,525	1,514	1,011	60.0	40.0	0.4	0.3	0.6
Fraud	9,632	5,222	4,410	54.2	45.8	1.4	1.0	2.5
Embezzlement	531	265	266	49.9	50.1	0.1	0.1	0.2
Stolen property; buying, receiving, possessing	4,143	3,270	873	78.9	21.1	0.6	0.7	0.5
Vandalism	8,454	6,803	1,651	80.5	19.5	1.2	1.4	0.9
Weapons; carrying, possessing, etc.	6,912	6,265	647	90.6	9.4	1.0	1.2	0.4
Prostitution and commercialized vice	224	151	73	67.4	32.6	*	*	*
Sex offenses (except forcible rape and prostitution)	3,201	2,990	211	93.4	6.6	0.5	0.6	0.1
Drug abuse violations	99,677	74,017	25,660	74.3	25.7	14.7	14.7	14.7
Gambling	158	103	55	65.2	34.8	*	*	*
Offenses against the family and children	8,961	6,633	2,328	74.0	26.0	1.3	1.3	1.3
Driving under the influence	152,085	115,958	36,127	76.2	23.8	22.5	23.1	20.7
Liquor laws	15,600	10,791	4,809	69.2	30.8	2.3	2.1	2.8
Drunkenness	13,423	10,165	3,258	75.7	24.3	2.0	2.0	1.9
Disorderly conduct	16,278	11,620	4,658	71.4	28.6	2.4	2.3	2.7
Vagrancy	331	259	72	78.2	21.8	*	*	*
All other offenses (except traffic)	213,089	156,583	56,506	73.5	26.5	31.5	31.2	32.4
Suspicion	161	114	47	70.8	29.2	*	*	*
Curfew and loitering law violations	249	150	99	60.2	39.8	*	*	0.1

* = Less than one-tenth of 1 percent.
1 Because of rounding, the percentages may not sum to 100.   2 Violent crimes are offenses of murder and nonnegligent manslaughter, rape, robbery, and aggravated assault. Property crimes are offenses of burglary, larceny-theft, motor vehicle theft, and arson.   3 The rape figures in this table are an aggregate total of the data submitted using both the revised and legacy Uniform Crime Reporting definitions.

Table 50. Arrests, Nonmetropolitan Counties, Distribution by Race, 2015

(Number, percent; 2,054 agencies; 2015 estimated population 21,302,367.)

Offense charged	Total arrests						Percent distribution[1]					
	Total	White	Black	American Indian or Alaskan Native	Asian	Native Hawaiian or Other Pacific Islander	Total	White	Black	American Indian or Alaskan Native	Asian	Native Hawaiian or Other Pacific Islander
Total	667,049	559,826	85,234	17,779	3,993	217	100.0	83.9	12.8	2.7	0.6	*
Violent crime[2]	20,607	16,663	3,033	839	60	12	100.0	80.9	14.7	4.1	0.3	0.1
Murder and nonnegligent manslaughter	598	426	157	10	4	1	100.0	71.2	26.3	1.7	0.7	0.2
Rape[3]	1,543	1,306	165	64	6	2	100.0	84.6	10.7	4.1	0.4	0.1
Robbery	1,294	826	435	32	1	0	100.0	63.8	33.6	2.5	0.1	0.0
Aggravated assault	17,172	14,105	2,276	733	49	9	100.0	82.1	13.3	4.3	0.3	0.1
Property crime[2]	44,102	37,864	5,144	957	130	7	100.0	85.9	11.7	2.2	0.3	*
Burglary	12,549	10,671	1,568	292	17	1	100.0	85.0	12.5	2.3	0.1	*
Larceny-theft	27,202	23,440	3,180	483	93	6	100.0	86.2	11.7	1.8	0.3	*
Motor vehicle theft	3,782	3,261	345	158	18	0	100.0	86.2	9.1	4.2	0.5	0.0
Arson	569	492	51	24	2	0	100.0	86.5	9.0	4.2	0.4	0.0
Other assaults	55,719	46,967	6,830	1,767	129	26	100.0	84.3	12.3	3.2	0.2	*
Forgery and counterfeiting	2,496	2,032	415	36	11	2	100.0	81.4	16.6	1.4	0.4	0.1
Fraud	9,510	7,919	1,437	117	28	9	100.0	83.3	15.1	1.2	0.3	0.1
Embezzlement	528	469	53	5	1	0	100.0	88.8	10.0	0.9	0.2	0.0
Stolen property; buying, receiving, possessing	4,107	3,285	713	99	10	0	100.0	80.0	17.4	2.4	0.2	0.0
Vandalism	8,390	7,103	970	279	36	2	100.0	84.7	11.6	3.3	0.4	*
Weapons; carrying, possessing, etc.	6,833	5,343	1,297	157	35	1	100.0	78.2	19.0	2.3	0.5	*
Prostitution and commercialized vice	220	177	29	4	10	0	100.0	80.5	13.2	1.8	4.5	0.0
Sex offenses (except forcible rape and prostitution)	3,177	2,772	334	58	12	1	100.0	87.3	10.5	1.8	0.4	*
Drug abuse violations	97,813	80,643	14,742	1,850	550	28	100.0	82.4	15.1	1.9	0.6	*
Gambling	156	102	27	6	14	7	100.0	65.4	17.3	3.8	9.0	4.5
Offenses against the family and children	8,908	7,364	1,371	142	22	9	100.0	82.7	15.4	1.6	0.2	0.1
Driving under the influence	148,452	125,766	16,647	4,050	1,951	38	100.0	84.7	11.2	2.7	1.3	*
Liquor laws	14,983	13,646	723	519	94	1	100.0	91.1	4.8	3.5	0.6	*
Drunkenness	13,363	11,961	843	512	37	10	100.0	89.5	6.3	3.8	0.3	0.1
Disorderly conduct	16,078	13,044	2,127	837	66	4	100.0	81.1	13.2	5.2	0.4	*
Vagrancy	329	259	65	4	1	0	100.0	78.7	19.8	1.2	0.3	0.0
All other offenses (except traffic)	210,871	176,107	28,381	5,529	795	59	100.0	83.5	13.5	2.6	0.4	*
Suspicion	161	122	37	1	0	1	100.0	75.8	23.0	0.6	0.0	0.6
Curfew and loitering law violations	246	218	16	11	1	0	100.0	88.6	6.5	4.5	0.4	0.0

Table 50. Arrests, Nonmetropolitan Counties, Distribution by Race, 2015—Continued

(Number, percent; 2,054 agencies; 2015 estimated population 21,302,367.)

Offense charged	Arrests under 18						Percent distribution[1]					
	Total	White	Black	American Indian or Alaskan Native	Asian	Native Hawaiian or Other Pacific Islander	Total	White	Black	American Indian or Alaskan Native	Asian	Native Hawaiian or Other Pacific Islander
Total	29,355	24,306	3,994	961	83	11	100.0	82.8	13.6	3.3	0.3	*
Violent crime[2]	1,248	959	230	57	2	0	100.0	76.8	18.4	4.6	0.2	0.0
Murder and nonnegligent manslaughter	23	14	9	0	0	0	100.0	60.9	39.1	0.0	0.0	0.0
Rape[3]	237	215	14	8	0	0	100.0	90.7	5.9	3.4	0.0	0.0
Robbery	95	51	41	3	0	0	100.0	53.7	43.2	3.2	0.0	0.0
Aggravated assault	893	679	166	46	2	0	100.0	76.0	18.6	5.2	0.2	0.0
Property crime[2]	4,062	3,267	634	146	14	1	100.0	80.4	15.6	3.6	0.3	*
Burglary	1,372	1,073	223	74	1	1	100.0	78.2	16.3	5.4	0.1	0.1
Larceny-theft	2,112	1,711	352	40	9	0	100.0	81.0	16.7	1.9	0.4	0.0
Motor vehicle theft	476	390	56	27	3	0	100.0	81.9	11.8	5.7	0.6	0.0
Arson	102	93	3	5	1	0	100.0	91.2	2.9	4.9	1.0	0.0
Other assaults	4,724	3,653	923	135	7	6	100.0	77.3	19.5	2.9	0.1	0.1
Forgery and counterfeiting	39	28	10	1	0	0	100.0	71.8	25.6	2.6	0.0	0.0
Fraud	103	85	17	1	0	0	100.0	82.5	16.5	1.0	0.0	0.0
Embezzlement	9	9	0	0	0	0	100.0	100.0	0.0	0.0	0.0	0.0
Stolen property; buying, receiving, possessing	261	177	81	3	0	0	100.0	67.8	31.0	1.1	0.0	0.0
Vandalism	1,541	1,291	188	48	14	0	100.0	83.8	12.2	3.1	0.9	0.0
Weapons; carrying, possessing, etc.	345	273	61	9	2	0	100.0	79.1	17.7	2.6	0.6	0.0
Prostitution and commercialized vice	18	17	1	0	0	0	100.0	94.4	5.6	0.0	0.0	0.0
Sex offenses (except forcible rape and prostitution)	482	415	57	9	1	0	100.0	86.1	11.8	1.9	0.2	0.0
Drug abuse violations	3,589	3,112	356	107	13	1	100.0	86.7	9.9	3.0	0.4	*
Gambling	5	1	4	0	0	0	100.0	20.0	80.0	0.0	0.0	0.0
Offenses against the family and children	171	151	14	6	0	0	100.0	88.3	8.2	3.5	0.0	0.0
Driving under the influence	820	752	32	29	7	0	100.0	91.7	3.9	3.5	0.9	0.0
Liquor laws	3,226	3,030	77	110	8	1	100.0	93.9	2.4	3.4	0.2	*
Drunkenness	173	161	9	3	0	0	100.0	93.1	5.2	1.7	0.0	0.0
Disorderly conduct	2,078	1,504	502	69	3	0	100.0	72.4	24.2	3.3	0.1	0.0
Vagrancy	15	14	0	1	0	0	100.0	93.3	0.0	6.7	0.0	0.0
All other offenses (except traffic)	6,124	5,115	780	216	11	2	100.0	83.5	12.7	3.5	0.2	*
Suspicion	76	74	2	0	0	0	100.0	97.4	2.6	0.0	0.0	0.0
Curfew and loitering law violations	246	218	16	11	1	0	100.0	88.6	6.5	4.5	0.4	0.0

Table 50. Arrests, Nonmetropolitan Counties, Distribution by Race, 2015—Continued

(Number, percent; 2,054 agencies; 2015 estimated population 21,302,367.)

Offense charged	Arrests 18 and over						Percent distribution[1]					
	Total	White	Black	American Indian or Alaskan Native	Asian	Native Hawaiian or Other Pacific Islander	Total	White	Black	American Indian or Alaskan Native	Asian	Native Hawaiian or Other Pacific Islander
Total	637,694	535,520	81,240	16,818	3,910	206	100.0	84.0	12.7	2.6	0.6	*
Violent crime[2]	19,359	15,704	2,803	782	58	12	100.0	81.1	14.5	4.0	0.3	0.1
Murder and nonnegligent manslaughter	575	412	148	10	4	1	100.0	71.7	25.7	1.7	0.7	0.2
Rape[3]	1,306	1,091	151	56	6	2	100.0	83.5	11.6	4.3	0.5	0.2
Robbery	1,199	775	394	29	1	0	100.0	64.6	32.9	2.4	0.1	0.0
Aggravated assault	16,279	13,426	2,110	687	47	9	100.0	82.5	13.0	4.2	0.3	0.1
Property crime[2]	40,040	34,597	4,510	811	116	6	100.0	86.4	11.3	2.0	0.3	*
Burglary	11,177	9,598	1,345	218	16	0	100.0	85.9	12.0	2.0	0.1	0.0
Larceny-theft	25,090	21,729	2,828	443	84	6	100.0	86.6	11.3	1.8	0.3	*
Motor vehicle theft	3,306	2,871	289	131	15	0	100.0	86.8	8.7	4.0	0.5	0.0
Arson	467	399	48	19	1	0	100.0	85.4	10.3	4.1	0.2	0.0
Other assaults	50,995	43,314	5,907	1,632	122	20	100.0	84.9	11.6	3.2	0.2	*
Forgery and counterfeiting	2,457	2,004	405	35	11	2	100.0	81.6	16.5	1.4	0.4	0.1
Fraud	9,407	7,834	1,420	116	28	9	100.0	83.3	15.1	1.2	0.3	0.1
Embezzlement	519	460	53	5	1	0	100.0	88.6	10.2	1.0	0.2	0.0
Stolen property; buying, receiving, possessing	3,846	3,108	632	96	10	0	100.0	80.8	16.4	2.5	0.3	0.0
Vandalism	6,849	5,812	782	231	22	2	100.0	84.9	11.4	3.4	0.3	*
Weapons; carrying, possessing, etc.	6,488	5,070	1,236	148	33	1	100.0	78.1	19.1	2.3	0.5	*
Prostitution and commercialized vice	202	160	28	4	10	0	100.0	79.2	13.9	2.0	5.0	0.0
Sex offenses (except forcible rape and prostitution)	2,695	2,357	277	49	11	1	100.0	87.5	10.3	1.8	0.4	*
Drug abuse violations	94,224	77,531	14,386	1,743	537	27	100.0	82.3	15.3	1.8	0.6	*
Gambling	151	101	23	6	14	7	100.0	66.9	15.2	4.0	9.3	4.6
Offenses against the family and children	8,737	7,213	1,357	136	22	9	100.0	82.6	15.5	1.6	0.3	0.1
Driving under the influence	147,632	125,014	16,615	4,021	1,944	38	100.0	84.7	11.3	2.7	1.3	*
Liquor laws	11,757	10,616	646	409	86	0	100.0	90.3	5.5	3.5	0.7	0.0
Drunkenness	13,190	11,800	834	509	37	10	100.0	89.5	6.3	3.9	0.3	0.1
Disorderly conduct	14,000	11,540	1,625	768	63	4	100.0	82.4	11.6	5.5	0.5	*
Vagrancy	314	245	65	3	1	0	100.0	78.0	20.7	1.0	0.3	0.0
All other offenses (except traffic)	204,747	170,992	27,601	5,313	784	57	100.0	83.5	13.5	2.6	0.4	*
Suspicion	85	48	35	1	0	1	100.0	56.5	41.2	1.2	0.0	1.2
Curfew and loitering law violations	NA	NA	NA	NA	NA	NA	NA	NA	NA	NA	NA	NA

NA = Not available.
* = Less than one-tenth of one percent.   1 Because of rounding, the percentages may not sum to 100.   2 Violent crimes are offenses of murder and nonnegligent manslaughter, rape, robbery, and aggravated assault. Property crimes are offenses of burglary, larceny-theft, motor vehicle theft, and arson.   3 The rape figures in this table are an aggregate total of the data submitted using both the revised and legacy Uniform Crime Reporting definitions.

Table 51. Arrests, Nonmetropolitan Counties, Distribution by Ethnicity, 2015

(Number, percent; 2,054 agencies; 2015 estimated population 21,302,367.)

Offense charged	Total arrests			Percent distribution[1]			Arrests under 18		
	Total[2]	Hispanic or Latino	Not Hispanic or Latino	Total[2]	Hispanic or Latino	Not Hispanic or Latino	Total[2]	Hispanic or Latino	Not Hispanic or Latino
Total	475,512	38,430	437,082	100.0	8.1	91.9	22,245	3,121	19,124
Violent crime[3]	14,930	1,285	13,645	100.0	8.6	91.4	848	90	758
Murder and nonnegligent manslaughter	406	32	374	100.0	7.9	92.1	13	2	11
Rape[4]	1,021	109	912	100.0	10.7	89.3	143	8	135
Robbery	928	59	869	100.0	6.4	93.6	74	3	71
Aggravated assault	12,575	1,085	11,490	100.0	8.6	91.4	618	77	541
Property crime[3]	33,811	1,928	31,883	100.0	5.7	94.3	2,946	228	2,718
Burglary	9,537	538	8,999	100.0	5.6	94.4	1,012	83	929
Larceny-theft	21,058	1,132	19,926	100.0	5.4	94.6	1,508	100	1,408
Motor vehicle theft	2,804	235	2,569	100.0	8.4	91.6	354	43	311
Arson	412	23	389	100.0	5.6	94.4	72	2	70
Other assaults	42,692	2,654	40,038	100.0	6.2	93.8	3,506	241	3,265
Forgery and counterfeiting	1,831	141	1,690	100.0	7.7	92.3	30	2	28
Fraud	6,827	360	6,467	100.0	5.3	94.7	75	7	68
Embezzlement	384	11	373	100.0	2.9	97.1	8	0	8
Stolen property; buying, receiving, possessing	3,111	168	2,943	100.0	5.4	94.6	203	21	182
Vandalism	6,886	376	6,510	100.0	5.5	94.5	1,293	106	1,187
Weapons; carrying, possessing, etc.	5,119	385	4,734	100.0	7.5	92.5	247	19	228
Prostitution and commercialized vice	169	15	154	100.0	8.9	91.1	2	0	2
Sex offenses (except forcible rape and prostitution)	2,256	216	2,040	100.0	9.6	90.4	337	23	314
Drug abuse violations	68,086	6,881	61,205	100.0	10.1	89.9	3,686	1,481	2,205
Gambling	133	15	118	100.0	11.3	88.7	1	0	1
Offenses against the family and children	6,415	450	5,965	100.0	7.0	93.0	111	7	104
Driving under the influence	90,599	7,052	83,547	100.0	7.8	92.2	574	57	517
Liquor laws	10,581	981	9,600	100.0	9.3	90.7	2,372	202	2,170
Drunkenness	12,291	1,584	10,707	100.0	12.9	87.1	156	26	130
Disorderly conduct	10,517	661	9,856	100.0	6.3	93.7	1,394	94	1,300
Vagrancy	132	36	96	100.0	27.3	72.7	6	3	3
All other offenses (except traffic)	158,443	13,207	145,236	100.0	8.3	91.7	4,229	498	3,731
Suspicion	78	8	70	100.0	10.3	89.7	0	0	0
Curfew and loitering law violations	221	16	205	100.0	7.2	92.8	221	16	205

Table 51. Arrests, Nonmetropolitan Counties, Distribution by Ethnicity, 2015—Continued

(Number, percent; 2,054 agencies; 2015 estimated population 21,302,367.)

Offense charged	Percent distribution[1]			Arrests 18 and over			Percent distribution[1]		
	Total[2]	Hispanic or Latino	Not Hispanic or Latino	Total[2]	Hispanic or Latino	Not Hispanic or Latino	Total[2]	Hispanic or Latino	Not Hispanic or Latino
Total	100.0	14.0	86.0	453,267	35,309	417,958	100.0	7.8	92.2
Violent crime[3]	100.0	10.6	89.4	14,082	1,195	12,887	100.0	8.5	91.5
Murder and nonnegligent manslaughter	100.0	15.4	84.6	393	30	363	100.0	7.6	92.4
Rape[4]	100.0	5.6	94.4	878	101	777	100.0	11.5	88.5
Robbery	100.0	4.1	95.9	854	56	798	100.0	6.6	93.4
Aggravated assault	100.0	12.5	87.5	11,957	1,008	10,949	100.0	8.4	91.6
Property crime[3]	100.0	7.7	92.3	30,865	1,700	29,165	100.0	5.5	94.5
Burglary	100.0	8.2	91.8	8,525	455	8,070	100.0	5.3	94.7
Larceny-theft	100.0	6.6	93.4	19,550	1,032	18,518	100.0	5.3	94.7
Motor vehicle theft	100.0	12.1	87.9	2,450	192	2,258	100.0	7.8	92.2
Arson	100.0	2.8	97.2	340	21	319	100.0	6.2	93.8
Other assaults	100.0	6.9	93.1	39,186	2,413	36,773	100.0	6.2	93.8
Forgery and counterfeiting	100.0	6.7	93.3	1,801	139	1,662	100.0	7.7	92.3
Fraud	100.0	9.3	90.7	6,752	353	6,399	100.0	5.2	94.8
Embezzlement	100.0	0.0	100.0	376	11	365	100.0	2.9	97.1
Stolen property; buying, receiving, possessing	100.0	10.3	89.7	2,908	147	2,761	100.0	5.1	94.9
Vandalism	100.0	8.2	91.8	5,593	270	5,323	100.0	4.8	95.2
Weapons; carrying, possessing, etc.	100.0	7.7	92.3	4,872	366	4,506	100.0	7.5	92.5
Prostitution and commercialized vice	100.0	0.0	100.0	167	15	152	100.0	9.0	91.0
Sex offenses (except forcible rape and prostitution)	100.0	6.8	93.2	1,919	193	1,726	100.0	10.1	89.9
Drug abuse violations	100.0	40.2	59.8	64,400	5,400	59,000	100.0	8.4	91.6
Gambling	100.0	0.0	100.0	132	15	117	100.0	11.4	88.6
Offenses against the family and children	100.0	6.3	93.7	6,304	443	5,861	100.0	7.0	93.0
Driving under the influence	100.0	9.9	90.1	90,025	6,995	83,030	100.0	7.8	92.2
Liquor laws	100.0	8.5	91.5	8,209	779	7,430	100.0	9.5	90.5
Drunkenness	100.0	16.7	83.3	12,135	1,558	10,577	100.0	12.8	87.2
Disorderly conduct	100.0	6.7	93.3	9,123	567	8,556	100.0	6.2	93.8
Vagrancy	100.0	50.0	50.0	126	33	93	100.0	26.2	73.8
All other offenses (except traffic)	100.0	11.8	88.2	154,214	12,709	141,505	100.0	8.2	91.8
Suspicion				78	8	70	100.0	10.3	89.7
Curfew and loitering law violations	100.0	7.2	92.8	NA	NA	NA	NA	NA	NA

NA = Not available.

1 Because of rounding, the percentages may not sum to 100.   2 The ethnicity totals are representative of those agencies that provided ethnicity breakdowns. Not all agencies provide ethnicity data; therefore, the race and ethnicity totals will not be equal.   3 Violent crimes are offenses of murder and nonnegligent manslaughter, rape, robbery, and aggravated assault. Property crimes are offenses of burglary, larceny-theft, motor vehicle theft, and arson.   4 The rape figures in this table are an aggregate total of the data submitted using both the revised and legacy Uniform Crime Reporting definitions.

Table 52. Arrest Trends, Suburban Areas,[1] 2014–2015

(Number, percent change; 6,241 agencies; 2015 estimated population 99,661,743; 2015 estimated population 99,579,617.)

	Number of persons arrested								
	Total, all ages			Under 18 years of age			18 years of age and over		
Offense charged	2014	2015	Percent change	2014	2015	Percent change	2014	2015	Percent change
Total[2]	3,149,177	3,038,957	-3.5	272,159	251,500	-7.6	2,877,018	2,787,457	-3.1
Violent crime[3]	116,281	117,794	+1.3	12,399	12,131	-2.2	103,882	105,663	+1.7
Murder and nonnegligent manslaughter	2,155	2,261	+4.9	153	122	-20.3	2,002	2,139	+6.8
Rape[4]	5,414	5,897	+8.9	904	1,019	+12.7	4,510	4,878	+8.2
Robbery	18,501	18,894	+2.1	3,330	3,306	-0.7	15,171	15,588	+2.7
Aggravated assault	90,211	90,742	+0.6	8,012	7,684	-4.1	82,199	83,058	+1.0
Property crime[3]	413,008	391,914	-5.1	56,216	51,314	-8.7	356,792	340,600	-4.5
Burglary	62,899	56,311	-10.5	9,507	8,636	-9.2	53,392	47,675	-10.7
Larceny-theft	330,929	314,685	-4.9	43,257	39,041	-9.7	287,672	275,644	-4.2
Motor vehicle theft	16,602	18,657	+12.4	2,469	2,825	+14.4	14,133	15,832	+12.0
Arson	2,578	2,261	-12.3	983	812	-17.4	1,595	1,449	-9.2
Other assaults	285,590	282,746	-1.0	38,970	38,029	-2.4	246,620	244,717	-0.8
Forgery and counterfeiting	17,013	16,715	-1.8	409	346	-15.4	16,604	16,369	-1.4
Fraud	43,970	41,162	-6.4	1,250	1,234	-1.3	42,720	39,928	-6.5
Embezzlement	4,560	4,376	-4.0	107	156	+45.8	4,453	4,220	-5.2
Stolen property; buying, receiving, possessing	26,638	25,168	-5.5	2,714	2,559	-5.7	23,924	22,609	-5.5
Vandalism	53,126	51,721	-2.6	13,137	12,377	-5.8	39,989	39,344	-1.6
Weapons; carrying, possessing, etc.	33,028	34,833	+5.5	5,084	4,849	-4.6	27,944	29,984	+7.3
Prostitution and commercialized vice	5,092	4,558	-10.5	101	70	-30.7	4,991	4,488	-10.1
Sex offenses (except forcible rape and prostitution)	15,457	14,836	-4.0	2,824	2,696	-4.5	12,633	12,140	-3.9
Drug abuse violations	452,480	438,339	-3.1	35,551	31,559	-11.2	416,929	406,780	-2.4
Gambling	925	915	-1.1	78	71	-9.0	847	844	-0.4
Offenses against the family and children	35,401	34,644	-2.1	889	927	+4.3	34,512	33,717	-2.3
Driving under the influence	367,384	348,777	-5.1	2,148	1,991	-7.3	365,236	346,786	-5.1
Liquor laws	95,394	78,864	-17.3	18,294	14,640	-20.0	77,100	64,224	-16.7
Drunkenness	102,713	94,631	-7.9	1,889	1,638	-13.3	100,824	92,993	-7.8
Disorderly conduct	116,515	108,372	-7.0	22,665	21,171	-6.6	93,850	87,201	-7.1
Vagrancy	4,345	4,534	+4.3	252	256	+1.6	4,093	4,278	+4.5
All other offenses (except traffic)	953,284	937,069	-1.7	50,209	46,497	-7.4	903,075	890,572	-1.4
Suspicion	341	247	-27.6	46	49	+6.5	295	198	-32.9
Curfew and loitering law violations	6,973	6,989	+0.2	6,973	6,989	+0.2	NA	NA	NA

NA = Not available.
1 Suburban areas include law enforcement agencies in cities with less than 50,000 inhabitants and county law enforcement agencies that are within a Metropolitan Statistical Area. Suburban areas exclude all metropolitan agencies associated with a principal city.   2 Does not include suspicion.   3 Violent crimes are offenses of murder and nonnegligent manslaughter, rape, robbery, and aggravated assault. Property crimes are offenses of burglary, larceny-theft, motor vehicle theft, and arson.   4 The rape figures in this table are aggregate totals of the data submitted based on both the legacy and revised Uniform Crime Reporting definitions.

Table 53. Arrests, Suburban Areas,[1] Distribution by Age, 2015

(Number, percent; 7,022 agencies; 2015 estimated population 111,227,944.)

Offense charged	Total, all ages	Ages under 15	Ages under 18	Ages 18 and over	Under 10	10–12	13–14	15	16	17	18	19	20
Total	3,484,757	77,999	288,994	3,195,763	2,277	16,897	58,825	53,287	70,265	87,443	124,472	133,481	131,265
Total percent distribution[2]	100.0	2.2	8.3	91.7	0.1	0.5	1.7	1.5	2.0	2.5	3.6	3.8	3.8
Violent crime[3]	133,451	3,964	13,793	119,658	117	927	2,920	2,619	3,410	3,800	4,726	4,711	4,671
Violent crime percent distribution[2]	100.0	3.0	10.3	89.7	0.1	0.7	2.2	2.0	2.6	2.8	3.5	3.5	3.5
Murder and nonnegligent manslaughter	2,713	17	153	2,560	0	2	15	19	43	74	138	146	149
Rape[4]	6,639	441	1,128	5,511	9	129	303	207	219	261	340	324	281
Robbery	21,909	667	3,879	18,030	7	68	592	785	1,131	1,296	1,613	1,393	1,200
Aggravated assault	102,190	2,839	8,633	93,557	101	728	2,010	1,608	2,017	2,169	2,635	2,848	3,041
Property crime[3]	458,610	16,241	60,516	398,094	344	3,330	12,567	11,701	15,108	17,466	20,987	19,047	17,263
Property crime percent distribution[2]	100.0	3.5	13.2	86.8	0.1	0.7	2.7	2.6	3.3	3.8	4.6	4.2	3.8
Burglary	63,491	2,898	9,781	53,710	85	576	2,237	1,993	2,361	2,529	3,254	3,050	2,574
Larceny-theft	371,823	12,124	46,598	325,225	210	2,478	9,436	8,789	11,704	13,981	16,699	15,131	13,802
Motor vehicle theft	20,720	685	3,209	17,511	9	66	610	741	923	860	938	806	816
Arson	2,576	534	928	1,648	40	210	284	178	120	96	96	60	71
Other assaults	327,735	16,320	43,261	284,474	535	4,335	11,450	8,409	9,329	9,203	8,117	8,272	8,808
Forgery and counterfeiting	19,346	31	374	18,972	0	4	27	34	97	212	531	721	818
Fraud	47,639	281	1,425	46,214	6	41	234	253	339	552	1,033	1,329	1,531
Embezzlement	5,050	14	174	4,876	0	4	10	6	52	102	222	285	285
Stolen property; buying, receiving, possessing	28,868	629	2,999	25,869	9	99	521	632	800	938	1,269	1,213	1,136
Vandalism	59,966	5,207	14,004	45,962	223	1,372	3,612	2,566	2,979	3,252	3,000	2,662	2,303
Weapons; carrying, possessing, etc.	39,175	1,996	5,433	33,742	95	582	1,319	913	1,153	1,371	1,667	1,708	1,590
Prostitution and commercialized vice	5,413	15	83	5,330	0	4	11	15	13	40	109	150	197
Sex offenses (except forcible rape and prostitution)	16,661	1,437	3,027	13,634	70	347	1,020	551	505	534	572	542	513
Drug abuse violations	488,748	5,274	35,134	453,614	38	705	4,531	5,322	9,079	15,459	27,335	28,540	26,048
Gambling	982	10	76	906	0	4	6	15	24	27	28	26	38
Offenses against the family and children	37,718	477	1,248	36,470	110	96	271	205	241	325	370	413	503
Driving under the influence	387,181	47	2,236	384,945	11	1	35	79	478	1,632	4,802	7,398	9,249
Liquor laws	90,670	1,450	16,327	74,343	5	88	1,357	2,341	4,604	7,932	16,600	16,900	13,035
Drunkenness	109,959	209	1,760	108,199	6	16	187	224	422	905	2,501	2,987	2,957
Disorderly conduct	127,083	9,164	24,880	102,203	241	2,253	6,670	5,262	5,377	5,077	4,744	4,225	4,115
Vagrancy	5,324	88	270	5,054	4	24	60	50	61	71	180	159	143
All other offenses (except traffic)	1,086,779	13,015	53,802	1,032,977	443	2,374	10,198	10,044	13,745	16,998	25,652	32,174	36,045
Suspicion	277	9	50	227	0	6	3	8	17	16	27	19	17
Curfew and loitering law violations	8,122	2,121	8,122	NA	20	285	1,816	2,038	2,432	1,531	NA	NA	NA

Table 53. Arrests, Suburban Areas,[1] Distribution by Age, 2015—Continued

(Number, percent; 7,022 agencies; 2015 estimated population 111,227,944.)

Offense charged	21	22	23	24	25–29	30–34	35–39	40–44	45–49	50–54	55–59	60–64	65 and over
Total	132,107	133,528	134,944	133,971	583,435	471,805	352,833	259,831	223,069	181,691	110,728	51,435	37,168
Total percent distribution[2]	3.8	3.8	3.9	3.8	16.7	13.5	10.1	7.5	6.4	5.2	3.2	1.5	1.1
Violent crime[3]	5,080	4,971	4,966	4,906	21,440	17,650	13,447	9,972	8,590	6,714	4,127	1,924	1,763
Violent crime percent distribution[2]	3.8	3.7	3.7	3.7	16.1	13.2	10.1	7.5	6.4	5.0	3.1	1.4	1.3
Murder and nonnegligent manslaughter	139	138	131	134	452	347	242	140	125	114	78	38	49
Rape[4]	251	235	165	204	745	755	574	500	371	328	189	114	135
Robbery	1,203	995	961	877	3,434	2,301	1,443	921	792	506	252	87	52
Aggravated assault	3,487	3,603	3,709	3,691	16,809	14,247	11,188	8,411	7,302	5,766	3,608	1,685	1,527
Property crime[3]	16,788	16,390	16,677	16,145	73,808	59,701	42,754	30,234	26,523	20,586	11,917	5,392	3,882
Property crime percent distribution[2]	3.7	3.6	3.6	3.5	16.1	13.0	9.3	6.6	5.8	4.5	2.6	1.2	0.8
Burglary	2,622	2,434	2,445	2,267	10,543	8,368	5,726	3,402	3,090	2,194	1,077	441	223
Larceny-theft	13,327	13,106	13,404	13,064	59,452	48,195	34,818	25,371	22,333	17,643	10,485	4,820	3,575
Motor vehicle theft	776	776	773	763	3,565	2,889	2,042	1,343	976	621	281	90	56
Arson	63	74	55	51	248	249	168	118	124	128	74	41	28
Other assaults	10,124	10,703	10,852	10,908	49,468	42,832	34,550	27,105	23,145	18,767	11,121	5,212	4,490
Forgery and counterfeiting	656	753	781	866	3,768	3,109	2,307	1,619	1,302	953	485	195	108
Fraud	1,464	1,608	1,640	1,739	8,633	7,347	6,029	4,573	3,701	2,673	1,614	711	589
Embezzlement	256	235	230	193	857	654	484	393	327	233	128	57	37
Stolen property; buying, receiving, possessing	1,179	1,133	1,182	1,119	5,266	4,213	2,941	1,873	1,470	996	525	222	132
Vandalism	2,334	2,321	2,216	2,008	8,266	6,266	4,505	3,082	2,604	2,152	1,218	584	441
Weapons; carrying, possessing, etc.	1,732	1,707	1,651	1,698	6,530	4,810	3,303	2,282	1,780	1,408	932	498	446
Prostitution and commercialized vice	223	228	241	228	1,019	781	607	476	377	327	177	122	68
Sex offenses (except forcible rape and prostitution)	501	453	447	400	1,753	1,661	1,477	1,180	1,105	1,081	731	513	705
Drug abuse violations	24,349	23,694	22,848	21,954	87,004	64,532	43,806	28,307	22,876	17,331	9,619	3,796	1,575
Gambling	9	23	18	15	100	120	92	105	106	79	83	41	23
Offenses against the family and children	667	819	914	1,114	6,480	7,054	6,408	4,569	3,286	2,198	1,035	405	235
Driving under the influence	14,926	16,197	17,008	17,179	71,142	54,793	41,734	34,161	31,176	28,160	19,378	10,081	7,561
Liquor laws	2,048	1,472	1,247	1,135	4,336	3,677	2,924	2,540	2,580	2,560	1,828	868	593
Drunkenness	4,468	4,038	3,855	3,674	16,111	14,063	11,356	9,723	10,322	10,492	6,838	3,237	1,577
Disorderly conduct	5,036	4,663	4,327	4,119	16,729	13,104	10,217	8,215	7,680	6,779	4,402	2,097	1,751
Vagrancy	143	167	153	170	804	644	477	405	475	526	333	193	82
All other offenses (except traffic)	40,113	41,938	43,683	44,394	199,889	164,770	123,395	89,003	73,634	57,664	34,233	15,286	11,104
Suspicion	11	15	8	7	32	24	20	14	10	12	4	1	6
Curfew and loitering law violations	NA	NA	NA	NA	NA	NA	NA	NA	NA	NA	NA	NA	NA

NA = Not available.
1 Suburban areas include law enforcement agencies in cities with less than 50,000 inhabitants and county law enforcement agencies that are within a Metropolitan Statistical Area Suburban areas exclude all metropolitan agencies associated with a principal city.   2 Because of rounding, the percentages may not sum to 100.   3 Violent crimes are offenses of murder and nonnegligent manslaughter, rape, robbery, and aggravated assault. Property crimes are offenses of burglary, larceny-theft, motor vehicle theft, and arson.   4 The rape figures in this table are an aggregate total of the data submitted using both the revised and legacy Uniform Crime Reporting definitions.

Table 54. Arrests, Suburban Areas,[1] Persons Under 15, 18, 21, and 25 Years of Age, 2015

(Number, percent; 7,022 agencies; 2015 estimated population 111,227,944.)

Offense charged	Total, all ages	Number of persons arrested				Percent of total all ages			
		Under 15	Under 18	Under 21	Under 25	Under 15	Under 18	Under 21	Under 25
Total	3,484,757	77,999	288,994	678,212	1,212,762	2.2	8.3	19.5	34.8
Violent crime[2]	133,451	3,964	13,793	27,901	47,824	3.0	10.3	20.9	35.8
Murder and nonnegligent manslaughter	2,713	17	153	586	1,128	0.6	5.6	21.6	41.6
Rape[3]	6,639	441	1,128	2,073	2,928	6.6	17.0	31.2	44.1
Robbery	21,909	667	3,879	8,085	12,121	3.0	17.7	36.9	55.3
Aggravated assault	102,190	2,839	8,633	17,157	31,647	2.8	8.4	16.8	31.0
Property crime[2]	458,610	16,241	60,516	117,813	183,813	3.5	13.2	25.7	40.1
Burglary	63,491	2,898	9,781	18,659	28,427	4.6	15.4	29.4	44.8
Larceny-theft	371,823	12,124	46,598	92,230	145,131	3.3	12.5	24.8	39.0
Motor vehicle theft	20,720	685	3,209	5,769	8,857	3.3	15.5	27.8	42.7
Arson	2,576	534	928	1,155	1,398	20.7	36.0	44.8	54.3
Other assaults	327,735	16,320	43,261	68,458	111,045	5.0	13.2	20.9	33.9
Forgery and counterfeiting	19,346	31	374	2,444	5,500	0.2	1.9	12.6	28.4
Fraud	47,639	281	1,425	5,318	11,769	0.6	3.0	11.2	24.7
Embezzlement	5,050	14	174	966	1,880	0.3	3.4	19.1	37.2
Stolen property; buying, receiving, possessing	28,868	629	2,999	6,617	11,230	2.2	10.4	22.9	38.9
Vandalism	59,966	5,207	14,004	21,969	30,848	8.7	23.4	36.6	51.4
Weapons; carrying, possessing, etc.	39,175	1,996	5,433	10,398	17,186	5.1	13.9	26.5	43.9
Prostitution and commercialized vice	5,413	15	83	539	1,459	0.3	1.5	10.0	27.0
Sex offenses (except forcible rape and prostitution)	16,661	1,437	3,027	4,654	6,455	8.6	18.2	27.9	38.7
Drug abuse violations	488,748	5,274	35,134	117,057	209,902	1.1	7.2	24.0	42.9
Gambling	982	10	76	168	233	1.0	7.7	17.1	23.7
Offenses against the family and children	37,718	477	1,248	2,534	6,048	1.3	3.3	6.7	16.0
Driving under the influence	387,181	47	2,236	23,685	88,995	*	0.6	6.1	23.0
Liquor laws	90,670	1,450	16,327	62,862	68,764	1.6	18.0	69.3	75.8
Drunkenness	109,959	209	1,760	10,205	26,240	0.2	1.6	9.3	23.9
Disorderly conduct	127,083	9,164	24,880	37,964	56,109	7.2	19.6	29.9	44.2
Vagrancy	5,324	88	270	752	1,385	1.7	5.1	14.1	26.0
All other offenses (except traffic)	1,086,779	13,015	53,802	147,673	317,801	1.2	5.0	13.6	29.2
Suspicion	277	9	50	113	154	3.2	18.1	40.8	55.6
Curfew and loitering law violations	8,122	2,121	8,122	8,122	8,122	26.1	100.0	100.0	100.0

* = Less than one-tenth of one percent.
1 Suburban areas include law enforcement agencies in cities with less than 50,000 inhabitants and county law enforcement agencies that are within a Metropolitan Statistical Area. Suburban areas exclude all metropolitan agencies associated with a principal city.   2 Violent crimes are offenses of murder and nonnegligent manslaughter, rape, robbery, and aggravated assault. Property crimes are offenses of burglary, larceny-theft, motor vehicle theft, and arson.   3 The rape figures in this table are an aggregate total of the data submitted using both the revised and legacy Uniform Crime Reporting definitions.

Table 55. Arrests, Suburban Areas,[1] Distribution by Sex, 2015

(Number, percent; 7,022 agencies; 2015 estimated population 111,227,944.)

Offense charged	Number of persons arrested			Percent male	Percent female	Percent distribution[2]		
	Total	Male	Female			Total	Male	Female
Total	3,484,757	2,528,170	956,587	72.5	27.5	100.0	100.0	100.0
Violent crime[3]	133,451	106,843	26,608	80.1	19.9	3.8	4.2	2.8
Murder and nonnegligent manslaughter	2,713	2,362	351	87.1	12.9	0.1	0.1	*
Rape[4]	6,639	6,473	166	97.5	2.5	0.2	0.3	*
Robbery	21,909	18,769	3,140	85.7	14.3	0.6	0.7	0.3
Aggravated assault	102,190	79,239	22,951	77.5	22.5	2.9	3.1	2.4
Property crime[3]	458,610	282,607	176,003	61.6	38.4	13.2	11.2	18.4
Burglary	63,491	52,431	11,060	82.6	17.4	1.8	2.1	1.2
Larceny-theft	371,823	211,887	159,936	57.0	43.0	10.7	8.4	16.7
Motor vehicle theft	20,720	16,187	4,533	78.1	21.9	0.6	0.6	0.5
Arson	2,576	2,102	474	81.6	18.4	0.1	0.1	*
Other assaults	327,735	234,291	93,444	71.5	28.5	9.4	9.3	9.8
Forgery and counterfeiting	19,346	12,682	6,664	65.6	34.4	0.6	0.5	0.7
Fraud	47,639	29,276	18,363	61.5	38.5	1.4	1.2	1.9
Embezzlement	5,050	2,548	2,502	50.5	49.5	0.1	0.1	0.3
Stolen property; buying, receiving, possessing	28,868	22,542	6,326	78.1	21.9	0.8	0.9	0.7
Vandalism	59,966	47,643	12,323	79.5	20.5	1.7	1.9	1.3
Weapons; carrying, possessing, etc.	39,175	35,278	3,897	90.1	9.9	1.1	1.4	0.4
Prostitution and commercialized vice	5,413	2,254	3,159	41.6	58.4	0.2	0.1	0.3
Sex offenses (except forcible rape and prostitution)	16,661	15,368	1,293	92.2	7.8	0.5	0.6	0.1
Drug abuse violations	488,748	374,163	114,585	76.6	23.4	14.0	14.8	12.0
Gambling	982	625	357	63.6	36.4	*	*	*
Offenses against the family and children	37,718	28,244	9,474	74.9	25.1	1.1	1.1	1.0
Driving under the influence	387,181	287,842	99,339	74.3	25.7	11.1	11.4	10.4
Liquor laws	90,670	63,072	27,598	69.6	30.4	2.6	2.5	2.9
Drunkenness	109,959	87,390	22,569	79.5	20.5	3.2	3.5	2.4
Disorderly conduct	127,083	90,387	36,696	71.1	28.9	3.6	3.6	3.8
Vagrancy	5,324	4,133	1,191	77.6	22.4	0.2	0.2	0.1
All other offenses (except traffic)	1,086,779	795,304	291,475	73.2	26.8	31.2	31.5	30.5
Suspicion	277	227	50	81.9	18.1	*	*	*
Curfew and loitering law violations	8,122	5,451	2,671	67.1	32.9	0.2	0.2	0.3

* = Less than one-tenth of one percent.
1 Suburban areas include law enforcement agencies in cities with less than 50,000 inhabitants and county law enforcement agencies that are within a Metropolitan Statistical Area. Suburban areas exclude all metropolitan agencies associated with a principal city.   2 Because of rounding, the percentages may not sum to 100.   3 Violent crimes are offenses of murder and nonnegligent manslaughter, rape, robbery, and aggravated assault. Property crimes are offenses of burglary, larceny-theft, motor vehicle theft, and arson.   4 The rape figures in this table are an aggregate total of the data submitted using both the revised and legacy Uniform Crime Reporting definitions.

Table 56. Arrests, Suburban Areas,[1] Distribution by Race, 2015

(Number, percent; 7,014 agencies; 2015 estimated population 111,221,322.)

Offense charged	Total arrests						Percent distribution[2]					
	Total	White	Black	American Indian or Alaskan Native	Asian	Native Hawaiian or Other Pacific Islander	Total	White	Black	American Indian or Alaskan Native	Asian	Native Hawaiian or Other Pacific Islander
Total	3,463,539	2,530,862	854,028	35,162	37,867	5,620	100.0	73.1	24.7	1.0	1.1	0.2
Violent crime[3]	132,820	88,171	41,603	1,263	1,461	322	100.0	66.4	31.3	1.0	1.1	0.2
Murder and nonnegligent manslaughter	2,707	1,464	1,153	18	65	7	100.0	54.1	42.6	0.7	2.4	0.3
Rape[4]	6,590	4,887	1,552	56	82	13	100.0	74.2	23.6	0.8	1.2	0.2
Robbery	21,838	10,686	10,879	79	137	57	100.0	48.9	49.8	0.4	0.6	0.3
Aggravated assault	101,685	71,134	28,019	1,110	1,177	245	100.0	70.0	27.6	1.1	1.2	0.2
Property crime[3]	455,850	323,741	123,032	3,700	4,719	658	100.0	71.0	27.0	0.8	1.0	0.1
Burglary	63,254	46,334	15,795	348	643	134	100.0	73.3	25.0	0.6	1.0	0.2
Larceny-theft	369,377	259,904	102,050	3,157	3,854	412	100.0	70.4	27.6	0.9	1.0	0.1
Motor vehicle theft	20,653	15,470	4,711	180	188	104	100.0	74.9	22.8	0.9	0.9	0.5
Arson	2,566	2,033	476	15	34	8	100.0	79.2	18.6	0.6	1.3	0.3
Other assaults	326,033	232,588	86,806	3,033	3,179	427	100.0	71.3	26.6	0.9	1.0	0.1
Forgery and counterfeiting	19,225	12,131	6,752	76	254	12	100.0	63.1	35.1	0.4	1.3	0.1
Fraud	47,234	31,562	14,872	252	524	24	100.0	66.8	31.5	0.5	1.1	0.1
Embezzlement	5,026	3,120	1,817	21	67	1	100.0	62.1	36.2	0.4	1.3	*
Stolen property; buying, receiving, possessing	28,768	19,766	8,542	184	254	22	100.0	68.7	29.7	0.6	0.9	0.1
Vandalism	59,542	44,247	14,092	575	588	40	100.0	74.3	23.7	1.0	1.0	0.1
Weapons; carrying, possessing, etc.	39,020	25,418	12,931	213	388	70	100.0	65.1	33.1	0.5	1.0	0.2
Prostitution and commercialized vice	5,383	3,257	1,687	14	421	4	100.0	60.5	31.3	0.3	7.8	0.1
Sex offenses (except forcible rape and prostitution)	16,571	12,737	3,457	133	223	21	100.0	76.9	20.9	0.8	1.3	0.1
Drug abuse violations	486,020	357,875	119,531	2,960	4,953	701	100.0	73.6	24.6	0.6	1.0	0.1
Gambling	980	521	344	8	96	11	100.0	53.2	35.1	0.8	9.8	1.1
Offenses against the family and children	37,502	24,956	11,704	575	259	8	100.0	66.5	31.2	1.5	0.7	*
Driving under the influence	384,447	322,243	50,622	3,645	7,382	555	100.0	83.8	13.2	0.9	1.9	0.1
Liquor laws	89,580	74,748	10,988	2,405	1,327	112	100.0	83.4	12.3	2.7	1.5	0.1
Drunkenness	109,595	92,639	14,394	1,320	1,102	140	100.0	84.5	13.1	1.2	1.0	0.1
Disorderly conduct	126,236	86,549	36,800	1,778	1,013	96	100.0	68.6	29.2	1.4	0.8	0.1
Vagrancy	5,313	3,713	1,552	12	33	3	100.0	69.9	29.2	0.2	0.6	0.1
All other offenses (except traffic)	1,080,043	764,805	290,411	12,929	9,539	2,359	100.0	70.8	26.9	1.2	0.9	0.2
Suspicion	274	149	102	11	10	2	100.0	54.4	37.2	4.0	3.6	0.7
Curfew and loitering law violations	8,077	5,926	1,989	55	75	32	100.0	73.4	24.6	0.7	0.9	0.4

Table 56. Arrests, Suburban Areas,[1] Distribution by Race, 2015—Continued

(Number, percent; 7,014 agencies; 2015 estimated population 111,221,322.)

Offense charged	Arrests under 18						Percent distribution[2]					
	Total	White	Black	American Indian or Alaskan Native	Asian	Native Hawaiian or Other Pacific Islander	Total	White	Black	American Indian or Alaskan Native	Asian	Native Hawaiian or Other Pacific Islander
Total	286,685	193,565	87,451	2,501	2,709	459	100.0	67.5	30.5	0.9	0.9	0.2
Violent crime[3]	13,714	7,221	6,283	76	102	32	100.0	52.7	45.8	0.6	0.7	0.2
Murder and nonnegligent manslaughter	152	75	75	1	1	0	100.0	49.3	49.3	0.7	0.7	0.0
Rape[4]	1,113	804	285	12	10	2	100.0	72.2	25.6	1.1	0.9	0.2
Robbery	3,867	1,263	2,566	5	21	12	100.0	32.7	66.4	0.1	0.5	0.3
Aggravated assault	8,582	5,079	3,357	58	70	18	100.0	59.2	39.1	0.7	0.8	0.2
Property crime[3]	60,009	36,334	22,466	407	703	99	100.0	60.5	37.4	0.7	1.2	0.2
Burglary	9,730	5,941	3,618	55	97	19	100.0	61.1	37.2	0.6	1.0	0.2
Larceny-theft	46,171	27,659	17,539	331	571	71	100.0	59.9	38.0	0.7	1.2	0.2
Motor vehicle theft	3,187	2,013	1,122	17	29	6	100.0	63.2	35.2	0.5	0.9	0.2
Arson	921	721	187	4	6	3	100.0	78.3	20.3	0.4	0.7	0.3
Other assaults	42,986	26,433	15,848	330	309	66	100.0	61.5	36.9	0.8	0.7	0.2
Forgery and counterfeiting	371	240	124	3	3	1	100.0	64.7	33.4	0.8	0.8	0.3
Fraud	1,395	795	565	14	21	0	100.0	57.0	40.5	1.0	1.5	0.0
Embezzlement	173	102	68	2	1	0	100.0	59.0	39.3	1.2	0.6	0.0
Stolen property; buying, receiving, possessing	2,985	1,438	1,494	24	27	2	100.0	48.2	50.1	0.8	0.9	0.1
Vandalism	13,872	10,133	3,475	127	132	5	100.0	73.0	25.1	0.9	1.0	*
Weapons; carrying, possessing, etc.	5,413	3,471	1,844	31	59	8	100.0	64.1	34.1	0.6	1.1	0.1
Prostitution and commercialized vice	83	47	34	1	0	1	100.0	56.6	41.0	1.2	0.0	1.2
Sex offenses (except forcible rape and prostitution)	3,003	2,286	671	23	21	2	100.0	76.1	22.3	0.8	0.7	0.1
Drug abuse violations	34,851	27,715	6,322	351	380	83	100.0	79.5	18.1	1.0	1.1	0.2
Gambling	75	36	35	2	2	0	100.0	48.0	46.7	2.7	2.7	0.0
Offenses against the family and children	1,236	824	366	30	16	0	100.0	66.7	29.6	2.4	1.3	0.0
Driving under the influence	2,210	2,006	144	28	30	2	100.0	90.8	6.5	1.3	1.4	0.1
Liquor laws	16,152	14,525	1,124	272	200	31	100.0	89.9	7.0	1.7	1.2	0.2
Drunkenness	1,739	1,508	173	38	16	4	100.0	86.7	9.9	2.2	0.9	0.2
Disorderly conduct	24,720	14,110	10,249	153	184	24	100.0	57.1	41.5	0.6	0.7	0.1
Vagrancy	267	122	141	0	4	0	100.0	45.7	52.8	0.0	1.5	0.0
All other offenses (except traffic)	53,306	38,277	14,005	533	424	67	100.0	71.8	26.3	1.0	0.8	0.1
Suspicion	48	16	31	1	0	0	100.0	33.3	64.6	2.1	0.0	0.0
Curfew and loitering law violations	8,077	5,926	1,989	55	75	32	100.0	73.4	24.6	0.7	0.9	0.4

Table 56. Arrests, Suburban Areas,[1] Distribution by Race, 2015—Continued

(Number, percent; 7,014 agencies; 2015 estimated population 111,221,322.)

Offense charged	Arrests 18 and over						Percent distribution[2]					
	Total	White	Black	American Indian or Alaskan Native	Asian	Native Hawaiian or Other Pacific Islander	Total	White	Black	American Indian or Alaskan Native	Asian	Native Hawaiian or Other Pacific Islander
Total	3,176,854	2,337,297	766,577	32,661	35,158	5,161	100.0	73.6	24.1	1.0	1.1	0.2
Violent crime[3]	119,106	80,950	35,320	1,187	1,359	290	100.0	68.0	29.7	1.0	1.1	0.2
Murder and nonnegligent manslaughter	2,555	1,389	1,078	17	64	7	100.0	54.4	42.2	0.7	2.5	0.3
Rape[4]	5,477	4,083	1,267	44	72	11	100.0	74.5	23.1	0.8	1.3	0.2
Robbery	17,971	9,423	8,313	74	116	45	100.0	52.4	46.3	0.4	0.6	0.3
Aggravated assault	93,103	66,055	24,662	1,052	1,107	227	100.0	70.9	26.5	1.1	1.2	0.2
Property crime[3]	395,841	287,407	100,566	3,293	4,016	559	100.0	72.6	25.4	0.8	1.0	0.1
Burglary	53,524	40,393	12,177	293	546	115	100.0	75.5	22.8	0.5	1.0	0.2
Larceny-theft	323,206	232,245	84,511	2,826	3,283	341	100.0	71.9	26.1	0.9	1.0	0.1
Motor vehicle theft	17,466	13,457	3,589	163	159	98	100.0	77.0	20.5	0.9	0.9	0.6
Arson	1,645	1,312	289	11	28	5	100.0	79.8	17.6	0.7	1.7	0.3
Other assaults	283,047	206,155	70,958	2,703	2,870	361	100.0	72.8	25.1	1.0	1.0	0.1
Forgery and counterfeiting	18,854	11,891	6,628	73	251	11	100.0	63.1	35.2	0.4	1.3	0.1
Fraud	45,839	30,767	14,307	238	503	24	100.0	67.1	31.2	0.5	1.1	0.1
Embezzlement	4,853	3,018	1,749	19	66	1	100.0	62.2	36.0	0.4	1.4	*
Stolen property; buying, receiving, possessing	25,783	18,328	7,048	160	227	20	100.0	71.1	27.3	0.6	0.9	0.1
Vandalism	45,670	34,114	10,617	448	456	35	100.0	74.7	23.2	1.0	1.0	0.1
Weapons; carrying, possessing, etc.	33,607	21,947	11,087	182	329	62	100.0	65.3	33.0	0.5	1.0	0.2
Prostitution and commercialized vice	5,300	3,210	1,653	13	421	3	100.0	60.6	31.2	0.2	7.9	0.1
Sex offenses (except forcible rape and prostitution)	13,568	10,451	2,786	110	202	19	100.0	77.0	20.5	0.8	1.5	0.1
Drug abuse violations	451,169	330,160	113,209	2,609	4,573	618	100.0	73.2	25.1	0.6	1.0	0.1
Gambling	905	485	309	6	94	11	100.0	53.6	34.1	0.7	10.4	1.2
Offenses against the family and children	36,266	24,132	11,338	545	243	8	100.0	66.5	31.3	1.5	0.7	*
Driving under the influence	382,237	320,237	50,478	3,617	7,352	553	100.0	83.8	13.2	0.9	1.9	0.1
Liquor laws	73,428	60,223	9,864	2,133	1,127	81	100.0	82.0	13.4	2.9	1.5	0.1
Drunkenness	107,856	91,131	14,221	1,282	1,086	136	100.0	84.5	13.2	1.2	1.0	0.1
Disorderly conduct	101,516	72,439	26,551	1,625	829	72	100.0	71.4	26.2	1.6	0.8	0.1
Vagrancy	5,046	3,591	1,411	12	29	3	100.0	71.2	28.0	0.2	0.6	0.1
All other offenses (except traffic)	1,026,737	726,528	276,406	12,396	9,115	2,292	100.0	70.8	26.9	1.2	0.9	0.2
Suspicion	226	133	71	10	10	2	100.0	58.8	31.4	4.4	4.4	0.9
Curfew and loitering law violations	NA	NA	NA	NA	NA	NA	NA	NA	NA	NA	NA	NA

NA = Not available.
* = Less than one-tenth of one percent.
1 Suburban areas include law enforcement agencies in cities with less than 50,000 inhabitants and county law enforcement agencies that are within a Metropolitan Statistical Area. Suburban areas exclude all metropolitan agencies associated with a principal city.   2 Because of rounding, the percentages may not sum to 100.   3 Violent crimes are offenses of murder and nonnegligent manslaughter, rape, robbery, and aggravated assault. Property crimes are offenses of burglary, larceny-theft, motor vehicle theft, and arson.   4 The rape figures in this table are an aggregate total of the data submitted using both the revised and legacy Uniform Crime Reporting definitions.

Table 57. Arrests, Suburban Areas,[1] Distribution by Ethnicity, 2015

(Number, percent; 7,014 agencies; 2015 estimated population 111,221,322.)

Offense charged	Total arrests			Percent distribution[2]			Arrests under 18		
	Total[3]	Hispanic or Latino	Not Hispanic or Latino	Total[3]	Hispanic or Latino	Not Hispanic or Latino	Total[3]	Hispanic or Latino	Not Hispanic or Latino
Total	2,546,353	436,187	2,110,166	100.0	17.1	82.9	202,691	39,071	163,620
Violent crime[4]	100,315	22,338	77,977	100.0	22.3	77.7	9,966	2,115	7,851
Murder and nonnegligent manslaughter	1,862	450	1,412	100.0	24.2	75.8	100	40	60
Rape[5]	4,559	1,157	3,402	100.0	25.4	74.6	749	134	615
Robbery	16,113	3,069	13,044	100.0	19.0	81.0	2,794	581	2,213
Aggravated assault	77,781	17,662	60,119	100.0	22.7	77.3	6,323	1,360	4,963
Property crime[4]	321,808	42,943	278,865	100.0	13.3	86.7	40,634	7,263	33,371
Burglary	49,381	7,995	41,386	100.0	16.2	83.8	7,219	1,516	5,703
Larceny-theft	254,264	30,380	223,884	100.0	11.9	88.1	30,487	5,062	25,425
Motor vehicle theft	16,153	4,279	11,874	100.0	26.5	73.5	2,198	571	1,627
Arson	2,010	289	1,721	100.0	14.4	85.6	730	114	616
Other assaults	235,989	35,928	200,061	100.0	15.2	84.8	31,326	5,973	25,353
Forgery and counterfeiting	13,911	2,222	11,689	100.0	16.0	84.0	298	54	244
Fraud	33,682	3,306	30,376	100.0	9.8	90.2	897	124	773
Embezzlement	3,574	328	3,246	100.0	9.2	90.8	132	18	114
Stolen property; buying, receiving, possessing	20,103	3,829	16,274	100.0	19.0	81.0	1,976	419	1,557
Vandalism	45,359	6,833	38,526	100.0	15.1	84.9	10,851	1,840	9,011
Weapons; carrying, possessing, etc.	29,620	6,597	23,023	100.0	22.3	77.7	4,031	1,072	2,959
Prostitution and commercialized vice	3,939	627	3,312	100.0	15.9	84.1	56	9	47
Sex offenses (except forcible rape and prostitution)	11,948	2,753	9,195	100.0	23.0	77.0	2,003	382	1,621
Drug abuse violations	370,911	66,848	304,063	100.0	18.0	82.0	26,334	6,066	20,268
Gambling	743	117	626	100.0	15.7	84.3	59	16	43
Offenses against the family and children	26,740	3,228	23,512	100.0	12.1	87.9	657	104	553
Driving under the influence	307,024	70,992	236,032	100.0	23.1	76.9	1,693	335	1,358
Liquor laws	62,513	7,862	54,651	100.0	12.6	87.4	11,889	1,388	10,501
Drunkenness	91,688	21,519	70,169	100.0	23.5	76.5	1,555	594	961
Disorderly conduct	83,029	9,726	73,303	100.0	11.7	88.3	16,245	2,313	13,932
Vagrancy	3,709	542	3,167	100.0	14.6	85.4	121	34	87
All other offenses (except traffic)	774,282	126,396	647,886	100.0	16.3	83.7	36,683	7,722	28,961
Suspicion	217	27	190	100.0	12.4	87.6	36	4	32
Curfew and loitering law violations	5,249	1,226	4,023	100.0	23.4	76.6	5,249	1,226	4,023

Table 57. Arrests, Suburban Areas,[1] Distribution by Ethnicity, 2015—Continued

(Number, percent; 7,014 agencies; 2015 estimated population 111,221,322.)

Offense charged	Percent distribution[2]			Arrests 18 and over			Percent distribution[2]		
	Total[3]	Hispanic or Latino	Not Hispanic or Latino	Total[3]	Hispanic or Latino	Not Hispanic or Latino	Total[3]	Hispanic or Latino	Not Hispanic or Latino
Total	100.0	19.3	80.7	2,343,662	397,116	1,946,546	100.0	16.9	83.1
Violent crime[4]	100.0	21.2	78.8	90,349	20,223	70,126	100.0	22.4	77.6
Murder and nonnegligent manslaughter	100.0	40.0	60.0	1,762	410	1,352	100.0	23.3	76.7
Rape[5]	100.0	17.9	82.1	3,810	1,023	2,787	100.0	26.9	73.1
Robbery	100.0	20.8	79.2	13,319	2,488	10,831	100.0	18.7	81.3
Aggravated assault	100.0	21.5	78.5	71,458	16,302	55,156	100.0	22.8	77.2
Property crime[4]	100.0	17.9	82.1	281,174	35,680	245,494	100.0	12.7	87.3
Burglary	100.0	21.0	79.0	42,162	6,479	35,683	100.0	15.4	84.6
Larceny-theft	100.0	16.6	83.4	223,777	25,318	198,459	100.0	11.3	88.7
Motor vehicle theft	100.0	26.0	74.0	13,955	3,708	10,247	100.0	26.6	73.4
Arson	100.0	15.6	84.4	1,280	175	1,105	100.0	13.7	86.3
Other assaults	100.0	19.1	80.9	204,663	29,955	174,708	100.0	14.6	85.4
Forgery and counterfeiting	100.0	18.1	81.9	13,613	2,168	11,445	100.0	15.9	84.1
Fraud	100.0	13.8	86.2	32,785	3,182	29,603	100.0	9.7	90.3
Embezzlement	100.0	13.6	86.4	3,442	310	3,132	100.0	9.0	91.0
Stolen property; buying, receiving, possessing	100.0	21.2	78.8	18,127	3,410	14,717	100.0	18.8	81.2
Vandalism	100.0	17.0	83.0	34,508	4,993	29,515	100.0	14.5	85.5
Weapons; carrying, possessing, etc.	100.0	26.6	73.4	25,589	5,525	20,064	100.0	21.6	78.4
Prostitution and commercialized vice	100.0	16.1	83.9	3,883	618	3,265	100.0	15.9	84.1
Sex offenses (except forcible rape and prostitution)	100.0	19.1	80.9	9,945	2,371	7,574	100.0	23.8	76.2
Drug abuse violations	100.0	23.0	77.0	344,577	60,782	283,795	100.0	17.6	82.4
Gambling	100.0	27.1	72.9	684	101	583	100.0	14.8	85.2
Offenses against the family and children	100.0	15.8	84.2	26,083	3,124	22,959	100.0	12.0	88.0
Driving under the influence	100.0	19.8	80.2	305,331	70,657	234,674	100.0	23.1	76.9
Liquor laws	100.0	11.7	88.3	50,624	6,474	44,150	100.0	12.8	87.2
Drunkenness	100.0	38.2	61.8	90,133	20,925	69,208	100.0	23.2	76.8
Disorderly conduct	100.0	14.2	85.8	66,784	7,413	59,371	100.0	11.1	88.9
Vagrancy	100.0	28.1	71.9	3,588	508	3,080	100.0	14.2	85.8
All other offenses (except traffic)	100.0	21.1	78.9	737,599	118,674	618,925	100.0	16.1	83.9
Suspicion	100.0	11.1	88.9	181	23	158	100.0	12.7	87.3
Curfew and loitering law violations	100.0	23.4	76.6	NA	NA	NA	NA	NA	NA

NA = Not available.
1 Suburban areas include law enforcement agencies in cities with less than 50,000 inhabitants and county law enforcement agencies that are within a Metropolitan Statistical Area. Suburban areas exclude all metropolitan agencies associated with a principal city. 2 Because of rounding, the percentages may not sum to 100. 3 The ethnicity totals are representative of those agencies that provided ethnicity breakdowns. Not all agencies provide ethnicity data; therefore, the race and ethnicity totals will not be equal. 4 Violent crimes are offenses of murder and nonnegligent manslaughter, rape, robbery, and aggravated assault. Property crimes are offenses of burglary, larceny-theft, motor vehicle theft, and arson. 5 The rape figures in this table are an aggregate total of the data submitted using both the revised and legacy Uniform Crime Reporting definitions.

SECTION V

LAW ENFORCEMENT PERSONNEL

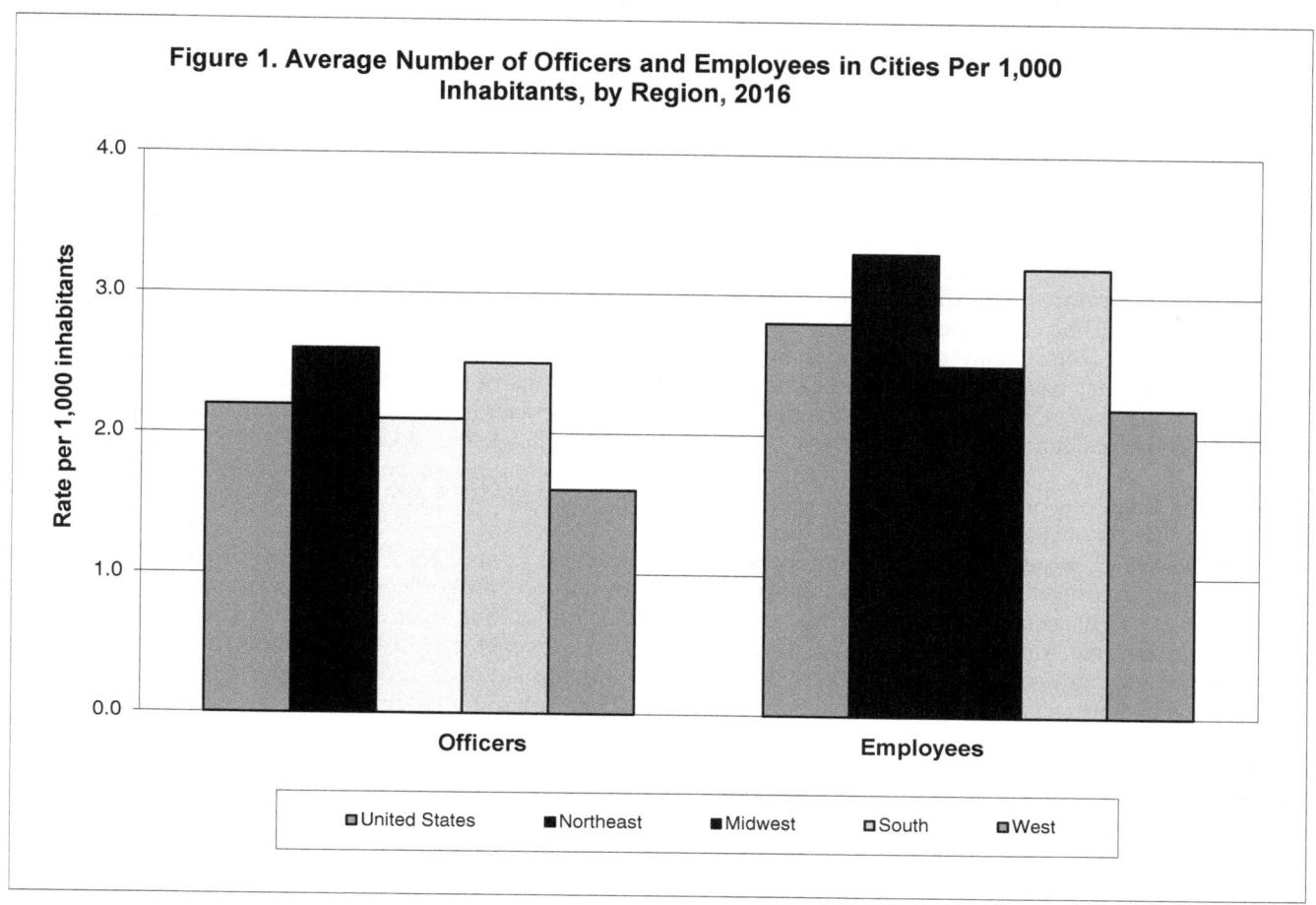

Figure 1. Average Number of Officers and Employees in Cities Per 1,000 Inhabitants, by Region, 2016

The Uniform Crime Reporting (UCR) program defines law enforcement officers as individuals who ordinarily carry a firearm and a badge, have full arrest powers, and are paid from government funds set aside specifically for sworn law enforcement representatives. Because of law enforcement's varied service requirements and functions, as well as the distinct demographic traits and characteristics of jurisdictions, readers should use caution when comparing staffing levels between agencies based on police employment data from the UCR program. In addition, the data presented here reflect existing staff levels and should not be interpreted as preferred officer strengths recommended by the Federal Bureau of Investigation (FBI). Also, readers should note that the totals given for sworn officers for any particular agency reflect both patrol officers on the street and officers assigned to various other duties, such as administrative and investigative positions and assignments to special teams.

Each year, law enforcement agencies across the United States report the total number of sworn law enforcement officers and civilians in their agencies as of October 31 to the UCR program. Civilian employees include personnel such as clerks, radio dispatchers, meter attendants, stenographers, jailers, correctional officers, and mechanics, (provided that they are full-time employees of the agency).

This section of *Crime in the United States* presents those data as the number and rate of law enforcement officers and civilian employees throughout the United States. In 2016, 652,936 sworn officers and 280,206 civilians provided law enforcement services to more than 273 million people nationwide. These law enforcement personnel were employed by 13,217 state, city, university/college, metropolitan/nonmetropolitan county, and other designated law enforcement agencies. Of the slightly less than 1 million law enforcement employees, 73.5 percent were male. (Table 60)

The data in this section are broken down by geographic region and division, population group, state, city, university/college, metropolitan/nonmetropolitan county, and other law enforcement agency groups. (Information about geographic regions and divisions and population groups can be found in Appendix III.) UCR program staff compute the rate of sworn officers and law enforcement employees by taking the number of employees (sworn officers only or in combination with civilians), dividing by the population for which the agency provides law enforcement service, and multiplying by 1,000.

The demographic traits and characteristics of a jurisdiction affect its requirements for law enforcement service. For instance, a village between two large cities may require more law enforcement than a community of the same size with no urban center nearby. A town with legal gambling may have different law enforcement needs than a town near a military base. A city largely made up of college students may have different law enforcement needs than a city whose residents are mainly retirees.

Similarly, the functions of law enforcement agencies are diverse. Employees of these agencies patrol local streets and major highways, protect citizens in the nation's smallest towns and largest cities, and conduct investigations on offenses at the local and state levels. State police in one area may enforce traffic laws on state highways and interstates; in another area, they may be responsible for investigating violent crimes. Sheriff's departments may collect tax monies, serve as the enforcement authority for local and state courts, administer jail facilities, or carry out some combination of these duties. This has an impact on an agency's staffing levels.

Because of the differing service requirements and functions, care should be taken when drawing comparisons between and among the staffing levels of law enforcement agencies. The data in this section are not intended as recommended or preferred officer strength; they should be used merely as guides. Adequate staffing levels can be determined only after careful study of the conditions that affect the service requirements in a particular jurisdiction.

Rate

The UCR program computes these rates by taking the number of employees, dividing by the population of the agency's jurisdiction, and multiplying by 1,000.

An examination of the 2016 law enforcement employee data by population group showed that the nation's cities had a collective rate of 2.8 law enforcement employees per 1,000 inhabitants. Cities with fewer than 10,000 inhabitants had the highest rate of law enforcement employees, with a rate of 4.8 per 1,000 inhabitants. Cities with 15,000 to 49,999 inhabitants, 50,000 to 99,999 inhabitants, and 100,000 to 249,999 inhabitants had the lowest rates of law enforcement employees (2.1 per 1,000 in population each). The nation's largest cities, those with 250,000 or more inhabitants, averaged 3.4 law enforcement employees for every 1,000 inhabitants. (Table 58) These rates are either static or not significantly different from their 2015 levels.

Sworn Personnel

An analysis of the 2016 data showed that law enforcement agencies in the cities in the Northeast and the South had the highest rate of sworn officers—2.6 and 2.5 per 1,000 inhabitants, respectively—followed by the Midwest (2.1), and the West (1.6). (Table 59)

Males accounted for 87.9 percent of all full-time sworn law enforcement officers in 2016. Cities with populations of 1 million and over employed the highest percentage (17.8 percent) of full-time female officers. Of the city population groups, cities with populations of 10,000 to 24,999 inhabitants employed the highest percentage (91.7 percent) of male officers. In metropolitan counties, 86.7 percent of officers were male, and in nonmetropolitan counties, 92.0 percent of officers were male. (Table 60)

Civilian Employees

Civilian employees provide a myriad of services to the nation's law enforcement and criminal justice agencies. Among other duties, they dispatch officers, provide administrative and record keeping support, and query local, state, and national databases.

In 2016, 30.0 percent of all law enforcement employees in the nation were civilians. Male employees accounted for 40.0 percent of all full-time civilian law enforcement employees in 2016. In cities, civilians made up 22.4 percent of law enforcement agency employees. Civilians made up 40.9 percent of law enforcement employees in metropolitan counties, 41.1 percent of law enforcement employees in nonmetropolitan counties, and 34.2 percent of law enforcement employees in suburban areas. (Table 60)

Table 58. Full-Time Law Enforcement Employees,[1] by Region and Geographic Division and Population Group, 2016

(Number, rate per 1,000 inhabitants.)

Region/geographic division	Total (10,126 cities; population 192,569,624)	Group I (79 cities, 250,000 and over; population 59,221,977)	Group II (200 cities, 100,000 to 249,999; population 29,632,582)	Group III (433 cities, 50,000 to 99,999; population 30,220,472)	Group IV (773 cities, 25,000 to 49,999; population 26,885,069)	Group V (1,597 cities, 10,000 to 24,999; population 25,434,997)	Group VI (7,044 cities, under 10,000; population 21,174,527)	Total city agencies	2016 estimated city population
Total									
Number of employees	543,105	199,810	63,555	62,534	57,020	57,987	102,199	10,126	192,569,624
Average number of employees per 1,000 inhabitants	2.8	3.4	2.1	2.1	2.1	2.3	4.8		
Northeast									
Number of employees	150,352	66,610	8,428	15,399	18,309	18,553	23,053	2,628	45,116,740
Average number of employees per 1,000 inhabitants	3.3	5.6	2.9	2.4	2.2	2.1	3.6		
New England									
Number of employees	34,056	2,678	4,468	6,281	7,068	6,931	6,630	795	12,871,266
Average number of employees per 1,000 inhabitants	2.6	4.0	3.0	2.3	2.2	2.3	3.8		
Middle Atlantic									
Number of employees	116,296	63,932	3,960	9,118	11,241	11,622	16,423	1,833	32,245,474
Average number of employees per 1,000 inhabitants	3.6	5.7	2.9	2.4	2.1	2.0	3.5		
Midwest									
Number of employees	94,374	31,832	7,333	11,733	11,890	13,012	18,574	2,537	37,123,846
Average number of employees per 1,000 inhabitants	2.5	3.7	2.0	1.8	1.9	2.0	3.3		
East North Central									
Number of employees	60,559	24,326	3,669	7,089	8,645	7,761	9,069	1,309	23,081,262
Average number of employees per 1,000 inhabitants	2.6	4.0	2.0	1.9	1.9	2.0	3.1		
West North Central									
Number of employees	33,815	7,506	3,664	4,644	3,245	5,251	9,505	1,228	14,042,584
Average number of employees per 1,000 inhabitants	2.4	2.9	2.0	1.7	1.9	2.1	3.6		
South									
Number of employees	184,239	52,351	27,507	19,997	17,872	19,962	46,550	3,587	57,655,948
Average number of employees per 1,000 inhabitants	3.2	2.9	2.5	2.5	2.5	2.9	6.9		
South Atlantic									
Number of employees	89,129	23,469	12,958	10,855	9,079	9,520	23,248	1,635	24,823,862
Average number of employees per 1,000 inhabitants	3.6	3.7	2.6	2.6	2.7	3.0	8.0		
East South Central									
Number of employees	25,156	4,093	4,200	2,582	3,111	3,513	7,657	653	7,286,658
Average number of employees per 1,000 inhabitants	3.5	3.1	2.9	2.7	2.6	3.1	6.3		
West South Central									
Number of employees	69,954	24,789	10,349	6,560	5,682	6,929	15,645	1,299	25,545,428
Average number of employees per 1,000 inhabitants	2.7	2.4	2.2	2.3	2.3	2.6	5.9		
West									
Number of employees	114,140	49,017	20,287	15,405	8,949	6,460	14,022	1,374	52,673,090
Average number of employees per 1,000 inhabitants	2.2	2.4	1.7	1.6	1.7	2.0	5.9		
Mountain									
Number of employees	41,165	15,909	7,076	4,823	3,654	2,473	7,230	614	16,789,215
Average number of employees per 1,000 inhabitants	2.5	2.4	2.0	1.9	1.9	2.3	6.1		
Pacific									
Number of employees	72,975	33,108	13,211	10,582	5,295	3,987	6,792	760	35,883,875
Average number of employees per 1,000 inhabitants	2.0	2.3	1.6	1.5	1.6	1.9	5.7		

1 Full-time law enforcement employees include civilians.

Table 59. Full-Time Law Enforcement Officers, by Region and Geographic Division, and Population Group, 2016

(Number, rate per 1,000 inhabitants.)

Region/geographic division	Total (10,126 cities; population 192,569,624)	Group I (79 cities, 250,000 and over; population 59,221,977)	Group II (200 cities, 100,000 to 249,999; population 29,632,582)	Group III (433 cities, 50,000 to 99,999; population 30,220,472)	Group IV (773 cities, 25,000 to 49,999; population 26,885,069)	Group V (1,597 cities, 10,000 to 24,999; population 25,434,997)	Group VI (7,044 cities, under 10,000; population 21,174,527)	Total city agencies	2016 estimated city population
Total									
Number of officers	421,459	152,607	48,534	48,450	45,582	47,148	79,138	10,126	192,569,624
Average number of officers per 1,000 inhabitants	2.2	2.6	1.6	1.6	1.7	1.9	3.7		
Northeast									
Number of officers	118,398	48,245	7,103	12,744	15,469	15,777	19,060	2,628	45,116,740
Average number of officers per 1,000 inhabitants	2.6	4.0	2.5	1.9	1.8	1.8	2.9		
New England									
Number of officers	28,015	2,125	3,791	5,373	5,924	5,607	5,195	795	12,871,266
Average number of officers per 1,000 inhabitants	2.2	3.2	2.5	2.0	1.9	1.8	3.0		
Middle Atlantic									
Number of officers	90,383	46,120	3,312	7,371	9,545	10,170	13,865	1,833	32,245,474
Average number of officers per 1,000 inhabitants	2.8	4.1	2.4	1.9	1.8	1.7	2.9		
Midwest									
Number of officers	78,550	27,129	6,115	9,505	9,583	10,766	15,452	2,537	37,123,846
Average number of officers per 1,000 inhabitants	2.1	3.1	1.6	1.5	1.5	1.7	2.8		
East North Central									
Number of officers	51,479	21,368	3,156	5,810	7,007	6,492	7,646	1,309	23,081,262
Average number of officers per 1,000 inhabitants	2.2	3.5	1.7	1.6	1.5	1.7	2.6		
West North Central									
Number of officers	27,071	5,761	2,959	3,695	2,576	4,274	7,806	1,228	14,042,584
Average number of officers per 1,000 inhabitants	1.9	2.2	1.6	1.4	1.5	1.7	3.0		
South									
Number of officers	141,967	40,913	20,912	15,357	14,000	15,740	35,045	3,587	57,655,948
Average number of officers per 1,000 inhabitants	2.5	2.3	1.9	1.9	2.0	2.3	5.2		
South Atlantic									
Number of officers	69,077	17,848	10,036	8,421	7,253	7,664	17,855	1,635	24,823,862
Average number of officers per 1,000 inhabitants	2.8	2.8	2.0	2.0	2.2	2.4	6.1		
East South Central									
Number of officers	19,802	3,376	3,219	2,028	2,482	2,770	5,927	653	7,286,658
Average number of officers per 1,000 inhabitants	2.7	2.5	2.2	2.1	2.1	2.4	4.9		
West South Central									
Number of officers	53,088	19,689	7,657	4,908	4,265	5,306	11,263	1,299	25,545,428
Average number of officers per 1,000 inhabitants	2.1	1.9	1.6	1.7	1.7	2.0	4.2		
West									
Number of officers	82,544	36,320	14,404	10,844	6,530	4,865	9,581	1,374	52,673,090
Average number of officers per 1,000 inhabitants	1.6	1.8	1.2	1.2	1.2	1.5	4.2		
Mountain									
Number of officers	29,548	11,466	5,142	3,394	2,748	1,873	4,925	614	16,789,215
Average number of officers per 1,000 inhabitants	1.8	1.8	1.4	1.4	1.4	1.7	4.2		
Pacific									
Number of officers	52,996	24,854	9,262	7,450	3,782	2,992	4,656	760	35,883,875
Average number of officers per 1,000 inhabitants	1.5	1.8	1.1	1.1	1.2	1.4	3.9		

Table 60. Full-Time Law Enforcement Employees, by Population Group, Percent Male and Female, 2016

(Number, percent.)

Population group	Total law enforcement employees (number)	Law enforcement employees (percent)		Total officers (number)	Officers (percent)		Civilians (number) Total civilians	Civilians (percent)		Agencies (number)	Population, 2016, estimated
		Male	Female		Male	Female		Male	Female		
Total Agencies	933,142	73.5	26.5	652,936	87.9	12.1	280,206	40.0	60.0	13,217	277,638,758
Total Cities	543,105	75.3	24.7	421,459	87.7	12.3	121,646	32.4	67.6	10,126	192,569,624
Group I (250,000 and over)	199,810	71.7	28.3	152,607	83.4	16.6	47,203	34.0	66.0	79	59,221,977
1,000,000 and over (Group I subset)	110,936	70.3	29.7	83,800	82.2	17.8	27,136	33.6	66.4	11	27,658,777
500,000 to 999,999 (Group I subset)	46,843	75.1	24.9	36,642	85.0	15.0	10,201	39.5	60.5	21	15,316,228
250,000 to 499,999 (Group I subset)	42,031	71.8	28.2	32,165	84.7	15.3	9,866	29.6	70.4	47	16,246,972
Group II (100,000 to 249,999)	63,555	73.7	26.3	48,534	88.3	11.7	15,021	26.4	73.6	200	29,632,582
Group III (50,000 to 99,999)	62,534	75.8	24.2	48,450	89.4	10.6	14,084	28.8	71.2	433	30,220,472
Group IV (25,000 to 49,999)	57,020	78.2	21.8	45,582	90.8	9.2	11,438	28.0	72.0	773	26,885,069
Group V (10,000 to 24,999)	57,987	79.7	20.3	47,148	91.7	8.3	10,839	27.5	72.5	1,597	25,434,997
Group VI (under 10,000)	102,199	78.9	21.1	79,138	90.3	9.7	23,061	39.8	60.2	7,044	21,174,527
Metropolitan Counties	282,756	70.1	29.9	166,532	86.7	13.3	116,224	46.2	53.8	1,257	63,585,694
Nonmetropolitan Counties	107,281	73.4	26.6	64,945	92.0	8.0	42,336	44.7	55.3	1,834	21,483,440
Suburban Areas[1]	434,964	73.2	26.8	286,120	88.3	11.7	148,844	44.1	55.9	7,050	116,271,221

1 Suburban areas include law enforcement agencies in cities with less than 50,000 inhabitants and county law enforcement agencies that are within a Metropolitan Statistical Area. Suburban areas exclude all metropolitan agencies associated with a principal city. The agencies associated with suburban areas also appear in other groups within this table.

Table 61. Full-Time Civilian Law Enforcement Employees, by Population Group, 2015

(Number, percent.)

Population group	Civilian employees (percent)	Agencies (number)	Population, 2015, estimated
Total Agencies	30.4	13,160	273,099,970
Total Cities	22.4	10,075	187,551,939
Group I (250,000 and over)	24.0	76	56,116,904
1,000,000 and over (Group I subset)	25.6	10	24,675,984
500,000 to 999,999 (Group I subset)	21.3	23	16,678,441
250,000 to 499,999 (Group I subset)	23.5	43	14,762,479
Group II (100,000 to 249,999)	23.7	195	28,956,838
Group III (50,000 to 99,999)	22.2	419	29,206,031
Group IV (25,000 to 49,999)	20.1	764	26,443,466
Group V (10,000 to 24,999)	18.4	1,612	25,662,681
Group VI (under 10,000)	22.3	7,009	21,166,019
Metropolitan Counties	40.9	1,238	63,774,885
Nonmetropolitan Counties	41.0	1,847	21,773,146
Suburban Areas[1]	34.1	7,034	116,427,469

1 Suburban areas include law enforcement agencies in cities with less than 50,000 inhabitants and county law enforcement agencies that are within a Metropolitan Statistical Area. Suburban areas exclude all metropolitan agencies associated with a principal city. The agencies associated with suburban areas also appear in other groups within this table.

Table 62. Full-Time Law Enforcement Employees, by Selected State and City, 2016

(Number.)

State/city	Population	Total law enforcement employees	Total officers	Total civilians
ALABAMA				
Abbeville	2,608	17	9	8
Alabaster	33,040	80	61	19
Albertville	21,525	69	45	24
Andalusia	9,071	36	25	11
Anniston	22,205	107	87	20
Arab	8,334	34	26	8
Ardmore	1,390	11	7	4
Ashford	2,161	6	5	1
Ashland	1,974	14	9	5
Athens	25,603	59	48	11
Atmore	10,021	27	22	5
Attalla	5,870	27	22	5
Auburn	63,871	116	110	6
Bay Minette	9,281	29	22	7
Bayou La Batre	2,607	18	13	5
Boaz	9,729	35	24	11
Brewton	5,441	32	24	8
Brighton	2,846	8	4	4
Brookwood	1,821	5	5	0
Brundidge	1,972	12	7	5
Butler	1,781	7	7	0
Camden	1,916	8	7	1
Centre	3,586	12	11	1
Centreville	2,691	6	6	0
Chatom	1,227	4	4	0
Chickasaw	5,927	26	21	5
Citronelle	3,884	12	8	4
Coaling	1,646	4	4	0
Collinsville	1,971	8	4	4
Creola	1,961	9	5	4
Crossville	1,845	5	5	0
Cullman	15,459	72	51	21
Dadeville	3,136	13	12	1
Daleville	5,109	27	16	11
Daphne	25,564	74	50	24
Decatur	55,374	148	133	15
Demopolis	7,089	30	24	6
Dora	1,947	12	7	5
Dothan	69,071	233	161	72
Douglas	761	4	4	0
Eclectic	1,034	8	8	0
Elba	3,894	24	14	10
Enterprise	28,227	70	52	18
Eufaula	12,503	51	31	20
Evergreen	3,742	25	19	6
Fairfield	10,869	30	21	9
Fairhope	19,470	59	36	23
Falkville	1,266	10	9	1
Fayette	4,465	12	12	0
Flomaton	1,405	13	8	5
Florala	1,971	3	3	0
Florence	40,160	130	105	25
Foley	17,639	90	61	29
Fort Payne	14,156	43	38	5
Fultondale	9,188	33	26	7
Gardendale	13,675	41	31	10
Georgiana	1,654	13	8	5
Glencoe	5,150	8	8	0
Goodwater	1,318	8	4	4
Gordo	1,675	4	4	0
Grove Hill	1,481	5	5	0
Gulf Shores	11,340	65	47	18
Guntersville	8,421	46	34	12
Haleyville	4,072	16	11	5
Hartford	2,651	13	8	5
Hartselle	14,540	29	28	1
Headland	4,778	19	11	8
Helena	18,525	27	22	5
Hoover	85,601	227	165	62
Hueytown	15,632	47	38	9
Huntsville	192,587	606	500	106
Irondale	12,439	43	35	8
Jacksons Gap	798	3	3	0
Killen	979	4	4	0
Kimberly	2,931	14	4	10
Lafayette	2,989	15	13	2
Lanett	6,451	27	25	2
Level Plains	2,012	4	4	0
Lexington	721	4	4	0
Lincoln	6,579	19	17	2
Lineville	2,306	11	7	4
Loxley	1,817	18	13	5
Luverne	2,843	16	11	5
Madison	47,729	106	80	26

Table 62. Full-Time Law Enforcement Employees, by Selected State and City, 2016—Continued

(Number.)

State/city	Population	Total law enforcement employees	Total officers	Total civilians
Maplesville	703	5	5	0
Mentone	369	1	1	0
Millbrook	15,446	42	32	10
Mobile	249,921	736	496	240
Montevallo	6,716	17	13	4
Montgomery	199,565	614	503	111
Mountain Brook	20,737	69	56	13
Mount Vernon	1,508	6	6	0
Munford	1,253	1	1	0
Napier Field	346	2	2	0
Northport	25,045	77	59	18
Ohatchee	1,144	3	3	0
Oneonta	6,624	20	19	1
Opelika	30,180	104	84	20
Opp	6,657	30	21	9
Orange Beach	5,932	67	47	20
Oxford	21,234	72	61	11
Ozark	14,679	38	33	5
Pelham	23,162	84	69	15
Phenix City	38,521	108	84	24
Pine Hill	910	4	4	0
Pleasant Grove	10,293	20	15	5
Powell	957	1	1	0
Prattville	35,698	92	83	9
Priceville	3,291	5	5	0
Prichard	22,299	53	33	20
Rainbow City	9,573	33	23	10
Rainsville	5,047	16	12	4
Ranburne	410	2	2	0
Red Bay	3,125	12	8	4
Roanoke	5,993	29	22	7
Robertsdale	6,019	25	14	11
Saraland	13,967	57	40	17
Sardis City	1,764	4	4	0
Scottsboro	14,711	68	44	24
Skyline	837	2	1	1
Snead	844	4	4	0
Southside	8,602	19	13	6
Spanish Fort	8,312	24	20	4
Steele	1,085	3	3	0
St. Florian	475	2	2	0
Sumiton	2,400	15	7	8
Summerdale	1,181	7	7	0
Thomaston	395	1	1	0
Town Creek	1,058	3	3	0
Trinity	2,170	7	7	0
Troy	18,985	78	55	23
Trussville	21,229	68	55	13
Tuscaloosa	99,925	352	274	78
Tuskegee	8,623	28	17	11
Uniontown	2,364	9	8	1
Valley	9,465	30	28	2
Vernon	1,876	8	8	0
Warrior	3,204	18	11	7
Weaver	3,101	11	8	3
Wedowee	807	8	8	0
Wetumpka	8,280	38	30	8
ALASKA				
Anchorage	299,097	497	356	141
Bethel	6,522	19	9	10
Bristol Bay Borough	870	10	4	6
Cordova	2,186	11	6	5
Craig	1,256	11	5	6
Dillingham	2,419	19	7	12
Fairbanks	32,456	43	37	6
Haines	2,535	9	4	5
Homer	5,613	22	11	11
Hoonah	757	8	4	4
Juneau	32,964	82	50	32
Kenai	7,770	26	17	9
Ketchikan	8,221	32	20	12
Klawock	766	4	4	0
Kodiak	6,274	39	18	21
Kotzebue	3,290	19	11	8
Nome	3,846	15	8	7
North Pole	2,201	14	13	1
North Slope Borough	9,710	74	47	27
Palmer	6,959	28	13	15
Petersburg	3,162	11	7	4
Sand Point	1,080	5	4	1
Seward	2,813	23	9	14
Sitka	8,836	27	13	14
Skagway	1,075	11	4	7
Soldotna	4,619	15	13	2

Table 62. Full-Time Law Enforcement Employees, by Selected State and City, 2016—Continued

(Number.)

State/city	Population	Total law enforcement employees	Total officers	Total civilians
St. Paul	512	10	4	6
Unalaska	4,517	28	12	16
Valdez	3,847	19	10	9
Wasilla	9,585	52	25	27
Whittier	213	4	4	0
Wrangell	2,380	13	6	7
ARIZONA				
Apache Junction	38,506	87	57	30
Avondale	81,605	183	122	61
Benson	4,851	20	11	9
Bisbee	5,132	14	11	3
Buckeye	64,563	112	86	26
Bullhead City	39,426	113	71	42
Camp Verde	11,213	28	19	9
Casa Grande	51,995	97	77	20
Chandler	265,922	497	329	168
Chino Valley	11,202	30	22	8
Clarkdale	4,271	9	8	1
Clifton	3,774	11	4	7
Colorado City	4,834	10	7	3
Coolidge	12,387	43	31	12
Cottonwood	11,932	54	31	23
Douglas	16,398	40	27	13
Eagar	4,863	8	6	2
El Mirage	34,376	54	40	14
Eloy	17,110	40	26	14
Flagstaff	71,179	150	102	48
Florence	31,130	37	29	8
Fredonia	1,320	3	3	0
Gilbert	255,899	341	227	114
Glendale	242,938	542	419	123
Globe	7,366	22	19	3
Goodyear	82,018	132	96	36
Hayden	993	6	6	0
Holbrook	5,012	15	13	2
Huachuca City	1,735	12	5	7
Jerome	458	4	4	0
Kearny	2,055	8	3	5
Kingman	29,069	71	54	17
Lake Havasu City	53,746	103	68	35
Mammoth	1,499	5	3	2
Marana	42,808	116	88	28
Maricopa	49,627	86	65	21
Mesa	478,277	1,221	804	417
Miami	1,776	10	7	3
Nogales	20,143	68	53	15
Oro Valley	44,089	128	100	28
Page	7,516	28	17	11
Paradise Valley	14,155	40	32	8
Parker	3,045	13	10	3
Patagonia	886	3	3	0
Payson	15,351	47	26	21
Peoria	174,797	275	184	91
Phoenix	1,586,611	3,706	2,762	944
Pima	2,554	6	6	0
Pinetop-Lakeside	4,354	19	14	5
Prescott	42,321	81	68	13
Prescott Valley	42,900	81	61	20
Quartzsite	3,615	12	11	1
Safford	9,717	25	21	4
Sahuarita	25,792	50	43	7
San Luis	32,227	54	35	19
Scottsdale	240,885	633	401	232
Sedona	10,457	37	22	15
Show Low	10,892	40	28	12
Sierra Vista	42,988	94	70	24
Snowflake-Taylor	9,835	22	13	9
Somerton	15,196	27	19	8
South Tucson	5,727	20	18	2
Springerville	1,952	9	7	2
St. Johns	3,482	9	6	3
Superior	2,963	9	8	1
Surprise	130,679	181	127	54
Tempe	178,654	493	355	138
Thatcher	5,019	12	11	1
Tolleson	7,105	41	29	12
Tombstone	1,298	10	7	3
Tucson	533,663	1,168	870	298
Wellton	2,944	7	6	1
Wickenburg	6,835	23	16	7
Willcox	3,511	17	9	8
Williams	3,140	21	13	8
Winslow	9,581	31	21	10
Yuma	94,696	258	170	88

Table 62. Full-Time Law Enforcement Employees, by Selected State and City, 2016—Continued

(Number.)

State/city	Population	Total law enforcement employees	Total officers	Total civilians
ARKANSAS				
Alexander	2,841	6	6	0
Alma	5,595	21	13	8
Arkadelphia	10,755	29	23	6
Ashdown	4,434	13	11	2
Ash Flat	1,060	4	4	0
Atkins	3,056	8	7	1
Augusta	2,024	6	6	0
Austin	3,723	4	4	0
Bald Knob	2,910	9	6	3
Barling	4,748	12	12	0
Batesville	10,732	24	23	1
Bay	1,815	3	3	0
Bearden	884	1	1	0
Beebe	8,269	27	18	9
Bella Vista	28,274	40	27	13
Benton	34,920	90	64	26
Bentonville	46,458	98	68	30
Berryville	5,386	14	12	2
Bethel Heights	2,512	7	6	1
Black Rock	618	1	1	0
Blytheville	14,523	49	37	12
Bono	2,257	4	4	0
Booneville	3,872	13	9	4
Bradford	760	2	2	0
Brinkley	2,837	15	10	5
Brookland	3,245	5	5	0
Bryant	20,687	48	39	9
Bull Shoals	1,929	3	3	0
Cabot	25,927	53	42	11
Caddo Valley	602	4	4	0
Camden	11,191	42	26	16
Cammack Village	744	4	4	0
Caraway	1,268	3	3	0
Carlisle	2,176	9	5	4
Cave City	1,861	4	4	0
Cave Springs	3,369	7	7	0
Centerton	12,584	22	20	2
Charleston	2,475	5	5	0
Cherokee Village	4,583	9	8	1
Clarendon	1,475	5	4	1
Clarksville	9,482	22	18	4
Clinton	2,526	8	7	1
Conway	66,104	166	126	40
Corning	3,122	12	8	4
Cotter	947	2	2	0
Crossett	5,166	27	17	10
Damascus	382	2	2	0
Danville	2,338	6	5	1
Dardanelle	4,642	17	10	7
Decatur	1,787	6	6	0
Dell	206	1	1	0
De Queen	6,724	16	14	2
Dermott	2,688	13	7	6
Des Arc	1,624	4	4	0
De Valls Bluff	581	1	1	0
De Witt	3,162	13	9	4
Diamond City	781	1	1	0
Diaz	1,235	2	2	0
Dierks	1,084	3	3	0
Dover	1,401	5	5	0
Dumas	4,253	20	11	9
Dyer	857	1	1	0
El Dorado	18,297	68	51	17
Elkins	3,005	6	6	0
England	2,752	15	11	4
Etowah	325	1	1	0
Eudora	2,070	6	4	2
Eureka Springs	2,084	16	12	4
Fairfield Bay	2,254	17	7	10
Farmington	6,852	12	11	1
Fayetteville	84,726	169	123	46
Flippin	1,331	7	6	1
Fordyce	3,979	14	9	5
Forrest City	14,544	42	32	10
Fort Smith	88,573	189	141	48
Gassville	2,144	4	4	0
Gentry	3,443	10	8	2
Glenwood	2,125	2	2	0
Gosnell	3,261	7	7	0
Gravette	3,253	10	9	1
Greenbrier	5,416	15	9	6
Green Forest	2,769	13	10	3
Greenland	1,406	4	4	0

Table 62. Full-Time Law Enforcement Employees, by Selected State and City, 2016—Continued

(Number.)

State/city	Population	Total law enforcement employees	Total officers	Total civilians
Greenwood	9,372	21	20	1
Greers Ferry	867	4	3	1
Gurdon	2,132	5	4	1
Guy	721	2	2	0
Hamburg	2,772	6	5	1
Hampton	1,274	3	3	0
Hardy	756	3	3	0
Harrisburg	2,304	6	5	1
Harrison	13,178	43	31	12
Hazen	1,392	6	5	1
Heber Springs	7,144	24	15	9
Helena-West Helena	10,898	33	21	12
Higginson	659	1	1	0
Highfill	641	3	3	0
Highland	1,056	3	3	0
Hope	9,852	31	25	6
Hot Springs	35,716	130	102	28
Hoxie	2,660	4	4	0
Hughes	1,302	3	3	0
Jacksonville	28,684	86	72	14
Jasper	446	1	1	0
Johnson	3,683	13	12	1
Jonesboro	75,230	182	155	27
Judsonia	2,028	4	3	1
Keiser	694	1	1	0
Kensett	1,650	3	3	0
Lake City	2,374	4	4	0
Lakeview	723	2	2	0
Lake Village	2,388	16	10	6
Lamar	1,680	3	3	0
Lavaca	2,425	3	3	0
Leachville	1,845	4	3	1
Lepanto	1,824	7	3	4
Lewisville	1,161	1	1	0
Lincoln	2,468	5	5	0
Little Flock	2,781	6	6	0
Little Rock	198,800	639	525	114
Lonoke	4,248	16	11	5
Lowell	8,812	24	18	6
Luxora	1,088	2	2	0
Magnolia	11,642	23	21	2
Malvern	11,016	24	22	2
Mammoth Spring	968	2	2	0
Mansfield	1,088	4	4	0
Marianna	3,701	24	12	12
Marion	12,270	30	27	3
Marked Tree	2,489	10	6	4
Marmaduke	1,238	4	4	0
Marvell	1,022	7	4	3
Maumelle	18,068	41	32	9
Mayflower	2,473	11	9	2
McCrory	1,577	5	5	0
McGehee	3,866	25	10	15
McRae	679	2	2	0
Mena	5,635	15	14	1
Menifee	306	1	1	0
Mineral Springs	1,152	2	2	0
Monette	1,533	3	3	0
Monticello	9,860	28	21	7
Morrilton	6,733	26	23	3
Mountain Home	12,305	34	26	8
Mountain View	2,856	11	10	1
Mulberry	1,630	3	3	0
Murfreesboro	1,569	3	3	0
Nashville	4,450	17	16	1
Newport	7,733	19	13	6
North Little Rock	67,344	215	178	37
Ola	1,246	4	3	1
Osceola	7,138	38	25	13
Ozark	3,572	11	9	2
Pangburn	602	2	2	0
Paragould	28,254	59	48	11
Paris	3,427	14	9	5
Parkin	1,047	2	2	0
Pea Ridge	5,331	15	14	1
Perryville	1,426	5	5	0
Piggott	3,619	8	8	0
Pine Bluff	43,976	173	143	30
Plainview	596	1	1	0
Plumerville	801	4	4	0
Pocahontas	6,405	15	14	1
Pottsville	3,131	9	7	2
Prairie Grove	5,345	10	10	0
Prescott	3,103	10	9	1
Quitman	738	4	4	0

Table 62. Full-Time Law Enforcement Employees, by Selected State and City, 2016—Continued

(Number.)

State/city	Population	Total law enforcement employees	Total officers	Total civilians
Ravenden	446	1	1	0
Redfield	1,593	7	6	1
Rison	1,270	3	3	0
Rogers	64,616	139	98	41
Rose Bud	482	3	2	1
Russellville	29,366	57	51	6
Salem	1,635	3	3	0
Searcy	24,452	65	50	15
Shannon Hills	3,926	5	5	0
Sheridan	4,858	30	14	16
Sherwood	30,676	95	67	28
Siloam Springs	16,277	46	31	15
Springdale	79,288	200	142	58
Stamps	1,525	5	2	3
Star City	2,163	6	5	1
St. Charles	220	1	1	0
Stuttgart	9,002	29	22	7
Sulphur Springs	529	3	3	0
Swifton	748	1	1	0
Texarkana	30,429	104	80	24
Trumann	7,118	25	18	7
Tuckerman	1,739	5	4	1
Tyronza	741	2	2	0
Van Buren	23,133	57	44	13
Vilonia	4,568	9	9	0
Waldron	3,406	10	9	1
Walnut Ridge	4,630	8	8	0
Ward	4,835	11	10	1
Warren	5,767	19	12	7
Weiner	683	1	1	0
West Fork	2,587	5	5	0
West Memphis	24,818	96	76	20
White Hall	5,114	17	15	2
Wynne	8,161	20	18	2
CALIFORNIA				
Alameda	79,597	110	81	29
Albany	19,975	32	24	8
Alhambra	86,035	125	84	41
Alturas	2,549	7	7	0
Anaheim	353,504	562	408	154
Anderson	10,273	23	17	6
Angels Camp	3,755	7	6	1
Antioch	112,090	123	95	28
Arcadia	58,816	91	66	25
Arcata	17,913	38	25	13
Arroyo Grande	18,280	30	26	4
Arvin	21,195	30	22	8
Atascadero	30,108	38	28	10
Atherton	7,218	27	19	8
Atwater	29,437	34	27	7
Auburn	14,078	27	20	7
Avenal	12,941	17	15	2
Azusa	50,393	94	57	37
Bakersfield	378,788	530	390	140
Baldwin Park	77,400	98	65	33
Banning	31,191	43	27	16
Barstow	23,894	54	36	18
Bear Valley	5,464	12	6	6
Beaumont	45,249	56	38	18
Bell	36,347	45	33	12
Bell Gardens	43,316	72	50	22
Belmont	27,492	44	30	14
Belvedere	2,131	8	7	1
Benicia	28,400	49	33	16
Berkeley	122,651	263	175	88
Beverly Hills	35,018	184	117	67
Bishop	3,793	16	10	6
Blythe	18,961	31	21	10
Brawley	26,076	50	36	14
Brea	42,465	95	61	34
Brentwood	60,512	83	62	21
Brisbane	4,807	18	15	3
Broadmoor	4,411	11	10	1
Buena Park	83,768	121	81	40
Burbank	105,720	234	154	80
Burlingame	30,792	56	36	20
Calexico	40,336	35	23	12
California City	13,244	26	16	10
Calipatria	7,384	3	3	0
Calistoga	5,364	14	9	5
Campbell	41,457	67	42	25
Capitola	10,241	29	21	8
Carlsbad	115,040	150	103	47
Carmel	3,931	24	14	10

Table 62. Full-Time Law Enforcement Employees, by Selected State and City, 2016—Continued

(Number.)

State/city	Population	Total law enforcement employees	Total officers	Total civilians
Cathedral City	54,317	74	49	25
Central Marin	35,265	46	41	5
Ceres	48,372	62	46	16
Chico	91,122	137	86	51
Chino	87,081	159	107	52
Chowchilla	18,487	24	16	8
Chula Vista	270,175	305	225	80
Citrus Heights	87,811	134	88	46
Claremont	36,553	61	37	24
Clayton	12,057	12	10	2
Clearlake	15,165	28	23	5
Cloverdale	8,848	22	15	7
Clovis	105,865	162	100	62
Coalinga	16,282	32	21	11
Colma	1,534	24	18	6
Colton	55,100	72	46	26
Colusa	5,926	9	8	1
Concord	129,903	201	150	51
Corcoran	22,111	29	17	12
Corning	7,522	19	12	7
Corona	166,534	225	158	67
Coronado	24,974	63	42	21
Costa Mesa	113,816	172	112	60
Cotati	7,479	15	10	5
Covina	49,222	87	59	28
Crescent City	6,622	10	9	1
Culver City	39,880	153	100	53
Cypress	49,557	69	53	16
Daly City	107,640	133	100	33
Davis	68,087	91	60	31
Delano	52,656	69	50	19
Del Rey Oaks	1,700	6	6	0
Desert Hot Springs	28,573	30	24	6
Dinuba	24,156	49	38	11
Dixon	19,592	24	19	5
Dos Palos	5,158	8	7	1
Downey	114,704	150	106	44
East Palo Alto	29,957	40	33	7
El Cajon	104,483	179	121	58
El Centro	44,213	71	48	23
El Cerrito	25,222	47	40	7
Elk Grove	169,742	211	128	83
El Monte	117,354	152	108	44
El Segundo	17,113	73	56	17
Emeryville	12,060	51	38	13
Escalon	7,601	11	10	1
Escondido	152,897	211	156	55
Etna	712	3	3	0
Eureka	26,981	71	47	24
Exeter	10,589	18	16	2
Fairfax	7,662	16	11	5
Fairfield	114,521	169	114	55
Farmersville	10,812	15	13	2
Ferndale	1,368	4	4	0
Firebaugh	8,484	15	11	4
Folsom	77,245	95	70	25
Fontana	209,531	275	185	90
Fort Bragg	7,292	21	15	6
Fortuna	12,013	22	15	7
Foster City	34,081	50	36	14
Fountain Valley	57,291	80	59	21
Fowler	6,397	13	12	1
Fremont	235,881	282	180	102
Fresno	524,796	1,013	748	265
Fullerton	141,968	210	141	69
Galt	25,638	49	33	16
Gardena	60,770	119	95	24
Garden Grove	176,230	218	159	59
Gilroy	54,130	87	62	25
Glendale	202,903	328	232	96
Glendora	52,380	86	51	35
Gonzales	8,533	13	10	3
Grass Valley	12,961	24	21	3
Greenfield	17,343	21	18	3
Gridley	6,584	19	14	5
Grover Beach	13,686	26	18	8
Guadalupe	7,365	13	11	2
Gustine	5,801	12	10	2
Hanford	55,973	77	53	24
Hawthorne	89,299	136	88	48
Hayward	161,122	310	194	116
Healdsburg	11,830	26	17	9
Hemet	84,838	92	62	30
Hercules	25,553	22	20	2
Hermosa Beach	19,930	62	34	28

Table 62. Full-Time Law Enforcement Employees, by Selected State and City, 2016—Continued

(Number.)

State/city	Population	Total law enforcement employees	Total officers	Total civilians
Hillsborough	11,575	33	25	8
Hollister	37,953	33	27	6
Huntington Beach	204,071	334	214	120
Huntington Park	59,692	86	51	35
Huron	6,852	17	10	7
Imperial	17,582	22	18	4
Indio	89,201	99	63	36
Inglewood	112,059	219	175	44
Ione	6,860	6	6	0
Irvine	266,663	301	213	88
Irwindale	1,440	35	28	7
Jackson	4,649	11	10	1
Kensington	5,364	10	10	0
Kerman	14,654	22	19	3
King City	14,111	17	13	4
Kingsburg	11,905	17	14	3
Laguna Beach	23,486	83	49	34
La Habra	62,483	99	69	30
Lakeport	4,817	13	12	1
Lake Shastina	2,546	3	3	0
La Mesa	60,681	97	68	29
La Palma	15,975	25	19	6
La Verne	33,011	60	40	20
Lemoore	25,875	38	31	7
Lincoln	47,206	27	20	7
Lindsay	13,533	19	14	5
Livermore	89,553	133	89	44
Livingston	14,076	25	17	8
Lodi	65,067	97	67	30
Lompoc	44,541	68	45	23
Long Beach	476,476	1,173	806	367
Los Alamitos	11,774	26	23	3
Los Altos	31,000	42	27	15
Los Angeles	4,007,905	12,692	9,850	2,842
Los Banos	37,738	62	37	25
Los Gatos	30,947	54	37	17
Madera	64,753	78	60	18
Mammoth Lakes	7,891	13	10	3
Manhattan Beach	35,955	105	66	39
Manteca	77,104	86	59	27
Marina	21,539	35	28	7
Martinez	38,541	45	33	12
Marysville	12,241	25	18	7
McFarland	14,263	16	13	3
Mendota	11,481	16	14	2
Menlo Park	33,726	67	47	20
Merced	83,106	125	89	36
Mill Valley	14,491	26	20	6
Milpitas	79,990	109	85	24
Modesto	212,880	300	214	86
Monrovia	37,637	82	51	31
Montclair	39,085	68	47	21
Montebello	64,206	99	66	33
Monterey	28,506	61	43	18
Monterey Park	61,710	98	69	29
Moraga	17,505	12	11	1
Morgan Hill	44,015	59	39	20
Morro Bay	10,719	19	17	2
Mountain View	81,726	129	86	43
Mount Shasta	3,277	12	9	3
Murrieta	111,043	128	89	39
Napa	81,115	110	69	41
National City	61,550	120	86	34
Nevada City	3,167	12	10	2
Newark	45,893	77	55	22
Newman	11,037	15	12	3
Newport Beach	87,482	228	140	88
Novato	56,263	80	56	24
Oakdale	22,572	32	22	10
Oakland	424,998	1,046	750	296
Oceanside	177,340	278	204	74
Ontario	172,606	339	254	85
Orange	141,841	213	143	70
Orange Cove	9,706	12	11	1
Orland	7,587	13	11	2
Oroville	16,322	44	24	20
Oxnard	209,048	337	227	110
Pacifica	39,650	35	33	2
Pacific Grove	15,795	24	14	10
Palm Springs	47,909	127	88	39
Palo Alto	67,317	137	79	58
Palos Verdes Estates	13,730	35	29	6
Paradise	26,532	33	19	14
Parlier	15,262	11	10	1
Pasadena	143,288	357	234	123

Table 62. Full-Time Law Enforcement Employees, by Selected State and City, 2016—Continued

(Number.)

State/city	Population	Total law enforcement employees	Total officers	Total civilians
Paso Robles	31,939	44	31	13
Petaluma	60,933	82	58	24
Piedmont	11,515	27	19	8
Pinole	19,451	33	22	11
Pismo Beach	8,264	31	19	12
Pittsburg	70,663	96	77	19
Placentia	52,800	68	45	23
Placerville	10,705	26	18	8
Pleasant Hill	35,140	57	41	16
Pleasanton	81,464	110	77	33
Pomona	154,109	261	154	107
Porterville	56,421	86	60	26
Port Hueneme	22,570	27	21	6
Red Bluff	14,138	38	24	14
Redding	91,918	131	98	33
Redlands	71,485	118	80	38
Redondo Beach	68,447	143	92	51
Redwood City	87,046	116	91	25
Reedley	25,828	40	27	13
Rialto	103,893	142	105	37
Richmond	110,868	242	177	65
Ridgecrest	29,003	50	32	18
Rio Dell	3,390	5	5	0
Rio Vista	8,554	14	12	2
Ripon	15,318	31	22	9
Riverside	325,896	503	350	153
Rocklin	62,006	79	55	24
Rohnert Park	42,723	85	59	26
Roseville	132,566	183	125	58
Ross	2,492	8	8	0
Sacramento	495,471	954	652	302
Salinas	158,729	191	134	57
San Bernardino	217,303	360	215	145
San Bruno	43,613	65	49	16
Sand City	391	10	9	1
San Diego	1,413,414	2,522	1,815	707
San Fernando	25,194	41	27	14
San Francisco	871,155	2,892	2,296	596
San Gabriel	40,580	64	49	15
Sanger	25,078	37	33	4
San Jose	1,041,844	1,352	939	413
San Leandro	91,870	131	90	41
San Luis Obispo	47,774	78	55	23
San Marino	13,528	30	25	5
San Mateo	104,802	148	111	37
San Pablo	30,674	67	46	21
San Rafael	59,435	86	65	21
San Ramon	76,901	81	65	16
Santa Ana	337,419	523	310	213
Santa Barbara	92,519	205	140	65
Santa Clara	128,179	215	144	71
Santa Cruz	64,969	115	93	22
Santa Maria	106,200	166	111	55
Santa Monica	93,921	374	204	170
Santa Paula	30,784	38	30	8
Santa Rosa	176,383	251	172	79
Sausalito	7,198	24	19	5
Scotts Valley	12,016	26	19	7
Seal Beach	24,721	45	30	15
Seaside	34,827	46	37	9
Sebastopol	7,734	19	14	5
Selma	24,641	38	30	8
Shafter	18,608	38	26	12
Sierra Madre	11,212	18	15	3
Signal Hill	11,677	47	34	13
Simi Valley	127,252	177	122	55
Soledad	24,805	21	17	4
Sonora	4,802	17	10	7
South Gate	96,791	118	79	39
South Lake Tahoe	21,765	56	37	19
South Pasadena	26,256	49	35	14
South San Francisco	67,995	110	80	30
Stallion Springs	2,628	3	3	0
St. Helena	6,142	18	13	5
Stockton	308,348	610	412	198
Suisun City	29,768	33	21	12
Sunnyvale	154,108	278	209	69
Susanville	14,798	19	17	2
Sutter Creek	2,484	4	4	0
Taft	9,543	26	16	10
Tehachapi	12,770	24	15	9
Tiburon	9,263	16	13	3
Torrance	149,078	309	208	101
Tracy	87,844	126	85	41
Truckee	16,326	34	22	12

Table 62. Full-Time Law Enforcement Employees, by Selected State and City, 2016—Continued

(Number.)

State/city	Population	Total law enforcement employees	Total officers	Total civilians
Tulare	62,902	109	72	37
Tulelake	990	1	1	0
Turlock	73,031	117	78	39
Tustin	81,642	131	87	44
Ukiah	15,897	49	32	17
Union City	75,501	104	75	29
Upland	76,956	96	69	27
Vacaville	97,671	150	99	51
Vallejo	122,293	150	110	40
Ventura	110,228	165	125	40
Vernon	114	51	39	12
Visalia	131,186	200	135	65
Walnut Creek	69,860	118	85	33
Watsonville	54,110	86	68	18
Weed	2,479	13	8	5
West Covina	108,950	156	93	63
Westminster	92,582	115	79	36
Westmorland	2,275	5	5	0
West Sacramento	53,532	89	69	20
Wheatland	3,775	9	8	1
Whittier	87,860	167	120	47
Williams	5,208	9	7	2
Willits	4,856	16	11	5
Willows	6,053	10	9	1
Winters	7,120	13	11	2
Woodlake	7,727	9	8	1
Woodland	59,190	75	61	14
Yreka	7,559	20	14	6
Yuba City	67,198	78	52	26
COLORADO				
Alamosa	9,927	27	23	4
Arvada	117,186	215	158	57
Aspen	6,926	36	27	9
Ault	1,642	6	5	1
Aurora	366,477	810	670	140
Avon	6,532	19	17	2
Basalt	3,900	12	11	1
Bayfield	2,611	8	8	0
Black Hawk	126	34	23	11
Blue River	915	2	1	1
Boulder	109,189	267	176	91
Breckenridge	4,971	31	23	8
Brighton	38,363	88	63	25
Broomfield	66,953	209	108	101
Brush	5,456	14	11	3
Buena Vista	2,790	9	8	1
Burlington	3,624	8	7	1
Calhan	790	3	3	0
Campo	104	2	2	0
Canon City	16,390	40	32	8
Carbondale	6,728	17	15	2
Castle Rock	57,109	93	69	24
Cedaredge	2,170	8	6	2
Centennial	111,479	171	137	34
Center	2,196	14	8	6
Central City	736	2	2	0
Cherry Hills Village	6,649	28	23	5
Collbran	702	2	2	0
Colorado Springs	464,113	924	645	279
Columbine Valley	1,381	6	6	0
Commerce City	55,341	120	96	24
Cortez	8,761	49	29	20
Craig	8,724	26	21	5
Crested Butte	1,599	8	6	2
Cripple Creek	1,147	26	18	8
Dacono	4,925	13	10	3
De Beque	496	4	4	0
Del Norte	1,588	4	3	1
Delta	8,778	20	17	3
Denver	699,259	1,799	1,483	316
Dillon	972	9	8	1
Durango	18,248	65	55	10
Eagle	6,715	12	11	1
Eaton	5,045	10	8	2
Edgewater	5,330	18	17	1
Elizabeth	1,411	6	5	1
Englewood	33,657	100	71	29
Erie	22,115	27	25	2
Estes Park	6,335	30	19	11
Evans	21,975	38	35	3
Fairplay	681	3	3	0
Federal Heights	12,563	36	24	12
Firestone	12,375	26	21	5
Florence	3,861	12	11	1

Table 62. Full-Time Law Enforcement Employees, by Selected State and City, 2016—Continued

(Number.)

State/city	Population	Total law enforcement employees	Total officers	Total civilians
Fort Collins	164,670	292	206	86
Fort Lupton	7,903	16	14	2
Fort Morgan	11,313	31	26	5
Fountain	28,115	62	51	11
Fowler	1,141	3	3	0
Fraser/Winter Park	2,205	10	9	1
Frederick	12,045	20	17	3
Frisco	3,108	15	10	5
Fruita	12,825	18	16	2
Georgetown	1,052	3	3	0
Glendale	5,396	36	25	11
Glenwood Springs	9,978	31	24	7
Golden	20,616	64	43	21
Granby	1,880	7	6	1
Grand Junction	60,628	197	111	86
Greeley	102,491	196	145	51
Greenwood Village	16,024	89	63	26
Gunnison	6,110	30	14	16
Gypsum	7,012	3	3	0
Haxtun	926	3	3	0
Hayden	1,847	6	4	2
Holyoke	2,237	3	3	0
Hotchkiss	895	3	3	0
Hudson	1,477	3	3	0
Hugo	737	2	2	0
Idaho Springs	1,730	8	7	1
Ignacio	723	7	6	1
Johnstown	16,143	20	18	2
Kersey	1,602	4	4	0
Kiowa	753	4	4	0
Kremmling	1,461	4	4	0
Lafayette	28,421	48	38	10
La Junta	6,919	17	10	7
Lakeside	8	7	6	1
Lakewood	154,553	417	263	154
Lamar	7,479	33	19	14
La Salle	2,070	8	8	0
La Veta	752	2	2	0
Leadville	2,656	10	9	1
Limon	1,917	6	5	1
Littleton	47,288	95	70	25
Lochbuie	5,516	10	9	1
Log Lane Village	873	2	2	0
Lone Tree	13,593	49	42	7
Longmont	93,268	204	137	67
Louisville	20,814	38	32	6
Loveland	76,936	149	103	46
Mancos	1,388	4	4	0
Manitou Springs	5,397	18	16	2
Manzanola	416	2	2	0
Meeker	2,344	6	6	0
Milliken	6,551	11	9	2
Monte Vista	4,262	17	14	3
Montrose	19,054	50	36	14
Monument	6,497	17	14	3
Morrison	436	10	9	1
Mountain View	532	8	8	0
Mountain Village	1,412	9	6	3
Mount Crested Butte	833	9	8	1
Nederland	1,534	6	5	1
New Castle	4,706	9	8	1
Northglenn	39,890	79	60	19
Oak Creek	894	3	3	0
Olathe	1,790	4	4	0
Ouray	1,008	6	6	0
Pagosa Springs	1,763	8	7	1
Palisade	2,654	10	8	2
Palmer Lake	2,621	2	2	0
Paonia	1,395	4	4	0
Parachute	1,110	5	4	1
Parker	50,409	113	72	41
Platteville	3,737	6	6	0
Pueblo	109,927	250	195	55
Rangely	2,378	10	5	5
Ridgway	987	3	3	0
Rifle	9,613	24	20	4
Rocky Ford	3,801	8	8	0
Salida	5,516	17	15	2
Sanford	846	1	1	0
Sheridan	6,113	34	31	3
Silt	3,069	6	6	0
Silverthorne	4,530	16	14	2
Simla	635	2	2	0
Snowmass Village	2,935	13	10	3
South Fork	359	2	2	0

Table 62. Full-Time Law Enforcement Employees, by Selected State and City, 2016—Continued

(Number.)

State/city	Population	Total law enforcement employees	Total officers	Total civilians
Springfield	1,385	4	4	0
Steamboat Springs	12,512	37	24	13
Sterling	14,087	25	20	5
Stratton	659	1	1	0
Telluride	2,434	15	10	5
Thornton	136,451	245	180	65
Timnath	3,234	7	6	1
Trinidad	7,990	31	22	9
Vail	5,496	61	29	32
Walsenburg	2,871	10	8	2
Walsh	512	1	1	0
Westminster	114,514	247	174	73
Wheat Ridge	31,389	102	75	27
Wiggins	893	2	2	0
Windsor	22,404	27	23	4
Woodland Park	7,226	28	19	9
Wray	2,382	7	6	1
Yuma	3,612	8	7	1
CONNECTICUT				
Ansonia	18,776	49	42	7
Avon	18,464	41	32	9
Berlin	20,695	55	42	13
Bethel	19,712	50	37	13
Bloomfield	20,801	59	47	12
Branford	28,168	62	49	13
Bridgeport	148,180	433	376	57
Bristol	60,445	143	118	25
Brookfield	17,278	43	33	10
Canton	10,337	20	15	5
Cheshire	29,259	59	47	12
Clinton	13,008	36	27	9
Coventry	12,437	19	14	5
Cromwell	14,041	33	25	8
Danbury	85,335	151	146	5
Darien	21,995	57	49	8
Derby	12,660	36	34	2
East Hampton	12,839	17	15	2
East Hartford	50,733	153	123	30
East Haven	28,879	56	52	4
Easton	7,649	17	15	2
East Windsor	11,443	34	26	8
Enfield	44,258	114	94	20
Fairfield	61,889	113	107	6
Farmington	25,684	61	45	16
Glastonbury	34,724	75	57	18
Granby	11,301	20	15	5
Greenwich	62,970	178	151	27
Groton	9,189	34	27	7
Groton Long Point	512	5	5	0
Groton Town	29,910	64	59	5
Guilford	22,343	40	33	7
Hamden	61,138	135	108	27
Hartford	123,736	430	398	32
Madison	18,212	41	27	14
Manchester	57,957	135	104	31
Meriden	59,812	125	113	12
Middlebury	7,645	13	11	2
Middletown	46,580	122	109	13
Milford	53,752	138	116	22
Monroe	19,898	56	43	13
Naugatuck	31,469	68	57	11
New Britain	72,720	169	161	8
New Canaan	20,509	51	45	6
New Haven	130,425	509	454	55
Newington	30,610	64	51	13
New London	27,092	92	77	15
New Milford	27,111	62	50	12
Newtown	28,105	48	44	4
North Branford	14,234	27	22	5
North Haven	23,777	58	49	9
Norwalk	88,989	217	177	40
Norwich	39,771	102	88	14
Old Saybrook	10,145	32	25	7
Orange	13,940	53	43	10
Plainfield	15,015	22	18	4
Plainville	17,782	45	37	8
Plymouth	11,731	30	24	6
Portland	9,369	12	11	1
Putnam	9,331	18	15	3
Redding	9,317	23	17	6
Ridgefield	25,358	48	42	6
Rocky Hill	20,085	48	36	12
Seymour	16,462	43	41	2
Shelton	41,638	61	52	9

Table 62. Full-Time Law Enforcement Employees, by Selected State and City, 2016—Continued

(Number.)

State/city	Population	Total law enforcement employees	Total officers	Total civilians
Simsbury	24,519	47	37	10
Southington	43,948	89	68	21
South Windsor	25,803	52	38	14
Stamford	130,116	315	267	48
Stonington	18,337	48	37	11
Stratford	52,841	107	100	7
Suffield	15,641	22	17	5
Thomaston	7,570	28	16	12
Torrington	34,626	87	76	11
Trumbull	36,741	86	75	11
Vernon	28,915	64	49	15
Wallingford	44,840	90	69	21
Waterbury	108,491	316	272	44
Waterford	19,236	54	47	7
Watertown	21,792	48	39	9
West Hartford	62,979	146	128	18
West Haven	54,800	138	123	15
Weston	10,425	17	16	1
Westport	28,198	75	62	13
Wethersfield	26,306	61	48	13
Willimantic	17,766	48	43	5
Wilton	18,845	47	45	2
Winchester	10,750	24	19	5
Windsor	28,998	67	54	13
Windsor Locks	12,543	32	25	7
Wolcott	16,666	32	23	9
Woodbridge	8,864	31	23	8
DELAWARE				
Bethany Beach	1,193	11	9	2
Blades	1,377	3	3	0
Bridgeville	2,297	8	5	3
Camden	3,512	9	8	1
Cheswold	1,424	3	3	0
Clayton	3,165	10	9	1
Dagsboro	875	4	4	0
Delaware City	1,750	5	4	1
Delmar	1,757	13	12	1
Dewey Beach	378	10	8	2
Dover	37,824	136	105	31
Ellendale	422	1	1	0
Elsmere	6,149	13	12	1
Felton	1,423	4	4	0
Fenwick Island	425	6	6	0
Frankford	950	1	1	0
Georgetown	7,177	20	18	2
Greenwood	1,086	5	4	1
Harrington	3,719	13	12	1
Laurel	4,150	16	15	1
Lewes	3,065	13	12	1
Middletown	20,666	35	31	4
Milford	10,392	40	30	10
Millsboro	4,286	13	12	1
Milton	2,875	8	8	0
Newark	34,297	88	71	17
New Castle	5,392	17	16	1
Newport	1,059	10	9	1
Ocean View	2,075	10	9	1
Rehoboth Beach	1,485	27	17	10
Seaford	7,725	35	22	13
Selbyville	2,440	7	6	1
Smyrna	11,573	29	22	7
South Bethany	507	8	7	1
Wilmington	72,183	360	302	58
Wyoming	1,497	4	4	0
DISTRICT OF COLUMBIA				
Washington	681,170	4,352	3,753	599
FLORIDA				
Alachua	9,900	31	22	9
Altamonte Springs	43,499	114	98	16
Apalachicola	2,291	8	7	1
Apopka	49,796	128	94	34
Arcadia	7,893	19	15	4
Astatula	1,938	6	6	0
Atlantic Beach	13,302	37	25	12
Atlantis	2,126	19	14	5
Auburndale	15,356	41	33	8
Aventura	38,009	119	80	39
Bal Harbour Village	2,955	36	24	12
Bartow	19,322	58	36	22
Bay Harbor Islands	6,117	29	22	7
Belleair	4,017	14	12	2
Belle Isle	6,835	16	15	1

Table 62. Full-Time Law Enforcement Employees, by Selected State and City, 2016—Continued

(Number.)

State/city	Population	Total law enforcement employees	Total officers	Total civilians
Belleview	4,813	16	14	2
Biscayne Park	3,243	10	10	0
Blountstown	2,495	14	10	4
Boca Raton	94,931	287	182	105
Bonifay	2,712	6	6	0
Bowling Green	2,916	7	7	0
Boynton Beach	75,141	202	148	54
Bradenton	55,518	145	118	27
Bradenton Beach	1,257	10	10	0
Brooksville	7,881	26	23	3
Bunnell	2,856	11	9	2
Cape Coral	179,631	306	221	85
Casselberry	27,220	57	48	9
Cedar Key	703	3	3	0
Chattahoochee	3,059	11	10	1
Chiefland	2,213	14	12	2
Chipley	3,557	12	11	1
Clearwater	113,904	352	231	121
Clermont	33,158	71	65	6
Clewiston	7,579	25	17	8
Cocoa	17,825	87	63	24
Cocoa Beach	11,669	50	33	17
Coconut Creek	60,633	130	96	34
Cooper City	36,900	77	59	18
Coral Gables	51,980	229	160	69
Coral Springs	131,159	290	193	97
Cottondale	894	3	3	0
Crescent City	1,533	6	5	1
Crestview	23,749	60	48	12
Cross City	1,702	5	5	0
Dade City	7,061	29	22	7
Dania	31,806	75	68	7
Davenport	3,677	12	11	1
Davie	102,692	248	184	64
Daytona Beach	65,495	250	218	32
Daytona Beach Shores	4,417	36	28	8
Deerfield Beach	80,713	132	122	10
De Funiak Springs	5,927	27	20	7
DeLand	30,881	74	56	18
Delray Beach	67,400	213	155	58
Doral	58,309	158	118	40
Edgewater	21,729	35	30	5
Edgewood	2,856	16	13	3
El Portal	2,509	8	8	0
Eustis	20,292	51	38	13
Fernandina Beach	12,489	37	32	5
Flagler Beach	4,946	17	15	2
Fort Lauderdale	181,218	662	508	154
Fort Myers	76,579	238	179	59
Fort Pierce	44,987	133	108	25
Fort Walton Beach	22,314	54	40	14
Fruitland Park	4,548	15	14	1
Gainesville	131,242	360	299	61
Green Cove Springs	7,352	20	15	5
Groveland	12,192	33	26	7
Gulf Breeze	6,435	24	17	7
Gulfport	12,384	34	30	4
Gulf Stream	846	12	12	0
Haines City	23,278	57	44	13
Hallandale	39,960	129	92	37
Havana	1,674	13	9	4
Hialeah	239,451	324	260	64
Hialeah Gardens	24,370	54	38	16
Highland Beach	3,767	15	14	1
Holly Hill	12,002	31	27	4
Homestead	67,700	152	112	40
Howey-in-the-Hills	1,179	6	6	0
Indialantic	2,861	15	10	5
Indian Creek Village	92	14	10	4
Indian Harbour Beach	8,523	27	20	7
Indian River Shores	4,209	22	19	3
Interlachen	1,346	4	4	0
Jacksonville	880,557	2,947	1,758	1,189
Jacksonville Beach	23,418	81	62	19
Jasper	4,099	8	7	1
Jennings	869	2	2	0
Juno Beach	3,532	17	15	2
Jupiter	64,273	142	114	28
Jupiter Inlet Colony	454	6	6	0
Jupiter Island	901	24	16	8
Kenneth City	5,095	13	12	1
Key Biscayne	13,113	44	33	11
Key Colony Beach	862	5	5	0
Key West	25,976	118	92	26
Kissimmee	71,197	220	126	94

Table 62. Full-Time Law Enforcement Employees, by Selected State and City, 2016—Continued

(Number.)

State/city	Population	Total law enforcement employees	Total officers	Total civilians
Lady Lake	14,877	34	27	7
Lake Alfred	5,568	14	10	4
Lake City	12,186	54	38	16
Lake Clarke Shores	3,586	12	11	1
Lake Hamilton	1,370	7	6	1
Lake Helen	2,700	5	4	1
Lakeland	105,766	353	237	116
Lake Mary	16,506	59	42	17
Lake Placid	2,172	10	8	2
Lake Wales	15,819	48	43	5
Lantana	11,239	37	29	8
Largo	81,402	182	140	42
Lauderdale-by-the-Sea	6,541	26	24	2
Lauderdale Lakes	35,222	41	39	2
Lauderhill	72,504	123	98	25
Lawtey	717	2	2	0
Leesburg	22,313	82	58	24
Lighthouse Point	11,256	41	32	9
Live Oak	6,946	22	18	4
Longboat Key	7,343	26	18	8
Longwood	14,171	47	42	5
Lynn Haven	20,496	36	26	10
Madison	2,849	15	14	1
Maitland	17,824	51	44	7
Manalapan	458	12	10	2
Marco Island	17,947	37	34	3
Margate	58,030	140	105	35
Marianna	9,464	22	17	5
Mascotte	5,549	13	12	1
Melbourne	80,900	211	152	59
Melbourne Beach	3,243	11	10	1
Melbourne Village	697	5	5	0
Mexico Beach	1,187	8	7	1
Miami	449,469	1,559	1,201	358
Miami Beach	93,165	492	394	98
Miami Springs	14,620	53	41	12
Midway	3,325	5	5	0
Milton	9,788	25	19	6
Miramar	140,288	272	203	69
Monticello	2,393	13	9	4
Mount Dora	13,796	51	34	17
Naples	21,917	98	67	31
Neptune Beach	7,316	27	20	7
New Port Richey	16,038	58	41	17
New Smyrna Beach	24,658	57	44	13
Niceville	15,142	34	26	8
North Bay Village	8,552	36	26	10
North Lauderdale	44,229	58	51	7
North Miami	62,974	160	114	46
North Miami Beach	44,442	140	106	34
North Palm Beach	13,023	31	30	1
North Port	63,386	127	98	29
Oakland	2,890	12	11	1
Oakland Park	44,903	96	85	11
Ocala	58,596	231	159	72
Ocean Ridge	1,928	21	16	5
Ocoee	45,330	89	77	12
Orange City	11,262	28	23	5
Orange Park	8,763	29	21	8
Orlando	277,719	915	715	200
Ormond Beach	41,325	82	61	21
Palatka	10,362	38	30	8
Palm Bay	108,823	212	155	57
Palm Beach	8,702	93	62	31
Palm Beach Gardens	53,811	159	108	51
Palm Beach Shores	1,221	15	11	4
Palmetto	13,371	47	34	13
Palm Springs	22,581	68	44	24
Panama City	38,847	131	95	36
Panama City Beach	12,844	77	58	19
Parker	4,661	10	9	1
Parkland	31,571	45	40	5
Pembroke Pines	169,156	298	218	80
Pensacola	53,424	200	140	60
Perry	7,063	22	20	2
Pinellas Park	52,113	121	101	20
Plantation	94,075	252	165	87
Plant City	37,949	84	67	17
Ponce Inlet	3,183	14	12	2
Port Orange	60,546	99	85	14
Port Richey	2,779	19	13	6
Port St. Joe	3,441	8	8	0
Port St. Lucie	182,365	289	229	60
Punta Gorda	18,466	49	34	15
Quincy	7,760	33	25	8

Table 62. Full-Time Law Enforcement Employees, by Selected State and City, 2016—Continued

(Number.)

State/city	Population	Total law enforcement employees	Total officers	Total civilians
Riviera Beach	34,304	150	107	43
Rockledge	26,967	71	50	21
Sanibel	7,395	39	25	14
Sarasota	55,732	209	163	46
Satellite Beach	10,737	30	21	9
Sea Ranch Lakes	739	11	7	4
Sebastian	24,441	52	34	18
Sebring	10,516	39	35	4
Sewall's Point	2,180	10	9	1
South Daytona	12,653	32	26	6
South Miami	12,354	55	50	5
South Palm Beach	1,437	8	8	0
Springfield	9,550	24	19	5
Starke	5,390	20	19	1
St. Augustine	14,359	62	49	13
St. Cloud	47,289	117	79	38
St. Petersburg	259,510	759	548	211
Stuart	16,640	70	44	26
Sunrise	94,400	231	175	56
Tallahassee	191,564	437	372	65
Tamarac	65,516	99	81	18
Tampa	375,904	1,212	951	261
Tarpon Springs	24,834	61	48	13
Tavares	15,741	28	25	3
Temple Terrace	25,972	66	50	16
Tequesta	6,003	23	18	5
Titusville	45,723	123	86	37
Trenton	2,079	4	3	1
Umatilla	3,751	9	8	1
Valparaiso	5,023	15	11	4
Venice	22,514	57	44	13
Vero Beach	16,589	71	52	19
Village of Pinecrest	19,692	78	54	24
Virginia Gardens	2,508	8	7	1
Wauchula	4,936	17	13	4
West Melbourne	21,156	44	37	7
West Miami	7,163	22	18	4
West Palm Beach	108,074	365	278	87
White Springs	773	10	10	0
Wildwood	6,788	43	33	10
Williston	2,741	18	11	7
Wilton Manors	12,535	48	33	15
Windermere	3,320	14	13	1
Winter Garden	41,556	100	71	29
Winter Haven	38,488	112	86	26
Winter Park	30,359	110	80	30
Winter Springs	35,100	65	51	14
Zephyrhills	14,833	45	30	15
GEORGIA				
Abbeville	2,796	5	5	0
Adairsville	4,804	18	16	2
Adel	5,313	23	21	2
Alamo	3,374	4	4	0
Alapaha	653	2	1	1
Albany	74,330	186	162	24
Alma	3,548	12	10	2
Alto	1,166	3	1	2
Americus	15,838	39	33	6
Aragon	1,241	4	3	1
Arcade	1,801	3	3	0
Ashburn	3,757	18	16	2
Athens-Clarke County	123,934	292	228	64
Atlanta	472,579	2,140	1,694	446
Auburn	7,621	23	16	7
Austell	7,204	32	23	9
Avondale Estates	3,175	11	11	0
Bainbridge	12,473	46	44	2
Baldwin	3,287	14	7	7
Barnesville	6,611	19	17	2
Baxley	4,452	12	11	1
Berlin	559	1	1	0
Blackshear	3,608	16	13	3
Blairsville	542	8	7	1
Bloomingdale	2,778	15	12	3
Blythe	697	1	1	0
Braselton	9,912	17	16	1
Bremen	6,380	22	20	2
Brookhaven	52,442	85	77	8
Brunswick	16,309	63	59	4
Byron	5,222	23	19	4
Cairo	9,772	24	21	3
Calhoun	16,439	49	42	7
Camilla	5,080	18	16	2
Canton	25,985	50	45	5

Table 62. Full-Time Law Enforcement Employees, by Selected State and City, 2016—Continued
(Number.)

State/city	Population	Total law enforcement employees	Total officers	Total civilians
Carrollton	26,593	76	63	13
Centerville	7,657	18	15	3
Chatsworth	4,362	17	15	2
Claxton	2,324	9	8	1
Clayton	2,250	12	12	0
Cleveland	3,828	16	15	1
Cochran	4,234	14	13	1
College Park	14,724	117	91	26
Conyers	16,004	84	64	20
Coolidge	526	2	1	1
Cordele	10,907	35	26	9
Covington	14,077	66	55	11
Cumming	5,772	24	15	9
Dallas	13,135	29	20	9
Dalton	33,989	96	83	13
Danielsville	579	3	3	0
Darien	1,842	10	10	0
Davisboro	1,989	2	2	0
Dawson	4,315	23	16	7
Decatur	22,449	51	39	12
Doerun	772	4	4	0
Donalsonville	2,680	13	9	4
Douglasville	33,287	122	97	25
Dublin	16,195	63	57	6
Duluth	29,720	93	78	15
Dunwoody	49,232	64	54	10
Eastman	5,232	15	13	2
Eatonton	6,528	22	15	7
Elberton	4,432	22	20	2
Ellaville	1,892	6	6	0
Ellijay	1,691	10	10	0
Emerson	1,546	11	9	2
Enigma	1,285	3	3	0
Eton	902	3	3	0
Fairburn	14,151	44	37	7
Fairmount	739	6	5	1
Fayetteville	17,157	46	41	5
Fitzgerald	9,001	28	23	5
Flowery Branch	6,895	18	16	2
Folkston	5,349	7	6	1
Forest Park	19,570	89	68	21
Forsyth	4,042	18	13	5
Fort Oglethorpe	9,911	29	27	2
Fort Valley	8,374	29	23	6
Franklin	964	8	8	0
Franklin Springs	1,195	2	2	0
Gainesville	39,425	111	98	13
Glennville	5,068	15	13	2
Glenwood	737	2	2	0
Gordon	1,946	11	6	5
Gray	3,271	14	13	1
Greensboro	3,411	22	18	4
Grovetown	13,469	28	21	7
Guyton	1,891	4	4	0
Hahira	2,928	8	7	1
Hampton	7,451	18	16	2
Harlem	3,026	8	7	1
Hartwell	4,523	26	20	6
Hazlehurst	4,189	17	13	4
Helen	536	9	8	1
Hiram	3,840	18	15	3
Hoboken	531	2	1	1
Hogansville	3,126	21	14	7
Holly Springs	11,034	28	27	1
Homeland	861	7	7	0
Homerville	2,487	13	11	2
Jackson	4,966	14	12	2
Jesup	9,525	29	27	2
Johns Creek	84,629	81	72	9
Jonesboro	4,752	39	31	8
Kennesaw	34,204	75	58	17
Kingsland	16,597	35	33	2
Kingston	657	1	1	0
Lafayette	7,185	24	22	2
LaGrange	30,931	100	84	16
Lake City	2,752	20	19	1
Lakeland	3,314	7	5	2
Lake Park	729	4	4	0
Lawrenceville	30,913	94	70	24
Leary	583	2	1	1
Leslie	384	4	3	1
Lilburn	12,854	38	30	8
Locust Grove	5,862	23	20	3
Loganville	11,409	33	30	3
Lyons	4,372	20	18	2

Table 62. Full-Time Law Enforcement Employees, by Selected State and City, 2016—Continued

(Number.)

State/city	Population	Total law enforcement employees	Total officers	Total civilians
Madison	4,034	17	15	2
Manchester	4,068	15	10	5
Marietta	59,516	175	137	38
McIntyre	615	5	5	0
McRae-Helena	8,786	12	11	1
Metter	4,107	11	10	1
Midville	262	1	1	0
Midway	1,992	6	6	0
Milledgeville	19,072	68	44	24
Millen	2,889	10	10	0
Milton	38,551	41	37	4
Montezuma	3,141	13	11	2
Mountain City	1,056	3	3	0
Mount Zion	1,743	4	4	0
Nashville	4,834	17	14	3
Newnan	38,137	93	79	14
Nicholls	3,378	3	2	1
Norcross	16,929	58	42	16
Norman Park	961	3	2	1
Oakwood	4,218	16	14	2
Oxford	2,210	4	4	0
Palmetto	4,780	17	15	2
Patterson	755	2	2	0
Peachtree City	35,387	68	63	5
Pelham	3,669	13	12	1
Pine Mountain	1,368	10	8	2
Pooler	24,006	55	49	6
Porterdale	1,494	4	4	0
Port Wentworth	8,177	32	27	5
Poulan	793	6	5	1
Powder Springs	15,004	33	30	3
Quitman	3,863	18	16	2
Remerton	1,127	9	8	1
Reynolds	1,016	8	6	2
Richland	1,502	7	7	0
Richmond Hill	12,520	39	32	7
Ringgold	3,722	11	11	0
Riverdale	16,142	52	38	14
Rochelle	1,109	6	4	2
Rockmart	4,322	20	18	2
Rome	36,278	97	89	8
Roswell	95,684	196	141	55
Royston	2,574	15	13	2
Sandersville	5,724	21	18	3
Sandy Springs	107,685	144	127	17
Sardis	957	5	5	0
Savannah-Chatham Metropolitan	241,296	821	570	251
Senoia	4,233	17	15	2
Sky Valley	264	2	2	0
Smyrna	57,152	127	90	37
Snellville	20,025	56	44	12
Sparks	1,999	3	3	0
Sparta	1,275	10	4	6
Springfield	2,903	7	6	1
Statesboro	31,176	80	61	19
Statham	2,647	6	5	1
Stillmore	527	1	1	0
St. Marys	18,102	33	30	3
Stone Mountain	6,171	19	18	1
Summerville	4,442	17	16	1
Suwanee	19,432	45	36	9
Swainsboro	7,512	24	21	3
Sylvania	2,527	13	11	2
Sylvester	6,019	23	19	4
Talbotton	874	2	2	0
Tallapoosa	3,170	11	10	1
Tallulah Falls	168	2	2	0
Tennille	1,826	3	3	0
Thunderbolt	2,641	12	10	2
Tifton	16,799	46	38	8
Toccoa	8,252	28	27	1
Trenton	2,226	8	8	0
Tybee Island	3,124	33	24	9
Tyrone	7,243	19	17	2
Valdosta	55,880	157	135	22
Vidalia	10,721	43	29	14
Vienna	3,735	9	7	2
Villa Rica	15,095	48	40	8
Walthourville	3,957	6	5	1
Warner Robins	74,419	146	104	42
Warwick	404	6	5	1
Watkinsville	2,877	8	8	0
Waverly Hall	842	3	3	0
Waycross	13,934	62	52	10
West Point	3,785	23	15	8

Table 62. Full-Time Law Enforcement Employees, by Selected State and City, 2016—Continued

(Number.)

State/city	Population	Total law enforcement employees	Total officers	Total civilians
Whigham	480	4	3	1
Willacoochee	1,395	6	5	1
Winder	15,652	42	37	5
Winterville	1,182	2	2	0
Woodland	361	1	1	0
Woodstock	31,243	55	50	5
Wrens	2,026	8	7	1
Wrightsville	3,620	6	5	1
Zebulon	1,150	6	6	0
HAWAII				
Honolulu	995,572	2,537	2,042	495
IDAHO				
Aberdeen	1,915	7	4	3
American Falls	4,291	10	8	2
Bellevue	2,296	5	5	0
Blackfoot	11,700	30	27	3
Boise	220,749	363	272	91
Bonners Ferry	2,549	7	7	0
Buhl	4,305	9	8	1
Caldwell	52,792	78	64	14
Chubbuck	14,515	33	19	14
Coeur d'Alene	50,155	98	80	18
Cottonwood	925	1	1	0
Emmett	6,617	14	13	1
Filer	2,724	6	6	0
Fruitland	5,170	15	9	6
Garden City	11,667	35	27	8
Gooding	3,497	9	7	2
Grangeville	3,156	6	6	0
Hagerman	866	1	1	0
Hailey	8,175	14	13	1
Heyburn	3,250	8	7	1
Homedale	2,554	6	6	0
Idaho City	472	1	1	0
Idaho Falls	59,615	132	87	45
Jerome	11,234	21	18	3
Kamiah	1,269	4	4	0
Kellogg	2,061	7	7	0
Ketchum	2,732	15	11	4
Kimberly	3,680	9	8	1
Lewiston	32,665	63	41	22
McCall	3,139	14	12	2
Meridian	94,113	115	92	23
Montpelier	2,493	5	5	0
Moscow	25,307	43	35	8
Mountain Home	13,627	31	26	5
Nampa	91,520	167	112	55
Orofino	3,056	6	5	1
Osburn	1,503	2	2	0
Parma	2,101	4	4	0
Payette	7,360	16	14	2
Pinehurst	1,573	2	2	0
Pocatello	54,462	127	88	39
Ponderay	1,138	7	6	1
Post Falls	31,026	70	43	27
Preston	5,214	8	7	1
Priest River	1,761	7	5	2
Rathdrum	7,681	16	13	3
Rexburg	28,112	40	32	8
Rigby	4,040	8	7	1
Rupert	5,736	13	12	1
Salmon	3,019	8	8	0
Sandpoint	7,931	20	17	3
Shelley	4,321	8	8	0
Shoshone	1,492	5	5	0
Soda Springs	2,921	7	7	0
Spirit Lake	2,117	7	6	1
St. Anthony	3,423	6	5	1
St. Maries	2,310	4	4	0
Sun Valley	1,426	11	10	1
Twin Falls	48,083	102	71	31
Weiser	5,281	15	12	3
Wilder	1,640	4	4	0
ILLINOIS				
Addison	37,246	119	66	53
Altamont	2,306	5	5	0
Alton	26,829	75	58	17
Annawan	854	1	1	0
Antioch	14,302	29	26	3
Arlington Heights	76,077	136	108	28
Arthur	2,288	6	6	0
Assumption	1,106	1	1	0

Table 62. Full-Time Law Enforcement Employees, by Selected State and City, 2016—Continued

(Number.)

State/city	Population	Total law enforcement employees	Total officers	Total civilians
Athens	1,928	4	4	0
Auburn	4,788	9	5	4
Batavia	26,558	46	40	6
Berkeley	5,201	20	17	3
Bethalto	9,314	18	14	4
Bloomington	78,604	161	125	36
Bolingbrook	74,471	124	109	15
Bourbonnais	18,552	31	24	7
Braidwood	6,160	17	14	3
Brookfield	18,935	34	29	5
Buffalo Grove	41,511	74	63	11
Burnham	4,209	12	10	2
Burr Ridge	10,863	30	27	3
Byron	3,628	7	6	1
Cairo	2,402	12	7	5
Cambridge	2,104	1	1	0
Camp Point	1,123	1	1	0
Campton Hills	11,390	6	6	0
Canton	14,116	29	20	9
Carbondale	26,373	83	67	16
Carlinville	5,615	17	12	5
Carlyle	3,211	8	7	1
Carol Stream	40,473	82	60	22
Carthage	2,534	4	4	0
Cary	17,903	29	26	3
Caseyville	4,003	13	12	1
Centreville	4,970	10	10	0
Champaign	87,071	141	119	22
Charleston	21,067	34	31	3
Chenoa	3,199	5	5	0
Chester	8,590	11	8	3
Chicago	2,725,153	13,135	11,954	1,181
Chicago Ridge	14,383	35	31	4
Chillicothe	6,253	14	11	3
Christopher	2,771	6	6	0
Cicero	83,807	176	150	26
Clarendon Hills	8,724	15	14	1
Coal City	5,469	11	10	1
Cobden	1,136	3	3	0
Colfax	1,043	1	1	0
Columbia	10,288	22	16	6
Countryside	6,015	27	24	3
Crest Hill	21,211	30	28	2
Crete	8,171	18	17	1
Creve Coeur	5,235	10	8	2
Crystal Lake	40,374	69	60	9
Darien	22,285	40	34	6
Decatur	72,694	189	158	31
De Kalb	43,034	77	62	15
Delavan	1,622	3	3	0
De Pue	1,726	3	3	0
De Soto	1,571	4	3	1
Divernon	1,153	3	3	0
Dixon	15,246	34	30	4
Downers Grove	49,894	98	71	27
Dupo	3,881	6	6	0
Earlville	1,619	3	3	0
East Hazel Crest	1,545	11	9	2
East Peoria	23,008	60	48	12
Edwardsville	25,133	56	42	14
Effingham	12,660	35	21	14
Elgin	112,886	246	182	64
Elk Grove Village	33,255	105	89	16
Elmhurst	46,318	89	67	22
Elmwood	2,088	2	2	0
Elwood	2,253	11	10	1
Erie	1,543	2	2	0
Eureka	5,388	6	6	0
Evanston	75,716	227	166	61
Evergreen Park	19,836	80	62	18
Fairfield	5,019	13	9	4
Farmington	2,305	5	5	0
Fox Lake	10,495	25	22	3
Frankfort	18,822	32	28	4
Freeburg	4,218	11	10	1
Freeport	24,257	63	45	18
Galena	3,276	11	10	1
Genoa	5,197	8	7	1
Germantown	1,285	1	1	0
Gibson City	3,408	8	6	2
Gifford	1,117	1	1	0
Gilman	1,743	2	2	0
Glenview	48,008	74	69	5
Granite City	28,899	69	56	13
Greenfield	1,010	2	2	0

Table 62. Full-Time Law Enforcement Employees, by Selected State and City, 2016—Continued

(Number.)

State/city	Population	Total law enforcement employees	Total officers	Total civilians
Gurnee	31,014	90	60	30
Hanover Park	38,402	81	56	25
Henry	2,301	5	4	1
Herrin	12,985	26	19	7
Herscher	1,547	3	3	0
Hickory Hills	14,134	32	25	7
Highland	9,827	26	19	7
Hillsboro	5,635	8	8	0
Hillsdale	509	1	1	0
Hinckley	2,056	3	3	0
Hinsdale	17,790	25	23	2
Hodgkins	1,862	23	21	2
Hoffman Estates	52,177	103	88	15
Homer	1,199	1	1	0
Hometown	4,340	4	1	3
Homewood	19,379	43	38	5
Hopedale	839	1	1	0
Ina	2,365	2	2	0
Island Lake	8,079	14	13	1
Itasca	8,825	24	21	3
Jacksonville	19,039	45	41	4
Johnsburg	6,303	12	10	2
Joliet	147,886	330	263	67
Kankakee	26,509	72	68	4
Kenilworth	2,563	12	9	3
Kewanee	12,460	29	22	7
Kincaid	1,424	3	2	1
Kingston	1,154	2	2	0
Kirkland	1,732	3	3	0
Ladd	1,231	2	2	0
La Grange	15,754	38	28	10
Lake Villa	8,849	18	17	1
Lake Zurich	20,051	51	34	17
La Salle	9,194	23	22	1
Lawrenceville	4,428	7	7	0
Lemont	16,927	30	27	3
Le Roy	3,585	7	7	0
Lexington	2,058	2	2	0
Lincolnwood	12,655	40	33	7
Lindenhurst	14,408	17	14	3
Lisle	23,063	41	32	9
Lombard	43,866	82	68	14
Loves Park	23,349	37	34	3
Lovington	1,104	2	2	0
Lyons	10,719	19	13	6
Macomb	18,402	29	26	3
Marengo	7,467	15	13	2
Marissa	1,833	4	4	0
Maroa	1,727	3	3	0
Maryville	7,978	13	13	0
Mattoon	18,026	42	38	4
McHenry	26,581	57	46	11
Mendota	7,173	18	15	3
Metropolis	6,290	19	14	5
Milledgeville	973	2	2	0
Moline	42,517	98	79	19
Monee	5,068	15	13	2
Monmouth	9,261	28	17	11
Morris	14,507	28	25	3
Morrison	4,137	6	6	0
Morton	16,310	28	22	6
Mount Carmel	6,982	15	10	5
Mount Carroll	1,602	3	3	0
Mount Morris	2,854	5	4	1
Mount Prospect	54,839	102	82	20
Mount Zion	5,865	11	9	2
Moweaqua	1,736	2	2	0
Mundelein	31,685	70	51	19
Neoga	1,609	3	3	0
New Athens	1,930	4	4	0
New Lenox	26,085	41	37	4
Newton	2,807	7	6	1
Niles	29,886	68	55	13
Normal	54,727	93	81	12
Norridge	14,629	49	35	14
Oak Brook	8,130	43	40	3
Oakbrook Terrace	2,169	23	19	4
Oak Forest	28,088	52	41	11
Oak Lawn	56,791	124	108	16
Okawville	1,392	3	3	0
Olney	8,984	14	13	1
Orion	1,818	2	2	0
Orland Park	59,009	124	98	26
Ottawa	18,263	50	35	15
Palestine	1,324	2	2	0

Table 62. Full-Time Law Enforcement Employees, by Selected State and City, 2016—Continued

(Number.)

State/city	Population	Total law enforcement employees	Total officers	Total civilians
Palos Hills	17,578	34	31	3
Park City	7,357	14	11	3
Park Forest	21,947	48	40	8
Park Ridge	37,805	66	54	12
Pawnee	2,707	6	6	0
Pekin	33,052	64	54	10
Peotone	4,114	10	9	1
Pingree Grove	7,162	7	6	1
Plano	11,358	18	16	2
Pontiac	11,771	18	17	1
Pontoon Beach	5,598	20	14	6
Posen	5,992	20	18	2
Princeton	7,534	19	17	2
Prophetstown	1,999	2	2	0
Quincy	40,799	83	70	13
Raleigh	348	1	1	0
Red Bud	3,564	6	6	0
Richmond	1,904	5	5	0
Riverwoods	3,639	8	8	0
Robinson	7,616	14	13	1
Rockdale	1,942	5	5	0
Rockford	147,363	323	288	35
Rolling Meadows	24,205	57	50	7
Roscoe	10,523	14	13	1
Roselle	23,037	36	29	7
Rosemont	4,206	99	77	22
Round Lake Beach	27,796	38	37	1
Round Lake Heights	2,713	5	5	0
Roxana	1,472	7	6	1
Royalton	1,135	3	3	0
Rushville	2,927	4	4	0
Salem	7,249	23	15	8
Sandoval	1,221	3	3	0
Sauget	151	11	11	0
Savanna	2,845	7	7	0
Schiller Park	11,807	39	32	7
Seneca	2,278	6	5	1
Shawneetown	1,150	3	3	0
Silvis	7,487	21	15	6
Sleepy Hollow	3,354	8	7	1
South Beloit	7,639	15	14	1
South Chicago Heights	4,137	10	9	1
South Elgin	22,436	35	31	4
South Jacksonville	3,248	6	5	1
South Pekin	1,115	2	2	0
Springfield	116,563	268	241	27
Spring Valley	5,269	12	10	2
St. Anne	1,213	3	3	0
St. Charles	33,556	63	52	11
Steger	9,502	19	15	4
St. Elmo	1,402	3	3	0
Stickney	6,785	23	16	7
Stonington	882	2	2	0
Streator	13,082	26	24	2
Tolono	3,483	2	2	0
Urbana	42,461	68	54	14
Vernon Hills	26,574	71	42	29
Vienna	1,696	3	3	0
Walnut	1,338	2	2	0
Warren	1,366	4	3	1
Wauconda	13,843	27	25	2
Waukegan	88,337	189	150	39
Wenona	975	2	2	0
West Chicago	27,490	51	46	5
West Dundee	7,406	18	16	2
Westmont	24,992	40	35	5
Wheaton	53,848	82	66	16
Wheeling	38,158	95	60	35
White Hall	2,389	7	5	2
Willow Springs	5,701	10	7	3
Winnebago	2,995	6	6	0
Wood Dale	13,943	44	35	9
Wood River	10,225	24	18	6
Worth	10,781	27	24	3
Zion	24,067	59	46	13
INDIANA				
Auburn	13,010	24	23	1
Avon	17,076	25	23	2
Bremen	4,561	17	12	5
Clinton	4,799	9	8	1
Columbia City	8,873	18	17	1
East Chicago	28,503	101	94	7
Edinburgh	4,560	13	12	1
Elkhart	52,505	142	120	22

Table 62. Full-Time Law Enforcement Employees, by Selected State and City, 2016—Continued

(Number.)

State/city	Population	Total law enforcement employees	Total officers	Total civilians
Elwood	8,427	18	17	1
Evansville	119,908	305	281	24
Fairmount	2,832	6	5	1
Frankfort	15,987	33	31	2
Gas City	5,931	10	10	0
Greenwood	56,502	66	58	8
Hammond	77,005	234	207	27
Highland	22,783	45	38	7
Hobart	28,223	71	62	9
Indianapolis	866,351	1,806	1,612	194
Jeffersonville	47,327	87	82	5
Kendallville	9,942	24	19	5
La Porte	21,891	49	43	6
Mishawaka	48,267	121	107	14
Mooresville	9,675	27	21	6
Munster	22,865	42	37	5
New Whiteland	5,991	7	6	1
North Vernon	6,599	19	16	3
Portage	36,715	74	67	7
Portland	6,183	16	12	4
Scottsburg	6,655	14	14	0
Sellersburg	8,723	18	16	2
Seymour	19,762	56	40	16
South Bend	101,621	284	240	44
Tell City	7,253	20	12	8
Valparaiso	32,796	55	50	5
Vincennes	17,937	42	38	4
Walkerton	2,289	10	6	4
Warsaw	14,657	43	37	6
Westfield	38,186	50	45	5
Whitestown	6,850	13	12	1
Whiting	4,848	20	18	2
Winchester	4,732	13	13	0
Zionsville	26,877	30	29	1
IOWA				
Adel	4,356	10	9	1
Albia	3,840	7	6	1
Algona	5,453	14	10	4
Altoona	17,503	29	26	3
Ames	66,333	76	52	24
Anamosa	5,454	9	8	1
Ankeny	59,236	62	54	8
Arnolds Park	1,255	6	5	1
Atlantic	6,781	13	12	1
Audubon	1,988	4	4	0
Belle Plaine	2,464	5	5	0
Belmond	2,303	5	5	0
Bettendorf	35,946	52	45	7
Bloomfield	2,611	7	6	1
Blue Grass	1,724	2	2	0
Boone	12,702	19	18	1
Buffalo	1,304	3	3	0
Burlington	25,376	47	43	4
Camanche	4,320	6	6	0
Carlisle	4,225	7	6	1
Carroll	9,940	16	15	1
Carter Lake	3,791	11	10	1
Cedar Falls	41,651	41	40	1
Cedar Rapids	131,181	280	214	66
Centerville	5,343	17	11	6
Chariton	4,194	5	4	1
Charles City	7,417	21	14	7
Cherokee	4,983	9	8	1
Clarinda	5,386	11	10	1
Clarion	2,752	7	6	1
Clear Lake	7,555	22	16	6
Clinton	25,906	46	40	6
Clive	17,836	27	24	3
Colfax	2,043	4	4	0
Coralville	20,957	37	33	4
Council Bluffs	62,642	129	109	20
Cresco	3,826	7	7	0
Creston	7,860	15	11	4
Davenport	103,118	178	158	20
Decorah	7,864	21	13	8
Denison	8,335	17	12	5
Des Moines	211,501	446	343	103
De Witt	5,226	12	11	1
Dubuque	59,026	108	101	7
Dyersville	4,231	6	6	0
Eagle Grove	3,389	7	7	0
Eldora	2,696	4	4	0
Eldridge	6,348	10	9	1
Emmetsburg	3,795	7	6	1

Table 62. Full-Time Law Enforcement Employees, by Selected State and City, 2016—Continued

(Number.)

State/city	Population	Total law enforcement employees	Total officers	Total civilians
Estherville	5,947	12	12	0
Evansdale	4,824	8	7	1
Fairfield	9,982	21	14	7
Forest City	3,994	8	8	0
Fort Dodge	24,557	46	40	6
Fort Madison	10,654	21	19	2
Garner	3,104	5	5	0
Glenwood	5,250	11	10	1
Grinnell	9,127	17	15	2
Grundy Center	2,715	4	4	0
Hampton	4,256	8	7	1
Harlan	4,982	9	8	1
Hawarden	2,552	4	4	0
Hiawatha	7,235	14	14	0
Humboldt	4,579	6	6	0
Independence	6,041	12	11	1
Indianola	15,601	22	20	2
Iowa City	75,527	103	80	23
Iowa Falls	5,186	14	10	4
Jefferson	4,176	7	7	0
Johnston	21,635	29	27	2
Keokuk	10,577	27	24	3
Knoxville	7,239	15	14	1
Le Claire	4,029	8	7	1
Le Mars	9,750	15	14	1
Leon	1,890	4	3	1
Lisbon	2,212	1	1	0
Manchester	5,051	16	10	6
Maquoketa	5,961	18	11	7
Marengo	2,511	4	4	0
Marion	37,845	57	45	12
Marshalltown	27,628	58	41	17
Mason City	27,230	51	46	5
Missouri Valley	2,668	6	6	0
Monticello	3,832	7	6	1
Mount Pleasant	8,389	16	14	2
Mount Vernon	4,482	6	6	0
Muscatine	24,010	43	40	3
Nevada	6,836	10	8	2
New Hampton	3,430	6	6	0
New Sharon	1,290	1	1	0
Newton	15,102	27	22	5
North Liberty	16,458	21	20	1
Norwalk	10,371	14	13	1
Oelwein	6,104	15	10	5
Ogden	2,041	3	3	0
Onawa	2,859	6	6	0
Orange City	6,225	7	7	0
Osage	3,659	7	6	1
Osceola	4,976	12	11	1
Oskaloosa	11,626	18	16	2
Ottumwa	24,543	47	38	9
Pella	10,368	24	18	6
Perry	8,160	19	12	7
Pleasant Hill	9,415	20	18	2
Polk City	4,524	6	6	0
Prairie City	1,715	3	3	0
Princeton	937	1	1	0
Red Oak	5,424	11	9	2
Rock Valley	3,762	5	5	0
Sac City	2,129	4	4	0
Sergeant Bluff	4,579	9	8	1
Sheldon	5,067	7	7	0
Sigourney	1,995	3	3	0
Sioux Center	7,544	7	7	0
Sioux City	82,819	150	125	25
Spencer	11,211	28	18	10
Spirit Lake	5,049	10	9	1
Storm Lake	10,959	23	19	4
Story City	3,439	6	6	0
Tama	2,809	5	5	0
Tipton	3,196	7	6	1
Toledo	2,176	5	5	0
Urbandale	45,012	59	51	8
Vinton	5,128	9	8	1
Walcott	1,639	3	3	0
Washington	7,437	12	11	1
Waterloo	68,470	133	124	9
Waukee	20,186	22	20	2
Waukon	3,701	7	7	0
Waverly	10,104	17	16	1
Webster City	7,768	17	12	5
West Burlington	3,055	10	9	1
West Des Moines	65,631	78	63	15
Williamsburg	3,221	6	6	0

Table 62. Full-Time Law Enforcement Employees, by Selected State and City, 2016—Continued

(Number.)

State/city	Population	Total law enforcement employees	Total officers	Total civilians
Wilton	2,808	4	4	0
Windsor Heights	4,893	11	10	1
Winterset	5,170	8	8	0
KANSAS				
Abilene	6,501	17	14	3
Altamont	1,041	3	3	0
Andale	1,004	2	2	0
Andover	12,937	33	26	7
Anthony	2,224	6	5	1
Argonia	485	1	1	0
Arkansas City	12,085	28	24	4
Arma	1,445	5	5	0
Atchison	10,654	24	23	1
Attica	584	1	1	0
Atwood	1,187	3	3	0
Augusta	9,304	34	25	9
Baldwin City	4,698	11	10	1
Basehor	5,563	13	11	2
Bel Aire	7,574	13	12	1
Belle Plaine	1,610	4	4	0
Belleville	1,894	4	4	0
Beloit	3,784	6	6	0
Benton	875	2	2	0
Blue Rapids	976	2	2	0
Bonner Springs	7,625	27	25	2
Buhler	1,330	3	3	0
Burlington	2,604	9	7	2
Burrton	894	2	2	0
Caldwell	1,023	2	2	0
Caney	2,054	11	6	5
Canton	731	1	1	0
Carbondale	1,388	2	2	0
Cawker City	453	1	1	0
Cedar Vale	525	1	1	0
Chanute	9,279	20	18	2
Chapman	1,372	2	2	0
Cheney	2,170	7	7	0
Cherokee	713	1	1	0
Cherryvale	2,203	6	6	0
Chetopa	1,074	4	4	0
Clay Center	4,140	7	6	1
Clearwater	2,547	6	5	1
Coffeyville	9,555	30	21	9
Colby	5,418	18	12	6
Coldwater	802	1	1	0
Columbus	3,116	9	8	1
Colwich	1,388	3	3	0
Concordia	5,183	16	9	7
Conway Springs	1,231	2	2	0
Council Grove	2,068	8	7	1
Derby	23,708	55	45	10
Dodge City	27,997	63	43	20
Eastborough	767	6	6	0
Edwardsville	4,377	18	17	1
El Dorado	12,913	28	27	1
Elkhart	2,011	2	2	0
Ellinwood	2,053	5	5	0
Ellis	2,065	5	5	0
Ellsworth	3,043	7	6	1
Elwood	1,181	2	2	0
Erie	1,097	5	4	1
Eudora	6,424	11	10	1
Fairway	3,987	11	9	2
Fort Scott	7,792	29	20	9
Fredonia	2,296	7	6	1
Frontenac	3,419	11	7	4
Galena	2,901	10	9	1
Galva	882	1	1	0
Garden City	27,038	91	62	29
Garden Plain	907	3	3	0
Garnett	3,229	8	8	0
Girard	2,754	7	6	1
Goddard	4,782	13	12	1
Goodland	4,450	10	9	1
Grandview Plaza	1,656	7	7	0
Greensburg	799	1	1	0
Halstead	2,094	6	5	1
Harper	1,383	3	3	0
Haven	1,221	3	3	0
Havensville	150	1	1	0
Hays	21,206	32	30	2
Haysville	11,288	32	25	7
Herington	2,371	7	6	1
Hesston	3,832	7	6	1

Table 62. Full-Time Law Enforcement Employees, by Selected State and City, 2016—Continued

(Number.)

State/city	Population	Total law enforcement employees	Total officers	Total civilians
Hiawatha	3,080	9	8	1
Hill City	1,465	4	4	0
Hillsboro	2,845	5	5	0
Hoisington	2,607	7	6	1
Holcomb	2,167	4	3	1
Holton	3,250	7	7	0
Holyrood	430	1	1	0
Horton	1,711	10	6	4
Howard	609	1	1	0
Hugoton	3,974	8	6	2
Humboldt	1,838	5	4	1
Hutchinson	41,439	109	72	37
Independence	8,860	25	17	8
Inman	1,358	3	3	0
Iola	5,425	18	17	1
Junction City	24,780	66	45	21
Kansas City	151,623	425	339	86
Kechi	2,013	5	4	1
Kingman	3,070	7	7	0
Kiowa	1,009	2	2	0
La Cygne	1,104	2	2	0
La Harpe	536	2	1	1
Lake Quivira	941	1	1	0
Lansing	11,860	16	15	1
Larned	3,950	8	8	0
Lawrence	95,149	184	151	33
Leavenworth	36,100	75	52	23
Leawood	35,139	77	56	21
Lenexa	53,376	128	88	40
Liberal	20,785	51	36	15
Lindsborg	3,369	6	5	1
Linn Valley	806	3	3	0
Little River	541	1	1	0
Louisburg	4,266	11	10	1
Lyndon	1,016	2	2	0
Lyons	3,721	7	6	1
Macksville	536	1	1	0
Maize	4,564	11	10	1
Maple Hill	622	1	1	0
Marion	1,825	6	5	1
Marquette	618	1	1	0
Marysville	3,329	9	8	1
McLouth	849	1	1	0
McPherson	13,146	36	31	5
Meade	1,605	4	3	1
Medicine Lodge	1,986	4	4	0
Melvern	361	1	1	0
Merriam	11,337	37	32	5
Minneapolis	1,996	5	5	0
Mission	9,523	31	29	2
Mission Hills	3,621	3	3	0
Moran	513	1	1	0
Mound City	677	1	1	0
Moundridge	1,689	4	4	0
Mulberry	504	1	1	0
Mulvane	6,347	19	14	5
Neodesha	2,333	8	7	1
Newton	19,226	41	36	5
North Newton	1,811	3	3	0
Norton	2,830	7	6	1
Oakley	2,104	11	6	5
Oberlin	1,758	5	5	0
Olathe	135,977	194	166	28
Osage City	2,825	7	7	0
Osawatomie	4,267	17	12	5
Osborne	1,358	3	3	0
Oswego	1,755	5	5	0
Ottawa	12,334	32	27	5
Overbrook	1,018	1	1	0
Overland Park	189,104	298	243	55
Oxford	1,019	3	3	0
Paola	5,509	21	15	6
Park City	7,671	16	14	2
Parsons	10,016	32	23	9
Peabody	1,131	2	2	0
Perry	905	1	1	0
Pittsburg	20,439	74	50	24
Plainville	1,893	5	5	0
Pleasanton	1,168	2	2	0
Prairie Village	21,958	54	41	13
Pratt	6,854	22	15	7
Protection	495	1	1	0
Quinter	955	1	1	0
Roeland Park	6,845	15	13	2
Rose Hill	4,007	9	8	1

Table 62. Full-Time Law Enforcement Employees, by Selected State and City, 2016—Continued

(Number.)

State/city	Population	Total law enforcement employees	Total officers	Total civilians
Russell	4,537	8	8	0
Sabetha	2,589	9	4	5
Salina	47,805	98	73	25
Scott City	3,840	12	7	5
Sedgwick	1,709	2	2	0
Seneca	2,041	5	5	0
Shawnee	65,603	109	89	20
South Hutchinson	2,576	9	7	2
Spearville	811	1	1	0
Spring Hill	6,090	13	11	2
Stafford	976	3	3	0
Sterling	2,285	5	5	0
St. Francis	1,300	3	2	1
St. George	991	1	1	0
St. Marys	2,668	5	5	0
Stockton	1,321	6	6	0
Tonganoxie	5,295	13	12	1
Topeka	127,166	334	282	52
Troy	984	1	1	0
Udall	728	2	2	0
Valley Center	7,302	16	15	1
Valley Falls	1,150	3	3	0
Victoria	1,229	2	2	0
Wa Keeney	1,803	5	5	0
Wakefield	973	1	1	0
Waterville	646	1	1	0
Wathena	1,330	2	2	0
Wellington	7,954	20	17	3
Wellsville	1,810	4	4	0
Westwood	2,314	8	7	1
Wichita	391,399	794	612	182
Wilson	755	1	1	0
Winfield	12,176	31	25	6
Yates Center	1,315	3	3	0
KENTUCKY				
Adairville	888	1	1	0
Alexandria	9,112	19	16	3
Anchorage	2,434	14	10	4
Auburn	1,354	2	2	0
Beaver Dam	3,640	5	5	0
Benton	4,346	8	8	0
Berea	15,135	34	32	2
Booneville	75	1	1	0
Bowling Green	64,561	151	116	35
Brownsville	824	3	3	0
Burgin	966	2	2	0
Burkesville	1,511	6	6	0
Burnside	845	6	5	1
Butler	583	1	1	0
Campbellsville	11,357	22	20	2
Carrollton	3,877	17	10	7
Catlettsburg	1,798	8	8	0
Cave City	2,411	7	7	0
Central City	5,875	12	12	0
Clinton	1,306	5	5	0
Cold Spring	6,217	9	9	0
Covington	41,094	116	108	8
Crab Orchard	832	2	1	1
Cumberland	2,078	6	6	0
Dry Ridge	2,208	5	5	0
Eddyville	2,582	5	5	0
Edgewood	8,801	15	15	0
Edmonton	1,562	6	6	0
Elkhorn City	928	2	1	1
Elsmere	8,563	14	13	1
Erlanger	22,952	40	39	1
Ferguson	944	1	1	0
Flemingsburg	2,902	7	7	0
Fort Thomas	16,436	22	21	1
Fort Wright	5,801	13	13	0
Frankfort	27,926	59	56	3
Greensburg	2,116	5	5	0
Hardinsburg	2,332	5	5	0
Harrodsburg	8,399	30	19	11
Hawesville	1,006	1	1	0
Henderson	28,904	81	60	21
Highland Heights	7,216	11	10	1
Hillview	8,177	14	14	0
Hodgenville	3,259	7	7	0
Jackson	2,138	11	8	3
Jamestown	1,805	4	4	0
Jeffersontown	27,006	59	49	10
Jenkins	2,077	3	3	0
La Center	1,004	2	2	0

Table 62. Full-Time Law Enforcement Employees, by Selected State and City, 2016—Continued

(Number.)

State/city	Population	Total law enforcement employees	Total officers	Total civilians
Lakeside Park-Crestview Hills	6,159	12	11	1
Lancaster	3,873	11	10	1
Lawrenceburg	11,140	22	14	8
Lebanon	5,710	24	15	9
Leitchfield	6,904	19	18	1
Louisa	2,452	6	6	0
Loyall	648	2	2	0
Marion	2,976	11	6	5
Maysville	8,780	33	25	8
Middlesboro	9,615	28	24	4
Monticello	6,071	12	11	1
Morgantown	2,480	6	6	0
Mount Sterling	7,268	22	20	2
Mount Washington	14,162	19	18	1
New Haven	893	1	1	0
Owensboro	59,359	136	90	46
Paducah	24,836	79	71	8
Paris	9,883	23	22	1
Pioneer Village	2,866	5	5	0
Powderly	729	2	2	0
Princeton	6,142	15	14	1
Prospect	4,918	7	6	1
Radcliff	22,346	49	35	14
Richmond	33,965	61	47	14
Russell Springs	2,525	10	9	1
Russellville	7,073	21	20	1
Scottsville	4,446	26	18	8
Shepherdsville	12,098	31	29	2
Smiths Grove	740	1	1	0
Southgate	3,871	8	8	0
Springfield	3,093	13	8	5
Stanford	3,668	13	13	0
Taylor Mill	6,793	11	10	1
Taylorsville	1,035	5	4	1
Tompkinsville	2,277	13	10	3
Uniontown	960	2	2	0
Vanceburg	1,445	6	6	0
West Buechel	1,277	11	11	0
West Point	856	4	4	0
Wilder	3,099	12	12	0
Williamsburg	5,324	14	13	1
Woodburn	381	2	2	0
LOUISIANA				
Abbeville	12,471	39	37	2
Addis	4,808	12	11	1
Alexandria	47,936	190	157	33
Baker	13,655	28	24	4
Baldwin	2,328	14	6	8
Ball	3,989	9	7	2
Basile	1,815	13	7	6
Baton Rouge	228,389	814	641	173
Berwick	4,732	13	12	1
Blanchard	2,941	6	5	1
Bogalusa	11,882	51	34	17
Bossier City	69,384	200	161	39
Breaux Bridge	8,446	23	20	3
Broussard	11,998	32	28	4
Brusly	2,823	10	10	0
Bunkie	4,044	9	5	4
Carencro	8,763	26	24	2
Clarence	486	2	1	1
Clinton	1,564	9	7	2
Coushatta	1,832	8	7	1
Covington	10,178	44	36	8
Crowley	13,119	39	37	2
Denham Springs	10,107	36	27	9
De Quincy	3,147	12	12	0
De Ridder	10,939	30	24	6
Epps	834	2	1	1
Erath	2,106	11	7	4
Eunice	10,291	45	32	13
Farmerville	3,849	13	9	4
Ferriday	3,348	21	21	0
Fisher	225	1	1	0
Florien	628	3	3	0
Folsom	808	4	4	0
Franklinton	3,769	22	20	2
French Settlement	1,132	3	3	0
Golden Meadow	2,052	5	3	2
Gonzales	10,860	46	41	5
Gramercy	3,430	10	9	1
Greenwood	3,184	10	9	1
Gretna	17,908	133	100	33

Table 62. Full-Time Law Enforcement Employees, by Selected State and City, 2016—Continued

(Number.)

State/city	Population	Total law enforcement employees	Total officers	Total civilians
Hammond	20,576	106	80	26
Harahan	9,364	25	22	3
Haughton	3,306	13	12	1
Houma	34,410	98	81	17
Ida	214	1	1	0
Independence	1,820	8	8	0
Iowa	3,266	17	13	4
Jena	3,420	7	7	0
Jennings	10,140	33	26	7
Kaplan	4,619	17	11	6
Kenner	67,164	232	167	65
Kentwood	2,368	10	10	0
Killian	1,324	4	3	1
Kinder	2,436	16	11	5
Krotz Springs	1,203	7	4	3
Lafayette	128,923	315	257	58
Lake Arthur	2,742	10	10	0
Lake Charles	76,864	186	183	3
Lake Providence	3,666	11	6	5
Leesville	6,270	28	26	2
Lutcher	3,341	3	3	0
Mamou	3,170	16	14	2
Mandeville	12,423	48	36	12
Mansfield	4,937	17	17	0
Many	2,778	13	13	0
Marion	753	1	1	0
Marksville	5,499	27	19	8
Monroe	49,677	180	137	43
Montgomery	721	3	3	0
Moreauville	899	5	4	1
Natchitoches	18,332	67	55	12
New Orleans	397,208	1,403	1,171	232
Oak Grove	1,650	6	6	0
Olla	1,385	2	2	0
Patterson	6,105	26	26	0
Pearl River	2,553	17	12	5
Pineville	14,379	72	72	0
Plaquemine	6,825	28	24	4
Ponchatoula	7,168	29	23	6
Port Allen	5,116	21	20	1
Port Vincent	750	3	3	0
Rayne	8,031	24	21	3
Rayville	3,658	16	14	2
Ringgold	1,420	5	5	0
Ruston	22,416	49	35	14
Scott	9,092	25	24	1
Shreveport	196,467	711	524	187
Slidell	28,107	99	67	32
Springhill	5,064	17	16	1
Sterlington	2,689	9	9	0
St. Francisville	1,689	8	8	0
St. Gabriel	7,183	19	12	7
Sulphur	20,142	62	41	21
Tallulah	6,930	14	14	0
Thibodaux	14,588	65	45	20
Vidalia	4,076	39	30	9
Ville Platte	7,234	46	31	15
Vinton	3,344	13	11	2
Walker	6,351	24	20	4
Welsh	3,226	20	18	2
Westlake	4,626	17	17	0
West Monroe	12,942	69	67	2
White Castle	1,814	17	15	2
Wilson	571	4	4	0
Zachary	16,753	43	41	2
MAINE				
Ashland	1,222	2	2	0
Auburn	22,836	61	53	8
Augusta	18,347	58	43	15
Baileyville	1,444	4	4	0
Bangor	32,264	92	76	16
Bar Harbor	5,339	18	13	5
Bath	8,269	24	19	5
Belfast	6,685	16	15	1
Berwick	7,567	13	12	1
Biddeford	21,285	75	53	22
Boothbay Harbor	2,158	7	6	1
Brewer	9,185	22	20	2
Bridgton	5,405	8	8	0
Brownville	1,189	2	2	0
Brunswick	20,544	43	29	14
Bucksport	4,927	12	8	4
Buxton	8,171	10	5	5
Calais	2,953	5	5	0

Table 62. Full-Time Law Enforcement Employees, by Selected State and City, 2016—Continued

(Number.)

State/city	Population	Total law enforcement employees	Total officers	Total civilians
Camden	4,863	12	10	2
Cape Elizabeth	9,364	14	13	1
Caribou	7,747	16	15	1
Carrabassett Valley	772	2	2	0
Clinton	3,291	2	2	0
Cumberland	7,821	13	11	2
Damariscotta	2,214	6	5	1
Dexter	3,775	4	4	0
Dixfield	2,462	2	2	0
Dover-Foxcroft	4,004	5	5	0
East Millinocket	2,986	2	2	0
Eastport	1,254	4	4	0
Eliot	6,362	9	8	1
Ellsworth	7,881	20	17	3
Fairfield	6,505	11	10	1
Falmouth	12,154	26	18	8
Farmington	7,401	14	13	1
Fort Fairfield	3,330	4	4	0
Fort Kent	3,940	9	5	4
Freeport	8,407	16	14	2
Fryeburg	3,385	5	5	0
Gardiner	5,558	13	12	1
Gorham	17,346	26	24	2
Gouldsboro	1,739	2	2	0
Greenville	1,582	3	2	1
Hallowell	2,303	5	5	0
Hampden	7,414	12	11	1
Holden	3,077	3	3	0
Houlton	5,835	17	11	6
Islesboro	567	1	1	0
Jay	4,750	8	7	1
Kennebunk	11,289	24	22	2
Kennebunkport	3,586	17	12	5
Kittery	9,686	24	18	6
Lewiston	36,126	91	80	11
Limestone	2,202	3	3	0
Lincoln	5,020	7	6	1
Lisbon	8,823	18	12	6
Livermore Falls	3,118	6	6	0
Machias	2,096	4	4	0
Madawaska	3,803	7	6	1
Mechanic Falls	2,990	5	5	0
Mexico	2,590	5	5	0
Milbridge	1,283	2	2	0
Millinocket	4,332	6	6	0
Milo	2,242	2	2	0
Monmouth	4,008	4	4	0
Mount Desert	2,074	10	6	4
Newport	3,224	6	6	0
North Berwick	4,672	9	8	1
Norway	4,911	10	9	1
Oakland	6,119	11	10	1
Ogunquit	916	11	10	1
Old Orchard Beach	8,807	23	21	2
Old Town	7,583	18	17	1
Orono	10,772	17	16	1
Oxford	4,034	9	8	1
Paris	5,085	8	7	1
Phippsburg	2,234	1	1	0
Pittsfield	4,051	5	5	0
Portland	67,041	216	157	59
Presque Isle	9,075	21	16	5
Rangeley	1,149	3	3	0
Richmond	3,394	4	4	0
Rockland	7,227	20	18	2
Rockport	3,392	7	6	1
Rumford	5,646	11	10	1
Sabattus	5,038	8	7	1
Saco	19,197	44	32	12
Sanford	20,914	43	39	4
Scarborough	19,851	58	40	18
Searsport	2,627	3	3	0
Skowhegan	8,454	13	13	0
South Berwick	7,454	13	9	4
South Portland	25,674	59	53	6
Southwest Harbor	1,774	9	5	4
Thomaston	2,776	5	5	0
Topsham	8,748	17	13	4
Van Buren	2,037	3	3	0
Veazie	1,855	4	4	0
Waldoboro	4,954	8	7	1
Washburn	1,578	2	2	0
Waterville	16,370	41	31	10
Wells	10,174	30	22	8
Westbrook	18,078	41	39	2

Table 62. Full-Time Law Enforcement Employees, by Selected State and City, 2016—Continued

(Number.)

State/city	Population	Total law enforcement employees	Total officers	Total civilians
Wilton	3,922	6	6	0
Windham	17,983	29	26	3
Winslow	7,506	15	14	1
Winthrop	5,888	14	9	5
Wiscasset	3,638	5	4	1
Yarmouth	8,584	14	13	1
York	12,927	36	26	10
MARYLAND				
Aberdeen	15,704	51	41	10
Annapolis	39,703	153	109	44
Baltimore	618,385	2,908	2,512	396
Baltimore City Sheriff		201	156	45
Bel Air	10,200	42	32	10
Berlin	4,537	17	12	5
Berwyn Heights	3,311	9	8	1
Bladensburg	9,735	26	19	7
Boonsboro	3,457	6	5	1
Bowie	58,631	80	63	17
Brentwood	3,219	6	5	1
Brunswick	6,162	12	12	0
Cambridge	12,524	49	46	3
Capitol Heights	4,620	11	9	2
Centreville	4,696	12	12	0
Chestertown	5,067	15	14	1
Cheverly	6,546	15	12	3
Chevy Chase Village	2,080	17	11	6
Colmar Manor	1,482	4	3	1
Cottage City	1,383	3	3	0
Crisfield	2,642	14	11	3
Cumberland	19,995	54	50	4
Delmar	3,068	13	12	1
Denton	4,337	13	12	1
District Heights	6,204	12	11	1
Easton	16,689	54	46	8
Edmonston	1,532	7	5	2
Elkton	15,837	45	40	5
Fairmount Heights	1,585	1	1	0
Federalsburg	2,646	7	7	0
Forest Heights	2,598	9	7	2
Frederick	70,316	186	148	38
Frostburg	8,601	20	15	5
Fruitland	5,287	20	19	1
Glenarden	6,390	14	12	2
Greenbelt	24,511	63	45	18
Greensboro	1,864	2	2	0
Hagerstown	40,567	114	101	13
Hampstead	6,365	11	10	1
Hancock	1,548	4	3	1
Havre de Grace	13,604	45	36	9
Hurlock	2,036	10	9	1
Hyattsville	18,666	50	38	12
Landover Hills	1,828	6	5	1
La Plata	9,201	19	18	1
Laurel	26,424	85	64	21
Luke	63	1	1	0
Manchester	4,820	6	6	0
Morningside	2,104	8	7	1
Mount Rainier	8,552	21	17	4
New Carrollton	12,914	27	21	6
North East	3,734	12	11	1
Oakland	1,868	2	2	0
Ocean City	7,045	126	96	30
Ocean Pines	12,207	18	14	4
Oxford	615	3	3	0
Perryville	4,451	13	12	1
Pocomoke City	4,124	23	16	7
Princess Anne	3,299	13	12	1
Ridgely	1,611	5	5	0
Rising Sun	2,860	6	6	0
Riverdale Park	7,373	28	19	9
Rock Hall	1,302	4	4	0
Salisbury	33,417	114	90	24
Seat Pleasant	4,826	17	13	4
Smithsburg	3,000	4	3	1
Snow Hill	2,082	6	6	0
St. Michaels	1,048	9	8	1
Sykesville	4,409	8	7	1
Takoma Park	17,905	58	40	18
Taneytown	6,749	15	14	1
Thurmont	6,507	15	13	2
Trappe	1,015	1	1	0
University Park	2,688	9	8	1
Upper Marlboro	671	3	3	0
Westminster	18,683	53	42	11

Table 62. Full-Time Law Enforcement Employees, by Selected State and City, 2016—Continued

(Number.)

State/city	Population	Total law enforcement employees	Total officers	Total civilians
MASSACHUSETTS				
Abington	16,201	27	25	2
Acton	23,770	54	43	11
Acushnet	10,466	21	19	2
Adams	8,131	17	16	1
Agawam	28,844	57	47	10
Andover	35,558	71	51	20
Aquinnah	331	4	4	0
Arlington	45,004	84	66	18
Ashburnham	6,206	16	11	5
Ashby	3,242	9	5	4
Ashland	17,689	29	25	4
Attleboro	44,225	91	79	12
Auburn	16,508	46	35	11
Avon	4,505	15	11	4
Ayer	8,078	26	18	8
Barnstable	43,974	128	113	15
Barre	5,491	9	8	1
Becket	1,759	4	4	0
Bedford	14,280	38	29	9
Belchertown	14,985	22	18	4
Bellingham	16,922	40	33	7
Belmont	25,637	60	46	14
Berkley	6,678	8	8	0
Berlin	3,038	14	10	4
Bernardston	2,096	3	3	0
Beverly	41,303	72	68	4
Billerica	42,965	78	65	13
Blackstone	9,079	20	17	3
Bolton	5,210	13	12	1
Boston	673,880	2,678	2,125	553
Bourne	19,577	47	40	7
Boxborough	5,223	17	11	6
Boxford	8,271	11	11	0
Boylston	4,551	13	10	3
Braintree	37,673	92	77	15
Brewster	9,888	29	24	5
Brockton	95,189	208	187	21
Brookline	59,033	159	129	30
Buckland	1,857	2	2	0
Burlington	26,083	73	65	8
Cambridge	111,030	322	277	45
Canton	22,962	42	42	0
Carlisle	5,300	13	10	3
Carver	11,600	18	13	5
Charlton	13,430	22	18	4
Chatham	6,119	26	21	5
Chelmsford	35,251	64	52	12
Chelsea	40,096	119	110	9
Cheshire	3,143	1	1	0
Chicopee	56,887	136	132	4
Chilmark	926	5	5	0
Clinton	13,780	28	24	4
Cohasset	8,538	19	18	1
Concord	20,189	46	36	10
Dalton	6,642	11	10	1
Danvers	27,997	58	46	12
Dartmouth	34,630	88	70	18
Dedham	25,402	59	57	2
Deerfield	4,994	10	9	1
Dennis	13,905	52	45	7
Dighton	7,430	13	12	1
Douglas	8,741	19	15	4
Dover	6,008	17	16	1
Dracut	31,586	45	39	6
Dudley	11,558	15	14	1
Dunstable	3,471	9	8	1
East Bridgewater	14,390	23	21	2
Eastham	4,886	22	16	6
Easthampton	16,026	33	27	6
East Longmeadow	16,267	27	26	1
Easton	23,918	39	31	8
Egremont	1,207	3	3	0
Erving	1,771	5	5	0
Essex	3,675	10	9	1
Everett	46,754	110	101	9
Fairhaven	16,120	31	25	6
Fall River	88,371	265	218	47
Falmouth	31,382	59	55	4
Fitchburg	40,391	94	78	16
Foxborough	17,491	44	36	8
Framingham	71,422	158	144	14
Franklin	33,264	54	46	8
Freetown	9,199	18	18	0

Table 62. Full-Time Law Enforcement Employees, by Selected State and City, 2016—Continued

(Number.)

State/city	Population	Total law enforcement employees	Total officers	Total civilians
Georgetown	8,623	16	12	4
Gloucester	29,836	52	47	5
Goshen	1,073	2	2	0
Grafton	18,613	22	18	4
Granby	6,375	13	9	4
Granville	1,628	2	1	1
Great Barrington	6,870	16	15	1
Greenfield	17,456	44	34	10
Groton	11,372	25	19	6
Groveland	6,776	13	10	3
Hadley	5,372	15	11	4
Hamilton	8,181	18	13	5
Hampden	5,227	15	11	4
Hanson	10,666	25	20	5
Hardwick	4,019	4	4	0
Harwich	12,112	37	34	3
Hatfield	3,302	3	3	0
Haverhill	62,851	104	92	12
Hingham	23,204	52	50	2
Holbrook	11,047	22	21	1
Holland	2,505	2	2	0
Holliston	14,656	27	22	5
Holyoke	40,738	144	120	24
Hopedale	5,938	16	12	4
Hopkinton	16,960	32	23	9
Hudson	19,931	45	33	12
Ipswich	13,863	28	23	5
Kingston	13,378	31	24	7
Lakeville	11,417	22	17	5
Lancaster	8,150	12	11	1
Lanesboro	2,972	6	6	0
Lawrence	80,622	147	129	18
Leicester	11,355	23	18	5
Lenox	4,971	10	10	0
Leominster	41,547	83	67	16
Lexington	33,643	61	47	14
Lincoln	7,550	19	13	6
Littleton	10,074	24	18	6
Longmeadow	15,876	32	26	6
Lowell	111,027	336	239	97
Ludlow	21,484	44	38	6
Lunenburg	11,438	14	14	0
Lynn	92,443	200	181	19
Malden	61,102	114	101	13
Mansfield	23,681	48	35	13
Marblehead	20,563	39	30	9
Marion	5,098	16	16	0
Marlborough	39,899	77	65	12
Marshfield	25,696	49	46	3
Mashpee	14,122	42	35	7
Mattapoisett	6,282	19	19	0
Maynard	10,745	26	21	5
Medford	57,367	105	103	2
Medway	13,289	28	22	6
Melrose	28,070	47	47	0
Mendon	6,033	17	12	5
Merrimac	6,859	11	7	4
Methuen	49,912	111	93	18
Middleboro	24,490	47	41	6
Middleton	9,852	16	14	2
Milford	28,606	54	45	9
Millbury	13,532	24	19	5
Millville	3,228	6	5	1
Montague	8,242	16	16	0
Nahant	3,484	13	12	1
Nantucket	11,036	51	34	17
Natick	36,777	69	56	13
Needham	30,733	55	46	9
New Bedford	94,524	297	255	42
Newton	89,116	195	149	46
Norfolk	11,991	24	18	6
North Adams	13,162	34	29	5
Northampton	28,521	69	63	6
North Andover	29,853	51	40	11
North Attleboro	29,013	58	44	14
Northborough	15,109	27	20	7
Northbridge	16,638	27	19	8
Northfield	2,984	4	4	0
North Reading	15,712	32	31	1
Norton	19,445	30	29	1
Norwell	11,030	26	21	5
Norwood	29,058	68	57	11
Orange	7,615	13	12	1
Orleans	5,810	27	22	5
Oxford	13,895	28	22	6

Table 62. Full-Time Law Enforcement Employees, by Selected State and City, 2016—Continued

(Number.)

State/city	Population	Total law enforcement employees	Total officers	Total civilians
Palmer	12,171	26	19	7
Paxton	4,874	19	17	2
Peabody	52,501	111	92	19
Pelham	1,332	4	2	2
Pepperell	12,242	16	15	1
Petersham	1,243	2	2	0
Phillipston	1,751	2	2	0
Pittsfield	43,031	114	96	18
Plainville	9,178	24	19	5
Plymouth	59,088	134	119	15
Plympton	2,922	9	9	0
Princeton	3,465	7	6	1
Provincetown	2,959	25	19	6
Quincy	93,437	238	210	28
Randolph	33,807	61	59	2
Raynham	13,818	35	27	8
Reading	25,779	55	42	13
Rehoboth	12,033	28	23	5
Revere	53,514	107	98	9
Rochester	5,522	12	12	0
Rockport	7,222	20	16	4
Rowley	6,343	16	12	4
Royalston	1,271	1	1	0
Salem	42,888	106	100	6
Sandwich	20,312	45	35	10
Saugus	28,131	72	58	14
Scituate	18,462	38	33	5
Seekonk	15,159	39	37	2
Sharon	18,200	34	31	3
Sheffield	3,179	6	6	0
Sherborn	4,317	15	15	0
Shrewsbury	36,874	57	45	12
Somerset	18,223	37	30	7
Somerville	80,899	142	127	15
Southborough	10,048	22	17	5
Southbridge	16,819	42	36	6
South Hadley	17,748	30	25	5
Southwick	9,758	23	18	5
Spencer	11,782	21	17	4
Springfield	154,102	523	419	104
Sterling	7,993	14	13	1
Stockbridge	1,936	7	6	1
Stoneham	22,045	44	37	7
Stoughton	28,583	59	52	7
Stow	7,197	11	11	0
Sturbridge	9,520	25	19	6
Sudbury	19,035	34	25	9
Sunderland	3,652	5	5	0
Sutton	9,292	21	16	5
Swampscott	14,551	34	32	2
Swansea	16,418	36	30	6
Taunton	56,720	120	114	6
Templeton	8,169	14	9	5
Tewksbury	31,160	74	59	15
Tisbury	4,129	15	14	1
Topsfield	6,590	12	11	1
Townsend	9,585	16	15	1
Truro	1,999	17	12	5
Tyngsboro	12,397	32	26	6
Uxbridge	13,916	23	18	5
Wakefield	27,080	46	45	1
Walpole	25,187	53	40	13
Waltham	63,613	170	143	27
Wareham	22,422	59	47	12
Watertown	34,655	71	67	4
Wayland	13,760	32	23	9
Webster	16,842	32	30	2
Wellesley	29,049	45	39	6
Wellfleet	2,737	19	13	6
Wenham	5,198	11	10	1
Westborough	18,984	31	29	2
West Brookfield	3,778	6	5	1
Westfield	41,700	88	81	7
Westford	24,103	49	45	4
Westminster	7,595	14	13	1
West Newbury	4,582	13	8	5
Weston	12,147	34	25	9
Westport	15,798	32	28	4
West Springfield	28,689	93	84	9
West Tisbury	2,927	10	9	1
Westwood	16,285	40	31	9
Weymouth	56,149	108	92	16
Whitman	14,852	27	26	1
Wilbraham	14,684	28	27	1
Williamsburg	2,466	1	1	0

Table 62. Full-Time Law Enforcement Employees, by Selected State and City, 2016—Continued

(Number.)

State/city	Population	Total law enforcement employees	Total officers	Total civilians
Williamstown	7,591	14	11	3
Wilmington	23,667	50	48	2
Winchendon	10,727	19	14	5
Winchester	22,523	46	38	8
Winthrop	18,216	33	31	2
Woburn	39,638	80	75	5
Worcester	184,595	485	435	50
Wrentham	11,614	22	21	1
Yarmouth	23,299	73	61	12
MICHIGAN				
Adrian	20,600	30	28	2
Adrian Township	6,316	1	1	0
Akron	391	1	1	0
Albion	8,155	17	16	1
Allegan	5,086	10	9	1
Allen Park	27,284	43	40	3
Alma	9,159	16	15	1
Almont	2,734	7	6	1
Alpena	10,119	19	17	2
Ann Arbor	117,688	151	125	26
Argentine Township	6,591	6	5	1
Armada	1,747	2	2	0
Auburn Hills	22,933	53	48	5
Au Gres	853	1	1	0
Bad Axe	2,989	8	7	1
Bangor	1,843	5	5	0
Baraga	1,985	2	2	0
Baroda-Lake Township	3,774	4	4	0
Barry Township	3,413	2	2	0
Bath Township	12,552	13	12	1
Battle Creek	60,904	125	109	16
Bay City	33,725	53	49	4
Beaverton	1,044	2	2	0
Belding	5,772	8	8	0
Bellaire	1,062	3	3	0
Belleville	3,860	10	8	2
Bellevue	1,277	2	2	0
Benton Harbor	9,963	25	20	5
Benton Township	14,413	26	22	4
Berkley	15,328	34	27	7
Berrien Springs-Oronoko Township	9,085	9	8	1
Beverly Hills	10,455	27	26	1
Big Rapids	10,389	17	16	1
Birch Run	1,465	6	5	1
Birmingham	21,012	42	32	10
Blackman Township	37,522	35	34	1
Blissfield	3,239	5	5	0
Bloomfield Hills	4,031	27	24	3
Bloomfield Township	42,313	74	54	20
Boyne City	3,785	8	7	1
Breckenridge	1,301	1	1	0
Bridgeport Township	9,993	11	10	1
Bridgman	2,251	5	5	0
Brighton	7,643	19	17	2
Bronson	2,333	4	4	0
Brown City	1,264	2	2	0
Brownstown Township	30,864	39	32	7
Buchanan	4,344	10	9	1
Buena Vista Township	8,158	10	9	1
Burton	28,563	43	40	3
Cadillac	10,372	17	15	2
Calumet	698	1	1	0
Cambridge Township	5,645	4	4	0
Canton Township	89,861	119	82	37
Capac	1,842	1	1	0
Carleton	2,335	3	2	1
Caro	4,074	7	7	0
Carrollton Township	5,781	6	6	0
Carson City	1,090	2	2	0
Caspian-Gaastra	1,190	1	1	0
Cass City	2,343	4	4	0
Cassopolis	1,721	5	5	0
Center Line	8,332	23	19	4
Central Lake	932	1	1	0
Charlevoix	2,546	8	7	1
Charlotte	9,051	18	16	2
Cheboygan	4,709	8	8	0
Chelsea	5,254	14	10	4
Chesterfield Township	44,963	55	41	14
Chikaming Township	3,090	5	5	0
Chocolay Township	5,952	5	4	1
Clare	3,071	8	8	0
Clawson	12,053	18	17	1
Clayton Township	7,156	4	4	0

Table 62. Full-Time Law Enforcement Employees, by Selected State and City, 2016—Continued

(Number.)

State/city	Population	Total law enforcement employees	Total officers	Total civilians
Clay Township	8,844	19	16	3
Clinton	2,260	4	4	0
Clinton Township	100,514	102	93	9
Clio	2,516	4	4	0
Coldwater	10,827	20	17	3
Coleman	1,198	1	1	0
Coloma Township	6,388	10	7	3
Colon	1,156	3	3	0
Columbia Township	7,424	5	5	0
Constantine	2,062	3	3	0
Corunna	3,386	3	3	0
Covert Township	2,824	7	7	0
Croswell	2,318	6	6	0
Crystal Falls	1,404	2	2	0
Davison	4,927	7	6	1
Davison Township	19,029	20	18	2
Dearborn	94,646	246	189	57
Dearborn Heights	55,852	95	83	12
Decatur	1,759	4	4	0
Denton Township	5,358	6	6	0
Detroit	669,673	2,855	2,350	505
DeWitt Township	14,686	17	16	1
Dowagiac	5,849	15	14	1
Dryden Township	4,773	4	4	0
Dundee	4,004	2	2	0
Durand	3,317	6	6	0
East Grand Rapids	11,436	30	28	2
East Jordan	2,376	4	4	0
East Lansing	48,451	67	54	13
Eastpointe	32,701	41	37	4
Eaton Rapids	5,226	9	8	1
Eau Claire	617	1	1	0
Ecorse	9,213	18	17	1
Elk Rapids	1,611	5	5	0
Elkton	774	2	2	0
Emmett Township	11,604	16	14	2
Erie Township	4,374	4	3	1
Escanaba	12,278	40	29	11
Essexville	3,381	8	8	0
Evart	1,853	2	2	0
Fair Haven Township	1,051	1	1	0
Farmington	10,553	24	23	1
Farmington Hills	81,649	137	100	37
Fennville	1,401	1	1	0
Fenton	11,383	18	14	4
Ferndale	20,232	48	38	10
Flat Rock	9,917	18	18	0
Flint	97,548	117	103	14
Flint Township	30,460	43	38	5
Flushing	8,028	10	10	0
Flushing Township	10,235	6	6	0
Forsyth Township	6,196	9	8	1
Fowlerville	2,898	7	6	1
Frankenmuth	5,037	7	7	0
Frankfort	1,283	3	3	0
Franklin	3,254	10	10	0
Fraser	14,667	48	37	11
Fremont	4,027	7	6	1
Fruitport Township	13,879	9	9	0
Gaines Township	6,177	1	1	0
Galesburg	2,050	4	4	0
Garden City	26,781	30	28	2
Gaylord	3,662	10	9	1
Genesee Township	20,393	14	12	2
Gerrish Township	2,922	7	7	0
Gibraltar	4,509	9	8	1
Gladstone	4,802	11	10	1
Gladwin	2,869	4	4	0
Grand Beach	278	4	4	0
Grand Blanc	7,940	19	16	3
Grand Blanc Township	36,598	46	39	7
Grand Haven	11,196	33	30	3
Grand Ledge	7,790	14	14	0
Grand Rapids	196,538	335	276	59
Grandville	16,070	26	24	2
Grant	880	1	1	0
Grayling	1,836	8	8	0
Green Oak Township	18,722	17	15	2
Greenville	8,438	19	17	2
Grosse Ile Township	10,123	23	17	6
Grosse Pointe	5,198	22	22	0
Grosse Pointe Farms	9,188	41	32	9
Grosse Pointe Park	11,160	38	33	5
Grosse Pointe Shores	2,920	17	17	0
Grosse Pointe Woods	15,699	32	27	5

Table 62. Full-Time Law Enforcement Employees, by Selected State and City, 2016—Continued

(Number.)

State/city	Population	Total law enforcement employees	Total officers	Total civilians
Hamburg Township	21,714	18	17	1
Hampton Township	9,401	11	10	1
Hamtramck	21,929	35	30	5
Hancock	4,537	8	8	0
Harbor Beach	1,621	4	4	0
Harbor Springs	1,203	6	5	1
Harper Woods	13,764	32	28	4
Hart	2,093	4	4	0
Hartford	2,604	5	5	0
Hastings	7,274	15	13	2
Hazel Park	16,636	37	33	4
Hesperia	935	2	2	0
Highland Park	10,810	8	7	1
Hillsdale	8,139	14	13	1
Holland	33,867	65	57	8
Holly	6,186	8	8	0
Home Township	1,350	1	1	0
Hopkins	608	1	1	0
Houghton	8,020	10	9	1
Howell	9,533	19	17	2
Hudson	2,229	2	2	0
Huntington Woods	6,360	18	16	2
Huron Township	15,622	24	18	6
Imlay City	3,569	8	8	0
Inkster	24,548	29	25	4
Ionia	11,370	18	16	2
Iron Mountain	7,482	12	12	0
Iron River	2,881	4	4	0
Ironwood	4,929	11	10	1
Ishpeming	6,485	10	9	1
Jackson	33,060	58	46	12
Jonesville	2,213	3	3	0
Kalamazoo	76,389	259	216	43
Kalamazoo Township	24,534	38	31	7
Kalkaska	2,042	4	3	1
Keego Harbor	3,040	4	4	0
Kentwood	51,897	81	68	13
Kingsford	5,057	17	17	0
Kinross Township	7,536	2	2	0
Lake Angelus	298	1	1	0
Lake Linden	985	1	1	0
Lake Odessa	2,032	3	3	0
Lake Orion	3,065	5	4	1
Lakeview	1,011	2	2	0
L'Anse	1,920	4	4	0
Lansing	115,199	213	188	25
Lansing Township	8,148	16	15	1
Lapeer	8,782	22	20	2
Lathrup Village	4,147	9	9	0
Laurium	1,933	4	4	0
Lawton	1,860	5	5	0
Lennon	499	1	1	0
Leslie	1,869	3	3	0
Lexington	1,119	3	3	0
Lincoln Park	36,808	46	40	6
Lincoln Township	14,500	12	11	1
Linden	3,811	5	5	0
Litchfield	1,343	2	2	0
Livonia	94,226	186	147	39
Lowell	3,931	6	5	1
Ludington	8,054	15	14	1
Luna Pier	1,380	2	2	0
Mackinac Island	479	5	5	0
Mackinaw City	802	6	6	0
Madison Heights	30,297	58	46	12
Madison Township	8,464	5	5	0
Mancelona	1,361	1	1	0
Manistee	6,057	12	12	0
Manistique	2,960	7	7	0
Manton	1,389	1	1	0
Marenisco Township	1,681	1	1	0
Marine City	4,124	4	4	0
Marlette	1,787	4	4	0
Marquette	21,283	37	33	4
Marshall	7,038	15	15	0
Marysville	9,722	16	14	2
Mason	8,461	13	12	1
Mattawan	1,938	5	5	0
Mayville	914	1	1	0
Melvindale	10,348	24	23	1
Mendon	859	2	2	0
Menominee	8,344	17	16	1
Meridian Township	42,700	44	39	5
Metamora Township	4,241	4	4	0
Michiana	183	3	3	0

Table 62. Full-Time Law Enforcement Employees, by Selected State and City, 2016—Continued

(Number.)

State/city	Population	Total law enforcement employees	Total officers	Total civilians
Midland	42,263	48	46	2
Milan	6,012	13	9	4
Milford	16,707	20	18	2
Millington	1,030	2	2	0
Monroe	19,971	43	38	5
Montague	2,362	5	5	0
Montrose Township	7,524	10	9	1
Morenci	2,181	2	2	0
Morrice	891	2	2	0
Mount Morris	2,941	4	4	0
Mount Morris Township	20,502	31	28	3
Mount Pleasant	26,069	35	29	6
Mundy Township	14,562	19	16	3
Munising	2,278	4	4	0
Muskegon	38,442	82	74	8
Muskegon Heights	10,785	23	20	3
Muskegon Township	17,791	15	14	1
Napoleon Township	6,764	12	12	0
Nashville	1,635	4	4	0
Negaunee	4,584	9	9	0
Newaygo	1,951	5	5	0
New Baltimore	12,409	18	17	1
New Buffalo	1,875	8	7	1
New Era	444	1	1	0
Niles	11,282	24	16	8
Northfield Township	8,617	11	10	1
North Muskegon	3,779	8	8	0
Northville	6,019	13	13	0
Northville Township	28,890	38	27	11
Norton Shores	24,256	31	29	2
Norway	2,789	6	6	0
Novi	59,441	84	62	22
Oak Park	29,838	61	49	12
Olivet	1,611	2	2	0
Ontwa Township-Edwardsburg	6,481	6	6	0
Orchard Lake	2,428	12	10	2
Oscoda Township	6,838	11	10	1
Otsego	3,998	7	6	1
Ovid	1,614	2	2	0
Owosso	14,605	18	17	1
Oxford	3,554	7	4	3
Paw Paw	3,441	9	8	1
Pentwater	843	3	3	0
Perry	2,088	4	4	0
Petoskey	5,731	20	19	1
Pigeon	1,158	1	1	0
Pinckney	2,439	6	6	0
Pinconning	1,264	1	1	0
Pittsfield Township	38,704	57	40	17
Plainwell	3,826	9	8	1
Pleasant Ridge	2,562	6	6	0
Plymouth	8,865	16	15	1
Plymouth Township	26,870	48	30	18
Portage	48,550	74	54	20
Port Austin	638	1	1	0
Port Huron	29,182	69	54	15
Portland	3,929	6	6	0
Potterville	2,619	4	4	0
Prairieville Township	3,409	3	2	1
Quincy	1,638	3	3	0
Raisin Township	7,577	6	5	1
Reading	1,052	1	1	0
Redford Township	47,218	65	56	9
Reed City	2,383	5	5	0
Richfield Township, Genesee County	8,315	11	9	2
Richfield Township, Roscommon County	3,628	5	4	1
Richland	793	3	3	0
Richland Township, Saginaw County	3,961	3	3	0
Richmond	5,882	11	9	2
River Rouge	7,480	20	18	2
Riverview	12,127	25	23	2
Rochester	13,050	28	21	7
Rockford	6,218	11	10	1
Rockwood	3,183	6	6	0
Rogers City	2,692	6	6	0
Romeo	3,630	11	8	3
Romulus	23,315	51	39	12
Roosevelt Park	3,820	5	5	0
Roseville	47,704	72	69	3
Royal Oak	59,367	93	78	15
Saginaw	48,942	61	53	8
Saginaw Township	39,421	46	41	5
Saline	9,158	17	13	4
Sandusky	2,580	6	5	1
Sault Ste. Marie	13,763	25	23	2

Table 62. Full-Time Law Enforcement Employees, by Selected State and City, 2016—Continued

(Number.)

State/city	Population	Total law enforcement employees	Total officers	Total civilians
Schoolcraft	1,574	3	3	0
Scottville	1,213	2	2	0
Sebewaing	1,679	3	3	0
Shelby	2,010	3	3	0
Shelby Township	78,427	85	66	19
Shepherd	1,505	2	2	0
Somerset Township	4,580	3	3	0
Southfield	73,438	150	121	29
Southgate	29,158	40	36	4
South Haven	4,352	21	17	4
South Lyon	11,801	17	16	1
South Rockwood	1,635	2	2	0
Sparta	4,346	6	6	0
Spaulding Township	2,041	1	1	0
Spring Arbor Township	8,097	2	2	0
Springport Township	2,148	2	2	0
Standish	1,442	1	1	0
Stanton	1,414	1	1	0
St. Charles	1,940	2	2	0
St. Clair	5,368	7	7	0
St. Clair Shores	59,938	86	81	5
Sterling Heights	132,523	165	145	20
St. Ignace	2,376	6	5	1
St. Johns	7,916	11	10	1
St. Joseph	8,271	23	21	2
St. Joseph Township	9,850	12	11	1
St. Louis	7,212	7	6	1
Stockbridge	1,235	2	2	0
Sturgis	10,876	24	19	5
Sumpter Township	9,265	16	14	2
Swartz Creek	5,531	9	8	1
Sylvan Lake	1,798	4	4	0
Tawas	4,515	5	4	1
Taylor	61,290	90	74	16
Tecumseh	8,353	15	13	2
Thomas Township	11,505	7	7	0
Three Rivers	7,738	18	16	2
Tittabawassee Township	9,782	6	5	1
Traverse City	15,330	30	29	1
Trenton	18,294	34	33	1
Troy	83,743	149	102	47
Tuscarora Township	2,946	8	7	1
Ubly	822	1	1	0
Unadilla Township	3,405	3	3	0
Union City	1,581	5	5	0
Utica	4,980	18	14	4
Van Buren Township	28,090	55	40	15
Vassar	2,605	4	4	0
Vernon	753	1	1	0
Vicksburg	3,298	7	6	1
Walker	24,874	38	34	4
Walled Lake	7,132	6	6	0
Warren	135,620	235	196	39
Waterford Township	73,308	70	53	17
Watervliet	1,684	3	3	0
Wayland	4,184	7	6	1
Wayne	16,989	21	21	0
West Bloomfield Township	66,123	103	70	33
West Branch	2,054	5	4	1
Westland	81,625	107	81	26
White Cloud	1,378	2	2	0
Whitehall	2,712	8	8	0
White Lake Township	31,135	36	26	10
White Pigeon	1,513	4	4	0
Williamston	3,888	6	6	0
Wixom	13,796	23	20	3
Wolverine Lake	4,397	6	6	0
Woodhaven	12,478	29	27	2
Wyandotte	25,029	46	32	14
Wyoming	75,917	102	87	15
Yale	1,896	3	3	0
Ypsilanti	20,019	34	29	5
Zeeland	5,650	11	10	1
Zilwaukee	1,562	2	2	0
MINNESOTA				
Aitkin	2,031	8	7	1
Akeley	431	1	1	0
Albany	2,661	5	4	1
Albert Lea	17,604	29	27	2
Alexandria	12,006	27	23	4
Annandale	3,317	5	5	0
Anoka	17,389	38	28	10
Appleton	1,328	3	3	0
Apple Valley	51,648	60	52	8

Table 62. Full-Time Law Enforcement Employees, by Selected State and City, 2016—Continued

(Number.)

State/city	Population	Total law enforcement employees	Total officers	Total civilians
Arlington	2,157	3	2	1
Ashby	428	1	1	0
Atwater	1,122	2	2	0
Austin	24,529	36	33	3
Avon	1,481	4	3	1
Babbitt	1,528	4	4	0
Barnesville	2,581	5	5	0
Baudette	1,055	2	2	0
Baxter	7,993	15	14	1
Bayport	3,763	5	5	0
Becker	4,730	7	6	1
Belgrade/Brooten	1,504	2	2	0
Belle Plaine	6,968	11	9	2
Bemidji	14,690	35	33	2
Benson	3,045	8	7	1
Big Lake	10,421	14	12	2
Blackduck	778	2	2	0
Blaine	63,115	70	59	11
Blooming Prairie	1,993	3	3	0
Bloomington	87,134	148	118	30
Blue Earth	3,216	5	5	0
Bovey	813	2	2	0
Braham	1,765	3	3	0
Brainerd	13,327	29	23	6
Breckenridge	3,270	6	6	0
Breezy Point	2,356	7	6	1
Breitung Township	607	2	2	0
Brooklyn Center	30,893	60	48	12
Brooklyn Park	79,800	133	103	30
Brownton	734	1	1	0
Buffalo	16,134	21	18	3
Buffalo Lake	682	2	2	0
Burnsville	61,697	83	74	9
Caledonia	2,772	5	4	1
Cambridge	8,515	16	15	1
Canby	1,693	3	3	0
Cannon Falls	4,057	10	8	2
Centennial Lakes	10,937	18	16	2
Champlin	24,048	31	26	5
Chaska	25,483	28	25	3
Chisholm	4,983	13	12	1
Clara City	1,312	2	2	0
Cloquet	12,064	24	22	2
Cold Spring/Richmond	5,547	10	9	1
Coleraine	2,005	2	2	0
Columbia Heights	19,754	32	26	6
Coon Rapids	62,380	70	63	7
Corcoran	5,586	9	8	1
Cottage Grove	36,164	48	41	7
Crookston	7,765	17	15	2
Crosby	2,336	7	7	0
Crosslake	2,222	5	5	0
Crystal	23,102	35	31	4
Danube	463	1	1	0
Dawson/Boyd	1,590	3	3	0
Dayton	5,185	7	6	1
Deephaven	3,880	8	7	1
Deer River	934	4	4	0
Detroit Lakes	9,075	17	15	2
Dilworth	4,437	7	6	1
Duluth	86,090	183	149	34
Eagan	66,698	83	70	13
Eagle Lake	2,933	2	2	0
East Grand Forks	8,649	25	23	2
East Range	3,665	8	8	0
Eden Prairie	64,037	93	67	26
Eden Valley	1,035	1	1	0
Edina	50,577	72	51	21
Elbow Lake	1,138	2	2	0
Elko New Market	4,831	4	4	0
Elk River	24,150	42	32	10
Elmore	632	1	1	0
Ely	3,398	8	7	1
Eveleth	3,665	11	10	1
Fairfax	1,160	2	2	0
Fairmont	10,137	19	16	3
Faribault	23,708	41	34	7
Farmington	23,060	27	24	3
Fergus Falls	13,312	28	23	5
Floodwood	521	4	3	1
Forest Lake	19,867	27	25	2
Fountain	408	1	1	0
Fridley	27,811	45	41	4
Fulda	1,229	2	2	0
Gaylord	2,233	4	4	0

Table 62. Full-Time Law Enforcement Employees, by Selected State and City, 2016—Continued

(Number.)

State/city	Population	Total law enforcement employees	Total officers	Total civilians
Gilbert	1,791	7	7	0
Glencoe	5,495	9	8	1
Glenwood	2,571	6	5	1
Golden Valley	21,454	41	31	10
Goodview	4,168	5	4	1
Grand Rapids	11,181	23	20	3
Granite Falls	2,719	6	5	1
Hallock	948	1	1	0
Hastings	22,627	32	28	4
Hawley	2,203	4	4	0
Hector	1,062	2	2	0
Hermantown	9,761	19	16	3
Hibbing	16,176	29	26	3
Hill City	594	1	1	0
Hokah	556	1	1	0
Hopkins	18,169	36	27	9
Houston	964	2	2	0
Howard Lake	2,052	3	3	0
Hutchinson	13,867	34	22	12
International Falls	6,107	12	11	1
Inver Grove Heights	35,049	44	39	5
Isanti	5,493	10	9	1
Isle	790	3	3	0
Janesville	2,253	3	3	0
Jordan	6,203	11	9	2
Kasson	6,157	9	8	1
Keewatin	1,046	2	2	0
Kimball	777	3	3	0
La Crescent	4,820	8	7	1
Lake City	5,021	11	10	1
Lake Crystal	2,522	3	3	0
Lakefield	1,648	3	3	0
Lakes Area	9,322	15	13	2
Lake Shore	1,026	2	2	0
Lakeville	61,581	64	55	9
Lamberton	785	1	1	0
Lester Prairie	1,678	3	3	0
Le Sueur	3,988	8	7	1
Lewiston	1,562	2	2	0
Lino Lakes	21,212	30	27	3
Litchfield	6,643	10	9	1
Little Falls	8,611	16	14	2
Long Prairie	3,325	6	6	0
Lonsdale	3,873	9	8	1
Madelia	2,240	4	4	0
Madison Lake	1,110	2	2	0
Mankato	41,300	65	56	9
Maple Grove	69,783	79	66	13
Mapleton	1,726	3	3	0
Maplewood	41,071	55	50	5
Marshall	13,645	25	21	4
Medina	6,216	11	10	1
Melrose	3,620	5	4	1
Menahga	1,346	3	3	0
Mendota Heights	11,252	18	17	1
Milaca	2,871	5	4	1
Minneapolis	416,751	1,018	847	171
Minneota	1,357	1	1	0
Minnesota Lake	654	1	1	0
Minnetonka	52,055	69	52	17
Minnetrista	9,675	15	13	2
Montevideo	5,184	11	10	1
Montgomery	2,907	5	4	1
Moorhead	42,507	72	56	16
Moose Lake	2,747	5	4	1
Morris	5,367	10	8	2
Mounds View	13,063	20	18	2
Mountain Lake	2,119	4	4	0
Nashwauk	965	3	3	0
New Brighton	22,521	33	28	5
New Hope	21,168	43	34	9
New Prague	7,631	12	10	2
New Richland	1,185	1	1	0
New Ulm	13,293	25	22	3
North Branch	10,233	13	11	2
Northfield	20,445	27	22	5
North Mankato	13,553	15	14	1
North St. Paul	12,495	19	17	2
Oakdale	28,211	38	32	6
Oak Park Heights	4,912	11	10	1
Olivia	2,333	4	4	0
Onamia	861	3	3	0
Orono	19,799	31	27	4
Ortonville	1,796	4	4	0
Osakis	1,715	3	3	0

Table 62. Full-Time Law Enforcement Employees, by Selected State and City, 2016—Continued

(Number.)

State/city	Population	Total law enforcement employees	Total officers	Total civilians
Osseo	2,817	6	5	1
Ostrander	254	1	1	0
Owatonna	25,760	39	36	3
Park Rapids	3,963	10	9	1
Paynesville	2,434	5	5	0
Pequot Lakes	2,259	6	5	1
Pike Bay	1,635	3	3	0
Pine River	923	3	3	0
Plainview	3,217	8	7	1
Plymouth	76,996	88	72	16
Preston	1,294	3	3	0
Princeton	4,668	13	11	2
Prior Lake	25,767	28	25	3
Proctor	3,070	8	7	1
Ramsey	26,273	27	24	3
Red Wing	16,442	32	27	5
Redwood Falls	5,024	13	11	2
Renville	1,199	3	3	0
Richfield	36,410	50	42	8
Robbinsdale	14,510	28	24	4
Rochester	113,306	193	137	56
Rogers	12,847	21	18	3
Roseau	2,735	6	5	1
Rosemount	23,717	25	22	3
Roseville	35,954	56	48	8
Rushford	1,709	3	3	0
Sartell	16,943	21	18	3
Sauk Centre	4,367	7	6	1
Sauk Rapids	13,545	17	16	1
Savage	31,118	40	32	8
Shakopee	40,524	56	47	9
Silver Bay	1,799	5	5	0
Silver Lake	807	2	2	0
Slayton	2,035	4	4	0
Sleepy Eye	3,414	7	7	0
South Lake Minnetonka	12,247	16	13	3
South St. Paul	20,452	31	28	3
Springfield	2,052	5	5	0
Spring Grove	1,286	2	2	0
Spring Lake Park	6,484	13	11	2
St. Anthony	9,150	26	23	3
Staples	2,867	7	6	1
Starbuck	1,258	4	4	0
St. Charles	3,703	5	5	0
St. Cloud	67,341	132	105	27
St. Francis	7,442	12	10	2
Stillwater	19,051	24	20	4
St. James	4,441	8	7	1
St. Joseph	6,924	9	8	1
St. Louis Park	48,770	67	53	14
St. Paul	303,920	796	627	169
St. Paul Park	5,399	9	9	0
St. Peter	11,763	18	13	5
Thief River Falls	8,776	18	16	2
Tracy	2,108	3	3	0
Tri-City	1,425	3	3	0
Two Harbors	3,546	9	8	1
Virginia	8,564	21	21	0
Wabasha	2,437	8	7	1
Wadena	4,194	9	8	1
Waite Park	7,551	19	16	3
Walker	925	3	3	0
Warroad	1,804	5	4	1
Waseca	9,207	18	16	2
Wayzata	6,627	14	13	1
Wells	2,231	4	4	0
West Concord	772	1	1	0
West Hennepin	5,575	11	9	2
West St. Paul	19,762	32	29	3
Wheaton	1,351	3	3	0
White Bear Lake	25,484	37	28	9
Willmar	19,641	36	32	4
Windom	4,532	10	9	1
Winnebago	1,368	3	3	0
Winona	27,001	42	38	4
Winsted	2,285	4	4	0
Woodbury	69,032	79	67	12
Worthington	13,151	34	22	12
Wyoming	7,816	11	10	1
Zumbrota	3,385	5	5	0
MISSISSIPPI				
Aberdeen	5,358	18	13	5
Ackerman	1,472	5	5	0
Amory	7,022	28	21	7

Table 62. Full-Time Law Enforcement Employees, by Selected State and City, 2016—Continued

(Number.)

State/city	Population	Total law enforcement employees	Total officers	Total civilians
Biloxi	45,952	177	127	50
Byhalia	1,247	13	10	3
Byram	11,511	38	27	11
D'Iberville	11,795	38	36	2
Florence	4,407	23	15	8
Fulton	4,101	10	10	0
Gautier	18,566	47	36	11
Gulfport	72,668	207	153	54
Hernando	15,793	43	33	10
Horn Lake	27,077	67	50	17
Jackson	170,070	641	409	232
Laurel	18,894	73	51	22
Madison	26,119	86	67	19
McComb	12,632	57	33	24
Meridian	39,364	102	78	24
Ocean Springs	17,688	53	38	15
Oxford	23,052	81	68	13
Pascagoula	22,091	90	62	28
Pass Christian	5,690	23	20	3
Petal	10,747	31	26	5
Picayune	10,631	50	34	16
Ridgeland	24,406	89	62	27
Summit	1,677	8	7	1
Waveland	6,382	18	18	0
Wiggins	4,577	21	16	5
MISSOURI				
Adrian	1,611	3	3	0
Advance	1,369	3	3	0
Anderson	1,980	6	6	0
Annapolis	343	1	1	0
Arbyrd	482	1	1	0
Archie	1,205	3	3	0
Arnold	21,461	55	48	7
Ash Grove	1,465	5	5	0
Ashland	3,895	7	6	1
Aurora	7,471	24	17	7
Ava	2,924	12	7	5
Ballwin	30,609	59	48	11
Bates City	219	1	1	0
Battlefield	6,083	8	8	0
Bella Villa	739	4	4	0
Bellefontaine Neighbors	10,788	29	26	3
Bel-Nor	1,479	6	6	0
Bel-Ridge	2,719	13	12	1
Belton	23,170	58	41	17
Berkeley	9,063	35	27	8
Bertrand	786	1	1	0
Bethany	3,122	5	5	0
Billings	1,092	4	4	0
Birch Tree	658	1	1	0
Bismarck	1,491	3	3	0
Bloomfield	1,897	5	5	0
Blue Springs	54,445	141	98	43
Bolivar	10,790	27	21	6
Bonne Terre	7,175	11	11	0
Boonville	8,423	27	21	6
Bourbon	1,620	4	4	0
Bowling Green	5,400	11	8	3
Branson	11,593	58	43	15
Branson West	434	7	7	0
Braymer	842	1	1	0
Breckenridge Hills	4,709	16	15	1
Brentwood	8,058	29	27	2
Bridgeton	11,835	60	49	11
Brookfield	4,324	17	10	7
Bucklin	442	1	1	0
Buckner	3,065	9	8	1
Buffalo	3,031	7	6	1
Butler	4,067	14	9	5
Butterfield Village	464	1	1	0
Cabool	2,126	11	7	4
California	4,415	9	8	1
Calverton Park	1,287	7	7	0
Camdenton	3,907	18	15	3
Cameron	9,817	23	16	7
Campbell	1,908	3	3	0
Canton	2,391	5	4	1
Cape Girardeau	39,738	118	81	37
Cardwell	682	2	2	0
Carl Junction	7,780	16	11	5
Carrollton	3,610	8	8	0
Carterville	1,843	5	5	0
Carthage	14,300	36	27	9
Caruthersville	5,887	19	19	0

Table 62. Full-Time Law Enforcement Employees, by Selected State and City, 2016—Continued

(Number.)

State/city	Population	Total law enforcement employees	Total officers	Total civilians
Cassville	3,311	11	11	0
Center	505	1	1	0
Centralia	4,226	14	9	5
Charleston	5,797	19	14	5
Chesterfield	47,939	100	90	10
Chillicothe	9,495	22	14	8
Claycomo	1,475	9	9	0
Clayton	15,873	57	49	8
Cleveland	663	2	1	1
Clever	2,592	4	4	0
Clinton	8,878	23	22	1
Cole Camp	1,101	2	2	0
Columbia	121,143	182	150	32
Concordia	2,378	6	6	0
Conway	774	1	1	0
Cottleville	5,151	12	10	2
Country Club Village	2,465	2	2	0
Crane	1,337	1	1	0
Crestwood	11,977	32	26	6
Creve Coeur	18,367	54	48	6
Crocker	1,061	4	4	0
Crystal City	4,845	22	16	6
Crystal Lakes	346	2	1	1
Cuba	3,380	14	13	1
Delta	440	1	1	0
Desloge	4,916	11	11	0
De Soto	6,512	19	14	5
Des Peres	8,611	51	40	11
Dexter	8,014	23	18	5
Diamond	930	2	2	0
Dixon	1,486	10	6	4
Doniphan	1,990	11	8	3
Doolittle	600	1	1	0
Drexel	954	2	2	0
Duenweg	1,300	3	3	0
Duquesne	1,730	10	9	1
East Prairie	3,150	9	6	3
Edina	1,095	1	1	0
Edmundson	838	11	10	1
Eldon	4,646	15	14	1
El Dorado Springs	3,559	12	7	5
Ellisville	9,318	24	23	1
Ellsinore	448	2	2	0
Elsberry	1,996	3	3	0
Essex	457	1	1	0
Eureka	10,681	25	21	4
Excelsior Springs	11,562	35	24	11
Exeter	775	1	1	0
Fair Grove	1,472	5	5	0
Fair Play	464	1	1	0
Farmington	18,564	34	26	8
Fayette	2,705	7	7	0
Ferguson	21,032	47	39	8
Ferrelview	464	1	1	0
Festus	12,157	35	25	10
Florissant	52,266	108	85	23
Fordland	818	2	2	0
Foristell	523	6	6	0
Forsyth	2,446	7	6	1
Fredericktown	4,097	13	11	2
Frontenac	3,872	21	20	1
Fulton	12,973	33	27	6
Gallatin	1,736	1	1	0
Garden City	1,621	4	4	0
Gerald	1,313	5	5	0
Gideon	1,031	2	2	0
Gladstone	27,138	58	43	15
Glendale	5,928	14	11	3
Goodman	1,230	2	2	0
Gower	1,496	3	3	0
Grain Valley	13,484	25	21	4
Granby	2,127	5	5	0
Grandview	25,412	60	51	9
Greenfield	1,306	4	4	0
Greenwood	5,641	9	9	0
Hamilton	1,692	4	4	0
Hannibal	17,825	48	37	11
Hardin	537	1	1	0
Harrisonville	9,975	29	21	8
Hartville	592	2	2	0
Hayti	2,759	10	9	1
Hazelwood	25,655	78	67	11
Herculaneum	4,030	12	11	1
Hermann	2,365	12	7	5
Higginsville	4,638	15	9	6

Table 62. Full-Time Law Enforcement Employees, by Selected State and City, 2016—Continued

(Number.)

State/city	Population	Total law enforcement employees	Total officers	Total civilians
Highlandville	967	2	2	0
Hillsboro	3,121	9	7	2
Hillsdale	1,520	12	11	1
Holcomb	602	2	2	0
Holden	2,265	6	5	1
Hollister	4,515	19	13	6
Hornersville	630	3	3	0
Houston	2,081	6	6	0
Howardville	364	3	1	2
Humansville	1,036	1	1	0
Huntsville	1,516	1	1	0
Iberia	745	3	3	0
Independence	117,335	257	184	73
Indian Point	511	2	2	0
Iron Mountain Lake	713	1	1	0
Ironton	1,379	3	3	0
Jackson	15,092	31	23	8
Jasper	927	10	10	0
Jefferson City	43,171	125	88	37
Jonesburg	722	1	1	0
Joplin	52,001	146	102	44
Kahoka	2,013	3	3	0
Kansas City	478,364	1,875	1,356	519
Kearney	9,629	18	17	1
Kennett	10,610	30	22	8
Kimberling City	2,290	7	6	1
Kinloch	299	10	4	6
Kirksville	17,521	28	25	3
Kirkwood	27,793	75	61	14
Knob Noster	2,771	12	7	5
Laddonia	510	1	1	0
Ladue	8,612	32	26	6
La Grange	941	4	4	0
Lake Lotawana	2,029	8	6	2
Lake Ozark	1,795	17	11	6
Lakeshire	1,427	4	4	0
Lake St. Louis	15,534	40	31	9
Lake Tapawingo	723	3	3	0
Lake Waukomis	908	2	2	0
Lake Winnebago	1,146	5	5	0
Lamar	4,330	13	11	2
Lanagan	410	3	3	0
La Plata	1,330	3	3	0
Lathrop	2,042	10	10	0
Laurie	929	5	5	0
Lawson	2,397	6	5	1
Leadington	457	5	4	1
Leadwood	1,227	5	5	0
Lebanon	14,721	41	29	12
Lee's Summit	95,821	193	139	54
Leeton	562	1	1	0
Lexington	4,573	10	9	1
Liberal	714	1	1	0
Liberty	30,699	54	40	14
Licking	3,113	5	5	0
Lilbourn	1,126	2	2	0
Lincoln	1,169	3	3	0
Linn	1,423	4	4	0
Linn Creek	244	1	1	0
Lone Jack	1,139	6	6	0
Louisiana	3,284	11	5	6
Macon	5,427	12	10	2
Malden	4,092	16	14	2
Manchester	18,256	42	39	3
Mansfield	1,254	5	5	0
Maplewood	7,931	34	31	3
Marceline	2,139	8	7	1
Marionville	2,181	3	3	0
Marshall	13,031	33	26	7
Marshfield	7,230	11	10	1
Marston	472	1	1	0
Marthasville	1,155	2	2	0
Maryland Heights	27,374	95	78	17
Maryville	11,855	24	20	4
Matthews	628	2	2	0
Maysville	1,090	1	1	0
Memphis	1,831	3	3	0
Merriam Woods	1,764	2	2	0
Mexico	11,691	34	32	2
Milan	1,831	4	4	0
Miller	684	8	8	0
Miner	956	12	7	5
Moberly	13,900	38	27	11
Moline Acres	2,428	7	6	1
Monett	9,006	23	20	3

Table 62. Full-Time Law Enforcement Employees, by Selected State and City, 2016—Continued

(Number.)

State/city	Population	Total law enforcement employees	Total officers	Total civilians
Monroe City	2,432	8	8	0
Montgomery City	2,714	5	5	0
Morehouse	916	2	2	0
Moscow Mills	2,585	5	5	0
Mound City	1,040	2	2	0
Mountain Grove	4,662	14	11	3
Mountain View	2,662	8	8	0
Mount Vernon	4,531	11	11	0
Neosho	12,218	27	25	2
Nevada	8,230	23	19	4
Newburg	448	2	2	0
New Florence	720	1	1	0
New Franklin	1,081	5	4	1
New Haven	2,097	7	7	0
New London	967	1	1	0
New Madrid	2,988	8	8	0
Nixa	21,377	35	29	6
Noel	1,822	3	3	0
Normandy	7,618	32	31	1
North Kansas City	4,387	45	34	11
Northwoods	4,187	20	18	2
Oak Grove	7,956	16	15	1
Oakland	1,382	75	61	14
Oakview Village	394	3	3	0
O'Fallon	86,093	151	117	34
Olivette	7,893	24	22	2
Oregon	763	1	1	0
Oronogo	2,433	5	5	0
Orrick	804	3	3	0
Osage Beach	4,449	37	24	13
Osceola	909	3	3	0
Overland	15,940	58	42	16
Owensville	2,616	6	6	0
Ozark	19,366	37	33	4
Pacific	7,192	25	19	6
Pagedale	3,312	6	5	1
Palmyra	3,617	8	7	1
Park Hills	8,676	16	15	1
Parkville	6,450	18	17	1
Peculiar	4,937	10	9	1
Perry	696	1	1	0
Perryville	8,431	30	25	5
Pevely	5,682	20	14	6
Piedmont	1,976	7	7	0
Pierce City	1,277	4	4	0
Pilot Grove	760	1	1	0
Pilot Knob	707	2	2	0
Pineville	784	5	5	0
Platte City	4,859	11	10	1
Platte Woods	403	1	1	0
Plattsburg	2,286	6	6	0
Pleasant Hill	8,320	20	14	6
Pleasant Hope	614	1	1	0
Pleasant Valley	3,074	15	10	5
Polo	533	1	1	0
Poplar Bluff	17,309	63	48	15
Potosi	2,637	10	9	1
Purdy	1,103	2	2	0
Queen City	592	1	1	0
Qulin	452	1	1	0
Raymore	20,600	41	29	12
Raytown	29,377	72	53	19
Republic	16,219	27	22	5
Rich Hill	1,325	3	3	0
Richland	1,815	7	6	1
Richmond	5,558	13	11	2
Richmond Heights	8,466	40	39	1
Risco	325	1	1	0
Riverside	3,192	33	24	9
Riverview	2,831	10	10	0
Rockaway Beach	871	2	2	0
Rock Hill	4,648	11	10	1
Rock Port	1,217	3	3	0
Rogersville	3,436	8	7	1
Rolla	20,093	57	35	22
Salem	4,998	17	12	5
Salisbury	1,550	5	4	1
Savannah	5,115	7	6	1
Scott City	4,518	17	12	5
Sedalia	21,536	64	46	18
Seligman	838	3	2	1
Senath	1,700	3	3	0
Seneca	2,409	4	4	0
Seymour	1,975	3	3	0
Shelbina	1,627	6	5	1

Table 62. Full-Time Law Enforcement Employees, by Selected State and City, 2016—Continued

(Number.)

State/city	Population	Total law enforcement employees	Total officers	Total civilians
Shrewsbury	6,197	22	20	2
Sikeston	16,455	75	63	12
Silex	309	1	1	0
Slater	1,827	5	4	1
Smithville	9,403	16	16	0
Southwest City	956	3	3	0
Sparta	1,798	1	1	0
Springfield	168,307	418	344	74
St. Ann	12,925	56	42	14
St. Charles	69,364	152	110	42
Steele	2,091	5	5	0
Steelville	1,711	6	6	0
Ste. Genevieve	4,486	10	10	0
St. James	4,130	10	9	1
St. John	6,454	24	22	2
St. Joseph	76,577	169	125	44
St. Louis	314,507	1,632	1,194	438
St. Marys	345	1	1	0
Stover	1,070	3	3	0
St. Peters	57,835	113	89	24
Strafford	2,366	7	7	0
St. Robert	6,112	22	16	6
Sturgeon	914	2	2	0
Sugar Creek	3,315	22	17	5
Sullivan	7,143	25	18	7
Summersville	500	2	2	0
Sunset Hills	8,548	33	26	7
Sweet Springs	1,463	3	3	0
Tarkio	1,459	3	3	0
Thayer	2,248	11	7	4
Town and Country	11,158	32	30	2
Trenton	5,874	16	10	6
Troy	11,730	26	24	2
Truesdale	730	1	1	0
Union	11,092	25	23	2
University City	35,002	96	68	28
Urbana	405	2	2	0
Velda City	1,400	11	10	1
Verona	601	1	1	0
Versailles	2,432	10	10	0
Viburnum	656	2	2	0
Vienna	594	1	1	0
Vinita Park	1,887	55	53	2
Walnut Grove	787	3	3	0
Warrensburg	20,136	38	35	3
Warrenton	8,147	22	20	2
Warsaw	2,093	7	7	0
Warson Woods	1,957	8	8	0
Washington	14,065	33	30	3
Waverly	819	1	1	0
Waynesville	5,467	13	12	1
Weatherby Lake	1,872	5	5	0
Webb City	11,192	26	22	4
Webster Groves	23,216	47	45	2
Wellsville	1,138	2	2	0
Wentzville	36,938	84	63	21
West Plains	12,334	32	28	4
Wheaton	699	2	2	0
Willard	5,485	13	12	1
Willow Springs	2,142	7	6	1
Winfield	1,439	3	3	0
Winona	1,305	8	4	4
Woodson Terrace	4,074	19	17	2
Wright City	3,511	12	11	1
MONTANA				
Baker	2,063	5	5	0
Belgrade	8,146	18	15	3
Billings	111,447	176	148	28
Boulder	1,213	3	3	0
Bozeman	44,739	70	62	8
Bridger	733	2	2	0
Chinook	1,233	4	4	0
Colstrip	2,359	11	7	4
Columbia Falls	5,175	9	9	0
Columbus	2,072	5	4	1
Conrad	2,594	5	5	0
Cut Bank	3,023	8	7	1
Deer Lodge	2,938	7	6	1
Dillon	4,224	9	8	1
East Helena	2,065	5	5	0
Ennis	895	1	1	0
Fort Benton	1,459	4	4	0
Fromberg	445	1	1	0
Glasgow	3,442	11	8	3

Table 62. Full-Time Law Enforcement Employees, by Selected State and City, 2016—Continued

(Number.)

State/city	Population	Total law enforcement employees	Total officers	Total civilians
Glendive	5,608	13	9	4
Great Falls	59,717	130	88	42
Hamilton	4,659	15	14	1
Havre	9,896	27	21	6
Helena	31,052	70	48	22
Hot Springs	548	2	2	0
Kalispell	22,470	48	38	10
Laurel	6,986	17	13	4
Libby	2,646	6	6	0
Livingston	7,364	12	12	0
Manhattan	1,656	3	3	0
Miles City	8,878	16	16	0
Missoula	71,860	130	104	26
Plains	1,053	3	3	0
Polson	4,744	16	15	1
Red Lodge	2,242	7	6	1
Ronan City	1,998	5	5	0
Sidney	7,190	11	11	0
Stevensville	1,940	3	3	0
Thompson Falls	1,334	4	4	0
Troy	876	4	4	0
West Yellowstone	1,353	12	6	6
Whitefish	7,226	19	16	3
Wolf Point	2,901	8	7	1
NEBRASKA				
Albion	1,577	3	3	0
Alliance	8,533	21	14	7
Ashland	2,577	5	4	1
Aurora	4,499	9	8	1
Bayard	1,136	4	4	0
Beatrice	12,340	35	22	13
Bellevue	56,294	108	92	16
Bennington	1,712	2	2	0
Blair	7,969	19	17	2
Broken Bow	3,551	6	5	1
Central City	2,876	6	5	1
Chadron	5,761	21	15	6
Columbus	22,911	49	33	16
Crete	7,047	13	12	1
Emerson	814	2	2	0
Fairbury	3,718	7	6	1
Falls City	4,173	13	9	4
Fremont	26,490	42	37	5
Gering	8,297	18	16	2
Gothenburg	3,503	6	5	1
Grand Island	51,980	102	85	17
Hastings	24,872	53	39	14
Holdrege	5,575	16	10	6
Imperial	2,054	4	4	0
Kearney	33,471	69	56	13
Kimball	2,388	4	4	0
La Vista	16,973	39	34	5
Lexington	10,044	23	21	2
Lincoln	281,138	465	327	138
Lyons	808	2	2	0
Madison	2,365	4	3	1
Milford	2,110	4	4	0
Minatare	796	2	2	0
Minden	3,023	5	5	0
Mitchell	1,658	4	4	0
Neligh	1,513	3	3	0
Norfolk	24,389	57	40	17
North Platte	24,092	65	40	25
Ogallala	4,538	10	9	1
Omaha	446,163	926	798	128
O'Neill	3,642	8	7	1
Ord	2,051	3	3	0
Plainview	1,216	3	3	0
Plattsmouth	6,454	17	14	3
Ralston	6,003	16	14	2
Randolph	916	1	1	0
Schuyler	6,160	10	8	2
Scottsbluff	14,747	35	30	5
Scribner	844	2	2	0
Sidney	6,983	16	14	2
St. Paul	2,369	4	4	0
Superior	1,869	4	4	0
Tekamah	1,727	4	4	0
Tilden	936	1	1	0
Valentine	2,857	6	5	1
Wahoo	4,508	6	6	0
Walthill	776	1	1	0
Waterloo	1,086	3	3	0
Wayne	5,549	11	7	4

Table 62. Full-Time Law Enforcement Employees, by Selected State and City, 2016—Continued

(Number.)

State/city	Population	Total law enforcement employees	Total officers	Total civilians
West Point	3,367	7	6	1
Wilber	1,873	3	3	0
Wymore	1,406	3	3	0
York	7,885	22	16	6
NEVADA				
Boulder City	15,661	41	30	11
Carlin	2,291	7	6	1
Elko	20,687	44	37	7
Fallon	8,433	33	22	11
Henderson	291,584	588	350	238
Las Vegas Metropolitan Police Department	1,592,178	4,855	3,326	1,529
Lovelock	1,876	5	4	1
Mesquite	17,969	47	34	13
North Las Vegas	238,554	414	268	146
Reno	244,554	375	311	64
Sparks	97,269	156	110	46
West Wendover	4,271	23	13	10
Winnemucca	7,978	25	22	3
Yerington	3,067	6	5	1
NEW HAMPSHIRE				
Alexandria	1,625	2	2	0
Alstead	1,911	2	2	0
Alton	5,338	14	12	2
Amherst	11,272	24	18	6
Antrim	2,662	6	5	1
Ashland	2,055	5	5	0
Atkinson	6,817	7	6	1
Auburn	5,368	10	8	2
Barnstead	4,615	5	5	0
Barrington	8,894	11	10	1
Bedford	22,407	47	34	13
Belmont	7,315	19	16	3
Bennington	1,471	2	2	0
Berlin	9,241	31	22	9
Bethlehem	2,558	5	5	0
Boscawen	3,950	8	7	1
Bow	7,779	12	10	2
Bradford	1,664	3	3	0
Brentwood	4,786	6	6	0
Bristol	3,076	10	9	1
Brookline	5,256	9	8	1
Campton	3,300	8	7	1
Candia	3,905	7	6	1
Canterbury	2,401	2	2	0
Carroll	745	4	4	0
Center Harbor	1,099	3	3	0
Charlestown	4,969	8	5	3
Chester	4,962	7	6	1
Claremont	12,913	24	19	5
Colebrook	2,167	5	5	0
Concord	42,610	89	78	11
Conway	9,915	33	23	10
Danville	4,466	7	6	1
Deerfield	4,436	7	6	1
Deering	1,924	2	2	0
Derry	33,249	64	51	13
Dover	31,054	73	50	23
Dublin	1,541	4	3	1
Dunbarton	2,799	4	4	0
Durham	17,078	23	20	3
Effingham	1,533	2	2	0
Enfield	4,544	8	7	1
Epping	6,927	17	16	1
Epsom	4,654	6	5	1
Exeter	14,635	36	27	9
Farmington	6,841	15	14	1
Fitzwilliam	2,328	3	3	0
Franconia	1,120	3	3	0
Franklin	8,446	27	19	8
Freedom	1,486	2	2	0
Fremont	4,648	5	4	1
Gilford	7,182	24	18	6
Gilmanton	3,780	6	5	1
Goffstown	18,000	41	29	12
Gorham	2,622	10	7	3
Grantham	2,953	5	4	1
Greenland	3,943	7	7	0
Hampstead	8,588	8	8	0
Hampton	15,358	43	34	9
Hampton Falls	2,303	4	4	0
Hancock	1,635	3	3	0
Hanover	11,430	30	19	11

Table 62. Full-Time Law Enforcement Employees, by Selected State and City, 2016—Continued

(Number.)

State/city	Population	Total law enforcement employees	Total officers	Total civilians
Haverhill	4,641	9	8	1
Henniker	4,934	9	8	1
Hillsborough	5,974	19	13	6
Hinsdale	3,876	8	7	1
Holderness	2,095	5	5	0
Hollis	7,814	15	14	1
Hooksett	14,232	36	25	11
Hopkinton	5,614	7	7	0
Hudson	24,997	65	48	17
Jackson	814	1	1	0
Jaffrey	5,270	12	11	1
Keene	23,244	55	41	14
Kensington	2,133	5	4	1
Kingston	6,144	9	8	1
Laconia	16,300	48	38	10
Lancaster	3,322	9	7	2
Lebanon	13,668	44	31	13
Lee	4,403	8	7	1
Lincoln	1,721	14	9	5
Lisbon	1,569	3	3	0
Litchfield	8,482	13	11	2
Littleton	5,905	13	10	3
Londonderry	25,439	70	56	14
Loudon	5,455	8	7	1
Lyndeborough	1,706	1	1	0
Madison	2,521	4	4	0
Manchester	110,353	288	231	57
Marlborough	2,064	2	2	0
Meredith	6,396	18	14	4
Merrimack	25,675	52	40	12
Middleton	1,788	3	3	0
Milford	15,317	30	25	5
Milton	4,583	9	8	1
Mont Vernon	2,485	3	3	0
Moultonborough	4,008	10	10	0
Nashua	88,252	235	174	61
New Boston	5,524	8	7	1
Newbury	2,184	4	4	0
New Durham	2,662	4	4	0
Newfields	1,700	4	4	0
New Hampton	2,215	6	6	0
Newington	777	11	10	1
New Ipswich	5,212	6	5	1
New London	4,678	13	8	5
Newmarket	8,911	19	12	7
Newport	6,337	17	12	5
Newton	4,927	8	7	1
Northfield	4,805	10	9	1
North Hampton	4,435	12	11	1
Northumberland	2,145	3	3	0
Northwood	4,281	9	8	1
Nottingham	4,977	6	5	1
Orford	1,246	1	1	0
Ossipee	4,229	10	9	1
Pelham	13,384	28	20	8
Pembroke	7,118	11	9	2
Peterborough	6,469	13	11	2
Pittsfield	4,068	6	6	0
Plainfield	2,350	3	3	0
Plaistow	7,612	22	15	7
Plymouth	6,639	18	12	6
Portsmouth	21,612	79	60	19
Raymond	10,324	23	15	8
Rindge	5,822	8	7	1
Rochester	30,096	68	55	13
Rollinsford	2,527	4	4	0
Rye	5,396	10	9	1
Salem	28,949	77	63	14
Sanbornton	2,979	7	6	1
Sandown	6,348	7	7	0
Sandwich	1,307	2	2	0
Seabrook	8,804	34	27	7
Somersworth	11,757	32	26	6
South Hampton	809	2	2	0
Springfield	1,313	2	2	0
Strafford	4,090	5	5	0
Stratham	7,403	11	10	1
Sugar Hill	567	1	1	0
Sunapee	3,408	5	5	0
Thornton	2,491	4	3	1
Tilton	3,588	18	16	2
Troy	2,075	3	3	0
Wakefield	5,629	12	11	1
Warner	2,877	5	4	1
Waterville Valley	246	7	6	1

Table 62. Full-Time Law Enforcement Employees, by Selected State and City, 2016—Continued

(Number.)

State/city	Population	Total law enforcement employees	Total officers	Total civilians
Weare	8,937	10	9	1
Webster	1,894	2	2	0
Wilton	3,692	8	7	1
Winchester	4,189	7	6	1
Windham	14,625	27	20	7
Wolfeboro	6,198	18	13	5
Woodstock	1,374	5	5	0
NEW JERSEY				
Aberdeen Township	18,562	42	35	7
Absecon	8,298	30	25	5
Allendale	6,849	20	15	5
Allenhurst	490	13	9	4
Allentown	1,824	6	5	1
Alpine	1,918	12	12	0
Andover Township	5,979	17	12	5
Asbury Park	15,757	90	87	3
Atlantic City	39,202	397	278	119
Atlantic Highlands	4,297	19	14	5
Audubon	8,669	18	17	1
Avalon	1,273	29	21	8
Avon-by-the-Sea	1,774	11	11	0
Barnegat Township	22,272	51	49	2
Barrington	6,752	16	15	1
Bay Head	971	9	8	1
Bayonne	66,629	284	182	102
Beach Haven	1,168	13	11	2
Beachwood	11,219	20	18	2
Bedminster Township	8,239	17	15	2
Belleville	36,258	120	111	9
Bellmawr	11,380	23	21	2
Belmar	5,694	29	22	7
Belvidere	2,593	6	6	0
Bergenfield	27,646	52	49	3
Berkeley Heights Township	13,548	31	25	6
Berkeley Township	41,684	88	66	22
Berlin	7,544	18	17	1
Berlin Township	5,419	18	17	1
Bernards Township	27,024	43	38	5
Bernardsville	7,802	24	18	6
Beverly	2,555	7	7	0
Blairstown Township	5,791	6	6	0
Bloomfield	48,215	146	121	25
Bloomingdale	8,290	17	16	1
Bogota	8,397	20	15	5
Boonton	8,414	25	21	4
Boonton Township	4,359	13	13	0
Bordentown City	3,873	13	13	0
Bordentown Township	12,049	25	23	2
Bound Brook	10,494	29	24	5
Bradley Beach	4,261	21	18	3
Branchburg Township	14,676	27	26	1
Brick Township	74,818	196	134	62
Bridgeton	24,982	75	60	15
Bridgewater Township	45,251	82	74	8
Brielle	4,753	15	14	1
Brigantine	9,156	48	35	13
Brooklawn	1,919	6	6	0
Buena	4,520	11	9	2
Burlington City	9,785	33	30	3
Burlington Township	22,867	51	42	9
Butler	7,691	17	16	1
Byram Township	7,969	14	14	0
Caldwell	7,933	22	22	0
Cape May	3,496	26	21	5
Carlstadt	6,277	28	26	2
Carney's Point Township	7,809	18	17	1
Carteret	24,316	65	57	8
Cedar Grove Township	12,603	29	29	0
Chatham	8,954	23	19	4
Chatham Township	10,555	23	21	2
Cherry Hill Township	71,079	166	139	27
Chesilhurst	1,626	9	8	1
Chester	1,671	7	6	1
Chesterfield Township	7,534	11	10	1
Chester Township	7,940	17	16	1
Cinnaminson Township	16,871	24	24	0
Clark Township	15,609	51	40	11
Clayton	8,511	17	16	1
Clementon	4,913	13	12	1
Cliffside Park	24,977	50	48	2
Clifton	86,324	178	145	33
Clinton	2,645	10	10	0
Clinton Township	12,933	23	22	1
Closter	8,674	19	19	0

Table 62. Full-Time Law Enforcement Employees, by Selected State and City, 2016—Continued

(Number.)

State/city	Population	Total law enforcement employees	Total officers	Total civilians
Collingswood	13,943	27	23	4
Colts Neck Township	10,018	21	20	1
Cranbury Township	3,958	18	17	1
Cranford Township	24,324	68	53	15
Cresskill	8,815	26	22	4
Deal	735	22	18	4
Delanco Township	4,592	12	11	1
Delaware Township	4,478	8	7	1
Delran Township	16,739	34	30	4
Demarest	5,051	12	12	0
Denville Township	16,759	40	30	10
Deptford Township	30,400	69	64	5
Dover	18,290	37	33	4
Dumont	18,010	39	31	8
Dunellen	7,434	17	16	1
Eastampton Township	6,005	16	15	1
East Brunswick Township	49,016	110	84	26
East Greenwich Township	10,473	17	15	2
East Hanover Township	11,233	38	34	4
East Newark	2,707	8	8	0
East Orange	64,787	262	205	57
East Rutherford	9,166	38	37	1
East Windsor Township	27,537	49	43	6
Eatontown	12,264	45	37	8
Edgewater	12,079	33	30	3
Edgewater Park Township	8,769	15	14	1
Edison Township	102,679	226	177	49
Egg Harbor City	4,238	12	11	1
Egg Harbor Township	43,971	110	85	25
Elizabeth	129,096	388	293	95
Elk Township	4,122	13	12	1
Elmer	1,334	2	2	0
Elmwood Park	20,348	46	41	5
Emerson	7,716	23	20	3
Englewood	28,677	110	84	26
Englewood Cliffs	5,397	26	25	1
Englishtown	1,979	8	8	0
Essex Fells	2,157	13	13	0
Evesham Township	45,581	85	76	9
Ewing Township	36,435	94	75	19
Fairfield Township, Essex County	7,561	40	37	3
Fair Haven	6,010	13	13	0
Fair Lawn	33,646	72	59	13
Fairview	14,497	34	31	3
Fanwood	7,677	18	17	1
Far Hills	930	6	6	0
Flemington	4,654	14	13	1
Florence Township	12,805	27	25	2
Florham Park	11,794	38	32	6
Fort Lee	36,739	110	90	20
Franklin	4,814	17	16	1
Franklin Lakes	10,902	27	22	5
Franklin Township, Gloucester County	16,551	29	26	3
Franklin Township, Hunterdon County	3,237	6	6	0
Franklin Township, Somerset County	66,791	124	104	20
Freehold Borough	11,941	31	28	3
Freehold Township	35,736	69	65	4
Frenchtown	1,389	3	3	0
Galloway Township	37,280	81	59	22
Garfield	31,895	76	66	10
Garwood	4,352	20	16	4
Gibbsboro	2,228	10	10	0
Glassboro	19,245	50	45	5
Glen Ridge	7,647	34	23	11
Glen Rock	12,014	23	22	1
Gloucester City	11,247	31	29	2
Gloucester Township	63,484	147	125	22
Green Brook Township	7,266	24	23	1
Greenwich Township, Gloucester County	4,824	21	19	2
Greenwich Township, Warren County	5,527	9	9	0
Guttenberg	11,701	28	26	2
Hackensack	44,968	138	119	19
Hackettstown	9,549	19	18	1
Haddonfield	11,323	23	21	2
Haddon Heights	7,482	16	15	1
Haddon Township	14,439	27	26	1
Haledon	8,432	18	18	0
Hamburg	3,131	10	8	2
Hamilton Township, Atlantic County	26,824	73	50	23
Hamilton Township, Mercer County	88,665	205	169	36
Hammonton	14,585	35	29	6
Hanover Township	14,468	37	30	7
Harding Township	3,900	12	11	1
Hardyston Township	7,991	24	18	6
Harrington Park	4,830	11	11	0

Table 62. Full-Time Law Enforcement Employees, by Selected State and City, 2016—Continued

(Number.)

State/city	Population	Total law enforcement employees	Total officers	Total civilians
Harrison	15,788	46	35	11
Harrison Township	13,023	18	17	1
Harvey Cedars	340	8	8	0
Hasbrouck Heights	12,239	32	30	2
Haworth	3,469	13	12	1
Hawthorne	19,031	35	31	4
Hazlet Township	20,050	50	42	8
Helmetta	2,231	7	7	0
High Bridge	3,538	7	7	0
Highland Park	14,346	35	28	7
Highlands	4,838	19	16	3
Hightstown	5,491	14	13	1
Hillsborough Township	40,037	65	52	13
Hillsdale	10,569	22	19	3
Hillside Township	21,981	70	59	11
Hi-Nella	854	12	12	0
Hoboken	54,095	145	126	19
Ho-Ho-Kus	4,161	19	15	4
Holland Township	5,137	7	6	1
Holmdel Township	16,651	50	41	9
Hopatcong	14,388	31	24	7
Hopewell Township	18,570	38	30	8
Howell Township	52,306	102	86	16
Independence Township	5,502	10	9	1
Irvington	54,430	195	158	37
Island Heights	1,664	5	5	0
Jackson Township	56,563	105	87	18
Jamesburg	6,028	17	13	4
Jefferson Township	21,418	45	37	8
Jersey City	266,179	1,279	865	414
Keansburg	9,828	43	34	9
Kearny	42,208	115	109	6
Kenilworth	8,229	30	25	5
Keyport	7,126	23	17	6
Kinnelon	10,367	17	16	1
Lacey Township	28,540	57	43	14
Lakehurst	2,696	14	12	2
Lakewood Township	100,269	153	121	32
Lambertville	3,817	13	10	3
Laurel Springs	1,870	7	7	0
Lavallette	1,789	16	12	4
Lawnside	2,898	9	8	1
Lawrence Township, Mercer County	33,023	62	58	4
Lebanon Township	6,356	8	7	1
Leonia	9,224	20	17	3
Lincoln Park	10,327	29	23	6
Linden	42,100	153	127	26
Lindenwold	17,340	44	41	3
Linwood	6,950	17	16	1
Little Egg Harbor Township	20,686	59	43	16
Little Falls Township	14,478	30	26	4
Little Ferry	10,970	29	26	3
Little Silver	5,901	20	16	4
Livingston Township	29,788	79	68	11
Lodi	24,841	47	44	3
Logan Township	5,939	19	18	1
Long Beach Township	3,015	49	37	12
Long Branch	30,959	103	82	21
Long Hill Township	8,749	25	23	2
Longport	884	12	12	0
Lopatcong Township	8,281	15	14	1
Lower Alloways Creek Township	1,702	13	11	2
Lower Township	21,982	57	44	13
Lumberton Township	12,400	20	18	2
Lyndhurst Township	22,530	54	51	3
Madison	16,098	36	28	8
Magnolia	4,267	11	11	0
Mahwah Township	26,588	60	52	8
Manalapan Township	40,407	57	54	3
Manasquan	5,798	21	16	5
Manchester Township	43,525	86	68	18
Mansfield Township, Burlington County	8,578	14	13	1
Mansfield Township, Warren County	7,461	15	14	1
Mantoloking	244	10	9	1
Mantua Township	14,939	28	26	2
Manville	10,424	27	24	3
Maple Shade Township	18,927	36	32	4
Maplewood Township	24,743	73	63	10
Margate City	6,214	37	27	10
Marlboro Township	40,764	103	73	30
Matawan	8,851	22	21	1
Maywood	9,804	26	22	4
Medford Lakes	4,072	10	9	1
Medford Township	23,481	34	30	4
Mendham	4,979	12	11	1

Table 62. Full-Time Law Enforcement Employees, by Selected State and City, 2016—Continued

(Number.)

State/city	Population	Total law enforcement employees	Total officers	Total civilians
Mendham Township	5,846	15	14	1
Merchantville	3,751	15	13	2
Metuchen	13,879	33	28	5
Middlesex Borough	13,923	31	29	2
Middle Township	18,555	63	49	14
Middletown Township	65,919	135	112	23
Midland Park	7,330	16	15	1
Millburn Township	20,310	59	53	6
Milltown	7,044	19	16	3
Millville	28,177	85	74	11
Monmouth Beach	3,233	10	9	1
Monroe Township, Gloucester County	36,805	73	67	6
Monroe Township, Middlesex County	44,923	72	55	17
Montclair	38,108	121	104	17
Montgomery Township	23,160	35	29	6
Montvale	8,519	24	22	2
Montville Township	21,801	43	37	6
Moonachie	2,790	20	17	3
Moorestown Township	20,530	37	32	5
Morris Plains	5,615	19	17	2
Morristown	18,544	59	55	4
Morris Township	22,555	47	42	5
Mountain Lakes	4,291	14	13	1
Mountainside	6,887	27	22	5
Mount Arlington	5,324	15	14	1
Mount Ephraim	4,609	13	12	1
Mount Holly Township	9,483	24	21	3
Mount Laurel Township	41,828	69	61	8
Mount Olive Township	29,095	56	47	9
Mullica Township	6,089	13	12	1
Neptune City	4,790	19	17	2
Neptune Township	27,505	83	73	10
Netcong	3,240	9	9	0
Newark	281,450	1,383	1,113	270
New Brunswick	57,158	179	144	35
Newfield	1,522	5	5	0
New Hanover Township	8,218	3	3	0
New Milford	16,804	36	34	2
New Providence	12,461	26	24	2
Newton	7,950	28	23	5
North Arlington	15,921	35	28	7
North Bergen Township	63,113	130	120	10
North Brunswick Township	42,777	98	81	17
North Caldwell	6,732	20	15	5
Northfield	8,502	21	20	1
North Haledon	8,529	21	17	4
North Hanover Township	7,594	11	10	1
North Plainfield	22,135	51	44	7
Northvale	4,876	13	13	0
North Wildwood	3,874	36	28	8
Norwood	5,869	16	15	1
Nutley Township	28,673	86	74	12
Oakland	13,176	27	23	4
Oaklyn	3,963	16	15	1
Ocean City	11,287	73	58	15
Ocean Gate	2,004	9	8	1
Oceanport	5,718	16	15	1
Ocean Township, Monmouth County	27,070	74	61	13
Ocean Township, Ocean County	8,927	26	18	8
Ogdensburg	2,266	6	6	0
Old Bridge Township	67,238	117	90	27
Old Tappan	6,039	14	13	1
Oradell	8,222	22	21	1
Orange	30,470	118	97	21
Palisades Park	20,861	40	32	8
Palmyra	7,296	19	18	1
Paramus	26,958	108	87	21
Park Ridge	8,927	20	19	1
Parsippany-Troy Hills Township	53,447	124	103	21
Passaic	70,972	180	154	26
Paterson	147,265	478	383	95
Paulsboro	5,937	20	18	2
Peapack and Gladstone	2,603	9	8	1
Pemberton Borough	1,378	7	6	1
Pemberton Township	27,739	43	38	5
Pennington	2,586	6	5	1
Pennsauken Township	35,402	81	73	8
Penns Grove	4,908	15	15	0
Pennsville Township	12,720	22	22	0
Pequannock Township	15,425	36	31	5
Perth Amboy	52,767	144	119	25
Phillipsburg	14,435	37	36	1
Pine Beach	2,149	8	7	1
Pine Hill	10,514	24	21	3
Pine Valley	12	6	6	0

Table 62. Full-Time Law Enforcement Employees, by Selected State and City, 2016—Continued

(Number.)

State/city	Population	Total law enforcement employees	Total officers	Total civilians
Piscataway Township	58,181	105	85	20
Pitman	8,830	17	16	1
Plainfield	51,221	152	126	26
Plainsboro Township	23,621	47	35	12
Pleasantville	20,855	65	51	14
Plumsted Township	8,511	15	14	1
Pohatcong Township	3,224	13	12	1
Point Pleasant	18,502	43	33	10
Point Pleasant Beach	4,519	28	22	6
Pompton Lakes	11,164	24	20	4
Princeton	29,660	70	52	18
Prospect Park	5,940	18	17	1
Rahway	29,797	82	73	9
Ramsey	15,145	38	32	6
Randolph Township	25,877	41	36	5
Raritan	8,268	19	18	1
Raritan Township	22,011	36	33	3
Readington Township	15,893	25	23	2
Red Bank	12,187	47	40	7
Ridgefield	11,380	29	27	2
Ridgefield Park	13,107	35	28	7
Ridgewood	25,617	46	43	3
Ringwood	12,427	24	20	4
Riverdale	4,409	20	16	4
River Edge	11,671	28	25	3
Riverside Township	7,980	14	14	0
Riverton	2,741	6	6	0
River Vale Township	10,053	21	19	2
Robbinsville Township	14,209	34	27	7
Rochelle Park Township	5,683	24	20	4
Rockaway	6,471	15	14	1
Rockaway Township	24,655	61	50	11
Roseland	5,857	24	24	0
Roselle	21,669	70	57	13
Roselle Park	13,669	40	34	6
Roxbury Township	23,425	45	42	3
Rumson	6,886	20	16	4
Runnemede	8,322	17	15	2
Rutherford	18,717	41	38	3
Saddle Brook Township	14,108	34	30	4
Saddle River	3,256	22	17	5
Salem	4,849	19	17	2
Sayreville	45,141	96	84	12
Scotch Plains Township	24,144	49	45	4
Sea Bright	1,331	11	11	0
Sea Girt	1,807	11	11	0
Sea Isle City	2,080	28	22	6
Seaside Heights	2,886	38	25	13
Seaside Park	1,541	15	13	2
Secaucus	19,528	76	65	11
Ship Bottom	1,128	12	11	1
Shrewsbury	4,199	21	16	5
Somerdale	5,496	15	14	1
Somers Point	10,667	37	30	7
Somerville	12,198	34	32	2
South Amboy	8,843	27	25	2
South Bound Brook	4,624	13	12	1
South Brunswick Township	45,862	106	80	26
South Hackensack Township	2,469	22	19	3
South Harrison Township	3,116	5	5	0
South Orange	16,332	51	44	7
South Plainfield	24,349	67	52	15
South River	16,391	70	34	36
South Toms River	3,737	12	11	1
Sparta Township	19,049	44	31	13
Spotswood	8,477	25	21	4
Springfield	17,764	46	42	4
Springfield Township	3,343	10	9	1
Spring Lake	2,959	13	13	0
Spring Lake Heights	4,648	12	12	0
Stafford Township	26,972	71	51	20
Stanhope	3,372	10	9	1
Stone Harbor	830	19	17	2
Stratford	6,974	17	15	2
Summit	22,078	51	46	5
Surf City	1,201	10	10	0
Teaneck Township	40,988	105	89	16
Tenafly	14,877	40	34	6
Tewksbury Township	5,862	11	10	1
Tinton Falls	17,747	42	41	1
Toms River Township	90,504	187	160	27
Totowa	10,948	32	28	4
Trenton	83,644	381	246	135
Tuckerton	3,374	12	11	1
Union Beach	5,476	18	15	3

Table 62. Full-Time Law Enforcement Employees, by Selected State and City, 2016—Continued

(Number.)

State/city	Population	Total law enforcement employees	Total officers	Total civilians
Union City	69,345	249	162	87
Union Township	58,109	182	133	49
Upper Saddle River	8,369	21	17	4
Ventnor City	10,455	50	37	13
Vernon Township	22,359	38	30	8
Verona	13,523	35	30	5
Vineland	60,823	157	132	25
Voorhees Township	29,235	58	49	9
Waldwick	10,134	24	19	5
Wallington	11,731	23	22	1
Wall Township	26,033	91	66	25
Wanaque	11,937	30	25	5
Warren Township	16,051	37	30	7
Washington Township, Bergen County	9,381	22	20	2
Washington Township, Gloucester County	47,477	84	77	7
Washington Township, Morris County	18,696	33	30	3
Washington Township, Warren County	6,430	28	27	1
Watchung	5,925	37	30	7
Waterford Township	10,720	26	23	3
Wayne Township	55,023	141	114	27
Weehawken Township	14,284	61	48	13
Wenonah	2,237	7	7	0
Westampton Township	8,707	25	22	3
West Amwell Township	2,767	7	7	0
West Caldwell Township	11,057	30	26	4
West Deptford Township	21,257	46	43	3
Westfield	30,427	71	58	13
West Long Branch	7,975	22	21	1
West Milford Township	26,734	51	44	7
West New York	53,813	119	109	10
West Orange	47,374	111	97	14
Westville	4,189	12	11	1
West Wildwood	566	5	5	0
West Windsor Township	28,482	59	47	12
Westwood	11,252	30	25	5
Wharton	6,593	22	20	2
Wildwood	5,115	49	39	10
Wildwood Crest	3,162	26	20	6
Willingboro Township	31,195	75	65	10
Winfield Township	1,509	8	8	0
Winslow Township	38,724	79	72	7
Woodbridge Township	102,124	252	194	58
Woodbury	9,937	32	29	3
Woodbury Heights	2,985	8	7	1
Woodcliff Lake	5,925	19	18	1
Woodland Park	12,594	28	25	3
Woodlynne	2,922	7	7	0
Wood-Ridge	8,335	27	22	5
Woodstown	3,529	11	9	2
Woolwich Township	12,675	24	23	1
Wyckoff Township	17,242	25	25	0
NEW MEXICO				
Alamogordo	30,768	76	56	20
Angel Fire	1,104	6	5	1
Artesia	12,180	46	27	19
Aztec	6,031	17	14	3
Belen	7,127	23	20	3
Bernalillo	8,946	23	21	2
Bloomfield	7,163	23	18	5
Bosque Farms	3,823	14	13	1
Capitan	1,373	3	3	0
Carlsbad	29,538	89	62	27
Carrizozo	931	4	3	1
Clayton	2,735	13	7	6
Cloudcroft	683	3	3	0
Clovis	39,725	79	54	25
Corrales	8,530	18	15	3
Cuba	736	5	4	1
Dexter	1,273	6	5	1
Edgewood	3,819	11	8	3
Espanola	10,030	36	23	13
Estancia	1,586	7	3	4
Eunice	3,182	13	8	5
Farmington	42,270	169	131	38
Gallup	23,528	70	56	14
Grants	9,245	22	19	3
Hatch	1,596	9	8	1
Hobbs	39,349	128	94	34
Hurley	1,249	5	3	2
Jal	2,234	14	7	7
Las Cruces	102,349	256	182	74
Las Vegas	13,256	53	33	20
Logan	951	4	4	0

Table 62. Full-Time Law Enforcement Employees, by Selected State and City, 2016—Continued

(Number.)

State/city	Population	Total law enforcement employees	Total officers	Total civilians
Lordsburg	2,485	11	9	2
Los Alamos	17,667	70	33	37
Los Lunas	15,398	40	36	4
Magdalena	906	3	3	0
Mesilla	1,869	7	7	0
Milan	3,248	12	6	6
Moriarty	1,786	11	9	2
Portales	11,921	28	22	6
Questa	1,750	4	3	1
Raton	6,058	19	10	9
Red River	476	9	4	5
Rio Rancho	95,454	233	135	98
Roswell	48,556	103	79	24
Ruidoso	7,683	34	22	12
Ruidoso Downs	2,548	12	6	6
Santa Clara	1,629	5	4	1
Santa Fe	84,663	213	166	47
Santa Rosa	2,641	13	7	6
San Ysidro	195	2	2	0
Springer	924	3	3	0
Taos	5,746	23	17	6
Texico	1,114	2	2	0
Truth or Consequences	6,000	13	12	1
Tularosa	2,863	11	6	5
NEW YORK				
Addison Town and Village	2,541	3	3	0
Akron Village	2,840	1	1	0
Albany	98,617	433	336	97
Albion Village	5,984	11	11	0
Alfred Village	4,039	5	5	0
Allegany Village	1,726	3	2	1
Altamont Village	1,721	1	1	0
Amherst Town	120,436	179	149	30
Amity Town and Belmont Village	2,210	1	1	0
Amityville Village	9,477	23	22	1
Amsterdam	17,891	42	40	2
Arcade Village	1,971	5	5	0
Ardsley Village	4,674	19	19	0
Asharoken Village	653	3	3	0
Attica Village	2,457	3	3	0
Auburn	26,854	71	66	5
Avon Village	3,308	4	4	0
Baldwinsville Village	7,805	12	11	1
Ballston Spa Village	5,366	5	5	0
Batavia	14,931	33	30	3
Bath Village	5,605	11	9	2
Beacon	14,291	36	34	2
Bedford Town	18,063	44	39	5
Binghamton	45,780	145	131	14
Blooming Grove Town	11,907	14	12	2
Bolivar Village	998	1	1	0
Boonville Village	2,034	3	3	0
Brant Town	2,064	1	1	0
Briarcliff Manor Village	8,066	20	20	0
Brighton Town	36,889	44	38	6
Brockport Village	8,355	16	15	1
Bronxville Village	6,460	23	21	2
Buffalo	257,446	900	693	207
Cairo Town	6,437	1	1	0
Caledonia Village	2,136	3	3	0
Cambridge Village	1,822	6	6	0
Camden Village	2,196	2	2	0
Camillus Town and Village	24,622	26	24	2
Canajoharie Village	2,149	4	4	0
Canandaigua	10,407	24	22	2
Canastota Village	4,638	6	5	1
Canisteo Village	2,191	3	3	0
Canton Village	6,619	10	9	1
Carmel Town	34,355	38	31	7
Carthage Village	3,575	3	3	0
Catskill Village	3,840	14	13	1
Cayuga Heights Village	3,840	7	6	1
Cazenovia Village	2,861	5	4	1
Centre Island Village	409	7	7	0
Cheektowaga Town	78,100	162	126	36
Chester Town	7,941	14	14	0
Chester Village	3,907	14	13	1
Chittenango Village	4,855	3	1	2
Clarkstown Town	82,171	181	157	24
Clayton Village	1,950	3	3	0
Cobleskill Village	4,545	12	12	0
Coeymans Town	7,420	5	4	1
Cohoes	16,615	37	33	4
Colchester Town	2,015	1	1	0

Table 62. Full-Time Law Enforcement Employees, by Selected State and City, 2016—Continued

(Number.)

State/city	Population	Total law enforcement employees	Total officers	Total civilians
Colonie Town	80,075	150	111	39
Cooperstown Village	1,780	5	4	1
Corning	10,841	24	20	4
Cornwall-on-Hudson Village	2,955	3	3	0
Cornwall Town	9,589	11	9	2
Cortland	18,856	46	43	3
Crawford Town	9,202	10	9	1
Croton-on-Hudson Village	8,308	22	20	2
Cuba Town	3,153	4	4	0
Dansville Village	4,525	5	5	0
Deerpark Town	7,749	3	3	0
Delhi Village	3,173	4	4	0
Depew Village	15,116	34	29	5
Deposit Village	1,586	1	1	0
DeWitt Town	25,616	48	44	4
Dobbs Ferry Village	11,180	28	26	2
Dolgeville Village	2,119	2	2	0
Dryden Village	2,137	4	4	0
Dunkirk	11,991	38	37	1
East Aurora-Aurora Town	13,823	20	15	5
Eastchester Town	20,150	48	46	2
East Fishkill Town	29,316	38	29	9
East Greenbush Town	16,483	31	22	9
East Hampton Town	19,950	92	68	24
East Hampton Village	1,130	27	23	4
Eden Town	7,670	5	4	1
Ellenville Village	4,070	12	11	1
Ellicott Town	5,140	12	12	0
Ellicottville	1,598	3	3	0
Elmira Heights Village	3,959	10	10	0
Elmira Town	5,786	4	4	0
Elmsford Village	4,838	19	19	0
Endicott Village	12,944	30	28	2
Evans Town	16,234	30	24	6
Fairport Village	5,350	11	10	1
Fallsburg Town	11,966	20	20	0
Floral Park Village	15,986	48	34	14
Florida Village	2,912	1	1	0
Fort Edward Village	3,258	5	5	0
Fort Plain Village	2,232	4	4	0
Frankfort Town	4,925	3	3	0
Frankfort Village	2,490	4	4	0
Franklinville Village	1,670	2	2	0
Fredonia Village	10,604	18	14	4
Freeport Village	43,419	115	98	17
Fulton City	11,483	34	33	1
Garden City Village	22,656	64	51	13
Gates Town	28,669	35	30	5
Geddes Town	10,349	17	15	2
Geneseo Village	8,199	8	8	0
Geneva	13,033	35	33	2
Glen Cove	27,480	54	50	4
Glens Falls	14,212	29	27	2
Glenville Town	21,754	24	22	2
Gloversville	14,908	30	28	2
Goshen Town	8,515	9	9	0
Goshen Village	5,384	20	17	3
Gouverneur Village	3,769	9	6	3
Gowanda Village	2,622	2	2	0
Granville Village	2,451	6	6	0
Great Neck Estates Village	2,839	15	12	3
Greece Town	96,975	105	99	6
Greenburgh Town	45,745	140	112	28
Greene Village	1,488	1	1	0
Greenwich Village	1,738	6	6	0
Greenwood Lake Village	3,104	6	5	1
Groton Village	2,402	1	1	0
Guilderland Town	34,405	48	35	13
Hamburg Town	46,028	78	61	17
Hamburg Village	9,608	14	13	1
Hamilton Village	4,166	5	5	0
Hancock Village	966	2	2	0
Harriman Village	2,486	7	7	0
Harrison Town	28,518	74	63	11
Hastings-on-Hudson Village	8,044	21	21	0
Haverstraw Town	37,756	69	64	5
Hempstead Village	55,870	140	118	22
Herkimer Village	7,478	19	19	0
Highland Falls Village	3,829	9	7	2
Holley Village	1,721	2	2	0
Hoosick Falls Village	3,419	1	1	0
Hornell	8,289	23	22	1
Horseheads Village	6,653	10	10	0
Hudson	6,381	29	25	4
Hudson Falls Village	7,170	14	14	0

Table 62. Full-Time Law Enforcement Employees, by Selected State and City, 2016—Continued

(Number.)

State/city	Population	Total law enforcement employees	Total officers	Total civilians
Hunter Town	2,634	3	3	0
Huntington Bay Village	1,431	4	4	0
Ilion Village	7,877	20	18	2
Inlet Town	322	3	2	1
Interlaken Village	627	1	1	0
Irondequoit Town	50,874	60	49	11
Irvington Village	6,643	23	22	1
Ithaca	30,937	74	66	8
Jamestown	29,879	68	59	9
Johnson City Village	14,699	38	33	5
Johnstown	8,282	23	21	2
Kenmore Village	15,110	25	25	0
Kensington Village	1,189	6	6	0
Kent Town	13,274	25	20	5
Kingston	23,360	76	71	5
Kirkland Town	8,279	5	5	0
Lake Placid Village	2,453	15	12	3
Lake Success Village	3,072	25	22	3
Lakewood-Busti	4,509	13	12	1
Lancaster Town	37,418	64	49	15
Larchmont Village	6,186	28	25	3
Le Roy Village	4,269	7	7	0
Lewisboro Town	12,862	3	3	0
Lewiston Town and Village	16,009	11	10	1
Liberty Village	4,090	16	14	2
Little Falls	4,757	11	10	1
Liverpool Village	2,284	5	5	0
Lloyd Harbor Village	3,695	13	12	1
Lloyd Town	10,568	13	10	3
Long Beach	33,591	85	68	17
Lowville Village	3,406	6	6	0
Lynbrook Village	19,579	58	50	8
Macedon Town and Village	8,911	6	5	1
Malone Village	5,726	13	13	0
Malverne Village	8,579	23	23	0
Mamaroneck Town	12,292	39	38	1
Mamaroneck Village	19,460	56	50	6
Marlborough Town	8,682	10	8	2
Massena Village	10,571	24	19	5
Maybrook Village	3,356	4	4	0
Mechanicville	5,160	12	10	2
Medina Village	5,781	12	11	1
Menands Village	4,000	14	11	3
Middleport Village	1,778	4	4	0
Middletown	27,752	75	64	11
Mohawk Village	2,611	4	4	0
Monroe Village	8,680	21	17	4
Montgomery Village	4,782	4	4	0
Monticello Village	6,438	25	23	2
Moriah Town	3,585	2	2	0
Mount Hope Town	6,899	4	4	0
Mount Morris Village	2,883	5	5	0
Mount Pleasant Town	26,903	47	41	6
Mount Vernon	68,881	261	192	69
Newark Village	8,786	18	17	1
New Berlin Town	1,548	2	2	0
Newburgh	28,171	99	86	13
Newburgh Town	30,933	56	46	10
New Castle Town	18,167	38	36	2
New Hartford Town and Village	20,441	24	20	4
New Paltz Town and Village	14,214	25	21	4
New Rochelle	80,389	211	152	59
New Windsor Town	26,835	48	38	10
New York	8,566,917	51,399	36,228	15,171
New York Mills Village	3,303	4	4	0
Niagara Falls	48,675	178	157	21
Niagara Town	8,080	6	5	1
Niskayuna Town	22,171	29	27	2
Nissequogue Village	1,762	2	2	0
North Castle Town	12,390	34	32	2
North Greenbush Town	12,232	19	17	2
Northport Village	7,387	21	17	4
North Syracuse Village	6,861	11	10	1
North Tonawanda	30,634	51	47	4
Norwich	6,929	20	20	0
Ocean Beach Village	81	4	4	0
Ogdensburg	10,840	30	25	5
Ogden Town	20,257	15	12	3
Old Brookville Village	2,230	33	25	8
Old Westbury Village	4,678	31	26	5
Olean	13,765	40	34	6
Olive Town	4,331	1	1	0
Oneonta City	13,857	28	23	5
Orangetown Town	37,962	86	82	4
Orchard Park Town	29,721	39	31	8

Table 62. Full-Time Law Enforcement Employees, by Selected State and City, 2016—Continued

(Number.)

State/city	Population	Total law enforcement employees	Total officers	Total civilians
Oswego City	17,717	54	47	7
Owego Village	3,705	7	6	1
Oyster Bay Cove Village	4,313	14	14	0
Palmyra Village	3,390	6	5	1
Peekskill	24,129	64	54	10
Pelham Manor Village	5,614	22	21	1
Pelham Village	7,074	28	25	3
Penn Yan Village	4,988	13	12	1
Perry Village	3,487	3	3	0
Piermont Village	2,585	8	8	0
Plattsburgh City	19,765	58	51	7
Pleasantville Village	7,205	22	22	0
Port Chester Village	29,750	63	61	2
Port Dickinson Village	1,585	5	4	1
Port Jervis	8,565	31	30	1
Port Washington	19,272	63	55	8
Potsdam Village	9,744	16	13	3
Poughkeepsie	30,262	125	91	34
Poughkeepsie Town	39,222	91	80	11
Pound Ridge Town	5,275	2	1	1
Pulaski Village	2,299	1	1	0
Quogue Village	995	14	13	1
Ramapo Town	92,620	117	95	22
Rensselaer City	9,441	33	27	6
Riverhead Town	33,818	103	85	18
Rochester	209,643	864	747	117
Rockville Centre Village	24,229	64	55	9
Rome	32,345	76	74	2
Rosendale Town	5,927	2	1	1
Rotterdam Town	29,352	43	40	3
Rouses Point Village	2,161	1	1	0
Rye	16,108	41	36	5
Rye Brook Village	9,658	27	26	1
Sag Harbor Village	2,305	15	13	2
Salamanca	5,545	17	17	0
Sands Point Village	2,767	20	20	0
Saranac Lake Village	5,248	12	12	0
Saratoga Springs	28,005	86	73	13
Saugerties Town	19,128	28	24	4
Scarsdale Village	18,026	49	44	5
Schenectady	65,138	171	146	25
Schodack Town	11,730	11	10	1
Scotia Village	7,725	14	13	1
Seneca Falls Town	8,808	19	17	2
Shandaken Town	2,986	4	4	0
Shawangunk Town	14,098	4	4	0
Shelter Island Town	2,423	11	9	2
Sherrill	3,066	3	3	0
Sidney Village	3,729	8	7	1
Skaneateles Village	2,479	1	1	0
Sodus Village	1,743	1	1	0
Solvay Village	6,394	15	14	1
Southampton Town	51,191	126	94	32
Southampton Village	3,296	44	30	14
South Glens Falls Village	3,593	6	6	0
South Nyack Village	3,539	6	6	0
Southold Town	20,114	74	52	22
Spring Valley Village	32,844	58	51	7
St. Johnsville Village	1,687	1	1	0
Stony Point Town	15,599	26	25	1
Suffern Village	11,053	24	20	4
Syracuse	143,925	484	415	69
Tonawanda	14,864	33	27	6
Tonawanda Town	57,698	151	103	48
Troy	49,876	139	126	13
Tuckahoe Village	6,673	26	23	3
Tupper Lake Village	3,560	9	9	0
Tuxedo Park Village	605	5	4	1
Ulster Town	12,264	26	23	3
Utica	60,879	180	163	17
Vestal Town	28,253	37	34	3
Walden Village	6,810	16	13	3
Wallkill Town	28,540	40	39	1
Walton Village	2,901	5	5	0
Warsaw Village	3,357	5	5	0
Warwick Town	18,345	36	31	5
Washingtonville Village	5,765	16	14	2
Waterford Town and Village	8,439	11	8	3
Waterloo Village	5,012	8	7	1
Watertown	26,765	68	65	3
Watervliet	10,208	24	24	0
Watkins Glen Village	1,860	3	3	0
Waverly Village	4,231	11	10	1
Wayland Village	1,804	1	1	0
Webb Town	1,817	5	5	0

Table 62. Full-Time Law Enforcement Employees, by Selected State and City, 2016—Continued

(Number.)

State/city	Population	Total law enforcement employees	Total officers	Total civilians
Webster Town and Village	44,487	36	32	4
Wellsville Village	4,506	11	10	1
Westfield Village	3,066	5	5	0
Westhampton Beach Village	1,790	18	15	3
West Seneca Town	45,752	81	68	13
Whitehall Village	2,574	3	3	0
White Plains	58,767	201	191	10
Whitesboro Village	3,680	5	5	0
Whitestown Town	9,275	6	6	0
Windham Town	1,674	2	2	0
Woodbury Town	10,917	20	16	4
Woodstock Town	5,865	10	10	0
Yonkers	202,075	696	613	83
Yorktown Town	37,287	63	54	9
Yorkville Village	2,625	3	3	0
NORTH CAROLINA				
Aberdeen	7,549	30	28	2
Ahoskie	4,883	18	14	4
Albemarle	16,024	56	48	8
Andrews	1,746	6	5	1
Angier	5,097	14	14	0
Apex	47,324	91	74	17
Archdale	11,593	30	24	6
Asheboro	26,230	79	71	8
Asheville	89,546	263	200	63
Atlantic Beach	1,503	17	16	1
Aurora	522	1	1	0
Ayden	5,078	22	18	4
Badin	1,983	5	5	0
Bailey	564	2	2	0
Bakersville	450	1	1	0
Bald Head Island	174	19	18	1
Banner Elk	1,163	9	8	1
Beaufort	4,244	16	15	1
Beech Mountain	320	14	10	4
Belhaven	1,586	11	8	3
Belmont	10,593	39	30	9
Benson	3,648	14	13	1
Bessemer City	5,591	13	12	1
Bethel	1,628	5	5	0
Beulaville	1,335	3	3	0
Biltmore Forest	1,461	14	13	1
Biscoe	1,689	9	8	1
Black Creek	767	2	2	0
Black Mountain	8,368	22	18	4
Bladenboro	1,721	5	5	0
Blowing Rock	1,303	12	11	1
Boiling Spring Lakes	5,873	13	12	1
Boiling Springs	4,681	8	8	0
Boone	18,374	47	35	12
Boonville	1,204	5	5	0
Brevard	7,747	31	24	7
Bridgeton	437	1	1	0
Broadway	1,271	4	4	0
Brookford	374	1	1	0
Bryson City	1,466	9	8	1
Bunn	366	3	3	0
Burgaw	4,147	13	12	1
Burlington	52,760	161	121	40
Burnsville	1,653	8	8	0
Butner	7,781	39	32	7
Cameron	297	1	1	0
Candor	838	3	3	0
Canton	4,188	18	13	5
Cape Carteret	2,080	8	8	0
Carolina Beach	6,223	31	29	2
Carrboro	21,478	40	37	3
Carthage	2,416	11	10	1
Cary	164,835	223	185	38
Caswell Beach	428	4	4	0
Chadbourn	1,782	8	7	1
Chapel Hill	60,004	127	104	23
Charlotte-Mecklenburg[1]	896,379	2,302	1,743	559
Cherryville	6,018	19	14	5
China Grove	4,187	13	13	0
Chocowinity	821	3	3	0
Claremont	1,368	10	9	1
Clayton	19,968	46	43	3
Cleveland	874	5	5	0
Clinton	8,789	30	26	4
Clyde	1,247	4	4	0
Coats	2,467	6	6	0
Columbus	994	11	10	1
Concord	89,446	194	166	28

Table 62. Full-Time Law Enforcement Employees, by Selected State and City, 2016—Continued

(Number.)

State/city	Population	Total law enforcement employees	Total officers	Total civilians
Conover	8,261	29	27	2
Conway	760	2	2	0
Cooleemee	974	3	3	0
Cornelius	28,756	77	62	15
Cramerton	4,361	15	15	0
Creedmoor	4,487	19	15	4
Dallas	4,656	17	13	4
Davidson	12,469	18	17	1
Dobson	1,570	7	7	0
Drexel	1,864	5	5	0
Duck	386	10	9	1
Dunn	9,804	42	37	5
Durham	263,716	679	490	189
East Bend	597	2	2	0
East Spencer	1,552	5	5	0
Eden	15,343	49	45	4
Edenton	4,822	21	19	2
Elizabeth City	17,852	68	56	12
Elizabethtown	3,577	18	17	1
Elkin	4,067	21	17	4
Elon	10,150	17	16	1
Emerald Isle	3,731	18	17	1
Enfield	2,407	10	9	1
Erwin	4,730	10	9	1
Fair Bluff	912	3	3	0
Fairmont	2,703	7	5	2
Farmville	4,776	22	18	4
Fayetteville	202,200	601	442	159
Fletcher	7,660	17	16	1
Forest City	7,246	33	31	2
Four Oaks	2,075	6	6	0
Foxfire Village	984	3	3	0
Franklin	3,947	18	17	1
Franklinton	2,156	8	8	0
Fremont	1,284	4	4	0
Fuquay-Varina	25,249	44	38	6
Garner	28,508	70	62	8
Garysburg	963	2	2	0
Gaston	1,051	3	3	0
Gastonia	75,118	192	170	22
Gibsonville	6,843	17	16	1
Glen Alpine	1,497	3	3	0
Goldsboro	35,871	101	89	12
Graham	14,712	40	37	3
Granite Falls	4,651	17	14	3
Granite Quarry	3,002	8	8	0
Greensboro	288,618	786	681	105
Greenville	91,766	222	178	44
Grifton	2,683	6	6	0
Hamlet	6,430	23	19	4
Havelock	20,283	30	24	6
Haw River	2,420	7	7	0
Henderson	15,249	54	45	9
Hendersonville	13,954	53	41	12
Hertford	2,148	9	8	1
Hickory	40,437	138	103	35
Highlands	939	14	13	1
High Point	111,435	268	222	46
Hillsborough	6,475	28	27	1
Holden Beach	642	8	8	0
Holly Ridge	2,300	11	10	1
Holly Springs	32,862	60	49	11
Hope Mills	16,268	40	36	4
Hot Springs	562	1	1	0
Hudson	3,710	15	14	1
Huntersville	53,932	91	85	6
Indian Beach	115	5	5	0
Jackson	475	1	1	0
Jacksonville	66,686	143	115	28
Jefferson	1,605	4	4	0
Jonesville	2,251	11	10	1
Kannapolis	46,867	106	79	27
Kenansville	872	3	3	0
Kenly	1,472	8	8	0
Kernersville	23,943	87	68	19
Kill Devil Hills	7,132	35	29	6
King	7,091	23	20	3
Kings Mountain	10,785	40	32	8
Kinston	21,268	68	59	9
Kitty Hawk	3,482	18	16	2
Knightdale	14,875	29	27	2
Kure Beach	2,106	12	11	1
Lake Lure	1,182	10	9	1
Lake Royale	2,670	5	5	0
Lake Waccamaw	1,464	5	5	0

Table 62. Full-Time Law Enforcement Employees, by Selected State and City, 2016—Continued

(Number.)

State/city	Population	Total law enforcement employees	Total officers	Total civilians
Landis	3,121	10	10	0
Laurel Park	2,341	7	7	0
Laurinburg	15,423	40	37	3
Leland	18,842	31	30	1
Lenoir	17,822	60	48	12
Lexington	19,407	62	55	7
Liberty	2,688	11	10	1
Lilesville	499	1	1	0
Lillington	3,532	13	12	1
Lincolnton	10,981	38	33	5
Littleton	641	3	3	0
Locust	2,973	12	12	0
Long View	4,901	16	16	0
Louisburg	3,582	13	12	1
Lowell	3,674	8	8	0
Lumberton	21,683	93	83	10
Madison	2,187	17	16	1
Maggie Valley	1,273	11	10	1
Magnolia	951	1	1	0
Maiden	3,379	15	14	1
Manteo	1,401	8	7	1
Marion	7,827	27	26	1
Marshall	876	3	3	0
Mars Hill	2,320	5	5	0
Marshville	2,684	8	8	0
Matthews	31,401	68	55	13
Maxton	2,454	13	9	4
Mayodan	2,469	14	14	0
Maysville	1,003	3	3	0
Mebane	14,201	34	30	4
Micro	493	1	1	0
Middlesex	812	4	4	0
Mint Hill	26,221	34	31	3
Misenheimer	715	5	5	0
Mocksville	5,170	22	21	1
Monroe	34,978	95	82	13
Montreat	723	5	5	0
Mooresville	36,482	98	79	19
Morehead City	9,477	45	40	5
Morganton	16,656	85	60	25
Morrisville	24,976	35	34	1
Mount Airy	10,345	47	36	11
Mount Gilead	1,180	7	7	0
Mount Holly	14,284	40	31	9
Mount Olive	4,752	21	19	2
Murfreesboro	3,038	7	6	1
Murphy	1,613	11	9	2
Nags Head	2,938	25	23	2
Nashville	5,459	16	15	1
Navassa	1,668	3	3	0
New Bern	30,137	103	81	22
Newland	684	5	5	0
Newport	4,841	9	9	0
Newton	13,049	43	36	7
Newton Grove	577	3	3	0
Norlina	1,074	5	5	0
North Topsail Beach	736	11	10	1
Northwest	776	2	2	0
North Wilkesboro	4,215	25	24	1
Norwood	2,397	8	7	1
Oakboro	1,877	5	5	0
Oak Island	7,651	23	21	2
Ocean Isle Beach	608	13	12	1
Old Fort	911	3	3	0
Oriental	882	1	1	0
Oxford	8,794	31	29	2
Parkton	440	1	1	0
Pembroke	3,009	18	14	4
Pikeville	695	4	4	0
Pilot Mountain	1,462	8	7	1
Pinebluff	1,467	3	3	0
Pinehurst	15,948	30	25	5
Pine Knoll Shores	1,368	7	7	0
Pine Level	1,893	5	5	0
Pinetops	1,308	4	4	0
Pineville	8,626	47	36	11
Pink Hill	538	2	2	0
Pittsboro	4,287	11	11	0
Plymouth	3,618	15	14	1
Polkton	3,526	2	2	0
Princeton	1,302	4	4	0
Raeford	4,907	18	17	1
Raleigh	460,593	875	729	146
Ramseur	1,703	6	6	0
Randleman	4,160	15	15	0

Table 62. Full-Time Law Enforcement Employees, by Selected State and City, 2016—Continued

(Number.)

State/city	Population	Total law enforcement employees	Total officers	Total civilians
Ranlo	3,581	8	8	0
Red Springs	3,434	15	14	1
Reidsville	13,991	48	43	5
Richlands	1,720	8	8	0
Rich Square	891	1	1	0
River Bend	3,153	6	6	0
Roanoke Rapids	15,273	43	39	4
Robbins	1,195	3	3	0
Robersonville	1,412	8	8	0
Rockingham	9,155	39	34	5
Rockwell	2,148	6	6	0
Rocky Mount	55,431	202	160	42
Rolesville	6,962	20	19	1
Rose Hill	1,672	5	5	0
Rowland	1,052	7	6	1
Roxboro	8,331	35	31	4
Rutherfordton	4,173	15	14	1
Salisbury	34,121	76	69	7
Saluda	705	4	4	0
Sanford	29,347	105	82	23
Scotland Neck	1,948	7	6	1
Seagrove	229	1	1	0
Selma	6,351	26	24	2
Seven Devils	201	6	6	0
Shallotte	4,066	14	13	1
Sharpsburg	1,999	8	8	0
Shelby	20,168	85	72	13
Siler City	8,498	24	19	5
Smithfield	12,235	40	37	3
Snow Hill	1,570	6	6	0
Southern Pines	13,778	44	35	9
Southern Shores	2,897	13	12	1
Southport	3,617	11	11	0
Sparta	1,718	6	6	0
Spencer	3,296	14	13	1
Spindale	4,252	10	10	0
Spring Hope	1,311	6	6	0
Spring Lake	13,490	37	34	3
Spruce Pine	2,131	11	11	0
Stallings	15,569	26	21	5
Stanfield	1,491	5	4	1
Stanley	3,712	12	11	1
Stantonsburg	789	4	4	0
Star	874	4	4	0
Statesville	26,557	92	72	20
Stoneville	1,034	4	4	0
St. Pauls	2,422	18	13	5
Sugar Mountain	197	5	5	0
Sunset Beach	3,847	13	13	0
Surf City	2,256	20	19	1
Swansboro	3,250	11	10	1
Sylva	2,623	14	14	0
Tabor City	3,910	11	10	1
Tarboro	11,113	33	27	6
Taylorsville	2,078	11	11	0
Taylortown	825	3	3	0
Thomasville	27,117	72	66	6
Topsail Beach	424	9	8	1
Trent Woods	4,192	6	6	0
Troutman	2,576	14	14	0
Troy	3,411	12	11	1
Tryon	1,631	10	8	2
Valdese	4,455	13	12	1
Vanceboro	998	2	2	0
Vass	756	4	4	0
Wadesboro	5,541	26	20	6
Wagram	801	1	1	0
Wake Forest	39,996	83	68	15
Wallace	3,979	19	15	4
Walnut Creek	866	2	2	0
Warrenton	861	6	5	1
Warsaw	3,191	16	14	2
Washington	9,796	39	29	10
Waxhaw	14,367	26	24	2
Waynesville	9,801	42	34	8
Weaverville	3,988	15	14	1
Weldon	1,574	14	13	1
Wendell	6,368	17	16	1
West Jefferson	1,309	8	8	0
Whispering Pines	3,187	9	8	1
Whitakers	721	2	2	0
White Lake	778	6	6	0
Whiteville	5,635	24	22	2
Wilkesboro	3,527	23	21	2
Williamston	5,467	22	21	1

Table 62. Full-Time Law Enforcement Employees, by Selected State and City, 2016—Continued

(Number.)

State/city	Population	Total law enforcement employees	Total officers	Total civilians
Wilmington	117,852	331	260	71
Wilson	49,734	124	109	15
Wilson's Mills	2,527	5	5	0
Windsor	3,819	9	9	0
Winfall	600	1	1	0
Wingate	3,930	7	7	0
Winston-Salem	243,507	699	536	163
Winterville	9,502	18	17	1
Woodfin	6,411	14	14	0
Woodland	733	1	1	0
Wrightsville Beach	2,581	25	23	2
Yadkinville	2,918	14	13	1
Youngsville	1,228	11	10	1
Zebulon	5,074	19	18	1
NORTH DAKOTA				
Arnegard	129	2	2	0
Belfield	1,115	3	2	1
Berthold	510	1	1	0
Beulah	3,450	7	6	1
Bismarck	73,248	145	115	30
Bowman	1,764	4	4	0
Burlington	1,208	2	2	0
Carrington	2,073	5	5	0
Cavalier	1,233	4	4	0
Devils Lake	7,394	18	16	2
Dickinson	25,130	55	36	19
Ellendale	1,281	2	2	0
Emerado	434	1	1	0
Fargo	121,217	183	160	23
Fessenden	471	1	1	0
Grafton	4,237	10	9	1
Grand Forks	57,853	99	84	15
Harvey	1,779	4	4	0
Hazen	2,504	4	4	0
Hillsboro	1,576	2	2	0
Jamestown	15,417	36	31	5
Kenmare	1,080	3	3	0
Killdeer	1,392	5	5	0
Kulm	342	1	1	0
Lamoure	920	5	4	1
Lincoln	3,776	4	4	0
Lisbon	2,146	3	3	0
Mandan	22,011	42	35	7
Medora	138	3	3	0
Minot	51,265	108	81	27
Napoleon	785	2	2	0
New Town	2,656	7	6	1
Northwood	924	2	2	0
Oakes	1,786	2	2	0
Powers Lake	313	2	2	0
Rolla	1,333	4	4	0
Rugby	2,841	4	4	0
Sherwood	253	1	1	0
South Heart	459	3	3	0
Stanley	3,079	5	5	0
Steele	707	1	1	0
Surrey	1,462	4	4	0
Thompson	1,009	1	1	0
Tioga	1,738	8	6	2
Valley City	6,680	13	12	1
Wahpeton	7,927	16	14	2
Watford City	8,819	20	17	3
West Fargo	35,389	61	51	10
Williston	29,929	69	50	19
Wishek	986	2	2	0
OHIO				
Ada	5,782	9	8	1
Akron	197,257	484	449	35
Alliance	22,012	52	40	12
American Township	12,254	1	1	0
Amherst	12,156	26	20	6
Aurora	15,897	36	28	8
Barberton	26,172	44	42	2
Bath Township, Summit County	9,896	25	19	6
Bay Village	15,346	27	23	4
Beavercreek	46,490	61	47	14
Beaver Township	6,492	14	11	3
Bedford	12,678	36	31	5
Bellefontaine	13,073	36	29	7
Bellville	1,863	4	4	0
Belpre	6,484	16	11	5
Bexley	13,775	36	30	6
Blanchester	4,249	7	7	0

Table 62. Full-Time Law Enforcement Employees, by Selected State and City, 2016—Continued

(Number.)

State/city	Population	Total law enforcement employees	Total officers	Total civilians
Blue Ash	12,169	41	34	7
Bluffton	4,127	7	7	0
Bowling Green	31,404	52	37	15
Brecksville	13,390	38	30	8
Brooklyn	10,841	37	32	5
Brookville	5,902	12	11	1
Brunswick	34,774	53	40	13
Butler Township	7,856	14	14	0
Cambridge	10,341	27	22	5
Canal Fulton	5,489	11	10	1
Canfield	7,323	22	15	7
Carey	3,570	12	8	4
Catawba Island Township	3,539	4	4	0
Celina	10,383	21	16	5
Centerville	23,853	54	40	14
Chagrin Falls	4,003	12	11	1
Chester Township	10,371	12	12	0
Cincinnati	298,880	1,292	1,051	241
Circleville	13,930	27	21	6
Clearcreek Township	15,322	15	14	1
Cleveland	386,227	1,678	1,444	234
Cleveland Heights	44,696	104	95	9
Clyde	6,233	22	18	4
Coitsville Township	1,344	2	2	0
Coldwater	4,501	9	8	1
Columbiana	6,269	15	11	4
Conneaut	12,689	24	17	7
Copley Township	17,653	23	21	2
Cortland	6,894	9	9	0
Defiance	16,697	32	29	3
Delaware	38,658	59	52	7
Delhi Township	29,573	32	30	2
Dublin	45,860	91	63	28
East Cleveland	17,240	31	26	5
Eastlake	18,166	32	23	9
Elyria	53,633	94	79	15
Englewood	13,455	27	20	7
Euclid	47,416	98	92	6
Evendale	2,766	22	19	3
Fairborn	33,587	59	45	14
Fairfield	42,810	79	61	18
Fairfield Township	22,417	19	19	0
Fairport Harbor	3,093	6	5	1
Findlay	41,156	82	64	18
Forest Park	18,669	42	36	6
Fort Recovery	1,430	2	2	0
Fostoria	13,119	27	21	6
Gahanna	34,859	68	53	15
Genoa Township	26,415	26	24	2
Georgetown	4,436	7	7	0
Germantown	5,495	12	11	1
German Township, Montgomery County	2,893	4	4	0
Glenwillow	926	4	4	0
Grandview Heights	7,502	22	17	5
Gratis	855	2	2	0
Grove City	40,161	78	61	17
Groveport	5,813	24	23	1
Hamilton	62,423	120	111	9
Hamilton Township, Warren County	22,670	18	16	2
Harrison	10,819	24	21	3
Heath	10,528	25	18	7
Highland Heights	8,402	30	23	7
Hinckley Township	8,041	10	9	1
Hiram	1,238	2	2	0
Holland	1,698	9	9	0
Independence	7,132	44	31	13
Indian Hill	5,801	25	20	5
Jamestown	2,034	4	4	0
Kalida	1,566	1	1	0
Kent	29,995	56	42	14
Kettering	55,384	99	73	26
Lakewood	50,349	122	100	22
Lancaster	39,959	84	67	17
Lebanon	20,726	36	26	10
Lexington	4,715	13	9	4
Lima	37,715	102	84	18
Lithopolis	1,401	3	3	0
Lordstown	3,278	13	9	4
Louisville	9,115	12	11	1
Lyndhurst	13,624	35	27	8
Madison	3,182	5	4	1
Mansfield	46,656	116	82	34
Mariemont	3,431	11	10	1
Marysville	22,952	43	36	7
Mason	33,026	51	46	5

Table 62. Full-Time Law Enforcement Employees, by Selected State and City, 2016—Continued

(Number.)

State/city	Population	Total law enforcement employees	Total officers	Total civilians
Maumee	13,875	56	42	14
Mechanicsburg	1,591	5	5	0
Medina	26,280	46	36	10
Mentor	46,852	110	81	29
Mentor-on-the-Lake	7,375	13	8	5
Miamisburg	20,000	37	34	3
Miami Township, Montgomery County	29,140	45	38	7
Middlefield	2,694	11	10	1
Middletown	48,768	103	68	35
Milan	1,343	3	3	0
Milford	6,910	19	17	2
Milton Township	2,470	5	5	0
Minerva	3,670	13	9	4
Minerva Park	1,327	7	6	1
Mingo Junction	3,299	4	4	0
Montgomery	10,558	22	20	2
Moreland Hills	3,303	16	15	1
Mount Vernon	16,685	33	30	3
Napoleon	8,566	19	14	5
New Albany	10,340	26	19	7
New Bremen	2,961	7	7	0
Newcomerstown	3,789	8	5	3
New Franklin	14,285	19	13	6
New London	2,366	5	5	0
Newton Falls	4,628	3	3	0
Niles	18,538	37	32	5
North Canton	17,435	29	22	7
North Ridgeville	33,095	47	38	9
Northwood	5,376	23	18	5
Norton	12,026	16	15	1
Norwalk	16,792	29	23	6
Oberlin	8,342	25	18	7
Olmsted Falls	8,859	10	10	0
Oregon	20,055	58	45	13
Ottawa	4,385	8	8	0
Perkins Township	11,844	23	22	1
Perrysburg Township	12,813	29	23	6
Pierce Township	11,559	16	15	1
Plain City	4,318	8	8	0
Port Clinton	5,939	18	13	5
Powell	13,273	21	19	2
Reynoldsburg	37,406	71	53	18
Richfield	3,713	24	17	7
Richmond Heights	10,445	25	19	6
Rittman	6,598	11	8	3
Rossford	6,547	16	15	1
Russell Township	5,250	10	9	1
Russellville	539	3	3	0
Sabina	2,530	5	5	0
Salem	11,943	21	21	0
Sandusky	25,078	49	47	2
Sebring	4,240	9	5	4
Seven Hills	11,661	17	16	1
Shaker Heights	27,478	82	60	22
Sharonville	13,819	48	40	8
Shawnee Hills	746	4	4	0
Shawnee Township	12,173	18	12	6
Sidney	20,797	46	36	10
Silver Lake	2,524	8	8	0
Solon	22,971	64	47	17
South Euclid	21,686	43	35	8
South Point	3,917	8	8	0
South Russell	3,827	9	9	0
Springboro	18,379	28	24	4
Springdale	11,175	39	33	6
Springfield	59,503	132	120	12
Springfield Township, Hamilton County	36,527	54	47	7
Springfield Township, Mahoning County	6,446	10	10	0
Steubenville	18,137	44	38	6
St. Henry	2,529	3	3	0
St. Marys	8,256	20	15	5
Stow	34,792	47	39	8
St. Paris	2,014	1	1	0
Streetsboro	16,364	37	29	8
Strongsville	44,626	85	71	14
Sugarcreek	2,236	6	6	0
Sugarcreek Township	8,283	18	17	1
Tallmadge	17,502	28	25	3
Thornville	997	1	1	0
Toledo	278,366	652	592	60
Troy	25,745	44	42	2
Uhrichsville	5,403	8	8	0
Union Township, Clermont County	47,933	62	48	14
University Heights	13,131	34	29	5
Utica	2,206	3	3	0

Table 62. Full-Time Law Enforcement Employees, by Selected State and City, 2016—Continued

(Number.)

State/city	Population	Total law enforcement employees	Total officers	Total civilians
Valley View, Cuyahoga County	2,007	20	18	2
Vandalia	15,073	38	30	8
Van Wert	10,794	29	21	8
Walton Hills	2,236	18	13	5
Washington Court House	13,986	23	18	5
Waterville	5,511	12	11	1
West Carrollton	12,944	25	23	2
West Chester Township	61,080	106	83	23
Westerville	38,808	102	74	28
West Jefferson	4,291	15	11	4
West Salem	1,491	2	2	0
Whitehall	18,804	58	46	12
Whitehouse	4,528	10	10	0
Wickliffe	12,506	38	28	10
Wooster	26,883	43	40	3
Xenia	26,037	67	41	26
Youngstown	64,181	193	149	44
OKLAHOMA				
Achille	513	4	2	2
Ada	17,390	38	34	4
Allen	935	2	2	0
Altus	19,093	49	39	10
Alva	5,227	12	10	2
Anadarko	6,702	21	16	5
Antlers	2,336	9	4	5
Apache	1,426	3	3	0
Ardmore	25,315	70	51	19
Arkoma	1,912	5	3	2
Atoka	3,055	16	15	1
Barnsdall	1,203	2	2	0
Bartlesville	36,753	83	61	22
Beaver	1,442	2	2	0
Beggs	1,242	7	4	3
Bernice	561	2	2	0
Bethany	19,690	41	30	11
Big Cabin	261	5	4	1
Bixby	25,453	36	27	9
Blackwell	6,837	23	16	7
Blanchard	8,461	15	10	5
Boise City	1,103	2	2	0
Bristow	4,251	15	11	4
Broken Arrow	108,088	188	138	50
Broken Bow	4,133	19	14	5
Cache	2,944	6	6	0
Caddo	1,055	2	2	0
Calera	2,262	11	10	1
Caney	197	5	3	2
Canton	612	3	3	0
Carnegie	1,695	7	4	3
Carney	664	3	2	1
Cashion	857	3	3	0
Catoosa	7,145	16	15	1
Chandler	3,189	13	9	4
Checotah	3,246	13	9	4
Chelsea	1,970	3	3	0
Cherokee	1,574	3	3	0
Chickasha	16,579	40	30	10
Choctaw	12,382	19	18	1
Chouteau	2,088	9	8	1
Claremore	19,076	49	37	12
Clayton	790	5	5	0
Cleveland	3,209	7	7	0
Clinton	9,675	27	18	9
Coalgate	1,849	6	6	0
Colbert	1,191	5	2	3
Collinsville	6,678	15	11	4
Comanche	1,618	5	5	0
Cordell	2,917	6	5	1
Coweta	9,589	23	15	8
Crescent	1,550	8	4	4
Cushing	7,874	23	16	7
Davenport	822	1	1	0
Davis	2,816	11	9	2
Del City	22,152	45	35	10
Depew	483	2	2	0
Dewar	866	1	1	0
Dewey	3,511	12	11	1
Dibble	830	2	2	0
Drumright	2,874	5	5	0
Duncan	23,188	64	48	16
Durant	17,566	45	41	4
Edmond	91,869	158	119	39
Elgin	3,146	5	5	0
Elk City	12,939	41	27	14

Table 62. Full-Time Law Enforcement Employees, by Selected State and City, 2016—Continued

(Number.)

State/city	Population	Total law enforcement employees	Total officers	Total civilians
El Reno	18,872	53	32	21
Enid	52,240	122	98	24
Eufaula	2,960	11	8	3
Fairfax	1,344	4	2	2
Fairview	2,672	9	6	3
Forest Park	1,089	6	4	2
Fort Gibson	4,068	11	10	1
Frederick	3,645	12	9	3
Geary	1,309	12	6	6
Glenpool	13,717	28	21	7
Goodwell	1,331	4	4	0
Grandfield	959	1	1	0
Grove	6,773	29	21	8
Guthrie	11,486	34	24	10
Guymon	12,001	22	15	7
Haileyville	773	3	3	0
Harrah	6,061	11	10	1
Hartshorne	1,997	5	5	0
Haskell	1,974	6	6	0
Healdton	2,774	6	5	1
Heavener	3,321	9	8	1
Hennessey	2,212	8	4	4
Henryetta	5,732	18	12	6
Hinton	3,252	6	6	0
Hobart	3,596	13	7	6
Holdenville	5,743	14	9	5
Hollis	1,950	12	7	5
Hominy	3,499	8	4	4
Hooker	2,009	3	3	0
Howe	787	2	1	1
Hugo	5,206	23	16	7
Hulbert	605	3	3	0
Hydro	958	3	3	0
Idabel	7,006	25	19	6
Jay	2,479	12	8	4
Jenks	21,535	29	21	8
Jones	3,000	7	7	0
Kellyville	1,147	3	3	0
Kiefer	1,960	4	4	0
Kingfisher	4,912	13	11	2
Kingston	1,638	6	6	0
Krebs	1,958	8	6	2
Lahoma	659	2	2	0
Lamont	410	1	1	0
Lawton	96,420	235	167	68
Lexington	2,161	11	6	5
Lindsay	2,829	12	6	6
Locust Grove	1,403	8	4	4
Lone Grove	5,243	11	7	4
Luther	1,611	4	4	0
Madill	3,957	12	11	1
Mangum	2,894	16	6	10
Mannford	3,131	14	8	6
Marietta	2,750	7	6	1
Marlow	4,580	16	10	6
Maysville	1,234	4	3	1
McAlester	18,300	48	45	3
McLoud	4,633	10	9	1
Medicine Park	456	2	2	0
Meeker	1,177	6	5	1
Miami	13,620	38	29	9
Midwest City	57,797	125	92	33
Minco	1,661	4	4	0
Moore	61,511	93	88	5
Mooreland	1,298	2	2	0
Morris	1,458	3	3	0
Mounds	1,182	3	3	0
Mountain View	764	2	2	0
Muldrow	3,248	13	8	5
Muskogee	38,293	111	90	21
Mustang	20,813	33	23	10
Newcastle	9,816	18	17	1
Newkirk	2,242	5	5	0
Nichols Hills	3,921	20	16	4
Nicoma Park	2,483	5	5	0
Ninnekah	1,043	4	3	1
Noble	6,699	17	12	5
Norman	122,143	237	176	61
North Enid	938	4	4	0
Nowata	3,747	9	7	2
Oilton	1,015	2	2	0
Okemah	3,249	12	8	4
Oklahoma City	641,681	1,381	1,113	268
Okmulgee	12,177	26	24	2
Oologah	1,185	4	4	0

Table 62. Full-Time Law Enforcement Employees, by Selected State and City, 2016—Continued

(Number.)

State/city	Population	Total law enforcement employees	Total officers	Total civilians
Owasso	35,551	73	55	18
Pauls Valley	6,163	18	13	5
Pawhuska	3,590	13	9	4
Pawnee	2,153	6	5	1
Perkins	2,862	8	8	0
Perry	5,091	20	12	8
Piedmont	7,420	11	9	2
Pocola	4,026	11	8	3
Ponca City	24,647	74	52	22
Porum	711	3	3	0
Poteau	8,770	31	25	6
Prague	2,466	17	8	9
Pryor Creek	9,455	27	22	5
Purcell	6,405	22	20	2
Ringling	996	2	2	0
Roland	3,604	10	7	3
Rush Springs	1,283	4	4	0
Salina	1,381	5	5	0
Sallisaw	8,530	28	20	8
Sand Springs	19,961	42	32	10
Sapulpa	20,667	53	40	13
Sawyer	316	3	3	0
Sayre	4,858	13	8	5
Seiling	887	2	2	0
Seminole	7,531	12	10	2
Shawnee	31,560	75	52	23
Skiatook	8,005	23	19	4
Snyder	1,336	3	3	0
South Coffeyville	771	7	5	2
Spencer	4,049	7	7	0
Sperry	1,281	2	2	0
Spiro	2,167	4	4	0
Stigler	2,783	13	9	4
Stillwater	49,637	111	72	39
Stilwell	4,026	17	12	5
Stonewall	475	2	2	0
Stratford	1,537	4	4	0
Stringtown	400	1	1	0
Stroud	2,782	15	8	7
Sulphur	5,130	12	10	2
Tahlequah	16,764	49	34	15
Talala	277	2	2	0
Talihina	1,091	10	5	5
Tecumseh	6,662	13	12	1
The Village	9,493	28	22	6
Tishomingo	3,080	8	7	1
Tonkawa	3,111	11	7	4
Tryon	504	1	1	0
Tulsa	405,748	912	747	165
Tushka	300	3	3	0
Tuttle	6,974	15	10	5
Union City	2,004	6	6	0
Valley Brook	784	14	8	6
Valliant	744	4	3	1
Verdigris	4,428	5	4	1
Vian	1,383	9	6	3
Vici	731	3	2	1
Vinita	5,621	22	15	7
Wagoner	8,787	20	15	5
Walters	2,486	4	4	0
Warner	1,619	3	3	0
Warr Acres	10,505	30	24	6
Washington	637	3	2	1
Watonga	3,002	10	8	2
Watts	308	3	2	1
Waukomis	1,381	4	4	0
Waurika	1,974	8	7	1
Waynoka	974	4	3	1
Weatherford	12,399	31	21	10
Webbers Falls	597	4	4	0
Weleetka	984	5	5	0
West Siloam Springs	839	9	9	0
Westville	1,554	9	5	4
Wetumka	1,238	5	4	1
Wewoka	3,449	8	7	1
Wilburton	2,653	7	6	1
Wilson	1,731	8	5	3
Woodward	13,223	27	24	3
Wright City	741	3	2	1
Wyandotte	333	6	5	1
Wynnewood	2,226	6	5	1
Yale	1,222	6	3	3
Yukon	26,546	61	43	18

Table 62. Full-Time Law Enforcement Employees, by Selected State and City, 2016—Continued

(Number.)

State/city	Population	Total law enforcement employees	Total officers	Total civilians
OREGON				
Albany	52,544	89	61	28
Ashland	21,017	42	29	13
Astoria	9,655	24	16	8
Aumsville	4,101	6	5	1
Baker City	9,741	18	15	3
Bandon	3,125	8	7	1
Beaverton	97,907	171	134	37
Bend	89,244	115	87	28
Black Butte		8	7	1
Boardman	3,378	11	10	1
Brookings	6,506	21	14	7
Burns	2,748	4	4	0
Canby	17,395	29	25	4
Cannon Beach	1,704	10	8	2
Carlton	2,080	4	3	1
Central Point	18,161	31	25	6
Clatskanie	1,761	5	4	1
Coburg	1,059	3	2	1
Columbia City	1,960	1	1	0
Condon	681	1	1	0
Coos Bay	16,224	37	24	13
Coquille	3,857	7	6	1
Corvallis	56,061	90	56	34
Cottage Grove	10,025	24	16	8
Dallas	15,411	20	17	3
Eagle Point	8,987	12	11	1
Enterprise	1,883	4	4	0
Eugene	164,883	323	188	135
Fairview	9,350	16	14	2
Florence	8,685	20	12	8
Forest Grove	24,433	36	31	5
Gearhart	1,536	3	3	0
Gervais	2,663	6	5	1
Gladstone	12,083	20	17	3
Gold Beach	2,284	7	6	1
Grants Pass	37,317	85	53	32
Gresham	111,491	153	122	31
Hermiston	17,280	38	27	11
Hillsboro	104,440	185	133	52
Hines	1,517	3	3	0
Hood River	7,719	16	14	2
Hubbard	3,323	6	5	1
Independence	9,355	18	14	4
Jacksonville	2,903	6	5	1
John Day	1,667	10	4	6
Junction City	5,935	14	8	6
Keizer	38,165	43	36	7
King City	3,804	7	6	1
Klamath Falls	22,296	41	36	5
La Grande	13,071	34	19	15
Lake Oswego	38,860	66	42	24
Lebanon	16,487	38	26	12
Lincoln City	8,588	32	21	11
Madras	6,735	11	10	1
Malin	804	7	7	0
Manzanita	627	4	4	0
McMinnville	34,242	43	37	6
Medford	80,794	137	100	37
Milton-Freewater	7,029	17	11	6
Milwaukie	20,935	42	38	4
Molalla	9,064	15	13	2
Monmouth	10,131	13	12	1
Mount Angel	3,448	9	7	2
Myrtle Creek	3,466	11	9	2
Myrtle Point	2,514	5	5	0
Newberg-Dundee	26,105	49	35	14
Newport	10,328	24	19	5
North Bend	9,669	25	16	9
North Plains	2,131	2	2	0
Oakridge	3,212	6	5	1
Ontario	10,925	25	22	3
Oregon City	36,485	52	45	7
Pendleton	16,927	27	23	4
Philomath	4,602	10	9	1
Phoenix	4,578	8	7	1
Pilot Rock	1,514	2	2	0
Portland	642,129	1,150	908	242
Prineville	9,595	29	16	13
Rainier	1,921	6	5	1
Redmond	29,164	45	36	9
Rockaway Beach	1,354	4	4	0
Rogue River	2,246	7	5	2
Roseburg	22,159	39	35	4
Salem	166,508	312	190	122
Sandy	14,104	21	17	4

Table 62. Full-Time Law Enforcement Employees, by Selected State and City, 2016—Continued

(Number.)

State/city	Population	Total law enforcement employees	Total officers	Total civilians
Scappoose	7,005	11	10	1
Seaside	6,556	25	15	10
Sherwood	19,486	27	24	3
Silverton	9,860	18	17	1
Springfield	61,164	96	65	31
Stayton	8,028	15	13	2
St. Helens	13,184	15	13	2
Sutherlin	7,932	17	14	3
Sweet Home	9,337	22	15	7
Talent	6,483	10	8	2
The Dalles	15,413	25	22	3
Tigard	51,885	88	73	15
Tillamook	5,003	11	10	1
Toledo	3,521	12	7	5
Tualatin	27,370	45	37	8
Turner	2,010	2	2	0
Umatilla	7,026	13	11	2
Vernonia	2,139	5	4	1
Warrenton	5,340	12	11	1
West Linn	26,889	33	29	4
Winston	5,396	9	8	1
Woodburn	25,395	42	34	8
Yamhill	1,109	4	3	1
PENNSYLVANIA				
Abington Township, Montgomery County	55,623	114	92	22
Adams Township, Butler County	13,531	11	11	0
Adams Township, Cambria County	5,710	6	6	0
Akron	4,014	4	4	0
Albion	1,459	3	3	0
Alburtis	2,552	4	4	0
Aldan	4,168	5	5	0
Aleppo Township	1,903	17	14	3
Aliquippa	9,150	19	18	1
Allegheny Township, Blair County	6,652	8	7	1
Allegheny Township, Westmoreland County	8,213	10	9	1
Allentown	120,615	240	220	20
Altoona	45,158	69	61	8
Ambler	6,517	13	12	1
Ambridge	6,822	8	8	0
Amity Township	12,884	13	12	1
Annville Township	4,835	10	8	2
Archbald	6,951	18	18	0
Arnold	4,956	8	8	0
Ashland	2,718	2	2	0
Ashley	2,714	2	2	0
Aspinwall	2,756	7	6	1
Aston Township	16,828	18	16	2
Athens	3,234	4	4	0
Athens Township	5,058	11	10	1
Avalon	4,630	6	5	1
Avoca	2,661	2	2	0
Avonmore Boro	976	1	1	0
Baden	4,018	3	3	0
Baldwin Borough	19,828	25	24	1
Baldwin Township	1,962	5	5	0
Bally	1,105	2	2	0
Bangor	5,189	11	10	1
Beaver	4,399	12	11	1
Beaver Falls	8,598	19	18	1
Beaver Meadows	837	1	1	0
Bedford	2,724	5	5	0
Bedminster Township	7,123	7	6	1
Bell Acres	1,396	3	3	0
Bellefonte	6,260	13	10	3
Bellevue	8,229	18	15	3
Bellwood	1,779	1	1	0
Ben Avon	1,776	17	14	3
Ben Avon Heights	377	17	14	3
Bensalem Township	60,362	122	99	23
Berlin	2,003	2	2	0
Bern Township	6,967	12	12	0
Bernville	950	1	1	0
Berwick	10,170	15	14	1
Bethel Park	32,077	44	38	6
Bethel Township, Berks County	4,136	3	3	0
Bethlehem	74,869	148	148	0
Bethlehem Township	23,869	36	35	1
Biglerville	1,211	2	2	0
Birdsboro	5,158	8	7	1
Birmingham Township	4,272	3	3	0
Blairsville	3,304	4	4	0
Blair Township	4,564	4	4	0
Blakely	6,289	6	6	0

Table 62. Full-Time Law Enforcement Employees, by Selected State and City, 2016—Continued

(Number.)

State/city	Population	Total law enforcement employees	Total officers	Total civilians
Blawnox	1,413	3	3	0
Bloomsburg Town	14,532	20	16	4
Blossburg	1,512	2	2	0
Bonneauville	1,832	1	1	0
Boyertown	4,043	8	7	1
Brackenridge	3,201	4	4	0
Braddock Hills	1,857	2	2	0
Bradford	8,459	18	18	0
Bradford Township	4,814	5	5	0
Branch Township	1,774	2	2	0
Brecknock Township, Berks County	4,636	5	5	0
Brentwood	9,486	16	14	2
Briar Creek Township	3,005	4	4	0
Bridgeport	4,565	10	9	1
Bridgeville	5,081	9	8	1
Bridgewater	690	2	2	0
Brighton Township	8,434	8	8	0
Bristol	9,539	14	12	2
Bristol Township	53,978	68	61	7
Brockway	2,034	3	2	1
Brookhaven	8,090	8	7	1
Brookville	3,855	7	7	0
Brownsville	2,285	2	2	0
Bryn Athyn	1,397	5	5	0
Buckingham Township	20,440	22	20	2
Buffalo Township	7,258	5	5	0
Buffalo Valley Regional	12,284	16	15	1
Bushkill Township	8,430	17	16	1
Butler	13,198	24	23	1
Butler Township, Butler County	16,713	23	21	2
Butler Township, Luzerne County	9,713	11	10	1
Butler Township, Schuylkill County	5,657	4	4	0
Caernarvon Township, Berks County	4,074	8	7	1
California	7,004	8	7	1
Caln Township	14,167	21	20	1
Cambria Township	5,885	4	4	0
Cambridge Springs	2,528	3	3	0
Camp Hill	7,929	13	12	1
Canonsburg	8,909	17	17	0
Canton	1,910	3	3	0
Carbondale	8,503	9	9	0
Carlisle	19,225	33	30	3
Carnegie	7,923	12	11	1
Carrolltown	810	2	2	0
Carroll Township, Washington County	5,539	2	2	0
Carroll Township, York County	6,309	11	11	0
Carroll Valley	3,954	5	4	1
Castle Shannon	8,219	16	15	1
Catasauqua	6,543	9	8	1
Catawissa	1,506	3	3	0
Cecil Township	12,059	20	19	1
Center Township	11,750	15	14	1
Centerville	3,178	2	2	0
Central Berks Regional	9,458	15	14	1
Central Bucks Regional	15,380	30	27	3
Chambersburg	20,770	36	33	3
Charleroi Regional	6,630	7	7	0
Chartiers Township	7,960	12	12	0
Cheltenham Township	37,064	78	70	8
Chester	34,109	103	93	10
Chester Township	4,130	12	11	1
Cheswick	1,727	1	1	0
Chippewa Township	8,192	9	8	1
Churchill	2,973	10	10	0
Clairton	6,661	9	9	0
Clarion	6,284	9	8	1
Clarks Summit	6,336	5	5	0
Claysville	806	3	3	0
Clearfield	5,996	7	7	0
Cleona	2,146	4	4	0
Clifton Heights	6,691	11	10	1
Clymer	1,307	1	1	0
Coaldale	2,181	3	3	0
Coal Township	10,480	12	11	1
Coatesville	13,157	33	29	4
Cochranton	1,104	2	2	0
Colebrookdale District	6,007	11	9	2
Collegeville	5,327	8	8	0
Collier Township	8,096	17	16	1
Collingdale	8,794	9	8	1
Colonial Regional	20,361	26	24	2
Columbia	10,385	20	17	3
Conemaugh Township, Cambria County	1,910	2	2	0
Conemaugh Township, Somerset County	6,961	6	6	0
Conewago Township, Adams County	7,200	10	9	1

Table 62. Full-Time Law Enforcement Employees, by Selected State and City, 2016—Continued

(Number.)

State/city	Population	Total law enforcement employees	Total officers	Total civilians
Conewango Township	3,422	4	4	0
Conneaut Lake Regional	3,505	4	3	1
Connellsville	7,492	15	14	1
Conoy Township	3,472	17	15	2
Conshohocken	7,979	21	19	2
Conway	2,145	4	4	0
Conyngham	1,874	3	3	0
Coopersburg	2,428	7	7	0
Coplay	3,236	4	4	0
Coraopolis	5,573	13	9	4
Cornwall	4,249	7	6	1
Corry	6,384	12	11	1
Coudersport	2,469	4	4	0
Covington Township	2,265	3	3	0
Crafton	6,316	10	9	1
Cranberry Township	30,940	31	27	4
Crescent Township	2,601	2	2	0
Cresson	1,619	10	10	0
Cresson Township	2,562	6	5	1
Croyle Township	2,274	1	1	0
Cumberland Township, Adams County	6,243	6	6	0
Cumberland Township, Greene County	6,385	3	3	0
Cumru Township	15,385	22	21	1
Curwensville	2,461	2	2	0
Dallas	2,779	4	4	0
Dallas Township	9,333	10	10	0
Dalton	1,204	2	2	0
Danville	4,686	8	6	2
Darby	10,687	18	17	1
Darby Township	9,329	14	13	1
Decatur Township	4,850	2	2	0
Delmont	2,631	4	4	0
Derry	2,576	2	2	0
Derry Township, Dauphin County	25,044	58	39	19
Dickson City	5,839	10	9	1
Donegal Township	2,432	3	3	0
Donora	4,641	6	6	0
Dormont	8,440	14	13	1
Douglass Township, Berks County	3,554	5	5	0
Douglass Township, Montgomery County	10,475	12	11	1
Downingtown	7,957	19	16	3
Doylestown Township	17,539	22	20	2
Dublin Borough	2,171	2	2	0
Du Bois	7,561	13	13	0
Duboistown	1,208	5	1	4
Dunbar	1,014	1	1	0
Duncansville	1,198	1	1	0
Dunmore	13,247	17	17	0
Duquesne	5,528	13	12	1
Duryea	4,935	4	4	0
East Bangor	1,655	1	1	0
East Berlin	1,537	1	1	0
East Bethlehem Township	2,288	1	1	0
East Brandywine Township	8,642	16	15	1
East Cocalico Township	10,502	15	14	1
East Coventry Township	6,767	8	7	1
East Deer Township	1,470	1	1	0
East Earl Township	6,848	8	8	0
Eastern Adams Regional	7,403	6	6	0
Eastern Pike Regional	4,614	11	10	1
East Fallowfield Township	7,590	7	7	0
East Franklin Township	3,949	1	1	0
East Hempfield Township	24,462	37	33	4
East Lampeter Township	17,090	38	35	3
East Lansdowne	2,665	5	3	2
East Marlborough Township	7,334	1	1	0
East McKeesport	2,671	3	3	0
East Norriton Township	14,171	30	28	2
Easton	26,938	66	62	4
East Pennsboro Township	21,712	22	21	1
East Penn Township	2,785	1	1	0
East Pikeland Township	7,411	8	8	0
East Pittsburgh	1,789	1	1	0
Easttown Township	10,644	14	13	1
East Union Township	1,591	2	2	0
East Whiteland Township	10,711	22	20	2
Ebensburg	3,175	4	4	0
Economy	9,389	13	12	1
Eddystone	2,407	10	9	1
Edgewood	3,059	9	9	0
Edgeworth	1,668	13	4	9
Edinboro	6,316	8	8	0
Edwardsville	4,716	13	12	1
Elizabeth	2,006	2	2	0
Elizabethtown	11,592	19	17	2

Table 62. Full-Time Law Enforcement Employees, by Selected State and City, 2016—Continued

(Number.)

State/city	Population	Total law enforcement employees	Total officers	Total civilians
Elizabeth Township	13,216	12	12	0
Elkland	1,771	2	2	0
Ellwood City	7,561	12	10	2
Emmaus	11,398	21	19	2
Emporium	1,908	2	2	0
Emsworth	2,413	17	14	3
Ephrata	13,955	36	32	4
Erie	99,019	191	169	22
Etna	3,391	7	7	0
Evans City-Seven Fields Regional	4,599	3	3	0
Everett	1,745	3	3	0
Exeter	5,585	2	2	0
Exeter Township, Berks County	25,930	31	29	2
Exeter Township, Luzerne County	2,360	1	1	0
Fairchance	1,925	1	1	0
Fairview Township, Luzerne County	4,486	6	6	0
Fairview Township, York County	17,312	16	13	3
Falls Township, Bucks County	33,823	60	52	8
Fawn Township	2,348	1	1	0
Ferguson Township	19,222	24	22	2
Ferndale	1,544	1	1	0
Findlay Township	5,637	22	15	7
Fleetwood	4,085	5	5	0
Folcroft	6,643	12	11	1
Ford City	2,857	1	1	0
Forest City	1,789	2	2	0
Forest Hills	6,428	9	9	0
Forks Township	15,390	22	21	1
Forty Fort	4,109	4	4	0
Forward Township	3,336	1	1	0
Foster Township, McKean County	4,191	5	5	0
Fountain Hill	4,635	9	8	1
Fox Chapel	5,381	11	11	0
Frackville	3,715	5	5	0
Franconia Township	13,272	11	10	1
Franklin	6,255	23	17	6
Franklin Park	14,600	12	11	1
Franklin Township, Beaver County	3,970	3	3	0
Franklin Township, Carbon County	4,134	4	4	0
Franklin Township, Columbia County	588	4	4	0
Frazer Township	1,159	2	2	0
Freedom Township	3,418	3	3	0
Freeland	3,446	5	4	1
Freemansburg	2,611	2	2	0
Freeport	1,730	1	1	0
Galeton	1,119	1	1	0
Gallitzin	1,828	1	1	0
Geistown	2,353	3	3	0
Gettysburg	7,608	12	11	1
Girard	3,007	4	4	0
Glassport	4,408	5	5	0
Glenolden	7,177	11	10	1
Granville Township	5,046	10	8	2
Greencastle	4,051	5	4	1
Greenfield Township, Blair County	4,075	4	4	0
Greensburg	14,419	38	28	10
Green Tree	5,089	11	10	1
Greenville	5,794	8	7	1
Greenwood Township	1,912	1	1	0
Grove City	8,169	12	11	1
Hamburg	4,420	7	6	1
Hampden Township	29,684	26	25	1
Hampton Township	18,504	19	18	1
Hanover	15,537	28	25	3
Hanover Township, Luzerne County	10,901	16	16	0
Harmar Township	3,100	9	8	1
Harmony Township	3,100	5	5	0
Harrisburg	48,996	155	133	22
Harrison Township	10,448	21	18	3
Harveys Lake	2,763	3	3	0
Hastings	2,206	2	2	0
Hatboro	7,420	17	14	3
Hatfield Township	20,925	26	24	2
Haverford Township	49,168	82	70	12
Hazleton	24,725	41	37	4
Hegins Township	3,457	2	2	0
Heidelberg	1,228	3	3	0
Heidelberg Township, Berks County	1,740	1	1	0
Hellam Township	8,666	10	8	2
Hellertown	5,809	11	10	1
Hemlock Township	2,266	6	6	0
Hempfield Township, Mercer County	3,705	7	6	1
Hermitage	15,958	32	29	3
Highspire	2,374	13	13	0
Hilltown Township	15,308	20	17	3

Table 62. Full-Time Law Enforcement Employees, by Selected State and City, 2016—Continued

(Number.)

State/city	Population	Total law enforcement employees	Total officers	Total civilians
Hollidaysburg	5,782	9	7	2
Homer City	1,642	2	2	0
Homestead	3,104	12	11	1
Honesdale	4,185	5	5	0
Honey Brook	1,766	1	1	0
Hooversville	613	1	1	0
Hopewell Township	12,466	15	14	1
Horsham Township	26,669	47	40	7
Hughesville	2,093	3	3	0
Hummelstown	4,565	8	7	1
Huntingdon	7,017	12	12	0
Independence Township, Beaver County	2,442	1	1	0
Indiana	14,122	24	22	2
Indiana Township	7,267	10	10	0
Indian Lake	388	5	5	0
Ingram	3,271	4	4	0
Irwin	3,838	4	4	0
Ivyland	1,055	2	2	0
Jackson Township, Butler County	3,708	10	8	2
Jackson Township, Cambria County	4,180	2	2	0
Jackson Township, Luzerne County	4,648	2	2	0
Jeannette	9,274	17	14	3
Jefferson Hills Borough	11,505	17	16	1
Jefferson Township, Mercer County	1,875	2	2	0
Jenkins Township	4,453	3	3	0
Jermyn	2,082	1	1	0
Jessup	4,460	6	3	3
Jim Thorpe	4,614	8	7	1
Johnsonburg	2,351	2	2	0
Johnstown	21,227	41	38	3
Kane	3,588	3	3	0
Kennedy Township	8,211	10	8	2
Kennett Square	6,188	15	12	3
Kennett Township	8,294	6	5	1
Kidder Township	1,935	6	6	0
Kilbuck Township	689	17	14	3
Kingston	12,894	21	19	2
Kingston Township	6,963	11	11	0
Kiskiminetas Township	4,611	9	9	0
Kittanning	3,858	9	8	1
Kline Township	1,387	2	1	1
Knox	1,091	2	2	0
Koppel	739	2	2	0
Kulpmont	2,838	1	1	0
Kutztown	5,032	14	12	2
Lake City	2,952	3	3	0
Lancaster	59,340	148	124	24
Lancaster Township, Butler County	2,520	2	2	0
Langhorne Borough	1,594	1	1	0
Lansdale	16,558	32	23	9
Lansdowne	10,643	18	15	3
Lansford	3,771	5	5	0
Larksville	4,442	4	4	0
Laureldale	3,882	4	4	0
Lawrence Park Township	3,830	9	8	1
Lawrence Township, Clearfield County	7,489	9	8	1
Lebanon	25,549	44	41	3
Leechburg	2,055	3	3	0
Leetsdale	1,195	4	4	0
Leet Township	1,616	2	2	0
Lehighton	5,279	11	10	1
Lehigh Township, Northampton County	10,344	13	12	1
Lehman Township	3,474	3	3	0
Lewistown	8,260	15	14	1
Liberty	2,514	1	1	0
Ligonier	1,534	2	2	0
Ligonier Township	6,525	5	5	0
Limerick Township	18,939	27	25	2
Lincoln	1,059	4	2	2
Linesville	990	6	6	0
Lititz	9,232	17	14	3
Littlestown	4,486	9	8	1
Lock Haven	9,572	17	15	2
Locust Township	1,414	4	4	0
Logan Township	12,313	18	16	2
Lower Allen Township	19,206	23	20	3
Lower Burrell	11,408	18	17	1
Lower Frederick Township	4,901	3	3	0
Lower Gwynedd Township	11,574	19	18	1
Lower Heidelberg Township	6,059	11	10	1
Lower Makefield Township	32,793	42	38	4
Lower Merion Township	58,234	146	131	15
Lower Moreland Township	13,261	26	21	5
Lower Paxton Township	48,582	66	59	7
Lower Pottsgrove Township	12,194	19	17	2

Table 62. Full-Time Law Enforcement Employees, by Selected State and City, 2016—Continued

(Number.)

State/city	Population	Total law enforcement employees	Total officers	Total civilians
Lower Providence Township	26,333	33	31	2
Lower Salford Township	15,415	20	18	2
Lower Saucon Township	10,764	17	15	2
Lower Southampton Township	19,185	33	30	3
Lower Swatara Township	8,881	16	14	2
Lower Windsor Township	7,486	10	9	1
Lykens	1,755	1	1	0
Macungie	3,146	5	5	0
Mahanoy City	4,053	3	3	0
Mahanoy Township	3,348	1	1	0
Mahoning Township, Carbon County	4,211	6	6	0
Mahoning Township, Lawrence County	2,943	2	2	0
Mahoning Township, Montour County	4,275	7	6	1
Malvern	3,527	6	5	1
Manheim	4,871	18	17	1
Manheim Township	39,930	75	63	12
Manor	3,310	3	3	0
Manor Township, Lancaster County	20,778	21	19	2
Mansfield	3,395	5	5	0
Marcus Hook	2,397	5	4	1
Marietta	2,612	17	15	2
Marion Township, Beaver County	899	2	2	0
Marlborough Township	3,332	3	3	0
Marple Township	23,805	32	29	3
Mars	1,650	1	1	0
Martinsburg	1,903	2	2	0
Marysville	2,535	2	2	0
Masontown	3,389	5	5	0
Mayfield	1,723	2	2	0
McAdoo	2,187	3	3	0
McCandless	28,902	30	28	2
McDonald Borough	2,085	5	5	0
McKeesport	21,156	55	52	3
McKees Rocks	5,992	10	9	1
McSherrystown	3,072	4	4	0
Meadville	12,999	28	22	6
Mechanicsburg	9,003	14	13	1
Media	5,370	22	14	8
Mercer	1,923	4	4	0
Mercersburg	1,557	2	2	0
Meshoppen	1,452	2	2	0
Meyersdale	2,063	6	6	0
Middleburg	1,313	3	2	1
Middlesex Township, Butler County	5,640	4	4	0
Middlesex Township, Cumberland County	7,364	10	9	1
Middletown	9,153	12	11	1
Middletown Township	45,408	62	56	6
Midland	2,552	3	3	0
Mifflinburg	3,516	10	9	1
Mifflin County Regional	16,889	14	14	0
Milford	972	2	2	0
Millbourne	1,162	1	1	0
Millcreek Township, Erie County	54,089	78	62	16
Millcreek Township, Lebanon County	5,600	2	2	0
Millersburg	2,532	3	2	1
Millersville	8,471	15	13	2
Millvale	3,678	4	4	0
Milton	6,908	9	8	1
Minersville	4,232	5	5	0
Mohnton	3,034	4	4	0
Monaca	5,631	7	7	0
Monessen	7,438	12	11	1
Monongahela	4,172	11	8	3
Monroeville	28,142	53	44	9
Montgomery	1,553	1	1	0
Montgomery Township	26,272	45	36	9
Montour Township	1,314	3	3	0
Montrose	1,509	1	1	0
Moon Township	25,845	34	28	6
Moore Township	9,235	11	10	1
Moosic	5,758	10	10	0
Morris-Cooper Regional	5,562	1	1	0
Morrisville	8,581	13	11	2
Morton	2,700	5	4	1
Moscow	1,947	3	3	0
Mount Carmel	5,698	8	8	0
Mount Carmel Township	3,057	6	6	0
Mount Holly Springs	2,038	2	2	0
Mount Joy	8,204	13	12	1
Mount Lebanon	32,692	54	45	9
Mount Oliver	3,344	10	10	0
Mount Pleasant	4,346	4	4	0
Mount Pleasant Township	3,510	4	4	0
Mount Union	2,387	5	5	0

Table 62. Full-Time Law Enforcement Employees, by Selected State and City, 2016—Continued

(Number.)

State/city	Population	Total law enforcement employees	Total officers	Total civilians
Muhlenberg Township	20,181	30	30	0
Muncy	2,424	2	2	0
Muncy Township	1,091	2	2	0
Munhall	11,216	22	21	1
Murrysville	20,142	23	21	2
Nanticoke	10,218	15	14	1
Nanty Glo	2,575	1	1	0
Narberth	4,314	5	5	0
Neshannock Township	9,319	8	8	0
Nether Providence Township	13,827	15	14	1
Neville Township	1,065	17	14	3
Newberry Township	15,470	18	16	2
New Bethlehem	2,741	2	2	0
New Brighton	8,991	9	7	2
New Britain Township	11,269	13	12	1
New Cumberland	7,297	10	9	1
New Garden Township	12,113	13	12	1
New Hanover Township	12,814	10	9	1
New Holland	5,439	15	14	1
New Hope	2,507	11	9	2
New Kensington	12,636	22	22	0
Newport Township	5,399	2	2	0
New Sewickley Township	7,454	9	9	0
Newtown	2,217	5	5	0
Newtown Township, Bucks County	22,914	32	28	4
Newtown Township, Delaware County	12,864	19	17	2
New Wilmington	2,190	5	5	0
Norristown	34,425	82	67	15
Northampton	9,846	14	12	2
Northampton Township	39,559	47	41	6
North Belle Vernon	1,892	2	2	0
North Braddock	4,773	3	3	0
North Catasauqua	2,824	5	5	0
North Cornwall Township	7,811	9	9	0
North Coventry Township	8,054	12	11	1
North East, Erie County	4,148	7	7	0
Northeastern Regional	11,655	13	12	1
Northern Berks Regional	13,228	15	14	1
Northern Cambria Borough	3,625	2	2	0
Northern Lancaster County Regional	34,756	26	24	2
Northern Regional	34,787	31	29	2
Northern York Regional	68,894	53	49	4
North Fayette Township	14,733	24	19	5
North Franklin Township	4,601	10	10	0
North Hopewell Township	2,798	3	3	0
North Huntingdon Township	30,787	34	28	6
North Londonderry Township	8,420	10	9	1
North Middleton Township	11,542	11	10	1
North Sewickley Township	5,513	1	1	0
North Strabane Township	14,523	20	19	1
Northumberland	3,715	5	5	0
North Versailles Township	12,322	24	19	5
North Wales	3,254	4	4	0
Northwest Lancaster County Regional	19,732	18	16	2
Norwood	5,899	7	6	1
Oakmont	6,472	7	7	0
O'Hara Township	8,591	15	14	1
Ohio Township	6,401	17	14	3
Ohioville	3,461	2	2	0
Oil City	10,057	22	16	6
Old Forge	7,996	5	5	0
Old Lycoming Township	5,059	12	11	1
Oley Township	3,736	3	3	0
Olyphant	5,102	3	3	0
Orangeville Area	1,750	1	1	0
Orwigsburg	2,983	4	4	0
Overfield Township	2,847	1	1	0
Oxford	5,449	12	11	1
Paint Township	5,110	2	1	1
Palmerton	5,282	9	8	1
Palmer Township	21,492	36	34	2
Palmyra	7,476	9	8	1
Palo Alto	1,005	1	1	0
Parkesburg	3,705	9	8	1
Parkside	2,335	3	3	0
Parks Township	2,626	2	2	0
Patterson Township	2,962	4	4	0
Patton	1,665	2	2	0
Patton Township	16,027	20	18	2
Penbrook	2,968	7	7	0
Penndel	2,200	1	1	0
Penn Hills	41,841	53	50	3
Pennridge Regional	11,029	15	13	2
Penn Township, Butler County	4,941	4	3	1
Penn Township, Perry County	3,184	2	2	0

Table 62. Full-Time Law Enforcement Employees, by Selected State and City, 2016—Continued

(Number.)

State/city	Population	Total law enforcement employees	Total officers	Total civilians
Penn Township, Westmoreland County	19,632	23	21	2
Penn Township, York County	16,243	24	22	2
Pequea Township	4,778	8	8	0
Perkasie	8,464	19	17	2
Perryopolis	1,717	2	2	0
Peters Township	22,274	23	21	2
Philadelphia	1,570,826	7,995	6,313	1,682
Phoenixville	16,695	31	30	1
Pine Creek Township	3,302	2	2	0
Pine Grove	2,134	2	2	0
Pitcairn	3,236	3	3	0
Pittsburgh	302,443	976	908	68
Pittston	7,635	9	9	0
Pittston Township	3,395	4	4	0
Plains Township	9,743	19	18	1
Pleasant Hills	8,248	20	18	2
Plum	27,576	30	24	6
Plumstead Township	13,735	18	16	2
Plymouth	5,809	4	4	0
Plymouth Township, Montgomery County	17,887	51	45	6
Pocono Mountain Regional	42,284	46	41	5
Pocono Township	10,723	19	18	1
Point Township	3,695	5	5	0
Polk	790	2	2	0
Portage	2,484	2	2	0
Port Carbon	1,803	2	2	0
Portland	508	2	2	0
Port Vue	3,733	2	2	0
Pottstown	22,719	59	46	13
Pottsville	13,703	23	23	0
Pringle	967	20	19	1
Prospect Park	6,486	9	9	0
Pulaski Township, Lawrence County	3,323	2	2	0
Punxsutawney	5,841	12	9	3
Pymatuning Township	3,158	7	6	1
Quakertown	8,831	20	18	2
Quarryville	2,762	4	4	0
Raccoon Township	2,992	4	4	0
Radnor Township	31,625	46	42	4
Ralpho Township	4,301	6	6	0
Rankin	2,084	1	1	0
Reading	87,834	182	160	22
Reading Township	5,855	2	2	0
Redstone Township	5,425	3	3	0
Reilly Township	700	2	2	0
Renovo	1,229	1	1	0
Reserve Township	3,285	4	4	0
Reynoldsville	2,700	2	2	0
Rice Township	3,544	6	6	0
Richland Township, Bucks County	13,176	15	13	2
Richland Township, Cambria County	12,140	19	18	1
Ridgway	3,863	6	5	1
Ridley Park	7,041	12	10	2
Ridley Township	31,110	37	32	5
Riverside	1,909	3	3	0
Roaring Brook Township	1,936	1	1	0
Roaring Spring	2,528	3	3	0
Robeson Township	7,387	6	5	1
Robinson Township, Allegheny County	13,813	31	29	2
Rochester	3,551	7	6	1
Rochester Township	2,726	4	4	0
Rockledge	2,540	4	4	0
Ross Township	30,858	45	43	2
Rostraver Township	11,130	17	16	1
Royalton	1,048	5	5	0
Royersford	4,771	8	7	1
Rush Township	3,310	3	3	0
Sadsbury Township, Chester County	3,908	2	2	0
Salem Township, Luzerne County	4,197	5	5	0
Salisbury Township	13,762	19	17	2
Sandy Lake	651	1	1	0
Sandy Township	10,699	11	10	1
Saxonburg	1,485	1	1	0
Saxton	701	1	1	0
Sayre	6,418	13	10	3
Schuylkill Haven	5,189	8	8	0
Schuylkill Township, Chester County	8,587	13	11	2
Scottdale	4,226	6	6	0
Scott Township, Allegheny County	16,848	23	22	1
Scott Township, Columbia County	5,081	6	6	0
Scott Township, Lackawanna County	4,812	3	3	0
Scranton	77,332	170	150	20
Selinsgrove	5,820	7	6	1
Sewickley	4,364	9	8	1

Table 62. Full-Time Law Enforcement Employees, by Selected State and City, 2016—Continued

(Number.)

State/city	Population	Total law enforcement employees	Total officers	Total civilians
Sewickley Heights	821	5	3	2
Shaler Township	28,467	28	26	2
Shamokin	7,124	11	10	1
Shamokin Dam	1,710	3	3	0
Sharon Hill	5,703	10	9	1
Sharpsburg	3,388	5	5	0
Shenandoah	4,835	4	4	0
Shenango Township, Lawrence County	7,323	7	7	0
Shenango Township, Mercer County	3,810	7	7	0
Shillington	5,263	8	7	1
Shinglehouse	1,086	1	1	0
Shippensburg	5,568	10	9	1
Shippingport	210	2	2	0
Shiremanstown	1,582	2	2	0
Shohola Township	2,332	1	1	0
Silver Spring Township	16,884	22	21	1
Sinking Spring	4,121	5	5	0
Slate Belt Regional	12,358	23	23	0
Slatington	4,285	6	6	0
Slippery Rock	3,605	4	4	0
Smethport	1,584	2	2	0
Smith Township	4,402	4	4	0
Solebury Township	8,628	16	14	2
Somerset	5,985	8	7	1
Souderton	6,771	6	5	1
South Abington Township	9,010	12	11	1
South Annville Township	2,939	2	2	0
South Beaver Township	2,656	4	4	0
South Buffalo Township	2,593	2	2	0
South Centre Township	4,197	4	4	0
South Coatesville	1,461	2	2	0
South Connellsville Borough	1,928	1	1	0
Southern Regional Lancaster County	3,863	8	8	0
Southern Regional York County	13,766	16	14	2
South Fayette Township	15,723	18	17	1
South Fork	866	1	1	0
South Greensburg	2,042	2	2	0
South Heidelberg Township	7,386	8	8	0
South Lebanon Township	9,796	8	7	1
South Londonderry Township	7,807	9	7	2
South Park Township	13,463	15	14	1
South Pymatuning Township	2,615	3	3	0
Southwestern Regional	17,774	15	14	1
Southwest Greensburg	2,073	2	2	0
Southwest Regional, Fayette County	7,688	4	4	0
South Whitehall Township	19,797	37	35	2
South Williamsport	6,261	9	7	2
Spring City	3,322	3	3	0
Springdale	3,369	3	3	0
Springdale Township	1,615	4	4	0
Springettsbury Township	26,931	35	32	3
Springfield Township, Bucks County	5,036	5	5	0
Springfield Township, Delaware County	24,438	37	32	5
Springfield Township, Montgomery County	19,603	30	28	2
Spring Garden Township	12,977	21	18	3
Spring Township, Berks County	27,517	30	29	1
Spring Township, Centre County	7,693	9	8	1
State College	58,119	65	55	10
St. Clair Boro	2,869	5	5	0
Steelton	5,921	12	11	1
St. Marys City	12,577	15	14	1
Stonycreek Township	2,695	3	3	0
Stowe Township	6,247	6	6	0
Strasburg	2,925	4	4	0
Stroud Area Regional	34,242	59	52	7
Sugarcreek	5,085	3	3	0
Sugarloaf Township, Luzerne County	4,111	5	5	0
Sugar Notch	970	7	1	6
Summerhill Township	2,354	2	2	0
Summit Hill	2,937	6	4	2
Sunbury	9,607	19	15	4
Susquehanna Regional	8,334	17	15	2
Susquehanna Township, Dauphin County	24,846	44	42	2
Swarthmore	6,214	9	9	0
Swatara Township	24,916	52	49	3
Sweden Township	853	1	1	0
Swissvale	8,829	15	15	0
Swoyersville	4,969	5	5	0
Sykesville	1,131	1	1	0
Tamaqua	6,777	7	6	1
Tarentum	4,449	8	7	1
Tatamy	1,128	1	1	0
Taylor	5,979	7	7	0
Telford	4,860	7	6	1

Table 62. Full-Time Law Enforcement Employees, by Selected State and City, 2016—Continued

(Number.)

State/city	Population	Total law enforcement employees	Total officers	Total civilians
Throop	3,934	6	6	0
Tiadaghton Valley Regional	6,554	11	10	1
Tilden Township	3,591	3	3	0
Tinicum Township, Bucks County	3,957	5	5	0
Tinicum Township, Delaware County	4,113	19	17	2
Titusville	5,349	10	10	0
Towamencin Township	18,409	26	23	3
Towanda	2,792	7	7	0
Trafford	3,127	3	3	0
Trainer	1,847	4	4	0
Tredyffrin Township	29,601	47	42	5
Troy	1,259	2	2	0
Tullytown	1,856	7	6	1
Tulpehocken Township	3,309	3	3	0
Tunkhannock	1,770	3	3	0
Tunkhannock Township, Wyoming County	6,254	6	6	0
Turtle Creek	5,257	4	4	0
Tyrone	5,330	14	11	3
Union City	3,197	3	2	1
Uniontown	9,919	21	20	1
Union Township, Lawrence County	4,985	7	7	0
Upland	3,254	6	5	1
Upper Allen Township	19,815	23	22	1
Upper Burrell Township	2,260	2	2	0
Upper Chichester Township	17,054	23	22	1
Upper Darby Township	82,896	145	126	19
Upper Dublin Township	26,333	46	40	6
Upper Macungie Township	23,396	30	28	2
Upper Makefield Township	8,267	16	15	1
Upper Merion Township	28,661	80	64	16
Upper Moreland Township	24,270	41	35	6
Upper Nazareth Township	6,795	9	8	1
Upper Perkiomen	6,869	10	9	1
Upper Pottsgrove Township	5,511	9	8	1
Upper Providence Township, Delaware County	10,510	15	15	0
Upper Providence Township, Montgomery County	23,927	30	28	2
Upper Saucon Township	16,451	22	21	1
Upper Southampton Township	15,114	25	22	3
Upper St. Clair Township	19,726	36	29	7
Upper Uwchlan Township	11,603	11	11	0
Upper Yoder Township	5,210	13	13	0
Uwchlan Township	19,274	22	21	1
Valley Township	7,803	6	6	0
Vandergrift	4,999	9	8	1
Vandling	716	2	2	0
Vernon Township	5,449	2	2	0
Verona	2,436	4	3	1
Versailles	1,492	2	2	0
Walnutport	2,059	3	3	0
Warminster Township	32,577	48	43	5
Warren	9,264	21	15	6
Warrington Township	24,044	32	29	3
Warwick Township, Bucks County	14,741	18	17	1
Washington, Washington County	13,421	33	31	2
Washington Township, Fayette County	3,740	4	4	0
Washington Township, Franklin County	14,631	12	10	2
Washington Township, Northampton County	5,180	5	5	0
Washington Township, Westmoreland County	7,216	7	7	0
Watsontown	2,315	5	5	0
Waverly Township	1,708	3	3	0
Waynesboro	10,902	18	16	2
Waynesburg	4,021	11	8	3
Weatherly	2,450	4	4	0
Wellsboro	3,295	7	7	0
Wesleyville	3,204	8	7	1
West Brandywine Township	7,482	6	6	0
West Brownsville	971	2	1	1
West Caln Township	9,097	2	2	0
West Carroll Township	1,234	2	2	0
West Chester	20,129	60	47	13
West Conshohocken	1,393	12	11	1
West Deer Township	11,975	12	11	1
West Earl Township	8,195	6	6	0
Western Berks Regional	2,549	6	5	1
West Fallowfield Township	2,602	2	2	0
Westfield	1,048	2	2	0
West Goshen Township	23,398	34	30	4
West Grove Borough	2,860	3	3	0
West Hazleton	4,485	4	3	1
West Hempfield Township	16,538	23	20	3

Table 62. Full-Time Law Enforcement Employees, by Selected State and City, 2016—Continued

(Number.)

State/city	Population	Total law enforcement employees	Total officers	Total civilians
West Hills Regional	10,302	12	11	1
West Homestead	1,917	7	6	1
West Lampeter Township	16,029	16	15	1
West Mahanoy Township	2,761	3	3	0
West Manchester Township	18,880	30	27	3
West Manheim Township	8,371	9	9	0
West Mead Township	5,121	2	2	0
West Mifflin	20,028	39	33	6
West Newton	2,527	2	2	0
West Norriton Township	15,799	30	27	3
West Penn Township	4,327	2	2	0
West Pikeland Township	4,097	4	4	0
West Pike Run	1,556	1	1	0
West Pittston	4,753	2	2	0
West Pottsgrove Township	3,885	9	8	1
West Reading	4,186	14	12	2
West Sadsbury Township	2,481	5	5	0
West Salem Township	3,463	8	7	1
West Shore Regional	7,734	13	12	1
Westtown-East Goshen Regional	32,687	33	30	3
West View	6,668	13	11	2
West Vincent Township	5,133	7	6	1
West Whiteland Township	18,482	28	26	2
West York	4,560	8	8	0
Whitehall	13,812	26	21	5
Whitehall Township	27,426	50	45	5
Whitemarsh Township	17,721	39	34	5
White Oak	7,758	13	12	1
Whitpain Township	19,237	38	30	8
Wiconisco Township	1,189	1	1	0
Wilkes-Barre	40,640	92	81	11
Wilkes-Barre Township	2,921	15	14	1
Wilkinsburg	15,692	27	23	4
Wilkins Township	6,283	12	12	0
Williamsburg	1,216	1	1	0
Williamsport	29,163	55	51	4
Willistown Township	10,987	19	17	2
Wilson	7,758	13	12	1
Windber	3,938	3	2	1
Womelsdorf	2,860	1	1	0
Woodward Township	2,408	2	2	0
Wrightsville	2,285	4	4	0
Wyoming	3,038	4	4	0
Wyomissing	10,473	23	22	1
Yardley	2,442	3	3	0
Yeadon	11,537	14	13	1
York	44,017	120	105	15
York Area Regional	55,292	48	44	4
Youngsville	1,653	2	2	0
Zelienople	3,689	10	9	1
RHODE ISLAND				
Barrington	16,218	30	23	7
Bristol	22,229	48	38	10
Burrillville	16,357	29	22	7
Central Falls	19,277	47	37	10
Charlestown	7,762	24	19	5
Coventry	34,967	69	55	14
Cranston	81,162	176	147	29
Cumberland	34,708	54	43	11
East Greenwich	13,120	42	34	8
East Providence	47,456	111	92	19
Foster	4,713	13	9	4
Glocester	10,037	20	15	5
Hopkinton	8,093	19	14	5
Jamestown	5,494	19	14	5
Johnston	29,322	80	67	13
Lincoln	21,770	42	34	8
Little Compton	3,505	13	9	4
Middletown	16,035	41	37	4
Narragansett	15,600	52	39	13
Newport	24,077	93	77	16
New Shoreham	1,046	8	4	4
North Kingstown	26,120	53	44	9
North Providence	32,540	78	61	17
North Smithfield	12,377	27	26	1
Pawtucket	71,640	170	138	32
Portsmouth	17,362	38	35	3
Providence	179,340	511	423	88
Richmond	7,621	18	13	5
Scituate	10,587	23	16	7
Smithfield	21,660	55	41	14
South Kingstown	30,872	70	52	18
Tiverton	15,768	41	29	12
Warren	10,460	27	22	5

Table 62. Full-Time Law Enforcement Employees, by Selected State and City, 2016—Continued

(Number.)

State/city	Population	Total law enforcement employees	Total officers	Total civilians
Warwick	81,481	218	167	51
Westerly	22,675	60	49	11
West Greenwich	6,132	17	12	5
West Warwick	28,777	63	52	11
Woonsocket	41,511	114	92	22
SOUTH CAROLINA				
Abbeville	5,177	21	20	1
Aiken	30,800	114	86	28
Allendale	3,064	8	8	0
Anderson	27,522	128	91	37
Aynor	689	6	5	1
Bamberg	3,341	12	10	2
Barnwell	4,561	16	15	1
Batesburg-Leesville	5,457	24	20	4
Beaufort	13,477	55	48	7
Belton	4,374	12	12	0
Bennettsville	8,514	34	30	4
Bethune	347	1	1	0
Bishopville	3,237	13	11	2
Blacksburg	1,889	12	11	1
Blackville	2,273	6	5	1
Bluffton	17,498	56	50	6
Bonneau	508	4	2	2
Branchville	983	3	2	1
Briarcliffe Acres	544	1	1	0
Burnettown	2,795	2	2	0
Camden	7,132	33	25	8
Cameron	414	1	1	0
Cayce	13,729	74	57	17
Central	5,165	9	8	1
Chapin	1,578	7	7	0
Charleston	135,153	530	430	100
Cheraw	5,766	27	25	2
Chesnee	907	5	5	0
Chester	5,462	22	20	2
Chesterfield	1,450	5	5	0
Clemson	15,767	39	29	10
Clinton	8,664	41	34	7
Clio	682	2	2	0
Clover	5,874	25	20	5
Columbia	134,489	424	338	86
Conway	21,874	53	49	4
Cottageville	733	6	6	0
Coward	749	1	1	0
Cowpens	2,288	7	5	2
Darlington	6,130	32	29	3
Denmark	3,274	11	10	1
Dillon	6,648	24	21	3
Due West	1,238	5	5	0
Duncan	3,350	19	17	2
Easley	20,911	55	44	11
Edgefield	4,762	9	9	0
Edisto Beach	415	7	7	0
Ehrhardt	499	3	2	1
Elgin	1,510	6	6	0
Elloree	677	3	3	0
Estill	1,933	10	9	1
Fairfax	1,787	7	6	1
Florence	38,382	120	92	28
Folly Beach	2,806	30	17	13
Forest Acres	10,654	33	26	7
Fort Lawn	862	3	2	1
Fort Mill	14,150	49	43	6
Fountain Inn	8,450	32	19	13
Gaffney	12,568	41	36	5
Gaston	1,662	3	3	0
Georgetown	9,044	39	35	4
Gifford	270	4	2	2
Goose Creek	41,540	90	63	27
Great Falls	1,923	5	5	0
Greeleyville	405	2	2	0
Greenville	65,686	230	182	48
Greenwood	23,250	60	56	4
Greer	28,927	72	54	18
Hampton	2,637	12	12	0
Hanahan	22,357	39	32	7
Hardeeville	5,893	22	20	2
Harleyville	699	4	4	0
Hartsville	7,837	37	33	4
Hemingway	427	4	3	1
Holly Hill	1,230	6	6	0
Honea Path	3,737	14	13	1
Inman	2,294	10	8	2
Irmo	12,240	26	23	3

Table 62. Full-Time Law Enforcement Employees, by Selected State and City, 2016—Continued

(Number.)

State/city	Population	Total law enforcement employees	Total officers	Total civilians
Isle of Palms	4,419	24	17	7
Iva	1,288	10	10	0
Jackson	1,774	4	4	0
Jamestown	82	5	4	1
Johnsonville	1,509	6	5	1
Johnston	2,345	8	8	0
Jonesville	856	4	4	0
Kingstree	3,155	13	10	3
Lake City	6,809	23	19	4
Lamar	968	4	4	0
Lancaster	9,039	39	27	12
Lane	471	3	1	2
Latta	1,345	7	7	0
Laurens	9,173	31	27	4
Lexington	20,597	53	51	2
Liberty	3,242	15	10	5
Loris	2,630	12	8	4
Lyman	3,456	10	9	1
Manning	4,023	17	16	1
Marion	6,674	21	18	3
Mauldin	25,540	60	49	11
McBee	853	1	1	0
McColl	2,049	7	7	0
McCormick	2,540	7	7	0
Moncks Corner	10,298	29	26	3
Mount Pleasant	84,277	167	146	21
Mullins	4,491	24	22	2
Myrtle Beach	31,864	300	219	81
Newberry	10,338	34	30	4
New Ellenton	2,134	4	3	1
Nichols	356	3	2	1
Ninety Six	2,050	7	5	2
North	737	3	3	0
North Augusta	22,755	88	62	26
North Charleston	110,490	394	327	67
North Myrtle Beach	15,945	103	73	30
Olanta	571	2	2	0
Olar	236	1	1	0
Orangeburg	13,365	84	58	26
Pacolet	2,373	7	7	0
Pamplico	1,249	2	2	0
Pawleys Island	108	5	5	0
Pelion	708	4	3	1
Pickens	3,183	13	13	0
Pine Ridge	2,263	7	3	4
Port Royal	12,417	23	22	1
Prosperity	1,204	3	3	0
Ridgeland	3,991	14	13	1
Ridgeville	1,811	2	2	0
Rock Hill	72,589	194	150	44
Salem	148	3	3	0
Salley	420	1	1	0
Saluda	3,603	13	11	2
Santee	930	6	6	0
Scranton	864	1	1	0
Seneca	8,308	50	37	13
Simpsonville	21,223	45	34	11
Society Hill	545	1	1	0
South Congaree	2,404	7	6	1
Spartanburg	38,083	138	115	23
Springdale	2,814	7	7	0
Springfield	499	1	1	0
St. George	2,197	10	10	0
St. Matthews	1,978	8	7	1
St. Stephen	1,829	6	6	0
Sullivans Island	1,940	11	10	1
Summerton	959	5	5	0
Summerville	50,154	115	94	21
Sumter	40,864	158	110	48
Surfside Beach	4,372	25	19	6
Swansea	904	3	2	1
Tega Cay	10,032	27	24	3
Travelers Rest	5,074	22	16	6
Turbeville	798	4	3	1
Union	7,981	34	31	3
Wagener	827	5	5	0
Walhalla	4,254	14	13	1
Walterboro	5,253	35	27	8
Ware Shoals	2,175	10	9	1
West Columbia	16,193	62	50	12
Westminster	2,493	11	11	0
West Pelzer	914	4	3	1
West Union	313	2	2	0
Whitmire	1,466	7	6	1
Williamston	4,161	17	16	1

Table 62. Full-Time Law Enforcement Employees, by Selected State and City, 2016—Continued

(Number.)

State/city	Population	Total law enforcement employees	Total officers	Total civilians
Williston	3,007	11	10	1
Winnsboro	3,316	21	20	1
Woodruff	4,137	11	10	1
York	8,058	39	32	7
SOUTH DAKOTA				
Aberdeen	28,498	54	45	9
Alcester	752	2	2	0
Avon	567	1	1	0
Beresford	1,969	4	4	0
Box Elder	9,607	12	11	1
Brandon	10,042	13	12	1
Brookings	23,971	47	34	13
Canton	3,380	5	5	0
Clark	1,033	2	2	0
Deadwood	1,255	15	12	3
Eagle Butte	1,355	3	3	0
Elk Point	1,854	4	4	0
Faith	414	2	2	0
Flandreau	2,296	7	6	1
Freeman	1,284	2	2	0
Gregory	1,247	3	3	0
Groton	1,518	4	4	0
Hot Springs	3,507	8	7	1
Huron	13,459	36	26	10
Jefferson	511	1	1	0
Kadoka	718	1	1	0
Lead	2,974	6	5	1
Lennox	2,304	4	4	0
Leola	437	1	1	0
Madison	7,411	12	11	1
Menno	593	1	1	0
Milbank	3,162	7	7	0
Miller	1,427	4	4	0
Mitchell	15,749	30	27	3
Mobridge	3,465	16	8	8
North Sioux City	2,772	9	8	1
Parkston	1,483	3	3	0
Philip	747	2	2	0
Pierre	14,068	40	26	14
Rapid City	74,573	143	114	29
Scotland	816	1	1	0
Sioux Falls	175,152	276	239	37
Sisseton	2,451	7	7	0
Spearfish	11,429	31	21	10
Springfield	1,947	2	2	0
Sturgis	6,699	18	15	3
Summerset	2,329	3	3	0
Tea	5,064	6	6	0
Tripp	627	1	1	0
Tyndall	1,046	2	2	0
Vermillion	10,774	19	18	1
Wagner	1,593	5	5	0
Watertown	22,186	59	38	21
Webster	1,785	5	5	0
Winner	2,805	10	10	0
Yankton	14,575	29	26	3
TENNESSEE				
Adamsville	2,245	6	5	1
Alamo	2,486	5	5	0
Alcoa	9,503	49	41	8
Alexandria	978	3	3	0
Algood	3,770	14	14	0
Ardmore	1,213	11	7	4
Ashland City	4,650	13	11	2
Athens	13,717	31	29	2
Atoka	9,176	20	19	1
Baileyton	431	2	2	0
Baneberry	526	1	1	0
Bartlett	58,897	155	120	35
Baxter	1,388	6	6	0
Bean Station	3,085	7	7	0
Belle Meade	3,021	21	15	6
Bells	2,449	4	4	0
Benton	1,275	6	6	0
Berry Hill	549	18	14	4
Big Sandy	540	1	1	0
Blaine	1,869	2	2	0
Bluff City	1,719	8	8	0
Bolivar	5,032	24	22	2
Bradford	1,004	5	5	0
Brentwood	42,739	73	58	15
Brighton	3,018	6	6	0
Bristol	26,656	88	69	19

Table 62. Full-Time Law Enforcement Employees, by Selected State and City, 2016—Continued

(Number.)

State/city	Population	Total law enforcement employees	Total officers	Total civilians
Brownsville	9,795	39	34	5
Bruceton	1,426	2	2	0
Burns	1,475	1	1	0
Calhoun	496	2	2	0
Camden	3,574	17	13	4
Carthage	2,273	12	8	4
Caryville	2,182	6	6	0
Celina	1,494	8	6	2
Centerville	3,574	23	13	10
Chapel Hill	1,471	6	6	0
Charleston	681	3	3	0
Chattanooga	177,801	523	434	89
Church Hill	6,714	11	10	1
Clarksville	152,526	348	282	66
Cleveland	44,423	103	85	18
Clifton	2,657	5	5	0
Clinton	10,091	40	33	7
Collegedale	11,245	22	22	0
Collierville	49,531	137	99	38
Collinwood	972	4	4	0
Columbia	37,219	97	85	12
Cookeville	32,292	90	70	20
Coopertown	4,426	4	3	1
Cornersville	1,227	2	2	0
Covington	9,039	36	35	1
Cowan	1,698	3	3	0
Cross Plains	1,725	2	2	0
Crossville	11,514	43	40	3
Crump	1,394	4	4	0
Cumberland City	300	2	2	0
Dandridge	2,949	12	11	1
Dayton	7,421	19	18	1
Decatur	1,571	6	6	0
Decaturville	869	1	1	0
Decherd	2,439	12	11	1
Dickson	15,501	48	43	5
Dover	1,465	5	5	0
Dresden	2,879	10	9	1
Dunlap	5,167	14	12	2
Dyer	2,262	7	6	1
Dyersburg	16,711	63	55	8
Eagleville	661	3	3	0
East Ridge	21,311	42	37	5
Elizabethton	13,672	40	36	4
Elkton	563	2	2	0
Englewood	1,529	6	5	1
Erin	1,288	5	5	0
Erwin	5,959	14	14	0
Estill Springs	2,043	6	6	0
Ethridge	476	1	1	0
Etowah	3,503	11	10	1
Fairview	8,440	19	18	1
Fayetteville	7,182	27	25	2
Franklin	74,771	139	128	11
Friendship	668	1	1	0
Gainesboro	954	5	4	1
Gallatin	35,154	92	71	21
Gallaway	654	1	1	0
Gatlinburg	4,229	53	44	9
Germantown	39,311	123	100	23
Gibson	370	4	3	1
Gleason	1,399	5	5	0
Goodlettsville	23,358	55	40	15
Gordonsville	1,203	6	6	0
Grand Junction	299	2	2	0
Graysville	1,517	5	4	1
Greenbrier	6,807	15	14	1
Greeneville	15,101	53	51	2
Greenfield	2,108	7	6	1
Halls	2,164	7	6	1
Harriman	6,195	17	16	1
Henderson	6,597	15	15	0
Hendersonville	56,965	132	105	27
Henry	467	1	1	0
Hohenwald	3,650	16	15	1
Hollow Rock	693	1	1	0
Hornbeak	406	1	1	0
Humboldt	8,287	35	29	6
Huntingdon	3,912	16	12	4
Huntland	852	5	5	0
Jacksboro	1,935	5	5	0
Jackson	66,990	256	212	44
Jamestown	1,945	9	9	0
Jasper	3,323	8	8	0
Jefferson City	8,549	29	27	2

Table 62. Full-Time Law Enforcement Employees, by Selected State and City, 2016—Continued

(Number.)

State/city	Population	Total law enforcement employees	Total officers	Total civilians
Jellico	2,244	7	6	1
Johnson City	66,511	177	148	29
Jonesborough	5,338	21	17	4
Kenton	1,213	3	3	0
Kimball	1,398	9	9	0
Kingsport	53,059	153	113	40
Kingston	5,823	13	12	1
Kingston Springs	2,773	5	4	1
Knoxville	186,583	465	377	88
Lafayette	5,088	22	15	7
La Follette	6,977	30	21	9
La Vergne	35,228	66	53	13
Lawrenceburg	10,595	39	35	4
Lebanon	31,125	93	74	19
Lenoir City	9,175	24	22	2
Lewisburg	11,552	31	30	1
Lexington	7,859	32	27	5
Livingston	4,073	22	17	5
Lookout Mountain	1,887	21	16	5
Loretto	1,752	4	4	0
Loudon	5,800	15	14	1
Madisonville	4,823	20	17	3
Manchester	10,596	35	32	3
Martin	10,859	38	29	9
Maryville	28,661	56	50	6
Mason	1,594	4	3	1
Maynardville	2,343	4	4	0
McEwen	1,693	5	5	0
McKenzie	5,294	18	13	5
McMinnville	13,789	36	32	4
Memphis	656,434	2,385	1,978	407
Middleton	652	3	3	0
Milan	7,803	29	23	6
Millersville	6,748	16	12	4
Millington	11,002	41	30	11
Minor Hill	525	2	2	0
Monteagle	1,174	6	6	0
Monterey	2,858	7	6	1
Morristown	29,576	92	85	7
Moscow	528	4	4	0
Mountain City	2,463	8	8	0
Mount Carmel	5,424	4	4	0
Mount Juliet	33,048	70	55	15
Mount Pleasant	4,835	12	12	0
Munford	6,140	19	17	2
Murfreesboro	129,730	267	218	49
Nashville Metropolitan	668,685	1,708	1,398	310
Newbern	3,341	21	13	8
New Johnsonville	1,884	6	5	1
New Market	1,371	3	3	0
Newport	6,812	32	27	5
New Tazewell	2,943	9	9	0
Niota	718	4	3	1
Nolensville	7,164	6	6	0
Norris	1,655	11	7	4
Oakland	7,670	15	14	1
Oak Ridge	29,296	71	55	16
Obion	1,065	2	2	0
Oliver Springs	3,238	14	10	4
Oneida	3,701	17	12	5
Paris	10,143	37	26	11
Parsons	2,331	7	7	0
Petersburg	549	2	2	0
Pigeon Forge	6,230	69	57	12
Pikeville	1,642	3	3	0
Piperton	1,667	8	8	0
Pittman Center	578	3	3	0
Plainview	2,049	1	1	0
Pleasant View	4,327	5	5	0
Portland	12,502	36	27	9
Pulaski	7,572	28	26	2
Puryear	668	1	1	0
Red Bank	11,789	26	24	2
Red Boiling Springs	1,146	5	5	0
Ridgely	1,690	5	5	0
Ridgetop	2,021	6	6	0
Ripley	8,129	31	24	7
Rockwood	5,400	17	16	1
Rocky Top	1,764	9	6	3
Rogersville	4,374	13	12	1
Rossville	790	5	5	0
Rutherford	1,101	5	4	1
Rutledge	1,200	5	5	0
Savannah	7,035	20	18	2
Scotts Hill	985	2	2	0

Table 62. Full-Time Law Enforcement Employees, by Selected State and City, 2016—Continued

(Number.)

State/city	Population	Total law enforcement employees	Total officers	Total civilians
Selmer	4,507	19	17	2
Sevierville	16,843	64	50	14
Sharon	911	1	1	0
Shelbyville	21,511	52	42	10
Signal Mountain	8,577	18	16	2
Smithville	4,662	15	14	1
Smyrna	48,016	100	77	23
Sneedville	1,338	1	1	0
Soddy-Daisy	13,215	36	29	7
Somerville	3,095	11	11	0
South Carthage	1,337	4	4	0
South Fulton	2,243	6	6	0
South Pittsburg	3,115	8	8	0
Sparta	5,131	15	14	1
Spencer	1,640	2	2	0
Spring City	1,998	9	9	0
Springfield	16,873	39	34	5
Spring Hill	37,599	52	48	4
Sunbright	544	2	2	0
Surgoinsville	1,785	1	1	0
Sweetwater	5,957	20	19	1
Tazewell	2,301	6	6	0
Tellico Plains	955	6	6	0
Tiptonville	4,331	7	7	0
Townsend	453	3	3	0
Tracy City	1,433	5	5	0
Trenton	4,108	20	15	5
Trezevant	838	1	1	0
Trimble	620	1	1	0
Troy	1,307	4	4	0
Tullahoma	19,229	42	37	5
Tusculum	2,667	2	2	0
Union City	10,506	42	34	8
Vonore	1,496	9	9	0
Wartburg	901	5	5	0
Wartrace	661	2	1	1
Watertown	1,524	5	5	0
Waverly	4,089	13	12	1
Waynesboro	2,380	6	6	0
Westmoreland	2,308	11	7	4
White Bluff	3,442	5	5	0
White House	11,419	25	22	3
White Pine	2,250	11	10	1
Whiteville	4,502	5	5	0
Whitwell	1,731	6	6	0
Winchester	8,545	25	23	2
Winfield	948	1	1	0
Woodbury	2,779	9	8	1
TEXAS				
Abernathy	2,728	5	5	0
Addison	16,067	68	59	9
Alamo	19,409	39	30	9
Alamo Heights	8,248	35	22	13
Alice	19,464	47	37	10
Allen	101,020	179	120	59
Alpine	5,939	16	11	5
Alton	16,137	21	16	5
Alvin	26,100	76	47	29
Amarillo	200,141	411	343	68
Andrews	14,428	20	19	1
Angleton	19,546	48	36	12
Anna	12,233	16	15	1
Anson	2,315	5	5	0
Aransas Pass	8,603	39	26	13
Arcola	1,679	6	6	0
Argyle	4,047	8	8	0
Athens	12,802	30	24	6
Atlanta	5,594	17	12	5
Aubrey	3,527	6	6	0
Austin	956,911	2,361	1,807	554
Azle	11,854	33	25	8
Baird	1,481	2	2	0
Balch Springs	25,474	53	36	17
Ballinger	3,767	9	7	2
Bangs	1,575	3	3	0
Bartonville	1,702	4	4	0
Bastrop	8,447	25	22	3
Bay City	17,595	63	41	22
Bayou Vista	1,603	6	6	0
Baytown	77,224	235	163	72
Beaumont	118,283	317	254	63
Bedford	49,803	126	76	50
Bee Cave	6,891	20	19	1
Beeville	13,362	34	25	9

Table 62. Full-Time Law Enforcement Employees, by Selected State and City, 2016—Continued

(Number.)

State/city	Population	Total law enforcement employees	Total officers	Total civilians
Bellmead	10,212	31	20	11
Bellville	4,296	12	11	1
Belton	20,988	45	35	10
Benbrook	22,906	47	38	9
Bertram	1,398	3	3	0
Beverly Hills	2,034	13	9	4
Big Sandy	1,380	5	5	0
Big Spring	29,189	51	34	17
Bishop	3,154	10	6	4
Blanco	1,913	7	7	0
Blue Mound	2,509	11	7	4
Boerne	14,368	51	38	13
Bogata	1,103	4	4	0
Bonham	10,070	27	18	9
Borger	12,894	29	27	2
Bovina	1,750	3	3	0
Bowie	5,108	20	15	5
Boyd	1,362	7	7	0
Brady	5,560	17	9	8
Brazoria	3,082	12	8	4
Breckenridge	5,556	19	12	7
Bremond	919	3	3	0
Brenham	16,736	38	33	5
Bridge City	7,959	21	15	6
Bridgeport	6,466	21	14	7
Brookshire	5,203	20	16	4
Brookside Village	1,577	4	4	0
Brownfield	9,750	24	19	5
Brownsville	185,583	354	244	110
Bryan	83,286	178	141	37
Buda	15,449	20	18	2
Bullard	2,906	11	10	1
Bulverde	4,999	16	15	1
Burkburnett	11,088	25	19	6
Burleson	45,116	82	61	21
Burnet	6,288	17	16	1
Cactus	3,198	10	8	2
Caddo Mills	1,497	5	5	0
Caldwell	4,318	11	10	1
Calvert	1,144	4	4	0
Cameron	5,445	16	11	5
Canyon	15,212	26	23	3
Carthage	6,858	23	17	6
Castle Hills	4,485	29	21	8
Castroville	2,960	10	9	1
Cedar Hill	49,215	87	64	23
Cedar Park	69,051	116	80	36
Celina	8,074	17	16	1
Center	5,218	25	18	7
Cibolo	28,077	37	32	5
Cisco	3,769	11	8	3
Clarksville	3,170	7	4	3
Cleburne	30,069	70	52	18
Cleveland	7,893	27	16	11
Clifton	3,344	8	7	1
Clute	11,490	30	22	8
Clyde	3,784	8	7	1
Cockrell Hill	4,340	21	15	6
Coleman	4,334	17	10	7
College Station	110,785	187	130	57
Colleyville	26,038	49	43	6
Collinsville	1,700	3	3	0
Colorado City	4,111	13	7	6
Columbus	3,625	12	11	1
Comanche	4,171	12	11	1
Combes	3,089	8	8	0
Commerce	9,062	23	17	6
Conroe	71,111	162	118	44
Converse	22,782	51	36	15
Coppell	41,654	69	62	7
Copperas Cove	33,237	67	45	22
Corpus Christi	327,948	625	444	181
Corrigan	1,529	19	13	6
Corsicana	23,974	45	36	9
Crandall	3,318	14	14	0
Crane	4,013	13	7	6
Crockett	6,480	16	14	2
Crosbyton	1,692	3	3	0
Crowell	850	1	1	0
Crowley	15,272	40	29	11
Crystal City	7,566	13	9	4
Cuero	7,167	16	15	1
Cumby	792	3	3	0
Daingerfield	2,432	8	7	1
Dalhart	8,455	19	15	4

Table 62. Full-Time Law Enforcement Employees, by Selected State and City, 2016—Continued

(Number.)

State/city	Population	Total law enforcement employees	Total officers	Total civilians
Dallas	1,320,939	3,829	3,279	550
Dalworthington Gardens	2,395	17	12	5
Danbury	1,788	4	4	0
Decatur	6,621	30	25	5
Deer Park	34,156	83	56	27
De Kalb	1,653	5	5	0
Del Rio	36,177	76	60	16
Denison	23,237	58	44	14
Denton	134,054	217	161	56
Denver City	4,949	13	8	5
DeSoto	53,143	120	65	55
Devine	4,775	13	9	4
Diboll	5,399	19	14	5
Dickinson	20,131	44	29	15
Dilley	4,290	9	8	1
Dimmitt	4,153	9	7	2
Double Oak	3,118	8	8	0
Driscoll	754	5	4	1
Dublin	3,667	12	8	4
Dumas	15,051	30	24	6
Duncanville	40,075	66	54	12
Eagle Lake	3,652	11	10	1
Eagle Pass	29,257	78	63	15
Early	2,842	9	7	2
Eastland	3,799	12	10	2
Edgewood	1,452	4	4	0
Edinburg	86,535	195	141	54
Edna	5,855	12	10	2
El Campo	11,604	39	31	8
Electra	2,695	13	8	5
Elgin	9,229	26	20	6
El Paso	687,193	1,236	1,013	223
Elsa	6,861	23	17	6
Ennis	19,096	44	36	8
Euless	54,791	132	84	48
Everman	6,399	18	14	4
Fairfield	2,905	13	8	5
Fair Oaks Ranch	7,723	22	20	2
Fairview	8,685	15	15	0
Farmers Branch	33,571	100	68	32
Farmersville	3,474	12	10	2
Farwell	1,301	2	2	0
Ferris	2,552	15	10	5
Florence	1,249	2	2	0
Floresville	7,499	19	17	2
Flower Mound	72,600	121	81	40
Floydada	2,729	6	6	0
Forney	19,252	42	28	14
Fort Worth	851,849	2,007	1,566	441
Fredericksburg	11,205	34	30	4
Freer	2,718	10	6	4
Friendswood	39,402	78	58	20
Friona	3,849	10	6	4
Frisco	162,917	247	166	81
Fulton	1,580	1	1	0
Gainesville	16,349	56	42	14
Galena Park	11,209	23	18	5
Galveston	50,667	179	143	36
Ganado	2,116	3	3	0
Garden Ridge	3,971	13	12	1
Garland	238,859	454	326	128
Gatesville	15,717	26	17	9
Georgetown	67,436	117	80	37
George West	2,670	10	9	1
Giddings	5,102	16	12	4
Gilmer	5,246	19	15	4
Gladewater	6,427	20	14	6
Glenn Heights	12,185	18	15	3
Godley	1,082	6	6	0
Gonzales	7,609	29	21	8
Gorman	1,045	2	2	0
Graham	8,857	25	23	2
Granbury	9,683	38	33	5
Grand Prairie	190,270	384	257	127
Grand Saline	3,130	7	7	0
Granger	1,536	2	2	0
Granite Shoals	5,104	9	9	0
Grapeland	1,404	3	3	0
Greenville	26,689	73	54	19
Gregory	2,012	5	5	0
Groesbeck	4,299	8	8	0
Groves	15,680	21	19	2
Gun Barrel City	6,048	19	13	6
Hallettsville	2,601	8	7	1
Haltom City	44,558	84	71	13

Table 62. Full-Time Law Enforcement Employees, by Selected State and City, 2016—Continued

(Number.)

State/city	Population	Total law enforcement employees	Total officers	Total civilians
Hamilton	2,908	8	7	1
Hamlin	2,026	8	5	3
Harlingen	65,913	170	130	40
Hawkins	1,296	4	4	0
Hearne	4,459	18	12	6
Heath	8,400	20	19	1
Hedwig Village	2,724	23	17	6
Helotes	8,855	22	20	2
Hemphill	1,209	4	4	0
Hempstead	7,403	23	19	4
Hereford	14,941	33	27	6
Hewitt	14,384	35	23	12
Hidalgo	13,943	45	34	11
Highland Park	9,316	71	57	14
Highland Village	16,357	40	30	10
Hill Country Village	1,083	11	11	0
Hitchcock	7,753	26	19	7
Hollywood Park	3,338	13	12	1
Hondo	9,178	24	21	3
Hooks	2,739	7	7	0
Horizon City	19,808	40	23	17
Horseshoe Bay	3,585	21	19	2
Houston	2,334,348	6,632	5,182	1,450
Howe	2,840	6	6	0
Hubbard	1,359	5	5	0
Hughes Springs	1,780	9	9	0
Humble	15,770	80	57	23
Huntington	2,145	6	6	0
Huntsville	41,390	65	58	7
Hurst	39,345	121	75	46
Hutchins	5,809	23	17	6
Hutto	24,160	31	28	3
Idalou	2,343	4	4	0
Indian Lake	642	2	2	0
Ingleside	9,769	32	24	8
Ingram	1,828	7	6	1
Iowa Park	6,338	17	11	6
Irving	240,765	482	330	152
Italy	1,904	7	5	2
Itasca	1,621	6	6	0
Jacinto City	10,825	24	19	5
Jacksboro	4,410	9	8	1
Jacksonville	14,950	38	28	10
Jamaica Beach	1,059	6	6	0
Jarrell	1,209	3	3	0
Jasper	7,617	26	20	6
Jefferson	2,038	8	7	1
Jersey Village	7,954	28	26	2
Johnson City	2,021	5	5	0
Jones Creek	2,076	3	3	0
Jonestown	2,074	8	7	1
Joshua	6,101	14	12	2
Jourdanton	4,355	11	10	1
Junction	2,421	5	5	0
Karnes City	3,437	10	9	1
Katy	16,589	69	52	17
Kaufman	7,245	21	17	4
Keene	6,206	18	13	5
Keller	47,047	84	48	36
Kemah	2,028	20	16	4
Kenedy	3,444	12	11	1
Kennedale	7,910	22	20	2
Kermit	6,596	19	13	6
Kerrville	23,287	68	52	16
Kilgore	15,258	49	37	12
Killeen	143,248	353	252	101
Kingsville	26,227	67	47	20
Kirbyville	2,128	6	6	0
Knox City	1,194	2	2	0
Kress	681	1	1	0
Kyle	37,407	59	34	25
Lacy-Lakeview	6,629	26	17	9
La Feria	7,349	13	13	0
Lago Vista	6,643	23	16	7
La Grange	4,728	14	14	0
La Grulla	1,709	8	6	2
Laguna Vista	3,223	9	8	1
La Joya	4,350	16	11	5
Lake Dallas	8,053	19	14	5
Lake Jackson	27,676	59	44	15
Lakeside	1,401	3	3	0
Lakeview, Harrison County	6,454	16	12	4
Lakeway	14,771	45	31	14
Lake Worth	4,870	35	26	9
La Marque	16,191	35	29	6

Table 62. Full-Time Law Enforcement Employees, by Selected State and City, 2016—Continued

(Number.)

State/city	Population	Total law enforcement employees	Total officers	Total civilians
Lamesa	9,429	24	18	6
Lampasas	7,898	31	18	13
Lancaster	39,219	57	48	9
La Porte	35,410	106	75	31
Laredo	259,325	546	473	73
La Vernia	1,312	7	7	0
La Villa	2,632	10	8	2
Lavon	3,045	10	9	1
League City	101,436	156	114	42
Leander	40,650	60	43	17
Levelland	13,997	33	22	11
Lewisville	105,762	219	149	70
Lexington	1,183	4	3	1
Liberty	9,169	26	18	8
Linden	1,978	6	5	1
Little Elm	41,421	51	47	4
Littlefield	6,033	19	12	7
Livingston	5,140	25	18	7
Llano	3,356	9	8	1
Lockhart	13,590	34	25	9
Lone Star	1,514	5	4	1
Longview	82,632	186	172	14
Lorena	1,745	6	5	1
Lubbock	252,900	526	392	134
Lufkin	36,581	99	75	24
Luling	5,838	19	12	7
Lumberton	12,500	20	17	3
Lyford	2,605	4	4	0
Lytle	2,946	8	7	1
Madisonville	4,681	15	13	2
Magnolia	1,932	17	15	2
Malakoff	2,292	6	6	0
Manor	8,200	28	24	4
Mansfield	65,882	225	95	130
Manvel	8,645	20	14	6
Marble Falls	6,323	32	19	13
Marlin	5,626	16	12	4
Marshall	23,876	67	47	20
Mathis	5,062	14	8	6
McAllen	142,227	408	262	146
McKinney	169,689	234	189	45
Melissa	8,132	11	11	0
Memorial Villages	12,282	45	32	13
Mercedes	16,830	38	31	7
Mesquite	145,786	300	218	82
Mexia	7,393	26	16	10
Midland	137,780	239	181	58
Midlothian	23,085	63	43	20
Mineola	4,649	19	13	6
Mineral Wells	14,391	37	28	9
Mission	84,380	193	148	45
Missouri City	75,607	131	102	29
Monahans	7,854	17	12	5
Mont Belvieu	5,482	18	11	7
Morgans Point Resort	4,257	9	8	1
Moulton	911	4	4	0
Mount Pleasant	16,058	45	32	13
Muleshoe	5,193	13	8	5
Munday	1,347	2	2	0
Murphy	21,175	34	23	11
Nacogdoches	34,079	87	63	24
Nash	3,177	8	8	0
Nassau Bay	4,118	12	12	0
Navasota	7,545	27	20	7
Nederland	17,240	38	24	14
Needville	3,088	7	7	0
New Boston	4,666	16	11	5
New Braunfels	73,334	142	117	25
New Deal	805	2	1	1
Nixon	2,482	7	5	2
Nolanville	4,876	10	10	0
Normangee	695	1	1	0
Northeast	2,535	8	8	0
Northlake	2,329	11	11	0
North Richland Hills	70,409	186	110	76
Oak Ridge	180	2	2	0
Oak Ridge North	3,181	17	17	0
Odessa	123,209	220	166	54
O'Donnell	803	1	1	0
Olmos Park	2,420	14	13	1
Olney	3,159	7	6	1
Olton	2,121	5	5	0
Omaha	986	2	2	0
Onalaska	1,770	8	8	0
Orange	19,493	56	40	16

Table 62. Full-Time Law Enforcement Employees, by Selected State and City, 2016—Continued

(Number.)

State/city	Population	Total law enforcement employees	Total officers	Total civilians
Overton	2,532	12	7	5
Ovilla	3,933	10	9	1
Oyster Creek	1,136	11	7	4
Palacios	4,617	16	11	5
Palestine	18,194	54	37	17
Palmer	2,064	10	9	1
Palmhurst	2,714	18	13	5
Palm Valley	1,291	5	5	0
Palmview	5,763	37	27	10
Pampa	18,228	30	28	2
Panhandle	2,321	4	4	0
Pantego	2,558	16	11	5
Paris	24,706	86	61	25
Pasadena	154,648	345	268	77
Patton Village	1,632	18	17	1
Pearland	112,814	215	161	54
Pearsall	10,151	17	15	2
Pecos	9,669	41	19	22
Pelican Bay	1,653	4	4	0
Penitas	4,785	15	13	2
Perryton	9,354	24	14	10
Pflugerville	58,975	109	82	27
Pharr	77,744	164	125	39
Pilot Point	4,140	9	8	1
Pinehurst	2,078	8	6	2
Pittsburg	4,622	12	9	3
Plainview	20,667	40	33	7
Plano	288,242	512	350	162
Pleasanton	10,013	29	22	7
Port Aransas	4,055	30	19	11
Port Arthur	55,510	148	112	36
Port Isabel	5,015	25	18	7
Portland	16,340	42	27	15
Port Lavaca	12,458	23	17	6
Port Neches	12,741	22	19	3
Poteet	3,450	12	11	1
Pottsboro	2,267	9	8	1
Prairie View	6,538	7	6	1
Primera	4,748	9	8	1
Prosper	17,634	28	19	9
Queen City	1,466	6	6	0
Ralls	1,890	3	3	0
Rancho Viejo	2,502	8	8	0
Raymondville	11,104	23	14	9
Red Oak	12,278	26	24	2
Refugio	2,850	10	9	1
Reno	3,302	5	5	0
Richardson	113,216	248	155	93
Richland Hills	8,159	22	17	5
Richmond	12,245	38	28	10
Richwood	3,895	9	9	0
Riesel	1,021	3	3	0
Rio Bravo	4,819	1	1	0
Rio Grande City	14,518	39	28	11
Rio Hondo	2,453	7	7	0
River Oaks	7,782	22	17	5
Roanoke	7,707	40	29	11
Robinson	11,674	27	21	6
Robstown	11,596	32	24	8
Rockdale	5,619	16	10	6
Rockport	10,725	30	27	3
Rockwall	43,542	100	80	20
Rollingwood	1,570	9	9	0
Roma	10,310	36	28	8
Rosenberg	36,360	92	70	22
Round Rock	119,308	227	158	69
Rowlett	61,047	102	76	26
Royse City	11,914	17	16	1
Rusk	5,630	13	12	1
Sabinal	1,721	5	4	1
Sachse	25,467	42	28	14
Saginaw	22,540	42	34	8
Salado	2,140	5	5	0
San Angelo	101,870	193	162	31
San Antonio	1,498,642	2,819	2,152	667
San Augustine	1,989	8	7	1
San Benito	24,535	51	43	8
San Diego	4,350	8	7	1
Sanger	7,913	14	13	1
San Juan	37,075	58	47	11
San Marcos	64,380	143	103	40
San Saba	3,004	5	5	0
Sansom Park Village	4,892	14	13	1
Santa Anna	1,022	3	3	0
Santa Fe	13,172	26	21	5

Table 62. Full-Time Law Enforcement Employees, by Selected State and City, 2016—Continued

(Number.)

State/city	Population	Total law enforcement employees	Total officers	Total civilians
Schertz	39,225	72	51	21
Schulenburg	2,941	9	8	1
Seagoville	16,085	29	20	9
Seagraves	2,836	7	5	2
Sealy	6,469	21	20	1
Seguin	28,319	78	56	22
Selma	10,027	31	28	3
Seminole	7,656	14	12	2
Seven Points	1,447	12	8	4
Shamrock	2,007	7	3	4
Shavano Park	3,631	17	16	1
Shenandoah	2,914	24	23	1
Sherman	41,139	83	61	22
Shoreacres	1,624	6	6	0
Silsbee	6,693	21	15	6
Sinton	5,756	12	11	1
Smithville	4,159	18	11	7
Snyder	11,882	23	20	3
Socorro	33,447	41	29	12
Somerset	1,814	3	3	0
Sonora	2,841	7	5	2
Sour Lake	1,765	8	7	1
South Houston	17,650	40	29	11
Southlake	30,644	69	62	7
Southmayd	1,019	3	3	0
South Padre Island	2,895	34	25	9
Southside Place	1,859	13	8	5
Spearman	3,378	4	4	0
Springtown	2,841	15	11	4
Spring Valley	4,289	24	19	5
Spur	1,183	2	2	0
Stafford	18,602	65	48	17
Stagecoach	589	2	2	0
Stamford	2,944	7	6	1
Stanton	3,032	5	5	0
Stephenville	20,787	54	37	17
Stratford	2,085	3	3	0
Sugar Land	90,088	175	151	24
Sullivan City	4,223	12	8	4
Sulphur Springs	16,227	39	28	11
Sunrise Beach Village	734	5	5	0
Sunset Valley	708	14	13	1
Sweeny	3,780	8	8	0
Sweetwater	10,785	30	24	6
Taft	3,104	9	8	1
Tahoka	2,551	4	4	0
Taylor	16,979	36	25	11
Teague	3,575	8	8	0
Temple	73,411	178	144	34
Terrell	17,211	57	37	20
Texarkana	37,442	99	87	12
Texas City	48,095	82	61	21
The Colony	42,925	89	58	31
Thorndale	1,313	3	3	0
Thrall	936	3	3	0
Three Rivers	1,996	11	10	1
Tioga	874	2	2	0
Tool	2,274	11	7	4
Trinity	2,744	11	6	5
Trophy Club	12,645	20	16	4
Troup	1,986	9	8	1
Troy	1,883	6	6	0
Tulia	4,716	16	8	8
Tye	1,263	5	5	0
Tyler	105,044	238	190	48
University Park	25,103	53	39	14
Uvalde	16,619	54	38	16
Valley Mills	1,171	3	3	0
Van	2,695	8	8	0
Van Alstyne	3,406	14	9	5
Venus	3,366	10	9	1
Vernon	10,495	25	18	7
Victoria	68,603	142	107	35
Vidor	10,991	32	24	8
Waco	133,790	334	241	93
Waelder	1,115	4	4	0
Wake Village	5,466	8	7	1
Waller	2,559	11	10	1
Wallis	1,303	6	6	0
Waxahachie	34,152	76	59	17
Weimar	2,163	8	7	1
Weslaco	39,987	90	66	24
West	2,898	8	8	0
West Columbia	3,941	17	11	6
West Lake Hills	3,364	18	13	5

Table 62. Full-Time Law Enforcement Employees, by Selected State and City, 2016—Continued

(Number.)

State/city	Population	Total law enforcement employees	Total officers	Total civilians
West Orange	3,459	11	9	2
Westover Hills	729	13	9	4
West Tawakoni	1,654	6	3	3
West University Place	15,932	33	24	9
Westworth	2,687	20	15	5
Wharton	8,706	33	24	9
Whitehouse	8,286	15	15	0
White Oak	6,317	20	16	4
Whitesboro	3,931	13	8	5
White Settlement	17,267	42	31	11
Whitewright	1,638	5	5	0
Whitney	2,103	8	7	1
Wichita Falls	104,685	284	199	85
Willis	6,401	18	16	2
Willow Park	5,130	13	12	1
Wills Point	3,551	10	10	0
Wilmer	3,978	17	12	5
Windcrest	5,877	36	26	10
Wink	1,087	2	2	0
Winnsboro	3,354	14	9	5
Winters	2,563	5	5	0
Wolfforth	4,371	12	11	1
Woodbranch	1,396	4	2	2
Woodville	2,457	10	9	1
Woodway	8,836	43	31	12
Wortham	1,019	4	4	0
Wylie	47,772	66	61	5
Yoakum	6,059	19	12	7
UTAH				
Alta	391	8	4	4
American Fork/Cedar Hills	39,028	42	35	7
Big Water	465	1	1	0
Blanding	3,876	5	5	0
Bluffdale	11,765	8	8	0
Bountiful	44,003	53	36	17
Brian Head	87	5	5	0
Brigham City	18,914	27	23	4
Cedar City	30,441	40	36	4
Centerfield	1,389	1	1	0
Centerville	17,204	23	18	5
Clearfield	30,783	42	31	11
Clinton	21,567	16	15	1
Cottonwood Heights	34,493	52	42	10
Draper	47,696	47	39	8
East Carbon	1,548	3	3	0
Enoch	6,348	8	4	4
Ephraim	7,009	5	5	0
Fairview	1,265	1	1	0
Farmington	23,505	20	17	3
Garland	2,449	3	3	0
Grantsville	10,253	15	13	2
Harrisville	6,347	10	9	1
Heber	14,954	24	19	5
Helper	2,094	6	5	1
Hildale	2,959	13	7	6
Hurricane	15,869	25	23	2
Kanab	4,406	7	6	1
Kaysville	31,055	29	26	3
La Verkin	4,220	4	4	0
Layton	75,482	107	75	32
Lehi	60,806	53	47	6
Lindon	10,958	17	15	2
Logan	50,767	84	55	29
Lone Peak	28,862	24	21	3
Mantua	741	5	5	0
Mapleton	9,479	9	8	1
Minersville	861	1	1	0
Moab	5,262	19	14	5
Monticello	2,085	3	3	0
Mount Pleasant	3,306	4	4	0
Murray	49,758	90	75	15
Myton	653	1	1	0
Naples	2,320	6	5	1
Nephi	5,594	12	10	2
North Ogden	18,654	22	19	3
North Park	15,088	12	10	2
North Salt Lake	20,572	25	20	5
Ogden	85,930	156	128	28
Orem	95,640	116	85	31
Park City	8,231	46	31	15
Parowan	2,951	5	5	0
Payson	19,738	21	20	1
Perry	4,739	8	7	1
Pleasant Grove	38,984	35	27	8

Table 62. Full-Time Law Enforcement Employees, by Selected State and City, 2016—Continued

(Number.)

State/city	Population	Total law enforcement employees	Total officers	Total civilians
Pleasant View	9,548	10	8	2
Price	8,310	20	17	3
Provo	115,739	149	103	46
Richfield	7,597	17	15	2
Riverdale	8,699	22	19	3
Roosevelt	7,179	11	10	1
Roy	38,167	44	38	6
Salem	7,696	11	10	1
Salina	2,527	4	4	0
Salt Lake City	193,918	542	435	107
Sandy	94,601	143	109	34
Santa Clara/Ivins	15,107	17	15	2
Santaquin/Genola	12,289	12	11	1
Saratoga Springs	27,211	41	31	10
Smithfield	11,015	12	11	1
South Jordan	70,226	58	50	8
South Ogden	17,026	24	20	4
South Salt Lake	25,022	68	57	11
Spanish Fork	38,529	37	32	5
Springdale	561	5	5	0
Springville	32,825	35	25	10
St. George	81,755	155	107	48
Stockton	644	1	1	0
Sunset	5,191	9	8	1
Syracuse	28,011	23	21	2
Tooele	33,448	49	38	11
Tremonton	8,333	12	10	2
Vernal	11,687	25	22	3
Washington	25,564	26	24	2
Wellington	1,607	2	2	0
West Bountiful	5,559	10	9	1
West Jordan	113,595	146	112	34
West Valley	137,558	231	191	40
Willard	1,789	2	2	0
Woods Cross	11,600	19	16	3
VERMONT				
Barre	8,687	27	19	8
Barre Town	7,791	7	6	1
Bellows Falls	3,030	11	10	1
Bennington	15,265	31	23	8
Berlin	2,802	8	7	1
Bradford	2,760	2	2	0
Brandon	3,801	8	7	1
Brattleboro	11,607	37	22	15
Bristol	3,955	3	3	0
Burlington	42,454	134	96	38
Castleton	4,572	5	5	0
Chester	3,069	5	4	1
Colchester	17,437	35	27	8
Dover	1,095	7	6	1
Essex	21,217	31	25	6
Fair Haven	2,614	4	4	0
Hardwick	2,925	8	7	1
Hartford	9,747	30	22	8
Hinesburg	4,508	5	5	0
Killington	786	2	2	0
Ludlow	1,923	5	5	0
Lyndonville	1,187	3	3	0
Manchester	4,310	12	9	3
Middlebury	8,570	16	14	2
Milton	10,921	17	16	1
Montpelier	7,542	26	17	9
Morristown	5,452	11	11	0
Newport	4,415	14	12	2
Northfield	6,044	7	6	1
Norwich	3,369	5	4	1
Pittsford	2,858	1	1	0
Randolph	4,788	6	6	0
Richmond	4,134	6	6	0
Royalton	2,741	2	2	0
Rutland	15,698	46	34	12
Rutland Town	4,009	3	3	0
Shelburne	7,887	19	10	9
South Burlington	18,962	49	40	9
Springfield	9,132	21	16	5
St. Albans	6,799	28	22	6
St. Johnsbury	7,414	18	12	6
Stowe	4,474	11	11	0
Swanton	6,500	7	7	0
Thetford	2,603	2	2	0
Waterbury	5,120	2	2	0
Weathersfield	2,765	2	2	0
Williston	9,556	14	11	3
Wilmington	1,825	8	6	2

Table 62. Full-Time Law Enforcement Employees, by Selected State and City, 2016—Continued

(Number.)

State/city	Population	Total law enforcement employees	Total officers	Total civilians
Windsor	3,447	10	10	0
Winhall	753	7	6	1
Winooski	7,178	20	16	4
Woodstock	2,971	8	5	3
VIRGINIA				
Abingdon	8,105	28	25	3
Alexandria	155,319	409	317	92
Altavista	3,478	13	13	0
Amherst	2,206	4	4	0
Appalachia	1,655	5	5	0
Ashland	7,559	28	25	3
Bedford	6,556	25	23	2
Berryville	4,323	8	7	1
Big Stone Gap	5,378	14	13	1
Blacksburg	44,528	71	61	10
Blackstone	3,467	12	9	3
Bloxom	384	1	1	0
Bluefield	5,247	22	17	5
Boykins	539	2	2	0
Bridgewater	5,939	9	9	0
Bristol	16,908	72	52	20
Broadway	3,831	5	5	0
Brookneal	1,120	2	2	0
Buena Vista	6,576	17	16	1
Burkeville	408	1	1	0
Cape Charles	1,019	3	3	0
Cedar Bluff	1,064	3	3	0
Charlottesville	46,979	157	124	33
Chase City	2,285	10	9	1
Chatham	1,482	3	3	0
Chesapeake	236,570	501	387	114
Chilhowie	1,733	6	6	0
Chincoteague	2,909	14	10	4
Christiansburg	22,134	65	59	6
Clarksville	1,199	8	7	1
Clifton Forge	3,713	12	10	2
Clintwood	1,309	4	4	0
Coeburn	1,982	8	8	0
Colonial Beach	3,589	11	10	1
Colonial Heights	17,814	56	52	4
Covington	5,570	27	17	10
Crewe	2,225	6	5	1
Culpeper	17,733	52	44	8
Damascus	799	4	4	0
Danville	41,686	132	124	8
Dayton	1,598	7	6	1
Dublin	2,719	9	8	1
Dumfries	5,263	6	5	1
Elkton	2,826	7	6	1
Emporia	5,382	32	22	10
Exmore	1,443	6	6	0
Fairfax City	24,173	83	63	20
Falls Church	14,124	41	31	10
Farmville	8,159	28	26	2
Franklin	8,423	37	25	12
Fredericksburg	28,823	91	66	25
Front Royal	15,193	47	37	10
Galax	6,858	40	24	16
Gate City	1,937	5	5	0
Glade Spring	1,452	3	3	0
Glen Lyn	116	1	1	0
Gordonsville	1,595	7	7	0
Gretna	1,243	3	3	0
Grottoes	2,776	6	6	0
Grundy	970	6	6	0
Halifax	1,243	5	5	0
Hampton	135,504	393	271	122
Harrisonburg	52,972	113	95	18
Haymarket	2,019	7	6	1
Haysi	470	2	2	0
Herndon	24,806	70	55	15
Hillsville	2,666	14	13	1
Honaker	1,382	4	3	1
Hopewell	22,204	80	61	19
Hurt	1,269	2	2	0
Independence	923	2	2	0
Jonesville	968	4	4	0
Kenbridge	1,220	5	5	0
Kilmarnock	1,428	5	5	0
La Crosse	586	1	1	0
Lawrenceville	1,019	6	6	0
Lebanon	3,323	13	12	1
Leesburg	53,016	83	68	15
Lexington	7,264	19	17	2

Table 62. Full-Time Law Enforcement Employees, by Selected State and City, 2016—Continued

(Number.)

State/city	Population	Total law enforcement employees	Total officers	Total civilians
Louisa	1,633	6	6	0
Luray	4,817	13	12	1
Lynchburg	80,215	198	172	26
Manassas	42,267	119	92	27
Manassas Park	15,912	43	34	9
Marion	5,956	22	20	2
Martinsville	13,553	51	46	5
Middleburg	835	6	6	0
Middletown	1,324	3	3	0
Mount Jackson	2,051	5	5	0
Narrows	1,940	5	5	0
New Market	2,220	5	5	0
Newport News	181,676	547	410	137
Norfolk	245,734	811	718	93
Norton	3,911	25	17	8
Occoquan	1,042	1	1	0
Onancock	1,260	5	5	0
Onley	516	5	5	0
Orange	4,992	16	14	2
Parksley	840	3	3	0
Pearisburg	2,655	7	7	0
Pembroke	1,073	3	3	0
Pennington Gap	1,793	9	8	1
Petersburg	32,293	120	93	27
Pocahontas	376	4	4	0
Poquoson	11,975	25	24	1
Portsmouth	95,813	312	231	81
Pound	957	5	5	0
Pulaski	8,855	31	27	4
Purcellville	9,547	16	14	2
Quantico	548	1	1	0
Radford	17,504	49	37	12
Remington	634	1	1	0
Rich Creek	744	1	1	0
Richlands	5,443	22	17	5
Richmond	222,430	802	680	122
Roanoke	99,978	292	245	47
Rocky Mount	4,803	23	21	2
Salem	25,396	85	62	23
Saltville	2,022	6	6	0
Shenandoah	2,334	6	5	1
Smithfield	8,418	25	21	4
South Boston	7,944	31	28	3
South Hill	4,503	18	16	2
Stanley	1,649	3	3	0
Staunton	24,399	62	46	16
Stephens City	1,962	3	3	0
St. Paul	910	6	6	0
Strasburg	6,622	19	17	2
Suffolk	88,342	243	182	61
Tangier	726	1	1	0
Tappahannock	2,387	10	9	1
Tazewell	4,378	17	15	2
Timberville	2,618	6	6	0
Victoria	1,668	4	4	0
Vienna	16,679	48	37	11
Vinton	8,266	25	23	2
Virginia Beach	453,017	951	779	172
Warrenton	9,953	26	24	2
Warsaw	1,492	4	4	0
Waverly	2,057	11	6	5
Waynesboro	21,464	53	42	11
Weber City	1,251	4	4	0
West Point	3,336	10	9	1
Williamsburg	15,256	40	37	3
Winchester	27,363	96	72	24
Windsor	2,681	6	6	0
Wise	3,093	13	12	1
Woodstock	5,277	18	16	2
Wytheville	8,097	39	29	10
WASHINGTON				
Aberdeen	16,155	48	35	13
Airway Heights	8,425	19	18	1
Algona	3,166	7	7	0
Anacortes	16,532	33	26	7
Arlington	19,142	28	23	5
Asotin	1,287	3	3	0
Auburn	78,400	128	108	20
Bainbridge Island	23,998	22	18	4
Battle Ground	19,734	26	22	4
Bellevue	142,238	215	175	40
Bellingham	86,005	174	113	61
Black Diamond	4,420	9	8	1
Blaine	5,130	13	11	2

Table 62. Full-Time Law Enforcement Employees, by Selected State and City, 2016—Continued

(Number.)

State/city	Population	Total law enforcement employees	Total officers	Total civilians
Bonney Lake	20,449	32	27	5
Bothell	43,828	84	58	26
Bremerton	39,862	67	55	12
Brewster	2,350	6	5	1
Brier	6,753	8	7	1
Buckley	5,077	12	10	2
Burien	50,934	74	52	22
Burlington	8,680	32	27	5
Camas	22,350	29	26	3
Carnation	1,890	3	2	1
Castle Rock	2,197	6	5	1
Centralia	16,785	36	27	9
Chehalis	7,417	22	17	5
Cheney	11,703	21	15	6
Chewelah	2,607	6	5	1
Clarkston	7,330	15	14	1
Cle Elum	2,812	8	7	1
Clyde Hill	3,279	9	8	1
Colfax	2,883	6	6	0
College Place	9,114	13	10	3
Colville	4,728	12	10	2
Connell	5,747	6	6	0
Cosmopolis	1,583	6	5	1
Coulee Dam	1,092	3	3	0
Covington	19,529	24	18	6
Des Moines	31,523	43	32	11
Dupont	9,593	13	12	1
Duvall	7,876	13	12	1
East Wenatchee	13,746	24	21	3
Eatonville	2,930	5	4	1
Edgewood	9,918	9	8	1
Edmonds	41,705	63	54	9
Ellensburg	19,148	36	29	7
Elma	3,020	8	7	1
Enumclaw	11,709	30	17	13
Ephrata	8,116	18	15	3
Everett	108,988	226	187	39
Everson	4,128	7	6	1
Federal Way	96,338	159	130	29
Ferndale	13,338	22	19	3
Fife	10,134	40	30	10
Fircrest	6,728	8	8	0
Forks	3,787	12	5	7
Gig Harbor	9,124	18	16	2
Goldendale	3,439	8	7	1
Grand Coulee	2,064	7	7	0
Grandview	11,230	22	17	5
Granger	3,792	6	6	0
Hoquiam	8,342	24	23	1
Issaquah	37,308	61	33	28
Kalama	2,410	7	6	1
Kelso	11,897	31	27	4
Kenmore	22,340	18	14	4
Kennewick	79,837	106	91	15
Kent	128,604	188	139	49
Kettle Falls	1,596	4	3	1
Kirkland	88,627	130	94	36
Kittitas	1,439	3	3	0
La Center	3,159	10	8	2
Lacey	47,215	58	50	8
Lake Forest Park	13,369	23	19	4
Lake Stevens	31,440	33	27	6
Lakewood	60,153	112	96	16
Langley	1,085	4	4	0
Liberty Lake	9,187	12	11	1
Long Beach	1,359	7	6	1
Longview	36,854	69	58	11
Lynden	13,834	19	15	4
Lynnwood	37,217	102	70	32
Mabton	2,300	4	4	0
Maple Valley	26,304	24	19	5
Marysville	68,172	88	64	24
Mattawa	4,568	4	4	0
McCleary	1,612	3	3	0
Medina	3,278	9	8	1
Mercer Island	25,527	35	31	4
Mill Creek	20,419	27	22	5
Milton	7,785	14	13	1
Monroe	18,247	43	33	10
Montesano	3,875	9	8	1
Morton	1,129	3	3	0
Moses Lake	22,372	40	32	8
Mountlake Terrace	21,212	33	26	7
Mount Vernon	34,521	54	42	12
Moxee	3,911	5	5	0

Table 62. Full-Time Law Enforcement Employees, by Selected State and City, 2016—Continued

(Number.)

State/city	Population	Total law enforcement employees	Total officers	Total civilians
Mukilteo	21,416	31	26	5
Napavine	1,794	2	2	0
Newcastle	11,576	12	9	3
Normandy Park	6,733	7	6	1
Oak Harbor	22,795	36	24	12
Ocean Shores	5,721	13	12	1
Odessa	864	2	2	0
Olympia	50,972	95	67	28
Omak	4,854	13	11	2
Oroville	1,674	6	5	1
Orting	7,594	11	11	0
Othello	7,893	21	14	7
Pacific	7,228	14	12	2
Palouse	1,027	3	3	0
Pasco	71,077	83	71	12
Pe Ell	634	1	1	0
Port Angeles	19,525	58	31	27
Port Orchard	13,897	25	23	2
Port Townsend	9,378	15	13	2
Poulsbo	10,199	20	17	3
Prosser	5,895	14	13	1
Pullman	33,456	40	29	11
Puyallup	40,167	77	56	21
Quincy	7,482	25	17	8
Raymond	2,804	7	6	1
Reardan	551	1	1	0
Redmond	61,893	123	79	44
Renton	101,908	146	117	29
Republic	1,072	2	2	0
Richland	55,475	76	62	14
Ridgefield	6,852	10	9	1
Ritzville	1,663	4	4	0
Roy	809	2	2	0
Royal City	2,234	3	3	0
Ruston	808	3	3	0
Sammamish	53,387	40	32	8
SeaTac	28,466	60	43	17
Seattle	700,313	1,946	1,384	562
Sedro Woolley	10,860	20	17	3
Selah	7,753	18	15	3
Sequim	6,868	22	19	3
Shelton	9,830	20	18	2
Shoreline	55,905	73	53	20
Snohomish	9,773	20	18	2
Snoqualmie	13,713	25	21	4
Soap Lake	1,586	5	4	1
South Bend	1,609	5	4	1
Spokane	214,028	400	307	93
Spokane Valley	95,923	102	101	1
Springdale	273	1	1	0
Stanwood	6,888	13	11	2
Steilacoom	6,257	10	9	1
Sumas	1,386	7	6	1
Sumner	9,753	23	19	4
Sunnyside	16,387	51	28	23
Tacoma	209,914	371	336	35
Tenino	1,761	3	2	1
Tieton	1,264	3	2	1
Toledo	727	5	4	1
Tonasket	1,012	5	4	1
Toppenish	8,997	22	13	9
Tukwila	20,195	94	77	17
Tumwater	19,569	33	28	5
Twisp	946	2	2	0
Union Gap	6,031	19	16	3
University Place	33,196	16	15	1
Vancouver	174,912	235	193	42
Walla Walla	32,326	71	46	25
Wapato	5,067	18	15	3
Warden	2,743	5	4	1
Washougal	15,527	25	20	5
Wenatchee	33,920	47	38	9
Westport	2,011	8	7	1
West Richland	14,127	21	18	3
White Salmon	2,364	7	6	1
Winthrop	425	2	1	1
Woodinville	11,953	19	15	4
Woodland	5,902	12	10	2
Yakima	94,111	183	140	43
Yelm	8,780	14	12	2
Zillah	3,157	8	7	1
WEST VIRGINIA				
Alderson	1,181	3	3	0
Anmoore	753	2	2	0

Table 62. Full-Time Law Enforcement Employees, by Selected State and City, 2016—Continued

(Number.)

State/city	Population	Total law enforcement employees	Total officers	Total civilians
Ansted	1,394	3	2	1
Athens	933	1	1	0
Barboursville	4,091	22	20	2
Barrackville	1,324	3	2	1
Beckley	16,940	73	54	19
Belington	1,935	3	3	0
Belle	1,202	4	4	0
Benwood	1,350	6	6	0
Berkeley Springs	606	2	2	0
Bethlehem	2,410	4	4	0
Bluefield	10,298	36	28	8
Bradshaw	302	1	1	0
Bramwell	362	2	2	0
Bridgeport	8,402	33	29	4
Buckhannon	5,662	11	10	1
Burnsville	496	2	2	0
Cameron	895	3	3	0
Capon Bridge	363	3	2	1
Cedar Grove	943	2	2	0
Ceredo	1,377	9	5	4
Chapmanville	1,199	3	3	0
Charleston	49,429	187	163	24
Charles Town	6,030	16	14	2
Chesapeake	1,492	3	3	0
Chester	2,481	6	5	1
Clarksburg	16,067	45	41	4
Clendenin	1,179	3	3	0
Danville	648	1	1	0
Davy	378	1	1	0
Delbarton	533	3	3	0
Dunbar	7,612	16	15	1
Eleanor	1,599	2	2	0
Elkins	7,235	12	11	1
Fairmont	18,733	40	34	6
Fairview	415	1	1	0
Farmington	377	2	1	1
Fayetteville	2,885	10	9	1
Follansbee	2,870	7	7	0
Fort Gay	678	3	3	0
Gary	874	2	2	0
Gassaway	901	1	1	0
Gauley Bridge	591	3	1	2
Gilbert	419	2	2	0
Glasgow	872	3	3	0
Glen Dale	1,452	11	6	5
Glenville	1,542	4	3	1
Grafton	5,145	7	6	1
Grantsville	546	3	3	0
Grant Town	619	1	1	0
Granville	3,362	13	13	0
Hamlin	1,120	2	2	0
Handley	339	1	1	0
Harpers Ferry/Bolivar	1,361	3	2	1
Harrisville	1,757	1	1	0
Hinton	2,500	6	5	1
Huntington	48,540	116	105	11
Hurricane	6,534	18	16	2
Iaeger	270	1	1	0
Kenova	3,058	13	8	5
Kermit	377	1	1	0
Keyser	5,212	14	9	5
Kimball	175	1	1	0
Kingwood	2,963	2	2	0
Lewisburg	3,971	14	12	2
Logan	1,625	9	8	1
Lumberport	861	2	2	0
Mabscott	1,365	3	3	0
Madison	2,900	6	6	0
Man	694	3	3	0
Mannington	2,079	4	4	0
Marmet	1,440	7	7	0
Martinsburg	17,789	51	44	7
Mason	937	3	3	0
Matewan	461	1	1	0
Matoaka	219	1	1	0
McMechen	1,826	3	3	0
Milton	2,683	8	7	1
Monongah	1,100	1	1	0
Montgomery	1,588	4	3	1
Moorefield	2,467	9	8	1
Morgantown	31,109	76	65	11
Moundsville	8,644	20	16	4
Mount Hope	1,371	5	4	1
Mullens	1,445	4	4	0
New Cumberland	1,055	2	2	0

Table 62. Full-Time Law Enforcement Employees, by Selected State and City, 2016—Continued

(Number.)

State/city	Population	Total law enforcement employees	Total officers	Total civilians
New Haven	1,527	4	3	1
New Martinsville	5,190	15	11	4
Nitro	6,729	17	16	1
Nutter Fort	1,570	6	6	0
Oak Hill	8,104	19	15	4
Oceana	1,285	4	4	0
Paden City	2,483	5	4	1
Parkersburg	30,913	76	68	8
Parsons	1,424	1	1	0
Paw Paw	490	2	1	1
Pennsboro	1,068	1	1	0
Petersburg	2,543	2	2	0
Philippi	3,320	6	6	0
Piedmont	829	1	1	0
Pineville	621	3	3	0
Point Pleasant	4,262	10	9	1
Pratt	583	1	1	0
Princeton	6,017	23	21	2
Rainelle	1,480	5	4	1
Ranson	5,053	13	12	1
Ravenswood	3,837	12	11	1
Rhodell	169	2	1	1
Richwood	1,966	2	2	0
Ridgeley	637	2	1	1
Ripley	3,255	10	9	1
Rivesville	946	1	1	0
Romney	1,759	4	3	1
Ronceverte	1,749	6	6	0
Salem	1,544	3	3	0
Shepherdstown	2,064	6	5	1
Shinnston	2,164	7	7	0
Sistersville	1,361	4	4	0
Smithers	786	3	2	1
Sophia	1,313	4	4	0
South Charleston	12,957	45	42	3
Spencer	2,175	6	6	0
St. Albans	10,635	25	23	2
Star City	2,054	7	7	0
St. Marys	1,859	4	4	0
Stonewood	1,758	3	3	0
Summersville	3,459	17	16	1
Sutton	982	1	1	0
Sylvester	152	1	1	0
Terra Alta	1,496	2	2	0
Triadelphia	766	1	1	0
Vienna	10,537	20	17	3
War	760	2	2	0
Wayne	1,373	2	2	0
Webster Springs	725	5	4	1
Weirton	19,067	42	38	4
Welch	1,899	7	6	1
Wellsburg	2,685	8	7	1
West Logan	395	1	1	0
West Milford	616	2	2	0
Weston	4,078	7	5	2
Westover	4,267	7	7	0
Wheeling	27,486	77	68	9
White Hall	665	4	4	0
White Sulphur Springs	2,438	8	7	1
Whitesville	469	2	2	0
Williamson	2,968	10	8	2
Williamstown	2,977	8	7	1
Winfield	2,364	6	6	0
WISCONSIN				
Adams	1,879	5	5	0
Albany	1,018	3	3	0
Algoma	3,079	4	4	0
Alma	742	1	1	0
Altoona	7,446	14	13	1
Amery	2,816	6	6	0
Antigo	7,801	18	15	3
Appleton	74,439	137	110	27
Arcadia	3,004	4	4	0
Ashland	8,005	20	19	1
Ashwaubenon	17,219	60	54	6
Athens	1,094	1	1	0
Balsam Lake	988	1	1	0
Bangor	1,498	3	3	0
Baraboo	12,174	34	28	6
Barneveld	1,233	1	1	0
Barron	3,303	6	6	0
Bayfield	478	3	3	0
Bayside	4,417	14	13	1
Beaver Dam	16,640	35	31	4

Table 62. Full-Time Law Enforcement Employees, by Selected State and City, 2016—Continued

(Number.)

State/city	Population	Total law enforcement employees	Total officers	Total civilians
Belleville	2,433	6	5	1
Beloit	36,878	77	65	12
Beloit Town	7,672	12	10	2
Berlin	5,400	13	12	1
Big Bend	1,318	3	3	0
Black River Falls	3,557	10	9	1
Blair	1,348	3	3	0
Blanchardville	817	1	1	0
Bloomer	3,515	7	6	1
Bloomfield	6,253	6	6	0
Blue Mounds	955	2	1	1
Boscobel	3,181	6	6	0
Boyceville	1,106	1	1	0
Brandon-Fairwater	1,221	2	1	1
Brillion	3,138	8	8	0
Brodhead	3,291	12	8	4
Brookfield	38,043	88	70	18
Brookfield Township	6,093	11	11	0
Brown Deer	12,101	35	32	3
Burlington	10,669	26	20	6
Butler	1,822	8	7	1
Caledonia	24,681	35	32	3
Campbellsport	1,970	2	2	0
Campbell Township	4,419	4	4	0
Cashton	1,095	4	2	2
Cedarburg	11,488	28	20	8
Chenequa	606	9	8	1
Chetek	2,185	6	5	1
Chilton	3,886	6	6	0
Chippewa Falls	14,109	26	23	3
Cleveland	1,464	3	2	1
Clinton	2,138	5	5	0
Clintonville	4,434	15	11	4
Colby-Abbotsford	4,078	7	6	1
Colfax	1,161	2	2	0
Columbus	4,996	12	10	2
Cornell	1,435	2	2	0
Cottage Grove	6,954	12	11	1
Crandon	1,852	4	3	1
Cross Plains	4,072	6	5	1
Cuba City	2,049	5	4	1
Cudahy	18,338	40	31	9
Cumberland	2,142	5	5	0
Dane	1,146	2	1	1
Darlington	2,397	5	5	0
Deforest	9,674	21	18	3
Delafield	7,194	16	14	2
Delavan	9,992	27	22	5
Delavan Town	5,337	12	11	1
De Pere	24,896	39	35	4
Dodgeville	4,645	10	10	0
Durand	1,831	3	3	0
Eagle River	1,356	6	6	0
Eagle Village	1,978	2	2	0
East Troy	4,298	7	7	0
Eau Claire	68,084	134	99	35
Edgar	1,459	1	1	0
Edgerton	5,554	11	10	1
Eleva	676	1	1	0
Elkhart Lake	962	3	3	0
Elkhorn	9,859	17	15	2
Ellsworth	3,180	5	5	0
Elm Grove	6,222	24	16	8
Elroy	1,359	3	3	0
Evansville	5,268	10	9	1
Everest Metropolitan	17,318	29	25	4
Fall Creek	1,315	2	2	0
Fall River	1,675	2	2	0
Fennimore	2,485	5	5	0
Fitchburg	28,588	61	49	12
Fond du Lac	42,907	80	73	7
Fontana	1,702	7	6	1
Fort Atkinson	12,433	25	19	6
Fox Lake	1,470	3	2	1
Fox Point	6,754	17	16	1
Fox Valley Metro	21,515	31	29	2
Franklin	36,313	75	59	16
Frederic	1,099	1	1	0
Freedom	6,098	2	2	0
Galesville	1,565	4	4	0
Geneva Town	5,050	8	7	1
Genoa City	3,026	6	5	1
Germantown	20,042	43	33	10
Gillett	1,346	3	3	0
Gilman	395	2	1	1

Table 62. Full-Time Law Enforcement Employees, by Selected State and City, 2016—Continued

(Number.)

State/city	Population	Total law enforcement employees	Total officers	Total civilians
Glendale	12,846	48	43	5
Grafton	11,532	29	22	7
Grand Chute	22,463	35	30	5
Grand Rapids	7,466	8	6	2
Grantsburg	1,279	3	3	0
Green Bay	105,452	228	189	39
Greendale	14,367	38	29	9
Greenfield	37,405	75	57	18
Green Lake	989	3	3	0
Hales Corners	7,758	19	16	3
Hartford	14,377	28	24	4
Hartland	9,239	18	16	2
Hayward	2,287	8	7	1
Hazel Green	1,245	4	2	2
Highland	843	1	1	0
Hillsboro	1,422	2	2	0
Hobart-Lawrence	13,793	9	8	1
Holmen	9,760	12	11	1
Horicon	3,697	8	7	1
Hortonville	2,714	6	5	1
Hudson	13,740	27	24	3
Hurley	1,484	7	6	1
Independence	1,342	3	3	0
Iron Ridge	899	1	1	0
Iron River	1,128	1	1	0
Jackson	6,877	12	11	1
Janesville	64,234	108	97	11
Jefferson	7,935	17	14	3
Juneau	2,669	5	4	1
Kaukauna	15,928	27	26	1
Kenosha	99,954	208	199	9
Kewaskum	4,117	8	8	0
Kewaunee	2,862	6	6	0
Kiel	3,720	7	7	0
Kohler	2,108	8	7	1
Kronenwetter	7,714	8	7	1
La Crosse	52,498	109	92	17
Ladysmith	3,147	9	8	1
La Farge	773	1	1	0
Lake Delton	2,975	22	20	2
Lake Geneva	7,803	32	23	9
Lake Hallie	6,546	9	8	1
Lake Mills	5,816	12	10	2
Lancaster	3,760	9	8	1
Linn Township	2,404	6	6	0
Lodi	3,052	6	5	1
Lomira	2,376	4	3	1
Luxemburg	2,562	2	2	0
Madison	252,136	580	476	104
Manawa	1,306	3	3	0
Manitowoc	32,877	73	63	10
Maple Bluff	1,344	5	5	0
Marathon City	1,513	2	2	0
Marinette	10,771	28	24	4
Marion	1,213	3	3	0
Markesan	1,406	3	3	0
Marshall Village	3,940	9	8	1
Marshfield	18,530	47	39	8
Mauston	4,365	9	8	1
Mayville	4,958	9	8	1
McFarland	8,290	18	16	2
Medford	4,335	10	9	1
Menasha	17,609	37	30	7
Menomonee Falls	36,218	73	57	16
Menomonie	16,308	34	27	7
Mequon	24,114	47	38	9
Merrill	9,150	25	22	3
Middleton	19,263	48	38	10
Milton	5,601	13	11	2
Milwaukee	600,193	2,328	1,889	439
Mineral Point	2,496	5	5	0
Minocqua	4,438	16	11	5
Mishicot	1,401	2	2	0
Mondovi	2,631	4	4	0
Monona	8,288	24	20	4
Monroe	10,794	36	26	10
Montello	1,449	3	2	1
Mosinee	4,038	8	7	1
Mount Horeb	7,479	12	11	1
Mount Pleasant	26,286	53	48	5
Mukwonago	7,795	21	14	7
Mukwonago Town	8,147	7	6	1
Muscoda	1,259	3	3	0
Muskego	24,876	45	36	9
Neenah	25,850	51	41	10

Table 62. Full-Time Law Enforcement Employees, by Selected State and City, 2016—Continued

(Number.)

State/city	Population	Total law enforcement employees	Total officers	Total civilians
Neillsville	2,399	7	6	1
New Berlin	39,873	78	67	11
New Glarus	2,170	4	4	0
New Holstein	3,213	7	6	1
New Lisbon	2,473	4	4	0
New London	7,148	19	17	2
New Richmond	8,913	17	16	1
Niagara	1,580	4	4	0
North Fond du Lac	5,003	10	9	1
North Hudson	3,832	5	4	1
Oak Creek	35,337	78	56	22
Oconomowoc	16,480	29	22	7
Oconomowoc Lake	615	7	6	1
Oconomowoc Town	8,662	11	10	1
Oconto	4,468	9	9	0
Oconto Falls	2,823	5	5	0
Omro	3,560	7	6	1
Onalaska	18,600	29	26	3
Oregon	10,189	17	15	2
Osceola	2,502	6	5	1
Oshkosh	66,654	112	98	14
Osseo	1,703	4	4	0
Owen	929	3	3	0
Palmyra	1,775	3	3	0
Park Falls	2,311	14	7	7
Pepin	787	1	1	0
Peshtigo	3,416	7	6	1
Pewaukee Village	8,207	20	18	2
Phillips	1,371	5	5	0
Plainfield	829	2	2	0
Platteville	12,859	26	20	6
Pleasant Prairie	20,928	37	33	4
Plover	12,360	22	19	3
Plymouth	8,518	15	15	0
Portage	10,394	26	22	4
Port Washington	11,633	25	20	5
Poynette	2,485	5	4	1
Prairie du Chien	5,731	13	12	1
Prescott	4,197	10	9	1
Princeton	1,180	3	3	0
Pulaski	3,552	8	7	1
Racine	77,536	215	191	24
Reedsburg	9,605	27	20	7
Rhinelander	7,477	19	16	3
Rib Lake	891	1	1	0
Rice Lake	8,391	17	17	0
Richland Center	4,980	13	11	2
Rio	1,041	2	2	0
Ripon	7,694	20	14	6
Ripon Town	1,392	1	1	0
River Falls	15,314	27	24	3
River Hills	1,606	11	11	0
Rome Town	2,692	7	6	1
Rosendale	1,038	1	1	0
Rothschild	5,342	12	10	2
Sauk Prairie	4,640	15	13	2
Saukville	4,465	13	11	2
Seymour	3,437	6	6	0
Shawano	9,095	22	20	2
Sheboygan	48,710	101	82	19
Sheboygan Falls	7,849	15	14	1
Shiocton	921	1	1	0
Shorewood	13,319	27	23	4
Shorewood Hills	2,149	8	6	2
Siren	773	3	2	1
Slinger	5,232	11	10	1
South Milwaukee	21,212	39	33	6
Sparta	9,708	21	19	2
Spencer	1,920	3	3	0
Spooner	2,565	8	7	1
Spring Green	1,655	4	3	1
Stanley	3,560	5	5	0
St. Croix Falls	2,048	6	5	1
Stevens Point	26,587	48	44	4
St. Francis	9,580	21	20	1
Stoughton	13,148	28	22	6
Strum	1,127	2	2	0
Sturgeon Bay	8,925	22	20	2
Sturtevant	6,958	9	8	1
Summit	4,828	10	10	0
Sun Prairie	32,943	69	52	17
Superior	26,451	61	56	5
Theresa	1,204	2	2	0
Thiensville	3,167	7	6	1
Three Lakes	2,124	5	5	0

Table 62. Full-Time Law Enforcement Employees, by Selected State and City, 2016—Continued

(Number.)

State/city	Population	Total law enforcement employees	Total officers	Total civilians
Tomah	9,398	22	20	2
Tomahawk	3,189	9	8	1
Town of East Troy	4,094	12	6	6
Town of Madison	6,878	15	14	1
Town of Menasha	19,083	31	25	6
Trempealeau	1,632	2	2	0
Twin Lakes	6,119	18	13	5
Two Rivers	11,259	27	24	3
Verona	12,942	23	21	2
Viroqua	4,364	11	9	2
Walworth	2,843	7	6	1
Washburn	2,043	5	5	0
Waterloo	3,345	9	8	1
Watertown	23,816	51	38	13
Waukesha	72,223	150	118	32
Waunakee	13,556	21	19	2
Waupaca	6,001	15	14	1
Waupun	11,342	16	15	1
Wausau	39,091	81	72	9
Wautoma	2,120	6	5	1
Wauwatosa	47,771	113	87	26
West Allis	60,558	153	126	27
West Bend	31,791	70	53	17
Westby	2,276	3	3	0
Westfield	1,221	2	2	0
West Milwaukee	4,206	24	19	5
West Salem	5,055	8	7	1
Whitefish Bay	14,087	25	24	1
Whitehall	1,570	4	4	0
Whitewater	14,752	34	24	10
Wild Rose	694	2	2	0
Williams Bay	2,605	7	6	1
Winneconne	2,458	11	5	6
Wisconsin Dells	2,702	19	14	5
Wisconsin Rapids	17,802	41	37	4
Woodruff	1,979	6	5	1
WYOMING				
Afton	1,983	4	4	0
Buffalo	4,640	22	13	9
Casper	61,343	129	93	36
Cheyenne	64,046	123	102	21
Cody	9,842	24	21	3
Diamondville	738	4	3	1
Douglas	6,617	25	17	8
Evanston	12,087	30	25	5
Evansville	2,999	10	8	2
Gillette	33,218	78	51	27
Glenrock	2,603	13	7	6
Green River	12,477	32	27	5
Greybull	1,886	6	5	1
Hanna	809	1	1	0
Jackson	10,713	37	30	7
Kemmerer	2,757	7	7	0
Lander	7,699	20	19	1
Laramie	32,411	71	46	25
Mills	3,854	17	13	4
Moorcroft	1,072	4	3	1
Newcastle	3,537	16	8	8
Pine Bluffs	1,149	1	1	0
Powell	6,491	24	17	7
Rawlins	9,004	28	18	10
Riverton	10,905	41	28	13
Rock Springs	24,161	58	46	12
Saratoga	1,675	9	4	5
Sheridan	17,956	44	28	16
Sundance	1,289	3	3	0
Thermopolis	2,967	11	6	5
Torrington	6,676	24	17	7
Wheatland	3,665	9	8	1
Worland	5,348	11	10	1

1 The employee data presented in this table for Charlotte-Mecklenburg represent only Charlotte-Mecklenburg Police Department and exclude Mecklenburg County Sheriff's Office.

Table 63. Full-Time Law Enforcement Employees, by Selected State and University or College, 2016

(Number.)

State and university/college	Student enrollment[1]	Law enforcement employees	Officers	Civilians
ALABAMA				
Bishop State Community College	3,111	9	7	2
Jacksonville State University	8,314	18	13	5
Northwest-Shoals Community College	3,700	6	4	2
Troy University	17,765	29	27	2
Tuskegee University	2,996	24	10	14
University of Alabama				
Huntsville	7,866	23	16	7
Tuscaloosa	37,098	105	87	18
University of Montevallo	3,031	21	10	11
University of North Alabama	7,078	16	14	2
University of South Alabama	16,211	36	30	6
University of West Alabama	4,032	14	9	5
Wallace Community College, Selma	1,591	6	3	3
ALASKA				
University of Alaska				
Anchorage	16,762	17	11	6
Fairbanks	8,638	12	6	6
ARIZONA				
Arizona State University, Main Campus	90,906	154	86	68
Arizona Western College	7,514	13	8	5
Central Arizona College	5,849	9	8	1
Northern Arizona University	29,021	34	21	13
Pima Community College	26,880	49	29	20
University of Arizona	42,595	112	59	53
Yavapai College	7,385	10	7	3
ARKANSAS				
Arkansas State University				
Beebe	3,935	6	5	1
Jonesboro	13,410	23	19	4
Newport	2,651	1	1	0
Arkansas Tech University	12,054	17	16	1
Henderson State University	3,527	9	8	1
Southern Arkansas University	4,095	10	8	2
Southern Arkansas University Tech	1,650	3	3	0
University of Arkansas				
Fayetteville	26,754	53	37	16
Little Rock	11,891	48	29	19
Medical Sciences	3,021	52	40	12
Monticello	3,643	9	8	1
Pine Bluff	2,658	16	12	4
University of Central Arkansas	11,754	37	27	10
CALIFORNIA				
Allan Hancock College	10,949	10	5	5
California State Polytechnic University				
Pomona	23,717	41	18	23
San Luis Obispo	20,944	35	19	16
California State University				
Bakersfield	9,228	21	13	8
Channel Islands	6,167	29	15	14
Chico	17,220	27	16	11
Dominguez Hills	14,635	25	19	6
East Bay	15,528	24	13	11
Fresno	24,136	37	23	14
Fullerton	38,948	40	26	14
Long Beach	37,446	42	26	16
Los Angeles	27,680	28	17	11
Monterey Bay	7,102	27	15	12
Northridge	41,548	35	20	15
Sacramento	30,284	36	22	14
San Bernardino	20,024	26	14	12
San Jose	32,773	70	26	44
San Marcos	12,793	26	21	5
Stanislaus	9,282	19	11	8
College of the Sequoias	11,266	6	5	1
Contra Costa Community College	34,910	34	22	12
Cuesta College	9,600	12	7	5
El Camino College	24,001	32	23	9
Foothill-De Anza College	37,960	13	10	3
Humboldt State University	8,790	20	12	8
Irvine Valley College	13,183	14	9	5
Marin Community College	5,490	6	4	2
Pasadena Community College	27,050	11	6	5
Riverside Community College	37,594	24	18	6
San Bernardino Community College	19,121	18	8	10
San Diego State University	34,254	49	24	25
San Francisco State University	30,256	47	24	23
San Jose/Evergreen Community College	17,136	15	7	8
Santa Rosa Junior College	22,411	26	13	13
Sonoma State University	9,408	21	14	7
State Center Community College District	32,533	17	11	6

Table 63. Full-Time Law Enforcement Employees, by Selected State and University or College, 2016—Continued

(Number.)

State and university/college	Student enrollment[1]	Law enforcement employees	Officers	Civilians
University of California				
Berkeley	38,189	125	58	67
Davis	35,186	73	46	27
Irvine	30,836	59	41	18
Los Angeles	41,908	99	58	41
Merced	6,685	21	12	9
Riverside	21,385	44	31	13
San Diego	32,906	69	36	33
San Francisco	3,107	139	53	86
Santa Barbara	23,497	54	39	15
Santa Cruz	17,868	29	17	12
Ventura County Community College District	34,022	17	16	1
West Valley-Mission College	17,375	13	9	4
COLORADO				
Adams State University	3,404	6	5	1
Arapahoe Community College	10,004	12	8	4
Auraria Higher Education Center[2]		45	27	18
Colorado School of Mines	6,054	11	10	1
Colorado State University, Fort Collins	30,614	46	32	14
Fort Lewis College	3,707	10	8	2
Pikes Peak Community College	13,311	20	18	2
Red Rocks Community College	7,789	9	6	3
University of Colorado				
University of Colorado	33,056	74	38	36
Boulder	11,988	30	16	14
Colorado Springs	23,671	62	25	37
Denver	12,216	24	16	8
CONNECTICUT				
Central Connecticut State University	12,086	26	19	7
Eastern Connecticut State University	5,261	24	14	10
Southern Connecticut State University	10,473	33	27	6
University of Connecticut				
Health Center[2]		45	19	26
Storrs, Avery Point and Hartford[2]		88	77	11
Western Connecticut State University	5,826	18	12	6
Yale University	12,385	104	87	17
DELAWARE				
Delaware State University	4,288	39	15	24
University of Delaware	22,852	75	49	26
FLORIDA				
Florida A&M University	9,928	36	30	6
Florida Atlantic University	30,380	60	36	24
Florida Gulf Coast University	14,833	26	18	8
Florida International University	49,782	83	56	27
Florida SouthWestern State College	15,709	22	11	11
New College of Florida	861	17	11	6
Pensacola State College	9,840	11	9	2
Santa Fe College	14,767	22	16	6
Tallahassee Community College	12,445	23	12	11
University of Central Florida	62,953	130	72	58
University of Florida	50,645	127	82	45
University of North Florida	15,675	39	29	10
University of South Florida				
St. Petersburg	4,739	22	16	6
Tampa	42,067	68	51	17
University of West Florida	12,763	27	19	8
GEORGIA				
Abraham Baldwin Agricultural College	3,393	14	13	1
Agnes Scott College	902	16	9	7
Albany State University	3,492	42	26	16
Andrew College	311	2	2	0
Armstrong State University	7,103	23	15	8
Augusta Technical College	4,490	3	3	0
Augusta University	8,333	62	45	17
Bainbridge State College	2,401	8	5	3
Berry College	2,245	18	13	5
Chattahoochee Technical College	9,817	13	10	3
Dalton State College	5,044	16	13	3
Emory University	13,788	70	52	18
Georgia College and State University	6,889	23	17	6
Georgia Gwinnett College	11,468	26	22	4
Georgia Institute of Technology	25,034	97	71	26
Georgia Military College	7,876	5	3	2
Georgia Southern University	20,459	51	40	11
Georgia Southwestern State University	2,755	13	13	0
Georgia State University	32,058	261	120	141
Gordon State College	4,084	13	12	1
Gwinnett Technical College	6,959	2	1	1
Kennesaw State University	33,252	106	57	49
Mercer University	8,600	31	22	9

Table 63. Full-Time Law Enforcement Employees, by Selected State and University or College, 2016—Continued

(Number.)

State and university/college	Student enrollment[1]	Law enforcement employees	Officers	Civilians
Middle Georgia State University	7,676	31	29	2
Morehouse College	2,167	22	7	15
Savannah State University	4,800	58	29	29
Southern Crescent Technical College	4,867	5	5	0
South Georgia State College	2,648	11	8	3
Spelman College	2,144	31	18	13
University of Georgia	36,130	105	83	22
University of North Georgia	17,289	41	32	9
University of West Georgia	12,834	38	27	11
Valdosta State University	11,302	29	21	8
Wesleyan College	708	9	9	0
West Georgia Technical College	6,431	7	7	0
ILLINOIS				
Illinois Central College	9,704	20	7	13
John Wood Community College	2,016	5	4	1
Joliet Junior College	14,944	22	13	9
Lincoln Land Community College	6,447	15	13	2
Parkland College	8,147	18	15	3
Prairie State College	4,699	12	12	0
Rend Lake College	2,303	3	3	0
Southern Illinois University				
Carbondale	17,292	56	37	19
Edwardsville	14,265	47	37	10
School of Medicine[2]		7	7	0
Triton College	11,684	13	8	5
University of Illinois, Springfield	5,402	22	15	7
INDIANA				
Indiana University				
Bloomington	48,514	39	38	1
Southeast	6,173	12	10	2
Purdue University	40,472	51	35	16
IOWA				
Iowa State University	35,714	50	36	14
University of Iowa	30,844	64	36	28
University of Northern Iowa	11,981	17	14	3
KANSAS				
Butler Community College	8,950	10	8	2
Emporia State University	6,094	9	8	1
Fort Hays State University	14,210	8	8	0
Garden City Community College	2,099	2	2	0
Kansas City Kansas Community College	5,625	18	17	1
Kansas State University	24,146	41	21	20
University of Kansas, Main Campus	27,259	60	23	37
Washburn University	6,615	21	17	4
KENTUCKY				
Murray State University	10,998	16	16	0
Northern Kentucky University	14,699	20	15	5
Transylvania University	1,053	11	9	2
Western Kentucky University	20,063	30	21	9
LOUISIANA				
Louisiana State University				
Baton Rouge	31,524	70	54	16
Health Sciences Center, New Orleans	2,791	32	32	0
Health Sciences Center, Shreveport	891	44	29	15
Shreveport	4,428	8	7	1
McNeese State University	8,153	15	9	6
Nicholls State University	6,158	13	9	4
Northwestern State University	9,179	22	22	0
Southeastern Louisiana University	14,581	28	24	4
Southern University and A&M College				
New Orleans	2,792	15	15	0
Shreveport	3,174	10	9	1
Tulane University	12,485	109	79	30
University of Louisiana, Monroe	8,804	20	19	1
University of New Orleans	8,423	20	19	1
MAINE				
University of Maine				
Farmington	2,016	5	4	1
Orono	10,922	26	17	9
University of Southern Maine	7,739	18	10	8
MARYLAND				
Bowie State University	5,430	27	14	13
Coppin State University	3,108	31	22	9
Frostburg State University	5,756	22	18	4
Hagerstown Community College	4,276	2	2	0
Morgan State University	7,725	59	37	22
Salisbury University	8,671	30	17	13

Table 63. Full-Time Law Enforcement Employees, by Selected State and University or College, 2016—Continued

(Number.)

State and university/college	Student enrollment[1]	Law enforcement employees	Officers	Civilians
St. Mary's College	1,735	16	3	13
Towson University	22,284	53	36	17
University of Baltimore	6,229	30	19	11
University of Maryland				
Baltimore City	6,329	140	53	87
Baltimore County	13,839	34	25	9
College Park	38,140	127	83	44
Eastern Shore	4,465	18	14	4
MASSACHUSETTS				
Amherst College	1,795	19	14	5
Assumption College	2,675	25	18	7
Babson College	3,057	29	20	9
Becker College	2,153	18	12	6
Bentley University	5,552	33	22	11
Boston College	14,354	69	48	21
Boston University	32,158	68	53	15
Brandeis University	5,752	25	22	3
Bridgewater State University	11,089	22	19	3
Bristol Community College	8,761	9	8	1
Bunker Hill Community College	13,142	16	15	1
Cape Cod Community College	3,627	3	3	0
Clark University	3,485	14	12	2
College of the Holy Cross	2,729	26	19	7
Dean College	1,363	15	1	14
Emerson College	4,479	23	20	3
Endicott College	4,695	21	17	4
Fisher College	1,959	8	7	1
Fitchburg State University	6,598	21	16	5
Framingham State University	6,398	19	15	4
Gordon College	2,045	5	5	0
Greenfield Community College	2,050	5	4	1
Harvard University	29,652	99	77	22
Holyoke Community College	6,285	28	27	1
Massachusetts Bay Community College	4,859	7	7	0
Massachusetts College of Art	1,990	31	11	20
Massachusetts College of Liberal Arts	1,641	15	10	5
Massachusetts Institute of Technology	11,331	61	58	3
Massasoit Community College	7,637	19	17	2
Merrimack College	3,620	18	14	4
Mount Holyoke College	2,215	52	38	14
Mount Wachusett Community College	4,074	11	10	1
Northeastern University	19,940	94	62	32
North Shore Community College	6,961	22	20	2
Quinsigamond Community College	8,064	17	14	3
Regis College	1,954	9	7	2
Salem State University	9,215	23	19	4
Springfield College	3,241	21	15	6
Springfield Technical Community College	6,286	19	16	3
Stonehill College	2,400	22	16	6
Tufts University, Medford	11,137	81	43	38
University of Massachusetts				
Amherst	29,269	69	60	9
Dartmouth	8,916	34	24	10
Harbor Campus, Boston	17,030	38	26	12
Medical Center, Worcester	1,079	32	27	5
Wellesley College	2,510	19	14	5
Wentworth Institute of Technology	4,576	20	13	7
Western New England University	3,912	29	17	12
Westfield State University	6,496	25	19	6
Wheaton College	1,598	15	12	3
Worcester Polytechnic Institute	6,573	24	18	6
MICHIGAN				
Central Michigan University	26,825	37	23	14
Delta College	9,291	8	5	3
Eastern Michigan University	21,824	43	34	9
Ferris State University	14,715	17	13	4
Grand Rapids Community College	14,926	17	13	4
Grand Valley State University	25,325	22	18	4
Kalamazoo Valley Community College	8,836	9	6	3
Kellogg Community College	5,081	2	2	0
Kirtland Community College	1,628	1	1	0
Lansing Community College	14,851	16	12	4
Macomb Community College	22,182	33	27	6
Michigan State University	50,538	113	85	28
Michigan Technological University	7,218	15	12	3
Mott Community College	8,617	15	12	3
Northern Michigan University	8,303	24	21	3
Oakland Community College	21,061	26	25	1
Oakland University	20,261	28	21	7
Saginaw Valley State University	9,633	9	8	1
Schoolcraft College	11,687	11	9	2
University of Michigan				
Ann Arbor	43,651	76	59	17

Table 63. Full-Time Law Enforcement Employees, by Selected State and University or College, 2016—Continued

(Number.)

State and university/college	Student enrollment[1]	Law enforcement employees	Officers	Civilians
Dearborn	9,066	25	10	15
Flint	8,470	32	19	13
Western Michigan University	23,529	40	32	8
MINNESOTA				
University of Minnesota				
Duluth	10,878	10	8	2
Morris	1,856	5	3	2
Twin Cities	50,678	63	51	12
MISSISSIPPI				
Coahoma Community College	2,148	8	7	1
Mississippi State University	20,873	47	37	10
University of Mississippi				
Medical Center[2]		90	58	32
Oxford	23,212	44	28	16
MISSOURI				
Jefferson College	4,705	7	7	0
Metropolitan Community College	17,821	37	27	10
Mineral Area College	4,388	4	4	0
Missouri Southern State University	5,783	8	7	1
Missouri University of Science and Technology	8,886	22	12	10
Missouri Western State University	5,513	12	10	2
Southeast Missouri State University	11,987	23	17	6
St. Charles Community College	6,865	14	11	3
St. Louis Community College				
Florissant Valley[2]		11	9	2
Meramec	18,902	14	11	3
Truman State University	6,208	12	10	2
University of Central Missouri	14,395	24	18	6
University of Missouri				
Columbia	35,424	62	40	22
Kansas City	16,685	39	26	13
St. Louis	16,738	27	21	6
MONTANA				
Montana State University	15,236	31	18	13
NEBRASKA				
Metropolitan Community College, Douglas County	14,812	22	17	5
University of Nebraska				
Kearney	6,747	11	10	1
Lincoln	25,260	60	34	26
NEVADA				
College of Southern Nevada	33,313	40	19	21
University of Nevada				
Las Vegas	28,600	57	39	18
Reno	20,898	38	30	8
NEW HAMPSHIRE				
University of New Hampshire	15,351	31	17	14
NEW JERSEY				
Brookdale Community College	13,835	13	12	1
Essex County College	10,954	66	10	56
Kean University	14,112	43	21	22
Middlesex County College	11,662	17	12	5
Monmouth University	6,394	41	19	22
Montclair State University	20,465	47	37	10
New Jersey Institute of Technology	11,325	65	33	32
Princeton University	8,138	100	32	68
Rowan University	16,155	85	32	53
Rutgers University				
Camden	6,408	93	19	74
Newark	11,720	200	61	139
New Brunswick	49,428	122	68	54
Stevens Institute of Technology	6,359	22	20	2
Stockton University	8,674	26	18	8
The College of New Jersey	7,406	30	18	12
William Paterson University	10,862	43	29	14
NEW MEXICO				
Eastern New Mexico University	5,725	9	8	1
New Mexico Military Institute	428	5	5	0
University of New Mexico	27,285	57	40	17
Western New Mexico University	3,354	7	6	1
NEW YORK				
Cornell University	21,904	70	45	25
Ithaca College	6,769	33	16	17
State University of New York				
Albany	17,178	58	39	19

Table 63. Full-Time Law Enforcement Employees, by Selected State and University or College, 2016—Continued

(Number.)

State and university/college	Student enrollment[1]	Law enforcement employees	Officers	Civilians
Binghamton	16,913	48	32	16
Buffalo	29,796	69	56	13
Downstate Medical Center	1,858	103	25	78
Stony Brook	25,272	143	68	75
Upstate Medical Center	1,480	106	18	88
State University of New York Agricultural and Technical College				
Alfred	3,699	15	10	5
Canton	3,140	9	8	1
Cobleskill	2,441	11	10	1
Farmingdale	8,648	31	21	10
Morrisville	2,940	14	12	2
State University of New York College				
Brockport	8,161	18	16	2
Buffalo	10,330	35	32	3
Cortland	6,926	24	18	6
Environmental Science and Forestry	2,222	9	8	1
Fredonia	4,842	16	15	1
Geneseo	5,699	22	15	7
New Paltz	7,751	25	21	4
Old Westbury	4,353	21	16	5
Oneonta	6,119	26	17	9
Optometry	381	15	6	9
Oswego	7,937	27	21	6
Plattsburgh	5,718	19	15	4
Potsdam	3,904	12	9	3
Technology	3,457	13	11	2
Utica-Rome	2,779	16	11	5
NORTH CAROLINA				
Appalachian State University	17,932	42	25	17
Beaufort County Community College	1,820	3	3	0
Belmont Abbey College	1,495	4	4	0
Davidson College	1,784	10	9	1
Duke University	15,984	153	61	92
East Carolina University	28,289	64	51	13
Elizabeth City State University	1,585	21	11	10
Elon University	6,631	24	16	8
Fayetteville State University	6,104	56	19	37
Methodist University	2,474	24	11	13
North Carolina Agricultural and Technical State University	10,852	42	16	26
North Carolina Central University	8,011	51	25	26
North Carolina School of the Arts	970	22	15	7
North Carolina State University, Raleigh	34,015	66	52	14
Queens University	2,286	11	8	3
Saint Augustine's University	810	20	1	19
University of North Carolina				
Asheville	3,891	22	15	7
Chapel Hill	29,084	107	53	54
Charlotte	27,983	48	38	10
Greensboro	19,393	53	34	19
Pembroke	6,441	21	17	4
Wilmington	14,918	44	30	14
Wake Forest University	7,837	47	23	24
Western Carolina University	10,340	19	19	0
Winston-Salem State University	5,107	40	15	25
NORTH DAKOTA				
Bismarck State College	4,078	3	2	1
North Dakota State College of Science	3,123	4	3	1
North Dakota State University	14,516	26	17	9
University of North Dakota	14,951	21	19	2
OHIO				
Bowling Green State University	16,908	30	22	8
Columbus State Community College	25,983	50	29	21
Miami University	19,076	34	25	9
Notre Dame College	2,094	11	9	2
Ohio State University, Columbus	58,663	57	47	10
Ohio University	29,157	36	29	7
Otterbein University	2,808	10	9	1
Sinclair Community College	18,136	22	18	4
University of Cincinnati	36,042	134	68	66
University of Toledo	20,377	41	33	8
Wright State University	17,070	27	18	9
OKLAHOMA				
Cameron University	5,177	13	13	0
East Central University	4,444	6	5	1
Langston University	2,543	16	12	4
Northeastern Oklahoma A&M College	2,107	6	6	0
Northeastern State University, Tahlequah	8,251	19	15	4
Oklahoma City University	2,991	12	8	4

Table 63. Full-Time Law Enforcement Employees, by Selected State and University or College, 2016—Continued

(Number.)

State and university/college	Student enrollment[1]	Law enforcement employees	Officers	Civilians
Oklahoma State University				
Main Campus	25,930	45	34	11
Okmulgee	2,617	7	6	1
Tulsa	787	8	6	2
Rogers State University	4,081	9	9	0
Seminole State College	1,839	2	2	0
Southeastern Oklahoma State University	3,754	6	5	1
Southwestern Oklahoma State University	5,113	7	6	1
Tulsa Community College	17,160	34	27	7
University of Central Oklahoma	16,910	28	17	11
University of Oklahoma				
Health Sciences Center	3,389	60	39	21
Norman	27,428	67	40	27
OREGON				
Portland State University	27,488	29	10	19
University of Oregon	24,032	42	23	19
PENNSYLVANIA				
Bloomsburg University	9,737	21	16	5
California University	7,854	21	17	4
Cheyney University	711	16	9	7
Clarion University	5,368	14	8	6
Dickinson College	2,420	20	14	6
East Stroudsburg University	6,828	14	11	3
Edinboro University	6,548	15	14	1
Indiana University	13,835	31	21	10
Kutztown University	8,995	19	16	3
Lehigh University	7,054	35	26	9
Lock Haven University	4,607	12	9	3
Mansfield University	2,352	11	8	3
Millersville University	7,959	16	14	2
Moravian College	2,261	17	14	3
Pennsylvania State University				
Altoona	3,839	9	7	2
Beaver	705	6	6	0
Behrend	4,327	11	7	4
Berks	2,906	9	8	1
Brandywine	1,457	3	3	0
Greater Allegheny	577	5	5	0
Harrisburg	4,678	9	8	1
Hazleton	831	5	5	0
Mont Alto	893	5	5	0
Schuylkill	783	4	4	0
University Park	47,307	74	44	30
Wilkes-Barre	501	1	1	0
Worthington Scranton	1,034	2	2	0
Shippensburg University	7,048	18	16	2
Slippery Rock University	8,611	19	12	7
University of Pittsburgh				
Bradford	1,453	8	6	2
Greensburg	1,562	9	8	1
Johnstown	2,816	13	12	1
Pittsburgh	28,649	159	98	61
Titusville	346	7	6	1
West Chester University	16,597	22	22	0
RHODE ISLAND				
Brown University	9,458	94	53	41
University of Rhode Island	16,613	32	27	5
SOUTH CAROLINA				
Bob Jones University	3,005	4	4	0
Clemson University	22,698	45	34	11
Coastal Carolina University	10,263	82	33	49
College of Charleston	11,531	40	29	11
Columbia College	1,484	11	9	2
Denmark Technical College	1,043	6	1	5
Erskine College	761	3	2	1
Francis Marion University	3,947	14	9	5
Furman University	2,884	20	14	6
Greenville Technical College	12,280	17	9	8
Lander University	2,701	20	13	7
Medical University of South Carolina	2,992	77	56	21
Midlands Technical College	10,946	10	10	0
Orangeburg-Calhoun Technical College	2,774	5	5	0
Presbyterian College	1,379	8	7	1
South Carolina State University	3,054	22	12	10
Spartanburg Methodist College	771	4	4	0
The Citadel	3,506	16	14	2
Tri-County Technical College	6,128	13	8	5
Trident Technical College	15,043	30	24	6
University of South Carolina				
Aiken	3,448	7	6	1
Beaufort	1,980	11	11	0
Columbia	33,724	83	65	18

Table 63. Full-Time Law Enforcement Employees, by Selected State and University or College, 2016—Continued

(Number.)

State and university/college	Student enrollment[1]	Law enforcement employees	Officers	Civilians
Upstate	5,996	15	14	1
Winthrop University	6,031	20	14	6
SOUTH DAKOTA				
South Dakota State University	12,576	17	12	5
TENNESSEE				
Austin Peay State University	10,099	26	17	9
Chattanooga State Community College	9,374	15	8	7
Christian Brothers University	1,842	18	6	12
Cleveland State Community College	3,509	4	3	1
East Tennessee State University	14,334	26	19	7
Jackson State Community College	4,746	5	4	1
Lincoln Memorial University	3,983	24	8	16
Middle Tennessee State University	22,511	42	33	9
Motlow State Community College	5,256	2	2	0
Northeast State Community College	6,084	8	8	0
Pellissippi State Community College	10,325	12	4	8
Roane State Community College	5,861	7	7	0
Southwest Tennessee Community College	9,135	20	17	3
Tennessee State University	9,167	44	30	14
Tennessee Technological University	10,900	21	13	8
University of Memphis	20,585	70	41	29
University of Tennessee				
Chattanooga	11,387	26	16	10
Health Science Center	3,075	53	22	31
Knoxville	27,845	93	53	40
Martin	6,827	15	11	4
University of the South	1,797	14	10	4
Vanderbilt University	12,567	268	97	171
Volunteer State Community College	8,098	12	9	3
Walters State Community College	5,947	9	7	2
TEXAS				
Abilene Christian University	4,544	15	14	1
Alamo Community College District	57,165	91	75	16
Alvin Community College	5,114	13	11	2
Amarillo College	9,936	12	11	1
Angelo State University	8,483	16	11	5
Austin College	1,255	7	6	1
Baylor Health Care System[3]		169	58	111
Baylor University, Waco	16,787	56	36	20
Brookhaven College	10,553	26	16	10
Central Texas College	19,562	8	7	1
College of the Mainland	4,013	7	7	0
El Paso Community College	28,764	43	36	7
Grayson College	4,591	6	5	1
Hardin-Simmons University	2,112	8	7	1
Houston Baptist University	3,160	16	13	3
Houston Community College	56,522	111	72	39
Lamar University, Beaumont	14,965	59	26	33
Laredo Community College	8,749	24	22	2
McLennan Community College	8,305	14	9	5
Midwestern State University	6,043	14	9	5
Mountain View College	8,539	12	12	0
North Lake College	9,871	25	24	1
Paris Junior College	4,999	4	4	0
Prairie View A&M University	8,315	24	19	5
Rice University	6,719	48	31	17
Southern Methodist University	11,643	37	29	8
South Plains College	9,126	6	6	0
Southwestern University	1,515	7	6	1
Stephen F. Austin State University	12,606	49	26	23
St. Mary's University	3,625	21	17	4
Sul Ross State University	2,967	10	8	2
Tarleton State University	12,330	19	15	4
Texas A&M International University	7,192	29	19	10
Texas A&M University				
Central Texas	2,466	11	7	4
College Station	63,813	132	65	67
Commerce	12,928	31	20	11
Corpus Christi	11,661	32	17	15
Galveston[2]		10	9	1
Kingsville	9,207	21	16	5
San Antonio	4,564	18	12	6
Texas Christian University	10,323	56	32	24
Texas Southern University	8,965	76	31	45
Texas State Technical College				
Harlingen[2]		13	10	3
Waco[2]		12	11	1
West Texas[2]		5	5	0
Texas State University, San Marcos	37,979	46	33	13
Texas Tech University, Lubbock	35,859	133	60	73
Texas Woman's University	15,286	45	16	29
Trinity University	2,438	26	18	8

Table 63. Full-Time Law Enforcement Employees, by Selected State and University or College, 2016—Continued

(Number.)

State and university/college	Student enrollment[1]	Law enforcement employees	Officers	Civilians
Tyler Junior College	10,934	26	20	6
University of Houston				
Central Campus	42,704	119	50	69
Clearlake	8,906	30	17	13
Downtown Campus	14,262	41	23	18
University of Mary Hardin-Baylor	3,898	15	12	3
University of North Texas				
Denton	37,299	60	39	21
Health Science Center	2,382	21	12	9
University of Texas				
Arlington	41,988	100	35	65
Austin	50,950	163	89	74
Brownsville	4,029	70	35	35
Dallas	24,554	70	27	43
El Paso	23,397	56	27	29
Health Science Center, Tyler[2]		29	8	21
Houston	5,115	356	96	260
Permian Basin	6,077	25	15	10
San Antonio	28,787	119	47	72
Southwestern Medical School	2,295	141	43	98
Tyler	8,785	29	12	17
West Texas A&M University	9,489	21	15	6
UTAH				
Brigham Young University	33,469	42	30	12
Southern Utah University	8,881	6	5	1
University of Utah	31,592	129	37	92
Utah State University				
Eastern[2]		2	2	0
Logan	28,622	18	12	6
Utah Valley University	33,211	13	11	2
Weber State University	25,955	13	11	2
VERMONT				
University of Vermont	12,815	33	21	12
VIRGINIA				
Bridgewater College	1,834	13	7	6
Christopher Newport University	5,172	27	18	9
College of William and Mary	8,484	28	20	8
Eastern Virginia Medical School	1,096	47	21	26
Emory and Henry College	1,117	6	2	4
Ferrum College	1,334	8	8	0
George Mason University	33,929	50	41	9
Germanna Community College	6,993	7	3	4
Hampton University	4,269	44	22	22
James Madison University	21,227	40	31	9
J. Sargeant Reynolds Community College	10,889	21	13	8
Longwood University	5,087	28	19	9
Lord Fairfax Community College	7,002	4	4	0
Norfolk State University	5,107	45	17	28
Northern Virginia Community College	52,078	57	45	12
Old Dominion University	24,672	63	51	12
Radford University	9,743	32	25	7
Richard Bland College	2,255	5	4	1
Thomas Nelson Community College	9,316	10	8	2
University of Mary Washington	4,647	22	16	6
University of Richmond	4,181	34	22	12
University of Virginia	23,883	118	54	64
University of Virginia's College at Wise	2,027	10	9	1
Virginia Commonwealth University	30,918	120	88	32
Virginia Military Institute	1,717	12	11	1
Virginia Polytechnic Institute and State University	32,663	64	47	17
Virginia State University	4,696	34	21	13
Virginia Western Community College	7,932	9	9	0
WASHINGTON				
Central Washington University	11,993	16	14	2
Eastern Washington University	12,361	18	17	1
Evergreen State College	4,190	15	9	6
University of Washington	45,408	81	42	39
Washington State University				
Pullman	29,686	23	18	5
Vancouver[2]		6	3	3
Western Washington University	15,332	20	15	5
WEST VIRGINIA				
Bluefield State College	1,486	2	2	0
Concord University	2,507	9	6	3
Fairmont State University	4,041	12	9	3
Glenville State College	1,732	5	3	2
Marshall University	13,621	21	20	1
Potomac State College	1,475	7	6	1
Shepherd University	3,861	12	10	2
West Liberty University	2,341	5	5	0

Table 63. Full-Time Law Enforcement Employees, by Selected State and University or College, 2016—Continued

(Number.)

State and university/college	Student enrollment[1]	Law enforcement employees	Officers	Civilians
West Virginia State University	3,166	8	5	3
West Virginia Tech	1,263	7	7	0
West Virginia University	28,776	79	56	23
WISCONSIN				
University of Wisconsin				
Eau Claire	10,592	11	11	0
Green Bay	6,784	11	10	1
La Crosse	10,490	15	12	3
Madison	42,716	117	60	57
Milwaukee	26,726	45	33	12
Oshkosh	14,051	14	11	3
Parkside	4,412	13	9	4
Platteville	8,945	10	8	2
River Falls	5,949	5	5	0
Stevens Point	9,265	5	3	2
Stout	9,554	11	9	2
Superior	2,497	7	2	5
Whitewater	12,360	16	14	2
WYOMING				
University of Wyoming	12,648	24	14	10

1 The student enrollment figures provided by the United States Department of Education are for the 2015 school year, the most recent available. The enrollment figures include full-time and part-time students.   2 Student enrollment figures were not available.

Table 64. Full-Time Law Enforcement Employees, by Selected State Metropolitan and Nonmetropolitan Counties, 2016

(Number.)

State/county	Total law enforcement employees	Total officers	Total civilians
ALABAMA			
Metropolitan Counties			
Autauga	74	37	37
Baldwin	288	115	173
Bibb	12	11	1
Calhoun	55	50	5
Chilton	32	28	4
Elmore	108	48	60
Etowah	156	61	95
Geneva	27	13	14
Hale	27	11	16
Henry	20	16	4
Houston	152	62	90
Lauderdale	42	36	6
Lee	176	79	97
Limestone	117	47	70
Lowndes	37	17	20
Mobile	541	188	353
Montgomery	169	129	40
Pickens	33	9	24
Russell	128	40	88
St. Clair	56	48	8
Tuscaloosa	204	101	103
Walker	83	34	49
Nonmetropolitan Counties			
Bullock	13	6	7
Clay	26	10	16
Cleburne	27	10	17
Conecuh	39	13	26
Coosa	25	11	14
Covington	28	25	3
Dale	49	25	24
Dallas	50	23	27
Escambia	66	27	39
Greene	32	14	18
Lamar	18	7	11
Macon	35	12	23
Marion	31	15	16
Marshall	73	39	34
Pike	28	17	11
Talladega	101	38	63
Tallapoosa	57	25	32
Winston	28	10	18
ARIZONA			
Metropolitan Counties			
Cochise	116	81	35
Coconino	239	56	183
Maricopa	3,397	706	2,691
Mohave	250	80	170
Pima	1,465	512	953
Pinal	352	155	197
Yavapai	171	110	61
Yuma	310	72	238
Nonmetropolitan Counties			
Apache	70	31	39
Gila	190	44	146
Graham	76	23	53
Greenlee	42	12	30
La Paz	85	30	55
Navajo	141	56	85
Santa Cruz	87	35	52
ARKANSAS			
Metropolitan Counties			
Benton	218	135	83
Cleveland	12	7	5
Craighead	121	45	76
Crawford	70	33	37
Crittenden	143	40	103
Faulkner	164	47	117
Garland	184	56	128
Grant	17	14	3
Jefferson	115	43	72
Lincoln	21	9	12
Little River	29	12	17
Lonoke	67	31	36
Madison	19	9	10
Miller	68	24	44
Perry	21	11	10
Poinsett	37	10	27

Table 64. Full-time Law Enforcement Employees, by Selected State Metropolitan and Nonmetropolitan Counties, 2016—Continued

(Number.)

State/county	Total law enforcement employees	Total officers	Total civilians
Pulaski	516	125	391
Saline	93	48	45
Sebastian	161	41	120
Washington	274	150	124
Nonmetropolitan Counties			
Arkansas	50	11	39
Ashley	36	17	19
Baxter	52	32	20
Boone	52	25	27
Bradley	7	5	2
Calhoun	12	6	6
Carroll	23	20	3
Chicot	11	7	4
Clark	27	13	14
Clay	26	10	16
Cleburne	42	23	19
Columbia	39	22	17
Conway	41	18	23
Cross	42	18	24
Dallas	25	6	19
Desha	7	6	1
Drew	10	9	1
Franklin	24	11	13
Fulton	13	5	8
Greene	30	22	8
Hempstead	48	18	30
Howard	24	11	13
Independence	58	32	26
Izard	35	19	16
Jackson	38	15	23
Johnson	45	16	29
Lafayette	24	19	5
Lawrence	24	11	13
Lee	10	5	5
Logan	30	13	17
Marion	17	15	2
Mississippi	94	39	55
Monroe	16	6	10
Montgomery	19	11	8
Nevada	29	22	7
Newton	17	7	10
Ouachita	44	17	27
Pike	22	8	14
Polk	27	14	13
Pope	83	33	50
Prairie	21	7	14
Randolph	11	10	1
Scott	27	8	19
Searcy	14	7	7
Sevier	34	16	18
Sharp	32	14	18
St. Francis	37	17	20
Stone	22	11	11
Union	63	36	27
Van Buren	38	20	18
White	96	52	44
Woodruff	14	5	9
CALIFORNIA			
Metropolitan Counties			
Alameda	1,564	1,003	561
Butte	269	94	175
Contra Costa	957	633	324
El Dorado	349	154	195
Fresno	1,104	406	698
Imperial	286	190	96
Kern	1,137	826	311
Kings	271	75	196
Los Angeles	16,721	9,316	7,405
Madera	107	79	28
Marin	291	191	100
Merced	223	88	135
Monterey	416	295	121
Napa	139	100	39
Orange	3,622	1,745	1,877
Placer	513	244	269
Riverside	3,939	2,003	1,936
Sacramento	1,923	1,247	676
San Benito	54	26	28
San Bernardino	3,059	1,855	1,204
San Diego	4,254	2,569	1,685
San Francisco	1,027	830	197

Table 64. Full-time Law Enforcement Employees, by Selected State Metropolitan and Nonmetropolitan Counties, 2016—Continued

(Number.)

State/county	Total law enforcement employees	Total officers	Total civilians
San Joaquin	699	274	425
San Luis Obispo	396	295	101
San Mateo	681	330	351
Santa Barbara	617	452	165
Santa Clara	1,655	1,257	398
Santa Cruz	332	142	190
Shasta	216	153	63
Solano	526	124	402
Sonoma	331	232	99
Stanislaus	611	456	155
Sutter	133	105	28
Tulare	747	531	216
Ventura	1,247	756	491
Yolo	263	89	174
Yuba	162	118	44
Nonmetropolitan Counties			
Alpine	17	13	4
Amador	86	45	41
Calaveras	101	49	52
Colusa	65	33	32
Del Norte	55	24	31
Glenn	55	22	33
Humboldt	235	182	53
Inyo	71	35	36
Lake	135	53	82
Lassen	81	59	22
Mariposa	71	56	15
Mendocino	165	123	42
Modoc	28	19	9
Mono	38	21	17
Nevada	155	63	92
Plumas	65	33	32
Sierra	17	11	6
Siskiyou	108	86	22
Tehama	113	79	34
Trinity	44	35	9
Tuolumne	126	62	64
COLORADO			
Metropolitan Counties			
Adams	540	355	185
Arapahoe	515	226	289
Boulder	373	211	162
Clear Creek	73	29	44
Douglas	470	309	161
Elbert	44	37	7
El Paso	795	506	289
Gilpin	57	40	17
Jefferson	811	531	280
Larimer	365	245	120
Mesa	206	98	108
Park	56	31	25
Pueblo	347	92	255
Teller	70	45	25
Weld	351	144	207
Nonmetropolitan Counties			
Alamosa	44	27	17
Archuleta	33	14	19
Baca	12	4	8
Bent	27	13	14
Chaffee	54	20	34
Cheyenne	9	5	4
Conejos	30	10	20
Costilla	9	6	3
Crowley	13	6	7
Custer	23	10	13
Delta	65	34	31
Dolores	8	5	3
Eagle	74	42	32
Fremont	115	52	63
Garfield	136	53	83
Grand	51	24	27
Gunnison	31	13	18
Hinsdale	5	4	1
Huerfano	23	10	13
Jackson	7	3	4
Kiowa	6	5	1
Kit Carson	31	7	24
Lake	27	12	15
La Plata	129	103	26
Las Animas	31	13	18

Table 64. Full-time Law Enforcement Employees, by Selected State Metropolitan and Nonmetropolitan Counties, 2016—Continued

(Number.)

State/county	Total law enforcement employees	Total officers	Total civilians
Lincoln	22	21	1
Logan	52	19	33
Mineral	6	4	2
Moffat	37	34	3
Montezuma	70	29	41
Montrose	98	44	54
Morgan	51	17	34
Otero	23	20	3
Ouray	7	7	0
Phillips	4	4	0
Pitkin	58	23	35
Prowers	30	10	20
Rio Blanco	27	11	16
Rio Grande	34	14	20
Routt	49	40	9
Saguache	19	8	11
San Juan	3	3	0
San Miguel	36	16	20
Sedgwick	7	6	1
Summit	59	50	9
Washington	45	9	36
Yuma	24	9	15
DELAWARE			
New Castle County Police Department	483	367	116
FLORIDA			
Metropolitan Counties			
Baker	145	39	106
Bay	273	207	66
Charlotte	406	294	112
Citrus	419	220	199
Clay	545	268	277
Collier	884	567	317
Escambia	665	411	254
Flagler	250	189	61
Gadsden	68	42	26
Gilchrist	49	27	22
Gulf	40	27	13
Highlands	323	137	186
Hillsborough	3,273	1,181	2,092
Indian River	456	180	276
Jefferson	62	25	37
Lee	1,527	702	825
Leon	378	253	125
Manatee	1,109	724	385
Marion	718	502	216
Martin	495	276	219
Nassau	239	158	81
Orange	2,097	1,447	650
Osceola	610	395	215
Palm Beach	3,397	1,533	1,864
Santa Rosa	379	194	185
Sarasota	942	406	536
Seminole	1,148	572	576
St. Johns	608	277	331
Sumter	287	211	76
Volusia	719	422	297
Wakulla	111	69	42
Walton	374	250	124
Nonmetropolitan Counties			
Bradford	54	36	18
Calhoun	30	21	9
DeSoto	123	60	63
Dixie	73	26	47
Glades	100	29	71
Hardee	100	72	28
Holmes	52	25	27
Jackson	79	59	20
Levy	152	79	73
Liberty	40	17	23
Madison	78	41	37
Monroe	501	195	306
Okeechobee	171	125	46
Putnam	204	101	103
Suwannee	111	61	50
Taylor	75	32	43
Union	20	14	6
Washington	60	37	23

Table 64. Full-time Law Enforcement Employees, by Selected State Metropolitan and Nonmetropolitan Counties, 2016—Continued

(Number.)

State/county	Total law enforcement employees	Total officers	Total civilians
GEORGIA			
Metropolitan Counties			
Barrow	165	116	49
Bartow	206	193	13
Bibb	540	454	86
Brantley	47	19	28
Brooks	38	22	16
Butts	89	52	37
Carroll	191	107	84
Cherokee	379	335	44
Clarke	165	134	31
Clayton	460	163	297
Clayton County Police Department	403	345	58
Cobb County Police Department	708	649	59
Columbia	344	242	102
Coweta	237	160	77
Crawford	32	14	18
Dawson	92	58	34
DeKalb	766	564	202
DeKalb County Police Department	954	727	227
Dougherty	235	226	9
Dougherty County Police Department	49	40	9
Douglas	335	295	40
Echols	9	7	2
Effingham	139	76	63
Fayette	216	143	73
Floyd County Police Department	77	72	5
Forsyth	406	332	74
Fulton	931	737	194
Glynn County Police	124	116	8
Gwinnett County Police Department	939	667	272
Hall	411	263	148
Haralson	79	71	8
Harris	73	71	2
Heard	36	19	17
Henry County Police Department	244	208	36
Jones	73	53	20
Madison	65	43	22
Marion	14	5	9
McIntosh	63	39	24
Meriwether	53	29	24
Oconee	88	55	33
Paulding	273	238	35
Peach	57	32	25
Spalding	168	136	32
Terrell	32	30	2
Walker	101	63	38
Walton	190	172	18
Worth	33	29	4
Nonmetropolitan Counties			
Baldwin	124	58	66
Banks	60	57	3
Ben Hill	53	48	5
Bulloch	111	101	10
Camden	125	66	59
Clay	6	5	1
Clinch	16	11	5
Coffee	105	51	54
Cook	47	40	7
Decatur	60	48	12
Dodge	56	20	36
Dooly	75	33	42
Early	46	25	21
Elbert	55	29	26
Emanuel	40	33	7
Evans	16	9	7
Fannin	49	46	3
Gilmer	98	76	22
Gordon	137	80	57
Grady	42	18	24
Hancock	40	25	15
Hart	51	31	20
Irwin	21	13	8
Jackson	165	97	68
Jeff Davis	41	26	15
Jefferson	44	41	3
Johnson	17	9	8
Laurens	105	87	18
Pierce	49	18	31
Polk	75	37	38
Polk County Police Department	40	36	4
Putnam	64	32	32

Table 64. Full-time Law Enforcement Employees, by Selected State Metropolitan and Nonmetropolitan Counties, 2016—Continued

(Number.)

State/county	Total law enforcement employees	Total officers	Total civilians
Quitman	7	5	2
Rabun	53	51	2
Schley	8	4	4
Screven	20	19	1
Seminole	31	16	15
Stephens	64	38	26
Talbot	17	11	6
Taylor	21	20	1
Thomas	84	80	4
Tift	107	91	16
Treutlen	22	12	10
Troup	80	73	7
Turner	41	21	20
Union	54	49	5
Upson	68	35	33
Ware	144	39	105
Warren	8	8	0
Washington	51	46	5
Wayne	69	32	37
Webster	5	5	0
Wheeler	12	7	5
Wilkes	40	25	15
Wilkinson	30	18	12
HAWAII			
Metropolitan Counties			
Maui Police Department	486	372	114
Nonmetropolitan Counties			
Hawaii Police Department	559	431	128
Kauai Police Department	197	150	47
IDAHO			
Metropolitan Counties			
Ada	438	140	298
Bannock	66	42	24
Boise	23	13	10
Bonneville	102	67	35
Butte	11	4	7
Canyon	159	69	90
Franklin	15	10	5
Gem	22	13	9
Jefferson	33	19	14
Kootenai	167	93	74
Nez Perce	45	22	23
Owyhee	20	12	8
Nonmetropolitan Counties			
Adams	13	6	7
Bear Lake	13	6	7
Benewah	15	7	8
Bingham	53	34	19
Blaine	42	36	6
Bonner	71	40	31
Boundary	19	8	11
Camas	6	4	2
Caribou	17	9	8
Cassia	52	32	20
Clark	7	3	4
Clearwater	18	11	7
Custer	15	8	7
Elmore	42	21	21
Fremont	28	20	8
Gooding	21	16	5
Idaho	30	20	10
Jerome	22	17	5
Latah	36	25	11
Lemhi	10	8	2
Lewis	8	5	3
Lincoln	8	7	1
Madison	35	21	14
Minidoka	29	19	10
Oneida	14	8	6
Payette	32	16	16
Power	17	9	8
Shoshone	26	17	9
Teton	19	11	8
Twin Falls	69	42	27
Valley	26	16	10
Washington	21	13	8
ILLINOIS			
Metropolitan Counties			
Cook	6,106	1,800	4,306
Ford	25	23	2

Table 64. Full-time Law Enforcement Employees, by Selected State Metropolitan and Nonmetropolitan Counties, 2016—Continued

(Number.)

State/county	Total law enforcement employees	Total officers	Total civilians
Grundy	49	31	18
Henry	63	22	41
Jackson	87	28	59
Kane	268	76	192
Kankakee	172	46	126
Kendall	108	52	56
Macoupin	43	20	23
Madison	161	81	80
Marshall	24	8	16
McHenry	345	88	257
McLean	134	50	84
Monroe	34	16	18
Sangamon	199	64	135
Williamson	82	27	55
Nonmetropolitan Counties			
Brown	7	7	0
Clay	16	10	6
Cumberland	14	5	9
Douglas	20	10	10
Effingham	46	19	27
Fulton	39	20	19
Hancock	19	8	11
Iroquois	24	13	11
Jefferson	53	19	34
Jo Daviess	37	18	19
Livingston	69	28	41
Logan	27	19	8
McDonough	25	13	12
Morgan	32	14	18
Ogle	77	28	49
Perry	32	12	20
Putnam	13	8	5
Saline	46	12	34
Scott	5	2	3
Whiteside	48	20	28
INDIANA			
Metropolitan Counties			
Allen	299	127	172
Brown	40	14	26
Clark	151	41	110
Floyd	112	32	80
Hancock	73	39	34
Howard	133	34	99
Newton	38	16	22
Shelby	93	32	61
Vigo	42	39	3
Warrick	78	39	39
Wells	16	16	0
Nonmetropolitan Counties			
Blackford	30	9	21
Fulton	27	12	15
Gibson	41	16	25
Greene	45	18	27
Jay	41	13	28
Steuben	54	21	33
Tipton	33	13	20
Wabash	42	16	26
IOWA			
Metropolitan Counties			
Benton	31	12	19
Black Hawk	137	95	42
Bremer	32	12	20
Dallas	58	24	34
Dubuque	87	72	15
Grundy	16	12	4
Guthrie	14	9	5
Harrison	11	10	1
Johnson	90	68	22
Jones	24	10	14
Linn	188	121	67
Madison	16	8	8
Mills	27	11	16
Plymouth	31	11	20
Polk	459	127	332
Pottawattamie	200	54	146
Scott	153	43	110
Story	85	31	54
Warren	36	20	16
Washington	36	17	19
Woodbury	129	38	91

Table 64. Full-time Law Enforcement Employees, by Selected State Metropolitan and Nonmetropolitan Counties, 2016—Continued

(Number.)

State/county	Total law enforcement employees	Total officers	Total civilians
Nonmetropolitan Counties			
Adair	13	5	8
Adams	11	6	5
Allamakee	17	9	8
Appanoose	15	7	8
Audubon	10	6	4
Boone	29	11	18
Buchanan	28	13	15
Buena Vista	34	13	21
Butler	18	12	6
Calhoun	11	6	5
Carroll	22	9	13
Cass	12	9	3
Cedar	36	13	23
Cerro Gordo	73	20	53
Cherokee	20	7	13
Chickasaw	15	8	7
Clarke	20	7	13
Clay	23	10	13
Clayton	26	12	14
Clinton	43	25	18
Crawford	15	10	5
Davis	6	5	1
Decatur	17	6	11
Delaware	20	13	7
Des Moines	47	20	27
Dickinson	19	9	10
Emmet	18	9	9
Fayette	37	12	25
Floyd	18	11	7
Franklin	10	7	3
Fremont	26	9	17
Greene	16	7	9
Hamilton	26	10	16
Hancock	11	11	0
Hardin	31	11	20
Henry	30	11	19
Howard	16	9	7
Humboldt	15	9	6
Ida	17	10	7
Iowa	28	12	16
Jackson	17	10	7
Jasper	46	17	29
Jefferson	29	27	2
Keokuk	11	6	5
Kossuth	25	10	15
Lee	35	15	20
Louisa	28	11	17
Lucas	12	5	7
Lyon	26	12	14
Mahaska	23	9	14
Marion	36	15	21
Marshall	55	19	36
Mitchell	16	7	9
Monona	18	8	10
Monroe	14	5	9
Montgomery	19	8	11
Muscatine	70	21	49
O'Brien	28	9	19
Osceola	13	9	4
Page	16	8	8
Palo Alto	17	8	9
Pocahontas	15	7	8
Ringgold	12	6	6
Sac	19	8	11
Shelby	15	9	6
Sioux	40	14	26
Tama	22	13	9
Taylor	13	9	4
Union	12	6	6
Van Buren	11	5	6
Wapello	44	12	32
Wayne	15	6	9
Webster	32	16	16
Winneshiek	23	10	13
Worth	25	13	12
Wright	20	9	11
KANSAS			
Metropolitan Counties			
Butler	98	65	33
Douglas	148	76	72
Harvey	21	19	2

Table 64. Full-time Law Enforcement Employees, by Selected State Metropolitan and Nonmetropolitan Counties, 2016—Continued

(Number.)

State/county	Total law enforcement employees	Total officers	Total civilians
Jackson	30	22	8
Jefferson	37	23	14
Johnson	598	448	150
Kingman	21	8	13
Leavenworth	85	64	21
Linn	29	19	10
Miami	48	26	22
Osage	44	21	23
Pottawatomie	41	29	12
Riley County Police Department	193	107	86
Wabaunsee	23	8	15
Nonmetropolitan Counties			
Allen	28	11	17
Anderson	9	9	0
Atchison	23	13	10
Barber	10	4	6
Barton	41	18	23
Bourbon	11	10	1
Brown	22	8	14
Chase	9	5	4
Cherokee	47	18	29
Cheyenne	4	4	0
Clark	10	5	5
Clay	18	7	11
Cloud	10	9	1
Coffey	19	13	6
Cowley	44	22	22
Crawford	67	28	39
Decatur	3	3	0
Dickinson	31	18	13
Edwards	10	6	4
Elk	10	5	5
Ellis	19	19	0
Ellsworth	18	8	10
Ford	38	23	15
Franklin	33	29	4
Geary	87	34	53
Gove	5	4	1
Grant	8	3	5
Gray	18	12	6
Greeley	7	3	4
Hodgeman	8	4	4
Jewell	10	6	4
Kearny	20	11	9
Kiowa	19	7	12
Labette	31	18	13
Lane	9	4	5
Lincoln	13	8	5
Logan	4	4	0
Marion	9	8	1
Marshall	20	9	11
McPherson	22	19	3
Meade	18	7	11
Mitchell	21	8	13
Montgomery	41	29	12
Morris	12	7	5
Morton	11	6	5
Nemaha	21	9	12
Ness	13	7	6
Norton	10	5	5
Osborne	14	7	7
Ottawa	19	5	14
Pawnee	13	12	1
Phillips	13	8	5
Pratt	15	9	6
Rawlins	7	2	5
Republic	11	10	1
Rice	9	7	2
Rush	12	7	5
Russell	11	10	1
Saline	99	37	62
Scott	4	4	0
Seward	39	14	25
Sheridan	3	3	0
Sherman	6	4	2
Smith	5	5	0
Stafford	9	4	5
Stevens	19	8	11
Thomas	7	6	1
Trego	6	4	2
Wallace	8	4	4
Washington	7	7	0

Table 64. Full-time Law Enforcement Employees, by Selected State Metropolitan and Nonmetropolitan Counties, 2016—Continued

(Number.)

State/county	Total law enforcement employees	Total officers	Total civilians
Wichita	9	4	5
Wilson	14	10	4
Woodson	13	8	5
KENTUCKY			
Metropolitan Counties			
Allen	18	16	2
Boone	140	133	7
Boyd	31	27	4
Bullitt	53	38	15
Butler	8	6	2
Clark	17	13	4
Daviess	41	37	4
Grant	18	16	2
Greenup	18	15	3
Jefferson	290	238	52
Larue	6	5	1
Meade	18	10	8
Oldham	16	12	4
Trigg	10	7	3
Warren	87	38	49
Woodford	11	8	3
Nonmetropolitan Counties			
Bath	7	5	2
Breckinridge	10	7	3
Carlisle	3	2	1
Casey	8	6	2
Cumberland	6	4	2
Fleming	7	6	1
Graves	19	16	3
Grayson	11	8	3
Green	12	4	8
Harlan	21	17	4
Hart	9	6	3
Johnson	12	10	2
Knott	9	6	3
Laurel	59	35	24
Lewis	7	5	2
Livingston	6	5	1
Logan	19	17	2
Madison	31	28	3
Marion	10	7	3
McCracken	47	41	6
McCreary	4	3	1
Menifee	4	4	0
Metcalfe	13	10	3
Montgomery	17	15	2
Muhlenberg	15	13	2
Muhlenberg County Police Department	1	1	0
Pike	16	8	8
Rowan	13	11	2
Russell	11	9	2
Todd	5	4	1
Whitley	19	13	6
LOUISIANA			
Metropolitan Counties			
Acadia	101	68	33
Ascension	324	270	54
Bossier	403	328	75
Caddo	684	418	266
Calcasieu	880	648	232
Cameron	79	69	10
De Soto	30	24	6
East Baton Rouge	852	739	113
East Feliciana	54	54	0
Grant	75	33	42
Iberia	271	188	83
Iberville	145	95	50
Jefferson	1,432	627	805
Lafayette	796	569	227
Lafourche	350	267	83
Livingston	280	280	0
Ouachita	401	401	0
Plaquemines	209	209	0
Pointe Coupee	98	46	52
Rapides	508	414	94
St. Bernard	266	244	22
St. Charles	394	276	118
St. Helena	45	31	14
St. James	99	60	39
St. John the Baptist	239	237	2

Table 64. Full-time Law Enforcement Employees, by Selected State Metropolitan and Nonmetropolitan Counties, 2016—Continued

(Number.)

State/county	Total law enforcement employees	Total officers	Total civilians
St. Martin	182	113	69
St. Tammany	749	418	331
Tangipahoa	238	119	119
Terrebonne	306	306	0
Union	50	35	15
Vermilion	128	103	25
Webster	60	38	22
West Baton Rouge	196	150	46
West Feliciana	69	69	0
Nonmetropolitan Counties			
Allen	64	26	38
Assumption	80	52	28
Avoyelles	273	217	56
Beauregard	87	69	18
Bienville	70	42	28
Caldwell	30	30	0
Catahoula	115	22	93
Claiborne	92	41	51
Concordia	261	27	234
East Carroll	46	16	30
Evangeline	28	14	14
Franklin	98	98	0
Jackson	178	42	136
Jefferson Davis	75	75	0
La Salle	135	30	105
Lincoln	76	60	16
Madison	34	34	0
Morehouse	144	48	96
Natchitoches	180	75	105
Red River	59	32	27
Richland	133	117	16
Sabine	89	60	29
St. Landry	200	147	53
St. Mary	102	102	0
Tensas	36	19	17
Vernon	164	62	102
Washington	84	71	13
West Carroll	21	10	11
Winn	29	17	12
MAINE			
Metropolitan Counties			
Androscoggin	32	19	13
Cumberland	71	59	12
Penobscot	36	32	4
Sagadahoc	21	19	2
York	33	30	3
Nonmetropolitan Counties			
Aroostook	27	21	6
Franklin	21	20	1
Hancock	20	19	1
Kennebec	23	20	3
Knox	22	22	0
Lincoln	25	23	2
Oxford	28	26	2
Piscataquis	8	7	1
Somerset	25	22	3
Waldo	21	19	2
Washington	13	11	2
MARYLAND			
Metropolitan Counties			
Allegany	31	28	3
Anne Arundel	96	72	24
Anne Arundel County Police Department	960	698	262
Baltimore County	85	73	12
Baltimore County Police Department	2,092	1,833	259
Calvert	147	122	25
Carroll	141	113	28
Cecil	106	89	17
Charles	423	295	128
Frederick	236	176	60
Harford	380	285	95
Howard	69	53	16
Howard County Police Department	659	476	183
Montgomery	180	140	40
Montgomery County Police Department	1,904	1,365	539
Prince George's	331	247	84
Prince George's County Police Department	1,888	1,675	213
Queen Anne's	66	60	6
Somerset	29	25	4

516 CRIME IN THE UNITED STATES (BERNAN PRESS)

Table 64. Full-time Law Enforcement Employees, by Selected State Metropolitan and Nonmetropolitan Counties, 2016—Continued

(Number.)

State/county	Total law enforcement employees	Total officers	Total civilians
St. Mary's	264	115	149
Washington	246	100	146
Wicomico	108	87	21
Worcester	60	51	9
Nonmetropolitan Counties			
Caroline	34	30	4
Dorchester	42	38	4
Garrett	57	31	26
Kent	28	25	3
Talbot	35	32	3
MICHIGAN			
Metropolitan Counties			
Barry	54	30	24
Bay	76	32	44
Berrien	158	74	84
Calhoun	181	86	95
Cass	70	33	37
Clinton	61	26	35
Eaton	127	70	57
Genesee	247	113	134
Ingham	164	91	73
Jackson	128	52	76
Kalamazoo	218	130	88
Kent	531	207	324
Lapeer	79	50	29
Livingston	147	52	95
Macomb	508	241	267
Midland	70	32	38
Monroe	154	74	80
Montcalm	42	17	25
Muskegon	108	47	61
Oakland	1,042	859	183
Ottawa	235	145	90
Saginaw	129	66	63
St. Clair	185	75	110
Van Buren	103	56	47
Washtenaw	303	128	175
Wayne	920	629	291
Nonmetropolitan Counties			
Alcona	29	12	17
Alger	18	9	9
Allegan	19	10	9
Alpena	27	13	14
Antrim	45	20	25
Arenac	26	13	13
Baraga	13	6	7
Benzie	33	15	18
Branch	35	14	21
Charlevoix	36	20	16
Cheboygan	37	20	17
Chippewa	32	15	17
Clare	31	21	10
Crawford	25	15	10
Delta	30	14	16
Dickinson	29	12	17
Emmet	47	25	22
Gladwin	41	16	25
Gogebic	24	16	8
Grand Traverse	122	64	58
Gratiot	40	25	15
Hillsdale	32	22	10
Houghton	30	21	9
Huron	46	20	26
Ionia	56	24	32
Iosco	22	5	17
Iron	19	10	9
Isabella	49	22	27
Kalkaska	34	15	19
Keweenaw	6	6	0
Lake	53	14	39
Leelanau	50	20	30
Lenawee	104	41	63
Luce	4	4	0
Mackinac	28	13	15
Manistee	38	16	22
Marquette	61	22	39
Mason	40	20	20
Mecosta	52	24	28
Menominee	15	15	0
Missaukee	26	13	13

Table 64. Full-time Law Enforcement Employees, by Selected State Metropolitan and Nonmetropolitan Counties, 2016—Continued

(Number.)

State/county	Total law enforcement employees	Total officers	Total civilians
Montmorency	13	13	0
Newaygo	27	24	3
Oceana	35	21	14
Ogemaw	36	18	18
Ontonagon	5	5	0
Osceola	36	17	19
Oscoda	16	10	6
Otsego	25	12	13
Presque Isle	26	13	13
Roscommon	39	24	15
Sanilac	28	25	3
Schoolcraft	9	2	7
Shiawassee	51	21	30
St. Joseph	58	27	31
Tuscola	47	22	25
Wexford	48	23	25
MINNESOTA			
Metropolitan Counties			
Anoka	256	129	127
Benton	70	24	46
Blue Earth	69	31	38
Carlton	52	22	30
Carver	148	77	71
Chisago	85	40	45
Clay	71	34	37
Dakota	185	82	103
Dodge	37	24	13
Fillmore	30	19	11
Hennepin	792	321	471
Houston	33	13	20
Isanti	56	21	35
Le Sueur	33	19	14
Mille Lacs	84	34	50
Nicollet	41	14	27
Olmsted	176	71	105
Polk	44	32	12
Ramsey	384	210	174
Scott	128	43	85
Sherburne	278	82	196
Sibley	24	12	12
Stearns	185	68	117
St. Louis	253	105	148
Wabasha	45	17	28
Washington	237	101	136
Wright	228	136	92
Nonmetropolitan Counties			
Aitkin	48	17	31
Becker	56	21	35
Beltrami	70	29	41
Big Stone	7	5	2
Brown	37	14	23
Cass	70	39	31
Chippewa	18	8	10
Clearwater	24	10	14
Cook	20	12	8
Cottonwood	22	10	12
Crow Wing	123	37	86
Douglas	82	33	49
Faribault	26	10	16
Freeborn	73	23	50
Goodhue	102	39	63
Grant	12	7	5
Hubbard	44	18	26
Itasca	71	30	41
Jackson	26	14	12
Kanabec	47	19	28
Kandiyohi	103	33	70
Kittson	10	5	5
Koochiching	20	10	10
Lac Qui Parle	12	7	5
Lake	30	17	13
Lake of the Woods	12	6	6
Lincoln	13	6	7
Lyon	48	17	31
Mahnomen	20	13	7
Marshall	22	12	10
Martin	33	14	19
McLeod	54	22	32
Meeker	46	21	25
Morrison	51	20	31
Mower	70	22	48

Table 64. Full-time Law Enforcement Employees, by Selected State Metropolitan and Nonmetropolitan Counties, 2016—Continued

(Number.)

State/county	Total law enforcement employees	Total officers	Total civilians
Murray	16	9	7
Nobles	34	13	21
Norman	10	7	3
Otter Tail	82	35	47
Pennington	30	8	22
Pine	81	31	50
Pipestone	24	14	10
Pope	15	8	7
Red Lake	11	8	3
Redwood	29	12	17
Renville	35	14	21
Rice	51	25	26
Rock	17	12	5
Roseau	20	10	10
Steele	28	22	6
Stevens	16	8	8
Swift	17	8	9
Todd	32	15	17
Traverse	14	6	8
Wadena	20	10	10
Waseca	28	13	15
Watonwan	15	7	8
Wilkin	16	7	9
Winona	72	20	52
Yellow Medicine	10	10	0
MISSISSIPPI			
Metropolitan Counties			
Hancock	122	68	54
Harrison	326	109	217
Hinds	383	116	267
Lamar	77	39	38
Marshall	48	27	21
Nonmetropolitan Counties			
Adams	73	39	34
Choctaw	14	8	6
Claiborne	28	12	16
Grenada	14	12	2
Jones	51	46	5
Kemper	17	11	6
Lauderdale	123	48	75
Marion	22	18	4
Scott	66	25	41
Stone	22	18	4
Sunflower	44	38	6
Warren	42	39	3
Washington	47	34	13
MISSOURI			
Metropolitan Counties			
Andrew	28	15	13
Bates	43	19	24
Bollinger	16	11	5
Boone	75	58	17
Buchanan	108	77	31
Caldwell	13	6	7
Callaway	26	23	3
Cape Girardeau	82	42	40
Cass	86	68	18
Christian	82	46	36
Clay	197	124	73
Clinton	21	17	4
Cole	84	52	32
Dallas	22	16	6
DeKalb	11	6	5
Franklin	136	109	27
Greene	334	129	205
Jackson	128	93	35
Jasper	134	86	48
Jefferson	221	150	71
Lafayette	52	43	9
Lincoln	108	50	58
McDonald	30	24	6
Moniteau	12	7	5
Newton	68	35	33
Osage	12	9	3
Platte	127	83	44
Polk	30	17	13
St. Charles	46	32	14
St. Charles County Police Department	167	130	37
St. Louis County Police Department	1,160	880	280
Warren	60	36	24
Webster	34	18	16

Table 64. Full-time Law Enforcement Employees, by Selected State Metropolitan and Nonmetropolitan Counties, 2016—Continued

(Number.)

State/county	Total law enforcement employees	Total officers	Total civilians
Nonmetropolitan Counties			
Adair	27	12	15
Atchison	10	5	5
Audrain	45	35	10
Barry	38	25	13
Benton	26	18	8
Butler	43	20	23
Camden	97	58	39
Carroll	8	7	1
Carter	14	9	5
Cedar	30	11	19
Chariton	15	9	6
Clark	11	4	7
Cooper	10	9	1
Crawford	37	23	14
Daviess	7	6	1
Dent	19	12	7
Douglas	11	6	5
Dunklin	20	12	8
Gasconade	10	9	1
Gentry	5	5	0
Grundy	16	6	10
Henry	41	26	15
Hickory	14	8	6
Holt	10	5	5
Howard	13	9	4
Howell	37	28	9
Iron	17	12	5
Johnson	57	31	26
Knox	4	3	1
Laclede	30	23	7
Lawrence	34	26	8
Lewis	12	6	6
Linn	7	6	1
Livingston	10	9	1
Macon	18	12	6
Maries	13	10	3
Marion	40	16	24
Mercer	9	3	6
Miller	18	15	3
Monroe	9	8	1
Montgomery	19	17	2
Morgan	43	27	16
New Madrid	16	13	3
Nodaway	15	13	2
Oregon	11	7	4
Ozark	14	9	5
Pemiscot	43	18	25
Perry	38	26	12
Pettis	50	25	25
Phelps	65	24	41
Pike	22	8	14
Pulaski	34	21	13
Ralls	10	9	1
Randolph	44	25	19
Reynolds	10	9	1
Ripley	10	9	1
Saline	37	23	14
Schuyler	7	4	3
Scotland	6	2	4
Scott	50	24	26
Shannon	8	4	4
Shelby	10	5	5
St. Clair	73	21	52
Ste. Genevieve	64	45	19
St. Francois	69	56	13
Stoddard	28	12	16
Stone	58	48	10
Sullivan	5	4	1
Taney	54	38	16
Texas	12	11	1
Vernon	35	20	15
Washington	35	22	13
Wayne	17	7	10
Worth	4	3	1
Wright	13	6	7
MONTANA			
Metropolitan Counties			
Carbon	17	10	7
Cascade	143	35	108

Table 64. Full-time Law Enforcement Employees, by Selected State Metropolitan and Nonmetropolitan Counties, 2016—Continued

(Number.)

State/county	Total law enforcement employees	Total officers	Total civilians
Golden Valley	2	2	0
Missoula	184	52	132
Yellowstone	158	51	107
Nonmetropolitan Counties			
Beaverhead	39	11	28
Blaine	14	8	6
Broadwater	28	10	18
Carter	3	3	0
Chouteau	22	9	13
Custer	17	6	11
Daniels	4	2	2
Dawson	51	6	45
Deer Lodge	28	19	9
Fallon	9	4	5
Fergus	21	8	13
Flathead	114	56	58
Gallatin	110	55	55
Garfield	4	3	1
Glacier	25	13	12
Granite	6	6	0
Hill	30	12	18
Jefferson	24	12	12
Judith Basin	5	4	1
Lake	45	22	23
Lewis and Clark	79	45	34
Liberty	7	5	2
Madison	24	11	13
McCone	10	4	6
Meagher	9	3	6
Mineral	17	7	10
Musselshell	10	9	1
Park	25	15	10
Phillips	11	7	4
Pondera	10	9	1
Powder River	4	4	0
Powell	10	5	5
Prairie	4	3	1
Ravalli	82	31	51
Richland	39	11	28
Roosevelt	41	17	24
Rosebud	24	12	12
Sanders	19	12	7
Sheridan	10	8	2
Silver Bow	101	51	50
Stillwater	17	9	8
Sweet Grass	13	7	6
Teton	12	9	3
Toole	20	12	8
Treasure	2	2	0
Valley	23	7	16
Wheatland	11	6	5
NEBRASKA			
Metropolitan Counties			
Cass	75	54	21
Dixon	14	8	6
Douglas	199	125	74
Hall	40	31	9
Hamilton	18	9	9
Howard	11	5	6
Lancaster	106	87	19
Sarpy	199	134	65
Saunders	20	11	9
Seward	17	15	2
Washington	52	28	24
Nonmetropolitan Counties			
Adams	30	16	14
Antelope	16	5	11
Arthur	1	1	0
Banner	1	1	0
Blaine	1	1	0
Boone	12	5	7
Box Butte	19	5	14
Boyd	3	3	0
Brown	9	5	4
Buffalo	45	26	19
Burt	5	5	0
Butler	18	10	8
Cedar	6	6	0
Chase	8	4	4
Cherry	6	5	1

Table 64. Full-time Law Enforcement Employees, by Selected State Metropolitan and Nonmetropolitan Counties, 2016—Continued

(Number.)

State/county	Total law enforcement employees	Total officers	Total civilians
Cheyenne	21	9	12
Clay	12	7	5
Colfax	18	10	8
Cuming	6	5	1
Custer	8	7	1
Dawes	14	7	7
Dawson	63	26	37
Deuel	6	5	1
Dodge	23	20	3
Dundy	9	5	4
Fillmore	13	7	6
Franklin	7	3	4
Frontier	9	5	4
Furnas	14	8	6
Gage	27	15	12
Garfield	2	2	0
Gosper	6	5	1
Grant	1	1	0
Greeley	3	2	1
Harlan	8	4	4
Hayes	2	1	1
Hitchcock	8	4	4
Holt	10	4	6
Hooker	2	2	0
Jefferson	16	9	7
Johnson	11	6	5
Kearney	10	5	5
Keith	8	7	1
Keya Paha	1	1	0
Kimball	9	4	5
Knox	14	5	9
Lincoln	57	24	33
Madison	61	33	28
McPherson	1	1	0
Morrill	14	9	5
Nance	11	7	4
Nemaha	10	10	0
Nuckolls	8	5	3
Otoe	29	15	14
Pawnee	4	3	1
Perkins	8	7	1
Platte	69	20	49
Red Willow	21	6	15
Rock	7	3	4
Saline	24	17	7
Scotts Bluff	25	17	8
Sheridan	15	5	10
Sherman	6	5	1
Thurston	11	6	5
Wayne	4	4	0
Webster	9	6	3
Wheeler	1	1	0
York	27	10	17
NEVADA			
Metropolitan Counties			
Carson City	93	93	0
Storey	27	25	2
Washoe	691	407	284
Nonmetropolitan Counties			
Churchill	45	39	6
Douglas	98	98	0
Elko	79	66	13
Esmeralda	17	12	5
Eureka	14	8	6
Humboldt	56	35	21
Lander	21	21	0
Lincoln	30	23	7
Mineral	23	17	6
Nye	123	95	28
Pershing	16	13	3
White Pine	31	25	6
NEW HAMPSHIRE			
Metropolitan Counties			
Rockingham	51	26	25
Strafford	29	15	14
Nonmetropolitan Counties			
Carroll	22	12	10
Cheshire	22	9	13
Grafton	23	9	14
Merrimack	34	20	14

Table 64. Full-time Law Enforcement Employees, by Selected State Metropolitan and Nonmetropolitan Counties, 2016—Continued

(Number.)

State/county	Total law enforcement employees	Total officers	Total civilians
NEW JERSEY			
Metropolitan Counties			
Atlantic	133	110	23
Bergen	585	502	83
Burlington	89	71	18
Camden	187	155	32
Camden County Police Department	463	410	53
Cape May	148	134	14
Cumberland	63	56	7
Essex	522	449	73
Gloucester	109	92	17
Hudson	347	222	125
Hunterdon	32	28	4
Mercer	183	141	42
Middlesex	225	182	43
Monmouth	691	438	253
Morris	122	92	30
Ocean	278	139	139
Passaic	698	557	141
Salem	262	221	41
Somerset	225	166	59
Sussex	147	117	30
Union	249	205	44
Warren	23	19	4
NEW MEXICO			
Metropolitan Counties			
Dona Ana	203	143	60
Sandoval	15	12	3
Santa Fe	121	94	27
Valencia	61	55	6
Nonmetropolitan Counties			
Catron	13	8	5
Chaves	46	37	9
Colfax	11	11	0
Curry	26	18	8
De Baca	5	5	0
Eddy	72	60	12
Guadalupe	6	5	1
Hidalgo	11	9	2
Lea	69	59	10
Lincoln	33	23	10
Luna	39	31	8
Mora	7	5	2
Otero	61	38	23
Quay	8	7	1
San Miguel	13	9	4
Sierra	16	14	2
Socorro	15	12	3
Taos	26	22	4
Union	7	5	2
NEW YORK			
Metropolitan Counties			
Albany	172	113	59
Broome	62	53	9
Chemung	49	44	5
Dutchess	129	99	30
Erie	197	147	50
Herkimer	16	6	10
Jefferson	57	40	17
Livingston	78	51	27
Madison	44	34	10
Monroe	334	279	55
Nassau	3,218	2,450	768
Niagara	155	111	44
Oneida	113	87	26
Onondaga	247	215	32
Ontario	114	70	44
Orleans	39	26	13
Oswego	85	68	17
Putnam	100	86	14
Rensselaer	43	35	8
Rockland	149	77	72
Saratoga	152	110	42
Schenectady	17	11	6
Schoharie	31	17	14
Suffolk	386	262	124
Suffolk County Police Department	3,040	2,521	519
Tioga	55	35	20

Table 64. Full-time Law Enforcement Employees, by Selected State Metropolitan and Nonmetropolitan Counties, 2016—Continued

(Number.)

State/county	Total law enforcement employees	Total officers	Total civilians
Tompkins	46	40	6
Ulster	59	56	3
Warren	104	67	37
Wayne	69	63	6
Westchester Public Safety	354	283	71
Nonmetropolitan Counties			
Allegany	45	26	19
Cattaraugus	81	57	24
Cayuga	37	33	4
Chautauqua	111	61	50
Clinton	25	25	0
Columbia	67	52	15
Cortland	41	36	5
Delaware	24	16	8
Essex	15	15	0
Franklin	18	8	10
Fulton	40	25	15
Genesee	78	50	28
Greene	32	28	4
Hamilton	6	5	1
Lewis	26	17	9
Montgomery	49	26	23
Otsego	20	17	3
Schuyler	21	18	3
Seneca	39	31	8
Steuben	50	39	11
St. Lawrence	33	31	2
Sullivan	42	42	0
Wyoming	31	30	1
NORTH CAROLINA			
Metropolitan Counties			
Alamance	255	117	138
Alexander	71	39	32
Brunswick	261	154	107
Buncombe	393	247	146
Burke	110	88	22
Cabarrus	310	183	127
Caldwell	113	103	10
Catawba	194	145	49
Chatham	132	100	32
Craven	126	73	53
Cumberland	603	303	300
Currituck	96	63	33
Davidson	180	124	56
Davie	86	56	30
Durham	463	181	282
Edgecombe	134	54	80
Forsyth	474	206	268
Franklin	123	74	49
Gaston	206	119	87
Gaston County Police Department	215	123	92
Gates	13	13	0
Guilford	612	267	345
Haywood	125	68	57
Henderson	203	134	69
Hoke	122	63	59
Iredell	203	147	56
Johnston	186	114	72
Jones	29	18	11
Lincoln	158	107	51
Madison	43	24	19
Mecklenburg[1]	1,084	294	790
Nash	140	88	52
New Hanover	488	349	139
Onslow	264	126	138
Orange	140	94	46
Pamlico	50	22	28
Pender	110	64	46
Person	83	46	37
Pitt	310	130	180
Randolph	229	176	53
Rockingham	142	95	47
Rowan	185	124	61
Stokes	66	46	20
Union	285	203	82
Wake	967	378	589
Wayne	223	118	105
Yadkin	76	39	37
Nonmetropolitan Counties			
Alleghany	33	17	16

Table 64. Full-time Law Enforcement Employees, by Selected State Metropolitan and Nonmetropolitan Counties, 2016—Continued

(Number.)

State/county	Total law enforcement employees	Total officers	Total civilians
Anson	60	32	28
Ashe	62	30	32
Avery	49	25	24
Beaufort	90	55	35
Bertie	36	23	13
Bladen	85	53	32
Camden	21	18	3
Carteret	92	63	29
Caswell	52	35	17
Cherokee	67	31	36
Chowan	34	17	17
Clay	44	17	27
Cleveland	173	103	70
Columbus	118	75	43
Dare	144	65	79
Duplin	111	76	35
Graham	30	17	13
Greene	49	23	26
Halifax	94	62	32
Harnett	218	122	96
Hertford	53	23	30
Hyde	20	14	6
Jackson	76	53	23
Lee	106	67	39
Lenoir	121	62	59
Macon	76	50	26
Martin	40	37	3
McDowell	63	44	19
Mitchell	20	18	2
Montgomery	55	30	25
Moore	131	74	57
Northampton	54	31	23
Pasquotank	66	45	21
Perquimans	15	13	2
Polk	46	36	10
Richmond	88	56	32
Robeson	218	130	88
Rutherford	137	80	57
Sampson	133	90	43
Scotland	63	37	26
Stanly	90	87	3
Surry	105	77	28
Swain	47	27	20
Transylvania	82	60	22
Tyrrell	18	12	6
Vance	81	40	41
Warren	67	36	31
Washington	52	22	30
Watauga	76	45	31
Wilkes	127	71	56
Wilson	151	91	60
Yancey	38	18	20
NORTH DAKOTA			
Metropolitan Counties			
Burleigh	113	52	61
Cass	162	110	52
Grand Forks	40	33	7
Morton	58	33	25
Oliver	5	4	1
Sioux	1	1	0
Nonmetropolitan Counties			
Adams	6	5	1
Barnes	9	8	1
Benson	4	4	0
Billings	6	6	0
Bottineau	15	11	4
Bowman	5	4	1
Burke	5	4	1
Cavalier	11	6	5
Dickey	5	4	1
Divide	7	7	0
Dunn	18	15	3
Eddy	5	4	1
Emmons	6	5	1
Foster	3	3	0
Golden Valley	5	4	1
Grant	4	4	0
Griggs	3	3	0
Hettinger	5	4	1
Kidder	3	3	0
Lamoure	5	4	1

Table 64. Full-time Law Enforcement Employees, by Selected State Metropolitan and Nonmetropolitan Counties, 2016—Continued

(Number.)

State/county	Total law enforcement employees	Total officers	Total civilians
Logan	3	3	0
McHenry	8	8	0
McIntosh	3	3	0
McKenzie	63	31	32
McLean	39	24	15
Mercer	33	18	15
Mountrail	22	13	9
Nelson	6	5	1
Pembina	18	12	6
Pierce	38	3	35
Ramsey	7	6	1
Ransom	5	4	1
Renville	5	5	0
Richland	35	18	17
Rolette	19	10	9
Sargent	5	4	1
Sheridan	3	3	0
Slope	2	2	0
Stark	30	25	5
Steele	3	3	0
Stutsman	13	11	2
Towner	5	5	0
Traill	13	8	5
Walsh	19	11	8
Ward	90	39	51
Wells	3	3	0
Williams	80	40	40

OHIO
Metropolitan Counties

Allen	147	68	79
Brown	43	27	16
Carroll	35	21	14
Delaware	202	93	109
Fairfield	142	114	28
Fulton	24	22	2
Greene	141	63	78
Licking	206	84	122
Lorain	77	66	11
Madison	40	32	8
Medina	138	55	83
Miami	108	49	59
Perry	19	13	6
Pickaway	85	41	44
Portage	142	76	66
Richland	128	42	86
Summit	406	332	74
Union	55	37	18
Warren	183	94	89

Nonmetropolitan Counties

Ashland	77	49	28
Ashtabula	71	31	40
Athens	33	27	6
Champaign	29	26	3
Darke	66	28	38
Erie	85	42	43
Fayette	43	26	17
Hancock	92	36	56
Highland	47	30	17
Holmes	53	30	23
Knox	62	47	15
Marion	50	28	22
Monroe	27	20	7
Muskingum	110	73	37
Ottawa	63	44	19
Paulding	29	20	9
Scioto	76	37	39
Washington	87	43	44
Wyandot	28	15	13

OKLAHOMA
Metropolitan Counties

Canadian	104	61	43
Cleveland	160	58	102
Comanche	41	31	10
Cotton	12	6	6
Creek	98	37	61
Garfield	69	26	43
Grady	29	19	10
Le Flore	20	14	6
Lincoln	32	15	17
Logan	61	30	31

Table 64. Full-time Law Enforcement Employees, by Selected State Metropolitan and Nonmetropolitan Counties, 2016—Continued

(Number.)

State/county	Total law enforcement employees	Total officers	Total civilians
McClain	34	21	13
Oklahoma	642	463	179
Okmulgee	17	16	1
Osage	73	40	33
Pawnee	26	9	17
Rogers	80	53	27
Sequoyah	53	23	30
Tulsa	631	223	408
Wagoner	70	32	38
Nonmetropolitan Counties			
Adair	9	9	0
Alfalfa	9	6	3
Atoka	23	8	15
Beaver	15	7	8
Beckham	40	14	26
Blaine	14	6	8
Bryan	17	15	2
Caddo	34	15	19
Carter	56	18	38
Cherokee	28	22	6
Choctaw	20	8	12
Cimarron	7	3	4
Coal	9	6	3
Craig	28	12	16
Custer	37	14	23
Delaware	43	17	26
Dewey	16	6	10
Ellis	18	8	10
Garvin	36	19	17
Grant	10	6	4
Greer	6	2	4
Harmon	4	3	1
Harper	8	5	3
Haskell	18	7	11
Hughes	7	6	1
Jackson	35	12	23
Jefferson	17	6	11
Johnston	24	7	17
Kay	24	16	8
Kingfisher	18	8	10
Kiowa	16	7	9
Latimer	13	6	7
Love	24	9	15
Major	13	5	8
Marshall	26	6	20
Mayes	54	28	26
McCurtain	21	16	5
McIntosh	43	15	28
Murray	13	6	7
Muskogee	99	34	65
Noble	24	9	15
Nowata	16	7	9
Okfuskee	16	6	10
Ottawa	36	15	21
Payne	91	36	55
Pittsburg	26	14	12
Pontotoc	41	18	23
Pottawatomie	29	25	4
Pushmataha	4	3	1
Roger Mills	13	8	5
Seminole	38	18	20
Stephens	36	21	15
Texas	35	12	23
Tillman	24	4	20
Washita	31	9	22
Woods	8	7	1
Woodward	37	12	25
OREGON			
Metropolitan Counties			
Benton	78	65	13
Clackamas	468	362	106
Columbia	45	14	31
Deschutes	229	79	150
Jackson	168	121	47
Josephine	57	42	15
Lane	253	176	77
Linn	187	137	50
Marion	349	92	257
Multnomah	774	115	659
Polk	65	26	39
Yamhill	85	68	17

Table 64. Full-time Law Enforcement Employees, by Selected State Metropolitan and Nonmetropolitan Counties, 2016—Continued

(Number.)

State/county	Total law enforcement employees	Total officers	Total civilians
Nonmetropolitan Counties			
Baker	32	30	2
Clatsop	52	25	27
Coos	87	57	30
Crook	35	16	19
Curry	36	22	14
Douglas	145	109	36
Gilliam	7	6	1
Grant	8	8	0
Harney	18	12	6
Hood River	46	25	21
Jefferson	38	33	5
Klamath	72	25	47
Lake	20	20	0
Lincoln	84	28	56
Sherman	7	6	1
Tillamook	58	30	28
Umatilla	83	24	59
Union	34	20	14
Wallowa	12	6	6
Wasco	29	17	12
Wheeler	4	4	0
PENNSYLVANIA			
Metropolitan Counties			
Adams	14	11	3
Allegheny	186	153	33
Allegheny County Police Department	273	215	58
Beaver	27	24	3
Berks	108	97	11
Blair	29	25	4
Butler	30	27	3
Cumberland	34	28	6
Erie	45	38	7
Franklin	23	18	5
Lancaster	54	48	6
Lycoming	23	17	6
Mercer	19	15	4
Monroe	43	26	17
Montgomery	130	104	26
Northampton	66	60	6
Pike	23	19	4
Washington	32	29	3
Westmoreland	61	53	8
Wyoming	5	3	2
York	104	104	0
Nonmetropolitan Counties			
Bedford	11	10	1
Bradford	11	9	2
Clarion	11	8	3
Elk	6	5	1
Greene	10	8	2
Indiana	19	16	3
Jefferson	9	8	1
Lawrence	23	18	5
Schuylkill	19	15	4
Snyder	7	7	0
Tioga	8	6	2
Union	9	8	1
Warren	12	10	2
Wayne	16	13	3
SOUTH CAROLINA			
Metropolitan Counties			
Aiken	246	136	110
Anderson	390	220	170
Beaufort	317	219	98
Berkeley	268	150	118
Calhoun	32	30	2
Charleston	722	267	455
Chester	119	49	70
Darlington	132	61	71
Dorchester	271	140	131
Edgefield	64	37	27
Fairfield	51	46	5
Florence	229	190	39
Greenville	536	439	97
Horry	365	71	294
Horry County Police Department	284	242	42
Jasper	36	31	5
Kershaw	72	59	13

Table 64. Full-time Law Enforcement Employees, by Selected State Metropolitan and Nonmetropolitan Counties, 2016—Continued

(Number.)

State/county	Total law enforcement employees	Total officers	Total civilians
Lancaster	164	112	52
Laurens	70	63	7
Lexington	437	281	156
Pickens	135	114	21
Richland	597	493	104
Saluda	62	21	41
Spartanburg	343	314	29
Sumter	135	109	26
Union	33	30	3
York	315	158	157
Nonmetropolitan Counties			
Abbeville	61	29	32
Allendale	14	12	2
Bamberg	13	13	0
Barnwell	64	28	36
Cherokee	92	55	37
Chesterfield	55	44	11
Clarendon	59	52	7
Colleton	109	47	62
Dillon	47	36	11
Georgetown	164	76	88
Greenwood	155	79	76
Hampton	40	33	7
Marion	59	32	27
Marlboro	25	21	4
McCormick	34	16	18
Newberry	102	51	51
Oconee	163	91	72
Orangeburg	121	85	36
Williamsburg	71	29	42
SOUTH DAKOTA			
Metropolitan Counties			
Custer	12	11	1
Lincoln	20	18	2
McCook	8	7	1
Meade	45	18	27
Minnehaha	207	72	135
Pennington	384	94	290
Turner	10	8	2
Union	28	8	20
Nonmetropolitan Counties			
Aurora	4	3	1
Beadle	25	5	20
Bennett	5	3	2
Bon Homme	8	3	5
Brookings	22	14	8
Brown	59	16	43
Brule	10	4	6
Buffalo	1	1	0
Butte	14	5	9
Campbell	2	2	0
Charles Mix	20	6	14
Clark	3	3	0
Clay	14	8	6
Codington	28	10	18
Corson	4	4	0
Davison	10	7	3
Day	5	3	2
Deuel	6	5	1
Dewey	4	3	1
Douglas	4	4	0
Edmunds	4	4	0
Fall River	8	6	2
Faulk	11	4	7
Grant	8	4	4
Gregory	4	3	1
Hamlin	6	5	1
Hand	3	2	1
Hanson	4	3	1
Harding	3	2	1
Hughes	48	6	42
Hutchinson	3	3	0
Hyde	2	2	0
Jackson	3	2	1
Jerauld	5	4	1
Jones	2	2	0
Kingsbury	6	5	1
Lake	13	7	6
Lawrence	37	13	24
Lyman	5	4	1

Table 64. Full-time Law Enforcement Employees, by Selected State Metropolitan and Nonmetropolitan Counties, 2016—Continued

(Number.)

State/county	Total law enforcement employees	Total officers	Total civilians
Marshall	11	6	5
McPherson	3	3	0
Mellette	5	4	1
Miner	4	3	1
Moody	8	3	5
Perkins	7	6	1
Potter	3	2	1
Roberts	34	5	29
Sanborn	3	3	0
Spink	13	8	5
Stanley	6	5	1
Sully	3	3	0
Todd	1	1	0
Tripp	4	3	1
Walworth	13	5	8
Yankton	32	12	20
Ziebach	2	2	0
TENNESSEE			
Metropolitan Counties			
Anderson	169	60	109
Blount	281	152	129
Bradley	219	115	104
Campbell	92	47	45
Cannon	36	18	18
Carter	127	124	3
Cheatham	79	39	40
Chester	46	15	31
Crockett	36	17	19
Dickson	133	65	68
Fayette	87	44	43
Grainger	45	22	23
Hamblen	106	41	65
Hamilton	403	164	239
Hartsville/Trousdale	41	20	21
Hawkins	119	59	60
Hickman	47	24	23
Jefferson	104	53	51
Knox	954	433	521
Loudon	78	47	31
Macon	54	27	27
Madison	262	110	152
Marion	56	28	28
Maury	158	83	75
Montgomery	350	105	245
Morgan	44	21	23
Polk	49	22	27
Roane	76	43	33
Robertson	152	51	101
Rutherford	426	228	198
Sequatchie	44	23	21
Shelby	1,809	613	1,196
Smith	58	26	32
Sullivan	274	123	151
Sumner	285	96	189
Tipton	99	60	39
Unicoi	40	24	16
Union	51	31	20
Washington	220	97	123
Williamson	249	160	89
Wilson	250	114	136
Nonmetropolitan Counties			
Bedford	90	40	50
Benton	60	20	40
Bledsoe	40	15	25
Carroll	65	24	41
Claiborne	110	38	72
Clay	26	15	11
Cocke	71	38	33
Coffee	130	47	83
Cumberland	109	52	57
Decatur	28	13	15
DeKalb	48	26	22
Dyer	88	36	52
Fentress	45	18	27
Franklin	71	43	28
Gibson	84	37	47
Giles	66	32	34
Greene	155	59	96
Grundy	38	16	22
Hancock	34	12	22
Hardeman	68	28	40

Table 64. Full-time Law Enforcement Employees, by Selected State Metropolitan and Nonmetropolitan Counties, 2016—Continued

(Number.)

State/county	Total law enforcement employees	Total officers	Total civilians
Hardin	50	22	28
Haywood	43	19	24
Henderson	71	32	39
Henry	67	34	33
Houston	25	11	14
Humphreys	40	23	17
Jackson	37	14	23
Johnson	42	19	23
Lake	22	9	13
Lauderdale	66	19	47
Lawrence	100	55	45
Lewis	16	15	1
Lincoln	82	32	50
Marshall	51	26	25
McMinn	74	32	42
McNairy	37	17	20
Meigs	37	18	19
Monroe	55	49	6
Moore	34	14	20
Obion	55	23	32
Overton	57	24	33
Perry	30	14	16
Pickett	12	8	4
Putnam	146	69	77
Rhea	55	54	1
Scott	66	29	37
Sevier	214	106	108
Stewart	51	20	31
Van Buren	19	9	10
Warren	96	49	47
Wayne	49	14	35
Weakley	44	21	23
White	64	29	35
TEXAS			
Metropolitan Counties			
Aransas	72	26	46
Archer	20	9	11
Armstrong	8	4	4
Austin	71	43	28
Bandera	64	27	37
Bastrop	211	76	135
Bell	309	104	205
Bowie	42	35	7
Brazoria	341	129	212
Brazos	227	99	128
Burleson	43	17	26
Caldwell	96	32	64
Callahan	12	5	7
Cameron	501	114	387
Clay	23	12	11
Collin	470	156	314
Comal	283	151	132
Coryell	75	33	42
Crosby	14	5	9
Dallas	2,243	423	1,820
Ector	229	80	149
Ellis	220	80	140
El Paso	1,012	253	759
Falls	26	7	19
Fort Bend	800	549	251
Goliad	29	14	15
Grayson	160	65	95
Gregg	256	106	150
Hardin	67	29	38
Hays	301	144	157
Hidalgo	773	280	493
Hood	138	53	85
Hudspeth	41	14	27
Hunt	139	46	93
Irion	12	5	7
Jefferson	435	169	266
Johnson	146	93	53
Kaufman	232	82	150
Kendall	81	48	33
Lampasas	37	17	20
Liberty	75	52	23
Lubbock	499	212	287
McLennan	378	97	281
Medina	71	33	38
Midland	198	77	121
Montgomery	789	461	328
Newton	21	11	10

Table 64. Full-time Law Enforcement Employees, by Selected State Metropolitan and Nonmetropolitan Counties, 2016—Continued

(Number.)

State/county	Total law enforcement employees	Total officers	Total civilians
Nueces	298	53	245
Oldham	11	6	5
Orange	131	63	68
Parker	126	89	37
Potter	219	98	121
Randall	196	88	108
Robertson	31	13	18
Rockwall	108	34	74
Rusk	78	41	37
San Patricio	115	54	61
Smith	369	172	197
Tarrant	1,337	371	966
Taylor	233	83	150
Tom Green	163	61	102
Travis	1,630	345	1,285
Victoria	204	114	90
Waller	86	61	25
Webb	331	267	64
Wichita	211	82	129
Williamson	510	224	286
Wilson	79	33	46
Wise	142	64	78
Nonmetropolitan Counties			
Anderson	74	36	38
Andrews	36	14	22
Angelina	112	49	63
Baylor	8	3	5
Bee	51	21	30
Blanco	30	12	18
Borden	3	2	1
Bosque	41	20	21
Brewster	15	14	1
Briscoe	3	3	0
Brooks	35	11	24
Brown	68	29	39
Burnet	132	45	87
Calhoun	62	25	37
Camp	18	7	11
Cass	36	21	15
Castro	19	6	13
Cherokee	73	34	39
Childress	21	5	16
Cochran	12	6	6
Coke	6	5	1
Comanche	31	11	20
Concho	12	7	5
Crane	11	6	5
Dawson	19	7	12
Delta	23	11	12
Dickens	7	3	4
Dimmit	70	31	39
Duval	46	26	20
Eastland	31	12	19
Edwards	12	6	6
Erath	60	21	39
Fayette	49	26	23
Floyd	11	7	4
Foard	4	3	1
Franklin	25	11	14
Frio	40	19	21
Gaines	37	16	21
Garza	35	8	27
Glasscock	5	4	1
Gonzales	55	20	35
Gray	43	13	30
Grimes	56	31	25
Hale	69	69	0
Hamilton	14	7	7
Hansford	13	7	6
Hardeman	11	7	4
Hartley	5	5	0
Haskell	12	4	8
Hemphill	14	7	7
Hill	68	33	35
Hockley	26	11	15
Hopkins	65	25	40
Houston	48	21	27
Howard	57	21	36
Hutchinson	33	13	20
Jack	29	11	18
Jackson	34	12	22
Jasper	66	18	48

Table 64. Full-time Law Enforcement Employees, by Selected State Metropolitan and Nonmetropolitan Counties, 2016—Continued

(Number.)

State/county	Total law enforcement employees	Total officers	Total civilians
Jim Wells	70	64	6
Karnes	66	32	34
Kenedy	18	11	7
Kent	7	3	4
Kerr	94	45	49
Kimble	13	8	5
Kinney	15	7	8
Knox	9	3	6
Lamar	76	27	49
Lamb	32	13	19
La Salle	139	25	114
Lavaca	34	15	19
Lee	42	14	28
Leon	46	28	18
Limestone	89	23	66
Lipscomb	10	6	4
Llano	50	26	24
Madison	31	13	18
Marion	12	11	1
Matagorda	74	38	36
Maverick	95	39	56
McCulloch	13	6	7
McMullen	12	10	2
Milam	60	19	41
Mills	18	7	11
Mitchell	20	5	15
Montague	29	8	21
Moore	49	17	32
Morris	22	9	13
Motley	2	2	0
Nacogdoches	86	40	46
Nolan	36	12	24
Ochiltree	20	8	12
Panola	61	39	22
Parmer	18	6	12
Pecos	37	22	15
Polk	107	48	59
Presidio	27	8	19
Rains	27	11	16
Reagan	22	14	8
Real	10	5	5
Red River	25	13	12
Reeves	49	21	28
Refugio	36	13	23
Roberts	6	5	1
Runnels	26	6	20
Sabine	19	9	10
San Augustine	19	8	11
San Jacinto	66	36	30
San Saba	10	5	5
Schleicher	11	5	6
Scurry	38	9	29
Shackelford	12	4	8
Starr	108	48	60
Stephens	20	7	13
Sterling	4	4	0
Stonewall	9	3	6
Swisher	10	4	6
Terry	37	12	25
Trinity	17	11	6
Upton	20	10	10
Uvalde	69	32	37
Val Verde	65	44	21
Van Zandt	71	30	41
Walker	83	40	43
Ward	33	14	19
Wharton	75	44	31
Wheeler	22	10	12
Wilbarger	18	7	11
Willacy	45	16	29
Winkler	30	9	21
Wood	60	24	36
Yoakum	21	9	12
Young	36	11	25
UTAH			
Metropolitan Counties			
Box Elder	83	28	55
Cache	146	55	91
Davis	312	145	167
Juab	26	14	12
Morgan	12	10	2
Salt Lake County Unified Police Department	580	427	153

Table 64. Full-time Law Enforcement Employees, by Selected State Metropolitan and Nonmetropolitan Counties, 2016—Continued

(Number.)

State/county	Total law enforcement employees	Total officers	Total civilians
Tooele	90	34	56
Utah	378	145	233
Washington	159	44	115
Weber	70	70	0
Nonmetropolitan Counties			
Beaver	70	23	47
Carbon	54	29	25
Daggett	25	10	15
Duchesne	58	24	34
Emery	39	27	12
Garfield	29	13	16
Grand	31	17	14
Iron	78	37	41
Kane	46	14	32
Millard	54	34	20
Piute	5	4	1
Rich	10	4	6
San Juan	28	12	16
Sanpete	58	20	38
Sevier	24	22	2
Summit	98	60	38
Uintah	79	25	54
Wasatch	55	28	27
Wayne	6	5	1
VERMONT			
Metropolitan Counties			
Chittenden	17	15	2
Franklin	9	9	0
Grand Isle	1	1	0
Nonmetropolitan Counties			
Addison	6	6	0
Bennington	15	12	3
Caledonia	12	9	3
Essex	2	2	0
Lamoille	24	11	13
Orange	16	10	6
Orleans	9	7	2
Rutland	16	12	4
Washington	13	11	2
Windham	18	13	5
Windsor	14	13	1
VIRGINIA			
Metropolitan Counties			
Albemarle County Police Department	156	128	28
Amelia	28	17	11
Amherst	44	44	0
Appomattox	23	22	1
Arlington County Police Department	464	361	103
Augusta	82	71	11
Bedford	91	83	8
Botetourt	119	96	23
Buckingham	26	19	7
Campbell	68	59	9
Caroline	68	48	20
Charles City	16	10	6
Chesterfield County Police Department	605	503	102
Clarke	27	15	12
Craig	15	10	5
Culpeper	96	82	14
Dinwiddie	53	51	2
Fairfax County Police Department	1,617	1,414	203
Fauquier	147	122	25
Floyd	32	22	10
Fluvanna	49	35	14
Franklin	94	73	21
Frederick	140	124	16
Giles	34	23	11
Gloucester	98	83	15
Goochland	47	36	11
Greene	42	25	17
Hanover	254	237	17
Henrico County Police Department	807	639	168
Isle of Wight	52	48	4
James City County Police Department	102	96	6
King William	32	19	13
Loudoun	642	531	111
Mathews	18	11	7
Montgomery	117	107	10
Nelson	22	18	4

Table 64. Full-time Law Enforcement Employees, by Selected State Metropolitan and Nonmetropolitan Counties, 2016—Continued

(Number.)

State/county	Total law enforcement employees	Total officers	Total civilians
New Kent	48	32	16
Powhatan	61	42	19
Prince George County Police Department	79	54	25
Prince William County Police Department	744	611	133
Pulaski	48	46	2
Rappahannock	18	17	1
Roanoke County Police Department	155	141	14
Rockingham	78	62	16
Scott	37	30	7
Spotsylvania	230	181	49
Stafford	240	173	67
Sussex	48	43	5
Warren	70	53	17
Washington	80	59	21
York	94	86	8
Nonmetropolitan Counties			
Accomack	68	57	11
Alleghany	65	46	19
Bath	19	12	7
Bland	18	10	8
Brunswick	38	27	11
Buchanan	46	33	13
Carroll	42	36	6
Charlotte	36	33	3
Cumberland	22	17	5
Dickenson	25	14	11
Essex	21	10	11
Grayson	32	26	6
Greensville	34	21	13
Halifax	38	31	7
Henry	131	118	13
Highland	12	7	5
King and Queen	20	12	8
King George	58	40	18
Lancaster	38	29	9
Lee	34	34	0
Louisa	64	47	17
Lunenburg	19	13	6
Madison	34	21	13
Mecklenburg	52	50	2
Middlesex	42	30	12
Northampton	84	66	18
Northumberland	33	22	11
Nottoway	24	14	10
Orange	49	40	9
Page	72	55	17
Patrick	69	54	15
Pittsylvania	141	122	19
Prince Edward	31	31	0
Richmond	23	15	8
Rockbridge	40	37	3
Russell	50	35	15
Shenandoah	62	57	5
Smyth	45	45	0
Southampton	80	68	12
Surry	21	11	10
Tazewell	82	58	24
Westmoreland	54	40	14
Wise	65	49	16
Wythe	46	37	9
WASHINGTON			
Metropolitan Counties			
Asotin	30	13	17
Benton	71	58	13
Chelan	73	57	16
Clark	211	134	77
Columbia	9	8	1
Cowlitz	47	41	6
Douglas	33	27	6
Franklin	85	27	58
King	321	230	91
Kitsap	140	117	23
Pend Oreille	34	14	20
Pierce	328	268	60
Skagit	117	54	63
Skamania	20	17	3
Snohomish	341	273	68
Spokane	182	119	63
Stevens	53	26	27
Thurston	215	83	132
Walla Walla	33	26	7

Table 64. Full-time Law Enforcement Employees, by Selected State Metropolitan and Nonmetropolitan Counties, 2016—Continued

(Number.)

State/county	Total law enforcement employees	Total officers	Total civilians
Whatcom	187	86	101
Yakima	81	55	26
Nonmetropolitan Counties			
Adams	35	16	19
Clallam	43	35	8
Ferry	17	11	6
Garfield	15	8	7
Grant	66	50	16
Grays Harbor	73	60	13
Island	45	38	7
Jefferson	45	23	22
Kittitas	71	32	39
Klickitat	39	20	19
Lewis	50	35	15
Lincoln	24	14	10
Mason	96	52	44
Okanogan	35	30	5
Pacific	42	13	29
San Juan	32	20	12
Wahkiakum	19	8	11
Whitman	21	18	3
WEST VIRGINIA			
Metropolitan Counties			
Berkeley	68	60	8
Boone	29	24	5
Brooke	27	17	10
Cabell	63	43	20
Clay	8	3	5
Fayette	38	34	4
Hampshire	23	19	4
Hancock	32	29	3
Jefferson	33	27	6
Kanawha	135	100	35
Lincoln	7	6	1
Marshall	35	32	3
Mineral	16	14	2
Monongalia	42	39	3
Ohio	36	34	2
Preston	22	20	2
Putnam	61	42	19
Raleigh	65	48	17
Wayne	24	20	4
Wirt	3	3	0
Nonmetropolitan Counties			
Barbour	10	9	1
Braxton	9	8	1
Calhoun	3	2	1
Doddridge	10	8	2
Gilmer	4	4	0
Grant	11	8	3
Greenbrier	32	31	1
Hardy	15	13	2
Harrison	53	51	2
Jackson	22	14	8
Lewis	21	15	6
Logan	22	20	2
Marion	47	32	15
Mason	33	19	14
McDowell	16	14	2
Mercer	38	27	11
Mingo	29	21	8
Monroe	8	8	0
Morgan	12	11	1
Nicholas	27	21	6
Pendleton	3	3	0
Pleasants	7	6	1
Pocahontas	13	8	5
Randolph	19	14	5
Ritchie	10	6	4
Roane	9	6	3
Summers	7	6	1
Taylor	15	8	7
Tucker	7	5	2
Tyler	11	10	1
Upshur	14	12	2
Webster	5	4	1
Wetzel	14	12	2
Wyoming	20	20	0

Table 64. Full-time Law Enforcement Employees, by Selected State Metropolitan and Nonmetropolitan Counties, 2016—Continued

(Number.)

State/county	Total law enforcement employees	Total officers	Total civilians
WISCONSIN			
Metropolitan Counties			
Brown	320	158	162
Calumet	53	25	28
Chippewa	70	51	19
Columbia	109	41	68
Dane	533	435	98
Douglas	77	29	48
Eau Claire	109	41	68
Fond du Lac	122	58	64
Green	44	32	12
Iowa	37	20	17
Kenosha	330	119	211
Kewaunee	34	32	2
La Crosse	112	42	70
Marathon	180	68	112
Milwaukee	615	298	317
Oconto	58	26	32
Outagamie	179	73	106
Ozaukee	99	78	21
Pierce	56	48	8
Racine	214	136	78
Rock	208	99	109
Sheboygan	181	71	110
St. Croix	88	80	8
Washington	167	70	97
Waukesha	356	158	198
Winnebago	186	128	58
Nonmetropolitan Counties			
Adams	58	28	30
Ashland	42	33	9
Barron	68	31	37
Bayfield	43	20	23
Buffalo	25	11	14
Burnett	33	17	16
Clark	47	25	22
Crawford	29	23	6
Dodge	169	69	100
Door	65	52	13
Dunn	55	27	28
Florence	20	12	8
Forest	37	17	20
Grant	50	28	22
Green Lake	41	16	25
Iron	20	20	0
Jackson	49	23	26
Jefferson	115	93	22
Juneau	53	41	12
Lafayette	32	31	1
Langlade	40	19	21
Lincoln	65	30	35
Manitowoc	94	63	31
Marinette	63	32	31
Marquette	42	42	0
Menominee	10	9	1
Monroe	52	23	29
Oneida	86	37	49
Pepin	18	7	11
Polk	70	28	42
Portage	101	48	53
Price	30	20	10
Richland	32	32	0
Rusk	30	27	3
Sauk	143	47	96
Sawyer	48	26	22
Shawano	111	39	72
Taylor	39	18	21
Trempealeau	55	25	30
Vernon	44	24	20
Vilas	70	35	35
Walworth	201	80	121
Washburn	22	14	8
Waupaca	101	40	61
Waushara	54	24	30
Wood	70	40	30
WYOMING			
Metropolitan Counties			
Laramie	155	50	105
Natrona	163	60	103
Nonmetropolitan Counties			
Albany	43	40	3

Table 64. Full-time Law Enforcement Employees, by Selected State Metropolitan and Nonmetropolitan Counties, 2016—Continued

(Number.)

State/county	Total law enforcement employees	Total officers	Total civilians
Big Horn	27	12	15
Campbell	66	43	23
Carbon	33	17	16
Crook	21	15	6
Fremont	36	33	3
Hot Springs	12	10	2
Johnson	31	29	2
Lincoln	42	26	16
Park	50	18	32
Platte	13	10	3
Sheridan	57	38	19
Sublette	32	28	4
Sweetwater	99	43	56
Uinta	48	35	13
Washakie	16	14	2
Weston	8	8	0
Menominee	0	0	0
Monroe	16	0	1
Oneida	24	0	0
Pepin	3	0	1
Polk	99	0	1
Portage	15	0	1
Price	1	0	1
Richland	0	0	0
Rusk	23	1	1
Sauk	27	0	0
Sawyer	19	1	1
Shawano	26	1	1
Taylor	17	0	0
Trempealeau	9	0	1
Vernon	7	0	0
Vilas	8	0	1
Walworth	10	0	0
Washburn	17	0	1
Waupaca	82	1	3
Waushara	23	0	2
Wood	5	0	2
WYOMING			
Metropolitan Counties			
Laramie	70	3	1
Natrona	56	0	3
Nonmetropolitan Counties			
Albany	9	0	1
Big Horn	2	0	1
Campbell	126	2	3
Carbon	8	0	0
Crook	1	0	0
Fremont	25	0	0
Goshen	27	0	0
Hot Springs	1	0	0
Johnson	5	0	0
Lincoln	19	0	2
Park	30	0	0
Platte	1	0	0
Sheridan	27	0	0
Sublette	3	0	0
Sweetwater	25	0	5
Uinta	4	0	0
Washakie	0	0	0
Weston	1	0	0

1 The employee data presented in this table for Mecklenburg represent only Mecklenburg County Sheriff's Office employees and exclude Charlotte-Mecklenburg Police Department employees.

SECTION VI

HATE CRIMES

Figure 1. Percent Distribution of Single-Bias Hate Crime Incidents, 2016

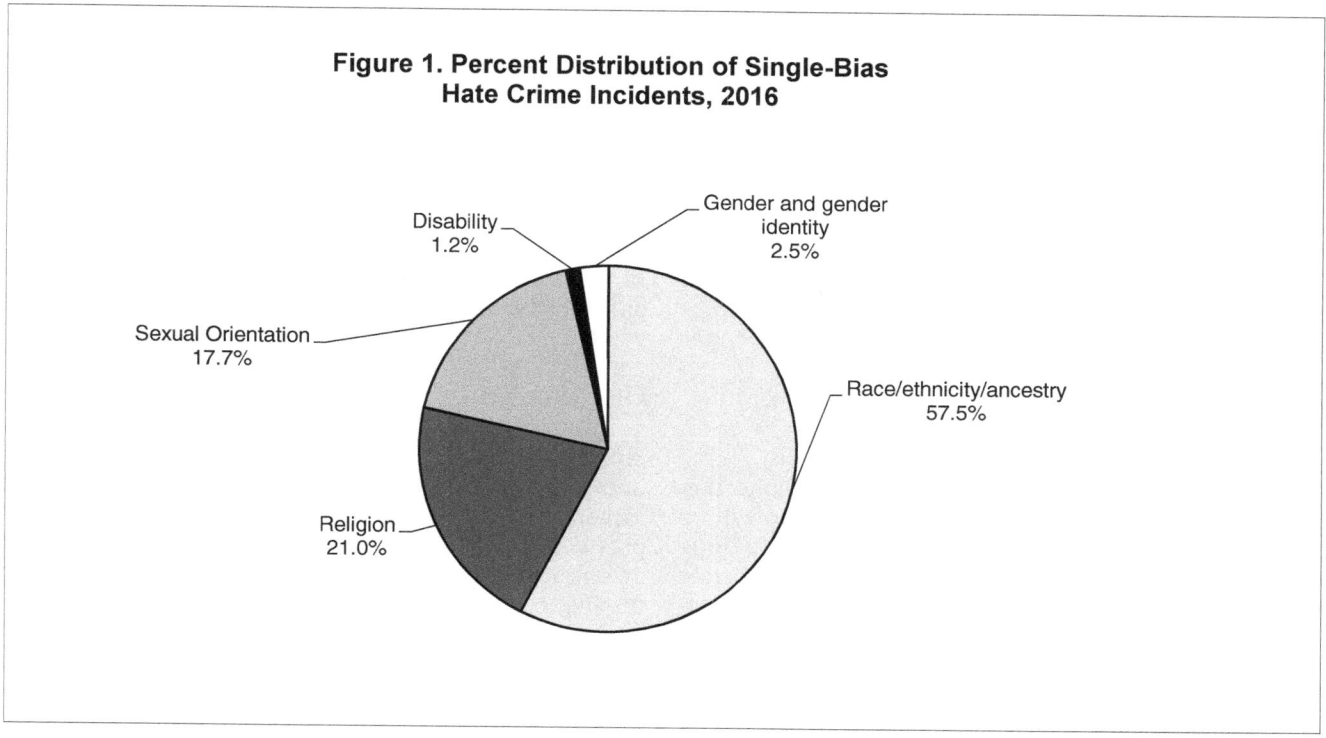

Disability 1.2%

Gender and gender identity 2.5%

Sexual Orientation 17.7%

Race/ethnicity/ancestry 57.5%

Religion 21.0%

The Federal Bureau of Investigation (FBI) began the procedures for implementing, collecting, and managing hate crime data after Congress passed the Hate Crime Statistics Act in 1990. This act required the collection of data "about crimes that manifest evidence of prejudice based on race, religion, sexual orientation, or ethnicity." Beginning in 2013, law enforcement agencies could submit hate crime data in accordance with a number of program modifications. In 1994, the Hate Crime Statistics Act was amended to include bias against persons with disabilities. The Church Arson Prevention Act, which was signed into law in July 1996, removed the sunset clause from the original statute and mandated that the collection of hate crime data become a permanent part of the UCR program. In 2009, Congress further amended the Hate Crime Statistics Act by passing the Matthew Shepard and James Byrd, Jr., Hate Crime Prevention Act. The amendment includes the collection of data for crimes motivated by bias against a particular gender and gender identity, as well as for crimes committed by, and crimes directed against, juveniles. In response to the Shepard/Byrd Act, the FBI modified its data collection so that reporting agencies could indicate whether hate crimes were committed by, or directed against, juveniles.

Definitions

Hate crimes include any crime motivated by bias against race, religion, sexual orientation, ethnicity/national origin, and/or disability. Because motivation is subjective, it is sometimes difficult to know with certainty whether a crime resulted from the offender's bias. Moreover, the presence of bias alone does not necessarily mean that a crime can be considered a hate crime. Only when law enforcement investigation reveals sufficient evidence to lead a reasonable and prudent person to conclude that the offender's actions were motivated, in whole or in part, by his or her bias should an incident be reported as a hate crime.

Starting with the 2015 data, incidents motivated by race and ethnicity are grouped in the new "Race/Ethnicity/Ancestry" single-bias category. New subcategories include anti-Arab, anti-Hispanic or Latino (the former ethnicity designation), and anti-other race/ethnicity/ancestry. Under "Anti-Religion," new subcategories include anti-Mormon, anti-Jehovah's Witness, anti-Eastern Orthodox (Russian/Greek/other), anti-Buddhist, anti-Hindu, and anti-Sikh.

Data Collection

The UCR (Uniform Crime Reporting) program collects data about both single-bias and multiple-bias hate crimes. A single-bias incident is defined as an incident in which one or more offense types are motivated by the same bias. A multiple-bias incident is defined as an incident in which more than one offense type occurs and at least two offense types are motivated by different biases.

A table enumerating selected places in the United States that did not report hate crimes in 2016 is available at https://ucr.fbi.gov/hate-crime/2016/tables/table-14/table_14_hate_crime_zero_data_submitted_per_quarter_by_state_and_agency_2016-.xls.xlsx/view.

Important Note: Rape

In 2013, the FBI UCR Program initiated the collection of rape data under a revised definition and removed the term "forcible" from the offense name. The changes bring uniformity to the offense in both the Summary Reporting System (SRS) and the National Incident-Based Reporting System (NIBRS) by capturing data (1) without regard to gender, (2) including penetration of any bodily orifice by any object or body part, and (3) including offenses where physical force is not involved. The UCR Program now defines rape as follows:

- **Rape (revised):** Penetration, no matter how slight, of the vagina or anus with any body part or object, or oral penetration by a sex organ of another person, without the consent of the victim. This includes the offenses of rape, sodomy, and sexual assault with an object.

- **Rape (legacy):** The carnal knowledge of a female forcibly and against her will.

The offenses of fondling, incest, and statutory rape are included in the Crimes Against Persons, Other category.

Beginning January 1, 2017, the UCR Program discontinued collecting rape data via the SRS according to the historical, legacy definition. Only rape data submitted under the revised definition will be published for 2017 and subsequent years. This change will not affect agencies that submit rape data via NIBRS.

CRIMES AGAINST PERSONS, PROPERTY, OR SOCIETY

The UCR program's data collection guidelines stipulate that a hate crime may involve multiple offenses, victims, and offenders within one incident; therefore, the Hate Crime Statistics program is incident-based. According to UCR counting guidelines:

- One offense is counted for each victim in *crimes against persons*

- One offense is counted for each offense type in *crimes against property*

- One offense is counted for each offense type in *crimes against society*

VICTIMS

In the UCR program, the victim of a hate crime may be an individual, a business, an institution, or society as a whole.

OFFENDERS

According to the UCR program, the term *known offender* does not imply that the suspect's identity is known; rather, the term indicates that some aspect of the suspect was identified, thus distinguishing the suspect from an unknown offender. Law enforcement agencies specify the number of offenders, and when possible, the race of the offender or offenders as a group.

RACE/ETHNICITY

The UCR program uses the following racial designations in its Hate Crime Statistics program: White; Black; American Indian or Alaskan Native; Asian; Native Hawaiian or Other Pacific Islander; and Multiple Races, Group. In addition, the UCR program uses the ethnic designations of Hispanic or Latino and Not Hispanic or Latino.

The law enforcement agencies that voluntarily participate in the Hate Crime Statistics program collect details about an offender's bias motivation associated with 11 offense types already being reported to the UCR program: murder and nonnegligent manslaughter, rape, aggravated assault, simple assault, and intimidation (crimes against persons); and robbery, burglary, larceny-theft, motor vehicle theft, arson, and destruction/damage/vandalism (crimes against property). The law enforcement agencies that participate in the UCR program via the National Incident-Based Reporting System (NIBRS) collect data about additional offenses for *crimes against persons* and *crimes against property*. These data appear in the category of other. These agencies also collect hate crime data for the category called *crimes against society*, which includes drug or narcotic offenses, gambling offenses, prostitution offenses, and weapon law violations.

National Volume and Percent Distribution

In 2016, 1,776 law enforcement agencies (out of 15,254 participating agencies) reported 6,121 hate crime incidents involving 7,321 offenses. Of these, 6,063 were single-bias offenses. An analysis of the single-bias incidents revealed that 57.5 percent were racially/ethnically/ancestrally motivated, 21.0 percent were motivated by religious bias, 17.7 percent resulted from sexual orientation bias, 2.5 percent were motivated by gender and gender-identity bias, and 1.2 percent were prompted by a disability bias. (Table 65)

The majority of the 3,310 hate crime offenses that were racially/ethnically/ancestrally motivated resulted from an anti-Black bias (50.2 percent) followed by an anti-White basis (20.7 percent). Bias against people of more than one race accounted for 4.2 percent of offenses, while anti-Asian bias also accounted for 3.1 percent of racially motivated offenses, anti-Native Hawaiian and Other Pacific Islander accounted for 0.2 percent of these offenses, and anti-American Indian or Alaska Native bias accounted for 3.8 percent of these offenses. Anti-Arab offenses accounted for 1.3 percent of the total, while anti-Hispanic or Latino offenses comprised 10.6 percent of the total. Anti-Other Race/Ethnicity/Ancestry accounted for 5.8 percent of the total. (Table 65)

Hate crimes motivated by religious bias accounted for 1,244 offenses reported by law enforcement. A breakdown of these offenses revealed 54.2 percent were motivated by anti-Jewish bias, followed by 24.8 percent by anti-Islamic (Muslim) bias. Approximately 3.1 percent of incidents were anti-multiple religions or groups, 4.1 percent had an anti-Catholic bias, 1.3 percent were anti-Protestant, 0.4 percent were anti-atheism/agnosticism/etc., and the remainder of the offenses were based on biases against other religions (anti-Mormon, anti-Jehovah's Witness, anti-Eastern Orthodox, anti-other Christian, anti-Buddhist, anti-Hindu, and anti-Sikh). (Table 65)

Of the offenses based on sexual orientation, 21.5 percent were classified as having an anti-lesbian, gay, bisexual, or transgender (mixed group) bias; 62.8 percent were classified as having an anti-male homosexual bias; 11.6 percent had an anti-female homosexual basis; 2.2 percent had an anti-bisexual bias; and 1.9 percent had an anti-heterosexual bias. (Table 65)

Hate crime offenses committed based on disability totaled 76 offenses. The majority (47 incidents) were classified as anti-physical disability, with the rest (29 incidents) classified as anti-mental disability. (Table 65)

Of the 130 gender and gender identity bias offenses reported, 111 were anti-transgender and 19 were anti-gender nonconforming. Of the 36 gender bias offenses reported, 26 were anti-female and 10 were anti-male. (Table 65)

Crimes Against Persons

Law enforcement agencies reported 4,720 hate crime offenses against persons in 2016, up from 3,646 offenses in 2015. Approximately 44.7 percent involved intimidation, 35.7 percent involved simple assault, and 18.5 percent involved aggravated assault. In addition, there were 9 murders and 24 rapes (all submitted under the revised definition of rape). (Table 66)

Crimes Against Property

In 2014, hate crime offenses against property totaled 2,519. Approximately 75.9 percent of offenses involved destruction/damage or vandalism. The remaining 24.1 percent of crimes against property consisted of robbery, burglary, larceny-theft, motor vehicle theft, arson, destruction/damage/vandalism, and other crimes. (Table 66)

Table 65. Incidents, Offenses, Victims, and Known Offenders, by Bias Motivation, 2016

(Number.)

Bias motivation	Incidents	Offenses	Victims[1]	Known offenders[2]
Total	6,121	7,321	7,615	5,770
Single-Bias Incidents	6,063	7,227	7,509	5,727
Race/Ethnicity/Ancestry	3,489	4,229	4,426	3,383
Anti-White	720	876	909	831
Anti-Black or African American	1,739	2,122	2,220	1,588
Anti-American Indian or Alaska Native	154	161	169	118
Anti-Asian	113	131	137	123
Anti-Native Hawaiian or Other Pacific Islander	9	9	9	8
Anti-Multiple Races, Group	136	178	190	104
Anti-Arab	51	56	57	60
Anti-Hispanic or Latino	344	449	483	380
Anti-Other Race/Ethnicity/Ancestry	223	247	252	171
Religion	1,273	1,538	1,584	859
Anti-Jewish	684	834	862	421
Anti-Catholic	62	63	65	45
Anti-Protestant	15	20	22	12
Anti-Islamic (Muslim)	307	381	388	243
Anti-Other Religion	74	90	91	53
Anti-Multiple Religions, Group	34	48	48	20
Anti-Mormon	7	8	8	3
Anti-Jehovah's Witness	2	3	3	1
Anti-Eastern Orthodox (Russian, Greek, Other)	28	28	30	23
Anti-Other Christian	36	37	39	13
Anti-Buddhist	1	1	1	0
Anti-Hindu	10	12	12	11
Anti-Sikh	7	7	8	10
Anti-Atheism/Agnosticism/etc.	6	6	7	4
Sexual Orientation	1,076	1,218	1,255	1,225
Anti-Gay (Male)	675	765	787	806
Anti-Lesbian	124	141	147	127
Anti-Lesbian, Gay, Bisexual, or Transgender (Mixed Group)	234	262	271	254
Anti-Heterosexual	20	23	23	13
Anti-Bisexual	23	27	27	25
Disability	70	76	77	67
Anti-Physical	26	29	30	29
Anti-Mental	44	47	47	38
Gender	31	36	36	28
Anti-Male	7	10	10	7
Anti-Female	24	26	26	21
Gender Identity	124	130	131	165
Anti-Transgender	105	111	111	149
Anti-Gender Non-Conforming	19	19	20	16
Multiple-Bias Incidents[3]	58	94	106	43

1 The term *victim* may refer to an individual, business/financial institution, government entity, religious organization, or society/public as a whole.   2 The term known offender does not imply that the identity of the suspect is known, but only that an attribute of the suspect has been identified, which distinguishes him/her from an unknown offender.   3 A multiple-bias incident is an incident in which one or more offense types are motivated by two or more biases.

Table 66. Incidents, Offenses, Victims, and Known Offenders, by Offense Type, 2016

(Number.)

Offense type	Incidents[1]	Offenses	Victims[2]	Known offenders[3]
Total	6,121	7,321	7,615	5,770
Crimes against persons	3,765	4,720	4,720	4,353
Murder and nonnegligent manslaughter	5	9	9	9
Rape (revised definition)[4]	24	24	24	29
Rape (legacy definition)[5]	0	0	0	0
Aggravated assault	684	873	873	1,031
Simple assault	1,458	1,687	1,687	1,857
Intimidation	1,577	2,109	2,109	1,409
Other[6]	17	18	18	18
Crimes against property	2,519	2,519	2,813	1,618
Robbery	134	134	163	249
Burglary	123	123	138	87
Larceny-theft	231	231	253	173
Motor vehicle theft	20	20	21	14
Arson	39	39	51	33
Destruction/damage/vandalism	1,913	1,913	2,122	1,015
Other[6]	59	59	65	47
Crimes against society[6]	82	82	82	97

1 The actual number of incidents is 6,121. However, the column figures will not add to the total because incidents may include more than one offense type, and these are counted in each appropriate offense type category. 2 The term victim may refer to a person, business, institution, or society as a whole. 3 The term known offender does not imply that the identity of the suspect is known, but only that an attribute of the suspect has been identified, which distinguishes him/her from an unknown offender. The actual number of known offenders is 5,770. However, the column figures will not add to the total because some offenders are responsible for more than one offense type, and are, therefore, counted more than once in this table. 4 The figures shown in this row for the offense of rape include only those reported by law enforcement agencies that used the revised Uniform Crime Reporting (UCR) definition of rape. 5 The figures shown in this row for the offense of rape include only those reported by law enforcement agencies that used the legacy UCR definition of rape. 6 Includes additional offenses collected in the National Incident-Based Reporting System.

Table 67. Offenses, Known Offender's Race and Ethnicity, by Offense Type, 2016

(Number.)

Bias motivation	Total offenses	Known offender's race							Known offender's ethnicity[1]				Unknown offender
		White	Black or African American	American Indian or Alaska Native	Asian	Native Hawaiian or Other Pacific Islander	Group of multiple races	Unknown race	Hispanic or Latino	Not Hispanic or Latino	Group of multiple ethnicities	Unknown ethnicity	
Total	7,321	2,680	1,331	49	45	7	245	1,010	254	1,026	38	2,504	1,954
Crimes against persons	4,720	2,197	1,117	35	35	4	199	505	214	856	28	1,880	628
Murder and nonnegligent manslaughter	9	4	5	0	0	0	0	0	0	1	0	3	0
Rape (revised definition)[2]	24	9	6	2	0	0	0	3	2	2	1	14	4
Rape (legacy definition)[3]	0	0	0	0	0	0	0	0	0	0	0	0	0
Aggravated assault	873	395	268	9	7	1	63	56	69	179	9	313	74
Simple assault	1,687	764	513	17	9	3	93	184	90	377	14	654	104
Intimidation	2,109	1,015	322	7	19	0	43	262	52	288	4	893	441
Other[4]	18	10	3	0	0	0	0	0	1	9	0	3	5
Crimes against property	2,519	429	194	12	9	3	45	504	40	153	8	564	1,323
Robbery	134	25	67	3	0	0	13	11	10	30	1	47	15
Burglary	123	33	11	1	1	0	3	18	2	12	2	35	56
Larceny-theft	231	69	33	1	1	0	2	33	1	21	1	101	92
Motor vehicle theft	20	3	3	0	0	0	1	4	0	0	0	11	9
Arson	39	13	5	0	0	0	2	4	3	3	1	7	15
Destruction/damage/ vandalism	1,913	267	69	7	7	3	24	422	23	85	3	329	1,114
Other[4]	59	19	6	0	0	0	0	12	1	2	0	34	22
Crimes against society[4]	82	54	20	2	1	0	1	1	0	17	2	60	3

1 The sum of offenses by the known offender's ethnicity does not equal the sum of offenses by the known offender's race because not all law enforcement agencies that report offender race data also report offender ethnicity data.   2 The figures shown in the rape (revised definition) row include only those reported by law enforcement agencies that used the revised Uniform Crime Reporting (UCR) definition of rape.   3 The figures shown in the rape (legacy definition) row include only those reported by law enforcement agencies that used the legacy UCR definition of rape.   4 Includes additional offenses collected in the National Incident-Based Reporting System.

Table 68. Offenses, Offense Type, by Bias Motivation, 2016

(Number.)

Bias motivation	Total offenses	Crimes against persons						
		Murder and nonnegligent manslaughter	Rape (revised definition)[1]	Rape (legacy definition)[2]	Aggravated assault	Simple assault	Intimidation	Other[3]
Total	7,321	9	24	0	873	1,687	2,109	18
Single-Bias Incidents	7,227	9	23	0	866	1,677	2,074	17
Race/Ethnicity/Ancestry	4,229	7	10	0	548	1,002	1,320	5
Anti-White	876	5	5	0	120	241	188	2
Anti-Black or African American	2,122	2	2	0	273	455	782	2
Anti-American Indian or Alaska Native	161	0	1	0	8	17	36	0
Anti-Asian	131	0	0	0	15	40	45	0
Anti-Native Hawaiian or Other Pacific Islander	9	0	0	0	0	4	3	0
Anti-Multiple Races, Group	178	0	0	0	17	36	49	0
Anti-Arab	56	0	0	0	8	16	17	0
Anti-Hispanic or Latino	449	0	1	0	91	129	140	1
Anti-Other Race/Ethnicity/Ancestry	247	0	1	0	16	64	60	0
Religion	1,538	0	1	0	85	168	433	1
Anti-Jewish	834	0	0	0	12	61	238	0
Anti-Catholic	63	0	0	0	1	5	6	0
Anti-Protestant	20	0	0	0	1	3	1	0
Anti-Islamic (Muslim)	381	0	0	0	52	75	144	0
Anti-Other Religion	90	0	0	0	13	10	8	0
Anti-Multiple Religions, Group	48	0	0	0	2	4	21	0
Anti-Mormon	8	0	0	0	0	0	2	0
Anti-Jehovah's Witness	3	0	0	0	0	0	2	0
Anti-Eastern Orthodox (Russian, Greek, Other)	28	0	0	0	1	4	2	1
Anti-Other Christian	37	0	0	0	1	3	2	0
Anti-Buddhist	1	0	0	0	0	0	0	0
Anti-Hindu	12	0	0	0	1	2	6	0
Anti-Sikh	7	0	0	0	1	2	6	0
Anti-Atheism/Agnosticism/etc.	6	0	1	0	0	0	0	0
Sexual Orientation	1,218	1	9	0	197	414	289	4
Anti-Gay (Male)	765	1	1	0	126	281	183	3
Anti-Lesbian	141	0	4	0	23	46	37	0
Anti-Lesbian, Gay, Bisexual, or Transgender (Mixed Group)	262	0	4	0	45	71	59	1
Anti-Heterosexual	23	0	0	0	1	2	7	0
Anti-Bisexual	27	0	0	0	2	14	3	0
Disability	76	0	2	0	5	33	9	2
Anti-Physical	29	0	0	0	2	15	4	1
Anti-Mental	47	0	2	0	3	18	5	1
Gender	36	1	0	0	6	11	7	0
Anti-Male	10	1	0	0	0	7	1	0
Anti-Female	26	0	0	0	6	4	6	0
Gender Identity	130	0	1	0	25	49	16	5
Anti-Transgender	111	0	1	0	24	47	14	5
Anti-Gender Non-Conforming	19	0	0	0	1	2	2	0
Multiple-Bias Incidents[4]	94	0	1	0	7	10	35	1

Table 68. Offenses, Offense Type, by Bias Motivation, 2016—Continued

(Number.)

Bias motivation	Crimes against property							Crimes against society[3]
	Robbery	Burglary	Larceny-theft	Motor vehicle theft	Arson	Destruction/ damage/ vandalism	Other[3]	
Total	134	123	231	20	39	1,913	59	82
Single-Bias Incidents	131	122	227	20	38	1,882	59	82
Race/Ethnicity/Ancestry	71	75	149	14	13	916	46	53
Anti-White	30	22	78	6	2	122	24	31
Anti-Black or African American	14	17	14	2	7	537	5	10
Anti-American Indian or Alaska Native	0	18	31	4	0	29	12	5
Anti-Asian	2	4	5	0	0	18	0	2
Anti-Native Hawaiian or Other Pacific Islander	0	0	0	0	0	2	0	0
Anti-Multiple Races, Group	4	5	0	1	2	62	2	0
Anti-Arab	1	0	0	0	1	13	0	0
Anti-Hispanic or Latino	19	2	5	0	0	57	0	4
Anti-Other Race/Ethnicity/Ancestry	1	7	16	1	1	76	3	1
Religion	10	29	47	4	18	720	6	16
Anti-Jewish	3	9	15	1	4	489	1	1
Anti-Catholic	0	3	10	1	1	31	1	4
Anti-Protestant	0	1	4	0	1	8	0	1
Anti-Islamic (Muslim)	4	2	3	0	5	92	0	4
Anti-Other Religion	1	6	1	0	0	49	1	1
Anti-Multiple Religions, Group	1	1	1	1	2	15	0	0
Anti-Mormon	0	0	1	0	1	2	0	2
Anti-Jehovah's Witness	0	0	1	0	0	0	0	0
Anti-Eastern Orthodox (Russian, Greek, Other)	0	3	8	1	0	5	1	2
Anti-Other Christian	1	3	2	0	3	22	0	0
Anti-Buddhist	0	0	0	0	0	1	0	0
Anti-Hindu	0	0	0	0	0	2	0	1
Anti-Sikh	0	1	0	0	0	2	1	0
Anti-Atheism/Agnosticism/etc.	0	0	1	0	1	2	1	0
Sexual Orientation	38	10	17	2	6	221	4	6
Anti-Gay (Male)	28	6	6	0	1	126	0	3
Anti-Lesbian	0	2	3	0	2	23	1	0
Anti-Lesbian, Gay, Bisexual, or Transgender (Mixed Group)	10	1	1	1	3	64	1	1
Anti-Heterosexual	0	0	5	0	0	6	0	2
Anti-Bisexual	0	1	2	1	0	2	2	0
Disability	1	3	8	0	0	6	2	5
Anti-Physical	0	2	2	0	0	1	1	1
Anti-Mental	1	1	6	0	0	5	1	4
Gender	0	3	0	0	0	7	1	0
Anti-Male	0	1	0	0	0	0	0	0
Anti-Female	0	2	0	0	0	7	1	0
Gender Identity	11	2	6	0	1	12	0	2
Anti-Transgender	11	1	2	0	1	5	0	0
Anti-Gender Non-Conforming	0	1	4	0	0	7	0	2
Multiple-Bias Incidents[4]	3	1	4	0	1	31	0	0

1 The figures shown in this column for the offense of rape include only those reported by law enforcement agencies that used the revised Uniform Crime Reporting (UCR) definition of rape.   2 The figures shown in this column for the offense of rape include only those reported by law enforcement agencies that used the legacy UCR definition of rape.   3 Includes additional offenses collected in the National Incident-Based Reporting System.   4 A multiple-bias incident is an incident in which one or more offense types are motivated by two or more biases.

Table 69. Offenses, Known Offender's Race, by Bias Motivation, 2016

(Number.)

Bias motivation	Total offenses	Known offender's race						
		White	Black or African American	American Indian or Alaska Native	Asian	Native Hawaiian or Other Pacific Islander	Group of multiple races	Unknown race
Total	7321	2680	1331	49	45	7	245	1010
Single-Bias Incidents	7227	2661	1307	49	45	7	242	993
Race/Ethnicity/Ancestry	4229	1775	781	37	32	2	150	398
Anti-White	876	133	452	20	6	0	27	80
Anti-Black or African American	2122	1142	80	9	17	1	88	202
Anti-American Indian or Alaska Native	161	56	28	2	0	0	3	14
Anti-Asian	131	65	20	2	6	0	5	9
Anti-Native Hawaiian or Other Pacific Islander	9	4	4	0	0	0	0	0
Anti-Multiple Races, Group	178	54	33	0	1	0	9	17
Anti-Arab	56	32	6	0	1	0	3	6
Anti-Hispanic or Latino	449	228	114	2	0	1	12	24
Anti-Other Race/Ethnicity/Ancestry	247	61	44	2	1	0	3	46
Religion	1538	389	118	5	5	2	32	410
Anti-Jewish	834	156	34	4	0	0	12	300
Anti-Catholic	63	9	3	0	2	0	3	22
Anti-Protestant	20	11	2	0	0	0	0	3
Anti-Islamic (Muslim)	381	135	49	1	2	0	9	66
Anti-Other Religion	90	20	20	0	1	2	1	7
Anti-Multiple Religions, Group	48	20	1	0	0	0	4	4
Anti-Mormon	8	2	2	0	0	0	0	0
Anti-Jehovah's Witness	3	2	0	0	0	0	0	0
Anti-Eastern Orthodox (Russian, Greek, Other)	28	15	3	0	0	0	0	1
Anti-Other Christian	37	4	2	0	0	0	1	6
Anti-Buddhist	1	0	0	0	0	0	0	0
Anti-Hindu	12	9	0	0	0	0	1	0
Anti-Sikh	7	4	1	0	0	0	1	0
Anti-Atheism/Agnosticism/etc.	6	2	1	0	0	0	1	1
Sexual Orientation	1218	414	326	6	6	3	49	156
Anti-Gay (Male)	765	257	223	2	1	2	33	102
Anti-Lesbian	141	51	37	0	0	0	3	14
Anti-Lesbian, Gay, Bisexual, or Transgender (Mixed Group)	262	86	53	4	3	1	12	37
Anti-Heterosexual	23	12	1	0	2	0	1	0
Anti-Bisexual	27	8	12	0	0	0	0	3
Disability	76	35	16	1	1	0	1	6
Anti-Physical	29	14	8	0	1	0	1	2
Anti-Mental	47	21	8	1	0	0	0	4
Gender	36	18	9	0	0	0	1	4
Anti-Male	10	10	0	0	0	0	0	0
Anti-Female	26	8	9	0	0	0	1	4
Gender Identity	130	30	57	0	1	0	9	19
Anti-Transgender	111	27	54	0	0	0	9	14
Anti-Gender Non-Conforming	19	3	3	0	1	0	0	5
Multiple-Bias Incidents[2]	94	19	24	0	0	0	3	17

Table 69. Offenses, Known Offender's Race, by Bias Motivation, 2016—Continued

(Number.)

Bias motivation	Known offender's ethnicity[1]				Unknown offender
	Hispanic or Latino	Not Hispanic or Latino	Group of multiple ethnicities	Unknown ethnicity	
Total	254	1026	38	2504	1954
Single-Bias Incidents	252	998	38	2476	1923
Race/Ethnicity/Ancestry	135	662	22	1618	1054
Anti-White	22	169	9	393	158
Anti-Black or African American	82	267	5	808	583
Anti-American Indian or Alaska Native	1	3	0	92	58
Anti-Asian	6	28	3	40	24
Anti-Native Hawaiian or Other Pacific Islander	0	1	0	3	1
Anti-Multiple Races, Group	2	31	1	50	64
Anti-Arab	4	16	0	14	8
Anti-Hispanic or Latino	15	112	2	150	68
Anti-Other Race/Ethnicity/Ancestry	3	35	2	68	90
Religion	23	100	9	364	577
Anti-Jewish	9	16	4	152	328
Anti-Catholic	4	3	0	14	24
Anti-Protestant	0	8	0	6	4
Anti-Islamic (Muslim)	5	40	2	121	119
Anti-Other Religion	2	16	2	18	39
Anti-Multiple Religions, Group	0	4	0	21	19
Anti-Mormon	0	4	0	0	4
Anti-Jehovah's Witness	0	0	0	0	1
Anti-Eastern Orthodox (Russian, Greek, Other)	0	4	0	15	9
Anti-Other Christian	3	1	0	5	24
Anti-Buddhist	0	0	0	0	1
Anti-Hindu	0	2	0	5	2
Anti-Sikh	0	2	1	4	0
Anti-Atheism/Agnosticism/etc.	0	0	0	3	3
Sexual Orientation	80	177	7	406	258
Anti-Gay (Male)	63	126	6	209	145
Anti-Lesbian	6	24	0	34	36
Anti-Lesbian, Gay, Bisexual, or Transgender (Mixed Group)	10	20	1	140	66
Anti-Heterosexual	1	1	0	9	7
Anti-Bisexual	0	6	0	14	4
Disability	2	14	0	39	16
Anti-Physical	0	7	0	14	3
Anti-Mental	2	7	0	25	13
Gender	0	8	0	17	4
Anti-Male	0	2	0	8	0
Anti-Female	0	6	0	9	4
Gender Identity	12	37	0	32	14
Anti-Transgender	12	33	0	30	7
Anti-Gender Non-Conforming	0	4	0	2	7
Multiple-Bias Incidents[2]	2	28	0	28	31

1 The total number of offenses by the known offender's ethnicity do not equal the total number of offenses by the known offender's race because not all law enforcement agencies that report offender race data also report offender ethnicity data.   2 A multiple-bias incident is an incident in which one or more offense types are motivated by two or more biases.

Table 70. Offenses, Victim Type, by Offense Type, 2016

(Number.)

Offense type	Total offenses	Victim type					
		Individual	Business/financial institution	Government	Religious organization	Society/public[1]	Other/ unknown/ multiple
Total	7,321	5,954	406	224	160	82	495
Crimes against persons[2]	4,720	4,720	NA	NA	NA	NA	NA
Crimes against property	2,519	1,234	406	224	160	0	495
Robbery	134	121	0	0	0	0	13
Burglary	123	79	18	1	10	0	15
Larceny-theft	231	148	61	4	6	0	12
Motor vehicle theft	20	18	2	0	0	0	0
Arson	39	18	3	2	10	0	6
Destruction/damage/vandalism	1,913	809	311	213	134	0	446
Other[2]	59	41	11	4	0	0	3
Crimes against society[2]	82	NA	NA	NA	NA	82	NA

NA = Not available.
1 The victim type *society/public* is collected only in the National Incident-Based Reporting System (NIBRS).   2 Includes additional offenses collected in the NIBRS.

Table 71. Victims, Offense Type, by Bias Motivation, 2016

(Number.)

Bias motivation	Total victims[1]	Total number of adult victims[2]	Total number of juvenile victims[2]	Crimes against persons						
				Murder and nonnegligent manslaughter	Rape (revised definition)[3]	Rape (legacy definition)[4]	Aggravated assault	Simple assault	Intimidation	Other[5]
Total	7,615	4,311	565	9	24	0	873	1,687	2,109	18
Single-Bias Incidents	7,509	4,254	558	9	23	0	866	1,677	2,074	17
Race/Ethnicity/Ancestry	4,426	2,685	384	7	10	0	548	1,002	1,320	5
Anti-White	909	586	41	5	5	0	120	241	188	2
Anti-Black or African American	2,220	1,297	261	2	2	0	273	455	782	2
Anti-American Indian or Alaska Native	169	120	6	0	1	0	8	17	36	0
Anti-Asian	137	83	5	0	0	0	15	40	45	0
Anti-Native Hawaiian or Other Pacific Islander	9	9	0	0	0	0	0	4	3	0
Anti-Multiple Races, Group	190	99	12	0	0	0	17	36	49	0
Anti-Arab	57	45	0	0	0	0	8	16	17	0
Anti-Hispanic or Latino	483	302	46	0	1	0	91	129	140	1
Anti-Other Race/Ethnicity/Ancestry	252	144	13	0	1	0	16	64	60	0
Religion	1,584	587	91	0	1	0	85	168	433	1
Anti-Jewish	862	264	60	0	0	0	12	61	238	0
Anti-Catholic	65	15	2	0	0	0	1	5	6	0
Anti-Protestant	22	9	0	0	0	0	1	3	1	0
Anti-Islamic (Muslim)	388	200	17	0	0	0	52	75	144	0
Anti-Other Religion	91	29	3	0	0	0	13	10	8	0
Anti-Multiple Religions, Group	48	26	4	0	0	0	2	4	21	0
Anti-Mormon	8	4	1	0	0	0	0	0	2	0
Anti-Jehovah's Witness	3	1	0	0	0	0	0	0	2	0
Anti-Eastern Orthodox (Russian, Greek, Other)	30	15	2	0	0	0	1	4	2	1
Anti-Other Christian	39	10	0	0	0	0	1	3	2	0
Anti-Buddhist	1	0	0	0	0	0	0	0	0	0
Anti-Hindu	12	4	2	0	0	0	1	2	6	0
Anti-Sikh	8	5	0	0	0	0	1	1	1	0
Anti-Atheism/Agnosticism/etc.	7	5	0	0	1	0	0	0	0	0
Sexual Orientation	1,255	819	65	1	9	0	197	414	289	4
Anti-Gay (Male)	787	508	36	1	1	0	126	281	183	3
Anti-Lesbian	147	87	7	0	4	0	23	46	37	0
Anti-Lesbian, Gay, Bisexual, or Transgender (Mixed Group)	271	192	18	0	4	0	45	71	59	1
Anti-Heterosexual	23	16	0	0	0	0	1	2	7	0
Anti-Bisexual	27	16	4	0	0	0	2	14	3	0
Disability	77	58	8	0	2	0	5	33	9	2
Anti-Physical	30	24	0	0	0	0	2	15	4	1
Anti-Mental	47	34	8	0	2	0	3	18	5	1
Gender	36	24	3	1	0	0	6	11	7	0
Anti-Male	10	7	3	1	0	0	0	7	1	0
Anti-Female	26	17	0	0	0	0	6	4	6	0
Gender Identity	131	81	7	0	1	0	25	49	16	5
Anti-Transgender	111	75	6	0	1	0	24	47	14	5
Anti-Gender Non-Conforming	20	6	1	0	0	0	1	2	2	0
Multiple-Bias Incidents[6]	106	57	7	0	1	0	7	10	35	1

Table 71. Victims, Offense Type, by Bias Motivation, 2016—Continued

(Number.)

Bias motivation	Crimes against property							Crimes against society[5]
	Robbery	Burglary	Larceny-theft	Motor vehicle theft	Arson	Destruction/ damage/ vandalism	Other[5]	
Total	163	138	253	21	51	2,122	65	82
Single-Bias Incidents	160	135	249	21	49	2,082	65	82
Race/Ethnicity/Ancestry	92	83	164	15	24	1,051	52	53
Anti-White	39	25	87	6	4	129	27	31
Anti-Black or African American	16	17	16	3	13	624	5	10
Anti-American Indian or Alaska Native	0	20	34	4	0	29	15	5
Anti-Asian	2	6	5	0	0	22	0	2
Anti-Native Hawaiian or Other Pacific Islander	0	0	0	0	0	2	0	0
Anti-Multiple Races, Group	5	5	0	1	5	70	2	0
Anti-Arab	1	0	0	0	1	14	0	0
Anti-Hispanic or Latino	28	2	5	0	0	82	0	4
Anti-Other Race/Ethnicity/Ancestry	1	8	17	1	1	79	3	1
Religion	12	32	53	4	18	755	6	16
Anti-Jewish	3	10	18	1	4	513	1	1
Anti-Catholic	0	3	12	1	1	31	1	4
Anti-Protestant	0	1	4	0	1	10	0	1
Anti-Islamic (Muslim)	4	2	3	0	5	99	0	4
Anti-Other Religion	1	6	1	0	0	50	1	1
Anti-Multiple Religions, Group	1	1	1	1	2	15	0	0
Anti-Mormon	0	0	1	0	1	2	0	2
Anti-Jehovah's Witness	0	0	1	0	0	0	0	0
Anti-Eastern Orthodox (Russian, Greek, Other)	0	4	9	1	0	5	1	2
Anti-Other Christian	3	3	2	0	3	22	0	0
Anti-Buddhist	0	0	0	0	0	1	0	0
Anti-Hindu	0	0	0	0	0	2	0	1
Anti-Sikh	0	2	0	0	0	2	1	0
Anti-Atheism/Agnosticism/etc.	0	0	1	0	1	3	1	0
Sexual Orientation	44	10	18	2	6	251	4	6
Anti-Gay (Male)	32	6	7	0	1	143	0	3
Anti-Lesbian	0	2	3	0	2	29	1	0
Anti-Lesbian, Gay, Bisexual, or Transgender (Mixed Group)	12	1	1	1	3	71	1	1
Anti-Heterosexual	0	0	5	0	0	6	0	2
Anti-Bisexual	0	1	2	1	0	2	2	0
Disability	1	4	8	0	0	6	2	5
Anti-Physical	0	3	2	0	0	1	1	1
Anti-Mental	1	1	6	0	0	5	1	4
Gender	0	3	0	0	0	7	1	0
Anti-Male	0	1	0	0	0	0	0	0
Anti-Female	0	2	0	0	0	7	1	0
Gender Identity	11	3	6	0	1	12	0	2
Anti-Transgender	11	1	2	0	1	5	0	0
Anti-Gender Non-Conforming	0	2	4	0	0	7	0	2
Multiple-Bias Incidents[6]	3	3	4	0	2	40	0	0

Note: The aggregate of adult and juvenile individual victims does not equal the total number of victims because total victims include individuals, businesses, institutions, and society as a whole. In addition, the aggregate of adult and juvenile individual victims does not equal the aggregate of victims of crimes against persons because not all law enforcement agencies report the ages of individual victims.
1 A victim can be an individual, a business, an institution, or society as a whole.   2 The figures shown in this column are individual victims only.   3 The figures shown in this column for the offense of rape include only those reported by law enforcement agencies that used the revised Uniform Crime Reporting (UCR) definition of rape.   4 The figures shown in this column for the offense of rape include only those reported by law enforcement agencies that used the legacy UCR definition of rape.   5 Includes additional offenses collected in the National Incident-Based Reporting System.   6 A multiple-bias incident is an incident in which one or more offense types are motivated by two or more biases.

Table 72. Incidents, Victim Type, by Bias Motivation, 2016

(Number.)

Bias motivation	Total incidents	Victim type					
		Individual	Business/financial institution	Government	Religious organization	Society/public[1]	Other/unknown/ multiple
Total	6,121	4,779	391	220	146	63	522
Single-Bias Incidents	6,063	4,740	385	214	145	63	516
Race/Ethnicity/Ancestry	3,489	2,906	211	131	21	37	183
Religion	1,273	641	144	66	118	14	290
Sexual Orientation	1,076	992	26	13	6	5	34
Disability	70	64	0	0	0	5	1
Gender	31	29	1	1	0	0	0
Gender Identity	124	108	3	3	0	2	8
Multiple-Bias Incidents[2]	58	39	6	6	1	0	6

1 The victim type society/public is collected only in the National Incident-Based Reporting System.   2 A multiple-bias incident is an incident in which one or more offense types are motivated by two or more biases.

Table 73. Known Offenders,[1] by Known Offender's Race, Ethnicity, and Age, 2016

(Number.)

Race/ethnicity/age	Total
Race	
White	5,770
Black or African American	2,671
American Indian or Alaska Native	1,508
Asian	45
Native Hawaiian or Other Pacific Islander	46
Group of multiple races[2]	7
Unknown race	447
	1,046
Ethnicity[3]	
Hispanic or Latino	4,222
Not Hispanic or Latino	339
Group of multiple ethnicities[4]	1,101
Unknown ethnicity	97
	2,685
Age[3]	
Total known offenders 18 and over	4,100
Total known offenders under 18	3,435
	664

1 The term known offender does not imply that the identity of the suspect is known, but only that an attribute of the suspect has been identified, which distinguishes him/her from an unknown offender.   2 The term group of multiple races is used to describe a group of offenders of varying races.   3 The total number of known offenders by age and the total number of known offenders by ethnicity do not equal the total number of known offenders by race because not all law enforcement agencies report the age and/or ethnicity of the known offenders.   4 The term group of multiple ethnicities is used to describe a group of offenders of varying ethnicities.

Table 74. Incidents, Bias Motivation, by Location, 2016

(Number.)

Location	Total incidents	Bias motivation						Multiple-bias incidents[1]
		Race	Religion	Sexual orientation	Disability	Gender	Gender Identity	
Total	6,121	3,489	1,273	1,076	70	31	124	58
Abandoned/condemned structure	5	2	3	0	0	0	0	0
Air/bus/train terminal	94	60	11	16	2	0	2	3
Amusement park	1	0	0	1	0	0	0	0
Arena/stadium/fairgrounds/coliseum	6	4	1	1	0	0	0	0
ATM separate from bank	1	1	0	0	0	0	0	0
Auto dealership new/used	6	6	0	0	0	0	0	0
Bank/savings and loan	20	11	6	1	0	1	1	0
Bar/nightclub	96	49	3	43	0	0	0	1
Camp/campground	3	2	0	1	0	0	0	0
Church/synagogue/temple/mosque	241	36	194	8	0	0	0	3
Commercial office building	117	63	29	20	1	0	3	1
Community center	11	5	4	2	0	0	0	0
Construction site	19	12	7	0	0	0	0	0
Convenience store	88	57	16	11	0	1	3	0
Cyberspace	4	3	0	1	0	0	0	0
Daycare facility	2	2	0	0	0	0	0	0
Department/discount store	72	45	11	13	2	0	1	0
Dock/wharf/freight/modal terminal	3	2	1	0	0	0	0	0
Drug store/doctor's office/hospital	64	49	11	2	2	0	0	0
Farm facility	0	0	0	0	0	0	0	0
Field/woods	31	19	7	2	0	0	3	0
Gambling facility/casino/race track	3	3	0	0	0	0	0	0
Government/public building	111	73	24	10	1	2	0	1
Grocery/supermarket	62	46	7	8	0	0	1	0
Highway/road/alley/street/sidewalk	1,128	718	117	241	7	1	35	9
Hotel/motel/etc.	44	32	3	8	0	0	1	0
Industrial site	12	10	1	1	0	0	0	0
Jail/prison/penitentiary/corrections facility	61	42	3	13	1	1	0	1
Lake/waterway/beach	6	2	0	4	0	0	0	0
Liquor store	15	12	2	1	0	0	0	0
Military installation	0	0	0	0	0	0	0	0
Park/playground	98	66	13	12	2	1	2	2
Parking/drop lot/garage	351	222	50	68	3	0	5	3
Rental storage facility	9	5	3	0	0	0	1	0
Residence/home	1,670	1,008	249	327	32	11	24	19
Rest area	4	3	0	1	0	0	0	0
Restaurant	143	92	14	29	3	2	3	0
School/college[2]	146	67	52	24	0	1	0	2
School—college/university	210	107	61	36	1	0	5	0
School—elementary/secondary	248	155	48	29	6	1	2	7
Service/gas station	72	55	8	6	0	0	3	0
Shelter—mission/homeless	16	10	2	2	0	0	2	0
Shopping mall	8	6	2	0	0	0	0	0
Specialty store (TV, fur, etc.)	39	28	9	2	0	0	0	0
Other/unknown	777	297	301	132	7	8	27	5
Multiple locations	4	2	0	0	0	1	0	1

1 A *multiple-bias incident* is an incident in which one or more offense types are motivated by two or more biases. 2 The location designation School/college has been retained for agencies that have not updated their records management systems to include the new location designations of *School—college/university* and *School—elementary/secondary*, which allow for more specificity in reporting.

Table 75. Offenses, Offense Type, by Participating State, 2016

(Number.)

State	Total offenses	Crimes against persons						
		Murder and nonnegligent manslaughter	Rape (revised definition)[1]	Rape (legacy definition)[2]	Aggravated assault	Simple assault	Intimidation	Other[3]
Total	7,321	9	24	0	873	1,687	2,109	18
Alabama	17	0	0		0	2	11	0
Alaska	13	0	0		1	6	1	0
Arizona	291	0	0		41	65	112	0
Arkansas	15	0	0		1	5	2	0
California	1,142	0	1		191	240	308	0
Colorado	126	0	1		15	25	39	0
Connecticut	124	0	0		12	18	40	0
Delaware	19	0	0		1	7	5	1
District of Columbia	127	0	0		17	62	23	0
Florida	110	0	0		28	28	18	0
Georgia	46	0		0	6	16	12	0
Idaho	35	1	0		7	9	5	0
Illinois	122	0	1		23	32	31	0
Indiana	163	3	1	0	4	24	101	0
Iowa	21	0	0		4	2	8	0
Kansas	70	0	0		16	11	26	0
Kentucky	241	0	0		15	39	76	0
Louisiana	33	0	0		5	10	7	0
Maine	45	0	0		1	6	23	0
Maryland	40	0	0		11	11	0	0
Massachusetts	444	0	1		54	84	139	3
Michigan	459	0	3		62	96	179	2
Minnesota	165	0	0		28	52	47	0
Mississippi	10	0	0	0	0	3	0	0
Missouri	114	0	1		27	32	20	0
Montana	20	0	1		1	2	3	0
Nebraska	35	0	1	0	4	14	4	1
Nevada	49	0	1		13	18	3	0
New Hampshire	40	0	0		1	5	24	0
New Jersey	308	0	0		2	12	179	0
New Mexico	36	0	0	0	3	13	11	0
New York	598	0	1	0	61	209	0	0
North Carolina	208	0	0	0	27	47	70	0
North Dakota	8	0	0		1	4	3	0
Ohio	508	0	0	0	22	68	224	1
Oklahoma	35	0	2	0	2	7	15	0
Oregon	122	0	1	0	18	20	33	0
Pennsylvania	67	0	0		3	24	25	0
Rhode Island	13	0	0	0	0	4	0	0
South Carolina	23	0	0		4	5	4	0
South Dakota	21	0	0	0	1	9	2	0
Tennessee	190	0	0		18	62	44	1
Texas	224	5	0		42	57	53	5
Utah	72	0	2		2	22	2	1
Vermont	26	0	0		1	8	1	0
Virginia	150	0	2		10	52	31	0
Washington	482	0	2	0	52	111	133	3
West Virginia	48	0	2		10	16	2	0
Wisconsin	42	0	0	0	4	10	10	0
Wyoming	4	0	0		1	3	0	0
Guam	3	0	0		3	0	0	0

Table 75. Offenses, Offense Type, by Participating State, 2016—Continued

(Number.)

State	Crimes against property							Crimes against society[3]
	Robbery	Burglary	Larceny-theft	Motor vehicle theft	Arson	Destruction/ damage/ vandalism	Other[3]	
Total	134	123	231	20	39	1,913	59	82
Alabama	0	0	2	0	0	2	0	0
Alaska	1	0	0	0	1	3	0	0
Arizona	6	1	4	0	0	62	0	0
Arkansas	0	1	1	0	1	3	0	1
California	31	14	6	2	12	337	0	0
Colorado	4	1	1	0	1	39	0	0
Connecticut	1	1	7	0	0	39	1	5
Delaware	0	0	0	0	0	5	0	0
District of Columbia	6	0	2	0	0	17	0	0
Florida	4	0	0	0	1	31	0	0
Georgia	1	1	0	0	0	10	0	0
Idaho	0	0	0	0	0	13	0	0
Illinois	1	0	1	0	1	32	0	0
Indiana	1	0	0	0	0	23	1	5
Iowa	0	0	0	0	1	5	0	1
Kansas	0	2	4	0	0	9	2	0
Kentucky	4	11	20	4	2	61	7	2
Louisiana	0	2	3	0	0	4	0	2
Maine	0	0	1	0	0	14	0	0
Maryland	1	0	0	0	0	17	0	0
Massachusetts	2	4	14	0	3	136	2	2
Michigan	2	6	10	1	1	75	6	16
Minnesota	4	0	1	0	1	32	0	0
Mississippi	0	2	2	0	0	3	0	0
Missouri	7	2	1	2	1	20	0	1
Montana	0	2	4	1	0	4	1	1
Nebraska	1	0	0	0	0	8	0	2
Nevada	3	1	0	1	0	9	0	0
New Hampshire	0	0	0	0	0	10	0	0
New Jersey	3	2	2	0	0	108	0	0
New Mexico	1	2	0	0	0	6	0	0
New York	9	11	11	0	7	289	0	0
North Carolina	5	3	5	0	1	50	0	0
North Dakota	0	0	0	0	0	0	0	0
Ohio	6	22	58	5	0	84	15	3
Oklahoma	2	0	0	0	1	5	1	0
Oregon	1	2	1	0	0	43	1	2
Pennsylvania	0	1	2	0	2	10	0	0
Rhode Island	1	0	0	0	0	7	0	1
South Carolina	0	0	2	0	0	8	0	0
South Dakota	0	1	1	0	0	3	0	4
Tennessee	2	3	9	0	0	35	2	14
Texas	9	3	8	0	0	42	0	0
Utah	1	3	6	0	0	18	2	13
Vermont	0	1	4	0	0	11	0	0
Virginia	2	1	4	0	1	42	4	1
Washington	11	13	22	4	1	113	12	5
West Virginia	1	2	9	0	0	3	2	1
Wisconsin	0	2	3	0	0	13	0	0
Wyoming	0	0	0	0	0	0	0	0
Guam	0	0	0	0	0	0	0	0

1 The figures shown in this column for the offense of rape include only those reported by law enforcement agencies that used the revised Uniform Crime Reporting (UCR) definition of rape.   2 The figures shown in this column for the offense of rape include only those reported by law enforcement agencies that used the legacy UCR definition of rape.   3 Includes additional offenses collected in the National Incident-Based Reporting System.

Table 76. Agency Hate Crime Reporting, by Participating State and Territory, 2016

(Number.)

State	Number of participating agencies	Population covered	Agencies submitting incident reports	Total number of incidents reported
Total	15,254	289,814,003	1,776	6,121
Alabama	28	1,013,839	4	14
Alaska	32	738,566	3	11
Arizona	85	6,361,910	18	213
Arkansas	288	2,853,645	5	12
California	733	39,242,633	213	931
Colorado	229	5,519,770	37	104
Connecticut	106	3,576,452	42	106
Delaware	63	952,065	8	15
District of Columbia	2	681,170	2	115
Florida	46	8,988,095	44	96
Georgia	493	8,216,137	6	39
Idaho	111	1,683,140	14	27
Illinois	738	12,373,460	42	111
Indiana	164	2,874,580	24	78
Iowa	241	3,113,786	12	17
Kansas	343	2,591,338	30	49
Kentucky	405	4,427,530	79	206
Louisiana	139	3,560,451	10	26
Maine	199	1,331,479	14	40
Maryland	154	6,016,447	10	37
Massachusetts	351	6,637,616	84	391
Michigan	625	9,847,710	166	399
Minnesota	331	5,178,985	34	119
Mississippi	26	585,454	4	7
Missouri	612	6,089,857	24	88
Montana	109	1,042,048	10	20
Nebraska	235	1,846,626	7	31
Nevada	51	2,940,058	4	41
New Hampshire	174	1,275,170	19	28
New Jersey	507	8,942,857	117	282
New Mexico	18	576,958	2	26
New York	584	19,738,790	72	595
North Carolina	528	10,145,637	41	148
North Dakota	108	757,493	6	8
Ohio	562	9,573,452	115	442
Oklahoma	355	3,869,095	22	33
Oregon	170	3,547,910	28	104
Pennsylvania	1,463	12,644,372	20	61
Rhode Island	49	1,056,426	10	12
South Carolina	440	4,936,962	21	23
South Dakota	112	787,337	12	18
Tennessee	463	6,651,194	55	142
Texas	1,097	27,862,596	66	178
Utah	130	3,014,190	32	66
Vermont	90	624,594	15	25
Virginia	419	8,411,424	55	122
Washington	253	7,282,106	80	387
West Virginia	324	1,621,366	19	41
Wisconsin	414	5,652,781	18	34
Wyoming	55	556,446	1	3

Table 77. Hate Crime Incidents Per Bias Motivation and Quarter, by Selected State and Agency, 2016

(Number.)

State/agency	Number of incidents per bias motivation						Number of incidents per quarter				Population[1]
	Race/ Ethnicity/ Ancestry	Religion	Sexual orientation	Disability	Gender	Gender Identity	1st quarter	2nd quarter	3rd quarter	4th quarter	
ALABAMA											
Total	12	1	1	0	0	0					
Cities	12	1	1	0	0	0					
Birmingham	7	1	1	0	0	0	3	2	2	2	212,549
Florence	1	0	0	0	0	0	0	0	1	0	40,160
Foley	1	0	0	0	0	0	0	1	0	0	17,639
Hoover	3	0	0	0	0	0	1	0	1	1	85,601
ALASKA											
Total	11	0	0	0	0	0					
Cities	11	0	0	0	0	0					
Anchorage	4	0	0	0	0	0	1	0	2	1	299,097
Juneau	6	0	0	0	0	0	1	1	3	1	32,964
Wasilla	1	0	0	0	0	0	1	0	0	0	9,585
ARIZONA											
Total	110	50	53	1	0	0					
Cities	105	48	53	1	0	0					
Apache Junction	2	0	0	0	0	0	1	0	1	0	38,506
Chandler	2	2	0	0	0	0	1	0	1	2	265,922
Gilbert	1	0	0	0	0	0	1	0	0	0	255,899
Glendale	1	0	0	0	0	0	0	1	0	0	242,938
Mesa	3	0	2	0	0	0	3	0	0	2	478,277
Phoenix[2]	90	40	44	1	0	0	34	39	45	56	1,586,611
Prescott Valley	1	0	1	0	0	0	1	1			42,900
Sahuarita	1	0	0	0	0	0	0	0	0	1	25,792
Scottsdale	1	3	0	0	0	0	0		2	2	240,885
St. Johns	0	0	1	0	0	0	1	0	0	0	3,482
Tempe	0	0	1	0	0	0	1	0	0	0	178,654
Tucson	1	2	2	0	0	0	2	1	1	1	533,663
Williams	0	0	1	0	0	0	0	1	0	0	3,140
Yuma	2	1	1	0	0	0	1	1	2	0	94,696
Universities and Colleges	1	2	0	0	0	0					
Arizona State University, Main Campus	1	0	0	0	0	0	0	0	0	1	90,906
University of Arizona	0	2	0	0	0	0	0	2			42,595
Metropolitan Counties	4	0	0	0	0	0					
Maricopa	3	0	0	0	0	0		0	3	0	
Pima	1	0	0	0	0	0	0	1	0		
ARKANSAS											
Total	10	1	0	0	0	1					
Cities	5	1	0	0	0	1					
Fort Smith	3	1	0	0	0	0	2	0	0	2	88,573
Jacksonville	2	0	0	0	0	0	0	0	0	2	28,684
Little Rock	0	0	0	0	0	1	0	1	0	0	198,800
Metropolitan Counties	3	0	0	0	0	0					
Sebastian	3	0	0	0	0	0	0	1	0	2	
Nonmetropolitan Counties	2	0	0	0	0	0					
Sevier	2	0	0	0	0	0	0	0	2	0	
CALIFORNIA											
Total	522	171	208	2	3	27					
Cities	421	150	173	2	3	23					
Adelanto	1	0	1	0	0	0	0	1	1	0	33,479
Alameda	3	0	0	0	0	0	0	1	0	2	79,597
Alhambra	1	0	0	0	0	0	0	0	0	1	86,035
Anaheim	1	0	0	0	0	0	1	0	0	0	353,504
Antioch	2	0	0	0	0	0	0	0	2	0	112,090
Arcata	2	0	0	0	0	0	0	0	1	1	17,913
Azusa	2	0	0	0	0	0	2	0	0	0	50,393
Bakersfield	8	0	0	0	0	0	0	3	2	3	378,788
Baldwin Park	0	0	1	0	0	0	1	0	0	0	77,400
Bellflower	0	0	1	0	0	0	1	0	0	0	78,806
Berkeley	9	2	2	0	0	0	5	3	2	3	122,651
Beverly Hills	1	0	0	0	0	0	0	0	1	0	35,018
Brea	0	0	1	0	0	0	0	1	0	0	42,465
Buena Park	2	1	0	0	0	0	0	0	2	1	83,768
Burbank	1	0	0	0	0	0	0	0	1	0	105,720
Calabasas	3	0	0	0	0	0	1	0	2	0	24,492
Camarillo	1	0	0	0	0	0	0	1	0	0	68,072
Campbell	0	1	0	0	0	0	0	1	0	0	41,457
Capitola	1	0	0	0	0	0	0	0	0	1	10,241
Central Marin	2	0	0	0	0	0	0	1	1	0	35,265
Cerritos	0	0	1	0	0	0	0	0	1	0	50,159
Chico	3	0	0	0	0	0	0	1	0	2	91,122
Chino	2	0	1	0	0	0	0	1	1	1	87,081
Chino Hills	1	0	0	0	0	0	1	0	0	0	78,990
Chula Vista	1	2	2	0	0	0	1	1	3	0	270,175
Citrus Heights	1	0	1	0	0	0	1	0	0	1	87,811
Claremont	7	1	1	0	0	0	1	0	1	7	36,553

Table 77. Hate Crime Incidents Per Bias Motivation and Quarter, by Selected State and Agency, 2016—Continued

(Number.)

State/agency	Number of incidents per bias motivation						Number of incidents per quarter				
	Race/ Ethnicity/ Ancestry	Religion	Sexual orientation	Disability	Gender	Gender Identity	1st quarter	2nd quarter	3rd quarter	4th quarter	Population[1]
Clayton	0	0	2	0	0	0	0	2	0	0	12,057
Clearlake	1	0	0	0	0	0	0	0	0	1	15,165
Clovis	1	0	0	0	0	0	0	0	0	1	105,865
Coalinga	0	0	1	0	0	0	1	0	1	0	16,282
Compton	0	0	0	0	0	1	0	0	1	0	98,861
Concord	1	0	2	0	0	0	1	0	0	2	129,903
Culver City	0	0	1	0	0	0	0	1	0	0	39,880
Cupertino	2	1	0	0	0	0	0	0	3	0	60,948
Danville	0	1	0	0	0	0	1	0	0	0	44,897
Davis	5	1	1	0	0	1	2	0	1	5	68,087
Desert Hot Springs	0	0	1	0	0	0	0	1	0	0	28,573
Downey	1	0	0	0	0	0	0	1	0	0	114,704
East Palo Alto	0	0	1	0	0	0	0	0	0	1	29,957
Eastvale	0	1	0	0	0	0	0	1	0	0	60,115
Elk Grove	1	0	0	0	0	0	1	0	0	0	169,742
El Segundo	2	0	0	0	0	0	1	0	1	0	17,113
Encinitas	1	0	0	0	0	0	0	0	0	1	63,597
Escondido	1	0	0	0	0	0	0	1	0	0	152,897
Fairfield	1	1	1	0	0	0	2	0	1	0	114,521
Farmersville	0	1	0	0	0	0	0	0	1	0	10,812
Folsom	0	1	0	0	0	0	0	1	0	0	77,245
Fort Bragg	1	1	1	0	0	0	0	2	1	0	7,292
Fremont	1	0	0	0	0	0	1	0	0	0	235,881
Fresno	7	3	3	0	0	0	3	3	4	3	524,796
Fullerton	1	0	1	0	0	0	1	0	0	1	141,968
Garden Grove	1	1	0	0	0	0	1	0	0	1	176,230
Glendale	1	1	0	0	0	0	0	1	0	1	202,903
Hanford	0	1	0	0	0	0	0	1	0	0	55,973
Hawaiian Gardens	0	0	0	0	0	1	0	1	0	0	14,654
Hawthorne	0	1	0	0	0	0	0	0	0	1	89,299
Hayward	1	1	0	0	0	0	0	0	1	1	161,122
Highland	1	0	0	0	0	0	0	0	1	0	55,184
Hollister	0	0	1	0	0	0	0	0	1	0	37,953
Huntington Beach	3	3	0	0	0	0	1	1	3	1	204,071
Huntington Park	0	0	1	0	0	0	1	0	0	0	59,692
Irvine	2	0	0	0	0	0	1	0	0	1	266,663
Jurupa Valley	1	0	0	0	0	0	0	1	0	0	101,316
Kingsburg	1	0	0	0	0	0	1	0	0	0	11,905
Laguna Beach	1	0	0	0	0	0	0	0	0	1	23,486
La Habra	1	0	0	0	0	0	0	1	0	0	62,483
Lake Elsinore	1	0	1	0	0	0	1	1	0	0	63,907
Lakewood	3	0	1	0	0	0	2	0	1	1	81,921
La Mesa	2	1	0	0	0	0	0	0	1	2	60,681
La Mirada	0	2	0	0	0	0	0	2	0	0	49,715
Lancaster	5	0	2	0	0	1	1	4	1	2	161,963
La Puente	0	0	1	0	0	0	1	0	0	0	40,928
Loma Linda	1	0	0	0	0	0	0	1	0	0	24,190
Long Beach	2	2	3	0	0	1	2	0	3	3	476,476
Los Angeles	112	43	58	0	1	13	55	56	52	64	4,007,905
Malibu	2	0	0	0	0	0	1	0	0	1	13,030
Mammoth Lakes	1	0	0	0	0	0	0	1	0	0	7,891
Manteca	5	0	0	0	0	0	1	1	3	0	77,104
Merced	0	0	1	0	0	1	0	0	1	1	83,106
Modesto	6	4	1	0	0	0	2	4	2	3	212,880
Montclair	1	1	0	0	0	0	0	1	0	1	39,085
Monterey	1	0	0	0	0	0	0	0	0	1	28,506
Mountain View	0	1	0	0	0	0	1	0	0	0	81,726
Murrieta	0	0	0	0	1	0	0	0	0	1	111,043
Napa	0	0	1	0	0	0	0	0	0	1	81,115
National City	1	0	0	0	0	0	1	0	0	0	61,550
Newark	1	0	0	0	0	0	0	1	0	0	45,893
Norco	2	0	0	0	0	0	1	0	0	1	26,132
Norwalk	1	0	0	0	0	0	0	0	1	0	107,453
Novato	1	1	0	0	0	0	0	0	0	2	56,263
Oakland	3	3	3	0	0	0	3	2	2	2	424,998
Oceanside	2	2	3	0	0	0	1	3	1	2	177,340
Orange	1	0	0	0	0	0	0	0	1	0	141,841
Oxnard	4	1	1	0	0	0	2	1	1	2	209,048
Pacific Grove	1	0	0	0	0	0	0	1	0	0	15,795
Palmdale	6	2	0	0	0	0	5	0	2	1	159,441
Palm Springs	3	0	0	0	0	0	1	2	0	0	47,909
Palo Alto	3	1	0	0	0	0	1	2	1	0	67,317
Paradise	1	0	0	0	0	0	0	1	0	0	26,532
Parlier	0	0	1	0	0	0	0	1	0	0	15,262
Pasadena	1	1	0	0	0	0	1	0	1	0	143,288
Perris	0	1	0	0	0	0	0	0	0	1	76,260
Petaluma	1	0	0	0	0	0	1	0	0	0	60,933
Placentia	1	0	0	0	0	0	0	1	0	0	52,800
Pomona	2	1	2	0	0	0	2	1	2	0	154,109
Poway	0	0	1	0	0	0	0	0	0	1	50,606
Rancho Cucamonga	4	0	0	0	0	0	0	2	1	1	177,089

Table 77. Hate Crime Incidents Per Bias Motivation and Quarter, by Selected State and Agency, 2016—Continued

(Number.)

State/agency	Number of incidents per bias motivation						Number of incidents per quarter				Population[1]
	Race/ Ethnicity/ Ancestry	Religion	Sexual orientation	Disability	Gender	Gender Identity	1st quarter	2nd quarter	3rd quarter	4th quarter	
Rancho Palos Verdes	1	0	0	0	0	0	0	0	1	0	42,947
Redding	7	1	2	0	0	0	0	1	7	2	91,918
Redlands	4	0	2	0	0	0	1	2	3	0	71,485
Redwood City	2	0	2	0	0	0	0	0	1	3	87,046
Rialto	1	0	0	0	0	0	0	0	0	1	103,893
Richmond	4	0	0	0	0	0	0	1	1	2	110,868
Ridgecrest	1	0	0	0	0	0	0	1	0	0	29,003
Riverside	5	1	2	0	0	0	2	2	2	2	325,896
Roseville	7	4	0	0	0	0	0	1	4	6	132,566
Sacramento	2	0	4	0	0	0	4	1	1	0	495,471
Salinas	0	1	0	0	0	0	0	1	0	0	158,729
San Bernardino[2]	6	0	1	0	0	0	0	1	4	1	217,303
San Bruno	2	0	0	0	0	0	0	0	1	1	43,613
San Diego	16	7	12	0	0	0	7	10	6	12	1,413,414
San Fernando	0	1	1	0	0	0	1	0	0	1	25,194
San Francisco[2]	11	7	14	0	1	4	9	12	10	5	871,155
San Jose	10	7	2	0	0	0	5	1	4	9	1,041,844
San Leandro	15	3	3	1	0	0	4	5	5	8	91,870
San Luis Obispo	2	0	0	0	0	0	2	0	0	0	47,774
San Marcos	1	1	0	0	0	0	1	0	0	1	94,840
San Mateo	0	1	1	0	0	0	0	1	0	1	104,802
San Rafael	1	0	0	0	0	0	0	0	0	1	59,435
San Ramon	4	0	0	0	0	0	0	0	0	4	76,901
Santa Ana	2	3	1	0	0	0	3	2	0	1	337,419
Santa Clarita	6	4	0	0	0	0	3	1	2	4	219,611
Santa Cruz	7	3	2	0	0	0	4	1	2	5	64,969
Santa Monica	1	1	1	0	0	0	0	2	1	0	93,921
Santa Rosa	0	0	1	0	0	0	1	0	0	0	176,383
Santee	0	1	0	0	0	0	0	0	0	1	58,651
Sebastopol	1	0	0	0	0	0	0	1	0	0	7,734
Simi Valley	1	1	0	0	0	0	0	1	0	1	127,252
Solvang	0	0	1	0	0	0	0	0	1	0	5,844
Sonoma	1	0	0	0	0	0	1	0	0	0	11,113
Sonora	1	0	0	0	0	0	0	0	0	1	4,802
South Gate	0	1	1	0	0	0	0	0	1	1	96,791
South San Francisco	0	4	0	0	0	0	0	0	0	4	67,995
Stockton	2	0	0	1	0	0	0	0	2	1	308,348
Suisun City	1	0	0	0	0	0	0	1	0	0	29,768
Sunnyvale	0	1	0	0	0	0	0	1	0	0	154,108
Thousand Oaks	0	1	0	0	0	0	0	1	0	0	129,853
Torrance	0	1	0	0	0	0	0	0	1	0	149,078
Turlock	3	0	0	0	0	0	3	0	0	0	73,031
Twentynine Palms	1	0	0	0	0	0	0	0	0	1	26,213
Ukiah	0	0	1	0	0	0	0	1	0	0	15,897
Union City	0	0	1	0	0	0	0	1	0	0	75,501
Vacaville	1	0	0	0	0	0	1	0	0	0	97,671
Vallejo	2	0	0	0	0	0	0	0	1	1	122,293
Ventura	2	0	1	0	0	0	0	1	1	1	110,228
Victorville	1	0	1	0	0	0	0	1	0	1	123,438
Walnut Creek	1	1	1	0	0	0	0	1	1	1	69,860
Watsonville	0	1	0	0	0	0	1	0	0	0	54,110
West Covina	1	0	0	0	0	0	1	0	0	0	108,950
West Hollywood	2	0	5	0	0	0	0	2	2	3	36,594
Westminster	3	0	1	0	0	0	3	0	1	0	92,582
Wildomar	1	0	0	0	0	0	0	0	0	1	36,310
Windsor	2	0	0	0	0	0	1	0	0	1	27,594
Universities and Colleges	22	7	9	0	0	1					
California State Polytechnic University, San Luis Obispo	1	0	0	0	0	0	1	0	0	0	20,944
California State University:											
Dominguez Hills	4	0	0	0	0	0	2	0	0	2	14,635
Fullerton	0	0	1	0	0	0	0	1	0	0	38,948
Long Beach	2	0	0	0	0	0	0	0	2	0	37,446
San Jose	5	0	0	0	0	0	0	0	1	4	32,773
Stanislaus	0	0	1	0	0	0	1	0	0	0	9,282
Foothill-De Anza College	0	0	1	0	0	1	1	1	0	0	37,960
Humboldt State University	1	1	1	0	0	0	0	2	1	0	8,790
Riverside Community College	0	1	0	0	0	0	0	0	0	1	37,594
San Diego State University	3	0	0	0	0	0	1	1	0	1	34,254
University of California:											
Berkeley	1	2	1	0	0	0	1	1	0	2	38,189
Davis	1	0	0	0	0	0	1	0	0	0	35,186
Los Angeles	2	1	1	0	0	0	2	0	1	1	41,908
Riverside	0	1	0	0	0	0	1	0	0	0	21,385
San Diego	2	0	1	0	0	0	0	2	0	1	32,906
San Francisco	0	1	0	0	0	0	0	0	0	1	3,107
Santa Cruz	0	0	1	0	0	0	0	0	0	1	17,868
Ventura County Community College District	0	0	1	0	0	0	0	0	0	1	34,022
Metropolitan Counties	58	9	20	0	0	2					
Butte	0	0	1	0	0	0	0	0	1	0	

Table 77. Hate Crime Incidents Per Bias Motivation and Quarter, by Selected State and Agency, 2016—Continued

(Number.)

State/agency	Number of incidents per bias motivation						Number of incidents per quarter				Population[1]
	Race/ Ethnicity/ Ancestry	Religion	Sexual orientation	Disability	Gender	Gender Identity	1st quarter	2nd quarter	3rd quarter	4th quarter	
El Dorado	0	1	0	0	0	0	1	0	0	0	
Fresno	0	0	1	0	0	0	0	1	0	0	
Los Angeles	17	3	6	0	0	0	5	4	6	11	
Orange	2	0	0	0	0	0	2	0	0	0	
Riverside	3	0	1	0	0	1	0	1	3	1	
Sacramento	8	1	1	0	0	0	5	3	1	1	
San Bernardino	3	2	1	0	0	1	4	3	0	0	
San Diego	13	1	4	0	0	0	1	7	8	2	
San Mateo	1	1	1	0	0	0	1	1	1	0	
Santa Barbara	1	0	0	0	0	0	0	0	0	1	
Santa Clara	2	0	0	0	0	0	1	0	1	0	
Shasta	2	0	0	0	0	0	1	1	0	0	
Solano	1	0	0	0	0	0	0	0	1	0	
Sonoma	1	0	3	0	0	0	0	1	3	0	
Sutter	1	0	0	0	0	0	0	0	0	1	
Ventura	2	0	0	0	0	0	0	1	1	0	
Yuba	1	0	1	0	0	0	0	0	0	2	
Nonmetropolitan Counties	3	3	0	0	0	0					
Amador	0	1	0	0	0	0	0	0	1	0	
Humboldt	0	1	0	0	0	0	0	0	0	1	
Lake	1	0	0	0	0	0	0	1	0	0	
Mendocino	2	0	0	0	0	0	1	0	0	1	
Tuolumne	0	1	0	0	0	0	0	0	1	0	
Other Agencies	18	2	6	0	0	1					
California State Fair	1	0	0	0	0	0	0	0	1	0	
East Bay Regional Parks, Alameda County	0	1	0	0	0	0	0	0	0	1	
Fontana Unified School District	0	0	1	0	0	0	0	0	0	1	
Los Angeles Transportation Services Bureau[2]	10	0	4	0	0	1	7	2	3	3	
Port of San Diego Harbor	2	1	0	0	0	0	2	0	1	0	
San Francisco Bay Area Rapid Transit:											
Alameda County	2	0	0	0	0	0	1	0	0	1	
Contra Costa County	2	0	0	0	0	0	1	0	0	1	
Santa Clara Transit District	1	0	1	0	0	0	0	0	1	1	
COLORADO											
Total	67	19	23	0	0	0					
Cities	47	7	17	0	0	0					
Aspen	0	1	0	0	0	0	0	0	0	1	6,926
Aurora	15	0	3	0	0	0	1	3	6	8	366,477
Boulder	2	1	1	0	0	0	1	1	2	0	109,189
Breckenridge	0	0	1	0	0	0	0	0	1	0	4,971
Carbondale	1	0	0	0	0	0	0	1	0	0	6,728
Centennial	2	0	0	0	0	0	0	0	2	0	111,479
Colorado Springs	1	1	4	0	0	0	0	2	1	3	464,113
Delta	0	0	1	0	0	0	1	0	0	0	8,778
Denver	10	3	6	0	0	0	4	2	1	12	699,259
Dillon	0	1	0	0	0	0	0	0	0	1	972
Erie	1	0	0	0	0	0	0	0	1	0	22,115
Florence	1	0	0	0	0	0	0	0	1	0	3,861
Fort Collins	2	0	0	0	0	0	2	0	0	0	164,670
Fort Lupton	1	0	0	0	0	0	0	1	0	0	7,903
Fountain	0	0	1	0	0	0	0	0	0	1	28,115
Golden	1	0	0	0	0	0	0	0	1	0	20,616
Grand Junction	3	0	0	0	0	0	0	0	3	0	60,628
Longmont	3	0	0	0	0	0	0	0	1	2	93,268
Loveland	1	0	0	0	0	0	0	0	1	0	76,936
Nederland	1	0	0	0	0	0	0	0	1	0	1,534
Pueblo	1	0	0	0	0	0	0	0	0	1	109,927
Sterling	1	0	0	0	0	0	0	0	0	1	14,087
Universities and Colleges	2	3	3	0	0	0					
Auraria Higher Education Center[3]	0	0	1	0	0	0	0	1	0	0	
University of Colorado, Boulder	2	3	1	0	0	0	2	0	2	2	33,056
University of Northern Colorado	0	0	1	0	0	0	0	0	1	0	12,216
Metropolitan Counties	15	8	3	0	0	0					
Adams	1	0	0	0	0	0	0	0	1	0	
Arapahoe	2	1	2	0	0	0	0	3	1	1	
Boulder	1	1	0	0	0	0	0	0	0	2	
Douglas	2	0	0	0	0	0	0	0	1	1	
El Paso	1	0	0	0	0	0	1	0	0	0	
Larimer[2]	6	6	1	0	0	0	0	2	1	5	
Mesa	1	0	0	0	0	0	1	0	0	0	
Teller	1	0	0	0	0	0	0	1	0	0	
Nonmetropolitan Counties	3	1	0	0	0	0					
Custer	1	0	0	0	0	0	0	0	1	0	
Garfield	1	0	0	0	0	0	1	0	0	0	
San Juan	1	0	0	0	0	0	0	0	1	0	
Summit	0	1	0	0	0	0	0	0	0	1	

Table 77. Hate Crime Incidents Per Bias Motivation and Quarter, by Selected State and Agency, 2016—Continued

(Number.)

State/agency	Number of incidents per bias motivation						Number of incidents per quarter				Population[1]
	Race/ Ethnicity/ Ancestry	Religion	Sexual orientation	Disability	Gender	Gender Identity	1st quarter	2nd quarter	3rd quarter	4th quarter	
CONNECTICUT											
Total	62	30	14	0	0	0					
Cities	59	27	12	0	0	0					
Bloomfield	0	1	1	0	0	0	1	1	0	0	20,801
Bridgeport	5	1	0	0	0	0	0	4	2	0	148,180
Bristol	0	0	2	0	0	0	0	0	1	1	60,445
Clinton	1	0	0	0	0	0	0	0	1	0	13,008
Danbury	3	5	1	0	0	0	1	1	1	6	85,335
Darien	0	1	0	0	0	0	0	0	1	0	21,995
Greenwich	0	1	0	0	0	0	0	0	1	0	62,970
Groton	1	0	0	0	0	0	0	0	0	1	9,189
Groton Town	1	0	0	0	0	0	0	0	1	0	29,910
Guilford	1	0	0	0	0	0	1	0	0	0	22,343
Hartford	5	0	1	0	0	0	2	2	1	1	123,736
Ledyard	0	0	1	0	0	0	0	0	0	1	15,021
Madison	0	1	0	0	0	0	0	0	0	1	18,212
Manchester	6	0	1	0	0	0	1	2	1	3	57,957
Middletown	1	1	0	0	0	0	0	2	0	0	46,580
Naugatuck	1	0	0	0	0	0	0	1	0	0	31,469
New Haven	4	3	2	0	0	0	5	1	0	3	130,425
Newington	1	0	1	0	0	0	1	0	0	1	30,610
New London	0	2	0	0	0	0	2	0	0	0	27,092
Norwalk	5	2	0	0	0	0	1	5	0	1	88,989
Norwich	1	0	0	0	0	0	1	0	0	0	39,771
Old Saybrook	1	0	0	0	0	0	0	0	0	1	10,145
Ridgefield	0	1	0	0	0	0	0	0	0	1	25,358
Rocky Hill	0	1	0	0	0	0	0	0	0	1	20,085
Shelton	0	1	0	0	0	0	0	0	0	1	41,638
Southington	1	0	0	0	0	0	0	1	0	0	43,948
Stamford	5	1	2	0	0	0	4	2	1	1	130,116
Stratford	1	0	0	0	0	0	0	1	0	0	52,841
Torrington	1	2	0	0	0	0	0	1	1	1	34,626
Trumbull	1	0	0	0	0	0	1	0	0	0	36,741
Vernon	1	0	0	0	0	0	0	0	0	1	28,915
Wallingford	1	0	0	0	0	0	0	0	1	0	44,840
Waterbury	6	0	0	0	0	0	2	3	0	1	108,491
Waterford	0	1	0	0	0	0	0	0	1	0	19,236
West Hartford	1	1	0	0	0	0	0	0	0	2	62,979
Westport	2	0	0	0	0	0	0	2	0	0	28,198
Wethersfield	1	0	0	0	0	0	1	0	0	0	26,306
Willimantic	1	0	0	0	0	0	0	0	1	0	17,766
Woodbridge	0	1	0	0	0	0	0	0	1	0	8,864
Universities and Colleges	0	1	1	0	0	0					
Southern Connecticut State University	0	1	1	0	0	0	1	0	1	0	10,473
State Police Agencies	2	2	1	0	0	0					
Connecticut State Police	2	2	1	0	0	0	0	1	3	1	
Tribal Agencies	1	0	0	0	0	0					
Mashantucket Pequot Tribal	1	0	0	0	0	0	0	0	0	1	
DELAWARE											
Total	11	3	1	0	0	0					
Cities	3	1	0	0	0	0					
Camden	1	0	0	0	0	0	0	0	0	1	3,512
Newark	1	0	0	0	0	0	0	0	0	1	34,297
Rehoboth Beach	1	0	0	0	0	0	1	0	0	0	1,485
Smyrna	0	1	0	0	0	0	0	1	0	0	11,573
Metropolitan Counties	3	1	0	0	0	0					
New Castle County Police Department	3	1	0	0	0	0	1	0	2	1	
State Police Agencies	3	1	1	0	0	0					
State Police:											
Kent County	1	0	0	0	0	0	0	0	1	0	
New Castle County	2	1	1	0	0	0	1	2	0	1	
Other Agencies	2	0	0	0	0	0					
Park Rangers	2	0	0	0	0	0	0	0	0	2	
DISTRICT OF COLUMBIA											
Total	33	18	42	2	0	20					
Cities	26	18	40	1	0	19					
Washington	26	18	40	1	0	19	20	35	25	24	681,170
Other Agencies	7	0	2	1	0	1					
Metro Transit Police	7	0	2	1	0	1	0	4	3	4	
FLORIDA											
Total	43	19	32	1	0	1					
Cities	27	14	23	1	0	0					
Arcadia	1	0	0	0	0	0			1		7,893
Cape Coral	1	0	0	0	0	0				1	179,631
Casselberry	0	1	0	0	0	0			1		27,220
Cocoa	0	0	1	0	0	0	1				17,825

Table 77. Hate Crime Incidents Per Bias Motivation and Quarter, by Selected State and Agency, 2016—Continued

(Number.)

State/agency	Number of incidents per bias motivation						Number of incidents per quarter				Population[1]
	Race/ Ethnicity/ Ancestry	Religion	Sexual orientation	Disability	Gender	Gender Identity	1st quarter	2nd quarter	3rd quarter	4th quarter	
Coral Gables	1	0	0	0	0	0	1				51,980
Davie	3	1	1	0	0	0	2	3			102,692
Fort Myers	2	0	1	0	0	0	1		1	1	76,579
Gainesville	4	0	0	0	0	0	1			3	131,242
Homestead	1	0	1	0	0	0	2				67,700
Largo	1	0	1	0	0	0		1		1	81,402
Miami Beach	0	4	12	1	0	0	6	4	4	3	93,165
New Port Richey	2	0	0	0	0	0		2			16,038
North Miami	0	0	1	0	0	0		1			62,974
North Miami Beach	0	2	0	0	0	0		2			44,442
Oakland Park	0	0	1	0	0	0		1			44,903
Orlando	3	1	1	0	0	0		2	1	2	277,719
Palm Bay	3	1	0	0	0	0		2	1	1	108,823
Pinellas Park	1	0	0	0	0	0			1		52,113
Southwest Ranches	1	1	0	0	0	0	1		1		7,953
Sunrise	0	1	0	0	0	0		1			94,400
Tamarac	0	0	1	0	0	0	1				65,516
Tampa	2	0	1	0	0	0			2	1	375,904
Temple Terrace	0	0	1	0	0	0				1	25,972
Titusville	0	1	0	0	0	0	1				45,723
West Palm Beach	0	1	0	0	0	0			1		108,074
West Park	1	0	0	0	0	0	1				15,285
Universities and Colleges	1	0	0	0	0	0					
University of Florida	1	0	0	0	0	0			1		50,645
Metropolitan Counties	15	5	9	0	0	1					
Brevard	1	0	2	0	0	0		1	1	1	
Charlotte	1	0	0	0	0	0	1				
Clay	2	0	0	0	0	0	1			1	
Escambia	2	0	0	0	0	0	1	1			
Hillsborough	1	0	0	0	0	0			1		
Lake	1	0	0	0	0	0	1				
Lee	1	0	1	0	0	0	2				
Miami-Dade	0	1	0	0	0	0		1			
Orange	0	1	1	0	0	1	2			1	
Osceola	1	0	0	0	0	0	1				
Palm Beach	0	1	0	0	0	0				1	
Pasco	0	0	1	0	0	0				1	
Pinellas	1	0	1	0	0	0		2			
Seminole	0	1	0	0	0	0		1			
St. Johns	0	0	1	0	0	0			1		
St. Lucie	0	1	0	0	0	0			1		
Volusia	4	0	2	0	0	0		2	1	3	
GEORGIA											
Total	25	2	12	0	0	0					
Cities	1	0	5	0	0	0					
Atlanta	0	0	5	0	0	0	1	4	0	0	472,579
Conyers	1	0	0	0	0	0	0	0	0	1	16,004
Universities and Colleges	1	0	0	0	0	0					
University of Georgia	1	0	0	0	0	0	1	0	0	0	36,130
Metropolitan Counties	23	2	7	0	0	0					
Cobb County Police Department	19	2	4	0	0	0	6	7	12	0	
Fulton County Police Department	0	0	1	0	0	0	0	1	0	0	
Gwinnett County Police Department	4	0	2	0	0	0	2	1	3	0	
IDAHO											
Total	16	7	4	0	0	0					
Cities	13	6	3	0	0	0					
Blackfoot	0	0	1	0	0	0	0	0	1	0	11,700
Boise	0	2	1	0	0	0	1	1	1	0	220,749
Chubbuck	1	0	0	0	0	0	0	0	0	1	14,515
Coeur d'Alene	3	2	0	0	0	0	0	3	1	1	50,155
Meridian	1	1	0	0	0	0	0	0	0	2	94,113
Moscow	0	0	1	0	0	0	0	0	0	1	25,307
Mountain Home	1	0	0	0	0	0	0	0	0	1	13,627
Nampa	2	0	0	0	0	0	0	1	1	0	91,520
Payette	0	1	0	0	0	0	0	0	1	0	7,360
Pocatello	3	0	0	0	0	0	1	2	0	0	54,462
Twin Falls	2	0	0	0	0	0	0	2	0	0	48,083
Metropolitan Counties	2	1	1	0	0	0					
Ada	0	1	0	0	0	0	1	0	0	0	
Canyon	2	0	1	0	0	0	0	2	1	0	
Nonmetropolitan Counties	1	0	0	0	0	0					
Benewah	1	0	0	0	0	0	1	0	0	0	
ILLINOIS											
Total	73	13	21	0	1	3					
Cities	71	12	20	0	0	3					
Algonquin	2	0	0	0	0	0	0	1	1	0	30,673
Aurora	3	0	0	0	0	0	0	1	0	2	201,159

Table 77. Hate Crime Incidents Per Bias Motivation and Quarter, by Selected State and Agency, 2016—Continued

(Number.)

State/agency	Number of incidents per bias motivation						Number of incidents per quarter				Population[1]
	Race/ Ethnicity/ Ancestry	Religion	Sexual orientation	Disability	Gender	Gender Identity	1st quarter	2nd quarter	3rd quarter	4th quarter	
Berwyn	3	0	0	0	0	0	0	0	1	2	56,305
Bradley	3	0	0	0	0	0		1	1	1	15,561
Braidwood	1	0	0	0	0	0	0	0	1	0	6,160
Centralia	1	0	0	0	0	0	0	0	0	1	12,580
Champaign	1	0	1	0	0	0	0	0	1	1	87,071
Charleston	1	0	0	0	0	0	0	0	1	0	21,067
Chicago	26	9	14	0	0	2	5	19	10	17	2,725,153
Collinsville	1	0	0	0	0	0	0	0	0	1	24,599
Crete	0	0	1	0	0	0	0	0	0	1	8,171
Crystal Lake	1	0	0	0	0	0	1	0	0	0	40,374
De Kalb	1	0	0	0	0	0	0	0	1	0	43,034
Downers Grove	1	0	0	0	0	0	0	0	1	0	49,894
Effingham	1	1	0	0	0	0	0	0	0	2	12,660
Elk Grove Village	1	0	0	0	0	0	0	1	0	0	33,255
Flossmoor	1	0	0	0	0	0	0	0	1	0	9,479
Glenwood	1	0	0	0	0	0	0	0	1	0	8,996
Grayslake	1	0	0	0	0	0	1	0	0	0	20,916
Homewood	1	0	0	0	0	0	1	0	0	0	19,379
Joliet	1	0	1	0	0	0	0	0	1	1	147,886
Mokena	1	0	0	0	0	0	0	0	0	1	20,156
Monmouth	1	0	0	0	0	0	0	1	0	0	9,261
Morrison	0	0	1	0	0	0	0	1	0	0	4,137
New Lenox	1	0	0	0	0	0	0	0	0	1	26,085
Normal	3	0	0	0	0	0		0	2	1	54,727
Oak Lawn	1	0	0	0	0	0	1	0	0	0	56,791
Pekin	1	0	0	0	0	0	0	0	0	1	33,052
Peoria	1	0	0	0	0	0	1	0	0	0	115,099
Plainfield	1	1	0	0	0	0	0	0	0	2	43,063
Robinson	1	0	0	0	0	0	0	0	1	0	7,616
Rockford	3	0	2	0	0	0	1	2	1	1	147,363
Salem	1	0	0	0	0	0	0	1	0	0	7,249
Springfield	2	0	0	0	0	0	0	1	1	0	116,563
Urbana	0	1	0	0	0	0	0	0	0	1	42,461
West Chicago	1	0	0	0	0	0	0	0	1	0	27,490
Wheeling	0	0	0	0	0	1	1	0	0	0	38,158
Woodstock	1	0	0	0	0	0	0	0	0	1	25,259
Universities and Colleges	1	0	0	0	0	0					
Southern Illinois University, Carbondale	1	0	0	0	0	0	0	0	1	0	17,292
Metropolitan Counties	1	1	1	0	1	0					
Champaign	0	1	0	0	1	0	0	1	1	0	
Sangamon	1	0	0	0	0	0	0	0	0	1	
Will	0	0	1	0	0	0	0	1	0	0	
INDIANA											
Total	52	11	14	0	1	0					
Cities	42	5	11	0	0	0					
Anderson	0	0	1	0	0	0		1			55,134
Bloomington	7	0	2	0	0	0	3	1	1	4	84,772
Fort Wayne	2	0	2	0	0	0	1	1	1	1	261,642
Indianapolis	20	3	5	0	0	0	5	11	8	4	866,351
La Porte	2	0	0	0	0	0		2			21,891
Muncie	1	0	0	0	0	0	0	0	1	0	70,065
Munster	0	1	0	0	0	0	1				22,865
Plainfield	0	1	0	0	0	0	1	0	0		31,198
South Bend	10	0	0	0	0	0	3	2	5	0	101,621
Westville	0	0	1	0	0	0			1		5,641
Universities and Colleges	3	0	2	0	0	0					
Ball State University	1	0	0	0	0	0				1	21,196
Indiana University, Indianapolis	1	0	0	0	0	0		1			30,105
Purdue University	1	0	2	0	0	0	1	1	0	1	40,472
Metropolitan Counties	1	0	1	0	0	0					
Brown	0	0	1	0	0	0				1	
Porter	1	0	0	0	0	0			1		
Nonmetropolitan Counties	0	0	0	0	1	0					
Dubois	0	0	0	0	1	0	1				
State Police Agencies	6	6	0	0	0	0					
Indiana State Police	3	0	0	0	0	0			2	1	
State Police:											
Daviess County	0	1	0	0	0	0	0	0	0	1	
Marion County	1	1	0	0	0	0	0	1	0	1	
Monroe County	0	2	0	0	0	0	2	0	0	0	
Putnam County	1	0	0	0	0	0	0	0	1	0	
Scott County	1	0	0	0	0	0	0	1	0	0	
Vanderburgh County	0	1	0	0	0	0	0	0	1	0	
Washington County	0	1	0	0	0	0	0	1	0	0	
IOWA											
Total	13	2	2	0	0	0					
Cities	10	2	1	0	0	0					
Boone	1	0	0	0	0	0	0	0	1	0	12,702

Table 77. Hate Crime Incidents Per Bias Motivation and Quarter, by Selected State and Agency, 2016—Continued

(Number.)

State/agency	Race/Ethnicity/Ancestry	Religion	Sexual orientation	Disability	Gender	Gender Identity	1st quarter	2nd quarter	3rd quarter	4th quarter	Population[1]
Clinton	0	1	0	0	0	0	0	0	0	1	25,906
Des Moines	2	1	0	0	0	0	0	1	1	1	211,501
Dubuque	1	0	0	0	0	0	0	1	0	0	59,026
Iowa City	3	0	0	0	0	0	1	0	0	2	75,527
Newton	1	0	0	0	0	0	0	0	1	0	15,102
North Liberty	1	0	0	0	0	0	0	0	1	0	16,458
Oskaloosa	1	0	0	0	0	0	0	0	1	0	11,626
West Des Moines	0	0	1	0	0	0	0	0	0	1	65,631
Universities and Colleges	3	0	0	0	0	0					
Iowa State University	1	0	0	0	0	0	0	0	0	1	35,714
University of Iowa	2	0	0	0	0	0	0	0	0	2	30,844
Metropolitan Counties	0	0	1	0	0	0					
Linn	0	0	1	0	0	0	0	1	0	0	
KANSAS											
Total	36	5	5	3	0	0					
Cities	27	3	4	2	0	0					
Andover	1	0	0	0	0	0	0	0	0	1	12,937
Chanute	1	0	0	0	0	0	0	1	0	0	9,279
Coffeyville	0	0	0	1	0	0	0	0	1	0	9,555
Dodge City	2	0	0	1	0	0	1	1	1	0	27,997
Edwardsville	1	0	0	0	0	0	0	1	0	0	4,377
El Dorado	1	1	0	0	0	0	2	0	0	0	12,913
Elwood	1	0	0	0	0	0	0	0	1	0	1,181
Garden City	0	0	1	0	0	0	0	0	0	1	27,038
Hays	1	0	0	0	0	0	1	0	0	0	21,206
Hiawatha	1	0	0	0	0	0	0	1	0	0	3,080
Hutchinson	0	0	1	0	0	0	0	0	1	0	41,439
Independence	1	0	0	0	0	0	0	0	1	0	8,860
Lenexa	1	0	0	0	0	0	0	0	0	1	53,376
Newton	2	0	0	0	0	0	0	0	1	1	19,226
Oakley	1	0	0	0	0	0	0	1	0	0	2,104
Ottawa	1	0	0	0	0	0	0	0	0	1	12,334
Overland Park	2	2	0	0	0	0	2	0	1	1	189,104
Pittsburg	1	0	0	0	0	0	0	0	1	0	20,439
Pratt	1	0	0	0	0	0	0	1	0	0	6,854
Salina	3	0	0	0	0	0	0	0	1	2	47,805
Wichita	5	0	2	0	0	0	1	1	3	2	391,399
Universities and Colleges	3	0	0	0	0	0					
University of Kansas, Medical Center[3]	1	0	0	0	0	0	0	1	0	0	
Washburn University	1	0	0	0	0	0	0	0	0	1	6,615
Wichita State University	1	0	0	0	0	0	0	0	1	0	14,240
Metropolitan Counties	5	2	1	0	0	0					
Linn	1	0	0	0	0	0	0	0	0	1	
Riley County Police Department	2	1	1	0	0	0	2	1	1	0	
Shawnee	1	1	0	0	0	0	0	1	0	1	
Wabaunsee	1	0	0	0	0	0	0	0	1	0	
Nonmetropolitan Counties	1	0	0	1	0	0					
Greeley	0	0	0	1	0	0	0	0	1	0	
Reno	1	0	0	0	0	0	1	0	0	0	
KENTUCKY											
Total	135	43	22	2	1	3					
Cities	100	30	19	1	1	3					
Alexandria	1	0	0	0	0	0	0	1	0	0	9,112
Ashland	0	1	0	0	0	0	1	0	0	0	20,987
Audubon Park	1	0	0	0	0	0	1	0	0	0	1,515
Bellevue	1	0	1	0	0	0	0	0	0	2	5,879
Benton	0	1	1	0	0	0	0	0	0	2	4,346
Berea	2	1	0	0	0	0	1	0	1	1	15,135
Bowling Green	6	2	3	0	0	0	1	3	4	3	64,561
Cave City	1	0	0	0	0	0	0	1	0	0	2,411
Cloverport	1	0	0	0	0	0	0	0	1	0	1,157
Covington	4	3	3	0	0	0	2	3	3	2	41,094
Cynthiana	1	0	0	0	0	0	1	0	0	0	6,421
Elizabethtown	0	0	1	0	0	0	0	0	0	1	29,821
Elkton	0	1	0	0	0	0	1	0	0	0	2,181
Elsmere	2	0	1	0	0	0	1	1	0	1	8,563
Fort Mitchell	0	0	1	0	0	0	0	0	1	0	8,334
Frankfort	2	1	0	0	0	0	0	1	1	1	27,926
Franklin	2	0	0	0	0	0	0	0	1	1	8,852
Georgetown	3	0	0	0	0	0	1	1	1	0	33,007
Glasgow	1	0	1	0	0	0	0	1	1	0	14,560
Henderson	2	0	0	0	0	0	1	0	0	1	28,904
Highland Heights	0	1	0	0	0	0	0	0	0	1	7,216
Hopkinsville	5	0	0	0	0	0	3	1	0	1	32,222
Lakeside Park-Crestview Hills	0	0	1	0	0	0	0	0	0	1	6,159
Lancaster	1	0	0	0	0	0	1	0	0	0	3,873
Lexington	26	9	4	1	1	0	7	9	14	11	317,853
Louisville Metro	5	3	1	0	0	2	2	1	3	5	683,825

Table 77. Hate Crime Incidents Per Bias Motivation and Quarter, by Selected State and Agency, 2016—Continued

(Number.)

State/agency	Number of incidents per bias motivation						Number of incidents per quarter				Population[1]
	Race/Ethnicity/Ancestry	Religion	Sexual orientation	Disability	Gender	Gender Identity	1st quarter	2nd quarter	3rd quarter	4th quarter	
Loyall	1	0	0	0	0	0	0	0	0	1	648
Madisonville	2	2	0	0	0	0	4	0	0	0	19,467
Mayfield	2	0	0	0	0	0	1	0	1	0	10,086
Mount Washington	3	0	0	0	0	0	1	0	0	2	14,162
Murray	1	1	0	0	0	0	1	1	0	0	19,182
Nicholasville	5	1	0	0	0	0	2	0	3	1	30,093
Owensboro	4	0	0	0	0	0	1	0	0	3	59,359
Paducah	2	1	0	0	0	0	0	1	1	1	24,836
Paris	0	1	0	0	0	0	0	0	1	0	9,883
Radcliff	3	0	0	0	0	1	1	0	2	1	22,346
Richmond	1	0	0	0	0	0	0	0	0	1	33,965
Shelbyville	2	0	0	0	0	0	1	1	0	0	15,488
Shively	0	0	1	0	0	0	0	1	0	0	15,800
Stanton	0	1	0	0	0	0	0	0	1	0	2,651
St. Matthews	3	0	0	0	0	0	0	0	2	1	18,127
Versailles	1	0	0	0	0	0	0	1	0	0	25,923
Winchester	3	0	0	0	0	0	1	0	2	0	18,461
Universities and Colleges	3	1	2	0	0	0					
Eastern Kentucky University	1	0	0	0	0	0	0	1	0	0	16,844
Murray State University	0	1	0	0	0	0	0	0	0	1	10,998
University of Kentucky	1	0	0	0	0	0	0	0	0	1	29,727
University of Louisville	0	0	2	0	0	0	1	1	0	0	21,294
Western Kentucky University	1	0	0	0	0	0	0	0	1	0	20,063
Metropolitan Counties	14	4	1	1	0	0					
Boone	1	0	1	0	0	0	0	1	1	0	
Boyd	1	0	0	0	0	0	1	0	0	0	
Bracken	0	0	0	1	0	0	0	0	0	1	
Bullitt	4	0	0	0	0	0	0	2	2	0	
Campbell County Police Department	1	0	0	0	0	0	0	1	0	0	
Christian	1	0	0	0	0	0	0	0	1	0	
Daviess	1	1	0	0	0	0	0	0	0	2	
Hardin	1	0	0	0	0	0	1	0	0	0	
Jefferson	0	1	0	0	0	0	1	0	0	0	
Kenton	1	0	0	0	0	0	1	0	0	0	
Oldham County Police Department	1	0	0	0	0	0	0	0	1	0	
Pendleton	0	1	0	0	0	0	0	0	0	1	
Shelby	1	1	0	0	0	0	1	0	1	0	
Spencer	1	0	0	0	0	0	0	0	1	0	
Nonmetropolitan Counties	10	1	0	0	0	0					
Anderson	1	0	0	0	0	0	0	0	0	1	
Franklin	1	1	0	0	0	0	0	1	1	0	
Letcher	1	0	0	0	0	0	1	0	0	0	
Mason	1	0	0	0	0	0	0	0	0	1	
McCracken	1	0	0	0	0	0	1	0	0	0	
McCreary	1	0	0	0	0	0	0	1	0	0	
Muhlenberg County Police Department	2	0	0	0	0	0	2	0	0	0	
Nelson	1	0	0	0	0	0	0	0	1	0	
Wolfe	1	0	0	0	0	0	1	0	0	0	
State Police Agencies	5	6	0	0	0	0					
State Police:											
Bowling Green	1	3	0	0	0	0	0	0	2	2	
Harlan	0	1	0	0	0	0	0	1	0	0	
Hazard	2	0	0	0	0	0	0	0	1	1	
Henderson	1	1	0	0	0	0	0	0	2	0	
Mayfield	1	0	0	0	0	0	0	0	1	0	
Richmond	0	1	0	0	0	0	1	0	0	0	
Other Agencies	3	1	0	0	0	0					
Fayette County Schools	2	0	0	0	0	0	1	0	0	1	
Jefferson County School District	1	1	0	0	0	0	1	0	1	0	
LOUISIANA											
Total	20	3	4	0	0	0					
Cities	7	2	2	0	0	0					
Baton Rouge	2	0	1	0	0	0	0	0	1	2	228,389
New Orleans[2]	3	2	1	0	0	0	3	1	0	1	397,208
Thibodaux	1	0	0	0	0	0	0	0	1	0	14,588
Westlake	1	0	0	0	0	0	1	0	0	0	4,626
Metropolitan Counties	11	1	2	0	0	0					
Bossier	1	0	1	0	0	0	1	0	1	0	
Caddo	0	1	0	0	0	0	0	0	0	1	
St. Charles	6	0	0	0	0	0	0	0	6		
St. John the Baptist	4	0	1	0	0	0	0	3	2	0	
Nonmetropolitan Counties	2	0	0	0	0	0					
Avoyelles	1	0	0	0	0	0			1		
Madison	1	0	0	0	0	0	0	0	1	0	
MAINE											
Total	21	11	8	0	0	0					

Table 77. Hate Crime Incidents Per Bias Motivation and Quarter, by Selected State and Agency, 2016—Continued

(Number.)

State/agency	Number of incidents per bias motivation						Number of incidents per quarter				Population[1]
	Race/ Ethnicity/ Ancestry	Religion	Sexual orientation	Disability	Gender	Gender Identity	1st quarter	2nd quarter	3rd quarter	4th quarter	
Cities	16	10	6	0	0	0					
Augusta	0	1	1	0	0	0	1	0	1	0	18,347
Biddeford	0	1	0	0	0	0	0	0	1	0	21,285
Farmington	0	0	1	0	0	0	0	0	1	0	7,401
Lewiston	2	0	0	0	0	0	0	1	1	0	36,126
Lincoln	1	0	0	0	0	0	0	0	0	1	5,020
Old Orchard Beach	1	0	0	0	0	0	0	0	0	1	8,807
Portland	6	3	2	0	0	0	2	3	6	0	67,041
Saco	4	2	0	0	0	0	1	2	1	2	19,197
Sanford	1	0	1	0	0	0	0	1	0	1	20,914
Scarborough	0	1	0	0	0	0	0	1	0	0	19,851
South Portland	0	2	1	0	0	0	0	1	1	1	25,674
Waterville	1	0	0	0	0	0	0	0	0	1	16,370
Universities and Colleges	4	1	2	0	0	0					
University of Southern Maine	4	1	2	0	0	0	2	0	3	2	7,739
State Police Agencies	1	0	0	0	0	0					
State Police, Kennebec County	1	0	0	0	0	0	1	0	0	0	
MARYLAND											
Total	24	7	6	0	0	0					
Cities	2	0	3	0	0	0					
Baltimore	1	0	2	0	0	0	0	1	2	0	618,385
Laurel	1	0	1	0	0	0	0	2	0	0	26,424
Universities and Colleges	1	0	0	0	0	0					
University of Maryland, College Park	1	0	0	0	0	0	0	0	0	1	38,140
Metropolitan Counties	20	6	3	0	0	0					
Anne Arundel County Police Department	10	5	1	0	0	0	2	1	3	10	
Baltimore County Police Department	1	0	0	0	0	0	0	0	1	0	
Harford[2]	4	0	0	0	0	0	1	1	0	2	
Howard County Police Department	1	0	0	0	0	0	0		0	1	
Montgomery County Police Department	4	1	2	0	0	0	2		3	2	
State Police Agencies	0	1	0	0	0	0					
State Police, Anne Arundel County	0	1	0	0	0	0	0	0	0	1	
Other Agencies	1	0	0	0	0	0					
National Capitol Park Police, Montgomery County	1	0	0	0	0	0	0	1	0	0	
MASSACHUSETTS											
Total	212	94	76	8	8	16					
Cities	194	71	65	8	7	16					
Acton	2	0	0	0	0	1	1	2	0	0	23,770
Andover	2	1	0	0	0	0	1	2	0	0	35,558
Arlington[2]	9	1	0	1	0	0	2	4	3	1	45,004
Barnstable	0	0	3	1	0	0	1	0	3	0	43,974
Belmont	1	0	0	0	0	0	0	0	0	1	25,637
Beverly	2	1	0	0	0	0	1	1	1	0	41,303
Billerica	1	1	0	0	0	0	1	0	0	1	42,965
Boston[2]	75	16	28	1	0	9	29	34	27	30	673,880
Boxford	0	1	0	0	0	0	0	0	0	1	8,271
Braintree[2]	6	1	1	0	1	0	3	1	2	1	37,673
Cambridge[2]	16	6	4	0	0	0	5	7	3	10	111,030
Chelmsford	0	0	0	0	1	0	0	1	0	0	35,251
Chelsea	0	1	0	0	0	0	0	0	1	0	40,096
Chicopee	1	0	0	0	0	0	1	0	0	0	56,887
Cohasset	1	0	0	0	0	0	0	0	0	1	8,538
Danvers	0	3	0	0	0	0	0	0	1	2	27,997
Dartmouth	1	0	0	0	0	0	0	0	1	0	34,630
Dennis	2	0	0	0	0	0	0	0	1	1	13,905
Dudley	0	1	0	0	0	0	0	0	0	1	11,558
Everett[2]	7	1	0	0	0	0	1	0	4	3	46,754
Fitchburg	0	1	0	0	0	0	0	0	0	1	40,391
Framingham	3	0	0	0	0	0	1	1	1	0	71,422
Freetown	1	0	0	0	0	0	0	0	1	0	9,199
Greenfield	0	0	0	0	1	0	0	0	1	0	17,456
Haverhill[2]	3	1	2	0	0	0	0	1	1	3	62,851
Holliston	0	0	1	0	0	0	0	1	0	0	14,656
Hopkinton	0	2	1	0	0	0	1	2	0	0	16,960
Lancaster	0	0	1	0	0	0	1	0	0	0	8,150
Lawrence	0	0	1	0	0	0	0	0	0	1	80,622
Lenox	0	0	1	0	0	0	0	0	1	0	4,971
Lexington	1	1	0	0	0	0	0	0	2	0	33,643
Lowell	0	1	1	0	0	0	1	0	0	1	111,027
Lynn[2]	5	0	2	0	0	1	2	1	3	1	92,443
Malden	1	0	2	0	0	0	0	0	2	1	61,102
Manchester-by-the-Sea	0	0	0	1	0	0	0	0	1	0	5,387
Mansfield	1	0	0	0	0	0	0	0	0	1	23,681

Table 77. Hate Crime Incidents Per Bias Motivation and Quarter, by Selected State and Agency, 2016—Continued

(Number.)

State/agency	Race/ Ethnicity/ Ancestry	Religion	Sexual orientation	Disability	Gender	Gender Identity	1st quarter	2nd quarter	3rd quarter	4th quarter	Population[1]
Mattapoisett	1	0	0	0	0	0	0	1	0	0	6,282
Medford	3	0	0	0	0	0	0	0	1	2	57,367
Methuen[2]	2	1	0	0	0	0	0	0	2	0	49,912
Milford	1	0	0	0	0	0	0	0	0	1	28,606
Millbury	0	1	0	0	0	0	1	0	0	0	13,532
Milton	1	0	1	0	0	0	0	0	2	0	27,317
Nahant	1	0	1	0	0	0	1	1	0	0	3,484
Newburyport	1	0	0	0	0	0	0	1	0	0	18,011
Newton[2]	7	16	0	0	0	1	8	6	4	3	89,116
Northampton[2]	2	1	1	0	0	0	1	0	2	1	28,521
Pepperell	0	1	0	0	0	0	0	0	1	0	12,242
Pittsfield	1	0	0	0	0	0	0	0	0	1	43,031
Provincetown	0	0	1	0	0	0	0	1	0	0	2,959
Quincy	3	0	1	0	1	0	1	1	2	1	93,437
Randolph	3	0	0	0	0	0	0	1	2	0	33,807
Salem	1	1	3	0	0	0	0	2	3	0	42,888
Saugus	1	0	0	0	0	0	1	0	0	0	28,131
Sharon	0	0	0	0	1	0	0	0	0	1	18,200
Shelburne	0	0	0	1	0	0	0	0	0	1	1,839
Somerville	6	3	1	1	0	0	2	2	2	5	80,899
Southbridge	1	0	0	0	0	0	0	0	1	0	16,819
Springfield	7	0	3	0	0	0	3	1	4	2	154,102
Stoughton	0	1	0	0	0	0	0	0	1	0	28,583
Sturbridge	0	0	0	1	0	0	0	1	0	0	9,520
Sudbury	0	1	0	0	0	0	0	0	0	1	19,035
Swampscott	0	3	0	0	0	0	0	2	0	1	14,551
Taunton	3	0	1	0	1	0	2	1	2	0	56,720
Topsfield	1	0	0	0	0	0	1	0	0	0	6,590
Waltham	1	0	1	1	0	3	2	1	1	2	63,613
Watertown[2]	0	2	2	0	0	0	0	0	2	1	34,655
Westfield	0	0	1	0	0	0	0	1	0	0	41,700
West Tisbury	0	0	0	0	1	0	0	0	1	0	2,927
Williamstown	1	0	0	0	0	0	0	0	1	0	7,591
Worcester	5	0	0	0	0	1	0	1	2	3	184,595
Universities and Colleges	14	22	10	0	1	0					
Boston University[2]	5	11	4	0	1	0	3	3	9	4	32,158
Brandeis University	0	1	0	0	0	0	0	0	0	1	5,752
Bridgewater State University	0	0	1	0	0	0	1	0	0	0	11,089
Bristol Community College	1	0	0	0	0	0	0	0	0	1	8,761
Clark University	0	3	0	0	0	0	2	0	0	1	3,485
Hampshire College	1	0	0	0	0	0	0	0	0	1	1,410
Massachusetts Institute of Technology	0	1	0	0	0	0	1	0	0	0	11,331
Northeastern University	0	1	0	0	0	0		1			19,940
Salem State University	0	0	3	0	0	0	2	1	0	0	9,215
Tufts University, Suffolk[3]	0	1	0	0	0	0	0	1	0	0	
University of Massachusetts: Amherst[2]	6	4	2	0	0	0	6	4	1	0	29,269
Medical Center, Worcester	1	0	0	0	0	0	0	0	0	1	1,079
Other Agencies	4	1	1	0	0	0					
Massachusetts Bay Transportation Authority:											
Middlesex County	1	0	0	0	0	0	0	0	1		
Suffolk County	3	1	1	0	0	0	1	1	1	2	
MICHIGAN											
Total	282	47	59	6	5	0					
Cities	209	41	44	4	1	0					
Albion	2	1	0	0	0	0	0	0	0	3	8,155
Allegan	0	0	1	0	0	0	0	1	0	0	5,086
Ann Arbor	0	1	0	0	0	0	0	0	0	1	117,688
Auburn Hills	1	0	0	0	0	0	0	1	0	0	22,933
Battle Creek	3	0	0	0	0	0	0	1	1	1	60,904
Belleville	1	0	0	0	0	0	0	0	0	1	3,860
Benton Harbor	1	0	0	0	0	0	1	0	0	0	9,963
Benton Township	2	0	0	0	0	0	0	0	2	0	14,413
Berkley	1	0	0	0	0	0	0	0	1	0	15,328
Big Rapids	1	0	0	0	0	0	0	0	0	1	10,389
Birmingham	0	1	0	0	0	0	0	1	0	0	21,012
Blackman Township	3	0	0	0	0	0	0	0	2	1	37,522
Bloomfield Hills	1	1	0	0	0	0	0	1	0	1	4,031
Bloomfield Township	1	1	0	0	0	0	0	0	0	2	42,313
Buena Vista Township	2	0	0	0	0	0	0	1	1	0	8,158
Burton	1	0	0	0	0	0	0	0	1	0	28,563
Cadillac	1	0	0	0	0	0	0	0	0	1	10,372
Caro	1	0	0	0	0	0	0	0	0	1	4,074
Chesterfield Township	1	0	0	0	0	0	1	0	0	0	44,963
Clawson	2	0	0	0	0	0	0	0	1	1	12,053
Clinton Township	1	0	0	0	0	0	1	0	0	0	100,514
Clio	1	0	0	0	0	0	0	0	1	0	2,516
Coldwater	1	0	0	0	0	0	0	1	0	0	10,827

Table 77. Hate Crime Incidents Per Bias Motivation and Quarter, by Selected State and Agency, 2016—Continued

(Number.)

State/agency	Number of incidents per bias motivation						Number of incidents per quarter				
	Race/ Ethnicity/ Ancestry	Religion	Sexual orientation	Disability	Gender	Gender Identity	1st quarter	2nd quarter	3rd quarter	4th quarter	Population[1]
Commerce Township	1	0	0	0	0	0	0	0	1	0	38,218
Dearborn	7	4	3	0	0	0	3	5	5	1	94,646
Dearborn Heights	1	1	0	0	0	0	0	0	1	1	55,852
Detroit	16	1	13	2	0	0	6	6	7	13	669,673
East Lansing	2	1	0	0	0	0	2	0	0	1	48,451
Eastpointe	3	0	0	0	0	0	0	1	0	2	32,701
Eaton Rapids	1	0	0	0	0	0	0	0	1	0	5,226
Escanaba	1	0	0	0	1	0	0	0	2	0	12,278
Evart	1	0	0	0	0	0	0	0	1	0	1,853
Farmington	0	0	1	0	0	0	0	0	1	0	10,553
Ferndale	2	0	0	0	0	0	0	1	0	1	20,232
Flint	14	1	1	0	0	0	1	4	8	3	97,548
Flushing	0	0	1	0	0	0	0	1	0	0	8,028
Forsyth Township	1	0	0	0	0	0	1	0	0	0	6,196
Fruitport Township	1	0	0	0	0	0	0	0	1	0	13,879
Galesburg	2	0	0	0	0	0	0	1	0	1	2,050
Garden City	2	1	0	0	0	0	0	0	1	2	26,781
Gaylord	1	0	0	0	0	0	0	0	1	0	3,662
Genesee Township	0	0	1	0	0	0	1	0	0	0	20,393
Grand Rapids	2	0	0	0	0	0	0	1	0	1	196,538
Grandville	0	1	0	0	0	0	0	1	0	0	16,070
Grant	3	0	0	0	0	0	0	2	0	1	880
Grosse Pointe Park	1	0	1	0	0	0	0	0	1	1	11,160
Grosse Pointe Woods	1	0	0	0	0	0	0	1	0	0	15,699
Hampton Township	1	0	0	0	0	0	0	0	0	1	9,401
Hamtramck	3	2	0	0	0	0	2	2	1	0	21,929
Harper Woods	1	0	0	0	0	0	0	1	0	0	13,764
Hart	1	0	0	0	0	0	0	0	1	0	2,093
Hastings	1	0	0	0	0	0	0	1	0	0	7,274
Highland Park	5	1	1	0	0	0	1	0	3	3	10,810
Houghton	2	0	0	0	0	0	1	0	0	1	8,020
Huntington Woods	0	1	0	0	0	0	1	0	0	0	6,360
Huron Township	1	0	0	0	0	0	0	0	1	0	15,622
Independence Township	2	0	0	0	0	0	1	0	0	1	36,689
Inkster	3	2	1	0	0	0	2	1	2	1	24,548
Ishpeming	2	0	0	0	0	0	1	0	0	1	6,485
Kalamazoo	1	0	0	0	0	0	0	1	0	0	76,389
Lansing	1	1	0	0	0	0	2	0	0	0	115,199
Lapeer	1	0	1	0	0	0	1	0	1	0	8,782
Lawton	2	0	0	0	0	0	0	1	0	1	1,860
Leslie	1	0	0	0	0	0	0	1	0	0	1,869
Lincoln Park	1	0	0	0	0	0	0	1	0	0	36,808
Lincoln Township	2	0	0	0	0	0	0	0	0	2	14,500
Livonia	3	1	0	0	0	0	0	0	3	1	94,226
Ludington	3	0	0	0	0	0	0	2	1	0	8,054
Mackinac Island	0	0	1	0	0	0	0	1	0	0	479
Marysville	0	0	1	0	0	0	0	1	0	0	9,722
Mason	1	0	0	0	0	0	0	1	0	0	8,461
Melvindale	2	0	0	0	0	0	0	1	1	0	10,348
Meridian Township	4	1	1	0	0	0	2	0	0	4	42,700
Monroe	2	0	0	0	0	0	0	1	1	0	19,971
Montrose Township	0	1	1	0	0	0	0	2	0	0	7,524
Mount Pleasant	1	0	0	0	0	0	0	1	0	0	26,069
Muskegon	0	1	1	0	0	0	0	0	0	2	38,442
Muskegon Township	0	0	1	0	0	0	0	0	0	1	17,791
Niles	1	1	0	0	0	0	0	0	2	0	11,282
Norton Shores	3	0	0	0	0	0	0	1	1	1	24,256
Ontwa Township-Edwardsburg	0	0	1	0	0	0	0	0	1	0	6,481
Owosso	1	0	0	0	0	0	0	0	1	0	14,605
Oxford Township	1	0	0	0	0	0	1	0	0	0	18,164
Pittsfield Township	1	1	1	0	0	0	0	0	2	1	38,704
Plymouth	0	0	1	0	0	0	0	0	1	0	8,865
Plymouth Township	0	0	1	0	0	0	0	0	0	1	26,870
Pontiac	2	0	0	0	0	0	1	0	1	0	60,003
Portage	1	0	0	0	0	0	0	0	1	0	48,550
Port Huron	0	0	1	0	0	0	0	0	1	0	29,182
Redford Township	1	1	0	0	0	0	0	1	1	0	47,218
Richland	1	0	0	0	0	0	0	1	0	0	793
River Rouge	1	0	0	0	0	0	0	0	0	1	7,480
Rochester Hills	2	0	0	0	0	0	1	0	1	0	73,913
Romulus	4	0	0	0	0	0	0	2	1	1	23,315
Roseville	3	0	0	0	0	0	1	1	1	0	47,704
Royal Oak	1	0	0	0	0	0	1	0	0	0	59,367
Saginaw	3	1	1	0	0	0	2	2	0	1	48,942
Saginaw Township	2	0	0	0	0	0	0	1	1	0	39,421
Saline	1	0	0	0	0	0	0	0	1	0	9,158
Sault Ste. Marie	0	0	2	0	0	0	2	0	0	0	13,763
Shelby Township	3	0	1	0	0	0	0	1	1	2	78,427
Southfield	1	1	1	0	0	0	1	1	0	1	73,438
Southgate	3	0	1	0	0	0	1	2	1	0	29,158
South Lyon	2	0	0	0	0	0	0	1	1	0	11,801

Table 77. Hate Crime Incidents Per Bias Motivation and Quarter, by Selected State and Agency, 2016—Continued

(Number.)

State/agency	Number of incidents per bias motivation						Number of incidents per quarter				Population[1]
	Race/ Ethnicity/ Ancestry	Religion	Sexual orientation	Disability	Gender	Gender Identity	1st quarter	2nd quarter	3rd quarter	4th quarter	
St. Charles	1	1	0	0	0	0	0	0	2	0	1,940
St. Joseph Township	1	0	0	0	0	0	0	1	0	0	9,850
Sturgis	1	0	0	0	0	0	0	1	0	0	10,876
Taylor	3	0	0	0	0	0	0	1	1	1	61,290
Tittabawassee Township	1	0	0	0	0	0	0	0	1	0	9,782
Traverse City	4	3	0	0	0	0	0	2	2	3	15,330
Troy	7	0	0	0	0	0	0	1	3	3	83,743
Van Buren Township	2	0	2	0	0	0	0	0	2	2	28,090
Warren	7	1	0	2	0	0	2	2	2	4	135,620
Waterford Township	1	0	0	0	0	0	1	0	0	0	73,308
West Bloomfield Township	5	4	0	0	0	0	1	2	4	2	66,123
Wyoming	0	1	0	0	0	0	1	0	0	0	75,917
Universities and Colleges	16	4	3	0	0	0					
Eastern Michigan University	4	2	0	0	0	0	0	0	2	4	21,824
Grand Valley State University	0	0	1	0	0	0	0	0	1	0	25,325
Michigan State University	2	1	1	0	0	0	0	0	1	3	50,538
Mott Community College	1	0	0	0	0	0	0	0	1	0	8,617
Schoolcraft College	1	0	0	0	0	0	0	0	1	0	11,687
University of Michigan:											
Ann Arbor	6	1	1	0	0	0	2	2	1	3	43,651
Flint	1	0	0	0	0	0	0	0	0	1	8,470
Western Michigan University	1	0	0	0	0	0	0	0	1	0	23,529
Metropolitan Counties	24	0	8	1	1	0					
Barry	2	0	0	0	0	0	0	2	0	0	
Calhoun	1	0	1	0	0	0	0	0	2	0	
Eaton	1	0	0	0	0	0	0	0	1	0	
Genesee	1	0	0	0	0	0	0	0	0	1	
Ingham	2	0	0	0	0	0	0	2	0	0	
Jackson	3	0	0	0	0	0	0	0	3	0	
Kent	1	0	1	0	0	0	1	1	0	0	
Lapeer	2	0	1	0	0	0	2	0	0	1	
Livingston	0	0	0	1	1	0	1	0	0	1	
Macomb	1	0	0	0	0	0	0	1	0	0	
Monroe	3	0	0	0	0	0	0	1	1	1	
Montcalm	1	0	1	0	0	0	1	0	1	0	
Muskegon	1	0	0	0	0	0	0	0	1	0	
Oakland	0	0	2	0	0	0	1	0	1	0	
Saginaw	2	0	0	0	0	0	1	1	0	0	
St. Clair	0	0	1	0	0	0	0	0	0	1	
Van Buren	1	0	1	0	0	0	0	0	0	2	
Washtenaw	2	0	0	0	0	0	0	0	1	1	
Nonmetropolitan Counties	18	1	2	1	1	0					
Benzie	1	0	0	0	0	0	1	0	0	0	
Clare	1	0	0	0	0	0	0	0	1	0	
Emmet	1	0	0	0	0	0	0	1	0	0	
Gratiot	2	0	0	0	0	0	0	1	0	1	
Hillsdale	1	0	0	0	0	0	0	1	0	0	
Huron	1	0	0	0	0	0	0	0	0	1	
Ionia	1	0	0	0	0	0	0	0	1	0	
Luce	0	0	0	1	0	0	0	0	1	0	
Marquette	1	0	0	0	0	0	0	1	0	0	
Mason	1	0	0	0	0	0	0	0	0	1	
Mecosta	2	0	0	0	0	0	0	1	1	0	
Menominee	3	0	0	0	0	0	1	2	0	0	
Oceana	1	0	1	0	0	0	1	1	0	0	
Sanilac	1	0	0	0	0	0	0	0	1	0	
Tuscola	1	1	1	0	1	0	0	0	2	2	
State Police Agencies	14	1	2	0	2	0					
State Police:											
Ingham County	2	0	0	0	0	0	0	0	0	2	
Isabella County	3	0	2	0	0	0	1	1	2	1	
Jackson County	1	0	0	0	0	0	0	0	0	1	
Kent County	3	0	0	0	0	0	0	0	1	2	
Livingston County	0	1	0	0	1	0	0	0	0	2	
Mecosta County	1	0	0	0	0	0	0	1	0	0	
Muskegon County	0	0	0	0	1	0	1	0	0	0	
Oceana County	4	0	0	0	0	0	0	2	1	1	
Other Agencies	1	0	0	0	0	0					
Gerald R. Ford International Airport	1	0	0	0	0	0	0	0	1	0	
MINNESOTA											
Total	77	30	15	0	0	0					
Cities	71	28	15	0	0	0					
Blaine	2	0	0	0	0	0	1	0	0	1	63,115
Bloomington	1	0	0	0	0	0	0	0	0	1	87,134
Brooklyn Center	1	0	0	0	0	0	1	0	0	0	30,893
Brooklyn Park	8	1	1	0	0	0	4	2	2	2	79,800
Cottage Grove	2	0	0	0	0	0	1	1	0	0	36,164
Crystal	2	0	0	0	0	0	1	0	1	0	23,102
Eagan	2	0	0	0	0	0	0	0	0	2	66,698

Table 77. Hate Crime Incidents Per Bias Motivation and Quarter, by Selected State and Agency, 2016—Continued

(Number.)

State/agency	Race/ Ethnicity/ Ancestry	Religion	Sexual orientation	Disability	Gender	Gender Identity	1st quarter	2nd quarter	3rd quarter	4th quarter	Population[1]
Inver Grove Heights[2]	7	0	1	0	0	0	1	1	3	2	35,049
Little Falls	1	0	0	0	0	0	0	0	1	0	8,611
Mankato	3	0	2	0	0	0	0	0	2	3	41,300
Maplewood	2	0	0	0	0	0	1	0	0	1	41,071
Minneapolis	20	13	5	0	0	0	5	16	11	6	416,751
Minnetonka	0	2	0	0	0	0	1	1	0	0	52,055
Moorhead	0	0	1	0	0	0	1	0	0	0	42,507
New Hope	1	0	0	0	0	0	0	1	0	0	21,168
Oakdale[2]	1	1	0	0	0	0	0	1	0	0	28,211
Orono	0	1	0	0	0	0	0	1	0	0	19,799
Plymouth	4	1	1	0	0	0	2	1	2	1	76,996
Roseville[2]	1	1	1	0	0	0	0	1	1	0	35,954
Sauk Centre	0	1	0	0	0	0	0	1	0	0	4,367
Savage	0	1	0	0	0	0	0	1	0	0	31,118
South St. Paul	1	0	0	0	0	0	0	0	1	0	20,452
Spring Lake Park	1	0	0	0	0	0	0	0	0	1	6,484
St. Cloud	3	1	1	0	0	0	2	2	1		67,341
St. Louis Park	2	3	0	0	0	0	0	0	1	4	48,770
St. Paul	5	2	2	0	0	0	3	1	3	2	303,920
Wayzata	1	0	0	0	0	0	0	0	1	0	6,627
Universities and Colleges	0	1	0	0	0	0					
University of Minnesota, Twin Cities	0	1	0	0	0	0	0	0	0	1	50,678
Metropolitan Counties	5	0	0	0	0	0					
Carver	1	0	0	0	0	0	0	0	1	0	
Mille Lacs	1	0	0	0	0	0	1	0	0	0	
Ramsey	2	0	0	0	0	0	0	0	0	2	
Wright	1	0	0	0	0	0	0	1	0	0	
Nonmetropolitan Counties	1	0	0	0	0	0					
Crow Wing	1	0	0	0	0	0	1	0	0	0	
Other Agencies	0	1	0	0	0	0					
Minneapolis-St. Paul International Airport	0	1	0	0	0	0	0	1		0	
MISSISSIPPI											
Total	4	1	2	0	0	0					
Cities	3	1	1	0	0	0					
Biloxi	0	0	1	0	0	0	1	0	0	0	45,952
Olive Branch	3	1	0	0	0	0	1	0	0	3	36,513
Metropolitan Counties	0	0	1	0	0	0					
DeSoto	0	0	1	0	0	0	1	0	0	0	
Nonmetropolitan Counties	1	0	0	0	0	0					
Stone	1	0	0	0	0	0				1	
MISSOURI											
Total	65	13	10	0	1	0					
Cities	62	11	10	0	1	0					
Battlefield	1	0	0	0	0	0	0	0	1	0	6,083
Blue Springs	1	0	0	0	0	0	0	1	0	0	54,445
Bolivar	0	1	0	0	0	0	0	1	0	0	10,790
Branson	1	0	0	0	0	0	1	0	0	0	11,593
Bridgeton	0	0	1	0	0	0	0	0	0	1	11,835
Cameron	1	0	0	0	0	0	0	0	1	0	9,817
Chesterfield	1	1	0	0	0	0	2	0	0	0	47,939
Clayton	1	0	0	0	0	0	1	0	0	0	15,873
Columbia	5	0	2	0	0	0	0	1	5	1	121,143
Gladstone	1	0	0	0	0	0	0	0	1	0	27,138
Independence	1	0	1	0	0	0	1	1	0	0	117,335
Kansas City	33	6	4	0	0	0	7	7	16	13	478,364
Lee's Summit	1	0	0	0	1	0	0	1	1	0	95,821
Marionville	1	0	0	0	0	0	0	1	0	0	2,181
North Kansas City	1	0	0	0	0	0	0	0	0	1	4,387
Rolla	2	0	0	0	0	0	2	0	0	0	20,093
St. Charles	1	0	0	0	0	0	0	0	1	0	69,364
St. Joseph	0	0	1	0	0	0	0	1	0	0	76,577
St. Louis	8	1	0	0	0	0		3	3	3	314,507
St. Peters[2]	1	2	1	0	0	0	0	1	2	0	57,835
University City	1	0	0	0	0	0	1	0	0		35,002
Universities and Colleges	2	1	0	0	0	0					
University of Missouri:											
Kansas City	2	0	0	0	0	0	0	0	0	2	16,685
St. Louis	0	1	0	0	0	0	0	0	1	0	16,738
Metropolitan Counties	1	1	0	0	0	0					
St. Louis County Police Department	1	1	0	0	0	0	2	0	0	0	
MONTANA											
Total	10	5	4	0	1	0					
Cities	4	4	2	0	1	0					
Billings	2	1	1	0	0	0	3	0	0	1	111,447
Columbia Falls	0	0	0	0	1	0	1	0	0	0	5,175
Conrad	1	0	0	0	0	0	0	1	0	0	2,594

Table 77. Hate Crime Incidents Per Bias Motivation and Quarter, by Selected State and Agency, 2016—Continued

(Number.)

State/agency	Number of incidents per bias motivation						Number of incidents per quarter				Population[1]
	Race/ Ethnicity/ Ancestry	Religion	Sexual orientation	Disability	Gender	Gender Identity	1st quarter	2nd quarter	3rd quarter	4th quarter	
Havre	1	0	0	0	0	0	0	0	0	1	9,896
Helena	0	3	0	0	0	0	1	2	0	0	31,052
Whitefish	0	0	1	0	0	0	0	0	1	0	7,226
Nonmetropolitan Counties	6	1	2	0	0	0					
Big Horn	2	0	2	0	0	0	2	1	0	1	
Broadwater	1	0	0	0	0	0	0	0	1	0	
Lewis and Clark	3	0	0	0	0	0	0	0	3	0	
Richland	0	1	0	0	0	0	0	0	1	0	
NEBRASKA											
Total	23	4	3	0	1	0					
Cities	23	4	3	0	1	0					
Crete	2	0	0	0	0	0	2	0	0	0	7,047
Grand Island	2	0	0	0	0	0	1	1	0	0	51,980
Kearney	1	0	0	0	0	0	0	1	0	0	33,471
Lincoln	13	3	2	0	1	0	6	6	4	3	281,138
Norfolk	1	0	0	0	0	0	0	1	0	0	24,389
Omaha	4	1	0	0	0	0	3	0	2	0	446,163
Papillion	0	0	1	0	0	0	0	0	1	0	19,576
NEVADA											
Total	31	4	6	0	0	1					
Cities	31	4	6	0	0	1					
Henderson	9	1	1	0	0	0	2	4	3	2	291,584
Las Vegas Metropolitan Police Department[2]	19	1	5	0	0	1	3	10	2	10	1,592,178
North Las Vegas	3	1	0	0	0	0	0	1	3	0	238,554
Reno	0	1	0	0	0	0	0	0	0	1	244,554
NEW HAMPSHIRE											
Total	15	6	5	2	0	0					
Cities	15	6	4	2	0	0					
Belmont	1	0	0	0	0	0	1	0	0	0	7,315
Boscawen	0	0	1	0	0	0	0	1	0	0	3,950
Bow	1	0	0	0	0	0	0	0	1	0	7,779
Brookline	0	1	0	0	0	0	0	1	0	0	5,256
Claremont	1	0	0	0	0	0	0	1	0	0	12,913
Concord	1	0	1	0	0	0	0	1	1	0	42,610
Derry	1	0	0	0	0	0	0	0	0	1	33,249
Dover	0	0	0	1	0	0	1	0	0	0	31,054
Durham	0	1	0	0	0	0	0	0	0	1	17,078
Exeter	2	1	0	0	0	0	1	1	1	0	14,635
Farmington	2	0	1	0	0	0	0	0	3	0	6,841
Hillsborough	1	0	0	0	0	0	0	0	0	1	5,974
Keene	1	2	0	0	0	0	0	0	1	2	23,244
Laconia	1	1	0	1	0	0	0	2	0	1	16,300
Manchester	0	0	1	0	0	0	0	0	0	1	110,353
Pembroke	1	0	0	0	0	0	1	0	0	0	7,118
Sandown	1	0	0	0	0	0	0	0	0	1	6,348
Troy	1	0	0	0	0	0	0	0	1	0	2,075
Universities and Colleges	0	0	1	0	0	0					
University of New Hampshire	0	0	1	0	0	0	1	0	0	0	15,351
NEW JERSEY											
Total	137	110	34	1	0	0					
Cities	130	110	33	1	0	0					
Aberdeen Township	1	1	0	0	0	0		0	1	1	18,562
Allendale	0	1	0	0	0	0	0	1	0	0	6,849
Atlantic City	1	0	0	0	0	0	0	0	1	0	39,202
Bergenfield	0	1	0	0	0	0	0	1	0	0	27,646
Blairstown Township	1	1	0	0	0	0	0	2	0	0	5,791
Bloomfield	1	0	0	0	0	0	0	1	0	0	48,215
Brick Township	0	1	1	0	0	0		1	1	0	74,818
Cinnaminson Township	1	0	0	0	0	0	0	1	0	0	16,871
Colts Neck Township	0	0	1	0	0	0		0	1	0	10,018
Cresskill	0	1	0	0	0	0	0	1	0	0	8,815
Dunellen	0	1	0	0	0	0		0	0	1	7,434
East Brunswick Township	6	2	1	0	0	0		6	2	1	49,016
East Hanover Township	1	0	0	0	0	0		0	0	1	11,233
East Orange	1	0	0	0	0	0	1	0	0	0	64,787
East Rutherford	0	1	0	0	0	0	0	1	0	0	9,166
East Windsor Township	2	0	0	0	0	0		1	0	1	27,537
Edgewater	0	1	0	0	0	0	0	0	0	1	12,079
Edison Township	2	1	0	0	0	0		2	0	1	102,679
Evesham Township	4	1	1	0	0	0	2	1	1	2	45,581
Ewing Township	0	1	0	0	0	0		0	1	0	36,435
Florence Township	0	0	1	0	0	0	0	1	0	0	12,805
Fort Lee	1	1	1	0	0	0	1	0	1	1	36,739
Freehold Borough	2	0	0	0	0	0		0	0	2	11,941
Freehold Township	2	0	0	0	0	0		1	1	0	35,736
Galloway Township	0	1	0	0	0	0	0	0	1	0	37,280

Table 77. Hate Crime Incidents Per Bias Motivation and Quarter, by Selected State and Agency, 2016—Continued

(Number.)

State/agency	Number of incidents per bias motivation						Number of incidents per quarter				Population[1]
	Race/ Ethnicity/ Ancestry	Religion	Sexual orientation	Disability	Gender	Gender Identity	1st quarter	2nd quarter	3rd quarter	4th quarter	
Glassboro	1	1	1	0	0	0		1	0	2	19,245
Hackensack	2	2	1	0	0	0	2	2	0	1	44,968
Hamilton Township, Mercer County	0	2	0	0	0	0		2	0	0	88,665
Hammonton	0	1	0	0	0	0	0	0	1	0	14,585
Hanover Township	1	0	0	0	0	0		0	0	1	14,468
Harrison Township	0	1	1	0	0	0		1	0	1	13,023
Highland Park	2	1	0	0	0	0		3	0	0	14,346
Highlands	1	0	0	0	0	0		0	1	0	4,838
Hillsborough Township	1	0	0	0	0	0		0	0	1	40,037
Hoboken	2	0	1	0	0	0		0	1	2	54,095
Holmdel Township	0	3	0	0	0	0		1	0	2	16,651
Hopewell Township	0	1	0	0	0	0		0	0	1	18,570
Howell Township	4	6	1	0	0	0		3	7	1	52,306
Jackson Township	1	1	0	0	0	0		2	0	0	56,563
Jersey City	3	1	0	0	0	0		0	1	3	266,179
Keansburg	5	0	0	0	0	0		1	2	2	9,828
Lacey Township	0	1	0	0	0	0		0	1	0	28,540
Lakewood Township	3	14	0	0	0	0	2	6	7	2	100,269
Lindenwold	0	1	0	0	0	0	0	0	1	0	17,340
Linwood	0	1	0	0	0	0	0	0	1	0	6,950
Little Falls Township	2	0	1	0	0	0		0	0	3	14,478
Livingston Township	1	1	0	0	0	0	1	0	0	1	29,788
Lodi	0	1	0	0	0	0	0	1	0	0	24,841
Long Branch	2	1	0	0	0	0		0	0	3	30,959
Madison	0	1	0	0	0	0		1	0	0	16,098
Magnolia	1	1	0	0	0	0	0	1	1	0	4,267
Manalapan Township	0	3	1	0	0	0		1	0	3	40,407
Manasquan	1	0	0	0	0	0		0	0	1	5,798
Manchester Township	1	0	0	0	0	0		0	0	1	43,525
Medford Township	2	1	0	0	0	0	0	0	3		23,481
Metuchen	0	1	0	0	0	0		0	0	1	13,879
Middletown Township	1	0	0	0	0	0		0	0	1	65,919
Monmouth Beach	1	0	0	1	0	0		2	0	0	3,233
Montclair	2	2	2	0	0	0	2	0	0	4	38,108
Montville Township	1	0	0	0	0	0		1	0	0	21,801
Moonachie	1	0	0	0	0	0	0	0	0	1	2,790
Moorestown Township	0	1	0	0	0	0	0	0	1	0	20,530
Mount Arlington	1	0	0	0	0	0		0	1	0	5,324
Mount Laurel Township	0	2	0	0	0	0	0	0	1	1	41,828
Mount Olive Township	1	0	0	0	0	0		1	0	0	29,095
Neptune Township	8	0	4	0	0	0		3	7	2	27,505
Newark	0	2	1	0	0	0	2	0	0	1	281,450
New Brunswick	5	2	2	0	0	0		1	5	3	57,158
New Providence	0	1	0	0	0	0	0	1	0	0	12,461
Newton	0	1	0	0	0	0		0	0	1	7,950
North Brunswick Township	0	1	0	0	0	0		1	0	0	42,777
Northfield	1	1	0	0	0	0	0	0	2	0	8,502
North Haledon	1	0	0	0	0	0		1	0	0	8,529
Nutley Township	1	0	0	0	0	0	0	0	0	1	28,673
Ocean Township, Monmouth County	3	3	3	0	0	0		1	5	3	27,070
Paramus	0	1	0	0	0	0	0	1	0	0	26,958
Passaic	1	0	0	0	0	0		0	1	0	70,972
Pemberton Township	3	0	0	0	0	0	0	1	1	1	27,739
Pequannock Township	1	0	0	0	0	0		1	0	0	15,425
Piscataway Township	0	1	0	0	0	0		0	1	0	58,181
Plainsboro Township	0	1	0	0	0	0		0	0	1	23,621
Point Pleasant Beach	0	1	0	0	0	0		0	1	0	4,519
Pompton Lakes	1	0	0	0	0	0		0	1	0	11,164
Princeton	1	2	1	0	0	0		2	2	0	29,660
Randolph Township	0	2	0	0	0	0		2	0	0	25,877
Raritan Township	0	0	1	0	0	0		0	1	0	22,011
Readington Township	1	0	0	0	0	0		1	0	0	15,893
Robbinsville Township	0	1	0	0	0	0		0	0	1	14,209
Rockaway Township	0	1	0	0	0	0		0	0	1	24,655
Saddle Brook Township	0	1	0	0	0	0	1	0	0	0	14,108
Scotch Plains Township	1	0	0	0	0	0	0	0	1	0	24,144
Sea Isle City	1	0	0	0	0	0	0	0	1	0	2,080
Secaucus	2	1	1	0	0	0		0	3	1	19,528
Somerville	0	0	1	0	0	0		0	1	0	12,198
South Brunswick Township	3	11	1	0	0	0		4	5	6	45,862
South Orange	2	0	1	0	0	0	1	0	0	2	16,332
South River	0	1	0	0	0	0		1	0	0	16,391
Spotswood	1	0	0	0	0	0		1	0	0	8,477
Toms River Township	0	2	0	0	0	0		0	2	0	90,504
Trenton	1	0	0	0	0	0		0	1	0	83,644
Union Township	0	1	0	0	0	0	0	0	0	1	58,109
Vineland	2	2	0	0	0	0	0	0	0	4	60,823
Voorhees Township	2	0	0	0	0	0	1	0	0	1	29,235
Washington	1	0	0	0	0	0	0	0	0	1	6,508

Table 77. Hate Crime Incidents Per Bias Motivation and Quarter, by Selected State and Agency, 2016—Continued

(Number.)

State/agency	Number of incidents per bias motivation						Number of incidents per quarter				Population[1]
	Race/ Ethnicity/ Ancestry	Religion	Sexual orientation	Disability	Gender	Gender Identity	1st quarter	2nd quarter	3rd quarter	4th quarter	
Washington Township, Gloucester County	1	0	1	0	0	0		0	2	0	47,477
Washington Township, Warren County	1	0	0	0	0	0	0	0	0	1	6,430
West Deptford Township	1	0	0	0	0	0		1	0	0	21,257
West Long Branch	1	1	1	0	0	0		2	0	1	7,975
Winslow Township	1	0	0	0	0	0	0	0	0	1	38,724
Woodbridge Township	0	1	0	0	0	0		0	1	0	102,124
Woodbury	11	0	0	0	0	0		6	5		9,937
Woolwich Township	1	0	0	0	0	0		0	0	1	12,675
State Police Agencies	7	0	1	0	0	0					
State Police:											
Burlington County	1	0	1	0	0	0	1	0	1	0	
Cumberland County	1	0	0	0	0	0	0	0	1	0	
Salem County	1	0	0	0	0	0		1	0	0	
Sussex County	3	0	0	0	0	0	3	0	0	0	
Warren County	1	0	0	0	0	0	0	0	1	0	
NEW MEXICO											
Total	8	9	9	0	0	0					
Cities	8	9	9	0	0	0					
Albuquerque	7	9	9	0	0	0	2	2	11	10	561,560
Los Lunas	1	0	0	0	0	0		1			15,398
NEW YORK											
Total	155	311	99	1	5	24					
Cities	101	205	87	1	5	20					
Albany	1	0	0	0	0	0	0	1	0	0	98,617
Amherst Town	2	0	0	0	0	0	0	2	0	0	120,436
Auburn	0	1	0	0	0	0	0	0	1		26,854
Bedford Town	0	1	0	0	0	0	0	0	1	0	18,063
Binghamton	1	0	0	0	0	0	0	0	1	0	45,780
Brighton Town	1	0	0	0	0	0	0	1	0	0	36,889
Buffalo	5	0	1	0	0	1	1	1	4	1	257,446
Cheektowaga Town	1	0	0	0	0	0	0	0	0	1	78,100
Clarkstown Town	1	2	0	0	0	0	0	0	3	0	82,171
Colonie Town	0	1	0	0	0	0	0	0	1	0	80,075
Cooperstown Village	1	0	0	0	0	0	0	0	1	0	1,780
Crawford Town	1	0	0	0	0	0	0	0	0	1	9,202
Dobbs Ferry Village	0	1	0	0	0	0	0	1	0	0	11,180
Elmira	1	0	0	0	0	0	0	1	0	0	27,995
Glen Cove	0	0	1	0	0	0	0	1	0	0	27,480
Hamburg Town	1	0	0	0	0	0	1	0	0	0	46,028
Lake Placid Village	1	0	0	0	0	0	0	1	0	0	2,453
Larchmont Village	0	2	0	0	0	0	0	1	0	1	6,186
Middletown	0	1	0	0	0	0	0	1	0	0	27,752
Monroe Village	0	3	0	0	0	0	1	1	1	0	8,680
New Rochelle	1	4	0	0	0	0	1	0	0	4	80,389
New York	74	183	79	1	5	19	66	85	85	125	8,566,917
Niagara Falls	0	0	1	0	0	0	0	0	1	0	48,675
North Tonawanda	2	0	0	0	0	0	0	0	2	0	30,634
Norwich	1	0	0	0	0	0	0	0	0	1	6,929
Peekskill	0	0	1	0	0	0	1	0	0	0	24,129
Ramapo Town	1	1	1	0	0	0	1	1	1	0	92,620
Rochester	1	0	1	0	0	0	0	1	0	1	209,643
Saratoga Springs	0	1	0	0	0	0	0	0	0	1	28,005
Schenectady	0	1	0	0	0	0	0	0	0	1	65,138
Southampton Town	1	0	0	0	0	0	1	0	0	0	51,191
Spring Valley Village	0	1	0	0	0	0	0	0	1	0	32,844
Utica	0	0	1	0	0	0	0	1	0	0	60,879
Wellsville Village	1	0	0	0	0	0	0	0	0	1	4,506
Yonkers	2	2	1	0	0	0	0	1	1	3	202,075
Universities and Colleges	15	10	4	0	0	3					
Cornell University	0	0	2	0	0	0	0	1	1	0	21,904
State University of New York:											
Binghamton	1	0	1	0	0	0	0	1	1	0	16,913
Buffalo	1	3	0	0	0	3	3	3	0	1	29,796
Downstate Medical Center	0	0	1	0	0	0	0	0	1	0	1,858
State University of New York Agricultural and Technical College, Morrisville	4	2	0	0	0	0	0	0	6	0	2,940
State University of New York College:											
Brockport	1	0	0	0	0	0	0	0	1	0	8,161
Buffalo	1	1	0	0	0	0	1	0	0	1	10,330
Geneseo	2	1	0	0	0	0	0	0	0	3	5,699
New Paltz	3	0	0	0	0	0	0	0	0	3	7,751
Plattsburgh	1	1	0	0	0	0	1	0	0	1	5,718
Potsdam	1	0	0	0	0	0	0	0	0	1	3,904
Purchase	0	2	0	0	0	0	1	1	0	0	4,169

Table 77. Hate Crime Incidents Per Bias Motivation and Quarter, by Selected State and Agency, 2016—Continued

(Number.)

State/agency	Number of incidents per bias motivation						Number of incidents per quarter				Population[1]
	Race/ Ethnicity/ Ancestry	Religion	Sexual orientation	Disability	Gender	Gender Identity	1st quarter	2nd quarter	3rd quarter	4th quarter	
Metropolitan Counties	17	79	4	0	0	1					
Albany	1	0	0	0	0	0	0	0	0	1	
Monroe	1	1	0	0	0	0	2	0	0	0	
Nassau	7	45	0	0	0	0	8	10	9	25	
Oswego	1	0	0	0	0	0	0	0	0	1	
Saratoga	0	1	0	0	0	0	0	1	0	0	
Schoharie	0	1	0	0	0	0	1	0	0	0	
Suffolk County Police Department	7	30	4	0	0	1	10	12	8	12	
Westchester Public Safety	0	1	0	0	0	0	0	0	1	0	
Nonmetropolitan Counties	1	0	0	0	0	0					
Chenango	1	0	0	0	0	0	0	1	0		
State Police Agencies	10	5	4	0	0	0					
State Police:											
Albany County	1	1	1	0	0	0	0	0	0	3	
Chemung County	0	1	0	0	0	0	1	0	0	0	
Dutchess County	0	1	0	0	0	0	0	0	0	1	
Franklin County	0	0	1	0	0	0	0	0	1	0	
Jefferson County	1	0	1	0	0	0	0	1	0	1	
Montgomery County	1	0	0	0	0	0	0	0	0	1	
New York County	2	1	0	0	0	0	0	0	0	3	
Niagara County	0	0	1	0	0	0	0	0	0	1	
Orange County	0	1	0	0	0	0	1	0	0	0	
Oswego County	1	0	0	0	0	0	1	0	0	0	
Rockland County	1	0	0	0	0	0	0	1	0	0	
Schoharie County	1	0	0	0	0	0	0	1	0	0	
Wayne County	1	0	0	0	0	0	0	1	0	0	
Westchester County	1	0	0	0	0	0	0	0	0	1	
Other Agencies	11	12	0	0	0	0					
New York City Metropolitan Transportation Authority	11	11	0	0	0	0	3	2	2	15	
State Park, Finger Lakes Region	0	1	0	0	0	0	0	0	1	0	
NORTH CAROLINA											
Total	99	21	26	0	1	2					
Cities	75	17	24	0	0	1					
Apex	3	0	0	0	0	0	0	1	1	1	47,324
Asheville	1	0	2	0	0	0	1	0	2	0	89,546
Boone	0	0	1	0	0	0	0	1	0	0	18,374
Charlotte-Mecklenburg	16	3	8	0	0	0	6	11	5	5	896,379
Concord	0	1	0	0	0	0	0	0	1	0	89,446
Durham	2	1	0	0	0	0	0	1	1	1	263,716
Fayetteville	7	0	0	0	0	0	0	1	4	2	202,200
Gastonia	3	0	0	0	0	0	0	0	2	1	75,118
Greensboro	1	4	1	0	0	0	0	1	4	1	288,618
Greenville	1	0	4	0	0	1	2	2	1	1	91,766
Hickory	1	0	0	0	0	0	0	0	0	1	40,437
High Point	5	0	0	0	0	0	1	1	0	3	111,435
Huntersville	1	0	0	0	0	0	1	0	0	0	53,932
Jacksonville	0	0	1	0	0	0	0	0	1	0	66,686
Littleton	1	0	0	0	0	0	0	0	0	0	641
Morganton	4	0	0	0	0	0	0	0	1	3	16,656
Raleigh	15	7	6	0	0	0	8	6	9	5	460,593
Roanoke Rapids[2]	4	0	0	0	0	0	1	1	2	0	15,273
Rockingham	1	0	0	0	0	0	0	0	0	1	9,155
Rocky Mount	1	0	0	0	0	0	0	0	1	0	55,431
Salisbury	3	0	0	0	0	0	0	1	0	2	34,121
Siler City	1	0	0	0	0	0	0	0	0	1	8,498
Wilmington	4	1	0	0	0	0	2	1	1	1	117,852
Wilson	0	0	1	0	0	0	0	0	1	0	49,734
Universities and Colleges	4	1	2	0	0	1					
Duke University	0	1	0	0	0	0	0	0	0	1	15,984
East Carolina University	1	0	0	0	0	0	1	0	0	0	28,289
North Carolina Central University	0	0	1	0	0	1	0	0	1	1	8,011
North Carolina School of the Arts	2	0	0	0	0	0	1	1	0	0	970
University of North Carolina, Greensboro	1	0	1	0	0	0	0	1	0	1	19,393
Metropolitan Counties	15	2	0	0	0	0					
Forsyth	6	0	0	0	0	0	1	3	1	1	
Franklin	4	0	0	0	0	0	2	1	0	1	
Gaston County Police Department	1	0	0	0	0	0	0	0	1	0	
Iredell	2	0	0	0	0	0	1	0	0	1	
New Hanover	1	0	0	0	0	0	0	0	0	1	
Randolph	0	1	0	0	0	0	0	0	1	0	
Yadkin	1	1	0	0	0	0	1	0	0	1	
Nonmetropolitan Counties	4	1	0	0	1	0					
Jackson[2]	1	1	0	0	0	0	0	0	0	1	
Moore	0	0	0	0	1	0	1	0	0	0	
Sampson[2]	2	0	0	0	0	0	0	0	0	2	
Surry	1	0	0	0	0	0	0	0	0	1	

Table 77. Hate Crime Incidents Per Bias Motivation and Quarter, by Selected State and Agency, 2016—Continued

(Number.)

State/agency	Number of incidents per bias motivation						Number of incidents per quarter				Population[1]
	Race/ Ethnicity/ Ancestry	Religion	Sexual orientation	Disability	Gender	Gender Identity	1st quarter	2nd quarter	3rd quarter	4th quarter	
Other Agencies	1	0	0	0	0	0					
University of North Carolina Hospitals	1	0	0	0	0	0	0	0	1	0	
NORTH DAKOTA											
Total	7	1	0	0	0	0					
Cities	5	1	0	0	0	0					
Bismarck	2	0	0	0	0	0	0	0	0	2	73,248
Grand Forks	0	1	0	0	0	0	0	0	1	0	57,853
Watford City	2	0	0	0	0	0	0	0	1	1	8,819
Williston	1	0	0	0	0	0	0	0	1	0	29,929
Universities and Colleges	1	0	0	0	0	0					
University of North Dakota	1	0	0	0	0	0	0	0	1	0	14,951
Nonmetropolitan Counties	1	0	0	0	0	0					
Hettinger	1	0	0	0	0	0	0	0	0	1	
OHIO											
Total	336	35	60	9	1	1					
Cities	308	28	56	8	1	0					
Akron	3	0	1	0	0	0	1	2	1	0	197,257
Albany	0	0	1	0	0	0	0	0	0	1	918
Athens	1	0	0	0	0	0	0	0	1	0	25,203
Aurora	2	0	1	0	0	0	0	1	1	1	15,897
Barberton	1	0	0	0	0	0	0	0	0	1	26,172
Beaver Township	0	0	1	0	0	0	0	1	0	0	6,492
Bellbrook	0	1	0	1	0	0	2	0	0	0	7,074
Bellefontaine	1	0	1	0	0	0	0	1	1	0	13,073
Bexley	0	1	0	0	0	0	0	0	1	0	13,775
Blue Ash	1	1	1	0	1	0	3	0	0	1	12,169
Boardman[2]	1	0	0	0	0	0	0	1	0	0	39,692
Canton	1	0	0	0	0	0	0	1	0	0	71,652
Chillicothe	1	0	0	0	0	0	0	0	1	0	21,692
Cincinnati	32	2	8	0	0	0	7	10	10	15	298,880
Circleville	1	0	0	0	0	0	0	0	1	0	13,930
Cleveland	8	0	0	0	0	0	2	5	1	0	386,227
Colerain Township	4	0	0	0	0	0	3	1	0	0	58,907
Columbus[2]	123	10	18	0	0	0	42	29	49	31	862,515
Dayton	5	0	0	0	0	0	0	4	0	1	140,260
Defiance	1	0	0	0	0	0	0	0	0	1	16,697
Delhi Township	3	0	0	0	0	0	1	1	1	0	29,573
East Palestine	2	0	0	0	0	0	0	1	1	0	4,548
Elyria	2	0	1	0	0	0	1	2	0	0	53,633
Fairborn	1	0	1	0	0	0	1	0	0	1	33,587
Fairview Park	1	0	0	0	0	0	0	0	0	1	16,318
Findlay	0	1	0	0	0	0	1	0			41,156
Gahanna	2	1	0	0	0	0	1	2	0	0	34,859
Garfield Heights	0	0	1	0	0	0	1			0	27,938
Green Township	0	0	1	0	0	0	0	0	0	1	58,764
Greenville	1	0	0	0	0	0	0	1	0	0	12,962
Grove City	5	0	0	0	0	0	1	2	1	1	40,161
Hamilton	9	0	0	0	0	0	1	3	3	2	62,423
Heath	1	0	0	0	0	0	0	0	1	0	10,528
Hilliard	2	0	1	0	0	0	0	2	1	0	34,832
Huber Heights	3	0	1	1	0	0	1	1	2	1	38,180
Independence	1	0	0	0	0	0	0	0	0	1	7,132
Jackson Township, Stark County	2	0	1	0	0	0	2	0	1	0	40,780
Lockland	1	0	0	0	0	0	1	0	0	0	3,422
Lyndhurst	1	1	1	0	0	0	0	1	1	1	13,624
Mansfield	1	2	0	0	0	0	2	1	0	0	46,656
Marietta	1	0	0	0	0	0	0	1	0		13,867
Massillon	3	0	0	0	0	0	1	2	0	0	32,268
Maumee	0	1	0	0	0	0	0	0	1	0	13,875
Mayfield Heights	1	0	0	0	0	0	0	1	0	0	18,770
Medina Township	1	0	0	0	0	0	1	0	0	0	9,015
Miamisburg	0	1	0	0	0	0	0	1	0	0	20,000
Miami Township, Montgomery County	1	0	0	0	0	0	0	0	0	1	29,140
Monroe	1	0	0	0	0	0	0	1	0	0	15,933
Montgomery	1	0	0	0	0	0	1	0	0	0	10,558
Montpelier	1	0	0	0	0	0	1	0	0	0	3,980
Montville Township	1	0	0	0	0	0	0	1	0	0	11,815
Moraine	3	0	0	0	0	0	1	0	1	1	6,385
Mount Healthy	1	0	0	0	0	0	0	0	1	0	6,028
Napoleon	2	0	2	0	0	0	2	0	1	1	8,566
New Franklin	1	0	0	0	0	0	0	1	0	0	14,285
Newton Falls	1	0	0	0	0	0	0	0	1	0	4,628
North College Hill	0	0	1	0	0	0	0	0	1	0	9,320
Oberlin	0	1	0	0	0	0	0	0	0	1	8,342
Parma	1	2	0	0	0	0	1	1	0	1	79,576
Portsmouth	1	0	0	0	0	0	0	1	0		20,442
Powell	1	0	0	0	0	0	0	1	0	0	13,273
Reynoldsburg	1	0	0	0	0	0	0	0	1		37,406

Table 77. Hate Crime Incidents Per Bias Motivation and Quarter, by Selected State and Agency, 2016—Continued

(Number.)

State/agency	Number of incidents per bias motivation						Number of incidents per quarter				Population[1]
	Race/ Ethnicity/ Ancestry	Religion	Sexual orientation	Disability	Gender	Gender Identity	1st quarter	2nd quarter	3rd quarter	4th quarter	
Salem	0	0	0	4	0	0	1	0	3	0	11,943
Shelby	1	0	1	0	0	0	0	1	1	0	9,012
Sidney	2	0	1	0	0	0	0	1	2	0	20,797
South Euclid	1	0	0	0	0	0	0	1	0	0	21,686
Springfield Township, Hamilton County	0	0	1	0	0	0	0	1	0	0	36,527
Springfield Township, Summit County	1	0	1	0	0	0	0	1	0	1	17,813
Steubenville	1	0	0	0	0	0		0	1	0	18,137
Streetsboro	0	0	0	1	0	0	0	0	0	1	16,364
Toledo	31	0	4	0	0	0	3	3	17	12	278,366
Troy	0	0	2	0	0	0	2	0	0	0	25,745
Upper Arlington	1	0	0	0	0	0	1	0	0	0	35,150
Upper Sandusky	1	0	0	0	0	0	0	0	1	0	6,515
Urbana	9	0	0	0	0	0	0	0	0	9	11,482
Vienna Township	1	0	0	0	0	0	0	0	0	1	3,817
Wadsworth	1	0	0	0	0	0	0	0	1	0	21,910
Wapakoneta	2	1	0	0	0	0	0	1	1	1	9,815
Warren	1	0	0	0	0	0	0	0	0	1	40,005
West Chester Township	1	0	0	0	0	0	0	1	0	0	61,080
West Jefferson	0	0	0	1	0	0	0	0	1	0	4,291
Wilmington	1	1	0	0	0	0	0	1	1	0	12,443
Wooster	1	0	0	0	0	0	1	0	0	0	26,883
Xenia	1	0	0	0	0	0	1	0	0	0	26,037
Yellow Springs	1	1	0	0	0	0	1	1	0	0	3,857
Youngstown	2	0	1	0	0	0	0	1	2	0	64,181
Zanesville	1	0	2	0	0	0	1	0	1	1	25,494
Universities and Colleges	5	0	1	0	0	0					
Capital University	0	0	1	0	0	0	0	0	0	1	3,465
Kent State University	1	0	0	0	0	0			1		30,067
Ohio State University, Columbus	2	0	0	0	0	0	0	0	0	2	58,663
Otterbein University	1	0	0	0	0	0	0	1	0	0	2,808
University of Akron	1	0	0	0	0	0	0	0	1	0	23,101
Metropolitan Counties	13	4	3	1	0	1					
Butler	1	1	0	0	0	0	1	0	1	0	
Clark	0	1	1	0	0	0	0	2	0	0	
Clermont	0	1	0	0	0	0	0	1	0	0	
Delaware	1	0	0	0	0	0	0	0	1	0	
Geauga	1	0	0	0	0	0	0	0	0	1	
Greene	6	1	0	0	0	0	2	1	2	2	
Lawrence	1	0	0	0	0	0	0	0	1	0	
Lorain	0	0	0	0	0	1	0	0	1	0	
Montgomery	1	0	1	0	0	0	0	0	2	0	
Summit	1	0	0	0	0	0	0	0	1	0	
Trumbull	1	0	0	1	0	0	1	0	1	0	
Warren	0	0	1	0	0	0	1	0	0	0	
Nonmetropolitan Counties	7	2	0	0	0	0					
Ashland	1	0	0	0	0	0	0	1	0	0	
Ashtabula	1	0	0	0	0	0	0	0	1	0	
Champaign	1	0	0	0	0	0	0	0	0	1	
Fayette	0	1	0	0	0	0	0	1	0	0	
Gallia	1	0	0	0	0	0	0	0	1	0	
Highland	1	0	0	0	0	0	1	0	0	0	
Mercer	0	1	0	0	0	0	0	1	0	0	
Pike	1	0	0	0	0	0	0	1	0	0	
Ross	1	0	0	0	0	0	0	1	0	0	
Other Agencies	3	1	0	0	0	0					
Cleveland Metropolitan Park District	2	1	0	0	0	0	1	1	1	0	
Ohio Department of Natural Resources	1	0	0	0	0	0	0	0	1	0	
OKLAHOMA											
Total	20	5	5	3	0	0					
Cities	9	4	4	0	0	0					
Anadarko	1	0	0	0	0	0	0	0	1	0	6,702
Blanchard	0	1	0	0	0	0	0	1	0	0	8,461
Collinsville	2	0	0	0	0	0	0	1	0	1	6,678
Cushing	1	1	0	0	0	0	0	0	0	2	7,874
Heavener	0	0	1	0	0	0	1	0	0	0	3,321
Norman	1	0	1	0	0	0	1	0	1	0	122,143
Nowata	0	1	0	0	0	0	0	0	0	1	3,747
Oklahoma City	3	0	0	0	0	0	1	0	0	2	641,681
Perry	0	0	1	0	0	0	1	0	0	0	5,091
Tulsa	0	1	0	0	0	0	0	1	0	0	405,748
Union City	1	0	0	0	0	0	0	0	0	1	2,004
Woodward	0	0	1	0	0	0	0	0	0	1	13,223
Metropolitan Counties	6	1	0	0	0	0					
Lincoln	1	0	0	0	0	0	0	0	1	0	
Okmulgee	1	0	0	0	0	0	0	1	0	0	
Wagoner	4	1	0	0	0	0	1	0	3	1	

Table 77. Hate Crime Incidents Per Bias Motivation and Quarter, by Selected State and Agency, 2016—Continued

(Number.)

State/agency	Number of incidents per bias motivation						Number of incidents per quarter				Population[1]
	Race/ Ethnicity/ Ancestry	Religion	Sexual orientation	Disability	Gender	Gender Identity	1st quarter	2nd quarter	3rd quarter	4th quarter	
Nonmetropolitan Counties	5	0	1	3	0	0					
Craig	0	0	0	1	0	0	0	0	1	0	
Delaware	2	0	0	1	0	0	0	1	2	0	
Garvin	1	0	0	0	0	0	1	0	0	0	
Kingfisher	1	0	0	0	0	0	1	0	0	0	
Payne	0	0	0	1	0	0	0	0	0	1	
Seminole	0	0	1	0	0	0	1	0	0	0	
Woodward	1	0	0	0	0	0	0	0	1	0	
OREGON											
Total	61	23	17	2	0	1					
Cities	57	19	13	1	0	1					
Ashland	1	0	1	0	0	0	1	0	0	1	21,017
Beaverton	2	0	0	0	0	0	0	0	0	2	97,907
Coos Bay	0	1	0	0	0	0	0	0	1	0	16,224
Cornelius	1	0	0	0	0	0	0	0	0	1	12,402
Corvallis	1	1	0	0	0	0	1	1	0	0	56,061
Eugene	27	5	4	1	0	1	2	12	11	13	164,883
Gervais	0	0	1	0	0	0	1	0	0	0	2,663
Gresham	4	1	1	0	0	0	2	1	1	2	111,491
Hood River	0	1	0	0	0	0	1	0			7,719
Lincoln City	0	3	0	0	0	0	0	0	0	3	8,588
Medford	0	0	1	0	0	0	0	1	0	0	80,794
Newberg-Dundee	1	0	0	0	0	0	0	1	0	0	26,105
Oregon City	2	0	0	0	0	0	1	1	0	0	36,485
Portland	5	3	2	0	0	0	2	2	4	2	642,129
Salem	4	2	2	0	0	0	3	1	2	2	166,508
Springfield	6	1	0	0	0	0	2	1	2	2	61,164
Talent	1	0	0	0	0	0	0	1	0	0	6,483
Tigard	2	1	0	0	0	0	0	1	0	2	51,885
Tualatin	0	0	1	0	0	0	0	1	0	0	27,370
Metropolitan Counties	1	1	1	0	0	0					
Jackson	0	1	0	0	0	0	0	0	1	0	
Lane	1	0	0	0	0	0	0	1	0	0	
Washington	0	0	1	0	0	0	0	0	0	1	
Nonmetropolitan Counties	3	3	3	1	0	0					
Crook	1	0	1	0	0	0	2	0	0	0	
Hood River	0	1	0	0	0	0	1	0	0	0	
Jefferson	0	0	1	0	0	0	0	0	1	0	
Morrow	1	1	0	0	0	0	0	0	2	0	
Umatilla	0	1	1	1	0	0	0	0	2	1	
Union	1	0	0	0	0	0	0	1	0	0	
PENNSYLVANIA											
Total	40	9	11	1	0	0					
Cities	32	8	9	1	0	0					
Abington Township, Montgomery County	1	1	0	0	0	0	0	2	0	0	55,623
Camp Hill	1	0	0	0	0	0	0	0	1	0	7,929
Carlisle	0	0	1	0	0	0	0	1	0	0	19,225
Ferguson Township	1	0	0	0	0	0	0	1	0	0	19,222
Hamburg	1	0	0	0	0	0	0	0	0	1	4,420
Johnstown	1	0	0	0	0	0	1	0	0	0	21,227
Lancaster	1	0	0	0	0	0	0	1	0	0	59,340
Mechanicsburg	2	0	0	0	0	0	0	0	0	2	9,003
Philadelphia	7	4	7	0	0	0	3	3	2	10	1,570,826
Pittsburgh	11	2	1	0	0	0	2	2	6	4	302,443
Reading	1	0	0	0	0	0	1	0	0	0	87,834
Scranton	1	1	0	0	0	0	0	1	1	0	77,332
State College	2	0	0	1	0	0	2		1	0	58,119
Washington Township, Franklin County	1	0	0	0	0	0	1	0	0	0	14,631
Whitemarsh Township	1	0	0	0	0	0	0	0	1	0	17,721
Universities and Colleges	4	0	2	0	0	0					
Pennsylvania State University, University Park	4	0	2	0	0	0	5	0	0	1	47,307
Metropolitan Counties	1	0	0	0	0	0					
Allegheny	1	0	0	0	0	0	0	1	0	0	
State Police Agencies	3	1	0	0	0	0					
State Police:											
Delaware County	1	0	0	0	0	0	0	0	0	1	
Monroe County	0	1	0	0	0	0	1	0	0	0	
Skippack	2	0	0	0	0	0	0	0	0	2	
RHODE ISLAND											
Total	2	6	3	1	0	0					
Cities	2	4	1	0	0	0					
Cranston	0	1	0	0	0	0	0	1	0	0	81,162
Pawtucket	1	1	0	0	0	0	0	1	0	1	71,640
Portsmouth	0	1	0	0	0	0	0	0	1	0	17,362
Providence	0	0	1	0	0	0	0	1	0	0	179,340

Table 77. Hate Crime Incidents Per Bias Motivation and Quarter, by Selected State and Agency, 2016—Continued

(Number.)

State/agency	Number of incidents per bias motivation						Number of incidents per quarter				Population[1]
	Race/Ethnicity/Ancestry	Religion	Sexual orientation	Disability	Gender	Gender Identity	1st quarter	2nd quarter	3rd quarter	4th quarter	
South Kingstown	0	1	0	0	0	0	0	0	1	0	30,872
Tiverton	1	0	0	0	0	0	0	0	0	1	15,768
Universities and Colleges	0	2	1	0	0	0					
Brown University	0	1	1	0	0	0	1	1	0	0	9,458
University of Rhode Island	0	1	0	0	0	0	1	0	0	0	16,613
State Police Agencies	0	0	1	1	0	0					
State Police:											
Chepachet	0	0	0	1	0	0	1	0	0	0	
Lincoln	0	0	1	0	0	0	0	1	0	0	
SOUTH CAROLINA											
Total	18	1	3	1	0	0					
Cities	10	1	1	0	0	0					
Andrews	1	0	0	0	0	0	0	0	0	1	2,894
Blackville	0	1	0	0	0	0	1	0	0	0	2,273
Chester	1	0	0	0	0	0	0	0	1	0	5,462
Cottageville	1	0	0	0	0	0	0	0	1	0	733
Florence	0	0	1	0	0	0	0	1	0	0	38,382
Folly Beach	2	0	0	0	0	0	0	1	1	0	2,806
Greer	1	0	0	0	0	0	0	1	0	0	28,927
Moncks Corner	1	0	0	0	0	0	0	1	0	0	10,298
North Myrtle Beach	1	0	0	0	0	0	0	0	0	1	15,945
Pageland	1	0	0	0	0	0	0	1	0	0	2,745
Simpsonville	1	0	0	0	0	0	0	1	0	0	21,223
Universities and Colleges	2	0	0	1	0	0					
Clemson University	1	0	0	0	0	0	0	0	0	1	22,698
Coastal Carolina University	0	0	0	1	0	0	0	0	0	1	10,263
Trident Technical College	1	0	0	0	0	0	0	0	0	1	15,043
Metropolitan Counties	4	0	2	0	0	0					
Anderson	1	0	0	0	0	0	0	1	0	0	
Darlington	0	0	1	0	0	0	0	1	0	0	
Greenville	1	0	0	0	0	0	0	0	1	0	
Horry County Police Department	2	0	0	0	0	0	0	2	0	0	
Sumter	0	0	1	0	0	0	0	1	0	0	
Nonmetropolitan Counties	2	0	0	0	0	0					
Abbeville	1	0	0	0	0	0	1	0	0	0	
Georgetown	1	0	0	0	0	0	1	0	0	0	
SOUTH DAKOTA											
Total	6	2	5	3	0	2					
Cities	4	2	3	2	0	1					
Aberdeen	0	0	0	0	0	1	0	0	0	1	28,498
Brandon	0	1	0	0	0	0	0	1	0	0	10,042
Brookings	0	0	0	1	0	0	0	1	0	0	23,971
Chamberlain	0	0	1	0	0	0	0	1	0	0	2,383
Madison	0	0	1	0	0	0	0	0	1	0	7,411
Rapid City	2	0	0	1	0	0	0	1	1	1	74,573
Sioux Falls	2	1	1	0	0	0	0	2	0	2	175,152
Metropolitan Counties	2	0	1	1	0	0					
Meade	1	0	0	0	0	0	0	0	1	0	
Minnehaha	1	0	1	0	0	0	0	1	1	0	
Union	0	0	0	1	0	0	1	0	0	0	
Nonmetropolitan Counties	0	0	1	0	0	1					
Hamlin	0	0	1	0	0	0	0	1	0	0	
Jerauld	0	0	0	0	0	1	1	0	0	0	
TENNESSEE											
Total	93	18	25	6	0	0					
Cities	50	12	20	3	0	0					
Alcoa	4	0	2	0	0	0	0	0	1	5	9,503
Alexandria	2	0	0	0	0	0	0	0	2	0	978
Bristol	1	0	0	0	0	0	0	0	1	0	26,656
Chattanooga	1	2	0	0	0	0	1	1	0	1	177,801
Clarksville	1	0	0	0	0	0	0	0	0	1	152,526
Cleveland	4	0	0	0	0	0	1	0	2	1	44,423
Coopertown	0	0	1	0	0	0	1	0	0	0	4,426
Covington	0	1	0	1	0	0	0	1	1	0	9,039
Cowan	0	0	0	1	0	0	0	1	0	0	1,698
Dyersburg	1	0	0	0	0	0	0	0	0	1	16,711
East Ridge	1	0	0	0	0	0	0	0	1	0	21,311
Franklin	0	1	0	0	0	0	0	0	1	0	74,771
Gallaway	2	0	0	0	0	0	2	0	0	0	654
Greenbrier	1	0	0	0	0	0	1	0	0	0	6,807
Hendersonville	1	0	0	0	0	0	0	0	1	0	56,965
Humboldt	1	0	0	0	0	0	0	0	1	0	8,287
Jackson	2	1	0	0	0	0	1	0	2	0	66,990
Jamestown	7	0	0	0	0	0	7	0	0	0	1,945
Jasper	0	0	1	0	0	0	0	0	1	0	3,323
Johnson City	0	0	1	1	0	0	1	0	0	1	66,511
Kingsport	1	0	0	0	0	0	0	0	0	1	53,059
Knoxville	0	1	0	0	0	0	0	1	0	0	186,583

Table 77. Hate Crime Incidents Per Bias Motivation and Quarter, by Selected State and Agency, 2016—Continued

(Number.)

State/agency	Number of incidents per bias motivation						Number of incidents per quarter				Population[1]
	Race/ Ethnicity/ Ancestry	Religion	Sexual orientation	Disability	Gender	Gender Identity	1st quarter	2nd quarter	3rd quarter	4th quarter	
Lebanon	2	1	0	0	0	0	2	0	0	1	31,125
Lenoir City	1	0	0	0	0	0	0	0	0	1	9,175
Livingston	1	0	0	0	0	0	0	0	1	0	4,073
Memphis	1	1	7	0	0	0	3	3	2	1	656,434
Milan	1	0	0	0	0	0	0	1	0	0	7,803
Millington	1	0	0	0	0	0	0	1	0	0	11,002
Morristown	1	0	0	0	0	0	1	0	0	0	29,576
Murfreesboro[2]	2	0	1	0	0	0	0	1	1	1	129,730
Nashville Metropolitan	5	2	5	0	0	0	3	4	5	0	668,685
Newport	1	0	0	0	0	0	0	0	1	0	6,812
Oak Ridge	0	0	1	0	0	0	0	1	0	0	29,296
Pigeon Forge	2	1	0	0	0	0	1	2	0	0	6,230
Portland	0	1	0	0	0	0	0	0	1	0	12,502
Spring Hill	2	0	0	0	0	0	1	0	0	1	37,599
White House	0	0	1	0	0	0	1	0	0	0	11,419
Universities and Colleges	3	1	1	0	0	0					
Pellissippi State Community College	0	1	0	0	0	0	0	0	0	1	10,325
Tennessee Technological University	2	0	0	0	0	0	0	0	2	0	10,900
University of Tennessee, Knoxville	0	0	1	0	0	0	0	0	1	0	27,845
University of the South	1	0	0	0	0	0	1	0	0	0	1,797
Metropolitan Counties	28	4	4	3	0	0					
Anderson	1	0	0	0	0	0	0	0	1	0	
Bradley	2	0	1	0	0	0	1	0	1	1	
Dickson	2	0	0	0	0	0	0	2	0	0	
Hamblen	1	0	0	0	0	0	0	0	0	1	
Hamilton	2	4	1	1	0	0	3	2	0	3	
Knox	1	0	0	0	0	0	0	0	1	0	
Montgomery	1	0	0	0	0	0	0	0	0	1	
Roane	0	0	1	0	0	0	0	0	1	0	
Rutherford	1	0	0	0	0	0	0	0	0	1	
Shelby	16	0	0	2	0	0	6	5	2	5	
Sullivan	1	0	1	0	0	0	0	2	0	0	
Nonmetropolitan Counties	1	1	0	0	0	0					
Lawrence	0	1	0	0	0	0	0	0	0	1	
Sevier	1	0	0	0	0	0	1	0	0	0	
Other Agencies	11	0	0	0	0	0					
Department of Safety	11	0	0	0	0	0	1	1	7	2	
TEXAS											
Total	104	23	37	5	1	8					
Cities	91	17	28	4	1	8					
Arlington	4	1	0	0	0	0	0	2	2	1	392,666
Austin	10	2	6	0	0	1	7	6	4	2	956,911
Beaumont	4	0	0	0	0	0	3	0	0	1	118,283
Bedford	1	0	0	0	0	5	0	0	0	6	49,803
Borger	1	0	0	0	0	0	0	0	1	0	12,894
Burleson	1	0	0	0	0	0	0	1	0	0	45,116
Cedar Hill	1	0	0	0	0	0	0	0	1	0	49,215
Cedar Park	1	0	1	0	0	0	0	2	0	0	69,051
Center	0	0	0	0	1	0	0	0	0	1	5,218
College Station	0	1	0	0	0	0	0	0	1	0	110,785
Converse	0	0	0	1	0	0	0	1	0	0	22,782
Dallas	7	2	2	0	0	0	1	5	4	1	1,320,939
Denison	0	0	1	0	0	0	0	1	0	0	23,237
Denton	2	0	1	0	0	0	1	1	1	0	134,054
El Paso	0	0	1	0	0	0	0	0	0	1	687,193
Fort Worth	11	3	5	1	0	0	7	5	3	5	851,849
Frankston	1	0	0	0	0	0	0	1	0	0	1,163
Galveston	5	0	1	0	0	0	1	1	3	1	50,667
Gilmer	1	0	0	0	0	0	0	1	0	0	5,246
Grand Prairie	1	0	0	0	0	0	0	1	0	0	190,270
Hedwig Village	0	1	0	0	0	0	0	1	0	0	2,724
Houston	3	1	2	0	0	2	1	1	3	3	2,334,348
League City	1	0	0	0	0	0	0	1	0	0	101,436
Levelland	2	0	0	0	0	0	0	0	1	1	13,997
Lewisville	2	0	0	0	0	0	1	0	0	1	105,762
Livingston	1	0	0	0	0	0	1	0	0	0	5,140
Longview	2	0	0	1	0	0	0	0	1	2	82,632
McKinney	5	0	2	0	0	0	0	3	2	2	169,689
Odessa	2	1	0	0	0	0	1	0	1	1	123,209
Plano	1	0	0	0	0	0	0	0	1	0	288,242
Pleasanton	1	0	0	0	0	0	0	0	1	0	10,013
Reno	0	1	0	0	0	0	0	0	1	0	3,302
Rockwall	1	0	0	0	0	0	0	1	0	0	43,542
Round Rock	0	1	1	0	0	0	0	1	1	0	119,308
San Angelo	0	0	1	0	0	0	0	0	0	1	101,870
San Antonio	6	2	1	0	0	0	2	1	4	2	1,498,642
San Marcos	0	0	1	0	0	0	0	0	0	1	64,380
Seabrook	1	0	0	0	0	0	0	1	0	0	14,091

Table 77. Hate Crime Incidents Per Bias Motivation and Quarter, by Selected State and Agency, 2016—Continued

(Number.)

State/agency	Number of incidents per bias motivation						Number of incidents per quarter				Population[1]
	Race/ Ethnicity/ Ancestry	Religion	Sexual orientation	Disability	Gender	Gender Identity	1st quarter	2nd quarter	3rd quarter	4th quarter	
Sealy	1	0	0	0	0	0	0	1	0	0	6,469
Sugar Land	1	0	0	0	0	0	0	0	0	1	90,088
Teague	1	0	0	0	0	0	0	0	1	0	3,575
Temple	1	0	0	0	0	0	0	0	0	1	73,411
Texas City	2	0	0	0	0	0	0	0	0	2	48,095
Tomball	1	0	0	0	0	0	0	0	0	1	11,700
Tyler	2	0	1	1	0	0	1	3	0	0	105,044
Weslaco	1	0	1	0	0	0	0	2	0	0	39,987
Wichita Falls	1	1	0	0	0	0	0	1	0	1	104,685
Willis	1	0	0	0	0	0	0	0	1	0	6,401
Universities and Colleges	3	3	3	0	0	0					
Amarillo College	1	0	0	0	0	0	1	0	0	0	9,936
Baylor University, Waco	1	0	0	0	0	0	0	0	0	1	16,787
Southwestern University	0	0	2	0	0	0	0	0	0	2	1,515
Texas State Technical College, West Texas[3]	0	0	1	0	0	0	1	0	0	0	
Texas Tech University, Lubbock	1	0	0	0	0	0	0	0	0	1	35,859
Tyler Junior College	0	1	0	0	0	0	0	1	0	0	10,934
University of Texas, Dallas	0	2	0	0	0	0	2	0	0	0	24,554
Metropolitan Counties	7	3	3	1	0	0					
Bexar	1	0	0	0	0	0	1	0	0	0	
Lubbock	1	0	0	0	0	0	0	0	0	1	
Parker	0	0	1	1	0	0	0	1	1	0	
Travis	3	2	2	0	0	0	1	4	1	1	
Williamson	2	1	0	0	0	0	1	1	0	1	
Nonmetropolitan Counties	2	0	1	0	0	0					
Brewster	0	0	1	0	0	0	1	0	0	0	
San Jacinto	1	0	0	0	0	0	1	0	0	0	
Zavala	1	0	0	0	0	0	0	0	1	0	
Other Agencies	1	0	2	0	0	0					
Dallas-Fort Worth International Airport	0	0	1	0	0	0	0	0	1	0	
Hospital District, Dallas County	1	0	0	0	0	0	0	0	1	0	
Independent School District, El Paso	0	0	1	0	0	0	0	0	0	1	
UTAH											
Total	47	8	9	2	0	0					
Cities	31	6	7	1	0	0					
Bountiful	3	0	0	0	0	0	0	0	0	3	44,003
Centerville	1	0	0	0	0	0	0	0	1	0	17,204
Draper	0	1	0	0	0	0	0	1	0	0	47,696
Farmington	0	1	0	0	0	0	0	1	0	0	23,505
Grantsville	2	0	0	0	0	0	0	2	0	0	10,253
Helper	1	0	0	0	0	0	1	0	0	0	2,094
Hurricane	1	0	0	0	0	0	0	0	1	0	15,869
Layton	1	0	0	0	0	0	0	0	1	0	75,482
Lindon	1	0	0	0	0	0	0	0	0	1	10,958
Moab	1	0	0	0	0	0	0	0	1	0	5,262
North Ogden	2	0	0	0	0	0	0	1	1	0	18,654
Ogden[2]	3	0	4	1	0	0	1	1	3	3	85,930
Payson	1	0	1	0	0	0	1	1	0	0	19,738
Pleasant View	1	0	0	0	0	0	0	1	0	0	9,548
Roosevelt	0	0	1	0	0	0	0	0	0	1	7,179
Salt Lake City	1	0	0	0	0	0	0	0	1	0	193,918
Santa Clara/Ivins	0	1	0	0	0	0	0	0	0	1	15,107
Saratoga Springs	0	2	0	0	0	0	0	2	0	0	27,211
South Jordan	1	0	0	0	0	0	0	1	0	0	70,226
South Ogden	1	0	0	0	0	0	0	1	0	0	17,026
South Salt Lake	1	0	0	0	0	0	0	0	1	0	25,022
St. George	2	0	0	0	0	0	0	0	0	2	81,755
Tooele	2	0	1	0	0	0	1	2	0	0	33,448
West Jordan	2	0	0	0	0	0	0	0	2	0	113,595
West Valley	3	1	0	0	0	0	3	0	0	1	137,558
Universities and Colleges	2	0	1	0	0	0					
Brigham Young University	2	0	0	0	0	0	0	0	1	1	33,469
Utah State University, Logan	0	0	1	0	0	0	0	0	0	1	28,622
Metropolitan Counties	1	2	0	0	0	0					
Salt Lake County Unified Police Department	0	1	0	0	0	0	1	0	0	0	
Utah	1	0	0	0	0	0	0	0	1	0	
Washington	0	1	0	0	0	0	0	0	1	0	
State Police Agencies	10	0	0	0	0	0					
Utah Highway Patrol	10	0	0	0	0	0	3	3	1	3	
Other Agencies	3	0	1	1	0	0					
Utah Transit Authority	3	0	1	1	0	0	2	0	2	1	
VERMONT											
Total	16	5	3	1	0	0					
Cities	15	3	3	1	0	0					
Barre	1	0	0	0	0	0	0	0	1	0	8,687

Table 77. Hate Crime Incidents Per Bias Motivation and Quarter, by Selected State and Agency, 2016—Continued

(Number.)

State/agency	Number of incidents per bias motivation						Number of incidents per quarter				Population[1]
	Race/ Ethnicity/ Ancestry	Religion	Sexual orientation	Disability	Gender	Gender Identity	1st quarter	2nd quarter	3rd quarter	4th quarter	
Barre Town	1	0	0	0	0	0	0	1	0	0	7,791
Brandon	1	0	0	0	0	0	1	0	0	0	3,801
Burlington	2	1	2	0	0	0	2	0	1	2	42,454
Chester	0	0	0	1	0	0	0	1	0	0	3,069
Colchester	1	0	0	0	0	0	0	1	0	0	17,437
Middlebury	0	1	0	0	0	0	0	0	0	1	8,570
Milton	1	0	1	0	0	0	0	1	1	0	10,921
Rutland	0	1	0	0	0	0	0	0	0	1	15,698
Springfield	1	0	0	0	0	0	0	0	0	1	9,132
St. Albans	2	0	0	0	0	0	0	2	0	0	6,799
St. Johnsbury	4	0	0	0	0	0	0	3	0	1	7,414
Williston	1	0	0	0	0	0	0	0	0	1	9,556
Universities and Colleges	0	2	0	0	0	0					
University of Vermont	0	2	0	0	0	0	0	0	2	0	12,815
Nonmetropolitan Counties	1	0	0	0	0	0					
Lamoille	1	0	0	0	0	0	1	0	0	0	
VIRGINIA											
Total	76	21	22	3	0	0					
Cities	23	6	8	1	0	0					
Alexandria	0	0	2	0	0	0	0	1	1	0	155,319
Chesapeake	2	1	0	1	0	0	2	1	1	0	236,570
Clifton Forge	1	0	0	0	0	0	1	0	0	0	3,713
Covington	0	1	0	0	0	0	0	0	1	0	5,570
Front Royal	1	0	2	0	0	0	1	0	1	1	15,193
Hampton	1	0	0	0	0	0	0	1	0	0	135,504
Harrisonburg	3	1	0	0	0	0	1	0	3	0	52,972
Herndon	0	1	0	0	0	0	0	0	1	0	24,806
Manassas	1	0	0	0	0	0	0	0	1	0	42,267
Newport News	3	0	1	0	0	0	0	1	2	1	181,676
Norfolk	0	1	0	0	0	0	0	0	1	0	245,734
Portsmouth	3	0	0	0	0	0	0	1	1	1	95,813
Purcellville	1	0	0	0	0	0	0	0	1	0	9,547
Radford	1	0	0	0	0	0	0	0	0	1	17,504
Richmond	0	1	0	0	0	0	1	0	0	0	222,430
Rocky Mount	1	0	0	0	0	0	1	0	0	0	4,803
Virginia Beach	2	0	3	0	0	0	0	0	3	2	453,017
Waynesboro	1	0	0	0	0	0	1	0	0	0	21,464
Williamsburg	1	0	0	0	0	0	0	0	0	1	15,256
Woodstock	1	0	0	0	0	0	0	1	0	0	5,277
Universities and Colleges	6	1	3	0	0	0					
College of William and Mary	0	0	1	0	0	0	1	0	0	0	8,484
Emory and Henry College	1	0	0	0	0	0	0	1	0	0	1,117
George Mason University	0	1	0	0	0	0	1	0	0	0	33,929
Hampton University	1	0	0	0	0	0	0	0	1		4,269
Old Dominion University	2	0	0	0	0	0	2	0	0	0	24,672
Radford University	1	0	0	0	0	0	1	0	0	0	9,743
University of Virginia	0	0	1	0	0	0	0	0	0	1	23,883
Virginia Commonwealth University	1	0	1	0	0	0	0	0	0	2	30,918
Metropolitan Counties	42	12	7	0	0	0					
Albemarle County Police Department	3	0	1	0	0	0	1	2	1	0	
Amelia	1	0	0	0	0	0	0	0	1	0	
Arlington County Police Department	2	1	0	0	0	0	0	0	1	2	
Fairfax County Police Department	14	6	4	0	0	0	7	7	3	7	
Franklin	0	1	0	0	0	0	0	0	0	1	
Frederick	1	0	0	0	0	0	0	0	0	1	
Hanover	1	0	0	0	0	0	0	0	0	1	
Henrico County Police Department	0	1	0	0	0	0	1	0	0	0	
Loudoun	5	1	2	0	0	0	0	0	1	7	
Mathews	1	0	0	0	0	0	0	0	1	0	
Montgomery	0	1	0	0	0	0	1	0	0	0	
Powhatan	1	0	0	0	0	0	0	0	1	0	
Prince William County Police Department	5	1	0	0	0	0	1	0	2	3	
Spotsylvania	1	0	0	0	0	0	0	0	0	1	
Stafford	4	0	0	0	0	0	0	2	0	2	
Washington	2	0	0	0	0	0	0	1	1	0	
York	1	0	0	0	0	0	0	0	0	1	
Nonmetropolitan Counties	3	0	1	2	0	0					
Accomack	0	0	0	2	0	0	0	0	2	0	
Grayson	1	0	0	0	0	0	0	0	0	1	
Louisa	1	0	1	0	0	0	0	1	1	0	
Shenandoah	1	0	0	0	0	0	0	1	0	0	
State Police Agencies	2	2	3	0	0	0					
State Police:											
Chesapeake	1	0	0	0	0	0	0	0	1	0	
Fairfax County	0	1	1	0	0	0	0	1	0	1	

Table 77. Hate Crime Incidents Per Bias Motivation and Quarter, by Selected State and Agency, 2016—Continued

(Number.)

State/agency	Number of incidents per bias motivation						Number of incidents per quarter				Population[1]
	Race/ Ethnicity/ Ancestry	Religion	Sexual orientation	Disability	Gender	Gender Identity	1st quarter	2nd quarter	3rd quarter	4th quarter	
Goochland County	0	0	1	0	0	0	0	0	0	1	
Newport News	1	0	0	0	0	0	0	0	0	1	
Rockingham County	0	0	1	0	0	0	0	0	1	0	
Surry County	0	1	0	0	0	0	0	0	0	1	
WASHINGTON											
Total	239	61	70	2	3	14					
Cities	190	51	59	2	2	11					
Aberdeen	1	0	1	0	0	0	2	0	0	0	16,155
Algona	1	0	0	0	0	0	0	0	1	0	3,166
Arlington	1	0	0	0	0	0	0	0	0	1	19,142
Auburn	4	1	0	0	0	0	1	2	1	1	78,400
Bainbridge Island	0	0	1	0	0	0	0	0	1	0	23,998
Battle Ground	1	0	0	0	0	0	0	0	0	1	19,734
Bellevue	2	13	3	0	0	0	6	5	3	4	142,238
Bellingham	7	0	1	0	0	0	3	0	1	4	86,005
Bothell	1	0	0	0	0	0	0	0	0	1	43,828
Brier	1	0	0	0	0	0	1	0	0	0	6,753
Centralia	4	1	0	0	0	0	1	0	4	0	16,785
Darrington	1	0	0	0	0	0	1	0	0	0	1,381
Des Moines	1	0	0	0	0	0	0	0	0	1	31,523
Edmonds	4	1	0	0	0	0	0	0	3	2	41,705
Enumclaw	1	0	0	0	0	0	0	0	1	0	11,709
Everett	4	1	0	0	0	0	2	0	0	3	108,988
Federal Way	2	0	0	0	0	0	1	0	0	1	96,338
Forks	1	0	0	0	1	0	0	1	1	0	3,787
Granite Falls	0	0	1	0	0	0	0	0	1	0	3,516
Kent	8	3	5	0	0	0	3	5	5	3	128,604
Kettle Falls	1	0	0	0	0	0	0	0	1	0	1,596
Kirkland	1	0	0	0	0	0	0	1	0	0	88,627
Lake Forest Park	0	1	0	0	0	0	0	0	0	1	13,369
Lake Stevens	2	0	0	0	0	0	0	1	1	0	31,440
Lakewood	2	0	1	0	0	0	0	0	1	2	60,153
Longview[2]	5	2	0	0	0	0	2	1	1	2	36,854
Lynnwood	2	0	0	0	0	0	0	0	1	1	37,217
Marysville	2	1	0	0	0	1	2	0	1	1	68,172
Mill Creek	0	0	1	0	0	0	0	0	0	1	20,419
Milton	1	0	0	0	0	0	0	1	0	0	7,785
Mountlake Terrace	1	0	0	0	0	0	0	0	1	0	21,212
Mount Vernon	0	0	0	0	0	1	0	1	0	0	34,521
Mukilteo	0	1	0	0	0	0	0	1	0	0	21,416
Oak Harbor	2	0	0	1	0	0	0	2	1	0	22,795
Olympia	1	0	0	0	0	0	0	0	1	0	50,972
Orting	3	0	0	0	0	0	0	1	2	0	7,594
Pasco	1	0	0	0	0	0	0	1	0	0	71,077
Port Angeles	4	0	1	0	0	0	0	2	2	1	19,525
Port Townsend	0	1	0	0	0	0	0	0	0	1	9,378
Pullman	0	1	1	0	0	0	1	0	1	0	33,456
Puyallup	2	1	0	0	0	0	1	2	0	0	40,167
Redmond[2]	2	5	0	0	0	0	0	1	0	5	61,893
Renton	5	1	2	0	0	0	0	4	2	2	101,908
Richland	2	0	0	0	0	0	0	0	1	1	55,475
Sammamish	5	1	0	0	1	0	0	0	6	1	53,387
Seattle	64	12	33	0	0	9	30	27	33	28	700,313
Snohomish	1	0	0	0	0	0	0	0	1	0	9,773
Spokane	6	1	1	0	0	0	1	2	0	5	214,028
Spokane Valley	8	1	1	0	0	0	2	1	1	6	95,923
Stanwood	1	0	0	0	0	0	0	0	0	1	6,888
Tacoma	4	0	5	0	0	0	2	2	3	2	209,914
Tenino	1	0	0	0	0	0	0	0	1	0	1,761
Tukwila	1	0	0	0	0	0	1	0	0	0	20,195
Vancouver	4	0	0	0	0	0	0	4	0	0	174,912
Walla Walla	6	0	0	1	0	0	4	2	0	1	32,326
White Salmon	2	0	0	0	0	0	1	1	0	0	2,364
Woodinville	0	1	0	0	0	0	0	0	1	0	11,953
Yakima	3	1	1	0	0	0	0	2	1	2	94,111
Universities and Colleges	3	1	4	0	1	1					
Eastern Washington University	0	0	1	0	0	0	1	0	0	0	12,361
Evergreen State College	0	0	1	0	0	1	1	1	0	0	4,190
University of Washington	1	1	1	0	1	0	0	2	1	1	45,408
Washington State University, Pullman	1	0	0	0	0	0	1	0	0	0	29,686
Western Washington University	1	0	1	0	0	0	0	0	0	2	15,332
Metropolitan Counties	41	8	7	0	0	1					
Clark	1	0	0	0	0	0	0	0	0	1	
Cowlitz	2	1	2	0	0	0	1	0	3	1	
King	11	2	1	0	0	0	2	4	4	4	
Pierce	10	0	1	0	0	0	3	2	0	6	
Skagit	0	0	0	0	0	1	0	1	0	0	
Snohomish	4	2	0	0	0	0	2	2	1	1	
Spokane	1	0	0	0	0	0	0	0	0	1	

Table 77. Hate Crime Incidents Per Bias Motivation and Quarter, by Selected State and Agency, 2016—Continued

(Number.)

State/agency	Number of incidents per bias motivation						Number of incidents per quarter				Population[1]
	Race/ Ethnicity/ Ancestry	Religion	Sexual orientation	Disability	Gender	Gender Identity	1st quarter	2nd quarter	3rd quarter	4th quarter	
Walla Walla	0	1	0	0	0	0	0	0	1	0	
Whatcom[2]	8	2	3	0	0	0	5	3	3	2	
Yakima	4	0	0	0	0	0	0	1	1	2	
Nonmetropolitan Counties	3	1	0	0	0	1					
Grays Harbor	1	0	0	0	0	0	1	0	0	0	
Island	1	0	0	0	0	0	0	0	0	1	
Lewis	1	0	0	0	0	0	0	0	1	0	
Mason	0	1	0	0	0	0	0	0	1	0	
San Juan	0	0	0	0	0	1	0	0	0	1	
Tribal Agencies	1	0	0	0	0	0					
Lummi Tribal	1	0	0	0	0	0	0	0	0	1	
Other Agencies	1	0	0	0	0	0					
Port of Seattle	1	0	0	0	0	0	1	0	0	0	
WEST VIRGINIA											
Total	30	1	7	3	0	0					
Cities	20	1	6	2	0	0					
Beckley	1	0	0	0	0	0	0	0	1	0	16,940
Buckhannon	1	0	0	0	0	0	0	0	0	1	5,662
Charleston	10	1	4	0	0	0	4	5	4	2	49,429
Fairmont	0	0	0	1	0	0	1	0	0	0	18,733
Fayetteville	2	0	0	0	0	0	1	1	0	0	2,885
Huntington	0	0	1	1	0	0	1	1	0	0	48,540
Moundsville	1	0	0	0	0	0	1	0	0	0	8,644
Oak Hill	2	0	0	0	0	0	0	1	1	0	8,104
Parkersburg	0	0	1	0	0	0	1	0	0	0	30,913
Philippi	1	0	0	0	0	0	0	0	1	0	3,320
Ranson	1	0	0	0	0	0	0	1	0	0	5,053
Wheeling	1	0	0	0	0	0	0	1	0	0	27,486
Metropolitan Counties	7	0	1	1	0	0					
Berkeley	1	0	0	0	0	0	0	0	1	0	
Brooke	1	0	0	0	0	0	0	0	0	1	
Cabell	1	0	0	0	0	0	0	0	0	1	
Hancock	2	0	0	0	0	0	1	1	0	0	
Jefferson	1	0	0	0	0	0	0	0	0	1	
Kanawha	1	0	1	1	0	0	1	1	1	0	
Nonmetropolitan Counties	3	0	0	0	0	0					
Mason	3	0	0	0	0	0	0	0	2	1	
WISCONSIN											
Total	22	8	3	0	0	1					
Cities	18	7	3	0	0	1					
Appleton	1	0	0	0	0	0	1	0	0	0	74,439
Cross Plains	0	0	1	0	0	0	1	0	0	0	4,072
Fox Valley Metro	1	0	0	0	0	0	0	0	1	0	21,515
Green Bay	1	0	0	0	0	0	1	0	0	0	105,452
Hudson	0	0	1	0	0	0	0	0	0	1	13,740
Janesville	1	0	0	0	0	0	0	1	0	0	64,234
La Crosse	1	0	0	0	0	0	0	1	0	0	52,498
Madison	8	7	0	0	0	0	0	8	2	5	252,136
Manitowoc	1	0	0	0	0	0	0	1	0	0	32,877
Milwaukee	0	0	1	0	0	1	0	1	1	0	600,193
New Richmond	1	0	0	0	0	0	0	0	1	0	8,913
Onalaska	1	0	0	0	0	0	0	1	0	0	18,600
Osceola	1	0	0	0	0	0	0	0	0	1	2,502
Stoughton	1	0	0	0	0	0	0	0	0	1	13,148
Metropolitan Counties	3	1	0	0	0	0					
Fond du Lac	2	0	0	0	0	0	1	0	0	1	
Outagamie	1	0	0	0	0	0	0	0	1	0	
St. Croix	0	1	0	0	0	0	0	0	0	1	
Nonmetropolitan Counties	1	0	0	0	0	0					
Rusk	1	0	0	0	0	0	0	0	1	0	
WYOMING											
Total	3	0	0	0	0	0					
Cities	3	0	0	0	0	0					
Gillette	3	0	0	0	0	0	0	2	0	1	33,218

1 Population figures are published only for the cities. The figures listed for the universities and colleges are student enrollment and were provided by the United States Department of Education for the 2015 school year, the most recent available. The enrollment figures include full-time and part-time students.   2 Includes one incident reported with more than one bias motivation.   3 Student enrollment figures were not available.

APPENDIX I. METHODOLOGY

Submitting UCR data to the FBI is a collective effort on the part of city, university/college, county, state, tribal, and federal law enforcement agencies to present a nationwide view of crime. Participating agencies throughout the country voluntarily provide reports on crimes known to the police and on persons arrested. For the most part, agencies submit monthly crime reports, using uniform offense definitions, to a centralized repository within their state. The state UCR Program then forwards the data to the FBI's UCR Program. Agencies in states that do not have a state UCR Program submit their data directly to the FBI. Staff members review the information for accuracy and reasonableness. [The FBI distributes the data presentations, special studies, and other publications compiled from the data to all who are interested in knowing about crime in the nation.] The national UCR Program is housed in the Operational Programs (OP) Branch of the FBI's Criminal Justice Information Services (CJIS) Division. Within the OP Branch, four units (the Crime Statistics Management Unit [CSMU], the CJIS Audit Unit, the Multimedia Productions Group [MPG]), and the CJIS Training and Advisory Process [CTAP] Unit), are involved in the day-to-day administration of the program.

Criteria for State UCR programs

The criteria established for state programs ensure consistency and comparability in the data submitted to the national program, as well as regular and timely reporting. These criteria are:

1. A UCR Program must conform to the FBI UCR Program's submission standards, definitions, specifications, and required deadlines.

2. A UCR Program must establish data integrity procedures and have personnel assigned to assist contributing agencies in quality assurance practices and crime reporting procedures. Data integrity procedures should include crime trend assessments, offense classification verification, and technical specification validation.

3. A UCR Program's submissions must cover more than 50 percent of the law enforcement agencies within its established reporting domain and be willing to cover any and all UCR-contributing agencies that wish to use the UCR Program from within its domain. (An agency wishing to become a UCR Program must be willing to report for all of the agencies within the state.)

4. A UCR Program must furnish the FBI UCR Program with all of the UCR data collected by the law enforcement agencies within its domain.

These requirements do not prohibit the state from gathering other statistical data beyond the national collection.

Data Completeness and Quality

National program staff members contact the state UCR program in connection with crime-reporting matters and, when necessary and approved by the state, they contact individual contributors within the state. To fulfill its responsibilities in connection with the UCR program, the FBI reviews and edits individual agency reports for completeness and quality. Upon request, they conduct training programs within the state on law enforcement record-keeping and crime-reporting procedures. The FBI conducts an audit of each state's UCR data collection procedures once every three years, in accordance with audit standards established by the federal government. Should circumstances develop in which the state program does not comply with the aforementioned requirements, the national program may institute a direct collection of data from law enforcement agencies within the state.

During a review of publication processes, the UCR Program staff analyzed Web statistics from previous editions of *Crime in the United States* (*CIUS*) to determine the tables that users access the most. Based on these criteria, the UCR Program streamlined the 2016 edition by reducing the number of tables from 81 to 29. The publication, however, still presents the major topics (offenses known, clearances, and persons arrested) that readers have come to expect. On June 30, 2017, the UCR Program launched the Crime Data Explorer (CDE), which provides law enforcement and the general public with crime data at the agency, state, and national levels. Offering multiple pathways to reported crime data, the CDE provides data visualizations of high-level trends and incident data with more detailed perspectives through downloads and a system enabling developers to create software applications. Planned enhancements to the CDE include additional tools to create dynamic data presentations, progressing beyond the static data tables of *CIUS* and the National Incident-Based Reporting System (NIBRS).

Beginning January 1, 2017, the UCR Program discontinued collecting rape data via the SRS according to the legacy definition. Therefore, the 2016 editions of *CIUS* and *Hate Crime Statistics* are the final publications which include the legacy definition of rape. Only rape data submitted under the revised definition will be published for 2017 and subsequent years. This change did not affect agencies that submit rape data via NIBRS.

Reporting Procedures

Offenses known and value of property–Law enforcement agencies tabulate the number of Part I offenses reported based on records of all reports of crime received from victims, officers who discover infractions, or other sources, and submit these reports each month to the FBI directly or through their state UCR programs. Part I offenses include murder and nonnegligent manslaughter, forcible rape, robbery, aggravated assault, burglary, larceny-theft, motor vehicle theft, and arson. Each month, law enforcement agencies also submit to the FBI the value of property stolen and recovered in connection with the offenses and detailed information pertaining to criminal homicide.

Unfounded offenses and clearances—When, through investigation, an agency determines that complaints of crimes are unfounded or false, the agency eliminates that offense from its crime tally through an entry on the monthly report. The report also provides the total number of actual Part I offenses, the number of offenses cleared, and the number of clearances that involve only offenders under the age of 18. (Law enforcement can clear crimes in one of two ways: by the arrest of at least one person who is charged and turned over to the court for prosecution or by exceptional means—when some element beyond law enforcement's control precludes the arrest of a known offender.)

Persons arrested—In addition to reporting Part I offenses each month, law enforcement agencies also provide data on the age, sex, and race of persons arrested for Part I and Part II offenses. Part II offenses encompass all crimes, except traffic violations, that are not classified as Part I offenses.

Officers killed or assaulted—Each month, law enforcement agencies also report information to the UCR program regarding law enforcement officers killed or assaulted, and each year they report the number of full-time sworn and civilian law enforcement personnel employed as of October 31.

Hate crimes—At the end of each quarter, law enforcement agencies report summarized data on hate crimes; that is specific offenses that were motivated by an offender's bias against the perceived race, religion, ethnic or national origin, sexual orientation, or physical or mental disability of the victim. Those agencies participating in the UCR program's National Incident-Based Reporting System (NIBRS) submit hate crime data monthly.

Editing Procedures

The UCR program thoroughly examines each report it receives for arithmetical accuracy and for deviations in crime data from month to month and from present to past years that may indicate errors. UCR staff members compare an agency's monthly reports with its previous submissions and with reports from similar agencies to identify any unusual fluctuations in the agency's crime count. Considerable variations in crime levels may indicate modified records procedures, incomplete reporting, or changes in the jurisdiction's geopolitical structure.

Evaluation of trends—Data reliability is a high priority of the FBI, which brings any deviations or arithmetical adjustments to the attention of state UCR programs or the submitting agencies. Typically, FBI staff members study the monthly reports to evaluate periodic trends prepared for individual reporting units. Any significant increase or decrease becomes the subject of a special inquiry. Changes in crime reporting procedures or annexations that affect an agency's jurisdiction can influence the level of reported crime. When this occurs, the FBI excludes the figures for specific crime categories or totals, if necessary, from the trend tabulations.

Training for contributors—In addition to the evaluation of trends, the FBI provides training seminars and instructional materials on crime reporting procedures to assist contributors in complying with UCR standards. Throughout the country, representatives from the national program coordinate with representatives of state programs and law enforcement personnel and hold training sessions to explain the purpose of the program, the rules of uniform classification and scoring, and the methods of assembling the information for reporting. When an individual agency has specific problems with compiling its crime statistics and its remedial efforts are unsuccessful, personnel from the FBI's Criminal Justice Information Services Division may visit the contributor to aid in resolving the problems.

UCR Handbook—The national UCR program publishes the *Uniform Crime Reporting (UCR) Handbook*, which details procedures for classifying and scoring offenses and serves as the contributing agencies' basic resource for preparing reports. The national staff also produces letters to UCR contributors, state program bulletins, and UCR newsletters as needed. These publications provide policy updates and new information, as well as clarification of reporting issues.

The final responsibility for data submissions rests with the individual contributing law enforcement agency. Although the FBI makes every effort through its editing procedures, training practices, and correspondence to ensure the validity of the data it receives, the accuracy of the statistics depends primarily on the adherence of each contributor to the established standards of reporting. Deviations from these established standards that cannot be resolved by the national UCR program may be brought to the attention of the Criminal Justice Information Systems Committees of the International Association of Chiefs of Police and the National Sheriffs' Association.

NIBRS Conversion

Thirty-three state programs are certified to provide their UCR data in the expanded National Incident-Based Reporting System (NIBRS) format. For presentation in this book, the NIBRS data were converted to the historical Summary Reporting System data. The UCR program staff constructed the NIBRS database to allow for such conversion so that UCR's long-running time series could continue.

Crime Trends

By showing fluctuations from year to year, trend statistics offer the data user an added perspective from which to study crime. Percent change tabulations in this publication are computed only for reporting agencies that provided comparable data for the periods under consideration. The FBI excludes from the trend calculations all figures except those received for common months from common agencies. Also excluded are unusual fluctuations of data that the FBI determines are the result of such variables as improved records procedures, annexations, and so on.

Caution to Users

Data users should exercise care in making any direct comparison between data in this publication and those in prior issues of *Crime in the United States*. Because of differing levels of participation from year to year and

reporting problems that require the FBI to estimate crime counts for certain contributors, some data may not be comparable. In addition, this publication may contain updates to data provided in prior years' publications.

Offense Estimation

Some tables in this publication contain statistics for the entire United States. Because not all law enforcement agencies provide data for complete reporting periods, the FBI includes estimated crime numbers in these presentations. The FBI estimates data for three areas: Metropolitan Statistical Areas (MSAs), cities outside MSAs, and nonmetropolitan counties; and computes estimates for participating agencies that do not provide 12 months of complete data. For agencies supplying 3 to 11 months of data, the national UCR program estimates for the missing data by following a standard estimation procedure using the data provided by the agency. If an agency has supplied less than 3 months of data, the FBI computes estimates by using the known crime figures of similar areas within a state and assigning the same proportion of crime volumes to nonreporting agencies. The estimation process considers the following: population size covered by the agency; type of jurisdiction; for example, police department versus sheriff's office; and geographic location.

Estimation of State-Level Data

In response to various circumstances, the FBI calculates estimated offense totals for certain states. For example, some states do not provide forcible rape figures in accordance with UCR guidelines. In addition, problems at the state level have, at times, resulted in no useable data. Also, the conversion of the National Incident-Based Reporting System (NIBRS) data to Summary data has contributed to the need for unique estimation procedures.

APPENDIX II. OFFENSE DEFINITIONS

The Uniform Crime Reporting (UCR) program divides offenses into two groups. Contributing agencies submit information on the number of Part I offenses known to law enforcement; those offenses cleared by arrest or exceptional means; and the age, sex, and race of persons arrested for each of these offenses. Contributors provide only arrest data for Part II offenses. These are definitions of offenses set forth by the UCR.

The UCR program collects data on Part I offenses to measure the level and scope of crime occurring throughout the nation. The program's founders chose these offenses because (1) they are serious crimes, (2) they occur with regularity in all areas of the country, and (3) they are likely to be reported to police.

Part I offenses include criminal homicide, forcible rape, robbery, aggravated assault, burglary, larceny-theft, motor vehicle theft, and arson.

Criminal homicide—a.) Murder and nonnegligent manslaughter: the willful (nonnegligent) killing of one human being by another. Deaths caused by negligence, attempts to kill, assaults to kill, suicides, and accidental deaths are excluded. The program classifies justifiable homicides separately and limits the definition to (1) the killing of a felon by a law enforcement officer in the line of duty; or (2) the killing of a felon, during the commission of a felony, by a private citizen. b. Manslaughter by negligence: the killing of another person through gross negligence. Deaths of persons due to their own negligence, accidental deaths not resulting from gross negligence, and traffic fatalities are excluded.

Rape—In 2013, the FBI UCR Program initiated collection of rape data under a revised definition within the Summary Reporting System. Previously, offense data for forcible rape were collected under the legacy UCR definition: the carnal knowledge of a female forcibly and against her will. Beginning with the 2013 data year, the term "forcible" was removed from the offense title, and the definition was changed. The revised UCR definition of rape is: penetration, no matter how slight, of the vagina or anus with any body part or object, or oral penetration by a sex organ of another person, without the consent of the victim. Attempts or assaults to commit rape are also included; however, statutory rape and incest are excluded. All rape data submitted in 2015—whether collected under the revised definition or the legacy definition—are presented in this publication. However, because only two years of rape data have been collected under the revised definition, the overview presented here discusses only legacy definition rape data. The UCR Program counts one offense for each victim of a rape, attempted rape, or assault with intent to rape, regardless of the victim's age. Sexual relations without the victim's consent which involves a familial offender is counted as a rape and not an act of incest. All other crimes of a sexual nature are considered to be Part II offenses; as such, the UCR Program collects only arrest data for those crimes. The offense of statutory rape, in which no force is used but the female victim is under the age of consent, is included in the arrest total for the sex offenses category.

Beginning January 1, 2017, the UCR Program discontinued collecting rape data via the SRS according to the historical, legacy definition. Only rape data submitted under the revised definition will be published for 2017 and subsequent years. This change will not affect agencies that submit rape data via NIBRS.

Robbery—The taking or attempted taking of anything of value from the care, custody, or control of a person or persons by force or threat of force or violence and/or by putting the victim in fear.

Aggravated assault—An unlawful attack by one person upon another for the purpose of inflicting severe or aggravated bodily injury. This type of assault usually is accompanied by the use of a weapon or by means likely to produce death or great bodily harm. Simple assaults are excluded.

Burglary (breaking or entering)—The unlawful entry of a structure to commit a felony or a theft. Attempted forcible entry is included.

Larceny-theft (except motor vehicle theft)—The unlawful taking, carrying, leading, or riding away of property from the possession or constructive possession of another. Examples are thefts of bicycles or automobile parts and accessories, shoplifting, pocket-picking, or the stealing of any property or article that is not taken by force and violence or by fraud. Attempted larcenies are included. Embezzlement, confidence games, forgery, worthless checks, and the like, are excluded.

Motor vehicle theft—The theft or attempted theft of a motor vehicle. A motor vehicle is self-propelled and runs on land surface and not on rails. Motorboats, construction equipment, airplanes, and farming equipment are specifically excluded from this category.

Arson—Any willful or malicious burning or attempt to burn, with or without intent to defraud, a dwelling house, public building, motor vehicle, aircraft, personal property of another, and the like.

The **Part II** offenses for which only arrest data are collected, are:

Other assaults, also known as other assaults (simple)—Assaults and attempted assaults that are not of an aggravated nature and do not result in serious injury to the victim. Included in this category are stalking, intimidation, coercion, and hazing.

Forgery and counterfeiting—The altering, copying, or imitating of something, without authority or right, with the intent to deceive or defraud by passing the copy or thing altered or imitated as that which is original or genuine; or the selling, buying, or possession of an altered, copied, or imitated thing with the intent to deceive or defraud. Attempts are included.

Fraud—The intentional perversion of the truth for the purpose of inducing another person or other entity in reliance upon it to part with something of value or to surrender a legal right. Fraudulent conversion and obtaining of money or property by false pretenses. Confidence games and bad checks, except forgeries and counterfeiting, are included.

Embezzlement—The unlawful misappropriation or misapplication by an offender of money, property, or some other thing of value entrusted to that offender's care, custody, or control.

Stolen property; buying, receiving, possessing—Buying, receiving, possessing, selling, concealing, or transporting any property with the knowledge that it has been unlawfully taken, as by burglary, embezzlement, fraud, larceny, robbery, and the like. Attempts are included.

Vandalism—To willfully or maliciously destroy, injure, disfigure, or deface any public or private property, real or personal, without the consent of the owner or person having custody or control by cutting, tearing, breaking, marking, painting, drawing, covering with filth, or any other such means as may be specified by local law. Attempts are included.

Weapons; carrying, possessing, and the like—The violation of laws or ordinances prohibiting the manufacture, sale, purchase, transportation, possession, concealment, or use of firearms, cutting instruments, explosives, incendiary devices, or other deadly weapons. Attempts are included.

Prostitution and commercialized vice—The unlawful promotion of or participation in sexual activities for profit, including attempts. To solicit customers or transport persons for prostitution purposes; to own, manage, or operate a dwelling or other establishment for the purposes of providing a place where prostitution is performed; or to otherwise assist or promote prostitution.

Sex offenses (except forcible rape, prostitution, and commercialized vice)—Offenses against chastity, common decency, morals, and the like. Incest, indecent exposure, and statutory rape, as well as attempts are included.

Drug abuse violations—The violation of laws prohibiting the production, distribution, and/or use of certain controlled substances. The unlawful cultivation, manufacture, distribution, sale, purchase, use, possession, transportation, or importation of any controlled drug or narcotic substance. Arrests for violations of state and local laws, specifically those relating to the unlawful possession, sale, use, growing, manufacturing, and making of narcotic drugs. The following drug categories are specified: opium or cocaine and their derivatives (morphine, heroin, codeine); marijuana; synthetic narcotics—manufactured narcotics that can cause true addiction (demerol, methadone); and dangerous nonnarcotic drugs (barbiturates, benzedrine).

Gambling—To unlawfully bet or wager money or something else of value; assist, promote, or operate a game of chance for money or some other stake; possess or transmit wagering information; manufacture, sell, purchase, possess, or transport gambling equipment, devices, or goods; or tamper with the outcome of a sporting event or contest to gain a gambling advantage.

Offenses against the family and children—Unlawful nonviolent acts by a family member (or legal guardian) that threaten the physical, mental, or economic well-being or morals of another family member and that are not classifiable as other offenses, such as assault or sex offenses. Attempts are included.

Driving under the influence—Driving or operating a motor vehicle or common carrier while mentally or physically impaired as the result of consuming an alcoholic beverage or using a drug or narcotic.

Liquor laws—The violation of state or local laws or ordinances prohibiting the manufacture, sale, purchase, transportation, possession, or use of alcoholic beverages, not including driving under the influence and drunkenness. Federal violations are excluded.

Drunkenness—To drink alcoholic beverages to the extent that one's mental faculties and physical coordination are substantially impaired. Excludes driving under the influence.

Disorderly conduct—Any behavior that tends to disturb the public peace or decorum, scandalize the community, or shock the public sense of morality.

Vagrancy—The violation of a court order, regulation, ordinance, or law requiring the withdrawal of persons from the streets or other specified areas; prohibiting persons from remaining in an area or place in an idle or aimless manner; or prohibiting persons from going from place to place without visible means of support.

All other offenses—All violations of state or local laws not specifically identified as Part I or Part II offenses, except traffic violations.

Suspicion—Arrested for no specific offense and released without formal charges being placed.

Curfew and loitering laws (persons under 18 years of age)—Violations by juveniles of local curfew or loitering ordinances.

APPENDIX III. GEOGRAPHIC AREA DEFINITIONS

The program collects crime data and supplemental information that make it possible to generate a variety of statistical compilations, including data presented by reporting areas. These statistics enable data users to analyze local crime data in conjunction with those for areas of similar geographic location or population size. The reporting areas that the program uses in its data breakdowns include community types, population groups, and regions and divisions. For community types, the program considers proximity to metropolitan areas using the designations established by the U.S. Office of Management and Budget (OMB). (Generally, sheriffs, county police, and state police report crimes within counties but outside of cities; local police report crimes within city limits.) The number of inhabitants living in a locale (based on the U.S. Census Bureau's figures) determines the population group into which the program places it. For its geographic breakdowns, the program divides the United States into regions and divisions.

Regions and Divisions

The map below illustrates the nine divisions that make up the four regions of the United States. The program uses this widely recognized geographic organization when compiling the nation's crime data. The regions and divisions are as follows:

NORTHEAST

New England—Connecticut, Maine, Massachusetts, New Hampshire, Rhode Island, and Vermont

Middle Atlantic—New York, New Jersey, and Pennsylvania

MIDWEST

East North Central—Illinois, Indiana, Michigan, Ohio, and Wisconsin

West North Central—Iowa, Kansas, Minnesota, Missouri, Nebraska, North Dakota, and South Dakota

SOUTH

South Atlantic—Delaware, District of Columbia, Florida, Georgia, Maryland, North Carolina, South Carolina, Virginia, and West Virginia

East South Central—Alabama, Kentucky, Mississippi, and Tennessee

West South Central—Arkansas, Louisiana, Oklahoma, and Texas

WEST

Mountain—Arizona, Colorado, Idaho, Montana, Nevada, New Mexico, Utah, and Wyoming

Pacific—Alaska, California, Hawaii, Oregon, and Washington

Community Types

To assist data users who wish to analyze and present uniform statistical data about metropolitan areas, the program uses reporting units that represent major population centers. The program compiles data for the following three types of communities:

Metropolitan Statistical Areas (MSAs)—Each MSA contains a principal city or urbanized area with a population of at least 50,000 inhabitants. MSAs include the principal city, the county in which the city is located, and other adjacent counties that have a high degree of economic and social integration with the principal city and county (as defined by the OMB), which is measured through commuting. In the program, counties within an MSA are considered metropolitan counties. In addition, MSAs may cross state boundaries.

Some presentations in this publication refer to Metropolitan Divisions, which are subdivisions of an MSA that consists of a core with "a population of at least 2.5 million persons. A Metropolitan Division consists of one or more main/secondary counties that represent an employment center or centers, plus adjacent counties associated with the main county or counties through commuting ties," (*Federal Register* 65 [249]). Also, some tables reference suburban areas, which are subdivisions of MSAs that exclude the principal cities but include all the remaining cities (those having fewer than 50,000 inhabitants) and the unincorporated areas of the MSAs.

Because the elements that comprise MSAs, particularly the geographic compositions, are subject to change, the program discourages data users from making year-to-year comparisons of MSA data.

Cities Outside MSAs—Ordinarily, cities outside MSAs are incorporated areas. In 2013, cities outside MSAs made up 6.0 percent of the nation's population.

Nonmetropolitan Counties Outside MSAs—Most non-metropolitan counties are composed of unincorporated areas.

Metropolitan and nonmetropolitan community types are further illustrated in the following table:

Metropolitan	Nonmetropolitan
Principal cities (50,000+ inhabitants)	Cities outside metropolitan areas
Suburban cities	
Metropolitan counties	Nonmetropolitan counties

APPENDIX IV. THE NATION'S TWO CRIME MEASURES

The Department of Justice administers two statistical programs to measure the magnitude, nature, and impact of crime in the nation: the Uniform Crime Reporting (UCR) program and the National Crime Victimization Survey (NCVS). Each of these programs produces valuable information about aspects of the nation's crime problem. Because the UCR and NCVS programs are conducted for different purposes, use different methods, and focus on somewhat different aspects of crime, the information they produce together provides a more comprehensive panorama of the nation's crime problem than either could produce alone.

Uniform Crime Reporting (UCR) program

The UCR program, administered by the Federal Bureau of Investigation (FBI), was created in 1929 and collects information on the following crimes reported to law enforcement authorities: murder and nonnegligent manslaughter, forcible rape, robbery, aggravated assault, burglary, larceny-theft, motor vehicle theft, and arson. Law enforcement agencies also report arrest data for 20 additional crime categories.

The UCR program compiles data from monthly law enforcement reports and from individual crime incident records transmitted directly to the FBI or to centralized state agencies that report to the FBI. The program thoroughly examines each report it receives for reasonableness, accuracy, and deviations that may indicate errors. Large variations in crime levels may indicate modified records procedures, incomplete reporting, or changes in a jurisdiction's boundaries. To identify any unusual fluctuations in an agency's crime counts, the program compares monthly reports to previous submissions of the agency and to those for similar agencies.

The FBI annually publishes its findings in a preliminary release in the spring of the following calendar year, followed by a detailed annual report, *Crime in the United States*, issued in the fall. (The printed copy of *Crime in the United States* is now published by Bernan.) In addition to crime counts and trends, this report includes data on crimes cleared, persons arrested (age, sex, and race), law enforcement personnel (including the number of sworn officers killed or assaulted), and the characteristics of homicides (including age, sex, and race of victims and offenders; victim-offender relationships; weapons used; and circumstances surrounding the homicides). Other periodic reports are also available from the UCR program.

The state and local law enforcement agencies participating in the UCR program are continually converting to the more comprehensive and detailed National Incident-Based Reporting System (NIBRS).

The UCR program presents crime counts for the nation as a whole, as well as for regions, states, counties, cities, towns, tribal law enforcement areas, and colleges and universities. This allows for studies among neighboring jurisdictions and among those with similar populations and other common characteristics.

National Crime Victimization Survey

The NCVS, conducted by the Bureau of Justice Statistics (BJS), began in 1973. It provides a detailed picture of crime incidents, victims, and trends. After a substantial period of research, the BJS completed an intensive methodological redesign of the survey in 1993. It conducted this redesign to improve the questions used to uncover crime, update the survey methods, and broaden the scope of crimes measured. The redesigned survey collects detailed information on the frequency and nature of the crimes of rape, sexual assault, personal robbery, aggravated and simple assault, household burglary, theft, and motor vehicle theft. It does not measure homicide or commercial crimes (such as burglaries of stores).

Twice a year, Census Bureau personnel interview household members in a nationally representative sample of approximately 90,000 households (about 160,000 people). Households stay in the sample for 3 years, and new households rotate into the sample on an ongoing basis.

The NCVS collects information on crimes suffered by individuals and households, whether or not those crimes were reported to law enforcement. It estimates the proportion of each crime type reported to law enforcement, and it summarizes the reasons that victims give for reporting or not reporting.

The survey provides information about victims (age, sex, race, ethnicity, marital status, income, and educational level); offenders (sex, race, approximate age, and victim-offender relationship); and crimes (time and place of occurrence, use of weapons, nature of injury, and economic consequences). Questions also cover victims' experiences with the criminal justice system, self-protective measures used by victims, and possible substance abuse by offenders. Supplements are added to the survey periodically to obtain detailed information on specific topics, such as school crime.

The BJS published the first data from the redesigned NCVS in a June 1995 bulletin. The publication of NCVS data includes *Criminal Victimization in the United States*, an annual report that covers the broad range of detailed information collected by the NCVS. The bureau also publishes detailed reports on topics such as crime against women, urban crime, and gun use in crime. The National Archive of Criminal Justice Data at the University of Michigan archives the NCVS data files to help researchers perform independent analyses.

Comparing the UCR program and the NCVS

Because the BJS designed the NCVS to complement the UCR program, the two programs share many similarities. As much as their different collection methods permit, the two measure the same subset of serious crimes with the same definitions. Both programs cover rape, robbery, aggravated assault, burglary, theft, and motor vehicle theft; both define rape, robbery, theft, and motor vehicle theft virtually identically. (Although rape is defined analogously, the UCR program measures the crime against women only, and the NCVS measures it against both sexes.)

There are also significant differences between the two programs. First, the two programs were created to serve different purposes. The UCR program's primary objective is to provide a reliable set of criminal justice statistics for law enforcement administration, operation, and management. The BJS established the NCVS to provide previously unavailable information about crime (including crime not reported to police), victims, and offenders.

Second, the two programs measure an overlapping but nonidentical set of crimes. The NCVS includes crimes both reported and not reported to law enforcement. The NCVS excludes—but the UCR program includes—homicide, arson, commercial crimes, and crimes committed against children under 12 years of age. The UCR program captures crimes reported to law enforcement but collects only arrest data for simple assaults and sexual assaults other than forcible rape.

Third, because of methodology, the NCVS and UCR have different definitions of some crimes. For example, the UCR defines burglary as the unlawful entry or attempted entry of a structure to commit a felony or theft. The NCVS, not wanting to ask victims to ascertain offender motives, defines burglary as the entry or attempted entry of a residence by a person who had no right to be there.

Fourth, for property crimes (burglary, theft, and motor vehicle theft), the two programs calculate crime rates using different bases. The UCR program rates for these crimes are per capita (number of crimes per 100,000 persons), whereas the NCVS rates for these crimes are per household (number of crimes per 1,000 households).

Because the number of households may not grow at the same annual rate as the total population, trend data for rates of property crimes measured by the two programs may not be comparable. In addition, some differences in the data from the two programs may result from sampling variation in the NCVS and from estimating for non-responsiveness in the UCR program.

The BJS derives the NCVS estimates from interviewing a sample and are, therefore, subject to a margin of error. The bureau uses rigorous statistical methods to calculate confidence intervals around all survey estimates, and describes trend data in the NCVS reports as genuine only if there is at least a 90-percent certainty that the measured changes are not the result of sampling variation. The UCR program bases its data on the actual counts of offenses reported by law enforcement agencies. In some circumstances, the UCR program estimates its data for nonparticipating agencies or those reporting partial data. Apparent discrepancies between statistics from the two programs can usually be accounted for by their definitional and procedural differences, or resolved by comparing NCVS sampling variations (confidence intervals) of crimes said to have been reported to police with UCR program statistics.

For most types of crimes measured by both the UCR program and the NCVS, analysts familiar with the programs can exclude those aspects of crime not common to both from analysis. Resulting long-term trend lines can be brought into close concordance. The impact of such adjustments is most striking for robbery, burglary, and motor vehicle theft, whose definitions most closely coincide.

With robbery, the BJS bases the NCVS victimization rates on only those robberies reported to the police. It is also possible to remove UCR program robberies of commercial establishments, such as gas stations, convenience stores, and banks, from analysis. When users compare the resulting NCVS police-reported robbery rates and the UCR program noncommercial robbery rates, the results reveal closely corresponding long-term trends.

Conclusion

Each program has unique strengths. The UCR program provides a measure of the number of crimes reported to law enforcement agencies throughout the country. The program's Supplementary Homicide Reports provide the most reliable, timely data on the extent and nature of homicides in the nation. The NCVS is the primary source of information on the characteristics of criminal victimization and on the number and types of crimes not reported to law enforcement authorities.

By understanding the strengths and limitations of each program, it is possible to use the UCR program and NCVS to achieve a greater understanding of crime trends and the nature of crime in the United States. For example, changes in police procedures, shifting attitudes towards crime and police, and other societal changes can affect the extent to which people report and law enforcement agencies record crime. NCVS and UCR program data can be used in concert to explore why trends in reported and police-recorded crime may differ.